T0145376

Lecture Notes in Computer Science 10631

Commenced Publication in 1973
Founding and Former Series Editors:
Gerhard Goos, Juris Hartmanis, and Jan van Leeuwen

More information about this series at http://www.springer.com/series/7410

Sihan Qing · Chris Mitchell
Liqun Chen · Dongmei Liu (Eds.)

Information and Communications Security

19th International Conference, ICICS 2017
Beijing, China, December 6–8, 2017
Proceedings

 Springer

Editors
Sihan Qing
Chinese Academy of Sciences
   and Peking University
Beijing
China

Chris Mitchell
Royal Holloway, University of London
Egham, Surrey
UK

Liqun Chen
University of Surrey
Guildford, Surrey
UK

Dongmei Liu
Microsoft
Beijing
China

ISSN 0302-9743   ISSN 1611-3349   (electronic)
Lecture Notes in Computer Science
ISBN 978-3-319-89499-7   ISBN 978-3-319-89500-0   (eBook)
https://doi.org/10.1007/978-3-319-89500-0

Library of Congress Control Number: 2018939454

LNCS Sublibrary: SL4 – Security and Cryptology

Printed on acid-free paper

This Springer imprint is published by the registered company Springer International Publishing AG
part of Springer Nature
The registered company address is: Gewerbestrasse 11, 6330 Cham, Switzerland

More information about this series at http://www.springer.com/series/7410

Lecture Notes in Computer Science   10631

Commenced Publication in 1973
Founding and Former Series Editors:
Gerhard Goos, Juris Hartmanis, and Jan van Leeuwen

Preface

The 19th International Conference on Information and Communications Security (ICICS 2017) was held in Beijing, China, during December 6–8, 2017. The ICICS conference series is an established forum that brings together people from universities, research institutes, industry, and government institutions who work in a range of fields within information and communications security. The ICICS conferences give attendees the opportunity to exchange new ideas and investigate developments in the state of the art. In previous years, ICICS has taken place in Australia (1999), China (2015, 2013, 2011, 2009, 2007, 2005, 2003, 2001 and 1997), Hong Kong (2012, 2014), Singapore (2002, 2016), Spain (2010, 2004), UK (2008), and USA (2006). On each occasion, as on this one, the proceedings have been published in the Springer LNCS series.

In total, 188 manuscripts from 20 countries and districts were submitted to ICICS 2017, among which 43 regular and 14 short papers from 13 countries and districts were accepted. The accepted papers cover a wide range of disciplines within information security and applied cryptography. Each submission to ICICS 2017 was anonymously reviewed by at least three or four reviewers. We are very grateful to the Program Committee, which was composed of 72 members from 19 countries; we would like to thank them, as well as all the external reviewers, for their valuable contributions to the tough and time-consuming reviewing process. We also thank our two keynote speakers: Dr. K. P. Chow from the University of Hong Kong and Prof. Atsuko Miyaji from Osaka University of Japan.

ICICS 2017 was organized and hosted by the Institute of Information Engineering, Chinese Academy of Sciences (CAS), the Institute of Software and Microelectronics, Peking University, and the State Key Laboratory of Information Security of the Institute of Software, Chinese Academy of Sciences (CAS). ICICS 2017 was supported by the National Natural Science Foundation of China under Grant No. 61170282.

We would like to thank the authors who submitted their papers to ICICS 2017, and the attendees from all around the world. Finally, we would also like to thank Organizing Committee Chair Zhen Xu and co-chair Liming Wang for providing logistic support, Chao Zheng for managing the conference website and the EasyChair system, Publicity Chair Qingni Shen for making the wide distribution of the call for papers, and Publication Chair Dongmei Liu for her time and expertise in compiling the proceedings.

December 2017

Sihan Qing
Chris Mitchell
Liqun Chen

Organization

General Chair

Dan Meng   Institute of Information Engineering, Chinese Academy
of Sciences, China

Program Chairs

Sihan Qing   Chinese Academy of Sciences and Peking University, China
Chris Mitchell   Royal Holloway, University of London, UK
Liqun Chen   University of Surrey, UK

Organizing Committee

Zhen Xu (Chair)   Institute of Information Engineering, Chinese Academy
of Sciences, China
Liming Wang
(Vice Chair)   Institute of Information Engineering, Chinese Academy
of Sciences, China
Chao Zheng   SKLOIS, Institute of Information Engineering,
Chinese Academy of Sciences, China

Publicity Chair

Qingni Shen   Peking University, China

Publication Chair

Dongmei Liu   Microsoft, China

Program Committee

Man Ho Allen Au   The Hong Kong Polytechnic University, Hong Kong
Joonsang Baek   University of Wollongong, Australia
Zhenfu Cao   East China Normal University, China
Chin Chen Chang   Feng Chia University, Taiwan
Chi Chen   Institute of Information Engineering, Chinese Academy
of Sciences, China
Kefei Chen   Hangzhou Normal University, China
Liqun Chen   University of Surrey, UK
Zhong Chen   Peking University, China
K. P. Chow   The University of Hong Kong, Hong Kong
Frédéric Cuppens   Telecom Bretagne, France

Naccache David   Ecole Normale Superieure, France
Josep-Lluís   University of the Balearic Islands, Spain
  Ferrer-Gomila
Steven Furnell   University of Plymouth, UK
Debin Gao   Singapore Management University, Singapore
Dieter Gollmann   Hamburg University of Technology, Germany
Dawu Gu   Shanghai Jiao Tong University, China
Yong Guan   Iowa State University, USA
Jinguang Han   University of Surrey, UK
Shoichi Hirose   University of Fukui, Japan
Qiong Huang   South China Agricultural University, China
Xinyi Huang   Fujian Normal University, China
Chi Kwong Hui   The University of Hong Kong, Hong Kong
Lech Janczewski   The University of Auckland, New Zealand
Chunfu Jia   Nankai University, China
Sokratis K. Katsikas   Center for Cyber and Information Security, NTNU, Norway
Howon Kim   Pusan National University, South Korea
Kwangjo Kim   Korea Advanced Institute of Science and Technology, Korea
Byoungcheon Lee   Joongbu University, South Korea
Xinghua Li   Xidian University, China
Zichen Li   Beijing Institue Graphic Communication, China
Kaitai Liang   Manchester Metropolitan University, UK
Dongdai Lin   Institute of Information Engineering, Chinese Academy
                           of Sciences, China
Hua-Yi Lin   China University of Technology, Taiwan
Chris Mitchell   Royal Holloway, University of London, UK
Atsuko Miyaji   Japan Advanced Institute of Science and Technology, Japan
Takashi Nishide   University of Tsukuba, Japan
Takao Okubo   Institute of Information Security, Japan
Changgen Peng   Guizhou University, China
Raphael Phan   Loughborough University, Malaysia
Josef Pieprzyk   Queensland University of Technology, Australia
Jing Qin   Shandong University, China
Sihan Qing   Institute of Software, Chinese Academy of Sciences, China
Elizabeth Quaglia   Royal Holloway, University of London, UK
Kai Rannenberg   Goethe University Frankfurt, Germany
Bimal Roy   Indian Statistical Institute, Kolkata, India
Pierangela Samarati   Università degli Studi di Milano, Italy
Daniele Sgandurra   Information Security Group, Royal Holloway, UK
Qingni Shen   Peking University, China
Hung-Min Sun   National Tsing Hua University, Taiwan
Neeraj Suri   TU Darmstadt, Germany
Willy Susilo   University of Wollongong, Australia
Chunming Tang   Guangzhou University, China
Claire Vishik   Intel Corporation, UK
Guilin Wang   Huawei International Pte Ltd., Singapore

Huaxiong Wang	Nanyang Technological University, Singapore
Jingsong Wang	Tianjin University of Technology, China
Lihua Wang	National Institute of Information and Communications Technology, Japan
Liming Wang	Institute of Information Engineering, Chinese Academy of Sciences, China
Lina Wang	Wuhan University, China
Weiping Wen	Peking University, China
Jian Weng	Jinan University, China
Andreas Wespi	IBM Zurich Research Laboratory, Switzerland
Wenling Wu	Institute of Software, Chinese Academy of Sciences, China
Yingjie Wu	Fuzhou University, China
Yongdong Wu	Institute for Infocomm Research, Singapore
Zhenqiang Wu	Shaanxi Normal University, China
Shouhuai Xu	University of Texas at San Antonio, USA
Zhen Xu	Institute of Information Engineering, Chinese Academy of Sciences, China
Rui Xue	The Institute of Information Engineering, CAS, China
Min Yang	Fudan University, China
Alec Yasinsac	University of South Alabama, USA
Siu Ming Yiu	The University of Hong Kong, Hong Kong
Yong Yu	Shaanxi Normal University, China
Fangguo Zhang	Sun Yat-sen University, China
Hongli Zhang	Harbin Institute of Technology, China
Rui Zhang	Institute of Information Engineering, Chinese Academy of Sciences, China
Wentao Zhang	Institute of Information Engineering, Chinese Academy of Sciences, China
Chao Zheng	Institute of Information Engineering, Chinese Academy of Sciences, China
Yongbin Zhou	Institute of Information Engineering, Chinese Academy of Sciences, China

Additional Reviewers

Aminanto, Muhamad Erza	Chu, Cheng Kang	Jiang, Linzhi
Bao, Judong	Cui, Yuzhao	Kang, Xin
Chan, Raymond	Cuppens, Nora	Li, Baichuan
Chen, Haoyu	Fan, Limin	Li, Hongbo
Chen, Hua	Feng, Chao	Li, Huige
Chen, Zehong	Gong, Junqing	Li, Jiguo
Chen, Zhide	Guo, Qingwen	Li, Juanru
Cheng, Chen-Mou	Hamm, Peter	Li, Yannan
Choi, Rak Yong	Harborth, David	Li, Zhi
Chou, Tung	Huang, Jianye	Li, Zichen

Lin, Cheng-Jun
Liu, Jianghua
Liu, Xiangyu
Liu, Yuejun
Liu, Zhen
Liu, Zhiqiang
Long, Yu
Ma, Hui
Ma, Jinhua
Minaud, Brice
Mishra, Pradeep
Nakasho, Kazuhisa
Nan, Yuhong
Niu, Ben
Okumura, Shinya
Qin, Yu
Schmid, Michael
Schmitz, Christopher
Shen, Jiachen

Su, Chunhua
Sun, Hung-Min
Tan, Benjamin
    Hong Meng
Tan, Gaosheng
Tao, Yang
Tomasin, Stefano
Tsuchida, Hikaru
Wang, Fuqun
Wang, Haijiang
Wang, Huige
Wang, Licheng
Wang, Weijia
Wang, Yuntao
Wang, Zhu
Wei, Lifei
Wei, Yichen
Wen, Joy
Xiao, Yuting

Xie, Shaohao
Xu, Rui
Xu, Yanhong
Xue, Liang
Xv, Lingling
Yanai, Naoto
Yang, Rupeng
Yang, Wenbo
Yang, Yanjiang
Yuen, John
Zhang, Huang
Zhang, Juanyang
Zhang, Kai
Zhang, Lei
Zhang, Rocky
Zhang, Yuexin
Zhang, Zheng
Zhou, Shunfan

Contents

Attacks and Attacks Defense

Wireless Sensor Network Security

Security Applications

Malicious Code Defense and Mobile Security

IoT Security

Healthcare and Industrial Control System Security

Privacy Protection

Engineering Issues of Crypto

Cloud and E-commerce Security

Security Protocols

Formal Analysis and Randomness Test

Formal Analysis of a TTP-Free Blacklistable Anonymous Credentials System

Weijin Wang[1,2](✉), Jingbin Liu[1,2], Yu Qin[1], and Dengguo Feng[1,3]

[1] TCA, Institute of Software, Chinese Academy of Sciences, Beijing, China
{wangweijin,liujingbin,qin_yu,feng}@tca.iscas.ac.cn
[2] University of Chinese Academy of Sciences, Beijing, China
[3] SKLCS, Institute of Software, Chinese Academy of Sciences, Beijing, China

Abstract. This paper firstly introduces a novel security definition for BLAC-like schemes (BLAC represents TTP-free BLacklistable Anonymous Credentials) in symbolic model using applied pi calculus, which is suitable for automated reasoning via formal analysis tools. We model the definitions of some common security properties: authenticity, non-framebility, mis-authentication resistance and privacy (anonymity and unlinkability). The case study of these security definitions is demonstrated by modelling and analyzing BLACR (BLAC with Reputation) system. We verify these security properties by Blanchet's ProVerif and a ZKP (Zero-Knowledge Proof) compiler developed by Backes *et al.*. In particular, we analyze the express-lane authentication in BLACR. The analysis discovers a known attack that can be carried out by any potential user to escape from being revoked as he wishes. We provide a revised variant that can be proved successfully by ProVerif, which also indicates that the fix provided by ExBLACR (Extending BLACR) is incorrect.

Keywords: Formal analysis · Anonymous credential · ProVerif
BLACR

1 Introduction

Anonymous credentials allow users to obtain credentials on their identities and prove possession of these credentials anonymously. There are three parties in the anonymous credentials system: *users* obtain credentials from *issuers* (or GM, indicating Group Manager). They can then present these credentials to *verifiers* (or SP, indicating Service Provider) in an anonymous manner. The verifiers can check the validity of users' anonymous credentials but cannot identify them.

Practical solutions for anonymous credentials have been proposed, such as IBM's identity mixer [19] and TCG (Trusted Computing Group)'s DAA (Direct Anonymous Attestation) protocol [14,15], Microsoft's U-Prove [22], or Nymble system [21]. To avoid misbehavior, most of schemes introduce a TTP (Trust Third Party) to revoke misbehaved users. However, having a TTP capable of

© Springer International Publishing AG, part of Springer Nature 2018
S. Qing et al. (Eds.): ICICS 2017, LNCS 10631, pp. 3–16, 2018.
https://doi.org/10.1007/978-3-319-89500-0_1

deanonymizing or linking users' access may be dangerous. Recognizing this, elimination of such TTP while still supporting revocation is desired. In this spirit, many schemes had been proposed, such as EPID [16], BLAC [27], BLACR [8], ExBLACR [29], PEREA [6], PERM [7], PE(AR)^2 [32], FARB [30]. In these schemes, SP can punish users without the assistance of TTP, and the users must convince SP that they satisfy the predetermined authentication policy in a zero-knowledge way.

All these schemes are claimed to be provable secure except for U-Prove. However, computational security definitions of these schemes are very complex, thus making the proof of security error-prone. For example, Camenisch et al. [18] pointed out that the known security models of DAA are non-comprehensive and even insecure recently, and gave a security model under universally composable framework. BLACR system is also reported that a feasible attack exists [29]. Recognizing this, we tend to prove these complex schemes in another perspective, namely formal methods, which are widely used to verify cryptographic protocols. We think formal analysis can help us to find the logical errors of protocols and become a complement of the computational security proof.

Fortunately, formal analysis has shown its power to prove the complex security definitions although the formal analysis of anonymous credentials is relatively limited (almost for DAA). Arapinis et al. [4] presented a framework for analyzing the unlinkability and anonymity in the applied pi calculus. Arapinis et al. [2,3] make use of this framework to analyze the privacy of composing protocols using ProVerif [13]. Smyth et al. [25,26] introduced a definition of privacy for DAA schemes that was suited to automated reasoning by ProVerif. They discovered a vulnerability in the RSA-based DAA scheme and fixed it to meet their definition of privacy. Xi et al. [31] utilized ProVerif to analyze the DAA scheme in TPM 2.0. They put forward a definition of forward anonymity for DAA scheme in symbolic model. To deal with the complex zero-knowledge proof within equational theory, Backes et al. [10] presented an abstraction of zero-knowledge proof that is formalized by the applied pi calculus and developed a compiler to encode this abstraction into a rewriting system that is suited to ProVerif. They also performed an analysis for DAA using this approach and found a novel attack.

Contributions. In this paper, we present a novel definition for some common security properties of BLAC-like schemes via applied pi calculus. Specifically, we formalize authenticity, non-frameability and mis-authentication resistance as correspondence properties and privacy as equivalence properties using applied pi calculus (Sect. 2).

For a case study, we analyze BLACR system (Sect. 3). We model its subprotocols by applied pi processes and defined some main processes to analyze those security properties. Our analysis result shows that the BLACR holds these security properties in the normal-lane form (Sect. 3.4). Specially, we also model and analyze the express-lane authentication of BLACR (Sect. 3.5). This analysis shows an anticipative action if a user always does not trigger the revocation conditions but reports a known vulnerability when a user have potential to get revoked. This attack allows a user to escape from being revoked as he wishes after he owns a express-lane token, which disables the security policy of BLACR. Then we provide a revised variant that can be proved by ProVerif. The revision also shows that the fix provided by ExBLACR is incorrect.

2   Syntax and Security Definition

We adopt the process calculus of ProVerif [1,11,12,20], which is inspired by applied pi calculus [23] to define the security properties. Without ambiguity, we sometimes call it applied pi calculus instead of ProVerif calculus. Due to space limitation, the review of ProVerif calculus will be presented in the full version.

2.1   Syntax

Roughly speaking, a TTP-free blacklistable anonymous credentials system contains the following algorithms:

Initialization. This algorithm initializes the system parameters. The issuer constructs a signing key pair (pk_I, sk_I). If SP is not the issuer, then SP will construct its own key pair (pk_V, sk_V). Especially, the implementation-specific parameters will be defined, such as initializing the blacklist.

Registration. This algorithm is registration phase between the issuer and a legitimate user to enroll the user as a member in the group of registered users. Upon successful completion of this phase, The user obtains a credential signature cre on his secret value x.

Authentication. The user will generate a zero-knowledge proof to convince an SP that he has the right to obtain service. First, the user in possession of x proves that he holds a valid credential cre. Then the user convinces that he satisfies the authentication policy. Note that a *protocol transcript* τ (a ticket) must be seen by the SP to guarantee freshness and to block the authenticating user if necessary.

Verification. SP will check the validity of the received zero-knowledge proofs. If failed, the user will be blocked to access.

List Management. SP can manipulate the list with the transcript τ according to a specific authentication policy. In a reputation-based policy, the SP scores the user's action of the session with a transcript τ and executes the operation $add(L, (\tau, s))$ to add the score s to the current blacklist L.

2.2   Security Definition

In this section, we present the definitions of security properties in the symbolic model using applied pi calculus.

Assumptions and Notations. In this paper, we denote registration process as Register (for users) and Issue (for the issuer), and authentication process as Authenticate. Verification and list management processes can be combined together since they are all handled by SP, which is denoted as Verify. Initialization process will be encoded into the main process.

In process Register, event *registered* will be executed after the user successfully registers with the issuer and obtains a valid credential, otherwise, event *unregistered* will be executed. In process Authenticate, event *startAuth* represents a new authentication activated by the user. Event *acceptAuth* will be executed when the verification of zero-knowledge proofs succeeds in process Verify, and conversely, event *revoke* will be executed.

We assume that the adversary controls the execution of an arbitrary number of users in an arbitrary fashion except for learning their secret, as shown below:

ControlUsers $=!pub(id).!vp.$(Register $|$ $(p(cre).!$(Authenticate $|$ Judge))).

The adversary can choose any user (id) to run the processes Register and Authenticate. The restricted channel name p is used for delivering the credential of the user between registration and authentication.

Process Judge models the judgment of a user's state (for example, his current reputation score). We record two events in process Judge: event *satisfyPolicy* for a satisfied judgment; and event *notSatisfy* for a failure.

Authenticity. In a system with *authenticity*, an SP is assured to accept authentication only from users who satisfy the authentication policy. This definition can be parsed as the following statements:

1. SP accepts authentication from users who satisfy the authentication policy.
2. SP would never accept authentication from users who violate the policy.

Build on this understanding, we formalize *authenticity* as two correspondence properties using the events recorded in the processes.

Definition 1 (Authenticity).   Given   processes   ⟨Register, Issue, Authenticate, Verify, Judge⟩, we say authenticity is satisfied if the following correspondences are held:

$$event : acceptAuth \rightsquigarrow startAuth \& satisfyPolicy \text{ is } true.$$
$$event : acceptAuth \rightsquigarrow startAuth \& notSatisfy \text{ is } false.$$

The correspondence event:*acceptAuth* ⇝ *startAuth* & *satisfyPolicy* means that if the SP passes the verification and accepts the authentication from a user, then this user has started an authentication session and satisfied the authentication policy before. This means that the SP accepts the authentication from a user who has satisfied the policy, which is immediately corresponding to the statement 1. Similarly, the second failed correspondence is corresponding to statement 2.

Non-frameability. A user is framed if he satisfies the authentication policy, but is unable to successfully authenticate himself to an honest SP [8]. Hence, if a system satisfies *non-frameability*, then the situation that a user fails to authenticate to an honest SP but satisfies the policy should never happen.

Definition 2 (Non-frameability). Given processes in Definition 1, if correspondence event:*revoke* ⤳ *startAuth* & *satisfyPolicy* is false, non-framebility is satisfied.

This correspondence means that, if SP rejects an authentication, then the situation that a user has started this authentication session and satisfied the authentication policy would never happen, which is corresponding to the statement of non-frameability.

Mis-authentication Resistance. Mis-authentication takes place when an unregistered user successfully authenticates himself to an SP. In a system with *mis-authentication resistance*, an SP is assured to accept authentications only from registered users. we can parse this description into two statements.

1. The statement "a user successfully authenticates to an SP, but he never registered to the issuer before" is false.
2. The statement "if an SP accepts the authentication from a user, then before that, this user has registered with the issuer" is true.

Naturally, we formalize the statements into the following properties.

Definition 3 (Mis-authentication Resistance). If processes in Definition 1 are given, Mis-authentication resistance is satisfied when the following correspondences are held:

$$event : acceptAuth \rightsquigarrow startAuth \& unregistered \, is \, false.$$
$$event : acceptAuth \rightsquigarrow startAuth \& registered \, is \, true.$$

Privacy. The definition of privacy is twofold: *anonymity* and *unlinkability*, which is inspired by the formal definitions in [4].

Anonymity ensures that an adversary cannot see the difference between a system in which the user with a publicly known identity id_0 executes the analyzed processes and the system where id_0 is not present at all.

Definition 4 (Anonymity).   Given   processes   ⟨Register, Issue, Authenticate, Judge⟩, anonymity is satisfied if the following equivalence holds:

$(vid.vp.(\text{Register}|(p(cre).!(\text{Authenticate}|\text{Judge})))) \, |$
$(let \, id = id_0 \, in \, let \, p = int_0 \, in \, (\text{Register}|(p(cre).!(\text{Authenticate}|\text{Judge}))))$
$\approx$
$(!vid.vp.(\text{Register}|(p(cre).!(\text{Authenticate}|\text{Judge}))))$

Both sides of equivalence are of the same processes except that the left side executes the registration and authentication processes of the user id_0. That is to say, if the equivalence is held, then the adversary cannot tell whether or not the user id_0 has executed the registration and authentication processes.

Unlinkability ensures that a system in which the analyzed processes can be executed by a user multiple times looks the same to an adversary that the system in which the analyzed processes can be executed by the user at most once.

Definition 5 (Unlinkability). Given processes in Definition 4, unlinkability is satisfied if the following equivalence holds:

$$(!vid.vp.(\texttt{Register}|(p(cre).!(\texttt{Authenticate}|\texttt{Judge}))))$$
$$\approx$$
$$(!vid.vp.(\texttt{Register}|(p(cre).(\texttt{Authenticate}|\texttt{Judge}))))$$

The difference between two sides locates in the number of times that the authentication has been executed. On condition that this equivalence is satisfied, the adversary cannot distinguish the user executing the authentication multiple times from executing at most once.

3   Case Study: BLACR System

In this section, we model BLACR and automatically verify its security properties using formal analysis tool ProVerif. The review of ProVerif calculus and ZKP compiler are presented in the full version.

3.1   Primitives and Equational Theory

BLACR system employs BBS+ signature scheme, which is proposed by Au *et al.* [9]. In this section, we will introduce the primitives described by applied pi calculus and the associated equational theory.

We consider commitment $\texttt{commit}(x, y)$, where x is a message and y is a commitment factor (or blind factor). We also specify an open function together with the signature scheme for permitting signatures on committed values.

We consider BBS+ signature scheme $\texttt{bbssign}(m, \texttt{sk}(s))$, where m is a message to be signed, and s is a key seed to generate signing key pair $(\texttt{sk}(s), \texttt{pk}(s))$. We specify an open function $\texttt{open}(\texttt{bbssign}(\texttt{commit}(x, y),\ \texttt{sk}(s)),\ y)$ for opening the signature of a commitment. Again, we construct a verification function $\texttt{bbsver}(\texttt{open}(\texttt{bbssign}(\texttt{commit}(x, y),\ \texttt{sk}(s)),\ y),\ x,\ \texttt{pk}(s))$ for this signature. Moreover, a message recovery function $\texttt{getmess}(\texttt{open}(\texttt{bbssign}(\texttt{commit}(x,\ y),\ \texttt{sk}(s)),\ y))$ is provided to adversary for getting the signing message x.

We construct a zero-knowledge proof as function $\texttt{ZK}_{i,j}(\widetilde{M}, \widetilde{N}, F)$, where $\widetilde{M}$ is private component representing the knowledge to be proved, $\widetilde{N}$ denote the public component and F denotes a formula over those terms.

In summary, we construct a suitable signature Σ and define an equational theory E to capture the operations of cryptographic primitives. The signature can be defined as follows:

$$\Sigma = \Sigma_{\text{base}} \cup \Sigma_{ZK}, \text{ where}$$
$$\Sigma_{\text{base}} = \left\{ \begin{array}{l} \texttt{true},\texttt{false},\texttt{hash},\texttt{exp},\texttt{and},\texttt{or},\texttt{eq},\texttt{pk},\texttt{sk}, \\ \texttt{commit},\texttt{open},\texttt{bbssign},\texttt{bbsver},\texttt{getmess} \end{array} \right\}$$
$$\Sigma_{ZK} = \left\{ \texttt{ZK}_{i,j}, \texttt{Ver}_{i,j}, \texttt{Public}_i, \texttt{Formula}, \alpha_i, \beta_j | i,j \in N \right\}$$

For the signature Σ_{base}, functions $\texttt{true}$, $\texttt{false}$ are constant symbols; $\texttt{hash}$, $\texttt{pk}$, $\texttt{sk}$, $\texttt{getmess}$ are unary functions; $\texttt{exp}$, $\texttt{land}$, $\texttt{or}$, $\texttt{eq}$, $\texttt{commit}$, $\texttt{open}$, $\texttt{bbssign}$ are binary functions; $\texttt{bbsver}$ is ternary functions. The equation theory E_{base} associated with signature Σ_{base} is defined as follows:

$$\begin{aligned} E_{\text{base}} = \ & \texttt{and}(\texttt{true},\texttt{true}) = \texttt{true} \\ & \texttt{or}(\texttt{true},x) = \texttt{true} \\ & \texttt{or}(x,\texttt{true}) = \texttt{true} \\ & \texttt{eq}(x,x) = \texttt{true} \\ & \texttt{bbsver}(\texttt{open}(\texttt{bbssign}(\texttt{commit}(x,y),\texttt{sk}(s)),y),x,\texttt{pk}(s)) = \texttt{true} \\ & \texttt{getmess}(\texttt{open}(\texttt{bbssign}(\texttt{commit}(x,y),\texttt{sk}(s)),y)) = x \end{aligned}$$

Functions $\texttt{and}$, $\texttt{or}$, $\texttt{eq}$ are used for conjunction, disjunction and equality test respectively; $\texttt{hash}$ is used for hashing messages; $\texttt{exp}$ is used for the exponent operation. The rest functions are used for constructing and verifying BBS+ signature scheme.

3.2   Review of BLACR

In this section, we give a high-level description of the BLACR system. The initialization parameters include: the signing key pair $(\texttt{pk}(s_{iss}), \texttt{sk}(s_{iss}))$ of an issuer; the unique identity string sid of an SP; the number of categories m and the blacklist of each category with the thresholds TS_i. The registration process proceeds as follows.

1. The issuer sends a random challenge m_{reg} to a user.
2. The user generates a random number y and computes $C_x = \texttt{commit}(x,y)$. Then the user generates a signature proof of knowledge $\Pi_1 = SPK\{(x,y) : C_x = \texttt{commit}(x,y)\}(m_{reg})$. He sends a pair (C_x, Π_1) to the issuer.
3. The issuer computes a blind credential $bcre = \texttt{bbssign}(C_x, \texttt{sk}(s))$ if the verification of Π_1 is successful and then sends $bcre$ to the user.
4. The user opens the blind credential $cre = \texttt{open}(bcre, y)$. He outputs cre as his credential when the verification $\texttt{bbsver}(cre, x, \texttt{pk}(s))$ is true.

After the user obtains a credential cre, he can authentication to the SP multiple times using cre. The authentication process is presented below.

1. The SP sends to the user the lists for each category as well as their corresponding threshold values $\widetilde{TS} = (TS_1, ..., TS_m)$ and a random challenge m_{auth} as well as the policy Pol.

2. The user judges his reputation score s_i of each category by checking if the entries on the corresponding list belong to him. Then he tests if $s_i < TS_i$ so that *Pol* evaluates to 1.

3. If the test is successful, the user returns to the SP a pair (τ, Π_2, Π_3), where $\tau = (b, t = H(b||sid)^x)$ is the ticket associated with the current authentication session, and (Π_2, Π_3) is a pair of signature proof of knowledges. Π_2 is used to prove that τ is correctly formed with the credential *cre*: $SPK\{(x, r, cre) : C_x = \text{commit}(x, r), \text{bbsver}(cre, x, \text{pk}(s)) = \text{true}, t = \hat{b}^x\}(m_{auth})$, where $\hat{b} = H(b||sid)$; Π_3 is used to prove *Pol* evaluates to 1: $SPK\{(x, r, s_i) : C_x = \text{commit}(x, r), C_{s_{ij}} = \text{commit}(0)|_{j \notin user}, C_{s_{ij}} = \text{commit}(s_{ij})|_{j \in user}, C_{s_i} = C_{s_{i1}} \cdots C_{s_{iL}}, s_i < TS_i\}(m_{auth})$, where $j \in \{1, ..., L\}$ and L is the length of the corresponding list.

4. The SP verifies the proofs (Π_2, Π_3).

If verification of (Π_2, Π_3) is successful, SP can ensure that the user is a valid one to access the service.

BLACR also realizes a novel approach called express-lane authentication, which can expedite the authentication. To adapt this mechanism, SP should issue a token that is a signature on the aggregated reputation score prior to a time point upon a successful authentication. Then the user can use this token to convince his reputation score in that time instead of proving whether or not an entry belongs to him for every entry in the blacklist. However, using a token disables the SP's capability of unblacklisting since removing entries from blacklist would disable the validity of the token.

3.3   Processes for BLACR

We model the registration phase by a pair of processes ⟨Register, Issue⟩ presented in Fig. 1. We assume that every user has a unique id, which can be a limited resource such as IP, mobile phone number to prevent sybil attack. To model the secret value x bound to limited resource, we present a private function bind to construct the secret value $x = \text{bind}(id)$. We also assume that there is only one category for blacklist, thus there exists only one threshold value TS.

The user first generates a zero-knowledge proof $\Pi_1 = \text{ZK}(x, y; id, C_x, m_{reg}; F_{reg})$ to ensure the ownership of x with the formula $F_{reg} = \text{and}(\alpha_1 = \text{bind}(\beta_1), \beta_2 = \text{commit}(\alpha_1, \alpha_2))$. The issuer verifies the validity of Π_1. If the verification is successful, the issuer will check if this user is a sybil. We introduce a predicate *sybil* in the issuer process. The predicate *sybil* is true if and only if the user id has been marked sybil. For example, we could set $sybil = \text{or}(id = sybilid_1, id = sybilid_2)$ if $sybilid_1, sybilid_2$ have been marked sybil. For a valid id, the issuer signs the commitment C_x and sends the blind signature *bcre* to the user. The user will open the blind signature *bcre* and get a credential *cre*.

We model the authentication phase by a pair of processes ⟨Authenticate, Verify⟩ presented in Fig. 2. To generate zero-knowledge proofs, the user must know his reputation score. However, the calculus of ProVerif cannot afford to handle either the algebraic operations or the state transition, so we need a trick

```
Register =                                    Issue =
  c(m_reg).                                     vm_reg.c̄⟨m_reg⟩ .c((C_x, Pi_1)).
  let x = bind(id) in                           if public_2(Pi_1) = C_x then
  vy.let C_x = commit(x, y) in                  if public_3(Pi_1) = m_reg then
  let Pi_1 = ZK(x, y; id, C_x, m_reg; F_reg) in if Ver_{2,3}(F_reg, Pi_1) = true then
  c̄⟨(C_x, Pi_1)⟩ .c(bcre).                       let id = public_1(Pi_1) in
  let cre = open(bcre, y) in                    if sybil = true then 0 else
  if bbsver(cre, x, pk(s_iss)) = true then      let bcre = bbssign(C_x, sk(s_iss)) in
    event(registered).! p̄⟨cre⟩                  c̄⟨bcre⟩
  else
    event(unregistered)
```

Fig. 1. Process calculus for registration

to model the judgment process. We assume a trusted judgment process outputs the judged score for users. We set the judgment process as follows.

$$Judge = asg(s).$$
$$if\ s = TS\ then\ \mathsf{event}(\mathit{notSatisfy}).\overline{jud}\,\langle TS\rangle$$
$$else\ \mathsf{event}(\mathit{satisfyPolicy}).\overline{jud}\,\langle ltTS\rangle$$

In a satisfied score judgment, event *satisfyPolicy* is executed and a term $ltTS$ (means less than the threshold value TS) is sent on the private channel jud. Otherwise, event *notSatisfy* is executed and the threshold value TS is sent on the channel jud.

```
Authenticate =                         Verify =
  c(m_auth).vr.vb.vr_s                   vm_auth.c̄⟨(v_auth)⟩ .c((Pi_2, Pi_3)).
  let x = bind(id) in                    if public_2(Pi_2) = pk(s_iss) then
  let C_x = commit(x, r) in              if public_5(Pi_2) = hash((public_3(Pi_2),
  let h = hash((b, sid)) in                sid)) then
  let t = exp(h, x) in                   if public_6(Pi_2) = m_auth then
  let Pi_2 = ZK(x, r, cre; C_x, pk(s_iss), b, t, h,  if Ver_{3,6}(F_sig, Pi_2) = true then
    m_auth; F_sig) in                    let C_x = public_1(Pi_2) in
  jud(s).let C_s = commit(s, r_s) in     let b = public_3(Pi_2) in
  let Pi_3 = ZK(x, r, s, r_s; C_x, C_s, ltTS, m_auth;  let t = public_4(Pi_2) in
    F_Pol) in                            if public_1(Pi_3) = C_x then
  event(startAuth).c̄⟨(Pi_2, Pi_3)⟩       if public_3(Pi_3) = ltTS then
                                         if public_4(Pi_3) = m_auth then
                                         if Ver_{4,4}(F_Pol, Pi_3) = true then
                                           event(acceptAuth).! l̄t⟨(b, t)⟩
                                         else
                                           event(revoke)
```

Fig. 2. Process calculus of authentication

Then the user generates two zero-knowledge proofs: Π_2 with formula $F_{sig} =$ and(and($\beta_1 = \mathsf{commit}(\alpha_1, \alpha_2)$, bbsver($\alpha_3, \alpha_1, \beta_2$) = true), $\beta_4 = \exp(\beta_5, \alpha_1)$)

and Π_3 with formula $F_{Pol} = \text{and}(\text{and}(\beta_1 = \text{commit}(\alpha_1, \alpha_2), \beta_2 = \text{commit}(\alpha_3, \alpha_4)),$ $\beta_3 = \alpha_3)$. The process executes the event *startAuth* before it outputs $\langle \Pi_2, \Pi_3 \rangle$.

The process of SP verifies $\langle \Pi_2, \Pi_3 \rangle$ and executes the event *acceptAuth* when all verifications are passed, otherwise, it executes the event *revoke*. For a successful authentication, this process also "stores" the ticket (b, t) of current authentication by a private channel lt for further assigning reputation score.

3.4   Experiment Results

In this section, we examine the security properties defined in Sect. 2 using ProVerif. The processes above will be expressed as specifications of ZKP compiler and then be encoded into the inputs of ProVerif. The detailed specifications can be found in [28].

Security Properties as Correspondences. Security goals *Authenticity, Non-frameability* and *Mis-authentication resistance* are expressed by correspondences. To verify these properties, we implement a main process C-Process as follows:

> C-Process
> $vs_{iss}.vs_{ver}.vjud.vlt.let\ c = pub\ in\ (\overline{pub}\ \langle \text{pk}(s_{iss}) \rangle\ |\ \overline{pub}\ \langle \text{pk}(s_{ver}) \rangle\ |$
> (! issue) | (! (Verify | AssignScore)) | ControlUsers)

Note that we also initialize a key pair for the SP since we set $sid = \text{pk}(s_{ver})$ to identify the SP for computing the ticket.

Result 1. *Given the main process* C-Process, ProVerif *succeeds in proving the correspondence statements defined in Sect. 2.2. Hence, security properties Authenticity, Non-frameability and Mis-authentication resistance are held.*

Security Properties as Equivalence. Privacy of BLACR is expressed by biprocess. We identify two kinds of privacy: *anonymity* and *unlinkability*. We implement a main process A-Process to capture anonymity.

A-Process
$vs_{iss}.vs_{ver}.vjud.vlt.vint_0.vint_1.let\ c = pub\ in\ ($
$\overline{pub}\ \langle \text{pk}(s_{iss}) \rangle\ |\overline{pub}\ \langle \text{pk}(s_{ver}) \rangle\ |(!\text{Issue})\ |\text{Users}|$
$(let\ (id, p) = (id_0, int_0)\ in\ \text{Register})|(vid_1.let\ (id, p) = (id_1, int_1)\ in\ ($
  $\text{Register}|int_0(cre_0).int_1(cre_1).$
  $let\ (id, cre) = (\text{diff}[id_0, id_1], \text{diff}[cre_0, cre_1])\ in\ (\text{Authenticate}|\text{Judge})))$
$)$
where
  Users $=!vid.!vp.(\text{Register}|(p(cre).!(\text{Authenticate}|\text{Judge})))$

To adapt the definition of anonymity, we use the process Users instead of ControlUsers to capture arbitrary users except id_0 executing the processes.

Encoding anonymity in this way, we have the left side of diff representing an execution of publicly known id id_0, while the right side of diff represents an execution of unknown id id_1 (a restrict id). In fact, the right side of diff is a case of Users. Hence, it directly corresponds to the definition in Sect. 2.2 and we succeed in reducing the problem of proving anonymity to the diff-equivalence that can be verified by ProVerif.

Result 2. *Given the main process A-Process, ProVerif succeeds in proving the diff-equivalence, therefore, anonymity is satisfied.*

We also implement a main process U-Process to capture unlinkability.

> U-Process
> $vs_{iss}.vs_{ver}.vjud.vL.let\ c = pub\ in\ (\overline{pub}\ \langle \mathrm{pk}(s_{iss}) \rangle)\ |\overline{pub}\ \langle \mathrm{pk}(s_{ver}) \rangle\ |$
> (! issue) |Unlinkability)

where

Unlinkability =
$!vid_1.vint_1.((let\ (id, p) = (id_1, int_1)\ in\ \mathrm{Register})|(!vid_2.vint_2.($
$\quad (let\ (id, p) = (id_2, int_2)\ in\ \mathrm{Register})|(int_1(cre_1).int_2(cre_2).$
$\quad let\ (id, cre) = (\mathrm{diff}[id_1, id_2], \mathrm{diff}[cre_1, cre_2])\ in\ (\mathrm{Authenticate}|\mathrm{Judge}))\ ))$
$)$

Thinking inside this process, we have that the left side of the diff representing a user executes the system many time, while the right side represents the users execute the system at most once (The user id_2 is always different for each execution of processes of the user id_1).

Result 3. *Given the main process U-Process, ProVerif succeeds in proving the diff-equivalence, therefore, unlinkability is satisfied.*

3.5   Express-Lane Case in BLACR

To reward active users, BLACR offers express-lane authentication to speed up the authentication process. In the express-lane authentication, an SP additionally signs a credential (a token) on the score of previous time after the verification succeeds. This token will be used in the next authentication.

However, an additional state transition that ProVerif cannot deal with is introduced since a token generated by current authentication must be transferred to the next time for use. Hence we have to bring in another trick to adapt ProVerif. We divide the analysis into two scenarios: the first is the one that a user is honest people, thus always getting a valid token and proceeding as expectation; the second is the one that a user will be revoked and test if BLACR proceeds as expectation.

Since the processes are similar to the normal one, they will be omit for the space limitation. Specifically, we have presented the details in the full version.

Result 4. ProVerif *discovers an attack trace in the second express-lane authentication. As a consequence, we say that the token mechanism of BLACR does not work properly.*

The attack trace shows that a replay attack can be carried out by a malicious user as follows: in the second express-lane authentication, the user finds his aggregated reputation score does not satisfy the authentication policy. But he still proceeds in this way: he uses a preceding token that is enough to make the aggregate score satisfying the policy. This attack can happen since these tokens do not consist of any labels to distinguish each other.

In general, this attack can be applied to two scenarios violating the security policy: the first one is that a user can utilize an old token to escape from being revoked; the other is that a user in possession of a token can conduct an express-lane authentication at any time, regardless of whether he is an active user.

This attack can be fixed by refining the definition of token tk. The token must consist of the timestamp information t. We revise the processes with the timestamp and the verification is successful by ProVerif.

In fact, our solution in symbolic representation mode indicates that the fix presented in ExBLACR still does not work properly since the timestamp in the proving process of ExBLACR does not be revealed. In such way, a malicious user can still conduct the replay attack mentioned above, because the SP can just ensure the token tk is correct but can not know the timestamp t corresponding to this token.

4   Conclusion

This paper presents the definitions of some common security properties for BLAC-like systems in the symbolic model using applied pi calculus. We express these definitions as correspondence and equivalence properties. As a case study, we verify these properties in BLACR system. The analysis finds a known attack aiming at the token mechanism in the express-lane authentication. This revision with a successful verification in ProVerif also indicates that the fix provided by ExBLACR is incorrect.

Actually, our model is of approximate due to the nature of ProVerif. We think some other modelling method can also be under consideration to record state, such as multiset rewriting rules (Tamarin tool [24]) or stateful variant of applied pi calculus [5,17]. Another extension may be lying in research of composing protocols as mentioned in the introduction. These may be the future work.

Acknowledgements. The research presented in this paper is supported by the National Grand Fundamental Research 973 Program of China under Grant No.2013CB338003 and the National Natural Science Foundation of China under Grant Nos. 91118006, 61202414.

References

1. Abadi, M., Blanchet, B.: Analyzing security protocols with secrecy types and logic programs. J. ACM (JACM) **52**(1), 102–146 (2005)
2. Arapinis, M., Cheval, V., Delaune, S.: Verifying privacy-type properties in a modular way. In: CSF 2012, pp. 95–109. IEEE (2012)
3. Arapinis, M., Cheval, V., Delaune, S.: Composing security protocols: from confidentiality to privacy. In: Focardi, R., Myers, A. (eds.) POST 2015. LNCS, vol. 9036, pp. 324–343. Springer, Heidelberg (2015). https://doi.org/10.1007/978-3-662-46666-7_17
4. Arapinis, M., Chothia, T., Ritter, E., Ryan, M.: Analysing unlinkability and anonymity using the applied pi calculus. In: CSF 2010, pp. 107–121. IEEE (2010)
5. Arapinis, M., Phillips, J., Ritter, E., Ryan, M.D.: Statverif: verification of stateful processes. J. Comput. Secur. **22**(5), 743–821 (2014)
6. Au, M.H., Tsang, P.P., Kapadia, A.: PEREA: practical TTP-free revocation of repeatedly misbehaving anonymous users. ACM Trans. Inf. Syst. Secur. (TISSEC) **14**(4), 29 (2011)
7. Au, M.H., Kapadia, A.: PERM: practical reputation-based blacklisting without TTPs. In: CCS 2012, pp. 929–940. ACM (2012)
8. Au, M.H., Kapadia, A., Susilo, W.: BLACR: TTP-free blacklistable anonymous credentials with reputation. In: NDSS Symposium 2012: 19th Network & Distributed System Security Symposium, pp. 1–17. Internet Society (2012)
9. Au, M.H., Susilo, W., Mu, Y.: Constant-size dynamic k-TAA. In: De Prisco, R., Yung, M. (eds.) SCN 2006. LNCS, vol. 4116, pp. 111–125. Springer, Heidelberg (2006). https://doi.org/10.1007/11832072_8
10. Backes, M., Maffei, M., Unruh, D.: Zero-knowledge in the applied pi-calculus and automated verification of the direct anonymous attestation protocol. In: SP 2008, pp. 202–215. IEEE (2008)
11. Blanchet, B.: Automatic proof of strong secrecy for security protocols. In: SP 2004, pp. 86–100. IEEE (2004)
12. Blanchet, B., Abadi, M., Fournet, C.: Automated verification of selected equivalences for security protocols. In: 20th IEEE Symposium on Logic in Computer Science. Proceedings, pp. 331–340. IEEE (2005)
13. Blanchet, B., et al.: ProVerif: cryptographic protocol verifier in the formal model. http://prosecco.gforge.inria.fr/personal/bblanche/proverif/
14. Brickell, E., Camenisch, J., Chen, L.: Direct anonymous attestation. In: Proceedings of the 11th ACM Conference on Computer and Communications Security, pp. 132–145. ACM (2004)
15. Brickell, E., Chen, L., Li, J.: A new direct anonymous attestation scheme from bilinear maps. In: Lipp, P., Sadeghi, A.-R., Koch, K.-M. (eds.) Trust 2008. LNCS, vol. 4968, pp. 166–178. Springer, Heidelberg (2008). https://doi.org/10.1007/978-3-540-68979-9_13
16. Brickell, E., Li, J.: Enhanced privacy ID: a direct anonymous attestation scheme with enhanced revocation capabilities. In: Proceedings of the 2007 ACM Workshop on Privacy in Electronic Society, pp. 21–30. ACM (2007)
17. Bruni, A., Modersheim, S., Nielson, F., Nielson, H.R.: Set-pi: set membership p-calculus. In: CSF 2015, pp. 185–198. IEEE (2015)
18. Camenisch, J., Drijvers, M., Lehmann, A.: Universally composable direct anonymous attestation. In: Cheng, C.-M., Chung, K.-M., Persiano, G., Yang, B.-Y. (eds.) PKC 2016. LNCS, vol. 9615, pp. 234–264. Springer, Heidelberg (2016). https://doi.org/10.1007/978-3-662-49387-8_10

19. Camenisch, J., et al.: Specification of the identity mixer cryptographic library, version 2.3. 1, 7 December 2010
20. Cheval, V., Blanchet, B.: Proving more observational equivalences with ProVerif. In: Basin, D., Mitchell, J.C. (eds.) POST 2013. LNCS, vol. 7796, pp. 226–246. Springer, Heidelberg (2013). https://doi.org/10.1007/978-3-642-36830-1_12
21. Johnson, P.C., Kapadia, A., Tsang, P.P., Smith, S.W.: Nymble: anonymous IP-address blocking. In: Borisov, N., Golle, P. (eds.) PET 2007. LNCS, vol. 4776, pp. 113–133. Springer, Heidelberg (2007). https://doi.org/10.1007/978-3-540-75551-7_8
22. Paquin, C., Zaverucha, G.: U-prove cryptographic specification v1. 1. Technical report, revision 3. Microsoft Corporation (2013)
23. Ryan, M.D., Smyth, B.: Applied pi calculus. In: Cortier, V., Kremer, S. (eds.) Formal Models and Techniques for Analyzing Security Protocols, Chap. 6. IOS Press (2011)
24. Schmidt, B., Meier, S., Cremers, C., Basin, D.: Automated analysis of Diffie-Hellman protocols and advanced security properties. In: CSF 2012, pp. 78–94. IEEE (2012)
25. Smyth, B., Ryan, M., Chen, L.: Formal analysis of anonymity in ECC-based direct anonymous attestation schemes. In: Barthe, G., Datta, A., Etalle, S. (eds.) FAST 2011. LNCS, vol. 7140, pp. 245–262. Springer, Heidelberg (2012). https://doi.org/10.1007/978-3-642-29420-4_16
26. Smyth, B., Ryan, M.D., Chen, L.: Formal analysis of privacy in direct anonymous attestation schemes. Sci. Comput. Program. **111**, 300–317 (2015)
27. Tsang, P.P., Au, M.H., Kapadia, A., Smith, S.W.: BLAC: revoking repeatedly misbehaving anonymous users without relying on TTPs. ACM Trans. Inf. Syst. Secur. (TISSEC) **13**(4), 39 (2010)
28. Wang, W.: Proverif inputs for analyzing BLACR system. https://github.com/WangWeijin/Formal-analysis-of-BLACR-system
29. Wang, W., Feng, D., Qin, Y., Shao, J., Xi, L., Chu, X.: ExBLACR: extending BLACR system. In: Susilo, W., Mu, Y. (eds.) ACISP 2014. LNCS, vol. 8544, pp. 397–412. Springer, Cham (2014). https://doi.org/10.1007/978-3-319-08344-5_26
30. Xi, L., Feng, D.: FARB: fast anonymous reputation-based blacklisting without TTPs. In: Proceedings of the 13th Workshop on Privacy in the Electronic Society, pp. 139–148. ACM (2014)
31. Xi, L., Feng, D.: Formal analysis of DAA-related APIs in TPM 2.0. In: Au, M.H., Carminati, B., Kuo, C.-C.J. (eds.) NSS 2014. LNCS, vol. 8792, pp. 421–434. Springer, Cham (2014). https://doi.org/10.1007/978-3-319-11698-3_32
32. Yu, K.Y., Yuen, T.H., Chow, S.S.M., Yiu, S.M., Hui, L.C.K.: PE(AR)^2: privacy-enhanced anonymous authentication with reputation and revocation. In: Foresti, S., Yung, M., Martinelli, F. (eds.) ESORICS 2012. LNCS, vol. 7459, pp. 679–696. Springer, Heidelberg (2012). https://doi.org/10.1007/978-3-642-33167-1_39

An Efficiency Optimization Scheme for the On-the-Fly Statistical Randomness Test

Jiahui Shen[1,2,3], Tianyu Chen[1,2(✉)], Lei Wang[1,2], and Yuan Ma[1,2]

[1] Institute of Information Engineering, Chinese Academy of Sciences, Beijing, China
{shenjiahui,chentianyu,wanglei,mayuan}@iie.ac.cn
[2] Data Assurance and Communication Security Research Center,
Chinese Academy of Sciences, Beijing, China
[3] School of Cyber Security, University of Chinese Academy of Sciences,
Huairou, China

Abstract. In many cryptographic systems, random number can significantly influence its security. Although in practice random number generators (RNGs) are allowed to adopt only after strict analysis and security evaluation, the environmental factors also may lead the randomness of generated sequences to degrade. Therefore, on-the-fly statistical randomness test should be used to evaluate a candidate random sequence. Unfortunately, existing randomness test methods, such as the NIST test suite, are not well suitable to directly serve as on-the-fly test, because timely execution is usually not considered in their designs. In this paper, we propose a scheme to optimize the efficiency of randomness test suites, that is, providing the optimized order of the tests in a test suite, so that an unqualified sequence can be rejected as early as possible. This scheme finds out the optimized order by balancing the coverage, independence and time consumption of each test, and minimizing the average elimination time. We apply this optimization scheme on the revised NIST test suite as an instance. Experimental results on the sequences of 128 and 256 bits, demonstrate that the optimized efficiency approximates to the theoretical optimum and the scheme can be quickly implemented.

Keywords: On-the-fly statistical randomness test
Efficiency optimization · Execution order
Average elimination time used · Multi-attribute weight allocation

1 Introduction

Random number has numerous applications in a diverse set of areas ranging from statistics to cryptography. For cryptographic applications it is crucial to generate random bits which will be unpredictable even by the strongest adversary. The random sequence can be generated by two ways: true-random number generators (TRNGs) and pseudo-random number generators (PRNGs). Many studies have proved entropy source of random number generators (RNGs) is impressionable for many environmental condition changes [1], such as temperature,

© Springer International Publishing AG, part of Springer Nature 2018
S. Qing et al. (Eds.): ICICS 2017, LNCS 10631, pp. 17–35, 2018.
https://doi.org/10.1007/978-3-319-89500-0_2

humidity, tolerance of noise, ageing of components and so on. Besides, malicious attacks also impact the entropy source, such as the frequency injection attack [2]. Whether the attack or a great change of any of the above environment variables will induce some statistical weaknesses of the output of RNGs. However, how to evaluate the randomness of sequences still stir controversy today.

On-the-fly test is one of testing modes to evaluate the randomness of RNGs by several basic tests. Only the eligible random sequences can be used in cryptographic system. According to the requirements for online test in [3,4], we summarize the rules for on-the-fly test as follows.

- (R1) The on-the-fly test should reject sequences when any test fails, which is different from the requirement of traditional testing that collects the result of each test.
- (R2) On-the-fly test should detect statistical weaknesses of rejected sequences as early as possible, namely the delay introduced by an on-the-fly test should be short in order to meet the requirement of high efficiency.
- (R3) On-the-fly test is oriented towards such applications as cloud encryption/storage service, real-time encrypted communication, etc. Due to the time constraint of these applications, the length of sequences is usually relatively short, such as 128 bits for AES, 256 and 512 bits for hash functions.

A typical scenario is cloud service, for instance, unified authentication system. The cloud server is intended for a mass of clients, and there is a huge demand for random sequences. For security reasons, not only should each candidate sequences be tested by on-the-fly test before using, but a complete set of tests should be employed to get a reliable test result. However, if the execution of the on-the-fly test suite used is inefficient, it will directly reduce the operating speed of servers. Hence, on the premise of ensuring the reliability of test results, how to improve the testing efficiency (called *efficiency* for short) of on-the-fly test is the primary focus of this paper.

To detect all rejected sequences and ensure the reliability of test results, we commonly adopt statistical test suites as on-the-fly test instead of the basic tests. However, existing test suites are not adequate to on-the-fly test because of their inefficient execution. For example, the NIST test suite (i.e. SP 800-22 test suite) [5], which is widely used, traditionally executes tests in a default order and prints the result of all the tests. Due to rule (R1), efficient tests on sequence should reject one if any test fails. In fact it is often time-consuming for most rejected sequences to be eliminated by many tests execution order, and it does not coincide with rule (R2). This phenomenon is obvious in testing relatively "short sequences" particularly. Under the default execution order in the NIST, it may guarantee arrest unbalance sequences early via running frequency test at first, but efficiency is not optimal under this default order. Meanwhile, in line with rule (R3), some tests are excluded for incompatibility with the length requirement, such as binary matrix rank test, discrete Fourier transform test and maulers universal test, which require much longer sequences. In conclusion, the testing strategy of NIST needs to be fine-tuned to serve as on-the-fly test, and there is great potential to improve the efficiency through adjusting the execution order.

In this paper, we present three influence factors on test efficiency: coverage, independence and time consumption. The former two factors measure the ability to eliminate rejected sequences, and the independent coverage of a test to all other tests, respectively. The last one represents the execution time of a test, which can be got by experimental measurement. Nevertheless, it is difficult to calculate the exact values of the former two in theory. One method can traverse all the sequences of a specific length in experiment, but just for 20 or 30 bits [6]. In addition, even if we get values of the factors, it is also difficult to quantify the effects of them on efficiency. Because all factors should be considered together for the quantification, in fact there are opposite effects among the three factors, namely the larger the former two are (i.e. positive effect), the longer the last one is usually (i.e. negative effect). Based on these, we meet two challenges to obtain the optimized order: (1) acquiring the values of these factors of each test for sequence lengths 128, 256, *etc.* (2) quantifying the effects of the factors on efficiency comprehensively.

For efficiency improvement of on-the-fly test, in this paper we want to seek out an appropriate execution order. To attain this, we establish a model for evaluating efficiency. In this model, we identify influence factors on efficiency and present a metric. In consideration of the factors, we design an efficiency optimization scheme (called *optimization scheme* in the remainder). For instance, we utilize the NIST test suite to get values of these factors by random sampling method, and give a comprehensive verification for the feasibility. Then we adopt multi-attribute weight allocation to quantify the contribution of these factors to the efficiency. Finally, according to contributions, we present an optimized order for 128- or 256- bit sequences and evaluate its efficiency. Evaluation results indicate that our optimized order improves the testing efficiency by 33% in comparison with the NIST default order, and also approaches the optimum among all the possible orders.

Structure. The rest of this paper is organized as follows. In Sect. 2, we overview the related work on statistical tests and efficiency improvement methods. In Sect. 3, we establish the model for evaluation of efficiency and calculate the average elimination time by a metric. In Sect. 4, we design an optimization scheme for improving efficiency, and apply it to the NIST test suite as an instance. The evaluation on optimized results is shown in Sect. 5. We conclude our work and discuss the future work in Sect. 6.

2   Related Work

2.1   Standards for Statistical Randomness Test

There are a number of statistical test standards, including NIST SP 800-22 [5] and FIPS 140-2 [7,8] issued by NIST, AIS 31 [9] issued by Bundesamt für Sicherheit in der Informationstechnik (BSI), Diehard Battery [10] proposed by

Marsaglia, TestU01 [11] proposed by L'Ecuyer and Simard, *etc.* L'Ecuyer [12] studied some main techniques for theoretical and statistical tests. In our study, we focus on the efficiency optimization of NIST SP 800-22 test suite, because of the similar tests and testing strategy among these test suites. Meaning that, our optimization scheme is also suitable for other test suites as well as the SP 800-22.

In statistical test suites, tests are executed in a given execution order to test the sequences in series. In the NIST test suite, there is a default order [5] executed by the test: $\{T_1 - T_2 - T_{13} - T_3 - T_4 - T_5 - T_6 - T_7 - T_8 - T_9 - T_{12} - T_{14} - T_{15} - T_{11} - T_{10}\}$. And the serial number of tests is shown in Table 1. Note that the execution order does not influence the result of the NIST test suite, so we can adjust the order to find the optimized one.

Table 1. The 15 statistical randomness tests in SP 800-22

No.	T_1	T_2	T_3	T_4	T_5
Test	Frequency	Block frequency	Runs	Longest-run	Binary matrix rank
No.	T_6	T_7	T_8	T_9	T_{10}
Test	Discrete fourier transform	Non-overlapping TM	Overlapping TM	Maurer's universal	Linear complexity
No.	T_{11}	T_{12}	T_{13}	T_{14}	T_{15}
Test	Serial	Approximate entropy	Cumulative sums	Random excursions	Random excursions variant

2.2　Studies on the NIST Test Suite

The experimental result demonstrated the existence of statistical correlation in the NIST test suite [13]. Whereafter, Turan *et al.* identified the existence in theory [6]. They also got values of the correlation and independence by traversing all the sequences of length 20 and 30 bits. The statistical correlation could be quantified by the method in [14], where Fan *et al.* judged the degree of correlation between two tests by hypothesis testing, whose null hypothesis is that the two tests are independent of each other. Some works [15–18] studied on the design and correction for tests, and others [19,20] concerned about the assessment method for randomness. By comparison, the NIST test suite aims at testing the randomness of RNGs and leaves the efficiency out of consideration, and a RNG will be considered to be effective as long as the qualified rate of each test is not less than the preset threshold value. But relatively, the on-the-fly test aims at that (1) test efficiency should be efficient, and (2) each qualified sequence should pass the entire test suite.

2.3　Previous Optimization Methods

Suciu *et al.* [21] improved the efficiency of the NIST test suite by introducing the parallel computing based on the multicore architecture. After testing on different sizes of the sequence data, the experimental results showed a very significant speedup compared to the original version. Furthermore, Huang and Lai [22] provided a method to optimize the execution order of tests for efficiency, which is based on the conditional entropy of each test in the NIST test suite. However, the optimized result just stayed in the length range of 15 to 24 bits. In our optimization scheme, we can obtain the optimized order for the sequences between 128 and 256 bits, which is usually adopted as the length of the block by the block cipher. Chen *et al.* [23] proposed the prototype of the optimization scheme, and in this paper, we extended the previous work on efficiency evaluation and expanded the experimental principle and the process of proof.

3 Modeling for Testing Efficiency

In this section, we establish a model to evaluate the testing efficiency. We give priority to identifying the *influence factors* of testing efficiency, which are the basis of adjustment of the execution order. Then, we derive a *metric* for efficiency from these factors.

Testing Strategy of On-the-Fly Test. In the rules of on-the-fly test, we consider the sequence which can pass the entire test suite as the eligible. This is equivalent to eliminating the sequence which fails at least one test. So it is reasonable to terminate the testing when a test rejects the sample sequence, and this sequence is regarded as rejected afterwards. As shown in Fig. 1, the testing strategy is defined as follows: when a sample sequence $S_n = (\varepsilon_1, \varepsilon_2, \cdots, \varepsilon_n)$ is tested by one test suite, which the tests are executed in series by a given order. If the sequence is accepted by the currently executing test (i.e. $T_i(S_n) = Accept$), then the following test is being executed. The program of this test suite will not be terminated until the sequence is rejected by a test (i.e. $T_i(S_n) = reject$) or the test suite is finished under the execution order. The tests following the failed test do not need to be executed in the former case.

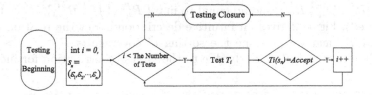

Fig. 1. The testing strategy of the randomness test

3.1 Influence Factors

We point out that there are three main influence factors for the testing efficiency, which are the *coverage*, *independence* and *time consumption*. We redeclare the concept of these factors as follows, and parts of the similar concepts have already been proposed in [22, 24, 25].

Definition 1 Coverage ($R_n^{T_i}$). *Coverage of the test T_i is defined as a set of all n-bit sequences that fail this test. The test whose coverage is larger has a stronger ability to eliminate the rejected sequence. The coverage of test T_i is larger than test T_j's, i.e. $|R_n^{T_i}| > |R_n^{T_j}|$.*

Definition 2 Independence ($R_n^{T_i} \setminus \bigcup_{k \neq i} R_n^{T_k}$). *Independence of the test T_i is defined as a set of all n-bit sequences that only fail this test, namely sequences in the set can pass all tests except this one. The test whose independence is larger has a stronger ability to detect the sequence with exclusive statistical weakness. The independence of test T_i is larger than test T_j's, i.e. $|R_n^{T_i} \setminus \bigcup_{k \neq i} R_n^{T_k}| > |R_n^{T_j} \setminus \bigcup_{k \neq j} R_n^{T_k}|$.*

Definition 3 Time Consumption ($t_n^{T_i}$). *Time consumption of the test T_i is the average time used of this test for testing a sequence with a given length n. Note that most of the $t_n^{T_i}$ for different T_i have notable difference.*

Effective Coverage. It is obvious that a test which has larger coverage, larger independence and smaller time consumption should be put at a fronter position. However, the three factors cannot be directly used to describe the efficiency of a specific order, thus we introduce the concept of effective coverage to give an intuitive explanation. Effective coverage is defined as the independent coverage of a test to the whole coverage of its all the previous tests *in a given execution order*. For example, the tests are executed under a specific order in a test suite, and set as $\{T_1 - T_2 - \cdots - T_N\}$. Then, the effective coverage of T_i is represented as $R_n^{T_i} \setminus \bigcup_{j=1}^{i-1} R_n^{T_j}$.

Since the influence of time consumption on efficiency is obvious, we analyze the influence of effective coverage under the assumption of the same time consumption. In order to reach the highest efficiency, for the above execution order, each position $i (= 1, 2, \cdots, N)$ should place such test to be sorted as which has the largest effective coverage. Illustrated with the n-bit sequences, the coverage of the ith test T_i is presented as $R_n^{T_i}$. The value of effective coverage of the ith test, i.e. $|R_n^{T_i} \setminus \bigcup_{j=1}^{i-1} R_n^{T_j}|$, should equal to $\max\{|R_n^{T_k} \setminus \bigcup_{j=1}^{i-1} R_n^{T_j}|\}$ (T_k is the test to be sorted). Figure 2 gives an intuitive description about the relation of tests T_i, T_j and T_k, and we presume the sorting of coverage is $T_i > T_j > T_k$. So test T_i should be executed firstly due to the largest contribution for increasing

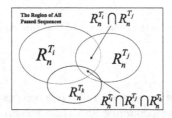

Fig. 2. The relation of reject region of tests

(effective) coverage of test suites. And next, we compare the effective coverage of test T_j to test T_k's. If $|R_n^{T_j} \setminus R_n^{T_i}| > |R_n^{T_k} \setminus R_n^{T_i}|$, test T_j should immediately follow with test T_i, and vice versa. Thus, the most efficient execution order should be $T_i \Rightarrow T_j \Rightarrow T_k$. It means that the larger the effective coverage is, the higher the efficiency is with identical time consumption. The analysis also indicates that the effective coverage is positive correlated with both the coverage and independence.

3.2 Metric of Efficiency

According to the above analysis, testing efficiency only depends on the *Total Elimination Time used (TET)* which is spent in eliminating the whole rejected sequences, and is independent of the time used on testing eligible sequences. Hence we only concern with how to shorten the *TET*. In fact, the proportion of the rejected sequences is considerable if the value of environment variables has great change, or some attacks work on the RNG. Therefore, it is significant to cut down this time cost. For the given order, if we follow the above notation and execution order, then the time used by a sample sequence of length n which is rejected by test T_m in the test suite is the partial sum $\sum_{i=1}^{m} t_n^{T_i}$. The cardinal number of effective coverage of test T_m is $|R_n^{T_m} \setminus \bigcup_{i=1}^{m-1} R_n^{T_i}|$, which is the number of sequences rejected by test T_m in this order. Thus, the expression of the *TET* is shown as Formula (1).

$$TET = t_n^{T_1}|R_n^{T_1}| + (t_n^{T_1} + t_n^{T_2})|R_n^{T_2} \setminus R_n^{T_1}| + \cdots + \sum_{i=1}^{N} t_n^{T_i}|R_n^{T_N} \setminus \bigcup_{j=1}^{N-1} R_n^{T_j}|$$

$$= t_n^{T_1}|R_n^{T_1}| + \sum_{m=2}^{N} \sum_{i=1}^{m} t_n^{T_i}|R_n^{T_m} \setminus \bigcup_{j=1}^{m-1} R_n^{T_j}| \tag{1}$$

Therefore, the *Average Elimination Time used (AET)* which can be utilized as an objective metric for testing efficiency is presented as follows.

$$AET = \frac{TET}{|\bigcup_{i=1}^{N} R_n^{T_i}|} \tag{2}$$

From Formula (1), the time consumption and effective coverage of each test under the given order are presented in each term. Both coverage and independence decide the size of effective coverage, which are shown from the second term to the $(N-1)^{th}$ term. In particular, the first and the Nth term only represent the coverage of test T_1 and the independence of test T_n, respectively. Thus, it further proves that efficiency is primarily determined by these three influence factors together.

4 Scheme Design for Optimization

In this section, we propose a novel optimization scheme for improving the testing efficiency. In our scheme, we mainly accomplish the weight allocation of the influence factors, which is one of the bases for adjustment of execution order, and the other bases are the value of the factors for each test. We will find out the optimized order of the SP 800-22 test suite by this scheme. Our optimization scheme is suitable for all the test suits, and the SP 800-22 is just adopted as a representation in this paper.

4.1   Scheme Design Overview

In general, the optimization scheme is composed of the following five steps, depicted in Fig. 3. Because the reliability of the optimized result relies on the sample size which is gotten by random sampling from all n-bit sequences ($n \in [128, 256]$), we select a size to start the experiment, and adjust the size based on the reliability of experimental results. The optimized order is obtained when the results are fixed in repeated experiments.

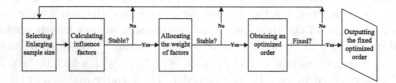

Fig. 3. The optimization scheme work flow

Step 1: selecting the size of samples from the entire sequence space. As we mentioned, the values of coverage and independence are derived from the experiments. However, for 128-bit or longer sequences, it is impossible to traverse the entire space. Therefore, we randomly select samples to obtain the (approximate) property of tests in the entire space. Also, we need to verify the result to confirm that the size of the samples is large enough to reflect the property.

Step 2: calculating the values of the influence factors. The chosen sequence samples are executed by all the tests, and we record the passing or failure status. Using these results, we figure out the set of samples that fail a specific test, i.e. coverage, and the set of samples that *only* fail the test, i.e. independence. In addition, the time consumption of these tests can be obtained from the timer of system where the tests are running.

Step 3: verifying the stability of the factor values for different sizes of samples. After choosing the number of samples, we repeat random sampling and calculate the factor values of the samples. If the calculated values are stable or almost stable each time, the chosen sample number is considered enough to reflect the property of the entire space. Otherwise, we enlarge the number until the stability appears.

Step 4: allocating the weights of the three factors. There is no explicit relationship among these factors, as they reflect different aspects of a test.

Hence, we need to allocate reasonable weights for these factors to merge them into one factor (called *contribution*) for measuring the efficiency. We employ a *multi-attribute weight allocation method* for influence factors which is based on fuzzy clustering analysis, rough set and information entropy (see Appendix A for details). We also need to verify the stability of the weights. **Step 5: obtaining optimized order.** Optimized order is obtained via reference to the contribution of tests to test suites. The stability of the order must be considered too. If it is not fixed, we should reselect a larger size of samples.

4.2   Experimental Statements

We apply our scheme to the SP 800-22 test suite as an instance. Statements for experimental parameter settings and environment of the optimization are described as follows.

- **Sample sequence:** In the following optimization and evaluation, sample sequences are generated from a commercial hardware RNG whose output can pass the SP 800-22 test suite successfully with the recommended testing requirements, and are *regenerated* in each experiment to ensure the reliability of results. In order to get several rejected sequences, we put the RNG into the adjustable environment. e.g., the temperature and supply voltage are adjustable. The length of sample sequences is in the range between 128 and 256 bits corresponding to the testing object of on-the-fly test. And in our optimization scheme, we ignore the three improper tests (binary matrix rank test, discrete Fourier transform test and maurers universal test) since the lengths adopted in optimization do not apply to them.
- **Applicability of the length in the NIST test suite:** As we known in the NIST test suite, it gives two approaches to interpret the empirical results: (i) the proportion of p-values that is greater than the significance level α and (ii) uniform distribution of p-values. Actually, most of the tests are applicable for smaller values of the sequence length n [5], if we do not analyze the empirical results by the second approach, like ours. Therefore, the relatively "short sequences" (128–256 bits) apply to the NIST test suite in this study.
- **Testbed:** The experiment is performed on a system with Intel Xeon CPU E3-1230 processor at 2 GB of RAM. The version 2.1 of the NIST test suite [26] is used.

4.3   Sample Size for Calculating Factors

We choose three types of sample size - $2^{15}, 2^{20}$ and 2^{25}, and it is not difficult to get these numbers of samples. For each size and each test, we respectively calculate the coverage size $|R_{128}^{T_i}|$ and independence $|R_{128}^{T_i} \setminus \bigcup_{j \neq i} R_{128}^{T_j}|$. The calculation is repeated 50 times to check the stability of the two factors under a certain sample size. Note that the factor - time consumption is unrelated with the sample size from experimental results, thus its value is constant. As the sizes of coverage and independence are proportional to the sample size, i.e., the more tested samples are, the more failed samples are. These values need to be normalized for a fair comparison. The normalized coverage value of test T_i is derived from $|R_{128}^{T_i}|/|\bigcup_{i=1}^{12} R_{128}^{T_i}|$, i.e., the ratio of the original coverage size of T_i to the size of entire sequences eliminated by any test. The normalized independence value of test T_i is derived from $|R_{128}^{T_i} \setminus \bigcup_{j \neq i} R_{128}^{T_j}|/|R_{128}^{T_i}|$, i.e., the ratio of the original independence size of T_i to the coverage size of T_i.

Table 2. Standard deviations of normalized coverage and independence of 128-bit sequences for different sample sizes

Test	Norm. Cov. ($\times 10^{-3}$)			Norm. Indep. ($\times 10^{-3}$)		
	Size					
	2^{15}	2^{20}	2^{25}	2^{15}	2^{20}	2^{25}
T_1	2.83	0.60	0.35	12.55	1.01	0.65
T_2	2.12	0.15	0.08	59.41	5.29	2.55
T_3	1.35	0.23	0.17	24.81	7.69	6.03
T_4	2.41	0.32	0.15	48.15	6.00	5.08
T_7	5.03	0.95	0.45	11.74	1.64	1.33
T_8	2.80	1.18	0.94	21.07	5.90	7.76
T_{10}	4.86	1.88	1.77	15.96	7.41	7.66
T_{11}	2.71	0.48	0.30	22.38	6.95	7.11
T_{12}	0.85	0.25	0.21	20.84	4.21	1.30
T_{13}	1.58	0.67	0.59	12.88	2.79	2.20
T_{14}	2.19	0.73	0.78	12.13	1.97	1.00
T_{15}	2.51	0.76	0.49	16.20	2.59	1.73

The standard variance comparison of normalized factors for the sample sizes of $2^{15}, 2^{20}$ and 2^{25} is shown in Table 2. Note that since the time consumption is independent of the sample size, it is not listed for comparison in Table 2. The stability (standard variance) under sample size 2^{20} or 2^{25} is several times better than that under 2^{15}, i.e., the sample size has a better performance in representing the entire sequence space. We also find that the standard deviation with sample size 2^{20} is close to that with 2^{25}, meaning that the sample size 2^{20} could be proper. Furthermore, we need to observe the stability (invariance) of the result of weight allocation and optimized order for each sample to determine which sample size is enough, which is explained in Sects. 4.4 and 4.5, respectively.

4.4 Weight Allocation for the Influence Factors

We elaborate on the optimization scheme by employing a multi-attribute weight allocation method for the influence factors. This method of multi-attribute weight allocation has obvious advantages in comparison with other incorporating subjective judgement or information entropy loss methods. Since there is no original information loss, this method can accurately determine the weight allocation of the factors through the amount of information contained by each factor in the original data. Furthermore, this method does not include any subjective factors to affect the weight allocation. So we can obtain a *reasonable* and *objective* result of the weight allocation.

Specifically, we use the 128-bit sample sequence and 2^{20} sample size to do this optimization experiment on the NIST test suite. The detailed procedure of the multi-attribute weight allocation is described in Appendix A. After repeating calculations 50 times, the identical result of weight allocation of the three factors is $w_1 = 0.2201$ for coverage, $w_2 = 0.3184$ for independence and $w_3 = 0.4615$ for time consumption. Similar to the factor values, the stability of the derived weight is also proportional to sample size. Then, the contribution of each test to the efficiency can be represented as

$$Contribution^{T_i} = \sum_{i-1}^{3}(f_i * w_i),$$ (3)

where f_1, f_2 and f_3 are the normalized values of coverage, independence and time consumption, respectively.

4.5 Optimized Order

According to the contribution values calculated for the 12 tests, the position of each test can be determined in execution order. Similar to the other two factors, the time consumption factor is normalized as $1 - t_{128}^{T_i}/\sum_{j=1}^{12} t_{128}^{T_j}$. Then we repeat the calculation 50 times to find the existence of a fixed optimized order for different sample sizes. We acquire that the derived order under sample size 2^{15} is unstable as expected. Specifically, there are 6 different optimized orders (including the correct order) in 50 experiments, namely under this sample size the obtained order is incorrect with nearly 83% probability in an experiment. As for the sample sizes 2^{20} and 2^{25}, the 50 derived orders are always consistent, which means that if only the sample size is greater than or equal to 2^{20}, it is enough to get a fixed order. In addition, the computation work can be reduced to such a small order of magnitude in comparison with larger sample size $2^{40}, 2^{50}$, *etc.* As a result, the fixed optimized order for 128 bits with sample size 2^{20} is shown in Table 3.

It is an interesting result that even if the No. 1 of each factor is non-overlapping TM test, linear complexity test and frequency test, their positions are only No. 4, No. 5 and No. 12 in the optimized order respectively, due to the poor performance in other two factors. On the contrary, the random excursions variant test is sorted as No. 1 in the optimized order with a good performance in each factor. Thus, for obtaining the optimized order, we should combine *multiple* factors to calculate the contribution of each test to test suites. We also calculate the sum of the coverage of these 12 tests like $\sum_i |R_{128}^{T_i}|$, and it is 0.304 of the

Table 3. The optimized execution order of NIST tests for 128 bits with sample size 2^{20}

Rank	Test	Norm. Cov.	Norm. Indep.	Norm. Time	Contr.
No. 1	Random excursions variant test (T_{15})	0.1947	0.7382	0.9261	0.7053
No. 2	Overlapping TM test (T_8)	0.1371	0.6793	0.9528	0.6862
No. 3	Random excursions test (T_{14})	0.1534	0.6668	0.9465	0.6829
No. 4	Non-overlapping TM test (T_7)	0.3260	0.7162	0.7180	0.6311
No. 5	Linear complexity test (T_{10})	0.2064	0.7386	0.6974	0.6024
No. 6	Runs test (T_3)	0.0347	0.4199	0.9771	0.5922
No. 7	Longest-run of ones in a block (T_4)	0.0298	0.4052	0.9741	0.5851
No. 8	Frequency test within a block (T_2)	0.0279	0.3547	0.9807	0.5717
No. 9	Serial test (T_{11})	0.0597	0.3846	0.9265	0.5632
No. 10	Approximate entropy test (T_{12})	0.0365	0.2205	0.9549	0.5189
No. 11	Cumulative sum test (T_{13})	0.0398	0.1161	0.9642	0.4907
No. 12	Frequency (monobit) test (T_1)	0.0331	0.0651	0.9817	0.4811

total samples, which indicates the necessity of shortening the elimination time used (TET).

Then we observe whether the order is changed for any other length of sequences. The optimized order obtained is stable for 256 bits as follows, but it is different from the optimized result for 128 bits. Besides, it seems that this sample size is suitable for 256-bit optimization because of the fixed optimized order. Note that we may need to increase sample size if the optimization is applied to longer sample sequences, such as 512 bits.

– The optimized order for 256-bit sequences with sample size 2^{20} and 2^{25}: $\{T_{15} - T_{14} - T_8 - T_7 - T_2 - T_3 - T_{11} - T_4 - T_{10} - T_{12} - T_{13} - T_1\}$.

The reason why different lengths can lead to the difference of optimized order is not only the change of time consumption, but also the coverage and independence are changed too. The change of coverage and independence result from that some of these tests will become stricter for testing sequences with different lengths, and the degree of strictness of other tests will not change. Furthermore, there is a strong correlation between time consumption and sequence length. With the growth of length, time consumption of testing a sequence will be increased, especially the time consumption of linear complexity test, which shows an exponential growth. This leads to an obviously decreasing contribution of such tests.

5   Evaluation

The *average elimination time used* (AET) is defined to precisely measure the efficiency of the test under a specific order. To evaluate the validity and efficiency of our scheme, we compare the AET result between the 20 bits and 128 bits, which is running under the most efficient order, i.e., optimal order, and our optimized order, shown in Table 4. The optimal order is found by traversing all the 12! possible orders with the sample size 2^{20}, and it takes 6 days to complete the process in our experimental platform. The result shows that the AET value of our optimized order approximates that of the optimal order.

Table 4. Comparison of AET for 20/128 bits with sample size 2^{20}

	20 bits	128 bits
Our order	26.7	113.3
Optimal order	26.3	109.6

Then, we run the test under the default order of SP 800-22 and our optimized order, with the sequence length 20/128/256 bits, respectively, and 2^{20} is still adopted as the sample size. The experimental result is shown in Table 5, which is calculated as the average value of about fifty rounds.

The efficiency under our optimized order is enhanced by 175.7% compared to the default order, with the 20-bit sequence length. In the case of 128 and 256-bit sequence length, the efficiency is increased by 33% and 20%, respectively. In compare with the AET of our optimized order and optimal order, the efficiency of our scheme is in close proximity to the most efficient one. Therefore, our optimization scheme provides a fast-implemented method to achieve the most optimized speed for on-the-fly statistical randomness test.

Table 5. Comparison of AET for 20/128/256 bits

	20 bits		128 bits		256 bits	
	Our order	SP 800-22 order	Our order	SP 800-22 order	Our order	SP 800-22 order
AET (μs)	26.7	73.6	113.3	150.7	192.9	230.5
Ratio	100.0%	275.7%	100%	133.01%	100%	119.5%

6   Conclusion and Future Work

On-the-fly test is employed in many cryptographic applications at present. The improvement of testing efficiency is a significant issue for the requirements of "on-the-fly". To solve this problem, we focus on the optimization of efficiency for testing sequences of length between 128 and 256 bits. In this work, we establish a model for evaluation of efficiency. In the model, we identify that the efficiency is primarily determined by three factors: coverage, independence and time consumption of tests. Based on the factors, we present a metric to evaluate the efficiency. In view of these factors, we propose a novel efficiency optimization scheme, and apply it to the NIST test suite as an instance. After the theoretical and experimental studies on optimization, we achieve a stable optimized execution order for sequence length 128 and 256 bits, respectively, and the sample size can be controlled in a small order of magnitude. The testing efficiency under optimized order is approximate to the global optimal one, which is 33% higher than the default order's in the NIST SP 800-22 test suite. For a given length, our optimization scheme can rapidly provide a quasi-optimal order by its fast implementation. In future, we would like to extend this scheme to longer sequences in on-the-fly tests, such as 512 or 1204 bits for RSA key generation.

Although, we have proved the existence of optimal order in theory, it would be still difficult to calculate this order experimentally. Because the sample space is too large to traverse, and the required sample size may be overlarge in random sampling. We are also working on the solution of optimized order from mathematical theory.

Acknowledgement. This work was partially supported by National Key R&D Plan No. 2016YFB0800504 and No. 2016QY02D0400, and National Natural Science Foundation of China No. U163620068.

Appendix A: Procedure of Multi-attribute Weight Allocation Method

Step 1. Initialization and Data Processing. Determine the objects to be processed and the attribute values of each object as the initial data. The objects are the statistical tests in SP 800-22, which denoted by $X = [x_1, x_2, \cdots, x_{12}]$ except three improper tests. The three influence factors, as the attribute, represent each test $T_j(j = 1, 2, \cdots, N)$, i.e. $x_j = [x_{1j}, x_{2j}, x_{3j}]$. Thus, after repeated experiments (50 times), the initial data in any one of them is $X = [x_{i,j}]_{3 \times 12}$ shown in Table 6, where the Inf_i represents the ith attribute for the sake of convenience in the introduction to this scheme, i.e. Inf_1 - Coverage, Inf_2 - Independence, Inf_3 - Time Consumption. The main testing parameter settings in partial tests are listed in Appendix B.

For removing the influence of the difference of dimension, the initial data should be normalized so that the processed results fall in the interval [0, 1]. The normalization formula which you choose depends on the practical situation.

Table 6. The initial data - the attribute values of tests in SP 800-22 for 128 bits with sample size 2^{20} for $\alpha = 0.01$ (**Example**)

Factor	Sample											
	T_1	T_2	T_3	T_4	T_7	T_8	T_{10}	T_{11}	T_{12}	T_{13}	T_{14}	T_{15}
Inf_1	10576	8919	11075	9507	104155	43816	65947	19063	11649	12701	49012	62223
Inf_2	688	3164	4650	3852	74600	29763	48708	7331	2569	1475	32683	45932
Inf_3 (μs)	5.30	5.59	6.65	7.52	81.79	13.7	87.76	21.32	13.07	10.39	15.51	21.42

We use the formula: $x'_{ij} = \dfrac{x_{ij} - \min_{1 \le j \le 12}\{x_{ij}\}}{\max_{1 \le j \le 12}\{x_{ij}\} - \min_{1 \le j \le 12}\{x_{ij}\}}$ to eliminate the influence of dimension and let the results fall in $[0, 1]$.

Step 2. Establishing the Fuzzy Similarity Matrix. According to multivariate analysis, we calculate the similarity degree $r_{ij} \in [0, 1](i, j = 1, 2, \cdots, 12)$ between test x'_i and test x'_j by the maximum and minimum method like

$$r_{ij} = \frac{\sum_{k=1}^{3}(x'_{ki} \wedge x'_{kj})}{\sum_{k=1}^{3}(x'_{ki} \vee x'_{kj})},$$

where r_{ij} is the element (i, j) in fuzzy similarity matrix, and define the notation $x'_{ki} \wedge x'_{kj} = min\{x'_{ki}, x'_{kj}\}, x'_{ki} \vee x'_{kj} = max\{x'_{ki}, x'_{kj}\}$.

Step 3. Dynamic Clustering Results. The dynamic clustering result is got from the maximal tree, whose vertexes and weights represent the tests and selectable maximal similarity degree between two tests respectively, under different threshold values. Based on the above fuzzy similarity matrix, the obtained maximal tree is shown in Fig. 4 by using the *Kruskal Method*.

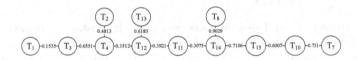

Fig. 4. The maximal tree of the initial data

From the weight on the branch of the maximal tree, we determine a series of proper threshold values $\lambda \in [0, 1]$. Cut off the branch whose weight is below λ so that we get a disconnected graph, and the connected branches form a class on this λ. Under different thresholds, the classifications of these 12 tests represented by their subscript are listed as follows, which is the dynamic clustering results. Refer to Table 1 for the serial number of tests.

- $0.8 < \lambda \le 1$, 11 classes: $\{1\}, \{2\}, \{3\}, \{4\}, \{7\}, \{8, 14\}, \{10\}, \{11\}, \{12\}, \{13\}, \{15\}$;
- $0.7 < \lambda \le 0.8$, 9 classes: $\{1\}, \{2\}, \{3\}, \{4\}, \{7, 10\}, \{8, 14, 15\}, \{11\}, \{12\}, \{13\}$;
- $0.5 < \lambda \le 0.7$, 6 classes: $\{1\}, \{2\}, \{3, 4\}, \{7, 8, 10, 14, 15\}, \{11\}, \{12, 13\}$;
- $0.4 < \lambda \le 0.5$, 5 classes: $\{1\}, \{2, 3, 4\}, \{7, 8, 10, 14, 15\}, \{11\}, \{12, 13\}$;
- $0.2 < \lambda \le 0.4$, 2 classes: $\{1\}, \{2, 3, 4, 7, 8, 10, 11, 12, 13, 14, 15\}$;
- $0.1 < \lambda \le 0.2$, 1 classes: $\{1, 2, 3, 4, 7, 8, 10, 11, 12, 13, 14, 15\}$.

Step 4. Determining the Optimum Threshold Value by F-Statistic. From the dynamic clustering results, we can get various classifications under different thresholds λ. To obtain the reasonable classification, we should find the best threshold by F- statistic. Based on the initial data matrix, let r be the number of classes under a given λ, n_i be the number of tests in the ith class, so

Table 7. The results of F- statistic

Threshold λ	0.9 or 0.8	0.7	0.6 or 0.5	0.4	0.3 or 0.2
The value of r	11	9	6	5	2
The degree of freedom $(r-1, n-r)$	$(10, 1)$	$(8, 3)$	$(5, 6)$	$(4, 7)$	$(1, 10)$
The calculated F	164.8	4.55	4.72	6.87	0.67
$F_{0.025}(r-1, n-r)$	968.6	14.54	5.99	5.52	6.94
$F - F_{0.025}(r-1, n-r)$	–	–	–	1.35	–

that the ith class is denoted by $\{x_1^{(i)}, x_2^{(i)}, \cdots, x_{n_i}^{(i)}\}$. The clustering center of the ith class is the vector $\bar{x}^{(i)} = (\bar{x}_1^{(i)}, \bar{x}_2^{(i)}, \bar{x}_3^{(i)})$, and the $\bar{x}_k^{(i)}$ is the mean of the kth attribute, i.e. $\bar{x}_k^{(i)} = \dfrac{1}{n_i} \sum_{j=1}^{n_i} x_{kj}^{(i)} (k = 1, 2, 3)$. So the F- statistic is calculated by

$$F = \frac{\sum_{i=1}^{r} n_i \sum_{k=1}^{3} (\bar{x}_k^{(i)} - \bar{x}_k)^2/(r-1)}{\sum_{i=1}^{r} \sum_{j=1}^{n_i} \sum_{k=1}^{3} (x_{kj}^{(i)} - \bar{x}_k^{(i)})^2/(n-r)} \sim F(r-1, n-r),$$

where the numerator and denominator indicate the distances between classes and the distances between samples in each class, respectively. Thus, for the given confidence level $1 - \alpha$, we obtain the F_α from the F- critical value table. Compared the calculated F to F_α, if $F > F_\alpha$, according to the variance theory of mathematical statistics, we believe that the differences among classes are obvious under this λ corresponding to the F. Moreover, if there are more than one candidate $F (>F_\alpha)$, we further find the maximum of the proportional $(F - F_\alpha)/F_\alpha$. This maximum means that the corresponding classification is the most reasonable. Table 7 shows the calculated results of F- statistic.

After calculating, only $\lambda = 0.4$ satisfies $F > F_\alpha(\alpha = 0.025)$. Therefore, the best classification is 5 classes: $\{1\}, \{2, 3, 4\}, \{7, 8, 10, 14, 15\}, \{11\}, \{12, 13\}$.

Step 5. Deleting Attribute. We delete the attribute in turn and get the altered initial data after an attribute deleted. Repeating the Steps 1–4, we enumerate the best classification of deleting each attribute, respectively. Notice that these best classification are also determined by the above method of F- statistic.

- Deleting Inf_1. $\{1\}, \{2, 3, 4\}, \{7, 10\}, \{8, 14, 15\}, \{11\}, \{12, 13\}$;
- Deleting Inf_2. $\{1\}, \{2\}, \{3, 4, 11, 12, 13\}, \{7, 8, 10, 14, 15\}$;
- Deleting Inf_3. $\{1, 2, 3, 4, 11, 12, 13\}, \{7, 8, 10, 14, 15\}$.

Step 6. Weight Quantification of Each Attribute. Assess the weight of attributes by the attribute importance rule in rough set and information entropy. Firstly, determine information entropy in the best classification of the initial data, denoted by $H(A)$. According to the concepts of conditional entropy and mutual information, if we can obtain most of the information about the best classification of the initial data from the best classification of the altered initial data after an attribute deleted, it means that this deleted attribute contains less information about the best classification of the initial data, and vice versa. Therefore, the amount of information of deleted i^{th} attribute Inf_i is anti-related to the mutual information $I(A; A - Inf_i)$ which is owned by the best classifications of both the initial data and the altered initial data after deleting the ith attribute. And the reciprocal of mutual information can be used to represent the relative amount of information of the deleted attribute [27]. Notice that the related theories are introduced in Appendix C. The expression of weight is

$$W_i = \frac{1}{I(A; A - Inf_i)}.$$

After calculating the weights, let the weight of each factor Inf_i be normalized as

$$w_i = \frac{W_i}{\sum_{j=1}^{3} W_j}.$$

Appendix B: Main Testing Parameter Setting

The main testing parameter settings of partial tests are shown in Table 8.

Table 8. The main testing parameter settings in partial tests in SP 800-22

Number	Test name	Testing parameter settings for different lengths		
		Parameter	$n = 128$	$n = 256$
1	Frequency Test within a block	The length of each block M	32	32
2	Non-overlapping TM Test	The length of template m	m = 5	m = 5
		The length of the substring M	M = 32	M = 32
3	Overlapping TM test	The length of template m	m = 5	m = 5
		The length of the substring M	M = 32	M = 32
4	Linear complexity test	The length of a block M	M = 128	M = 256
5	Serial test	The length of each block m	m = 4	m = 5
6	Approximate entropy test	The length of each block m	m = 2	m = 2

Appendix C: Definitions and Tools on Fuzzy Mathematics, Probability and Information

Definition 1 (Probability Distribution). *Let the partition X^* be derived from an equivalence relation X on domain of discourse U: $X^* = U/ind(X) = \{X_1, X_2, \cdots, X_n\}$, then the probability distribution of σ-Algebra which is the set of subsets based on X on U is*

$$\binom{X^*}{P} = \begin{bmatrix} X_1 & X_2 & \cdots & X_n \\ p(X_1) & p(X_2) & \cdots & p(X_n) \end{bmatrix},$$

where $p(X_i) = \frac{|X_i|}{|U|} (i = 1, 2, \cdots, n)$.

Definition 2 (Information Entropy). *A probabilistic approximation space* (U, X, P), *the indeterminacy of the system is represented by the entropy* $H(X^*)$ *of the system, i.e.*

$$H(X^*) = -\sum_{i=1}^{n} P(X_i) log_2 P(X_i),$$

where X^* *is the partition derived from* X *on* U: $X^* = U/ind(X) = \{X_1, X_2, \cdots, X_n\}$. *This entropy is called the initial entropy of the system.*

Definition 3 (Conditional Entropy). *If* Y *is another equivalence relation on the domain of discourse* U, *let* $Y^* = U/ind(Y) = \{Y_1, Y_2, \cdots, Y_m\}$, *then as the known knowledge* X^*, *the conditional entropy of the knowledge* Y^* *is*

$$H(Y^*|X^*) = -\sum_{i=1}^{n} P(X_i) \sum_{j=1}^{m} P(Y_j|X_i) log_2 P(Y_j|X_i).$$

Definition 4 (Mutual Information). *The mutual information between knowledge* X^* *and* Y^* *is*

$$I(X^*; Y^*) = H(X) - H(X|Y) = H(Y) - H(Y|X),$$

which represents the common information in X^* *and* Y^*.

References

1. Vasyltsov, I., Hambardzumyan, E., Kim, Y.-S., Karpinskyy, B.: Fast digital TRNG based on metastable ring oscillator. In: Oswald, E., Rohatgi, P. (eds.) CHES 2008. LNCS, vol. 5154, pp. 164–180. Springer, Heidelberg (2008). https://doi.org/10.1007/978-3-540-85053-3_11
2. Markettos, A.T., Moore, S.W.: The frequency injection attack on ring-oscillator-based true random number generators. In: Clavier, C., Gaj, K. (eds.) CHES 2009. LNCS, vol. 5747, pp. 317–331. Springer, Heidelberg (2009). https://doi.org/10.1007/978-3-642-04138-9_23
3. Fischer, V., Aubert, A., Bernard, F., et al.: True Random Number Generators in Configurable Logic Devices. Project ANR-ICTeR (2009)
4. Schindler, W.: Efficient online tests for true random number generators. In: Koç, Ç.K., Naccache, D., Paar, C. (eds.) CHES 2001. LNCS, vol. 2162, pp. 103–117. Springer, Heidelberg (2001). https://doi.org/10.1007/3-540-44709-1_10
5. Rukhin, A., Soto, J., Nechvatal, J., et al.: A statistical suite for random and pseudorandom number generators for cryptographic applications. NIST Special Publication 800-22, Washington, D.C., May 2001
6. Sönmez Turan, M., DoGanaksoy, A., Boztaş, S.: On independence and sensitivity of statistical randomness tests. In: Golomb, S.W., Parker, M.G., Pott, A., Winterhof, A. (eds.) SETA 2008. LNCS, vol. 5203, pp. 18–29. Springer, Heidelberg (2008). https://doi.org/10.1007/978-3-540-85912-3_2
7. NIST FIPS PUB: 140-2: Security Requirements for Cryptographic Modules. Washington, D.C., USA (2001)
8. Elaine, B., John, K.: Recommendation for random number generation using deterministic random bit generators. NIST Special Publication 800-90A, Washington, D.C., January 2012

9. Killmann, W., Schindler, W.: AIS 31: Functionality Classes and Evaluation Methodology for True (Physical) Random Number Generators. Version 3.1. T-Systems GEI GmbH and Bundesamt fr Sicherheit in der Informationstechnik (BSI), Bonn, Germany (2001)
10. Marsaglia, G.: The Marsaglia Random Number CDROM Including the Diehard Battery of Tests of Randomness (1995)
11. L'Ecuyer, P., Simard, R.J.: TestU01: AC library for empirical testing of random number generators. ACM Trans. Math. Softw. **33**(4) (2007)
12. L'Ecuyer, P.: Testing random number generators. In: Winter Simulation Conference, pp. 305–313. ACM Press (1992)
13. Hellekalek, P., Wegenkittl, S.: Empirical evidence concerning AES. ACM Trans. Model. Comput. Simul. **13**(4), 322–333 (2003)
14. Fan, L., Chen, H., Gao, S.: A general method to evaluate the correlation of randomness tests. In: Kim, Y., Lee, H., Perrig, A. (eds.) WISA 2013. LNCS, vol. 8267, pp. 52–62. Springer, Cham (2014). https://doi.org/10.1007/978-3-319-05149-9_4
15. Maurer, U.M.: A universal statistical test for random bit generators. J. Cryptol. **5**(2), 89–105 (1992)
16. Hamano, K., Kaneko, T.: Correction of overlapping template matching test included in NIST randomness test suite. IEICE Trans. **90–A**(9), 1788–1792 (2007)
17. Kim, S.-J., Umeno, K., Hasegawa, A.: Corrections of the NIST statistical test suite for randomness. IACR Cryptology ePrint Archive 2014:18–31 (2004)
18. Hamano, K.: The distribution of the spectrum for the discrete fourier transform test included in SP800-22. IEICE Trans. **88–A**(1), 67–73 (2005)
19. Pareschi, F., Rovatti, R., Setti, G.: On statistical tests for randomness included in the NIST SP800-22 test suite and based on the binomial distribution. IEEE Trans. Inf. Forensics Secur. **7**(2), 491–505 (2012)
20. Sulak, F., Doğanaksoy, A., Ege, B., Koçak, O.: Evaluation of randomness test results for short sequences. In: Carlet, C., Pott, A. (eds.) SETA 2010. LNCS, vol. 6338, pp. 309–319. Springer, Heidelberg (2010). https://doi.org/10.1007/978-3-642-15874-2_27
21. Suciu, A., Nagy, I., Marton, K., Pinca, I.: Parallel implementation of the NIST statistical test suite. In: Proceedings of the 2010 IEEE 6th International Conference on Intelligent Computer Communication and Processing (ICCP), pp. 363–368. Institute of Electrical and Electronic Engineers (2010)
22. Huang, J., Lai, X.: Measuring random tests by conditional entropy and optimal execution order. In: Chen, L., Yung, M. (eds.) INTRUST 2010. LNCS, vol. 6802, pp. 148–159. Springer, Heidelberg (2011). https://doi.org/10.1007/978-3-642-25283-9_10
23. Chen, T., Ma, Y., Lin, J., Wang, Z., Jing, J.: An efficiency optimization scheme for the on-the-fly statistical randomness test. In: Proceedings of the 2015 IEEE 2nd International Conference on Cyber Security and Cloud Computing (CSCloud), CSCLOUD 2015, pp. 515–517. IEEE Computer Society, Washington, D.C. (2015)
24. Soto, J.: Statistical testing of random number generators. In: Proceedings of the 22nd National Information Systems Security Conference (NISSC), vol. 10, pp. 12–23. NIST, Gaithersburg (1999)
25. Soto, J.: Randomness Testing of the AES Candidate Algorithms. NIST (1999). csrc.nist.gov
26. NIST: The NIST Statistical Test Suite (2010). http://csrc.nist.gov/groups/ST/toolkit/rng/documents/sts-2.1.2.zip
27. Chen, C.B., Wang, L.Y.: Rough set-based clustering with refinement using Shannon's entropy theory. Comput. Math. Appl. **52**(10–11), 1563–1576 (2006)

Signature Scheme and Key Management

FABSS: Attribute-Based Sanitizable Signature for Flexible Access Structure

Ruo Mo[1](✉), Jianfeng Ma[1], Ximeng Liu[2], and Qi Li[3]

[1] Xidian University, Xi'an, China
593430655@qq.com
[2] Singapore Management University, Singapore, Singapore
[3] Nanjing University of Posts and Telecommunications, Nanjing, China

Abstract. In the Electronic Health Record (EHR) system, digital signature is utilized to prevent the medical data from being tampered. However, users update their medical data frequently and have to sign these medical data from scratch after updating. Besides, traditional signature attests the identity of the individual signing the records, which leads to vast computation cost and the privacy leakage. In this paper, we obfuscate users identity information with attribute sets and introduce a semi-trusted participant–sanitizer to propose the Flexible Attribute-Based Sanitizable Signature (FABSS) scheme. We prove that our scheme is unforgeable under generic group model. Through comparison, the FABSS scheme not only reduces the users computation overhead, but also supports flexible access structures to implement expressively fine-grained access control.

Keywords: Flexible attribute-based access control
Sanitizable signature · Unforgeability · Anonymity
Information privacy

1 Instruction

The EHR system is considered as a sustainable solution for improving the quality of medical care, referring to the systematized collection of patient and population electronically-stored health information in a digital format. In the EHR system, it is important to guarantee the authentication and integrity of medical records, and thus digital signature is utilized in the EHR system. However, the secret signing key of the signature attests to the identity information of patients, such as names, ages which are not supposed to be shown to the public. With attribute based signature (ABS), patients sign the records with attributes signing key issued by attribute authorities according to the patients' attributes, such as $age : >45, profession : teacher, workunits : Xidian University$, etc. The signature attests not to the identities of patients but some of their attributes, which protects the identity privacy of patients and achieves anonymous authentication. Hence, ABS adapts to the EHR system.

© Springer International Publishing AG, part of Springer Nature 2018
S. Qing et al. (Eds.): ICICS 2017, LNCS 10631, pp. 39–50, 2018.
https://doi.org/10.1007/978-3-319-89500-0_3

In the system, the health data of patients are updated frequently. However, traditional digital signature including ABS prohibits any alteration of the original medical data once it is signed and has to be regenerated from scratch once parts of the original records are changed, which increases the computation overhead of users, leading to inefficiency. Sanitizable signature allows a semi-trusted party sanitizer to modify certain portions of the health records in the original signature. Thus, the signer needs to sign the records only once, which reduces the computation cost of the signer. In the sanitizing phase of the original signature, the sanitizer can generate the sanitized signature without interacting with the signer for signing keys, thus the sanitizer cannot forge the signature of the original signer. In addition, the process of sanitizing does not impact the verification.

In this paper, to address the efficiency and identity privacy problems in the EHR system, we propose a novel Flexible Attribute-Based Sanitizable Signature (FABSS) scheme. Specifically, major contributions of this paper are twofold.

- We introduce the sanitizable signature mechanism into present ABS with which patients sign the record with their attribute signing keys. When the records need to be updated, the patients deliver the original signature and the modifiable parts of the original message to the sanitizer, then the sanitizer can modify the message on the signature directly.
- Comparing with existing schemes, the FABSS scheme not only reduces the users computation overhead, but also preserves the anonymity and information privacy of users. Besides, the proposed scheme supports flexible access structure consisting of any AND, OR and threshold gates, which can provide expressively fine-grained access control.

1.1 Related Work

The notion of sanitizable signature was first proposed by Ateniese et al. [1], which allows a semi-trusted party sanitizer to modify certain portions of a signed message and produce a valid sanitized signature without interaction with the original signer for secret keys. Besides, They also define two necessary security requirements: (1) unforgeability, which means only legitimate signers can generate valid signatures. (2) information privacy, which means the sanitized message and corresponding signature should not reveal the original message. Nevertheless, they did not provide formal specifications for these properties. Brzuska et al. [2,3] introduced another security requirements unlinkability which prevents that one can link the sanitized message-signature pair of the same document and deduce the original message. Obviously, unlinkability is a variant of information privacy. Canard et al. [4] gave a generic construction of trapdoor sanitizable signatures which the candidate sanitizer cannot produce the sanitized signature until receiving the trapdoor from the signer. [5] utilized accountable chameleon hash and presented an accountable trapdoor sanitizable signature based on [4]. However, these schemes did not present a concrete construction of sanitizable signatures. Hence, several concrete sanitizable signature scheme [6–8] were proposed with thorough security proofs. Although these works make a significant contribution to the development of sanitizable signature, none of them considers the identity privacy of users and thus cannot be applied to EHR system.

ABS is converted from attribute-based encryption (ABE) [9,10]. Maji et al. [11] presented an ABS scheme which supported flexible access structure. However, the unforgeability proof of [11] was given under generic group model. In [12], Li et al. gave the construction of two efficient ABS schemes supporting threshold predicate in random oracle model and standard model, respectively. Okamoto and Takashima [13] proposed an ABS scheme for non-monotone access structure which introduced NOT gate into threshold access structure and was provably secure in the standard model. To achieve flexible access control as well as more secure level, [14,15] presented flexible ABS schemes in random oracle model and standard model, respectively. Concerning on the authority management of attributes, Li et al. [16] presented a formalized construction of multi-authority ABS scheme supporting threshold gates.

In this paper, we refer to two present ABSS schemes [17,18]. However, only [17] gave the concrete construction of ABSS. Thus, we compare our FABSS scheme with [17] and [8,12] to illustrate the advantage of our scheme in function and efficiency.

The remainder of this paper is organized as follows. The preliminary knowledge of our scheme is in Sect. 2. In Sect. 3 we define the algorithm model and security model. We propose the specific construction of FABSS scheme and corresponding security proof in Sects. 4 and 5, respectively. In Sect. 6 we compare our scheme with existing works and the paper is concluded in Sect. 7.

2   Preliminaries

2.1   Flexible Access Structure

The threshold access structure in ABS is composed of one threshold and several attributes. A user can generate a valid signature only if the size of the intersection of his attribute sets and the access structure attribute sets exceeds the threshold value. Simple access control can be achieved with threshold access structure, such as {'A' AND 'B' AND 'C'}, {'A' OR 'B' OR 'C'}.

The flexible access structure consists of a number of thresholds and attributes, in which each interior node is a threshold gate. Besides aforementioned structures, we can define expressive access control in large-scale attribute sets through changing the breadth and depth of the structure, such as {{'A' AND 'B'} OR 'C'}, {{'A' OR 'B'} AND 'C'}, etc.

2.2   Monotone Span Program

Suppose f is a monotone boolean function. A monotone span program over a field $\mathbb{F}$ for f is a $l \times t$ matrix $\mathbf{M}$, and f takes input as the mapping of each row of the matrix $\mathbf{M}$ with a labeling function $z(\cdot)$. The monotone span satisfies the following equation:

$$f(x_1, \ldots, x_n) = 1 \Leftrightarrow \exists v \in \mathbb{F}^{1 \times l} \ s.t. \ v\mathbf{M} = [1, 0, \ldots, 0] \text{ and } (\forall i : x_{z(i)} = 0 \Rightarrow v_i = 0).$$

Every monotone boolean function can be presented by some monotone span programs. The flexible attribute access structure is composed of several (t_i, l_i) threshold gates, meaning that we can obtain the secret from at least t_i of l_i attributes. The size of the matrix $\mathbf{M}$ depends on the specifications of these threshold gates. With i (t_i, l_i) threshold gates, we can construct a matrix $\mathbf{M}$ with length $l = \sum_i (l_i - 1) + 1$ and width $t = \sum_i (t_i - 1) + 1$.

2.3 Designated Instruction

The Designated Instruction (DI) refers to designated parts of the original message for updating. Let $m = m_1 m_2 \ldots m_n$, where m_k is defined as the bit at index k of message m. Let $DI \subseteq \{1, \ldots, n\}$ denote the set of the indexes that is going to be updated. Obviously, DI is classified into two groups, where $DI_1 = \{k \in DI : m_k = 0, \ m'_k = 1\}$, $DI_2 = \{k \in DI : m_k = 1, \ m'_k = 0\}$.

3 Algorithm Model and Security Model

3.1 Algorithm Model

The FABSS scheme is parametrized by five algorithms below.

$(Params, MSK) \leftarrow$ **Setup**(1^λ). Algorithm **Setup** takes a security parameter λ as input and outputs the public parameters $Params$ and the master secret key MSK.

$SK_\mathcal{A} \leftarrow$ **KeyGen**$(MSK, \mathcal{A})$. With the MSK, the **KeyGen** algorithm outputs the attribute private key $SK_\mathcal{A}$ based on the signing request of each patient on his attribute set $\mathcal{A} \subseteq \mathbb{A}$.

$\sigma \leftarrow$ **Sign**$(Params, SK_\mathcal{A}, m, f)$. The patient endorses a message m for the access structure f with his signing key $SK_\mathcal{A}$, resulting in the signature σ.

$accept/reject \leftarrow$ **Verify**$(Params, m, f, \sigma)$. The algorithm **Verify** allows the health professionals to verify whether the message is signed by a legitimate patient. It outputs $accept$ if the signature is valid, otherwise $reject$.

$(m', \sigma') \leftarrow$ **Sanitize**$(Params, m, \sigma, DI)$. According to the DI provided by the patient, the algorithm **Sanitize** outputs the sanitized message m' and corresponding signature σ'.

3.2 Security Model

Definition 1 (Correctness). *The FABSS scheme is correct if for $(Params, MSK) \leftarrow$ **Setup**, the message m, attribute sets $\mathcal{A}$ that satisfy the access structure f and the signing key $SK_\mathcal{A} \leftarrow$ **KeyGen**$(MSK, \mathcal{A})$,*

$$\textbf{Verify}(Params, m, f, \textbf{Sign}(params, SK_\mathcal{A}, m, f)) = \textbf{accept}.$$

Definition 2 (Unforgeability). *We prove the unforgeability under selective-predicate attack which is weaker than the adaptive predicate attack. The FABSS scheme is unforgeable under selective-predicate attack provided that the advantage of any polynomial-time adversary in the following experiment is negligible:*

- *The adversary chooses the challenge access structure f^*.*
- *The challenger runs $(Params, MSK) \leftarrow \textbf{Setup}$ and gives Params to the adversary.*
- *The adversary can make a polynomial bounded number of queries to oracles $\textbf{KeyGen}(MSK, \mathcal{A})$ and $\textbf{Sign}(Params, SK_{\mathcal{A}}, m, f)$.*
- *The adversary outputs the purported message-signature pair forgery (m^*, σ^*).*

The adversary wins if m^* is never queried to the $\textbf{Sign}$ oracle, and none of $\mathcal{A}$ queried to the $\textbf{KeyGen}$ oracle satisfy f, and $\textbf{Verify}(Params, m^*, f^*, \sigma^*) = $ accept.

Definition 3 (Anonymity). *Anonymity means that the signature would not reveal anything about the identity or attributes of the signer except the attributes in the access structure. The FABSS scheme is anonymous if for all access structure f, $(Params, MSK) \leftarrow \textbf{Setup}$, attributes $\mathcal{A}_1$ and $\mathcal{A}_2$ that satisfy f, attribute signing key $SK_{\mathcal{A}_1} \leftarrow \textbf{KeyGen}(MSK, \mathcal{A}_1)$ and $SK_{\mathcal{A}_2} \leftarrow \textbf{KeyGen}(MSK, \mathcal{A}_2)$, the distribution of $\sigma_{\mathcal{A}_1} \leftarrow \textbf{Sign}(Params, SK_{\mathcal{A}_1}, m, f)$ is identical to that of $\sigma_{\mathcal{A}_2} \leftarrow \textbf{Sign}(Params, SK_{\mathcal{A}_2}, m, f)$.*

Definition 4 (Information Privacy). *The FABSS scheme achieves information privacy if for all access structure f, $(Params, MSK) \leftarrow \textbf{Setup}(1^\lambda)$, attribute $\mathcal{A}$ satisfying f, $SK_{\mathcal{A}} \leftarrow \textbf{KeyGen}(MSK, \mathcal{A})$, message m_1, m_2 and a sanitized message m', where m' differs from m_1 and m_2 only at bits that are allowed to be sanitized, the distribution of $\sigma'_1 \leftarrow \textbf{Sanitize}(\textbf{Sign}(Params, SK_{\mathcal{A}}, m_1, f), Params, UI)$ and $\sigma'_2 \leftarrow \textbf{Sanitize}(\textbf{Sign}(Params, SK_{\mathcal{A}}, m_2, f), Params, UI)$ are identical.*

4   Our FABSS Scheme

Our scheme supports the access structure whose monotone span program $\mathbf{M}$ has width at most t_{max} which is an arbitrary number. $\mathbb{A} \subseteq \mathbb{Z}_p^*$ is the universe of all possible attributes in the access structure f. The original message $m = m_1 m_2 \ldots m_n \in \{0, 1\}^n$.

Setup: Let $\mathbb{G}_1, \mathbb{G}_2, \mathbb{G}_T$ be cyclic groups of prime order p. Choose a bilinear pairing $e : \mathbb{G}_1 \times \mathbb{G}_2 \to \mathbb{G}_T$ and random generators: $g_1 \leftarrow \mathbb{G}_1, g_{2_0}, \ldots, g_{2_{t_{max}}} \leftarrow \mathbb{G}_2$. Choose random $a_0, a, b \leftarrow \mathbb{Z}_p^*, u', u_1, \ldots, u_n \leftarrow \mathbb{Z}_p$ and set $A_0 = g_{2_0}^{a_0}, A_j = g_{2_j}^a$ and $B_j = g_{2_j}^b (\forall j \in [t_{max}]), U' = g_1^{u'}, U_k = g_1^{u_k} (\forall k \in [n])$. Public parameters are $g_{2_0}, \ldots, g_{2_{t_{max}}}, A_0, \ldots, A_{t_{max}}, B_0, \ldots, B_{t_{max}}, g_1, U', U_1, \ldots, U_n$. Master secret keys are a_0, a, b.

KeyGen: On inputting master secret keys and the attribute set $\mathcal{A} \subseteq \mathbb{A}$, choose random $K \leftarrow \mathbb{G}_1$ and set $K_0 = K^{1/a_0}, K_z = K^{1/(a+bz)} (\forall z \in \mathcal{A})$. The signing key is $SK_{\mathcal{A}} = (K, K_0, \{K_z \mid z \in \mathcal{A}\}$.

Sign: First convert the claim-predicate f into its corresponding monotone span program matrix $\mathbf{M} \in (\mathbb{Z}_p)^{l \times t}$, mapping each row of $\mathbf{M}$ with the row labeling function $z : [l] \to \mathbb{A}$. Then compute the vector v that corresponds to the desirable assignment for $\mathcal{A}$. Pick random $r \leftarrow \mathbb{Z}_p^*, r_1, \ldots, r_l \leftarrow \mathbb{Z}_p$ and compute $Y = K^r, S_i = (K_{z(i)}^{v_i})^r \cdot (U' \prod_{k=1}^n U_k^{m_k})^{r_i} (\forall i \in [l]), W = K_0^r, P_j = \prod_{i=1}^l (A_j B_j)^{\mathbf{M}_{i,j} \cdot r_i} (\forall j \in [t])$. The signature is $\sigma = (Y, W, S_1, \ldots, S_l, P_1, \ldots, P_t)$.

Verify: With $(Params, \sigma = (Y, W, S_1, \ldots, S_l, P_1, \ldots, P_t), m, f)$, the verifier first converts f into its corresponding monotone span program $\mathbf{M} \in (\mathbb{Z}_p)^{l \times t}$, with row labeling $z : [l] \to \mathbb{A}$. If $Y = 1$, the verifier outputs **reject**, otherwise checks $e(W, A_0) \overset{?}{=} e(Y, g_{2_0})$,

$$\prod_{i=1}^l e(S_i, (A_j B_j^{z(i)})^{\mathbf{M}_{i,j}}) \overset{?}{=} \begin{cases} e(Y, g_{2_1}) e(U' \prod_{k=1}^n U_k^{m_k}, P_1), & j = 1, \\ e(U' \prod_{k=1}^n U_k^{m_k}, P_j), & j > 1, \end{cases}$$

for each $j \in [t]$. The verifier returns **accept** if all the equations above hold, otherwise **reject**.

Sanitize: The sanitizer obtains σ and the DI from the signer. Pick random $\tilde{r}_1, \ldots, \tilde{r}_l \leftarrow \mathbb{Z}_p$ then compute $Y' = Y, S_i' = S_i \frac{\prod_{k \in I_1} U_k^{r_i}}{\prod_{k \in I_2} U_k^{r_i}} (U' \prod_{k=1}^n U_k^{m_k'})^{\tilde{r}_i} (\forall i \in [l]), W' = W, P_j' = P_j \prod_{i=1}^l (A_j B_j)^{\mathbf{M}_{i,j} \cdot \tilde{r}_i} (\forall j \in [t])$.

5 Security Analysis

Proof (Correctness). When the signature of either the original message or the sanitized message is signed by the signer whose attributes fit the access structure f, it can be successfully checked by the verification.

Verification:

$$e(W, A_0) = e(K_0^r, g_{2_0}^{a_0}) = e(K^r, g_{2_0}) = e(Y, g_{2_0}),$$

$$\prod_{i=1}^l e(S_i, (A_j B_j^{z(i)})^{\mathbf{M}_{i,j}}) = \prod_{i=1}^l e((K_{z(i)}^{v_i})^r \cdot (U' \prod_{k=1}^n U_k^{m_k})^{r_i}, g_{2_j}^{a + bz(i) \cdot \mathbf{M}_{i,j}})$$

$$= e((K^{\sum_{i=1}^l v_i \cdot \mathbf{M}_{i,j}})^r, g_{2_j}) \cdot e((U' \prod_{k=1}^n U_k^{m_k})^{r_i}, g_{2_j}^{(a + bz(i)) \cdot \mathbf{M}_{i,j}})$$

$$= \begin{cases} e(Y, g_{2_1}) e((U' \prod_{k=1}^n U_k^{m_k}), P_1), & j = 1, \\ e((U' \prod_{k=1}^n U_k^{m_k}), P_j), & j > 1. \end{cases}$$

Sanitization: From the definition of DI we note that $m_k' - m_k$ is 1 when $k \in I_1$, -1 when $k \in I_2$, and 0 otherwise. Thus we can conclude that

$$S_i' = S_i \frac{\prod_{k \in I_1} U_k^{r_i}}{\prod_{k \in I_2} U_k^{r_i}} (U' \prod_{k=1}^{n} U_k^{m_k'})^{\tilde{r}_i}$$

$$= (K_{z(i)}^{v_i})^r U'^{(r_i + \tilde{r}_i)} (\prod_{k=1}^{n} U_k^{m_k})^{r_i} (\prod_{k=1}^{n} U_k^{(m_k' - m_k)})^{\tilde{r}_i} (\prod_{k=1}^{n} U_k^{m_k'})^{\tilde{r}_i}$$

$$= (K_{z(i)}^{v_i})^r U'^{(r_i + \tilde{r}_i)} (\prod_{k=1}^{n} U_k^{m_k'})^{(r_i + \tilde{r}_i)},$$

$$P_j' = P_j \prod_{i=1}^{l} (A_j B_j)^{\mathbf{M}_{i,j} \cdot \tilde{r}_i} = \prod_{i=1}^{l} (A_j B_j)^{\mathbf{M}_{i,j} \cdot (\tilde{r}_i + r_i)}.$$

From the sanitization we can see that the distribution of the santized signature is identical to that of the original signature, so the verification fits both of them.   □

Proof (Unforgeability). We can prove that our FABSS scheme is unforgeable under selective-predicate attack in the generic group model. Here we present the full proof of unforgeability.

For $Y = K^r \leftarrow \mathbb{G}_1$ and $W = K_0^r = K^{r/a_0} \leftarrow \mathbb{G}_1$, we suppose $Y = g_1^y, W = g_1^{y/a_0}$. Similarly, suppose $S_i = g_1^{s_i}, P_j = g_{2_j}^{p_j}$. We can derive that $S_i = g_1^{\frac{yv_i}{a+bz(i)} + u'r_i + \sum_{k=1}^{n} u_k m_k r_i}, P_j = g_{2_j}^{\sum_{i=1}^{l}(a+bz(i))\mathbf{M}_{i,j} \cdot r_i}$. So $s_i = \frac{yv_i}{a+bz(i)} + u'r_i + \sum_{k=1}^{n} u_k m_k r_i, p_j = \sum_{i=1}^{l}(a + bz(i))\mathbf{M}_{i,j} \cdot r_i$. Then we get $s_i(a + bz(i))\mathbf{M}_{i,j} = yv_i\mathbf{M}_{i,j} + r_i(u' + \sum_{k=1}^{n} u_k m_k)(a + bz(i))\mathbf{M}_{i,j}$. Then $\sum_{i=1}^{l}(s_i(a+bz(i))\mathbf{M}_{i,j}) = \sum_{i=1}^{l}(yv_i\mathbf{M}_{i,j} + r_i(u' + \sum_{k=1}^{n} u_k m_k)(a+bz(i))\mathbf{M}_{i,j})$. We assume that $\sum_{i=1}^{l} v_i \cdot \mathbf{M}_{i,j} = \mathbf{d} = [1, 0, \ldots, 0]$, then we conclude that $p_j = \frac{1}{u' + \sum_{k=1}^{n} u_k m_k} \cdot [\sum_{i=1}^{l}(s_i(a + bz(i))\mathbf{M}_{i,j}) - yd_j]$.

Therefore, we can define that the oracle $\mathbf{Sign}(Params, SK_\mathcal{A}, m, f)$ generates signatures in the following way: Let $\mathbf{M} \in (\mathbb{Z}_p)^{l \times t}$ be the monotone span program for f, with row labeling function $z : [l] \to \mathbb{A}$.

- Pick random $s_1, \ldots, s_l \leftarrow \mathbb{Z}_p^*$.
- For all $j \in [t]$, compute $p_j = \frac{1}{u' + \sum_{k=1}^{n} u_k m_k} \cdot [\sum_{i=1}^{l}(s_i(a + bz(i))\mathbf{M}_{i,j}) - yd_j]$, where $\mathbf{d} = [1, 0, \ldots, 0]$.
- Output $\sigma = (g_1^y, g_1^{y/a_0}, g_1^{s_1}, \ldots, g_1^{s_l}, g_{2_1}^{p_1}, \ldots, g_{2_t}^{p_t})$.

We assume that there is an efficiently computable homomorphism between $\mathbb{G}_1$ and $\mathbb{G}_2$. For any generic-group adversary, the simulator registers each group element's discrete logarithm in the following formal variables: $\Sigma = \{a_0, a, b, u', \lambda_0\} \cup \{\lambda_j \mid j \in [t_{max}]\} \cup \{x_\mu \mid \mu \in [\Lambda]\} \cup \{s_i^{(q)}, y^{(q)} \mid q \in [\nu], i \in [l^{(q)}]\}$, where Λ is the number of queries made to the **KeyGen** oracle, ν is the number of **Sign** queries made by the adversary, and $l^{(q)}$ is the length of the monotone span program corresponding to the qth signature query.

The simulation associates each group element with aforementioned formal variables. For each group element in its collection, the simulator keeps track of its discrete logarithm and gives it to the adversary as the encoding of the group element. In the simulation, the group elements are expressed as follows:

Public key components are generated by **Setup**: 1, representing the generator g_1. λ_0, representing $g_{2_0} = g_1^{\lambda_0}$. $\lambda_0 a_0$, denoting $A_0 = g_1^{\lambda_0 a_0}$. $\{\lambda_j \mid j \in [t_{max}]\}$, indicating $g_{2_j} = g_1^{\lambda_j}$. $\{\lambda_j a \mid j \in [t_{max}]\}$, standing for $A_j = g_1^{\lambda_j a}$. $\{\lambda_j b \mid j \in [t_{max}]\}$, representing $B_j = g_1^{\lambda_j b}$. u', denoting $U' = g_1^{u'}$. $\{u_k \mid k \in [n]\}$, indicating $U_k = g_1^{u_k}$.

Signing key components are given by **KeyGen**. Let $\mathcal{A}_\mu$ be the μth set of attributes queried to **KeyGen**: x_μ, representing $K^{(\mu)} = g_1^{x_\mu}$. x_μ/a_0, denoting $K_0^{(\mu)} = g_1^{x_\mu/a_0}$. $\{x_\mu/(a+bz) \mid z \in \mathcal{A}_\mu\}$, indicating $K_z^{(\mu)} = g_1^{x_\mu/(a+bz)}$.

Sign queries. For the qth signature query on message $m^{(q)}$ under the predicate $f^{(q)}$ made by the adversary, let $\mathbf{M}^{(q)} \in (\mathbb{Z}_p)^{l^{(q)} \times t^{(q)}}$ be the monotone span program corresponding to $f^{(q)}$, with row labeling $z^{(q)} : [l^{(q)}] \rightarrow \mathbb{A}$: $\{s_i^{(q)} \mid i \in [l^{(q)}]\}$, representing $S_i^{(q)} = g_1^{s_i^{(q)}}$. $y^{(q)}$, denoting $Y^{(q)} = g_1^{y^{(q)}}$. $y^{(q)}/a_0$, standing for $W^{(q)} = g_1^{y^{(q)}/a_0}$. $\{p_j^{(q)} \mid j \in [t^{(q)}]\}$, where $p_j^{(q)} = \dfrac{\lambda_j}{u' + \sum_{k=1}^{n^{(q)}} u_k^{(q)} m_k^{(q)}} \cdot$ $\left[\sum_{i=1}^{l^{(q)}}(s_i^{(q)}(a + bz^{(q)}(i))\mathbf{M}_{i,j}) - y^{(q)} d_j\right]$, representing $P_j^{(q)} = g_1^{p_j^{(q)}}$.

Now the adversary outputs a forgery signature $\sigma^* = (g_1^{y^*}, g_1^{w^*}, g_1^{s_1^*}, \ldots, g_1^{s_{l^*}^*}, g_1^{p_1^*}, \ldots, g_1^{p_{t^*}^*})$ on a predicate f^* and message m^* such that $(m^*, f^*) \neq (m^{(q)}, f^{(q)})$ for all q. $\mathbf{M}^* \in (\mathbb{Z}_p)^{l^* \times t^*}$ is the corresponding monotone span program with row labeling $z^*(\cdot)$. The discrete logarithm of the forgery has to satisfy $y^* \neq 0, w^* \neq 0$, for $Y^* \neq 1, W^* \neq 1$ and $\sum_{i=1}^{l^*} s_i^* \mathbf{M}_{i,j}^*(a + bz^*(i))\lambda_j = y^* d_j \lambda_j + (u' + \sum_{k=1}^{n^*} u_k^* m_k^*)p_j^*$, these constraints can hold with non-negligible probability only if two sides of the equation are functionally equivalent.

Then we will prove if the two sides of the equation are functionally equivalent, there has to be a contradiction: there exists a $\mu_0 \in [\Lambda]$ such that $f^*(\mathcal{A}_{\mu_0}) = 1$. Namely, the adversary may generate a signature using the signing key $SK_{\mathcal{A}_{\mu_0}}$ that has been queried before but meets the new claim-predicate f^*, and thus the output is not a forgery.

Assume $\mathbb{L}(\Gamma)$ is the set of all multilinear polynomials over the set of terms Γ with coefficients in $\mathbb{Z}_p$. Let $\mathbb{H}(\Gamma) \subset \mathbb{L}(\Gamma)$ be the subset of homogeneous polynomial.

We know that $y^*, w^*, s_1^*, \ldots, s_{l^*}^*, p_1^*, \ldots, p_{t^*}^* \in \mathbb{L}(\Gamma)$, where $\Gamma = \{1, a_0, \lambda_0, u', u_k\} \cup \{\lambda_j, a\lambda_j, b\lambda_j \mid j \in [t_{max}]\} \cup \{x_\mu, x_\mu/a_0, x_\mu/(a+bz) \mid \mu \in [\Lambda], z \in \mathcal{A}_\mu\} \cup \{s_i^{(q)}, y^{(q)}, w^{(q)}, p_j^{(q)} \mid q \in [\nu], i \in [l^{(q)}], j \in [t^{(q)}]\}$. We can exclude certain terms by comparing terms between the equation, then for y^* we can get $y^* \in \mathbb{H}(\{x_\mu \mid \mu \in [\Lambda]\} \cup \{y^{(q)} \mid q \in [\nu]\})$. It is obvious that $\lambda_j \mid (u' + \sum_{k=1}^{n^*} u_k^* m_k^*)p_j^*$ and thus $\lambda_j \mid p_j^*$. So, $p_j^* \in \mathbb{H}(\{\lambda_j, a\lambda_j, b\lambda_j\} \cup \{p_j^{(q)} \mid q \in [\nu]\})$.

Suppose p_j^* has a λ_j term. Then the right side has monomials λ_j and $b\lambda_j$. Because y^* has no a or b term, $y^* d_j \lambda_j$ cannot contribute a λ_j monomial. Therefore $\sum_{i=1}^{l^*} s_i^* \mathbf{M}_{i,j}^*(a + bz^*(i))\lambda_j$ cannot contribute a monomial with λ_j alone, so $p_j^* \in \mathbb{H}(\{a\lambda_j, b\lambda_j\} \cup \{p_j^{(q)} \mid q \in [\nu]\})$.

Suppose p_j^* has a $p_j^{(q)}$ term. Then $(u' + \sum_{k=1}^{n^*} u_k^* m_k^*) p_j^*$ will contribute the term of $(\frac{u' + \sum_{k=1}^{n^*} u_k^* m_k^*}{u' + \sum_{k=1}^{n^{(q)}} u_k^{(q)} m_k^{(q)}}) \cdot p_j^{(q)}$. Since $\sum_{k=1}^{n^*} u_k^* m_k^* \neq \sum_{k=1}^{n^{(q)}} u_k^{(q)} m_k^{(q)}$ for any q, this is a proper rational. Neither y^* nor $\{s_i^*\}_{i \in l^*}$ can yield terms in the final equation with a factor of $\frac{u' + \sum_{k=1}^{n^*} u_k^* m_k^*}{u' + \sum_{k=1}^{n^{(q)}} u_k^{(q)} m_k^{(q)}}$. Hence, $p_j^* \in \mathbb{H}(\{a\lambda_j, b\lambda_j\})$.

Consider j_0 such that $d_{j_0} \neq 0$. As neither $(u' + \sum_{k=1}^{n^*} u_k^* m_k^*) p_{j_0}^*$ nor $\sum_{i=1}^{l^*} s_i^* \mathbf{M}_{i,j_0}^* (a + bz^*(i)) \lambda_{j_0}$ can contribute a monomial of this form, y^* cannot have a $y^{(q)}$ term. Therefore, $y^* \in \mathbb{H}(\{x_\mu \mid \mu \in [\Lambda]\})$. Finally we conclude that $p_j^* \in \mathbb{H}(\{a\lambda_j, b\lambda_j\}), y^* \in \mathbb{H}(\{x_\mu \mid \mu \in [\Lambda]\})$.

To make the expression equal, some parts of the left side have x_μ to fit y^* and the other parts do not have x_μ to satisfy p_j^*. So, we can break s_i^* up into two parts: one whose terms involve x_μ variables, and one whose terms do not. Suppose $s_i^* = t_i^*(X_i) + \delta^*(\Gamma \setminus X_i)$, where $X_i = \{\frac{x_\mu}{a + bz^*(i)} \mid z(i) \in \mathcal{A}_\mu, \mu \in [\Lambda]\}$ is to cancel out the term $(a + bz^*(i))$ from the left side. For $t_i^* \in \mathbb{H}(X_i)$, it is apparent for all $j \in [t]$ that $\sum_{i=1}^{l^*} t_i^* \mathbf{M}_{i,j}^*(a + bz^*(i)) = y^* d_j = y^* \sum_{i=1}^{l^*} v_i^* \mathbf{M}_{i,j}^*$, because of the equality of two sides of the equation, we get for all $i \in [l]$ that $t_i^* \mathbf{M}_{i,j}^*(a + bz^*(i)) = y^* v_i^* \mathbf{M}_{i,j}^*$.

Take account of any x_{μ_0} that has a non-zero coefficient in y^*. Construct v_i^*, for $i \in [l]$, by defining $v_i^* = \frac{1}{[x_{\mu_0}] y^*} \left[\frac{x_{\mu_0}}{a + bz^*(i)} \right] t_i^*$, where the $[x_{\mu_0}] y^*$ denotes the coefficient of the term x_{μ_0} in y^*, $\left[\frac{x_{\mu_0}}{a + bz^*(i)} \right] t_i^*$ denotes the coefficient of the term $\frac{x_{\mu_0}}{a + bz^*(i)}$ in t_i^*. v^* is a vector composed of constants, which satisfies the equation $v^* \mathbf{M}^* = [d_1, \ldots, d_t] = [1, 0, \ldots, 0]$. Further, when $v_i^* \neq 0$, the set $\mathcal{A}_{\mu_0}$ surely contains the attribute $z^*(i)$, which means $x_{z^*(i)} \neq 0$. By the properties of the monotone span program, it must be the case that $f^*(\mathcal{A}_{\mu_0}) = 1$, thus the signature is not a forgery.   □

Proof (Anonymity). In our construction, the signature will not reveal which attributes of the signer's attributes $\mathcal{A}$ are used to sign the message, because any attribute subset satisfying the access structure f can generate a valid signature. Thus, we only need to prove that the signer's identity among all users is kept anonymous even when $\mathcal{A} = \mathbb{A}$, where $\mathbb{A}$ is the attributes in f.

First, the challenger runs **Setup** to get the public parameters $Params$ and master secret keys MSK. The adversary outputs two attributes $\mathcal{A}_1$ and $\mathcal{A}_2$ satisfying f, and conducts **KeyGen** to get signing keys $SK_{\mathcal{A}_1} = (K_1, K_{0_1}, \{K_{z_1} \mid z \in \mathcal{A}_1\}$ and $SK_{\mathcal{A}_2} = (K_2, K_{0_2}, \{K_{z_2} \mid z \in \mathcal{A}_2\}$, respectively. Let $K_\theta, K_{0_\theta} = K_\theta^{1/a_0}, K_{z_\theta} = K_\theta^{1/(a+bz)}$ for each $z \in \mathcal{A}_\theta$, where $\theta \in \{1, 2\}$.

Then the adversary asks the challenger to generate a signature for message m^* with the signing key from either $SK_{\mathcal{A}_1}$ or $SK_{\mathcal{A}_2}$. The challenger chooses a random bit $b \in \{1, 2\}$ and outputs a signature $Y = K^r, W = K_0^r, S_i = K_{z(i)}^{v_i} \cdot (U' \prod_{k=1}^{n} U_k^{m_k})^{r_i}, P_j = \prod_{i=1}^{l} (A_j B_j)^{\mathbf{M}_{i,j} \cdot r_i}$ by the algorithm **Sign** with the signing key $SK_{\mathcal{A}_b} = (K_b, K_{0_b}, \{K_{z_b} \mid z \in \mathcal{A}_b\}$. On the basis of Monotone Span Program, it is obvious that it could be generated from either $SK_{\mathcal{A}_1}$ or

SK_{A_2}. Hence, if the signature is generated from SK_{A_1} for A_1, it could also be generated from SK_{A_2} for A_2. Thus, our FABSS scheme satisfies anonymity. $\square$

Proof (Information Privacy). From the construction of our scheme, the signature of message $m' = m'_1 m'_2 \ldots m'_n$ is $\sigma = (Y = K^r, S_i = (K^{v_i}_{z(i)})^r \cdot (U' \prod^n_{k=1} U^{m_k}_k)^{r_i} (\forall i \in [l]), W = K^r_0, P_j = \prod^l_{i=1}(A_j B^{z(i)}_j)^{M_{i,j} \cdot r_i} (\forall j \in [t]))$. The sanitized signature of message m_1 resulting in m' is $\sigma'_1 = (Y = K^r, \{S_i = (K^{v_i}_{z(i)})^r \cdot (U' \prod^n_{k=1} U^{m'_k}_k)^{r_i + \tilde{r}_i} : (\forall i \in [l])\}, W = K^r_0, \{P_j = \prod^l_{i=1}(A_j B^{z(i)}_j)^{M_{i,j} \cdot (r_i + \tilde{r}_i)} : (\forall j \in [t])\})$, where $r, r_i, \tilde{r}_i$ are random numbers. So the distribution of σ is identical to that of σ'_1. Similarly, the distribution is identical to σ'_2 of message m_2 resulting in m'. Hence, the distribution of σ'_1 and σ'_2 are identical and our scheme preserves the information privacy. $\square$

6   Performance Analysis

Through comparing with existing scheme functionally in Table 1, our FABSS scheme not only reduces the patients computation cost, but also preserves the privacy of patients. Meanwhile, the FABSS scheme achieves flexible access structure and fine-grained access control. Thus, our scheme applies to the EHR system.

Table 1. Functional analysis

	FABSS	ABSS [17]	ABS [12]	SS [8]
Reduce patients' computation cost	✓	✓	✗	✓
Flexible access structure	✓	✗	✗	✗
Anonymity	✓	✓	✓	✗
Fine-grained access control	✓	✓	✓	✗

In Table 2 we specify the efficiency of our scheme. For the ease of exposition we assume $\mathbb{G}_1, \mathbb{G}_2$ are symmetric, treating $\mathbb{G}_1$ as the base group and $\mathbb{G}_2$ as the bilinear group $\mathbb{G}_T$ in our scheme. In scheme [8,12,17], n denotes the sum of the attributes in the system, m is the length of the message, ω is the signers attributes, the threshold value is expressed by k and $d \geq k$. I is the order of UI. In our scheme, we first convert f into the matrix $\mathbf{M}^{l \times t}$, then denote the length and width of the matrix by l and t, respectively, where $l = n, t = k$. EX is the number of the exponent arithmetic and P is the number of the pairing arithmetic.

From Table 2 we find that our scheme exceeds in $Key.Size, Key.Gen, Sig.Size, Sansig.Size$ than that of [12,17] and is inferior to that of [8], because [8] does not consider the privacy of users and thus does not include the attribute sets. The size of $Params, MSK$ is similar to that of [12,17]. Furthermore, the computation cost of $Sig.Gen, Sansig.Gen$ and $Verify$ is longer than that of [8,17], which is due to the flexible access structure with matrix $\mathbf{M}$ and admissible.

Table 2. Efficiency analysis

	FABSS	ABSS [17]	ABS [12]	SS [8]
Params	$(3t + m + 5)\mathbb{G}_1$	$(m + n + 4)\mathbb{G}_1 + \mathbb{G}_2$	$(m + 3)\mathbb{G}_1 + \mathbb{G}_2$	$(m + 4)\mathbb{G}_1 + \mathbb{G}_2$
MSK	$3\mathbb{Z}_p$	$\mathbb{Z}_p$	$\mathbb{Z}_p$	$\mathbb{Z}_p$
Key.Size	$(\omega + 2)\mathbb{G}_1$	$2(\omega + d - 1)\mathbb{G}_1$	$2(\omega + d - 1)\mathbb{G}_1$	-
Key.Gen	$(\omega + 1)EX$	$3(\omega + d - 1)EX$	$3(\omega + d - 1)EX$	-
Sig.Size	$(l + t + 2)\mathbb{G}_1$	$2(n + d - k + 1)\mathbb{G}_1$	$(n + d - k + 2)\mathbb{G}_1$	$2\mathbb{G}_1$
Sansig.Size	$(l + t + 2)\mathbb{G}_1$	$2(n + d - k + 1)\mathbb{G}_1$	-	$2\mathbb{G}_1$
Sig.Gen	$(lt + 2l + m + 2)EX$	$(4n + 6d - 4k + m + 2)EX$	$(2(n + 2d - k) + m + 2)EX$	$(m + 3)EX$
Sansig.Gen	$(l(t + 1) + m + I)EX$	$(4(n + d - k) + m + I + 2)EX$	-	$(m + I + 2)EX$
Verify	$(tl + t + 3)P + (2tl + m)EX$	$2(n + d - k + 1)P + mEX$	$(n + d - k + 2)P + mEX$	$3P + mEX$

7 Conclusion

In order to reduce the computation cost and keep the identity privacy of users in the EHR system, we propose the Flexible Attribute-Based Sanitizable Signature (FABSS) scheme. Security demonstration shows that our scheme is unforgeable and preserves the anonymity and information privacy of the users. Compared with existing scheme, our scheme not only reduce the users' computation cost when data updating, but also supports flexible access structure defining expressive access control in large-scale users. Further efforts can be made on enhancing the security model of our FABSS scheme. In addition, we will exploit multi-authority FABSS scheme in which the attributes are assigned by different attribute authorities.

Acknowledgement. This work is supported by the National High Technology Research and Development Program (863 Program) (No. 2015AA016007, No. 2015AA017203), the Key Program of NSFC Grant (No. U1405255, No. U1135002), the National Natural Science Foundation of China (No. 61502248) and the NUPTSF (No. 215008). The authors would like to thank the editors and the anonymous reviewers for their constructive comments that would help us to improve this paper.

References

1. Ateniese, G., Chou, D.H., de Medeiros, B., Tsudik, G.: Sanitizable signatures. In: di Vimercati, S.C., Syverson, P., Gollmann, D. (eds.) ESORICS 2005. LNCS, vol. 3679, pp. 159–177. Springer, Heidelberg (2005). https://doi.org/10.1007/11555827_10
2. Brzuska, C., Fischlin, M., Freudenreich, T., Lehmann, A., Page, M., Schelbert, J., Schröder, D., Volk, F.: Security of sanitizable signatures revisited. In: Jarecki, S., Tsudik, G. (eds.) PKC 2009. LNCS, vol. 5443, pp. 317–336. Springer, Heidelberg (2009). https://doi.org/10.1007/978-3-642-00468-1_18
3. Brzuska, C., Fischlin, M., Lehmann, A., Schröder, D.: Unlinkability of sanitizable signatures. In: Nguyen, P.Q., Pointcheval, D. (eds.) PKC 2010. LNCS, vol. 6056, pp. 444–461. Springer, Heidelberg (2010). https://doi.org/10.1007/978-3-642-13013-7_26
4. Canard, S., Laguillaumie, F., Milhau, M.: Trapdoor sanitizable signatures and their application to content protection. In: Bellovin, S.M., Gennaro, R., Keromytis, A., Yung, M. (eds.) ACNS 2008. LNCS, vol. 5037, pp. 258–276. Springer, Heidelberg (2008). https://doi.org/10.1007/978-3-540-68914-0_16

5. Lai, J., Ding, X., Wu, Y.: Accountable trapdoor sanitizable signatures. In: Deng, R.H., Feng, T. (eds.) ISPEC 2013. LNCS, vol. 7863, pp. 117–131. Springer, Heidelberg (2013). https://doi.org/10.1007/978-3-642-38033-4_9

6. Miyazaki, K., Hanaoka, G., Imai, H.: Digitally signed document sanitizing scheme based on bilinear maps. In: Proceedings of the 2006 ACM Symposium on Information, Computer and Communications Security, pp. 343–354 (2006)

7. Yuen, T.H., Susilo, W., Liu, J.K., Mu, Y.: Sanitizable signatures revisited. In: Franklin, M.K., Hui, L.C.K., Wong, D.S. (eds.) CANS 2008. LNCS, vol. 5339, pp. 80–97. Springer, Heidelberg (2008). https://doi.org/10.1007/978-3-540-89641-8_6

8. Agrawal, S., Kumar, S., Shareef, A., Rangan, C.P.: Sanitizable signatures with strong transparency in the standard model. In: Bao, F., Yung, M., Lin, D., Jing, J. (eds.) Inscrypt 2009. LNCS, vol. 6151, pp. 93–107. Springer, Heidelberg (2010). https://doi.org/10.1007/978-3-642-16342-5_7

9. Goyal, V., Pandey, O., Sahai, A., Waters, B.: Attribute-based encryption for fine-grained access control of encrypted data. In: Proceedings of 13th ACM Conference on Computer and Communications Security, pp. 89–98 (2006)

10. Bethencourt, J., Sahai, A., Waters, B.: Ciphertext-policy attribute-based encryption. In: Proceedings of IEEE Symposium on Security and Privacy, pp. 321–334 (2007)

11. Maji, H.K., Prabhakaran, M., Rosulek, M.: Attribute-based signatures. In: Kiayias, A. (ed.) CT-RSA 2011. LNCS, vol. 6558, pp. 376–392. Springer, Heidelberg (2011). https://doi.org/10.1007/978-3-642-19074-2_24

12. Li, J., Au, M.H., Susilo, W., Xie, D., Ren, K.: Attribute-based signature and its applications. In: Proceedings of 5th ACM Symposium on Information, Computer and Communications Security, pp. 60–69 (2010)

13. Okamoto, T., Takashima, K.: Efficient attribute-based signatures for non-monotone predicates in the standard model. In: Catalano, D., Fazio, N., Gennaro, R., Nicolosi, A. (eds.) PKC 2011. LNCS, vol. 6571, pp. 35–52. Springer, Heidelberg (2011). https://doi.org/10.1007/978-3-642-19379-8_3

14. Su, J., Cao, D., Zhao, B., Wang, X., You, I.: ePASS: an expressive attribute-based signature scheme with privacy and an unforgeability guarantee for the internet of things. Future Gener. Comput. Syst. 33, 11–18 (2014)

15. Rao, Y.S., Dutta, R.: Efficient attribute-based signature and signcryption realizing expressive access structures. Int. J. Inf. Secur. 15, 81–109 (2016)

16. Li, J., Chen, X., Huang, X.: New attribute-based authentication and its application in anonymous cloud access service. Int. J. Web Grid Serv. 11, 125–141 (2015)

17. Liu, X., Ma, J., Xiong, J., Ma, J., Li, Q.: Attribute based sanitizable signature scheme. J. Commun. 34, 148–155 (2013)

18. Xu, L., Zhang, X., Wu, X., Shi, W.: ABSS: an attribute-based sanitizable signature for integrity of outsourced database with public cloud. In: Proceedings of 5th ACM Conference on Data and Application Security and Privacy, pp. 167–169 (2015)

SSUKey: A CPU-Based Solution Protecting Private Keys on Untrusted OS

Huorong Li[1,2,3], Wuqiong Pan[1,2(✉)], Jingqiang Lin[1,2], Wangzhao Cheng[1,2,3], and Bingyu Li[1,2,3]

[1] Data Assurance and Communication Security Research Center, Beijing, China
[2] State Key Laboratory of Information Security,
Institute of Information Engineering, CAS, Beijing, China
panwuqiong@iie.ac.cn
[3] School of Cyber Security, University of Chinese Academy of Sciences,
Beijing, China

Abstract. With more and more websites adopt private keys to authenticate users or sign digital payments in e-commerce, various solutions have been proposed to secure private keys – some of them employ extra specific hardware devices while most of them adopt security features provided by general OS. However, users are reluctant to extra devices and general OS is too complicated to protect itself, let alone the private keys on it. This paper proposes a software solution, SSUKey, adopting CPU security features to protect private keys against the vulnerabilities of OS. Firstly, threshold cryptography (TC) is employed to partition the private key into two shares and two Intel SGX enclaves on local client and remote server are used to secure the key shares respectively. Secondly, the two enclaves are carefully designed and configured to mitigate the vulnerabilities of Intel SGX, including side channel and rollback. Thirdly, an overall central private key management is designed to help users globally monitor the usage of private keys and detect abnormal behaviors. Finally, we implement SSUKey as a cryptography provider, apply it to file encryption and Transport Layer Security (TLS) download, and evaluate their performance. The experiment results show that the performance decline due to SSUKey is acceptable.

Keywords: Trusted Execution Environment (TEE) · Intel SGX
Trusted computing · Threshold cryptography · Key protection

1 Introduction

Digital signature is widely used in authentication, digital payment and online banking. According to Stratistics MRC, the Global Digital Signature Market is accounted for $662.4 million in 2016 [1]. Digital signature is based on asymmetric cryptography which has a pair of public key and private key. The private key represents the identity of an entity and is used to create digital signatures while

© Springer International Publishing AG, part of Springer Nature 2018
S. Qing et al. (Eds.): ICICS 2017, LNCS 10631, pp. 51–62, 2018.
https://doi.org/10.1007/978-3-319-89500-0_4

the public key is known to public and is used to verify the digital signatures. The private key should be kept secret.

At present the most effective way to protect private keys is using specific hardware devices, which have their own processors and storage isolated from host PC. This is adopted by Facebook, Google, GitHub, and Dropbox [2]. But users are reluctant to use specified hardware devices because they are inconvenient to carry and easy to lose. According to SafeNet Inc., the use of hardware-based authentication dropped from 60% in 2013 to 41% in 2014; conversely, the use of software-based authentication rose from 27% in 2013 to 40% in 2014 [3].

The security of software-based methods protecting private key relies on the security of privileged code, such as OS kernel and VMM (Virtual Machine Monitor). For example, [4,5] use hypervisor to provide isolation environment to protect sensitive data. However, privileged code had been found many serious vulnerabilities, for example, CVE-2015-2291, CVE-2017-0077, CVE-2016-0180 and CVE-2017-8468 for Windows kernel, CVE-2017-13715, CVE-2017-12146, CVE-2017-10663 and CVE-2016-10150 for Linux kernel, CVE-2009-1542, CVE-2016-7457 and CVE-2017-10918 for VMM, CVE-2016-8103, CVE-2016-5729 and CVE-2006-6730 for SMM, and may still have vulnerabilities.[1]

Intel Software Guard Extensions (SGX) [6–9] enables execution of security-critical application code, called enclaves, in isolation from the untrusted system software. It also provides enclaves processor-specific keys, such as the sealing key or the attestation key, which can be accessed by the enclaves. SGX is considered as a remarkable way to protect private keys when first proposed [7]. However, SGX has been found several vulnerabilities, such as cache-based side channel attack [10,11], page-based side channel attack [12], and rollback attack [9]. Although Intel has recently added support for monotonic counters (SGX counters) [13] that an enclave developer may use for rollback attack protection, this mechanism is likely vulnerable to bus tapping and flash mirroring attacks [14] since the non-volatile memory used to store the counters resides outside the processor package.

We propose a software solution, SSUKey, adopting Intel SGX to protect private keys against the vulnerabilities of OS. Especially, SSUKey employs ECC-based threshold cryptography (ECC-TC) to mitigate the vulnerabilities of SGX and enhance the security of SGX. Each private key is partitioned into two shares using ECC-TC, and the two key shares are protected using two Intel SGX enclaves on local client and remote server respectively. Since the two enclaves are carefully designed and the remote server can be carefully configured and well protected by additional mechanisms, such as advanced firewall, it is very difficult for an attacker to successfully perform side channel and rollback attacks on both the local client and the remote server enclaves. If the attacker only compromises one of them, threshold cryptography (TC) ensures that the attacker knows nothing about the private key. SSUKey also provides a central private key management. A user may use the same private key on different websites for con-

---

[1] All these vulnerabilities are published in Nation Vulnerability Database (NVD, https://nvd.nist.gov/).

venience. When the private key is compromised, our SSUKey can directly revoke the private key by the remote server immediately without having to inform all the websites respectively. The overall central private key management also help users globally monitor the usage of private keys and detect abnormal behaviors.

Windows CNG (Cryptography API: Next Generation), proposed by Microsoft, sets a standard interface for both cryptography provider and application. All Windows built-in applications (e.g., TLS, certificate tools, IE, Edge, IIS, etc.) use CNG to protect cryptographic keys and Microsoft recommends all Windows applications should use CNG to protect cryptographic keys. We implement our SSUKey complying with CNG, supporting SM2 (ECC algorithm) [15], SM3 (hash algorithm) [16], SM4 (symmetric algorithm) [17], PRF (pseudo random function) [18], and NIST hash-based DRBG (random number generation algorithm) [19]. As a proof-of-concept, we evaluate the single-thread performance of SSUKey on Intel NUC6 with i3-6100U CPU, which is designed low power (15 W). We first evaluate SSUKey by testing cryptographic operations. Compared to the software solution without any protection, the performance of verifying signatures, symmetric operations and hash operations almost does not change, while that of signing signatures declines from 481 Operations per second (Ops) to 110 Ops. Second, we evaluate SSUKey by testing it in real applications, file encryption and TLS download. Compared to the one without any protection, the performance of file encryption declines less than 3%, while that of TLS download (with 4 KB message) declines less than 1%. As the result, the performance decline due to SSUKey is acceptable.

In summary, we claim following main **contributions:**

- We propose and implement SSUKey, a CPU-based software solution protecting private keys against the vulnerabilities of OS, VMM, SMM, etc.
- Our SSUKey can mitigate the vulnerabilities of SGX, including side channel and rollback attacks, and add a useful function, an overall central private key management.
- We implement our SSUKey on Windows CNG, apply it to file encryption and TLS download, and evaluate the performance.

Intel CPU supports SGX starting with the Skylake microarchitecture, so our SSUKey can work on any new CPUs afterwards.

2   Assumptions

We consider a powerful adversary who controls all software except SSUKey on the target platform, including the OS. The adversary's aim is to compromise private keys. The adversary can block, delay, replay, read and modify all messages sent by SSUKey. Especially, the adversary can revert the sealed secrets in file system to previous state, i.e., rollback attack. The adversary can learn some information about the private keys by performing side channel attack [10,11].

The adversary cannot break through CPU and compromise SGX enclaves from inside. Specially the adversary cannot read or modify the enclave runtime memory and has no access to processor-specific keys, such as the sealing key or the attestation key. We also assume that it is very difficult to perform side channel or rollback attacks on both local client and remote server successfully, since the remote server is carefully configured and well protected by additional mechanisms, such as advanced firewall.

SSUKey ensures that the integrity, confidentiality and freshness of private keys. SSUKey does not aim to provide availability since the adversary controls the OS and denial-of-service (DoS) is always possible. SSUKey authenticates a user using the password entered by the user. But SSUKey does not protect the path between the input device like keyboard and the enclave. This function can be provided by SGXIO [20] which employs hypervisor to enhance the security of I/O path. Our SSUKey is compatible with SGXIO.

3   SSUKey Design

3.1   Architecture

Figure 1 shows our system overview. Our system consists of a remote server and some users' local platforms. Each local platform may run multiple user applications that host local client enclaves (CEs) which have an access to the user's cryptographic keys. The remote server runs a service that hosts a remote server enclave (SE) which assists CE to perform cryptographic operations cooperatively. The remote server is carefully configured and well protected by additional mechanisms, such as advanced firewall, intrusion detection system, and latest malware detection or anti-virus software. Both CE and SE run a share of ECC-TC algorithms and hold a share of corresponding cryptographic keys respectively.

Figure 2 gives the key components of our SSUKey architecture. Authentication and session management modules authenticate CE/SE to its counterpart and establish a trusted channel between CE and SE; sign/decrypt modules operate the cooperative ECC-TC algorithm shares and key management modules manage the key shares on CE/SE; authentication module authenticates user to CE; policy engine module checks while activity monitor module monitors the operation requests from CE overall; persistent storage stores the sealed key shares.

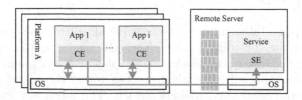

Fig. 1. System overview

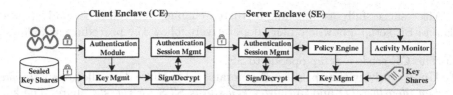

Fig. 2. SSUKey architecture

3.2 Trusted Channel Between CE and SE Establishment

A simple but effective protocol is proposed to establish a trusted channel between CE and SE with CE and SE authenticating each other. This protocol takes a few one-off steps to setup two asymmetric authentication key pairs. The one-off procedure proceeds as follows:

(1) During the first execution, SE generates an asymmetric authentication key pair SK_{SE}/PK_{SE}, and exports the public key. The public key is hard-coded to CE implementation.
(2) When a CE connects to SE for the first time, it generates an asymmetric authentication key pair SK_{CE}/PK_{CE}. The CE generates a SGX remote attestation report on the hash value of PK_{CE}. The report also includes the code measurement of the CE. After that, the CE encrypts PK_{CE} with SE's public key PK_{SE} and sends the ciphertext and the report to SE.
(3) Upon receiving the ciphertext and the report, SE verifies the report through attestation verification server typically provided by Intel, extracts the CE's public key PK_{CE}, and verifies whether the hash value of PK_{CE} matches that in the report.

On success, SE obtains the CE's public key (the CE has SE's public key hard-coded in its implementation). Specifically, SE is bounded with PK_{SE} and the CE is bounded with PK_{CE} since the key pairs can only be accessed from CE or SE respectively.

When a CE wants to connect to SE for the first time of current execution, the CE and SE use the raw public keys PK_{CE}/PK_{SE}, following the procedure specified in *RFC 7250: Using Raw Public Keys in Transport Layer Security (TLS) and Datagram Transport Layer Security (DTLS)* and TLS 1.3 [21], to establish a session key and use the established session key to protect all the subsequent messages between the CE and SE.

3.3 Key Setup

SSUKey adopts a 2-out-of-2 sharing scheme TC, Mediated SM2 [15,22], which partitions a private key into two shares. CE holds one share (denoted as d_{CE}) of the private key while SE holds the other share (denoted as d_{SE}). TC ensures that knowledge of one of the two key shares cannot not be used to derive the private key.

After successfully establishing a trusted channel between a CE and SE, the CE and SE setup a new key pair cooperatively follow the procedure as follows:

(1) The CE sends a *setup* opcode to SE.
(2) Upon receiving the opcode, SE generates a key share d_{SE}, allocates a *unique key identifier ID* and initializes *key status STS* for the key share. The key status can be one of three possible values, *valid*, *suspended*, and *revoked*, indicating the private key is available, suspended, and revoked respectively. A *suspended* key is not available until it is resumed while a *revoked* key is permanently not available. The key status is initialized *valid* when the key is created. After that, SE computes the public key share P_{SE} of d_{SE}.
(3) SE sends the ID and P_{SE} to the CE.
(4) Upon receiving the ID and P_{SE}, the CE generates the other key share d_{CE}, computes the public key P using P_{SE} and d_{CE}, and exports the public key.

The CE now has the public key P and a share of the private key d_{CE} while SE has the other share d_{SE} of the private key as well as the key identifier ID and the key status STS. The CE seals all the secrets (d_{CE}, P, and ID) two-fold – firstly, the secrets are sealed using user specific secret, such as password, and secondly, they are sealed using the CE's sealing key, which is derived from the code measurement of CE and the processor-specific secrets. The purpose of user specific secret is to authenticate the untrusted application that employs the CE and the application will be rejected to access the secrets if it fails to authenticate itself. After two-fold sealing the secrets, the CE saves the sealed secrets to persistent storage. The secrets on SE (ID, STS and d_{SE}) are saved in memory. When SE wants to store the secrets to non-volatile memory, SE seals them first and keeps the state of them in memory. The sealed secrets are protected from rollback attack as long as SE does not shut down since SE can maintain the state of the secrets itself. We explains more about rollback protection in Sect. 4.

3.4   Signature and Decryption

When a CE is starting, it firstly executes following steps in sequence. First, it loads the two-fold sealed secrets from persistent storage and extracts the key share d_{CE} and key identifier ID. Second, it establishes a trusted channel with SE. Once the trusted channel is established, the CE can trigger a signature or decryption operation by sending SE an opcode, *decrypt* or *sign*, as well as the message to be signed or decrypted. Upon receiving the opcode, SE signs or decrypts the message for the CE. The procedure proceeds as follows:

(1) The CE sends SE the key identifier ID, a *sign* or *decrypt* opcode, and the message.
(2) Upon receiving the ID and the opcode, SE checks the key policy, i.e., key status STS associated with the ID. If the key is available, SE signs or decrypts the message using d_{SE}.

(3) SE sends the result to the CE.
(4) Upon receiving the result, the CE continues signing or decrypting the result from SE using d_{CE} and obtains the final result, i.e., a signature or cleartext.

3.5 Key Management

SSUKey manages all private keys on SE. It globally monitors and analyzes the usage of private keys. For example, how frequent a private key is used, where a private key request is from, what a private key is typically used for (signing or decrypting), etc. Based on the private keys usage patterns, SE can detect abnormal behaviors. For example, the requested private key is far more frequent used in a short period. For another example, a signing operation requests a decrypting private key. If such abnormal behaviors are detected, SE suspends the associated private keys by setting key status to *suspended*. The private key owner will be informed next time when the CE requests to the suspended private key. This makes the owner aware of potential private key abusing. It is the owner's responsibility to confirm whether the suspended private key is still sound secure.

The private key owner can trigger a *resume* operation to resume a suspended private key, a *revoke* operation to revoke a suspended or unneeded private key, or a *sync* operation to synchronize current status of a private key. The procedure proceeds much like requesting a signature or decryption operation, except that it sends a key management opcode (*resume*, *revoke*, or *sync*) to SE. Upon receiving the opcode, SE updates the key status STS.

4 Security Analysis

The theoretical security of SSUKey is based on the security of ECC-TC [15,22] and the enclaves provided by Intel SGX. The adversary is allowed to attack from the very beginning of the private key being setup. The adversary has to compromise both two key shares on CE and SE separately to recover the private key. In this section, we mainly illustrate that the adversary cannot successfully compromise a private key by performing the most promising attacks on SSUKey, including tampering system memory, eavesdropping channels between CE and SE, performing side channel and rollback attacks on CE and SE.

Tamper-Proofing. The adversary cannot modify the code of CE and SE without being detected since any modification to the code will change the measurement of the code. A modified CE or SE will have a different code measurement comparing with the original one. CPU judges it as a different enclave. Thus, the modified CE or SE cannot access the secrets kept by the original one. The adversary cannot read or modify the runtime memory of CE and SE since the memory resides within the isolation region provided by SGX.

During the establishment of a session key between CE and SE, SE can authenticate the CE by verifying the signature of the session key signed by the CE's private key and the CE can confirm that only SE can decrypt the session key.

The adversary cannot masquerade as either CE or SE to establish a channel with the counterpart. Thus, a man-in-the-middle attack on SSUKey is not applicable. In addition, session hijack attack is disabled since the session key is immediately adopted once SE successfully authenticates the CE. The subsequent communication messages are transferred within the established trusted channel between CE and SE and the adversary cannot replay, read and modify the message.

Side Channel Protection. Intel SGX enclaves are vulnerable to side channel attack, for example, cached-based side channel attack [10,11] and page-based side channel attack [12]. CE and SE of our SSUKey are also threated by such attacks. A successful side channel attack on SSUKey has to extract the key shares from both the CE and SE. This is very difficult and almost impossible since the remote server that hosts SE is carefully configured and well protected by additional mechanisms. Compared with SE, the CE is more likely being attacked. If the key share d_{CE} on the CE is compromised due to side channel attack, TC ensures that the compromise of d_{CE} cannot be used to derive the private key.

SE verifies the CE's identity during the establishment of the trusted channel between the CE and SE. Thus, even though the adversary has compromised the d_{CE} on the CE, it cannot masquerade as the CE to request SE to help sign or decrypt a message. This makes SSUKey tolerant to the compromise of the key share d_{CE} on the CE.

Rollback Protection. Intel SGX enclaves are also vulnerable to rollback attack [9]. The adversary can exploit this vulnerability to break the freshness of the private key. A successful rollback attack on SSUKey has to revert the state of the two key shares from both the CE and SE. On the one hand, SE can be kept online almost all the time by a lot of ways (e.g., [23]), and the adversary cannot perform a rollback attack on SE successfully as long as SE does not shut down since SE can maintain the state of the secrets itself. On the other hand, when occasionally being restarted, for example, due to service update, SE can protect the secrets from rollback attack using SGX counters [13] or other useful solutions such as ROTE [24].

5   Evaluation

In this section, we describe our performance evaluation. We implemented our system consisting of two enclave libraries for CE and SE respectively, a remote service, and applications. The cryptographic library supports SM2 (Mediated SM2), SM3, SM4, KDF, and NIST hash-based DRBG. The enclave library for CE is implemented as a cryptography provider complying with Windows CNG. The internal distributed architecture of SSUKey is transparent to the applications. Both the applications and the remote service are running separately within a single thread atop Windows 10 on Intel NUC6 with i3-6100U CPU, which is designed low power (15 W). The applications connect to the remote service via local network (ping about 1.1 ms).

5.1   Cryptographic Operations Throughputs

The main performance metrics to measure are the throughputs of cryptographic operations including encryption, decryption, and signatures. A hash operation is included in a SM2 signature operation so we do not measure it alone.

We implemented several test cases for the cryptographic operations. We tested the test cases using (1) pure software implementation with neither enclaves nor Mediated SM2 and (2) our SSUKey implementation. For the symmetric encryption test case, it encrypted/decrypted the data repeatedly (data size varied from 0.5 KB to 256 KB). For the asymmetric encryption test case, it encrypted/decrypted the data repeatedly (data size varied from 16 B to 8 KB). For the signature test case, it signed/verified the data repeatedly (the data size varies from 16 B to 8 KB). We used data processed per second (MB/s) and operations per second (Ops) as the measuring unit to measure the throughputs of encryption and signatures respectively.

Figure 3a shows the performance of symmetric encryption/decryption. The throughputs are almost the same when data size is greater than 4 KB, while they are about 5–18% lower in SSUKey than that in the pure one when the data size is less than or equal to 4 KB. This is due to that data of small size weakens the throughput rate of a single operation and amplifies the influence from the overhead of enclave context switching.

The throughputs of asymmetric encryption and signature verification are almost the same. But the throughputs of asymmetric decryption and signature signing in SSUKey are about a quarter of that in the pure one, as shown in Figs. 3b and c (right figure is the logarithms of the throughputs to show the difference more clearly). This is as expected, since SSUKey adopts ECC-TC (i.e., Mediated SM2), and the procedure of using public keys (i.e., encrypting or verifying) is identical in both SSUKey and the pure one, while the procedure of using

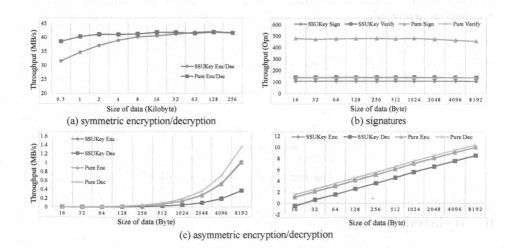

(a) symmetric encryption/decryption

(b) signatures

(c) asymmetric encryption/decryption

Fig. 3. The performance of cryptographic operations

private keys (i.e., signing or decrypting) in SSUKey adopts a sharing scheme but the pure one does not. The sharing scheme brings SSUKey much more time-consuming operations, e.g., point multiplication and large integer multiplication. Additionally, an asymmetric operation is generally considered much more time-consuming than that a symmetric operation and thus the overhead of enclave context switching is weakened in an asymmetric operation.

5.2 Applications Throughputs

Additionally, we evaluated our SSUKey in real-world scenarios, file encryption and TLS download. We implemented a file encryption application, a TLS server, and a TLS client that connected to and downloaded data (4 KB) from the TLS sever repeatedly. The TLS server acted as a download center and waited for the TLS client to connect.

We tested the file encryption application and the TLS client using (1) pure software implementation with neither enclaves nor Mediated SM2 and (2) our SSUKey implementation. The file encryption application encrypted/decrypted files repeatedly (file size varied from 0.5 MB to 256 MB). The TLS client connected to and downloaded data (4 KB) from the TLS sever repeatedly. We used the number of successful downloads per second (Ops) as the measuring unit to measure the throughput of TLS download.

Figure 4 shows the performance of file encryption. For file size greater than 8 MB, the throughput of file encryption in SSUKey is almost the same with that in the pure one, while it is 7–19% decline in SSUKey than that in the pure one when file size is less than or equal to 8 MB. As for TLS download, the performance is 72.04 Ops in SSUKey while 72.15 Ops in the pure one. The performance decline is less than 1%.

The results illustrates that our SSUKey imposes a moderate overhead to file encryption and has little influence on TLS download. We conclude that our SSUKey is acceptable.

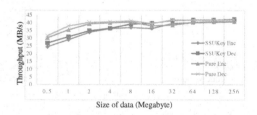

Fig. 4. The performance of file encryption

6 Related Work

TrustZone. ARM TrustZone (TZ) combines secure execution with trusted path support. It provides one secure world isolated against a normal world. The secure world operates a whole trusted stack, including security kernel, device drivers and applications. TZ allows device interrupts being directly routed into the secure world and thus supports generic trusted paths [25]. However, TZ does not distinguish between different secure application processes in hardware. It requires a security kernel for secure process isolation, management, attestation and similar. The prototype of SSUKey is promising to be migrated to TZ. Compared with SGX, TZ is more competent to offer generic trusted I/O path.

Rollback Protection. SGX counters [13] is a moderate and handy solution. It employs non-volatile memory to store the counter which is likely vulnerable to bus tapping and flash mirroring attacks [14]. It is not secure enough in our threat model since non-volatile memory resides outside the processor package. ROTE [24] is a more secure and promising solution than SGX counters. It adopts a distributed architecture and synchronizes the status of counters between distributed systems. This makes ROTE provide rollback protection counter as long as the status of the counter is kept on one or more systems. SSUKey is compatible with ROTE but we do not implement ROTE in this work.

7   Conclusion

In this paper, we have presented SSUKey, a CPU-based solution protecting private keys. Our main idea is to adopt Intel SGX to resist the vulnerabilities of privileged code, including OS kernel, and employ ECC-TC to mitigate the vulnerabilities of SGX, including side channel and rollback. We consider a powerful adversary that controls the OS and has even compromised one share of the private key. We provide a central key management function to help users globally monitor the usage of private keys and detect the abnormal behaviors, minimizing the risk of private key abusing. Our experiments demonstrate that our SSUKey is acceptable with a moderate performance decline when compared with the one without protection from SGX and TC.

Acknowledgments. We thank the anonymous reviewers for their helpful feedback. The work was partially supported by the National Basic Research 973 Program of China (No. 2014CB340603) and the National Natural Science Foundation of China (No. 61772518).

References

1. Stratistics MRC: Digital Signature - Global Market Outlook (2016–2022). http://www.strategymrc.com/report/digital-signature-market. Accessed Sept 2017
2. Services that Integrate with the YubiKey. https://www.yubico.com/solutions/#FIDO-U2F. Accessed Sept 2017
3. SafeNet Inc.: 2014 Authentication Survey Executive Summary. https://safenet.gemalto.com/news/2014/authentication-survey-2014-reveals-more-enterprises-adopting-multi-factor-authentication/. Accessed Sept 2017

4. Hofmann, O., et al.: InkTag: secure applications on an untrusted operating system, vol. 41, pp. 265–278. ACM (2013)
5. McCune, J., et al.: TrustVisor: efficient TCB reduction and attestation. In: 2010 IEEE Symposium on Security and Privacy (SP), pp. 143–158. IEEE (2010)
6. Anati, I., Gueron, S., Johnson, S., Scarlata, V.: Innovative technology for CPU based attestation and sealing. In: Proceedings of the 2nd International Workshop on Hardware and Architectural Support for Security and Privacy, vol. 13 (2013)
7. Hoekstra, M., et al.: Using innovative instructions to create trustworthy software solutions, p. 11 (2013)
8. McKeen, F., et al.: Innovative instructions and software model for isolated execution. In: HASP@ ISCA, p. 10 (2013)
9. Costan, V., Devadas, S.: Intel SGX explained. IACR Cryptology ePrint Archive, 2016:86 (2016)
10. Schwarz, M., et al.: Malware guard extension: using SGX to conceal cache attacks. arXiv preprint arXiv:1702.08719 (2017)
11. Brasser, F., et al.: Software grand exposure: SGX cache attacks are practical. arXiv preprint arXiv:1702.07521 (2017)
12. Xu, Y., Cui, W., Peinado, M.: Controlled-channel attacks: deterministic side channels for untrusted operating systems. In: 2015 IEEE Symposium on Security and Privacy (SP), pp. 640–656. IEEE (2015)
13. Intel: SGX documentation: SGX create monotonic counter. https://software.intel.com/en-us/node/709160. Accessed Sept 2017
14. Skorobogatov, S.: The bumpy road towards iPhone 5c NAND mirroring. arXiv preprint arXiv:1609.04327 (2016)
15. Shen, S. (ed.): SM2 Digital Signature Algorithm (draft 02) (2014). https://tools.ietf.org/html/draft-shen-sm2-ecdsa-02
16. Shen, S. (ed.): SM3 Hash function (draft 01) (2014). https://tools.ietf.org/html/draft-shen-sm3-hash-01
17. Tse, R.: The SM4 Block Cipher Algorithm and Its Modes of Operations (draft 01) (2014). https://tools.ietf.org/html/draft-ribose-cfrg-sm4-01
18. Dierks, T.: RFC 5246: the transport layer security (TLS) protocol. The Internet Engineering Task Force (2008)
19. Barker, E., Kelsey, J.: Recommendation of random number generation using deterministic random bit generators. NIST SP800-90A, June 2015
20. Weiser, S., Werner, M.: SGXIO: Generic Trusted I/O Path for Intel SGX. arXiv preprint arXiv:1701.01061 (2017)
21. Rescorla, E.: The Transport Layer Security (TLS) Protocol Version 1.3 (draft 21) (2017). https://tools.ietf.org/pdf/draft-ietf-tls-tls13-21.pdf
22. Lin, J., et al.: Signing and decrypting method and system applied to cloud computing and based on SM2 algorithm (2014). http://www.soopat.com/Patent/201410437599. CN Patent CN104243456A
23. Li, D., Morton, P., Li, T., Cole, B.: Cisco hot standby router protocol (HSRP) (1998)
24. Matetic, S., et al.: ROTE: rollback protection for trusted execution. IACR Cryptology ePrint Archive 2017:48 (2017)
25. Li, W., et al.: Building trusted path on untrusted device drivers for mobile devices. In: APSys 2014. ACM (2014)

Algorithms

The Reductions for the Approximating Covering Radius Problem

Wenwen Wang[1] and Kewei Lv[2,3(⊠)]

[1] Business School, University of Jinan, Jinan 250002, China
2010zywkk@sina.com
[2] State Key Laboratory of Information Security,
Institute of Information Engineering, Chinese Academy of Sciences,
Beijing 100093, China
lvkewei@iie.ac.cn
[3] Data Assurance Communication Security Research Center,
Chinese Academy of Sciences, Beijing 100093, China

Abstract. We establish the direct connection between CRP (Covering Radius Problem) and other lattice problems. We first prove that there is a polynomial-time rank-preserving reduction from approximating CRP to BDD$^\rho$ (Covering Bounded Distance Decoding Problem). Furthermore, we show that there are polynomial-time reductions from BDD$^\rho$ to approximating CVP (Closest Vector Problem) and SIVP (Shortest Independent Vector Problem), respectively. Hence, CRP reduces to CVP and SIVP under deterministic polynomial-time reductions.

Keywords: Lattice · Polynomial time reductions
Covering Radius Problem
Covering Bounded Distance Decoding Problem

1 Introduction

A lattice is the set of all integer combinations of n linearly independent vectors in $\mathbb{R}^m$, where n is the rank of the lattice, m is the dimension of the lattice, and the n linearly independent vectors are called a lattice basis. Successive minima are fundamental parameters of a lattice. The ith successive minimum $\lambda_i(\mathcal{L})$ ($i = 1, 2, \ldots, n$) of the lattice $\mathcal{L}$ is the least number r such that the sphere centered at the origin with radius r contains i linearly independent lattice vectors.

During recent decades, research on lattices has attracted many experts with a computational point of view. Some important lattice problems are defined below, where $\gamma \geq 1$ is a function of rank.

CVP (Closest Vector Problem): Given a lattice and a target vector, find a lattice point approximately closest to the target, i.e., a lattice point at a distance from the target that is at most γ times the distance of the closest lattice point.

SIVP (Shortest Independent Vector Problem): Given a lattice of rank n, find a maximal set of approximately shortest linearly independent lattice vectors, i.e., n linearly independent vectors of length at most $\gamma \cdot \lambda_n$.

© Springer International Publishing AG, part of Springer Nature 2018
S. Qing et al. (Eds.): ICICS 2017, LNCS 10631, pp. 65–74, 2018.
https://doi.org/10.1007/978-3-319-89500-0_5

The related complexity results for CVP and SIVP can be found in [1,4–7,13].

Another important lattice problem is the Covering Radius Problem (CRP). The exact CRP is in Π_2 at the second level of the polynomial hierarchy. CRP, given a lattice $\mathcal{L}$, asks for the maximum possible distance $\rho(\mathcal{L})$ from the lattice such that $\rho(\mathcal{L}) = \max\limits_{x \in span(\mathcal{L})} dist(x, \mathcal{L})$. Let $\rho(\mathcal{L})$ be the covering radius of the lattice $\mathcal{L}$. We can see that there is always a lattice point with distance $\rho(\mathcal{L})$ from the target. Micciancio [14] presented an approximation version of this problem, which is called the Covering Bounded Distance Decoding Problem (BDD^ρ), given a lattice $\mathcal{L}$ and a target point t, asks for a lattice point v such that $\|v - t\| \leq \gamma \cdot \rho(\mathcal{L})$. Micciancio [14] also proposed the approximation version of CRP, which given a lattice $\mathcal{L}$, the goal is to find a value $\hat{\rho}$ such that $\rho(\mathcal{L}) \leq \hat{\rho} \leq \gamma \cdot \rho(\mathcal{L})$.

In 2004, Micciancio [14] showed that finding collision of some hash function can be reduced to approximate CRP of lattices, where CRP only is used to connect the average and worst case complexity of lattice problems. Motivated by [7], Guruswami et al. [8] initiated the study of computation complexity for CRP (GapCRP), which given a lattice and some value r, we are supposed to decide if the covering radius is at most r. They showed that CRP_2 lies in AM, $CRP_{\sqrt{n/\log n}}$ lies in coAM and $CRP_{\sqrt{n}}$ lies in $NP \cap coNP$ which implies that under Karp reductions $CRP_{\sqrt{n}}$ is not NP-hard unless $NP = coNP$. But they did not give some hardness results for CRP [8]. Peikert [17] showed th $CRP_{\sqrt{n}}$ lies in coNP in the ℓ_p norm for $2 \leq p \leq \infty$. The first hardness result for CRP was presented by Haviv and Regev, they proved that there exists some constant such that it is Π_2-hard in the ℓ_p norm for any sufficiently large value of p [10]. In 2015, Haviv [9] proposed the Remote Set Problem (RSP) on lattices which given a lattice asks to find a set of points containing a point which is far from the lattice. Haviv proved that $GapCRP_{\sqrt{n/\log n}}$ is in NP, improving a result of [8].

Computing the covering radius of a lattice is a classic problem in the algorithm point of view, but it has received so far little attention from an algorithm point of view. In 2013, Micciancio and Voulgaris [15] gave a deterministic single exponential time algorithm for CRP using a randomized polynomial time reduction from [8].

We remark that to date virtually all known reduction for CRP is from the promise version (GapCRP) to other promise problems. Using the transference theorems [3], Micciancio and Goldwasser [16] gave the Karp reduction from $GapCRP_{\gamma n}$ to $GapSVP_\gamma$, and they proved that the hardness of GapCRP can be used to build provably secure cryptographic functions. In 2005, Guruswami et al. [8] proved that there exists a Karp reduction from $GapCRP_{\sqrt{n}}$ to the exact version of SIVP. In 2014, Haviv proved that if there exists a deterministic polynomial-time algorithm for RSP then there exists a deterministic polynomial-time Cook reduction from $GapCRP_{\gamma'}$ to $GapCVP_{\gamma'/\gamma}$ for some fixed γ' [9]. We have known CRP can related to CVP, but the connection is weaker. The covering radius corresponds to the worst case solution to CVP, because the covering radius of $\mathcal{L}$ is the smallest ρ such that CVP instance $(\mathcal{L}, t, \rho)$ has solution for any $t \in span(\mathcal{L})$. Given our limited understanding of the complexity of lattice approximation problem, it is natural to ask how CRP relate to other approximation lattice problems. Is CRP harder than others? In order to answer these questions, we will establish the reduction between CRP and other lattice problems. This can result in an exponential slow down in algorithm for CRP by applying the reductions. In this paper, we will initiate the study of the deterministic polynomial time reduction for the approximation version of CRP in [14].

In this paper, we give various deterministic polynomial time reductions between approximation CRP to other lattice approximation problems. Our main results show that approximating CRP reduces to approximating CVP and SIVP under deterministic polynomial-time reductions.

Firstly, we proved that there exists a deterministic polynomial-time reduction from $\text{CRP}_{\alpha \cdot \gamma}$ to BDD^ρ_γ which is related to Haviv's work. Given a lattice $\mathcal{L}(B) = \mathcal{L}(b_1, b_2, \ldots, b_n)$, the well known LLL algorithm [11] yields a deterministic polynomial-time algorithm for RSP [9]. That algorithm had been found a point $t = 1/2 \cdot b_n^* \in span(\mathcal{L}(B))$ whose distance from the lattice approximates the covering radius to within a factor $2^{n/2}$, where b_n^* is the component of $\tilde{b}_n$ orthogonal to $\tilde{b}_1, \ldots, \tilde{b}_{n-1}$ and $\tilde{B} = (\tilde{b}_1, \ldots, \tilde{b}_n)$ is a LLL reduced basis of lattice $\mathcal{L}(B)$. Let $\mathcal{L}$ be an instance of $\text{CRP}_{\alpha \cdot \gamma}$. Consider the BDD^ρ_γ instance $(\mathcal{L}, t)$ where $t = 1/2 \cdot b_n^*$. Call the BDD^ρ_γ oracle on instance $(\mathcal{L}, t)$ to obtain the solution to the $\text{CRP}_{\alpha \cdot \gamma}$. Moreover, there is a trivial reduction from BDD^ρ_γ to CVP_γ. Hence, we obtain that the deterministic polynomial-time rank-preserving reductions from $\text{CRP}_{\alpha \cdot \gamma}$ to CVP_γ where $\alpha = \lceil 2^{n/2} \rceil$.

Proving the reduction from $\text{CRP}_{\sqrt{3}\alpha}$ to SIVP_γ can also be broken down into two separated reductions, where $\alpha = \lceil 2^{n/2} \rceil, \gamma < \sqrt{2}$. We first give a deterministic polynomial-time reduction from $\text{BDD}^\rho_{\sqrt{3}}$ to SIVP_γ for any approximation factor $\gamma < \sqrt{2}$ and $\rho > \gamma/2 \cdot \lambda_n(\mathcal{L})$. By assuming that ρ is known, we construct the instance of SIVP_γ using ρ. The goal is to use the SIVP_γ oracle to return the solution to $\text{CRP}_{\sqrt{3}\alpha}$. Actually, we cannot obtain such a ρ exactly. Using the nearest plane algorithm for CVP [2], we can guess a good approximation for ρ to obtain the reduction from $\text{BDD}^\rho_{\sqrt{3} \cdot (1-1/n)^c}$ for some constant $c > 0$ to SIVP_γ. By giving the reduction from $\text{BDD}^\rho_{\sqrt{3}}$ to $\text{BDD}^\rho_{\sqrt{3} \cdot (1-1/n)^c}$, we can obtain that $\text{BDD}^\rho_{\sqrt{3}}$ can be reduced to SIVP_γ. Combining the reduction from $\text{CRP}_{\alpha \cdot \gamma}$ to BDD^ρ_γ which we have known, the approximating CRP can be reduced to approximating SIVP.

Organization. The paper is organized as follows. In Sect. 2, we introduce basic notations for lattices and some approximate versions of lattice problems. In Sect. 3, we study the relationship between CRP for BDD^ρ. In Sect. 4, we prove that the reduction CRP to CVP and SIVP.

2   Preliminaries

Notations. Let $\mathbb{R}^m$ be an m-dimensional Euclidean space. For every vector $x = (x_1, x_2, \ldots, x_m) \in \mathbb{R}^m$, the ℓ_2-norm of x is defined as $\|x\|_2 = \sqrt{\sum_{i=1}^m x_i^2}$.

The scalar product of two vectors x and y is $\langle x, y \rangle = \sum_i x_i y_i$. dist$(x, \mathcal{L})$ is the minimum Euclidean distance from $x \in \mathbb{R}^m$ to any vector in $\mathcal{L}$. All definitions and results in this paper are based on the ℓ_2 norm.

Lattice. A lattice $\mathcal{L}$ is the set of all linear combinations generated by n linearly independent vectors $b_1, \ldots, b_n$ in $\mathbb{R}^m (m \geq n)$, that is,

$$\mathcal{L} = \{\sum_{i=1}^{n} x_i b_i | x_i \in \mathbb{Z}, 1 \leq i \leq n\}.$$

The integer n is the rank of the lattice and m is the dimension of the lattice. The sequence of linearly independent vectors $b_1, \ldots, b_n \in \mathbb{R}^m$ is called a basis of the lattice. We can represent $b_1, \ldots, b_n$ as a matrix B with m rows and n columns, that is, $B = [b_1, \ldots, b_n] \in \mathbb{R}^{m \times n}$. The lattice $\mathcal{L}$ generated by a basis B is denoted by $\mathcal{L} = \mathcal{L}(B) = \{Bx : x \in \mathbb{Z}^n\}$. For a basis $B = [b_1, \ldots, b_n]$, we define the fundamental parallelepiped

$$\mathcal{P}(B) = \{\sum_{i=1}^{n} x_i b_i : 0 \leq x_i < 1\}.$$

Successive minima are fundamental constants of a lattice. The first successive minimum of a lattice $\mathcal{L}$, denoted by $\lambda_1(\mathcal{L})$, is the length of the shortest non-zero lattice vector, that is, $\lambda_1(\mathcal{L}) = min\{\|x\| : x \in \mathcal{L} \backslash \{0\}\}$. The ith minimum $\lambda_i(\mathcal{L})$ of a lattice $\mathcal{L}$ is the smallest value r such that $\mathcal{B}(0, r)$ contains i linearly independent lattice vectors, that is,

$$\lambda_i(\mathcal{L}) = min\{r : dim(span(\mathcal{L} \cap \mathcal{B}(0, r))) \geq i\}$$

where $\mathcal{B}(0, r)$ is an open ball of radius r centered at 0.

Another parameter associated with lattices is the covering radius. Formally, the covering radius $\rho(\mathcal{L})$ is defined as the maximum distance $dist(x, \mathcal{L})$:

$$\rho(\mathcal{L}) = \max_{x} dist(x, \mathcal{L})$$

where x ranges over the linear span of $\mathcal{L}$.

For any sequence of vectors $(b_1, \ldots, b_n)$, define the corresponding Gram-Schmidt orthogonalized vectors $b_1^*, \ldots, b_n^*$ by

$$b_i^* = b_i - \sum_{j=1}^{i-1} \mu_{i,j} b_j^*, \qquad \mu_{i,j} = \langle b_i, b_j^* \rangle / \langle b_j^*, b_j^* \rangle.$$

For every i, b_i^* is the component of b_i orthogonal to $b_1, \ldots, b_{i-1}$. In particular, $span(b_1, \ldots, b_n) = span(b_1^*, \ldots, b_n^*)$.

The following are several important lattice problems that we consider in this paper. Here we concentrate on the approximate version, where the approximation factor $\gamma \geq 1$ is a function of the rank n of the lattice.

Definition 1 (Closest Vector Problem). *CVP_γ: Given a lattice $\mathcal{L} \subseteq \mathbb{Q}^m$ and a target vector $t \in \mathbb{Q}^m$, find a lattice point v such that $dist(v,t) \leq \gamma \cdot dist(\mathcal{L}, t)$.*

Definition 2 (Shortest Independent Vector Problem). *$SIVP_\gamma$: Given a lattice $\mathcal{L} \subseteq \mathbb{Q}^m$ of rank n, find n linearly independent lattice vectors $s_1, s_2, \ldots, s_n$ such that $\|s_i\| \leq \gamma \cdot \lambda_n(\mathcal{L}), i = 1, 2, \ldots, n$.*

Definition 3 (Covering Radius Problem). *CRP_γ: Given a lattice $\mathcal{L} \subseteq \mathbb{Q}^m$, find a value $\hat{\rho}$ such that $\rho(\mathcal{L}) \leq \hat{\rho} \leq \gamma \cdot \rho(\mathcal{L})$.*

The promise problem associated to computing the covering radius is defined below.

Definition 4 ($GapCRP_\gamma$). *$(\mathcal{L}, r)$ is an instance of $GapCRP_\gamma$, where $\mathcal{L} \subseteq \mathbb{Q}^m$ is a lattice of rank n and $r \in \mathbb{Q}$ is a rational number, such that $(\mathcal{L}, r)$ is a YES instance if $\rho(\mathcal{L}) \leq r$ and a NO instance if $\rho(\mathcal{L}) > \gamma \cdot r$.*

The Covering Bounded Distance Decoding Problem was presented by Micciancio [14].

Definition 5 (Covering Bounded Distance Decoding Problem). *BDD_γ^ρ: Given a lattice $\mathcal{L} \subseteq \mathbb{Q}^m$ and a target vector $t \in \mathbb{Q}^m$, find a lattice point v such that $dist(v,t) \leq \gamma \cdot \rho(\mathcal{L})$.*

In the following, we will introduce the definition of RSP [9].

Definition 6 (Remote Set Problem). *An instance of $RSP_{d,\gamma}$ is a rank n lattice basis $\mathcal{L}$. The goal is to find a set $S \subseteq span(\mathcal{L})$ of size $|S| \leq d$ containing a point v such that $dist(v, \mathcal{L}) \geq \frac{1}{\gamma} \cdot \rho(\mathcal{L})$.*

The polynomial-time reductions presented in this paper relies on the following lemma.

Lemma 1 ([8]). *For any rank n lattice $\mathcal{L}$,*

$$\Pr_x(dist(x, \mathcal{L}) \geq \frac{\rho(\mathcal{L})}{2}) \geq 1/2$$

where x is chosen uniformly at random from $\mathcal{P}(\mathcal{L})$.

3   The Relationships Between CRP and Other Lattice Problems

3.1   Reducing CRP to BDD$^\rho$

Theorem 1. *For any approximation factor γ, there is a deterministic polynomial-time reduction from $CRP_{\alpha \cdot \gamma}$ to BDD_γ^ρ, where $\alpha = \lceil 2^{n/2} \rceil$.*

Proof. The reduction uses an idea that dates back to the result of Haviv [9].

Let $\mathcal{L}(B)$ be a lattice, $B = (b_1, b_2, \ldots, b_n)$ is a lattice basis. Using the LLL algorithm, we can obtain a reduced basis $\tilde{B} = (\tilde{b}_1, \ldots, \tilde{b}_n)$ such that for any pair of consecutive vectors b_i, b_{i+1}, $\|b_{i+1}^*\|^2 \geq 1/2 \cdot \|b_i^*\|^2$, where $b_1^*, \ldots, b_n^*$ are the Gram-Schmidt orthogonalized vectors of $\tilde{B}$. Clearly $\mathcal{L} = \tilde{\mathcal{L}} = \mathcal{L}(\tilde{B})$ and $\rho(\mathcal{L}) = \rho(\tilde{\mathcal{L}})$. Using the nearest plane algorithm for CVP [2], given a lattice $\tilde{\mathcal{L}}$ and a point $y \in span(\tilde{\mathcal{L}})$, we can always find a lattice point x, such that

$$\|x - y\| \leq \frac{1}{2} \cdot \sqrt{\sum_i \|b_i^*\|^2} \leq \frac{1}{2} \cdot \sqrt{\sum_i 2^{n-i} \|b_n^*\|^2} \leq 2^{n/2-1} \cdot \|b_n^*\|.$$

Then,

$$\rho(\mathcal{L}) = \rho(\tilde{\mathcal{L}}) \leq 2^{n/2-1} \|b_n^*\|.$$

Hence, we have

$$\|b_n^*\| \geq \frac{1}{2^{n/2-1}} \rho(\mathcal{L}).$$

On the other hand, let $y' = 1/2 \cdot b_n^* \in span(\tilde{\mathcal{L}})$. Since the project of every vector in $\tilde{\mathcal{L}}$ to $span(b_n^*)$ is $c \cdot b_n^*$ for some $c \in \mathbb{Z}$, we have

$$dist(\frac{1}{2} \cdot b_n^*, \tilde{\mathcal{L}}) \geq \frac{1}{2} \cdot \|b_n^*\| \geq \frac{1}{2} \cdot \frac{1}{2^{n/2-1}} \rho(\tilde{\mathcal{L}}) = \frac{1}{2^{n/2}} \rho(\tilde{\mathcal{L}}).$$

Let $t = y' = 1/2 \cdot b_n^* \in span(\mathcal{L})$, we have $dist(t, \mathcal{L}) \geq 1/2^{n/2} \rho(\mathcal{L})$.

Consider the $CRP_{\alpha \cdot \gamma}$ instance $\mathcal{L}$, the goal of the reduction is to use BDD_γ^ρ oracle to find a value $\hat{\rho}$ such that $\rho(\mathcal{L}) \leq \hat{\rho} \leq \gamma \cdot \rho(\mathcal{L})$. Call the BDD_γ^ρ oracle with the instance $(\mathcal{L}, t)$ to return a lattice point v such that $\|v - t\| \leq \gamma \cdot \rho(\mathcal{L})$, where $t = 1/2 \cdot b_n^*$. Then,

$$\frac{1}{2^{n/2}} \rho(\mathcal{L}) \leq dist(t, \mathcal{L}) \leq \|v - t\| \leq \gamma \cdot \rho(\mathcal{L}).$$

Hence, $\rho(\mathcal{L}) \leq \lceil 2^{n/2} \rceil \|v - t\| \leq \lceil 2^{n/2} \rceil \cdot \gamma \cdot \rho(\mathcal{L})$. Let $\alpha = \lceil 2^{n/2} \rceil \in \mathbb{Z}$, we have

$$\rho(\mathcal{L}) \leq \alpha \|v - t\| \leq \alpha \cdot \gamma \cdot \rho(\mathcal{L}).$$

Since $\alpha \|v - t\| = \|\alpha v - \alpha t\|$, $\alpha v \in \mathcal{L}$ and $\alpha t \in span(\mathcal{L})$, let $\hat{\rho} = dist(\alpha v, \alpha t) = \|\alpha v - \alpha t\|$, the value $\hat{\rho}$ can be found.

Theorem 2. *For any approximation factor γ, there is a probability polynomial-time reduction from $GapCRP_\gamma$ to $BDD_{\gamma/2}^\rho$.*

Proof. Let $(\mathcal{L}, r)$ be an instance of $GapCRP_\gamma$. We need to output YES if $\rho(\mathcal{L}) \leq r$ and NO if $\rho(\mathcal{L}) > \gamma \cdot r$.

We select a uniformly random point t from $\mathcal{P}(\mathcal{L})$. Feed the instance $(\mathcal{L}, t)$ to the $BDD_{\gamma/2}^\rho$ oracle and receive the answer $v \in \mathcal{L}$ such that $\|v - t\| \leq \gamma/2 \cdot \rho(\mathcal{L})$. If we have the case that $\|v - t\| \leq \gamma/2 \cdot r$, we output YES. Otherwise, we output NO.

If $(\mathcal{L}, r)$ is a YES instance of $GapCRP_\gamma$, i.e., $\rho(\mathcal{L}) \leq r$, then, there exists a lattice vector v such that $\|v - t\| \leq \gamma/2 \cdot \rho(\mathcal{L}) \leq \gamma/2 \cdot r$, it must be the vector that $BDD^\rho_{\gamma/2}$ oracle returns. So, the reduction outputs YES.

On the other hand, if $(\mathcal{L}, r)$ is a NO instance of $GapCRP_\gamma$, i.e., $\rho(\mathcal{L}) > \gamma \cdot r$. By Lemma 1, we select a random t from $\mathcal{P}(\mathcal{L})$, with probability at least $1/2$ that $dist(\mathcal{L}, t) \geq \rho(\mathcal{L})/2$. Hence, with probability at least $1/2$ that $dist(\mathcal{L}, t) \geq \gamma/2 \cdot r$, we output NO with probability $1/2$.

3.2   Reducing CRP to CVP and SIVP

Theorem 3. *For any approximation factor γ, there are the following Cook reductions between problem CVP and BDD:*

- *The problem $CVP_{2\gamma}$ can be reduced to BDD^ρ_γ;*
- *The problem BDD^ρ_γ can be reduced to CVP_γ.*

Proof. Let $(\mathcal{L}, t)$ be an instance of $CVP_{2\gamma}$. Call the BDD^ρ_γ oracle on the instance $(\mathcal{L}, t)$ to obtain a lattice point v that satisfies $\|v - t\| \leq \gamma \cdot \rho(\mathcal{L})$.

By Lemma 1, we can obtain $\Pr_{x \in \mathcal{P}(\mathcal{L})} (dist(x, \mathcal{L}) \geq \rho(\mathcal{L})/2) \geq 1/2$.

With a probability at least $1/2$, we can obtain $dist(t, \mathcal{L}) \geq \rho(\mathcal{L})/2$ for a target vector t (If $t \notin \mathcal{P}(\mathcal{L})$, let $x = t \mod \mathcal{L}$, then $dist(x, \mathcal{L}) = dist(t, \mathcal{L})$). So the oracle returns a vector $v = BDD^\rho_\gamma(\mathcal{L}, t)$ such that $\|v - t\| \leq \gamma \cdot \rho(\mathcal{L}) \leq 2\gamma \cdot dist(t, \mathcal{L})$ with probability $1/2$.

On the other hand, since $dist(t, \mathcal{L}) \leq \rho(\mathcal{L})$ and any solution to CVP_γ instance $(\mathcal{L}, t)$ is also a solution to $(\mathcal{L}, t)$ as BDD^ρ_γ instance, there is a trivial reduction from BDD^ρ_γ to CVP_γ.

Combining Theorem 1, we give the reduction from CRP to CVP.

Corollary 1. *For any approximation factor γ, there is a deterministic polynomial-time reduction from $CRP_{\alpha \cdot \gamma}$ to CVP_γ, where $\alpha = \lceil 2^{n/2} \rceil$.*

In the following, we will give a trivial reduction from solving BDD^ρ_γ to the slightly easier problem $BDD^\rho_{\gamma \cdot (1-1/n)^c}$ for any constant $c > 0$.

Corollary 2. *For any constant $c > 0$, there is a deterministic polynomial-time reduction from BDD^ρ_γ to $BDD^\rho_{\gamma \cdot (1-1/n)^c}$.*

Proof. Let $(\mathcal{L}, t)$ be an instance of BDD^ρ_γ. We use the $BDD^\rho_{\gamma \cdot (1-1/n)^c}$ oracle to find a lattice point v such that $dist(v, t) \leq \gamma \cdot (1-1/n)^c \cdot \rho$. We have $dist(v, t) \leq \gamma \cdot \rho$.

Next, we reduce BDD^ρ to SIVP. The idea is the reduction from the Bounded Distance Decoding (BDD) to Unique Shortest Vector (USVP) of Lyubashevsky and Micciancio [12].

Theorem 4. *For any $\gamma < \sqrt{2}$, there is a deterministic polynomial-time reduction from $BDD^\rho_{\sqrt{3}}$ to $SIVP_\gamma$, where $\rho(\mathcal{L}) = \max_{x \in span(\mathcal{L})} dist(x, \mathcal{L}) > \gamma/2 \cdot \lambda_n(\mathcal{L})$.*

Proof. Let $(\mathcal{L}, t)$ be an instance of $\text{BDD}^{\rho}_{\sqrt{3}}$ and $[b_1, \ldots, b_n]$ be a basis of $\mathcal{L}$.

First, let $u = dist(\mathcal{L}, t) = \min_{v \in \mathcal{L}} \|v - t\|, \rho = \rho(\mathcal{L})$. We do not know the exact value of ρ, but can guess a good-enough approximation at the end of the proof. For simplicity, we will assume that ρ is known. Let $\mathcal{L}'$ be the lattice generated by the matrix

$$B' = \begin{bmatrix} B & t \\ 0 & \rho \end{bmatrix} = \begin{bmatrix} b_1 \ldots b_n & t \\ 0 \ldots 0 & \rho \end{bmatrix} = [d_1, \ldots d_n, d_{n+1}].$$

We consider the lattice $\mathcal{L}' = \mathcal{L}(B')$ and invoke the SIVP_γ oracle on input $\mathcal{L}'$. The oracle return $n + 1$ linearly independent vectors $w_1, \ldots, w_{n+1}$ with $\|w_i\| \le \lambda_{n+1}(\mathcal{L}')$ for $i = 1, 2, \ldots, n + 1$ and at least one vector must depend on d_{n+1}. Assume that $w_{n+1} = \sum_{i=1}^{n+1} c_i d_i$, where for $i = 1, 2, \ldots, n, c_i \in \mathbb{Z}$, $c_{n+1} \in \mathbb{Z} \backslash \{0\}$, we have $\|w_{n+1}\|^2 \le \gamma^2 \lambda_{n+1}^2(\mathcal{L}')$. There are two cases:

1. $\lambda_{n+1}(\mathcal{L}') \le \sqrt{\mu^2 + \rho^2}$. If $|c_{n+1}| \ge 2$, then

$$4\rho^2 \le \|w_{n+1}\|^2 \le \gamma^2(\mu^2 + \rho^2).$$

Since $\mu \le \rho$, we can obtain $\gamma \ge \sqrt{2}$, contradicting the fact that $\gamma < \sqrt{2}$.

Hence, $|c_{n+1}| = 1$, without loss of generality, assume that $c_{n+1} = -1$, then

$$\|w_{n+1}\|^2 = \|\sum_{i=1}^{n+1} c_i b_i - t\|^2 + \rho^2 \le \gamma^2(\mu^2 + \rho^2).$$

We can obtain

$$\|\sum_{i=1}^{n} c_i b_i - t\|^2 \le \gamma^2(\mu^2 + \rho^2) - \rho^2 < 3\rho^2.$$

Then, there exists a lattice point $v = \sum_{i=1}^{n} c_i b_i$ such that $\|v - t\| < \sqrt{3}\rho$.

2. $\lambda_{n+1}(\mathcal{L}') > \sqrt{\mu^2 + \rho^2}$.

The lattice $\mathcal{L}$ contains n linearly independent vector $v_1, \ldots, v_n$ with $\|v_i\| \le \lambda_n(\mathcal{L})$ for $i = 1, \ldots, n$. Moreover, $(v_1, 0)^{\text{T}}, \ldots, (v_n, 0)^{\text{T}}, (v - t, \rho)^{\text{T}}$ are $n + 1$ linearly independent vector in $\mathcal{L}'$, where $v \in \mathcal{L}$ such that $\mu = dist(v, t)$. Clearly, we can see that $\lambda_n(\mathcal{L}) \ge \lambda_{n+1}(\mathcal{L}')$.

If $|c_{n+1}| \ge 2$, then

$$4\rho^2 \le \|w_{n+1}\|^2 \le \gamma^2 \lambda_{n+1}^2(\mathcal{L}') \le \gamma^2 \lambda_n^2(\mathcal{L}).$$

we have $\rho \le \gamma/2 \cdot \lambda_n(\mathcal{L})$, contradicting the fact that $\rho > \gamma/2 \cdot \lambda_n(\mathcal{L})$.

Hence, $|c_{n+1}| = 1$, assume that $c_{n+1} = -1$, then $\|w_{n+1}\|^2 = \|\sum_{i=1}^{n+1} c_i b_i - t\|^2 + \rho^2 \le \gamma^2 \lambda_n^2(\mathcal{L})$. We have

$$\|\sum_{i=1}^{n} c_i b_i - t\|^2 \le \gamma^2 \lambda_n^2(\mathcal{L}) - \rho^2 < (2\rho)^2 - \rho^2.$$

Then, there exists a lattice point $v = \sum_{i=1}^{n} c_i b_i$ such that $\|v - t\| < \sqrt{3}\rho$.

We now discuss to guess the ρ such that $\rho(\mathcal{L}) = \max_{x \in span(\mathcal{L})} dist(x, \mathcal{L})$. From Theorem 1, given a lattice $\mathcal{L}$, using the LLL algorithm, we can construct a reduced basis $\tilde{B} = (\tilde{b}_1, \ldots, \tilde{b}_n)$ such that for any pair of consecutive vectors $b_i, b_{i+1}, \|b_{i+1}^*\|^2 \geq 1/2 \cdot \|b_i^*\|^2$, where $b_1^*, \ldots, b_n^*$ are the Gram-Schmidt orthogonalized vectors. We can obtain that $\rho(\tilde{\mathcal{L}}) \leq 1/2 \cdot \sqrt{\sum_i \|b_i^*\|^2} \leq 2^{n/2-1}\|b_n^*\|$. Moreover, let $t = 1/2 \cdot b_n^* \in span(\tilde{\mathcal{L}})$, we have $\rho(\tilde{\mathcal{L}}) \geq 1/2 \cdot \|b_n^*\|$.

Hence, we obtain $\rho(\mathcal{L}) \in [1/2 \cdot \|b_n^*\|, 2^{n/2-1}\|b_n^*\|]$. So, we can find a $d = 1/2 \cdot \|b_n^*\|$ such that $d \in [2^{-n/2}\rho, \rho]$. In the polynomial-sized set $\{2^{n/2}d(1+1/n)^i : 0 \leq i \leq \log_{1+1/n} 2^{n/2}\}$, we can find at least one ρ such that $(1 - 1/n)\rho(\mathcal{L}) \leq \rho \leq (1 + 1/n)\rho(\mathcal{L})$ by trying all the possible values of ρ. We can then redo the above proof by appropriately modifying some terms by factors of $1 - 1/n$ or $1 + 1/n$ in order to satisfy the inequalities that appear. The result will from a slightly weaker problem $BDD^\rho_{\sqrt{3} \cdot (1-1/n)^c}$ to $SIVP_\gamma$, where $c > 0$ is some constant. By Corollary 2, we can obtain the reduction from $BDD^\rho_{\sqrt{3}}$ to $SIVP_\gamma$.

Combining Theorem 1, we have the following corollary.

Corollary 3. *For any approximation factor $\gamma < \sqrt{2}$, there is a deterministic polynomial-time reduction from $CRP_{\sqrt{3}\alpha}$ to $SIVP_\gamma$, where $\alpha = \lceil 2^{n/2} \rceil$.*

4 Conclusions

In our paper, we showed that there exists a polynomial-time reduction from $CRP_{\alpha \cdot \gamma}$ to BDD^ρ_γ. The reduction preserves the rank of the input lattice. But we do not know at present whether CRP and BDD^ρ are equivalent. We also proved that the reduction from approximating CRP to approximating CVP and SIVP. Considering the reduction from CRP to SIVP which preserves the approximation factor is also an interesting problem.

Acknowledgements. This work was supported by National Natural Key R&D Program of China (Grant No. 2017YFB0802502), the Science and Technology Plan Projects of University of Jinan (Grant No. XKY1714), the Doctoral Initial Foundation of the University of Jinan (Grant No. XBS160100335), the Social Science Program of the University of Jinan (Grant No. 17YB01).

References

1. Aharonov, D., Regev, O.: Lattice problems in NP intersect coNP. J. ACM **52**, 749–765 (2005). Preliminary version in FOCS 2004
2. Babai, L.: On Lovasz lattice reduction and the nearest lattice point problem. Combinatorica **6**(1), 1–13 (1986)
3. Banaszczyk, W.: New bounds in some transference theorems in the geometry of numbers. Math. Ann. **296**, 625–635 (1993)
4. Blömer, J., Naewe, S.: Sampling methods for shortest vectors, closest vectors and successive minima. Theor. Comput. Sci. **410**, 1648–1665 (2009)

5. Blöer, J., Seifert, J.P.: On the complexity of computing short linearly independent vectors and short bases in a lattice. In: 31th Annual ACM Symposium on Theory of Computing, pp. 711–720. ACM (1999)

6. Dubey, C., Holenstein, T.: Approximating the closest vector problem using an approximate shortest vector oracle. In: Goldberg, L.A., Jansen, K., Ravi, R., Rolim, J.D.P. (eds.) APPROX/RANDOM 2011. LNCS, vol. 6845, pp. 184–193. Springer, Heidelberg (2011). https://doi.org/10.1007/978-3-642-22935-0_16

7. Goldreich, O., Goldwasser, S.: On the limits of nonapproximability of lattice problems. J. Comput. Syst. Sci. **60**(3), 540–563 (2000)

8. Guruswami, V., Micciancio, D., Regev, O.: The complexity of the covering radius problem on lattices and codes. Comput. Complex. **14**(2), 90–121 (2005). Preliminary version in CCC 2004

9. Haviv, I.: The remote set problem on lattice. Comput. Complex. **24**, 103–131 (2015)

10. Haviv, I., Regev, O.: Hardness of the covering radius problem on lattices. Chicago J. Theor. Comput. Sci. **04**, 1–12 (2012)

11. Lenstra, A., Lenstra, H., Lovász, L.: Factoring polynomials with rational coefficients. Math. Ann. **261**, 515–534 (1982)

12. Lyubashevsky, V., Micciancio, D.: On bounded distance decoding, unique shortest vectors, and the minimum distance problem. In: Halevi, S. (ed.) CRYPTO 2009. LNCS, vol. 5677, pp. 577–594. Springer, Heidelberg (2009). https://doi.org/10.1007/978-3-642-03356-8_34

13. Micciancio, D.: Efficient reductions among lattice problems. In: 19th SODA Annual ACM-SIAM Symposium on Discrete Algorithm, pp. 84–98 (2008)

14. Micciancio, D.: Almost perfect lattices, the covering radius problem, and applications to Ajtai's connection factor. Electron. Colloq. Comput. Complex. **66**, 1–39 (2003)

15. Micciancio, D., Voulgaris, P.: A deterministic single exponential time algorithm for most lattice problems based on Voronoi cell computation. SIAM J. Comput. **42**(3), 1364–1391 (2013)

16. Micciancio, D., Goldwasser, S.: Complexity of Lattice Problems: A Cryptographic Perspective. The Kluwer International Series in Engineering and Computer Science, vol. 671. Kluwer Academic Publishers, Boston (2002)

17. Peikert, C.: Limits on the hardness of lattice problems in ℓ_p norms. Comput. Complex. **17**(2), 300–351 (2008)

Solving Discrete Logarithm Problem in an Interval Using Periodic Iterates

Jianing Liu[1,2,3] and Kewei Lv[1,2,3(✉)]

[1] State Key Laboratory of Information Security,
Institute of Information Engineering, Chinese Academy of Sciences,
Beijing, China
{liujianing,lvkewei}@iie.ac.cn
[2] Data Assurance and Communication Security Research Center,
Chinese Academy of Sciences, Beijing, China
[3] University of Chinese Academy of Sciences, Beijing, China

Abstract. The Pollard's kangaroos method can solve the discrete logarithm problem in an interval. We present an improvement of the classic algorithm, which reduces the cost of kangaroos' jumps by using the sine function to implement periodic iterates and giving some pre-computation. Our experiments show that this improvement is worthy of attention.

Keywords: Discrete logarithm problem · Pollard's kangaroos method
Pollard's rho method

1 Introduction

The discrete logarithm problem (DLP) in a group G is to find the integer n such that $g^n = h$ holds given $g, h \in G$. As one of the most important mathematical primitives in modern cryptography, there are some classic algorithms to solve it, such as the Pollard's rho method, the index calculus method, and the Pollard's kangaroos method as well [1]. It's interesting to study solving discrete logarithm problem of the given interval in the practical cryptography system. The discrete logarithm problem in an interval is defined as following:

Definition 1 (DLP in an interval). Let p be a prime number and G be a cyclic subgroup of order q in F_p^*. Given the generator g and an element h of G, and an integer N less than the order of g, it is assumed that there exists an unknown integer n in the interval $[0, N]$ such that $h = g^n$ holds. To compute n.

Indeed, some instances belonging to this case had been studied, such as the DLP with c-bit exponents (c-DLSE) [2–4], Boneh-Goh-Nissim homomorphic encryption scheme [5], counting points on curves or abelian varieties over finite fields [6], the analysis of the strong Diffie-Hellman problem [1, 7], and side-channel or small subgroup attacks [8, 9] and reference therein. Pollard's rho algorithm costs time $O(\sqrt{n})$ to solve it. [4] improves Pollard's kangaroos algorithm to solve DLP in an interval of size N with expected running time $(2 + O(1))\sqrt{N}$ group operations and polynomial storage. Galbraith et al. improve it by increasing the number of kangaroos showing that

S. Qing et al. (Eds.): ICICS 2017, LNCS 10631, pp. 75–80, 2018.
https://doi.org/10.1007/978-3-319-89500-0_6

when the number of kangaroos is four, total number of jumps is optimal and number of group operations is $(1.714 + O(1))\sqrt{N}$ [10]. [11] uses series of small integer multiplications to replace every multiplication of elements of a group, which reduces the cost of each jump in Pollard's rho algorithm and to determine to compute a complete multiplication according to whether some function values belong to the set of distinguished points or not. The definition of distinguished points is originally introduced in [12] for time-memory trade-off, which is some elements of group G satisfying a certain condition such that these points can be checked easily. [11] showed that when the related results meet the pre-defined distinguished point condition, we make a complete integer multiplication operation, thereby reducing the number of complete multiplications and time cost of each jump. A preprocessing storage size is $O\left((\log p)^{r+1} \cdot \log\log p\right)$ and running time is at least 10 times faster than the original algorithm.

Contribution. We use the sine-function to implement periodic iterates and give some pre-computation to reduce the cost of Pollard's kangaroos algorithm obviously. we can reduce $||p||^2$ bit operations of a complete integer multiplication to at most $d||\varepsilon|| ||\eta^2||$ bit operations, where $d = \log_\varepsilon p$. The pre-defined distinguished point condition is $[\eta - k, \eta]$, where $k = \log\eta + v$, v is an integer satisfying $0 \le v < \eta - \lfloor \log\eta \rfloor$. Furthermore, we also properly increase the number of kangaroos to reduce the total number of jumps, which improve both the time cost and the total number of jumps. Compared with the classic algorithm, the efficiency is noticeably improved.

2   Pollard's Kangaroos Algorithm

The Pollard's kangaroos algorithm [13] is based on random walk and each kangaroo jumps one step at a time. The main process is: First, fix a set of small integers of k elements $S = \{s_1, s_2, \ldots, s_k\}$, which is also considered as the set of the distances of jump steps such that the mean value of the elements of S is about $\sqrt{N}$ and k is a small integer. We randomly select some elements from group G to form the distinguished set $D = \{g_1, g_2, g_{3,\ldots,} g_t\}$, such that the size of D is approximately $|D|/|G| = \frac{c}{\sqrt{N}}$, where c is a constant and $c \gg 1$. Define a random map f from G to S. mA kangaroo's jumps corresponds to a sequence in G, $g_{i+1} = g_i g_i^{f(g)}$, $i = 0, 1, 2, \ldots$, starting from the given g_0. Let $d_0 = 0$, $d_{i+1} = d_i + f(g_i)$, $i = 0, 1, 2, \ldots$. Then, d_i is the sum of distances of first i jumps of kangaroo and $g_i = g_0 g_i^d$, $i = 0, 1, 2, \ldots$. The algorithm requires $2\sqrt{N}$ group operations and a small amount of additional storage space.

For each jump, we need to compute a complete integer multiplication between two group elements, which costs about $||p||^2$ bit operations. When the product belongs to the distinguished set D, the values related to this jump will be stored for collision detection; otherwise, the related values will not be stored. Thus, storage operations are not carried out every time, so it is not necessary to do a full product for each jump.

3   The Improved Pollard's Kangaroos Algorithm

In Pollard's kangaroos algorithm, the cost of each jump is complete multiplication operation of $\|p\|^2$ bits. We improve computational cost of jumps using pre-computation and periodic iterative functions, so that the total cost is reduced. Let p be a prime, n be an integer, and $G = <g>$ be a cyclic subgroup of order q of F_p^*. Given the generator g of G, element h and positive integer N, suppose there exists an unknown integer n in the interval $[0, N]$ such that $h = g^n$ holds, the algorithm to compute n is given in the following.

Let η denotes a small integer, we set $\Gamma = \{t_1, t_2, \ldots, t_\eta\}$, which is also considered as the set of the distances of jump steps and the mean value of the elements of Γ is about $\sqrt{N}$. Let the index set be $S = \{1, 2, \ldots, \eta\}$ and set $\{M_s = g^{t_s} | t_s \in \Gamma\}$. Fix a small positive integer l and precompute $M_l = \{M \cup \{1\}\}^l$. Initially, both tables L_t and L_w are null. We choose small integers d and ε such that $d = \lceil \log_\varepsilon p \rceil$. In order to facilitate the calculation of the discrete logarithm, we pre-calculate the M_l before the algorithm runs and store it in the appropriate table. The size of the set M_l does not exceed $\binom{l+\eta}{\eta}$.

Next, we define label function $\tau : G \to S$ such that $\tau(g) = \frac{g \bmod p}{p} \cdot \eta + 1$.

Given $x, y \in G$, for each $0 \le i \le d-1$, write

$$x = \sum_{i=0}^{d-1} x_i \varepsilon^i, \quad \text{where} \quad 0 \le x_i < \varepsilon \tag{1}$$

and

$$t_i = \varepsilon^i y \bmod 360, \quad \text{then } 0 \le t_i < 360. \tag{2}$$

Define the auxiliary label function $\bar{\tau} : G \times M_l \to S$

$$\bar{\tau}(x, y) = \sum_{i=0}^{d-1} x_i \lfloor |u \sin(t_i)| \rfloor \bmod \eta + 1 \tag{3}$$

where $u \ge \eta^2$, for the convenience of computation, u is taken as η^2. For any given $g \in G$ and $M \in M_l$, the time computing $\bar{\tau}(g, M)$ is much less than the cost of computing $g \cdot M$.

We define index function and auxiliary index function $\bar{s} : G \times M_l \to S$, such that $s : G \to S$ is a surjective and pre-image is approximately uniform,, and $\bar{s}(g, M) = s(gM)$. Let $\bar{s} = \bar{\tau}$. The pre-defined distinguished point condition is defined as the interval $[\eta - k, \eta]$, where $k = \lfloor \log \eta \rfloor + v$, $0 \le v < \eta - \lfloor \log \eta \rfloor$. Generally, the value of v is a small integer.

The jumping process of a kangaroo is a sequence table of G, G, $g_{i+1} = g_i \cdot M_{s(g_i)}$ for $i \ge 0$. The algorithm starts at an initial value $g_0 \in G$, and the initial $s_0 = s(g_0)$ is randomly selected from the set S. Since $g_1 = g_0 \cdot M_{s(g_0)}$, we can get the next index $s_1 = s(g_1) = s(g_0 M_{s(g_0)}) = \bar{s}(g_0, M_{s(g_0)})$ by calculating $\bar{s}(g_0, M_{s(g_0)})$ without computing $g_0 \cdot M_{s(g_0)}$. If the computed index value s_1 satisfies distinguished point condition, we can calculate $g_2 = g_0 \cdot M_{s_0} M_{s_1}$, $M_{s_0} M_{s_1} \in M_l$ has been pre-computed without computing $g_1 = g_0 \cdot M_{s_0}$. In the next process, for each iteration to complete a jump, the index value s_2, s_3, etc, can be calculated in the same way, and we do not compute the complete multiplication until that the pre-defined distinguished point condition is met, that is, the value of the function $\bar{s}$ falls in the interval $[\eta - k, \eta]$. At same time, we get the corresponding point $g_i = g_0 M_{s_0} \ldots M_{s_{i-1}}$, where $M_{s_0} \ldots M_{s_{i-1}} \in M_l$ has been basically pre-computed and can be obtained through look-up the table. If the collision has not occurred for l iterations, i.e., $g_{l+1} = g_0 M_{s_0} \ldots M_{s_l}$, the computed value of g_{l+1} will be stored in the table and the algorithm can be re-executed with g_{l+1} as a new starting point.

We denote two kangaroos as T and W. T and W jump respectively from the midpoint of the interval (i.e., $g_0 = g^{N/2}$) and $g_0' = h$ to the right side of the interval. The jumping process of T and W are alternately executed. The branches T and W randomly select the initial values $s_0 = s(g_0)$ and $s_0' = (g_0')$ from the set S respectively and set their own initial jumping points and initial distances of the jump step of the two branches be $g_0 = M_{s_0}$, $g = M_{s_0'}$ and $d_0(T) = 0$, $d_0(W) = 0$. When $i > 1$, we have $d_i(T) = \sum_{i=0}^{i-1} t_{s_i}$, $d_j(W) = \sum_{i=0}^{j-1} t_{s_j'}$. Let T_i and W_j denote the i and j-th jump of the two branches respectively. i and j start from 0. T_0, W_0, T_1, W_1, T_2, W_2,...,T_{i-1}, W_{i-1} are alternately executed. When the distinguished point condition is satisfied, the current jumping point's value of branch T or W will be computed. Then we can get the triplets that are $(g_i, d_i(T), T)$ or g, $d_j(W), W$ and store it into the corresponding table L_t or L_w at index g_i and g_j respectively. A collision occurs when g_i is accessed by a different type of branch kangaroo, so the value of $n = N/2 + d_i(T) - d_j(W)$ can be computed and the algorithm terminates.

Running Time. From Eq. (3), we can know the time of calculating $\bar{\tau}(x, y)$ includes d multiplications of modulo η, d-1 additions of modulo η, and d sinusoidal operations. Considering the time of calculating a sine operation as a constant C_0 and ignoring the relatively small cost of addition, time of computing $\bar{\tau}$ is about $d\mathrm{Mul}(||\eta||) + (\theta + 1/l)\mathrm{Mul}(||p||) + dC_0$, where θ is the probability that a point is a distinguished point, and l is the maximum number of iterations of the pre-process. Notice that the time of calculating sine function is neglected after processing in (2), the time of a jump is $d\mathrm{Mul}(||\eta||) + (\theta + 1/l)\mathrm{Mul}(||p||)$, where θ is the probability that a point is a distinguishable point, and l is the maximum number of iterations in the preprocessing table. Since the total number of jumps is $N/(2m) + 2m + 2/\theta$, the total time is $\{d\mathrm{Mul}(||\eta||) + (\theta + 1/l)\mathrm{Mul}(||p||)\} * \{N/(2m) + 2m + 2 \cdot 1/\theta\}$. From (1) and (3), we need about $d||\varepsilon|| ||\eta^2||$ bit operations required for a complete multiplication, obviously smaller than the $||p||^2$ bit operations required for a complete multiplication of the original algorithm. Usually we have the comparison results, seeing Table 1.

We can take the pre-defined distinguished point condition as $[\eta - k, \eta]$, the number of group operations is about $\log \eta / \eta (2 + O(1)) \sqrt{N}$. [10] improves the classic Pollard's kangaroos algorithm by increasing the number of kangaroos such that the total number of jumps is reduced and the probability of collision is increased. When the number of kangaroos is four, the total number of jumps is optimal and number of group operations is $(1.714 + O(1))\sqrt{N}$.

Table 1. Time contrast in case of Two Kangaroos

Algorithm	Number of group operations	Time cost of a jump	Computation cost
Pollard's	$(2 + O(1))\sqrt{N}$	$\mathrm{Mul}(\|p\|) + \|f\|$	$\|p\|^2$ bit operations of a jump
The improved	$\log\eta/\eta(2 + O(1))\sqrt{N}$	$d\mathrm{Mul}(\|\eta\|) + (\theta + 1/l)\mathrm{Mul}(\|p\|)$	$d\|\varepsilon\|\|\eta^2\|$ bit operations of a jump

4   Experiments on Improved Pollard's Kangaroos Algorithm

Given a 32-bit prime number $p = 2147483659$, $g = 29$, and take $\varepsilon = 8, N = 50$. Since $\sqrt{N} = 7$, here we set $\eta = 13$ and $\Gamma = \{1, 2, 3, \ldots, 13\}$. Then $k = \lfloor\log\eta\rfloor = 3$, so the interval $[\eta - k, \eta] = [10, 13]$. The distinguished point condition is $[10, 13]$. $M = \{g^1, g^2, \ldots, g^{13}\}$. Given $h = 44895682$, then our task is to seek x in the interval $[1, N]$ such that $29^x \bmod p = 44895682$. Here, we set $l = 3$ and precompute $M_l = \{\{29^1, 29^2, \ldots, 29^{13}\} \cup \{1\}\}^3$. We show some instances of experiment for different size primes p to display advantage of the improved algorithm in Table 2.

Table 2. Experiment cost

$\|p\|$	Prime p	Total number of jumps	Number of complete multiplications
64 bits	15509012368832652833	60	37
128 bits	292087288550973971472931860508592710703	73	42
256 bits	9244495511463549848558722622981797987364101890317331031445763518698 66679937827	115	62

5   Conclusion

In this paper, we improve Pollard's kangaroos algorithm using pre-defined distinguished point condition and periodic iterations. We reduce the cost of kangaroos' jumps by using the sine function to iterate periodically and pre- computation instead of multiplication between the elements of a group. The related function definition of the algorithm is not limited to a certain interval, the improved algorithm can be extended for the calculation of the discrete logarithm problem in the usual case.

Acknowledgements. This work is partially supported by National Key R&D Program of China (2017YFB0802502) and NSF (No. 61272039).

References

1. McCurley, K.: The discrete logarithm problem. In: Proceedings of the Symposium in Applied Mathematics, pp. 49–74. AMS (1990)
2. Gennaro, R.: An improved pseudo-random generator based on discrete log. In: Bellare, M. (ed.) CRYPTO 2000. LNCS, vol. 1880, pp. 469–481. Springer, Heidelberg (2000). https://doi.org/10.1007/3-540-44598-6_29
3. Patel, S., Sundaram, G.S.: An efficient discrete log pseudo random generator. In: Krawczyk, H. (ed.) CRYPTO 1998. LNCS, vol. 1462, pp. 304–317. Springer, Heidelberg (1998). https://doi.org/10.1007/BFb0055737
4. van Oorschot, P.C., Wiener, M.J.: On Diffie-Hellman key agreement with short exponents. In: Maurer, U. (ed.) EUROCRYPT 1996. LNCS, vol. 1070, pp. 332–343. Springer, Heidelberg (1996). https://doi.org/10.1007/3-540-68339-9_29
5. Boneh, D., Goh, E.-J., Nissim, K.: Evaluating 2-DNF formulas on ciphertexts. In: Kilian, J. (ed.) TCC 2005. LNCS, vol. 3378, pp. 325–341. Springer, Heidelberg (2005). https://doi.org/10.1007/978-3-540-30576-7_18
6. Gaudry, P., Schost, É.: A low-memory parallel version of Matsuo, Chao, and Tsujii's Algorithm. In: Buell, D. (ed.) ANTS 2004. LNCS, vol. 3076, pp. 208–222. Springer, Heidelberg (2004). https://doi.org/10.1007/978-3-540-24847-7_15
7. Cheon, J.H.: Security analysis of the strong Diffie-Hellman problem. In: Vaudenay, S. (ed.) EUROCRYPT 2006. LNCS, vol. 4004, pp. 1–11. Springer, Heidelberg (2006). https://doi.org/10.1007/11761679_1
8. Gopalakrishnan, K., Thériault, N., Yao, C.Z.: Solving discrete logarithms from partial knowledge of the key. In: Srinathan, K., Rangan, C.P., Yung, M. (eds.) INDOCRYPT 2007. LNCS, vol. 4859, pp. 224–237. Springer, Heidelberg (2007). https://doi.org/10.1007/978-3-540-77026-8_17
9. Lim, C.H., Lee, P.J.: A key recovery attack on discrete log-based schemes using a prime order subgroup. In: Kaliski, B.S. (ed.) CRYPTO 1997. LNCS, vol. 1294, pp. 249–263. Springer, Heidelberg (1997). https://doi.org/10.1007/BFb0052240
10. Galbraith, S.D., Pollard, J.M., Ruprai, R.S.: Computing discrete logarithm in an interval. Math. Comput. **82**(282), 1181–1195 (2013)
11. Cheon, J.H., Hong, J., Kim, M.: Speeding up the Pollard rho method on prime fields. In: Pieprzyk, J. (ed.) ASIACRYPT 2008. LNCS, vol. 5350, pp. 471–488. Springer, Heidelberg (2008). https://doi.org/10.1007/978-3-540-89255-7_29
12. Quisquater, J.-J., Delescaille, J.-P.: How easy is collision search? Application to DES. In: Quisquater, J.-J., Vandewalle, J. (eds.) EUROCRYPT 1989. LNCS, vol. 434, pp. 429–434. Springer, Heidelberg (1990). https://doi.org/10.1007/3-540-46885-4_43
13. Pollard, J.M.: Kangaroos, Monopoly and Discrete Logarithms. J. Cryptol. **4**, 437–447 (2000)

Distributed Pseudorandom Functions
for General Access Structures in NP

Bei Liang[✉] and Aikaterini Mitrokotsa

Chalmers University of Technology, Gothenburg, Sweden
{lbei,aikmitr}@chalmers.se

Abstract. Distributed pseudorandom functions (DPRFs) originally introduced by Naor, Pinkas and Reingold (EUROCRYPT '99) are pseudorandom functions (PRFs), whose computation is distributed to multiple servers. Although by distributing the function computation, we avoid single points of failures, this distribution usually implies the need for multiple interactions with the parties (servers) involved in the computation of the function. In this paper, we take distributed pseudorandom functions (DPRFs) even further, by pursuing a very natural direction. We ask if it is possible to construct *distributed PRFs* for a general class of access mechanism going beyond the threshold access structure and the access structure that can be described by a polynomial-size monotone span programs. More precisely, our contributions are two-fold and can be summarised as follows: *(i)* we introduce the notion of single round distributed PRFs for a general class of access structure (monotone functions in NP), *(ii)* we provide a provably secure general construction of distributed PRFs for every mNP access structure from puncturable PRFs based on indistinguishable obfuscation.

Keywords: Distributed pseudorandom functions
Puncturable PRFs · Function secret sharing

1 Introduction

Distributing the computation of a function is a rather important method employed in order to avoid performance bottlenecks as well as single point of failures due to security compromises or even increased demand (*i.e.*, overloaded servers). Investigating the distribution of trapdoor functions for public key cryptography has already received a lot of attention [2,3]. However, the computation of distributed functions that are useful in secret key cryptography *e.g.*, pseudorandom functions (PRFs) has received limited attention [7–9].

As a motivating example for the use of distributed PRFs, let us consider the scenario of a one-time password system (*e.g.*, RSA SecurID). Users obtain one-time passwords from this system by sending inputs. Each password should be random and independent from the other passwords, and asking the evaluating system on the same input twice should yield the same (random) output. In this

© Springer International Publishing AG, part of Springer Nature 2018
S. Qing et al. (Eds.): ICICS 2017, LNCS 10631, pp. 81–87, 2018.
https://doi.org/10.1007/978-3-319-89500-0_7

system, one assumes the existence of an authentication server, who has a secret key K and responds with PRF outputs $\mathsf{PRF}_K(x)$ that are used as the users' one-time passwords. Since the server knows the secret PRF key, this authentication server is a prime target for attacks. The natural solution to this problem is to distribute the role of the authentication server among many servers. This leads to the notion of *distributed PRFs (DPRFs)*.

In this paper, we investigate whether it is possible to construct distributed PRFs for a general class of access mechanism, going beyond the existing threshold access structure (*i.e.*, at least t-out-of-N servers are required to evaluate the PRF) and the access structure that can be described by a polynomial-size monotone span programs (*e.g.*, undirected connectivity in a graph).

More precisely our contributions are two-fold: *(i)* we introduce the notion of single round distributed PRFs for a general class of access structures (monotone functions in NP), *(ii)* we provide a provably secure general construction of distributed PRFs for every mNP access structure from puncturable PRFs based on indistinguishable obfuscation.

Distributed PRFs. *Distributed pseudorandom functions* (DPRFs), originally introduced by Naor *et al.* [7], provide the properties of regular PRFs (*i.e.*, indistinguishability from random functions) and the capability to evaluate the function f (approximate of a random function) among a set of distributed servers. More precisely, Naor *et al.* [7] considered the setting where the PRF secret key is split among N key servers and at least t servers are needed to evaluate the PRF. The distributed PRF in this setting is known as *distributed PRF* for threshold access structure. Very importantly, evaluating the PRF is done without reconstructing the key at a single location. Naor *et al.* [7] also presented constructions of DPRFs based on general monotone access structures, such as monotone symmetric branching programs (contact schemes), and monotone span programs.

Although some distributed PRFs (DPRFs) schemes have been proposed, all previous constructions have some limitations. Naor *et al.* [7] gave several efficient constructions of certain weak variants of DPRFs. One of their DPRF constructions requires the use of random oracles. To eliminate the use of random oracles, Nielsen [9] provided the first regular DPRF by distributing a slightly modified variant of the Naor-Reingold PRF [8]. Unfortunately, the resulting DPRF is highly interactive among the servers and requires a lot of rounds.

Boneh *et al.* [1] gave an efficient construction of DPRF for t-out-of-N threshold access structure from LWE using a key homomorphic PRF. Boneh *et al.* apply Shamir's t-out-of-N threshold secret sharing scheme [2] on top of their LWE-based key homomorphic PRF scheme, which results in an one-round DPRF with no interaction among the key servers. However, the question of constructing single round, non-interactive distributed PRFs that support more general access structures such as monotone functions in NP remained open prior to this work.

Our Contributions. In this work, we consider *single round distributed PRFs* for a more general class of access structures than the existing monotone access structures: monotone functions in NP, also known as mNP (firstly considered by Komargodski *et al.* [6]). An access structure that is defined by a function in mNP is called an mNP access structure. We also give a generic construction of distributed PRFs for every mNP access structure from puncturable PRFs based on indistinguishable obfuscation [4].

Intuitively, a single round distributed PRF for an mNP access structure is defined as follows: given an access structure, the setup algorithm outputs a public parameter PP and a secret key α which defines a PRF. On input the secret key α, there is an algorithm that allows to "split" α into many "shares" α_i and then to distribute the shares to a collection of servers. Using its own key, α_i, each server can compute a partial evaluation on input x. For the "qualified" subsets, there is a witness attesting to this fact and given the witness and the partial values of these "qualified" servers it should be possible to reconstruct the evaluation of PRF on input x. On the other hand, for the "unqualified" subsets there is no witness, and so it should not be possible to reconstruct the PRF on input x. For example, consider the Hamiltonian access structure. In this access structure, the parties correspond to edges of a complete undirected graph, and a set of parties X is said to be "qualified", if and only if the corresponding set of edges contains a Hamiltonian cycle and the set of parties knows a witness attesting to this fact.

Our central challenge is to reconstruct a function value on some input from a set of partial evaluations of the "qualified" servers. Prior solutions are based on specific PRFs with particular algebraic structures, in combination with Shamir's secret sharing scheme. These solutions employ the homomorphic property of the PRF to distribute the function value into different parts, from which in turn the PRF value can be reconstructed. Here, we explore a solution based on general PRFs with no algebraic structure. Our approach achieves these goals by employing program obfuscation. Both our general constructions of *distributed PRFs* are based on indistinguishability obfuscation [4] and we prove formally their security in the full version of this paper.

Overview of Our Techniques. We now give a high level overview of our technical approach. A formal treatment is given in the main body of the paper.

We propose a general method that makes any puncturable PRF to be a distributed PRF for any mNP access structure based on indistinguishability obfuscation [4]. Our basic scheme is rather easy to describe. Let $\mathbb{A} \in$ mNP be an access structure on N servers $S_1, \ldots, S_N$. Given the verification procedure $V_{\mathbb{A}}$ for an mNP access structure $\mathbb{A}$, a trusted third party samples the PRF key K as well as N PRF keys $K_1, \ldots, K_N$, and creates an obfuscated program $i\mathcal{O}(\mathsf{Prog})$ which with keys $K, K_1, \ldots, K_N$ and $V_{\mathbb{A}}$ hardwired, takes as input the valid witness w of the set of qualified servers $\Gamma \subseteq S_1, \ldots, S_N$, $\{\sigma_i\}_{i \in \Gamma}$ and x and checks if the condition $V_{\mathbb{A}}(\Gamma, w) = 1$ and $\sigma_i = \mathsf{PRF}(K_i, x)$ holds for every $i \in \Gamma$. If the condition holds, the program Prog outputs $\mathsf{PRF}(K, x)$; otherwise it outputs $\bot$. Each server's key is given as K_i. For input x, each server computes $\sigma_i = \mathsf{PRF}(K_i, x)$ and outputs σ_i as the partial share of the function value $\mathsf{PRF}(K, x)$. In order to reconstruct the function value on input x from a set of shares of qualified servers Γ, with witness w the client runs the public obfuscated program $i\mathcal{O}(\mathsf{Prog})$. We also show that the resulting distributed PRF remains selectively pseudorandom even when a set of unqualified servers $T \subseteq \{S_1, \ldots, S_N\}$, namely $T \notin \mathbb{A}$, are corrupted and the adversary is given the share of the servers that are uncorrupted on the inputs of its choice.

2   Preliminaries

2.1   Monotone-NP and Access Structures

A function $f : 2^{[n]} \to \{0, 1\}$ is said to be monotone if for every $\Gamma \subseteq [n]$, such that $f(\Gamma) = 1$ it also holds that $\forall \Gamma' \subseteq [n]$ such that $\Gamma \subseteq \Gamma'$ it holds that $f(\Gamma') = 1$.

A monotone Boolean circuit is a Boolean circuit with AND and OR gates (without negations). A non-deterministic circuit is a Boolean circuit whose inputs are divided into two parts: standard inputs and non-deterministic inputs. A non-deterministic circuit accepts a standard input if and only if there is some setting of the non-deterministic input that causes the circuit to evaluate to 1. A monotone non-deterministic circuit is a non-deterministic circuit, where the monotonicity requirement applies only to the standard inputs, that is, every path from a standard input wire to the output wire does not have a negation gate.

Definition 1 ([5]). *We say that a function L is in mNP if there exists a uniform family of polynomial-size monotone non-deterministic circuit that computes L.*

Lemma 1 ([5]). mNP $=$ NP $\cap$ mono, *where* mono *is the set of all monotone functions.*

Definition 2 (Access structure [6]). *An access structure $\mathbb{A}$ on $\mathcal{S}$ is a monotone set of subsets of $\mathcal{S}$. That is, for all $\Gamma \in \mathbb{A}$ it holds that $\Gamma \subseteq \mathcal{S}$ and for all $\Gamma \in \mathbb{A}$ and Γ' such that $\Gamma \subseteq \Gamma' \subseteq \mathcal{S}$ it holds that $\Gamma' \in \mathbb{A}$.*

We may think of $\mathbb{A}$ as a characteristic function $\mathbb{A} : 2^{\mathcal{P}} \to \{0, 1\}$ that outputs 1 given as input $\Gamma \subseteq \mathcal{S}$ if and only if Γ is in the access structure, namely $\Gamma \in \mathbb{A}$. We view $\mathbb{A}$ either as a function or as a language. Throughout this paper, we deal with distributed PRFs for access structures over N servers $\mathcal{S} = \mathcal{S}_N = \{S_1, \ldots, S_N\}$.

3   Distributed Pseudorandom Functions

We now formally define the syntax and security notion of distributed pseudorandom functions (DPRFs) for any mNP access structure $\mathbb{A}$ on N servers. It is a natural generalization of the definition of DPRFs given in [7] (which was proposed for threshold access structures).

Consider a PRF $F : \mathcal{K} \times \mathcal{X} \to \mathcal{Y}$ that can be computed by a deterministic polynomial time algorithm: on input $(K, x) \in \mathcal{K} \times \mathcal{X}$ the algorithm outputs $F(K, x) \in \mathcal{Y}$. To define distributed PRFs, we follow the partial exposition of Naor *et al.* [7]. The model comprises of N servers $S_1, \ldots, S_N$ and for each of the servers S_i the share space is $\mathcal{Z}_i$. Note we identify a server S_i with its index i.

Definition 3 (Distributed PRFs). *For $N \in \mathbb{N}$, let $\mathbb{A}$ be an mNP access structure on N servers $S_1, \ldots, S_N$. A distributed PRF for $\mathbb{A}$ is a tuple of polynomial time algorithms $\Pi =$ (Setup, Func, Gen, Eval, Comb) with the following syntax:*

- *Setup$(1^\lambda, N, V_{\mathbb{A}})$: On input the security parameter λ, the number N of servers and the verification procedure $V_{\mathbb{A}}$ for an mNP access structure $\mathbb{A}$ on N servers, the setup algorithm outputs the public parameters PP and a master secret key α.*
- *Func(α, x): On input the master secret key α and an input string $x \in \mathcal{X}$, the function evaluation algorithm outputs a function value $y \in \mathcal{Y}$.*
- *Gen(α): On input the master secret key α, the key generation algorithm outputs N keys, $(\alpha_1, \ldots, \alpha_N)$.*
- *Eval(i, α_i, x): On input a server index i, key α_i and input string $x \in \mathcal{X}$, the partial evaluation algorithm outputs a pair (x, y_i) where $y_i \in \mathcal{Z}_i$ is the server's S_i share of function value Func(α, x).*
- *Comb$(PP, V_{\mathbb{A}}, w, \{Eval(i, \alpha_i, x)\}_{i \in \Gamma})$: On input the public parameters PP, the verification procedure $V_{\mathbb{A}}$ for an mNP language $\mathbb{A}$, a witness w, and a set of shares $\{Eval(i, \alpha_i, x)\}_{i \in \Gamma}$ for a set of servers $\Gamma \subseteq \{S_1, \ldots, S_N\}$ where we recall that we identify a server S_i with its index i, the combining algorithm outputs a value $y \in \mathcal{Y} \cup \bot$;*

and satisfying the following correctness *and* pseudorandomness *requirements:*

Correctness: *If for all $\lambda, N \in \mathbb{N}$, any mNP access structure $\mathbb{A}$, any $x \in \mathcal{X}$, and any set of qualified servers $\Gamma \subseteq \{S_1, \ldots, S_N\}$ with valid witness w (i.e., $V_{\mathbb{A}}(\Gamma, w) = 1$), it holds that:*

$$\mathbf{Pr}[(PP, \alpha) \leftarrow Setup(1^\lambda, N, V_{\mathbb{A}}), (\alpha_1, \ldots, \alpha_N) \leftarrow Gen(\alpha) :$$
$$Comb(PP, V_{\mathbb{A}}, w, \{Eval(i, \alpha_i, x)\}_{i \in \Gamma}) = Func(\alpha, x)] = 1.$$

Selective Pseudorandomness: *Consider the following indistinguishability challenge experiment for corrupted servers $T \subseteq [N]$:*

1. *On input the security parameter 1^λ and number N, the adversary $\mathcal{A}$ outputs the challenge input x^*, an access structure $\mathbb{A} \in$ mNP and an unqualified set $T \subseteq [N]$ (that is, $T \notin \mathbb{A}$).*
2. *The challenger runs $(PP, \alpha) \leftarrow Setup(1^\lambda, N, V_{\mathbb{A}})$ and $(\alpha_1, \ldots, \alpha_N) \leftarrow Gen(\alpha)$, and publishes the public parameters PP to the adversary $\mathcal{A}$.*
3. *The challenger sends the corresponding keys $\{\alpha_i\}_{i \in T}$ to $\mathcal{A}$.*
4. *The adversary (adaptively) sends queries $x_1, \ldots, x_Q \in \mathcal{X}$ to the challenger, and for each query x_j the challenger responds with $Eval(i, \alpha_i, x_j)$ for all $i \in [N] \backslash T$.*
5. *The adversary submits a challenge query $x^* \notin \{x_1, \ldots, x_Q\}$ to the challenger. The challenger chooses a random bit $b \leftarrow \{0, 1\}$. If $b = 0$, the challenger returns a uniformly random $y^* \in \mathcal{Y}$ to the adversary. If $b = 1$, the challenger responds with $y^* = Func(\alpha, x^*)$.*
6. *The adversary continues to issue polynomially more queries of the form $x_j \neq x^*$, to which the challenger responds with $\{Eval(i, \alpha_i, x_j)\}_{i \in [N] \backslash T}$.*
7. *The adversary $\mathcal{A}$ outputs a bit $b' \in \{0, 1\}$.*

Let us denote by $Adv_{\Pi,\mathcal{A}}^{pseudo} := \Pr[b' = b] - 1/2$ the advantage of the adversary $\mathcal{A}$ in guessing b in the above experiment, where the probability is taken over the randomness of the challenger and of $\mathcal{A}$. We say the distributed PRFs Π for an mNP access structure $\mathbb{A}$ is selectively pseudorandom if there exists a negligible function $negl(\lambda)$ such that for all non-uniform PPT adversaries $\mathcal{A}$, it holds that $Adv_{\Pi,\mathcal{A}}^{pseudo} \leq negl(\lambda)$.

4   General Construction of Distributed PRFs

In this section, we describe our construction of DPRFs in details. The construction is parameterized over a security parameter λ and a number N, has input space $\mathcal{X} = \{0,1\}^{inp(\lambda)}$ and range space $\mathcal{Y} = \{0,1\}^{out(\lambda)}$ for some polynomial functions $inp(\cdot)$ and $out(\cdot)$. It relies on the following primitives:

- A puncturable PRF $(\mathsf{Setup}_{PRF}, \mathsf{Puncture}_{PRF}, \mathsf{Eval}_{PRF})$, that accepts inputs of length $inp(\lambda)$ and outputs strings of length $out(\lambda)$.
- N puncturable PRFs $(\mathsf{Setup}_{PRF_i}, \mathsf{Puncture}_{PRF_i}, \mathsf{Eval}_{PRF_i})$, for each $i \in [N]$, that accepts inputs of length $inp(\lambda)$ and outputs strings of length $\ell(\lambda)$.

Prog

Hardwired into the circuit: $V_{\mathbb{A}}$, K and $\{K_i\}_{i \in [N]}$.

Input to the circuit: $\{\sigma_i\}_{i \in \Gamma}$, x, w.

Algorithm:
1. Check $V_{\mathbb{A}}(\Gamma, w) = 1$. If it is true, go to the next step; else output $\perp$.
2. For all $i \in \Gamma$ check $\sigma_i = \mathsf{PRF}(K_i, x)$.
   If it is true, output $y = \mathsf{PRF}(K, x)$; else output $\perp$.

Fig. 1. The description of the programs Prog.

Our construction of a DPRF is composed of the following algorithms:

Setup$(1^\lambda, N, V_{\mathbb{A}})$: On input 1^λ, N and $V_{\mathbb{A}}$, it does as follows:
- sample PRF key $K \leftarrow \mathsf{Setup}_{PRF}(1^\lambda)$ and N keys $K_i \leftarrow \mathsf{Setup}_{PRF_i}(1^\lambda)$.
- create an obfuscated program $i\mathcal{O}(\mathsf{Prog})$, where the program Prog is defined in Fig. 1.
- set the secret key $\alpha = (K, \{K_i\}_{i \in [N]})$ and the public parameters $\mathsf{PP} = i\mathcal{O}(\mathsf{Prog})$.

Func(α, x): It parses $\alpha = (K, \{K_i\}_{i \in [N]})$. The function value for input $x \in \{0,1\}^{inp}$ is defined as: $\mathsf{Func}(\alpha, x) = \mathsf{PRF}(K, x) = y$.

Gen(α): It parses $\alpha = (K, \{K_i\}_{i \in [N]})$ and sets $\alpha_i = K_i$ for every $i \in [N]$, where α_i is the key used to compute the corresponding server's share of the function value.

Eval(i, α_i, x): It parses $\alpha_i = K_i$, computes $\sigma_i = \mathsf{PRF}(K_i, x)$ and outputs (σ_i, x), where σ_i is the server's S_i share of the function value $\mathsf{Func}(\alpha, x)$.

Comb$\big(\mathsf{PP}, V_{\mathbb{A}}, w, \{\mathbf{Eval}(i, \alpha_i, x)\}_{i \in \Gamma}\big)$: It parses $\mathsf{Eval}(i, \alpha_i, x) = (\sigma_i, x)$ for every $i \in \Gamma$ and runs $y \leftarrow i\mathcal{O}(\mathsf{Prog})(\{\sigma_i\}_{i \in \Gamma}, x, w)$ to obtain value y. Output y.

Theorem 1. *If $i\mathcal{O}$ is a secure indistinguishability obfuscator, $\mathsf{PRF}(K, \cdot)$ is a secure puncturable PRF, and for each $i \in [N]$ $\mathsf{PRF}(K_i, \cdot)$ is a secure puncturable PRF, then our distributed PRF given above is a selectively pseudorandom distributed PRF for the mNP access structure $\mathbb{A}$, as defined in Definition 3.*

The complete proof is provided in the full version of this article.

5   Conclusion

In this paper, we consider single round distributed PRFs for a more general class of access structures: monotone functions in NP. We also give a generic construction of distributed PRFs for every mNP access structure from puncturable PRFs based on indistinguishable obfuscation.

Acknowledgements. This work was partially supported by the People Programme (Marie Curie Actions) of the European Union's Seventh Framework Programme (FP7/2007-2013) under REA grant agreement n 608743 and the STINT grant IB 2015-6001.

References

1. Boneh, D., Lewi, K., Montgomery, H., Raghunathan, A.: Key homomorphic PRFs and their applications. In: Canetti, R., Garay, J.A. (eds.) CRYPTO 2013, Part I. LNCS, vol. 8042, pp. 410–428. Springer, Heidelberg (2013). https://doi.org/10.1007/978-3-642-40041-4_23
2. De Santis, A., Desmedt, Y., Frankel, Y., Yung, M.: How to share a function securely. In: Proceedings of STOC 1994, pp. 522–533. ACM, New York (1994)
3. Desmedt, Y., Frankel, Y.: Threshold cryptosystems. In: Brassard, G. (ed.) CRYPTO 1989. LNCS, vol. 435, pp. 307–315. Springer, New York (1990). https://doi.org/10.1007/0-387-34805-0_28
4. Garg, S., Gentry, C., Halevi, S., Raykova, M., Sahai, A., Waters, B.: Candidate indistinguishability obfuscation and functional encryption for all circuits. In: Proceedings of FOCS 2013, Washington, D.C., USA, pp. 40–49. IEEE Computer Society (2013)
5. Grigni, M., Sipser, M.: Monotone complexity (1990)
6. Komargodski, I., Naor, M., Yogev, E.: Secret-sharing for NP. J. Cryptol. **30**(2), 444–469 (2017)
7. Naor, M., Pinkas, B., Reingold, O.: Distributed pseudo-random functions and KDCs. In: Stern, J. (ed.) EUROCRYPT 1999. LNCS, vol. 1592, pp. 327–346. Springer, Heidelberg (1999). https://doi.org/10.1007/3-540-48910-X_23
8. Naor, M., Reingold, O.: Number-theoretic constructions of efficient pseudo-random functions. J. ACM (JACM) **51**(2), 231–262 (2004)
9. Nielsen, J.B.: A threshold pseudorandom function construction and its applications. In: Yung, M. (ed.) CRYPTO 2002. LNCS, vol. 2442, pp. 401–416. Springer, Heidelberg (2002). https://doi.org/10.1007/3-540-45708-9_26

Reducing Randomness Complexity
of Mask Refreshing Algorithm

Shuang Qiu[1,2], Rui Zhang[1,2(✉)], Yongbin Zhou[1,2], and Hailong Zhang[1]

[1] State Key Laboratory of Information Security, Institute of Information Engineering,
Chinese Academy of Sciences, Beijing 100093, China
{qiushuang,r-zhang,zhouyongbin,zhanghailong}@iie.ac.cn
[2] School of Cyber Security, University of Chinese Academy of Sciences,
Beijing 100049, China

Abstract. Among the existing countermeasures against side-channel analysis, masking is the most widely deployed one. In order to mask large functions (e.g. S-boxes), each basic operation of the function should be replaced with the d-th order secure operation. In this process, the multiplication with dependent inputs always exists, which may lead to security bias. In order to preserve the security of the dependent-input multiplication, a refreshing algorithm should be utilized to eliminate the dependence. Among the existing refreshing algorithms, only one proposal satisfying d-Strong Non-Interferent (d-SNI) can effectively solve the dependent-input issue. However, it suffers a low efficiency with a high randomness complexity. In this paper, we claim that the d-SNI refreshing algorithm is overqualified and a weaker refreshing algorithm can also ensure the security of the dependent-input multiplication. According to the property of the ISW multiplication, we prove that a refreshing algorithm satisfying a "conditional d-SNI" (weaker than d-SNI) can solve the dependent-input issue. In this way, we relax the security requirement of the refreshing algorithm. Based on this new security requirement, we propose a new refreshing algorithm satisfying conditional d-SNI. The randomness complexity of the new proposal is much lower than that of the original refreshing algorithm. As a validation, we implement the two refreshing algorithms on the 32-bit ARM core, and compare their random generations, clock cycles, and ROM consumptions. The comparison results indicate that our proposal outperforms the d-SNI refreshing algorithm in terms of both the randomness complexity and the arithmetic complexity, as significantly less random generations (33%–70% reduction), less clock cycles, and less ROM consumptions are involved in our proposal than in the d-SNI refreshing.

Keywords: Masking · Private circuit · Side-channel analysis
Ishai-Sahai-Wagner · Strong Non-Interferent

1 Introduction

Side Channel Analysis (SCA) [8,9] has become a serious threat to implementations of cryptographic algorithms. Among existing countermeasures, one of

© Springer International Publishing AG, part of Springer Nature 2018
S. Qing et al. (Eds.): ICICS 2017, LNCS 10631, pp. 88–101, 2018.
https://doi.org/10.1007/978-3-319-89500-0_8

the most widely used is masking [3–5,7,10–13]. A d-th order masking consists in splitting each secret-dependent intermediate variable x (called sensitive variable) into $d + 1$ shares $(x_0, x_1, \ldots, x_d)$, where $(x_1, \ldots, x_d)$ are randomly picked up. When d-th order masking is utilized to secure a block cipher, a so-called d-th order *masking scheme* should be designed to operate on those shares.

The first probing secure masking scheme is the ISW scheme [7], which works as a transformer mapping the AND and NOT gates to secure gates. In this way, they aim to map an S-box circuit to a randomized S-box circuit which satisfies the d-th order security. Rivain and Prouff apply the ISW transformers to secure the whole AES software implementation [13], by extending the ISW transformer to secure multiplication over $\mathbb{F}_2^n$. In this process, when the inputs of an ISW multiplication are related, the circuit may suffer joint leakage, which we call the "dependent-input issue" in the sequel. In order to solve the dependent-input issue, a so-called refreshing algorithm [5,6,13] should be inserted. Among the existing refreshing algorithms, the refreshing algorithm proposed in [6] is the only one which can actually solve the dependent-input issue. This refreshing algorithm satisfies d-SNI (Strong Non-Interference) [1], which we call the d-SNI refreshing in the sequel. It can be proved that the d-SNI refreshing algorithm can effectively eliminate the dependence of the input shares [1]. However, the d-SNI refreshing introduces exponential number of extra randomness, which may lead to a low efficiency. Therefore, improving the efficiency of the d-SNI refreshing, while maintaining the d-th order security of the dependent-input multiplication, is of great importance.

In [13], authors propose a refreshing algorithm which is very efficient with only d extra randomness. However, it only satisfies d-TNI (Tight Non-Interference) security [1], where d-TNI refreshing algorithms can hardly preserve the d-th order security of the dependent-input multiplication. In [2], a randomness reduction strategy for ISW multiplication is proposed. However, with this new strategy, the obtained algorithm only satisfies d-TNI security. d-TNI refreshing algorithm cannot solve the dependent-input issue.

In this paper, we claim that the d-SNI refreshing algorithm is overqualified when the multiplication is masked with ISW-like schemes [5,7,13]. According to the property of the ISW-like schemes, we relax the security requirement of the refreshing algorithm from d-SNI to conditional d-SNI (weaker than d-SNI). According to this new security requirement, we obtain a conditional d-SNI refreshing algorithm through search for security order $d \leq 11$, which requires less randomness generations than the original d-SNI refreshing algorithm. Finally, we implement the two refreshing algorithms on ARM, and compare the random generations and practical performances of both refreshing schemes.

Paper Organization. This paper is organized as follows. In Sect. 2, we give some useful notations and review the compositional security notions and the dependent-input issue. In Sect. 3, we prove that a refreshing algorithm satisfying conditional d-SNI can solve the dependent-input issue, and accordingly propose a conditional d-SNI refreshing algorithm. In Sect. 4, we compare the performances of our proposal with that of the d-SNI refreshing. In Sect. 5, we conclude this paper.

2 Preliminaries

2.1 Notations and Notions

$[n_1, n_2]$ denotes the integer set $\{n_1, n_1 + 1, \ldots, n_2\}$. For a set S, $|S|$ denotes the cardinality of S, and $\overline{S}$ denotes the complementary set of S. For a set S which can be represented as $S = \{s_1, s_2, \cdots, s_n\}$, $(a_i)_{i \in S}$ represents the set $\{a_{s_1}, a_{s_2}, \ldots, a_{s_n}\}$. Linear mapping is denoted as $\ell(\cdot)$. The arrow $\leftarrow$ represents to assign the value of the right variable to the left variable. $\xleftarrow{\$}$ represents to randomly pick one value from the set on the right and assign this value to the left variable. $\oplus$ denotes XOR operation on $\mathbb{F}_2$ (or $\mathbb{F}_2^n$), and $\cdot$ denotes AND operation on $\mathbb{F}_2$ (or $\mathbb{F}_2^n$). $\bigoplus_{i=1}^n$ represents the XOR sum, namely $\bigoplus_{i=1}^n x_i = x_1 \oplus x_2 \oplus \cdots \oplus x_n$. In this paper, the compositional security notions [1] are involved. We review them here.

Definition 1 (Simulatability). *Denote by* $P = \{p_1, \ldots, p_\ell\}$ *the set of* ℓ *intermediate variables of a multiplication algorithm. If there exists two sets* $I = \{i_1, \ldots, i_t\}$ *and* $J = \{j_1, \ldots, j_t\}$ *of* t *indices from set* $\{1, \ldots, d\}$ *and a random function S taking as input* $2t$ *bits and output* ℓ *bits such that for any fixed bits* $(a_i)_{0 \leq i \leq d}$ *and* $(b_j)_{0 \leq j \leq d}$, *the distributions of* $\{p_1, \ldots, p_\ell\}$ *and* $\{S(a_{i_1}, \ldots, a_{i_t}, b_{j_1}, \ldots, b_{j_t})\}$ *are identical, we say the set P can be simulated with at most* t *shares of each input* a_I *and* b_J.

Definition 2 (d-TNI). *An algorithm satisfies d-Tight-Non-Interferent (d-TNI) property if and only if every set of* $t \leq d$ *intermediate variables can be simulated with at most* t *shares of each input.*

Definition 3 (d-SNI). *An algorithm satisfies d-Strong-Non-Interferent (d-SNI) if and only if for every set* $\mathcal{I}$ *of* t_1 *probes on intermediate variables (i.e. no output shares) and every set* $\mathcal{O}$ *of* t_2 *probes on output shares such that* $t_1 + t_2 \leq d$, *the set* $\mathcal{I} \cup \mathcal{O}$ *can be simulated by only* t_1 *shares of each input.*

2.2 Dependent-Input Issue and Refreshing Algorithm

In the masked implementations of large functions, e.g. S-boxes, the "dependent-input issue" always exists and causes security biases. For the ISW scheme [7], the input shares $(a_i)_{i \in [0,d]}$ and $(b_i)_{i \in [0,d]}$ are required to be independent. Once the inputs are mutually dependent, i.e. $b = \ell(a)$, one can directly obtain the share of one input b_i utilizing the share of the other input a_i. In Fig. 1, x denotes the input, $\mathcal{O}$ denotes the set of observed output shares, $\mathcal{A}^1$ refers to the ISW multiplication, $\mathcal{I}^1$ denotes the observed internal variables in $\mathcal{A}^1$, and $\mathcal{S}_j^i$ denotes the set of shares from the j-th input of algorithm $\mathcal{A}^i$ utilized to simulate all further variables.

As is claimed in [13], the dependent-input multiplication in Fig. 1 can hardly preserve d-th order security. In fact, this conclusion can also be proved utilizing the aforementioned compositional security notions, as is shown in Proposition 1.

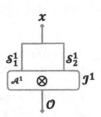

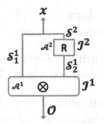

Fig. 1. The dependent-input multiplication.

Fig. 2. The dependent-input multiplication with a refreshing algorithm.

Proposition 1 (Dependent-Input Issue). *The circuit given in Fig. 1 with $\mathcal{A}^1$ being d-SNI is not necessarily d-TNI.*

Proof. The total number of variables used to attack the circuit is limited to d, i.e. $|\mathcal{I}^1| + |\mathcal{O}| \le d$. As in [1], we build the proof from right to left by simulating each algorithm. Algorithm $\mathcal{A}^1$ is d-SNI, thus $|\mathcal{S}_1^1|, |\mathcal{S}_2^1| \le |\mathcal{I}^1|$. Therefore, all the variables can be simulated with $|\mathcal{S}_1^1 \cup \mathcal{S}_2^1| \le |\mathcal{I}^1| + |\mathcal{I}^1|$ shares of input x. $|\mathcal{I}^1| + |\mathcal{I}^1|$ is not necessarily no more than d, thus the circuit in Fig. 1 is not necessarily d-TNI. $\square$

In order to deal with the dependent-input issue, a so-called "refreshing algorithm" should be inserted [13], as is illustrated in Fig. 2. In Fig. 2, $\mathcal{A}^1$ represents the ISW multiplication, and $\mathcal{A}^2$ represents the refreshing algorithm. The refreshing algorithm aims to eliminate the dependence of the inputs, and therefore solve the dependent-input issue. However, as is claimed by [5], the refreshing algorithm proposed in [13] is not secure enough and may lead to a security bias. This conclusion can also be verified utilizing the definition of d-SNI and d-TNI. The refreshing algorithm in [13] is d-TNI [1]. As is stated in Proposition 2, d-TNI refreshing algorithm cannot preserve the security of the dependent-input multiplication.

Proposition 2 (d-TNI Refreshing). *The circuit given in Fig. 2 with $\mathcal{A}^1$ being d-SNI multiplication and $\mathcal{A}^2$ being d-TNI refreshing algorithm is not necessarily d-TNI.*

Proof. The total number of variables used to attack the circuit is limited to d, i.e. $|\mathcal{I}^1| + |\mathcal{I}^2| + |\mathcal{O}| \le d$. As in [1], we build the proof from right to left by simulating each algorithm. Algorithm $\mathcal{A}^1$ is d-SNI, thus $|\mathcal{S}_1^1|, |\mathcal{S}_2^1| \le |\mathcal{I}^1|$. Algorithm $\mathcal{A}^2$ is d-TNI, thus $|\mathcal{S}^2| \le |\mathcal{I}^2| + |\mathcal{S}_2^1|$. Finally, all the variables can be simulated with $|\mathcal{S}_1^1 \cup \mathcal{S}^2| \le |\mathcal{I}^1| + |\mathcal{I}^1| + |\mathcal{I}^2|$ shares of input x. $|\mathcal{I}^1| + |\mathcal{I}^1| + |\mathcal{I}^2|$ is not necessarily no more than d, thus the circuit in Fig. 2 is not necessarily d-TNI. $\square$

2.3 d-SNI Refreshing Algorithm

In order to solve the dependent-input issue, the refreshing algorithm is required to be d-SNI. As is shown in Proposition 3, with a d-SNI refreshing algorithm, the dependent-input multiplication preserves d-th order security. The security proof is given in the full version of this paper.

Proposition 3 (d-SNI Refreshing). *The circuit given in Fig. 2 with $\mathcal{A}^1$ being d-SNI multiplication and $\mathcal{A}^2$ being d-SNI refreshing algorithm is d-SNI.*

To deal with the dependent-input issue, Duc *et al.* [6] propose a new refreshing algorithm satisfying d-SNI, which we call the d-SNI refreshing in the sequel. Although being proven to reach d-th order security when plugged in the dependent-input multiplication, it requires more random generations. The d-TNI refreshing algorithm [13] needs d random generations, while the d-SNI refreshing algorithm needs $d(d+1)/2$ random generations.

3   An Efficient Refreshing Algorithm with Less Random Generations

3.1   Dependent-Input Issue and Conditional d-SNI Refreshing

The implementation of a dependent-input multiplication is depicted in Fig. 2. The multiplication is masked utilizing the ISW-like scheme, which satisfies d-SNI [1]. In order to solve the dependent-input issue, one should ensure that the circuit in Fig. 2 satisfies d-th order security, i.e. d-SNI or d-TNI. As is shown in Proposition 3, if the refreshing algorithm satisfies d-SNI, the dependent-input multiplication (containing the multiplication and the refreshing algorithm) in Fig. 2 satisfies d-th order security.

In this section, we claimed that the refreshing algorithm is not necessarily d-SNI, and a weaker refreshing algorithm may also be secure. First, based on the property of the ISW multiplication (each intermediate leaks at most one share for each input), we propose a constraint on set $\mathcal{I}^1$.

Proposition 4. *In the circuit depicted in Fig. 2, we assume that $\mathcal{I}^1$ is the set of input variables and intermediate variables of $\mathcal{A}^1$ (the ISW multiplication), $\mathcal{I}^2$ is the set of input variables and intermediate variables of $\mathcal{A}^2$ (Algorithm 1). In $\mathcal{I}^1$, A denotes the set of indexes of multiplicand a, i.e. $\mathcal{S}_1^1$, and B denotes the set of indexes of multiplicand b, i.e. $\mathcal{S}_2^1$. Set $\mathcal{S}_1^1 \cup \mathcal{S}^2$ denotes the set of input shares used to simulate all further variables in the circuit. We give two constraints,*

1. $\mathcal{I}^1$ only contains $a_i \cdot b_j$, and involves no a_i or b_j (i.e. $|A| = |B| = |\mathcal{I}^1|$),
2. $A \cap B = \emptyset$,

For a given $\mathcal{I}^2$ and $t \leq d$, if every $\mathcal{I}^1$ satisfying the above constraints satisfies $|\mathcal{S}^2 \cup \mathcal{S}_1^1| \leq t$, then every $\mathcal{I}^1$ satisfies $|\mathcal{S}^2 \cup \mathcal{S}_1^1| \leq t$.

Proof. According to the description of ISW scheme, the intermediate variables of the ISW multiplication $\mathcal{I}^1$ may contain a_i, b_i, $a_i \cdot b_j$ and their linear combinations. In fact, each probes in $\mathcal{I}^1$ leaks at most two shares a_i and b_j [7,13]. As a result, according to set $\mathcal{I}^1$, we can retrieve $\bigoplus(a_i)_{i \in A} \bigoplus(b_i)_{i \in B}$. According to the description of the refreshing algorithm (Algorithm 1), set $\mathcal{I}^2$ contains r_i' ($r_i' = a_i \oplus b_i$), r_i, linear combinations of r_i and input shares a_i. Therefore, set $\mathcal{I}^2$ may depend on $\bigoplus(a_i \oplus b_i)_{i \in B}$. Finally, the probes in the circuit $\mathcal{I}^1 \cup \mathcal{I}^2$ can be simulated with at most $|A \cup B|$ shares of the input, as $\mathcal{S}_1^1 \cup \mathcal{S}^2 \subseteq (a_i)_{i \in A \cup B}$.

The proof can be divided in the following two steps, where $\mathbb{I}$ denotes the set of all possible $\mathcal{I}^1$, $\mathbb{I}|_{c1}$ denotes the set of all possible $\mathcal{I}^1$ satisfies the first constraint, and $\mathbb{I}|_{c1,c2}$ denotes the set of all possible $\mathcal{I}^1$ satisfies the first and second constraints.

1. **First, we prove that if there exists $\mathcal{I}^1 \in \mathbb{I}$ satisfying $|\mathcal{S}_1^1 \cup \mathcal{S}^2| > t$, there will exist $\mathcal{I}^{1'} \in \mathbb{I}|_{c1}$ which also satisfies $|\mathcal{S}_1^1 \cup \mathcal{S}^2| > t$.**

   Assume $\mathcal{I}^1 \in \mathbb{I}$ satisfying $|\mathcal{S}_2^1 \cup \mathcal{S}^2| > t$, where $\mathcal{I}^1$ contains a_i. According to $\mathcal{I}^1$, we construct $\mathcal{I}^{1'}$ by replacing a_i with $a_i \cdot b_j$. As there is no a_i or b_i involved in $\mathcal{I}^{1'}$, there exists $\mathcal{I}^{1'} \in \mathbb{I}|_{c1}$. As the involved indexes in $\mathcal{I}^{1'}$ is no less than that in $\mathcal{I}^1$, the input shares utilized to simulate $\mathcal{I}^{1'} \cup \mathcal{I}^2$ is no less than that utilized to simulate $\mathcal{I}^1 \cup \mathcal{I}^2$. Namely, $\mathcal{I}^{1'}$ also satisfies $|\mathcal{S}_1^1 \cup \mathcal{S}^2| > t$. Therefore, for each $\mathcal{I}^1 \in \mathbb{I}$ satisfying $|\mathcal{S}_1^1 \cup \mathcal{S}^2| > t$, we can always construct $\mathcal{I}^{1'} \in \mathbb{I}|_{c1}$ satisfying $|\mathcal{S}_1^1 \cup \mathcal{S}^2| > t$.

2. **Then, we prove that if there exists $\mathcal{I}^1 \in \mathbb{I}|_{c1}$ satisfying $|\mathcal{S}_1^1 \cup \mathcal{S}^2| > t$, there will exist $\mathcal{I}^{1'} \in \mathbb{I}|_{c1,c2}$ which also satisfies $|\mathcal{S}_1^1 \cup \mathcal{S}^2| > t$.**

   Assume $\mathcal{I}^1 \in \mathbb{I}|_{c1}$ satisfying $|\mathcal{S}_1^1 \cup \mathcal{S}^2| > t$, where $\mathcal{I}^1$ satisfies $A \cap B \neq \emptyset$. We denote by AB the intersection of set A and set B. According to $\mathcal{I}^1$, we can always construct $\mathcal{I}^{1'}$ by replacing $(b_i)_{i \in AB}$ with any element else. For $\mathcal{I}^{1'}$, $A' = A$, $B' = B \cap \overline{A}$, and thus $A' \cap B' = \emptyset$. Therefore, there exists $\mathcal{I}^{1'} \in \mathbb{I}|_{c1,c2}$. As the involved indexes in $\mathcal{I}^{1'}$ is no less than that in $\mathcal{I}^1$, the input shares utilized to simulate $\mathcal{I}^{1'} \cup \mathcal{I}^2$ is no less than that utilized to simulate $\mathcal{I}^1 \cup \mathcal{I}^2$. Namely, $\mathcal{I}^{1'}$ also satisfies $|\mathcal{S}_1^1 \cup \mathcal{S}^2| > t$. Therefore, for each $\mathcal{I}^1 \in \mathbb{I}$ satisfying $|\mathcal{S}_1^1 \cup \mathcal{S}^2| > t$, we can always construct $\mathcal{I}^{1'} \in \mathbb{I}|_{c1}$ satisfying $|\mathcal{S}_1^1 \cup \mathcal{S}^2| > t$.

Accordingly, we can deduce that if there exists $\mathcal{I}^1 \in \mathbb{I}$ satisfying $|\mathcal{S}_1^1 \cup \mathcal{S}^2| > t$, there will exist $\mathcal{I}^{1'} \in \mathbb{I}|_{c1,c2}$ which also satisfies $|\mathcal{S}_1^1 \cup \mathcal{S}^2| > t$. Namely, if every $\mathcal{I}^1 \in \mathbb{I}|_{c1,c2}$ satisfying the two constraints satisfies $|\mathcal{S}^2 \cup \mathcal{S}_1^1| \leq t$, then every $\mathcal{I}^1 \in \mathbb{I}$ satisfies $|\mathcal{S}^2 \cup \mathcal{S}_1^1| \leq t$. □

Proposition 5. *If the circuit in Fig. 2 is d-SNI when $\mathcal{I}^1$ satisfying the two constraints, the circuit is d-SNI.*

Proof. If the circuit in Fig. 2 is d-SNI when $\mathcal{I}^1$ satisfying the two constraints, there exists $|\mathcal{S}_1^1 \cup \mathcal{S}^2| \leq |\mathcal{I}^1| + |\mathcal{I}^2|$ on condition of the two constraints. According to Proposition 4, for arbitrary $\mathcal{I}^1$, there also exists $|\mathcal{S}_1^1 \cup \mathcal{S}^2| \leq |\mathcal{I}^1| + |\mathcal{I}^2|$. Namely, the circuit satisfies d-SNI. □

Proposition 6. *If the circuit in Fig. 2 is d-TNI when $\mathcal{I}^1$ satisfying the two constraints, the circuit is d-TNI.*

Proof. If the circuit in Fig. 2 is d-TNI when $\mathcal{I}^1$ satisfying the two constraints, there exists $|\mathcal{S}_1^1 \cup \mathcal{S}^2| \leq |\mathcal{I}^1| + |\mathcal{I}^2| + |\mathcal{O}|$ on condition of the two constraints. According to Proposition 4, for arbitrary $\mathcal{I}^1$, there also exists $|\mathcal{S}_1^1 \cup \mathcal{S}^2| \leq |\mathcal{I}^1| + |\mathcal{I}^2| + |\mathcal{O}|$. Namely, the circuit satisfies d-TNI. $\square$

Theorem 1 (Conditional d-SNI Refreshing). *If the refreshing algorithm satisfies d-SNI on condition of $|\mathcal{S}_2^1| \leq (d+1)/2$ and the multiplication algorithm is ISW-like scheme satisfying d-SNI (or d-TNI), the circuit in Fig. 2 preserves d-SNI (or d-TNI).*

Proof. According to Proposition 4, A and B satisfy $A \cap B = \emptyset$, and $|A| = |B|$. Accordingly, we can deduce that $|A| = |B| \leq (d+1)/2$, i.e. $|\mathcal{S}_2^1| \leq (d+1)/2$. For $|\mathcal{S}_2^1| \leq (d+1)/2$, if the refreshing algorithm is d-SNI, there exist $|\mathcal{S}^2| \leq |\mathcal{I}^2|$ on condition of the two constraints. Therefore, all the probes in the circuit can be simulated by $|\mathcal{S}_1^1 \cup \mathcal{S}^2| \leq |\mathcal{I}^1| + |\mathcal{I}^2|$ (or $|\mathcal{S}_1^1 \cup \mathcal{S}^2| \leq |\mathcal{I}^1| + |\mathcal{I}^2| + |\mathcal{O}|$) shares of x, which shows that the circuit is d-SNI (or d-TNI) on condition of $|\mathcal{S}_2^1| \leq (d+1)/2$. According to Propositions 5 and 6, the circuit in Fig. 2 satisfies d-SNI (or d-TNI). $\square$

According to Theorem 1, if the refreshing algorithm is d-SNI for $|\mathcal{S}_2^1| \leq (d+1)/2$, the dependent-input multiplication can preserve d-th order security and the dependent-input issue can be solved. This security requirement for the refreshing algorithm is weaker than d-SNI, which we call **the conditional d-SNI** in the sequel.

Algorithm 1. New Refreshing Algorithm.

Require:
  shares $(x_i)_{i \in [0,d]}$ satisfying $\bigoplus_i x_i = x$
Ensure:
  shares $(x_i')_{i \in [0,d]}$ satisfying $\bigoplus_i x_i' = x$
1: **for** $i = 1$ to $d + d_0$ **do**
2:   $r_i \xleftarrow{\$} \mathbb{F}_2^n$ ▷ Generate Random Bits
3: **end for**
4: $r_0 \leftarrow r_1$
5: **for** $i = 2$ to $d + d_0$ **do**
6:   $r_0 \leftarrow r_0 \oplus r_i$ ▷ Complete $r_0 = r_1 \oplus r_2 \oplus \cdots \oplus r_{d+d_0}$
7: **end for**
8: **for** $i = 1$ to d_0 **do**
9:   $r_{m(i)} \leftarrow r_{m(i)} \oplus r_{i+d}$ ▷ Complete $r_1, r_2, \cdots, r_d$
10: **end for**
11: **for** $i = 0$ to d **do**
12:   $r_i' \leftarrow r_i$ ▷ $r_i' = x_i \oplus x_i'$
13:   $x_i' \leftarrow x_i \oplus r_i'$ ▷ Refresh $x_0, x_1 \cdots, x_d$
14: **end for**
15: **return** $(x_0', x_1', \cdots, x_d')$

3.2   A New Refreshing Algorithm Satisfies Conditional d-SNI

In this section, we propose a new refreshing algorithm which achieves d-SNI on condition of $|\mathcal{S}_2^1| \leq (d+1)/2$. The description of the new refreshing algorithm is given in Algorithm 1. It can be seen as a two-step process. First, the first d random numbers $r_1, \ldots, r_d$ are added to shares $x_1, \ldots, x_d$ and x_0 in sequence. Then, the last d_0 random numbers are added to $x_1, \ldots, x_d$ according to $m(i)$, where $m(i)$ is a bijective function mapping $[1, d_0]$ to a d_0-element subset of $[1, d]$. We should search for suitable d_0 and $m(i)$, in order to make the refreshing algorithm be d-SNI on condition of $|\mathcal{S}_2^1| \leq (d+1)/2$ (Fig. 2).

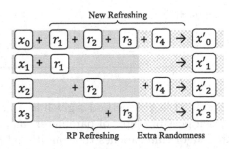

Fig. 3. An instance of the new scheme when $d = 3$.

Algorithm 2. The search method.

Require:
   The order of the mask refreshing, say d.
Ensure:
   Parameter d_0 and $m(i)$ which make the refreshing scheme satisfy $|\mathcal{S}_1^1 \cup \mathcal{S}^2| \leq |\mathcal{I}^1| + |\mathcal{I}^2|$.
 1: $d_0 \leftarrow 1$
 2: **while** do not find suitable $m(i)$ **do**
 3:    **for** every possible $m(i)$ **do**
 4:       **for** every possible $|\mathcal{S}_2^1| \leq (d+1)/2$ **do**
 5:          **for** every possible $\mathcal{S}^2 \subseteq \mathcal{S}_2^1$ **do**
 6:             $|\mathcal{I}_{min}^2| \leftarrow \mathsf{Sel}(\mathcal{S}_2^1, \mathcal{S}^2)$
 7:             **if** $|\mathcal{I}_{min}^2| < |\mathcal{S}^2|$ **then**
 8:                Break and jump to the first FOR-loop   ▷ If there exists leakage, try another $m(i)$
 9:             **end if**
10:          **end for**
11:       **end for**
12:       Break and output $m(i)$ and d_0 ▷ Find a suitable refreshing algorithm of order d
13:    **end for**
14:    $d_0 \leftarrow d_0 + 1$
15: **end while**

Algorithm 3. Sel.

Require:
    The set $\mathcal{S}_2^1$ and $\mathcal{S}^2$.
Ensure:
    The value of $|\mathcal{I}_{min}^2|$.
1: $T \leftarrow \bigoplus_{i \in B^*} r_i'$
2: $T' \leftarrow$ Rewritten(T) $\triangleright$ In the increasing order of the index of r_i
3: $m \leftarrow$ P(T') $\triangleright$ The number of the parts, m
4: $n \leftarrow$ NOA(T') $\triangleright$ The number of the non-overlap adjacent pairs, n
5: $\{k_1, k_2, \cdots, k_{t_0}\} \leftarrow$ OA(T') $\triangleright$ t_0 overlapping adjacent pairs, with each pair has k_t elements
6: $|\mathcal{I}_{min}^2| \leftarrow 2m - n$
7: **if** $t_0 \neq 0$ **then**
8:    **for** $t = 1$ to t_0 **do**
9:        **if** k_t is even **then**
10:            $|\mathcal{I}_{min}^2| \leftarrow |\mathcal{I}_{min}^2| - k_t/2$
11:        **else**
12:            $|\mathcal{I}_{min}^2| \leftarrow |\mathcal{I}_{min}^2| - (k_t + 1)/2$ $\triangleright$ Complete the computation
13:        **end if**
14:    **end for**
15: **end if**
16: **return** $|\mathcal{I}_{min}^2|$

Search Method. The detailed search method is given in Algorithm 2. According to Algorithm 2, we try each possible tuple of parameters d_0 and $m(i)$, and check if the obtained refreshing algorithm satisfies the conditional d-SNI. As is shown in Theorem 1, we only need to consider the case when $|\mathcal{S}_2^1| \leq (d+1)/2$. Moreover, if $b_i \notin \mathcal{S}_2^1$, the index i satisfies $a_i \notin \mathcal{S}^2$. Therefore, $\mathcal{S}^2 \subseteq \mathcal{S}_2^1$.

Accordingly, we do not need to search every possible $\mathcal{S}_2^1$ and $\mathcal{S}^2$, but only a subset. We utilize an algorithm Sel to judge if $|\mathcal{S}^2| \leq |\mathcal{I}^2|$ (the requirement of d-SNI) holds for any given $\mathcal{S}^2$ and $\mathcal{S}_2^1$. If this relation holds for every $|\mathcal{S}_1^2| \leq (d+1)/2$ and $\mathcal{S}^2 \subseteq \mathcal{S}_2^1$, we suggest this obtained refreshing algorithm is conditional d-SNI.

Algorithm Sel. The details of algorithm Sel is given in Algorithm 3. After each execution of Sel, one can obtain $|\mathcal{I}_{min}^2|$ for the given $\mathcal{S}_2^1$ and $\mathcal{S}^2$, where $\mathcal{I}_{min}^2$ is the smallest set of the intermediate variables $\mathcal{I}^2$ which makes $\mathcal{I}_{min}^2 \cup \mathcal{S}_1^1$ should be simulated with input shares $(x_i)_{i \in \mathcal{S}^2}$. If $|\mathcal{I}_{min}^2| \geq |\mathcal{S}^2|$, we can conclude that $|\mathcal{S}^2| \leq |\mathcal{I}^2|$ holds for $\mathcal{S}_2^1$ and $\mathcal{S}^2$. For each $\mathcal{S}_2^1$ satisfying $|\mathcal{S}_2^1| \leq (d+1)/2$, we execute algorithm Sel several times to judge if $|\mathcal{S}^2| \leq |\mathcal{I}^2|$ holds for every possible $\mathcal{S}^2$ and $\mathcal{S}_2^1$. Finally, we can judge if this refreshing algorithm satisfies the conditional d-SNI.

The description of Sel is given in Algorithm 3. In the sequel, we explain in detail how algorithm Sel maps $\mathcal{S}_2^1$ and $\mathcal{S}^2$ to $|\mathcal{I}_{min}^2|$. For $B^* \subseteq B$, according to $\mathcal{S}_2^1$, we can obtain $\bigoplus_{i \in B^*} b_i$, where $\bigoplus_{i \in B^*} b_i$ can be rewritten as $(\bigoplus_{i \in B^*} a_i) \oplus (\bigoplus_{i \in B^*} (a_i \oplus b_i))$. Then, if and only if we can obtain $\bigoplus_{i \in B^*} (a_i \oplus b_i)$ according to $\mathcal{I}^2$, the probes in $\mathcal{I}^2 \cup \mathcal{S}_2^1$ can be related to $(\bigoplus_{i \in B^*} a_i)$. Namely, $\mathcal{S}^2$ equals $(a_i)_{i \in B^*}$. Therefore, for a given $\mathcal{S}_2^1$ and a given $\mathcal{S}^2 = (a_i)_{i \in B^*}$, $\mathcal{S}^2$ should relate to $\bigoplus_{i \in B^*} (a_i \oplus b_i)$. To obtain the minimal set $\mathcal{I}_{min}^2$ is equivalent to reveal $\bigoplus_{i \in B^*} (a_i \oplus b_i)$ with minimal internal variables of the refreshing algorithm.

In the following, $\bigoplus_{i \in B^*} r_i'$ is called the "target" and it is denoted by T. Algorithm Sel aim to find the smallest subset $\mathcal{I}_{min}^2$, which satisfies $\bigoplus \mathcal{I}_{min}^2 = T$.

First, we rewrite the target T by processing function Rewritten(). According to Algorithm 1, each r_i' is the sum of several r_i. As a result, $T = \bigoplus_{i \in B^*} r_i'$ can be rewritten as the sum of several random numbers r_i. We re-sort these r_i in ascending order of i. The indexes are either "consecutive" or "inconsecutive". For example, if the target element $T = r_3 \oplus r_4 \oplus r_8 \oplus r_9 \oplus r_{10}$, then $r_3 \oplus r_4$ and $r_8 \oplus r_9 \oplus r_{10}$ are consecutive, and there is a missing r_5 between r_4 and r_6. Accordingly, we divide T into two consecutive parts, $(r_3 \oplus r_4) \oplus (r_8 \oplus r_9 \oplus r_{10})$. Till now, T is rewritten as T'. Subsequently, we count the number of parts in T' by processing $m = \mathsf{P}(T')$.

Then, we try to find the smallest set $\mathcal{I}^2_{min}$ which satisfies $\bigoplus \mathcal{I}^2_{min} = T'$. According to Algorithm 1, $\mathcal{I}^2$ contains two kinds of elements, $(r_i)_{i \in \{1,2,\cdots,d+d_0\}}$ and $\{r_1 \oplus r_2, r_1 \oplus r_2 \oplus r_3, \ldots, r_1 \oplus r_2 \oplus \cdots \oplus r_{d+d_0}\}$.[1] It is not hard to see that each consecutive part in T', i.e. $\bigoplus_{i=a}^{b} r_i$, can be rewritten as the sum of two elements in $\mathcal{I}^2$ (except for the case when $a = 1$), namely $\bigoplus_{i=a}^{b} r_i = (\bigoplus_{i=1}^{b} r_i) \oplus (\bigoplus_{i=1}^{a-1} r_i)$. In this way, we can always rewrite T' (with m parts) as a sum of $2m$ elements in $\mathcal{I}^2$ (when $a = 1$ for a part, T' can be written as $2m - 1$ elements). For instance, $(r_3 \oplus r_4) \oplus (r_8 \oplus r_9 \oplus r_{10})$ can be rewritten as $T' = (\bigoplus_{i=1}^{2} r_i) \oplus (\bigoplus_{i=1}^{4} r_i) \oplus (\bigoplus_{i=1}^{7} r_i) \oplus (\bigoplus_{i=1}^{9} r_i)$. That is to say, there always exists $\mathcal{I}^2_0 = \{\bigoplus_{i=1}^{2} r_i, \bigoplus_{i=1}^{4} r_i, \bigoplus_{i=1}^{7} r_i, \bigoplus_{i=1}^{9} r_i\}$ for any given $\{\mathcal{S}^1_2, \mathcal{S}^2\}$, satisfying $\bigoplus \mathcal{I}^2_0 = T'$, and $|\mathcal{I}^2| = 2m$ (or $2m - 1$).

Till now, we have mapped $\mathcal{S}^1_2$ and $\mathcal{S}^2$ to $|\mathcal{I}^2_0|$, but what we aim to find is the cardinality of the smallest set $\mathcal{I}^2_{min}$. Therefore, we should further decreasing the number of elements in $\mathcal{I}^2_0$. In $\mathcal{I}^2_0$, there may exist term $(\bigoplus_{m=1}^{i} r_m) \oplus (\bigoplus_{m=1}^{i-1} r_m)$ which can be written as r_i. We call $(\bigoplus_{m=1}^{i} r_m)$ and $(\bigoplus_{m=1}^{i-1} r_m)$ the adjacent pair. If there exists an adjacent pair, two probes $(\bigoplus_{m=1}^{i} r_m)$ and $(\bigoplus_{m=1}^{i-1} r_m)$ can be replaced with one probe r_i and therefore $|\mathcal{I}^2_0|$ can be reduced by 1. The adjacent pairs which are not mutually overlapped are denoted as the non-overlapping adjacent pair (Algorithm 3 NOA), while the adjacent pairs which are mutually overlapped are denoted as the overlapping adjacent pair (Algorithm 3 OA). The minimal cardinality $|\mathcal{I}^2_{min}|$ can be computed according to the following principles:

- If there does not exist any adjacent pair in $\mathcal{I}^2_0$, $|\mathcal{I}^2_{min}| = 2m$ (or $2m - 1$).
- If there exists some, say n, adjacent pairs in $\mathcal{I}^2_0$, and they do not overlap with each other, $|\mathcal{I}^2_{min}|$ should be decreased by n.
- If there exists a k-overlapping adjacent pair and k is even, $|\mathcal{I}^2_{min}|$ should be decreased by $(k-2)/2$. If there exists a k-overlapping adjacent pair and k is odd, $|\mathcal{I}^2_{min}|$ should be decreased by $(k-1)/2$.

To be clearer, we give a small instance of $T' = (r_1 \oplus r_2) \oplus (r_4 \oplus r_5) \oplus r_7$ in Fig. 4. As r_1 is included in T', $|\mathcal{I}^2_0| = 2m - 1 = 5$. Among the five elements in $\mathcal{I}^2_0$, there is one non-overlapping adjacent pair $\{\bigoplus_{i=1}^{2}, \bigoplus_{i=1}^{3}\}$ ($n = 1$), and one 3-overlapping adjacent pair $\{\bigoplus_{i=1}^{5}, \bigoplus_{i=1}^{6}, \bigoplus_{i=1}^{7}\}$ ($k = 3$). Therefore, according

---

[1] We do not utilize r_i'. The case when r_i' exists in $\mathcal{I}^2$ is checked through brute-force search.

to Algorithm Sel, we can obtain $|\mathcal{I}^2_{min}| = 2m - 1 - n - \frac{k-1}{2} = 3$. One case for $\mathcal{I}^2_{min}$ is $\{r_3, r_6, \bigoplus_{i=1}^{7} r_i\}$, and $r_3 \oplus r_6 \oplus \bigoplus_{i=1}^{7} r_i = T'$.

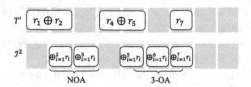

Fig. 4. A instance of $T' = (r_1 \oplus r_2) \oplus (r_4 \oplus r_5) \oplus r_7$.

Obtained $m(i)$ and d_0. With the search method in Algorithms 2 and 3, we obtain the conditional d-SNI refreshing algorithm for $d \leq 11$. In Table 1, we list part of the obtained $m(i)$ with minimum d_0 from order 3 to 11. We can hardly search for refreshing algorithms for order larger than 11, as the computational complexity will be much too high.

Table 1. The search results.

	d_0	$m(i)$
$d = 3$	1	(1), (2)
$d = 4$	1	(1), (2)
$d = 5$	3	(3, 2, 5), (3, 2, 4), (2, 3, 4), (2, 3, 5), (3, 1, 5), (3, 1, 4), (2, 1, 4), (2, 1, 5)
$d = 6$	3	(3, 5, 2), (3, 6, 2), (3, 4, 2), (3, 2, 5), (3, 2, 4), (3, 2, 6), (2, 5, 3), (2, 6, 3)
$d = 7$	4	(4, 3, 6, 2), (1, 4, 6, 3), (1, 4, 6, 2), (3, 4, 6, 2), (1, 4, 7, 3), (4, 1, 6, 2)
$d = 8$	5	(5, 4, 6, 3, 2), (2, 3, 5, 8, 4), (3, 2, 7, 4, 8), (5, 4, 8, 3, 2), (2, 6, 3, 4, 7), (4, 6, 2, 3, 8)
$d = 9$	7	(5, 4, 8, 3, 7, 9, 2), (3, 6, 1, 7, 4, 8, 2), (3, 7, 5, 4, 9, 6, 2), (2, 8, 5, 1, 7, 4, 9)
$d = 10$	7	(5, 4, 8, 3, 6, 10, 2), (2, 7, 5, 10, 3, 8, 4), (5, 9, 2, 8, 3, 10, 4) (5, 4, 8, 3, 6, 9, 2), (5, 2, 7, 8, 3, 9, 4), (5, 6, 2, 9, 4, 7, 3)
$d = 11$	9	(6, 2, 10, 5, 8, 3, 11, 9, 4)

4 Complexity Comparisons

In this section, we implement the refreshing algorithms on ARM, and verify the efficiency of our proposal by comparing the required random generations, clock cycles and ROM consumptions. For each algorithm (the d-SNI refreshing and our new proposal), we have six implementations for $d = 3, 4, \ldots, 8$. Codes were written in assembly language for an ARM-based 32-bit architecture. According to the comparison results, our proposal outperforms the d-SNI refreshing in terms of both the randomness complexity and the arithmetic complexity, as significantly less random generations, less clock cycles, and less ROM consumptions are involved in our proposal than in the d-SNI refreshing.

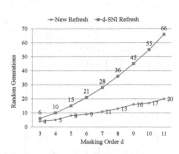

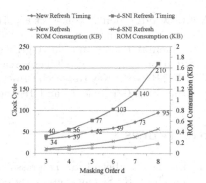

Fig. 5. The random complexity of the d-SNI refreshing and the new refreshing.

Fig. 6. Clock cycles and ROM consumptions (KBytes) of the new refreshing and the d-SNI refreshing.

First, we compare the random generations of the two refreshing schemes. For ISW-like masking schemes, the main overhead lies in the randomness generation. Random generations execute by calling a random generation module, which leads to significant time and storage consumptions. Therefore, decreasing the randomness generation is of crucial importance. The randomness complexities of the new refreshing algorithm and the d-SNI refreshing algorithm are compared in Fig. 5. We can see that the new refreshing makes a remarkable improvement and decreasing 33%–70% random generations than the d-SNI refreshing. Then, in order to verify the arithmetic complexity, we implemented two refreshing algorithms on 32-bit ARM core. As we have already compared the randomness complexity, the random generations are no longer executed in the implementations. The random numbers are assumed to be stored in ROM without considering its ROM consumption. The performances of the implementations, including clock cycles and ROM consumptions, are given in Fig. 6. According to Fig. 6, our proposal are better than the d-SNI refreshing in both timing performance and ROM consumption.

5 Conclusion and Future Work

The proposed refreshing algorithm satisfies a conditional d-SNI, which is weaker than d-SNI. In fact, this security notion is proposed specifically for the refreshing algorithm. We do not think it make sense for the multiplication algorithm. It is noteworthy that our work is different from the strategy proposed in [2]. Their scheme is designed for the multiplication and satisfies d-TNI security, while our scheme is designed for the refreshing algorithm and satisfies conditional d-SNI.

Our proposal is not a generic scheme for arbitrarily order d. We consider it an incredible future work to design a generic order refreshing satisfies the conditional d-SNI.

Acknowledgement. This work is partially supported by the National Natural Science Foundation of China (Grant Nos. 61632020, 61472416, 61602468, and 61772520), the Fundamental Theory and Cutting Edge Technology Research Program of Institute of Information Engineering, Chinese Academy of Sciences (Grant Nos. Y7Z0401102 and Y7Z0321102), the Key Research Project of Zhejiang Province (Grant No. 2017C01062), and the State Grid Science and Technology project No. JL71-15-038.

References

1. Barthe, G., Belaïd, S., Dupressoir, F., Fouque, P.-A., Grégoire, B., Strub, P.-Y., Zucchini, R.: Strong non-interference and type-directed higher-order masking. In: Proceedings of the 2016 ACM SIGSAC Conference on Computer and Communications Security, pp. 116–129. ACM (2016)
2. Belaïd, S., Benhamouda, F., Passelègue, A., Prouff, E., Thillard, A., Vergnaud, D.: Randomness complexity of private circuits for multiplication. In: Fischlin, M., Coron, J.-S. (eds.) EUROCRYPT 2016. LNCS, vol. 9666, pp. 616–648. Springer, Heidelberg (2016). https://doi.org/10.1007/978-3-662-49896-5_22
3. Bilgin, B., Gierlichs, B., Nikova, S., Nikov, V., Rijmen, V.: Higher-order threshold implementations. In: Sarkar, P., Iwata, T. (eds.) ASIACRYPT 2014. LNCS, vol. 8874, pp. 326–343. Springer, Heidelberg (2014). https://doi.org/10.1007/978-3-662-45608-8_18
4. Chari, S., Jutla, C.S., Rao, J.R., Rohatgi, P.: Towards sound approaches to counteract power-analysis attacks. In: Wiener, M. (ed.) CRYPTO 1999. LNCS, vol. 1666, pp. 398–412. Springer, Heidelberg (1999). https://doi.org/10.1007/3-540-48405-1_26
5. Coron, J.-S., Prouff, E., Rivain, M., Roche, T.: Higher-order side channel security and mask refreshing. In: Moriai, S. (ed.) FSE 2013. LNCS, vol. 8424, pp. 410–424. Springer, Heidelberg (2014). https://doi.org/10.1007/978-3-662-43933-3_21
6. Duc, A., Dziembowski, S., Faust, S.: Unifying leakage models: from probing attacks to noisy leakage. In: Nguyen, P.Q., Oswald, E. (eds.) EUROCRYPT 2014. LNCS, vol. 8441, pp. 423–440. Springer, Heidelberg (2014). https://doi.org/10.1007/978-3-642-55220-5_24
7. Ishai, Y., Sahai, A., Wagner, D.: Private circuits: securing hardware against probing attacks. In: Boneh, D. (ed.) CRYPTO 2003. LNCS, vol. 2729, pp. 463–481. Springer, Heidelberg (2003). https://doi.org/10.1007/978-3-540-45146-4_27
8. Kocher, P., Jaffe, J., Jun, B.: Differential power analysis. In: Wiener, M. (ed.) CRYPTO 1999. LNCS, vol. 1666, pp. 388–397. Springer, Heidelberg (1999). https://doi.org/10.1007/3-540-48405-1_25
9. Kocher, P.C.: Timing attacks on implementations of Diffie-Hellman, RSA, DSS, and other systems. In: Koblitz, N. (ed.) CRYPTO 1996. LNCS, vol. 1109, pp. 104–113. Springer, Heidelberg (1996). https://doi.org/10.1007/3-540-68697-5_9
10. Nassar, M., Souissi, Y., Guilley, S., Danger, J.-L.: RSM: a small and fast countermeasure for AES, secure against 1st and 2nd-order zero-offset SCAs. In: DATE 2012, pp. 1173–1178. IEEE (2012)
11. Nikova, S., Rechberger, C., Rijmen, V.: Threshold implementations against side-channel attacks and glitches. In: Ning, P., Qing, S., Li, N. (eds.) ICICS 2006. LNCS, vol. 4307, pp. 529–545. Springer, Heidelberg (2006). https://doi.org/10.1007/11935308_38

12. Reparaz, O., Bilgin, B., Nikova, S., Gierlichs, B., Verbauwhede, I.: Consolidating masking schemes. In: Gennaro, R., Robshaw, M. (eds.) CRYPTO 2015. LNCS, vol. 9215, pp. 764–783. Springer, Heidelberg (2015). https://doi.org/10.1007/978-3-662-47989-6_37

13. Rivain, M., Prouff, E.: Provably secure higher-order masking of AES. In: Mangard, S., Standaert, F.-X. (eds.) CHES 2010. LNCS, vol. 6225, pp. 413–427. Springer, Heidelberg (2010). https://doi.org/10.1007/978-3-642-15031-9_28

Applied Cryptography

A Plausibly Deniable Encryption Scheme Utilizing PUF's Thermo-Sensitivity

Changting Li[1,2,3], Zongbin Liu[2,3], Lingchen Zhang[2,3(✉)],
Cunqing Ma[2,3], and Liang Zheng[1,2,3]

[1] School of Cyber Security, University of Chinese Academy of Sciences,
Beijing, China
[2] Data Assurance and Communication Security Research Center, Beijing, China
[3] State Key Laboratory of Information Security,
Institute of Information Engineering, CAS, Beijing, China
{lichangting, liuzongbin, zhanglingchen, macunqing,
zhengliang}@iie.ac.cn

Abstract. Deniable encryption is proposed to protect sensitive data against adversaries, even when the user has been coerced to reveal his private keys and other random parameters. However, current deniable encryption schemes or techniques either require the user to remember some tedious random parameters used in encryption or demand special designs in the file system. Any abnormality in the user's behavior or in the file system tend to arouse suspicion, thus reduce the persuasion of the decrypted data. To cheat the adversary convincingly, we innovatively utilize the thermos-sensitivity of Physically Unclonable Functions (PUFs), to propose a novel and practical deniable encryption scheme, which enables the encryption system achieve deniability in a very covert way. The proposed scheme will automatically interpret the deniable ciphertext into different plaintexts at different temperatures and does not require any special designs in the file system. Furthermore, we successfully implement our scheme on Xilinx KC705 evaluation boards to prove its feasibility.

Keywords: Deniable encryption · Bistable Ring PUF
SRAM PUF · FPGA

1 Introduction

Conventional encryption schemes seldom think about situations when one or both two sides of communication are coerced to reveal their private information, e.g. private keys, nonce and other random parameters used in encryption. However, such situations can always be found in real world scenarios. For example, a man is taking a disk with encrypted sensitive documents through the Customs, but unfortunately the customs

The work is supported by a grant from the National Key Research and Development Program of China (Grant No. Y16A01602).

officer requires checking the content of his disk. In order to cheat the officer, the man would hope to convincingly deny the existence of the genuine plaintext.

One way to achieve this goal, is to explain the encrypted document into a fake innocuous one. Given this, Canetti, Dwork, Naor, and Ostrovsky firstly proposed intriguing Deniable Encryption in 1997 [1]. The main idea is to construct a fake randomness, maybe the key or some additional parameters required in the encryption, to reinterpret the ciphertext into a plausible fake plaintext. Though varieties of schemes have been proposed since then [14, 15, 18, 19], these schemes are limited in theoretical discussion. In order to satisfy information security requirements, all the theoretical schemes are suffering from extremely long length of ciphertext or key [1, 2].

In engineering practice, engineers seek another way to obtain deniability which is so called Plausibly Deniable Encryption. Plausibly Deniable Encryption aims to deny the existence of encrypted data with the help of engineering methods, e.g. TrueCrypt [3], Rubberhose filesystem [4], Steganographic File Systems [5–7, 17]. These schemes usually hide sensitive data in a hidden volume or a random-looking free space, but such schemes require some special designs in the filesystem and are under threat of flaws in the implementation [8] and forensic tools [9]. Moreover, the existence of such special designs in the file system is detectable.

No matter in theoretical discussion or in engineering practice, the basic idea to achieve deniability is the same: Though having been forced to hand in all the parameters used in encryption, the user is still able to retain a trapdoor information which is the radical difference between him and the adversary. The adversary without this trapdoor information, in spite of all the other parameters used in encryption he has had, he cannot tell whether the decrypted plaintext is a fake or a genuine one (in theoretical deniable encryption) or distinguish between a truly random sequence and a ciphertext (in plausibly deniable encryption). Therefore, the secrecy of the trapdoor information is even more important than the encrypt key in deniable encryption scenarios. This trapdoor information should be stored as covert as possible and to convincingly cheat the adversary, both the user's behavior and the encryption system should look normal enough not to arouse the adversary's suspicion.

On account of these, we propose a practical deniable encryption scheme which takes advantage of PUFs' thermo-sensitivity to implement deniable encryption in quite a covert way. Our scheme neither requires the user to remember or store any tedious trapdoor information, nor requires any special designs in the file system or extra inputs during decryption. Generally, PUF's sensitivity to temperature is regarded as an undesirable nature that undermines PUF's stability. However, we aware that if PUF's behavior varies with temperature, it may serve as a thermosensitive "hidden trigger" which can only be triggered in specific temperature range. In the proposed scheme, the PUF-based "hidden trigger" is able to perceive temperature variation, which makes the temperature become a vital and covert trapdoor information to determine whether to decrypt faithfully or not.

Details of the scheme will be described in Sect. 3 and we successfully implemented it on Xilinx KC705 evaluation boards to examine its feasibility. According to the experiment results, ciphertexts generated at extreme temperature (e.g. −40 °C or 60 ° C) will be decrypted as the prepared fake plaintext at room temperature (20 °C–30 °C).

In conclusion, our contributions are summarized as follows:

1. We take advantage of PUF's thermo-sensitivity, which is always thought to be an undesirable nature of PUF, to design a novel and practical deniable encryption scheme.
2. Our scheme enables the user to achieve deniability in a very covert way. The coerced user just needs to make sure the temperature of decryption environment is out of the "trigger range" in which the deniable ciphertext will be decrypted loyally. In addition, except one encryption key and ciphertexts, no extra input or extra operation is needed.
3. From the adversary's view, our encryption system works normally. The adversary is free to choose arbitrary text to invoke the encrypt and decrypt programs to examine our system and he will be convinced that the generated ciphertext is always decrypted loyally.

The rest of this paper is organized as follows. In Sect. 2 we describe working mechanisms and evaluations of PUFs and introduce our basic idea. Then we illustrate our scheme in Sect. 3 with performance analysis and present details of experiments on Xilinx KC705 evaluation boards in Sect. 4. Finally, we conclude in Sect. 5.

2 Preliminary

Before describing our design of PUF-based Deniable Encryption, we firstly introduce some backgrounds on PUFs and then elaborate where our inspiration comes from.

2.1 Physically Unclonable Functions

PUF as an emerging technique of physical roots of trust provides new solutions for authentication, tamper resistance, anti-counterfeiting, key generation and protection etc. [16]. Because of uncontrollable and inevitable influences of random variations during manufacturing process, no perfectly identical chips can be produced. Such subtle variations on products can be regarded as chips' physical "fingerprints" and PUFs aim to extract these "fingerprints" and translate them into unique secret sequences, the response, which can be utilized to serve cryptographic primitives.

Generally, each PUF entity can be described as a one-way function PUF: $C \rightarrow R$, where C is an input challenge set and R is the corresponding response set. For an PUF entity puf_i, its Challenge Response Pair (CRP) c_k and $r_i(c_k)$ should be unique and unpredictable, i.e. for different entities puf_i and $puf_j(i \neq j)$ with the same input c_k, their responses are different: $r_i(c_k) \neq r_j(c_k)$; and for the same PUF entity puf_i with different inputs c_{k1} and c_{k2}, its corresponding responses are different: $r_i(c_{k1}) \neq r_j(c_{k2})$. Besides, any adversary can neither predict a response before observing it, nor reversely derive its corresponding challenge.

To evaluate a PUF's performance, unpredictability, uniqueness and reliability are commonly investigated in the literature.

Unpredictability: An ideal PUF's unobserved response should be unpredictable, even if the adversary has observed enough CRPs of it. Providing every bit in a binary response sequence r $\in \{0,1\}^n$ is independent, min-entropy calculated as formula (1) offers a lower bound of responds' randomness in the worst case.

$$H_\infty(r) = \sum_{i=1}^{n} -\log_2(\max\{P(r_i = 1), P(r_i = 0)\}). \tag{1}$$

$P(r_i = 1)$ and $P(r_i = 0)$ are probabilities for the i_{th} bit of response to equal 1 and 0.

Reliability and Uniqueness: Assume we instantiate N_{puf} PUF entities, and invoke each of them with N_{chal} challenges, for each challenge we measure N_{meas} times. Thus, we obtain $N_{puf} \times N_{chal} \times N_{meas}$ response sequences. Equations (2) and (3) calculate the average intra-distance and average inter-distance respectively [13].

$$\mu_{intra} = \frac{2}{N_{puf} \cdot N_{chal} \cdot N_{meas} \cdot (N_{meas} - 1)} \sum_{\substack{j_1,j_2=1 \\ j_1 \neq j_2}}^{N_{meas}} \sum_{i=1}^{N_{puf}} \sum_{k=1}^{N_{chal}} HD(r_i^{j_1}(c_k), r_i^{j_2}(c_k)). \tag{2}$$

$$\mu_{inter} = \frac{2}{N_{puf} \cdot (N_{puf} - 1) \cdot N_{chal} \cdot N_{meas}} \sum_{\substack{i_1,i_2=1 \\ i_1 \neq i_2}}^{N_{puf}} \sum_{k=1}^{N_{chal}} \sum_{j=1}^{N_{meas}} HD(r_{i_1}^{j}(c_k), r_{i_2}^{j}(c_k)). \tag{3}$$

HD ($\cdot$) is a function counting the Hamming Distance (HD) between two PUF responses. Apparently, average intra-distance reflects the difference between each measurement (reliability) and average inter-distance demonstrates to what extent entities of the same PUF are different from each other (uniqueness). For a PUF design, its ideal inter-distance is 50%, while its intra-distance should be as low as possible.

Error Correcting Code (ECC): Because PUF's response is not perfectly reproductive, ECCs like Hamming code, Reed-Muller code, BCH code, repeating code etc., are widely adopted in PUF's application to guarantee that the same response is generated in every invoking. The enrollment and recovery process are shown in Fig. 1, generally the helper data can save in an unprotected NVM and the response security is guaranteed by the random number k in the enrollment process.

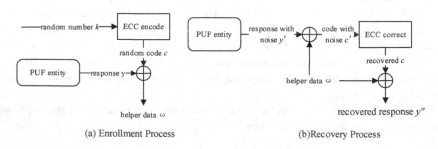

(a) Enrollment Process   (b)Recovery Process

Fig. 1. Enroll and recover PUF response with ECC

2.2   Inspiration and Basic Idea

For almost all the electric PUFs, temperature variation is one of the principal factors that undermine PUF's reliability. However, according to our survey, we notice that PUFs' behavior does not vary with temperature irregularly.

Daniel et al. in paper [10] investigated SRAM cells which showed no obvious tendency at 293 K and found that if a neutral-skewed SRAM cell at 293 K, whose power-up tendency is '0' at 273 K, is inclined to turn into '1' at 323 K and vice versa. They also noticed that this skew shift is monotonic with temperature. Resembling phenomena are also observed by Chen et al. who firstly proposed BR PUF [11]. According to their research, an intra-distance up to 5.81% was caused while temperature changed from room temperature to 85 °C, however, at each specific temperature the BR PUF showed high stability with a maximum distance of 0.76%. Figure 2 shows temperature variation on intra-distances and inter-distances of DAC PUF [20], which we think to be a good representation of PUFs' thermo-sensitivity. According to the blue curve, if we enroll a response at 25 °C and recover it at other temperature, as the temperature difference is enlarged gradually, the Hamming distance between the enrolled and recovered response sequence increases notably. However, from the green curve we can see that if we enroll and recover a response at every temperature respectively, the intra-distance will stable at a very low level.

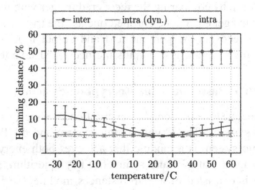

Fig. 2. Temperature variation on intra- and inter-distances of DAC PUF [20]

PUFs' such property suggests that if we choose an ECC algorithm with appropriate error correcting capability, we can control a PUF's responses only to be recovered within a temperature range, thereby utilize PUF to perceive temperature variations. If the enrolled response is recovered successfully, the ciphertext will be decrypted loyally, otherwise a prepared fake text will be output as the decrypted plaintext to cheat the adversary. This is the basic idea of the proposed deniable encryption scheme.

3 PUF-Based Deniable Encryption

The proposed scheme is a plan-ahead deniable encryption scheme, i.e. fake text is prepared before decryption. The basic idea is to let the cryptographic system vary its decryption result automatically under different temperature conditions. The scheme contains four programs.

- The **Enroll** program is responsible for recording environmental temperature in PUF's response sequence. As mentioned in Sect. 2.2, some PUFs' behavior stably varies with temperature, therefore, the enrolled response sequence can be regarded as a reflection of temperature and will serve as a "hidden trigger" which can only be successfully recovered in neighboring temperature range.
- The **Explain** program prepares alternative texts beforehand to generate deniable ciphertexts. The input of the **Explain** program are two texts m and m', where m is the genuine text and m' is the fake one which will take place of m as the decryption result to cheat the adversary.
- The **Encrypt** program also generates ciphertexts, but its ciphertexts can only be decrypted faithfully. Therefore, this program has only one input text m, the format of its ciphertext is analogous to that of the **Explain** program.
- The **Decrypt** program will selectively output genuine or fake plaintexts according to the temperature. While doing decryption, the **Decrypt** program checks the temperature condition by comparing the recovered trigger with the enrolled one. We call the recovered trigger equals the enrolled one as "the trigger is triggered". In this case, the program recovers the genuine text and output it as the final decryption result, otherwise, the program just outputs the decrypted fake text.

3.1 Overview of PUF-Based Deniable Encryption System

The hardware architecture of our deniable encryption module is shown in Fig. 3. It mainly contains two systems: The Cryptographic system and the PUF system.

The Cryptographic system is a module that achieves both encrypt function EN $(\cdot)$ and decrypt function DE $(\cdot)$ of a secure symmetric key algorithm, such as AES.

The PUF system is consisted of a PUF instances module, the ECC module and a nonvolatile memory. In the ECC module, there are two ECC algorithms with different error correcting capabilities. The weaker one ECC_{wk} only guarantees recovery of the "hidden trigger" in a narrow temperature range; while the stronger one ECC_{st} should make sure the random mask in the ciphertext can always be recovered under any condition.

3.2 Workflow

Enroll Program *Enrl* : $k \rightarrow (rsp_1, w_1)$. The **Enroll** program records current temperature in PUF's response sequence. It first uses the encryption key k as PUF's challenge and obtains a response sequence $rsp_1 = puf(k)$. rsp_1 will serve as the "hidden trigger" and be saved in the nonvolatile memory of the PUF module. Then the program calculates the helper data $w_1 = ECC_{wk}^{enrol}(rsp_1)$ and saves it as well.

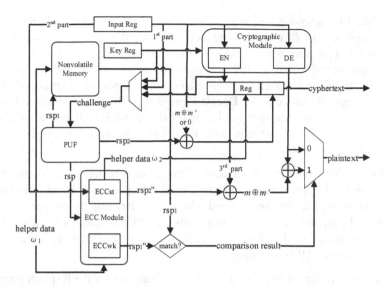

Fig. 3. The hardware architecture of the proposed deniable encryption module

Explain Program $Exp : (m, m') \rightarrow dc$. The **Explain** program generates deniable ciphertext dc with input (m, m'), m is the genuine text and m' is the fake one. First, the program encrypts the fake text normally with the symmetric key algorithm and acquires ciphertext $c' = EN(k, m')$. Then uses c' as PUF's challenge to get corresponding response sequence $rsp'_2 = puf(c')$. rsp'_2 serves as a random mask to hide the two texts' difference $m \oplus m'$. "$\oplus$" is the bit XOR operator. Finally, the helper data $w'_2 = ECC_{st}^{enrol}(rsp'_2)$ is calculated and forms the output deniable ciphertext: $dc = c' \| w'_2 \| (rsp'_2 \oplus m \oplus m')$.

Encrypt Program $Enc : m \rightarrow ec$. The **Encrypt** program generates ciphertext ec with one input text m. First, the program encrypts m with the encryption key k by the symmetric key algorithm, i.e. $c = EN(k, m)$, and uses this ciphertext as challenge to invoke the PUF and get corresponding response $rsp_2 = puf(c)$. Also, the helper data w_2 is calculated by ECC_{st} and the ciphertext $ec = c \| w_2 \| rsp_2$.

Decrypt Program $Dec : c_{in} \rightarrow m_{out}$. The **Decrypt** Program explains the input ciphertext c_{in} into certain plaintext m_{out}. First, the program divides c_{in} into three equilong parts $c_{in} = c'' \| w''_2 \| mk$ and decrypts c'' with the symmetric key algorithm to get $m_{temp} = DE(k, c'')$. Then the program invokes PUF with the encryption key k and recovers the acquired response with the saved helper data w_1 by the weaker ECC algorithm, i.e. $rsp''_1 = ECC_{wk}^{recov}(puf(k), w_1)$. If rsp''_1 dose not equal the saved trigger rsp_1, i.e. $rsp''_1 \neq rsp_1$, the program outputs m_{temp} directly; otherwise, it uses c'' to invoke the PUF and recover the obtained response with w''_2 by the stronger ECC algorithm, i.e. $rsp''_2 = ECC_{st}^{recov}(puf(c''), w''_2)$, finally outputs $m_{out} = m_{temp} \oplus rsp''_2 \oplus mk$.

3.3 Performance Analyses

Correctness: The deniable ciphertext dc can be correctly decrypted into the genuine text m by the **Decrypt** program under the enrolled temperature region, because the change of the PUF response rsp_1 that severs as the "hidden trigger" will be within the correction capability of ECC_{wk}. As long as the recovered response equals the enrolled one, the **Decrypt** program will extract the hidden information $m \oplus m'$ masked by rsp_2 (because there is: $rsp_2'' \oplus mk = rsp_2'' \oplus (rsp_2' \oplus m \oplus m') = m \oplus m'$) to reconstruct the genuine text. If the input ciphertext is generated by the **Encrypt** program, whether the trigger is "triggered" or not, the **Decrypt** program will always decrypt faithfully. Because $ec = c\|w_2\|rsp_2$ and rsp_2 can be regarded as a masked all-zero sequence. Any sequence doing bit XOR operation with the all-zero sequence equals itself, so the output will always be $DE(k, c)$.

Deniability: While operating under certain temperature which is out of the "trigger range", the deniable ciphertext dc, which is originally generated by the **Explain** program, will be decrypted into the prepared fake text m'. Because the change of response sequence is already out of the correction ability of ECC_{wk}, thus rsp_1 cannot be successfully recovered, i.e. the "hidden trigger" will not be "triggered", the **Decrypt** program just outputs $DE(k, c'')$ directly.

Security: As with respect to the first part of the ciphertext (in the **Explain** program is the fake text m', in the **Encrypt** program is the sole input m), the adversary has no way to derive the text protected by cryptographic algorithm. Owing to PUF's unpredictability and randomness, the random mask used in the third part makes the adversary unable to figure out the hidden difference $m \oplus m'$. As the second part, the helper data of the random mask, has nothing related to either text m or m', the security of the whole ciphertext in our scheme is guaranteed.

Practicability: The prime advantage of our scheme is that the user does not need any special manipulation to cheat the adversary. In our scheme, we hide the information $m \oplus m'$ that helps us to recover the genuine text in the ciphertext itself and utilize the temperature as the covert trapdoor information to achieve deniability. Therefore, no extra input is required during decryption and the enrolled temperature, under which the deniable ciphertexts are generated, is kept in the user's mind without a trace. The user just needs to make sure that the temperature of the environment, in which he may be compelled, is most likely to be out of the "trigger range". Furthermore, in our scheme, the **Encrypt** program and the **Decrypt** program are accessible to the adversary. The adversary can choose arbitrary plaintexts or ciphertexts to examine the loyalty of the encryption system, but as the ciphertext generated by the **Encrypt** program can only be decrypted loyally, from the view of the adversary, our deniable encryption system will always perform in a normal way.

4   Experiment and Result

4.1   Parameter Determination

The PUF in our proposed scheme is used for two main purposes: the "hidden trigger" and random mask generator. The "hidden trigger" is supposed to possess sufficient thermos-sensitivity, as well as relatively high reliability, while the random mask should possess adequate randomness to guarantee the security of the ciphertext.

The most important thing in the real design is to determine the weaker and the stronger ECC algorithms and their correction capabilities according to PUF's actual properties. We must investigate how much influence do temperature variations pose on the PUF's reliability, because if the ECC algorithm is too strong, the trigger would be unresponsive to temperature variation, then the deniable ciphertext will be decrypted faithfully in a large temperature range; if the ECC algorithm is too weak, the correctness of our scheme cannot be ensured.

We deploy1024 Bistable Ring PUFs (BR PUF) [11] on two KC705 boards respectively. To investigate the properties of this BR PUF, we exhaust all the challenges and measure every challenge for 32 times under 5 different temperature conditions (−40 °C, −20 °C, 25 °C, 40 °C and 60 °C). For each measurement, we can obtain 1024 response bits from each board, thus we totally acquire about 1 giga-bit data. According to formulas (2) and (3), we yield the PUF's average intra-distance and inter-distance are 5.00% and 44.34% respectively. This result suggests that this kind of BR PUF is able to generate a relatively stable trigger sequence and sufficiently different random masks with different configurations.

We further calculate the average intra-distances of responses generated under different temperatures and compare this temperature-influenced distribution with the original intra-distance distribution in Fig. 4. From the figure we can see, the whole distribution shifts rightwards, and the average intra-distance increases to 8.89%. As the weaker ECC algorithm must make sure the trigger sequence to be successfully recovered in a temperature range as narrow as possible, according to the original distribution, ECC that corrects sequences with 10% error bits is desirable. While the stronger one should be able to handle at least 18% error bit rate to recover the random mask at any temperature. Therefore, we chose (15, 11) Hamming Code (can correct 1-bit error in every 11 bits) as the weaker ECC and (1, 5) Reed-Muller Code [12] (can correct 7-bit error in every 32 bits) as the stronger one.

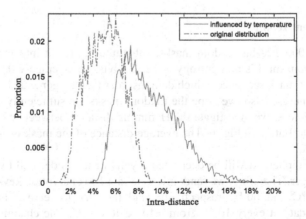

Fig. 4. The influence of temperature variation on intra-distance distribution

4.2   Implementation Details

The architecture of our evaluation system is shown in Fig. 5. We choose 128-bit AES as the symmetric key algorithm. To make the experiment more efficient, we output the generated "hidden trigger" and its corresponding helper data to the upper computer, rather than save them in a nonvolatile memory. Thus, at any specific temperature we can do enrollment and decrypt ciphertexts generated at other temperatures at the same time. The Microblaze, a soft microprocessor core designed for Xilinx FPGAs, is responsible for delivering commands and data between the upper computer and the hardware modules.

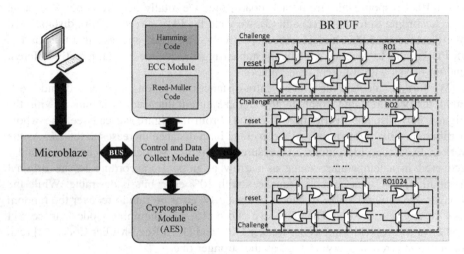

Fig. 5. The experimental evaluation system

4.3   Experiment Result

We generated 5000 128-bit random masks, substitute the result into formula (1) and acquire the random mask's min-entropy is 123.32 bits, i.e. averagely 0.96-bit entropy for each bit in the mask sequence, which demonstrates that the generated masks possess adequate randomness. Also, we hope the random masks are sufficiently different from each other. Therefore, we investigate the Hamming distance between every two masks and draw the distribution in Fig. 6. The average distance of the mask is 50.01%, which is quite desirable.

Whether the ciphertext will be decrypted loyally or not is decided by the recovery result of the trigger. Therefore, we randomly generate 100 encryption keys. Enroll them at −40 °C, 10 °C and 60 °C respectively, and then try to recover them with the enrolled helper data at every 10 °C from −40 °C to 60 °C. The changing patterns of recovery probability are drawn in Fig. 7, the x-coordinate is temperature and the y-coordinate represents recovery probability. For comparison, results on different boards are displayed separately.

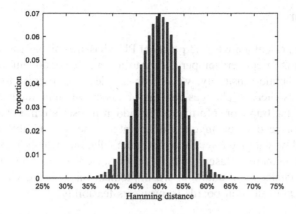

Fig. 6. The distributions of random masks' Hamming distances

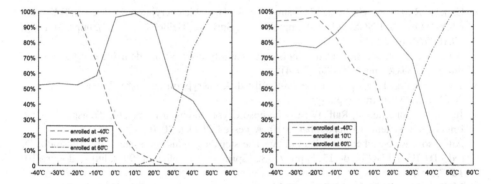

Fig. 7. Recovery probability under different circumstances

Comparing these two graphs, the changing trends of triggers' recovery probability on these two boards are the same on the whole. As the temperature difference is enlarging, the recovery probability declines obviously. With respect to changing patterns in the higher temperature region (10 °C–60 °C), we can see that triggers enrolled at 10 °C and 60 °C cannot be recovered when temperature difference reaches 50 °C. However, as lines tend to stay stable when temperature falls below −20 °C, triggers enrolled at 10 °C can still be recovered with a relatively high probability at −40 °C. Though the changing patterns at low temperatures are gentler, triggers enrolled at −40 °C are not likely to be recovered at room temperature (20 °C–30 °C). Considering heats emitted by electronic devices during working process, generating deniable ciphertexts at extreme low temperature could be a better choice.

5 Conclusion

In this paper, we present a novel and practical PUF-based deniable encryption scheme. Our key thought is to convert temperature into a covert trapdoor information, i.e. by utilizing PUF's thermo-sensitivity, we enable the decrypt program to perceive temperature variations thereby changes its output under different temperatures. In our scheme, because the trapdoor information is hidden in user's mind and as a physical factor it does not need to be invoked deliberately, the user is able to decrypt the ciphertext deniably without any abnormal manipulation, which makes the output plaintext more convincing. Based on this, we presented our architectural design and analysis its performances. In addition, we implement this scheme with BR PUFs on two Xilinx KC795 evaluation boards to prove its feasibility.

References

1. Canetti, R., Dwork, C., Naor, M., Ostrovsky, R.: Deniable encryption. In: Kaliski, B.S. (ed.) CRYPTO 1997. LNCS, vol. 1294, pp. 90–104. Springer, Heidelberg (1997). https://doi.org/10.1007/BFb0052229
2. Amit, S., Brent, W.: how to use indistinguishability obfuscation: deniable encryption, and more. In: STOC, pp. 475–484 (2014)
3. TrueCrypt.org. Free open source on-the-fly disk encryption software. Version 7.1a, July 2012. http://www.truecrypt.org/
4. Julian, A., Suelette, D., Ralf, W.: Rubberhose Cryptographically Deniable Transparent Disk Encryption System, 15 September 2010. Accessed 21 Oct. 2010
5. Anderson, R., Needham, R., Shamir, A.: The steganographic file system. In: Aucsmith, D. (ed.) IH 1998. LNCS, vol. 1525, pp. 73–82. Springer, Heidelberg (1998). https://doi.org/10.1007/3-540-49380-8_6
6. McDonald, A.D., Kuhn, M.G.: StegFS: a steganographic file system for linux. In: Pfitzmann, A. (ed.) IH 1999. LNCS, vol. 1768, pp. 463–477. Springer, Heidelberg (2000). https://doi.org/10.1007/10719724_32
7. HweeHwa, P., Kian-Lee, T., Xuan, Z.: Stegfs: a steganographic file system. In: 19th International Conference on Data Engineering, Proceedings, pp. 657–667. IEEE (2003)
8. Adal, C.: BestCrypt IV generation flaw. http://adal.chiriliuc.com/bc_iv_flaw.html
9. Robert, M.: Encrypted hard drives may not be safe. In: IDG News Service, 17 July 2010
10. Daniel, E.H., Wayne, P.B., Kevin, F.: Power-Up SRAM state as an identifying fingerprint and source of true random numbers. IEEE Trans. Comput. 58(9), 1198–1210 (2009)
11. Chen, Q., Csaba, G., Lugli, P., Schlichtmann, U., Ruhrmair, U.: The Bistable Ring PUF: a new architecture for strong Physical Unclonable functions. In: IEEE International Symposium on Hardware Oriented Security and Trust–HOST, pp. 134–141. IEEE (2011)
12. Sebastian, R.: Reed-Muller Codes, Carleton University (2003)
13. Roel, M.: Physically Unclonable Functions: Constructions, Properties and Applications. Katholieke Universiteit Leuven, Belgium (2012)
14. Klonowski, M., Kubiak, P., Kutyłowski, M.: Practical deniable encryption. In: Geffert, V., Karhumäki, J., Bertoni, A., Preneel, B., Návrat, P., Bieliková, M. (eds.) SOFSEM 2008. LNCS, vol. 4910, pp. 599–609. Springer, Heidelberg (2008). https://doi.org/10.1007/978-3-540-77566-9_52

15. Dürmuth, M., Freeman, D.M.: Deniable encryption with negligible detection probability: an interactive construction. In: Paterson, K.G. (ed.) EUROCRYPT 2011. LNCS, vol. 6632, pp. 610–626. Springer, Heidelberg (2011). https://doi.org/10.1007/978-3-642-20465-4_33
16. Tuyls, P., Škorić, B.: Strong authentication with physical unclonable functions. In: Petković, M., Jonker, W. (eds.) Security, Privacy, and Trust in Modern Data Management, pp. 133–148. Springer, Heidelberg (2007). https://doi.org/10.1007/978-3-540-69861-6_10
17. Katzenbeisser, S., Petitcolas, F.A.: Information Hiding Techniques for Steganography and Digital Watermarking. Artech House, Inc. (2000)
18. Howlader, J., Basu, S.: Sender-side public key deniable encryption scheme. In: International Conference on Advances in Recent Technologies in Communication and Computing, pp. 9–13. IEEE (2009)
19. Meng, B., Wang, J.Q.: An efficient receiver deniable encryption scheme and its applications. J. Netw. 5(6), 683–690 (2010)
20. Herkle, A., Becker, J., Ortmanns, M.: Exploiting weak PUFs from data converter nonlinearity—E.g., a multibit CT $\Delta\Sigma$ modulator. IEEE Trans. Circ. Syst. I Regul. Pap. 63(7), 994–1004 (2016)

Two Efficient Tag-Based Encryption Schemes on Lattices

Xueqing Wang[1,2](✉), Biao Wang[1,2], and Rui Xue[1,2](✉)

[1] State Key Laboratory of Information Security,
Institute of Information Engineering, Chinese Academy of Sciences,
Beijing 100093, China
{wangxueqing,wangbiao,xuerui}@iie.ac.cn
[2] School of Cyber Security, University of Chinese Academy of Sciences,
Beijing 100049, China

Abstract. Tag-based encryption (TBE) is a generalization of public-key encryption (PKE), in which both the encryption and the decryption algorithms take a tag as an extra input, which is potentially useful. However, in contrast to TBE schemes with various types of security and under traditional number-theoretic assumptions, as far as we know, there is only one lattice-based TBE scheme with selective-tag security, which, in fact, is under a variant of DLWE assumption.

In this paper, we propose two efficient TBE schemes, both of which have adaptive-tag security and are under the standard DLWE assumption. For efficiency, we adopt, in both schemes, a particular q-ary lattice equipped with efficient LWE inversion and preimage sampling algorithms, which are efficiently available for solving the related problems on a general q-ary lattice. The probabilistic partition technique is used to achieve the adaptive-tag security. On the other hand, we mainly embed the preimage sampling problem into the first scheme and the LWE inversion problem into the second one, the latter of which has a smaller modulus and a smaller approximation factor.

Our schemes can be applied to construct IND-CCA2 secure PKE schemes and to design protocols that securely realizes the secure message transmission functionality in a hybrid model. Additionally, our first scheme can also be used to construct an adaptively secure identity-based encryption (IBE) scheme with more efficient secret-key extraction algorithm than those in well-known IBE schemes.

Keywords: Tag-based encryption · DLWE · Adaptive security
Probabilistic partitioning technique · G-trapdoor

1 Introduction

The notion of tag-based encryption (TBE) was proposed by MacKenzie et al. [MRY04], while it was originated implicitly from Shoup [Sho01] (where the tag is called label). TBE is a generalization of public-key encryption (PKE), in which

© Springer International Publishing AG, part of Springer Nature 2018
S. Qing et al. (Eds.): ICICS 2017, LNCS 10631, pp. 118–131, 2018.
https://doi.org/10.1007/978-3-319-89500-0_10

the encryption and decryption algorithms both take a tag as an extra input. All the ECIES and RSA-OAEP submissions and Shoup's proposal for an ISO standard of PKE include the notion of a tag (in the first two it is called an encoding parameter), although no indication was given as to the role or function of a tag.

As an independent primitive, in contrast to PKE, TBE has an additional ability to attach a tag to the ciphertext during the encryption process, while the tag is generally not included in the ciphertext and is explicitly given to the decryption algorithm. Such an explicit treatment of a tag has some notational advantages, when we consider an adversary who tries to alter the tag without affecting the ciphertext. The security of TBE can be similarly defined as that of PKE, as well as adding another dimension selective/adaptive-tag indicating whether the adversary submits the target tag before receiving the public key (selective-tag), or in the challenge phase together with a pair of chosen messages (adaptive-tag). And thus its security notions include indistinguishability against selective-tag/adaptive-tag chosen-plaintext/(weak) lunch-time/(weak) chosen-ciphertext attacks, which can be abbreviated, respectively, to IND-sTag-CPA, IND-aTag-CPA, IND-sTag-wCCA1, IND-sTag-CCA1, IND-aTag-CCA1, IND-sTag-wCCA2, IND-sTag-CCA2, IND-aTag-wCCA2 and IND-aTag-CCA2. Note that w here is short for *weak*, which means that the adversary is not allowed to query the target tag instead of the pair of the target tag and the challenge ciphertext to the decryption oracle.

As a cryptographic tool, IND-sTag-wCCA2 secure TBE schemes, belongs to a more general class of cryptographic schemes than selectively secure identity-based encryption (IBE) schemes, are sufficient to construct CCA secure PKE schemes, according to [Kil06]. Note that IND-aTag-CCA2 secure TBE schemes are equivalent with IND-CCA2 secure PKE schemes. In addition, IND-aTag-wCCA2 secure TBE schemes can be used, with the technique in [MRY04], to construct protocols that realizes the secure message transmission functionality in the universal composition framework.

TBE is an interesting cryptographic primitive and a useful tool from the above description. As far, except that IND-sTag-wCCA2 (IND-aTag-wCCA2, IND-aTag-CCA2, respectively) secure TBE schemes can be obtained from IND-sID-CPA (IND-aID-CPA, IND-aID-CCA2, respectively) secure IBE schemes by the generic transformation in [Kil06], in the traditional number-theoretic field, there is also an IND-aTag-wCCA2 secure TBE scheme [MRY04] and two IND-sTag-wCCA2 secure TBE schemes [Kil06]. Unfortunately, in the lattice-based field, there is only one IND-sTag-wCCA2 secure lattice-based TBE scheme [SLLF15], which, in fact, is under a variant of DLWE assumption. Our goal here is to construct more efficient lattice-based TBE schemes with stronger security under standard assumptions.

1.1 Our Results

In this paper, we present two IND-aTag-wCCA2 secure TBE schemes TBE1 and TBE2 both under the standard DLWE assumption. We compare the schemes

Table 1. The comparison between our schemes and the one from [SLLF15]

Scheme	Modulus q	Approximation factor α^{-1}	Security
[SLLF15]	$\omega(n^{12})$	$\sqrt{m} \cdot \omega(n^{11})$	IND-sTag-wCCA2
TBE1	$\omega\left(p^2\ell \cdot m^{2.5} \cdot (\log n)^2\right)$	$p^2 \cdot \ell \cdot m^2 \cdot \omega\left(\log n\right)^2$	IND-aTag-wCCA2
TBE2	$\omega\left((\ell + \sqrt{m}) \cdot m \cdot \log n\right)$	$(\ell + \sqrt{m}) \cdot \sqrt{m} \cdot \omega\left(\log n\right)$	IND-aTag-wCCA2

Here n is the security parameter, $\mathbb{Z}_p$ is the message space of TBE1, ℓ is the bit length of the tag, $\ell_q := \lceil \log_2 q \rceil$ and $m = \mathcal{O}(n\ell_q)$.

with the one in [SLLF15] on some aspects in Table 1, which shows that our schemes are more efficient with smaller moduli, are under weaker lattice assumptions with smaller approximation factors, and are with stronger security, than the TBE scheme from [SLLF15].

The main idea for constructing our schemes is combining the probabilistic partition technique of [ABB10] for the adaptively secure IBE scheme, originated from the work [Wat05], and the $\mathbf{G}$-trapdoor as well as some efficient algorithms from [MP12]. In particular, an ingenious matrix, which comes from [Boy10], in the construction of [ABB10], is $\mathbf{A}_0 \| (\mathbf{B} + \sum_i \mathbf{id}[i]\mathbf{A}_i)$, where each entry of $\mathbf{id}$ is in $\{-1, 1\}$, whose trapdoor can be derived from that of $\mathbf{A}_0$, and is transformed, in the proof, into

$$\mathbf{A}_0 \| (\mathbf{A}_0 \sum_i \mathbf{id}[i]\mathbf{R}_i^* + (1 + \sum_i \mathbf{id}[i]h_i)\mathbf{B}), \tag{1}$$

by setting $\mathbf{A}_i := \mathbf{A}_0\mathbf{R}_i^* + h_i\mathbf{B}$, and the trapdoor of $\mathbf{B}$, instead of that of $\mathbf{A}_0$, is generated, the probabilistic partition for adaptively secure IBE is to separate the target identity $\mathbf{id}^*$ from the queried identities $\{\mathbf{id}_j\}$ by the term $1 + \sum_i \mathbf{id}[i]h_i$:

- If $1 + \sum_i \mathbf{id}^*[i]h_i = 0$, the trapdoor of $\mathbf{B}$ is not available, and the simulator's challenge can be embedded into the challenge ciphertext.
- If $1 + \sum_i \mathbf{id}_j[i]h_i \neq 0$, the trapdoor of $\mathbf{B}$ is used to generate that of matrix (1) and hence to generate the secret key for the queried identity $\mathbf{id}_j$.

According to [MP12], $\mathbf{R}_\mathbf{A}$ is a $\mathbf{G}$-trapdoor of $\mathbf{A} \in \mathbb{Z}_q^{n \times m}$ if $\mathbf{A} = \left(\bar{\mathbf{A}} \| (\mathbf{HG} - \bar{\mathbf{A}}\mathbf{R}_\mathbf{A})\right)$, where $\mathbf{H} \in \mathbb{Z}_q^{n \times n}$ is an invertible matrix, $\mathbf{G} \in \mathbb{Z}_q^{n \times w}$ is a primitive matrix, that is, its columns generate all of $\mathbb{Z}_q^n$ and $m \geq w \geq n$.

One of main challenges in the construction is that: If we retain $\mathbf{B}$, it is hard to extend the $\mathbf{G}$-trapdoor of $\mathbf{B}$ to obtain that of matrix (1) in use of efficient algorithms in [MP12]. However, we observe that if we replace $\mathbf{B}$ with $\mathbf{G}$ and sample each entry of $\mathbf{R}_i^*$ independently from a proper discrete Gaussian distribution instead of the uniform distribution over $\{-1, 1\}$ as in [ABB10], the ingenious matrix, in the proof of our constructions, will be $\mathbf{A_t} := \mathbf{A}_0 \| (\mathbf{A}_0 \sum_i \mathbf{t}[i]\mathbf{R}_i^* + (1 + \sum_i \mathbf{t}[i]h_i)\mathbf{G})$, where each entry of $\mathbf{t}$ is in $\{-1, 1\}$, and thus $- \sum_i \mathbf{t}[i]\mathbf{R}_i^*$ is just the trapdoor of matrix $\mathbf{A_t}$ when $(1 + \sum_i \mathbf{t}[i]h_i) \neq 0$ in case that q is a prime, which is key to simulating successfully without the trapdoor of $\mathbf{A}_0$. And $- \sum_i \mathbf{t}^*[i]\mathbf{R}_i^*$ is used to construct the artificial noise in the challenge ciphertext, which is a solution to make our schemes based on the DLWE assumption.

Additionally, we embed the preimage sampling problem into TBE1[1], which is the reason of adding an extra vector in the public key, and the LWE inversion problem into TBE2. And therefore, for the decryption of TBE1, a preimage sampling algorithm together with a trapdoor extension algorithm are enough.

It's more complex for the decryption of TBE2 since LWE samples are not generated in key generation as Regev encryption [Reg05], the secret key is a $\mathbf{G}$-trapdoor of the first part of LWE samples not the secret vector used to generate LWE samples and the message part will be lost if we execute the inversion algorithm on the second part of LWE samples (as the ciphertext, each entry of which is in $\mathbb{Z}_q$).

To overcome this obstacle, we observe that the inversion algorithm in [MP12] for $\Lambda(\mathbf{A}_t^T)$ is essentially that for $\Lambda(\mathbf{G}^T)$ by transforming the former into the latter in use of the trapdoor $\mathbf{R}_{\mathbf{A}_t}$ at first. To solve the above problem for TBE2, we map the message into an element in $\Lambda(\mathbf{G}^T)/2\Lambda(\mathbf{G}^T)$ and use a perturbed vector of $2\Lambda(\mathbf{A}_t)$ to hide the encoded message. And then in decryption, we get the transformed error by executing the first two steps of the inversion algorithm on the perturbed vector of $\Lambda(\mathbf{G}^T)$ and subtract it from the perturbed vector of $\Lambda(\mathbf{G}^T)/2\Lambda(\mathbf{G}^T)$, from which the message can be obtained by the inverse mapping. Note that the mapping is efficient to evaluate and to invert according to [MP12].

1.2 Applications

Adaptively Secure Identity-based Encryption. Although there is not, as far, a generic framework for transforming a TBE scheme into an IBE scheme, our scheme TBE1 can be easily transformed into an adaptively secure IBE scheme. For achieving this, we treat a tag as an identity, take the preimage vector of the vector in public key corresponding to the extended matrix for some identity as a secret key of the identity, and exploit the trapdoor extension algorithm and the preimage sampling algorithm to extract the key. Similar to those IBE schemes in [ZCZ16, Yam17], our derived IBE scheme is also an improved version of the adaptive one in [ABB10] (ABB-IBE). Specifically, Zhang et al. and Yamada used different techniques to make public parameters smaller and to make the DLWE assumption much stronger as well as the key extraction and the encryption more complex, which is a tradeoff. We just exploit $\mathbf{G}$-trapdoor and some related efficient algorithms to get a scheme with the most efficient key extraction algorithm. Their (variant of $\{0, 1\}$-message space) comparisons are presented in Table 2.

---

[1] Although it seems able to construct a TBE scheme by simply, based on the dual-Regev encryption [GPV08], duplicating the same number of the image vectors and the preimage vectors as the bit length of a tag in key generation and just sum the image vectors indexed by the tag during the encryption, such a scheme is only IND-aTag-CPA secure.

Table 2. The comparison of the Series of ABB-IBE

Scheme		Master Public Key	Secret-Key Extraction	Encryption	Modulus q	Approximation Factor α^{-1}
ABB-IBE		$\left(\mathbb{Z}_q^{n\times m}\right)^{\ell+2}\times\mathbb{Z}_q^n$	SampleLeft	Basic operations	$m^{2.5}\cdot\omega\left(\sqrt{\log n}\right)$	$\ell^2\cdot m^2\cdot\omega\left(\sqrt{\log n}\right)$
[ZCZ16](Type-II PHF)		$\begin{array}{c}\mathbb{Z}_q^{n\times m}\times\\\left(\mathbb{Z}_q^{n\times n\ell_q}\right)^{\mathcal{O}(\log n)+1}\times\\\mathbb{Z}_q^n\end{array}$	Eval + TrapExt + SamplePre	Eval + Basic operations	$\tilde{\mathcal{O}}(n^5m^2)$	$n^5m^{1.5}\cdot\omega\left(\sqrt{\log n}\right)$
[Yam17]	F_{MAH}	$\left(\mathbb{Z}_q^{n\times m}\right)^{\omega(\log^2 n)+2}\times\mathbb{Z}_q^n$	PubEval + TrapExt + SamplePre	PubEval + Basic operations	$\ell^2\cdot n^{7.5}m^6\cdot(\log n)^{3.5}$	$\ell^2\cdot n^3m^6\cdot\omega\left((\log n)^{3.5}\right)$
	F_{AFF}	$\left(\mathbb{Z}_q^{n\times m}\right)^{\omega(\log n)+2}\times\mathbb{Z}_q^n$	PubEval + TrapExt + SamplePre	PubEval + Basic operations	$\mathcal{O}\left(n^{7.5}m^2\cdot(\log n)^{3.5}\right)$	$\mathcal{O}\left(n^7m^2\cdot(\log n)^{3.5}\right)$
Our IBE ← TBE1		$\begin{array}{c}\mathbb{Z}_q^{n\times(m+n\ell_q)}\times\\\left(\mathbb{Z}_q^{n\times n\ell_q}\right)^\ell\times\mathbb{Z}_q^n\end{array}$	TrapExt + SamplePre	Basic operations	$\ell\cdot m^{2.5}\cdot(\log n)^2$	$\ell\cdot m^2\cdot\omega\left((\log n)^2\right)$

[1] n is the security parameter, ℓ is the bit length of the identity in ABB-IBE, F_{MAH}-case in [Yam17] and our scheme, and $m=\mathcal{O}(n\ell_q)$. SampleLeft is based on the preimage sampling algorithm from [GPV08], which, according to [MP12], is rather complex and not suitable for practice, in either runtime or the quality of its outputs and these drawbacks are overcome by SamplePre from [MP12]. Additionally, TrapExt from [MP12] is also efficient. Both Eval and PubEval are quite complex, whose details are referred to [ZCZ16] and [Yam17], respectively.

Chosen-Ciphertext Secure Public-Key Encryption. Kiltz [Kil06] proposed a transformation that turns an IND-sTag-wCCA2 secure TBE scheme into a IND-CCA2 secure PKE scheme, together with a strongly one-time secure signature or a strongly one-time secure message authentication code. So we can construct two IND-CCA2 PKE schemes from our schemes TBE1 and TBE2, respectively. In case of strongly one-time signature, our resulted IND-CCA2 secure PKE schemes also have smaller moduli and are under weaker lattice assumptions, than the one in [SLLF15], according to Table 1.

Secure Message Transmission Functionality. Intuitively, the secure message transmission functionality allows multiple parties to send messages to a single receiver with preserving the secrecy and the integrity of the message. MacKenzie et al. [MRY04] adopted their IND-aTag-wCCA2 secure TBE scheme to design a protocol that securely realizes this functionality in a hybrid model. With the same technique, we can design two protocols, realizing the functionality, by using our two schemes, respectively.

2   Preliminaries

2.1   Basic Notation

In this paper, we use bold lower case letters (e.g. $\mathbf{a}, \mathbf{b}$) to denote column vectors and bold upper case letters (e.g. $\mathbf{A}, \mathbf{B}$) to denote matrices. For a matrix $\mathbf{A}$, $\mathbf{A}^{-1}$, $\mathbf{A}^T$ denote its inversion and transposition, respectively, $\mathbf{A}[i,j]$ denotes the entry in the i-th row and the j-th column, $\|\mathbf{A}\|:=\max_{\mathbf{u}}\|\mathbf{A}\mathbf{u}\|$ for all unit vectors $\mathbf{u}$ and the norm of a vector $\mathbf{x}$ is defined as $\|\mathbf{x}\|:=\sqrt{\sum_i\mathbf{x}[i]^2}$, where

$\mathbf{x}[i]$ denotes the i-th entry of $\mathbf{x}$. For a positive integer n, let $\mathbf{I}_n$ denote the n-dimensional identity matrix. For an integer $q \geq 2$, the notation ℓ_q is $\lceil \log_2 q \rceil$. For a set S, then $s \xleftarrow{\$} S$ represents the operation of picking an element s from S uniformly at random. For $k \in \mathbb{N}$, then $[k]$ denotes the set $\{1, \ldots, k\}$. Let PPT short for probabilistic polynomial-time.

2.2 Lattices

In general, an m-dimensional lattice Λ is a discrete additive subgroup of $\mathbb{R}^m$. If Λ is generated as the set of all integer linear combinations of some k linearly independent vectors $\mathbf{b}_1, \ldots, \mathbf{b}_k$, then k is called the rank and $\mathbf{B} := (\mathbf{b}_1, \ldots, \mathbf{b}_k)$ is called a basis of Λ, i.e., $\Lambda = \{\mathbf{Bz} : \mathbf{z} \in \mathbb{Z}^k\}$. In case of $k = m$, $\Lambda \subseteq \mathbb{Z}^m$ is called a full-rank integer lattice.

In this paper, we focus on a particular family of so-called q-ary integer lattices, which contain $q\mathbb{Z}^m$ as a sublattice for any positive integer q. For positive integers n, m, q and a matrix $\mathbf{A} \in \mathbb{Z}_q^{n \times m}$, define the following full-rank m-dimensional q-ary lattices: $\Lambda^\perp(\mathbf{A}) := \{\mathbf{z} \in \mathbb{Z}^m : \mathbf{Az} = \mathbf{0} \mod q\}$, $\Lambda(\mathbf{A}^T) := \{\mathbf{z} \in \mathbb{Z}^m : \exists \, \mathbf{s} \in \mathbb{Z}_q^n \text{ s.t. } \mathbf{z} = \mathbf{A}^T\mathbf{s} \mod q\}$. For any $\mathbf{u} \in \mathbb{Z}_q^n$ admitting an integer solution $\mathbf{x}$ to $\mathbf{Ax} = \mathbf{u} \mod q$, define the coset (or "shifted" lattice): $\Lambda_\mathbf{u}^\perp(\mathbf{A}) := \{\mathbf{z} \in \mathbb{Z}^m : \mathbf{Az} = \mathbf{u} \mod q\} = \Lambda^\perp(\mathbf{A}) + \mathbf{x}$.

2.3 Discrete Gaussians

For any $\mathbf{c} \in \mathbb{R}^m$ and a positive parameter $s \in \mathbb{R}$, the m-dimensional Gaussian function $\rho_{\mathbf{c},s} : \mathbb{R}^m \to (0, 1]$ is defined as: $\rho_{\mathbf{c},s}(\mathbf{x}) := \exp(-\frac{\pi\|\mathbf{x}-\mathbf{c}\|^2}{s^2})$. For a lattice $\Lambda \subset \mathbb{R}^m$, the discrete Gaussian distribution over Λ with center $\mathbf{c}$ and parameter s is defined as $D_{\Lambda+\mathbf{c},s}(\mathbf{x}) := \frac{\rho_{\mathbf{c},s}(\mathbf{x})}{\rho_{\mathbf{c},s}(\Lambda)}$, where $\rho_{\mathbf{c},s}(\Lambda) = \sum_{\mathbf{x} \in \Lambda} \rho_{\mathbf{c},s}(\mathbf{x})$.

Combining the result of Lemma 3.1 in [GPV08] with Lemma 4.4 in [MR07], we have the following tail bound on discrete Gaussians.

Lemma 1. *Let $\Lambda \subset \mathbb{R}^m$ be a lattice with basis $\mathbf{B}$, $\mathbf{c} \in span(\Lambda) := \{\mathbf{Br} : \mathbf{r} \in \mathbb{R}^k\}$ and $s \geq \|\widetilde{\mathbf{B}}\| \cdot \omega(\sqrt{\log m})$, where $\widetilde{\mathbf{B}}$ is the Gram-Schmidt orthogonalization of $\mathbf{B}$, we have $\Pr_{\mathbf{x} \leftarrow D_{\Lambda+\mathbf{c},s}} [\|\mathbf{x}\| \geq s\sqrt{m}] = \mathrm{negl}(m)$.*

For positive $\alpha \in \mathbb{R}$, Ψ_α is defined to be the distribution on $\mathbb{T} := \mathbb{R}/\mathbb{Z}$ of a normal variable with mean 0 and standard deviation $\alpha/\sqrt{2\pi}$, reduced modulo 1. And its discretization $\bar{\Psi}_\alpha$ is the discrete distribution over $\mathbb{Z}_q$, for integer $q \geq 2$, of the random variable $\lfloor q \cdot X_{\Psi_\alpha} \rceil \mod q$, where X_{Ψ_α} has distribution Ψ_α.

2.4 Learning with Errors (LWE)

The LWE problem was introduced by Regev [Reg05]. Decisional LWE (DLWE) is defined as follows.

Definition 1 (DLWE). *For security parameter λ, let $n = n(\lambda)$ be an integer dimension, let an integer $q = q(\lambda) \geq 2$ be a modulus, and $\bar{\Psi}_\alpha$ be a noise distribution. The decisional learning with errors problem, denoted by $DLWE_{n,q,\bar{\Psi}_\alpha}$, is to distinguish the following two distributions: In the first distribution, denoted by $U(\mathbb{Z}_q^n \times \mathbb{Z}_q)$, one samples $(\mathbf{a}, b)$ uniformly from $\mathbb{Z}_q^n \times \mathbb{Z}_q$. In the second distribution, denoted by $A_{\mathbf{s}, \bar{\Psi}_\alpha}$ for uniformly random $\mathbf{s} \in \mathbb{Z}_q^n$, one samples $(\mathbf{a}, b) \in \mathbb{Z}_q^n \times \mathbb{Z}_q$ by sampling $\mathbf{a} \xleftarrow{\$} \mathbb{Z}_q^n$ uniformly at random, $e \leftarrow \bar{\Psi}_\alpha$, and setting $b = \langle \mathbf{a}, \mathbf{s} \rangle + e$. The $DLWE_{n,q,\bar{\Psi}_\alpha}$ assumption is that the $DLWE_{n,q,\bar{\Psi}_\alpha}$ problem is infeasible.*

There are known quantum [Reg05] and classical [Pei09] reductions between $DLWE_{n,q,\bar{\Psi}_\alpha}$ and approximating short vector problems on lattices. In particular, for $\alpha q \geq 2\sqrt{n}$, solving the $DLWE_{n,q,\bar{\Psi}_\alpha}$ problem is at least as hard as solving worst-case lattice problems with approximation factors of $\widetilde{\mathcal{O}}(n/\alpha)$.

2.5   Trapdoors for Lattices

It is much required to generate a (nearly) uniform parity-check matrix $\mathbf{A}$ together with some strong trapdoor for advanced lattice-based cryptographic schemes, including chosen-ciphertext secure encryption, "hash-and-sign" digital signature, identity-based encryption, et al.

In 1999, Ajtai [Ajt99] showed how to sample an essentially uniform $\mathbf{A}$, along with a relatively short trapdoor $\mathbf{S} \subset \Lambda^\perp(\mathbf{A})$. And later Micciancio and Goldwasser [MG02] and Gentry et al. [GPV08] successively improved the result slightly.

Lemma 2 (Trapdoor Generation I [Ajt99, GPV08]). *For any prime $q = \text{poly}(n)$ and any integer $m \geq 5n\ell_q$, there exists a PPT algorithm that, on input 1^n, outputs a matrix $\mathbf{A} \in \mathbb{Z}_q^{n \times m}$ and a full-rank set $\mathbf{S} \subset \Lambda^\perp(\mathbf{A})$, where the distribution of $\mathbf{A}$ is statistically close to uniform over $\mathbb{Z}_q^{n \times m}$ and the length $\|\mathbf{S}\| \leq L = m^{1+\varepsilon}$ for any $\varepsilon > 0$.*

In particular, by Lemma 7.1 in [MG02], given an arbitrary basis of $\Lambda^\perp(\mathbf{A})$, the full-rank set $\mathbf{S}$ can be converted efficiently to a good basis $\mathbf{T}$ such that $\|\widetilde{\mathbf{T}}\| \leq \|\widetilde{\mathbf{S}}\|$.

In 2011, Alwen and Peikert [AP11] elucidated and generalized Ajtai's algorithm to provide a basis of essentially optimal length.

Lemma 3 (Trapdoor Generation II [AP11]). *For any integer $q \geq 2$ and $m \geq 2n\ell_q^2$, there exists a PPT algorithm that, on inputs n, q and m, outputs a nearly uniform matrix $\mathbf{A} \in \mathbb{Z}_q^{n \times m}$ and a basis $\mathbf{S}$ of $\Lambda^\perp(\mathbf{A})$ with $\|\widetilde{\mathbf{S}}\| \leq 5\sqrt{n\ell_q}$.*

In 2012, Micciancio and Peikert [MP12] proposed a significantly more efficient algorithm, which essentially amounts to just one multiplication of two random matrices. For any positive integers n and $q \geq 2$, let $\mathbf{G} := \mathbf{I}_n \otimes \mathbf{g}^T \in \mathbb{Z}_q^{n \times n\ell_q}$, where $\mathbf{g}^T = (2^0, 2^1, \ldots, 2^{\ell_q - 1})$.[2]

---

[2] This $\mathbf{g}$ can be generalized into ones using other bases.

Lemma 4 (Trapdoor Generation III [MP12]). *For any positive integers $n, q \geq 2, m = \mathcal{O}(n\ell_q)$, there exists a PPT algorithm TrapGen that, on inputs a uniform matrix $\bar{\mathbf{A}} \in \mathbb{Z}_q^{n \times m}$ and an invertible matrix $\mathbf{H} \in \mathbb{Z}_q^{n \times n}$,[3] outputs a statistically near-uniform matrix $\mathbf{A} \in \mathbb{Z}_q^{n \times (m+n\ell_q)}$ and its $\mathbf{G}$-trapdoor $\mathbf{R} \in \mathbb{Z}^{m \times n\ell_q}$ w.r.t. $\mathbf{H}$, by firstly choosing each element of $\mathbf{R}$ independently from a proper discrete Gaussian distribution D over $\mathbb{Z}$, and then setting $\mathbf{A} := (\bar{\mathbf{A}} \| (\mathbf{HG} - \bar{\mathbf{A}}\mathbf{R}))$. Note that $\|\mathbf{R}\| \leq \mathcal{O}(\sqrt{m} + \sqrt{n\ell_q}) \cdot \omega(\sqrt{\log n}) = \mathcal{O}(\sqrt{n\ell_q}) \cdot \omega(\sqrt{\log n})$ except with probability $2^{-\Omega(m+n\ell_q)}$.*

Based on the above $\mathbf{G}$-trapdoor, Micciancio and Peikert constructed efficient parallel algorithms for preimage sampling over a shifted lattice, LWE inversion and trapdoor extension, respectively.

Lemma 5 (Preimage Sampling [MP12]). *For parameters given in Lemma 4, some $s \in \mathbb{R}$ and a uniformly random vector $\mathbf{u} \in \mathbb{Z}_q^n$, there exists a PPT algorithm SamplePre that, on inputs $\mathbf{R}, \bar{\mathbf{A}}, \mathbf{H}, \mathbf{u}, s$, outputs a vector $\mathbf{e}$, whose distribution is statistically close to $D_{\mathbb{Z}, s \cdot \omega(\sqrt{\log n})}^{m+n\ell_q}$, satisfying $(\bar{\mathbf{A}} \| (\mathbf{HG} - \bar{\mathbf{A}}\mathbf{R})) \cdot \mathbf{e} = \mathbf{u} \mod q$.*

Lemma 6 (LWE Inversion [MP12]). *For parameters given in Lemma 4, a vector $\mathbf{b} = \mathbf{A}^T \mathbf{s} + \mathbf{e}$ for any uniform $\mathbf{s} \in \mathbb{Z}_q^n$ and suitably small $\mathbf{e} \in \mathbb{Z}^{m+n\ell_q}$, there exists a PPT algorithm Invert that, on inputs $\mathbf{R}, \bar{\mathbf{A}}, \mathbf{H}, \mathbf{b}$, outputs $\mathbf{s}$ and $\mathbf{e}$, by first transforming the perturbed vector $\mathbf{b}$ w.r.t. $\Lambda(\mathbf{A}^T)$ into $\mathbf{b}' := (\mathbf{R}^T \| \mathbf{I}_{n\ell_q}) \cdot \mathbf{b}$ w.r.t. $\Lambda(\mathbf{G}^T)$, then obtaining the solution $(\mathbf{s}', \mathbf{e}')$ in use of the inversion algorithm for $\Lambda(\mathbf{G}^T)$, and finally computing $\mathbf{s} := (\mathbf{H}^{-1})^T \mathbf{s}'$, $\mathbf{e} := \mathbf{b} - \mathbf{A}^T \mathbf{s}$.*

Lemma 7 (Trapdoor Extension [MP12]). *For parameters given in Lemma 4, a uniform matrix $\mathbf{B} \in \mathbb{Z}_q^{n \times n\ell_q}$, there exists a PPT algorithm TrapExt that, on inputs a $\mathbf{G}$-trapdoor $\mathbf{R}$ for $\mathbf{A} \in \mathbb{Z}_q^{n \times m}$ w.r.t. some invertible $\mathbf{H}$, an extension $\mathbf{A}' = (\mathbf{A} \| \mathbf{B})$ of $\mathbf{A}$, an invertible $\mathbf{H}' \in \mathbb{Z}_q^{n \times n}$ and $s \in \mathbb{R}$, outputs a $\mathbf{G}$-trapdoor $\mathbf{R}'$ for $\mathbf{A}'$ w.r.t. $\mathbf{H}'$. Particularly, the i-th column of $\mathbf{R}'$ is sampling independently from a discrete Gaussian with parameter s over $\Lambda_{(\mathbf{H}'\mathbf{G}-\mathbf{B})[i]}^{\perp}(\mathbf{A})$ in use of $\mathbf{R}$, where $(\mathbf{H}'\mathbf{G} - \mathbf{B})[i]$ is the i-th column of $(\mathbf{H}'\mathbf{G} - \mathbf{B})$. Note that $\|\mathbf{R}'\| \leq s \cdot \mathcal{O}(\sqrt{m} + \sqrt{n\ell_q})$ except with negligible probability.*

2.6   Tag-Based Encryption

Informally, in a tag-based encryption scheme, both the encryption and decryption algorithms take an additional tag as input. A tag may be a binary string of appropriate length or has any particular internal structure. We recall its definition from [Kil06].

A tag-based encryption scheme, with message space $\mathcal{M}$ and tag space $\mathcal{T}$, consists of three polynomial-time algorithms (Gen, Enc, Dec) described as follows:

- Gen$(1^\lambda) \to (pk, sk)$: A probabilistic algorithm that takes the security parameter 1^λ as input, generates and outputs a pair of public key and private key (pk, sk).

---

[3] $\mathbf{H}$ here and below can be $\mathbf{I}_n$.

– Enc$(pk, t \in \mathcal{T}, \mu \in \mathcal{M}) \rightarrow c$: A probabilistic algorithm that takes the public key pk, a tag t and a message μ as input, generates and outputs a ciphertext c. Note that the tag is not explicitly contained in the ciphertext.
– Dec$(sk, t, c) \rightarrow \mu$: A deterministic or probabilistic algorithm that takes the secret key sk, a tag t and a ciphertext c as input, generates and outputs a message μ if t is valid and is just the tag used to generate c, and outputs $\perp$ meaning decryption failure otherwise.

The correctness and security are defined as follows:

– **Correctness.** For all $\lambda \in \mathbb{N}$, all tags $t \in \mathcal{T}$ and all messages $\mu \in \mathcal{M}$, we have $\Pr\left[\text{Dec}\left(sk, t, \text{Enc}\left(pk, t, \mu\right)\right) = \mu\right] = 1$, where the probability is taken over the choice of $(pk, sk) \leftarrow \text{Gen}(1^\lambda)$, and the coins of the algorithms in the expression.
– **Security.** Due to known applications of TBE, there is only some security definitions, IND-sTag-wCCA2, IND-aTag-wCCA2 and IND-aTag-CCA2, for TBE. In fact, other standard security definitions for TBE can be easily defined corresponding to those for PKE. In this paper, we focus on IND-aTag-wCCA2 security, which is defined as a game executed by a challenger $\mathcal{C}$ and a PPT adversary $\mathcal{A}$ interactively.

- **Key Generation Phase.** The challenger $\mathcal{C}$ calls $\text{Gen}(1^\lambda)$ to generate (pk, sk) and sends pk to the adversary $\mathcal{A}$.
- **Decryption Query Phase I.** On the query (t, c) from $\mathcal{A}$, $\mathcal{C}$ acts as the decryption oracle: Calls $\text{Dec}(sk, t, c)$ to generate a message μ or the failure symbol $\perp$ as the answer to $\mathcal{A}$.
- **Challenge Phase.** Once $\mathcal{A}$ submits t^* and a pair of messages (μ_0, μ_1) with the same length, $\mathcal{C}$ samples a random bit b, calls $\text{Enc}(pk, t^*, \mu_b)$ to generate the challenge ciphertext c^* and sends it to $\mathcal{A}$.
- **Decryption Query Phase II.** On the query (t, c) from $\mathcal{A}$, $\mathcal{C}$ checks whether $t = t^*$: if yes, $\mathcal{C}$ aborts the game and outputs a random bit; else, $\mathcal{C}$ answers to $\mathcal{A}$ as in the decryption query phase I.
- **Guess Phase.** Once $\mathcal{A}$ submits its guess b', $\mathcal{C}$ checks whether $b' = b$: if yes, it outputs 1, and outputs 0 otherwise.

The advantage of $\mathcal{A}$ is defined as

$$\mathbf{Adv}_{\mathcal{A}}^{\text{aTag-wCCA2}}(\lambda) := |\Pr[\mathcal{C} \text{ outputs } 1] - 1/2|, \qquad (2)$$

a TBE scheme is said to be IND-aTag-wCCA2 secure if the advantage function (2) is negligible for all PPT adversaries $\mathcal{A}$.

3   Tag-Based Encryption Scheme TBE1

In this section, we construct the first scheme TBE1, in which the preimage sampling problem is mainly embedded. Specifically, this scheme has an encryption similar to the dual-Regev encryption, where the relation $\mathbf{Ae} = \mathbf{u} \mod q$ is the core. And hence there is an image vector $\mathbf{u}$ in the public key, its corresponding

LWE value is used to hide the message, the tag is bound to the part of $\mathbf{A}$ and the preimage vector $\mathbf{e}$ will first be sampled for decryption.

Let n be the security parameter, a prime $q = \text{poly}(n)$, $\alpha \in (0,1)$ such that $\alpha q \geq 2\sqrt{n}$, $m = \mathcal{O}(n\ell_q)$ and D is the distribution used in Lemma 4. The tag space is $\mathcal{T} = \{0,1\}^{\ell}$ and the message space is $\mathbb{Z}_p$ for some $2 \leq p < q$.

- TBE1.Gen(1^n): Sample $\bar{\mathbf{A}}_0 \xleftarrow{\$} \mathbb{Z}_q^{n \times m}$ and run $(\mathbf{A}_0, \mathbf{T}_{\mathbf{A}_0}) \leftarrow \text{TrapGen}(\bar{\mathbf{A}}_0, \mathbf{I}_n)$, where $\mathbf{A}_0 := (\bar{\mathbf{A}}_0 \| (\mathbf{G} - \bar{\mathbf{A}}_0 \mathbf{T}_{\mathbf{A}_0}))$. Choose $\mathbf{A}_1, \ldots, \mathbf{A}_{\ell} \xleftarrow{\$} \mathbb{Z}_q^{n \times n\ell_q}$, $\mathbf{u} \xleftarrow{\$} \mathbb{Z}_q^n$, output $pk := (\mathbf{A}_0, \mathbf{A}_1, \ldots, \mathbf{A}_{\ell}, \mathbf{u})$ and $sk := \mathbf{T}_{\mathbf{A}_0}$.
- TBE1.Enc($pk, \mathbf{t} \in \mathcal{T}, \mu \in \mathbb{Z}_p$): Sample $\mathbf{s} \xleftarrow{\$} \mathbb{Z}_q^n$, $\mathbf{R}_i \leftarrow D^{(m+n\ell_q) \times n\ell_q}$ for $i \in [\ell]$, $x \leftarrow \bar{\Psi}_{\alpha}$, $\mathbf{y} \leftarrow \bar{\Psi}_{\alpha}^{m+n\ell_q}$, let $\mathbf{A}_{\mathbf{t}} := (\mathbf{A}_0 \| (\mathbf{G} + \sum_{i=1}^{\ell}(-1)^{\mathbf{t}[i]} \mathbf{A}_i)$, $\mathbf{R}_{\mathbf{t}} := \sum_{i=1}^{\ell}(-1)^{\mathbf{t}[i]} \mathbf{R}_i$, $\mathbf{z} := -\mathbf{R}_{\mathbf{t}}^T \mathbf{y}$, compute and output $\mathbf{c} := (\mathbf{u} \| \mathbf{A}_{\mathbf{t}})^T \mathbf{s} + (x, \mathbf{y}^T, \mathbf{z}^T)^T + (\mu \cdot \lfloor q/p \rfloor, \mathbf{0}_{1 \times (m+2n\ell_q)})^T \mod q$.
- TBE1.Dec($sk, \mathbf{t}, \mathbf{c}$): First derive a trapdoor $\mathbf{T}_{\mathbf{A}_{\mathbf{t}}} \leftarrow \text{TrapExt}(\mathbf{T}_{\mathbf{A}_0}, \mathbf{A}_{\mathbf{t}}, \mathbf{I}_n, \|\mathbf{T}_{\mathbf{A}_0}\|)$. And then sample $\mathbf{e}_{\mathbf{t}} \leftarrow \text{SamplePre}(\mathbf{T}_{\mathbf{A}_{\mathbf{t}}}, \mathbf{A}_{\mathbf{t}}, \mathbf{u}, \|\mathbf{T}_{\mathbf{A}_{\mathbf{t}}}\|)$, such that $\mathbf{A}_{\mathbf{t}} \mathbf{e}_{\mathbf{t}} = \mathbf{u} \mod q$, and compute $\delta := (1, -\mathbf{e}_{\mathbf{t}}^T) \cdot \mathbf{c}/q$. Finally find and output $\mu \in \mathbb{Z}_p$ such that $\delta - \mu/p$ is closest to 0 modulo 1.

Lemma 8 (Correctness). *Let a prime* $q = \omega(p^2\ell \cdot (n\ell_q)^{2.5} \cdot (\log n)^2)$ *and* $\alpha < (p^2\ell \cdot (n\ell_q)^2 \cdot \omega((\log n)^2))^{-1}$. *Then* TBE1.Dec *works with overwhelming probability.*

Proof. In the decryption algorithm, TrapExt and SamplePre are firstly called and their correctness are guaranteed by Lemmas 7 and 5 respectively. Subsequently, $(1, -\mathbf{e}_{\mathbf{t}}^T) \cdot \mathbf{c} = \mu \cdot (q/p) - \mu \cdot (q/p - \lfloor q/p \rfloor) + x - \mathbf{e}_{\mathbf{t}}^T (\mathbf{y}^T, \mathbf{z}^T)^T \mod q$, in which the error term is $-\mu \cdot (q/p - \lfloor q/p \rfloor) + x - (\mathbf{e}_{\mathbf{t},1} - \mathbf{R}\mathbf{e}_{\mathbf{t},2})^T \mathbf{y}$, if we parse $\mathbf{e}_{\mathbf{t}}$ as $(\mathbf{e}_{\mathbf{t},1}^T, \mathbf{e}_{\mathbf{t},2}^T)^T$.

According to Lemmas 1, 4 and 5, we have

$$\|\mathbf{e}_{\mathbf{t}}\| \leq \|\mathbf{T}_{\mathbf{A}_{\mathbf{t}}}\| \cdot \omega(\sqrt{\log n}) \cdot \sqrt{m + 2n\ell_q} \leq \mathcal{O}((n\ell_q)^{1.5}) \cdot \omega(\log n),$$

and since $\|\mathbf{R}\| \leq \ell \cdot \mathcal{O}(\sqrt{m + n\ell_q} + \sqrt{n\ell_q}) \cdot \omega(\sqrt{\log n}) = \ell \cdot \mathcal{O}(\sqrt{n\ell_q}) \cdot \omega(\sqrt{\log n})$ by Lemma 4, $\|\mathbf{e}_{\mathbf{t},1} - \mathbf{R}\mathbf{e}_{\mathbf{t},2}\| \leq \|\mathbf{e}_{\mathbf{t},1}\| + \|\mathbf{R}\mathbf{e}_{\mathbf{t},2}\| \leq \ell \cdot \mathcal{O}((n\ell_q)^2) \cdot \omega((\log n)^{1.5})$, and hence by Lemma 12 in [ABB10],

$$|(\mathbf{e}_{\mathbf{t},1} - \mathbf{R}\mathbf{e}_{\mathbf{t},2})^T \mathbf{y}| \leq \|\mathbf{e}_{\mathbf{t},1} - \mathbf{R}\mathbf{e}_{\mathbf{t},2}\| \cdot \alpha q \cdot \omega(\sqrt{\log(m + n\ell_q)})$$
$$+ \|\mathbf{e}_{\mathbf{t},1} - \mathbf{R}\mathbf{e}_{\mathbf{t},2}\| \cdot \sqrt{m + n\ell_q}/2,$$

and thus $|-\mu \cdot (q/p - \lfloor q/p \rfloor) + x - (\mathbf{e}_{\mathbf{t},1} - \mathbf{R}\mathbf{e}_{\mathbf{t},2})^T \mathbf{y}|$ is less than

$$p + \frac{2p^2\sqrt{n\ell_q}}{2p} + \frac{2p^2\ell \cdot (n\ell_q)^{2.5} \cdot \omega((\log n)^2)}{2p} + \ell \cdot \mathcal{O}((n\ell_q)^{2.5}) \cdot \omega((\log n)^{1.5}) < \frac{q}{2p},$$

therefore $|\delta - \mu/p| = |(1, -\mathbf{e}_{\mathbf{t}}^T) \cdot \mathbf{c}/q - \mu/p| = |\mu/p + 1/q \cdot (-\mu \cdot (q/p - \lfloor q/p \rfloor) + x - \mathbf{e}_{\mathbf{t}}^T (\mathbf{y}^T, \mathbf{z}^T)^T) - \mu/p| < 1/(2p)$,

so TBE1.Dec outputs μ as desired.   □

Theorem 1 (Security). *The above scheme TBE1 is IND-aTag-wCCA2 secure in the standard model if the $DLWE_{n,q,\bar{\Psi}_\alpha}$ assumption holds.*

Proof. To prove the theorem, we suppose that an arbitrary PPT adversary $\mathcal{A}$ against IND-aTag-wCCA2 security of TBE1. And we consider the following games, each of which is described as the modification from its previous one.

   Game 0. This is the original IND-aTag-wCCA2 security experiment between $\mathcal{A}$ and a challenger $\mathcal{C}$. In addition, $\mathcal{C}$ maintains a list T for storing queried tags.

   Game 1. In preparation for use of probabilistic partition technique, we slightly change the way that $\mathcal{C}$ generates the matrices $\mathbf{A}_i$ for all $i \in [\ell]$: At the key generation phase, $\mathcal{C}$ chooses $\mathbf{R}_i^*$ as in Game 0 and also chooses random scalar $h_i \in \mathbb{Z}_q$ uniformly, and then it uses $\mathbf{A}_0$ generated as in Game 0 to construct $\mathbf{A}_i$ as $\mathbf{A}_i := -\mathbf{A}_0\mathbf{R}_i^* + h_i\mathbf{G}$.

   Game 2. After receiving $\mathcal{A}$'s guess, we start to partition the challenge tag $\mathbf{t}^*$ from $\mathcal{A}$'s queried tags T by introducing the abort check with the abort-resistant function $H_\mathbf{h}(\mathbf{t}) := 1 + \sum_{i=1}^{\ell}(-1)^{\mathbf{t}[i]}h_i$, and then use an artificial abort to force the probability of aborting to be independent of $\mathcal{A}$'s particular queries, as in [Wat05, ABB10, ZCZ16].

   Game 3. $\mathcal{C}$ chooses $\mathbf{A}_0$ uniformly at random from $\mathbb{Z}_q^{n \times (m+n\ell_q)}$. For answering the decryption query on $(\mathbf{t}_i, \mathbf{c}_i)$, since

$$\mathbf{A_t} = (\mathbf{A}_0 \| (-\mathbf{A}_0 \sum_{i=1}^{\ell}(-1)^{\mathbf{t}[i]}\mathbf{R}_i^* + H_\mathbf{h}(\mathbf{t}) \cdot \mathbf{G})), \tag{3}$$

$\mathcal{C}$ first computes $H_\mathbf{h}(\mathbf{t}_i)$ and checks if $H_\mathbf{h}(\mathbf{t}_i) = 0$: If yes, it aborts the game and outputs a random bit; else, it computes $\mathbf{A_{t_i}}$ as in (3), uses its trapdoor $\sum_{j=1}^{\ell}(-1)^{\mathbf{t}_i[j]}\mathbf{R}_j^*$ to generate $\mathbf{e_{t_i}}$, and finally it exploits $\mathbf{e_{t_i}}$ to decrypt $\mathbf{c}_i$ and sends the result to $\mathcal{A}$.

   At the challenge phase, once receiving $\mathbf{t}^*$ from $\mathcal{A}$, $\mathcal{C}$ first computes $H_\mathbf{h}(\mathbf{t}^*)$ and checks whether it equals to 0: If not, it aborts the game and outputs a random bit; else, it generates a challenge ciphertext as in Game 2.

   At the guess phase, $\mathcal{C}$ just performs the artificial abort as in Game 2.

   Game 4. This game is identical to Game 3 except that the challenge ciphertext is chosen as a random element in $\mathbb{Z}_q^{m+2n\ell_q+1}$.

4   Tag-Based Encryption Scheme **TBE2** with Smaller Modulus and Approximation Factor

In this section, our second scheme TBE2 is presented. TBE2 has a smaller modulus, which is a key factor of efficiency, and a smaller approximation factor, which means a weaker lattice assumption, than TBE1. In particular, we mainly embed the LWE inversion problem without the image vector in the public key and hence the preimage sampling algorithm is not available. LWE samples are also generated freshly for hiding the message in the encryption, which has to be decrypted by recovering the secret vector or the noise.

The tag space is similar to that of TBE1. The message space is $\{0,1\}^{n\ell_q}$, according to [MP12], which can be mapped bijectively to the coset of $\Lambda(\mathbf{G}^T)/2\Lambda(\mathbf{G}^T)$ via a function $f : \{0,1\}^{n\ell_q} \to \mathbb{Z}^{n\ell_q}$. Note that f is efficient to evaluate and to invert and its inversion is denoted as f^{-1}.

- TBE2.Gen(1^n): Similar to TBE1.Gen(1^n) without sampling $\mathbf{u}$, output $pk :=$ $(\mathbf{A}_0, \mathbf{A}_1, \ldots, \mathbf{A}_\ell)$ and $sk := \mathbf{T}_{\mathbf{A}_0}$.
- TBE2.Enc($pk, \mathbf{t} \in \mathcal{T}, \boldsymbol{\mu} \in \{0,1\}^{n\ell_q}$): Sample $\mathbf{s} \xleftarrow{\$} \mathbb{Z}_q^n$, $\mathbf{e}_1 \leftarrow \bar{\Psi}_\alpha^{m+n\ell_q}$, $\mathbf{R}_i \leftarrow$ $D^{(m+n\ell_q) \times n\ell_q}$ for $i \in [\ell]$, where D is the distribution used in Lemma 4. Let $\mathbf{A}_t := (\mathbf{A}_0 \| (\mathbf{G} + \sum_{i=1}^{\ell}(-1)^{\mathbf{t}[i]}\mathbf{A}_i)), \mathbf{R}_t := \sum_{i=1}^{\ell}(-1)^{\mathbf{t}[i]}\mathbf{R}_i, \mathbf{e}_2 := -\mathbf{R}_t^T\mathbf{e}_1$, compute and output $\mathbf{c} := 2(\mathbf{A}_t^T\mathbf{s} \mod q) + (\mathbf{e}_1^T, \mathbf{e}_2^T)^T + (\mathbf{0}_{1 \times (m+n\ell_q)}, f(\boldsymbol{\mu})^T)^T$ $\mod 2q$.
- TBE2.Dec($sk, \mathbf{t}, \mathbf{c}$): Let $\mathbf{T}_{\mathbf{A}_t} \leftarrow$ TrapExt($\mathbf{T}_{\mathbf{A}_0}, \mathbf{A}_t, \mathbf{I}_n, \|\mathbf{T}_{\mathbf{A}_0}\|$), where $\mathbf{A}_0\mathbf{T}_{\mathbf{A}_t}$ $= \mathbf{G} - (\mathbf{G} + \sum_{i=1}^{\ell}(-1)^{\mathbf{t}[i]}\mathbf{A}_i) = -\sum_{i=1}^{\ell}(-1)^{\mathbf{t}[i]}\mathbf{A}_i$. And to compute $(\mathbf{z} \in \mathbb{Z}_q^n, \mathbf{e} \in \mathbb{Z}^{n\ell_q})$ as in Lemma 6 on inputs $(\mathbf{T}_{\mathbf{A}_t}, \mathbf{A}_t, \mathbf{c} \mod q)$ as follows:
  1. $\mathbf{b} := (\mathbf{T}_{\mathbf{A}_t}^T \| \mathbf{I}_{n\ell_q}) \cdot (\mathbf{c} \mod q)$ as a perturbed vector w.r.t. $\Lambda(\mathbf{G}^T)$;
  2. run the inversion algorithm for $\Lambda(\mathbf{G}^T)$, to get the inversion $(\mathbf{z}, \mathbf{e})$ for $\mathbf{b}$. If $\|\mathbf{e}\| \geq (\ell + \sqrt{n\ell_q}) \cdot \alpha q \cdot \mathcal{O}(\sqrt{n\ell_q}) \cdot \tilde{\omega}(\log n) + (\ell + \sqrt{n\ell_q}) \cdot \mathcal{O}(n\ell_q) \cdot \omega(\sqrt{\log n})$, output $\perp$. Compute $\mathbf{u} := (\mathbf{T}_{\mathbf{A}_t}^T \| \mathbf{I}_{n\ell_q}) \cdot (\mathbf{c} \mod 2q) - \mathbf{e}$, and output $f^{-1}(\mathbf{u})$.

Lemma 9 (Correctness). *Let* $q = \omega((\ell + \sqrt{n\ell_q}) \cdot n\ell_q \cdot \log n)$ *and* $\alpha < ((\ell + \sqrt{n\ell_q}) \cdot \sqrt{n\ell_q} \cdot \omega(\log n))^{-1}$. *Then TBE2.Dec works with overwhelming probability.*

The above lemma can be proved similarly as that for Lemma 8.

Theorem 2 (Security). *The above scheme TBE2 is IND-aTag-wCCA2 secure in the standard model if the* $\mathsf{DLWE}_{n,q,\bar{\Psi}_{\alpha'}}$ *assumption holds for* $\alpha' = \alpha/3 \geq 2\sqrt{n}/q$.

Proof. The proof is identical to that for Theorem 1 except that the difficulty of distinguishing from the latter two games is based on a particular form of discretized DLWE assumption: It is infeasible to distinguish the following two distributions for any uniform $\mathbf{s} \in \mathbb{Z}_q^n$, $U(\mathbb{Z}_q^n \times \mathbb{T}) := \{(\mathbf{a}, b)\}_{\mathbf{a} \xleftarrow{\$} \mathbb{Z}_q^n, b \xleftarrow{\$} \mathbb{T}}$ and $A_{\mathbf{s},\alpha'} :=$ $\{(\mathbf{a}, b := \langle \mathbf{a}, \mathbf{s} \rangle / q + e \mod 1)\}_{\mathbf{a} \xleftarrow{\$} \mathbb{Z}_q^n, e \leftarrow \bar{\Psi}_{\alpha'}}$, which can be transformed into the distributions over $\mathbb{Z}_q^n \times \mathbb{Z}_{2q}$ by the mapping $b \mapsto 2qb + D_{\mathbb{Z}-2qb, \sqrt{(\alpha q)^2 - (2\alpha' q)^2}}$ by Theorem 6.3 in [MP12]. $\square$

Acknowledgment. This work is supported by National Natural Science Foundation of China (No. 61402471, 61472414, 61602061, 61772514), and IIE's Cryptography Research Project.

References

[ABB10] Agrawal, S., Boneh, D., Boyen, X.: Efficient lattice (H)IBE in the standard model. In: Gilbert, H. (ed.) EUROCRYPT 2010. LNCS, vol. 6110, pp. 553–572. Springer, Heidelberg (2010). https://doi.org/10.1007/978-3-642-13190-5_28

[Ajt99] Ajtai, M.: Generating hard instances of the short basis problem. In: Wiedermann, J., van Emde Boas, P., Nielsen, M. (eds.) ICALP 1999. LNCS, vol. 1644, pp. 1–9. Springer, Heidelberg (1999). https://doi.org/10.1007/3-540-48523-6_1

[AP11] Alwen, J., Peikert, C.: Generating shorter bases for hard random lattices. Theory Comput. Syst. **48**(3), 535–553 (2011)

[Boy10] Boyen, X.: Lattice mixing and vanishing trapdoors: a framework for fully secure short signatures and more. In: Nguyen, P.Q., Pointcheval, D. (eds.) PKC 2010. LNCS, vol. 6056, pp. 499–517. Springer, Heidelberg (2010). https://doi.org/10.1007/978-3-642-13013-7_29

[GPV08] Gentry, C., Peikert, C., Vaikuntanathan, V.: Trapdoors for hard lattices and new cryptographic constructions. In: STOC 2008, pp. 197–206. ACM (2008)

[Kil06] Kiltz, E.: Chosen-ciphertext security from tag-based encryption. In: Halevi, S., Rabin, T. (eds.) TCC 2006. LNCS, vol. 3876, pp. 581–600. Springer, Heidelberg (2006). https://doi.org/10.1007/11681878_30

[MG02] Micciancio, D., Goldwasser, S.: Complexity of Lattice Problems, vol. 671, p. x,220. Springer, New York (2002). https://doi.org/10.1007/978-1-4615-0897-7

[MP12] Micciancio, D., Peikert, C.: Trapdoors for lattices: simpler, tighter, faster, smaller. In: Pointcheval, D., Johansson, T. (eds.) EUROCRYPT 2012. LNCS, vol. 7237, pp. 700–718. Springer, Heidelberg (2012). https://doi.org/10.1007/978-3-642-29011-4_41

[MR07] Micciancio, D., Regev, O.: Worst-case to average-case reductions based on gaussian measures. SIAM J. Comput. **37**(1), 267–302 (2007)

[MRY04] MacKenzie, P., Reiter, M.K., Yang, K.: Alternatives to non-malleability: definitions, constructions, and applications. In: Naor, M. (ed.) TCC 2004. LNCS, vol. 2951, pp. 171–190. Springer, Heidelberg (2004). https://doi.org/10.1007/978-3-540-24638-1_10

[Pei09] Peikert. C.: Public-key cryptosystems from the worst-case shortest vector problem. In: STOC 2009, pp. 333–342. ACM (2009)

[Reg05] Regev, O.: On lattices, learning with errors, random linear codes, and cryptography. In: STOC 2005, pp. 84–93 (2005)

[Sho01] Shoup, V.: A proposal for the ISO standard for public-key encryption (version 2.1). IACR E (2001)

[SLLF15] Sun, X., Li, B., Lu, X., Fang, F.: CCA secure public key encryption scheme based on LWE without gaussian sampling. In: Lin, D., Wang, X.F., Yung, M. (eds.) Inscrypt 2015. LNCS, vol. 9589, pp. 361–378. Springer, Cham (2016). https://doi.org/10.1007/978-3-319-38898-4_21

[Wat05] Waters, B.: Efficient identity-based encryption without random oracles. In: Cramer, R. (ed.) EUROCRYPT 2005. LNCS, vol. 3494, pp. 114–127. Springer, Heidelberg (2005). https://doi.org/10.1007/11426639_7

[Yam17] Yamada, S.: Asymptotically compact adaptively secure lattice IBEs and verifiable random functions via generalized partitioning techniques. In: Katz, J., Shacham, H. (eds.) CRYPTO 2017. LNCS, vol. 10403, pp. 161–193. Springer, Cham (2017). https://doi.org/10.1007/978-3-319-63697-9_6

[ZCZ16] Zhang, J., Chen, Y., Zhang, Z.: Programmable hash functions from lattices: short signatures and IBEs with small key sizes. In: Robshaw, M., Katz, J. (eds.) CRYPTO 2016. LNCS, vol. 9816, pp. 303–332. Springer, Heidelberg (2016). https://doi.org/10.1007/978-3-662-53015-3_11

Compact (Targeted Homomorphic) Inner Product Encryption from LWE

Jie Li[1,2,3], Daode Zhang[1,2,3(✉)], Xianhui Lu[1,2,3], and Kunpeng Wang[1,2,3]

[1] School of Cyber Security, University of Chinese Academy of Sciences,
Beijing, China
[2] State Key Laboratory of Information Security, Institute of Information Engineering,
Chinese Academy of Sciences, Beijing, China
{lijie,zhangdaode,luxianhui,wangkunpeng}@iie.ac.cn
[3] Science and Technology on Communication Security Laboratory, Beijing, China

Abstract. Inner product encryption (IPE) is a public-key encryption mechanism that supports fine-grained access control. Agrawal et al. (ASIACRYPT 2011) proposed the first IPE scheme from the Learning With Errors (LWE) problem. In their scheme, the public parameter size and ciphertext size are $O(un^2 \log^3 n)$ and $O(un \log^3 n)$, respectively. Then, Xagawa (PKC 2013) proposed the improved scheme with public parameter of size $O(un^2 \log^2 n)$ and ciphertext of size $O(un \log^2 n)$.

In this paper, we construct a more compact IPE scheme under the LWE assumption, which has public parameter of size $O(un^2 \log n)$ and ciphertext of size $O(un \log n)$. Thus our scheme improves the size of Xagawa's IPE scheme by a factor of $\log n$.

Inspired by the idea of Brakerski et al. (TCC 2016), we propose a targeted homomorphic IPE (THIPE) scheme based on our IPE scheme. Compared with Brakerski et al.'s scheme, our THIPE scheme has more compact public parameters and ciphertexts. However, our scheme can only apply to the inner product case, while in their scheme the predicate f can be any efficiently computable polynomial.

Keywords: Inner product encryption · Homomorphic encryption
Learning with errors

1 Introduction

Predicate encryption (PE) is a subclass of functional encryption that supports fine-grained access control. In the PE schemes, a receiver corresponding to the secret key sk_f which is associated with predicate f can decrypt the ciphertext c which is associated with the private attribute x if and only if $f(x) = 0$.

The inner product encryption (IPE) was firstly introduced by Katz et al. [10], which is a special case of PE. In the IPE scheme, the attribute x and predicate f are expressed as vectors $\boldsymbol{x}$ and $\boldsymbol{v}$, and $f(\boldsymbol{x}) = 0$ if and only if $\langle \boldsymbol{x}, \boldsymbol{v} \rangle = 0$. IPE has many useful application scenarios, such as it can support subset, conjunction

© Springer International Publishing AG, part of Springer Nature 2018
S. Qing et al. (Eds.): ICICS 2017, LNCS 10631, pp. 132–140, 2018.
https://doi.org/10.1007/978-3-319-89500-0_11

and range queries on encrypted data [8] and polynomial evaluation, CNF/DNF formulas [10].

At first, the IPE constructions [4,10–16] were based on bilinear groups and constructing IPE scheme from other assumption was left as an open problem. Until 2011, Agrawal et al. [2] proposed the first IPE scheme (denoted by AFV11) from the LWE assumption. One of the drawbacks of the scheme is that it has large sizes of public parameter (i.e., $O(un^2 \log^3 n)$) and ciphertext (i.e., $O(un \log^3 n)$) for $q = poly(n)$, where u is the dimension of the attribute vector, n is the security parameter. For efficiency, Xagawa[1] [17] improved the AFV11 IPE scheme and obtained a more compact IPE scheme (denoted by Xag13) with public parameter of size $O(un^2 \log^2 n)$ and ciphertext of size $O(un \log^2 n)$. Whether we can further compress the public parameter and ciphertext size to get a more compact IPE scheme is an interesting problem.

1.1 Our Contribution

In this paper, we mainly focus on the efficiency of the IPE scheme. We construct a selective security IPE scheme from the LWE assumption with compact parameters. Our scheme has smaller public parameter size (i.e., $O(un^2 \log n)$) and ciphertext size (i.e., $O(un \log n)$) for $q = poly(n)$ and improves both the public parameter size and the ciphertext size by a factor of $O(\log n)$ when compared with Xag13.

In addition, we further note that we can add homomorphic property to our IPE scheme. More formally, by using the technique proposed by Brakerski et al. [6], we obtain a targeted homomorphic IPE (THIPE) scheme which has more compact public parameters and ciphertexts than the scheme in [6] when only consider the inner product case. Note that, in Brakerski et al.'s scheme, the predicate f can be any efficiently computable polynomial.

In Table 1, we give a rough comparison of the sizes of public parameter and ciphertext, the modulus q, the approximate factor among the existing IPE schemes from LWE.

Table 1. Comparison of IPE schemes based on LWE.

IPE	Public parameter size	Ciphertext size	q	Approximation factor
AFV11 [2]	$O(un^2 \log^3 n)$	$O(un \log^3 n)$	$u^2 n^{3.5+5\delta} log^{2.5+2\delta} n$	$u^2 n^{4+5\delta} log^{1.5+\delta} n$
Xag13 [17]	$O(un^2 \log^2 n)$	$O(un \log^2 n)$	$u^2 n^{4.5+4\delta} log^{2.5+2\delta} n$	$u^2 n^{5+4\delta} log^{1.5+\delta} n$
This work	$O(un^2 \log n)$	$O(un \log n)$	$u^2 n^{6.5+4\delta} log^{0.5+2\delta} n$	$u^2 n^{7+4\delta} log^{-0.5+\delta} n$

Where u is the dimension of the attribute vector and $\delta > 0$ is a small constant.

1.2 Overview of Our Construction

Here we give the overview of our scheme. We first review the previous IPE scheme for $u = k\ell$ dimension attribute vector $\boldsymbol{x} = (x_{1,1}, \ldots, x_{1\ell}, \ldots, x_{k,1}, \ldots, x_{k,\ell})$ and

---

[1] Note that, when only consider the inner product case, the scheme in [7] is just as same as the scheme of Xagawa [17].

predicate vector $\boldsymbol{v} = (v_{1,1}, \ldots, v_{1\ell}, \ldots, v_{k,1}, \ldots, v_{k,\ell})$. We give a brief description of them and then we present our construction. For simplicity, we use the special case of $k = 1$ to demonstrate, that is $\boldsymbol{x} = (x_1, \ldots, x_\ell)$ and $\boldsymbol{v} = (v_1, \ldots, v_\ell)$.

Our Construction. We construct a compact IPE scheme based on [2,17] by using the technique of [1]. Let $\mathbf{G}_{n,2,m}$ be the gadget matrix with base 2 and matrix size $n \times m$. In our construction, we use two gadget matrices $\mathbf{G}_{n\ell,\ell',m}$ and $\mathbf{G}_{n,2,m}$ with different bases and matrix sizes as the critical tool to improve the efficiency.

In our construction, every public matrix can encode ℓ components of $\boldsymbol{x}$, where $\ell = O(\log n)$. That is, for $\boldsymbol{x} = (x_1, \ldots, x_\ell)$ and the corresponding $\mathbf{X}_i = x_i \mathbf{I}_n$ defined as before, let $\mathbf{X} = [\mathbf{X}_1 | \ldots | \mathbf{X}_\ell] \in \mathbb{Z}_q^{n \times n\ell}$, the encryption lattice is defined as

$$\Lambda_{\boldsymbol{x}} = \Lambda_q(\mathbf{A} | \mathbf{A}_1 + \mathbf{X}\mathbf{G}_{n\ell,\ell',m})$$

The corresponding ciphertext is a vector $CT = (\boldsymbol{c}, \boldsymbol{c}_1) \in (\mathbb{Z}_q^m)^2$.

For predicate vector $\boldsymbol{v} = (v_1, \ldots, v_\ell)$ and the corresponding $\mathbf{V}_i = v_i \mathbf{I}_n$ as before,

let $\mathbf{V} = \begin{pmatrix} v_1 \mathbf{I}_n \\ v_2 \mathbf{I}_n \\ \vdots \\ v_\ell \mathbf{I}_n \end{pmatrix} \in \mathbb{Z}_q^{n\ell \times n}$, we define the mapping $T_v : (\mathbb{Z}_q^m)^2 \to (\mathbb{Z}_q^m)^2$ by

$$T_v(\boldsymbol{c}, \boldsymbol{c}_1) = (\boldsymbol{c}, \boldsymbol{c}_1 \mathbf{G}_{n\ell,\ell',m}^{-1}(\mathbf{V}\mathbf{G}_{n,2,m}))$$

We denote $w = \langle \boldsymbol{x}, \boldsymbol{v} \rangle$ and let $\mathbf{W} = w\mathbf{I}_n$. And $T_v(\boldsymbol{c}, \boldsymbol{c}_1)$ is a vector close to the lattice

$$\Lambda_{v,x} = \Lambda_q(\mathbf{A} | \mathbf{A}_1 \mathbf{G}_{n\ell,\ell',m}^{-1}(\mathbf{V}\mathbf{G}_{n,2,m}) + \mathbf{W}\mathbf{G}_{n,2,m})$$

The secret key $\boldsymbol{r}$ is defined as a short basis of $\Lambda_q^\perp(\mathbf{A} | \mathbf{A}_1 \mathbf{G}_{n\ell,\ell',m}^{-1}(\mathbf{V}\mathbf{G}_{n,2,m}))$, so if $\langle \boldsymbol{x}, \boldsymbol{v} \rangle = 0$, then $\mathbf{W} = \boldsymbol{0}$, and thus the secret key $\boldsymbol{r}$ can decrypt the corresponding ciphertext.

Due to the fact that $n\ell \log_{\ell'} q = O(m) = O(n \log q)$, then $\ell = O(\log \ell')$. And ℓ' is a bit decomposition base of modulus $q = poly(n)$, thus $\ell' = O(n)$ and $\ell = O(\log n)$. So it's obvious that our IPE scheme improves the public parameter and ciphertext size by a factor of $\ell = O(\log n)$.

2 Preliminaries

2.1 Predicate Encryption

Predicate Encryption ([10]). For the set of attribute Σ and the class of the predicate $\mathcal{F}$, a predicate encryption scheme consists four algorithm Setup, KeyGen, Enc, Dec which are PPT algorithms such that:

- Setup uses the security parameter λ and outputs the master public key mpk and master secret key msk.
- KeyGen uses the master secret key msk and a predicate $f \in \mathcal{F}$ and outputs a secret key sk_f for f.
- Enc uses the master public key mpk and a attribute $I \in \Sigma$, outputs a ciphertexts C for message $\mu \in \mathcal{M}$.
- Dec takes as input the ciphertexts C and secret key sk_f. If $f(I) = 0$, it outputs μ; if $f(I) = 1$, it outputs a distinguished symbol $\bot$ with all but negligible probability.

Security. We say a PE scheme is weakly attribute hiding in the selective attribute setting if the adversary can't distinguish $\mathsf{Enc}(mpk, I_1, \mu_1)$ and $\mathsf{Enc}(mpk, I_2, \mu_2)$.

The definition of the weakly attribute hiding security is given in [10].

2.2 Lattices

For positive integers n, m, q, and a matrix $\mathbf{A} \in \mathbb{Z}_q^{n \times m}$, the m-dimensional integer lattices are defined as: $\Lambda_q(\mathbf{A}) = \{\mathbf{y} : \mathbf{y} = \mathbf{A}^{\mathrm{T}}\mathbf{s} \text{ for some } \mathbf{s} \in \mathbb{Z}^n\}$ and $\Lambda_q^{\perp}(\mathbf{A}) = \{\mathbf{y} : \mathbf{A}\mathbf{y} = \mathbf{0} \mod q\}$.

For $\mathbf{x} \in \Lambda$, define the Gaussian function $\rho_{s,\mathbf{c}}(\mathbf{x})$ over $\Lambda \subseteq \mathbb{Z}^m$ centered at $\mathbf{c} \in \mathbb{R}^m$ with parameter $s > 0$ as $\rho_{s,\mathbf{c}}(\mathbf{x}) = \exp(-\pi\|\mathbf{x} - \mathbf{c}\|/s^2)$. Let $\rho_{s,\mathbf{c}}(\Lambda) = \sum_{\mathbf{x} \in \Lambda} \rho_{s,\mathbf{c}}(\mathbf{x})$, and define the discrete Gaussian distribution over Λ as $\mathcal{D}_{\Lambda,s,\mathbf{c}}(\mathbf{x}) = \frac{\rho_{s,\mathbf{c}}(\mathbf{x})}{\rho_{s,\mathbf{c}}(\Lambda)}$, where $\mathbf{x} \in \Lambda$. For simplicity, $\rho_{s,0}$ and $\mathcal{D}_{\Lambda,s,0}$ are abbreviated as ρ_s and $\mathcal{D}_{\Lambda,s}$, respectively.

Lemma 1. *Let p, q, n, m be positive integers with $q \geq p \geq 2$ and q prime. There exists PPT algorithms such that*

- *[3,5]: $\mathsf{TrapGen}(n, m, q)$ a randomized algorithm that, when $m \geq 6n\lceil\log q\rceil$, outputs a pair $(\mathbf{A}, \mathbf{T_A}) \in \mathbb{Z}_q^{n \times m} \times \mathbb{Z}^{m \times m}$ such that $\mathbf{A}$ is statistically close to uniform in $\mathbb{Z}_q^{n \times m}$ and $\mathbf{T_A}$ is a basis of $\Lambda_q^{\perp}(\mathbf{A})$, satisfying $\|\widetilde{\mathbf{T_A}}\| \leq \mathcal{O}(\sqrt{n \log q})$ with overwhelming probability.*
- *[9]: $\mathsf{SampleLeft}(\mathbf{A}, \mathbf{B}, \mathbf{T_A}, \mathbf{u}, s)$ a randomized algorithm that, given a full rank matrix $\mathbf{A} \in \mathbb{Z}_q^{n \times m}$, a matrix $\mathbf{B} \in \mathbb{Z}_q^{n \times m}$, a basis $\mathbf{T_A}$ of $\Lambda_q^{\perp}(\mathbf{A})$, a vector $\mathbf{u} \in \mathbb{Z}_q^n$ and $\sigma \geq \|\widetilde{\mathbf{T_A}}\| \cdot \omega(\sqrt{\log(2m)})$, then outputs a vector $\mathbf{r} \in \mathbb{Z}_q^{2m}$ distributed statistically close to $\mathcal{D}_{\Lambda_q^{\mathbf{u}}(\mathbf{F}),s}$ where $\mathbf{F} = [\mathbf{A}|\mathbf{B}]$.*

3 Compact Inner Product Encryption from LWE

In this section, we propose a compact IPE scheme from LWE problem. For attribute vector $\mathbf{x} = (\mathbb{Z}_q^{\ell})^k$ and predicate vector $\mathbf{v} = (\mathbb{Z}_q^{\ell})^k$, we use $\mathbf{x} = (\mathbf{x}_1, \ldots, \mathbf{x}_k)$ and $\mathbf{v} = (\mathbf{v}_1, \ldots, \mathbf{v}_k)$ to denote them respectively and each $\mathbf{x}_i = (x_{i,1}, \ldots, x_{i,\ell}), \mathbf{v}_i = (v_{i,1}, \ldots, v_{i,\ell}) \in \mathbb{Z}_q^{\ell}$.

3.1   The Construction

Let λ be the security parameter and $u = k\ell$ be the dimension of predicate and attribute vectors. Set lattice parameters $n = n(\lambda), m = m(\lambda), q = q(\lambda)$ and Gaussian parameters $\alpha = \alpha(\lambda), s = s(\lambda)$, define $\ell' = 2^\ell$.

- IPE.Setup(1^λ): On input the security parameter λ, do:
  1. Use the algorithm TrapGen(n, m, q) to generate a matrix $\mathbf{A} \in \mathbb{Z}_q^{n \times m}$ and its trapdoor $\mathbf{T_A}$.
  2. Choose k uniformly random matrix $\mathbf{A}_i \in \mathbb{Z}_q^{n \times m}$ for $i = 1, \ldots, k$ and sample a uniformly random matrix $\mathbf{P} \in \mathbb{Z}_q^{n \times m}$.

  Output $mpk = (\mathbf{A}, \{\mathbf{A}_i\}_{i \in \{1, \ldots, k\}}, \mathbf{P})$ and $msk = \mathbf{T_A}$.
- IPE.KeyGen($mpk, msk, \boldsymbol{x}$): On input the master public key mpk and master secret key msk, and a predicate vector $\boldsymbol{v} = (\boldsymbol{v}_1, \ldots, \boldsymbol{v}_k) \in (\mathbb{Z}_q^\ell)^k$ where $\boldsymbol{v}_i = (v_{i,1}, \ldots, v_{i,\ell}) \in \mathbb{Z}_q^\ell$, do:

  1. For $i = 1, \ldots, \ell$, compute the matrices $\mathbf{V}_i' := \begin{pmatrix} v_{i,1}\mathbf{I}_n \\ v_{i,2}\mathbf{I}_n \\ \vdots \\ v_{i,\ell}\mathbf{I}_n \end{pmatrix} \in \mathbb{Z}_q^{\ell n \times n}$, and let

  $$\mathbf{V}_i := \mathbf{G}_{n\ell, \ell', m}^{-1}(\mathbf{V}_i' \cdot \mathbf{G}_{n,2,m})$$
  2. Define the matrices:

  $$\mathbf{B} := \sum_{i=1}^k \mathbf{A}_i \mathbf{V}_i \in \mathbb{Z}_q^{n \times m}$$

  3. Using msk to compute $\mathbf{U} \leftarrow$ SampleLeft($\mathbf{A}, \mathbf{B}, \mathbf{T_A}, \mathbf{P}, s$), it holds that $[\mathbf{A}|\mathbf{B}] \cdot \mathbf{U} = \mathbf{P} \mod q$, for $\mathbf{U} \in \mathbb{Z}_q^{2m \times m}$.

  Output the secret key $sk_v = \mathbf{U}$.
- IPE.Enc($mpk, \boldsymbol{x}, \mu$): On input the master public key mpk, the attribute vector $\boldsymbol{x} = (\boldsymbol{x}_1, \ldots, \boldsymbol{x}_k) \in (\mathbb{Z}_q^\ell)^k$, and a message $\mu \in \{0, 1\}$, do:
  1. For $i = 1, \ldots, k$, set the matrices $\mathbf{X}_i = [x_{i,1}\mathbf{I}_n | x_{i,2}\mathbf{I}_n | \ldots | x_{i,\ell}\mathbf{I}_n] \in \mathbb{Z}_q^{n \times n\ell}$.
  2. Choose a uniformly random vector $\boldsymbol{s} \in \mathbb{Z}_q^n$, and sample two noise vectors $\boldsymbol{e}, \boldsymbol{e}' \leftarrow \mathcal{D}_{\mathbb{Z}_q^m}$.
  3. For $i = 1, \ldots, k$, choose these random matrices $\mathbf{R}_i \in \{-1, 1\}^{m \times m}$. Then define noise vectors $\boldsymbol{e}_i^{\mathrm{T}} := \boldsymbol{e}^{\mathrm{T}}\mathbf{R}_i$.
  4. For $i = 1, \ldots, k$, compute the ciphertext

  $$\boldsymbol{c} := \boldsymbol{s}^{\mathrm{T}}\mathbf{A} + \boldsymbol{e}^{\mathrm{T}}, \boldsymbol{c}_i := \boldsymbol{s}^{\mathrm{T}}(\mathbf{A}_i + \mathbf{X}_i\mathbf{G}_{n\ell, \ell', m}) + \boldsymbol{e}_i^{\mathrm{T}}, \boldsymbol{c}' := \boldsymbol{s}^{\mathrm{T}}\mathbf{P} + \boldsymbol{e}' + (0, \ldots, 0, \lfloor\tfrac{q}{2}\rceil\mu)$$

  Output the ciphertext $CT := (\boldsymbol{c}, \{\boldsymbol{c}_i\}_{i \in \{1, \ldots k\}}, \boldsymbol{c}')$
- IPE.Dec(mpk, CT, sk_v): On input the master public key, a secret key $sk_v = \mathbf{U}$ for predicate vector $\boldsymbol{v}$ and the ciphertext $CT := (\boldsymbol{c}, \{\boldsymbol{c}_i\}_{i \in \{1, \ldots k\}}, \boldsymbol{c}')$, do:
  1. For $i = 1, \ldots, k$, compute the vector $\boldsymbol{c}_v = \sum_{i=1}^k \boldsymbol{c}_i \mathbf{V}_i$.
  2. Compute $\boldsymbol{z} \leftarrow \boldsymbol{c}' - [\boldsymbol{c}|\boldsymbol{c}_v] \cdot \mathbf{U} \mod q$.

  Output $\lfloor\tfrac{z_m}{q/2}\rceil \in \{0, 1\}$, if $\|(z_1, \ldots, z_{m-1})\|_\infty < q/4$; otherwise, output $\perp$.

3.2 Parameters

In Table 2, we set the parameters of the IPE scheme above.

Table 2. IPE parameters setting.

Variable	Description	Parameters setting
λ	Security parameter	
n	Row dimension of PK matrix	$n = \lambda$
m	Column dimension of PK matrix	$m = n^{1+\delta}$
q	Modulus	$q = k^2 n^{6.5+4\delta} log^{2.5+2\delta} n$
$k\ell$	Dimension of attribute vector	$\ell = \log n$
ℓ'	Base of gadget matrix $\mathbf{G}_{n\ell,\ell',m}$	$\ell' = n$
α	Gaussian parameter of error	$\alpha = \sqrt{n} log^{1+\delta} n$
s	Parameter of SampleLeft and SampleRight	$s = kn^{2.5+1.5\delta} log^{1.5+\delta} n$

3.3 Security

Theorem 1. *Suppose that $m \geq 6n \log q$, assuming the hardness of the decisional LWE problem, then the above inner product encryption scheme is weakly attribute hiding.*

4 A Single Targeted Homomorphic Compact IPE Scheme

In this section, we propose our single targeted homomorphic compact inner product encryption scheme from LWE. Inspired by the idea of [6], we add homomorphic property to our IPE scheme and get compact ciphertext and public parameter size. The construction of the scheme is as follows:

4.1 The THIPE Construction

Let λ be the security parameter and $u = k\ell$ be the length of predicate and attribute vectors. Set lattice parameters $n = n(\lambda), m = m(\lambda), q = q(\lambda)$ and Gaussian parameters $\alpha = \alpha(\lambda), s = s(\lambda)$, define $\ell' = 2^\ell$ and $M = (2m + 1)\lceil \log q \rceil$.

- THIPE.Setup(1^λ): On input a security parameter λ, do:
  1. Use the algorithm TrapGen(n, m, q) to generate a matrix $\mathbf{A}$ and its trapdoor $\mathbf{T_A}$.
  2. Choose $k+1$ uniformly random matrix $\mathbf{A}_i \in \mathbb{Z}_q^{n \times m}$ for $i = 0, 1, \ldots, k$ and sample a uniformly random vector $\boldsymbol{u} \in \mathbb{Z}_q^n$.

  Output $mpk = (\mathbf{A}, \mathbf{A}_0, \{\mathbf{A}_i\}_{i \in \{1,\ldots,k\}}, \boldsymbol{u})$ and $msk = \mathbf{T_A}$.

- THIPE.KeyGen($mpk, msk, \boldsymbol{x}$): On input the master public key mpk and master secret key msk, and a predicate vector $\boldsymbol{v} = (\boldsymbol{v}_1, \ldots, \boldsymbol{v}_k) \in (\mathbb{Z}_q^\ell)^k$ where $\boldsymbol{v}_i = (v_{i,1}, \ldots, v_{i,\ell}) \in \mathbb{Z}_q^\ell$, do:

  1. For $i = 1, \ldots, \ell$, compute the matrices $\mathbf{V}_i' := \begin{pmatrix} v_{i,1}\mathbf{I}_n \\ v_{i,2}\mathbf{I}_n \\ \vdots \\ v_{i,\ell}\mathbf{I}_n \end{pmatrix} \in \mathbb{Z}_q^{\ell n \times n}$, and let

     $\mathbf{V}_i := \mathbf{G}_{n\ell,\ell',m}^{-1}(\mathbf{V}_i' \cdot \mathbf{G}_{n,2,m})$
  2. Define the matrices:

     $$\mathbf{B} := \sum_{i=1}^{k} \mathbf{A}_i \mathbf{V}_i \in \mathbb{Z}_q^{n \times m}$$

  3. Using msk to compute $\boldsymbol{r}_1 \leftarrow \mathsf{SampleLeft}(\mathbf{A}, \mathbf{A}_0 + \mathbf{B}, \mathbf{T_A}, \boldsymbol{u}, s)$, it holds that $[\mathbf{A}|\mathbf{A}_0 + \mathbf{B}] \cdot \boldsymbol{r}_1 = \boldsymbol{u} \mod q$. For $\boldsymbol{r}^{\mathrm{T}} = [-\boldsymbol{r}_1^{\mathrm{T}}, 1]$, we have that $[\mathbf{A}|\mathbf{A}_0 + \mathbf{B}|\boldsymbol{u}] \cdot \boldsymbol{r} = \boldsymbol{0}$.

  Output the secret key $sk_v = \boldsymbol{r}$.
- THIPE.Enc($mpk, \boldsymbol{x}, \mu$): On input the master public key mpk, the attribute vector $\boldsymbol{x} = (\boldsymbol{x}_1, \ldots, \boldsymbol{x}_k) \in (\mathbb{Z}_q^\ell)^k$, and a message $\mu \in \{0, 1\}$, do:

  1. For $i = 1, \ldots, k$, set the matrices $\mathbf{X}_i = [x_{i,1}\mathbf{I}_n | x_{i,2}\mathbf{I}_n | \ldots | x_{i,\ell}\mathbf{I}_n] \in \mathbb{Z}_q^{n \times n\ell}$.
  2. Choose a uniformly random vector $\mathbf{S} \in \mathbb{Z}_q^{n \times M}$, and sample a noise matrix $\mathbf{E} \leftarrow \mathcal{D}_{\mathbb{Z}_q^{m \times M}, \alpha}$ and a noise vector $\boldsymbol{e} \leftarrow \mathcal{D}_{\mathbb{Z}_q^m, \alpha}$.
  3. For $i = 0, 1, \ldots, k$, choose these random matrices $\mathbf{R}_i \in \{-1, 1\}^{m \times m}$. Then define noise vectors $\mathbf{E}_i := \mathbf{R}_i^{\mathrm{T}} \mathbf{E}$.
  4. Compute the ciphertext as follows:

     $$\begin{pmatrix} \mathbf{C_A} \\ \mathbf{C}_0 \\ \mathbf{C_u} \end{pmatrix} = \begin{pmatrix} \mathbf{A}^{\mathrm{T}} \\ \mathbf{A}_0^{\mathrm{T}} \\ \boldsymbol{u}^{\mathrm{T}} \end{pmatrix} \cdot \mathbf{S} + \begin{pmatrix} \mathbf{E} \\ \mathbf{E}_0 \\ \boldsymbol{e} \end{pmatrix} + \mu \mathbf{G}_{2m+1,2,M}$$

  And for all $i = 1, \ldots, k$, we compute:

  $$\mathbf{C}_i = (\mathbf{A}_i + \mathbf{X}_i \mathbf{G}_{n\ell,\ell',m})^{\mathrm{T}} \mathbf{S} + \mathbf{E}_i$$

  Output the ciphertext $CT := (\mathbf{C_A}, \mathbf{C}_0, \mathbf{C_u}, \{\mathbf{C}_i\}_{i \in \{1, \ldots, k\}})$.
- THIPE.Trans($mpk, CT, \boldsymbol{v}$): For predicate vector $\boldsymbol{v}$ and ciphertext CT which corresponds to attribute $\boldsymbol{x}$, such that $\langle \boldsymbol{x}, \boldsymbol{v} \rangle = 0$. The evaluator then computes:

  $$\mathbf{C}_v = \sum_{i=1}^{k} \mathbf{V}_i^{\mathrm{T}} \mathbf{C}_i$$

Then the evaluator sets:

$$\mathbf{C} = \begin{pmatrix} \mathbf{C_A} \\ \mathbf{C}_0 + \mathbf{C}_v \\ \boldsymbol{c_u} \end{pmatrix} \in \mathbb{Z}_q^{(2m+1) \times M}$$

The ciphertext $\mathbf{C}$ is the final ciphertext that used to do homomorphic evaluation.

- THIPE.TEval($g, \mathbf{C}_1, \ldots, \mathbf{C}_t$): The ciphertexts $\mathbf{C}_i$ which are the outputs of THIPE.Trans are corresponding to the same predicate vector v that the evaluator knows in advance, it outputs $\mathbf{C}_g = \mathsf{Eval}(g, \mathbf{C}_1, \ldots, \mathbf{C}_t)$. In the process of evaluation, it computes NAND gate as:

$$\mathrm{NAND}(\mathbf{C}_1, \mathbf{C}_2) = \mathbf{G}_{2m+1,2,M} - \mathbf{C}_1(\mathbf{G}_{2m+1,2,M}^{-1}\mathbf{C}_2)$$

- THIPE.Dec($mpk, \mathbf{C}_g, sk_v$): On input the master public key, a secret key $sk_v = r$ for predicate vector v and the ciphertext $\mathbf{C}_g$, do:
  1. For $b = (0, \ldots, 0, \lfloor q/2 \rfloor)^{\mathrm{T}}$, compute $z \leftarrow r^{\mathrm{T}}\mathbf{C}_g\mathbf{G}_{2m+1,2,M}^{-1}(b) \mod q$
  2. Output 0, if $|z| < q/4$; otherwise, output 1.

5 Conclusion

In this work, we built a compact IPE scheme and a targeted homomorphic compact IPE scheme. We make use of two gadget matrix $\mathbf{G}_{n\ell,\ell',m}$ and $\mathbf{G}_{n,2,m}$ and decrease the public parameter size to $O(un^2 \log n)$, ciphertext size to $O(un \log n)$. Our IPE scheme improve the public parameters by a factor of $O(\log n)$ compared with [17].

Acknowledgments. We thank the anonymous ICICS'2017 reviewers for their helpful comments. This work is supported by the National Basic Research Program of China (973 project, No. 2014CB340603) and the National Nature Science Foundation of China (No. 61672030).

References

1. Apon, D., Fan, X., Liu, F.: Compact identity based encryption from LWE. http://eprint.iacr.org/2016/125
2. Agrawal, S., Freeman, D.M., Vaikuntanathan, V.: Functional encryption for inner product predicates from learning with errors. In: Lee, D.H., Wang, X. (eds.) ASIACRYPT 2011. LNCS, vol. 7073, pp. 21–40. Springer, Heidelberg (2011). https://doi.org/10.1007/978-3-642-25385-0_2
3. Ajtai, M.: Generating hard instances of the short basis problem. In: Wiedermann, J., van Emde Boas, P., Nielsen, M. (eds.) ICALP 1999. LNCS, vol. 1644, pp. 1–9. Springer, Heidelberg (1999). https://doi.org/10.1007/3-540-48523-6_1
4. Attrapadung, N., Libert, B.: Functional encryption for inner product: achieving constant-size ciphertexts with adaptive security or support for negation. In: Nguyen, P.Q., Pointcheval, D. (eds.) PKC 2010. LNCS, vol. 6056, pp. 384–402. Springer, Heidelberg (2010). https://doi.org/10.1007/978-3-642-13013-7_23
5. Alwen, J., Peikert, C.: Generating shorter bases for hard random lattices. Theory Comput. Syst. **48**, 535–553 (2011)
6. Brakerski, Z., Cash, D., Tsabary, R., Wee, H.: Targeted homomorphic attribute-based encryption. In: Hirt, M., Smith, A. (eds.) TCC 2016. LNCS, vol. 9986, pp. 330–360. Springer, Heidelberg (2016). https://doi.org/10.1007/978-3-662-53644-5_13

7. Boneh, D., Gentry, C., Gorbunov, S., Halevi, S., Nikolaenko, V., Segev, G., Vaikuntanathan, V., Vinayagamurthy, D.: Fully key-homomorphic encryption, arithmetic circuit ABE and compact Garbled circuits. In: Nguyen, P.Q., Oswald, E. (eds.) EUROCRYPT 2014. LNCS, vol. 8441, pp. 533–556. Springer, Heidelberg (2014). https://doi.org/10.1007/978-3-642-55220-5_30

8. Boneh, D., Waters, B.: Conjunctive, subset, and range queries on encrypted data. In: Vadhan, S.P. (ed.) TCC 2007. LNCS, vol. 4392, pp. 535–554. Springer, Heidelberg (2007). https://doi.org/10.1007/978-3-540-70936-7_29

9. Cash, D., Hofheinz, D., Kiltz, E., Peikert, C.: Bonsai trees, or how to delegate a lattice basis. In: Gilbert, H. (ed.) EUROCRYPT 2010. LNCS, vol. 6110, pp. 523–552. Springer, Heidelberg (2010). https://doi.org/10.1007/978-3-642-13190-5_27

10. Katz, J., Sahai, A., Waters, B.: Predicate encryption supporting disjunctions, polynomial equations, and inner products. In: Smart, N. (ed.) EUROCRYPT 2008. LNCS, vol. 4965, pp. 146–162. Springer, Heidelberg (2008). https://doi.org/10.1007/978-3-540-78967-3_9

11. Lewko, A., Okamoto, T., Sahai, A., Takashima, K., Waters, B.: Fully secure functional encryption: attribute-based encryption and (hierarchical) inner product encryption. In: Gilbert, H. (ed.) EUROCRYPT 2010. LNCS, vol. 6110, pp. 62–91. Springer, Heidelberg (2010). https://doi.org/10.1007/978-3-642-13190-5_4

12. Okamoto, T., Takashima, K.: Hierarchical predicate encryption for inner-products. In: Matsui, M. (ed.) ASIACRYPT 2009. LNCS, vol. 5912, pp. 214–231. Springer, Heidelberg (2009). https://doi.org/10.1007/978-3-642-10366-7_13

13. Okamoto, T., Takashima, K.: Fully secure functional encryption with general relations from the decisional linear assumption. In: Rabin, T. (ed.) CRYPTO 2010. LNCS, vol. 6223, pp. 191–208. Springer, Heidelberg (2010). https://doi.org/10.1007/978-3-642-14623-7_11

14. Okamoto, T., Takashima, K.: Achieving short ciphertexts or short secret-keys for adaptively secure general inner-product encryption. In: Lin, D., Tsudik, G., Wang, X. (eds.) CANS 2011. LNCS, vol. 7092, pp. 138–159. Springer, Heidelberg (2011). https://doi.org/10.1007/978-3-642-25513-7_11

15. Okamoto, T., Takashima, K.: Adaptively attribute-hiding (hierarchical) inner product encryption. In: Pointcheval, D., Johansson, T. (eds.) EUROCRYPT 2012. LNCS, vol. 7237, pp. 591–608. Springer, Heidelberg (2012). https://doi.org/10.1007/978-3-642-29011-4_35

16. Park, J.-H.: Inner-product encryption under standard assumptions. Des. Codes Crypt. 58, 235–257 (2011)

17. Xagawa, K.: Improved (Hierarchical) Inner-Product Encryption from Lattices. In: Kurosawa, K., Hanaoka, G. (eds.) PKC 2013. LNCS, vol. 7778, pp. 235–252. Springer, Heidelberg (2013). https://doi.org/10.1007/978-3-642-36362-7_15

Compact Inner Product Encryption
from LWE

Zhedong Wang[1,2], Xiong Fan[3(✉)], and Mingsheng Wang[1,2]

[1] State Key Laboratory of Information Security,
Institute of Information Engineering, Chinese Academy of Sciences, Beijing, China
{wangzhedong,wangmingsheng}@iie.ac.cn
[2] School of Cyber Security, University of Chinese Academy of Sciences,
Beijing, China
[3] Cornell University, Ithaca, NY, USA
xfan@cs.cornell.edu

Abstract. Predicate encryption provides fine-grained access control and has attractive applications. In this paper, We construct an compact inner product encryption scheme from the standard Learning with Errors (LWE) assumption that has compact public-key and achieves weakly attribute-hiding in the standard model. In particular, our scheme only needs two public matrices to support inner product over vector space $\mathbb{Z}_q^{\log \lambda}$, and $(\lambda/\log \lambda)$ public matrices to support vector space $\mathbb{Z}_q^\lambda$.

Our construction is the first compact functional encryption scheme based on lattice that goes beyond the very recent optimizations of public parameters in identity-based encryption setting. The main technique in our compact IPE scheme is a novel combination of IPE scheme of Agrawal, Freeman and Vaikuntanathan (Asiacrypt 2011), fully homomorphic encryption of Gentry, Sahai and Waters (Crypto 2013) and vector encoding schemes of Apon, Fan and Liu (Eprint 2017).

1 Introduction

Encryption has traditionally been regarded as a way to ensure confidentiality of an end-to-end communication. However, with the emergence of complex networks and cloud computing, recently the crypto community has been re-thinking the notion of encryption to address security concerns that arise in these more complex environments. *Functional encryption* [10,21], generalized from identity based encryption [8,23] and attribute based encryption [7,18], provides a satisfying solutions to this problem in theory. Two features provided by functional

Z. Wang and M. Wang—This work was supported by the National Science Foundation of China (No. 61772516).

X. Fan—This material is based upon work supported by IBM under Agreement 4915013672. Any opinions, findings, and conclusions or recommendations expressed in this material are those of the author(s) and do not necessarily reflect the views of the sponsors.

S. Qing et al. (Eds.): ICICS 2017, LNCS 10631, pp. 141–153, 2018.
https://doi.org/10.1007/978-3-319-89500-0_12

encryption are fine-grained access and computing on encrypted data. The fine-grained access part is formalized as a cryptographic notion, named *predicate encryption* [11,19]. In predicate encryption system, each ciphertext ct is associated with an attribute a while each secret key sk is associated with a predicate f. A user holding the key sk can decrypt ciphertext ct if and only if $f(a) = 0$. Moreover, the attribute a is kept hidden.

With several significant improvements on quantum computing, the community is working intensively on developing applications whose security holds even against quantum attacks. Lattice-based cryptography, the most promising candidate against quantum attacks, has matured significantly since the early works of Ajtai [3] and Regev [22]. Most cryptographic primitives, ranging from basic public-key encryption (PKE) [22] to more advanced schemes e.g., identity-based encryption (IBE) [1,12], attribute-based encryption (ABE) [9,17], fully-homomorphic encryption (FHE) [13], etc., can be built from now canonical lattice hardness assumptions, such as Regev's Learning with Errors (LWE). From the above facts, we can draw the conclusion that our understanding about instantiating different cryptographic primitives based on lattices is quite well. However, for improving the efficiency of existent lattice-based construction, e.g. reducing the size of public parameters and ciphertexts, or simplifying the decryption algorithm, our understanding is limited. Besides the theoretical interests in shrinking the size of ciphertext, as the main motivation of studying functional encryption comes from its potential deployment in complex networks and cloud computing, thus the size of transmitted data is a bottleneck of current lattice-based constructions. Combining all these, this brings us to the following open question:

Can we optimize the size of public parameters and ciphertexts of other functional encryption scheme beyond identity based encryption?

1.1 Our Contributions

We positively answer the above question by proposing the first lattice-based compact inner product encryption (IPE). Roughly speaking, in an IPE scheme, the secret key sk is associated with a predicate vector $v \in \mathbb{Z}_q^t$ and the ciphertext is associated with an attribute vector $w \in \mathbb{Z}_q^t$. The decryption works if and only if the inner product $\langle v, w \rangle = 0$. Despite this apparently restrictive structure, inner product predicates can support conjunction, subset and range queries on encrypted data [11], as well as disjunctions, polynomial evaluation, and CNF and DNF formulas [19]. Our construction can be summarized in the following informal theorem:

Theorem 1.1 (Main). *Under the standard Learning with Errors assumption, there is an IPE scheme satisfying weak attribute-hiding property for predicate/attribute vector of length $t = \log n$, where (1) the modulus q is a prime of size polynomial in the security parameter n, (2) ciphertexts consist of a vector in $\mathbb{Z}_q^{2m+1}$, where m is the lattice column dimension, and (3) the public parameters consists two matrices in $\mathbb{Z}_q^{n \times m}$ and a vector in $\mathbb{Z}_q^n$.*

Remark 1.2. Our technique only allows us to prove a weak form of anonymity ("attribute hiding"). Specifically, given a ciphertext ct and a number of keys that do not decrypt ct, the user cannot determine the attribute associated with ct. In the strong form of attribute hiding, the user cannot determine the attribute associated with ct even when given keys that do decrypt ct. The weakened form of attribute hiding we do achieve is nonetheless more that is required for ABE and should be sufficient for many applications of PE. See Sect. 2 for more detail.

We can also extend our compact IPE construction to support $t = \mathsf{poly}(n)$-length attribute vectors. Let $t' = t/\log n$, our IPE construction supporting $\mathsf{poly}(n)$-length vectors can be stated in the following corollary:

Corollary 1.3. *Under the standard Learning with Errors assumption, there is an IPE scheme with weak attribute-hiding property supporting predicate/attribute vector of length $t = \mathsf{poly}(n)$, where (1) the modulus q is a prime of size polynomial in the security parameter n, (2) ciphertexts consist of a vector in $\mathbb{Z}_q^{(t'+1)m+1}$, where m is the lattice column dimension and (3) the public parameters consists $(t' + 1)$ matrices in $\mathbb{Z}_q^{n \times m}$ and a vector in $\mathbb{Z}_q^n$.*

In addition to reducing the size of public parameters and ciphertexts, our decryption algorithm is computed in an Single-Instruction-Multiple-Data (SIMD) manner. In prior works [2,24], the decryption computes the inner product between the predicate vector and ciphertext by (1) decomposing the predicate vector, (2) multiplying-then-adding the corresponding vector bit and ciphertext, entry-by-entry. Our efficient decryption algorithm achieves the inner product by just one vector-matrix multiplication.

1.2   Our Techniques

Our high-level approach to compact inner product encryption from LWE begins by revisiting the first lattice-based IPE construction [2] and the novel fully homomorphic encryption proposed recently by Gentry et al. [15].

The Agrawal-Freeman-Vaikuntanathan IPE. We first briefly review the construction of IPE in [2]. Their construction relies on the algebraic structure of ABB-IBE [1] to solve "lattice matching" problem. Lattice matching means the lattice structure computed in decryption algorithm matches the structure used in key generation, and since the secret key is a *short* trapdoor of the desired lattice, thus the decryption succeeds. To encode a predicate vector $v \in \mathbb{Z}_q^t$ according to [2], the key generation first computes the r-ary decomposition of each entry of v as $v_i = \sum_{j=0}^k v_{ij} r^j$, and constructs the v-specific lattice as

$$[\mathbf{A}|\mathbf{A}_v] = [\mathbf{A}|\sum_{i=1}^t \sum_{j=0}^k v_{ij} \mathbf{A}_{ij}]$$

by "mixing" a *long* public matrices $(\mathbf{A}, \{\mathbf{A}_{ij}\}) \in \mathbb{Z}_q^{n \times m}$. The secret key sk_v is a short trapdoor of lattice $\Lambda_q^{\perp}([\mathbf{A}| \sum_{i=1}^{t} \sum_{j=0}^{k} v_{ij} \mathbf{A}_{ij}])$. To encode an attribute vector $\boldsymbol{w} \in \mathbb{Z}_q^t$, for $i \in [t], j \in [k]$, construct the $\boldsymbol{w}$-specific vector as

$$\boldsymbol{c}_{ij} = \boldsymbol{s}^{\mathsf{T}} (\mathbf{A}_{ij} + r^j w_i \mathbf{B}) + \mathsf{noise}$$

for a randomly chosen vector $\boldsymbol{s} \in \mathbb{Z}_q^n$ and a public matrix $\mathbf{B} \in \mathbb{Z}_q^{n \times m}$. To reduce the noise growth in the inner produce computation, decryption only needs to multiply-then-add the r-ary representation of v_{ij} to its corresponding $\boldsymbol{c}_{ij}$, as

$$\sum_{i=1}^{t} \sum_{j=0}^{k} v_{ij} \boldsymbol{r}_{ij} = \boldsymbol{s}^{\mathsf{T}} (\sum_{i=1}^{t} \sum_{j=0}^{k} v_{ij} \mathbf{A}_{ij} + \langle \boldsymbol{v}, \boldsymbol{w} \rangle \mathbf{B}) + \mathsf{noise}$$

when $\langle \boldsymbol{v}, \boldsymbol{w} \rangle = 0$, the $(\langle \boldsymbol{v}, \boldsymbol{w} \rangle \mathbf{B})$ part vanishes, thus the lattice computed after inner produce matches the $\mathbf{A}_v$ part in the key generation. Then the secret key sk_v can be used to decrypt the ciphertext. Therefore, the number of matrices in public parameters or vectors in ciphertext is quasilinear in the dimension of vectors.

Using GSW-FHE to compute inner product. Recent progress in fully homomorphic encryption [15] makes us re-think the process of computing inner product. We wonder whether we can use GSW-FHE [15] along with its simplification [4] to simplify the computing procedure. Recall ciphertext of message $x \in \mathbb{Z}_q$ in GSW-FHE can be view in the form $\mathsf{ct}_x = \mathbf{AR} + x\mathbf{G}$, where $\mathbf{A} \in \mathbb{Z}_q^{n \times m}$ is a LWE matrix, $\mathbf{R} \in \mathbb{Z}_q^{m \times m}$ is a random small matrix and $\mathbf{G}$ is the "gadget matrix" as first (explicitly) introduced in the work [20]. The salient point is that there is an efficiently computable function $\mathbf{G}^{-1}$, so that (1) $\mathsf{ct}_x \cdot \mathbf{G}^{-1}(y\mathbf{G}) = \mathsf{ct}_{xy}$, and (2) each entry in matrix $\mathbf{G}^{-1}(y\mathbf{G})$ is just 0 or 1, and thus has small norm. These two nice properties can shrink the size of public parameters (ciphertext) from quasilinear to linear. In particular, to encoding a predicate vector $\boldsymbol{v} \in \mathbb{Z}_q^t$, we construct the $\boldsymbol{v}$-specific lattice as

$$[\mathbf{A}|\mathbf{A}_v] = [\mathbf{A}| \sum_{i=1}^{t} \mathbf{A}_i \mathbf{G}^{-1}(v_i \mathbf{G})]$$

where the number of public matrices is $t + 1$. To encode an attribute vector $\boldsymbol{w} \in \mathbb{Z}_q^t$, for $i \in [t]$, construct the $\boldsymbol{w}$-specific vector as

$$\boldsymbol{c}_i = \boldsymbol{s}^{\mathsf{T}} (\mathbf{A}_i + w_i \mathbf{G}) + \mathsf{noise}$$

Then, we can compute the inner product as

$$\sum_{i=1}^{t} \boldsymbol{c}_i \cdot \mathbf{G}^{-1}(v_i \mathbf{G}) = \boldsymbol{s}^{\mathsf{T}} (\sum_{i=1}^{t} \mathbf{A}_i \mathbf{G}^{-1}(v_i \mathbf{G}) + \langle \boldsymbol{v}, \boldsymbol{w} \rangle \mathbf{G}) + \mathsf{noise}$$

Since $\mathbf{G}^{-1}(v_i \mathbf{G})$ is small norm, the decryption succeeds when $\langle \boldsymbol{v}, \boldsymbol{w} \rangle = 0$.

Achieving public parameters of two matrices. Our final step is to bring the size of public parameters (or ciphertext) to constant for $(t = \log \lambda)$-length vectors. Inspired by recent work [6] in optimizing size of public parameters in the IBE setting, we use their vector encoding method to further optimize our IPE construction. The vector encoding for encoding $\boldsymbol{v} \in \mathbb{Z}_q^t$ is

$$\mathbf{E}_{\boldsymbol{v}} = \left[v_1 \mathbf{I}_n | \cdots | v_t \mathbf{I}_n \right] \cdot \mathbf{G}_{tn,\ell,m}$$

where $\mathbf{G}_{tn,\ell,m} \in \mathbb{Z}_q^{tn \times m}$ is the generalized gadget matrix introduced in [6,20]. The dimension of this generalized gadget matrix $tn \times tn \log_\ell m$. By setting $t = \log q$ and $\ell = n$, we can obtain the similar column dimension as origin gadget matrix, i.e. $O(n \log q)$. Then the $\boldsymbol{v}$-specific lattice becomes

$$\mathbf{A}_{\boldsymbol{v}} = \mathbf{A}_1 \cdot \mathbf{G}_{dn,\ell,m}^{-1} \left(\begin{bmatrix} v_1 \mathbf{I}_n \\ \vdots \\ v_d \mathbf{I}_n \end{bmatrix} \cdot \mathbf{G}_{n,2,m} \right)$$

and the $\boldsymbol{w}$-specific ciphertext becomes

$$\boldsymbol{c} = \boldsymbol{s}^\mathsf{T} (\mathbf{A}_1 + \mathbf{E}_{\boldsymbol{w}}) + \mathsf{noise}$$

The inner product can be computed in an SIMD way, as

$$\boldsymbol{c} \cdot \mathbf{G}_{dn,\ell,m}^{-1} \left(\begin{bmatrix} v_1 \mathbf{I}_n \\ \vdots \\ v_d \mathbf{I}_n \end{bmatrix} \cdot \mathbf{G}_{n,2,m} \right) \approx \boldsymbol{s}^\mathsf{T} \left(\mathbf{A}_1 \cdot \mathbf{G}_{dn,\ell,m}^{-1} \left(\begin{bmatrix} v_1 \mathbf{I}_n \\ \vdots \\ v_d \mathbf{I}_n \end{bmatrix} \mathbf{G}_{n,2,m} \right) + \langle \boldsymbol{v}, \boldsymbol{w} \rangle \mathbf{G}_{n,2,m} \right)$$

As such, our final IPE system contains only two matrices $(\mathbf{A}, \mathbf{A}_1)$ (and a vector $\boldsymbol{u}$), and the ciphertext consists of two vectors. By carefully twisting the vector encoding and proof techniques shown in [2], we show our IPE construction satisfies weakly attribute-hiding. Our IPE system can also be extended in a "parallel repetition" manner to support $(t = \lambda)$-length vectors, as Corollary 1.3 states.

1.3   Related Work

In this section, we provide a comparison with the first IPE construction [2] and its follow-up improvement [24]. In [24], Xagawa used the "Full-Rank Difference encoding", proposed in [1] to map the vector $\mathbb{Z}_q^t$ to a matrix in $\mathbb{Z}_q^{n \times n}$. The size of public parameters (or ciphertext) in his scheme depends linearly on the length of predicate/attribute vectors, and the "Full-Rank Difference encoding" incurs more computation overhead than embedding GSW-FHE structure in IPE construction as described above. The detailed comparison is provided in Table 1 for length parameter $t = \log \lambda$.

Table 1. Comparison of lattice-based IPE scheme

Schemes	# of $\mathbb{Z}_q^{n \times m}$ mat. in $|\mathsf{pp}|$	# of $\mathbb{Z}_q^m$ vec. in $|\mathsf{ct}|$	LWE param $1/\alpha$
[2]	$O(\lambda \log \lambda)$	$O(\lambda \log \lambda)$	$O(\lambda^{3.5})$
[24]	$O(\lambda)$	$O(\lambda)$	$O(\lambda^4)$
Ours	2	2	$O(\lambda^4 \log \lambda)$

2 Preliminaries

Notation. Let λ be the security parameter, and let PPT denote probabilistic polynomial time. We use bold uppercase letters to denote matrices $\mathbf{M}$, and bold lowercase letters to denote vectors $\boldsymbol{v}$. We write $\widetilde{\mathbf{M}}$ to denote the Gram-Schmidt orthogonalization of $\mathbf{M}$. We write $[n]$ to denote the set $\{1, \ldots, n\}$, and $|\boldsymbol{t}|$ to denote the number of bits in the string $\boldsymbol{t}$. We denote the i-th bit $\boldsymbol{s}$ by $\boldsymbol{s}[i]$. We say a function $\mathsf{negl}(\cdot) : \mathbb{N} \to (0, 1)$ is negligible, if for every constant $c \in \mathbb{N}$, $\mathsf{negl}(n) < n^{-c}$ for sufficiently large n.

2.1 Inner Product Encryption

We recall the syntax and security definition of *inner product encryption* (IPE) [2,19]. IPE can be regarded as a generalization of predicate encryption. An IPE scheme $\Pi = (\mathsf{Setup}, \mathsf{KeyGen}, \mathsf{Enc}, \mathsf{Dec})$ can be described as follows:

$\mathsf{Setup}(1^\lambda)$: On input the security parameter λ, the setup algorithm outputs public parameters pp and master secret key msk.

$\mathsf{KeyGen}(\mathsf{msk}, \boldsymbol{v})$: On input the master secret key msk and a predicate vector $\boldsymbol{v}$, the key generation algorithm outputs a secret key $\mathsf{sk}_{\boldsymbol{v}}$ for vector $\boldsymbol{v}$.

$\mathsf{Enc}(\mathsf{pp}, \boldsymbol{w}, \mu)$: On input the public parameter pp and an attribute/message pair $(\boldsymbol{w}, \mu)$, it outputs a ciphertext $\mathsf{ct}_{\boldsymbol{w}}$.

$\mathsf{Dec}(\mathsf{sk}_{\boldsymbol{v}}, \mathsf{ct}_{\boldsymbol{w}})$: On input the secret key $\mathsf{sk}_{\boldsymbol{v}}$ and a ciphertext $\mathsf{ct}_{\boldsymbol{w}}$, it outputs the corresponding plaintext μ if $\langle \boldsymbol{v}, \boldsymbol{w} \rangle = 0$; otherwise, it outputs $\bot$.

Definition 2.1 (Correctness). *We say the IPE scheme described above is correct, if for any* $(\mathsf{msk}, \mathsf{pp}) \leftarrow \mathsf{Setup}(1^\lambda)$, *any message* μ, *any predicate vector* $\boldsymbol{v} \in \mathbb{Z}_q^d$, *and attribute vector* $\boldsymbol{w} \in \mathbb{Z}_q^d$ *such that* $\langle \boldsymbol{v}, \boldsymbol{w} \rangle = 0$, *we have* $\mathsf{Dec}(\mathsf{sk}_{\boldsymbol{v}}, \mathsf{ct}_{\boldsymbol{w}}) = \mu$, *where* $\mathsf{sk}_{\boldsymbol{w}} \leftarrow \mathsf{KeyGen}(\mathsf{msk}, \boldsymbol{v})$ *and* $\mathsf{ct}_{\boldsymbol{v}} \leftarrow \mathsf{Enc}(\mathsf{pp}, \boldsymbol{w}, \mu)$.

Security. For the weakly attribute-hiding property of IPE, we use the following experiment to describe it. Formally, for any PPT adversary $\mathcal{A}$, we consider the experiment $\mathbf{Expt}_{\mathcal{A}}^{\mathsf{IPE}}(1^\lambda)$:

- **Setup:** Adversary $\mathcal{A}$ sends two challenge attribute vectors $\boldsymbol{w}_0, \boldsymbol{w}_1 \in \mathbb{Z}_q^d$ to challenger. A challenger runs the $\mathsf{Setup}(1^\lambda)$ algorithm, and sends back the master public key pp.

– **Query Phase I:** Proceeding adaptively, the adversary $\mathcal{A}$ queries a sequence of predicate vectors $(\boldsymbol{v}_1, \ldots, \boldsymbol{v}_m)$ subject to the restriction that $\langle \boldsymbol{v}_i, \boldsymbol{w}_0 \rangle \neq 0$ and $\langle \boldsymbol{v}_i, \boldsymbol{w}_1 \rangle \neq 0$. On the i-th query, the challenger runs $\mathsf{sk}_{\boldsymbol{v}_i} \rightarrow \mathsf{KeyGen}(\mathsf{msk}, \boldsymbol{v}_i)$, and sends the result $\mathsf{sk}_{\boldsymbol{v}_i}$ to $\mathcal{A}$.

– **Challenge:** Once adversary $\mathcal{A}$ decides that Query Phase I is over, he outputs two length-equal messages (μ_0^*, μ_1^*) and sends them to challenger. In response, the challenger selects a random bit $b^* \in \{0, 1\}$, and sends the ciphertext $\mathsf{ct}^* \leftarrow \mathsf{Enc}(\mathsf{pp}, \boldsymbol{w}_{b^*}, \mu_{b^*})$ to adversary $\mathcal{A}$.

– **Query Phase II:** Adversary $\mathcal{A}$ continues to issue secret key queries $(\boldsymbol{v}_{m+1}, \ldots, \boldsymbol{v}_n)$ adaptively, subject to the restriction that $\langle \boldsymbol{v}_i, \boldsymbol{w}_0 \rangle \neq 0$ and $\langle \boldsymbol{v}_i, \boldsymbol{w}_1 \rangle \neq 0$. The challenger responds by sending back keys $\mathsf{sk}_{\boldsymbol{v}_i}$ as in Query Phase I.

– **Guess:** Adversary $\mathcal{A}$ outputs a guess $b' \in \{0, 1\}$.

We note that query phases I and II can happen polynomial times in terms of security parameter. The advantage of adversary $\mathcal{A}$ in attacking an IPE scheme Π is defined as:

$$\mathbf{Adv}_{\mathcal{A}}(1^\lambda) = \left| \Pr[b^* = b'] - \frac{1}{2} \right|,$$

where the probability is over the randomness of the challenger and adversary.

Definition 2.2 (Weakly attribute-hiding). *We say an IPE scheme Π is weakly attribute-hiding against chosen-plaintext attacks in selective attribute setting, if for all PPT adversaries $\mathcal{A}$ engaging in experiment $\mathbf{Expt}_{\mathcal{A}}^{\mathsf{IPE}}(1^\lambda)$, we have*

$$\mathbf{Adv}_{\mathcal{A}}(1^\lambda) \leq \mathsf{negl}(\lambda).$$

2.2 LWE and Sampling Algorithms over Lattices

Learning with Errors. The LWE problem was introduced by Regev [22], the works of [22] show that the LWE assumption is as hard as (quantum) solving GapSVP and SIVP under various parameter regimes.

Definition 2.3 (LWE). *For an integer $q = q(n) \geq 2$, and an error distribution $\chi = \chi(n)$ over $\mathbb{Z}_q$, the Learning With Errors problem $\mathsf{LWE}_{n,m,q,\chi}$ is to distinguish between the following pairs of distributions (e.g. as given by a sampling oracle $\mathcal{O} \in \{\mathcal{O}_s, \mathcal{O}_\$\}$):*

$$\{\mathbf{A}, \boldsymbol{s}^\mathsf{T} \mathbf{A} + \boldsymbol{x}^\mathsf{T}\} \ and \ \{\mathbf{A}, \boldsymbol{u}\}$$

where $\mathbf{A} \xleftarrow{\$} \mathbb{Z}_q^{n \times m}$, $\boldsymbol{s} \xleftarrow{\$} \mathbb{Z}_q^n$, $\boldsymbol{u} \xleftarrow{\$} \mathbb{Z}_q^m$, and $\boldsymbol{x} \xleftarrow{\$} \chi^m$.

Two-Sided Trapdoors and Sampling Algorithms. We will use the following algorithms to sample short vectors from specified lattices.

Lemma 2.4 [5,14]. *Let q, n, m be positive integers with $q \geq 2$ and sufficiently large $m = \Omega(n \log q)$. There exists a PPT algorithm $\mathsf{TrapGen}(q, n, m)$ that with overwhelming probability outputs a pair $(\mathbf{A} \in \mathbb{Z}_q^{n \times m}, \mathbf{T_A} \in \mathbb{Z}^{m \times m})$ such that $\mathbf{A}$ is statistically close to uniform in $\mathbb{Z}_q^{n \times m}$ and $\mathbf{T_A}$ is a basis for $\Lambda_q^{\perp}(\mathbf{A})$ satisfying*

$$\|\mathbf{T_A}\| \leq O(n \log q) \quad and \quad \|\widetilde{\mathbf{T_A}}\| \leq O(\sqrt{n \log q})$$

except with $\mathsf{negl}(n)$ probability.

Lemma 2.5 [1,12,14]. *Let $q > 2, m > n$. There are two sampling algorithms as follows:*

- *There is a PPT algorithm $\mathsf{SampleLeft}(\mathbf{A}, \mathbf{B}, \mathbf{T_A}, \mathbf{u}, s)$, taking as input: (1) a rank-n matrix $\mathbf{A} \in \mathbb{Z}_q^{n \times m}$, and any matrix $\mathbf{B} \in \mathbb{Z}_q^{n \times m_1}$, (2) a "short" basis $\mathbf{T_A}$ for lattice $\Lambda_q^{\perp}(\mathbf{A})$, a vector $\mathbf{u} \in \mathbb{Z}_q^n$, (3) a Gaussian parameter $s > \|\widetilde{\mathbf{T_A}}\| \cdot \omega(\sqrt{\log(m + m_1)})$. Then outputs a vector $\mathbf{r} \in \mathbb{Z}^{m+m_1}$ distributed statistically close to $\mathcal{D}_{\Lambda_q^u(\mathbf{F}),s}$ where $\mathbf{F} := [\mathbf{A}|\mathbf{B}]$.*
- *There is a PPT algorithm $\mathsf{SampleRight}(\mathbf{A}, \mathbf{B}, \mathbf{R}, \mathbf{T_B}, \mathbf{u}, s)$, taking as input: (1) a matrix $\mathbf{A} \in \mathbb{Z}_q^{n \times m}$, and a rank-$n$ matrix $\mathbf{B} \in \mathbb{Z}_q^{n \times m}$, a matrix $\mathbf{R} \in \mathbb{Z}_q^{m \times m}$, where $s_{\mathbf{R}} := \|\mathbf{R}\| = \sup_{\mathbf{x}:\|\mathbf{x}\|=1} \|\mathbf{Rx}\|$, (2) a "short" basis $\mathbf{T_B}$ for lattice $\Lambda_q^{\perp}(\mathbf{B})$, a vector $\mathbf{u} \in \mathbb{Z}_q^n$, (3) a Gaussian parameter $s > \|\widetilde{\mathbf{T_B}}\| \cdot s_{\mathbf{R}} \cdot \omega(\sqrt{\log m})$. Then outputs a vector $\mathbf{r} \in \mathbb{Z}^{2m}$ distributed statistically close to $\mathcal{D}_{\Lambda_q^u(\mathbf{F}),s}$ where $\mathbf{F} := (\mathbf{A}|\mathbf{AR} + \mathbf{B})$.*

Gadget Matrix. We now recall the gadget matrix [4,20], and the extended gadget matrix technique appeared in [6], that are important to our construction.

Definition 2.6. *Let $m = n \cdot \lceil \log q \rceil$, and define the gadget matrix*

$$\mathbf{G}_{n,2,m} = \mathbf{g} \otimes \mathbf{I}_n \in \mathbb{Z}_q^{n \times m}$$

where vector $\mathbf{g} = (1, 2, 4, \ldots, 2^{\lfloor \log q \rfloor}) \in \mathbb{Z}_q^{\lceil \log q \rceil}$, and $\otimes$ denotes tenser product. We will also refer to this gadget matrix as "powers-of-two" matrix. We define the inverse function $\mathbf{G}_{n,2,m}^{-1} : \mathbb{Z}_q^{n \times m} \to \{0,1\}^{m \times m}$ which expands each entry $a \in \mathbb{Z}_q$ of the input matrix into a column of size $\lceil \log q \rceil$ consisting of the bits of binary representations. We have the property that for any matrix $\mathbf{A} \in Z_q^{n \times m}$, it holds that $\mathbf{G}_{n,2,m} \cdot \mathbf{G}_{n,2,m}^{-1}(\mathbf{A}) = \mathbf{A}$.

As mentioned by [20] and explicitly described in [6], the results for $\mathbf{G}_{n,2,m}$ and its trapdoor can be extended to other integer powers or mixed-integer products. In this direction, we give a generalized notation for gadget matrices as follows:

3   Our Construction

In this section, we describe our compact IPE construction. Before diving into the details, we first revisit a novel encoding method implicitly employed in adaptively secure IBE setting in [6]. Consider the vector space $\mathbb{Z}_q^d$. For vector $\boldsymbol{v} = (v_1, \ldots, v_d) \in \mathbb{Z}_q^d$, we define the following encoding algorithm which maps a d-dimensional vector to an $n \times m$ matrix.

$$\mathsf{encode}(\boldsymbol{v}) = \mathbf{E}_{\boldsymbol{v}} = \left[v_1 \mathbf{I}_n | \cdots | v_d \mathbf{I}_n \right] \cdot \mathbf{G}_{dn,\ell,m} \qquad (1)$$

Similarly, we also define the encoding for an integer $a \in \mathbb{Z}_q$ as: $\mathsf{encode}(a) = \mathbf{E}_a = a\mathbf{G}_{n,2,m}$. The above encoding supports the vector space operations naturally, and our compact IPE construction relies on this property.

3.1 IPE Construction Supporting $\log(\lambda)$-Length Attributes

We describe our IPE scheme that each secret key is associated with a predicate vector $\boldsymbol{v} \in \mathbb{Z}_q^d$ (for some fixed $d = \log \lambda$), and each ciphertext will be associated with an attribute vector $\boldsymbol{w} \in \mathbb{Z}_q^d$. Decryption succeeds if and only if $\langle \boldsymbol{v}, \boldsymbol{w} \rangle = 0 \bmod q$. We further extend our IPE construction supporting $d = \mathsf{poly}(\lambda)$-length vectors in Sect. 3.3. The description of $\varPi = (\mathsf{Setup}, \mathsf{KeyGen}, \mathsf{Enc}, \mathsf{Dec})$ is as follows:

Setup$(1^\lambda, 1^d)$: On input the security parameter λ and length parameter d, the setup algorithm first sets the parameters (q, n, m, s) as below. We assume the parameters (q, n, m, s) are implicitly included in both pp and msk. Then it generates a random matrix $\mathbf{A} \in \mathbb{Z}_q^{n \times m}$ along with its trapdoor $\mathbf{T_A} \in \mathbb{Z}_q^{m \times m}$, using $(\mathbf{A}, \mathbf{T_A}) \leftarrow \mathsf{TrapGen}(q, n, m)$. Next sample a random matrix $\mathbf{B} \in \mathbb{Z}_q^{n \times m}$ and a random vector $\boldsymbol{u} \in \mathbb{Z}_q^n$. Output the public parameter pp and master secret key msk as

$$pp = (\mathbf{A}, \mathbf{B}, \boldsymbol{u}), \qquad \mathsf{msk} = (pp, \mathbf{T_A})$$

– KeyGen$(\mathsf{msk}, \boldsymbol{v})$: On input the master secret key msk and predictor vector $\boldsymbol{v} = (v_1, \ldots, v_d) \in \mathbb{Z}_q^d$, the key generation algorithm first sets matrix $\mathbf{B}_{\boldsymbol{v}}$ as

$$\mathbf{B}_{\boldsymbol{v}} = \mathbf{B} \cdot \mathbf{G}_{dn,\ell,m}^{-1} \left(\begin{bmatrix} v_1 \mathbf{I}_n \\ \vdots \\ v_d \mathbf{I}_n \end{bmatrix} \cdot \mathbf{G}_{n,2,m} \right)$$

Then sample a low-norm vector $\boldsymbol{r}_{\boldsymbol{v}} \in \mathbb{Z}^{2m}$ using algorithm SampleLeft$(\mathbf{A}, \mathbf{B}_{\boldsymbol{v}}, \boldsymbol{u}, s)$, such that $[\mathbf{A}|\mathbf{B}_{\boldsymbol{v}}] \cdot \boldsymbol{r}_{\boldsymbol{v}} = \boldsymbol{u} \bmod q$. Output secret key $\mathsf{sk}_{\boldsymbol{v}} = \boldsymbol{r}_{\boldsymbol{v}}$.
– Enc$(pp, \boldsymbol{w}, \mu)$: On input the public parameter pp, an attribute vector $\boldsymbol{w} = (w_1, \ldots, w_d) \in \mathbb{Z}_q^d$ and a message $\mu \in \{0, 1\}$, the encryption algorithm first chooses a random vector $\boldsymbol{s} \in \mathbb{Z}_q^n$ and a random matrix $\mathbf{R} \in \{-1, 1\}^{m \times m}$. Then encode the attribute vector $\boldsymbol{w}$ as in Eq. (1)

$$\mathbf{E}_{\boldsymbol{w}} = \left[w_1 \mathbf{I}_n | \cdots | w_d \mathbf{I}_n \right] \cdot \mathbf{G}_{dn,\ell,m}$$

Let the ciphertext $\mathsf{ct}_{\boldsymbol{w}} = (\boldsymbol{c}_0, \boldsymbol{c}_1, c_2) \in \mathbb{Z}_q^{2m+1}$ be

$$\boldsymbol{c}_0 = \boldsymbol{s}^\mathsf{T} \mathbf{A} + \boldsymbol{e}_0^\mathsf{T}, \quad \boldsymbol{c}_1 = \boldsymbol{s}^\mathsf{T} (\mathbf{B} + \mathbf{E}_{\boldsymbol{w}}) + \boldsymbol{e}_0^T \mathbf{R}, \quad c_2 = \boldsymbol{s}^\mathsf{T} \boldsymbol{u} + e_1 + \lceil q/2 \rceil \mu$$

where errors $\boldsymbol{e}_0 \leftarrow \mathcal{D}_{\mathbb{Z}^m, s}, e_1 \leftarrow \mathcal{D}_{\mathbb{Z}, s}$.

- $\mathsf{Dec}(\mathsf{sk}_v, \mathsf{ct}_w)$: On input the secret key $\mathsf{sk}_v = r_v$ and ciphertext $\mathsf{ct}_w = (c_0, c_1, c_2)$, if $\langle v, w \rangle \neq 0 \bmod q$, then output $\perp$. Otherwise, first compute

$$c_1' = c_1 \cdot \mathbf{G}_{dn,\ell,m}^{-1}\left(\begin{bmatrix} v_1 \mathbf{I}_n \\ \vdots \\ v_d \mathbf{I}_n \end{bmatrix} \cdot \mathbf{G}_{n,2,m} \right)$$

then output $\mathsf{Round}(c_2 - \langle (c_0, c_1'), r_v \rangle)$.

Lemma 3.1. *The IPE scheme Π described above is correct (c.f. Definition 2.1).*

Proof. When the predicate vector v and attribute vector w satisfies $\langle v, w \rangle = 0 \bmod q$, it holds that $c_1' = s^\mathsf{T} \mathbf{B}_v + e_0'$. Therefore, during decryption, we have

$$\mu' = \mathsf{Round}\left(\lceil q/2 \rceil \mu + \underbrace{e_1 - \langle (e_0, e_0'), r_v \rangle}_{\text{small}} \right) = \mu \in \{0, 1\}$$

The third equation follows if $(e_1 - \langle (e_0, e_0'), r_v \rangle)$ is indeed small, which holds w.h.p. by setting the parameters appropriately below. $\qquad\square$

Parameter Selection. To support $d = \log(\lambda)$-length predicate/attribute vectors, we set the system parameters according to Table 2, where $\epsilon > 0$ is an arbitrarily small constant.

Table 2. $\log(\lambda)$-length IPE Parameters Setting

Parameters	Description	Setting
λ	Security parameter	
n	Lattice row dimension	λ
m	Lattice column dimension	$n^{1+\epsilon}$
q	Modulus	$n^{3+\epsilon} m$
s	Sampling and error width	$n^{1+\epsilon}$
ℓ	Integer-base parameter	n

These values are chosen in order to satisfy the following constraints:

- To ensure correctness, we require $|e_1 - \langle (e_0, e_0'), r_v \rangle| < q/4$; Let $r_v = (r_1, r_2)$, here we can bound the dominating term:

$$|e_0'^\mathsf{T} r_2| \leq ||e_0'^\mathsf{T}|| \cdot ||r_2|| \approx s\sqrt{md\ell} \log_\ell q \cdot s\sqrt{m} = s^2 m n^{1+\epsilon} < q/4$$

- For $\mathsf{SampleLeft}$, we know $||\widetilde{\mathbf{T}_\mathbf{A}}|| = O(\sqrt{n \log(q)})$, thus this requires that the sampling width s satisfies $s > \sqrt{n \log(q)} \cdot \omega(\sqrt{\log(m)})$. For $\mathsf{SampleRight}$, we need $s > ||\widetilde{\mathbf{T}_{\mathbf{G}_{n,2,m}}}|| \cdot ||\mathbf{R}|| \omega(\sqrt{\log m}) = n^{1+\epsilon} \omega(\sqrt{\log m})$. To apply Regev's reduction, we need $s > \sqrt{n} \omega(\log(n))$ (s here is an absolute value, not a ratio). Therefore, we need $s > n^{1+\epsilon}$
- To apply the Leftover Hash Lemma, we need $m \geq (n+1) \log(q) + \omega(\log(n))$.

3.2 Security Proof

In this part, we show the weakly attribute-hiding property of our IPE construction. We adapt the simulation technique in [2] by plugin the encoding of vectors. Intuitively, to prove the theorem we define a sequences of hybrids against adversary $\mathcal{A}$ in the weak attribute-hiding experiment. The adversary $\mathcal{A}$ outputs two attribute vectors $\boldsymbol{w}_0$ and $\boldsymbol{w}_1$ at the beginning of each game, and at some point outputs two messages μ_0, μ_1. The first and last games correspond to real security game with challenge ciphertexts $\mathsf{Enc}(\mathsf{pp}, \boldsymbol{w}_0, \mu_0)$ and $\mathsf{Enc}(\mathsf{pp}, \boldsymbol{w}_1, \mu_1)$ respectively. In the intermediate games we use the "alternative" simulation algorithms $(\mathsf{Sim.Setup}, \mathsf{Sim.KeyGen}, \mathsf{Sim.Enc})$. During the course of the game the adversary can only request keys for predicate vector $\boldsymbol{v}_i$ such that $\langle \boldsymbol{v}_i, \boldsymbol{w}_0 \rangle \neq 0$ and $\langle \boldsymbol{v}_i, \boldsymbol{w}_1 \rangle \neq 0$. We first define the simulation algorithms $(\mathsf{Sim.Setup}, \mathsf{Sim.KeyGen}, \mathsf{Sim.Enc})$ in the following:

- $\mathsf{Sim.Setup}(1^\lambda, 1^d, \boldsymbol{w}^*)$: On input the security parameter λ, the length parameter d, and an attribute vector $\boldsymbol{w}^* \in \mathbb{Z}_q^d$, the simulation setup algorithm first chooses a random matrix $\mathbf{A} \leftarrow \mathbb{Z}_q^{n \times m}$ and a random vector $\boldsymbol{u} \leftarrow \mathbb{Z}_q^n$. Then set matrix

$$\mathbf{B} = \mathbf{A}\mathbf{R}^* - \mathbf{E}_{w^*}, \quad \mathbf{E}_{w^*} = \left[w_1^* \mathbf{I}_n | \cdots | w_d^* \mathbf{I}_n \right] \cdot \mathbf{G}_{dn,\ell,m}$$

where matrix $\mathbf{R}^*$ is chosen randomly from $\{-1, 1\}^{m \times m}$. Output $\mathsf{pp} = (\mathbf{A}, \mathbf{B}, \boldsymbol{u})$ and $\mathsf{msk} = \mathbf{R}^*$.
- $\mathsf{Sim.KeyGen}(\mathsf{msk}, \boldsymbol{v})$: On input the master secret key msk and a vector $\boldsymbol{v} \in \mathbb{Z}_q^d$, the simulation key generation algorithm sets matrix $\mathbf{R}_v$ and $\mathbf{B}_v$ as

$$\mathbf{R}_v = \left(\begin{bmatrix} v_1 \mathbf{I}_n \\ \vdots \\ v_d \mathbf{I}_n \end{bmatrix} \cdot \mathbf{G}_{n,2,m} \right), \quad \mathbf{B}_v = \mathbf{B} \cdot \mathbf{G}_{dn,\ell,m}^{-1}(\mathbf{R}_v)$$

Then sample a low-norm vector $\boldsymbol{r}_v \in \mathbb{Z}^{2m}$ using algorithm

$$\boldsymbol{r}_v \leftarrow \mathsf{SampleRight}(\mathbf{A}, \langle \boldsymbol{v}, \boldsymbol{w}^* \rangle \mathbf{G}_{n,2,m}, \mathbf{R}^* \mathbf{G}_{dn,\ell,m}^{-1}(\mathbf{R}_v), \mathbf{T}_{\mathbf{G}_{n,2,m}} \boldsymbol{u}, s)$$

such that $[\mathbf{A}|\mathbf{B}_v] \cdot \boldsymbol{r}_v = \boldsymbol{u} \bmod q$. Output secret key $\mathsf{sk}_v = \boldsymbol{r}_v$.
- $\mathsf{Sim.Enc}(\mathsf{pp}, \boldsymbol{w}^*, \mu)$: The simulation encryption algorithm is the same as the counterpart in the scheme, except the matrix $\mathbf{R}^*$ is used in generating the ciphertext instead of sampling a random matrix $\mathbf{R} \in \{-1, 1\}^{m \times m}$.

Due to the space limit, we include proof of the following theorem in full version.

Theorem 3.2. *Assuming the hardness of (n, q, χ)-LWE assumption, the IPE scheme described above is weakly attribute-hiding (c.f. Definition 2.2).*

3.3 IPE Construction Supporting poly(λ)-length Vectors

We also extend our IPE construction to support $t = \mathsf{poly}(\lambda)$-length vectors, which means the predicate and attribute vector are chosen in vector space $\mathbb{Z}_q^t$.

Intuitively speaking, our construction described below can be regarded as a $t' = \lceil t/d \rceil$ "parallel repetition" version of IPE construction for $d = \log(\lambda)$-length vectors. In particular, we encode every $\log(\lambda)$ part of the attribute vector $\boldsymbol{v}$, and then concatenate these encoding together as the encoding of $\boldsymbol{v}$. Due to space limit, we include the detailed scheme and proof in the full version.

References

1. Agrawal, S., Boneh, D., Boyen, X.: Efficient lattice (H) IBE in the standard model. In: Gilbert [16], pp. 553–572 (2010)
2. Agrawal, S., Freeman, D.M., Vaikuntanathan, V.: Functional encryption for inner product predicates from learning with errors. In: Lee, D.H., Wang, X. (eds.) ASIACRYPT 2011. LNCS, vol. 7073, pp. 21–40. Springer, Heidelberg (2011). https://doi.org/10.1007/978-3-642-25385-0_2
3. Ajtai, M.: Generating hard instances of lattice problems (extended abstract). In: 28th ACM STOC, pp. 99–108. ACM Press, May 1996
4. Alperin-Sheriff, J., Peikert, C.: Faster bootstrapping with polynomial error. In: Garay, J.A., Gennaro, R. (eds.) CRYPTO 2014. LNCS, vol. 8616, pp. 297–314. Springer, Heidelberg (2014). https://doi.org/10.1007/978-3-662-44371-2_17
5. Alwen, J., Peikert, C.: Generating shorter bases for hard random lattices. Theory Comput. Syst. **48**(3), 535–553 (2010)
6. Apon, D., Fan, X., Liu, F.-H,: Vector encoding over lattices and its applications. Cryptology ePrint Archive, Report 2017/455 (2017). http://eprint.iacr.org/2017/455
7. Bethencourt, J., Sahai, A., Waters, B.: Ciphertext-policy attribute-based encryption. In: 2007 IEEE Symposium on Security and Privacy, pp. 321–334. IEEE Computer Society Press, May 2007
8. Boneh, D., Franklin, M.: Identity-based encryption from the weil pairing. In: Kilian, J. (ed.) CRYPTO 2001. LNCS, vol. 2139, pp. 213–229. Springer, Heidelberg (2001). https://doi.org/10.1007/3-540-44647-8_13
9. Boneh, D., Gentry, C., Gorbunov, S., Halevi, S., Nikolaenko, V., Segev, G., Vaikuntanathan, V., Vinayagamurthy, D.: Fully key-homomorphic encryption, arithmetic circuit ABE and compact garbled circuits. In: Nguyen, P.Q., Oswald, E. (eds.) EUROCRYPT 2014. LNCS, vol. 8441, pp. 533–556. Springer, Heidelberg (2014). https://doi.org/10.1007/978-3-642-55220-5_30
10. Boneh, D., Sahai, A., Waters, B.: Functional encryption: definitions and challenges. In: Ishai, Y. (ed.) TCC 2011. LNCS, vol. 6597, pp. 253–273. Springer, Heidelberg (2011). https://doi.org/10.1007/978-3-642-19571-6_16
11. Boneh, D., Waters, B.: Conjunctive, subset, and range queries on encrypted data. In: Vadhan, S.P. (ed.) TCC 2007. LNCS, vol. 4392, pp. 535–554. Springer, Heidelberg (2007). https://doi.org/10.1007/978-3-540-70936-7_29
12. Cash, D., Hofheinz, D., Kiltz, E., Peikert, C.: Bonsai trees, or how to delegate a lattice basis. In: Gilbert [16], pp. 523–552 (2010)
13. Gentry, C.: Fully homomorphic encryption using ideal lattices. In: Mitzenmacher, M. (ed.) 41st ACM STOC, pp. 169–178. ACM Press, May/June 2009
14. Gentry, C., Peikert, C., Vaikuntanathan, V.: Trapdoors for hard lattices and new cryptographic constructions. In: Ladner, R.E., Dwork, C. (eds.) 40th ACM STOC, pp. 197–206. ACM Press, May 2008

15. Gentry, C., Sahai, A., Waters, B.: Homomorphic encryption from learning with errors: conceptually-simpler, asymptotically-faster, attribute-based. In: Canetti, R., Garay, J.A. (eds.) CRYPTO 2013. LNCS, vol. 8042, pp. 75–92. Springer, Heidelberg (2013). https://doi.org/10.1007/978-3-642-40041-4_5

16. Gilbert, H. (ed.): EUROCRYPT 2010. LNCS, vol. 6110. Springer, Heidelberg (2010). https://doi.org/10.1007/978-3-642-13190-5

17. Gorbunov, S., Vaikuntanathan, V., Wee, H.: Attribute-based encryption for circuits. In: Boneh, D., Roughgarden, T., Feigenbaum, J. (eds.) 45th ACM STOC, pp. 545–554. ACM Press, June 2013

18. Goyal, V., Pandey, O., Sahai, A., Waters, B.: Attribute-based encryption for fine-grained access control of encrypted data. In: Juels, A., Wright, R.N., De Capitani di Vimercati, S. (eds.) ACM CCS 2006, pp. 89–98. ACM Press, October/November 2006. Available as Cryptology ePrint Archive Report 2006/309

19. Katz, J., Sahai, A., Waters, B.: Predicate encryption supporting disjunctions, polynomial equations, and inner products. In: Smart, N. (ed.) EUROCRYPT 2008. LNCS, vol. 4965, pp. 146–162. Springer, Heidelberg (2008). https://doi.org/10.1007/978-3-540-78967-3_9

20. Micciancio, D., Peikert, C.: Trapdoors for lattices: simpler, tighter, faster, smaller. In: Pointcheval, D., Johansson, T. (eds.) EUROCRYPT 2012. LNCS, vol. 7237, pp. 700–718. Springer, Heidelberg (2012). https://doi.org/10.1007/978-3-642-29011-4_41

21. O'Neill, A.: Definitional issues in functional encryption. Cryptology ePrint Archive, Report 2010/556 (2010). http://eprint.iacr.org/2010/556

22. Regev, O.: On lattices, learning with errors, random linear codes, and cryptography. In: Gabow, H.N., Fagin, R. (eds.) 37th ACM STOC, pp. 84–93. ACM Press, May 2005

23. Shamir, A.: Identity-based cryptosystems and signature schemes. In: Blakley, G.R., Chaum, D. (eds.) CRYPTO 1984. LNCS, vol. 196, pp. 47–53. Springer, Heidelberg (1985). https://doi.org/10.1007/3-540-39568-7_5

24. Xagawa, K.: Improved (hierarchical) inner-product encryption from lattices. In: Kurosawa, K., Hanaoka, G. (eds.) PKC 2013. LNCS, vol. 7778, pp. 235–252. Springer, Heidelberg (2013). https://doi.org/10.1007/978-3-642-36362-7_15

Towards Tightly Secure Deterministic Public Key Encryption

Daode Zhang[1,2,3], Bao Li[1,2,3], Yamin Liu[1], Haiyang Xue[1(✉)], Xianhui Lu[1],
and Dingding Jia[1]

[1] School of Cyber Security, University of Chinese Academy of Sciences,
Beijing, China
{zhangdaode,lb}@is.ac.cn,
{liuyamin,xuehaiyang,luxianhui,jiadingding}@iie.ac.cn
[2] State Key Laboratory of Information Security, Institute of Information
Engineering, Chinese Academy of Sciences, Beijing, China
[3] Science and Technology on Communication Security Laboratory, Chengdu, China

Abstract. In this paper, we formally consider the construction of tightly secure deterministic public key encryption (D-PKE). Initially, we compare the security loss amongst the D-PKE schemes under the concrete assumptions and also analyze the tightness of generic D-PKE constructions. Furthermore, we prove that the CPA secure D-PKE scheme of Boldyreva et al. (Crypto'08) is tightly PRIV-IND-CPA secure for block-sources. Our security reduction improves the security loss of their scheme from $\mathcal{O}(n_{c^*})$ to $\mathcal{O}(1)$. Additionally, by upgrading the all-but-one trapdoor function (TDF) in the construction of Boldyreva et al. to all-but-n TDF defined by Hemenway et al. (Asiacrypt'11), we give general construction of PRIV-IND-$\frac{n}{2}$-CCA secure (i.e., the number of challenge ciphertexts n_{c^*} is bounded by $\frac{n}{2}$) D-PKE scheme for block-sources. And we observe that if the security reduction of the all-but-n TDF is tight, the D-PKE scheme can be tightly PRIV-IND-$\frac{n}{2}$-CCA secure. Finally, we prove that the all-but-n TDF given by Hemenway et al. is tightly secure, which results in the first tightly PRIV-IND-$\frac{n}{2}$-CCA secure D-PKE scheme for block-sources, based on the s-DCR assumption.

Keywords: Deterministic public key encryption
Tight security reduction · Lossy trapdoor functions · Standard model

1 Introduction

Currently, the formal way to prove the security of cryptographic primitives is providing a security reduction, i.e., any adversary A breaking the security of a scheme with advantage ε_A implies an adversary B that can solve the underlying hard problem with advantage ε_B. Specially, we call the quotient $L = \varepsilon_A/\varepsilon_B$ the security loss of a reduction. Naturally, we hope that the quotient L is small.

© Springer International Publishing AG, part of Springer Nature 2018
S. Qing et al. (Eds.): ICICS 2017, LNCS 10631, pp. 154–161, 2018.
https://doi.org/10.1007/978-3-319-89500-0_13

Tight Security Reduction. Standard security notions for public key encryption (PKE) schemes, e.g., IND-CCA security [6], only consider one user and one ciphertext. However, in the reality setting, the adversary can know at most n_u public keys of users and obtain at most n_{c*} challenge ciphertexts from per user. These two parameters can be very large, e.g., $n_u = n_{c*} = 2^{40}$. In general, L will depend on n_u and n_{c*} [1]. In order to compensate for the security loss, we have to increase the strength of the underlying intractability assumption which worsens the parameters of the encryption scheme and affects the performance of the implementation. For example, for encryption schemes from the Decisional Diffie-Hellman assumption over cyclic groups, we have to increase the size of the underlying groups, which in turn increases the running time of the implementation, as exponentiation in an l-bit group takes time about $\mathcal{O}(l^3)$ as stated in [7]. Hence, it is important to study tight security reductions where the security loss L is a small constant that in particular does not depend on parameters under the adversary's control, such as n_u, n_{c*}. In the case of CCA security, L should also be independent of the parameter n_c, which is the number of queries that the adversary can make to each decryption oracle at most.

Tight Security in Deterministic-PKE. Deterministic-PKE (D-PKE), namely, deterministic public-key encryption, was introduced by Bellare et al. [2], in which the encryption algorithm is deterministic.

Bellare et al. [2] defined a strongest possible security notion for D-PKE, called PRIV, over plaintext distributions with high min-entropy independent of the public key. The definition of PRIV considers a message block containing multi-plaintext. If the size of block is one, then the security definition is called PRIV1. The security notions of D-PKE evolved in a series of literatures [3–5,11]. Many D-PKE constructions have been proposed based on concrete assumptions as depicted in Fig. 1. These D-PKE constructions are all secure in the one-user, multi-ciphertext case. However, all of these constructions have a security loss about $\mathcal{O}(n_{c*})$.

Our Contributions. It seems that the tight security reduction of D-PKE has not been deliberately studied in literatures. We compare the security loss amongst the D-PKE schemes based on the concrete assumptions in Fig. 1. In this paper, we formally consider the construction of tightly secure D-PKE scheme which is either PRIV-IND-CPA or PRIV-IND-CCA secure for block-sources in the standard model.

We start from [4] which introduced two D-PKE schemes based on lossy TDFs and all-but-one TDFs [10]. One is PRIV1-IND-CPA secure and the other is PRIV1-IND-CCA secure, for block-sources. Initially, we prove that their PRIV1-IND-CPA secure D-PKE scheme is tightly PRIV-IND-CPA secure for block-sources. Our security reduction improves the security loss of this scheme from $\mathcal{O}(n_{c*})$ to $\mathcal{O}(1)$. So we can obtain tightly PRIV-IND-CPA secure D-PKE schemes for block-sources by instantiating D-PKE constructions based on the DDH, s-DCR, LWE assumption.

	CPA-schemes($n_u = 1, n_{c^*}$)	
Reference	security loss	assumption
BBO07 [2]	$\geq \mathcal{O}(n_{c^*})$	RSA+RO Model
BFO08 [4]	$\mathcal{O}(n_{c^*})$	DDH/s-DCR/LWE
BS11 [5]	$\mathcal{O}(n_{c^*})$	DLin
Wee12 [12]	$\mathcal{O}(n_{c^*})$	DDH/DLin/QR/s-DCR/LWE
XXZ12 [13]	$\mathcal{O}(n_{c^*})$	LWE
MPRS12 [9]	$\mathcal{O}(n_{c^*})$	DDH
Our Results of BFO08 [4]	$\mathcal{O}(1)$	DDH/s-DCR/LWE
	CCA-schemes ($n_u = 1, n_{c^*}, n_c$)	
BFO08 [4]	$\mathcal{O}(n_{c^*})$	DDH/s-DCR
Ours	bounded-$\mathcal{O}(1)$	s-DCR

Fig. 1. The security loss amongst the D-PKE schemes under the concrete assumptions.

However, their PRIV1-IND-CCA D-PKE scheme in [4] (The sect. 7.2) is not tightly PRIV-IND-CCA secure for block-sources. In their PRIV1-IND-CCA D-PKE scheme, the ciphertext of a message m contains an item as follows

$$\mathcal{F}_{abo}(ek_{abo}, \mathcal{H}_{cr}(k_{cr}, \mathcal{H}_{inv}(k_{inv}, m)), \mathcal{H}_{inv}(k_{inv}, m)),$$

where $\mathcal{F}_{abo}$ is a collection of all-but-one TDFs, $\mathcal{H}_{cr}$ is a family of collision-resistant hash functions, $\mathcal{H}_{inv}$ is a collection of pairwise-independent permutations with invertibility. Let function f be

$$f = \mathcal{F}_{abo}(ek_{abo}, \mathcal{H}_{cr}(k_{cr}, \cdot), \cdot) \quad \text{and} \quad ek_{abo} \xleftarrow{R} \mathcal{K}_{abo}(\mathcal{H}_{cr}(k_{cr}, \cdot)),$$

where $\mathcal{K}_{abo}$ is the key generation algorithm of $\mathcal{F}_{abo}$. According to the generalized "Crooked" leftover hash lemma, the statistical distance between $f(\mathcal{H}_{inv}(k_{inv}, m))$ and $f(h)$ is negligible, where $h \xleftarrow{\$} U_{inv}$ and U_{inv} denotes the uniform distribution on the range of $\mathcal{H}_{inv}$. So that $f(h)$ includes no information of the message m. In order to use the generalized "Crooked" leftover hash lemma, $\mathcal{H}_{cr}(k_{cr}, \mathcal{H}_{inv}(k_{inv}, m))$ and $\mathcal{H}_{cr}(k_{cr}, h)$ must belong to the lossy branch of the respective all-but-one TDF $\mathcal{F}_{abo}$. As a result, the security loss of their scheme is 2 times of the security loss of the all-but-one TDF $\mathcal{F}_{abo}$. However, the tight security reduction considers $n_{c^*} > 1$ challenge ciphertexts in the PRIV-IND-CCA security game for block-sources. Though PRIV1-IND-CCA and PRIV-IND-CCA are proved to be equivalent in [4], there is a security loss of $2 \cdot n_{c^*}$ due to the employment of the hybrid technique.

Furthermore, to address this problem, we upgrade the all-but-one TDF in the constructions of [4] to all-but-n TDF [8] whose number of the lossy branches is n. When the number of the lossy branches is two times of the number of the challenge ciphertexts, i.e., $n = 2 \cdot n_{c^*}$ (because we additionally need $\mathcal{H}_{cr}(k_{cr}, h)$ to be in the lossy branches of the all-but-n TDF), every challenge ciphertext can be evaluated on the lossy branches in the PRIV-IND-CCA security game for block-sources. In addition, apparently that if the security loss of the all-but-n

TDF is independent of n (tightly secure), then the security loss of the D-PKE scheme can also be independent of n_{c^*}, i.e., the D-PKE scheme can be tightly PRIV-IND-CCA secure for block-sources. However, because the number of the lossy branches of the all-but-n TDF in the construction is bounded by n, so that the number of the challenge ciphertexts n_{c^*} is bounded by $\frac{n}{2}$. As a result, our D-PKE schemes are only able to be tightly PRIV-IND-$\frac{n}{2}$-CCA secure for block-sources, where PRIV-IND-$\frac{n}{2}$-CCA security for block-sources is very similar to PRIV-IND-CCA security for block-sources except with the restriction the number of the challenge ciphertexts is bounded by $\frac{n}{2}$.

As aforementioned, the most important part of our constructions is to find tightly secure all-but-n TDFs. Finally, we prove that the all-but-n TDF given by Hemenway et al. [8] is tightly secure with a security loss of only 2. This improves their original security reduction which has a security loss of $2n$ due to the use of the hybrid technique. Applying this result to our constructions, we obtain the first D-PKE scheme which is tightly PRIV-IND-$\frac{n}{2}$-CCA secure for block-sources based on the s-DCR assumption.

2   Preliminaries

Notations. For a random variable X, we write $x \overset{R}{\leftarrow} X$ to denote sampling x according to X's distribution. For a random variable X, its min-entropy is defined as $H_\infty(X) = -\log(\max_x P_X(x))$. Given Y, the worst-case conditional min-entropy of X is $H_\infty(X|Y) = -\log(\max_{x,y} P_{X|Y=y}(x))$ and the average-case conditional min-entropy of X is $\tilde{H}_\infty(X|Y) = -\log(\sum_y P_Y(y) \cdot \max_x P_{X|Y=y}(x))$. A random variable $X \in \{0,1\}^l$ is called a (t,l)-source if it satisfies that $H_\infty(X) \geq t$. And a vector $\overrightarrow{X}$ is called a (t,l)-block-source of length n if it is a list of random variables $(X_1, \cdots, X_n)$ over $\{0,1\}^l$ and satisfies that $H_\infty(X_i|X_1, \cdots, X_{i-1}) \geq t$ for all $i \in [n] = \{1, \cdots, n\}$. The statistical distance between two distributions X, Y over a finite or countable domain D is $\triangle(X,Y) = \frac{1}{2}\sum_{w \in D}|P_X(w) - P_Y(w)|$. A hash function $\mathbf{H} = (\mathcal{K}, \mathcal{H})$ with range $\mathbb{R}$ is pairwise-independent if for all $x_1 \neq x_2 \in \{0,1\}^l$ and all $y_1, y_2 \in \mathbb{R}$, $\Pr[\mathcal{H}(K,x_1) = y_1 \wedge \mathcal{H}(K,x_2) = y_2 : K \overset{R}{\leftarrow} \mathcal{K}] \leq \frac{1}{|\mathbb{R}|^2}$. A hash function $\mathbf{H}(\mathcal{K}, \mathcal{H})$ is collision resistant if for all probabilistic polynomial-time adversary $\mathcal{A}$, the advantage $Adv_{\mathbf{H}}^{cr}(\mathcal{A})$ is negligible, where $Adv_{\mathbf{H}}^{cr} = \Pr\left[\mathcal{H}(K,x_1) = \mathcal{H}(K,x_2) \middle| K \overset{R}{\leftarrow} \mathcal{K}; (x_1, x_2) \overset{R}{\leftarrow} \mathcal{A}(K); \right]$.

Definition 1 *(Invertible Pairwise-Independent Permutation [4]). A pairwise-independent hash function $\mathbf{H}_{inv} = (\mathcal{K}_{inv}, \mathcal{H}_{inv})$ is an invertible pairwise-independent permutation if it satisfies the following two conditions: (1) **Invertible**. There exists a PPT algorithm $\mathcal{I}nv$ such that $\mathcal{I}nv(k_{inv}, \mathcal{H}_{inv}(k_{inv}, m)) = m$, where $m \in \{0,1\}^l$ and $k_{inv} \overset{R}{\leftarrow} \mathcal{K}_{inv}$; (2) **Permutable**. $\mathbf{H}_{inv}$ is a permutation.*

Definition 2 *(Lossy TDF [10]). A collection of $(l, l - r)$-lossy trapdoor function $\mathcal{LTDF}$ is defined by four probabilistic polynomial-time algorithms $(\mathcal{K}_{lt}, \widetilde{\mathcal{K}}_{lt}, \mathcal{F}_{lt}, \mathcal{F}_{lt}^{-1})$ satisfying the following properties. (1) $\widetilde{\mathcal{K}}_{lt}$ **induces a lossy**

function. When algorithm $\widetilde{\mathcal{K}}_{lt}(1^k)$ outputs $(\widetilde{ek}, \perp)$, $\mathcal{F}_{lt}$ on inputs $\widetilde{ek}$, $x \in \{0,1\}^l$ returns $\mathcal{F}_{lt}(\widetilde{ek}, x)$. In addition, we also require that the size of $\mathcal{F}_{lt}(\widetilde{ek}, \cdot)$ is bounded by 2^r for all $\widetilde{ek}$. **(2)** $\mathcal{K}_{lt}$ **induces an injective function with trap-door.** The key generation algorithm $\mathcal{K}_{lt}(1^k)$ outputs (ek, tk). Then $\mathcal{F}_{lt}$ takes ek and an input $x \in \{0,1\}^l$ to return an unique value $c = \mathcal{F}_{lt}(ek, x)$. Finally, on inputs $(tk, \mathcal{F}_{lt}(ek, x))$, $\mathcal{F}_{lt}^{-1}$ returns x or $\perp$. **(3) Security.** Let EK denote the fist random variable output by $\mathcal{K}_{lt}$, and let $\widetilde{EK}$ denote the first random variable output by $\widetilde{\mathcal{K}}_{lt}$. For all probabilistic polynomial-time adversary $\mathcal{A}$, the advantage of $\mathcal{A}$ in distinguishing EK from $\widetilde{EK}$, denoted by $Adv_{\mathcal{LTDF}}^{\mathrm{ind}}(\mathcal{A})$, is negligible, i.e., $EK \overset{c}{\approx} \widetilde{EK}$.

Definition 3 *(All-But-n TDF [8]).* *A collection of $(l, l-r)$ all-but-n trap-door function $\mathcal{ABN}$ with the branch set $\mathbb{B}$ is defined by a tuple of 3 probabilistic polynomial-time algorithms $(\mathcal{K}_{abn}, \mathcal{F}_{abn}, \mathcal{F}_{abn}^{-1})$ satisfying the properties below.* **(1)** $\mathcal{K}_{abn}$ **with a given lossy set** $\mathbb{I}$. *For any n-subset $\mathbb{I} \subseteq \mathbb{B}$, the key generation algorithm $\mathcal{K}_{abn}(\mathbb{I})$ returns (ek, tk). It requires that for each $b \in \mathbb{I}$, the size of $\mathcal{F}_{abn}(ek, b, \cdot)$ is bounded by 2^r for all ek. Additionally, for any branch $b \in \mathbb{B} \backslash \mathbb{I}$, $\mathcal{F}_{abn}(ek, b, \cdot)$ is an injective function on $\{0,1\}^l$, and $\mathcal{F}_{abn}^{-1}(tk, b, \mathcal{F}_{abn}(ek, b, x))$ $= x$ for all x.* **(2) Security.** *For any two distinct n-subsets $\mathbb{I}_0, \mathbb{I}_1 \subseteq \mathbb{B}$, let EK_0 denote the first random variable generated by $\mathcal{K}(\mathbb{I}_0)$ and EK_1 denote the first random variable generated by $\mathcal{K}(\mathbb{I}_1)$. For all probabilistic polynomial-time adversary $\mathcal{A}$, the advantage of $\mathcal{A}$ in distinguishing EK_0 from EK_1, denoted by $Adv_{\mathcal{ABN}}^{\mathrm{ind}}(\mathcal{A})$, is negligible, i.e., $EK_0 \overset{c}{\approx} EK_1$.*

If the quotient $L = Adv_{\mathcal{ABN}}^{\mathrm{ind}}(\mathcal{A})/Adv(\mathcal{A}')$ is a small constant, we say that the all-but-n TDF $\mathcal{ABN}$ is tightly secure, where $\mathcal{A}'$ is the adversary who attacks the underlying hard problem.

Definition 4 *(PRIV-IND Security for Block-Sources [4]).* *We say that an l-bit deterministic public encryption scheme $\mathcal{AE} = (\mathcal{K}, \mathcal{E}, \mathcal{D})$ is PRIV-IND secure for (t, l)-block-sources if for any (t, l)-block-sources $\overrightarrow{M_0}, \overrightarrow{M_1}$ of polynomial length n_{c^*} and all probabilistic polynomial-time adversary $\mathcal{A}$, the PRIV-IND-advantage*

$$Adv_{\mathcal{AE}}^{\mathrm{priv-ind}}(\mathcal{A}, \overrightarrow{M_0}, \overrightarrow{M_1}) = Guess_{\mathcal{AE}}(\mathcal{A}, \overrightarrow{M_0}) - Guess_{\mathcal{AE}}(\mathcal{A}, \overrightarrow{M_1})$$

of $\mathcal{A}$ against $\mathcal{AE}$ is negligible, where for $\beta \in \{0,1\}$

$$Guess_{\mathcal{AE}}(\mathcal{A}, \overrightarrow{M_\beta}) = \Pr\left[\mathcal{A}^{\mathcal{O}}(pk, \mathcal{E}(pk, \overrightarrow{m_\beta})) = 1 \middle| (pk, sk) \overset{R}{\leftarrow} \mathcal{K}; \overrightarrow{m_\beta} \overset{R}{\leftarrow} \overrightarrow{M_\beta}\right].$$

When $n_{c^*} = 1$, we call the scheme PRIV1-IND secure for block-sources; when $\mathcal{O}$ is the encryption oracle $\mathcal{E}(pk, \cdot)$, we call the scheme PRIV-IND-CPA secure for block-sources; when $\mathcal{O}$ includes the encryption and decryption oracle $\mathcal{E}(pk, \cdot) \vee \mathcal{D}(sk, \cdot)^{-\overrightarrow{c}^*}$, we call the scheme PRIV-IND-CCA secure for block-sources.

We also define a notion of PRIV-IND-q-CCA security for block-sources which is very similar to PRIV-IND-CCA security for block-sources except with the restriction that the length n_{c^*} of block-sources is bounded by q.

3 Tightly Secure D-PKE Constructions

Let $\mathbf{H}_{inv} = (\mathcal{K}_{inv}, \mathcal{H}_{inv})$ be an l-bit invertible pairwise-independent permutation with the inversion algorithm $\mathcal{I}nv$, and U_{inv} denote the uniform distribution on its range $\mathbb{R}_{inv} = \{0,1\}^l$. Let $\mathcal{LTDF} = (\mathcal{K}_{lt}, \widetilde{\mathcal{K}}_{lt}, \mathcal{F}_{lt}, \mathcal{F}_{lt}^{-1})$ be a collection of $(l, l-r_{lt})$ lossy TDF. Let $\mathcal{ABN} = (\mathcal{K}_{abn}, \mathcal{F}_{abn}, \mathcal{F}_{abn}^{-1})$ be a collection of $(l, l-r_{abn})$ all-but-n TDF with a branch set $\mathbb{B}$ and let $\mathbf{H}_{cr} = (\mathcal{K}_{cr}, \mathcal{H}_{cr})$ be an l-bit collision resistant hash function. And the range $\mathbb{R}_{cr} \subseteq \mathbb{B}$ of $\mathbf{H}_{cr}$ is bounded by $2^{r_{cr}}$.

Key Generation $\mathcal{K}_{cpa}(1^k)$	Encryption $\mathcal{E}_{cpa}(pk, m)$	Decryption $\mathcal{D}_{cpa}(sk, c)$
$k_{inv} \xleftarrow{R} \mathcal{K}_{inv}(1^k)$;	$h \leftarrow \mathcal{H}_{inv}(k_{inv}, m)$;	$h \leftarrow \mathcal{F}_{lt}^{-1}(tk_{lt}, c)$;
$(ek_{lt}, tk_{lt}) \xleftarrow{R} \mathcal{K}_{lt}(1^k)$;	$c \leftarrow \mathcal{F}_{lt}(ek_{lt}, h)$;	$m' \leftarrow \mathcal{I}nv(k_{inv}, h)$;
$pk := (k_{inv}, ek_{lt})$;	Return c.	Return m'.
$sk := (tk_{lt})$.		

(a) Tightly PRIV-IND-CCA Bounded-Secure D-PKE $\mathcal{AE}_{CCA}$ for Block-Sources

Key Generation $\mathcal{K}_{cca}(1^k)$	Encryption $\mathcal{E}_{cca}(pk, m)$	Decryption $\mathcal{D}_{cca}(sk, c = b\|c_1\|c_2)$
$k_{inv} \xleftarrow{R} \mathcal{K}_{inv}(1^k)$;	$h \leftarrow \mathcal{H}_{inv}(k_{inv}, m)$;	$h' \leftarrow \mathcal{F}_{lt}^{-1}(tk_{lt}, c_1)$;
$k_{cr} \xleftarrow{R} \mathcal{K}_{cr}(1^k)$;	$b \leftarrow \mathcal{H}_{cr}(k_{cr}, h)$;	$m' \leftarrow \mathcal{I}nv(k_{inv}, h')$;
$(ek_{lt}, tk_{lt}) \xleftarrow{R} \mathcal{K}_{lt}(1^k)$;	$c_1 \leftarrow \mathcal{F}_{lt}(ek_{lt}, h)$;	$c' \leftarrow \mathcal{E}(pk, m')$;
$\mathbb{I} = \{I_i, i \in [n]\}, I_i \xleftarrow{\$} \mathbb{B} \setminus \mathbb{R}_{cr}$;	$c_2 \leftarrow \mathcal{F}_{abn}(ek_{abn}, b, h)$;	If $c' = b\|c_1\|c_2$, return m',
$(ek_{abn}, tk_{abn}) \xleftarrow{R} \mathcal{K}_{abn}(\mathbb{I})$;	Return $b\|c_1\|c_2$.	Else return $\bot$.
$pk := (k_{inv}, k_{cr}, ek_{lt}, ek_{abn})$;		
$sk := (tk_{lt})$.		

(b) Tightly PRIV-IND-CCA Bounded-Secure D-PKE $\mathcal{AE}_{CCA}$ for Block-Sources

Fig. 2. Tightly secure D-PKE constructions

Theorem 1. *(1) Let $\mathcal{AE}_{CPA} = (\mathcal{K}, \mathcal{E}, \mathcal{D})$ be defined in Fig. 2(a). Then, the decryption algorithm can recover the message correctly. And for any probabilistic polynomial-time adversary $\mathcal{A}$, any (t,l)-block-sources $\overrightarrow{M_0}, \overrightarrow{M_1}$ of length n_{c^*}, there exists an adversary $\mathcal{A}_{lt}$ such that*

$$Adv_{\mathcal{AE}_{CPA}}^{priv-ind-cpa}(\mathcal{A}, \overrightarrow{M_0}, \overrightarrow{M_1}) \leq 2 \cdot Adv_{\mathcal{LTDF}}^{ind}(\mathcal{A}_{lt}) + 2n_{c^*} \cdot \epsilon, \qquad (1)$$

where $\epsilon \leq 2^{\frac{r_{lt}-2-t}{2}}$. (2) Let the D-PKE scheme $\mathcal{AE}_{CCA}$ be depicted in Fig. 2(b). Then the decryption algorithm can recover the message correctly. And for any probabilistic polynomial-time adversary $\mathcal{A}$, any (t,l)-block-sources $\overrightarrow{M_0}, \overrightarrow{M_1}$ of length $n_{c^*} \leq \frac{n}{2}$, there exist adversaries $\mathcal{A}_{cr}, \mathcal{A}_{lt}, \mathcal{A}_{abn}$ such that

$$\begin{aligned} &Adv_{\mathcal{AE}_{CCA}}^{priv-ind-\frac{n}{2}-cca}(\mathcal{A}, \overrightarrow{M_0}, \overrightarrow{M_1}) \\ &\leq 2 \cdot Adv_{\mathbf{H}_{cr}}^{cr}(\mathcal{A}_{cr}) + 2 \cdot Adv_{\mathcal{LTDF}}^{ind}(\mathcal{A}_{lt}) + 4 \cdot Adv_{\mathcal{ABN}}^{ind}(\mathcal{A}_{abn}) + 2n_{c^*} \cdot \epsilon, \end{aligned} \qquad (2)$$

where $\epsilon \leq 2^{\frac{r_{cr}+r_{lt}+r_{abn}-2-t}{2}}$. Additionally, if the all-but-n TDF $\mathcal{ABN}$ is tightly secure, then the D-PKE construction $\mathcal{AE}_{CCA}$ is tightly PRIV-IND-$\frac{n}{2}$-CCA *secure for block-sources. In the above, $\mathcal{A}_{cr}$ is the adversary who wants to find collisions of $\mathbf{H}_{cr}$, and $\mathcal{A}_{lt}$ (respectively, $\mathcal{A}_{abn}$) is the adversary who attacks the security of $\mathcal{LTDF}$ (respectively, $\mathcal{ABN}$).*

Tightly Secure All-But- n **TDF Under the s-DCR Assumption.** Look ahead, tightly PRIV-IND-$\frac{n}{2}$-CCA secure deterministic public-key encryption construction needs the primitive of tightly secure all-but-n TDF. In this paper, we also prove the all-but-n TDF given by [8] is tightly secure with a security loss of only 2. This improves their original security reduction which has a security loss of $2n$ due to the use of the hybrid technique. Please see more details in our full version paper.

Acknowledgments. We thank the anonymous ICICS'2017 reviewers for their helpful comments. This work is supported by the National Cryptography Development Fund MMJJ20170116 and the National Nature Science Foundation of China (Nos. 61602473, 61502480, 61672019, 61772522, 61379137, 61572495).

References

1. Bellare, M., Boldyreva, A., Micali, S.: Public-key encryption in a multi-user setting: security proofs and improvements. In: Preneel, B. (ed.) EUROCRYPT 2000. LNCS, vol. 1807, pp. 259–274. Springer, Heidelberg (2000). https://doi.org/10.1007/3-540-45539-6_18
2. Bellare, M., Boldyreva, A., O'Neill, A.: Deterministic and efficiently searchable encryption. In: Menezes, A. (ed.) CRYPTO 2007. LNCS, vol. 4622, pp. 535–552. Springer, Heidelberg (2007). https://doi.org/10.1007/978-3-540-74143-5_30
3. Bellare, M., Fischlin, M., O'Neill, A., Ristenpart, T.: Deterministic encryption: definitional equivalences and constructions without random oracles. In: Wagner, D. (ed.) CRYPTO 2008. LNCS, vol. 5157, pp. 360–378. Springer, Heidelberg (2008). https://doi.org/10.1007/978-3-540-85174-5_20
4. Boldyreva, A., Fehr, S., O'Neill, A.: On notions of security for deterministic encryption, and efficient constructions without random oracles. In: Wagner, D. (ed.) CRYPTO 2008. LNCS, vol. 5157, pp. 335–359. Springer, Heidelberg (2008). https://doi.org/10.1007/978-3-540-85174-5_19
5. Brakerski, Z., Segev, G.: Better security for deterministic public-key encryption: the auxiliary-input setting. In: Rogaway, P. (ed.) CRYPTO 2011. LNCS, vol. 6841, pp. 543–560. Springer, Heidelberg (2011). https://doi.org/10.1007/978-3-642-22792-9_31
6. Dolev, D., Dwork, C., Naor, M.: Non-malleable cryptography (extended abstract). In: STOC 1991, pp. 542–552
7. Gay, R., Hofheinz, D., Kiltz, E., Wee, H.: Tightly CCA-secure encryption without pairings. In: Fischlin, M., Coron, J.-S. (eds.) EUROCRYPT 2016. LNCS, vol. 9665, pp. 1–27. Springer, Heidelberg (2016). https://doi.org/10.1007/978-3-662-49890-3_1
8. Hemenway, B., Libert, B., Ostrovsky, R., Vergnaud, D.: Lossy encryption: constructions from general assumptions and efficient selective opening chosen ciphertext security. In: Lee, D.H., Wang, X. (eds.) ASIACRYPT 2011. LNCS, vol. 7073, pp. 70–88. Springer, Heidelberg (2011). https://doi.org/10.1007/978-3-642-25385-0_4

9. Mironov, I., Pandey, O., Reingold, O., Segev, G.: Incremental deterministic public-key encryption. In: Pointcheval, D., Johansson, T. (eds.) EUROCRYPT 2012. LNCS, vol. 7237, pp. 628–644. Springer, Heidelberg (2012). https://doi.org/10.1007/978-3-642-29011-4_37

10. Peikert, C., Waters, B.: Lossy trapdoor functions and their applications. In: STOC 2008, pp. 187–196

11. Raghunathan, A., Segev, G., Vadhan, S.: Deterministic public-key encryption for adaptively chosen plaintext distributions. In: Johansson, T., Nguyen, P.Q. (eds.) EUROCRYPT 2013. LNCS, vol. 7881, pp. 93–110. Springer, Heidelberg (2013). https://doi.org/10.1007/978-3-642-38348-9_6

12. Wee, H.: Dual projective hashing and its applications — lossy trapdoor functions and more. In: Pointcheval, D., Johansson, T. (eds.) EUROCRYPT 2012. LNCS, vol. 7237, pp. 246–262. Springer, Heidelberg (2012). https://doi.org/10.1007/978-3-642-29011-4_16

13. Xie, X., Xue, R., Zhang, R.: Deterministic public key encryption and identity-based encryption from lattices in the auxiliary-input setting. In: Visconti, I., De Prisco, R. (eds.) SCN 2012. LNCS, vol. 7485, pp. 1–18. Springer, Heidelberg (2012). https://doi.org/10.1007/978-3-642-32928-9_1

Efficient Inner Product Encryption
with Simulation-Based Security

Qingsong Zhao[1,4], Qingkai Zeng[1(✉)], and Ximeng Liu[2,3]

[1] State Key Laboratory for Novel Software Technology,
Department of Computer Science and Technology, Nanjing University,
Nanjing, China
zqk@nju.edu.cn
[2] College of Mathematics and Computer Science, Fuzhou University, Fuzhou, China
snbnix@gmail.com
[3] School of Information Systems, Singapore Management University,
Singapore, Singapore
[4] College of Information Science and Technology, Nanjing Agricultural University,
Nanjing, China
Qszhao@njau.edu.cn

Abstract. An inner product encryption (IPE) scheme is a special type of functional encryption where the decryption algorithm, given a ciphertext related to a vector x and a secret key to a vector y, computes the inner product $\langle x, y \rangle$. A function-hiding IPE scheme requires that the secret key reveals no unnecessary information on the vector y besides the privacy of the vector x. In this paper, we construct a function-hiding IPE scheme using the asymmetric bilinear pairing group setting of prime order. Compared with the existing similar schemes, our construction both reduces necessary storage complexity and computational complexity by a factor 2 or more and achieves simulation-based security, which is much stronger than indistinguishability-based security, under the External Decisional Linear assumption in the standard model.

Keywords: Functional encryption · Inner product
Function privacy · Simulation-based security

1 Introduction

Traditional public-key encryption provides all-or-nothing access to data: you can either recover the entire plaintext or reveal nothing from the ciphertext. Functional encryption (FE) [5,15] is a vast new paradigm for encryption which allows tremendous flexibility in accessing encrypted data. In functional encryption, a secret key sk_f embedded with a function f can be created from a master secret key msk. Then, given a ciphertext for x, a user learns $f(x)$ and reveals nothing else about x. In recent years, the cryptographic community has made great progress in research on the security of FE and construction for such schemes (see for instance [1,6,8–10] and any more).

© Springer International Publishing AG, part of Springer Nature 2018
S. Qing et al. (Eds.): ICICS 2017, LNCS 10631, pp. 162–171, 2018.
https://doi.org/10.1007/978-3-319-89500-0_14

There are two notions of security for a FE scheme, i.e., indistinguishability-based security and simulation-based security. The former one requires that an adversary cannot distinguish between ciphertexts of any two messages x_0, x_1 with access to a secret key sk_f for a function f such that $f(x_0) = f(x_1)$. In contrast, the latter one requires that the view of the adversary can be simulated by a simulator, given only access to the secret keys and the function evaluated on the corresponding messages. Note that simulation-based security is stronger than indistinguishability-based security such that there exists an indistinguishability-based secure FE scheme for a certain functionality which is not able to be proved secure under simulation-based security [5,15].

The traditional FE only considers data privacy and omits to protect the privacy of the function itself which is also crucial for practical applications. Consider the case where Bob wants to store his files in a cloud. Before uploading his files to the cloud, he employs a FE scheme to encrypt them avoiding leakage of data privacy and then he uploads the encryption form to the cloud. Later on, Bob wants to query his data by offering the cloud a key sk_f for a function f of his choice. However, if the FE scheme cannot support the privacy for the function, the key sk_f may reveal Bob's query f entirely to the cloud, which is not desirable when the function includes confidential information.

Due to the importance, some works are focus on function privacy of FE, and it was first studied in [16] in the private-key setting. It is later followed by the work of [6] in the private-key setting and that of [4] in the public-key setting. A intuitive definition of function privacy is one where function keys leak no unnecessary information on associated function. During the two scenarios of the public-key setting and the private-key setting, the degree to which function privacy can be satisfied differs dramatically. Specifically, a public-key FE scheme is inherent in leaking confidential information about the function. Note that an attacker who holds a secret key sk_f can always generate, on its own, the ciphertext for x_i for message x_i of her choice, and then use sk_f to learn $f(x_i)$. This can reveal non-trivial information about the function f. On the other hand, since an attacker holding a secret key sk_f cannot encrypt new messages in the private-key setting, such kind of attack is no longer applies.

Functional Encryption for Inner Product. Although FE supports the computation of general circuits relied on a wide spectrum of assumptions, there are two major problems with the state-of-the-art general FE constructions. First, the security of some constructions is only ensured so long as the adversary gets hold of a-priori bounded number of secret keys [9,10]. Second, some solutions rely on tools such as multilinear maps and indistinguishability obfuscation which are both impractical and founded on new security assumption undergone minimal scrutiny. It inspires us to explore constructions for firsthand and effective FE schemes for functionalities which focus on the inner product functionality as a first attempt [2,3,7,11,17,18].

In an inner product encryption (IPE) scheme, a ciphertext CT is related to a vector $x \in \mathbb{Z}_q^n$ of length n and a secret key SK to a vector $y \in \mathbb{Z}_q^n$ of length n. Given the ciphertext and the secret key, the decryption algorithm computes the inner product $\langle \boldsymbol{x}, \boldsymbol{y} \rangle = \sum_{i=1}^{n} x_i y_i$. In this paper, we consider IPE with function privacy, i.e., function-hiding inner product encryption.

Function-Hiding IPE. [2] presented adaptively secure schemes where the message x_0 and x_1 may be adaptively chosen at any point in time, based on the previously collected information. Bishop et al. [3] proposed a function-hiding IPE scheme under the Symmetric External Diffie-Hellman (SXDH) assumption, which satisfies an indistinguishability-based definition, and considered adaptive adversaries. However, the scheme is available in a rather weak and unrealistic security model which places limit on adversaries' queries. Recently, Datta et al. [7] developed a function-hiding IPE under the SXDH assumption where the additional restriction on adversaries' queries is removed. Tomida et al. [17] constructed a more efficient function-hiding IPE scheme than that of [7] under the External Decisional Linear (XDLIN) assumption. Kim et al. [11] put forth a fully-secure function-hiding IPE scheme with less parameter sizes and run-time complexity than in [3,7]. The scheme is proved simulation-based secure in the generic model of bilinear maps. For the first time Zhao et al. [18] presented a simulation-based secure functional-hiding IPE scheme under the SXDH assumption in the standard model. The scheme can tolerate an unbounded number of ciphertext queries and adaptive key queries.

Our Contribution. We construct a efficient simulation-based secure function-hiding IPE (SSFH-IPE) scheme in the standard model. We compare our scheme with related works in Table 1 where scalar multiplications on cyclic groups are involved in key generation algorithm and encryption algorithm, and paring operations on bilinear paring groups are involved in decryption algorithm. We achieve an outstanding reduction by a factor of 2 or more in computational complexity. Our scheme achieves $n + 6$ group elements in secret key and ciphertext, which also reduces storage complexity by a factor 2 or more. Hence, performance in the SSFH-IPE scheme is superior to that in the previous schemes in both storage complexity and computation complexity. Furthermore, our scheme is based on the XDLIN assumption which is weaker than the SXDH assumption. In more detail, the SXDH assumption relies on type 3 bilinear pairing groups, while the XDLIN assumption relies on any type of bilinear pairing groups [17]. Therefore from this angle, the SXDH assumption is stronger than the XDLIN assumption. Although the construction of [17] was proved to be indistinguishability-based secure under the XDLIN assumption and also succeeded in improving efficiency, both storage complexity and computation complexity of our scheme are better than that of [17] and our scheme achieves simulation-base security which is much stronger than indistinguishability-based security.

To guarantee correctness, our scheme requires that inner products are within a range of polynomial-size, which is consistent with other schemes in Table 1. As pointed out in [3], it is reasonable for statistical computations because the computations, like the average over a polynomial-size database, will naturally be contained within a polynomial range. In addition, our scheme is simulation-based secure against adversaries who hold in an unbounded number of ciphertext queries and adaptive key queries. Although very basic functionalities such as IBE

Table 1. Comparison of SSFH-IPE scheme. n is the dimension of vector. We have eight security notions xx-yy-zzz where xx $\in$ {one, many} refers to a single or multiple challenge ciphertexts; yy $\in$ {SEL, AD} refers to selectively or adaptively chosen ciphertext queries; zzz $\in$ {IND, SIM} refers to indistinguishability vs simulation-based security.

Scheme	Master secret key	Ciphertext secret key	Scalar multiplications	Pairing operations	Assum.	Security
BJK15 [3]	$8n^2 + 8$	$2n + 2$	$2n + 2$	$2n + 2$	SXDH	many-AD-IND
DDM16 [7]	$8n^2 + 12n + 28$	$4n + 8$	$4n + 8$	$4n + 8$	SXDH	many-AD-IND
TAO16 [17]	$4n^2 + 18n + 20$	$2n + 5$	$2n + 5$	$2n + 5$	XDLIN	many-AD-IND
ZZL17 [18]	$6n^2 + 10n + 24$	$2n + 4$	$2n + 4$	$2n + 4$	SXDH	many-AD-SIM
This work	$2n^2 + 18n + 36$	$n + 6$	$n + 6$	$n + 6$	XDLIN	many-AD-SIM

is simulation-based secure for a-priori bounded number of ciphertext queries in the standard model [1,5,15], it is possible for an unbounded number of ciphertext queries if adversaries have an underlying polynomial-size range.

Technical Overview. The SSFH-IPE scheme uses dual pairing vector spaces (DPVS) to construct, as in [3,7,17,18], which is bring forward by Okamoto and Takashima [13,14]. DPVS has the features of hidden linear subspaces in prime order bilinear group setting. A DPVS of dimension $n + 6$ is introduced in our construction, where n is the dimension of inner product vectors. Typically, we sample a pair of dual orthonormal bases $(\mathbb{B}, \mathbb{B}^*)$ and only use the $n + 4$ dimension $\mathbb{B}$ and the $n + 4$ dimension $\mathbb{B}^*$ to encode vector x and vector y respectively. Compared with the previous schemes, our scheme at least saves n dimensions of vector spaces. We preserve the remaining hidden dimensions of $\mathbb{B}$ and $\mathbb{B}^*$ for the security reduction. Specially, between two hybrid experiments, a hidden dimension can be used for reducing a difference of one coefficient in a secret key or a ciphertext to a XDLIN instance. In other words, the hidden dimension can be used to convert a corresponding coefficient to another coefficient in a secret key or a ciphertext, so that no PPT adversary can distinguish the two hybrid experiments.

2 Preliminaries

Let λ be the security parameter. If S is a set, $x \xleftarrow{\$} S$ denotes the process of choosing uniformly at random from S. Let $X = \{X_n\}_{n \in \mathbb{N}}$ and $Y = \{Y_n\}_{n \in \mathbb{N}}$ be distribution ensembles. We say that $X \approx_c Y$ are computationally indistinguishable between X and Y, if for all nonuniform probabilistic polynomial-time D and every $n \in \mathbb{N}$, the difference between $\Pr[D(X_n) = 1]$ and $\Pr[D(Y_n) = 1]$ is negligible. Let $negl(\lambda)$ be a negligible function in λ. Moreover, we write x to denote a vector $(x_1, \ldots, x_n) \in \mathbb{Z}_q^n$ of length n for some positive integer q and n. We use $\langle a, b \rangle$ to denote the inner product, $\sum_{i=1}^n a_i b_i \bmod q$, of vectors $a \in \mathbb{Z}_q^n$ and $b \in \mathbb{Z}_q^n$. We use upper case boldface to denote matrics. $\mathbf{X}^T$ denotes transpose of the matrix $\mathbf{X}$. $GL(n, \mathbb{Z}_q)$ denotes the general linear group of degree n over $\mathbb{Z}_q$. $\mathbb{Z}_q^{\times}$ denotes a set of integers $\{1, \ldots, q-1\}$.

Definition 1 (SSFH-IPE). *A SSFH-IPE scheme is composed of the four PPT algorithms defined as below. The setup algorithm* **SSFH-IPE.Setup** *receives as input the security parameter λ and n, which is vector length, and outputs a master secret key msk and public parameters pp. The encryption algorithm* **SSFH-IPE.Encrypt** *receives as input the master secret key msk, the public parameters pp and a vector $\boldsymbol{x} \in \mathbb{Z}_q^n$, and outputs a ciphertext $ct_{\boldsymbol{x}}$. The key generation algorithm* **SSFH-IPE.KeyGen** *receives as input the master secret key msk, the public parameters pp and a vector $\boldsymbol{y} \in \mathbb{Z}_q^n$, and outputs a secret key $sk_{\boldsymbol{y}}$. The decryption algorithm* **SSFH-IPE.Decrypt** *receives as input the public parameters pp, the ciphertext $ct_{\boldsymbol{x}}$ and a secret key $sk_{\boldsymbol{y}}$, and outputs either a value $m \in \mathbb{Z}_q$ or the dedicated symbol $\perp$.*

We make the following correctness requirement: for all (msk, pp) $\xleftarrow{\$}$ **SSFH-IPE.Setup**$(1^{\lambda}, n)$, all $\boldsymbol{x}, \boldsymbol{y} \in \mathbb{Z}_q^n$, for $ct_{\boldsymbol{x}} \xleftarrow{\$}$ **SSFH-IPE.Encrypt**(msk, pp, $\boldsymbol{x}$) and $sk_{\boldsymbol{y}} \xleftarrow{\$}$ **SSFH-IPE.KeyGen**(msk, pp, $\boldsymbol{y}$), we have that **SSFH-IPE.Decry-pt**(pp, $ct_{\boldsymbol{x}}$, $sk_{\boldsymbol{y}}$) is sure to output $\langle \boldsymbol{x}, \boldsymbol{y} \rangle$ whenever $\langle \boldsymbol{x}, \boldsymbol{y} \rangle \neq \perp$ with non-negligible probability. The correctness requires that it is $\langle \boldsymbol{x}, \boldsymbol{y} \rangle$ and not $\perp$ when $\langle \boldsymbol{x}, \boldsymbol{y} \rangle$ is from a fixed polynomial range of value inside $\mathbb{Z}_q$.

Definition 2 (Simulation-Based Security). *For a SSFH-IPE scheme, if there exits a PPT adversary $\mathcal{A} = (\mathcal{A}_1, \mathcal{A}_2)$ and a PPT simulator S, we define two experiments* $\boldsymbol{Real}_{\mathcal{A}}^{SSFH-IPE}(1^{\lambda})$ *and* $\boldsymbol{Ideal}_{\mathcal{A},S}^{SSFH-IPE}(1^{\lambda})$ *in Fig. 1. Let ℓ be the number of challenge messages output by $\mathcal{A}_1$ and p_1 be the number of secret key queries in the first stage. The oracles $\mathcal{O}$ and $\mathcal{O}'$ are defined as following:*

- *The oracle $\mathcal{O}(msk, \cdot) = SSFH\text{-}IPE.KeyGen(msk, \cdot, \cdot)$.*
- *The oracle $\mathcal{O}'(msk, st, \cdot)$ is the second stage of S, i.e., $S^{\langle \boldsymbol{x}_i, \boldsymbol{y}_j \rangle}(msk, st, \cdot)$ for $i \in [\ell], j \in [p_1]$, where $\boldsymbol{x}_i$ and $\boldsymbol{y}_j$ are inputs of the ith ciphertext query and the jth secret key query by $\mathcal{A}_1$ respectively.*

A SSFH-IPE scheme is simulation-based secure if there exists a PPT simulator S such that for all PPT adversaries $\mathcal{A}$,

$$\boldsymbol{Real}_{\mathcal{A}}^{SSFH-IPE}(1^{\lambda}) \approx_c \boldsymbol{Ideal}_{\mathcal{A},S}^{SSFH-IPE}(1^{\lambda}).$$

Definition 3 (Asymmetric Bilinear Pairing Groups). *We say an algorithm $\mathcal{G}_{abpg}(1^{\lambda})$ is an asymmetric bilinear group generator and it outputs a bilinear pairing group which is defined by the tuple $(q, \mathbb{G}_1, \mathbb{G}_2, \mathbb{G}_T, e)$, where q is a prime, $\mathbb{G}_1, \mathbb{G}_2, \mathbb{G}_T$ are cyclic groups of order q, and a bilinear pairing $e : \mathbb{G}_1 \times \mathbb{G}_2 \to \mathbb{G}_T$ with the following properties:*

1. *(Bilinearity) $\forall g_1 \in \mathbb{G}_1$, $g_2 \in \mathbb{G}_2$, $a, b \in \mathbb{Z}_q$, $e(g_1^a, g_2^b) = e(g_1, g_2)^{ab}$ and*
2. *(Non-degeneracy) $\exists g_1 \in \mathbb{G}_1$, $g_2 \in \mathbb{G}_2$ such that $e(g_1, g_2)$ has order q in $\mathbb{G}_T$.*

Experiment $\mathbf{Real}_{\mathcal{A}}^{\text{SSFH-IPE}}(1^\lambda)$:	Experiment $\mathbf{Ideal}_{\mathcal{A},S}^{\text{SSFH-IPE}}(1^\lambda)$:
$(\text{msk, pp}) \xleftarrow{\$} \text{SSFH-IPE.Setup}(1^\lambda, n)$	$(\text{msk}, st') \xleftarrow{\$} S(1^\lambda, n)$
$(\boldsymbol{x}, st) \xleftarrow{\$} \mathcal{A}_1^{\text{SSFH-IPE.KeyGen}(\text{msk},\cdot,\cdot)}(\text{pp})$	$(\boldsymbol{x}, st) \xleftarrow{\$} \mathcal{A}_1^{\text{SSFH-IPE.KeyGen}(\text{msk},\cdot,\cdot)}(\text{pp})$
$ct_{\boldsymbol{x}_i} \xleftarrow{\$} \text{SSFH-IPE.Encrypt}(\text{msk, pp}, \boldsymbol{x})$	$(\{ct_{\boldsymbol{x}_i}\}_{i \in [\ell]}) \xleftarrow{\$} S(\{\langle \boldsymbol{x}_i, \boldsymbol{y}_j \rangle\}_{i \in [\ell], j \in [p_1]})$
for $i \in [\ell]$	where $\boldsymbol{y}_1, ..., \boldsymbol{y}_{p_1}$ are key queries made by $\mathcal{A}_1$.
$\alpha \xleftarrow{\$} \mathcal{A}_2^{\mathcal{O}(\text{msk},\cdot,\cdot)}(\{ct_{\boldsymbol{x}_i}\}_{i \in [\ell]}, st)$	$\alpha \xleftarrow{\$} \mathcal{A}_2^{\mathcal{O}'(\text{msk}, st, \cdot)}(\{ct_{\boldsymbol{x}_i}\}_{i \in [\ell]}, st)$
$\text{output}(\alpha)$	$\text{output}(\alpha)$

Fig. 1. Real and ideal experiments.

Definition 4 (External Decisional Linear (XDLIN) Assumption).
$(q, \mathbb{G}_1, \mathbb{G}_2, \mathbb{G}_T, e)$ *is a tuple produced by* $\mathcal{G}_{abpg}(1^\lambda)$. *Consider the following problem: given the distributions* $\mathcal{G}_b^{\text{XDLIN}}(1^\lambda) = ((q, \mathbb{G}_1, \mathbb{G}_2, \mathbb{G}_T, e), \xi g_1, \kappa g_1, \delta \xi g_1,$
$\sigma \kappa g_1, \xi g_2, \kappa g_2, \delta \xi g_2, \sigma \kappa g_2, Y_b)$ *for* $b \in 0, 1$, *where* $\xi, \kappa, \delta, \sigma \xleftarrow{\$} \mathbb{Z}_q$, $Y_0 = (\delta + \sigma) g_c$,
$Y_1 = (\delta + \sigma + \rho) g_c$, $\rho \xleftarrow{\$} \mathbb{Z}_q$ *and* $c \in \{0, 1\}$, *output* $\mathcal{G}_0^{\text{XDLIN}}$ *if* b *is 0 and output*
$\mathcal{G}_1^{\text{XDLIN}}$ *otherwise. We refer to the problem as the External Decisional Linear (XDLIN) problem.*

For a PPT algorithm $\mathcal{A}$, *the advantage of* $\mathcal{A}$ *is defined as:*
$\text{Adv}_{\mathcal{A}}^{\text{XDLIN}}(\lambda) = |\Pr[\mathcal{A}(1^\lambda, \mathcal{G}_0^{\text{XDLIN}}) \to 1] - \Pr[\mathcal{A}(1^\lambda, \mathcal{G}_1^{\text{XDLIN}}(1^\lambda)) \to 1]|$.
If for all PPT algorithms $\mathcal{A}$, $\text{Adv}_{\mathcal{A}}^{\text{XDLIN}}(\lambda)$ *is negligible in* λ, *we say* $\mathcal{G}_b^{\text{XDLIN}}(1^\lambda)$ *satisfies the XDLIN assumption.*

Definition 5 (Dual Pairing Vector Spaces (DPVS)). *A dual pairing vector space (DPVS)* $(q, \mathbb{V}, \mathbb{V}^*, \mathbb{G}_T, \mathbb{A}, \mathbb{A}^*, E)$ *is directly defined by the tuple* $(q, \mathbb{G}_1, \mathbb{G}_2, \mathbb{G}_T, e) \xleftarrow{\$} \mathcal{G}_{abpg}(1^\lambda)$. $\mathbb{V} = \mathbb{G}_1^n$ *and* $\mathbb{V}^* = \mathbb{G}_2^n$ *over* $\mathbb{Z}_q^n$ *are* n *dimensional vector spaces.* $\mathbb{A} = \{\boldsymbol{a}_1, ..., \boldsymbol{a}_n\}$ *of* $\mathbb{V}$ *and* $\mathbb{A}^* = \{\boldsymbol{a}_1^*, ..., \boldsymbol{a}_n^*\}$ *of* $\mathbb{V}^*$ *are canonical bases, where* $\boldsymbol{a}_i = (0^{i-1}, g_1, 0^{n-i})$ *and* $\boldsymbol{a}_i^* = (0^{i-1}, g_2, 0^{n-i})$. $E : \mathbb{V} \times \mathbb{V}^* \to \mathbb{G}_T$ *is pairing which is defined by* $E(\boldsymbol{x}, \boldsymbol{y}) = \prod_{i=1}^n e(X_i, Y_i) \in \mathbb{G}_T$ *where* $\boldsymbol{x} = (X_1, ... X_n) \in \mathbb{V}$ *and* $\boldsymbol{y} = (Y_1, ... Y_n) \in \mathbb{V}^*$ *with the following properties:*

1. *(Bilinearity)* $E(a\boldsymbol{x}, b\boldsymbol{y}) = E(\boldsymbol{x}, \boldsymbol{y})^{ab}$ *for* $a, b \in \mathbb{Z}_q$ *and*
2. *(Non-degeneracy) if* $E(\boldsymbol{x}, \boldsymbol{y}) = 1$ *for all* $\boldsymbol{y} \in \mathbb{V}^*$, *then* $\boldsymbol{x} = \boldsymbol{0}$.

Let $(q, \mathbb{V}, \mathbb{V}^*, \mathbb{G}_T, \mathbb{A}, \mathbb{A}^*, E)$ *be the output of algorithm* $\mathcal{G}_{dpvs}(1^\lambda, n, (q, \mathbb{G}_1, \mathbb{G}_2, \mathbb{G}_T, e))$, *where* $n \in \mathbb{N}$.

We then describe random dual orthonormal basis generator $\mathcal{G}_{ob}(1^\lambda, n)$ as following:

$$\mathcal{G}_{ob}(1^\lambda, n) : (q, \mathbb{V}, \mathbb{V}^*, \mathbb{G}_T, \mathbb{A}, \mathbb{A}^*, E) \xleftarrow{\$} \mathcal{G}_{dpvs}(1^\lambda, n, (q, \mathbb{G}_1, \mathbb{G}_2, \mathbb{G}_T, e)),$$
$$\mathbf{B} = (\chi_{i,j}) \xleftarrow{\$} GL(n, \mathbb{Z}_q), (\phi_{i,j}) = \psi(\mathbf{B}^T)^{-1},$$
$$\boldsymbol{b}_i = \sum_{j=1}^n \chi_{i,j} \boldsymbol{a}_j, \mathbb{B} = \{\boldsymbol{b}_1, ..., \boldsymbol{b}_n\},$$

$$\boldsymbol{b}_i^* = \sum_{j=1}^n \phi_{i,j} \boldsymbol{a}_j^*, \quad \mathbb{B}^* = \{\boldsymbol{b}_1^*, ..., \boldsymbol{b}_n^*\}, \quad g_T = e(g_1, g_2)^\psi,$$
return $(\mathbb{B}, \mathbb{B}^*)$.

Let $(\boldsymbol{x})_{\mathbb{B}}$ denote $\sum_{i=1}^n x_i \boldsymbol{b}_i$, where $\boldsymbol{x} = (x_1, ..., x_n)^T \in \mathbb{Z}_q^n$ and $\mathbb{B} = \{\boldsymbol{b}_1, ..., \boldsymbol{b}_n\}$. Then we have

$$E((\boldsymbol{x})_{\mathbb{A}}, (\boldsymbol{y})_{\mathbb{A}^*}) = \prod_{i=1}^n e(x_i g_1, y_i g_2) = e(g_1, g_2)^{\sum_{i=1}^n x_i y_i} = e(g_1, g_2)^{\langle \boldsymbol{x}, \boldsymbol{y} \rangle}, \quad and$$

$$E((\boldsymbol{x}\mathbb{B}, (\boldsymbol{y})_{\mathbb{B}^*}) = E((\mathbf{B}\boldsymbol{x})_{\mathbb{A}}, (\psi(\mathbf{B}^T)^{-1}\boldsymbol{y})_{\mathbb{A}^*}) = e(g_1, g_2)^{\psi \mathbf{B}\boldsymbol{x} \cdot (\mathbf{B}^T)^{-1}\boldsymbol{y}} = g_T^{\langle \boldsymbol{x}, \boldsymbol{y} \rangle}.$$

3   SSFH-IPE Scheme

In this section, we present the construction of SSFH-IPE.

SSFH-IPE.Setup$(1^\lambda, \text{n}) \to (\text{msk, pp})$: The setup algorithm runs $(q, \mathbb{G}_1, \mathbb{G}_2, \mathbb{G}_T, e) \overset{\$}{\leftarrow} \mathcal{G}_{abpg}(1^\lambda)$. It then generates

$$(q, \mathbb{V}, \mathbb{V}^*, \mathbb{G}_T, \mathbb{A}, \mathbb{A}^*, E) \overset{\$}{\leftarrow} \mathcal{G}_{dpvs}(1^\lambda, n+6, (q, \mathbb{G}_1, \mathbb{G}_2, \mathbb{G}_T, e)) \text{ and}$$

$$(\mathbb{B} = \{\boldsymbol{b}_1, ..., \boldsymbol{b}_{n+6}\}, \mathbb{B}^* = \{\boldsymbol{b}_1^*, ..., \boldsymbol{b}_{n+6}^*\}) \overset{\$}{\leftarrow} \mathcal{G}_{ob}(1^\lambda, n+6).$$

The algorithm outputs msk= $(\widehat{\mathbb{B}}, \widehat{\mathbb{B}}^*)$, where $\widehat{\mathbb{B}} = \{\boldsymbol{b}_1, ..., \boldsymbol{b}_n, \boldsymbol{b}_{n+1}, \boldsymbol{b}_{n+2}, \boldsymbol{b}_{n+5}\}$, $\widehat{\mathbb{B}}^* = \{\boldsymbol{b}_1^*, ..., \boldsymbol{b}_n^*, \boldsymbol{b}_{n+3}^*, \boldsymbol{b}_{n+4}^*, \boldsymbol{b}_{n+6}^*\}$, and pp= $(q, \mathbb{V}, \mathbb{V}^*, \mathbb{G}_T, \mathbb{A}_1, \mathbb{A}_1^*, E)$.

SSFH-IPE.Encrypt(msk, pp, $\boldsymbol{x}$)$\to ct_{\boldsymbol{x}}$: The encryption algorithm samples $\alpha, \beta, \eta \overset{\$}{\leftarrow} \mathbb{Z}_q$ independently and uniformly at random and outputs

$$ct_{\boldsymbol{x}} = (\boldsymbol{x}, \alpha, \beta, 0, 0, \eta, 0)_{\mathbb{B}}.$$

SSFH-IPE.KeyGen(msk, pp, $\boldsymbol{y}$)$\to sk_{\boldsymbol{y}}$: The secret key generation algorithm samples $\theta, \gamma, \zeta \overset{\$}{\leftarrow} \mathbb{Z}_q$ independently and uniformly at random and outputs

$$sk_{\boldsymbol{y}} = (\boldsymbol{y}, 0, 0, \theta, \gamma, 0, \zeta)_{\mathbb{B}^*}.$$

SSFH-IPE.Decrypt (pp, $ct_{\boldsymbol{x}}, sk_{\boldsymbol{y}}) \to m \in \mathbb{Z}_q$ or $\perp$: The decryption algorithm outputs

$$d = E(ct_{\boldsymbol{x}}, sk_{\boldsymbol{y}}).$$

It then attempts to determine $m \in \mathbb{Z}_q$ such that $g_T^m = d$. If there is m that satisfies the equation, the algorithm outputs m. Otherwise, it outputs $\perp$. Due to a polynomial-size range of possible values for m, the decryption algorithm certainly runs in polynomial time.

Correctness. For any $ct_{\boldsymbol{x}}$ and $sk_{\boldsymbol{y}}$ by calling **SSFH-IPE.Encrypt**(msk, pp, $\boldsymbol{x}$) and **SSFH-IPE.KeyGen**(msk, pp, $\boldsymbol{y}$) respectively, the pairing evaluations in the decryption algorithm proceed as follows:

$$d = E(ct_{\boldsymbol{x}}, sk_{\boldsymbol{y}}) = E(g_1, g_2)^{\langle \boldsymbol{x}, \boldsymbol{y} \rangle} = g_T^{\langle \boldsymbol{x}, \boldsymbol{y} \rangle}.$$

If the decryption algorithm takes polynomial time in the size of the plaintext space, it will output $m = \langle \boldsymbol{x}, \boldsymbol{y} \rangle$ as desired.

Remark 1. We can easily notice that our scheme is malleable, where a ciphertext can be created from certain other ciphertexts. The scheme in [17] is also malleable, while it seems difficult to prove the schemes in [3,7,18] to be malleable.

4 Security Proof

Definition 6 (Problem 0). *Problem 0 is to guess* $b \in \{0,1\}$*, given* $((q, \mathbb{G}_1, \mathbb{G}_2,$ $\mathbb{G}_T, e), \mathbb{B}, \widehat{\mathbb{B}}^*, \boldsymbol{y}_b, \kappa g_1, \xi g_2)$*, where*

$$(q, \mathbb{G}_1, \mathbb{G}_2, \mathbb{G}_T, e) \xleftarrow{\$} \mathcal{G}_{abpg}(1^\lambda),$$
$$\mathbf{B} = (\chi_{i,j}) \xleftarrow{\$} GL(3, \mathbb{Z}_q),\ (\phi_{i,j}) = (\mathbf{B}^T)^{-1},$$
$$\kappa \xleftarrow{\$} \mathbb{Z}_q,\ \boldsymbol{b}_i = \kappa \sum_{j=1}^n \chi_{i,j} \boldsymbol{a}_j\ \text{for}\ i = 1, 2, 3,\ \mathbb{B} = \{\boldsymbol{b}_1, \boldsymbol{b}_2, \boldsymbol{b}_3\},$$
$$\xi \xleftarrow{\$} \mathbb{Z}_q,\ \boldsymbol{b}_i^* = \xi \sum_{j=1}^n \phi_{i,j} \boldsymbol{a}_j^*\ \text{for}\ i = 1, 3,\ \widehat{\mathbb{B}}^* = \{\boldsymbol{b}_1^*, \boldsymbol{b}_3^*\},$$
$$g_T = e(g_1, g_2)^{\kappa\xi},\ \delta, \sigma \xleftarrow{\$} \mathbb{Z}_q,\ \rho \xleftarrow{\$} \mathbb{Z}_q^\times,$$
$$\boldsymbol{y}_0 = (\delta, 0, \sigma)_\mathbb{B},\ \boldsymbol{y}_1 = (\delta, \rho, \sigma)_\mathbb{B}.$$

Definition 7 (Problem 1). *Problem 1 is to guess* $b \in \{0,1\}$*, given* $((q, \mathbb{G}_1, \mathbb{G}_2,$ $\mathbb{G}_T, e), \widehat{\mathbb{B}}, \widehat{\mathbb{B}}^*, \boldsymbol{Y}_b)$*, where*

$$(\mathbb{B}, \mathbb{B}^*, (q, \mathbb{G}_1, \mathbb{G}_2, \mathbb{G}_T, e)) \xleftarrow{\$} \mathcal{G}_{ob}(1^\lambda, n+6),$$
$$\widehat{\mathbb{B}} = \{\boldsymbol{b}_1, ..., \boldsymbol{b}_n, \boldsymbol{b}_{n+1}, \boldsymbol{b}_{n+2}, \boldsymbol{b}_{n+5}\},\ \widehat{\mathbb{B}}^* = \{\boldsymbol{b}_1^*, ..., \boldsymbol{b}_n^*, \boldsymbol{b}_{n+3}^*, \boldsymbol{b}_{n+4}^*, \boldsymbol{b}_{n+6}^*\},$$
$$\alpha, \beta \xleftarrow{\$} \mathbb{Z}_q,\ \eta \xleftarrow{\$} \mathbb{Z}_q^\times,$$
$$\boldsymbol{Y}_0 = (0^n, \alpha, \beta, 0, 0, \eta, 0)_\mathbb{B},\ \boldsymbol{Y}_1 = (0^n, \alpha, \beta, 0, 0, \eta, \zeta')_\mathbb{B}.$$

Definition 8 (Problem 2). *Problem 2 is to guess* $b \in \{0,1\}$*, given* $((q, \mathbb{G}_1, \mathbb{G}_2,$ $\mathbb{G}_T, e), \widehat{\mathbb{B}}, \widehat{\mathbb{B}}^*, \boldsymbol{Y}_b)$*, where*

$$(\mathbb{B}, \mathbb{B}^*, (q, \mathbb{G}_1, \mathbb{G}_2, \mathbb{G}_T, e)) \xleftarrow{\$} \mathcal{G}_{ob}(1^\lambda, n+6),$$
$$\widehat{\mathbb{B}} = \{\boldsymbol{b}_1, ..., \boldsymbol{b}_n, \boldsymbol{b}_{n+1}, \boldsymbol{b}_{n+2}, \boldsymbol{b}_{n+5}\},\ \widehat{\mathbb{B}}^* = \{\boldsymbol{b}_1^*, ..., \boldsymbol{b}_n^*, \boldsymbol{b}_{n+3}^*, \boldsymbol{b}_{n+4}^*, \boldsymbol{b}_{n+6}^*\},$$
$$\alpha, \beta, \eta \xleftarrow{\$} \mathbb{Z}_q,\ \zeta' \xleftarrow{\$} \mathbb{Z}_q^\times,$$
$$\boldsymbol{Y}_0 = (0^n, \alpha, \beta, 0, 0, \eta, \zeta')_\mathbb{B},\ \boldsymbol{Y}_1 = (0^n, \alpha, \beta, 0, 0, 0, \zeta')_\mathbb{B}.$$

Definition 9 (Problem 3). *Problem 3 is to guess* $b \in \{0,1\}$*, given* $((q, \mathbb{G}_1, \mathbb{G}_2,$ $\mathbb{G}_T, e), \widehat{\mathbb{B}}, \widehat{\mathbb{B}}^*, \boldsymbol{Y}_b^*)$*, where*

$$(\mathbb{B}, \mathbb{B}^*, (q, \mathbb{G}_1, \mathbb{G}_2, \mathbb{G}_T, e)) \xleftarrow{\$} \mathcal{G}_{ob}(1^\lambda, n+6),$$
$$\widehat{\mathbb{B}} = \{\boldsymbol{b}_1, ..., \boldsymbol{b}_n, \boldsymbol{b}_{n+1}, \boldsymbol{b}_{n+2}, \boldsymbol{b}_{n+5}\},\ \widehat{\mathbb{B}}^* = \{\boldsymbol{b}_1^*, ..., \boldsymbol{b}_n^*, \boldsymbol{b}_{n+3}^*, \boldsymbol{b}_{n+4}^*, \boldsymbol{b}_{n+6}^*\},$$
$$\theta, \gamma, \zeta \xleftarrow{\$} \mathbb{Z}_q,\ \eta' \xleftarrow{\$} \mathbb{Z}_q^\times,$$
$$\boldsymbol{Y}_0^* = (0^n, 0, 0, \theta, \gamma, 0, \zeta)_{\mathbb{B}^*},\ \boldsymbol{Y}_1^* = (0^n, 0, 0, \theta, \gamma, \eta', \zeta)_{\mathbb{B}^*}.$$

Definition 10 (Problem 4). *Problem 4 is to guess* $b \in \{0,1\}$*, given* $((q, \mathbb{G}_1, \mathbb{G}_2,$ $\mathbb{G}_T, e), \widehat{\mathbb{B}}, \widehat{\mathbb{B}}^*, \boldsymbol{Y}_b^*)$*, where*

$$(\mathbb{B}, \mathbb{B}^*, (q, \mathbb{G}_1, \mathbb{G}_2, \mathbb{G}_T, e)) \xleftarrow{\$} \mathcal{G}_{ob}(1^\lambda, n+6),$$
$$\widehat{\mathbb{B}} = \{\boldsymbol{b}_1, ..., \boldsymbol{b}_n, \boldsymbol{b}_{n+1}, \boldsymbol{b}_{n+2}, \boldsymbol{b}_{n+5}\},\ \widehat{\mathbb{B}}^* = \{\boldsymbol{b}_1^*, ..., \boldsymbol{b}_n^*, \boldsymbol{b}_{n+3}^*, \boldsymbol{b}_{n+4}^*, \boldsymbol{b}_{n+6}^*\},$$
$$\theta, \gamma, \zeta \xleftarrow{\$} \mathbb{Z}_q,\ \eta' \xleftarrow{\$} \mathbb{Z}_q^\times,$$
$$\boldsymbol{Y}_0^* = (0^n, 0, 0, \theta, \gamma, \eta', \zeta)_{\mathbb{B}^*},\ \boldsymbol{Y}_1^* = (0^n, 0, 0, \theta, \gamma, \eta', 0)_{\mathbb{B}^*}.$$

For a PPT adversary $\mathcal{A}$, the advantage of $\mathcal{A}$ for Problem n, where $n = 0, 1, 2, 3, 4$, is defined as:

$$\mathrm{Adv}_{\mathcal{A}}^{\mathrm{Prob}_n}(\lambda) = |\Pr[\mathrm{Exp}_{\mathcal{A}}^{P_0}(1^{\lambda}) = 1] - \Pr[\mathrm{Exp}_{\mathcal{A}}^{P_1}(1^{\lambda}) = 1]|,$$

where the instance is by definition P_0 if $b = 0$ and P_1 if $b = 1$.

Lemma 1 (Lemma 14 in the full version of [12]). *Suppose the XDLIN assumption holds in $\mathbb{G}_1$ and $\mathbb{G}_2$. Then for all PPT adversary $\mathcal{B}$, there is a adversary $\mathcal{A}$ such that $\mathrm{Adv}_{\mathcal{B}}^{\mathrm{Prob}_0}(\lambda) \leq \mathrm{Adv}_{\mathcal{A}}^{\mathrm{XDLIN}}(\lambda) + 5/q$.*

Lemma 2. *Suppose the XDLIN assumption holds in $\mathbb{G}_1$ and $\mathbb{G}_2$. Then for all PPT adversary $\mathcal{B}$, there is a adversary $\mathcal{A}$ such that $\mathrm{Adv}_{\mathcal{B}}^{\mathrm{Prob}_1}(\lambda) \leq \mathrm{Adv}_{\mathcal{A}}^{\mathrm{Prob}_0}(\lambda)$.*

Lemma 3. *Suppose the XDLIN assumption holds in $\mathbb{G}_1$ and $\mathbb{G}_2$. Then for all PPT adversary $\mathcal{B}$, there is a adversary $\mathcal{A}$ such that $\mathrm{Adv}_{\mathcal{B}}^{\mathrm{Prob}_2}(\lambda) \leq \mathrm{Adv}_{\mathcal{A}}^{\mathrm{Prob}_0}(\lambda)$.*

Lemma 4. *Suppose the XDLIN assumption holds in $\mathbb{G}_1$ and $\mathbb{G}_2$. Then for all PPT adversary $\mathcal{B}$, there is a adversary $\mathcal{A}$ such that $\mathrm{Adv}_{\mathcal{B}}^{\mathrm{Prob}_3}(\lambda) \leq \mathrm{Adv}_{\mathcal{A}}^{\mathrm{Prob}_0}(\lambda)$.*

Lemma 5. *Suppose the XDLIN assumption holds in $\mathbb{G}_1$ and $\mathbb{G}_2$. Then for all PPT adversary $\mathcal{B}$, there is a adversary $\mathcal{A}$ such that $\mathrm{Adv}_{\mathcal{B}}^{\mathrm{Prob}_4}(\lambda) \leq \mathrm{Adv}_{\mathcal{A}}^{\mathrm{Prob}_0}(\lambda)$.*

Theorem 1. *Under the XDLIN assumption the proposed scheme is many-AD-SIM-secure.*

The proofs of Lemmas 2–5 and **Theorem** 1 are given in the full version of this paper.

Acknowledgments. This work has been partly supported by National NSF of China under Grant No. 61772266, 61572248, 61431008.

References

1. Agrawal, S., Gorbunov, S., Vaikuntanathan, V., Wee, H.: Functional encryption: new perspectives and lower bounds. In: Canetti, R., Garay, J.A. (eds.) CRYPTO 2013. LNCS, vol. 8043, pp. 500–518. Springer, Heidelberg (2013). https://doi.org/10.1007/978-3-642-40084-1_28
2. Agrawal, S., Libert, B., Stehlé, D.: Fully secure functional encryption for inner products, from standard assumptions. In: Robshaw, M., Katz, J. (eds.) CRYPTO 2016. LNCS, vol. 9816, pp. 333–362. Springer, Heidelberg (2016). https://doi.org/10.1007/978-3-662-53015-3_12
3. Bishop, A., Jain, A., Kowalczyk, L.: Function-hiding inner product encryption. In: Iwata, T., Cheon, J.H. (eds.) ASIACRYPT 2015. LNCS, vol. 9452, pp. 470–491. Springer, Heidelberg (2015). https://doi.org/10.1007/978-3-662-48797-6_20
4. Boneh, D., Raghunathan, A., Segev, G.: Function-private identity-based encryption: hiding the function in functional encryption. In: Canetti, R., Garay, J.A. (eds.) CRYPTO 2013. LNCS, vol. 8043, pp. 461–478. Springer, Heidelberg (2013). https://doi.org/10.1007/978-3-642-40084-1_26

5. Boneh, D., Sahai, A., Waters, B.: Functional encryption: definitions and challenges. In: Ishai, Y. (ed.) TCC 2011. LNCS, vol. 6597, pp. 253–273. Springer, Heidelberg (2011). https://doi.org/10.1007/978-3-642-19571-6_16

6. Brakerski, Z., Segev, G.: Function-private functional encryption in the private-key setting. In: Dodis, Y., Nielsen, J.B. (eds.) TCC 2015. LNCS, vol. 9015, pp. 306–324. Springer, Heidelberg (2015). https://doi.org/10.1007/978-3-662-46497-7_12

7. Datta, P., Dutta, R., Mukhopadhyay, S.: Functional encryption for inner product with full function privacy. In: Cheng, C.-M., Chung, K.-M., Persiano, G., Yang, B.-Y. (eds.) PKC 2016. LNCS, vol. 9614, pp. 164–195. Springer, Heidelberg (2016). https://doi.org/10.1007/978-3-662-49384-7_7

8. De Caro, A., Iovino, V., Jain, A., O'Neill, A., Paneth, O., Persiano, G.: On the achievability of simulation-based security for functional encryption. In: Canetti, R., Garay, J.A. (eds.) CRYPTO 2013. LNCS, vol. 8043, pp. 519–535. Springer, Heidelberg (2013). https://doi.org/10.1007/978-3-642-40084-1_29

9. Goldwasser, S., Kalai, Y.T., Popa, R.A., Vaikuntanathan, V., Zeldovich, N.: Reusable garbled circuits and succinct functional encryption. In: STOC, pp. 555–564 (2013)

10. Gorbunov, S., Vaikuntanathan, V., Wee, H.: Functional encryption with bounded collusions via multi-party computation. In: Safavi-Naini, R., Canetti, R. (eds.) CRYPTO 2012. LNCS, vol. 7417, pp. 162–179. Springer, Heidelberg (2012). https://doi.org/10.1007/978-3-642-32009-5_11

11. Kim, S., Lewi, K., Mandal, A., Montgomery, H., Roy, A., Wu, D.J.: Function-hiding inner product encryption is practical. Cryptology ePrint Archive, Report 2016/440 (2016)

12. Okamoto, T., Takashima, K.: Fully secure functional encryption with general relations from the decisional linear assumption. In: Rabin, T. (ed.) CRYPTO 2010. LNCS, vol. 6223, pp. 191–208. Springer, Heidelberg (2010). https://doi.org/10.1007/978-3-642-14623-7_11

13. Okamoto, T., Takashima, K.: Homomorphic encryption and signatures from vector decomposition. In: Galbraith, S.D., Paterson, K.G. (eds.) Pairing 2008. LNCS, vol. 5209, pp. 57–74. Springer, Heidelberg (2008). https://doi.org/10.1007/978-3-540-85538-5_4

14. Okamoto, T., Takashima, K.: Hierarchical predicate encryption for inner-products. In: Matsui, M. (ed.) ASIACRYPT 2009. LNCS, vol. 5912, pp. 214–231. Springer, Heidelberg (2009). https://doi.org/10.1007/978-3-642-10366-7_13

15. O'Neill, A.: Definitional issues in functional encryption. Cryptology ePrint Archive, Report 2010/556 (2010)

16. Shen, E., Shi, E., Waters, B.: Predicate privacy in encryption systems. In: Reingold, O. (ed.) TCC 2009. LNCS, vol. 5444, pp. 457–473. Springer, Heidelberg (2009). https://doi.org/10.1007/978-3-642-00457-5_27

17. Tomida, J., Abe, M., Okamoto, T.: Efficient functional encryption for inner-product values with full-hiding security. In: Bishop, M., Nascimento, A.C.A. (eds.) ISC 2016. LNCS, vol. 9866, pp. 408–425. Springer, Cham (2016). https://doi.org/10.1007/978-3-319-45871-7_24

18. Zhao, Q., Zeng, Q., Liu, X., Xu, H.: Simulation-based security of function-hidinginner product encryption. Sci. China Inf. Sci. **61**, 048102 (2017). https://doi.org/10.1007/s11432-017-9224-9

Server-Aided Directly Revocable Ciphertext-Policy Attribute-Based Encryption with Verifiable Delegation

Gang Yu[1,2]($\boxtimes$), Xiaoxiao Ma[3]($\boxtimes$), Zhenfu Cao[2]($\boxtimes$), Weihua Zhu[1],
and Guang Zeng[1]

[1] State Key Laboratory of Mathematical Engineering and Advanced Computing,
Information Science and Technology Institute, Zhengzhou 450001, China
gyu1010@126.com, weihua1_2001@163.com, sunshine_zeng@sina.com
[2] Shanghai Key Lab for Trustworthy Computing, East China Normal University,
Shanghai 200062, China
zfcao@sei.ecnu.edu.cn
[3] Zheng Zhou Vocational University of Information and Technology,
Zhengzhou 450046, China
mxx1010@126.com

Abstract. Ciphertext-policy attribute-based encryption (CP-ABE) is a promising primitive for enforcing access control policies defined by data owner on outsourced data. We propose a novel primitive called server-aided directly revocable CP-ABE with verifiable delegation, denoted by sarCP-ABE. In sarCP-ABE, the workloads about revocation are delegated to an aide-server, and the data owner only needs to generate a normal ciphertext as in a pure CP-ABE system. A user can be directly revoked by updating a public revocation list. To prevent a revoked user from decrypting, the aide server can update the aide-ciphertext with current revocation list, and an auditor can publicly check the correctness of the updated aide-ciphertext. At last, the proposed scheme can be proved selectively secure against chosen-plaintext attack on both original and updated ciphertext.

Keywords: ABE · User revocation · Verifiable revocation delegation
LSSS

1 Introduction

Cloud Computing is a promising primitive which enables large amounts of resources to be easily accessible to cloud users. Although data storage on public cloud provides an ease of accessibility, it also raises concerns on data confidentiality. Due to poor scalability and complex key management, the traditional encryption schemes, such as identity based encryption, can't satisfy the requirements of various commercial applications that have a large amount of users.

© Springer International Publishing AG, part of Springer Nature 2018
S. Qing et al. (Eds.): ICICS 2017, LNCS 10631, pp. 172–179, 2018.
https://doi.org/10.1007/978-3-319-89500-0_15

Sahai and Waters [1] introduced the concept of attribute-based encryption (ABE). ABE can be divided into two kinds [2]: key-policy ABE (KP-ABE) and ciphertext-policy ABE (CP-ABE). In CP-ABE, without prior knowledge of who will decrypt the data, data owner encrypts data with an access policy, and a user can decrypt the ciphertext if and only if his/her attributes satisfy the access policy specified by the ciphertext. Pure CP-ABE is not sufficient for an access control system since users are not static, and users' access privileges should be revoked when they withdraw from the system.

Although, many revocable ABE schemes have been proposed to solve the revocation problem, the requirement of interaction between authority and non-revoked users in indirect revocation method [3–8], and the troublesome workloads related to a large revocation list for data owner in direct revocation method [9–13], limit the commercial applications of CP-ABE to a large extent.

In 2015, Shi et al. [14] gave a directly revocable KP-ABE scheme while the data owner still need to generate a ciphertext that is linear to the size of the revocation cover. In 2016, Cui et al. [15] proposed a server-aided indirect revocable ABE which delegates the overheads of data users resulted in key updates to a aide-server. In 2007, Yamada et al. [16] gave two generic constructions of recoverable ABE from ABE.

Inspired by the direct revocation method in [14], and aiming at alleviating the workloads of revocation for data owner, we propose a server-aided directly revocable CP-ABE with verifiable revocation delegation.

2   Preliminaries

Multilinear Maps. Let $\mathbb{G}_0, \mathbb{G}_1, ..., \mathbb{G}_{d+3}$ be cyclic groups of prime order p. Multilinear maps consist of $d + 3$ mappings $\{e_i : \mathbb{G}_0 \times \mathbb{G}_i \rightarrow \mathbb{G}_{i+1} | i = 0, ..., d + 2\}$, for $i = 0, ..., d + 2$, (i) if g_0 is a generator of $\mathbb{G}_0$, $g_{i+1} = e_i(g_0, g_i)$ is a generator of $\mathbb{G}_{i+1}$; (ii) $\forall a, b \in \mathbb{Z}_p$, $e_i(g_0^a, g_i^b) = e_i(g_0, g_i)^{ab}$; (iii) e_i can be efficiently computed.

$d + 4$ *Multilinear Decisional Diffie-Hellman Assumption (d + 4-MDDH).* Let $\mathcal{G}(\lambda) \rightarrow (p, \mathbb{G}_0, \mathbb{G}_1, ..., \mathbb{G}_{d+3}, e_0, e_1, ..., e_{d+2})$ be a generator of multilinear groups. Given $\vec{y} = g_0, g_0^{d_1}, g_0^{d_2}, g_0^{d_3}, g_0^c, g_0^{z_0}, ..., g_0^{z_d}$, where $z_0, ..., z_d, d_1, d_2, d_3$, $c \in_R \mathbb{Z}_p^*$ are unknown, there is no polynomial algorithm $\mathcal{A}$ that can distinguish $g_{d+3}^{cz_0 \cdots z_d d_1 d_2 d_3}$ from a random element $Z \in_R \mathbb{G}_{d+3}$ with a non-negligible advantage.

Subset Cover. Let $\mathcal{T}_{id}$ be a full binary tree, $depth(x)$ denote the depth of node x such that $depth(root) = 0$, $path(x) = \{x_{i_0}, ..., x_{i_{depth(x)}}\}$ denote the path from the root to node x. A list of revoked users R corresponds to a set of leaf nodes in $\mathcal{T}_{id}$. $\forall x \in R$, mark all nodes of $path(x)$, and subset cover $cover(R)$ is the set of unmarked nodes that are the direct children of marked nodes in $\mathcal{T}_{id}$, more details refer to [17].

3   Definition and Security Model

3.1   Definition

The sarCP-ABE scheme consists of eight algorithms.

Setup$(\lambda) \rightarrow (PP, MSK)$, takes a security parameter λ as input, and outputs the public parameters PP and master secret key MSK.

Server KeyGen$(PP) \rightarrow (SPK, SSK)$, takes PP as input, and outputs server's public key SPK and secret key SSK.

User KeyGen$(PP, SPK, id, S, MSK) \rightarrow SK_{id,S}$, takes as input PP, server's public key SPK, identity id, attributes S, master secret key MSK, and outputs secret key $SK_{id,S}$.

Encrypt$(PP, M, (\mathbb{W}, \rho)) \rightarrow CT$, takes as input PP, message M, access structure $(\mathbb{W}, \rho)$, and outputs a ciphertext CT.

Aide - Enc$(PP, CT, R, SSK) \rightarrow CT'$, takes as input PP, CT, SSK, revocation list R, and outputs an aide-ciphertext CT'.

Decrypt$(PP, CT, CT', SK_{id,S}, R) \rightarrow M$, takes as input PP, CT, CT', R, secret key $SK_{id,S}$ of identity id, and outputs a plaintext M if $id \notin R$ and S satisfies the access policy; else, outputs a reject symbol $\perp$.

Update$(PP, CT', R, R') \rightarrow C\hat{T}$, takes as input PP, CT', R, new revocation list R' such that $R \subset R'$, and outputs an updated aide-ciphertext $C\hat{T}$.

Verify$(PP, \text{SPK}, CT', C\hat{T}, R, R') \rightarrow 1$, takes as input PP, SPK, CT', R, $C\hat{T}, R'$, and outputs 1 if $C\hat{T}$ is correct; otherwise, outputs 0.

3.2   Security Model

Selective security for original ciphertext. The selective security against chosen-plaintext attack on original ciphertext, IND-s-CPA-OC in brief, is defined by following game between a challenger $\mathcal{C}$ and an adversary $\mathcal{A}$.

Init: $\mathcal{A}$ outputs a target access structure $(\mathbb{W}^*, \rho^*)$ that will be used to generate a challenge ciphertext.

Setup. $\mathcal{C}$ runs the Setup(λ) algorithm and gives the system public parameters PP to $\mathcal{A}$. $\mathcal{A}$ is allowed to generate the secret key of aide server, but it is asked to send the public key SPK to $\mathcal{C}$.

Phase 1. $\mathcal{A}$ makes KeyGen(id_i, S_i) queries for (id_1, S_1), ..., (id_{q_1}, S_{q_1}), $\mathcal{C}$ returns SK_{id_i, S_i} to $\mathcal{A}$.

Challenge. $\mathcal{A}$ submits two messages M_0, M_1 of equal length, an access structure $(\mathbb{W}^*, \rho^*)$, a revocation list R to $\mathcal{C}$. None of the sets S_1, ..., S_{q_1} from Phase 1 satisfies $(\mathbb{W}^*, \rho^*)$. $\mathcal{C}$ flips a random coin $\beta \in_R \{0, 1\}$ and generates the challenge ciphertext CT^* with M_β and aide-ciphertext CT'^* under revocation list R. At last, $\mathcal{C}$ returns CT^*, CT'^* to $\mathcal{A}$.

Phase 2. $\mathcal{A}$ makes KeyGen(id_i, S_i) queries for (id_{q_1+1}, S_{q_1+1}), ..., (id_q, S_q) as in Query Phase 1 with the restriction that S_{q_1+1}, ..., S_q should not satisfy the challenge access structure $(\mathbb{W}^*, \rho^*)$.

Guess. $\mathcal{A}$ outputs a guess bit $\beta' \in_R \{0, 1\}$ and wins the game if $\beta' = \beta$. The advantage of $\mathcal{A}$ is defined to be $Adv(\mathcal{A}) = |\Pr[\beta' = \beta] - 1/2|$.

Selective security for updated ciphertext. The selective security against chosen-plaintext attack on updated ciphertext, IND-s-CPA-UC in brief, is same as IND-s-CPA-OC except the challenge phase.

Challenge. $\mathcal{A}$ submits two messages M_0, M_1 of equal length, an access structure $(\mathbb{W}^*, \rho^*)$, a prior revocation list R, a new revocation list R' where $R \subset R'$

to $\mathcal{C}$. None of the sets $S_1, ..., S_{q_1}$ from Phase 1 satisfies $(\mathbb{W}^*, \rho^*)$. $\mathcal{C}$ flips a random coin $\beta \in_R \{0, 1\}$ and generates the challenge ciphertext CT^* with M_β and aide-ciphertext CT'^* under revocation list R, and then generates update aide-ciphertext $C\hat{T}^*$ under revocation list R'. At last, $\mathcal{C}$ returns $CT^*, C\hat{T}^*$ to $\mathcal{A}$.

Verifiability of revocation delegation. The verifiability of aide-ciphertext is defined by following game between a challenger $\mathcal{C}$ and an adversary $\mathcal{A}$.

Init, **Setup** and **Query Phase** are same as IND-s-CPA-OC.

Challenge. $\mathcal{A}$ submits a message M of equal length, an access structure $(\mathbb{W}^*, \rho^*)$, a prior revocation list R to $\mathcal{C}$. None of the sets $S_1, ..., S_{q_1}$ from Phase 1 satisfies $(\mathbb{W}^*, \rho^*)$. $\mathcal{C}$ generates ciphertext CT^* with M and aide-ciphertext CT'^* under revocation list R. At last, $\mathcal{C}$ returns CT^*, CT'^* to $\mathcal{A}$.

Guess. $\mathcal{A}$ generates update aide-ciphertext $C\hat{T}^*$ under revocation list R', where $R \subset R'$. $\mathcal{A}$ wins the game if $\text{Verify}(PP, CT'^*, C\hat{T}^*, R, R') \to 1$ and the distributions of $C\hat{T}^*$ and $C\tilde{T}$ are distinguishable, where $\text{Update}(PP, CT'^*, R, R') \to C\tilde{T}$ are normally produced by $\mathcal{C}$.

4   Our Construction

Let $\mathbb{U} = \{at_1, ..., at_{|\mathbb{U}|}\}$ be the attribute universe and $\mathbb{ID} = \{id_1, ..., id_{|\mathbb{ID}|}\}$ be the user universe in the system. Let d, such that $2^d = |\mathbb{ID}|$, be the depth for all leaves in the full binary tree of identities.

Setup$(\lambda) \to (PP, MSK)$: Given the security parameter λ, it generates $d + 3$ multilinear maps: $\{e_i : \mathbb{G}_0 \times \mathbb{G}_i \to \mathbb{G}_{i+1} | i = 0, ..., d + 2\}$, where $\mathbb{G}_0, \mathbb{G}_1, ..., \mathbb{G}_{d+3}$ are cyclic group of prime order p. Let g_0 be a random generator of $\mathbb{G}_0$, and then $g_{i+1} = e_i(g_0, g_i)$ is a generator of $\mathbb{G}_{i+1}$ for $i = 0, 1, ..., d + 2$. The authority chooses $\alpha, b \in_R \mathbb{Z}_p^*$ randomly and computes $g_{d+2}^\alpha, g_{d+2}^b$. For each attribute $at_i \in \mathbb{U}$, it selects $t_i \in_R \mathbb{Z}_p^*$ randomly and sets $T_i = g_0^{t_i}$. The authority chooses an efficient map $H : \{0, 1\}^* \to \mathbb{G}_0$. Let $\mathcal{T}_{id}$ denote a binary tree according to the revocation list R. At last, the authority sets master secret key as $MSK = \alpha, \{t_i, i = 1, ..., |\mathbb{U}|\}$ and publishes public parameters $PP = \{p, \mathbb{G}_0, \mathbb{G}_1, ..., \mathbb{G}_{d+3}, e_0, ..., e_{d+2}, T_1, ..., T_{|\mathbb{U}|}, g_0, g_{d+2}^b, e_{d+2}(g_0, g_{d+2})^\alpha, \mathbb{U},$ $\mathbb{ID}, H, d, \mathcal{T}_{id}\}$.

Server KeyGen$(PP) \to (SPK, SSK)$: The aide server randomly chooses $c \in_R \mathbb{Z}_p^*$, keeps secret key $SSK = c$ secretly and publishes public key $SPK = g_0^c$.

User KeyGen$(PP, SPK, id, S, MSK) \to SK_{id,S}$: The authority can generate the secret key $SK_{id,S} = (K, L, \{K_x : \forall x \in S\})$ as follows.

- Let $path(id) = \{x_{i_0}, ..., x_{i_d}\}$ and $P_{x_{i_0}} = e_0(g_0^b, H(x_{i_0}))$.
- For $k = 1$ to d, compute $P_{x_{i_k}} = e_k(P_{x_{i_{k-1}}}, H(x_{i_k}))$, let $P_{id} = e_{d+1}(P_{x_{i_d}}, g_0^c)$.
- Choose $a, r \in_R \mathbb{Z}_p^*$, compute $K = g_{d+2}^{\alpha-ar} P_{id}^r, L = g_0^r, K_i = g_{d+2}^{art_i^{-1}}, \forall at_i \in S$.

Encrypt$(PP, M, (\mathbb{W}, \rho)) \to CT$: Given a message M, access structure $(\mathbb{W}, \rho)$, where $\mathbb{W}$ is a $l \times k$ matrix and ρ is a map from each row $\mathbb{W}_i$ of $\mathbb{W}$ to an attribute $at_{\rho(i)}$, the data owner generates ciphertext $CT = (C, C', \{C_i\}_{i \in [l]})$ can be generated as follows.

- Choose $s, v_2, ..., v_k \in_R \mathbb{Z}_p^*$ randomly, and construct vector $\vec{v} = (s, v_2, \cdots, v_k)$.
- Compute $C = M \cdot e_{d+2}(g_0, g_{d+2})^{\alpha s}$, $C' = g_0^s$.
- For $i = 1, ..., l$, compute $C_i = T_i^{\lambda_i}$, where $\lambda_i = \mathbb{W}_i \cdot \vec{v}$.

Aided-Enc$(PP, CT, R, SSK) \rightarrow CT'$: Given CT, and a revocation list R, the aide-server generates aide-ciphertext $CT' = \{D_x : \forall x \in cover(R)\}$ as follows.

- Let $path(x) = \{x_{i_0}, ..., x_{i_{depth(x)}}\}$ and $P_{x_{i_0}} = e_0(g_0^b, H(x_{i_0}))$.
- For $k = 1$ to $depth(x)$, compute $P_{x_{i_k}} = e_k(P_{x_{i_{k-1}}}, H(x_{i_k}))$, let $P_x = P_{x_{i_{depth(x)}}}$.
- Compute $D_x = e_{depth(x)+1}(P_x, C')^c$.

Decrypt$(PP, CT, CT', SK_{id,S}, R) \rightarrow M$: If $id \notin R$ and S satisfies access structure $(\mathbb{W}, \rho)$, the message can be recovered as follows.

- Since $id \notin R$, there always exists $x \in (path(id) \cap cover(R))$. Let $path(id) = \{x_{i_0}, ..., x_{i_{depth(x)}}, ..., x_{i_d}\}$, where $x_{i_{depth(x)}} = x, x_{i_d} = id$. Let $Q'_{x_{i_{depth(x)}}} = D_x$, and for $k = depth(x) + 1$ to d compute $Q'_{x_{i_k}} = e_{k+1}(Q'_{x_{i_{k-1}}}, H(x_{i_k}))$. Then, $Q_{id} = Q'_{x_{i_d}} = P_{id}^s$. Since S satisfies $(\mathbb{W}, \rho)$, there exists $\{\omega_i : i \in I\}$ such that $\sum_{i \in I} \omega_i \mathbb{W}_i = (1, 0, ..., 0)$, where $I = \{i : at_{\rho(i)} \in S\}$.
- Computes $M = \dfrac{C \cdot e_{d+2}(L, Q_{id})}{e_{d+2}(C', K) \prod_{i \in I} e_{d+2}(K_i, C_i)^{\omega_i}}$.

Update$(PP, CT', R, R') \rightarrow C\hat{T}'$: Given an aide-ciphertext CT' under revocation list R and a new revocation list R' where $R \subset R'$, the updated aide-ciphertext $C\hat{T}' = \{\hat{D}_x : \forall x \in cover(R')\}$ can be generated as follows.

- For each $x' \in cover(R')$, if there exists $x \in cover(R)$ such that $x = x'$, let $\hat{D}_{x'} = D_x$;
- Else, there exists $x \in cover(R)$ that x is an ancestor of x'. Let $path(x') = path(x) \cup \{x_{i_{depth(x)+1}}, ..., x_{i_{depth(x')}}\}$ such that $x_{i_{depth(x)}} = x, x_{i_{depth(x')}} = x'$. Let $P'_{x_{i_{depth(x)}}} = D_x$, compute $P'_{x_{i_k}} = e_{k+1}(P'_{x_{i_{k-1}}}, H(x_{i_k}))$ for $k = depth(x) + 1, ..., depth(x')$, and let $\hat{D}_{x'} = P'_{x_{i_{depth(x')}}}$.

Verify$(PP, SPK, CT', C\hat{T}', R, R') \rightarrow 1$: The correctness of $C\hat{T}'$ can be publicly verified by an auditor as follows.

- For each $x \in cover(R)$, $path(x) = \{x_{i_0}, ..., x_{i_{depth(x)}}\}$, let $P_{x_{i_0}} = e_0(g_0^b, H(x_{i_0}))$; compute $P_{x_{i_k}} = e_k(P_{x_{i_{k-1}}}, H(x_{i_k}))$ for $k = 1$ to $depth(x)$; let $P_x = P_{x_{i_{depth(x)}}}$, compute $P'_x = e_{depth(x)+1}(P_x, C')$, and verify whether $e_{depth(x)+2}(D_x, g_0) = e_{depth(x)+2}(P'_x, g_0^c)$ holds or not. If not, output 0.
- Otherwise, for each $x \in cover(R) \cap cover(R')$, verify whether $\hat{D}_x = D_x$ holds or not. If not, output 0.

- Otherwise, for each $i \in [0, d]$, find out all the nodes $x_1, ..., x_k$ such that $x_t \in cover(R') - cover(R)$ where $depth(x_t) = i, t \in [0, k]$; choose $a_1, ..., a_k \in_R \mathbb{Z}_p$ at random, compute $P'_{x_t} = e_{depth(x_t)+1}(P_{x_t}, C')$ and verify

$$\prod_{t=1}^{k} e_{depth(x_t)+2}\left(\left(P'_{x_t}\right)^{a_t}, g_0^c\right) = e_{depth(x_t)+2}\left(g_0, \prod_{t=1}^{k}\left(\hat{D}_{x_t}\right)^{a_t}\right) \tag{1}$$

- If there exists $i \in [0, d]$ such that Eq. (1) does not hold, then output 0; otherwise, return 1.

5   Security Results

Due to space limitation, we only give the security results. The complete proof and efficiency analysis will be given in the full paper.

Theorem 1. *If the $d + 4$-MDDH assumption holds and the challenge matrix $\mathbb{W}^*$ is of size $l^* \times k^*$ such that $l^*, k^* \leq q$, there is no polynomial time adversary that can win the IND-s-CPA-OC game with non-negligible advantage ε.*

Theorem 2. *If $d + 4$-MDDH assumption holds, there is no polynomial adversary that can win the IND-s-CPA-UC game with non-negligible advantage ε.*

Theorem 3. *The proposed sarCP-ABE scheme can achieve verifiability of revocation delegation.*

6   Conclusion

In this paper, we introduce a new primitive, called server-aided directly revocable CP-ABE with verifiable revocation delegation to achieve efficient user revocation. We give the formal security model, propose a concrete sarCP-ABE scheme, and then prove that the proposed sarCP-ABE scheme is selectively secure under the security. The proposed sarCP-ABE scheme can support verifiable (complete) revocation delegation. Comparing with previous directly revocable ABE schemes, the workloads about revocation are delegated to the aide-server.

Acknowledgment. This work was supported in part by the National Natural Science Foundation of China (Nos. 61602512, 61632012, 61373154, 61371083, 61672239), in part by China Postdoctoral Science Foundation of China (No. 2016M591629), in part by National Key Research and Development Program (Nos. 2016YFB0800101 and 2016YFB0800100), Innovative Research Groups of the National Natural Science Foundation of China (No. 61521003).

References

1. Sahai, A., Waters, B.: Fuzzy identity-based encryption. In: Cramer, R. (ed.) EURO-CRYPT 2005. LNCS, vol. 3494, pp. 457–473. Springer, Heidelberg (2005). https://doi.org/10.1007/11426639_27
2. Goyal, V., Pandey, O., Sahai, A., Waters, B.: Attribute-based encryption for fine grained access control of encrypted data. In: Proceedings of the 13th ACM Conference on Computer and Communications Security, pp. 89–98. ACM (2006)
3. Pirretti, M., Traynor, P., McDaniel, P., Waters, B.: Secure attribute-based systems. In: Proceedings of the 13th ACM conference on Computer and communications security, pp. 99–112. ACM (2006)
4. Liang, X., Lu, R., Lin, X., Shen, X.: Ciphertext policy attribute based encryption with efficient revocation. Technical report, University of Waterloo (2010)
5. Ostrovsky R., Sahai A., Waters, B.: Attribute-based encryption with non-monotonic access structures. In: Proceedings of ACM Conference on Computer and Communication Security, pp. 195–203. ACM (2007)
6. Hur, J., Noh, D.: Attribute-based access control with efficient revocation in data outsourcing systems. IEEE Trans. Parallel Distrib. Syst. **22**(7), 1214–1221 (2011)
7. Sahai, A., Seyalioglu, H., Waters, B.: Dynamic credentials and ciphertext delegation for attribute-based encryption. In: Safavi-Naini, R., Canetti, R. (eds.) CRYPTO 2012. LNCS, vol. 7417, pp. 199–217. Springer, Heidelberg (2012). https://doi.org/10.1007/978-3-642-32009-5_13
8. Xie, X., Ma, H., Li, J., Chen, X.: New ciphertext-policy attribute-based access control with efficient revocation. In: Mustofa, K., Neuhold, E.J., Tjoa, A.M., Weippl, E., You, I. (eds.) ICT-EurAsia 2013. LNCS, vol. 7804, pp. 373–382. Springer, Heidelberg (2013). https://doi.org/10.1007/978-3-642-36818-9_41
9. Attrapadung, N., Imai, H.: Conjunctive broadcast and attribute-based encryption. In: Shacham, H., Waters, B. (eds.) Pairing 2009. LNCS, vol. 5671, pp. 248–265. Springer, Heidelberg (2009). https://doi.org/10.1007/978-3-642-03298-1_16
10. Yu, S., Wang, C., Ren, K., Lou, W.: Attribute based data sharing with attribute revocation. In: Proceedings of the 5th ACM Symposium on Information, Computer and Communications Security, pp. 261–270. ACM (2010)
11. Jahid, S., Mittal, P., Borisov, N.: EASiER: Encryption-based access control in social networks with efficient revocation. In: Proceedings of the 6th ACM Symposium on Information, Computer and Communications Security, pp. 411–415. ACM (2011)
12. Zhang, Y., Chen, X., Li, J., Li, H., Li, F.: FDR-ABE: attribute-based encryption with flexible and direct revocation. In: 5th International Conference on Intelligent Networking and Collaborative Systems-2013, pp. 38–45. IEEE (2013)
13. Naruse, T., Mohri, M., Shiraishi, Y.: Attribute-based encryption with attribute revocation and grant function using proxy re-encryption and attribute key for updating. In: Park, J., Stojmenovic, I., Choi, M., Xhafa, F. (eds.) Future Information Technology 2014. LNEE, vol. 276, pp. 119–125. Springer, Berlin, Heidelberg (2014). https://doi.org/10.1007/978-3-642-40861-8_18
14. Shi, Y., Zheng, Q., Liu, J., Han, Z.: Directly revocable key-policy attribute-based encryption with verifiable ciphertext delegation. Inf. Sci. **295**, 221–231 (2015)
15. Cui, H., Deng, R.H., Li, Y., Qin, B.: Server-aided revocable attribute-based encryption. In: Askoxylakis, I., Ioannidis, S., Katsikas, S., Meadows, C. (eds.) ESORICS 2016. LNCS, vol. 9879, pp. 570–587. Springer, Cham (2016). https://doi.org/10.1007/978-3-319-45741-3_29

16. Yamada, K., Attrapadung, N., Emura, K., Hanaoka, G., Tanaka, K.: Generic constructions for fully secure revocable attribute-based encryption. In: Foley, S.N., Gollmann, D., Snekkenes, E. (eds.) ESORICS 2017. LNCS, vol. 10493, pp. 532–551. Springer, Cham (2017). https://doi.org/10.1007/978-3-319-66399-9_29

17. Boldyreva, A., Goyal, V., Kumar, V. : Identity-based encryption with efficient revocation. In: Proceedings of the 15th ACM Conference on Computer and Communications Security, pp. 417–426. ACM (2008)

Practical Large Universe Attribute-Set Based Encryption in the Standard Model

Xinyu Feng[1,2], Cancan Jin[1,2], Cong Li[1,2], Yuejian Fang[1,2], Qingni Shen[1,2(✉)], and Zhonghai Wu[1,2]

[1] School of Software and Microelectronics, Peking University, Beijing, China
{xyf,jincancan1992,li.cong}@pku.edu.cn,
{fangyj,qingnishen,wuzh}@ss.pku.edu.cn
[2] National Engineering Research Center for Software Engineering, Peking University, Beijing, China

Abstract. Attribute-set based encryption is a promising branch of attribute-based encryption which deals with the case when many attributes are only meaningful in groups or in sets and helps to avoid the exponential growth of attributes. We propose a feasible and efficient attribute-set based encryption scheme which is large universe, unbounded and supports composite attributes, using linear secret sharing schemes as the underlying tool. Additionally, our construction has been proved to be selectively secure in the standard model while previous ones could only be proved to be secure in the generic group model.

Keywords: Attribute-set based encryption · Composite attribute
Large universe · Selective security

1 Introduction

In cloud computing system, the cloud service providers may be honest but curious about the customer data for the analysis of user behavior or advertising. A feasible solution is that owners encrypt sensitive data before uploading them. Compared with the traditional one-to-one encryption, Attribute-Based Encryption (ABE), as an excellent cryptographic access control mechanism, is quite preferable for data encryption and sharing based on the recipients' ability to satisfy a policy. ABE is an excellent cryptographic access control mechanism achieving the sharing of encrypted data. However, in many scenarios, separate attributes cannot give a good satisfaction for the various requirements, they are only meaningful when they are organized as the groups or sets.

There are mainly two types of ABE schemes: Ciphertext-Policy ABE (CP-ABE), where ciphertexts are associated with access policies and keys are associated with sets of attributes, and Key-Policy ABE (KP-ABE), where keys are associated with access policies and ciphertexts are associated with sets of attributes. In this work, we focus on the challenge how to organize attributes efficiently.

S. Qing et al. (Eds.): ICICS 2017, LNCS 10631, pp. 180–191, 2018.
https://doi.org/10.1007/978-3-319-89500-0_16

1. Attributes are often related with each other. Many attributes are only meaningful in groups or in sets.
2. Separate attributes cannot give a great satisfaction for various requirements in practice, which will lead to the consequence of a large number of repeated attributes in the access policy.

The concept of Attribute-set based encryption (ASBE) was first proposed by Bobba, et al. [5] in 2009. However, their construction is based on the access tree and proved secure in generic group model. The scheme [18] is constructed based on the [5] and also could only be proved secure in the generic model. In this work, we propose a new scheme which is more practical. Compared with the scheme of Bobba et al. [5], our scheme can achieve the properties of large universe and unbounded, and is constructed based on the Linear Secret Sharing Schemes (LSSS). Using the prime order groups and partition techniques [16], it is efficient and selectively secure in the standard model. In order to achieve the collusion attacks resistant ability, we use a different randomness to mask each component for each individual attribute and composite attribute set.

1.1 Related Work

Sahai and Waters first proposed the concept of Attribute-based Encryption [17] in 2005, as a generalization of Fuzzy Identity-based Encryption by using threshold gates as the access structure. Then ABE comes into two flavors, Key-Policy ABE (KP-ABE) and Ciphertext-Policy ABE (CP-ABE). Goyal et al. proposed the first KP-ABE scheme [7], which supports monotonic Boolean encryption policies. The first construction of CP-ABE was given by Bethencourt et al. [4], whose security proof was based on the generic group model. Okamoto et al. first gave a bounded fully secure construction in the standard model [9]. Until now many works have been presented to achieve the unbounded or large universe properties in ABE [8,13]. But most of them were somewhat limited such as restricting the expressiveness of policies or using random oracle model. In 2013, Rouselakis and Waters proposed a large universe and unbounded ABE scheme [16] and proved it to be selectively secure using the partitioning style techniques. Later in 2014, Wang and Feng proposed a large universe ABE scheme for lattices [20]. In 2016, Li et al. proposed a practical construction for large universe hierarchical ABE scheme [10] and Zhang et al. proposed an accountable large universe ABE scheme supporting monotone access structures [21].

There are many other schemes focus on the problem of how to organize attributes in ABE to make it practical and efficient. One study is hierarchical ABE (HABE) [6,11,12,19]. Another is ASBE. Note that ASBE is quite different from many existing HABE schemes in organizing attributes. Attributes in former is composite such as {University A, Master}, while in the latter they are hierarchical, that is, there is a relation between the superior and the subordinate. ASBE was first proposed by Bobba et al. [5] in 2009. In ASBE, attributes are organized into a recursive family of sets. In Bobba's work, access policy was based on binary access tree. A hierarchical attribute-set based encryption construction was proposed in 2012 [18]. Then in the following years between 2013 and 2015, many applications based on ASBE were proposed [1,2,14,15].

1.2 Our Contribution

We propose a practical Attribute-set based encryption scheme which is large universe, unbounded and supports composite attributes, we also prove our scheme to be selectively secure in the standard model.

We overcame the following difficulties to construct the CP-ASBE scheme.

- We used a different randomness to mask each component for each individual attribute and composite attribute set to achieve the collusion attacks resistant ability.
- To achieve an efficient ASBE construction, we improved the linear secret sharing schemes to support the composite attributes.
- We defined the formal security model, then by borrowing the idea of partition technique, we overcame the challenges appeared in security proof process and proved our scheme to be selective security in the standard model.

1.3 Organization

The remainder of the paper is organized as follows. Section 2 gives necessary background on bilinear maps, access structure, linear secret sharing schemes, algorithms and complexity assumptions. Then we formalize our CP-ASBE scheme and define its security model. We propose a construction of CP-ASBE with a formal security proof in Sects. 3 and 4. We give a belief conclusion in Sect. 5.

2 Preliminaries

Bilinear maps. Let $\mathbb{G}_0$ and $\mathbb{G}_1$ be two multiplicative cyclic groups of prime order p. Let g be a generator of $\mathbb{G}_0$ and e be a bilinear map, $e : \mathbb{G}_0 \times \mathbb{G}_0 \to \mathbb{G}_1$. The bilinear map e has the following properties:

1. Bilinearity: For all $u, v \in \mathbb{G}_0$ and $a, b \in \mathbb{Z}_p$, we have $e(u^a, v^b) = e(u, v)^{ab}$.
2. Non-degeneracy: $e(g, g) \neq 1$.

Linear Secret Sharing Schemes (LSSS) [3]. Some modifications will be made in LSSS to support composite attribute sets. First, a secret sharing scheme II over a set of parties $\mathcal{P}$ realizing access structure is linear over $\mathbb{Z}_p$ if

1. The share of a secret $s \in \mathbb{Z}_p$ for each attribute form a vector over $\mathbb{Z}_p$.

2. For each access structure $\mathbb{A}$ on U which is the attribute universe, there exists a matrix $M \in Z_p^{l \times n}$ with l rows and n columns, which is called the share-generating matrix and a function ρ, which is defined as the mapping from rows of M to attributes in U, i.e. $\rho : [l] \rightarrow \mathcal{U}$. For all $i = 1, \cdots, l$, the ith row of M is associated with an attribute $\rho(i)$. Let the function ρ define the party labeling row i as $\rho(i)$. To share the secret $s \in \mathbb{Z}_p$, we first consider the column vector $\boldsymbol{y} = (s, y_2, \cdots, y_n)^T$, where s is the secret to be shared, and $y_2, \cdots, y_n \in \mathbb{Z}_p$ are randomly chosen. Then $M\boldsymbol{y}$ is the vector of l shares of the secret s according to II. The share $(M\boldsymbol{y})_i$ belongs to party $\rho(i)$, that is, the attribute of $\rho(i)$.

According to [6], every LSSS enjoys the linear reconstruction property. Suppose II is an LSSS for the access structure $\mathbb{A}$. Let $\mathcal{S}$ be any authorized set if $\mathbb{A}(\mathcal{S}) = 1$, and let $I \subset \{1, 2, \cdots, l\}$ be defined as $I = \{i : \rho(i) \in \mathcal{S}\}$. Then there exist constants $\{d_i \in Z_p\}_{i \in I}$ such that, if $\{\lambda_i\}(i \in I)$ are valid shares of any secret s according to II, then $\sum_{i \in I} d_i \cdot \lambda_i = s$.

Furthermore, to support composite attribute sets, that is only attributes in the same set can be used to satisfy the access policy, one natural idea is to re-share the shares obtained from the outer set. Take the depth of key structure being 2, that is, $d = 2$ as an example, we will first generate a share $d_i(1 \le i \le k)$ of the secret for each attribute subset: $A_0, A_1, A_2, \cdots, A_k$. And then for each attribute subset A_i, it takes the share d_i as a new secret to share with the attributes $(a_{i1}, \cdots, a_{in_i})$ in it where n_i is the number of attributes in set A_i. When the depth of key structure is greater than d, iterate the process discussed above several times until there is no composite attribute subsets.

Algorithms. Our LU-CP-ASBE scheme consists of the following five algorithms:

- **Setup**$(1^\lambda) \rightarrow (PK, MK)$: This is a randomized algorithm that takes a security parameter $\lambda \in N$ encoded in unary, it generates the public parameters PK and master key MK.
- **KeyGen**$(PK, MK, \mathcal{S}) \rightarrow SK$: The private key generation algorithm is a randomized algorithm that takes as input the public parameters PK, the master key MK, and attribute set $\mathcal{S}$. It outputs a user's secret key SK.
- **Encrypt**$(PK, M, \mathbb{A}) \rightarrow CT$: This is a randomized algorithm that takes as input the public parameters PK, a plaintext message M, and an access structure $\mathbb{A}$. It outputs ciphertext CT.
- **Decrypt**$(PK, SK, CT) \rightarrow M$: The decryption algorithm takes as input the public parameters PK, a secret key SK of a user with a set of attributes $\mathcal{S}$, and a ciphertext CT that was encrypted under access structure $\mathbb{A}$. It outputs the message M if $\mathcal{S}$ satisfies $\mathbb{A}$. Otherwise, it outputs a symbol of $\perp$.

Assumption. Initially the challenger calls the groups generation algorithm with the security parameter as input and then picks a random group element $g \in \mathbb{G}_0$,

$q + 2$ random exponents $a, s, b_1, b_2, \cdots, b_q \in \mathbb{Z}_p$. Then he sends to the adversary the group description $(p, \mathbb{G}_0, \mathbb{G}_1, e)$ and all of the following terms:

$$g, g^s$$

$$g^{a^i}, g^{b^j}, g^{sb_j}, g^{a^i b_j}, g^{a^i b_j^2} \qquad\qquad \forall (i, j) \in [q, q]$$

$$g^{a^i b_j / b_{j'}^2} \qquad\qquad \forall (i, j, j') \in [2q, q, q] \text{ with } j \neq j'$$

$$g^{a^i / b_j} \qquad\qquad \forall (i, j) \in [2q, q] \text{ with } i \neq q + 1$$

$$g^{sa^i b_j / b_{j'}}, g^{sa^i b_j / b_{j'}^2} \qquad\qquad \forall (i, j, j') \in [q, q, q] \text{ with } j \neq j'$$

It is hard for the adversary to distinguish $e(g, g)^{sa^{q+1}} \in \mathbb{G}_1$ from an element which is randomly chosen from $\mathbb{G}_1$.

We say that the q-type assumption holds if no PPT adversary has a non-negligible advantage in solving the q-type problem.

Selective security model. We give the definition of the security model for our large universe CP-ASBE (LU-CP-ASBE) scheme. In our LU-CP-ASBE model, attributes are divided into simple attributes and composite attributes. Note that once some component in composite attribute sets satisfies the access structure, the associated user is said to be authorized. We described the security model by a game between an adversary $\mathcal{A}$ and a challenger $\mathcal{B}$ and is parameterized by the security parameter $\lambda \in \mathbb{N}$. The phases of the game are as follows:

- **Init**: The adversary $\mathcal{A}$ declares the access structure $\mathbb{A}^*$ which he wants to attack, and then sends it to the challenger $\mathcal{B}$.
- **Setup**: The challenger $\mathcal{B}$ runs the Setup(1^λ) algorithm and gives the public parameters PK to the adversary $\mathcal{A}$.
- **Phase 1**: The adversary $\mathcal{A}$ is allowed to issue queries for secret keys for users with sets of attributes $(\mathcal{S}_1), (\mathcal{S}_2), \cdots, (\mathcal{S}_{Q_1})$. For each $(\mathcal{S}_i)$, the challenger $\mathcal{B}$ calls KeyGen($PK, MK, \mathcal{S}_i$) $\to SK_i$ and sends SK_i to $\mathcal{A}$. The only restriction is that $\mathcal{S}_i$ does not satisfy $\mathbb{A}^*$.
- **Challenge**: The adversary $\mathcal{A}$ submits two equal length messages M_0 and M_1. The challenger $\mathcal{B}$ flips a random coin $b \in \{0, 1\}$, and encrypts M_b with $\mathbb{A}^*$. The ciphertext is passed to $\mathcal{A}$.
- **Phase 2**: Phase 1 is repeated.
- **Guess**: The adversary $\mathcal{A}$ outputs a guess b' of b.

The advantage of an adversary $\mathcal{A}$ in this game is defined as $|Pr[b' = b] - 1/2|$.

A CP-ASBE scheme is selectively secure if all probabilistic polynomial time (PPT) adversaries have negligible advantage in λ in the security game above.

3   Our Construction

In this section, we present the construction of LU-CP-ASBE scheme where the attributes are assumed to be divided into simple attributes and composite attributes. Composite attributes are expressed in the form of attribute sets. To prevent users from making the collusion attack, we use a unique random number to bind the attribute with the attribute set it belongs to. The public parameters consist of seven group elements (g, u, h, w, v, X, Y) where $X = w^\beta, Y = e(g, g)^\alpha$. These parameters are utilized in two layers, attribute layer (the u, h terms) and the secret sharing layer (the w term). Attribute layer provides a hash function to map arbitrary attributes as group elements. And the secret sharing layer is the main part to be modified for transforming CP-ABE into CP-ASBE. w term, the secret sharing layer, holds the secret randomness r associated with a user and the secret randomness r_{ij} associated with each attribute during key generation.

Let $\mathbb{G}_0$ be a bilinear group of prime order p, and let g be a generator of $\mathbb{G}_0$. In addition, let $e : \mathbb{G}_0 \times \mathbb{G}_0 \to \mathbb{G}_1$ denote the bilinear map. A security parameter λ will determine the size of the groups. We assume that users' attributes are elements in $\mathbb{Z}_p^*$, however, attributes can be any meaningful unique strings using a collision resistant hash function $H : \{0, 1\}^* \to \mathbb{Z}_p^*$.

Our construction follows.

- **Setup**$(1^\lambda, d = 2) \to (PK, MK)$. The input parameter d is the depth of key structures, which is decided at setup phase and restricted to be less than d. For convenience, here we show a scheme with the key structure depth of 2, although it can be easily extended to arbitrary depth.

  The algorithm calls the group generation algorithm $\mathcal{G}(1^\lambda)$ and gets the descriptions of the groups and the bilinear mapping $D = (p, \mathbb{G}_0, \mathbb{G}_1, e)$. Then it picks the random terms $g, u, h, w, v \in \mathbb{G}_0$ and $\alpha, \beta \in \mathbb{Z}_p$. The setup algorithm issues the public parameters PK as: (D, g, u, h, w, v, X, Y) and keeps the master key $MK(\alpha, \beta)$ as secret.

- **KeyGen**$(PK, MK, \mathcal{S} = \{A_0, \cdots, A_k\} \subseteq \mathbb{Z}_p) \to SK$. As what has been explained in Sect. 2, A_0 is the set of simple attributes in the outer set, and $A_i(i \in [1, k])$ are composite attribute sets in depth 1. Let $A_i = \{a_{i,1}, a_{i,2}, \cdots, a_{i,n_i}\}$, where $a_{i,j}$ denotes the jth attribute appearing in set A_i. The *KeyGen* algorithm first picks $k + 1$ random exponents $r, r_1, r_2, \cdots, r_k \in \mathbb{Z}_p$, r for the user u and $r_0, r_1, r_2, \cdots, r_k$ for each composite attribute set $A_i \in \mathcal{S}, 0 \leq i \leq k$. It also picks random exponent $r_{i,j}$ for each attribute in $\mathcal{S}$. Then calculate $K_0 = g^\alpha w^r$ and for each $\theta \in [0, k]$ calculate: $K_1^{\{\theta\}} = g^{r_\theta}, L^{\{\theta\}} = g^{\frac{r + r_\theta}{\beta}}, K_{i,2}^{\{\theta\}} = g^{r_{\theta,i}}, K_{i,3}^{\{\theta\}} = (u^{a_{\theta,i}} h)^{r_{\theta,i}} v^{-r_\theta}$.

  It outputs the secret key SK as: $(\mathcal{S}, K_0, \{K_1^{\{\theta\}}, L^{\{\theta\}}, K_{i,2}^{\{\theta\}}, K_{i,3}^{\{\theta\}}\}_{\theta \in [0,k], i \in [n_i]})$.

  Note that the operations on exponents are module the order p of the group, which is prime.

- **Encrypt**$(m, (M, \rho)) \to CT$. The encryption algorithm takes the plaintext message m and the access policy encoded by LSSS as input, where $M \in \mathbb{Z}_p^{l \times q}$ and ρ is a function mapping the row number to the corresponding attribute.

The encryption algorithm then randomly picks $\boldsymbol{y} = (s, y_2, \cdots, y_q) \in \mathbb{Z}_p^{q \times 1}$ and s is the random secret to be shared. The vector of shares is denoted as $\boldsymbol{\lambda} = (\lambda_1, \cdots, \lambda_l) = (\lambda_{01}, \cdots, \lambda_{0n_0}, \cdots, \lambda_{\gamma 1}, \cdots, \lambda_{\gamma n_\gamma})^T = M \cdot \boldsymbol{y}$.

It then chooses $\theta \cdot \tau$ random values $t_{\theta \tau} \in \mathbb{Z}_p$ and for every $\theta \in [0, \gamma], \tau \in [n_\theta]$ computes

$$C = me(g, g)^{\alpha s}, D_0 = g^s,$$
$$C_{\tau,1}^{\{\theta\}} = w^{\lambda_\mathcal{X}} v^{t_\mathcal{X}}, C_{\tau,2}^{\{\theta\}} = (u^{\rho(\mathcal{X})} h)^{-t_\mathcal{X}}, C_{\tau,3}^{\{\theta\}} = g^{t_\mathcal{X}}, \hat{C}_\tau^{\{\theta\}} = X^{\lambda_\mathcal{X}}$$

Then publishes the ciphertext CT as:

$$(C, (M, \rho), D_0, \{C_{\tau,1}^{\{\theta\}}, C_{\tau,2}^{\{\theta\}}, C_{\tau,3}^{\{\theta\}}, \hat{C}_\tau^{\{\theta\}}\}_{\theta \in [0,\gamma], \tau \in [n_\theta]}).$$

$\mathcal{X} \in [l]$ is the row number of each attribute where $\mathcal{X} = \sum_{i \in [0,\theta)} n_\theta + \tau$.

- **Decrypt**$(SK, CT) \to m$. The decryption algorithm first finds the set I of the attributes, $I = \{i : \rho(i) \in A\}$. Then if set I exists, there exists constant coefficient $\{d_i \in \mathbb{Z}_p\}_{i \in I}$ such that $\sum_{i \in I} d_i \cdot M_l = (1, 0, \cdots, 0)$, where M_l is the ith row of matrix M. Then we have $\sum_{i \in I} d_i \lambda_i = s$.

Function $\psi(i)$ defines subset $\dot{A}$ that $\rho(i)$ belongs to and function $\Phi(i)$ defines the position of $\rho(i)$ in $\dot{A}_{\psi(i)}$. Denote the set $\{i : i \in I \cap \psi(i)\}$ as I_θ. Now the decryption algorithm calculates

$$F = \prod_{\theta \in \psi(i)} \frac{\prod_{i \in I_\theta} e((\hat{C}_{\Phi(i)}^{\{\theta\}})^{d_i}, L^{\{\theta\}})}{\prod_{i \in I_\theta} (e(K_1^{\{\theta\}}, C_{\Phi(i),1}^{\{\theta\}}) e(K_{\tau,2}^{\{\theta\}}, C_{\Phi(i),2}^{\{\theta\}}) e(K_{\tau,3}^{\{\theta\}}, C_{\Phi(i),3}^{\{\theta\}}))^{d_i}}.$$

where τ is the index of the attribute $\rho(i)$ in subset A_θ. The algorithm outputs plaintext m as $C \cdot F/(D_0, K_0)$.
- **Correctness.**

$$F_\theta = \prod_{i \in I_\theta} (e(K_1^{\{\theta\}}, C_{\Phi(i),1}^{\{\theta\}}) e(K_{\tau,2}^{\{\theta\}}, C_{\Phi(i),2}^{\{\theta\}}) e(K_{\tau,3}^{\{\theta\}}, C_{\Phi(i),3}^{\{\theta\}}))^{d_i} = \prod_{i \in I_\theta} e(g, w)^{r_\theta d_i \lambda_i}$$

Translate F_θ to $F_{\theta'}$ by the following way.

$$F_{\theta'} = \frac{e(\prod_{i \in I_\theta} (\hat{C}_{\Phi(i)}^{\{\theta\}})^{d_i}, L^{\{\theta\}})}{F_\theta} = \frac{e(\prod_{i \in I_\theta} X^{d_i \lambda_i}, g^{\frac{r+r_\theta}{\beta}})}{\prod_{i \in I_\theta} e(g, w)^{r_\theta d_i \lambda_i}} = e(g, w)^{r \sum_{i \in I_\theta} d_i \lambda_i}$$

Then we have $F = \prod_{\theta \in \psi(i)} F_{\theta'} = e(g, w)^{r \sum_{i \in I} d_i \lambda_i} = e(g, w)^{rs}$ and $m = C \cdot F/(D_0, K_0) = me(g, g)^{\alpha s} e(g, w)^{rs}/e(g^s, g^\alpha w^r)$.

4 Selective Security Proof

In this section, we will give the concrete security proof of our LU-CP-ASBE scheme.

- **Theorem 1.** If the $q - 1$ assumption is selectively secure in polynomial time, then all PPT adversaries with a challenge matrix of size $l \times n$, where $l, n \leq q$, have a negligible advantage in selectively breaking our scheme.
- **Proof.** To prove the theorem, we will suppose that there exists a PPT adversary $\mathcal{A}$ with a challenge matrix that satisfies the restriction, which has a non-negligible advantage $Adv_{\mathcal{A}}$ in selectively breaking our scheme. Using the attacker, we will build a PPT simulator $\mathcal{B}$ that can challenge the $q-1$ assumption with a non-negligible advantage.
- **Init.** The adversary $\mathcal{A}$ declares a challenge access policy $\mathbb{A} = (M_*, \rho_*)$ which he wants to attack, and then sends it to the challenger $\mathcal{B}$. Each row of M_* will be labeled by an attribute and $\rho(i)$ denotes the label of ith row $\boldsymbol{M_*}$.
- **Setup.** $\mathcal{B}$ is supposed to generate the public parameters of system. It implicitly sets the master key to be $\alpha = a^{q+1} + \tilde{\alpha}, \beta = \tilde{\beta}/s$ where a, s and q are set in the assumption and $\tilde{\alpha}, \tilde{\beta}$ are random exponents known to $\mathcal{B}$. Notice that in this way α and β is correctly distributed and a is information-theoretically hidden from $\mathcal{A}$. Also $\mathcal{B}$ chooses $\tilde{v}, \tilde{u}, \tilde{h} \in \mathbb{Z}_p$ randomly, and gives the following public parameters PK to $\mathcal{A}$.

$$g = g, \ w = g^a, u = g^{\tilde{u}} \cdot \prod_{(j,k) \in [l,n]} (g^{a^k/b_j^2})^{M_{j,k}^*},$$

$$h = g^{\tilde{h}} \cdot \prod_{(j,k) \in [l,n]} (g^{a^k/b_j^2})^{-\rho^*(j)M_{j,k}^*}, v = g^{\tilde{v}} \cdot \prod_{(j,k) \in [l,n]} (g^{a^k/b_j})^{M_{j,k}^*},$$

$$e(g,g)^\alpha = e(g^a, g^{a^q}) \cdot e(g,g)^{\tilde{\alpha}}, X = w^\beta = g^{a\tilde{\beta}/s}.$$

- **Phase 1.** Now challenger $\mathcal{B}$ has to produce secret keys for tuples which consists of non-authorized attribute sets $\mathcal{S} = \{A_0, A_1, A_2, \cdots, A_k\}$, where $A_i = \{a_{i1}, a_{i2}, \cdots, a_{in_i}\}$. The only restriction is that $\mathcal{S}$ does not satisfy $\mathbb{A}^*$. Consequently, there exists a vector $\boldsymbol{d} = (d_1, d_2, \cdots, d_n)^T \in \mathbb{Z}_p^n$ such that $d_1 = -1$ and $\langle M_l^*, \boldsymbol{d} \rangle = 0$ for all $i \in I = \{i | i \in [l] \cap \rho^*(i) \in \mathcal{S}\}$. $\mathcal{B}$ computes $\boldsymbol{d}$ using linear algebra. Then $\mathcal{B}$ picks $\tilde{r}$ for the user and $\tilde{r}_\theta (\theta \in [k])$ for each attribute subset randomly from $\mathbb{Z}_p$, and for simplicity we let $\tilde{r}_0 = \tilde{r}$. Then $\mathcal{B}$ implicitly have

$$r = \tilde{r}_\theta - d_1 a^q - \cdots - d_n a^{q+1-n} = \tilde{r}_\theta - \sum_{i \in [n]} d_i a^{q+1-i} \ (\theta \in [0, k]),$$

$$r_\theta = \tilde{r}_\theta + d_1 a^q + \cdots + d_n a^{q+1-n} = \tilde{r}_\theta + \sum_{i \in [n]} d_i a^{q+1-i} \ (\theta \in [0, k]).$$

Each r_θ is properly distributed due to $\tilde{r}_\theta$. Then using the suitable terms from the assumption, $\mathcal{B}$ calculates:

$$K_0^{\{\theta\}} = g^\alpha w^{r_\theta} = g^{\tilde{\alpha}}(g^a)^{\tilde{r}_\theta}\prod_{i=2}^{n}(g^{a^{q+2-i}})^{d_i}, \quad K_1^{\{\theta\}} = g^{r_\theta} = g^{\tilde{r}_\theta}\prod_{i\in[n]}(g^{a^{q+1-i}})^{d_i},$$

$$L^{\{\theta\}} = g^{(r+r_\theta)/\beta} = g^{(\tilde{r}_0+\tilde{r}_\theta)s/\tilde{\beta}}.$$

Additionally, for each attribute $a_{\theta\tau}$ in attribute subset A_θ, $\mathcal{B}$ compute the terms $K_{i,2}^{\{\theta\}} = g^{r_{\theta,i}}$ and $K_{i,3}^{\{\theta\}} = (u^{a_{\theta,i}}h)^{r_{\theta,i}}v^{-r_\theta}$. The part v^{-r_θ} is

$$v^{-\tilde{r}_\theta}(g^{\tilde{v}}\cdot\prod_{(j,k)\in[l,n]}(g^{\frac{a^k}{b_j}})^{M^*_{j,k}})^{-\sum_{i\in[n]}d_i a^{q+1-i}}$$

$$= v^{-\tilde{r}_\theta}\prod_{i\in[n]}(g^{a^{q+1-i}})^{-\tilde{v}d_i}\cdot\prod_{(i,j,k)\in[n,l,n]}g^{-d_i M^*_{j,k}a^{q+1+k-i}/b_j}$$

$$= \underbrace{v^{-\tilde{r}_\theta}\prod_{i\in[n]}(g^{a^{q+1-i}})^{-\tilde{v}d_i}\cdot\prod_{(i,j,k)\in[n,l,n],i\neq k}(g^{\frac{a^{q+1+k-i}}{b_j}})^{-d_i M^*_{j,k}}}_{\Phi}$$

$$\cdot\prod_{(i,j)\in[n,l]}g^{-d_i M^*_{j,k}a^{q+1}/b_j}$$

$$= \Phi\cdot\prod_{j\in l}g^{-\langle M^*_j,d\rangle a^{q+1}/b_j} = \Phi\cdot\prod_{j\in l,\rho^*(j)\notin S}g^{-\langle M^*_j,d\rangle a^{q+1}/b_j}.$$

The Φ part can be calculated by the simulator using the assumption, while the second part cannot. Simulator $\mathcal{B}$ implicitly sets

$$r_{\theta,\tau} = \tilde{r}_{\theta,\tau} + r_\theta\cdot\sum_{i'\in[l],\rho^*(i')\notin S}\frac{b_{i'}}{a_{\theta\tau}-\rho^*(i')}$$

$$= \tilde{r}_{\theta,\tau} + \tilde{r}_\theta\cdot\sum_{i'\in[l],\rho^*(i')\notin S}\frac{b_{i'}}{a_{\theta\tau}-\rho^*(i')} + \sum_{\{i,i'\}\in[n,l],\rho^*(i')\notin S}\frac{d_i b_{i'}a^{q+1-i}}{a_{\theta\tau}-\rho^*(i')}.$$

where $r_{\theta,\tau}$ is properly distributed. Notice that $r_{\theta,\tau}$ is well defined only for attributes that has nothing to do with the policy, therefore, the denominators $a_{\theta\tau}-\rho^*(i')$ are non-zero. The $(u^{a_{\theta,i}}h)^{r_{\theta,i}}$ part in $K_{i,3}^{\{\theta\}}$ is computed as

$$(u^{a_{\theta,i}}h)^{\tilde{r}_{\theta,l}}\cdot(K_{i,2}^{\{\theta\}}/g^{\tilde{r}_{\theta,l}})^{\tilde{u}a_{\theta,i}+\tilde{h}}\cdot\prod_{(i',j,k)\in[l,l,n],\rho^*(i')\notin S}g^{\frac{\tilde{r}_\theta M^*_{j,k}b_{i'}a^k(a_{\theta,i}-\rho^*(j))}{b_j^2(a_{\theta\tau}-\rho^*(i'))}}$$

$$\cdot\prod_{(i,i',j,k)\in[n,l,l,n],\rho^*(i')\notin S}g^{\frac{M^*_{j,k}d_i b_{i'}a^{q+k+1-i}(a_{\theta,i}-\rho^*(j))}{b_j^2(a_{\theta\tau}-\rho^*(i'))}}$$

$$= \Psi\cdot\prod_{(i,j)\in[n,l],\rho^*(j)\notin S}g^{\frac{M^*_{j,i}d_i b_j a^{q+1}(a_{\theta,i}-\rho^*(j))}{b_j^2(a_{\theta\tau}-\rho^*(j))}} = \Psi\cdot\prod_{j\in[l],\rho^*(j)\notin S}g^{\frac{\langle M^*_j,d\rangle a^{q+1}}{b_j}}.$$

where Ψ and $K_{i,2}^{\{\theta\}}$ can be calculated using the terms in our assumption. The non-computable parts of $(u^{a_{\theta,i}}h)^{r_{\theta,i}}$ and $v^{-r_{\theta}}$ term can cancel with each other. In this way simulator $\mathcal{B}$ can calculate $K_{i,2}^{\{\theta\}}$ and $K_{i,3}^{\{\theta\}}$ and send the decryption key $SK = (\mathcal{S}, \{K_0^{\{\theta\}}, K_1^{\{\theta\}}, L^{\{\theta\}}, K_{i,2}^{\{\theta\}}, K_{i,3}^{\{\theta\}}\}_{\theta \in [0,k], i \in [n_\theta]})$ to $\mathcal{A}$.

- **Challenge.** The adversary $\mathcal{A}$ submits two equal length message m_0 and m_1. Then $\mathcal{B}$ flips a random coin $b \xleftarrow{\$} \{0,1\}$ and constructs $C = m_b T e(g,g)^{\tilde{\alpha}s}$ and $D_0 = g^s$ where T is the challenge term. Then $\mathcal{B}$ is supposed to generate the other components in ciphertext and it sets implicitly $\boldsymbol{y} = (s, sa + \tilde{y}_2, sa^2 + \tilde{y}_3, \cdots, sa^{n-1} + \tilde{y}_n)$ where $\tilde{y}_2, \tilde{y}_3, \cdots, \tilde{y}_n \xleftarrow{\$} Z_p$. Since $\boldsymbol{\lambda} = M^*\boldsymbol{y}$, we have that $\lambda_{\mathcal{X}} = \sum_{i \in [n]} M_{\mathcal{X},i}^* sa^{i-1} + \sum_{i=2}^n M_{\mathcal{X},i}^* \tilde{y}_l = \sum_{i \in [n]} M_{\mathcal{X},i}^* sa^{i-1} + \tilde{\lambda}_{\mathcal{X}}$ for each row $\mathcal{X} \in [l]$. And for each now $\mathcal{B}$ sets implicitly $t_{\mathcal{X}} = -sb_{\mathcal{X}}$ which is properly distributed. Using this, $\mathcal{B}$ calculates

$$C_{\tau,1}^{\{\theta\}} = w^{\lambda_{\mathcal{X}}} v^{t_{\mathcal{X}}}$$

$$= w^{\tilde{\lambda}_{\mathcal{X}}} \cdot \prod_{i \in [n]} g^{M_{\mathcal{X},i}^* sa^i} \cdot g^{-sb_{\mathcal{X}}\tilde{v}} \cdot \prod_{(j,k) \in [l,n]} g^{-\frac{sa^k b_{\mathcal{X}} M_{j,k}^*}{b_j}}$$

$$= w^{\tilde{\lambda}_{\mathcal{X}}} \cdot \prod_{i \in [n]} g^{M_{\mathcal{X},i}^* sa^i} \cdot g^{-sb_{\mathcal{X}}\tilde{v}} \cdot \prod_{k \in [n]} g^{-sa^k M_{\mathcal{X},k}^*} \cdot \prod_{(j,k) \in [l,n], j \neq \mathcal{X}} g^{-\frac{sa^k b_{\mathcal{X}} M_{j,k}^*}{b_j}}$$

$$= w^{\tilde{\lambda}_{\mathcal{X}}} \cdot (g^{sb_{\mathcal{X}}})^{-\tilde{v}} \cdot \prod_{(j,k) \in [l,n], j \neq \mathcal{X}} (g^{\frac{sa^k b_{\mathcal{X}}}{b_j}})^{-M_{j,k}^*},$$

$$C_{\tau,2}^{\{\theta\}} = (u^{\rho^*(\mathcal{X})}h)^{-t_{\mathcal{X}}}$$

$$= (g^{sb_{\mathcal{X}}})^{-(\tilde{u}\rho^*(\mathcal{X})+\tilde{h})} \cdot \left(\prod_{(j,k) \in [l,n]} g^{(\rho^*(\mathcal{X})-\rho^*(j))M_{j,k}^* a^k / b_j^2} \right)^{-sb_{\mathcal{X}}}$$

$$= (g^{sb_{\mathcal{X}}})^{-(\tilde{u}\rho^*(\mathcal{X})+\tilde{h})} \cdot \left(\prod_{(j,k) \in [l,n], j \neq \mathcal{X}} g^{sb_{\mathcal{X}} a^k / b_j^2} \right)^{-(\rho^*(\mathcal{X})-\rho^*(j))M_{j,k}^*},$$

$$C_{\tau,3}^{\{\theta\}} = (g^{sb_{\mathcal{X}}})^{-1},$$

$$\hat{C}_\theta = X^{\lambda_{\mathcal{X}}} = X^{\tilde{\lambda}_{\mathcal{X}}} \cdot \prod_{i \in [n]} g^{M_{\mathcal{X},i}^* s\tilde{\beta}/sa^i} = X^{\tilde{\lambda}_{\mathcal{X}}} \cdot \prod_{i \in [n]} (g^{a^i})^{M_{\mathcal{X},i}^* \tilde{\beta}}.$$

where $\mathcal{X} = \sum_{i=0}^\theta n_\theta + \tau$.

By using $t_{\mathcal{X}} = -sb_{\mathcal{X}}$, term v can cancel with the unknown powers of $w^{\lambda_{\mathcal{X}}}$ and similarly by using $\beta = \tilde{\beta}/s$, the unknown powers in $\hat{C}_\theta$ can also be canceled. Now there is nothing non-computable for $\mathcal{B}$ in terms $C_{i,2}^{\{\theta\}}, C_{i,3}^{\{\theta\}}$ and $\hat{C}_\theta$.

So far, $\mathcal{B}$ successfully generates the correct ciphertext under the access structure (M, ρ) using the suitable terms in our assumption and public parameters PK. Finally, $\mathcal{B}$ sends the challenged ciphertext CT

$$(C, (M,\rho), D_0, \{C_{\tau,1}^{\{\theta\}}, C_{\tau,2}^{\{\theta\}}, C_{\tau,3}^{\{\theta\}}\}_{\theta \in [0,m], \tau \in [n_\theta]}, \{\hat{C}_\theta\}_{\theta \in [m]})$$

to the attacker $\mathcal{A}$.

- **Phase 2.** Phase 1 is repeated.
- **Guess.** The adversary $\mathcal{A}$ is supposed to output a guess b' of b to $\mathcal{B}$. If $b' = b$, $\mathcal{B}$ outputs 0 and claim the challenge term is $T = e(g,g)^{a^{q+1}s}$, otherwise, it outputs 1 and the challenge term T is random.

Since the probability of $T = e(g,g)^{a^{q+1}s}$ equals $1/2$, $\mathcal{B}$ has an advantage of $Adv_{\mathcal{A}}/2$ to break the q-type security assumption.

5 Conclusion

In this paper, we proposed a feasible and efficient attribute-set based encryption scheme, which can be applied in the scenario where many attributes are only meaningful in groups or in sets as they describe users. Our scheme is large universe, unbounded and powerful in expressing complex access policies. Additionally, it is proved to be selectively secure under the q-type assumption.

Acknowledgement. This work is supported by the National Natural Science Foundation of China under Grant Nos. 61672062, 61232005, and the National High Technology Research and Development Program ("863" Program) of China under Grant No. 2015AA016009. We would like to thank Xing Zhang for valuable suggestions as well as Dan Li and Lingyun Guo for intensive modifications.

References

1. Aluvalu, R., Kamliya, V.: A survey on hierarchical attribute set based encryption (HASBE) access control model for cloud computing. Int. J. Comput. Appl. **112**(7), 4–7 (2015)
2. Ambrosin, M., Conti, M., Dargahi, T.: On the feasibility of attribute-based encryption on smartphone devices, pp. 49–54 (2015)
3. Beimel, A.: Secure schemes for secret sharing and key distribution. Int. J. Pure Appl. Math. (1996)
4. Bethencourt, J., Sahai, A., Waters, B.: Ciphertext-policy attribute-based encryption. In: IEEE Symposium on Security and Privacy, pp. 321–334 (2007)
5. Bobba, R., Khurana, H., Prabhakaran, M.: Attribute-sets: a practically motivated enhancement to attribute-based encryption. In: Backes, M., Ning, P. (eds.) ESORICS 2009. LNCS, vol. 5789, pp. 587–604. Springer, Heidelberg (2009). https://doi.org/10.1007/978-3-642-04444-1_36
6. Deng, H., Wu, Q., Qin, B., Domingo-Ferrer, J., Zhang, L., Liu, J., Shi, W.: Ciphertext-policy hierarchical attribute-based encryption with short ciphertexts. Inf. Sci. **275**(11), 370–384 (2014)
7. Goyal, V., Pandey, O., Sahai, A., Waters, B.: Attribute-based encryption for fine-grained access control of encrypted data. In: ACM Conference on Computer and Communications Security, pp. 89–98 (2006)
8. Lewko, A.: Tools for simulating features of composite order bilinear groups in the prime order setting. In: Pointcheval, D., Johansson, T. (eds.) EUROCRYPT 2012. LNCS, vol. 7237, pp. 318–335. Springer, Heidelberg (2012). https://doi.org/10.1007/978-3-642-29011-4_20

9. Lewko, A., Okamoto, T., Sahai, A., Takashima, K., Waters, B.: Fully secure functional encryption: attribute-based encryption and (hierarchical) inner product encryption. In: Gilbert, H. (ed.) EUROCRYPT 2010. LNCS, vol. 6110, pp. 62–91. Springer, Heidelberg (2010). https://doi.org/10.1007/978-3-642-13190-5_4

10. Li, C., Fang, Y., Zhang, X., Jin, C., Shen, Q., Wu, Z.: A practical construction for large universe hierarchical attribute-based encryption. Concurr. Comput. Pract. Exp. **29**(17) (2017)

11. Li, J., Wang, Q., Wang, C., Ren, K.: Enhancing attribute-based encryption with attribute hierarchy. Mob. Netw. Appl. **16**(5), 553–561 (2011)

12. Liu, J., Wan, Z., Gu, M.: Hierarchical attribute-set based encryption for scalable, flexible and fine-grained access control in cloud computing. In: Bao, F., Weng, J. (eds.) ISPEC 2011. LNCS, vol. 6672, pp. 98–107. Springer, Heidelberg (2011). https://doi.org/10.1007/978-3-642-21031-0_8

13. Okamoto, T., Takashima, K.: Fully secure unbounded inner-product and attribute-based encryption. In: Wang, X., Sako, K. (eds.) ASIACRYPT 2012. LNCS, vol. 7658, pp. 349–366. Springer, Heidelberg (2012). https://doi.org/10.1007/978-3-642-34961-4_22

14. Perumal, B., Rajasekaran, M.P., Duraiyarasan, S.: An efficient hierarchical attribute set based encryption scheme with revocation for outsourcing personal health records in cloud computing. In: International Conference on Advanced Computing and Communication Systems, pp. 1–5 (2014)

15. Ragesh, G.K., Baskaran, D.K.: Ragesh G K and Dr K Baskaran privacy preserving ciphertext policy attribute set based encryption (PP-CP-ASBE) scheme for patient centric data access control in cloud assisted WBANs, ACCIS 2014. In: ACCIS 2014. Elsevier (2014)

16. Rouselakis, Y., Waters, B.: Practical constructions and new proof methods for large universe attribute-based encryption. In: ACM SIGSAC Conference on Computer and Communications Security, pp. 463–474 (2013)

17. Sahai, A., Waters, B.: Fuzzy identity-based encryption. In: Cramer, R. (ed.) EUROCRYPT 2005. LNCS, vol. 3494, pp. 457–473. Springer, Heidelberg (2005). https://doi.org/10.1007/11426639_27

18. Wan, Z., Liu, J., Deng, R.H.: HASBE: a hierarchical attribute-based solution for flexible and scalable access control in cloud computing. IEEE Trans. Inf. Forensics Secur. **7**(2), 743–754 (2012)

19. Wang, G., Liu, Q., Wu, J.: Hierarchical attribute-based encryption for fine-grained access control in cloud storage services. In: ACM Conference on Computer and Communications Security, pp. 735–737 (2010)

20. Wang, S., Feng, F.: Large universe attribute-based encryption scheme from lattices. Comput. Sci. **17**(7), 327 (2014)

21. Zhang, Y., Li, J., Zheng, D., Chen, X., Li, H.: Accountable large-universe attribute-based encryption supporting any monotone access structures. In: Liu, J.K.K., Steinfeld, R. (eds.) ACISP 2016. LNCS, vol. 9722, pp. 509–524. Springer, Cham (2016). https://doi.org/10.1007/978-3-319-40253-6_31

Fully Secure Hidden Ciphertext-Policy Attribute-Based Proxy Re-encryption

Xinyu Feng[1,2], Cong Li[1,2], Dan Li[1,2], Yuejian Fang[1,2], and Qingni Shen[1,2(⊠)]

[1] School of Software and Microelectronics, Peking University, Beijing, China
{xyf,li.cong,lidan.sichuan.yaan}@pku.edu.cn,
{fangyj,qingnishen}@ss.pku.edu.cn
[2] National Engineering Research Center for Software Engineering,
Peking University, Beijing, China

Abstract. We propose a hidden ciphertext-policy attribute-based proxy re-encryption scheme. A data owner can delegate the capability of transforming a ciphertext under an access policy to another one with the same plaintext but different access policy to a semi-trusted proxy. Compared with traditional schemes, our scheme can hide the user's attributes information in the encryption and re-encryption process, which can obtain a better protection of the user's privacy. We also prove our scheme to be fully secure under standard assumptions using the dual system technique. As far as we know, this is the first scheme to achieve all these properties simultaneously.

Keywords: Attribute-based proxy re-encryption · Hidden policy
Fully secure · Delegation

1 Introduction

Attribute-based Encryption (ABE) which provides fine grained access control is a good solution to the secure sharing of cloud data. There are mainly two types of ABE schemes: the Key-Policy ABE (KP-ABE), where the ciphertexts are associated with sets of attributes while the keys are associated with access policies; the Ciphertext-Policy ABE (CP-ABE), where the keys are associated with sets of attributes and the ciphertexts are associated with access policies.

Attribute-based proxy re-encryption (AB-PRE) is an application of proxy cryptography in ABE [4,15,19,26]. AB-PRE schemes allow the data owner to delegate the capability of re-encryption to the semi-trusted proxy. In this way, the proxy is capable of running the re-encryption operation, which reduces the computation cost of the data owner. An authorized user is able to decrypt the re-encrypted data just using his/her own secret key and no additional component is needed. Moreover, no sensitive data can be revealed by the proxy. However, there exists a problem in current ciphertext-policy attribute-based proxy re-encryption (CP-AB-PRE) schemes [4,15,19,27]. In these schemes, the ciphertext policy which consists of the user's attributes is exposed to the proxy, thus the

© Springer International Publishing AG, part of Springer Nature 2018
S. Qing et al. (Eds.): ICICS 2017, LNCS 10631, pp. 192–204, 2018.
https://doi.org/10.1007/978-3-319-89500-0_17

proxy can get some information of attributes about both the owner and the user. A user's attributes may contain his/her sensitive information. These data relate to user privacy and should not be exposed to a third party.

To solve the problem mentioned above, we borrow the concept of hidden policy appeared in schemes [9,12,13,21,22] to propose a hidden ciphertext policy attribute-based proxy re-encryption scheme. By using our scheme, the proxy can obtain little sensitive data or privacy information of the user.

Our Contributions. By employing the AND-gates policy we propose the first fully secure hidden CP-AB-PRE scheme which can make a better protection of the user's privacy. Our scheme has the following properties:

- **Unidirectionality** (A ciphertext CT is able to be transformed to CT' but it cannot be transformed from CT').
- **Non-Interactivity** (The data owner is able to generate the re-encryption key by himself without any participation of the untrusted third party).
- **Multi-use** (The encrypted data can be re-encrypted for multiple times).
- **Master key security** (The proxy or the user doesn't need to obtain the data owner's secret key during the re-encryption and decryption process).
- **Re-encryption control** (The data owner can determine whether the encrypted data can be re-encrypted).
- **Collusion resistant** (Users are not able to combine their keys to obtain the plaintext which belongs to none of them).

Table 1 shows the comparison between our CP-AB-PRE scheme and other schemes on the main features.

Table 1. Comparison of features of AB-PRE schemes

Schemes	Liang et al. [15]	Luo et al. [19]	Do et al. [4]	Liang et al. [14]	Ours
Unidirectionality	√	√	√	√	√
Non-interactive	√	√	√	√	√
Multi-use	√	√	×	√	√
Master key security	√	√	√	√	√
Re-encryption control	√	√	×	√	√
Collusion resistant	√	√	√	√	√
Hidden policy	×	×	×	×	√
Fully secure	×	×	×	√	√

Related Work. Proxy re-encryption was first proposed by Blaze et al. [2], which can transform a key with the ciphertext into another key without revealing the secret key and the plaintext of the ciphertext. But there should be an unrealistic level of trust in the proxy to achieve the delegation because the sensitive information can be revealed during the re-encryption process. To solve this problem, Ateniese et al. proposed a new proxy re-encryption scheme in 2005 [1]. Green and

Ateniese presented an identity-based proxy re-encryption (IB-PRE) scheme in 2007 [5], but it only proved to be secure in the random oracle model. Then many improved IB-PRE schemes were proposed [3,7,16,20,23]. After ABE scheme was introduced, Guo et al. proposed the first AB-PRE scheme [26], which is also the first key-policy AB-PRE scheme, but this scheme exists in bidirectional property. Then Liang et al. proposed the first CP-AB-PRE scheme [15] and realized the *Multi-use* property, but as the times of re-encryption increases, the size of the encrypted ciphertext grows linearly. In 2010, Luo et al. presented a CP-AB-PRE scheme [19] which allows the data owner to decide whether re-encrypting the ciphertext or not. In the same year, Yu et al. introduced a new property of *Data confidentiality* in their paper [27], but their scheme has a problem of *Collusion Attack*. Do et al. proposed a new AB-PRE scheme to support the *Collusion resistant* property in 2011. There were also some other AB-PRE schemes proposed in 2011 [4,6,8,25]. After that, Liu et al. added the timestamp and proposed two AB-PRE schemes [17,18] which can prevent the revoked users to get access to the encrypted data. Later in 2012, Seo et al. introduced an AB-PRE scheme with a constant number of paring operations to save the computation cost [24]. However, none of the above schemes achieved fully security. In 2014, Liang et al. proposed a fully secure CP-AB-PRE scheme by integrating the dual system encryption technology [14], then in 2016, Li et al. proposed another fully secure scheme under the same system [11]. Until now, none of the previous CP-AB-PRE schemes has obtained the property of *Hidden Policy*. Therefore, we focus on this problem in this work.

Organization. This paper is organized as follows. We first give the relevant access structure, complexity assumptions and security model about CP-AB-PRE in Sect. 2. In Sect. 3, we introduce the construction of our hidden policy CP-AB-PRE scheme. In Sect. 4, we prove the full security of our scheme. Then in Sect. 5, we give a conclusion of our work.

2   Access Structure and Complexity Assumptions

2.1   Access Structure

We take AND-gates as the basic access policy in our scheme, where negative attributes and wildcards are supported. A negative attribute denotes a user shouldn't have this attribute and a wildcard means this attribute is out of consideration. Multi-valued attribute is also supported in our scheme.

We use the notation such as $W = [W_1, \cdots, W_n] = [1, 0, *, *, 0]$ where $n = 5$ to specify the ciphertext policy. The wildcard $*$ in the ciphertext policy means "not care" value, which can be considered as an AND-gate on all the attributes. For example, the above ciphertext policy means that the recipient who wants to decrypt must have the value 1 for W_1, 0 for W_2 and W_5, and the values for W_3 and W_4 do not matter in the AND-gate. A recipient with policy $[1, 0, 1, 0, 0]$ can decrypt the ciphertext, but a recipient with policy $[1, 1, 1, 0, 1]$ can not.

To support multi-valued attribute, we use the following notation. Given an attribute list $L = [v_{1,t_1}, v_{2,t_2}, \cdots, v_{n,t_n}]$ where t_i means the t_i^{th} attribute in attribute set L_i. For a ciphertext policy $W = [W_1, W_2, \cdots, W_n]$, L satisfies W if for all $i = 1, \cdots, n$, $v_{i,t_i} \in W_i$ or $W_i = *$, otherwise L does not satisfy W. We use the notation $L \models W$ to mean that L satisfies W.

2.2 Complexity Assumptions

The Basic Generic Group Assumption. Given a group generator $\mathcal{G}$, we define the following distribution:

$$\mathbb{G} = (N = p_1 p_2 p_3, G, G_T, e) \xleftarrow{R} \mathcal{G}, \ g_1 \in G_{p_1}, g_2, X_2, Y_2 \in G_{p_2}, g_3 \in G_{p_3}, \ \alpha, s \in \mathbb{Z}_N,$$

$$D = (\mathbb{G}, g_1, g_2, g_3, g_1^\alpha X_2, g_1^s Y_2), \ T_0 = e(g_1, g_1)^{\alpha s}, T_1 \in G_T.$$

We define the advantage of an algorithm $\mathcal{A}$ in breaking this assumption to be:

$$Adv_{\mathcal{G},\mathcal{A}}^1(\lambda) := |Pr[\mathcal{A}(D, T_0) = 1] - Pr[\mathcal{A}(D, T_1) = 1]|.$$

The General Subgroup Decision Assumption. We let $\mathcal{G}$ denote a group generator and $Z_0, Z_1, Z_2, \ldots, Z_k$ denote a collection of non-empty subsets of $\{1, 2, 3\}$ where each Z_i for $i \geq 2$ satisfies $\mathbb{G} = (N = p_1 p_2 p_3, G, G_T, e) \xleftarrow{R} \mathcal{G}$.

The Three Party Diffie-Hellman Assumption in a Subgroup. Given a group generator $\mathcal{G}$, we define the following distribution:

$$\mathbb{G} = (N = p_1 p_2 p_3, G, G_T, e) \xleftarrow{R} \mathcal{G}, \ g_1 \in G_{p_1}, \ g_2 \in G_{p_2}, \ g_3 \in G_{p_3}, \ x, y, z \in \mathbb{Z}_N,$$

$$D = (\mathbb{G}, g_1, g_2, g_3, g_2^x, g_2^y, g_2^z), \ T_0 = g_2^{xyz}, \ T1 \in G_{p_2}.$$

We define the advantage of an algorithm $\mathcal{A}$ in breaking this assumption to be:

$$Adv_{\mathcal{G},\mathcal{A}}^{3DH}(\lambda) := |Pr[\mathcal{A}(D, T_0) = 1] - Pr[\mathcal{A}(D, T_1) = 1]|.$$

We say that $\mathcal{G}$ satisfies The Three Party Diffie-Hellman Assumption if $Adv_{\mathcal{G},\mathcal{A}}^{3DH}(\lambda)$ is a negligible function of λ for any PPT algorithm $\mathcal{A}$.

The Source Group q-Parallel BDHE Assumption in a Subgroup. Given a group generator $\mathcal{G}$ and a positive integer q, we define the following distribution:

$$\mathbb{G} = (N = p_1 p_2 p_3, G, G_T, e) \xleftarrow{R} \mathcal{G}, \ g_1 \in G_{p_1}, g_2 \in G_{p_2}, g_3 \in G_{p_3}, \ c, d, f, b_1, \ldots, b_q \in \mathbb{Z}_N.$$

The adversary will be given:

$$D = (\mathbb{G}, g_1, g_2, g_3, g_2^f, g_2^{df}, g_2^c, g_2^{c^2}, \ldots, g_2^{c^q}, g_2^{c^{q+2}}, \ldots, g_2^{c^{2q}},$$

$$g_2^{\frac{c^i}{b_j}} \forall i \in [2q]\{q+1\}, j \in [q], g_2^{dfb_j} \forall j \in [q], g_2^{\frac{dfc^i b_{j'}}{b_j}} \forall i \in [q], j, j' \in [q] \ s.t. j \neq j').$$

We additionally define $T_0 = g_2^{dc^{q+1}}$, $T_1 \in G_{p_2}$.

We define the advantage of an algorithm $\mathcal{A}$ in breaking this assumption to be:

$$Adv_{\mathcal{G},\mathcal{A}}^q(\lambda) := |Pr[\mathcal{A}(D, T_0) = 1] - Pr[\mathcal{A}(D, T_1) = 1]|.$$

We say that $\mathcal{G}$ satisfies The Source Group q-Parallel BDHE Assumption in a Subgroup if $Adv_{\mathcal{G},\mathcal{A}}^q(\lambda)$ is a negligible function of λ for any PPT algorithm $\mathcal{A}$.

2.3 Security Model

The definition of full security for the CP-ABE system is described by a security game between a challenger and an attacker, which proceeds as follows:

- **Setup.** The challenger runs the *Setup* algorithm and sends the public parameters PP to the attacker and the challenger knows the master key MSK.
- **Phase 1.** The attacker adaptively makes queries for private keys corresponding to sets of attributes $S_1, \ldots, S_{Q_1}$ to the challenger. Each time, the challenger responds with a secret key obtained by running $KeyGen(MSK, PP, S_k)$. The attacker may also requests the re-encryption keys for access policies W', and the challenger will run the $RKGen(SK_L, W')$ algorithm to respond.
- **Challenge.** The attacker selects two messages M_0 and M_1 with the same length and an access structure W. The challenger flips a random coin $b \in \{0, 1\}$ and encrypts M_b under W to generate CT. It sends CT to the attacker.
- **Phase 2.** Phase 2 is similar to Phase 1 except that the attacker requests private keys corresponding to sets of attributes $S_{Q_1+1}, \ldots, S_Q$ adaptively. Notice that none of the attributes should satisfy the access structure W in the challenge phase.
- **Guess.** The attacker outputs a guess b' for b.

The advantage of an attacker in this game is defined to be $Pr[b = b'] - \frac{1}{2}$.

3 Our Construction

Setup($1^k, n$). A trusted authority generates a tuple $G = [p, G, G_T, g \in G, e]$ and random $w \in \mathbb{Z}_p^*$. For each attribute i where $1 \leq i \leq n$, the authority generates random values $\{a_{i,t}, b_{i,t} \in \mathbb{Z}_p^*\}_{1 \leq t \leq n_i}$ and random points $\{A_{i,t} \in G\}_{1 \leq t \leq n_i}$. It computes $Y = e(g, g)^w$. The public key PK and the master key MK is

$$PK = \{Y, p, G, G_T, g, e, \{\{A_{i,t}^{a_{i,t}}, A_{i,t}^{b_{i,t}}\}_{1 \leq t \leq n_i}\}_{1 \leq i \leq n}\},$$

$$MK = \{w, \{\{a_{i,t}, b_{i,t}\}_{1 \leq t \leq n_i}\}_{1 \leq i \leq n}\}.$$

KeyGen(MK,L). Let $L = [L_1, L_2, \ldots, L_n] = [v_{1,t_1}, v_{2,t_2}, \ldots, v_{n,t_n}]$ be the attribute list for the user who obtains the corresponding secret key. The trusted authority picks up random values $s_i, \lambda_i \in \mathbb{Z}_p^*$ and random elements $R, R_0, R_1, R_2 \in G_{p_3}$. For $1 \leq i \leq n$, sets $s = \sum_{i=1}^n s_i$, and computes $D_0 = g^{w-s}R$. For $1 \leq i \leq n$, the authority computes $D_{i,0} = g^{s_i}(A_{i,t_i})^{a_{i,t_i}b_{i,t_i}\lambda_i}R_0, D_{i,1} = g^{a_{i,t_i}\lambda_i}R_1, D_{i,2} = g^{b_{i,t_i}\lambda_i}R_2$. The secret key SK_L is formed as: $SK_L = \{D_0, \{D_{i,0}, D_{i,1}, D_{i,2}\}_{1 \leq i \leq n}\}$.

Encrypt(PK,M,W). An encryptor encrypts a message $M \in G_T$ under a ciphertext policy $W = [W_1, W_2, \ldots, W_n]$. It picks up a random value $r \in \mathbb{Z}_p^*$ and sets $\tilde{C} = MY^r, C_0 = g^r$, then picks up a random value $h \in \mathbb{Z}_p^*$ and computes

$C_0' = h^r$. For $1 \leq i \leq n$, it picks up random values $\{r_{i,t} \in \mathbb{Z}_p^*\}_{1 \leq t \leq n_i}$ and computes $C_{i,t,1}, C_{i,t,2}$ as follows: if $v_{i,t} \in W_i$, $C_{i,t,1} = (A_{i,t}^{b_{i,t}})^{r_{i,t}}, C_{i,t,2} = (A_{i,t}^{a_{i,t}})^{r-r_{i,t}}$ (*well-formed*); if $v_{i,t} \notin W_i$, $C_{i,t,1}, C_{i,t,2}$ are random (*mal-formed*). The ciphertext CT is: $CT = \{\tilde{C}, C_0, C_0', \{\{C_{i,t,1}, C_{i,t,2}\}_{1 \leq t \leq n_i}\}_{1 \leq i \leq n}\}$.

RKGen(SK_L, W). Let SK_L denote a valid secret key and W an access policy. To generate a re-encryption key for W, choose $d \in \mathbb{Z}_p$ and compute g^d, $D_{i,0}' = D_{i,0}h^d$. Set $D_0' = D_0, D_{i,1}' = D_{i,1}, D_{i,2}' = D_{i,2}$, and compute $\mathbb{C}$ which is the ciphertext of $E(g^d)$ under the access policy W, i.e., $\mathbb{C} = Encrypt(PK, E(g^d), W)$. The re-encryption key for W is $RK_{L \to W} = \{D_0', \{\{D_{i,j}'\}_{1 \leq j \leq 2}\}_{1 \leq i \leq n}, \mathbb{C}\}$.

Re-encrypt($RK_{L \to W'}, CT_W$). Let $RK_{L \to W'}$ be a valid re-encryption key for access policy W' and CT_W a well-formed ciphertext $\tilde{C}, C_0, C_0', \{\{C_{i,t,1}, C_{i,t,2}\}_{1 \leq t \leq n_i}\}_{1 \leq i \leq n}$, for $1 \leq i \leq n$, compute $E_i = \dfrac{e(C_0, D_{i,0}')}{e(C_{i,t,1}, D_{i,1}')e(C_{i,t,2}, D_{i,2}')} = e(g,g)^{rs_i}e(g,h)^{rd}$ then compute $\bar{C} = e(C_0, D_0')\prod_{i=1}^{n} E_i = e(g,g)^{wr}e(g,h)^{nrd}$, the re-encrypted ciphertext is formed as $CT' = \{\tilde{C}, C_0', \bar{C}, \mathbb{C}\}$.

Decrypt(CT_W, SK_L). The recipient tries decrypting the CT without knowing W using his/her SK_L as follows:

Assume $L = [L_1, L_2, \ldots, L_n] = [v_{1,t_1}, v_{2,t_2}, \ldots, v_{n,t_n}]$ is the user's attribute list.

- If CT is an original well-formed ciphertext, then for $1 \leq i \leq n$, $C_{i,1}' = C_{i,t,1}$, $C_{i,2}' = C_{i,t,2}$ where $L_i = v_{i,t_i}$, $M = \dfrac{\tilde{C}\prod_{i=1}^{n} e(C_{i,1}', D_{i,1})e(C_{i,2}', D_{i,2})}{e(C_0, D_0)\prod_{i=1}^{n} e(C_0, D_{i,0})}$.
- Else if CT is a re-encrypted well-formed ciphertext, then
  1. Decrypt $E(g^d)$ from $\mathbb{C}$ using the secret key SK_L and decode it to g^d.
  2. $M = \tilde{C} \cdot e(C_0', g^d)^n / \bar{C}$.

4   Security Proof

We prove our scheme fully secure using the dual system [10] under the *general subgroup decision assumption*, the *three party Diffie-Hellman assumption in a subgroup*, and the *source group q-parallel BDHE assumption in a subgroup*.

Let $Game_{real}$ denote the real security game defined in Sect. 2.3. We assume $g_2 \in G_{p_2}$ and give the definition of *semi-functional keys* and *semi-functional ciphertexts*.

- **Semi-function Keys.** Let $L = [L_1, L_2, \cdots, L_n] = [v_{1,t_1}, v_{2,t_2}, \cdots, v_{n,t_n}]$ be an attribute list. We first run the normal *KeyGen* algorithm to produce a normal key $D_0, \{D_{i,0}, D_{i,1}, D_{i,2}\}_{1 \leq i \leq n}$. Then we choose a random element $W \in G_{p_2}$ and generate the semi-functional key: $D_0W, \{D_{i,0}, D_{i,1}, D_{i,2}\}_{1 \leq i \leq n}$.

– **Semi-functional Ciphertexts.** Then we produce the semi-functional ciphertexts, we first run the normal *Encrypt* algorithm to produce a normal ciphertext which is formed as $\tilde{C}, C_0, C_0', C_{i,t,1}, C_{i,t,2}$. We assume $A_{i,t} = g^{u_{i,t}}$, so $C_{i,t,1} = (g^{u_{i,t}b_{i,t}})^{r_{i,t}}, C_{i,t,2} = (g^{u_{i,t}a_{i,t}})^{r-r_{i,t}}$. Then we choose random exponents $r', r_{i,t}' \in \mathbb{Z}_p^*$ and the semi-functional ciphertext is formed as:

$$\tilde{C}, C_0 g_2^{r'}, C_0' g_2^{r'}, C_{i,t,1} g_2^{u_{i,t}'b_{i,t}'r_{i,t}'}, C_{i,t,2} g_2^{u_{i,t}'a_{i,t}'(r'-r_{i,t}')}.$$

– **Game$_k$.** Let Q denote the total number of key queries from the attacker. In this game, the ciphertext given to the attacker is semi-functional as well as the first k keys. The remaining keys are normal.
We define some transitions to complete our security proof. At the beginning, we transit from $Game_{real}$ to $Game_0$, then from $Game_0$ to $Game_1$, and so on. We finally get the transition of $Game_{Q-1}$ to $Game_Q$. The ciphertext as well as all the keys given to the attacker are semi-functional in $Game_Q$. We then transit from $Game_Q$ to $Game_{final}$. $Game_{final}$ is similar to $Game_Q$ except that the ciphertext given to the attacker is a semi-functional encryption of a random message.
To complete the transition from $Game_{k-1}$ to $Game_k$, we define another two types of semi-functional keys as follows:

– **Nominal Semi-functional Keys.** The nominal semi-functional keys share the values $a_{i,t_i}', b_{i,t_i}', u_{i,t_i}'$ with the semi-function ciphertext. Then choose random exponents s' and s_i'. The nominal semi-functional keys are formed as:

$$D_0 g_2^{-s'}, D_{i,0} g_2^{s_i'+u_{i,t_i}'a_{i,t_i}'b_{i,t_i}'\lambda_i'}, D_{i,1} g_2^{a_{i,t_i}'\lambda_i'}, D_{i,2} g_2^{b_{i,t_i}'\lambda_i'}.$$

– **Temporary Semi-functional Keys.** The temporary semi-functional keys share the values $a_{i,t_i}', b_{i,t_i}', u_{i,t_i}'$ with the semi-function ciphertext. Then choose random $W \in G_{p_2}$ and random exponents s' and s_i'. The temporary semi-functional keys are formed as: $D_0 W, D_{i,0} g_2^{s_i'+u_{i,t_i}'a_{i,t_i}'b_{i,t_i}'\lambda_i'}, D_{i,1} g_2^{a_{i,t_i}'\lambda_i'}, D_{i,2} g_2^{b_{i,t_i}'\lambda_i'}.$
For any k $(1 \leq k \leq Q)$, we give the definition of $Game_k^N$ and $Game_k^T$:

– **Game$_k^N$.** $Game_k^N$ is similar to $Game_k$, except that the kth key given to the attacker is a nominal semi-functional key.

– **Game$_k^T$.** $Game_k^N$ is similar to $Game_k$, except that the kth key given to the attacker is a temporary semi-functional key. To achieve the transition from $Game_{k-1}$ to $Game_k$, we first transit from $Game_{k-1}$ to $Game_k^N$, then from $Game_k^N$ to $Game_k^T$ and finally from $Game_k^T$ to $Game_k$.
Then we give the following lemmas to realize our proof.

– **Lemma 1.** *There is no PPT attacker which can achieve a non-negligible difference in advantage between $Game_{real}$ and $Game_0$.*
We prove this lemma under the general subgroup decision assumption.

– **Proof.** Given a PPT attacker $\mathcal{A}$ achieving a non-negligible difference in advantage between $Game_{real}$ and $Game_0$, we will create a PPT algorithm $\mathcal{B}$

to break the general subgroup decision assumption. $\mathcal{B}$ is given g_1 which is a random element of G_{p_1}, g_3 which is a random element of G_{p_3}, and T which is either a random element of G_{p_1} or a random element of $G_{p_1 p_2}$. Due to the different values of T, $\mathcal{B}$ will simulate either $Game_{real}$ or $Game_0$ with $\mathcal{A}$.

$\mathcal{B}$ first runs the *Setup* algorithm and generates the public parameters:

$$N, p, G, G_T, g_1, e, Y = e(g_1, g_1)^w, \{\{A_{i,t}^{a_{i,t}} = g_1^{u_{i,t} a_{i,t}}, A_{i,t}^{b_{i,t}} = g_1^{u_{i,t} b_{i,t}}\}_{1 \le t \le n_i}\}_{1 \le i \le n}.$$

$A_{i,t}, w, u_{i,t}, a_{i,t}, b_{i,t}$ are selected randomly by $\mathcal{B}$, and the master key is known to $\mathcal{B}$. $\mathcal{B}$ sends the public parameters to $\mathcal{A}$. When $\mathcal{A}$ requests a secret key, or a re-encryption key, $\mathcal{B}$ runs the normal *KeyGen* algorithm or the normal *RKGen* algorithm to generate the requested one.

On the other hand, $\mathcal{A}$ is allowed to request a challenge ciphertext. $\mathcal{A}$ first selects two messages M_0 and M_1 with the same length, and an access policy W, then sends them to $\mathcal{B}$. $\mathcal{B}$ flips coin to choose a random bit b and then encrypts M_b ($b \in \{0,1\}$) under W as follows. It implicitly sets g^r equal to the G_{p_1} part of T. It also chooses $\tilde{r}_{i,t}, r'' \in \mathbb{Z}_N, \forall t \in [1, n_i], \forall i \in [1, n]$ and implicitly sets $r \tilde{r}_{i,t} = r_{i,t}$. The ciphertext is formed as:

$$\tilde{C} = M e(g_1, T)^w, C_0 = T, C_0' = T^{r''}, C_{i,t,1} = (T^{u_{i,t} b_{i,t}})^{\tilde{r}_{i,t}}, C_{i,t,2} = (T^{u_{i,t} a_{i,t}})^{1 - \tilde{r}_{i,t}}.$$

If $T \in G_{p_1}$, this is a properly distributed normal ciphertext, and $\mathcal{B}$ has properly simulated $Game_{real}$ with $\mathcal{A}$. If $T \in G_{p_1 p_2}$, then this is a semi-functional ciphertext, where $g_2^{r'}$ is the G_{p_2} part of T, $u_{i,t}'$ is equal to the value of $u_{i,t}$ modulo p_2, $a_{i,t}'$ is equal to the value of $a_{i,t}$ modulo p_2, $b_{i,t}'$ is equal to the value of $b_{i,t}$ modulo p_2, and $r' - r_{i,t}'$ is equal to the value of $1 - \tilde{r}_{i,t}$ modulo p_2. Then $\mathcal{B}$ has properly simulated $Game_0$ with $\mathcal{A}$.

- **Lemma 2.** *There is no PPT attacker which can achieve a non-negligible difference in advantage between $Game_{k-1}$ and $Game_k^N$ for any $k \in [1, Q]$.*

We prove this lemma under the general subgroup decision assumption.

- **Proof.** Given a PPT attacker $\mathcal{A}$ achieving a non-negligible difference in advantage between $Game_{k-1}$ and $Game_k^N$ for some k between 1 and Q, we will create a PPT algorithm $\mathcal{B}$ to break the general subgroup decision assumption. $\mathcal{B}$ is given $g_1, g_3, X_1 X_2, Y_2 Y_3, T$ where g_1, X_1 are generators of G_{p_1}, X_2 is a generator of G_{p_2}, g_3, Y_3 are generators of G_{p_3}, and T is either a random element of $G_{p_1} G_{p_3}$ or a random element of $G_{p_1 p_2 p_3}$. Due to the different values of T, $\mathcal{B}$ will simulate either $Game_{k-1}$ or $Game_k^N$ with $\mathcal{A}$.

$\mathcal{B}$ first runs the *Setup* algorithm and generates the public parameters:

$$N, p, G, G_T, g_1, e, Y = e(g_1, g_1)^w, \{A_{i,t}^{a_{i,t}} = g_1^{u_{i,t} a_{i,t}}, A_{i,t}^{b_{i,t}} = g_1^{u_{i,t} b_{i,t}}\}_{1 \le t \le n_i} \}_{1 \le i \le n}.$$

$A_{i,t}, w, u_{i,t}, a_{i,t}, b_{i,t}$ are selected randomly by $\mathcal{B}$, and the master key is known to $\mathcal{B}$. $\mathcal{B}$ sends the public parameters to $\mathcal{A}$. When $\mathcal{A}$ requests a secret key or a re-encryption key, $\mathcal{B}$ runs the normal *KeyGen* algorithm or the normal *RKGen* algorithm to generate the requested one.

In response to $\mathcal{A}$'s first $k-1$ key queries, $\mathcal{B}$ produces semi-functional keys as follows. It first runs the normal $KeyGen$ algorithm to produce a normal key $D_0, \{D_{i,0}, D_{i,1}, D_{i,2}\}_{1 \leq i \leq n}$, and then it chooses a random exponent $\tau \in \mathbb{Z}_N$ and the semi-functional key is formed as: $D_0(Y_2Y_3)^\tau, \{D_{i,0}, D_{i,1}, D_{i,2}\}_{1 \leq i \leq n}$. Then $\mathcal{B}$ runs the $RKGen$ algorithm and generates the re-encryption key:

$$D_0(Y_2Y_3)^\tau, \{D_{i,0}h^r, D_{i,1}, D_{i,2}\}_{1 \leq i \leq n}.$$

Here h is a random element of G_{p_1}, and r is a random element of $\mathbb{Z}_p^*$.

Then $\mathcal{B}$ generates the semi-functional challenge ciphertext as in $Lemma\ 1$, which is the ciphertext of M_b under policy W. It chooses random exponents $\tilde{r}_{i,t}, \forall i \in [1,n], t \in [1, n_i]$ and implicitly sets $g^r = X_1$, and $r\tilde{r}_{i,t} = r_{i,t}$. It chooses a random exponent r'', the semi-functional ciphertext is:

$$\tilde{C} = Me(g_1, X_1X_2)^w, \quad C_0 = X_1X_2, \quad C_0' = (X_1X_2)^{r''},$$
$$C_{i,t,1} = (X_1X_2)^{u_{i,t}b_{i,t}\tilde{r}_{i,t}}, \quad C_{i,t,2} = (X_1X_2)^{u_{i,t}a_{i,t}(1-\tilde{r}_{i,t})}.$$

We implicitly set $g_2^{r'} = X_2$, $u_{i,t}'$ is equal to the value of $u_{i,t}$ modulo p_2, $a_{i,t}'$ is equal to the value of $a_{i,t}$ modulo p_2, $b_{i,t}'$ is equal to the value of $b_{i,t}$ modulo p_2, and $r' - r_{i,t}'$ is equal to the value of $1 - \tilde{r}_{i,t}$ modulo p_2.

To produce the kth requested key for an attribute list L, $\mathcal{B}$ randomly chooses exponent $\tilde{\lambda}_i \in \mathbb{Z}_N$ and elements $R, R_0, R_1, R_2 \in G_{p_3}$. It sets:

$$D_0 = g^w T^{-s} R, D_{i,0} = T^{s_i} T^{u_{i,t}a_{i,t}b_{i,t}\tilde{\lambda}_i} R_0, D_{i,1} = T^{a_{i,t_i}\tilde{\lambda}_i} R_1, D_{i,2} = T^{b_{i,t_i}\tilde{\lambda}_i} R_2.$$

- **Lemma 3.** *There is no PPT attacker which can achieve a non-negligible difference in advantage between $Game_k^N$ and $Game_k^T$ for any $k \in [1, Q]$.*
  We prove this lemma under the three party Diffie-Hellman assumption.
- **Proof.** Given a PPT attacker $\mathcal{A}$ achieving a non-negligible difference in advantage between $Game_k^N$ and $Game_k^T$ for some k between 1 and Q_1, we will create a PPT algorithm $\mathcal{B}$ to break the three party Diffie-Hellman assumption in a subgroup. $\mathcal{B}$ is given $g_1, g_2, g_3, g_2^x, g_2^y, g_2^z, T$ where T is either g_2^{xyz} or a random element of G_{p_2}. Due to the different values of T, $\mathcal{B}$ will simulate either $Game_k^N$ or $Game_k^T$ with $\mathcal{A}$.
  $\mathcal{B}$ first runs the $Setup$ algorithm and generate the public parameters:

$$N, p, G, G_T, g_1, e, Y = e(g_1, g_1)^w, \{A_{i,t}^{a_{i,t}} = g_1^{u_{i,t}a_{i,t}}, A_{i,t}^{b_{i,t}} = g_1^{u_{i,t}b_{i,t}}\}_{1 \leq t \leq n_i} {}_{1 \leq i \leq n}.$$

$A_{i,t}, w, u_{i,t}, a_{i,t}, b_{i,t}$ are selected randomly by $\mathcal{B}$, and the master key is known to $\mathcal{B}$. $\mathcal{B}$ sends the public parameters to $\mathcal{A}$. When $\mathcal{A}$ requests a secret key, or a re-encryption key, $\mathcal{B}$ runs the normal $KeyGen$ algorithm or the normal $RKGen$ algorithm to generate the requested one.

In response to $\mathcal{A}$'s first $k-1$ key requests, $\mathcal{B}$ generates semi-functional keys by first run the normal $KeyGen$ algorithm and then multiplying D_0 by a random element of G_{p_2}.

To generate the kth key query by $\mathcal{A}$, $\mathcal{B}$ first run the normal $KeyGen$ algorithm to generate a normal key $D_0, \{D_{i,0}, D_{i,1}, D_{i,2}\}_{1 \leq i \leq n}$. It then chooses random exponents $s_i', u_{i,t}', a_{i,t}', b_{i,t}', \lambda_i' \in \mathbb{Z}_N$, the key is formed as:

$$D_0 T, D_{i,0} g_2^{s_i' + u_{i,t}' a_{i,t}' b_{i,t}' \lambda_i'}, D_{i,1} g_2^{a_{i,t}' \lambda_i'}, D_{i,2} g_2^{b_{i,t}' \lambda_i'}.$$

Then $\mathcal{B}$ runs the $RKGen$ algorithm and generates the re-encryption key:

$$D_0 T, D_{i,0} g_2^{s_i' + u_{i,t}' a_{i,t}' b_{i,t}' \lambda_i'} h^r, D_{i,1} g_2^{a_{i,t}' \lambda_i'}, D_{i,2} g_2^{b_{i,t}' \lambda_i'}.$$

If $T = g_2^{xyz}$, this will be a properly distributed nominal semi-functional key, and when T is random in G_{p2}, this will be a properly distributed temporary semi-functional key.

To generate the semi-functional challenge ciphertext for message M_b and access policy W. $\mathcal{B}$ first runs the normal $Encrypt$ algorithm to generate a normal ciphertext $\tilde{C}, C_0, C_0', \{\{C_{i,t,1}, C_{i,t,2}\}_{1 \leq t \leq n_i}\}_{1 \leq i \leq n}$. It then chooses random exponents $r', r_{i,t}' \in \mathbb{Z}_p^*$. The semi-functional ciphertext is formed as:

$$\tilde{C} = Me(g,g)^{wr}, C_0 g_2^{r'}, C_0' g_2^{r'}, C_{i,t,1} g_2^{u_{i,t} b_{i,t} r_{i,t}'}, C_{i,t,2} g^{u_{i,t} a_{i,t} r_{i,t}'}.$$

- **Lemma 4.** *There is no PPT attacker which can achieve a non-negligible difference in advantage between $Game_k^T$ and $Game_k$ for any k from 1 to Q. We prove this lemma under the general subgroup decision assumption.*
- **Proof.** The proof of this lemma is similar to Lemma 2, except that $\mathcal{B}$ uses $Y_2 Y_3$ to place a random G_{p2} component on the D_0 part of the kth key to make it a semi-functional key in the case that T has no G_{p2} component.
- **Lemma 5.** *There is no PPT attacker which can achieve a non-negligible difference in advantage between $Game_Q$ and $Game_{final}$.*
  We prove this lemma under the basic generic group assumption.
- **Proof.** Given a PPT attacker $\mathcal{A}$ achieving a non-negligible difference in advantage between $Game_Q$ and $Game_{final}$, we will create a PPT algorithm $\mathcal{B}$ to break the basic generic group assumption. $\mathcal{B}$ is given $g_1, g_2, g_3, g_1^w X_2, g_1^r Y_2, T$ where T is either $e(g_1, g_1)^{wr}$ or a random element of G_{p2}. Due to the different values of T, $\mathcal{B}$ will simulate either $Game_Q$ or $Game_{final}$ with $\mathcal{A}$.
  $\mathcal{B}$ first runs the $Setup$ algorithm and generate the public parameters:

$$N, p, G, G_T, g_1, e, Y = e(g_1, g_1)^w, \{A_{i,t}^{a_{i,t}} = g_1^{u_{i,t} a_{i,t}}, A_{i,t}^{b_{i,t}} = g_1^{u_{i,t} b_{i,t}}\}_{1 \leq t \leq n_i}\}_{1 \leq i \leq n}.$$

In response to $\mathcal{A}$'s requests for a key under an attribute list L, $\mathcal{B}$ generates the semi-functional key as follows. It chooses random exponents $r', \tilde{r}_{i,t}$ and random elements $R, R_0, R_1, R_2 \in G_{p3}$. The semi-functional key is formed as:

$$D_0 = (g_1^w X_2) g_1^{-s} R g_2^{r'}, D_{i,0} = g_1^{s_i} g_1^{u_{i,t} a_{i,t} b_{i,t} \lambda_i} R_0, D_{i,1} = g^{a_{i,t} \lambda_i} R_1, D_{i,2} = g^{b_{i,t} \lambda_i} R_2.$$

Then $\mathcal{B}$ runs the $RKGen$ algorithm and generates the re-encryption key:

$$D_0 = (g_1^w X_2) g_1^{-s} R g_2^{r'}, D_{i,0} = g_1^{s_i} g_1^{u_{i,t} a_{i,t} b_{i,t} \lambda_i} h^r R_0, D_{i,1} = g^{a_{i,t} \lambda_i} R_1, D_{i,2} = g^{b_{i,t} \lambda_i} R_2.$$

To generate the semi-functional ciphertext for M_b under access policy W, $\mathcal{B}$ chooses random exponents $\tilde{r}_{i,t}, r'$ and implicitly sets $r = r'\tilde{r}_{i,t}$, the semi-functional ciphertext is formed as:

$$\tilde{C} = M_b T, C_0 = g_1^{r'} Y_2, C_0' = h^{r'} Y_2,$$

$$C_{i,t,1} = (g_1^{r'} Y_2)^{u_{i,t} b_{i,t} \tilde{r}_{i,t}}, C_{i,t,2} = (g_1^{r'} Y_2)^{u_{i,t} a_{i,t}(1-\tilde{r}_{i,t})}.$$

In this semi-functional ciphertext, $g_2^{r'}$ equals Y_2, $u_{i,t}'$ equals $u_{i,t}$, $a_{i,t}'$ equals $a_{i,t}$, $b_{i,t}'$ equals $b_{i,t}$, $1 - \tilde{r}_{i,t}$ equals $r - r_{i,t}$ for each i, t modulo p_2. If $T = e(g_1, g_1)^{\alpha s}$ this is a properly distributed semi-functional encryption of M_b, and $\mathcal{B}$ has properly simulated $Game_q$. If T is a random element of G_T, then this is a properly distributed semi-functional encryption of a random message, and $\mathcal{B}$ has properly simulated $Game_{final}$.

5 Conclusion

In this work, we propose a hidden ciphertext-policy attribute-based proxy re-encryption scheme, which solves the problem of privacy leaking during the re-encryption process. In addition, we further prove our scheme to be fully secure in the standard model. In the future work, we intend to design a new CP-AB-PRE scheme to reduce the computation cost of the re-encryption process and provide a more expressive ability.

Acknowledgement. This work is supported by the National Natural Science Foundation of China under Grant No. 61672062, 61232005, and the National High Technology Research and Development Program ("863" Program) of China under Grant No. 2015AA016009.

References

1. Ateniese, G., Fu, K., Green, M., Hohenberger, S.: Improved proxy re-encryption schemes with applications to secure distributed storage. ACM Trans. Inf. Syst. Secur. **9**(1), 1–30 (2006)
2. Blaze, M., Bleumer, G., Strauss, M.: Divertible protocols and atomic proxy cryptography. In: Nyberg, K. (ed.) EUROCRYPT 1998. LNCS, vol. 1403, pp. 127–144. Springer, Heidelberg (1998). https://doi.org/10.1007/BFb0054122
3. Chu, C.-K., Tzeng, W.-G.: Identity-based proxy re-encryption without random oracles. In: Garay, J.A., Lenstra, A.K., Mambo, M., Peralta, R. (eds.) ISC 2007. LNCS, vol. 4779, pp. 189–202. Springer, Heidelberg (2007). https://doi.org/10.1007/978-3-540-75496-1_13
4. Do, J.M., Song, Y.J., Park, N.: Attribute based proxy re-encryption for data confidentiality in cloud computing environments. In: First ACIS/JNU International Conference on Computers, Networks, Systems and Industrial Engineering, pp. 248–251 (2011)

5. Green, M., Ateniese, G.: Identity-based proxy re-encryption. In: Katz, J., Yung, M. (eds.) ACNS 2007. LNCS, vol. 4521, pp. 288–306. Springer, Heidelberg (2007). https://doi.org/10.1007/978-3-540-72738-5_19

6. Green, M., Hohenberger, S., Waters, B.: Outsourcing the decryption of ABE ciphertexts. In: Usenix Conference on Security, pp. 34–34 (2011)

7. Hohenberger, S., Rothblum, G.N., Shelat, A., Vaikuntanathan, V.: Securely obfuscating re-encryption. In: Vadhan, S.P. (ed.) TCC 2007. LNCS, vol. 4392, pp. 233–252. Springer, Heidelberg (2007). https://doi.org/10.1007/978-3-540-70936-7_13

8. Hur, J., Noh, D.K.: Attribute-based access control with efficient revocation in data outsourcing systems. IEEE Trans. Parallel Distrib. Syst. 22(7), 1214–1221 (2011)

9. Lai, J., Deng, R.H., Li, Y.: Fully secure cipertext-policy hiding CP-ABE. In: Bao, F., Weng, J. (eds.) ISPEC 2011. LNCS, vol. 6672, pp. 24–39. Springer, Heidelberg (2011). https://doi.org/10.1007/978-3-642-21031-0_3

10. Lewko, A., Waters, B.: New proof methods for attribute-based encryption: achieving full security through selective techniques. In: Safavi-Naini, R., Canetti, R. (eds.) CRYPTO 2012. LNCS, vol. 7417, pp. 180–198. Springer, Heidelberg (2012). https://doi.org/10.1007/978-3-642-32009-5_12

11. Li, H., Pang, L.: Efficient and adaptively secure attribute-based proxy reencryption scheme. Int. J. Distrib. Sens. Netw. 12, 1–12 (2016)

12. Li, J., Ren, K., Zhu, B., Wan, Z.: Privacy-aware attribute-based encryption with user accountability. In: Samarati, P., Yung, M., Martinelli, F., Ardagna, C.A. (eds.) ISC 2009. LNCS, vol. 5735, pp. 347–362. Springer, Heidelberg (2009). https://doi.org/10.1007/978-3-642-04474-8_28

13. Li, X., Gu, D., Ren, Y., Ding, N., Yuan, K.: Efficient ciphertext-policy attribute based encryption with hidden policy. In: Xiang, Y., Pathan, M., Tao, X., Wang, H. (eds.) IDCS 2012. LNCS, vol. 7646, pp. 146–159. Springer, Heidelberg (2012). https://doi.org/10.1007/978-3-642-34883-9_12

14. Liang, K., Man, H.A., Liu, J.K., Susilo, W., Wong, D.S., Yang, G., Yu, Y., Yang, A.: A secure and efficient ciphertext-policy attribute-based proxy re-encryption for cloud data sharing. Future Gener. Comput. Syst. 52(C), 95–108 (2015)

15. Liang, X., Cao, Z., Lin, H., Shao, J.: Attribute based proxy re-encryption with delegating capabilities. In: AISACCS Pages, pp. 276–286 (2009)

16. Libert, B., Vergnaud, D.: Unidirectional chosen-ciphertext secure proxy re-encryption. IEEE Trans. Inf. Theory 57(3), 1786–1802 (2011)

17. Liu, Q., Tan, C.C., Wu, J., Wang, G.: Reliable re-encryption in unreliable clouds. In: Global Communications Conference, GLOBECOM 2011, 5–9 December 2011, Houston, Texas, USA, pp. 1–5 (2011)

18. Liu, Q., Wang, G., Wu, J.: Time-based proxy re-encryption scheme for secure data sharing in a cloud environment. Inf. Sci. 258(3), 355–370 (2014)

19. Luo, S., Hu, J., Chen, Z.: Ciphertext policy attribute-based proxy re-encryption. In: Soriano, M., Qing, S., López, J. (eds.) ICICS 2010. LNCS, vol. 6476, pp. 401–415. Springer, Heidelberg (2010). https://doi.org/10.1007/978-3-642-17650-0_28

20. Matsuo, T.: Proxy re-encryption systems for identity-based encryption. In: Takagi, T., Okamoto, T., Okamoto, E., Okamoto, T. (eds.) Pairing 2007. LNCS, vol. 4575, pp. 247–267. Springer, Heidelberg (2007). https://doi.org/10.1007/978-3-540-73489-5_13

21. Nishide, T., Yoneyama, K., Ohta, K.: Attribute-based encryption with partially hidden encryptor-specified access structures. In: Bellovin, S.M., Gennaro, R., Keromytis, A., Yung, M. (eds.) ACNS 2008. LNCS, vol. 5037, pp. 111–129. Springer, Heidelberg (2008). https://doi.org/10.1007/978-3-540-68914-0_7

22. Phuong, T.V.X., Yang, G., Susilo, W.: Hidden ciphertext policy attribute-based encryption under standard assumptions. IEEE Trans. Inf. Forensics Secur. **11**(1), 35–45 (2015)
23. Ran, C., Hohenberger, S.: Chosen-ciphertext secure proxy re-encryption. In: ACM Conference on Computer and Communications Security, CCS 2007, Alexandria, Virginia, USA, pp. 185–194, October 2007
24. Seo, H.J., Kim, H.: Attribute-based proxy re-encryption with a constant number of pairing operations. J. Inf. Commun. Converg. Eng. **10**(1), 53–60 (2012)
25. Seo, H., Kim, H.: Zigbee security for visitors in home automation using attribute based proxy re-encryption. In: IEEE International Symposium on Consumer Electronics, pp. 304–307 (2011)
26. Guo, S., Zeng, Y., Wei, J., Xu, Q.: Attribute-based re-encryption scheme in the standard model. Wuhan Univ. J. Nat. Sci. **13**(5), 621–625 (2008)
27. Yu, S., Wang, C., Ren, K., Lou, W.: Achieving secure, scalable, and fine-grained data access control in cloud computing. In: Conference on Information Communications, pp. 534–542 (2010)

Identity-Based Group Encryption Revisited

Kanika Gupta[1(✉)], S. Sharmila Deva Selvi[1], C. Pandu Rangan[1], and Shubham Sopan Dighe[2]

[1] Theoretical Computer Science Lab,
Department of Computer Science and Engineering,
Indian Institute of Technology Madras, Chennai, India
kanika12@gmail.com
[2] National Institute of Technology, Trichy, India

Abstract. In this paper, we focus on identity-based group encryption. We have revisited "Identity-Based Group Encryption (IBGE)" proposed by Xiling et al. Their scheme claims to achieve anonymity of the receiver. We have shown that the zero-knowledge proof they have used leaks much more information, due to which the verifier who is honest but curious will be able to identify the designated recipient.

Keywords: Group encryption · Identity-based

1 Introduction

Group Encryption (GE) is an encryption analogue of group signature. A GE scheme enables a sender to send a ciphertext to a member of group and satisfies the verifier that the ciphertext belongs to some member of the group. The focus of this paper is on the GE scheme in identity-based paradigm. There is only one identity-based group encryption system reported in the literature, and that was proposed in 2016 by Xiling et al. [2], which claims to achieve anonymity of the receiver. We take a closer look at their protocol. We show that an honest but curious verifier will be able to identify the designated recipient by using the information exchanged between the sender and verifier during the execution of a zero-knowledge protocol. Hence, this breaks the claimed anonymity of the construction in [2].

2 Overview of Xiling-IBGE Scheme

Xiling-IBGE involves five parties - a Group Manager (GM) who manages the group and traces the actual receiver in case of a dispute, a group of authorised users who receive messages from a sender by maintaining receiver anonymity, a sender who can be any one from within the group or outside and has secret messages to be sent to the authorised users, a verifier who proves that the encrypted

© Springer International Publishing AG, part of Springer Nature 2018
S. Qing et al. (Eds.): ICICS 2017, LNCS 10631, pp. 205–209, 2018.
https://doi.org/10.1007/978-3-319-89500-0_18

identity and the identity that forms the ciphertext are identical and a PKG who issues private keys to the users. The procedures involved are-

ParaGen: Let the user's identity be $ID \in Z_p$, $\mathbb{G}$ and $\mathbb{G}_T$ be two groups of order p, e: $\mathbb{G} \times \mathbb{G} \to \mathbb{G}_T$ be an admissible bilinear map, $\bar{\mathbb{G}}$ be an abelian group of order p in which the DDH problem is hard. PKG chooses random $g, h \leftarrow \mathbb{G}$ and a random $\alpha \leftarrow Z_p$, sets $g_1 \leftarrow g^\alpha$, chooses $g_2, g_3, t \leftarrow \bar{\mathbb{G}}$, and a universal hash function H. The public parameters are $(g, g_1, h, g_2, g_3, t, H)$ and the master secret key is α.

GKGen: This procedure chooses random $x_1, x_2, y_1, y_2, z \leftarrow Z_p$, computes $w = g_2^{x_1} g_3^{x_2}$, $d = g_2^{y_1} g_3^{y_2}$, $l = g_2^z$. Group public key and secret keys are (g_2, g_3, w, d, l) and (x_1, x_2, y_1, y_2, z) respectively.

UKGen: For every user, PKG chooses a random $r \leftarrow Z_p$, and calculates the user's secret key $SK_{ID} = (r, h_{ID})$, where $h_{ID} = (hg^{-r})^{1/(\alpha - ID)}$. The user registers his identity with the group manager.

Encryption: This procedure can be divided into two sub procedures:-

1. Message encryption: Given plaintext $m \in \mathbb{G}_T$, and member's identity ID, choose random $s \leftarrow Z_p$. Then compute the ciphertext as

$$C_1 = (g_1^s g^{-s \cdot ID}, e(g, g)^s, m \cdot e(g, h)^{-s}) = (C_{10}, C_{11}, C_{12}) \quad (1)$$

2. Member's identity encryption: Choose random $n \leftarrow Z_p$, and compute $k_1 = g_2^n$, $k_2 = g_3^n$, $\psi = l^n t^{ID}$, $\epsilon = H(k_1, k_2, \psi)$, $v = w^n d^{n\epsilon}$. The ciphertext is

$$C_2 = (k_1, k_2, \psi, v) \quad (2)$$

The sender sends ciphertext $C = (C_1, C_2)$ to the group.

Zero Knowledge Proof (ZKP): To prove that the ID "hidden" in ψ is identical to the ID used in C_{10} of the ciphertext, a zero-knowledge proof is constructed. It proves that the ciphertext is well formed. This proof is between the verifier and the sender and is based on *Groth-Sahai's* [1] zero-knowledge proof.

The protocol is denoted by

$$ZK\left\{s, n, ID \middle| C_{10} = g_1^s g^{-s \cdot ID}, \ C_{11} = e(g, g)^s, k_1 = g_2^n, k_2 = g_3^n, \ \psi = l^n t^{ID}, \ v = w^n d^{n\epsilon}\right\}$$

The zero knowledge proof has been converted into an equivalent form as follows-

$$ZK\left\{s, n, ID \middle| \begin{array}{l} C_{10} = g_1^s g^{-s \cdot ID}, \ C_{11} = e(g, g)^s, k_1 = g_2^n, k_2 = g_3^n, \\ \psi = l^n t^{ID}, \ v = w^n d^{n\epsilon}, A = \psi^s, A = A_1 A_2, \\ A_1 = l^{ns}, A_2^{-1} = t^{-s \cdot ID}, k = k_1^s, k = g_2^{ns} \end{array}\right\}$$

The protocol is a 3-move protocol as discussed below-

1. Prover chooses $\bar{s}, \bar{ID}, \bar{n}$ randomly and computes $\bar{C}_{10} = g_1^{\bar{s}} g^{-\bar{s} \cdot \bar{ID}}$, $\bar{C}_{11} = e(g, g)^{\bar{s}}$, $\bar{k}_1 = g_2^{\bar{n}}$, $\bar{k}_2 = g_3^{\bar{n}}$, $\bar{\psi} = l^{\bar{n}} t^{\bar{ID}}$, $\bar{v} = w^{\bar{n}} d^{\bar{n}\epsilon}$, $\bar{A} = \psi^{\bar{s}}$, $\bar{A} = \bar{A}_1 \bar{A}_2$, $\bar{A}_1 = l^{\bar{n}\bar{s}}$, $\bar{A}_2^{-1} = t^{-\bar{s} \cdot \bar{ID}}$, $\bar{k} = \bar{k}_1^{\bar{s}}$, $\bar{k} = g_2^{\bar{n}\bar{s}}$ and sends these to the verifier.

2. The verifier chooses a random $c \in Z_p$ and sends to the verifier.
3. The prover computes $r_1 \equiv \bar{s} + cs \ mod \ p$, $r_2 \equiv \bar{n} + cn \ mod \ p$, $r_3 \equiv \bar{ID} + c \cdot ID \ mod \ p$, $r_4 \equiv -\bar{s} \cdot \bar{ID} - cs \cdot ID \ mod \ p$, $r_5 \equiv \bar{n}\bar{s} + c \cdot ns \ mod \ p$ and responds to the verifier.
4. The verifier checks if $\psi^{r_1} \stackrel{?}{=} A^c \bar{A}$, $k_1^{r_1} \stackrel{?}{=} k^c \bar{k}$, $e(g,g)^{r_1} \stackrel{?}{=} C_{11}^c \bar{C}_{11}$, $g_2^{r_2} \stackrel{?}{=} k_1^c \bar{k}_1$, $g_3^{r_2} \stackrel{?}{=} k_2^c \bar{k}_2$, $(wd^\epsilon)^{r_2} \stackrel{?}{=} v^c \bar{v}$, $l^{r_2} t^{r_3} \stackrel{?}{=} \psi^c \bar{\psi}$, $g_1^{r_1} g^{r_4} \stackrel{?}{=} \bar{C}_{10} C_{10}^c$, $t^{r_4} \stackrel{?}{=} A_2^{-1}(A_2^{-1})^c$, $l^{r_5} \stackrel{?}{=} A_1^c \bar{A}_1$, $g_2^{r_5} \stackrel{?}{=} k^c \bar{k}$. The verifier outputs 1 if all the checks hold true, otherwise it outputs 0.

Note 1. *In the non-interactive version of the protocol, the sender sends* $C_3 = (r_1, r_2, r_3, r_4, r_5)$ *and a hash value* $\bar{H}(C_1, C_2, \bar{C}_{10}, \bar{C}_{11}, \bar{k}_1, \bar{k}_2, \bar{\psi}, \bar{v}, \bar{A}, \bar{A}_1, \bar{A}_2, A_2^{-1}, \bar{k}) = c$ *in addition to the ciphertext* (C_1, C_2)*. The verifier independently carries out appropriate tests using the values in* C_3 *and the hash value and concludes on the correctness of* (C_1, C_2)*.*

Decryption: To decrypt the message, user uses the ciphertext (C_1, C_2), and his private key $SK_{ID} = (r, h_{ID})$ to compute $m = C_{12} \cdot e(C_{10}, h_{ID}) \cdot C_{11}^r$.

3   Attack Based on Interactive Zero-Knowledge Proof

Let a sender encrypt a message m to a specific user with identity ID_r and let (C_1, C_2) be the ciphertext generated by the sender where

$$C_1 = (g_1^s g^{-s \cdot ID_r}, \ e(g,g)^s, \ m \cdot e(g,h)^{-s}) = (C_{10}, C_{11}, C_{12})$$
$$C_2 = (k_1, k_2, \psi, v) \tag{3}$$

where (k_1, k_2, ψ, v) are defined as in Eq. (2).

Note that during the execution of zero-knowledge protocol between the prover and verifier, the verifier obtains the following values -

$$c \in Z_p, \ r_1 \equiv \bar{s} + cs \ mod \ p, \ r_2 \equiv \bar{n} + cn \ mod \ p, \ r_3 \equiv \bar{ID} + c \cdot ID_r \ mod \ p,$$
$$r_4 \equiv -\bar{s} \cdot \bar{ID} - cs \cdot ID_r \ mod \ p, \ r_5 \equiv \bar{n}\bar{s} + c \cdot ns \ mod \ p$$

Now with the obtained c, r_1, r_3, r_4 from the sender and C_{11} in Eq. (3), we show that the verifier will be able to identify the actual receiver.

For each identity ID_i in the group, the verifier performs the procedure PROC as shown below.

PROC $(ID_i, c, r_1, r_3, r_4, C_{11})$

1. Compute $g^{r_1 \cdot ID_i + r_4}$
2. Compute $\left(e(g,g)^{r_1} \cdot (C_{11})^{-c} \right) = \left(e(g,g)^{r_1} \cdot (e(g,g)^s)^{-c} \right) = e(g,g)^{r_1 - sc} = e(g,g)^{\bar{s}}$
3. Compute $e(g,g)^{\bar{s} \cdot r_3}$
4. Compute $X = e(g, g^{r_1 \cdot ID_i + r_4}) \cdot e(g,g)^{\bar{s} \cdot r_3})$

5. Compute $Y = e(g, g)^{\bar{s} \cdot ID_i(c+1)}$
6. Now check,

$$X \stackrel{?}{=} Y \tag{4}$$

Return the identity ID_r for which (4) holds true.

Now we show that the check in (4) holds true only for the correct recipient ID_r.

Valid Recipient: $(ID_i = ID_r)$

1. $X = e(g, g^{r_1 \cdot ID_r + r_4}) \cdot e(g, g)^{\bar{s} \cdot r_3})$, where

$$\begin{aligned}
g^{r_1 \cdot ID_r + r_4} &= g^{(\bar{s}+cs) \cdot ID_r - \bar{s} \cdot \bar{ID} - cs \cdot ID_r} \\
&= g^{\bar{s} ID_r + cs \cdot ID_r - \bar{s} \cdot \bar{ID} - cs \cdot ID_r} \\
&= g^{\bar{s}(ID_r - \bar{ID})}
\end{aligned}$$

and $e(g, g)^{\bar{s} \cdot r_3} = e(g, g)^{\bar{s}(\bar{ID} + c \cdot ID_r)}$
Hence,

$$\begin{aligned}
X &= e(g, g^{\bar{s}(ID_r - \bar{ID})}) \cdot e(g, g)^{\bar{s}(\bar{ID} + c \cdot ID_r)} \\
&= e(g, g)^{\bar{s} ID_r - \bar{s} \bar{ID} + \bar{s} \bar{ID} + c \bar{s} ID_r} = e(g, g)^{\bar{s} \cdot ID_r(c+1)}
\end{aligned}$$

2. $Y = e(g, g)^{\bar{s} \cdot ID_r(c+1)}$
3. Check $X \stackrel{?}{=} Y$ returns true.

Invalid Recipient: $(\forall \ ID_i = ID_x \neq ID_r)$

1. $X = e(g, g^{r_1 \cdot ID_x + r_4}) \cdot e(g, g)^{\bar{s} \cdot r_3})$, where

$$\begin{aligned}
g^{r_1 \cdot ID_x + r_4} &= g^{(\bar{s}+cs) \cdot ID_x - \bar{s} \cdot \bar{ID} - cs \cdot ID_r} \\
&= g^{\bar{s}(ID_x - \bar{ID}) + sc(ID_x - ID_r)}
\end{aligned}$$

and

$$e(g, g)^{\bar{s} \cdot r_3} = e(g, g)^{\bar{s}(\bar{ID} + c \cdot ID_r)}$$

Hence,

$$\begin{aligned}
X &= e(g, g^{\bar{s}(ID_x - \bar{ID}) + sc(ID_x - ID_r)}) \cdot e(g, g)^{\bar{s}(\bar{ID} + c \cdot ID_r)} \\
&= e(g, g)^{\bar{s} ID_x - \bar{s} \bar{ID} + sc \cdot ID_x - sc \cdot ID_r + \bar{s} \bar{ID} + \bar{s} c \cdot ID_r} \\
&= e(g, g)^{\bar{s}(ID_x + c \cdot ID_r) + sc(ID_x - ID_r)}
\end{aligned}$$

2. $Y = e(g, g)^{\bar{s} \cdot ID_x(c+1)}$
3. Check $X \stackrel{?}{=} Y$ returns false.

4 Attack on Non-interactive Protocol of Xiling-IBGE Scheme

The authors have proposed an alternate encryption mechanism in which the interactive zero-knowledge proof is converted into a non-interactive protocol using a hash function $\bar{H}$. In this protocol, the sender does not need to interact with the verifier during encryption.

The resulting ciphertext for this alternate encryption is $C = (C_1, C_2, C_3)$ where $C_3 = (r_1, r_2, r_3, r_4, r_5)$ and r_1, r_2, r_3, r_4, r_5 are defined in step (3) of Sect. 3. The sender computes a hash value

$$\bar{H}(C_1, C_2, \bar{C}_{10}, \bar{C}_{11}, \bar{k}_1, \bar{k}_2, \bar{\psi}, \bar{v}, \bar{A}, \bar{A}_1, \bar{A}_2, \bar{A}_2^{-1}) = c,$$

where the values C_1, C_2 are defined in Eqs. (1), (2) respectively and $\bar{C}_{10}, \bar{C}_{11}, \bar{k}_1, \bar{k}_2, \bar{\psi}, \bar{v}, \bar{A}, \bar{A}_1, \bar{A}_2, \bar{A}_2^{-1}$ are defined in Eq. (4), and sends c to the verifier. Hence, all the steps in procedure PROC can be executed by the verifier using the ciphertext C and the hash value to break the anonymity of the receiver.

References

1. Groth, J., Sahai, A.: Efficient non-interactive proof systems for bilineargroups. In: Electronic Colloquium on Computational Complexity (ECCC), vol. 14, no. 053 (2007)
2. Luo, X., Ren, Y., Liu, J., Hu, J., Liu, W., Wang, Z., Xu, W., Wu, Q.: Identity-based group encryption. In: Liu, J.K., Steinfeld, R. (eds.) ACISP 2016. LNCS, vol. 9723, pp. 87–102. Springer, Cham (2016). https://doi.org/10.1007/978-3-319-40367-0_6

Compact Hierarchical IBE from Lattices in the Standard Model

Daode Zhang[1,2,3], Fuyang Fang[4(✉)], Bao Li[1,2,3], Haiyang Xue[1], and Bei Liang[5]

[1] School of Cyber Security, University of Chinese Academy of Sciences,
Beijing, China
{zhangdaode,lb}@is.ac.cn, xuehaiyang@iie.ac.cn
[2] State Key Laboratory of Information Security,
Institute of Information Engineering, Beijing, China
[3] Science and Technology on Communication Security Laboratory,
Chengdu, China
[4] Information Science Academy, China Electronics Technology Group Corporation,
Beijing, China
fuyang_fang@163.com
[5] Chalmers University of Technology, Gothenburg, Sweden
lbei@chalmers.se

Abstract. At Crypto'10, Agrawal *et al.* proposed a lattice-based selectively secure Hierarchical Identity-based Encryption (HIBE) scheme (ABB10b) with small ciphertext on the condition that λ (the length of identity at each level) is small in the standard model. In this paper, we present another lattice-based selectively secure HIBE scheme with depth d, using a gadget matrix $\mathbf{G}' \in \mathbb{Z}_q^{n \times n\lceil \log_b q \rceil}$ with enough large $b = 2^d$ to replace the matrix $\mathbf{B} \in \mathbb{Z}_q^{n \times m}$ in the HIBE scheme proposed by Agrawal *et al.* at Eurocrypt'10. In our HIBE scheme, not only the size of ciphertext at level ℓ is $O(\frac{d+\ell}{\lambda d})$ larger than the size in ABB10b and at least $O(\ell)$ smaller than the sizes in the previous HIBE schemes except ABB10b, but also the size of the master public key is at least $O(d)$ times smaller than the previous schemes.

Keywords: Lattices · Hierarchical identity-based encryption
Selectively secure · Compact public parameters

1 Introduction

Hierarchical identity-based encryption (HIBE) proposed by Horwitz *et al.* [7,8] is an extension of identity-based encryption (IBE)[12], in which arbitrary string can be as the public key. In a HIBE scheme, an identity at level k of the hierarchy tree is provided with a private key from its parent identity and also can delegate private keys to its descendant identities, but cannot decrypt the message intended for other identities.

HIBE from Lattices: The first lattice-based HIBE scheme based on the Learning with Errors (LWE) problem [11] proposed by Cash *et al.* [5], using the basis

© Springer International Publishing AG, part of Springer Nature 2018
S. Qing et al. (Eds.): ICICS 2017, LNCS 10631, pp. 210–221, 2018.
https://doi.org/10.1007/978-3-319-89500-0_19

delegation technique for lattices. Agrawal *et al.* [1] proposed SampleLeft and SampleRight algorithms, then extended them and obtained another basis delegation technique, with which they constructed an efficient HIBE scheme with selective security in the standard model. However, the above basis delegation techniques will increase the dimension of lattice involved, as well as the size of ciphertext. Later, Agrawal *et al.* [2] proposed a different delegation mechanism, called "in place" delegation technique, which preserves the dimension of lattices. With this technique, they constructed two HIBE schemes with and without random oracles, and the dimension of lattices involved for all nodes in the hierarchy remained unchanged. Nevertheless, as they said in [2], the construction in the standard model was competitive with previous schemes in [1,5] only when the bits of identity ($|id_i| = \lambda$) at level i in the hierarchy is small, e.g., $\lambda = 1$ at each level. Furthermore, as the length of identity increases, e.g., $\lambda = n$, the sizes of ciphertext, private key and master public key will be worse than the parameters in [1]. With the "in place" delegation technique, Fang *et al.* also utilized the Learning with Rounding (LWR) assumption [3,4] over small modulus to construct HIBE schemes. Thus, they possess the same restrictions as [2]. Micciancio and Peikert [10] introduced the notion of **G**-trapdoor for lattices and proposed an efficient trapdoor delegation for lattices. With this technique, they can decrease the public key and ciphertext by 4 factors and the size of the delegated trapdoor grows only linearly with the dimension of lattices in the hierarchy, rather than quadratically in [1], but the ciphertext will be increased by $nk \log q$ bits node by node.

1.1 Our Contributions and Techniques

We apply a gadget matrix $\mathbf{G}' \in \mathbb{Z}_q^{n \times nk}$ defined in [10] into the basis delegation technique in [1] to construct a selectively secure HIBE scheme with small parameter based on the LWE problem in the standard model, where $k = \lceil \log_b q \rceil$, $b = 2^d$ and d is the maximum depth of the HIBE scheme.

The public parameter in our HIBE scheme needs to contain one matrix of the same dimension as $\mathbf{G}'$ (i.e., about $n \log_b q$) and the size of ciphertext is $n \log_b q \log q \approx \frac{1}{d} \cdot n \log^2 q$ for each level of the hierarchy. However, we obtain this improvement at the cost of increasing the size of private key. Thus, the parameters in our HIBE are the trade-off of the sizes of the public parameter and private keys. Next, we compare our scheme with the previous schemes in following Table 1.

From Table 1, the advantages of our HIBE scheme are:

1. The size of the master public key in [1,10] is reduced by a factor of $O(d)$;
2. The sizes of the ciphertext and lattice dimension at level ℓ are $\frac{d}{d+\ell} \cdot \ell = O(\ell)$ times smaller than the sizes in [1,10] and $\frac{d+\ell}{d} < 2$ times larger than the sizes in [2] on the condition that $\lambda = 1$. In particular, the parameters in ABB10b except the private key are competitive with our HIBE scheme only when $\lambda = 1$.

Table 1. Comparison of Lattice-based selective-id secure HIBE schemes in the standard model. In this table, d is the maximum depth of HIBE schemes and ℓ be the depth of the identity in query. $|ct|$ denotes the size of ciphertext at level ℓ. $|mpk|$ denotes the the size of the master public key in scheme. $|\mathsf{SK}_{id}|$ denotes the size of the private key at level ℓ. Error rate $(1/\alpha)$ denotes the security of LWE problem. The last columns denotes the lattice dimension involved at level ℓ. In order to compare the HIBE schemes, we let λ be the number of bits in each component of the identity.

Schemes	$|ct|$	$|mpk|$	$|\mathsf{SK}_{id}|$	Error rate $1/\alpha$	Lattice dimension
[5]	$\tilde{O}(\lambda\ell nd^2)$	$\tilde{O}(\lambda n^2 d^3)$	$\tilde{O}(\lambda^2\ell^3 n^2 d^2)$	$\tilde{O}(d^d(\lambda n)^{d/2})$	$\tilde{O}(\lambda\ell nd)$
[1]	$\tilde{O}(\ell nd^2)$	$\tilde{O}(n^2 d^3)$	$\tilde{O}(\ell^3 n^2 d^2)$	$\tilde{O}(d^d n^{d/2})$	$\tilde{O}(\ell nd)$
[2]	$\tilde{O}(\lambda^2 nd^2)$	$\tilde{O}(\lambda^3 n^2 d^3)$	$\tilde{O}(\lambda^3\ell n^2 d^2)$	$\tilde{O}((\lambda dn)^{\lambda d + d/2})$	$\tilde{O}(\lambda nd)$
[10]	$\tilde{O}(\ell nd^2)$	$\tilde{O}(n^2 d^3)$	$\tilde{O}(\ell n^2 d^2)$	$\tilde{O}(d^d n^{d/2})$	$\tilde{O}(\ell nd)$
Our HIBE	$\tilde{O}(nd(d+\ell))$	$\tilde{O}(n^2 d^2)$	$\tilde{O}((\frac{d}{\log n}+\ell)n^2(d+\ell)^2)$	$\tilde{O}((4d)^{d/2}n^{d/2})$	$\tilde{O}(n(d+\ell))$

And the disadvantages of our scheme are

1. The size of the private key at level ℓ is $\frac{d+\ell\log n}{\ell\log n} \cdot (\frac{d+\ell}{d})^2 = O(\frac{d}{\ell\log n}+1)$ times larger than [10] and the maximum ratio can reach to $O(\frac{d}{\log n}+1)$when $\ell = 1$.
2. The error rate $1/\alpha$ is lightly smaller than the sizes in $[1,10]$ when $d > 4$.

Analysis: Before explaining why this modification works, let us firstly describe the reason that the sizes of ciphertexts in $[1,10]$ increase as mentioned above. In [1], the identity-based encryption matrix for identity $\boldsymbol{id} = (\boldsymbol{id}_1,\cdots,\boldsymbol{id}_\ell) \in (\{0,1\}^\lambda)^\ell$ is

$$\mathbf{F}_{id} = [\mathbf{A}|\mathbf{A}_1 + \mathsf{H}(\boldsymbol{id}_1)\mathbf{B}|\cdots|\mathbf{A}_\ell + \mathsf{H}(\boldsymbol{id}_\ell)\mathbf{B}] \in \mathbb{Z}_q^{n\times(\ell+1)m}$$

where $\mathbf{A}, \mathbf{A}_1,\cdots, \mathbf{A}_\ell, \mathbf{B} \in \mathbb{Z}_q^{n\times m}$ and $m = O(n\log q)$. The difference in [10] is that the matrix $\mathbf{B}$ is replaced by a gadget matrix $\mathbf{G} \in \mathbb{Z}_q^{n\times nk}$, that is,

$$\mathbf{F}_{id} = [\mathbf{A}|\mathbf{A}_1 + \mathsf{H}(\boldsymbol{id}_1)\mathbf{G}|\cdots|\mathbf{A}_\ell + \mathsf{H}(\boldsymbol{id}_\ell)\mathbf{G}|\mathbf{A}_{\ell+1}] \in \mathbb{Z}_q^{n\times(m+(\ell+1)nk)}$$

where $\mathbf{A} \in \mathbb{Z}_q^{n\times m}$, $\mathbf{A}_1,\cdots, \mathbf{A}_\ell \in \mathbb{Z}_q^{n\times\ell k}$ and $k = \lceil\log q\rceil$. Obviously, the ciphertext in $[1,10]$ will increase $m = O(n\log q)$ and $k = n\lceil\log q\rceil$ elements in $\mathbb{Z}_q$ to each level in the hierarchy, respectively.

The size of the public parameters of the HIBE scheme in [10] is

$$(m + dnk)n\log q = (O(n\log q) + dnk)n\log q = (O(1) + d)\cdot n^2\log^2 q$$

where d is the maximum depth of the HIBE scheme and $O(1)$ here satisfies $O(1) \geq 2$ is a small constant. That is, the parameter d plays the important role on the size of the public parameters.

The straight modification is to replace $\mathbf{B}$ and $\mathbf{G}$ with another matrix, which has a short basis as trapdoor but with smaller columns. We know that the gadget matrix $\mathbf{G}$ has special structure that can be simply modified. The widely used version of $\mathbf{G}$ is defined as

$$\mathbf{G} = \mathbf{g}^t \otimes \mathbf{I}_n \in \mathbb{Z}_q^{n \times nk}$$

where $\mathbf{g}^t = (1, 2, \cdots, 2^{k-1})$ and $k = \lceil \log q \rceil$. Lattice $\Lambda^\perp(\mathbf{G})$ has a short basis $\mathbf{S}$ and $\|\tilde{\mathbf{S}}\| \le \sqrt{5}$. In fact, a generalized notion of gadget $\mathbf{G}$ provided in [10] is defined as

$$\mathbf{G} = \mathbf{g}^t \otimes \mathbf{I}_n \in \mathbb{Z}_q^{n \times nk}$$

where $\mathbf{g}^t = (1, b, \cdots, b^{k-1})$ and $k = \lceil \log_b q \rceil$. Then lattice $\Lambda^\perp(\mathbf{G}')$ has a short basis $\mathbf{S}'$ and $\|\tilde{\mathbf{S}}'\| \le \sqrt{b^2 + 1}$.

If we let b be large enough, then k can be small enough. How small should be k to choose in the HIBE scheme? What we want is that the item dbk is approximate $n \log q$. If we set $b = 2^d$, then we have

$$dnk = dn\lceil \log_b q \rceil = dn(\frac{1}{d} \log q + e) = n \log q + dne$$

where $e \in [-1/2, 1/2)$ and the modulus q in $[1, 10]$ is at least $\tilde{O}(n^{d/2})$ and $\log q = O(d \cdot \log n) \gg de$. Therefore, we have $dnk \approx n \log q$ and we can imply that

$$(m + dnk)n \log q = O(n^2 \log^2 q)$$

When using the gadget matrix $\mathbf{G}'$, the identity-based encryption matrix is similar with [10]. However, we do not adopt the DelTrap algorithm to delegate the private key for identities. Because the Gaussian parameter σ_ℓ in DelTrap algorithm requires that $\sigma_\ell \ge s_1(\mathbf{R}_{id_{\ell-1}}) \cdot \|\tilde{\mathbf{S}}'\|\omega(\sqrt{\log n})$ and then the output $s_1(\mathbf{R}_{id_\ell}) \le \sigma_\ell \cdot \sqrt{m}$ will be proportion to $\|\tilde{\mathbf{S}}'\|^\ell = 2^{\ell d}$ which could be larger than q. Therefore, we still utilize the SampleBasisRight algorithm in the security proof.

The cost of this modification is that the norm of basis increases from $\sqrt{5}$ to $\sqrt{b^2 + 1}$, which will affect the bound of Gaussian parameter of SampleBasisRight algorithm in the security of proof. The Gaussian parameter σ_ℓ of SampleBasisRight algorithm in level ℓ should satisfy

$$\sigma_\ell \ge s_1(\mathbf{R}_{id}) \cdot \|\tilde{\mathbf{S}}'\| \cdot \omega(\sqrt{\log n}) \ for \ \ell = 1, \cdots, d$$

It seems that $\sigma_\ell \gg s_1(\mathbf{R}_{id}) \cdot \sqrt{5} \cdot \omega(\sqrt{\log n}) = s_1(\mathbf{R}) \cdot \|\tilde{\mathbf{S}}\| \cdot \omega(\sqrt{\log n})$, which maybe deteriorate the parameters of our HIBE scheme. Fortunately, this intuition is not true for our scheme.

In the Subsect. 3.2 for the correctness of our scheme, we give the bound that the Gaussian parameter $\sigma_{\ell+1}$ at level $\ell + 1$ should satisfy

$$\sigma_{\ell+1} \ge s_1(\mathbf{R}_{id}) \cdot \|\tilde{\mathbf{S}}'\| \cdot (m + \ell nk)^{\frac{\ell}{2}} \cdot \omega(\log^{\frac{\ell}{2}}(m + \ell nk))$$

to meet the conditions of SampleBasisLeft and SampleBasisRight algorithms, where $s_1(\mathbf{R}_{id}) \le O(\sqrt{m + \ell nk})$. Meanwhile, the correctness requires that

$$\alpha_\ell q\omega(\sqrt{\log n}) + \alpha_\ell q \sigma_\ell(m + \ell nk)^{3/2} \cdot \omega(\sqrt{\log(m + \ell nk)}) \le q/5$$

and the hardness of LWE requires that $\alpha_\ell q \geq 2\sqrt{n}$.

Without loss of generality, we can set $m = 2n \log q$. Hence, the modulus q should satisfy

$$q \geq \sqrt{n} \cdot (m + knd)^{(d+3)/2} \cdot b \cdot \omega(\log^{\frac{d}{2}}(m + knd))$$
$$\Rightarrow q \geq \sqrt{n} \cdot (2m)^{d/2} \cdot 2^d \cdot \omega(\log^{\frac{d}{2}}(2m))$$
$$\Rightarrow q \geq \sqrt{n} \cdot (dn \log n)^{d/2} \cdot 2^d \cdot \omega(\log^{\frac{d}{2}}(2m))$$
$$\Rightarrow q \geq \tilde{O}((4d)^{d/2} \cdot n^{d/2})$$

which is sufficient for our HIBE scheme and lightly smaller than the sizes of q in [1,10] if $d > 4$.

Furthermore, we decrease the columns of $\mathbf{G}$ from $n\lceil \log q \rceil$ to $n\lceil \log_b q \rceil$ so that the sizes of ciphertext and the master key increase linearly with $n\lceil \log_b q \rceil$, rather than m in [1] or $n\lceil \log q \rceil$ in [10] for each hierarchy and $m + \ell nk < m + dnk < 2m = O(dn \log n)$. This is why the sizes of ciphertext and the master key decrease by about ℓ and d factors, respectively.

2   Preliminaries

Let n be the security parameter and we use $negl(n)$ to denote an arbitrary negligible function $f(n)$ where $f(n) = o(n^{-c})$ for every fixed constant c. We say that a probability is *overwhelming* if it is $1 - negl(n)$. We use $poly(n)$ and $\widetilde{O}(n)$ to denote an unspecified function $f(n) = O(n^c)$ and $f(n) = O(n \cdot log^c n)$ respectively for some constant c. We use $A \approx_{c(s)} B$ to denote a distribution A is computationally (statistically) indistinguishable from a distribution B. Let $\mathbb{Z}_q$ be a q-ary finite field for a prime $q \geq 2$. The $s_1(\mathbf{R})$ are called the singular values of $\mathbf{R}$ and $s_1(\mathbf{R}) = \max_u \|\mathbf{R}u\| = \max_u \|\mathbf{R}^t u\| \leq \|\mathbf{R}\|, \|\mathbf{R}^t\|$, where the maximum are taken over all unit vectors u. Let $a \xleftarrow{\$} \mathbb{Z}_q$ denote that a is randomly chosen from $\mathbb{Z}_q$.

2.1   Hierarchical IBE

An identity-based encryption (IBE) scheme with the message space $\mathcal{M}$ can be defined by a tuple of PPT algorithms (KeyGen, Extract, Enc, Dec) as below:

- KeyGen$(1^n) \rightarrow (mpk, msk)$: The probabilistic algorithm KeyGen(1^n) generates (mpk, msk), which denotes public key and master key respectively.
- Extract$(mpk, msk, id) \rightarrow SK_{id}$: The Extract algorithm uses the master key to extract a private key SK_{id} corresponding to a given identity id.
- Enc$(mpk, id, m) \rightarrow c$: Given a message $m \in \mathcal{M}$ and an identity id, the probabilistic algorithm Enc uses the public key mpk to encrypt the message with respect to the identity id and outputs a ciphertext c.
- Dec$(SK_{id}, id, c) \rightarrow m \ or \perp$: Given a ciphertext c with respect to an identity id, the deterministic algorithm Dec uses the private key SK_{id} to recover the message m. When the ciphertext c is invalid, the algorithm outputs $\perp$.

In a HIBE scheme of depth d, there is a fifth algorithm Derive, which takes as input an identity $id = \{i_1, ..., i_\ell\}$ at depth $\ell \leq d$ and the private key $\mathsf{SK}_{id_{\ell-1}}$ of the parent identity $id_{\ell-1} = \{i_1, ..., i_{\ell-1}\}$ at depth $\ell - 1 > 0$ and outputs the private key Sk_{id} for identity id. In such an HIBE scheme, identities are vectors.

For an (H)IBE system described above, the correctness is that: for any message $m \in \mathcal{M}$, id and (mpk, msk) generated by $\mathsf{KeyGen}(1^n)$, c is the ciphertext output by the $\mathsf{Enc}(mpk, id, m)$ algorithm, then the $\mathsf{Dec}(\mathsf{SK}_{id}, id, c)$ will output m with overwhelming probability.

2.2   Security Definition

HIBE Security. For a HIBE system, besides the requirement of correctness, it also needs to achieve other security requirements. In the following, we will simply define selective security and adaptive security for a HIBE system. Let $\mathcal{A}$ be any non-uniform probability polynomial time adversary, the security experiment of selective security (INDr-sID-CPA) is defined as follows:

- Init: The adversary $\mathcal{A}$ is given the maximum hierarchy depth d and announces a target identity $id^* = \{i_1, ..., i_t\}$ of depth $t < d$.
- KeyGen: The simulator $\mathcal{S}$ generates the KeyGen algorithm to generate the public parameter mpk and master key msk and sends mpk to adversary $\mathcal{A}$.
- Query1: The adversary $\mathcal{A}$ makes queries on identity $id_1, ..., id_k$, where no one is a prefix of id^*. The simulator returns the private key Sk_{id_i} responding to each query on identity id_i by calling the Extract algorithm.
- Challenge Ciphertext: When the phase of Query1 is over and the adversary $\mathcal{A}$ sends a challenge message $m \in \mathcal{M}$ to $\mathcal{S}$. The simulator $\mathcal{S}$ chooses a random bit $b \in \{0, 1\}$ and a random c' from the ciphertext space. If $b = 0$, then $\mathcal{S}$ generates the challenge ciphertext c^* by calling $\mathsf{Enc}(mpk, id^*, m)$ with message m; Otherwise, $\mathcal{S}$ sends c' as the challenge ciphertext c^* to $\mathcal{A}$.
- Query2: The adversary makes additional adaptive private key queries as in the phase of Query1 and the simulator proceeds as before.
- Guess: Finally, the adversary outputs a guess $b' \in \{0, 1\}$ and wins if $b' = b$.

Definition 1. *Let $\mathcal{A}$ be a PPT adversary in above INDr-sID-CPA experiment attacking the HIBE scheme, the advantage of adversary $\mathcal{A}$ is defined as*

$$\mathbf{Adv}_{\mathrm{HIBE}, \mathcal{A}}^{indr\text{-}sid\text{-}cpa} \triangleq \left| \mathbf{Pr}[b' = b] - \frac{1}{2} \right|$$

We say an HIBE scheme of depth d is selective secure if for any INDr-sID-CPA adversaries $\mathcal{A}$ there is

$$\mathbf{Adv}_{\mathrm{HIBE}, \mathcal{A}}^{indr\text{-}sid\text{-}cpa} \leq negl(n)$$

2.3 The Gadget Matrix G

In this section, we will recall a parity-check matrix $\mathbf{G}$ used in [10], where $\mathbf{G}$ is defined as:

$$\mathbf{G} = \mathbf{I}_n \otimes \mathbf{g}^t \in \mathbb{Z}^{n \times nk}, k = \lceil \log_b q \rceil$$

where $\mathbf{g}^t = (1, b, b^2, ..., b^{k-1}) \in \mathbb{Z}^k$ is a special vector, $\mathbf{I}_n \in \mathbb{Z}^{n \times n}$ is the identity matrix and $\otimes$ denotes the tensor product.

For the lattice $\Lambda^\perp(\mathbf{g}^t)$, we have a good basis $\mathbf{T}$ as follows, and then $\mathbf{S} = \mathbf{I}_n \otimes \mathbf{T} \in \mathbb{Z}^{nk \times nk}$ is the basis of $\Lambda^\perp(\mathbf{G})$, that is,

$$\mathbf{T} := \begin{bmatrix} b & & & q_0 \\ -1 & b & & q_1 \\ & \ddots & & \vdots \\ & & b & q_{k-2} \\ & & -1 & q_{k-1} \end{bmatrix} \in \mathbb{Z}^{k \times k}, \mathbf{S} := \mathbf{I} \otimes \mathbf{T} = \begin{bmatrix} \mathbf{T} & & & \\ & \mathbf{T} & & \\ & & \ddots & \\ & & & \mathbf{T} \\ & & & \mathbf{T} \end{bmatrix} \in \mathbb{Z}^{nk \times nk}$$

where $q_0, ..., q_{k-1} \in [0, b)^k$ is decomposition of $q = \Sigma_i (b^i \cdot q_i)$ with base b.

There are some properties of this gadget matrix $\mathbf{G}$ proposed in [10]:

- **Short Basis:** $\mathbf{S}$ is the basis of lattice $\Lambda^\perp(\mathbf{G})$ with $\|\tilde{\mathbf{S}}\| \leq \sqrt{b^2 + 1}$.
- **Inverting simply:** The function $\mathbf{g_G}(s, e) = \mathbf{G}^t s + e \bmod q$ can be inverted in quasi-linear time $O(n \cdot \log^c n)$ for any $s \in \mathbb{Z}_q^n$ and $e \leftarrow \chi^m$ such that $e \in \mathcal{P}_{1/2}(q \cdot \mathbf{S}^{-t})$ or $e \in \mathcal{P}_{1/2}(q \cdot \tilde{\mathbf{S}}^{-t})$.

2.4 Some Algorithms

In this subsection, we will recall some algorithms: the trapdoor generation algorithm GenTrap in [10], the preimage sampling algorithms SamplePre with a short basis in [6] and SampleD with a trapdoor $\mathbf{R}$ in [10] and the extensions of preimage sampling algorithms SampleLeft and SampleRight in [1]. The concrete algorithms were described as follows.

Lemma 1 ([10]). *Let $n, q > 2$, $m = O(n \log q)$ be integers, then there exists a polynomial time algorithm GenTrap(n, m, q) outputs a vector $\mathbf{A} \in \mathbb{Z}_q^{n \times m}$ and a matrix $\mathbf{T_A} \in \mathbb{Z}^{m \times m}$, where $\mathbf{T_A}$ is a basis for $\Lambda^\perp(\mathbf{A})$ such that $\mathbf{A}$ is statistically close to uniform and $\|\widetilde{\mathbf{T_A}}\| = O(\sqrt{n \log q})$.*

Lemma 2 ([6]). *Let $n, q > 2$, $w > n$, $m = O(n \log q)$ be integers. Given $\mathbf{A} \in \mathbb{Z}_q^{n \times m}$, a matrix $\mathbf{T_A} \in \mathbb{Z}^{m \times m}$ is a basis for $\Lambda^\perp(\mathbf{A})$, a vector $\mathbf{u} \in \mathbb{Z}_q^n$ and a Gaussian parameter $\sigma \geq \|\widetilde{\mathbf{T_A}}\| \cdot \omega(\sqrt{\log(m + w)})$, then there exists a polynomial time algorithm SamplePre$(\mathbf{A}, \mathbf{u}, \mathbf{T_A}, \sigma)$ outputs a vector $e \in \mathbb{Z}^m$ sampled from a distribution which is statistically close to $D_{\Lambda^\perp(\mathbf{A}), \sigma, \mathbf{u}}$ and satisfies $\mathbf{A} * e = \mathbf{u}$.*

Lemma 3 ([10]). *Let $n, q, w > n$ be integers, $m = O(n \log q)$ and $k = \lceil \log_b q \rceil$ for $2 < b < q$. Given $\mathbf{A} \in \mathbb{Z}_q^{n \times m}$, $\mathbf{R} \in \mathbb{Z}^{m \times \ell}$, $\mathbf{A}' = \mathbf{AR} + \mathbf{HG} \in \mathbb{Z}_q^{n \times nk}$ and a vector $\mathbf{u} \in \mathbb{Z}_q^n$, a matrix $\mathbf{S} \in \mathbb{Z}^{nk \times nk}$ such that $\mathbf{S}$ is a basis for $\Lambda^\perp(\mathbf{G})$ and a*

Gaussian parameter $\sigma \geq \sqrt{s_1(\mathbf{R})^2 + 1} \cdot \|\widetilde{\mathbf{S}}\| \cdot \omega(\sqrt{\log(m + nk)})$, then there exists a polynomial time algorithm SampleD$(\mathbf{A}, \mathbf{R}, \mathbf{A}', \boldsymbol{u}, \mathbf{S}, \sigma)$ *outputs a vector $\boldsymbol{e} \in \mathbb{Z}^{m+kn}$ sampled from a distribution which is statistically close to $D_{\Lambda^\perp([\mathbf{A}|\mathbf{A}']), \sigma, \boldsymbol{u}}$ and satisfies $[\mathbf{A}|\mathbf{A}'] * \boldsymbol{e} = \boldsymbol{u}$.*

Lemma 4 ([1,5]). *Let n, $q > 2$, $w > n$, $m = O(n \log q)$ be integers. Given $\mathbf{A} \in \mathbb{Z}_q^{n \times m}$, $\mathbf{A}' \in \mathbb{Z}_q^{n \times w}$ and a vector $\boldsymbol{u} \in \mathbb{Z}_q^n$, a matrix $\mathbf{T_A} \in \mathbb{Z}^{m \times m}$ is a basis for $\Lambda^\perp(\mathbf{A})$ and a Gaussian parameter $\sigma \geq \|\widetilde{\mathbf{T_A}}\| \cdot \omega(\sqrt{\log(m + w)})$, then there exists a polynomial time algorithm* SampleLeft$(\mathbf{A}, \mathbf{A}', \boldsymbol{u}, \mathbf{T_A}, \sigma)$ *outputs a vector $\boldsymbol{e} \in \mathbb{Z}^{m+w}$ sampled from a distribution which is statistically close to $D_{\Lambda^\perp([\mathbf{A}|\mathbf{A}']), \sigma, \boldsymbol{u}}$ and satisfies $[\mathbf{A}|\mathbf{A}'] * \boldsymbol{e} = \boldsymbol{u}$.*

Lemma 5 ([1,9]). *Let n, $q > 2$, $w > n$, $m = O(n \log q)$ be integers. Given $\mathbf{A} \in \mathbb{Z}_q^{n \times m}$, $\mathbf{R} \in \mathbb{Z}^{m \times w}$, $\mathbf{B} \in \mathbb{Z}_q^{n \times w}$, $\mathbf{A}' = \mathbf{AR} + \mathbf{B} \in \mathbb{Z}_q^{n \times w}$, a vector $\boldsymbol{u} \in \mathbb{Z}_q^n$ and a matrix $\mathbf{T_B} \in \mathbb{Z}^{w \times w}$ is a basis for $\Lambda^\perp(\mathbf{B})$ and a Gaussian parameter $\sigma \geq \|\widetilde{\mathbf{T_B}}\| \cdot s_1(\mathbf{R}) \cdot \omega(\sqrt{\log w})$, then there exists a polynomial time algorithm* SampleRight$(\mathbf{A}, \mathbf{R}, \mathbf{A}', \boldsymbol{u}, \mathbf{T_B}, \sigma)$ *outputs a vector $\boldsymbol{e} \in \mathbb{Z}^{m+w}$ sampled from a distribution which is statistically close to $D_{\Lambda^\perp([\mathbf{A}|\mathbf{A}']), \sigma, \boldsymbol{u}}$ and satisfies $[\mathbf{A}|\mathbf{A}'] * \boldsymbol{e} = \boldsymbol{u}$.*

2.5 Trapdoor Delegation Algorithms

In this subsection, we will recall several trapdoor delegation algorithms. The SampleBasisLeft and SampleBasisRight algorithms were extensions of SampleLeft and SampleRight in [1]. Micciancio and Peikert [10] introduced another trapdoor delegation algorithm DelTrap with a trapdoor $\mathbf{R}$. The concrete algorithms are described as follows.

Lemma 6 ([1]). *Let n, $q > 2$, $w > n$, $m = O(n \log q)$ be integers. Given $\mathbf{A} \in \mathbb{Z}_q^{n \times m}$, $\mathbf{A}' \in \mathbb{Z}_q^{n \times w}$, a matrix $\mathbf{T_A} \in \mathbb{Z}^{m \times m}$ is a basis for $\Lambda^\perp(\mathbf{A})$ and a Gaussian parameter $\sigma \geq \|\widetilde{\mathbf{T_A}}\| \cdot \omega(\sqrt{\log(m + w)})$, then there exists a polynomial time algorithm* SampleBasisLeft$(\mathbf{A}, \mathbf{A}', \mathbf{T_A}, \sigma)$ *outputs a basis $\mathbf{T}$ for lattice $\Lambda^\perp([\mathbf{A}|\mathbf{A}'])$ and satisfies $\|\widetilde{\mathbf{T}}\| \leq \sigma\sqrt{(m + w)}$.*

Lemma 7 ([1]). *Let n, $q > 2$, $m = O(n \log q)$ be integers. Given $\mathbf{A} \in \mathbb{Z}_q^{n \times m}$ and the identity-based encryption matrix for $\boldsymbol{id} = (\boldsymbol{id}_1, \cdots, \boldsymbol{id}_\ell)$ is*

$$\mathbf{F}_{id} = [\mathbf{A}|\mathbf{AR}_1 + \mathsf{H}(\boldsymbol{id}_1)\mathbf{B}| \cdots |\mathbf{AR}_\ell + \mathsf{H}(\boldsymbol{id}_\ell)\mathbf{B}] \in \mathbb{Z}_q^{n \times (\ell+1)m}$$

Let $\mathbf{R}_\ell = (\mathbf{R}_1 | \cdots | \mathbf{R}_\ell)$ and $h_{id} = [\mathsf{H}(\boldsymbol{id}_1 - \boldsymbol{id}_1^*)\mathbf{B}| \cdots |\mathsf{H}(\boldsymbol{id}_\ell - \boldsymbol{id}_\ell^*)\mathbf{B}] \in \mathbb{Z}_q^{n \times \ell m}$. The matrix $\mathbf{T_B} \in \mathbb{Z}^{m \times m}$ is a basis for $\Lambda^\perp(\mathbf{B})$ and a Gaussian parameter $\sigma \geq \|\widetilde{\mathbf{T_B}}\| \cdot s_1(\mathbf{R}_\ell) \cdot \omega(\sqrt{\log m})$, then there exists a polynomial time algorithm SampleBasisRight$(\mathbf{A}, \mathbf{R}_\ell, \mathbf{F}_{id}, \mathbf{T_B}, \sigma)$ *outputs a basis $\mathbf{T}$ for lattice $\Lambda^\perp(\mathbf{F}_{id})$ and satisfies $\|\widetilde{\mathbf{T}}\| \leq \sigma\sqrt{(\ell+1)m}$.*

In our work, we will use the gadget matrix $\mathbf{G}'$ instead of the matrix $\mathbf{B}$ in the SampleBasisRight algorithm and use the algorithm SampleD instead of SampleRight in the SampleBasisRight algorithm. Because the $\mathbf{G}'$ is rank n and $\mathbf{S}'$ is a short basis for $\Lambda^\perp(\mathbf{G}')$, we can obtain the following corollary.

Corollary 1. *Let $n, q > 2, w > n, m = O(n \log q)$ be integers. Given $\mathbf{A} \in \mathbb{Z}_q^{n \times m}$ and the identity-based encryption matrix for $\mathbf{id} = (\mathbf{id}_1, \cdots, \mathbf{id}_\ell)$ is*

$$\mathbf{F}_{id} = [\mathbf{A}|\mathbf{A}\mathbf{R}_1 + \mathsf{H}(\mathbf{id}_1 - \mathbf{id}_1^*)\mathbf{G}'|\cdots|\mathbf{A}\mathbf{R}_\ell + \mathsf{H}(\mathbf{id}_\ell - \mathbf{id}_\ell^*)\mathbf{G}'] \in \mathbb{Z}_q^{m+\ell nk}$$

Let $\mathbf{R}_\ell = (\mathsf{R}_1|\cdots|\mathsf{R}_\ell)$ and $h_{id} = [\mathsf{H}(\mathbf{id}_1 - \mathbf{id}_1^*)\mathbf{G}'|\cdots|\mathsf{H}(\mathbf{id}_\ell - \mathbf{id}_\ell^*)\mathbf{G}'] \in \mathbb{Z}_q^{n \times \ell nk}$. The matrix $\mathbf{S}' \in \mathbb{Z}^{nk \times nk}$ is a basis for $\Lambda^\perp(\mathbf{G}')$ and a Gaussian parameter $\sigma \geq \|\widetilde{\mathbf{S}'}\| \cdot s_1(\mathbf{R}_\ell) \cdot \omega(\sqrt{\log nk})$, then there exists a polynomial time algorithm $\mathsf{SampleBasisRight}(\mathbf{A}, \mathbf{R}_\ell, \mathbf{F}_{id}, \mathbf{S}', \sigma)$ outputs a basis $\mathbf{T}$ for lattice $\Lambda^\perp([\mathbf{A}|\mathbf{A}'])$ and satisfies $\|\widetilde{\mathbf{T}}\| \leq \sigma\sqrt{m + \ell nk}$.

Proof. When we replace the matrix $\mathbf{B}$ with the gadget matrix $\mathbf{G}'$ and set the Gaussian parameter $\sigma \geq \|\widetilde{\mathbf{S}'}\| \cdot s_1(\mathbf{R}_\ell) \cdot \omega(\sqrt{\log nk})$, then output of the algorithms $\mathsf{SampleRight}$ and $\mathsf{SampleD}$ are the same. Therefore, the $\mathsf{SampleBasisRight}$ algorithm will output the short basis for $\mathbf{F}_{id}$. $\square$

Lemma 8 ([10]). *Let $n, q > 2, m = O(n \log q)$ be integers. Given $\mathbf{A} \in \mathbb{Z}_q^{n \times m}$ and $\mathbf{R} \in \mathbb{Z}^{m \times nk}$ is a $\mathbf{G}$-trapdoor for $\mathbf{A}$, let $\mathbf{A}' = [\mathbf{A}|\mathbf{A}_1] \in \mathbb{Z}_q^{n \times (m+k')}$, a tag $\mathbf{H} \in \mathbb{Z}_q^{n \times n}$ and a Gaussian parameter $\sigma \geq \sqrt{s_1(\mathbf{R})^2 + 1} \cdot s_1(\sqrt{\Sigma_\mathbf{G}})$, then there exists a polynomial time algorithm $\mathsf{DelTrap}(\mathbf{A}, \mathbf{R}, \mathbf{A}', \sigma)$ outputs a trapdoor $\mathbf{R}' \in \mathbb{Z}_q^{m \times k'}$ for $\mathbf{A}'$ with tag $\mathbf{H}'$ such that $\mathbf{A}\mathbf{R}' = \mathbf{H}'\mathbf{G}' - \mathbf{A}_1$ and satisfies $s_1(\mathbf{R}') \leq \sigma \cdot O(\sqrt{m} + \sqrt{k'})$, where $\mathbf{G}'$ is set by base b and $k' = \lceil \log_b q \rceil$.*

3   Hierarchical IBE with Compact Ciphertext from LWE

In this section, we will introduce our HIBE scheme based on the LWE problem. In the construction, we will utilize the function defined in [1,10] that encodes the identities into matrices and satisfies the "unit differences" property: for any $\mathbf{id}_i \neq \mathbf{id}_j$, $\mathsf{H}(\mathbf{id}_i) - \mathsf{H}(\mathbf{id}_j) = \mathsf{H}(\mathbf{id}_i - \mathbf{id}_j)$ is invertible and $\mathsf{H}(\mathbf{0}) = \mathbf{0}$. Moreover, the parity-check matrix $\mathbf{G}'$ in our construction is defined as $\mathbf{G}' = \mathbf{g}^t \otimes \mathbf{I}_n \in \mathbb{Z}^{n \times nk}$, where $\mathbf{g}^t = (1, b, b^2, ..., b^{k-1}) \in \mathbb{Z}^k$, $b = 2^d$ and $k = \lceil \log_b q \rceil$. And $\mathbf{S}'$ is a short basis of lattice $\Lambda^\perp(\mathbf{G}')$ with $\|\widetilde{\mathbf{S}'}\| \leq \sqrt{b^2 + 1}$.

3.1   The HIBE Construction

- $\mathsf{KeyGen}(1^n, q) \rightarrow (pk, sk)$: The algorithm calls $(\mathbf{A}, \mathbf{T}_\mathbf{A}) \xleftarrow{\$} \mathsf{GenTrap}(n, m, q)$ to generate $\mathbf{A} \in \mathbb{Z}_q^{n \times m}$ and a matrix $\mathbf{T}_\mathbf{A}$ is a short basis for lattice $\Lambda^\perp(\mathbf{A})$, then randomly samples d matrices $\mathbf{A}_1, \cdots, \mathbf{A}_d \xleftarrow{\$} \mathbb{Z}_q^{n \times nk}$ and a vector $\boldsymbol{u} \xleftarrow{\$} \mathbb{Z}_q^n$. Therefore, the master public key mpk and the master secret key msk are

$$mpk = (\mathbf{A}, \mathbf{A}_1, \cdots, \mathbf{A}_d, \boldsymbol{u}) \in \mathbb{Z}_q^{n \times (m+dnk+1)}; \ msk = \mathbf{T}_\mathbf{A}.$$

- $\mathsf{Derive}(mpk, \mathbf{id}|\mathbf{id}_\ell, \mathsf{SK}_{id}) \rightarrow \mathsf{SK}_{id|id_\ell}$: Given the master public key mpk, a private key SK_{id} for identity $\mathbf{id} = \{\mathbf{id}_1, \cdots, \mathbf{id}_{\ell-1}\}$ at depth $\ell - 1$ as inputs, the algorithm works as follows:

1. Let $\mathbf{A}_{id} = [\mathbf{A}_1 + \mathsf{H}(id_1)\mathbf{G}'|\cdots|\mathbf{A}_{\ell-1} + \mathsf{H}(id_{\ell-1})\mathbf{G}']$ and $\mathbf{F}_{id} = [\mathbf{A}|\mathbf{A}_{id}]$, then SK_{id} is a short basis for lattice $\Lambda_q^\perp(\mathbf{F}_{id})$;
2. Let $\mathbf{F}_{id|id_\ell} = [\mathbf{F}_{id}|\mathbf{A}_\ell + \mathsf{H}(id_\ell)\mathbf{G}']$;
3. Construct short basis for lattice $\Lambda_q^\perp(\mathbf{F}_{id|id_\ell})$ by invoking

$$\mathbf{S} \leftarrow \mathsf{SampleBasisLeft}(\mathbf{A}_{id}, \mathbf{A}_\ell + \mathsf{H}(id_\ell)\mathbf{G}', \mathsf{SK}_{id}, \sigma_\ell)$$

4. Output $\mathsf{SK}_{id|id_\ell} = \mathbf{S}$ as the private key for identity $id|id_\ell$.
- $\mathsf{Encrypt}(mpk, id, m) \to c$: Given the master public key mpk, the identity id and message $m \in \{0,1\}$ as inputs, the algorithm works as follows:
1. For identity $id = \{id_1, \cdots, id_\ell\}$, compute

$$\mathbf{A}_{id} = [\mathbf{A}_1 + \mathsf{H}(id_1)\mathbf{G}'|\cdots|\mathbf{A}_\ell + \mathsf{H}(id_\ell)\mathbf{G}'] \in \mathbb{Z}_q^{n \times \ell nk}$$

and $\mathbf{F}_{id} = [\mathbf{A}|\mathbf{A}_{id}] \in \mathbb{Z}_q^{n \times (m+\ell nk)}$;
2. Choose a uniformly randomness $\boldsymbol{s} \xleftarrow{\$} \mathbb{Z}_q^n$;
3. Choose a uniformly random matrix $\mathsf{R} \xleftarrow{\$} \{-1,1\}^{m \times \ell nk}$;
4. Choose $(x_0, \boldsymbol{x}_1) \leftarrow D_{\mathbb{Z}, \alpha \ell q} \times D_{\mathbb{Z}, \alpha \ell q}^m$, then set $\boldsymbol{x}_2^t = \boldsymbol{x}_1^t \mathsf{R} \in \mathbb{Z}_q^{\ell nk}$ and compute

$$\begin{cases} c_0 = \boldsymbol{s}^t \boldsymbol{u} + x_0 + \lfloor q/2 \rfloor \cdot \boldsymbol{m} \\ c_1 = \boldsymbol{s}^t \mathbf{F}_{id} + [\boldsymbol{x}_1^t|\boldsymbol{x}_2^t] = \boldsymbol{s}^t[\mathbf{A}|\mathbf{A}_{id}] + [\boldsymbol{x}_1^t|\boldsymbol{x}_2^t] \end{cases}$$

5. Output the ciphertext $\boldsymbol{c}^t = (c_0, \boldsymbol{c}_1^t) \in \mathbb{Z}_q \times \mathbb{Z}_q^{m+\ell nk}$.
- $\mathsf{Decrypt}(\boldsymbol{c}, id, \mathsf{SK}_{id}) \to \boldsymbol{m}$ or $\bot$: Given the ciphertext $\boldsymbol{c}$ and the private key SK_{id} for identity id as input, the algorithm works as follows:
1. Parse $\boldsymbol{c}^t = (c_0, \boldsymbol{c}_1^t)$, if $\boldsymbol{c}$ cannot parse in this way, output $\bot$;
2. Compute $\mathbf{A}_{id}, \mathbf{F}_{id}$ as before;
3. Let $\tau_\ell = \sigma_\ell \cdot \sqrt{m+\ell nk} \cdot \omega(\sqrt{\log(m+\ell nk)}) \geq \|\widetilde{\mathsf{SK}_{id}}\| \cdot \omega(\sqrt{\log(m+\ell nk)})$ and sample $\boldsymbol{e}_{id} \in \mathbb{Z}^{m+\ell nk}$ as

$$\boldsymbol{e}_{id} \leftarrow \mathsf{SamplePre}(\mathbf{F}_{id}, \mathsf{SK}_{id}, \tau_\ell, \boldsymbol{u})$$

s.t. $\mathbf{F}_{id}\boldsymbol{e}_{id} = \boldsymbol{u}$;
4. Compute $w = c_0 - c_1\boldsymbol{e}_{id}$;
5. Compute and output the message $\boldsymbol{m} = \lfloor \frac{w}{q/2} \rceil \pmod 2$.

3.2 Parameters and Correctness

In this subsection, we will describe the requirement of parameters which meets the correctness and security of the above HIBE scheme, then we will propose a set of parameters.

Lemma 9 (Correctness). *Assume the parameters* $n, m, q, \ell, \alpha_\ell, \sigma_\ell, \tau_\ell$ *satisfy the condition* $\alpha_\ell q \omega(\sqrt{\log n}) + \alpha_\ell q \sigma_\ell (m + \ell nk)^{3/2} \cdot \omega(\log(m + \ell nk)) \leq q/5$ *with all but negligible probability, then the* Dec *algorithm of the above HIBE will have negligible decryption error.*

Proof. For a valid ciphertext c of message m, the Dec algorithm computes

$$c_0 - c_1^t e_{id} = \lfloor \tfrac{q}{2} \rfloor m + x_0 - [x_1^t | x_2^t] e_{id}.$$

Thus, on the condition that $\|x_0 - [x_1^t|x_2^t]e_{id}\| \leq q/5$, the Dec algorithm can recover the message m correctly. Since $x_0 \leftarrow D_{\mathbb{Z},\alpha_\ell q}$, we have $\|x_0\| \leq \alpha_\ell q \omega(\sqrt{\log n})$ with all but negligible probability. Because $\mathsf{R} \xleftarrow{\$} \{-1,1\}^{m \times \ell nk}$, then we have $\|\mathsf{R}\| \leq O(\sqrt{m + \ell nk})$. Since $e_{id}^t = (e_1^t, e_2^t)$ is sampled by $\mathsf{SamplePre}(\mathbf{F}_{id}, \mathsf{SK}_{id}, \tau_\ell, u)$, let $\tau_\ell = \sigma_\ell \cdot \sqrt{m + \ell nk} \cdot \omega(\sqrt{\log(m + \ell nk)}) \geq \widetilde{\|\mathsf{SK}_{id}\|} \cdot \omega(\sqrt{\log(m + \ell nk)})$, we have $\|e_{id}\| \leq \tau_\ell \cdot \sqrt{m + \ell nk}$ with overwhelming probability. In addition, we have $\|e_1 + \mathsf{R} \cdot e_2\| \leq \|e_1\| + \|\mathsf{R} \cdot e_2\| \leq \sigma_\ell(m + \ell nk)^{3/2} \cdot \omega(\sqrt{\log(m + \ell nk)})$. Since $x_1 \leftarrow D_{\mathbb{Z},\alpha_\ell q}^m$, then we have $\|x_1^t(e_1 + \mathsf{R} \cdot e_2)\| \leq \|e_1 + \mathsf{R} \cdot e_2\| \cdot \alpha_\ell q \omega(\sqrt{\log m}) \leq \alpha_\ell q \sigma_\ell (m + \ell nk)^{3/2} \cdot \omega(\log(m + \ell nk))$. Therefore, the error item during the process of decryption is bounded by

$$\|x_0 - [x_1^t|x_2^t]e_{id}\| \leq \alpha_\ell q \omega(\sqrt{\log n}) + \alpha_\ell q \sigma_\ell (m + \ell nk)^{3/2} \cdot \omega(\log(m + \ell nk))$$

with all but negligible probability. Under the assumption in the lemma, the Dec algorithm of the above HIBE will have negligible decryption error. That completes the proof. □

To satisfy the requirement of correctness and security, taking n as security parameter, we set the parameters as

$$m = O(n \log q) = O(dn \log n) \quad , \quad q = \tilde{O}((4d)^{d/2} n^{d/2})$$
$$\sigma_\ell = 2^d (m + \ell nk)^{\frac{\ell}{2}} \omega(\log^{\frac{\ell}{2}}(m + \ell nk)) \quad , \quad 1/\alpha_\ell = \sigma_\ell (m + \ell nk)^{3/2} \omega(\log(m + \ell nk))$$

The parameters	The sizes (bits)
mpk	$(m + dnk + 1)n \log q = \tilde{O}(d^2 n^2)$
SK_{id} at level ℓ	$(m + \ell nk)^2 \log(\sigma_\ell \sqrt{m + \ell nk}) = \tilde{O}((\frac{d}{\log n} + \ell) \cdot (d + \ell)^2 n^2)$
$\mathbf{ct}$ at level ℓ	$(m + \ell nk) \log q = \tilde{O}(nd(d + \ell))$
Error rate at level ℓ	$\tilde{O}(2^d d^{(\ell+3)/2} n^{(\ell+3)/2})$

4 Conclusion

In this paper, we introduce a trade off of the sizes of public parameter and ciphertext and the size of private key in the selective-secure LWE-based HIBE scheme in the standard model. We obtain this trade-off by adjusting the base of the gadget matrix $\mathbf{G} \in \mathbb{Z}_q^{n \times n \lceil \log_b q \rceil}$ defined in [10]. By setting $b = 2^d$, the size of the master public key and ciphertext at level ℓ can de reduced by a factor of $O(d)$ and $O(\ell)$ respectively, at the cost of increasing the size of private key by a factor of $O(\frac{d}{\ell \log n} + 1)$. And the parameters in ABB10b scheme except the private key is competitive with our HIBE scheme only when $\lambda = 1$.

Acknowledgments. We thank the anonymous ICICS'2017 reviewers for their helpful comments. This work is supported by the National Cryptography Development Fund MMJJ20170116 and the National Nature Science Foundation of China (No. 61602473, No. 61502480, No. 61672019, No. 61772522, No. 61379137, No. 61572495) and National Basic Research Programm of China (973 project, No. 2014CB340603).

References

1. Agrawal, S., Boneh, D., Boyen, X.: Efficient lattice (H)IBE in the standard model. In: Gilbert, H. (ed.) EUROCRYPT 2010. LNCS, vol. 6110, pp. 553–572. Springer, Heidelberg (2010). https://doi.org/10.1007/978-3-642-13190-5_28

2. Agrawal, S., Boneh, D., Boyen, X.: Lattice basis delegation in fixed dimension and shorter-ciphertext hierarchical IBE. In: Rabin, T. (ed.) CRYPTO 2010. LNCS, vol. 6223, pp. 98–115. Springer, Heidelberg (2010). https://doi.org/10.1007/978-3-642-14623-7_6

3. Banerjee, A., Peikert, C., Rosen, A.: Pseudorandom functions and lattices. In: Pointcheval, D., Johansson, T. (eds.) EUROCRYPT 2012. LNCS, vol. 7237, pp. 719–737. Springer, Heidelberg (2012). https://doi.org/10.1007/978-3-642-29011-4_42

4. Bogdanov, A., Guo, S., Masny, D., Richelson, S., Rosen, A.: On the hardness of learning with rounding over small modulus. In: Kushilevitz, E., Malkin, T. (eds.) TCC 2016. LNCS, vol. 9562, pp. 209–224. Springer, Heidelberg (2016). https://doi.org/10.1007/978-3-662-49096-9_9

5. Cash, D., Hofheinz, D., Kiltz, E., Peikert, C.: Bonsai trees, or how to delegate a lattice basis. In: Gilbert, H. (ed.) EUROCRYPT 2010. LNCS, vol. 6110, pp. 523–552. Springer, Heidelberg (2010). https://doi.org/10.1007/978-3-642-13190-5_27

6. Gentry, C., Peikert, C., Vaikuntanathan, V.: Trapdoors for hard lattices and new cryptographic constructions. In: STOC 2008, pp. 197–206 (2008)

7. Gentry, C., Silverberg, A.: Hierarchical ID-based cryptography. In: Zheng, Y. (ed.) ASIACRYPT 2002. LNCS, vol. 2501, pp. 548–566. Springer, Heidelberg (2002). https://doi.org/10.1007/3-540-36178-2_34

8. Horwitz, J., Lynn, B.: Toward hierarchical identity-based encryption. In: Knudsen, L.R. (ed.) EUROCRYPT 2002. LNCS, vol. 2332, pp. 466–481. Springer, Heidelberg (2002). https://doi.org/10.1007/3-540-46035-7_31

9. Katsumata, S., Yamada, S.: Partitioning via non-linear polynomial functions: more compact IBEs from ideal lattices and bilinear maps. In: Cheon, J.H., Takagi, T. (eds.) ASIACRYPT 2016. LNCS, vol. 10032, pp. 682–712. Springer, Heidelberg (2016). https://doi.org/10.1007/978-3-662-53890-6_23

10. Micciancio, D., Peikert, C.: Trapdoors for lattices: simpler, tighter, faster, smaller. In: Pointcheval, D., Johansson, T. (eds.) EUROCRYPT 2012. LNCS, vol. 7237, pp. 700–718. Springer, Heidelberg (2012). https://doi.org/10.1007/978-3-642-29011-4_41

11. Regev, O.: On lattices, learning with errors, random linear codes, and cryptography. In: STOC 2005, pp. 84–93 (2005)

12. Shamir, A.: Identity-based cryptosystems and signature schemes. In: Blakley, G.R., Chaum, D. (eds.) CRYPTO 1984. LNCS, vol. 196, pp. 47–53. Springer, Heidelberg (1985). https://doi.org/10.1007/3-540-39568-7_5

Attacks and Attacks Defense

Methods for Increasing the Resistance of Cryptographic Designs Against Horizontal DPA Attacks

Ievgen Kabin[✉], Zoya Dyka, Dan Kreiser, and Peter Langendoerfer

IHP, Im Technologiepark 25, 15236 Frankfurt (Oder), Germany
{kabin,dyka,kreiser,langendoerfer}
@ihp-microelectronics.com

Abstract. Side channel analysis attacks, especially horizontal DPA and DEMA attacks, are significant threats for cryptographic designs. In this paper we investigate to which extend different multiplication formulae and randomization of the field multiplier increase the resistance of an ECC design against horizontal attacks. We implemented a randomized sequence of the calculation of partial products for the field multiplication in order to increase the security features of the field multiplier. Additionally, we use the partial polynomial multiplier itself as a kind of countermeasure against DPA attacks. We demonstrate that the implemented classical multiplication formula can increase the inherent resistance of the whole ECC design. We also investigate the impact of the combination of these two approaches. For the evaluation we synthesized all these designs for a 250 nm gate library technologies, and analysed the simulated power traces. All investigated protection means help to decrease the success rate of attacks significantly: the correctness of the revealed key was decreased from 99% to 69%.

Keywords: Elliptic curve cryptography (ECC)
Elliptic curve (EC) point multiplication · Field multiplication
Side channel analysis (SCA) · Differential power analysis (DPA) attacks
Horizontal attacks

1 Introduction

Wireless Sensor Networks (WSNs) and the Internet of Things (IoT) are emerging technologies and are used in application fields such as telemedicine, automation control and monitoring of critical infrastructures. These application fields require the data to be kept confidential and/or to ensure the integrity of transmitted data.

RSA and Elliptic curve cryptography (ECC) are asymmetric cryptographic approaches. Both can be applied not only for encryption and decryption of messages but also for digital signature operations and for key exchange. To reduce the time and energy consumption of computation, asymmetric cryptographic algorithms are implemented in hardware, as cryptographic accelerators. The area of cryptographic accelerators defines its production costs as well as its energy consumption per clock cycle, so it has to be as small as possible. As ECC uses by far smaller keys than RSA, it

© Springer International Publishing AG, part of Springer Nature 2018
S. Qing et al. (Eds.): ICICS 2017, LNCS 10631, pp. 225–235, 2018.
https://doi.org/10.1007/978-3-319-89500-0_20

provides an energy efficient kind of public key cryptography and is well suited for WSNs and for the IoT. In this type of networks the risk of side channel analysis (SCA) attacks needs to be taken serious. Due to the need of saving energy i.e. sleeping intervals and due to the nature of wireless connections devices can be stolen unnoticed, analysed in a labor and brought back. So, the devices or better the implementations of cryptographic operations need to be as resistant to SCA attacks as possible.

In ECC each cryptographic key pair consists of a private and a public component. As the security of the ECC is based on keeping the private key secret the goal of an attacker is to reveal this key. The most often applied attacks are power analysis (PA) attacks or electromagnetic analysis (EMA) attacks. The attacker measures the current through the crypto-accelerator or its electromagnetic emanation while a cryptographic operation using the private key or other sensitive data is performed. For ECC the core operation is the elliptic curve point multiplication with a scalar, denoted as kP operation. P is a point of the elliptic curve (EC) and k is a scalar. For the ECDSA signature generation [1] the critical operation is a kG multiplication, i.e. a multiplication of the EC basis point G with a random number k. If an attacker can reveal the scalar k, the private key Key used for a signature generation can be easy calculated as follows:

$$Key = \frac{s \cdot k - e}{r} \bmod \varepsilon$$

Here e is a hash value of the message to be signed; numbers r and s are components of the digital signature and ε is the order of the EC basis point G, respectively to [1, 2]. The numbers r, s and the message itself are transmitted to a receiver, i.e. the attacker knows these numbers. Additionally, the point G and its order ε are parameters of the EC, i.e. they are known to the attacker, as well.

kP algorithms implemented in hardware process the scalar k bitwise. Thus, the processing of each key bit takes a certain time, here denoted as a slot. The shape of a slot in a measured trace depends on the circuit of the ECC design, on the value of the processed key bit and on the data processed in the slot. This means that the measured traces can be used for revealing the scalar k. Horizontal attacks [3], i.e. attacks based on a statistical analysis of a single trace, are significant threats for cryptographic devices, especially due to the fact that the traditional randomization methods such as randomization of the scalar k, blinding of the EC point P or randomization of the projective coordinates of point P [4] do not provide any kind of protection.

1.1   Contribution of this Paper

In this paper we report on the impact of using a classical multiplication formula on the success of the low-cost horizontal DPA attack, that is described in [5–8]. Additionally we randomized the sequence of calculation of partial products by each field multiplication as described in [5]. The idea to randomize the sequence was proposed in [15, 16]. In [15, 16] it was evaluated only for a field multiplier. As reported in [5] this randomization increases the resistance of ECC designs against horizontal attacks but is not sufficient as a single countermeasure. In consequence we combined this approach with applying of the classical multiplication formula for the calculation of partial products.

To evaluate these countermeasures we performed the horizontal attack as described in [5] against different ECC designs using simulated power traces for 250 nm gate library technologies.

The rest of this paper is structured as follows. In Sect. 2 we describe investigated kP designs. In Sect. 3 we explain shortly how we performed the horizontal low-cost DPA attack using the difference of the means and how we evaluated the success of attacks. The results of the attacks are evaluated in Sect. 4. Conclusions are given in Sect. 5.

2   Investigated kP Designs

1987 Montgomery proposed an algorithm for the kP calculation [9]. 1998 Lopez and Dahab showed that the Montgomery kP algorithm can be performed using only the x-coordinate of the point P if P is a point on EC over $GF(2^n)$ [10]. Additionally, they proposed to use special projective coordinates of the EC point P to avoid the most complex operation, i.e. the division of elements of Galois fields. These optimizations reduced the execution time and the energy consumption of the kP calculation significantly. The Montgomery algorithm using projective Lopez-Dahab coordinates is a time and energy efficient solution and due to this fact this algorithm is the one mostly used for implementing the EC point multiplication in hardware. The most referenced version of the Montgomery kP algorithm is [11]. The kP operation according to this algorithm, can be performed using only 6 multiplications, 5 squarings and 3 additions of Galois field elements for each key bit, except of the most significant bit $k_{l-1} = 1$. The length of the operands depends on the chosen security level. We experimented with a kP design for EC B-233, recommended by NIST [1]. The maximal length l of operands is up to 233 bits in our designs.

The Montgomery kP algorithm has the same sequence of operations for the processing of each key bit, independently of its value. Such implementations are resistant against SPA attacks. A possibility to increase the inherent resistance of the Montgomery kP implementations against SCA attacks (not only against simple ones), is to increase the noise level in the analysed power profile. As reported in [7] the field multiplier can be the source of the noise if itself is resistant against SCA attacks. The *write to register* operations are most analysed ones while an attack is performed. If these operations are executed in parallel to the field multiplications the analysis becomes by far more complex. Thus, implementations exploiting parallel execution of operations of the kP algorithm are inherently more resistant against PA attacks. Additionally, the execution of many operations in parallel reduces the execution time of the cryptographic operations and increases the efficiency of the design.

Our kP design is a balanced and efficient implementation of the kP algorithm based on Algorithm 2 published in [7], that is a modification of the Montgomery kP algorithm.

2.1   Basic Design: Balanced, Efficient, Resistant Against SPA and HCCA

The structure of our kP designs is shown in Fig. 1.

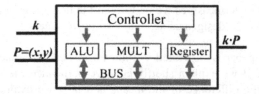

Fig. 1. Structure of our kP design.

The block Controller manages the sequence of the field operations. It controls the data flow between the other blocks and defines which operation has to be performed in the current clock cycle. Depending on the signals of the Controller the block ALU performs addition or squaring of its operands. Our design comprises of only one block MULT to calculate the product of 233 bit long operands. The multiplication is the most complex field operation. In our implementation it takes 9 clock cycles to calculate the product according to a fixed calculation plan using the iterative Karatsuba multiplication method as described in [12]. In each of the 9 clock cycles one partial polynomial product of two 59 bit long operands A_j and B_j (with $1 \leq j \leq 9$) is calculated and accumulated to the product including reduction.

Figure 2 shows the structure of our field multiplier for 233 bit long operands. It consists of a Partial Multiplier (PM) for 59 bit long operands. The field multiplier takes 9 clock cycles to calculate the product using a 59 bit partial multiplier. The PM takes 1 clock cycle to calculate the polynomial product of 59 bit long operands and is implemented as a combination of 3 multiplication methods (MMs). The 2-segment iterative Karatsuba multiplication formula [14] was applied for 60-bit long multiplicands. The gate complexity of this multiplier is $GC_{2m} = 3 \cdot GC_m + (7m - 3)_{XOR}$. Here m is the length of segments $m = 60/2 = 30$ and GC_m is the gate complexity of the internal m-bit partial multipliers. Thus, the 59 bit partial multiplier contains of 3 internal multipliers: two of them for 30 bit long operands and one multiplier for 29 bit long operands.

All these internal multipliers are implemented identically, using the 6-segment iterative Winograd multiplication formula [14], which gate complexity is: $GC_{6m} = 18 \cdot GC_m + (72m - 19)_{XOR}$, with $m = 30/6 = 5$ bits. Corresponding to the 6-segment iterative Winograd multiplication formula the 30-bit multiplier consists of 18 internal multipliers of 5-bit long operands. Each of these small multipliers was implemented using the classical multiplication formula with $n = 5$:

$$C = A \cdot B = \sum_{i=0}^{2n-2} c_i \cdot t^i, \text{ with } c_i = \bigoplus_{i=k+l} a_k \cdot b_l, \forall k, l < n. \tag{1}$$

The gate complexity of each of the 5-bit classical multiplier is $GC_5 = 25_{\&} + 16_{XOR}$, i.e. $5^2 = 25$ AND gates and $4^2 = 16$ XOR gates.

Applying the described combination of 3 multiplication methods, the gate complexity of the 59-bit partial multiplier is $GC_{59} = 1350_{\&} + 2094_{XOR}$. This PM is area optimized for the applied technology. The minimal possible processing time per key bit

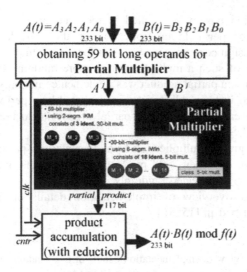

$A(t)=A_3 A_2 A_1 A_0$ $B(t)=B_3 B_2 B_1 B_0$
233 bit   233 bit

Fig. 2. Structure of the field multiplier for 233 bit long operands.

in our implementation is equal to the time needed to execute 6 field multiplications (here taking 9 clock cycles each), i.e. 54 clock cycles. This is achieved by implementing all arithmetic and *write to register* operations in parallel to the multiplications.

Our Basic Design is inherent resistant against Horizontal Collision Correlation Analysis (HCCA) attacks introduced in [13]. This is achieved by using the iterative 4-segment Karatsuba MM:

- the number of calculated partial products is small (only 9);
- the length of operands for each partial multiplication is big, $w = 59$;
- operands for partial product calculation using the iterative Karatsuba MM are different, that is not the case if the classical MM as assumed in [13] is applied.

2.2 Design with Randomized Sequence of PMs

Usually a field product of long operands is calculated as a sum of partial products of partial operands of smaller length. In each clock cycle one partial product is calculated and accumulated according to a fixed scheduled calculation sequence often denoted as accumulation plan. In [15, 16] it was proposed to randomize the calculation sequence of the partial products, i.e. to re-schedule the calculation plan for each new field multiplication with the goal to increase the resistance of the field multiplier against SCA attacks. In [5] this method was evaluated as a countermeasure against horizontal DPA attacks using an execution of a kP operation. If the multiplication formula consists of n partial products, there exist $n!$ different permutations of this sequence. One of these permutations can be selected randomly for the calculation of each field multiplication.

The field reduction has to be applied to the accumulation register and can be performed either once per field multiplication or after calculating of each partial product. The latter design consumes more power for the calculation of the filed product but the power shape of such a multiplication is more random. The partial reduction after each calculation of a partial product was implemented not only in [15, 16] but also in the design reported in [17]. All designs investigated here perform the reduction of the product after the calculation of each partial product to increase the noise and to reduce the success of SCA attacks.

In our Basic Design the multiplication formula contains 9 partial products of 59 bit long operands, i.e. for each new field product calculation one out of 9! possible calculation sequences can be selected randomly.

Table 1 gives an overview of implementation details of our design and the implementation described in [15, 16].

Table 1. Overview of implementation details of two randomized multipliers

Parameters	Design [15, 16]	Our design
Field multiplier for	$GF(2^r)$-elements	$GF(2^r)$-elements
Lengths of multiplicands	$r = 192$	$r = 233$
Irreducible polynomial	Not given	$f(t) = t^{233} + t^{74} + 1$
#segments	6	4
Applied multiplication formula	eMSK$_{6=2*3}$	4-segment iterative Karatsuba MM
Partial multiplier for	32 bit long operands	59 bit long operands
#partial multiplications	18	9
#possible permutations	18!	9!

The smaller number of possible permutations in our design compared to the one described in [15, 16] means that our multiplier is more vulnerable to collision-based attacks. They are a kind of vertical attacks and can be prevented using traditional randomization countermeasures [4]. In this work we concentrate on the prevention of horizontal DPA attacks. The area and energy consumption of a partial multiplier for 59-bit long operands are significantly higher than those of a multiplier for 32 bit long operands. Thus, the 59-bit partial multiplier can be more effective as a noise source and by that as a means against horizontal DPA attacks.

2.3   Design with Classical PM

The next design we used in our experiments was Basic Design (see Sect. 2.1) but here the partial multiplier was implemented using the classical multiplication formula only, i.e. it implements formula (1) for the length of the partial multiplicands $n = 59$.

The gate complexity (GC) of this multiplier, i.e. the amount of *AND* and *XOR* gates which are necessary to implement its functionality corresponding to formula (1) is n^2 *AND* gates and $(n-1)^2$ *XOR* gates, i.e.: $GC_{59} = 3481_\& + 3364_{XOR}$.

The gate complexity of such a multiplier is the biggest one of all potential multipliers. All other multiplication methods, like Karatsuba or eMSK multiplication formulae, were developed with the goal to reduce the (gate) complexity of the classical multiplication formula. On the one hand the gate complexity is a disadvantage of the classical multiplication method because it results in an increased chip area, price and energy consumption. But on the other hand the increased energy consumption and especially its fluctuation mean an increased noise level for an attacker, if it analyses the activity of the other blocks. Due to this fact, using the classical MM for the implementation of the partial multiplier can be an advantage, because it increases the inherent robustness of *kP* designs against SCA attacks.

2.4 Design with Classical PM and Randomized Sequence of PMs

The PM was implemented using the classical MM as it was done for the design introduced in Sect. 2.3. The sequence of the partial multiplications was re-scheduled for each new field multiplication as described for the design introduced in Sect. 2.2. Thus, our 4th implemented design is a combination of both approaches for increasing the resistance against SCA attacks.

3 Horizontal DPA Using the Difference of the Means

To perform a horizontal DPA attack we prepared the power traces as follows:

- We fragmented the power trace in time slots. Each time slot corresponds to the processing of a bit of the used scalar k. In the rest of the paper we denoted the scalar k as key. For our analysis we selected only time slots where key bits were processed in the main loop of the Montgomery kP algorithm. In our experiments with a 232 bit long randomly generated key k the slots correspond to k_j with $0 \leq j \leq 229$. I. e. we excluded the processing of the two most significant bits of the key from the analysis. In our implementation one time slot consists of 54 clock cycles.
- We averaged the power per clock cycle to represent the clock cycle in the analysis by only one power value, i.e. we compressed the trace.

We performed our horizontal DPA attack using the difference of the means applied to the compressed traces as follows:

1. Using the 230 time slots we calculated the arithmetical mean of all values with the same number i, which is the number of the clock cycle $(1 \leq i \leq 54)$ within the time slot, and different number j:

$$\overline{p^i} = \frac{1}{230} \sum_{j=0}^{229} p_j^i \tag{2}$$

Thus, the 54 calculated values $\overline{p^i}$ define the mean power profile of slots.

2. For each i we obtained one key candidate $k^{candidate\_i}$ using the following assumption: the jth bit of the key candidate is 1 if in the slot with number j the value with number i – i.e. the value p_j^i – is smaller than or equal to the average value $\overline{p^i}$. Else the jth bit of the ith key candidate is 0:

$$k_j^{candidate\_i} = \begin{cases} 1, & \text{if } p_j^i \leq \overline{p^i} \\ 0, & \text{if } p_j^i > \overline{p^i} \end{cases} \tag{3}$$

To evaluate the success of the attack we compared all extracted key candidates with the scalar k that was really processed. For each key candidate we calculated its relative correctness as follows:

$$\delta_1 = \frac{number\_of\_correct\_extracted\_bits\_of\_k^{candidate\_i}}{230} \cdot 100\% \tag{4}$$

The range of the correctness δ_1 is between 0 and 100%.

If a key candidate was extracted with a correctness close to 0%, it means that our assumption in Eq. (3) is wrong and the opposite assumption will be correct. Thus, the relative correctness $\delta_1 = 0$ of the key candidate obtained using assumption (3) will correspond to correctness $\delta_1 = 100\%$ if the opposite assumption is used. Taking this fact into account we can calculate the correctness as follow:

$$\delta = 50\% + |50\% - \delta_1| \tag{5}$$

Thus, we define the correctness as a value between 50% and 100%. For the attacker the worst-case of the attack results is a correctness of 50% which means the *difference of means* test cannot even provide a slight hint whether the key bit processed is more likely a '1' or a '0'. The worst-case from the attacker's point of view is the ideal case from the designer's point of view. We denote it as the "ideal case" in the rest of the paper.

Figure 3 shows attack results i.e. relative correctness δ for the key candidates extracted using PTs of our Basic Design, simulated for the 250 nm technology. In order to demonstrate that well-known countermeasures [4] are not effective against horizontal DPA, we applied point blinding, key randomization and a combination of both as countermeasures with the goal to randomize the data processed in our Basic Design. The red bars show the result of the attack for the Basic Design without randomized inputs. The green, the yellow and the black bars show the analysis results when traditional countermeasures [4] are applied.

Figure 4 shows all key candidates given in Fig. 3 sorted in descending order of correctness. According to that each key candidate got a new index displayed at the x axis. This representation helps to compare the analysis results.

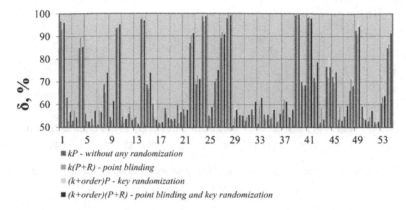

Fig. 3. Results of attacks against *kP* executions with and without traditional randomization countermeasure. All PTs were simulated for our Basic Design using the 250 nm technology. (Color figure online)

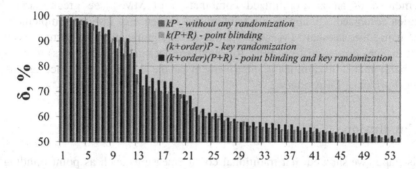

Fig. 4. Correctness of key candidates from Fig. 3 sorted in descending order; according to that each key candidate got a new index displayed at the *x* axis. The one with the highest correctness is now number 1, the one with the lowest number 54. The blue horizontal line at 50% shows the ideal case. (Color figure online)

Comparing attack results displayed in Figs. 3 and 4 shows clearly that the traditional randomization countermeasures do not provide any protection against horizontal SCA attacks.

4   Discussion of the Results for Investigated Designs

In this section we discuss the analysis results of the power shape randomization strategies introduced in Sect. 2. We synthesized the 4 designs described in Sect. 2 for a 250 nm technology. Then we simulated the designs using PrimeTime [18] to get power traces which we then analysed to evaluate the effectiveness of the randomization strategies for the complete *kP* designs. All 4 power traces were simulated using the same inputs, i.e. the key *k* and EC point *P*. Figure 5 shows the analysis results.

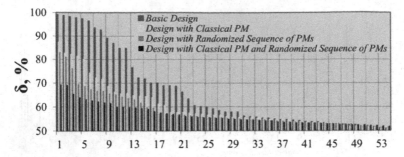

Fig. 5. Attack results: correctness of the extracted keys sorted in descending order. (Color figure online)

The results of the analysis show that the implementation of the partial multiplier using the classical multiplication formula has a significant impact on the resistance of the *kP* design against horizontal DPA (see yellow bars in Fig. 5). This effect is similar to the randomization of the calculation sequence of partial products if the PM is implemented as an area-optimized combination of MMs (see green bars). Both strategies combined, i.e. applying a randomized sequence of PMs and implementation of PM using the classical MM increases this effect significantly: the correctness of the extraction was decreased from 99% for our Basic Design (see blue bars) to 69% (see black bars) that is a significant improvement of the design's resistance against the applied horizontal DPA attack.

5 Conclusion

In this paper we showed that traditional countermeasures such as point blinding and key randomization provide almost no protection against horizontal DPA attacks (see Figs. 3 and 4 in Sect. 3). In order to prevent horizontal DPA attacks from being successful we investigated alternative means to increase the resistance of the *kP* designs: randomizing the calculation sequence of the partial products and implementing the partial multiplier using the classical multiplication formula. We showed that the impact of both countermeasures on the success of horizontal DPA attacks is similar. Especially a combination of these approaches can significantly increase the inherent resistance of ECC designs against horizontal attacks: the correctness of the revealed key was decreased from 99% to 69% (see Fig. 5 in Sect. 4).

Acknowledgments. The work presented here was partly supported by the German Ministry of Research and Education (BMBF) within the ParSec project, grant agreement no. 16KIS0219K.

References

1. Federal Information Processing Standard (FIPS) 186-4, Digital Signature Standard; Request for Comments on the NIST-Recommended Elliptic Curves (2015)

2. Johnson, D., Menezes, A., Vanstone, S.: The elliptic curve digital signature algorithm (ECDSA). IJIS **1**, 36–63 (2001)
3. Clavier, C., Feix, B., Gagnerot, G., Roussellet, M., Verneuil, V.: Horizontal correlation analysis on exponentiation. In: Soriano, M., Qing, S., López, J. (eds.) ICICS 2010. LNCS, vol. 6476, pp. 46–61. Springer, Heidelberg (2010). https://doi.org/10.1007/978-3-642-17650-0_5
4. Coron, J.-S.: Resistance against differential power analysis for elliptic curve cryptosystems. In: Koç, Ç.K., Paar, C. (eds.) CHES 1999. LNCS, vol. 1717, pp. 292–302. Springer, Heidelberg (1999). https://doi.org/10.1007/3-540-48059-5_25
5. Kabin, I., Dyka, Z., Kreiser, D., Langendoerfer, P.: Evaluation of resistance of ECC designs protected by different randomization countermeasures against horizontal DPA attacks. In: Proceedings of IEEE East-West Design Test Symposium (EWDTS2017) (2017)
6. Kabin, I., Dyka, Z., Kreiser, D., Langendoerfer, P.: Attack against montgomery kP implementation: horizontal address-bit DPA? In: Proceedings of the WiP Session of Euromicro Conference on Digital System Design (DSD2017) (2017)
7. Dyka, Z., Bock, E.A., Kabin, I., Langendoerfer, P.: Inherent resistance of efficient ECC designs against SCA attacks. In: 2016 8th IFIP International Conference on New Technologies, Mobility and Security (NTMS), pp. 1–5 (2016)
8. Kabin, I., Dyka, Z., Kreiser, D., Langendoerfer, P.: On the influence of hardware technologies on the vulnerability of protected ECC implementations. In: Proceedings of the WiP Session of Euromicro Conference on Digital System Design (DSD2016) (2016)
9. Montgomery, P.L.: Speeding the Pollard and elliptic curve methods of factorization. Math. Comp. **48**, 243–264 (1987)
10. López, J., Dahab, R.: Fast multiplication on elliptic curves over $GF(2^m)$ without precomputation. In: Koç, Çetin K., Paar, C. (eds.) CHES 1999. LNCS, vol. 1717, pp. 316–327. Springer, Heidelberg (1999). https://doi.org/10.1007/3-540-48059-5_27
11. Hankerson, D., López Hernandez, J., Menezes, A.: Software implementation of elliptic curve cryptography over binary fields. In: Koç, Ç.K., Paar, C. (eds.) CHES 2000. LNCS, vol. 1965, pp. 1–24. Springer, Heidelberg (2000). https://doi.org/10.1007/3-540-44499-8_1
12. Dyka, Z., Langendoerfer, P.: Area efficient hardware implementation of elliptic curve cryptography by iteratively applying Karatsuba's method. In: Design, Automation and Test in Europe, vol. 3, pp. 70–75 (2005)
13. Bauer, A., Jaulmes, E., Prouff, E., Wild, J.: Horizontal collision correlation attack on elliptic curves. In: Lange, T., Lauter, K., Lisoněk, P. (eds.) SAC 2013. LNCS, vol. 8282, pp. 553–570. Springer, Heidelberg (2014). https://doi.org/10.1007/978-3-662-43414-7_28
14. Dyka, Z.: Analysis and prediction of area- and energy-consumption of optimized polynomial multipliers in hardware for arbitrary $GF(2^n)$ for elliptic curve cryptography. Dissertation thesis, BTU Cottbus-Senftenberg (2013). https://opus4.kobv.de/opus4-btu/frontdoor/index/index/docId/2634
15. Madlener, F., Sötttinger, M., Huss, S.A.: Novel hardening techniques against differential power analysis for multiplication in GF(2ⁿ). In: 2009 International Conference on Field-Programmable Technology, pp. 328–334. IEEE (2009)
16. Stöttinger, M., Madlener, F., Huss, S.A.: Procedures for securing ECC implementations against differential power analysis using reconfigurable architectures. In: Platzner, M., Teich, J., Wehn, N. (eds.) Dynamically Reconfigurable Systems, pp. 395–415. Springer, Dordrecht (2010). https://doi.org/10.1007/978-90-481-3485-4_19
17. Dyka, Z., Wittke, C., Langendoerfer, P.: Clockwise randomization of the observable behaviour of crypto ASICs to counter side channel attacks. In: 2015 Euromicro Conference on Digital System Design, pp. 551–554 (2015)
18. Synopsis. PrimeTime. http://www.synopsys.com/Tools/

New Certificateless Public Key Encryption Secure Against Malicious KGC Attacks in the Standard Model

Wenjie Yang[1], Jian Weng[1(✉)], and Futai Zhang[2]

[1] College of Cyber Security/College of Information Science and Technology,
Jinan University, Guangzhou 510632, China
njnuywj@163.com, cryptjweng@gmail.com
[2] School of Computer Science and Technology,
Nanjing Normal University, Nanjing 210046, China
zhangfutai@njnu.edu.cn

Abstract. It is an interesting and challenging task to design an efficient certificateless encryption (CLE) scheme whose security can be proved without using random oracles. Although some CLE schemes claimed secure in the standard model have been available in the literature, we find most of the concrete constructions are in fact insecure. In this paper, we first demonstrate the insecurity of the CLE scheme introduced by Hwang and Liu in 2008. We show how a type II adversary breaks the indistinguishability of ciphertexts under chosen ciphertext attacks. We then propose a new concrete CLE scheme. Our new scheme can resist public key replacement attacks as well as malicious key generation center (KGC) attacks. We rigorously prove the security of our construction under the Decisional Bilinear Diffie-Hellman assumption in the standard model.

Keywords: Certificateless encryption scheme
Malicious KGC attack · Standard model

1 Introduction

Certificateless public key cryptography (CL-PKC), which was originally introduced by Al-Riyami and Paterson [1], represents an interesting and potentially useful balance between identity-based cryptography (ID-PKC) and public key cryptography (PKC) based on public key infrastructure (PKI). It eliminates the key escrow associated with identity-based cryptography without requiring the introduction of public key certificates. In CL-PKC, a key generation center (KGC) is involved in issuing partial private keys computed from the master secret for users. Each user also independently generates a secret value and the corresponding public key for itself. Cryptographic operations can then be performed successfully only when both a user partial private key and its secret value are obtained. An attacker who knows only one of them should not be able to impersonate the user to carry out any cryptographic operation such as decrypting or signing.

© Springer International Publishing AG, part of Springer Nature 2018
S. Qing et al. (Eds.): ICICS 2017, LNCS 10631, pp. 236–247, 2018.
https://doi.org/10.1007/978-3-319-89500-0_21

Since the KGC is no longer fully trusted, there are two different types of adversaries [1,8] in CL-PKC. A Type I adversary is able to compromise a user secret value and/or replace the user public key with some values chosen by the adversary. However, it does not know the user partial private key and the master secret key. Comparing with a Type I adversary, a Type II adversary knows the master secret key (and hence knows the partial private key of any user), but does not know the user secret value or being able to replace the user public key. Up to now, a number of CLE schemes [1,4,6,7,10,14,18] that can withstand the attacks of both types of adversaries have been available.

In 2007, Au et al. introduced the original concept of malicious key generation center [3] in CL-PKC. They pointed out that the malicious KGC is an important but seemingly previously neglected security concern in CL-PKC. In their improved security model, they allow the malicious KGC to launch the Type II attack at the beginning of the system initialization. That is the KGC may maliciously generate (by setting some trapdoors) the master public/secret key pair so that it may compromise the security of the resulting certificateless cryptosystem. As we no longer fully trust the KGC, a secure CL-PKC system should require that the KGC cannot get a non-negligible advantage in attacking a certificateless cryptosystem even if it is malicious. As all of those CLE schemes proposed before 2007 have an implicit assumption that the KGC always generates the master public/secret key pair honestly according to the scheme specification in their security model, most of them are insecure against malicious KGC attacks.

Since the introduction of malicious KGC, some attentions have been paid to the construction of secure CL-PKC systems which can withstand malicious KGC attacks. Several papers in this line of research have been available (The summary from the Table 1). In 2007, Huang et al. introduced the earliest secure generic CLE scheme (HW Scheme) [11] without random oracle. In 2008, Hwang et al. proposed a concrete CLE scheme (Hwang scheme) [13] in the standard model and claimed that their scheme was secure against the malicious KGC attack. Unfortunately, Zhang et al. later pointed out that Hwang scheme could not withstand the key replacement attack in [20]. Although Hwang et al. especially emphasize that their scheme could resist malicious KGC attacks, we find that the Hwang scheme is not secure against a traditional type II adversary/malicious KGC. In 2009, Zhang et al. presented a CLE scheme (ZW scheme) with a shorter public key without using random oracle. They proved the security of their scheme in the standard model and claimed it could resist malicious KGC attacks. Regrettably, Shen et al. [15] remarked that Zhang et al.'s security proof is not sound and their security conclusion is wrong. They showed that the ZW scheme is vulnerable to attacks of an ordinary type II adversary let alone malicious KGC attacks. In 2010, Huang et al. also proposed an improved generic CLE scheme [12] in the standard model. Unfortunately, they still did not give a concrete CLE scheme. As far as we know, until 2014, Yang et al. [19] constructed a CLE scheme secure against malicious KGC without random oracles (YZ scheme). Nevertheless, its security depends on the total number of partial private key extraction queries made by an adversary. So, it seems that there are few concrete secure CLE schemes withstanding malicious KGC attacks.

Table 1. Security comparison

CLE scheme		Type I	Type II*	Type II	Standard
Generic	HW scheme	Y	Y	Y	Y
Concrete	LQ scheme	Y	Y	Y	N
	Hwang scheme	N	N	N	Y
	ZW scheme	Y	N	N	Y
	YZ scheme	Y	Y	Y	Y
	Our scheme	Y	Y	Y	Y

Type II*: Honest-but-curious KGC. Type II: Malicious-but-passive KGC. Standard: Standard model.

In this paper, we first demonstrate that Hwang et al.'s security proof in [13] is not sound by giving concrete Type II attacks according to their security model. We then present a new CLE scheme and rigorously prove that our construction is secure against both Type I adversaries and malicious KGCs under the Decisional Bilinear Diffie-Hellman assumption without random oracles.

Note that, it seems to be somewhat *self-contradictory* [11] if we require a certificateless encryption scheme to be secure against both the Type I adversaries with access to the strong decryption oracle and the malicious KGC adversaries. The reason is as follows. If a type I adversary is allowed to assess the strong decryption oracle, the challenger (who knows the master secret) can successfully answer the decryption queries without knowing the secret value corresponding to the public key used in producing the ciphertext. Then, employing the same strategy as the strong decryption oracle for type I adversaries, the malicious KGC should also be able to decrypt any ciphertext. Based on this observation, in our security model, if the public key has been replaced, when making some decryption queries or private key extraction queries, the Type I adversaries are required to provide the corresponding secret value to the challenger. That is, the Type I adversary cannot access to the strong decryption oracle.

The rest of this paper is organized as follows. Some preliminaries and the security notions for CLE schemes are given in Sect. 2. Then, the insecurity of the Hwang scheme against type II adversaries is analyzed in Sect. 3. Our new CLE scheme is put forward in Sect. 4. And in Sect. 5 we give security analysis and performance analysis of our new scheme. Finally we present our conclusions in Sect. 6.

2   Preliminaries

We briefly introduce some basic notions used in this paper, namely bilinear pairings, complexity assumptions and the basic concepts of certificateless public key encryption schemes.

2.1   Bilinear Pairings and Complexity Assumptions

Definition 1 (Bilinear Pairing). *Suppose G and G_T are two multiplicative cyclic groups of the same prime order p. We call a map $\hat{e} : G \times G \to G_T$ a bilinear pairing (or a bilinear map) if it satisfies the following conditions:*

1. *Bilinearity: $\hat{e}(u^a, v^b) = \hat{e}(u,v)^{ab}$ for all $u, v \in G$ and all $a, b \in Z_p^*$.*
2. *Non-degeneracy: $\hat{e}(u,u) \neq 1$ for some $u \in G$.*
3. *Computability: for any $u, v \in G$, $\hat{e}(u,v)$ can be computed efficiently.*

Next, we recall the following intractability assumptions related to the security of our scheme.

Definition 2 (Decisional Bilinear Diffie-Hellman (DBDH) Assumption). *Let $(G, G_T, \hat{e})$ be groups and a bilinear map as in definition 1. Let $a, b, c, z \in Z_p^*$ be chosen at random and g be a generator of G. The (t, ϵ)-DBDH assumption in $(G, G_T, \hat{e})$ is that no probabilistic polynomial-time algorithm $\mathcal{A}$ can distinguish the tuple $(A = g^a, B = g^b, C = g^c, \hat{e}(g,g)^{abc})$ from the tuple $(A = g^a, B = g^b, C = g^c, \hat{e}(g,g)^z)$ with a non-negligible advantage ϵ in time t, where the advantage of $\mathcal{A}$ is defined as*

$$Adv_{\mathcal{A}}^{DBDH} = |Pr[\mathcal{A}(g, g^a, g^b, g^c, \hat{e}(g,g)^{abc}) = 1]$$
$$-Pr[\mathcal{A}(g, g^a, g^b, g^c, \hat{e}(g,g)^z) = 1]|$$

Definition 3 (Collision Resistant (CR) Assumption). *A hash function $H \leftarrow \mathcal{H}(k)$ is collision resistant if for all PPT algorithms $\mathcal{A}$ the advantage*

$$Adv_A^{CR}(k) = Pr[H(x) = H(y) \wedge x \neq y | (x,y) \leftarrow \mathcal{A}(1^k, H) \wedge H \leftarrow \mathcal{H}(k)]$$

is negligible as a function of the security parameter.

2.2   Security Definitions

A certificateless public key encryption scheme [1] is specified by seven algorithms: **Setup**(1^k), **ExtPPriK**(mpk, msk, ID), **SetSecV**(mpk, ID), **SetPubK**(mpk, sv_{ID}), **SetPriK**(mpk, sv_{ID}, d_{ID}), **Encrypt**(mpk, PK_{ID}, ID, M), **Decrypt**(mpk, SK_{ID}, C). The description of each algorithm is as follows:

- **Setup**(1^k): Taking a security parameter k as input, the KGC runs this probabilistic polynomial time (PPT) algorithm to output a randomly chosen master secret key msk and a master public key mpk.
- **ExtPPriK**(mpk, msk, ID): Taking the master public key mpk, the master secret key msk, and a user's identity ID as input, the KGC runs this PPT algorithm to generate the partial private key d_{ID} for the user with identity ID.
- **SetSecV**(mpk, ID): Taking the master public key mpk and a user's identity ID as input, the user with identity ID runs this PPT algorithm to output a secret value sv_{ID}.

- **SetPubK**(mpk, ID, sv_{ID}): Taking the master public key mpk and the user's secret value sv_{ID} as input, the user with identity ID runs this algorithm to output a public key PK_{ID}.
- **SetPriK**(mpk, sv_{ID}, d_{ID}): Taking the master public key mpk, the user's secret key sv_{ID}, and the user's partial private key d_{ID} as input, the user with identity ID runs this PPT algorithm to generate a private key SK_{ID}.
- **Encrypt**(mpk, PK_{ID}, ID, M): Taking a plaintext M, the master public key mpk, a user's identity ID and its public key PK_{ID} as input, a sender runs this PPT algorithm to create a ciphertext C.
- **Decrypt**(mpk, SK_{ID}, C): Taking the master public key mpk, the user's private key SK_{ID}, and a ciphertext C as input, the user as a recipient runs this *deterministic algorithm* to get a decryption σ, which is either a plaintext message or a "reject" message.

IND-CLE-CCA2 security:

As defined in [1], there are two types of security for a CLE scheme, Type I security and Type II security, along with two types of adversaries, $\mathcal{A}_I$ and $\mathcal{A}_{II}$ [1] respectively. The original model believes that the KGC honestly generates the master public key and master secret key pairs. However, in our security model, the KGC can maliciously generate them [3] by setting some trapdoors. Therefore, we allow a type II adversary generate all public parameters in any way it favours, which matches better with the original motivation of the CL-PKC.

Definition 4 (IND-CLE-CCA2). *A certificateless public key encryption scheme is semantically secure against an adaptive chosen cipher-text attack (IND-CLE-CCA2 secure) if no PPT adversary $\mathcal{A}$ of Type I or Type II has a non-negligible advantage in the following game played against the challenger:*

(1) If $\mathcal{A}$ is a Type I attacker, the challenger takes a security parameter k and runs the Setup algorithm of the CLE scheme. It gives $\mathcal{A}$ the master public key mpk, and keeps the master secret key msk to itself. Otherwise, the challenger invokes $\mathcal{A}$ (type II adversary, it may be a malicious KGC)to get mpk and msk.
(2) $\mathcal{A}$ is given access to the following oracles:
   Request Public Key $\mathcal{O}_{PubK}(ID)$: With a user's ID as input, the oracle computes $sv_{ID} = SetSecV(mpk, ID)$ and $PK_{ID} = SetPubK(mpk, ID, sv_{ID})$. It returns PK_{ID} to $\mathcal{A}$.
   Extract Partial Private Key $\mathcal{O}_{ParPriK}(ID)$: With a user's ID as input, compute $d_{ID} = ExtPPriK (mpk, msk, ID)$. Return d_{ID} to $\mathcal{A}$. (Note that this is only useful to a Type I attacker.)
   Extarct Private Key $\mathcal{O}_{PriK}(ID)$: With a user's ID as input, compute $SK_{ID} = SetPriK(mpk, d_{ID}, sv_{ID})$, then return it to $\mathcal{A}$. Note that if the corresponding public key has been replaced by the Type I attacker, when making the private key request query, the attacker $\mathcal{A}$ is required to provide the corresponding secret value sv_{ID} to the challenger.

Replace Public Key $\mathcal{O}_{RepPK}(ID, PK_{ID})$**:** With a user's identity ID and a valid public key PK_{ID} as input, replace the public key of user ID with PK_{ID} and return $\top$ if PK_{ID} is not a valid public key. Otherwise, return $\bot$. (Note that this is only useful to a Type I attacker.)

Request Decrypt $\mathcal{O}_{Dec}(ID, PK_{ID}, C)$**:** On input an identity ID, a public key PK_{ID}, together With a ciphertext C, compute $m = Decrypt(mpk, SK_{ID}, C)$ and return it to $\mathcal{A}$ if σ is a valid ciphertext, where SK_{ID} is the secret key corresponding to PK_{ID}. Otherwise, return $\bot$. Note that if the corresponding public key has been replaced, the Type I attacker is required to provide the corresponding secret value sv_{ID} to the challenger $\mathcal{C}$ in order to correctly decrypt the ciphertext under the replaced public key.

(3) After making the oracle queries a polynomial number of times, $\mathcal{A}$ outputs and submits two messages (M_0, M_1), together with an identity ID^*. The challenger picks a random bit b from $\{0, 1\}$ and computes the challenging ciphertext $C^* = Encrypt(mpk, PK_{ID^*}, ID^*, M_b)$ and delivers it to $\mathcal{A}$.

(4) $\mathcal{A}$ makes a new sequence of queries as in Step(2).

(5) $\mathcal{A}$ outputs a bit b' as its guess to b. $\mathcal{A}$ wins the game if $b' = b$ and the following conditions are satisfied:
   - At any time, ID^* has not been submitted to extract the private key.
   - In Step(4), $\mathcal{O}_{Dec}(ID^*, PK_{ID^*}, C^*)$ has not been submitted for Decryption.
   - With a Type I attacker, ID^* has not been submitted to both the Replace Public Key before Step(3) and the Extract Partial Private Key at any step.

We define $\mathcal{A}$'s advantage in this game as

$$Adv_{CLE}^{IND-CCA2}(\mathcal{A}) = |Pr[b' = b] - \frac{1}{2}|$$

3 Security Analysis of Hwang Scheme

In this section, we show that the Hwang scheme [13] is insecure against the attack of ordinary type II adversaries, and hence cannot withstand malicious KGC attacks.

3.1 Review of Hwang Scheme

Setup(1^k)**:** The KGC chooses groups G and G_T of prime order p such that a pairing $\hat{e} : G \times G \to G_T$ can be constructed and selects a generator g of G. It picks random values $\alpha, \beta, \mu', \mu_1, \ldots, \mu_n, \nu', \nu_1, \ldots, \nu_n$ in Z_p^* and computes $g_1 = g^\alpha$, $h = \hat{e}(g^\alpha, g^\beta)$, $u' = g^{\mu'}$, $u_1 = g^{\mu_1}, \ldots, u_n = g^{\mu_n}$, $v' = g^{\nu'}$, $v_1 = g^{\nu_1}, \ldots, v_n = g^{\nu_n}$, where n is the length of an identity in binary string representation. Let $H : \{0, 1\}^* \to \{0, 1\}^n$ be a collision-resistant hash function. The master public key is $mpk = (\hat{e}, G, G_T, g, g_1, h, u', u_1, \ldots, u_n, v', v_1, \ldots, v_n, H)$ and the master secret key is $msk = (\alpha, \beta, \mu', \mu_1, \ldots, \mu_n, \nu', \nu_1, \ldots, \nu_n)$.

ExtPPriK(mpk, msk, ID): Let ID be a bit string of length n and $ID[i]$ be its i-th bit. Let $\mathcal{U} \subset \{1, 2, \ldots, n\}$ be the set of indices i such that $ID[i] = 1$. The KGC picks a random value $r \in Z_p^*$ and computes

$$d_{ID} = (psk_1, psk_2) = (g_1^\beta \cdot F_u(ID)^r, g^r) \qquad where \quad F_u(ID) = u' \prod_{i \in \mathcal{U}} u_i.$$

d_{ID} is secretly delivered to the user with identity ID as its partial private key.

SetSecV(mpk, ID): The user with identity ID Picks at random an $x_{ID} \in Z_p^*$ as its secret value sv_{ID}.

SetPubK(mpk, ID, sv_{ID}): The user with identity ID computes its public key $pk_{ID} = (X_{ID}, \sigma_{ID})$, where $X_{ID} = h^{x_{ID}}$ and σ_{ID} is the Schnorr one-time signature using x_{ID} as the signing key and $(h, X_{ID} = h^{x_{ID}})$ as the verification key. (The message can be any arbitrary string which can be included in mpk. The signature can be generated using the technique of Fiat-Shamir transform without random oracles as described in [5].)

SetPriK(mpk, sv_{ID}, d_{ID}): The user ID picks r' randomly from Z_p^* and computes the private key $SK_{ID} = (sk_1, sk_2)$ as

$$(sk_1, sk_2) = (psk_1^{x_{ID}} \cdot F_u(ID)^{r'}, psk_2^{x_{ID}} \cdot g^{r'}) = (g_1^{\beta x_{ID}} \cdot F_u(ID)^{rx_{ID}+r'}, g^{rx_{ID}+r'}).$$

Encrypt(mpk, PK_{ID}, ID, m): To encrypt $m \in G_T$, first check whether the public key X_{ID} is correctly formed, by checking whether σ_{ID} is a valid signature using (h, X_{ID}) as the verification key. If not, output $\perp$ and abort the algorithm. Otherwise, select a random value $s \in Z_p^*$ and compute

$$C = (C_0, C_1, C_2, C_3) = (m \cdot (X_{ID})^s, g^s, F_u(ID)^s, F_v(w)^s)$$

where $w = H(C_0, C_1, C_2, ID, PK_{ID}) \in \{0, 1\}^n$ and $F_v(w) = v' \prod_{j=1}^n v_j^{w_j}$.

Decrypt(mpk, SK_{ID}, C): For a ciphertext $C = (C_0, C_1, C_2, C_3)$, check that

$$\hat{e}(C_1, F_u(ID) \cdot F_v(w)) = \hat{e}(g, C_2 C_3)$$

where $w = H(C_0, C_1, C_2, ID, PK_{ID}) \in \{0, 1\}^n$. If not, output $\perp$. Otherwise, compute

$$m = C_0 \cdot \hat{e}(C_2, sk_2) / \hat{e}(C_1, sk_1).$$

3.2   Analysis of Hwang Scheme

Hwang et al. [13] claimed their scheme is semantically secure even in the strengthened model considering the malicious KGC attack. Unfortunately, their conclusion is not sound. We show a concrete type II attack to their scheme which indicates Hwang scheme is vulnerable to type II adversaries including malicious KGCs. Our attack is depicted as follows.

- If the adversary $\mathcal{A}_{II}$ is an ordinary type II adversary, the challenger $\mathcal{C}$ takes a security parameter k and runs the **Setup** algorithm. It gives $\mathcal{A}_{II}$ the master secret key msk and publishes the master public key mpk. If the adversary $\mathcal{A}_{II}$ is a malicious KGC, the challenger $\mathcal{C}$ invokes $\mathcal{A}_{II}$ to get mpk and msk.
- In phase 1, adversary $\mathcal{A}_{II}$ needs not to issue any query.
- In the challenge phase, the adversary $\mathcal{A}_{II}$ picks uniformly at random an identity ID^* and two plaintexts $M_0, M_1 \in G_T^2$. Then, $\mathcal{A}_{II}$ is given a challenge ciphertext $C^* = Encrypt(mpk, pk_{ID^*}, ID^*, M_\gamma)$, where γ is the random bit chosen from $\{0,1\}$ by the challenger. Recall that $\mathcal{A}_{II}$'s goal is to correctly guess the value γ. Note that according to algorithm $Encrypt$, the ciphertext $C^* = (C_0^*, C_1^*, C_2^*, C_3^*)$ is of the following form:

$$C_0^* = M_\gamma \cdot (X_{ID^*})^s, C_1^* = g^s, C_2^* = F_u(ID^*)^s, C_3^* = F_v(w_\gamma^*)^s = (v' \prod_{j \in W^*_\gamma} v_j)^s$$

where $s \in_R Z_p^*$, $w_\gamma^* = H(C_0^*, C_1^*, C_2^*, ID^*, pk_{ID^*}) \in \{0,1\}^n$ and $W_\gamma^* = \{j|w_\gamma^*[j] = 1, 1, 2, \ldots, n\}$.

- In phase 2, adversary $\mathcal{A}_{II}$ first randomly picks $s' \in Z_p^*$ and generates another ciphertext $C' = (C_0', C_1', C_2', C_3')$ with

$$C_0' = C_0^* \cdot (X_{ID})^{s'}, C_1' = C_1^* \cdot g^{s'}, C_2' = C_2^* \cdot F_u(ID^*)^{s'},$$

$$C_3' = (C_1')^{v' + \sum_{j \in W_\gamma'} v_j} = F_v(w_\gamma')^{s+s'},$$

where $w_\gamma' = H(C_0', C_1', C_2', ID^*, pk_{ID^*}) \in \{0,1\}^n$ and $W_\gamma' = \{j|w_\gamma'[j] = 1, j = 1, 2, \ldots, n\}$.

Note that $C' = (C_0', C_1', C_2', C_3')$ is another valid ciphertext of message M_γ encrypted under identity ID and the public key PK_{ID}.

Next, the adversary $\mathcal{A}_{II}$ issues a decryption query $\mathcal{O}_{Dec}(ID^*, PK_{ID^*}, C')$. That is it submits the ciphertext C' to the challenger for decryption under the identity ID^* and the public key PK_{ID^*}. Recall that according to the restrictions specified in the security model, it is legal for $\mathcal{A}_{II}$ to issue such a query since $C^* \neq C'$. So, the challenger has to return the underlying message M_γ to $\mathcal{A}_{II}$. With M_γ, adversary $\mathcal{A}_{II}$ can certainly know the value γ, and then wins in the game. Thus, the Hwang scheme is insecure against chosen ciphertext attack of a type II adversary including malicious KGC.

4 Our CLE Scheme

Our new scheme below is motivated from the identity-based encryption scheme proposed by Waters [16]. In our scheme, the user partial private key and the user secret value are generated and used fully independently, while retaining high efficiency. Intuitively, an attacker cannot re-random or decrypt any ciphertext instead of the user if the attacker just has one of the two parts.

Setup(1^k): Let (G, G_T) be bilinear map groups of prime order $p > 2^k$ and let g be a generator of G. Set $g_1 = g^\alpha$, for a random $\alpha \in Z_p^*$, and pick at random a group element $g_2 \in G$ and vectors $(u', u_1, \ldots, u_n)$, $(v', v_1, \ldots, v_n) \in G^{n+1}$. These vectors define the hash functions

$$F_u(ID) = u' \prod_{j=1}^{n} u_j^{ID_j} \quad and \quad F_v(w) = v' \prod_{j=1}^{n} v_j^{w_j}$$

where $ID = ID_1 ID_2 \ldots ID_n$ and $w = w_1 w_2 \ldots w_n$ are bit-strings of length n. The KGC also selects a collision-resistant hash function $H : \{0, 1\}^* \to \{0, 1\}^n$. The master public key is $mpk = (g, g_1, g_2, u', u_1, \ldots, u_n, v', v_1, \ldots, v_n)$, the message space is G_T, and the master secret is $msk = g_2^\alpha$.

ExtPPriK(mpk, msk, ID): Pick at random $r \in Z_p^*$ and return $d_{ID} = (d_0, d_1) = (g_2^\alpha \cdot F_u(ID)^r, g^r)$.

SetSecV(mpk, ID): Pick at random $x_0, x_1 \in_R Z_p^*$ and return $sv_{ID} = (x_0, x_1)$.

SetPubK(mpk, ID, sv_{ID}): Return $PK_{ID} = (pk_0, pk_1) = (g^{x_0}, g^{x_1})$.

SetPriK(mpk, sv_{ID}, d_{ID}): Set $SK_{ID} = (sv_{ID}, d_{ID}) = (x_0, x_1, d_0, d_1)$.

Encrypt(mpk, PK_{ID}, ID, M): To encrypt $M \in_R G_T$, parse PK_{ID} as (pk_0, pk_1). Choose $s, t \in_R Z_p^*$ uniformly at random and compute

$$\begin{aligned} C &= (C_0, C_1, C_2, C_3, C_4) \\ &= (M \cdot \hat{e}(pk_0, pk_1)^{-t} \cdot \hat{e}(g_1, g_2)^s, \hat{e}(g, g)^t, g^s, F_u(ID)^s, F_v(w)^s), \end{aligned}$$

where $w = H(C_0, C_1, C_2, C_3, PK_{ID}, ID, \hat{e}(pk_0, g)^t)$.

Decrypt(mpk, SK_{ID}, C): Parse C as $(C_0, C_1, C_2, C_3, C_4)$ and the private key SK_{ID} as (x_0, x_1, d_0, d_1). Then compute

$$K = C_1^{x_0} = \hat{e}(g, g)^{t x_0} = \hat{e}(pk_0, g)^t, \text{ and } w = H(C_0, C_1, C_2, C_3, PK_{ID},$$
$ID, K)$. Check that

$$\hat{e}(C_2, F_u(ID) \cdot F_v(w)) \overset{?}{=} \hat{e}(g, C_3 \cdot C_4).$$

Reject C if the equation does not hold. Otherwise, return

$$M = C_0 \cdot K^{x_1} \cdot \hat{e}(C_3, d_1) \cdot \hat{e}(C_2, d_0)^{-1}.$$

5   Analysis of the Scheme

5.1   Correctness

The correctness of the scheme can be directly verified by the following equations.

$$\begin{aligned} \hat{e}(C_2, F_u(ID) \cdot F_v(w)) &= \hat{e}(g^s, F_u(ID) \cdot F_v(w)) \\ &= \hat{e}(g, F_u(ID)^s \cdot F_v(w)^s) \\ &= \hat{e}(g, C_3 \cdot C_4), \end{aligned}$$

and

$$C_0 \cdot K^{x_1} \cdot \hat{e}(C_3, d_1) \cdot \hat{e}(C_2, d_0)^{-1}$$
$$= C_0 \cdot (\hat{e}(pk_0, g)^t)^{x_1} \cdot \hat{e}(F_u(ID)^s, g^r) \cdot \hat{e}(g^s, g_2^\alpha \cdot F_u(ID)^r)^{-1}$$
$$= C_0 \cdot \hat{e}(pk_0, pk_1)^t \cdot \hat{e}(g_1, g_2)^{-s}$$
$$= M \cdot \hat{e}(pk_0, pk_1)^{-t} \cdot \hat{e}(g_1, g_2)^s \cdot \hat{e}(pk_0, pk_1)^t \cdot \hat{e}(g_1, g_2)^{-s}$$
$$= M.$$

5.2 Security

For more details about security analysis, the readers are referred to the full version of this paper.

5.3 Performance Analysis

Here, we compare the major computational cost and security properties of our scheme with some available concrete CLE schemes that are claimed to be secure against malicious KGC attacks. The comparison is listed in Table 1. All the schemes involve three major operations: Pairing, Multiplication and Exponentiation (in G and G_T). For ease of analysis, we only count the number of those operations in the Encrypt and Decrypt phases. For the security properties, we consider the confidentiality against the Type I adversaries and the Type II adversaries respectively. Note that, in the table, the symbol (n) in pairing column denotes the number of pairing operations is independent of the message and can be pre-computed.

Table 2. Performance analysis

CLE scheme	Multiplication		Exponentiation		Pairing		Type I	Type II
	Enc	Dec	Enc	Dec	Enc	Dec		
Hwang scheme	$2n+1$	$2n+3$	4	0	0	4	N	N
ZW scheme	3	4	6	4	(4)	2	Y	N
Our scheme	$2n+2$	$2n+5$	7	2	(4)	4	Y	Y

Table 2 shows that, although the computational cost of our scheme is relatively high, our scheme overcomes the security weaknesses of the previous schemes [13,20]. On the face of it, the ZW scheme has the advantages of a short public key and a higher computational efficiency. Unfortunately, the ZW scheme is not only insecure against type II adversaries, but also relies on *a stronger assumption*.

6 Conclusion

In this paper, we have shown that the CLE scheme introduced by Hwang and Liu is vulnerable to the attacks from the type II adversaries including malicious KGC. Furthermore, we have put forward a new concrete CLE scheme and proved its security against both types of adversaries including malicious KGC. Our security proofs have been rigorously presented in the standard model under the Decisional Bilinear Diffie-Hellman assumption.

Acknowledgments. This work was supported by National Science Foundation of China (Grant Nos. 61373158, 61472165 and 61732021), Guangdong Provincial Engineering Technology Research Center on Network Security Detection and Defence (Grant No. 2014B090904067), Guangdong Provincial Special Funds for Applied Technology Research and Development and Transformation of Important Scientific and Technological Achieve (Grant No. 2016B010124009), the Zhuhai Top Discipline– Information Security, Guangzhou Key Laboratory of Data Security and Privacy Preserving, Guangdong Key Laboratory of Data Security and Privacy Preserving.

References

1. Al-Riyami, S.S., Paterson, K.G.: Certificateless public key cryptography. In: Laih, C.-S. (ed.) ASIACRYPT 2003. LNCS, vol. 2894, pp. 452–473. Springer, Heidelberg (2003). https://doi.org/10.1007/978-3-540-40061-5_29
2. Al-Riyami, S.S., Paterson, K.G.: CBE from CL-PKE: a generic construction and efficient schemes. In: Vaudenay, S. (ed.) PKC 2005. LNCS, vol. 3386, pp. 398–415. Springer, Heidelberg (2005). https://doi.org/10.1007/978-3-540-30580-4_27
3. Au, M., Chen, J., Liu, J., Mu, Y., Wong, D., Yang G.: Malicious KGC attacks in certificateless cryptography. In: Deng, R., Samarati, P. (eds.) ASIACCS 2007, pp. 302–311. ACM Press (2007)
4. Baek, J., Safavi-Naini, R., Susilo, W.: Certificateless public key encryption without pairing. In: Zhou, J., Lopez, J., Deng, R.H., Bao, F. (eds.) ISC 2005. LNCS, vol. 3650, pp. 134–148. Springer, Heidelberg (2005). https://doi.org/10.1007/11556992_10
5. Bellare, M., Shoup, S.: Two-tier signatures, strongly unforgeable signatures, and fiat-shamir without random oracles. In: Okamoto, T., Wang, X. (eds.) PKC 2007. LNCS, vol. 4450, pp. 201–216. Springer, Heidelberg (2007). https://doi.org/10.1007/978-3-540-71677-8_14
6. Bentahar, K., Farshim, P., Malone-Lee, J., Smart, N.: Generic construction of identity-based and certificateless KEMs. Cryptology ePrint Archive: Report 2005/058 (2005). http://eprint.iacr.org/2005/058
7. Cheng, Z., Comley, R.: Efficient certificateless public key encryption. Cryptology ePrint Archive: Report 2005/012 (2005). http://eprint.iacr.org/2005/012
8. Dent, A.: A survey of certificateless encryption schemes and security models. Cryptology ePrint Archive, Report 2006/211 (2006)
9. Dent, A.W., Libert, B., Paterson, K.G.: Certificateless encryption schemes strongly secure in the standard model. In: Cramer, R. (ed.) PKC 2008. LNCS, vol. 4939, pp. 344–359. Springer, Heidelberg (2008). https://doi.org/10.1007/978-3-540-78440-1_20

10. Huang, X., Susilo, W., Mu, Y., Zhang, F.: On the security of certificateless signature schemes from Asiacrypt 2003. In: Desmedt, Y.G., Wang, H., Mu, Y., Li, Y. (eds.) CANS 2005. LNCS, vol. 3810, pp. 13–25. Springer, Heidelberg (2005). https://doi.org/10.1007/11599371_2

11. Huang, Q., Wong, D.S.: Generic certificateless encryption in the standard model. In: Miyaji, A., Kikuchi, H., Rannenberg, K. (eds.) IWSEC 2007. LNCS, vol. 4752, pp. 278–291. Springer, Heidelberg (2007). https://doi.org/10.1007/978-3-540-75651-4_19

12. Huang, Q., Wong, D.: Generic certificateless encryption secure against malicious-but-passive KGC attacks in the standard model. J. Comput. Sci. Technol. **25**(4), 807–826 (2010)

13. Hwang, Y., Liu, J.: Certificateless public key encryption secure against malicious KGC attacks in the standard model. J. Univ. Comput. Sci. **14**(3), 463–480 (2008)

14. Libert, B., Quisquater, J.-J.: On constructing certificateless cryptosystems from identity based encryption. In: Yung, M., Dodis, Y., Kiayias, A., Malkin, T. (eds.) PKC 2006. LNCS, vol. 3958, pp. 474–490. Springer, Heidelberg (2006). https://doi.org/10.1007/11745853_31

15. Shen, L., Zhang, F., Li, S.: Cryptanalysis of a certificateless encryption scheme in the standard model. In: 4th International Conference on Intelligent Networking and Collaborative Systems, INCos 2012 (2012)

16. Waters, B.: Efficient identity-based encryption without random oracles. In: Cramer, R. (ed.) EUROCRYPT 2005. LNCS, vol. 3494, pp. 114–127. Springer, Heidelberg (2005). https://doi.org/10.1007/11426639_7

17. Weng, J., Yao, G., Deng, R., Chen, M., Li, X.: Cryptanalysis of a certificateless signcryption scheme in the standard model. Inf. Sci. **181**(3), 661–667 (2011)

18. Yum, D.H., Lee, P.J.: Generic construction of certificateless signature. In: Wang, H., Pieprzyk, J., Varadharajan, V. (eds.) ACISP 2004. LNCS, vol. 3108, pp. 200–211. Springer, Heidelberg (2004). https://doi.org/10.1007/978-3-540-27800-9_18

19. Yang, W., Zhang, F., Shen, L.: Efficient certificateless encryption withstanding attacks from malicious KGC without using random oracles. Secur. Commun. Netw. **7**(2), 445–454 (2014)

20. Zhang, G., Wang, X.: Certificateless encryption scheme secure in standard model. Tsinghua Sci. Technol. **14**(4), 452–459 (2009)

A Lattice Attack on Homomorphic NTRU with Non-invertible Public Keys

Soyoung Ahn[1], Hyang-Sook Lee[1]([⊠]) (iD), Seongan Lim[2]([⊠]) (iD),
and Ikkwon Yie[3]([⊠])

[1] Department of Mathematics, Ewha Womans University, Seoul, Korea
syahn921@gmail.com, hsl@ewha.ac.kr
[2] Institute of Mathematical Sciences, Ewha Womans University, Seoul, Korea
seongannym@ewha.ac.kr
[3] Department of Mathematics, Inha University, Incheon, Korea
ikyie@inha.ac.kr

Abstract. In 2011, Stehlé and Steinfeld modified the original NTRU to
get a provably IND-CPA secure NTRU under the hardness assumption of
standard worst-case problems over ideal lattices. In 2012, López-Alt et al.
proposed the first multikey fully homomorphic encryption scheme based
on the IND-CPA secure NTRU. Interestingly, this homomorphic NTRU
and subsequent homomorphic variants of NTRU removed the condition
'invertible public key' of the underlying IND-CPA secure NTRU. In this
paper, we investigate the security influence of using non-invertible public
key in the homomorphic NTRU. As a result, we present how to mount
a lattice attack to message recovery for the homomorphic NTRU when
the public key is non-invertible. Our result suggests that using invertible
public keys in the homomorphic NTRU is necessary for its security.

Keywords: NTRU · Homomorphic NTRU · IND-CPA security
Lattices · LLL algorithm

1 Introduction

The NTRU encryption scheme designed by Hoffstein et al. [6] is considered as
a reasonable alternative to the public key encryption schemes based on either
integer factorization or discrete logarithm. Since its first introduction, minor
changes of the parameter to avoid known attacks have been added. Even with
its computational efficiency and standardization of the NTRU [11], a provably
secure version was not known until Stehlé et al. proposed a modification of the
original NTRU in the year 2011 [10]. The IND-CPA security of their modification is proven in the standard model under the hardness assumption of standard
worst-case problems over ideal lattices [10]. Reflecting the continued progress
in the research on quantum computing, researches on transitioning to quantum
resistant algorithms become very active. Moreover, NIST has initiated a standardization process in post-quantum cryptography. The IND-CPA secure version
of NTRU could be a strong candidate for the standardization of post-quantum
public key encryption. The security proof of the IND-CPA secure NTRU was

© Springer International Publishing AG, part of Springer Nature 2018
S. Qing et al. (Eds.): ICICS 2017, LNCS 10631, pp. 248–254, 2018.
https://doi.org/10.1007/978-3-319-89500-0_22

given in [10] under the assumption that the public key is an invertible polynomial in $R_q = \mathbb{Z}[x]/\langle q, x^n+1\rangle$, however, no such result is known for 'non-invertible' public key. López-Alt et al. observed that the IND-CPA secure NTRU can be made fully homomorphic and proposed the first multikey homomorphic encryption scheme for a bounded number of users [8]. Notably, the homomorphic NTRU [8] and its subsequent versions [3,9] do not assume invertible public keys. If q is a prime number and n is a power of 2 with $q = 1 \bmod 2n$, then there is a ring isomorphism between R_q and $\mathbb{Z}_q^n$ and the number of non-invertible elements in R_q is $q^n - (q-1)^n$.

In this paper, we investigate the security influence of using non-invertible public key in the homomorphic NTRU. We present a very effective lattice attack for message recovery on the homomorphic NTRU when the public key is not invertible. The message space of the homomorphic NTRU is $\{0,1\}$ which implies that the IND-CPA security is equivalent to the security against the message recovery attack. We interpret the message recovery attack as solving a system of linear equations under some condition over a finite field $\mathbb{Z}_q$ using $\beta(x) = \frac{x^n+1}{\gcd(h(x),x^n+1)} \in \mathbb{Z}_q[x]$ for any non-invertible public key $pk = h(x)$. For a proof of successful message recovery in general, we used a sequence of sublattices of the target lattice and showed that there is an optimal sublattice which gives the desired short vector by the LLL algorithm if the degree of $\deg \beta(x) \leq \frac{\log q}{4}$ in the homomorphic NTRU. Moreover, it is known that the actual shortest output vector of the LLL algorithm could be much shorter than its theoretical bound. In fact, our experiments using MLLL(Modified LLL) in [4] give much shorter vector than the theoretical bound and this suggests that avoiding $\beta(x)$ to have small degree is not enough to guarantee the security of the homomorphic NTRU under message recovery attack. Therefore we conclude that setting the public key of the homomorphic NTRU as an invertible polynomial in R_q is desirable since the security against message recovery attack is a minimal requirement for encryption scheme. We note that some lattice attacks called by the subfield attacks on NTRU cryptosystem were proposed by Cheon et al. [5] and Albrecht et al. [1] and the goal of the subfield attack is to recover private key which can be understood as a short vector of the NTRU lattice. Their subfield attacks are based on the fact that there exist subfields that allow to reduce the dimension of the NTRU lattice and successful when the modulus q is exponential in n. Contrary to [1,5], the goal of our lattice attack is the message recovery when the public key is non-invertible.

The rest of the paper is organized as follows. In Sect. 2, we review some basics of this paper. In Sect. 3, we show that how to mount the message recovery attack to be successful if the public key is not invertible. In Sect. 4, we conclude our paper.

2 Preliminaries

2.1 The Basic Scheme of Homomorphic NTRU

The homomorphic NTRU is defined on the ring $R_q = \mathbb{Z}[x]/\langle q, x^n + 1\rangle$ for q is a prime number and n is a power of two. Any element $k(x) \in R_q$ is represented as $k(x) = \sum_{i=0}^{n-1} k_i x^i$, where $-\frac{q}{2} < k_i < \frac{q}{2}$. For the ring $R = \mathbb{Z}[x]/\langle x^n + 1 \rangle$, we denote $k(x) \leftarrow \chi_\epsilon$ for an appropriate distribution χ_ϵ and each coefficient $|k_i| \leq \epsilon$ of $k(x)$ if $k(x) \leftarrow \chi_\epsilon$. In the homomorphic version in [8], it is assumed that $q = 2^{n^\delta}$ with $0 < \delta < 1$ and the message space is $\{0,1\}$ while it was considered that $q = poly(n)$ with the message space $\{0,1\}^n$ in the proven IND-CPA secure version [10]. The basic scheme of the homomorphic NTRU consists of three polynomial time algorithms $\mathsf{KeyGen}, \mathsf{Enc}, \mathsf{Dec}$).

$\mathsf{KeyGen}(1^\kappa)$: Sample polynomials $\tilde{f}(x)$, $g(x) \leftarrow \chi_\epsilon$, repeat sampling $\tilde{f}(x)$ until $f(x) := 2\tilde{f}(x) + 1$ is invertible in R_q and denote the inverse of $f(x)$ in R_q as $(f(x))^{-1}$. Output $pk = h(x) := 2g(x)(f(x))^{-1} \pmod{q, x^n + 1}$ and $sk = f(x)$.

$\mathsf{Enc}(pk, m \in \{0,1\})$: Sample polynomials $s(x)$, $e(x) \leftarrow \chi_\epsilon$, and output $c(x) := h(x)s(x) + 2e(x) + m \pmod{q, x^n + 1}$.

$\mathsf{Dec}(sk, c)$: Compute $\mu(x) = f(x)c(x) \pmod{q, x^n + 1}$, and output $m' = \mu(x) \pmod 2$.

2.2 Lattices and LLL Algorithm

The lattice L is an additive subgroup of $\mathbb{R}^m$ that is $\mathbb{Z}$-generated by a set of n linearly independent vectors $\{\mathbf{b}_1, ..., \mathbf{b}_n\}$ in $\mathbb{R}^m$. We say n as the dimension of the lattice L which is denoted by $\dim(L)$. For a given lattice L, there is a geometric invariant called the minimum of the lattice and there are several computational problems related to the minimum.

Definition 1 (Minimum). *The (first) minimum of a lattice L is the norm of a shortest non-zero vector in L and denoted as $\lambda_1(L) = \min_{\mathbf{v} \in L \setminus \{\mathbf{0}\}} \|\mathbf{v}\|_2$ where $\|\cdot\|_2$ is the Euclidean norm of the vector.*

In [2], Ajtai proved that for a given lattice L, the problem of finding a vector of the minimum norm, which is called as the Shortest Vector Problem(SVP), is NP-hard. A relaxed SVP is a problem of finding a vector which is no longer than a factor of γ to the first minimum and these problems are often refer to as the approximate SVP$_\gamma$. Note that if γ increases, the problem gets easier. There is no known efficient algorithm solving the SVP$_\gamma$ for small γ in a lattice in arbitrary dimension even in quantum computer. The LLL algorithm is a polynomial time algorithm for SVP$_\gamma$ with $\gamma = 2^{\frac{n-1}{2}}$ [7]. Moreover, in theoretical view, the shortest vector $\mathbf{v}$ of the output vector of LLL algorithm for n dimensional lattice L satisfies that $\|\mathbf{v}\|_2 \leq 2^{\frac{n-1}{4}} \det(L)^{1/n}$. We note that the input of LLL algorithm should be a basis of the lattice. The MLLL is modified from LLL so that it works on any set of generating set of vectors of integer lattices [4].

3 Message Recovery of Homomorphic NTRU with Non-invertible Public Keys

The IND-CPA security of homomorphic NTRU was proven when the public key $h(x) = \frac{2g(x)}{f(x)} \in R_q$ is invertible in [10]. In this section, we consider the case that the public key $h(x)$ is not invertible in R_q. Because q is prime, we see that $\mathbb{Z}_q[x]$ is a unique factorization domain. If $h(x)$ is not invertible in R_q, then $\gcd(h(x), x^n + 1) = d(x) \neq 1$ in $\mathbb{Z}_q[x]$. Therefore, we see that $x^n + 1 = \beta(x)d(x)$ and $\gcd(\beta(x), h(x)) = 1$ in $\mathbb{Z}_q[x]$. Since $x^n + 1$ divides $\beta(x)h(x)$, we see that $\beta(x)h(x) = 0$ in R_q. For a given ciphertext $c(x) = h(x)s(x) + 2e(x) + m$, we see that $w(x) = \beta(x)c(x) \bmod (q, x^n + 1) = \beta(x)(2e(x) + m) \bmod (q, x^n + 1)$. In the homomorphic NTRU, the plaintext is chosen from $\{0, 1\}$, and therefore, its IND-CPA security is equivalent to the security in message recovery attack. Therefore, the IND-CPA adversarial goal is to recover $m \in \{0, 1\}$ from

$$w(x) = \beta(x)(2e(x) + m) \bmod (q, x^n + 1), \tag{1}$$

while m and $e(x)$ are unknown and $w(x)$ and $\beta(x)$ are known.

3.1 A Sufficient Condition for Message Recovery

For $\beta(x) = \frac{x^n + 1}{\gcd(h(x), x^n + 1)} = \sum_{i=0}^{\ell} \beta_i x^i \in \mathbb{Z}_q[x]$, we consider the following matrix $[B] \in \mathbb{Z}^{n \times n}$:

$$[B] = \begin{bmatrix} \beta_0 & \cdots & \cdots & \beta_\ell & \cdots & 0 \\ \vdots & \ddots & & & \ddots & \vdots \\ 0 & \cdots & \beta_0 & \cdots & \cdots & \beta_\ell \\ -\beta_\ell & \cdots & 0 & \beta_0 & \cdots & \beta_{\ell-1} \\ & \ddots & & & \ddots & \\ -\beta_1 & \cdots & -\beta_\ell & 0 & \cdots & \beta_0 \end{bmatrix} = \begin{bmatrix} \mathbf{b}_{n-1} \\ \vdots \\ \mathbf{b}_\ell \\ \mathbf{b}_{\ell-1} \\ \vdots \\ \mathbf{b}_0 \end{bmatrix} \tag{2}$$

Note that the Eq. (1) can be represented by using matrices over $\mathbb{Z}_q$ for $e(x) = \sum_{i=0}^{n-1} e_i x^i$ and $w(x) = \sum_{i=0}^{n-1} w_i x^i$:

$$\mathbf{w} = [B] \cdot (2\mathbf{e} + \mathbf{m}) \bmod q \tag{3}$$

with $\mathbf{w} = [w_{n-1}, \ldots, w_0]^T$; $2\mathbf{e} + \mathbf{m} = [2e_{n-1}, \ldots, 2e_1, 2e_0 + m]^T$. Again, Eq. (3) of matrices can be written as

$$w_i = \langle \mathbf{b}_i, 2\mathbf{e} + \mathbf{m} \rangle \bmod q \text{ for all } i = 0, \ldots, n-1,$$

where $\langle \cdot, \cdot \rangle$ is the usual inner product of two vectors in $\mathbb{Z}^n$.

Theorem 1. *Suppose that $\mathbf{b}_i$'s are given as in Eq. (2) and a vector $\eta = (\eta_0, \ldots, \eta_{n-1}) \in \mathbb{Z}^n$ is known to satisfy the following condition:*

$$\text{Condition(*)} \begin{cases} (i) & \eta = \sum_{i=0}^{n-1} \lambda_i \mathbf{b}_i \bmod q \text{ for } \lambda_i \in \mathbb{Z} \\ (ii) & |\eta_i| < \frac{q}{4n\epsilon + 2} \text{ for all } i = 0, 1, \ldots, n-1 \\ (iii) & \eta_{n-1} = 1 \bmod 2 \end{cases}$$

For any given ciphertext $c(x)$, the plaintext $m \in \{0, 1\}$ can be recovered by $m = (\sum_{i=0}^{n-1} \lambda_i w_i \bmod q) \bmod 2$, where $w(x) = \beta(x)c(x) \bmod (q, x^n + 1) = \sum_{i=0}^{n-1} w_i x^i$.

Proof. For a given vector $\eta = (\eta_0, \ldots, \eta_{n-1}) = \sum_{i=0}^{n-1} \lambda_i \mathbf{b}_i \bmod q$ with the Condition(*) holds, we have

$$\sum_{i=0}^{n-1} \lambda_i w_i \bmod q = \left\langle \sum_{i=0}^{n-1} \lambda_i \mathbf{b}_i, 2\mathbf{e} + \mathbf{m} \right\rangle \bmod q = \left(\sum_{i=0}^{n-1} 2e_i \eta_i \right) + m\eta_{n-1} \bmod q.$$

From the assumptions $|\eta_i| < \frac{q}{4n\epsilon+2}$, $|e_i| \leq \epsilon$ and $m \in \{0,1\}$, we see that

$$\left| \left(\sum_{i=0}^{n-1} 2e_i \eta_i \right) + m\eta_{n-1} \right| < 2n\epsilon \frac{q}{4n\epsilon + 2} + \frac{q}{4n\epsilon + 2} = \frac{q(2n\epsilon + 1)}{4n\epsilon + 2} = q/2.$$

Therefore, we have $\sum_{i=0}^{n-1} \lambda_i w_i \bmod q = \left(\sum_{i=0}^{n-1} 2e_i \eta_i \right) + m\eta_{n-1}$, which implies that $(\sum_{i=0}^{n-1} \lambda_i w_i \bmod q) \bmod 2 = m$. □

Note that Theorem 1 works for any solution $(\lambda_i)_{0 \leq i \leq n-1}$ which is easy to compute from η by a simple linear algebra over $\mathbb{Z}_q$. Therefore, for a successful message recovery attack, it is enough to get a vector $\eta \in \mathbb{Z}^n$ that satisfies Condition(*).

3.2   A Lattice Attack for the Message Recovery

Now we present how to apply a lattice reduction algorithm, to find such a short vector η that is described in Theorem 1.

For the vectors $\mathbf{b}_i$'s as given in Eq. (2), we consider the lattice $L_B = \{\zeta \in \mathbb{Z}^n | \zeta = \sum_{i=0}^{n-1} x_i \mathbf{b}_i \bmod q$ for some $x_i \in \mathbb{Z}\}$. Now we describe the process of finding a short vector in L_B that satisfies Condition(*) in two ways. Firstly, we apply a lattice reduction algorithm MLLL [4] for the linearly dependent generating set of vectors

$$S = \{(q, 0, \ldots, 0), (0, q, 0, \ldots, 0), \ldots, (0, \ldots, 0, q), \mathbf{b}_{n-1}, \ldots, \mathbf{b}_0\} \subset \mathbb{Z}^n.$$

From our experiments, we see that the algorithm MLLL outputs a short vector with Condition(*) holds if the degree ℓ of $\beta(x)$ is small. However, the only thing we can prove on the size of the shortest vector of the output of MLLL is that it is at least smaller than $2^{\frac{n-1}{4}} (\det L_B)^{\frac{1}{n}} \leq 2^{\frac{n-1}{4}} q^{\frac{\ell}{n}}$ from the LLL reducedness of the output. This does not give enough reason why a short vector from the output of MLLL satisfies the Condition(*).

Now we present a method of finding a short vector in L_B that with Condition(*) holds provably if the degree $\ell \leq \frac{\log_2 q}{4}$. We consider a sequence of sublattices $L_{\ell+1} \subset L_{\ell+2} \subset \cdots \subset L_n \subset L_B$), where $L_i(\ell+1 \leq i \leq n)$ is generated by the row vectors of $B_i \in \mathbb{Z}^{i \times n}$ which are defined as follows:

$$B_i = \begin{bmatrix} 0 \cdots 0 & q & \cdots & 0 & 0 & \cdots & 0 \\ \vdots & \vdots & \ddots & & \vdots & & \vdots \\ 0 \cdots 0 & 0 & \cdots & q & 0 & \cdots & 0 \\ 0 \cdots 0 & \beta_0 & \cdots & \beta_{\ell-1} & 1 & \cdots & 0 \\ \vdots & \vdots & \ddots & & \ddots & \ddots & \vdots \\ 0 \cdots 0 & 0 & \cdots & \beta_0 & \cdots & \beta_{\ell-1} & 1 \end{bmatrix} = [0_{i \times (n-i)} | B'_{i,\text{red}}], \quad B'_{i,\text{red}} \in \mathbb{Z}^{i \times i}$$

Let $L_{B'_{i,\text{red}}} \subset \mathbb{Z}^i$ be the lattice generated by the row vectors of $B'_{i,\text{red}}$ for $i = \ell + 1, ..., n$. If $\eta_{\text{red}} = (\eta'_{n-i}, ..., \eta'_{n-1}) \in L_{B'_{i,\text{red}}}$ is a short vector that satisfies Condition(*) then $\eta = (\eta_j)_{0 \le j \le (n-1)}$ is a short vector in L_B that satisfies Condition(*), where $\eta_j = 0$ if $0 \le j \le (n-i-1)$ and $\eta_j = \eta'_j$ if $n-i \le j \le n-1$. From [4], we see that the shortest vector $\mathbf{v}'_i \in L_{B'_{i,\text{red}}}$ of the output of the LLL algorithm for the lattice generated by the row vectors of $B'_{i,\text{red}}$ satisfies that

$$||\mathbf{v}'_i|| \le ||\mathbf{v}'_i||_2 \le 2^{\frac{i-1}{4}} \det(B'_{i,\text{red}})^{1/i} = 2^{\frac{i-1}{4}} q^{\frac{\ell}{i}}.$$

By setting $\log_2 q = \tau$, we have a sequence of vectors $\mathbf{v}_i \in L_B$ with $||\mathbf{v}_i|| \le 2^{\frac{i-1}{4}+\frac{\ell\tau}{i}}$ for $i = \ell+1, ..., n$. From a simple calculation over real numbers using the derivatives, we see that the function $f(i) = 2^{\frac{i-1}{4}+\frac{\ell\tau}{i}}$ has its minimum $2^{-1/4+\sqrt{\ell\tau}}$ at $i = 2\sqrt{\ell\tau}$. For simplicity, we assume that $\kappa = 2\sqrt{\ell\tau}$ is an integer. Therefore, the LLL algorithm applied on $L_{B'_{\kappa,\text{red}}}$ on the basis consists of the row vectors of $B'_{\kappa,\text{red}}$ gives a vector $\mathbf{v} \in L_B$ with $||\mathbf{v}|| \le 2^{-1/4+\sqrt{\ell\tau}}$.

Now we want to show that this vector satisfies Condition(*) as long as the last component is an odd number. For this, it is enough to show that $2^{-1/4+\sqrt{\ell\tau}} \le \frac{q}{4n\epsilon+2}$. From the equality $2^{-1/4+\sqrt{\ell\tau}} = 2^{-1/4}q^{\sqrt{\frac{\ell}{\tau}}}$, it is enough to show that $2^{-1/4}(4n\epsilon + 2) \le q^{1-\sqrt{\frac{\ell}{\tau}}}$. In particular, if q is subexponential in n as in the homomorphic NTRU, one can assume that $2^{-1/4}(4n\epsilon + 2) \le q^{1/2}$. Moreover, if $\ell \le \frac{\log_2 q}{4} = \frac{\tau}{4}$, we clearly have $q^{1/2} \le q^{1-\sqrt{\frac{\ell}{\tau}}}$ and thus $2^{-1/4}(4n\epsilon+2) \le q^{1-\sqrt{\frac{\ell}{\tau}}}$. Therefore, we conclude that $2^{-1/4+\sqrt{\ell\tau}} \le \frac{q}{4n\epsilon+2}$ if $\ell \le \frac{\log_2 q}{4}$.

Note that the condition $\ell \le \frac{\log_2 q}{4}$ to guarantee the desired shortness of the vector $\mathbf{v}$ is deduced from the theoretical bound of the shortest vector of the output of the LLL algorithm. It is known that the actual shortest vector of the LLL algorithm is shorter than the theoretical bound in general. Moreover, as in the example of the following section, the method using MLLL gives a shorter vector than the method using the sublattice. This suggests that the message recovery attack can be successful for much larger ℓ's. Therefore, setting $h(x)$ as an invertible polynomial in R_q is more appropriate than avoiding $\beta(x)$ with successful lattice reduction attack using sublattice as described above.

4   Conclusion

The IND-CPA security of the homomorphic NTRU is proven when the public key is invertible in R_q [10]. However, no result on the security of the homomorphic NTRU is known when the public key is not invertible. In this paper, we show that if the public key is not invertible in the homomorphic NTRU, then one can use a lattice reduction algorithm effectively to recover the plaintext of any ciphertext. Therefore, we conclude that the public key of homomorphic NTRU should be invertible in the ring R_q to guarantee the IND-CPA security of homomorphic variants of NTRU [3,8,9].

Acknowledgement. Hyang-Sook Lee and Seongan Lim were supported by Basic Science Research Program through the National Research Foundation of Korea (NRF) funded by the Ministry of Science, ICT and Future Planning (Grant Number: 2015R1A2A1A15054564). Seongan Lim was also supported by Basic Science Research Program through the NRF funded by the Ministry of Science, ICT and Future Planning (Grant Number: 2016R1D1A1B01008562). Ikkwon Yie was supported by Basic Science Research Program through the NRF funded by the Ministry of Science, ICT and Future Planning (Grant Number: 2017R1D1A1B03034721).

References

1. Albrecht, M., Bai, S., Ducas, L.: A subfield lattice attack on overstretched NTRU assumptions. In: Robshaw, M., Katz, J. (eds.) CRYPTO 2016. LNCS, vol. 9814, pp. 153–178. Springer, Heidelberg (2016). https://doi.org/10.1007/978-3-662-53018-4_6
2. Ajtai, M.: The shortest vector problem in L_2 is NP-hard for randomized reductions. In: STOC 1998, pp. 10–19 (1998)
3. Bos, J.W., Lauter, K., Loftus, J., Naehrig, M.: Improved security for a ring-based fully homomorphic encryption scheme. In: Proceedings of IMA International Conference 2013, pp. 45–64 (2013)
4. Bremner, M.R.: Lattice Basis Reduction-An Introduction to the LLL Algorithm and its Applications. CRC Press, Boca Raton (2012)
5. Cheon, J.H., Jeong, J., Lee, C.: An algorithm for NTRU problems and cryptanalysis of the GGH multilinear map without an encoding of zero. Cryptology ePrint Archive, Report 2016/139 (2016)
6. Hoffstein, J., Pipher, J., Silverman, J.H.: NTRU: a ring-based public key cryptosystem. In: Buhler, J.P. (ed.) ANTS 1998. LNCS, vol. 1423, pp. 267–288. Springer, Heidelberg (1998). https://doi.org/10.1007/BFb0054868
7. Lenstra, A.K., Lenstra, H.W., Lovász, L.: Factoring polynomials with rational coefficients. Mahtematische Ann. **261**, 513–534 (1982)
8. Lopez-Alt, A., Tromer, E., Vaikuntanathan, V.: On-the-fly multyparty computation on the cloud via multikey fully homomorphic encryption. In: STOC 2012, pp. 1219–1234 (2012)
9. Rohloff, K., Cousins, D.B.: A scalable implementation of fully homomorphic encryption built on NTRU. In: Böhme, R., Brenner, M., Moore, T., Smith, M. (eds.) FC 2014. LNCS, vol. 8438, pp. 221–234. Springer, Heidelberg (2014). https://doi.org/10.1007/978-3-662-44774-1_18
10. Stehlé, D., Steinfeld, R.: Making NTRU as secure as worst-case problems over ideal lattices. In: Paterson, K.G. (ed.) EUROCRYPT 2011. LNCS, vol. 6632, pp. 27–47. Springer, Heidelberg (2011). https://doi.org/10.1007/978-3-642-20465-4_4
11. Security Inovation: NTRU PKCS Tutorial. https://www.securityinnovation.com

Practical Range Proof for Cryptocurrency Monero with Provable Security

Kang Li[1,2], Rupeng Yang[2,3(✉)], Man Ho Au[1,2], and Qiuliang Xu[3]

[1] Research Institute for Sustainable Urban Development,
The Hong Kong Polytechnic University, Hong Kong, China
kang.li@connect.polyu.hk
[2] Department of Computing, The Hong Kong Polytechnic University,
Hong Kong, China
csallen@comp.polyu.edu.hk
[3] School of Computer Science and Technology, Shandong University,
Jinan 250101, China
orbbyrp@gmail.com, xql@sdu.edu.cn

Abstract. With a market cap of about 1.5 billion US dollar, Monero is one of the most popular crypto-currencies at present. Much of its growing popularity can be attributed to its unique privacy feature. Observing that no formal security analysis is presented, we initiate a formal study on Monero's core protocol. In this study, we revisit the design rationale of an important component of Monero, namely, range proof. Our analysis shows that the range proof may not be a proof-of-knowledge even if the underlying building block, ring signature, is secure. Specifically, we show that if a certain secure ring signature scheme is used, it is impossible to construct a witness extractor unless the Computational Diffie-Hellman problem is equivalent to the Discrete Logarithm problem. This shows that the design rationale is to possibly flawed. Then, we present a new range proof protocol that enjoys a few advantages. Firstly, it is a zero-knowledge proof-of-knowledge protocol. Secondly, it is compatible with the Monero's wallet and algebraic structure and thus does not require extensive modification in the codebase. Finally, the efficiency is comparable to Monero's version which does not admit a formal security proof.

1 Introduction

Research on crypto-currency begins in the 80's, when Chaum [5] proposed the first electronic cash scheme. As the first and also the most popular decentralized cryptocurrency, Bitcoin was created in 2009 [9]. Achieving security and privacy simultaneously have been the design goal for most of these schemes since then. However, bitcoin does not offer a strong privacy as all transactions are publicly broadcast and replicated through the bitcoin blockchain. Any data on bitcoin blockchain could be collected and mined to derive some information that may undermine the user privacy.

In order to tackle the privacy issues of bitcoin, a new open-source decentralized cryptocurrency, called Monero, is created in April 2014. Firstly, it uses

© Springer International Publishing AG, part of Springer Nature 2018
S. Qing et al. (Eds.): ICICS 2017, LNCS 10631, pp. 255–262, 2018.
https://doi.org/10.1007/978-3-319-89500-0_23

linkable ring signature to obscure the original of a transaction and thus provide better payer privacy. Secondly, it utilises single-use, randomised version of the receiver's public key, called stealth address, to provide better payee privacy. Finally, In order to hide the wallet balance is not stored in plain. Instead, they are hidden using commitment schemes. As wallet balance is stored in committed forms, RingCT requires the sender to issue a proof that (1) the input of a ringCT transaction is equal to that of the output; and (2) the balance of each wallet involved is within the range of permitted values. The second part is a range proof and its importance has been explained in detail in the Monero white paper [10]. Briefly, the cryptographic primitives of Monero work in a cyclic group of known order q. Then, a commitment of -1 is equivalent to $q - 1$. Thus, a sender with 1 dollar in his wallet could send a transaction with the output of 2 and $q - 1$ if range proof is not performed. By requiring the sender to prove that all commitments involved are confined within a small range, the above attack can be prevented.

Despite being one of the most important components and accounts for over 50% of the total bandwidth of a ringCT transaction, the range proof employed in ringCT is not well-studied. This range proof combines bit decomposition technique with ring signatures in an unconventional way [8]. The Monero white paper [10] proposed a new ring signature called ANSL, and discussed two other options, namely, a well-studied scheme from Abe et al. [1], and a newly proposed scheme called Borromean ring signature [8] but no formal security analysis regarding the range proof instantiated from these ring signatures is given.

1.1 Overview of Our Contributions

We initiate the study of the range proof design employed by Monero and showed that their way to create range proof from bit decomposition technique and ring signatures does not guarantee security. Instead of pointing out that there is no formal security proof and thus the security is unclear, we give a very strong evidence that the design is flawed.

To achieve this goal, we give a counterexample. First, we present a secure and anonymous ring signature scheme. Then, we use this ring signature scheme as a building block to construct a range proof. The most challenging part is to show that, even if non-blackbox simulation technique is allowed, the resulting range proof is not sound (more concretely, it is not a proof-of-knowledge). We solve this challenge by relating the existence of the witness extractor to the relationship between the computational Diffie-Hellman problem (CDH) and the Discrete Logarithm problem (DL). In fact, we show that if the resulting protocol is a proof-of-knowledge, then the CDH problem and the DL problem are equivalent. Since it is highly unlikely, we give a very strong evidence that the resulting protocol is not a proof-of-knowledge. This supports the claim that the design is flawed. As a side result, we observe that the range proof offers witness indistinguishability if the underlying ring signature scheme is anonymous.

Our second contribution is to give a range proof that is provably a zero-knowledge proof-of-knowledge protocol which is fully compatible with Monero's architecture. In addition, the efficiency is comparable to the current Monero's range proof.

Remarks. We would like remark that our results do not imply Monero is broken. Firstly, perhaps a witness-indistinguishable proof, instead of a zero-knowledge proof-of-knowledge, provides sufficient security guarantee. Secondly, while the range proof is not a zero-knowledge proof-of-knowledge, it may be the case that the overall ringCT protocol can still be proven secure. However, this will involve a comprehensive analysis of the protocol and we leave it as an open problem to actually quantify the security and privacy guarantee of the current version of Monero.

1.2   Related Works

A range proof protocol is basically used to prove that a committed value lies in a specified interval range. It is often applied in various cryptographic protocols, such as e-voting or anonymous credential scenarios, to ensure anonymity and privacy. The problem of range proof has been studied extensively. In [7], an exact range proof relying on the fact that a number lies in $[0, 2^n]$ iff it can be represented as a n bits binary string is given. Our range proof for Monero is also adapted from this range proof. Subsequently, many efficient range proof protocols for exact range have been proposed. However, we argue that these improved constructions do not suit Monero's application scenario. The range proof presented in [3] work only in unknown order groups, and the range proof presented in [4] works in bilinear groups, while Monero works in the classical Elliptical-Curve groups not supporting bilinear operations. The range proof presented in [6] is more efficient than ours only when the interval $[0, H]$ satisfies the condition that H is not a power of 2, which is not the case in Monero.

2   Analysis of the Range Proof in Monero

2.1   Review of Monero's Range Proof

Let g, h be two random generators of a cyclic group $\mathbb{G}$ of prime order q. The common input is a Pedersen commitment C, and an interval $[0, 2^{\ell} - 1]$ for some integer ℓ such that $\ell < |q|$. The prover's private input include (u, r). The goal of the prover is to convince the verifier that u lies in an interval $[0, 2^{\ell} - 1]$. Let $\Pi = (\mathsf{KeyGen}, \mathsf{Sign}, \mathsf{Verify})$ be a ring signature scheme such that output of KeyGen is of the form (h^x, x).

- The prover first conducts a binary decomposition of u and r. That is, it finds $u_i \in \{0, 1\}$ for $i = 0$ to $\ell - 1$ such that $u = \sum_{i=0}^{\ell-1} 2^i u_i$. Next, it chooses $r_i \in_R \mathbb{Z}_q$ uniformly at random, and compute $r_{\ell-1} = r - \sum_{i=0}^{\ell-2} r_i$. It computes $C_i = g^{2^i u_i} h^{r_i}$ for $i = 0$ to $\ell - 1$. Note that the set of $\{C_i\}_{i=0}^{\ell-1}$ satisfies the following equation:

$$C = \prod_{i=0}^{\ell-1} C_i$$

- Let $M = H(C, C_0, \ldots, C_{\ell-1})$ for some hash function H. For each i, the prover generates a ring signature on the ring $\mathcal{R}_i = \{C_i, C_i/g^{2^i}\}$ by invoking $\sigma_i = \Pi.\mathsf{Sign}(\mathcal{R}_i, r_i, M)$. The range proof π for C is $(C_0, \sigma_0, \ldots, C_{\ell-1}, \sigma_{\ell-1})$.
- Upon receiving a proof π, the verifier computes $M = H(C, C_0, \ldots, C_{\ell-1})$ and outputs accept if and only the following holds:

$$
\begin{aligned}
C &= \textstyle\prod_{i=0}^{\ell-1} C_i \\
1 &= \Pi.\mathsf{Verify}(\{C_0, C_0/g\}, M, \sigma_0) \\
&\;\;\vdots \\
1 &= \Pi.\mathsf{Verify}(\{C_{\ell-1}, C_{\ell-1}/g^{2^{\ell-1}}\}, M, \sigma_{\ell-1})
\end{aligned}
$$

Discussions. The monero range proof follows the folklore approach in bit decomposition while replacing the standard 0/1 OR proof for each commitment C_i with a range signature. The design philosophy, as explained in [8] is that: "If C was a commitment to 1 then I do not know its discrete log, but C' becomes a commitment to 0 and I do know its discrete log (just the blinding factor). If C was a commitment to 0 I know its discrete log, and I don't for C'. If it was a commitment to any other amount, none of the results will be zero and I won't be able to sign".

After confirming C_i can only be a commitment to 0 or 2^i, the equation $C = \prod_{i=0}^{\ell-1}$ assures the verifier that C is a commitment to a number between 0 to $2^\ell - 1$.

2.2 Analysis of Monero's Range Proof

This is one of the core results of this paper in which we illustrate a flaw in the above design philosophy. As no security analysis is provided in [8] nor [10], the ring signature-based range proof may not be secure. Here we give evidence to support our claim by instantiating the ring signature-based range proof with a secure ring signature scheme, and show that existence of an extractor, in any setting, for the resulting range proof implies that the CDH problem is equivalent to the DL problem. Essentially it means it is highly unlikely that such an extractor can be constructed.

BKM Ring Signature. First, we review the ring signature scheme from [2]. The BKM scheme works in group equipped with a bilinear map, $\hat{e} : \mathbb{G} \times \mathbb{G} \to \mathbb{G}_T$.

- KeyGen. Randomly picks a value $x \in_R \mathbb{Z}_q$, computes $Y = h^x$. Also, pick a hash function $H : \{0,1\}^* \to \mathbb{G}$. The public key is Y, H and the secret key is x.
- Sign. Let the input ring be (Y_0, H_0) and (Y_1, H_1). Without loss of generality, assume the signing key is x_0 such that $Y_0 = h^{x_0}$. To sign message M, the signer randomly picks $r \in_R \mathbb{Z}_q$ and computes the signature $\sigma = (\sigma_1, \sigma_2)$

$$
\sigma_1 = Y_1^{x_0}(H_0(M)H_1(M))^r, \quad \sigma_2 = h^r.
$$

– Verify. On input ring $\mathcal{R} = \{(Y_0, H_0), Y_1, H_1\}$, message M, signature (σ_1, σ_2), the verifier outputs 1 if and only if:

$$\hat{e}(Y_0, Y_1)\hat{e}(\sigma_2, H_0(M)H_1(M)) = \hat{e}(\sigma_1, h),$$

and outputs 0 otherwise.

As shown in [2], this ring signature scheme is unforgeable under the CDH assumption in the standard model when H is a Waters' hash function.

An Impossibility Result. Denote by $(\mathcal{P}, \mathcal{V})$ the non-interactive ring signature-based range proof using BKM ring signature as a building block.

We show that it is impossible to construct ppt extractor $\mathcal{E}$ for $(\mathcal{P}, \mathcal{V})$ capable of extracting witness r from proof Π such that $\mathcal{V}(\Pi)$ outputs accept. More formally, we prove that if ppt $\mathcal{E}$ exists, it is possible to show that the CDH problem is equivalent to the DL problem in the bilinear group pair.

Theorem 1. *If ppt $\mathcal{E}$ exists for $(\mathcal{P}, \mathcal{V})$, we show how to construct simulator $\mathcal{S}$ that can solve the DL problem given a CDH oracle.*

Proof. We consider the case when $\ell = 1$, i.e., the ring signature-based range proof of which the value committed is either 0 or 1. Assume $(\mathcal{P}, \mathcal{V})$ is an non-interactive zero-knowledge proof-of-knowledge system,

$$NIZKPoK\{(r) : C = h^r \vee C/g = h^r\}.$$

It means there exists ppt $\mathcal{E}$ which can extracts from any $\mathcal{P}'$ capable of outputting valid proofs (i.e. proof accepted by $\mathcal{V}$). We show how to construct ppt $\mathcal{S}$, having access to a CDH oracle, which can solve the DL problem through interaction with $\mathcal{E}$.

$\mathcal{S}$ receives Y as a problem instance and its goal is to output r such that $Y = h^r$. It flips a coin $b \in \{0, 1\}$ and set $C = g^b Y$. Then, it invoked its CDH oracle on input $C, C/g$ to obtain a value Z. It computes $M = C$, generates a random $t \in_R$, uses Z, t to produce a proof π as follows: Compute $\sigma_1 = Z(H_0(M)H_1(M))^t, \sigma_2 = h^t$. Output $\sigma = (\sigma_1, \sigma_2)$ as the proof that $C = h^{r'} \vee C = gh^{r'}$. Invoke $\mathcal{E}$ on σ to obtain witness r' satisfying $C = h^{r'}$ or $C = gh^{r'}$. In both cases ($b = 0$ and $b = 1$), $\mathcal{S}$ outputs r' as the solution to the DL problem. Now if $b = 0$, then $\mathcal{S}$ succeeds if $C = h^{r'}$, and if $b = 1$, then $\mathcal{S}$ succeeds if $C = gh^{r'}$. Since b is hidden from $\mathcal{E}$, with probability $1/2$, $\mathcal{S}$ is able to solve the DL problem. □

Under the assumption that CDH $\not\Leftrightarrow$ DL, the above theorem implies that no $\mathcal{E}$ exists. In other words, $(\mathcal{P}, \mathcal{V})$ cannot be a proof-of-knowledge.

Additional Observations. It is straightforward to say that $(\mathcal{P}, \mathcal{V})$ is a proof (but not a proof of knowledge) because the statement $C = h^r \vee C/g = h^r$ is always true. Furthermore, $(\mathcal{P}, \mathcal{V})$ is witness-indistinguishable because the underlying ring signature is anonymous. However, it is not clear how a zero-knowledge simulator could be constructed and thus it is unclear whether or not $(\mathcal{P}, \mathcal{V})$ is zero-knowledge.

Thus, we conclude that $(\mathcal{P}, \mathcal{V})$ is a witness-indistinguishable proof, but not a witness-indistinguishable proof-of-knowledge, that C is a commitment to 0 or 1. Whether or not it is zero-knowledge remains unclear.

3   The Improved Range Proof for Monero

Let g, h be two random generators of $\mathbb{G}$, which can be sampled with some public randomness and also serve as the public key of the Peterson commitment. Let $\mathbb{H}$ be a cryptographic hash function. The common reference string of the range proof is $crs = (\mathbb{G}, q, g, h, \mathbb{H})$. The range proof Π consists of two algorithms, which are described as follows:

- **Prove.** On input an integer l and a commitment $C = g^u h^r$ as well as the value u and the randomness r for the commitment, where $u \in [0, 2^l - 1]$.
  1. The prove algorithm decomposes the value u into a binary vector $\boldsymbol{u} = (u_0, \ldots, u_{l-1})$, where $u_i \in \{0, 1\}$ for $i \in [0, l-1]$, and $u = \sum_{i=0}^{l-1} 2^i u_i$.
  2. It samples $r_0, \ldots r_{l-2}$ uniformly from $\mathbb{Z}_q$ and computes $r_{l-1} = r - \sum_{i=0}^{l-2} r_i$.
  3. It generates l commitments $C_0, \ldots C_{l-1}$, where $C_i = g^{2^i u_i} h^{r_i}$ for $i \in [0, l-1]$.
  4. It sets $C_{i,0} = C_i$ and computes $C_{i,1} = C_i / g^{2^i}$ for $i \in [0, l-1]$.
  5. For $i \in [0, l-1]$, it samples $c_{i,\bar{u}_i}, \alpha_i, z_{i,\bar{u}_i} \xleftarrow{\$} \mathbb{Z}_q$, and computes $T_{i,u_i} = h^{\alpha_i}$ and $T_{i,\bar{u}_i} = h^{z_{i,\bar{u}_i}} C_{i,\bar{u}_i}^{c_{i,\bar{u}_i}}$.
  6. It computes the challenge $c = \mathbb{H}(C, C_0, \ldots, C_{l-1}, T_{0,0}, T_{0,1}, \ldots, T_{l-1,0}, T_{l-1,1})$, and for $i \in [0, l-1]$, it computes $c_{i,u_i} = c - c_{i,\bar{u}_i} \mod q$, and $z_{i,u_i} = \alpha_i - c_{i,u_i} r_i$.
  7. It outputs the proof $\pi = (\{C_i\}_{i \in [0,l-2]}, \{c_{i,0}, c_{i,1}\}_{i \in [0,l-1]}, \{z_{i,0}, z_{i,1}\}_{i \in [0,l-1]})$.
- **Verify.** On input an integer l, a commitment C, and a proof π.
  1. The verify algorithm computes $C_{l-1} = C / (\prod_{i=0}^{l-2} C_i)$.
  2. For $i \in [0, l-1]$, it computes $C_i' = C_i / g^{2^i}$, $T_{i,0} = h^{z_{i,0}} C_i^{c_{i,0}}$ and $T_{i,1} = h^{z_{i,1}} C_i'^{c_{i,1}}$.
  3. It computes $c = \mathbb{H}(C, C_0, \ldots, C_{l-1}, T_{0,0}, T_{0,1}, \ldots, T_{l-1,0}, T_{l-1,1})$.
  4. It outputs 1 iff $c = c_{i,0} + c_{i,1} \mod q$ for all $i \in [0, l-1]$, outputs 0 otherwise.

3.1   Security Analysis

Theorem 1. *The range proof Π is a secure range proof, namely, a secure NIZKPoK system proving that the prover knows an open of a commitment that lies in a particular interval, assuming that $\mathbb{H}$ is modelled as the random oracle.*

Proof Sketch. The range proof proposed in this section is similar to the range proof presented in [7]. The main difference is that in [7], each commitment C_i is a commitment of u_i, while in our range proof it is a commitment of $2^i u_i$. We remark that our modification will not affect the security of the range proof since these two types of commitments are interconvertible, i.e., given a commitment of u_i (or $2^i u_i$), one can easily generate a commitment of $2^i u_i$ (or u_i). We illustrate this in more details in the full version of this paper.

3.2 Efficiency Analysis

We count the number of exponentiations needed by the prover and the verifier to compute and verify a proof respectively. For a range of $[0, 2^\ell]$, the proof effort is linear in ℓ. This is the same as Monero asymptotically. The following Table 1 shows the comparison of our scheme with Monero using the ANSL ring signature as a building block. We would like to remark that there is no formal security analysis for the range proof of Monero. Our range proof can be optimised using the trick that a multi-base exponentiation with 2 bases can be computed in roughly 1.1 times as a single base exponentiation. Comparing with the folklore binary decomposition technique, our protocol saves one commitment in terms of space complexity. As shown in the improved protocol, the proof π only includes the commitment $C_0, \ldots, C_{I-2}$. This trick works because the verifier could derive C_{l-1} using the equation that $C_{l-1} = C/(\prod_{i=0}^{l-2} C_i)$. In other words, our protocol has a slight edge compared with Monero in the sense that one less commitment is needed. The saving is quite small in practice since $\ell = 64$ in Monero's range proof.

Table 1. Efficiency of our range proof

	Prover	Verifier
This paper	5ℓ	4ℓ
This paper (optimised)	3.1ℓ	2.2ℓ
Monero (ANSL)	3ℓ	$2\ell + 2$

4 Conclusion

In this paper, we studied the range proof protocol employed in Monero. Firstly, we pointed out that the design philosophy of this range proof does not guarantee its security. Secondly, we designed a new range proof protocol and presented a formal security proof. And, it is also illustrated that the efficiency is comparable to that of Monero. Moreover, the improved protocol is compatible with Monero's wallet and the algebraic structure. Therefore, our proposed range proof protocol is secure and practical.

Acknowledgement. This work was supported by the National Natural Science Foundation of China (Grant No. 61602396, U1636205, 61572294, 61632020).

References

1. Abe, M., Ohkubo, M., Suzuki, K.: 1-out-of-n signatures from a variety of keys. In: Zheng, Y. (ed.) ASIACRYPT 2002. LNCS, vol. 2501, pp. 415–432. Springer, Heidelberg (2002). https://doi.org/10.1007/3-540-36178-2_26
2. Bender, A., Katz, J., Morselli, R.: Ring signatures: stronger definitions, and constructions without random oracles. Cryptology ePrint Archive, Report 2005/304 (2005). http://eprint.iacr.org/2005/304
3. Boudot, F.: Efficient proofs that a committed number lies in an interval. In: Preneel, B. (ed.) EUROCRYPT 2000. LNCS, vol. 1807, pp. 431–444. Springer, Heidelberg (2000). https://doi.org/10.1007/3-540-45539-6_31
4. Chaabouni, R., Lipmaa, H., Shelat, A.: Additive combinatorics and discrete logarithm based range protocols. In: Steinfeld, R., Hawkes, P. (eds.) ACISP 2010. LNCS, vol. 6168, pp. 336–351. Springer, Heidelberg (2010). https://doi.org/10.1007/978-3-642-14081-5_21
5. Chaum, D.: Blind signatures for untraceable payments. In: Chaum, D., Rivest, R.L., Sherman, A.T. (eds.) Advances in Cryptology, pp. 199–203. Springer, Boston (1983). https://doi.org/10.1007/978-1-4757-0602-4_18
6. Lipmaa, H., Asokan, N., Niemi, V.: Secure Vickrey auctions without threshold trust. In: Blaze, M. (ed.) FC 2002. LNCS, vol. 2357, pp. 87–101. Springer, Heidelberg (2003). https://doi.org/10.1007/3-540-36504-4_7
7. Mao, W.: Guaranteed correct sharing of integer factorization with off-line shareholders. In: Imai, H., Zheng, Y. (eds.) PKC 1998. LNCS, vol. 1431, pp. 60–71. Springer, Heidelberg (1998). https://doi.org/10.1007/BFb0054015
8. Maxwell, G.: Confidential transactions. Web, June 2015
9. Nakamoto, S.: Bitcoin: a peer-to-peer electronic cash system. White paper (2009). https://bitcoin.org/bitcoin.pdf
10. Noether, S., Mackenzie, A., Monero Core Team: Ring confidential transactions. Monero research lab report MRL-0005, February 2016

Wireless Sensor Network Security

Modeling Key Infection
in Large-Scale Sensor Networks

Feiyang Peng, Zhihong Liu(✉), Yong Zeng, and Jialei Wang

School of Cyber Engineering, Xidian University, Xi'an, China
liuzhihong@mail.xidian.edu.cn

Abstract. Key infection is a lightweight security protocol suitable for large-scale sensor networks. In this paper, we first derive a probabilistic model to analyze the security of key infection, then propose a group based key infection to improve its security performance.

Keywords: Key management · Key infection · Secrecy amplification
Sensor networks

1 Introduction

Typically, a sensor network is composed of a large number of sensor nodes; each sensor node is a small, inexpensive wireless device with limited battery power, memory storage, data processing capacity and short radio transmission range. Additionally, sensor networks are often operated on an unattended mode and sensors are not tamper resistant. This makes sensor networks more vulnerable than traditional wireless networks.

The first practical key predistribution scheme [1,2] for sensor networks is random key pre-distribution scheme introduced by Eschenauer and Gligor [3] and was investigated by Yağan and Makowski [4]. A major advantage of this scheme is the exclusion of the base station in key management. Another category scheme is location based key pre-distribution [5,6], which takes advantage of sensor deployment information to improve the network performance. Location based schemes can reach the same connectivity with fewer keys stored in sensors than previous schemes.

In this paper, we are interested in very simple sensors and a large number of them in a network. The number is such that it is infeasible to deploy every sensor node manually. Deployment in batches implies self-organizing network that is automatically and autonomously established upon physical deployment. Large number of sensors make it also hard to change code or data stored in every sensor, it is much easier to mass-produce sensors that are identical even on firmware and data level.

Key infection [7] is a lightweight security protocol suitable for large-scale sensor networks and is based on the assumption that, during the network deployment phase, the adversary can monitor only a fixed percentage of communication channels. Sensors simply broadcast keys in clear to all their neighbors. The plaintext key exchange is not much useful in common scenarios but when this process starts in hundred thousands instances at a time, it becomes extremely difficult for the adversary to compromise large fraction keys of the network.

To analyze key infection protocol, we propose a probability model of key infection. This model can help designers to evaluate key infection and adapt it to their needs. Then, a group based key infection protocol is proposed to improve the security performance of key infection.

2   Network Model and Security Assumptions

We consider a large-scale uniformly and densely distributed sensor network that monitors a vast terrain via a large number of static sensors, which can be deployed through approaches such as aerial scattering. No topology information is available before deployment. Eavesdroppers are also distributed uniformly over the same field. As depicted in Fig. 1, a sensor transmits a key in plaintext to its neighbor, any eavesdropper located in the transmission range can learn this key. However, a global passive adversary that can monitor all communications everywhere in the deployment region at all times is a too-strong security model. We adopt the attacker model [7] as follows:

- The attacker can deploy some eavesdroppers in the field and is able to monitor only a small proportion of the communications of the sensor network during the deployment phase. After key exchange is complete, she is able to monitor all communications at will;
- The attacker is passive, and does not execute active attacks (such as jamming or flooding) during the deployment phase.

Throughout the sequel, sensors are deployed randomly with locations assumed to be drawn independently from the uniform distribution in the field. The distance between two sensors i and j is denoted as $\|i - j\|$.

Let $\mathbf{X}$ be the point in the field, for $r \geq 0$, let $\mathbb{R}_i(r) = \{\mathbf{X} : \|\mathbf{X} - i\| \leq r\}$ for the disk of radius r centered at i, and in a slight abuse of notation, for

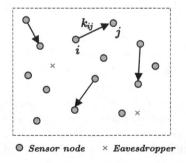

○ *Sensor node*   × *Eavesdropper*

Fig. 1. Example of key infection.

any $r_1, r_2 \geq 0$, write $\mathbb{R}_{ij}(r_1, r_2) = \{\mathbf{X} : \|\mathbf{X} - i\| \leq r_1 \text{ and } \|\mathbf{X} - j\| \leq r_2\}$ for the overlap region of $\mathbb{R}_i(r_1)$ and $\mathbb{R}_j(r_2)$, write $\mathbb{R}_{i\bar{j}}(r_1, r_2) = \{\mathbf{X} : \|\mathbf{X} - i\| \leq r_1 \text{ and } \|\mathbf{X} - j\| > r_2\}$ for the region $\mathbb{R}_i(r_1)\backslash\mathbb{R}_j(r_2)$, write $\mathbb{R}_{ij\bar{k}}(r_1, r_2, r_3) = \{\mathbf{X} : \|\mathbf{X} - i\| \leq r_1, \|\mathbf{X} - j\| \leq r_2 \text{ and } \|\mathbf{X} - k\| > r_3\}$ for the region $\mathbb{R}_{ij}(r_1, r_2)\backslash\mathbb{R}_k(r_3)$. If $r_1 = r_2 = r$, write $\mathbb{R}_{ij}(r_1, r_2) = \mathbb{R}_{ij}(r)$ for short. We also write $\mathbb{A}_i(r)$ for the area of region $\mathbb{R}_i(r)$, $\mathbb{A}_{ij}(r_1, r_2)$ for the area of region $\mathbb{R}_{ij}(r_1, r_2)$. In an extension of this notation, $\mathbb{A}_{ij\bar{k}}(r_1, r_2, r_3)$ denotes the area of the region $\mathbb{R}_{ij\bar{k}}(r_1, r_2, r_3) = \mathbb{R}_{ij}(r_1, r_2)\backslash\mathbb{R}_k(r_3)$.

3   Background of Key Infection

Basic Key Infection. The idea of basic key infection (B-KI) [7] is to propagate keying material after deployment: each sensor simply chooses a key and broadcasts it in plaintext to its neighbors.

Assume sensor i, when it comes to rest after deployment, broadcasts a key k_i and is heard by sensor j. Sensor j then generates a key k_{ji} and sends to i: $\{j, k_{ji}\}_{k_i}$. Later on, the key k_{ji} can be used to protect communication link between sensors i and j.

Whispering Key Infection. Whispering key infection (W-KI) [7] makes a small change to improve the performance of the basic key infection. Instead of each sensor broadcasting a key as loudly as it can, it starts off transmitting very quietly and steadily increases the power until a response is heard. This whispering key infection ensures that two sensors W_1 or W_2 within the range of each other will exchange a secure key provided that an eavesdropper is further away from either W_1 or W_2 than the distance between W_1 and W_2.

Secrecy Amplification. Secrecy amplification (SA-KI) [7] utilizes multipath key establishment to improve the security of basic key infection. Suppose that sensors W_1, W_2, and W_3 are neighbors. W_1 and W_2 share key k_{12}, W_1 and W_3 share key k_{13}, W_2 and W_3 share key k_{23}. To amplify the secrecy of key k_{12}, W_1 ask W_3 to exchange an additional key with W_2 as following:

$$W_1 \rightarrow W_3 : \{W_1, W_2, N_1\}_{k_{13}}$$
$$W_3 \rightarrow W_2 : \{W_1, W_2, N_1\}_{k_{23}}$$
$$W_2 \text{ computes} : k'_{12} = H(k_{12}\|N_1)$$
$$W_2 \rightarrow W_1 : \{N_1, N_2\}_{k'_{12}}$$
$$W_1 \rightarrow W_2 : \{N_2\}_{k'_{12}}$$

where N_1 and N_2 are nonces, $\{M\}_{k_i}$ represents the encrypted message M using key k_i, and $H(.)$ is a hash function. After the protocol terminates, W_1 and W_2 update their key from k_{12} to $k'_{12} = H(k_{12}\|N_1)$.

4   Probability Model of Key Infection

4.1   Basic Key Infection

Let n sensors with communication radius R be distributed over a field of size
S, t be the number of eavesdroppers in the field. As depicted in Fig. 2, two
adjacent sensors i and j exploit B-KI to establish a secure key. The adversary, in
order to eavesdrop the key setup process, should place at least one eavesdropper
in region $\mathbb{R}_{ij}(R)$, or one eavesdropper in region $\mathbb{R}_{i\bar{j}}(R)$ and another in region
$\mathbb{R}_{\bar{i}j}(R)$ simultaneously.

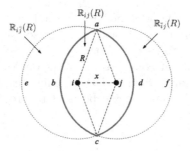

Fig. 2. Two adjacent sensors i and j in B-KI.

Let $\|i - j\| = x$, the cumulative distribution function of x is given by
$F(x) = \mathbf{P}\{\|i - j\| \leq x\} = x^2/R^2$, and its probability density function is
$f(x) = F'(x) = 2x/R^2$. The area of the overlap region $\mathbb{R}_{ij}(R)$ is $\mathbb{A}_{ij}(R) = 2R^2 \cos^{-1} \frac{x}{2R} - x\sqrt{R^2 - \frac{x^2}{4}}$, and its expectation is

$$\mathbf{E}[\mathbb{A}_{ij}(R)] = \int_0^R \mathbb{A}_{ij}(R) \frac{2x}{R^2} \, dx = \left(\pi - \frac{3\sqrt{3}}{4}\right) R^2 \approx 0.5865\pi R^2.$$

Therefore, the probability $\mathbf{P}\{b\}$ that there are exactly b eavesdroppers in the
overlap region $\mathbb{R}_{ij}(R)$ is

$$\mathbf{P}\{b\} = \binom{t}{b} \left(\frac{\mathbf{E}[\mathbb{A}_{ij}(R)]}{S}\right)^b \left(1 - \frac{\mathbf{E}[\mathbb{A}_{ij}(R)]}{S}\right)^{t-b},$$

and the probability of at least one eavesdropper located inside the interior of
region $\mathbb{R}_{ij}(R)$ is

$$\mathbf{P}_{\mathbb{R}_{ij}(R)} = 1 - \mathbf{P}\{b = 0\} = 1 - \left(1 - \frac{\mathbf{E}[\mathbb{A}_{ij}(R)]}{S}\right)^t$$

$$\approx 1 - \left(1 - \frac{0.5865\pi R^2}{S}\right)^t.$$

Let n' denote the average number of neighbors of a sensor. Because the sensors are distributed over the field uniformly, when $n \gg n'$ and $S \gg \pi R^2$, we have $\frac{\pi R^2}{S} = \frac{n'+1}{n} \approx \frac{n'}{n}$. It follows that, the probability $\mathbf{P}_{\mathbb{R}_{ij}(R)}$ can be approximated as $\mathbf{P}_{\mathbb{R}_{ij}(R)} = 1 - (1 - 0.5865 \cdot \frac{n'}{n})^t$.

Again, as estimated above, we can obtain $\mathbf{E}[\mathbb{A}_{i\bar{j}}(R)] = \mathbf{E}[\mathbb{A}_{\bar{i}j}(R)] = \pi R^2 - \mathbf{E}[\mathbb{A}_{ij}(R)] = 0.4135\pi R^2$, and

$$\mathbf{P}_{\mathbb{R}_{i\bar{j}}(R)} = \mathbf{P}_{\mathbb{R}_{\bar{i}j}(R)} = 1 - \left(1 - 0.4135 \cdot \frac{n'}{n}\right)^t.$$

Let $\mathbb{B}_{ij}$, $\mathbb{B}_{i\bar{j}}$, and $\mathbb{B}_{\bar{i}j}$ be events that the adversary has placed eavesdroppers in regions $\mathbb{R}_{ij}(R)$, $\mathbb{R}_{i\bar{j}}(R)$, and $\mathbb{R}_{\bar{i}j}(R)$, respectively. Clearly, $\mathbb{B}_{ij}$, $\mathbb{B}_{i\bar{j}}$, and $\mathbb{B}_{\bar{i}j}$ are independent. Therefore, the event $\mathbb{B}$ that the link key between i and j is broken in B-KI is $\mathbb{B} = \mathbb{B}_{ij} \cup (\mathbb{B}_{i\bar{j}} \cap \mathbb{B}_{\bar{i}j})$. Therefore

$$\mathbf{P}\{\mathbb{B}\} = \mathbf{P}\{\mathbb{B}_{ij}\} + \mathbf{P}\{\mathbb{B}_{i\bar{j}}\mathbb{B}_{\bar{i}j}\} - \mathbf{P}\{\mathbb{B}_{ij}\mathbb{B}_{i\bar{j}}\mathbb{B}_{\bar{i}j}\}.$$

Thus, as to the basic key infection B-KI, the outage probability $\mathbf{P}_{B-KI}$ that the link key between a pair of sensors is compromised, is equal to the probability that event $\mathbb{B}$ occurs. More preciously,

$$\mathbf{P}_{B-KI} = \mathbf{P}_{\mathbb{R}_{ij}(R)} + \mathbf{P}_{\mathbb{R}_{i\bar{j}}(R)} \cdot \mathbf{P}_{\mathbb{R}_{\bar{i}j}(R)} - \mathbf{P}_{\mathbb{R}_{ij}(R)} \cdot \mathbf{P}_{\mathbb{R}_{i\bar{j}}(R)} \cdot \mathbf{P}_{\mathbb{R}_{\bar{i}j}(R)}.$$

It will be convenient to introduce a new notation, $\varphi(x_1, x_2, \ldots, x_n) = \varphi(x_1) \cdot \varphi(x_2) \cdots \varphi(x_n)$, where $\varphi(x) = 1 - (1 - x \cdot \frac{n'}{n})^t$. Then, the outage probability $\mathbf{P}_{B-KI}$ can be expressed as

$$\mathbf{P}_{B-KI} = \varphi(0.5865) + \varphi^2(0.4135) - \varphi(0.5865)\varphi^2(0.4135). \tag{1}$$

4.2   Whispering Key Infection

Whispering key infection (W-KI) [7] makes a small change to improve the performance of the basic key infection. Sensor starts off transmitting very quietly and steadily increases the power until a response is heard. We begin by considering the case (denoted as W-KI(2)) that both parties exploit whispering key infection to establish a link key. Consider Fig. 3(a), where $\|i - j\| = x$, we have $\mathbb{A}_{ij}(x) = (\frac{2\pi}{3} - \frac{\sqrt{3}}{2})x^2$, and its expectation

$$\mathbf{E}[\mathbb{A}_{ij}(x)] = \int_0^R \mathbb{A}_{ij}(x) \frac{2x}{R^2} \mathrm{d}x = \left(\frac{\pi}{3} - \frac{\sqrt{3}}{4}\right) R^2 \approx 0.1955\pi R^2.$$

Again, we have $\mathbb{A}_{i\bar{j}}(x) = \mathbb{A}_{\bar{i}j}(x) = (\frac{\pi}{3} + \frac{\sqrt{3}}{2})x^2$, and

$$\mathbf{E}[\mathbb{A}_{i\bar{j}}(x)] = \mathbf{E}[\mathbb{A}_{\bar{i}j}(x)] = \int_0^R \mathbb{A}_{ij}(x) \frac{2x}{R^2} \mathrm{d}x = \left(\frac{\pi}{6} + \frac{\sqrt{3}}{4}\right) R^2 \approx 0.3045\pi R^2.$$

For two parties whispering key infection, W-KI(2), the outage probability $\mathbf{P}_{W-KI(2)}$ that the key is compromised is

$$\mathbf{P}_{W-KI(2)} = \mathbf{P}_{\mathbb{R}_{ij}(x)} + \mathbf{P}_{\mathbb{R}_{\bar{i}j}(x)}\mathbf{P}_{\mathbb{R}_{\bar{i}j}(x)} - \mathbf{P}_{\mathbb{R}_{ij}(x)}\mathbf{P}_{\mathbb{R}_{i\bar{j}}(x)}\mathbf{P}_{\mathbb{R}_{\bar{i}j}(x)}$$
$$= \varphi(0.1955) + \varphi^2(0.3045) - \varphi(0.1955)\varphi^2(0.3045) \qquad (2)$$

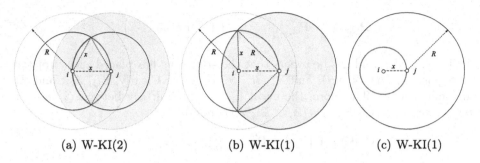

(a) W-KI(2)   (b) W-KI(1)   (c) W-KI(1)

Fig. 3. Two adjacent sensors in W-KI(2) and W-KI(1).

Now considering the case that only one party applies whispering key infection, denoted as W-KI(1). As depicted in Fig. 3(b) and (c), sensor i uses whispering key infection to communicate with sensor j, but j communicates with i using the maximum communication radius R. In this case, the area of the lenticular overlap region $\mathbb{R}_{ij}(x, R)$ is

$$\mathbb{A}_{ij}(x, R) = \begin{cases} \pi x^2 & 0 < x \leq \frac{R}{2}, \\ g(x) & \frac{R}{2} < x \leq R. \end{cases}$$

where, $g(x) = 2x^2 \sin^{-1}\frac{R}{2x} + R^2 \cos^{-1}\frac{R}{2x} - \frac{R}{2}\sqrt{4x^2 - R^2}$.

$$\mathbf{E}[\mathbb{A}_{ij}(x, R)] = \int_0^R \mathbb{A}_{ij}(x, R)\frac{2x}{R^2}\mathrm{d}x = \int_0^{\frac{R}{2}} \pi x^2 \frac{2x}{R^2}\mathrm{d}x + \int_{\frac{R}{2}}^R g(x)\frac{2x}{R^2}\mathrm{d}x \approx 0.2932\pi R^2.$$

When $R/2 < x \leq R$, $\mathbb{A}_{i\bar{j}}(x, R) = \pi x^2 - g(x)$. So we have

$$\mathbf{E}[\mathbb{A}_{i\bar{j}}(x, R)] = \int_{\frac{R}{2}}^R \mathbb{A}_{i\bar{j}}(x, R)\frac{2x}{R^2}\mathrm{d}x \approx 0.2068\pi R^2,$$

$$\mathbf{E}[\mathbb{A}_{\bar{i}j}(x, R)] = \pi R^2 - \mathbf{E}[\mathbb{A}_{ij}(x, R)] = 0.7068\pi R^2.$$

In consequence, the probability that a key is broken in W-KI(1) is

$$\mathbf{P}_{W-KI(1)} = \mathbf{P}_{\mathbb{R}_{ij}(x,R)} + \mathbf{P}_{\mathbb{R}_{i\bar{j}}(x,R)} \cdot \mathbf{P}_{\mathbb{R}_{\bar{i}j}(x,R)}$$
$$- \mathbf{P}_{\mathbb{R}_{ij}(x,R)} \cdot \mathbf{P}_{\mathbb{R}_{i\bar{j}}(x,R)} \cdot \mathbf{P}_{\mathbb{R}_{\bar{i}j}(x,R)}$$
$$= \varphi(0.2932) + \varphi(0.2068, 0.7068)$$
$$- \varphi(0.2932, 0.2068, 0.7068). \qquad (3)$$

4.3   Secrecy Amplification

Secrecy amplification (SA-KI) [7] utilizes multipath key establishment to make the adversary's job harder. As depicted in Fig. 4, sensors i, j use intermediate sensor k to update their initial key. The communication radius is R, the distances between i and j, i and k, j and k are x, y, z, respectively. We first estimate the area of overlap region $\mathbb{R}_{ijk}(R)$ among three neighboring sensors.

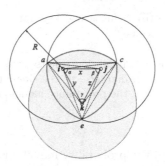

Fig. 4. Three adjacent sensors i, j, and k in SA-KI.

Let $\alpha = \angle cie$, $\beta = \angle aje$, and $\gamma = \angle akc$. Then, $\alpha = \cos^{-1}\frac{x}{2R} + \cos^{-1}\frac{y}{2R} - \cos^{-1}\frac{x^2+y^2-z^2}{2xy}$, $\beta = \cos^{-1}\frac{x}{2R} + \cos^{-1}\frac{z}{2R} - \cos^{-1}\frac{x^2+z^2-y^2}{2xz}$, $\gamma = \cos^{-1}\frac{y}{2R} + \cos^{-1}\frac{z}{2R} - \cos^{-1}\frac{y^2+z^2-x^2}{2yz}$, and the area of $\triangle ace$ is $S_{\triangle ace} = \sqrt{l(l-ce)(l-ae)(l-ac)}$, where $l = \frac{1}{2}(ce + ae + ac)$, $ce = 2R\sin(\alpha/2)$, $ae = 2R\sin(\beta/2)$, $ac = 2R\sin(\gamma/2)$.

The area of region $\mathbb{R}_{ijk}(R)$ shown in Fig. 4 is $\mathbb{A}_{ijk}(R) = S_{\triangle ace} + \frac{R^2}{2}(\alpha + \beta + \gamma - \sin\alpha - \sin\beta - \sin\gamma)$, and

$$\mathbf{E}[\mathbb{A}_{ijk}(R)] = \iiint_0^R \mathbb{A}_{ijk}(R)f(x)f(y)f(z)\mathrm{d}x\mathrm{d}y\mathrm{d}z \approx 0.4942\pi R^2,$$

where $f(x) = 2x/R^2$, $f(y) = 2y/R^2$, and $f(z) = 2z/R^2$.

According to Subsect. 4.1, $\mathbf{E}[\mathbb{A}_{ij}(R)] = \mathbf{E}[\mathbb{A}_{ik}(R)] = \mathbf{E}[\mathbb{A}_{jk}(R)] = 0.5865\pi R^2$, $\mathbf{E}[\mathbb{A}_{i\bar{j}}(R)] = \mathbf{E}[\mathbb{A}_{\bar{i}j}(R)] = 0.4135\pi R^2$, $\mathbf{E}[\mathbb{A}_{ij\bar{k}}(R)] = \mathbf{E}[\mathbb{A}_{ij}(R)] - \mathbf{E}[\mathbb{A}_{ijk}(R)] = 0.5865\pi R^2 - 0.4942\pi R^2 = 0.0923\pi R^2$, $\mathbf{E}[\mathbb{A}_{\bar{i}\bar{j}k}(R)] = \pi R^2 - \mathbf{E}[\mathbb{A}_{ik}(R)] - \mathbf{E}[\mathbb{A}_{jk}(R)] + \mathbf{E}[\mathbb{A}_{ijk}(R)] = 0.3212\pi R^2$.

Let events $\mathbf{A} = \mathbb{B}_{ijk}$, $\mathbf{B} = \mathbb{B}_{ij}$, $\mathbf{C} = \mathbb{B}_{\bar{i}j}$, $\mathbf{D} = \mathbb{B}_{\bar{i}\bar{j}k}$, and $\mathbf{E} = \mathbb{B}_{ij\bar{k}}$, the event $\mathbb{B}$ that a key is broken after secrecy amplification is $\mathbb{B} = \mathbf{A} \cup (\mathbf{BCD}) \cup (\mathbf{DE})$. Therefore, the outage probability of SA-KI is

$$\mathbf{P}_{SA-KI} = \mathbf{P}\{\mathbb{B}\} = \mathbf{P}\{\mathbf{A}\} + \mathbf{P}\{\mathbf{BCD}\} + \mathbf{P}\{\mathbf{DE}\} - \mathbf{P}\{\mathbf{ABCD}\}$$
$$- \mathbf{P}\{\mathbf{ADE}\} - \mathbf{P}\{\mathbf{BCDE}\} + \mathbf{P}\{\mathbf{ABCDE}\}$$
$$= \varphi(a) + \varphi(b,c,d) + \varphi(d,e) - \varphi(a,b,c,d)$$
$$- \varphi(a,d,e) - \varphi(b,c,d,e) + \varphi(a,b,c,d,e). \tag{4}$$

where $a = 0.4942$, $b = c = 0.4135$, $d = 0.3212$, and $e = 0.0923$.

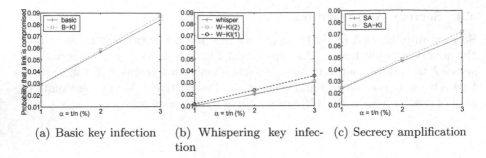

(a) Basic key infection   (b) Whispering key infec- (c) Secrecy amplification
                                tion

Fig. 5. The outage probability of simulation results [7] vs. the probability model. For each subfigure, the solid line with marker + is the simulation results given in [7], the dotted line represents the result of the probability model proposed in this paper. Here, $n' = 5$, $\alpha = t/n$.

The analytical results of the probability model for key infection are given in Fig. 5. Our results of probability model approximate to the simulation results in [7]. Therefore, this model can help designers to evaluate key infection and adapt it to their needs.

5   Group Based Key Infection

In practice, it is quite common that sensors are deployed in groups. Consider several canisters of sensors deployed via an artillery shell into enemy territory, sensors within a canister are more likely to be close to each other *a priori*. In this section, we present a group based key infection scheme, G-KI, to improve the security of key infection.

Group Based Key Infection. The scheme consists of two steps:

> *Step 1: In-group key establishment.* Before deployment, sensors are first pre-arranged into small groups, and sensors apply key infection to establish pairwise keys with all the other sensors in the same group.
> *Step 2: Cross-group key establishment.* After deployment, if two adjacent sensors have not established a secret key, they use key infection to negotiate a key. Secrecy amplification could be applied jointly if needed.

Evaluation of G-KI. Group based key infection is trivially secure if an adversary arrives after the cross-group key establishment phase. Only link between two sensors belong to different groups can be broken by eavesdroppers. In our analysis and simulations, we use the following setup:

- The number of sensors in the network is $n = 1080$. The deployment area is $500\,\text{m} \times 500\,\text{m}$, and is divided into a grid of size $36 = 6 \times 6$. The center of

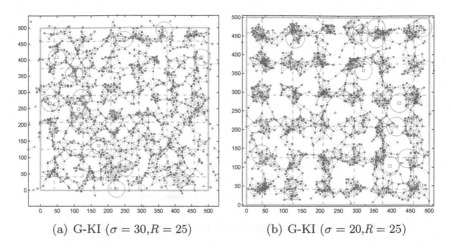

(a) G-KI ($\sigma = 30, R = 25$)　　　(b) G-KI ($\sigma = 20, R = 25$)

Fig. 6. Deployment examples of G-KI with different σ. Red squares and blue circles denote eavesdroppers and sensors, respectively. Red lines are the links compromised by the adversary, blue dot lines are the secure links. The big red circles are eavesdropping regions of eavesdroppers. (Color figure online)

each grid cell is the deployment point. Any sensor in the deployment group G_i follows a two-dimensional Gaussian distribution centered at a deployment point (x_i, y_i) with the standard deviation σ.

Figure 6 shows two deployment examples of G-KI with different σ. Figure 7 illustrates the probability that a link key is compromised for different standard deviation σ and communication radius R. Clearly, smaller σ, lower the probability that a link key is compromised. This indicates that G-KI can improve the security of key infection as long as the nodes in a group are close to each other after deployment.

Assume two sensors i and j which belong to the same group G_k are deployed independently from the two-dimensional Gaussian distribution centered at a deployment point (a_k, b_k) with location $(\mathbf{X}_i, \mathbf{Y}_i)$ and $(\mathbf{X}_j, \mathbf{Y}_j)$ respectively. For $\mathbf{X}_i$, $\mathbf{X}_j$, $\mathbf{Y}_i$, and $\mathbf{Y}_j$ are independent normal random variables which have the distributions $\mathbf{X}_i, \mathbf{X}_j \sim \mathcal{N}(a_k, \sigma^2)$, $\mathbf{Y}_i, \mathbf{Y}_j \sim \mathcal{N}(b_k, \sigma^2)$, then, random variables $\mathbf{X} = \mathbf{X}_i - \mathbf{X}_j \sim \mathcal{N}(0, 2\sigma^2)$, $\mathbf{Y} = \mathbf{Y}_i - \mathbf{Y}_j \sim \mathcal{N}(0, 2\sigma^2)$, and

$$f_{\mathbf{X},\mathbf{Y}}(x,y) = \frac{1}{4\pi\sigma} e^{-\frac{x^2+y^2}{4\sigma^2}}, -\infty < x, y < \infty$$

Therefore, the distance between nodes i and j, $\mathbf{Z} = \sqrt{\mathbf{X}^2 + \mathbf{Y}^2}$ has the *Rayleigh* distribution, $\mathbf{Z} = \sqrt{\mathbf{X}^2 + \mathbf{Y}^2} \sim Rayleigh(\sqrt{2}\sigma)$, and the probability distribution function of $\mathbf{Z}$ is given by $F_{\mathbf{Z}}(z) = 1 - e^{-\frac{z^2}{4\sigma^2}}$, $(z \geq 0)$. Therefore, the probability that two sensors in the same group are adjacent after deployment is $\mathbf{P}\{\mathbf{Z} \leq R\} = 1 - e^{-\frac{R^2}{4\sigma^2}}$.

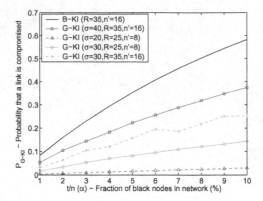

Fig. 7. Probability that a link is compromised in G-KI.

As Fig. 6 depicted, when the deviation σ increases, the sensors are more evenly distributed, but the benefits introduced by G-KI diminish monotonically, because the sensors in the same group are not close to each other. An appropriate σ is a trade-off between the security and the suitable distribution of the network.

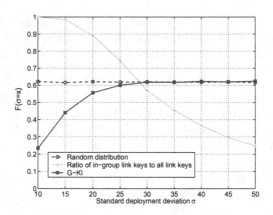

Fig. 8. How a distribution of G-KI with different deviation σ approximates random distribution in the field.

To tackle this contradiction, we evaluate how the distribution of sensors approximates to the random distribution over the deployment field. We first divide the whole deployment field into very small equal size cells, and calculate the deviation $Var(\sigma = x)$ of the number of sensors in each cell[1] when

---

[1] In our simulation, the field is divided into 50×50 square cells $cell(i,j), 1 \le i \le 50, 1 \le j \le 50$ with equal size. The number of sensors in each cell is calculated except the cells located at edges. Let the number of sensors in $cell(i,j)$ is $|cell(i,j)|$, the $Var(\sigma = x)$ is estimated as following: $\mu = \frac{1}{48 \times 48} \sum_{i=2}^{49} \sum_{j=2}^{49} |cell(i,j)|$, $Var(\sigma = x) = \frac{1}{48 \times 48} \sum_{i=2}^{49} \sum_{j=2}^{49} (\mu - |cell(i,j)|)^2$.

$\sigma = x$. Then, we define a function $F(x) = e^{-Var(\sigma=x)}$. If $F(x_1) > F(x_2)$, the distribution with $\sigma = x_1$ is more approximate to random distribution than the distribution with $\sigma = x_2$. Figure 8 depicts the simulation results of $F(x)$ with different σ. When $\sigma \geq 30$, the distribution of G-KI asymptotic approximates to random distribution.

6   Conclusions

Although key infection may seem extremely counterintuitive, it is remarkably simple and efficient. As can be anticipated, a one-fit-all solution does not work for all kinds of sensor networks, key infection provides a viable way to trade off security for cost and usability. Our probability model can help network designers to evaluate the security of key infection and adapt it to their needs. On occasions where more security is needed, group based key infection can be applied to further improve its security performance.

Acknowledgments. This work was supported by the National Key Research and Development Program of China (2016YFB0800601), the National Natural Science Foundation of China (61671360, 61173135), and in part by the Natural Science Basic Research Plan in Shaanxi Province of China (2017JM6082).

References

1. Ding, J., Bouabdallah, A., Tarokh, V.: Key pre-distributions from graph-based block designs. IEEE Sens. J. **16**(6), 1842–1850 (2016)
2. Bechkit, W., Challal, Y., Bouabdallah, A., Tarokh, V.: A highly scalable key pre-distribution scheme for wireless sensor networks. IEEE Trans. Wirel. Commun. **12**(2), 948–959 (2013)
3. Eschenauer, L., Gligor, V.: A key-management scheme for distributed sensor networks, In: Proceedings of the 9th ACM Conference on Computer and Communications Security, pp. 41–47. ACM Press, Washington (2002)
4. Yağan, O., Makowski, A.M.: Wireless sensor networks under the random pairwise key predistribution scheme: can resiliency be achieved with small key rings? IEEE/ACM Trans. Netw. **24**(6), 3383–3396 (2016)
5. Du, W., Deng, J., Han, Y.S., Chen, S., Varshney, P.K.: A key management scheme for wireless sensor networks using deployment knowledge. In: INFOCOM 2004, pp. 586–597. IEEE Press, New York (2004)
6. Choi, J., Bang, J., Kim, L., Ahn, M., Kwon, T.: Location-based key management strong against insider threats in wireless sensor networks. IEEE Syst. J. **11**(2), 494–502 (2017)
7. Anderson, R., Chan, H., Perrig, A.: Key infection: smart trust for smart dust. In: IEEE International Conference on Network Protocols, pp. 206–215. IEEE Press, New York (2004)

SDN-Based Secure Localization in Heterogeneous WSN

Meigen Huang[✉] and Bin Yu

Zhengzhou Information Science and Technology Institute,
Zhengzhou 450001, China
huang_meigen@163.com, byu2009@163.com

Abstract. There is a big security risk in traditional distributed localization without protecting the location and identity privacy of anchor nodes. Thus, based on software-defined networking (SDN), we propose a security localization mechanism for heterogeneous wireless sensor networks (WSN). After obtaining the state of sensor nodes in data plane, SDN controller runs the complementary range-based and range-free positional algorithms in a centralized way. At the same time, the difference of transmission power of heterogeneous sensor nodes is taken into account. The security analysis and experimental results show that the mechanism can reduce the positioning error while ensuring the privacy of anchor nodes.

Keywords: Wireless Sensor Networks (WSN)
Software-Defined Networking (SDN) · Secure localization · RSSI
DV-Hop

1 Introduction

The rapid development of Internet of Things (IoT) [1,2] makes wireless sensor networks (WSN) [3] face great challenges in heterogeneous interconnection and network management. The introduction of software-defined networking (SDN) has brought the dawn to solve this problem [4,5]. Centralized control is one of the core feature of SDN. Constructing network global view is the basis task of control plane [6], where the sensor node location information is the priority among priorities. On the one hand, the valuable sensing information must be associated with the location, and which is an important guarantee of quality of service (QoS). On the other hand, with the paradigm of "sensing as a service", location information is a significant foundation for the distribution and deployment of sensing services [7].

In distributed WSN, the sensor nodes localization method is usually divided into two kinds of range-based and range-free technologies [8]. Note that the

M. Huang—This work is supported by Key Laboratory of Information Assurance Technology Open Fund under granted no. KJ-15-104.

localization in this paper refers to the planar positioning of sensor node itself. The range-based localization refers to achieve location by using certain means to measure the distance between nodes, which including received signal strength indicator (RSSI), signal transmission time or angle [9–11]. With ease of implementation and no additional hardware, the RSSI-based method becomes the preferred localization technology in WSN. The range-free positioning indicates some properties of sensor nodes are used to obtain location, such as neighbors or hops [12,13]. This approach reduces the localization cost by sacrificing positioning accuracy, and is generally applicable to large-scale networks. Among them, the most classic one is hop-based DV-Hop algorithm [14].

Although there are large divergences in the above two methods, the basic process is essentially the same. First, the blind node (the sensor node to be positioned) acquires the distance (expressed as RSSI or hops, etc.) with the anchor node (the reference node with known location) through the range-based or range-free methods. Then, the anchor node publishes its own location information as a reference to blind node. Finally, the blind node calculates the position through plane geometry relation.

However, the above procedure does not take into account the anchor node location and identity privacy, and it is a big security threaten. The malicious node can pretend to be the blind node to eavesdrop the location information of anchor node. As the next step, it can destroy the network positioning capabilities by targeted physical destruction or signal interference. In turn, the malicious node can affect the positioning accuracy and QoS by impersonating anchor node to publish the fictitious location information [15]. In addition, the transmission power and radius of sensor nodes are different in heterogeneous WSN, and the RSSI- or hop-based distance may have notable errors, so the node localization accuracy is confronted with great challenges [16].

As far as the authors know, there is no related research using SDN to solve the security location problem in WSN, and only [17,18] using SDN method to program the activation state of anchor nodes. Although the node localization accuracy and network energy consumption are well balanced, it is still belonging to distributed positioning with the privacy leak problem. In view of this, we propose a centralized security localization mechanism based on SDN for heterogeneous WSN. In which, the localization algorithm is run on the SDN controller, thus ensuring the security of sensitive information such as anchor node location and identity. In addition, in the distance calculation process, the positioning accuracy is greatly enhanced by considering the transmission power of heterogeneous sensor nodes. Relative to sensor nodes, many capabilities of SDN controller like energy, computing, storage, communication, etc., are generally considered unrestricted. Therefore, the mechanism can effectively reduce the sensor node positioning load.

The outline of the rest of this paper is organized as follows: Sect. 2 gives a general introduction to the secure localization model. And the corresponding algorithm is detailedly described in Sect. 3. Section 4 analyzes the security and performance of the mechanism. Experimental design and results analysis is elaborated in Sect. 5 and summed up in Sect. 6.

2   Secure Localization Model

According to SDN paradigm, a security localization model is designed for heterogeneous WSN, as shown in Fig. 1. The model is mainly divided into control plane and data plane, in which SDN controller realizes the logical control of sensor nodes through the control link (essentially belongs to southbound interface protocol, such as Sensor OpenFlow [4], etc.).

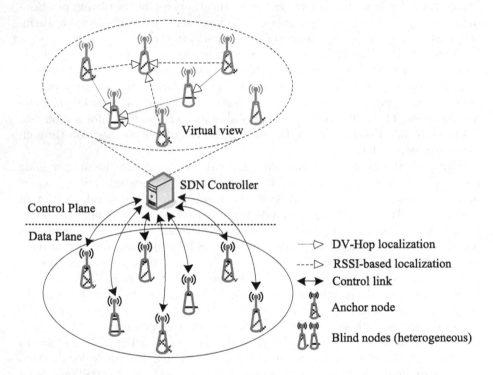

Fig. 1. Secure localization model

The data plane includes anchor and blind nodes. The anchor nodes can obtain its own position information by coordinates presetting or GPS positioning, so as to provide reference for the blind nodes. Considering heterogeneous factor, we design two classes of blind nodes. The same point is that they are sensor nodes to be located and can communicate with each other. And the difference between them is in the level of residual energy, communication radius and transmission power [19].

Limitations of space, we only designed a single controller, but can be extended to a logic unified control plane with multi-controllers. SDN controller is the key of security localization mechanism, the ultimate goal is to achieve the virtual view (part of the network global view) which all the sensor nodes are accurately positioned. It is necessary to illustrate that the position similarity between virtual view and data plane reflects the mechanism performance. At the same time, the security embodied in the virtual view too. By using centralized localization instead of traditional distributed one, SDN controller can protect the sensitive information in positional process, thus effectively resisting multiple attacks from malicious node for location based services. In the choice of centralized positioning algorithm, considering the diversity of traditional location technology, we only select two popular algorithms from range-based and range-free classes respectively, namely RSSI-based and DV-Hop algorithms.

3   Secure Localization Algorithm

According to the above model, the secure location algorithm includes state acquisition and centralized positioning. Among them, the former is the basis of mechanism security, and the latter is the key to algorithm efficiency.

3.1   State Acquisition

After the network is deployed, SDN controller first constructs the quaternion $LT = \langle ID, GP, SP, NT \rangle$ with the status information related to the sensor node location in data plane through control link. Where ID stands for the sensor node identity, GP represents the node location information (the blind node is empty) in the form of plane coordinates, and SP indicates the node transmission power (dBm). In the end, $NT = (\langle ID, LS \rangle, \langle ID, LS \rangle, \cdots)$ is the node neighbor table as linked list, where LS means the link quality with neighbor node in the form of RSSI.

In order to facilitate the calculation, the LSs of heterogeneous sensor nodes are preprocessed. The wireless signal propagation model commonly used in WSN is log-normal distribution model [20]. In the model, SP has the positive correlation with LS, as shown in Eq. (1), where $P_L(d)$ is the path loss when distance is d.

$$P_L(d) = SP - LS \tag{1}$$

It can be seen that SDN controller can normalize all the LSs by the minimum transmit power (SP_{min}) among all the sensor nodes, as shown in Eq. (2), and the amended LS denoted as LS'.

$$LS' = LS - (SP - SP_{min}) \tag{2}$$

Therefore, the preprocessing process is as follows: SDN controller traverses the NT in LT, then fixes the LS using formula (2) and rewrites the LS' to the corresponding $\langle ID, LS \rangle$ in each loop.

3.2   Centralized Positioning

After completing the state acquisition phase, SDN controller begins to perform centralized positioning to build a virtual view that actually reflects the data plane location information. In general, the node communication radius is not the same in heterogeneous WSN. In addition, there is a certain randomness with the node position by throwing deployment. Therefore, two types of positioning algorithm, namely RSSI-based and DV-Hop, shown in Fig. 2, with a view to the joint application to improve the positioning accuracy.

In Fig. 2, (a) is the RSSI-based localization algorithm, and three-or more anchor nodes can be used to calculate the location of blind nodes in the form of trajectory intersection, as shown in Eq. (3). Where the distance d is calculated using the log-normal distribution model [20]. Note that if the intersection located a small area, then the center of mass can be regarded as the final result. In general, this algorithm has high positioning accuracy and is well suited for dense areas of anchor nodes deployment (the more concentrated the anchor nodes, the higher the positioning accuracy).

$$\begin{cases} (x - x_1)^2 + (y - y_1)^2 = d_1^2 \\ (x - x_2)^2 + (y - y_2)^2 = d_2^2 \\ (x - x_3)^2 + (y - y_3)^2 = d_3^2 \end{cases} \tag{3}$$

(b) is the DV-Hop localization algorithm in the range-free class. Its main idea is taking the product of average estimated distance (ED) per hop and the number of hops as the final estimation distance between blind and anchor nodes. Thus,

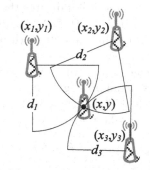

(a) RSSI-based localization

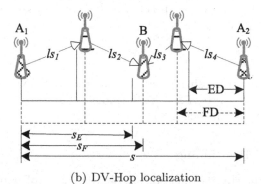

(b) DV-Hop localization

Fig. 2. Localization algorithms

it can be used as a supplement to RSSI-based algorithm for the areas where the anchor nodes are sparser. In order to improve the positioning accuracy of DV-Hop, this paper adopts the fixed distance (FD) by RSSI replace of ED per hop. As shown in Fig. 2(b), the number of hops between the anchor nodes A_1 and A_2 is 4, the distance is s, and the number of hops between blind node B and A_1 or A_2 are 2, so the traditional DV-Hop algorithm estimates the distance from B to A_1 or A_2 are $s_E = s \times 2/4$. Obviously, the positioning error arises. Therefore, we use the ratio relation between LSs to correct each hop distance, and the distance between B and A_1 (S_F) is shown in Eq. (4). Similarly, the distance between B and A_2 can be calculated.

$$s_F = \frac{ls_1 + ls_2}{ls_1 + ls_2 + ls_3 + ls_4} \times s \tag{4}$$

The algorithm flow chart is shown in Fig. 3. Among them, "Build LT" and "Amend LS" belong to the state acquisition phase, "RSSI-based Localization" and "DV-Hop Localization" are implemented in the centralized positioning stage, and "Complete Virtual View" is the final result of the algorithm.

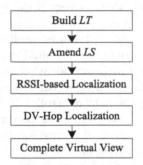

Fig. 3. Algorithm flow chart

4   Security and Performance Analysis

This section mainly analyzes the security and performance of the proposed algorithm. To our mind, the high security is the advantage, and the high performance is the prerequisite for our scheme.

4.1   Security Analysis

The design motivation of the security localization mechanism is to protect the anchor node location and identity privacy. Note that we assume that SDN controller with its control links is secure and sensor nodes can be effectively authenticated. On the basis of this, the algorithm adopts centralized positioning method. In the state acquisition stage, SDN controller treats all the nodes equally, avoiding the need for anchor nodes to broadcast their own location and identity in the distributed positioning technology. Thus, the attacker cannot get through eavesdropping to obtain the anchor node location, but also difficult to locate the anchor node through traffic analysis attack, and then capture or tamper is not feasible too. In other words, the probability of discovery anchor node through eavesdropping or traffic analysis attacks is equal to the one that the random selection node among all the sensor nodes is an anchor node. In addition, the attacker disguised as an anchor node is bound to be recognized by SDN controller.

Obviously, due to the openness of WSN deployment with its wireless channel, the attackers can physically capture all the sensor nodes, but the attack cost is huge, the actual feasibility is not high. It is worth mentioning that this mechanism cannot resist certain attacks aimed at the transmission signal to increase the positioning error, such as the installation of obstacles to reduce the LS between the neighbors. Such attacks in the distributed positioning method is also difficult to withstand.

4.2 Performance Analysis

The algorithm performance mainly includes three aspects: storage, calculation and communication. However, there is very little demand for storage resources in the positioning process, so it is not to be considered.

Towards calculation overhead, distributed positioning mechanism (including RSSI-based and DV-Hop algorithms), the blind nodes are required to perform certain operations to calculate their own location information. In our algorithm, the anchor and blind nodes do not need to run any action, all the computational overhead are concentrated in the SDN controller. Typically, SDN controller runs on the resourceful server, and the computing power can be considered infinity. Therefore, the computational cost of secure localization mechanism is better than that of distributed positioning method.

Wireless communication is the largest energy source of sensor nodes [21], which has a large impact on the lifetime of WSN. Figure 2 is used as a reference to compare the communication overhead, as shown in Table 1.

Obviously, the centralized localization advantage is very obvious in the communication overhead. For (a) and (b), the security localization mechanism can save 25% and 40% of communication cost than distributed positioning method respectively. Note that this is an analysis within five or less nodes. Typically, the number of nodes in WSN is very large, for example, ZigBee network can

Table 1. Comparison of communication overhead

		(a) RSSI-based	(b) DV-Hop
Centralization	Anchor node	12 bits	8 bits
	Blind node	6 bits	4 bits
Distributed	Anchor node	6 bits	8 bits
	Blind node	18 bits	12 bits

accommodate up to 65535 nodes [22]. Therefore, the communication cost of distributed positioning method may have a great impact on the network energy consumption in a large-scaled network.

5   Experiments and Results

The experiment is based on SDN-WISE architecture [23] and COOJA simulator [24]. During the construction of network global view, SDN-WISE only considers the connection relation of sensor nodes, but doesn't take the location information into account. Therefore, this paper builds the virtual view by adding new security module in SDN controller.

5.1   Experimental Deployment

The experimental network is randomly deployed in the planar area of $200 \times 200 \, \text{m}^2$, and the node transmission radius is set to 50 m. The number of nodes is regard as independent variables, from 30 to 110 with increment is 20, to analyze the effect of network size on the performance of the localization algorithm. In addition, the ratio of anchor nodes is also as a variable, taking 10%, 30% and 50% respectively, to analyze the influence of the number of anchor nodes on the network positioning accuracy. Considering the difference of transmission power between heterogeneous sensor nodes, 60% node is set to 1.0 dBm, and the remaining 40% nodes is randomly set to -1.5 dBm or 4.5 dBm. To simplify the analysis, we assume the transmit power has no effect on the transmission distance (there are quadratic curve relationship in theory). In addition, the node initial power is set to 9×10^6 mC (approximately equal to the power of 2 AAA batteries). The parameter settings are shown in Table 2.

Table 2. Parameter settings

Parameters	Value
Deployment area	$200 \times 200 \, \text{m}^2$
Transmission radius	50 m
Initial power	9×10^6 mC
Number of nodes	From 30 to 110 with increment is 20
Anchor node ratio	10%, 30% and 50%
Transmission power	1.0 dBm (60%), -1.5 dBm (20%) and 4.5 dBm (20%)

5.2   Experimental Results

(1) Energy Consumption
The comparison of energy consumption in centralization and distributed positioning methods is shown in Fig. 4. In which, the X- and Y-axes are the number of

sensor nodes and network average residual energy respectively, the black polyg-
onal line represents the proposed centralized positioning algorithm, and the blue
one stand for the distributed positioning using DV-Hop Algorithm. In addition,
the percentage data in explanatory text means the anchor node ratio.

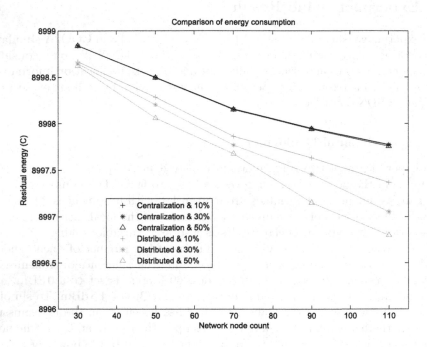

Fig. 4. Comparison of energy consumption (Color figure online)

It can be seen from Fig. 4 that the centralized localization algorithm is superior to the distributed one in energy consumption. With the increase in the
number of network nodes, it is natural that the time and energy required for
network positioning are correspondingly raised. However, the dissipation energy
in the distributed method is relatively fast. In addition, with the increase in the
proportion of anchor nodes, the energy consumption in centralized localization
is only slightly increased, while the raise in distributed positioning is very obvious. The fundamental reason is that the energy consumption of our mechanism
is mainly reflected in the state acquisition phase. At the same time, for all the
nodes are treated equally by SDN controller, thus it is only need to transfer the
location data of additional anchor nodes. On the contrary, DV-Hop algorithm
will in the full use of the anchor nodes to improve the positioning accuracy,
naturally wasting more network energy.

(2) Positioning Accuracy
In this paper, we take the concept of overall positioning accuracy, that is, the
sum of all the location deviation distance divided by the product of network

node count and communication radius, recorded as P_a, as shown in Eq. (5). Note that the deviation distance of unsuccessful positioning node is the same as node transmission radius.

$$P_a = \frac{\sum |p, \tilde{p}|}{NR} \tag{5}$$

Where p and $\tilde{p}$ are the true and calculated node locations respectively, $|\bullet|$ denotes as the Euclidean distance, N represents the number of blind nodes, and R is the node transmission radius.

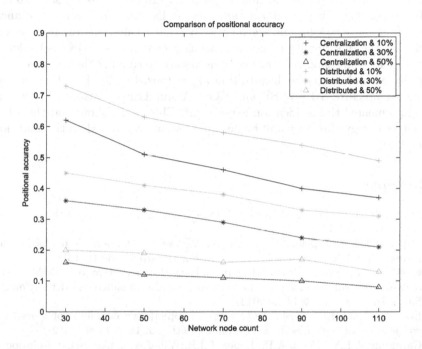

Fig. 5. Comparison of positioning accuracy

The positioning accuracy is shown in Fig. 5, and the drawing notes are the same as those shown in Fig. 4, which are no longer explained. Obviously, the security localization mechanism is better than the distributed positioning scheme, and the advantages are more prominent when the anchor nodes are deployed sparse. The reason is that this mechanism joint uses a variety of positioning algorithms (This paper enumerates only RSSI-based and DV-Hop methods). In the meantime, the transmission power is adopted to amend the link quality, and further applied to reduce the DV-Hop positioning error. In addition, as a whole, the more anchor node deployment, the higher the positioning accuracy, and when the proportion reaches 50%, the positioning error can be less than 0.1. Therefore, this scheme can effectively improve the positioning performance of heterogeneous WSN.

6   Summary

In the traditional distributed positioning method, the anchor node must broadcast its own location and identity information to assist the blind node positioning process. However, this approach makes the anchor node easily become the attack target, such as malicious nodes launching eavesdropping attacks to obtain anchor node location, and then can be implemented targeted manual capture or signal interference. To change this situation, we adopt SDN paradigm to transfer the distributed positioning process to SDN controller, so as to effectively protect the privacy information such as location and identity of anchor nodes. The above conclusions are verified by security analysis. In addition, after modifying the link quality of heterogeneous sensor nodes, SDN controller can improve the positioning accuracy of blind nodes by running the complementary range-based and range-free localization algorithms. Finally, based on the open source architecture SDN-WISE and COOJA simulation platform, we designed and implemented the verification experiment. The results show that the scheme has better energy efficiency and higher positioning accuracy than the traditional method.

References

1. Miorandi, D., Sicari, S., Pellegrini, F.D., Chlamtac, I.: Internet of things. Ad Hoc Netw. **10**, 1497–1516 (2012)
2. Capella, J.V., Campelo, J.C., Bonastre, A., Ors, R.: A reference model for monitoring IoT WSN-based applications. Sensors **16**, 1816–1836 (2016)
3. Ovsthus, K., Kristensen, L.M.: An industrial perspective on wireless sensor networks—a survey of requirements, protocols, and challenges. IEEE Commun. Surv. Tutor. **16**, 1391–1412 (2014)
4. Luo, T., Tan, H.P., Quek, T.Q.S.: Sensor OpenFlow: enabling software-defined wireless sensor networks. IEEE Commun. Lett. **16**, 1896–1899 (2012)
5. Caraguay, Á.L.V., Peral, A.B., López, L.I.B., Villalba, L.J.G.: SDN: evolution and opportunities in the development IoT applications. Int. J. Distrib. Sens. Netw. **2014**, 1–10 (2014)
6. Kreutz, D., Ramos, F.M.V., Verissimo, P.E., Rothenberg, C.E., Azodolmolky, S., Uhlig, S.: Software-defined networking: a comprehensive survey. Proc. IEEE **103**, 14–76 (2015)
7. Perera, C., Zaslavsky, A., Christen, P., Georgakopoulos, D.: Sensing as a service model for smart cities supported by Internet of Things. Trans. ETT **25**, 81–93 (2014)
8. Han, G., Xu, H., Duong, T.Q., Jiang, J., Hara, T.: Localization algorithms of wireless sensor networks: a survey. Telecommun. Syst. **52**, 2419–2436 (2013)
9. Shao, J.F., Tian, W.Z.: Energy-efficient RSSI-based localization for wireless sensor networks. IEEE Commun. Lett. **18**, 973–976 (2014)
10. Shao, H.J., Zhang, X.P., Wang, Z.: Efficient closed-form algorithms for AOA based self-localization of sensor nodes using auxiliary variables. IEEE Trans. Signal Process. **62**, 2580–2594 (2014)
11. Go, S., Chong, J.: Improved TOA-based localization method with BS selection scheme for wireless sensor networks. ETRI J. **37**, 707–716 (2015)

12. Ma, D., Meng, J.E., Wang, B.: Analysis of hop-count-based source-to-destination distance estimation in wireless sensor networks with applications in localization. IEEE Trans. Veh. Technol. **59**, 2998–3011 (2010)
13. García-Otero, M., Población-Hernández, A.: Secure neighbor discovery in wireless sensor networks using range-free localization techniques. Int. J. Distrib. Sens. Netw. **2012**, 178–193 (2012)
14. Gui, L., Val, T., Wei, A., Dalce, R.: Improvement of range-free localization technology by a novel DV-Hop protocol in wireless sensor networks. Ad Hoc Netw. **24**, 55–73 (2015)
15. Li, P., Yu, X., Xu, H., Qian, J., Dong, L., Nie, H.: Research on secure localization model based on trust valuation in wireless sensor networks. Secur. Commun. Netw. **2017**, 1–12 (2017)
16. Assaf, A.E., Zaidi, S., Affes, S., Kandil, N.: Low-cost localization for multihop heterogeneous wireless sensor networks. IEEE Trans. Wirel. Commun. **15**, 472–484 (2016)
17. Zhu, Y., Zhang, Y., Xia, W., Shen, L.: A software-defined network based node selection algorithm in WSN localization. In: IEEE Vehicular Technology Conference, pp. 1–5. IEEE Press, New York (2016)
18. Zhu, Y., Yan, F., Zhang, Y., Zhang, R., Shen, L.: SDN-based anchor scheduling scheme for localization in heterogeneous WSNs. IEEE Commun. Lett. **21**, 1127–1130 (2017)
19. Liu, X., Evans, B.G., Moessner, K.: Energy-efficient sensor scheduling algorithm in cognitive radio networks employing heterogeneous sensors. IEEE Trans. Veh. Technol. **64**, 1243–1249 (2015)
20. Peng, R., Sichitiu, M.L.: Probabilistic localization for outdoor wireless sensor networks. ACM SIGMOBILE Mob. Comput. Commun. Rev. **11**, 53–64 (2007)
21. Anastasi, G., Conti, M., Francesco, M.D., Passarella, A.: Energy conservation in wireless sensor networks: a survey. Ad Hoc Netw. **7**, 537–568 (2009)
22. Gill, K., Yang, S.H., Yao, F., Lu, X.: A ZigBee-based home automation system. IEEE Trans. Consum. Electron. **55**, 422–430 (2009)
23. Galluccio, L., Milardo, S., Morabito, G., Palazzo, S.: SDN-WISE: design, prototyping and experimentation of a stateful SDN solution for WIreless SEnsor networks. In: 2015 IEEE Conference on Computer Communications, INFOCOM, pp. 513–521. IEEE Press, New York (2015)
24. Osterlind, F., Dunkels, A., Eriksson, J., Finne, N., Voigt, T.: Cross-level sensor network simulation with COOJA. In: 2006 IEEE Conference on Local Computer Networks, pp. 641–648. IEEE Press, New York (2006)

Security Applications

A PUF and Software Collaborative Key Protection Scheme

Changting Li[1,2,3], Zongbin Liu[2,3(✉)], Lingchen Zhang[2,3],
Cunqing Ma[2,3], and Liang Zheng[1,2,3]

[1] School of Cyber Security, University of Chinese Academy of Sciences,
Beijing, China
[2] Data Assurance and Communication Security Research Center, Beijing, China
[3] State Key Laboratory of Information Security, Institute of Information
Engineering, CAS, Beijing, China
{lichangting, liuzongbin, zhanglingchen,
macunqing, zhengliang}@iie.ac.cn

Abstract. PUF-based key generation provides an alternative to address key storage problems. However, PUFs seem helpless in preventing the generated key from being stolen by malicious code and PUF itself is under threat of probing by adversaries. In this paper, we propose a cost-effective key protection scheme which protects against software leakage of the generated key through all stages of chip's development. In the proposed scheme, PUF primitives and device's firmware are bound together to generate the private key, therefore, the successful recovery of the key proves not only the legality of the hardware device but also the integrity of the bound firmware, which secures the operating environment of the generated key. Besides, a hash module in our scheme controls the PUF's input and output which restricts the access to PUF instance thereby further boosts the system's security.

Keywords: Key protection · Physically Unclonable Function · Controlled PUF

1 Introduction

Theoretically, authentication schemes and protocols are based on the assumption that the key stored in the non-volatile memory (NVM) is secure [1]. Unfortunately, this is quite difficult to achieve in practice. Physical attacks, e.g. side channel attack and reverse engineering, would result in key exposure and security breaks. Moreover, software attacks like malicious software and viruses, can also steal the private key. In industry, the natural idea for protecting against private key exposure through invasive physical attacks is to create a tamper sensing area to store the key information [2]. However, such methods are always complex and have not solved the essential problem that the private key is still permanently stored in the non-volatile memory.

Z. Liu—The work is supported by a grant from the National Key Research and Development Program of China (Grant No. Y16A01602).

Physically Unclonable Functions (PUFs) have been introduced to provide a more cost-effective alternative for key protection. Based on the idea that "There are no two identical leaves in the world", PUFs extract and reflect the entity's "hardware finger-prints" into their unique challenge-response behavior. Invoking a PUF instance with different challenges, it correspondingly returns different instance-specific response sequences that can be used for cryptographic purpose. PUF's such challenge-response behavior is determined directly by its physical structures. During the manufacturing process, varieties of random and uncontrollable factors would leave subtle differences on every entity, therefore, there cannot be perfectly identical products created. For example, even produced by the same production line with the most advanced control technology, every SRAM cell has its own preference of power-on state (logic '1' or '0'); the actual frequencies of nominally identical ring oscillators vary from each other; the arrival order of signals that go through similar propagation paths varies on different chips. These examples are also mechanisms of SRAM PUF [3, 4], Ring Oscillator PUF (RO PUF) [6–8] and Arbiter PUF [5, 9, 10] respectively.

As physical features extracted by PUFs are inherent and permanent, keys derived from PUFs can be generated anytime when it is strictly needed. Such keys only exist in the security system for a short period and disappear when power-off. In addition, many PUFs are tamper sensitive, invasive attacks may change PUFs' behavior notably and irreversibly, which implies that any attempts to probe the PUF instance by invasive methods is meanwhile taking risk of destroying the key material it contains.

However, PUF just address storage problems, keys derived from PUFs are still faced with disclosure threats. The prime threat that has long impaired PUF-base key protection is the leakage caused by malwares. Though the PUF-based key disappears when power-off, malicious code can also steal it during the working process. Another threat comes from the leakage of PUFs' Challenge Response Pairs (CRPs). Because keys are directly derived from PUFs' response sequences, it is crucial to prevent PUFs' CRP set from being observed completely. However, due to specialization of labor in society, PUFs are always threatened to be observed by cooperative companies or malicious employers during the manufacturing process.

In this paper, we implement a cost-effective key protection scheme, which secures the system through all stages of development.

1. We utilize PUF to bind the chip's hardware and firmware with its private key to authenticate both legality of the device and integrity of the running operating system thereby secure the operating environment of the generated key;
2. We take advantage of the concept of Controlled PUF (CPUF) and use a hash module to enhance the security of PUF's CRP set;
3. We adopt module reuse technique to make our scheme cost-effective and prove the scheme's feasibility by implementation on Xilinx KC705 evaluation boards.

The rest of the paper is organized as follows. We firstly introduce CPUFs and PUF-based key generation in Sect. 2. Then we illustrate our scheme with security discussions in Sect. 3. In Sect. 4 we present detail designs of the scheme we implement on Xilinx KC705 evaluation boards. Finally, we conclude in Sect. 5.

2 Related Work

2.1 Controlled PUFs

A PUF's CRP set contains all the secret with which the PUF can sever as a physical root of trust. Unfortunately, almost all popular electric PUFs used in practice are so called "Weak PUF". These PUFs have limited CRPs, which can be totally observed with low cost. In addition, path-delay based PUFs, e.g. Arbiter PUF and Ring Oscillator PUF, are proved to be vulnerable to modeling and machine learning attacks [11–13]. If a PUF's behavior has been penetrated, the key derived from it is also exposed.

To overcome the inborn defect of "Weak PUF", Blaise et al. proposed Controlled PUF (CPUF) [14], which enhances PUF's resistance to being modeled and broaden the application range of "Weak PUFs". A CPUF is a combination of a PUF and an inseparable circuit, which usually implements an encryption or hash algorithm. This circuit governs the PUF's input and output, which is so called "control". The input control restricts the selection of challenges, which is very effective in protecting the PUF from modeling attacks that adaptively choose challenges. The output control prevents the adversary from probing the PUF, because it hides the physical output of the PUF and the adversary can only obtain indirect sequences derived from PUF's responses [15] (Fig. 1).

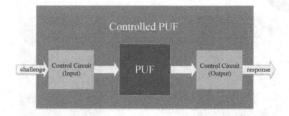

Fig. 1. Using control to improve a "Weak PUF"

2.2 PUF-Based Key Generation

PUF-base key generator is usually consisted of two parts: a secure sketch and an entropy accumulator [16–19].

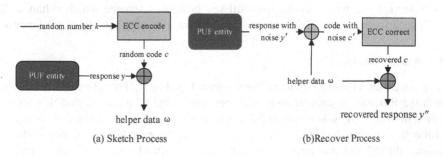

Fig. 2. Secure sketch of code-off construction

The secure sketch guarantees the perfect reproduction of the key derived from PUF's response. It is usually implemented by an Error Correcting Code (ECC) algorithm as Fig. 2 demonstrates. To ensure correctness of the key's recovery, the correcting capability of the ECC should be carefully designed according to PUF's reliability. During the sketch process, some redundant information ω will be produced. This redundant information ω is called "helper data" and can help recover the noisy response in the recover process. Generally, the helper data is stored in an NVM without any protection, the worst estimation of remaining entropy considering the helper data being revealed is $H_\infty(y) - (\#c - \#r)$, where $H_\infty(y)$ is the min-entropy of the enrolled response sequence y, $\#c$ is the code length of ECC and $\#r$ is the bit number of the encoded random number r.

Though PUF's response sequences are supposed to be random and unpredictable, they are in fact not nearly-uniform bit strings that satisfy the security requirement for a secret key. Therefore, an entropy accumulator is demanded to extract high quality random keys from response sequences that only possess limited entropy per bit. A secure hash algorithm is often applied as an entropy accumulator and the construction of PUF-based key generator is shown in Fig. 3.

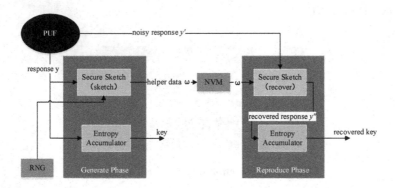

Fig. 3. Construction of PUF-based key generator

3   PUF and Software Collaborative Key Protection Scheme

In this section, we will elaborate our full key protection scheme which enhances the PUF's security and meanwhile authenticates the integrity and legality of the firmware.

3.1   Attack Model

The considered attack scenario is demonstrated in Fig. 4. Providing the NVM that stores the firmware is unprotected; other peripherals are all authenticated that none of them will leak PUF's key materials. With respect to the stored legal firmware we assume it is well behaved, i.e. it will not output the private key or key materials, besides, during the running process it carefully checks received commands or requirements to avoid buffer overflow attacks. Under these assumptions, we mainly consider the following three phases of adversaries that either have access to the PUF instance or have chance to tamper the firmware.

- **When chips are just produced:** The chip manufacturer has physical contact with the chip, which means the chip's physical features are easy to be investigated by the chip manufacturer.
- **During the software development phase:** At this stage, the bootloader and softwares have not been locked, cooperative companies or malicious employees may have chances to run malicious codes that read and send the PUF's CRPs or even the generated keys out of the chip.
- **When chips have hit the market:** When the firmware and bootloader have been locked, the most likely way for adversaries to inject malicious codes is to attack the unprotected NVM and break the secure boot system. We don't consider dynamic code injection like buffer overflow attack, for such problems are more concerned with secure software development. We assume the only approach for adversaries to inject malicious code is the NVM that stores the firmware.

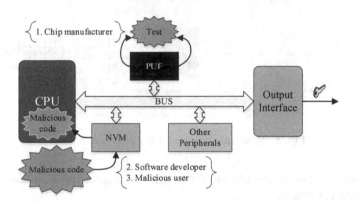

Fig. 4. Attack model

3.2 Our Scheme

The architecture of the proposed scheme is demonstrated in Fig. 5. The enhanced PUF module is consisted of a hash module, a secure sketch module and a conventional electric PUF instance.

Firstly, to keep the generated key free from injected malicious code, we aim to bind the private key with the legal firmware, consequently any subtle variation in the firmware code will lead to the failure of the key's recovery thus we can ensure that the legal key only appears when the firmware has been authenticated successfully. To achieve this goal, we condense the firmware code with the hash module. Then this hashed firmware sequence would be used as challenges to invoke the PUF instance and the obtained corresponding response sequences would serve as key generation materials. To guarantee the consistency of the running and the input firmware code, the PUF module have direct access to the NVM that stores the firmware code, i.e. firmware code is read directly by hardware logic without modification.

This hash module also serves as an entropy accumulator to form a PUF-base key generator with the secure sketch module and PUF instance. The secure sketch guarantees the generated key's reproducibility. Regarding the PUF instance, considering PUF's responses fluctuate randomly at every measurement, PUF itself can be regarded as a physical random source. Therefore, Except for offering instance-specific materials to generate the private key, PUF meanwhile forms a random number generator (RNG) with the hash module to serve the secure sketch in the key generation phase.

In addition, we notice that the PUF's input challenges and output responses have all been processed by the hash module, i.e. our design has naturally possessed CPUF structure, which strengthens PUF's resistance to adversaries like the chip manufacturer who have chance to read PUF's CRPs directly.

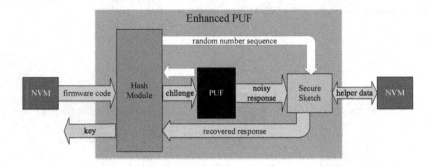

Fig. 5. Schematic diagram of the proposed scheme

The working flow of our key protection scheme is described as follows:

Key Generation Phase:

1. Directly read the firmware code (e.g. bootloader and the software code) from the NVM;
2. Calculate the hash value of the firmware code;
3. Use the obtained hash value as PUF's challenge to invoke the PUF instance and acquire a response sequence y;
4. Invoke the PUF instance multiple times to get a long response sequence y_r, hash this sequence to create a random number sequence r;
5. Sketch the response sequence y with obtained random number sequence r and save the generated helper data w in an NVM;
6. Hash the response sequence y to get the final private key pk and output it.

Key Recovery Phase:

1. Directly read the firmware code from the NVM;
2. Calculate the hash value of the firmware code;

3. Use the obtained hash value as PUF's challenge to invoke the PUF instance and acquire a noisy response sequence y';
4. Load helper data w;
5. Recover the noisy response y' with the helper data w and acquire the recovered response sequence y'';
6. Hash the recovered y'' to get the recovered private key pk' and output it.

3.3 Discussion and Analysis

Our scheme improves conventional PUF-based key protection scheme from two main aspects. On one hand, we bind the legal firmware strictly with the generated private key to protect the key throughout the chip's lifetime. During the manufacturing and software development stages, before the valid firmware is completed, there is no legal private key observed. After the software development stage, the system is sensitive to any change of the firmware code, because according to hash function's properties, even one-bit change in the firmware code will lead to a completely different hash result, i.e. a completely different challenge and finally a completely different key. Therefore, the successful recovery of the private key in return verifies the integrity and legality of the operating system by which it will be used.

On the other hand, the hash function and the PUF has naturally constructed a CPUF, thus prevent adversaries from probing the PUF instance. To investigate the enhanced PUF, the adversary should either be able to construct an input of the hash algorithm to generate a specific challenge, or to reversely derive the PUF's response from the hashed result. Therefore, adversary who can successfully investigate the enhanced PUF is equivalent to possessing the ability to break the hash algorithm.

Furthermore, PUF's inherent instance-specific behavior ensures the key's uniqueness and the reproduction of the key in return proves the identity of the hardware.

To ensure the generated key pk to be successfully reproduced and possess sufficient entropy, two requirements must be satisfied: correctness requirement and security requirement. Before analysis we should build a proper model of PUF's response.

PUF's Response Model: Providing every bit of the response sequence is independent. The actually measured response can be modeled as

$$Y_{meas} = Y_{ihrt}(INS, CHA) \oplus E \qquad (1)$$

Where INS is the PUF instance set and CHA is the challenge set. Y_{ihrt} represents PUF instance's inherent physical features. For $\forall y_{ihrt}(ins, cha) \in Y_{ihrt}$, $y_{ihrt}(ins, cha)$ is decided by the instance's random characters and the input challenge, it is invariable at each measurement; E is the summation of random variations (e.g. voltage and temperature fluctuations, thermal noise etc.) during the measurement, it changes at every measurement, i.e. $\forall i \neq j$, there is $e_i \neq e_j$. We assume PUF's bit error rate is p_e.

Correctness: To ensure the key's correct recovery, the error correcting capability of ECC algorithm in the secure sketch must be sufficiently strong. The lower bound of required error correcting capability is determined by the noise rate between the enrolled response y and reproduced response y'.

Assume that at the i_{th} measurement, the obtained response sequence $y_i = y_{ihrt}(ins, cha) \oplus e_i$, then for arbitrary two measurements $y_{i1} = y_{ihrt}(ins, cha) \oplus e_{i1}$ and $y_{i2} = y_{ihrt}(ins, cha) \oplus e_{i2}$, $i1 \neq i2$, the difference between y_{i1} and y_{i1} is $e_{i1} \oplus e_{i2}$, which is a Bernoulli distribution with probability $2p_e - 2p_e^2$. Therefore, the number of different bits between y_{i1} and y_{i1} is a binomial distribution with probability $2p_e - 2p_e^2$. Assume the ECC's parameters are $[n, k, t]$, i.e. it contains 2^k different codewords of length n bits, which are each at least $2t - 1$ bits apart, the correctness requires that:

$$\sum_{i=0}^{t} f_{bino}(t, n, 2p_e - 2p_e^2) \geq 1 - p_{fail}. \tag{2}$$

where $f_{bino}(t, n, p) = \binom{n}{t} p^t (1 - p)^{n-t}$, p_{fail} is the permitted failure probability for key's recovery, usually $p_{fail} = 10^{-6}$ in the industry.

Security: As we have assumed that every bit in a binary response sequence $r \in \{0, 1\}^n$ is independent, min-entropy calculated as formula (3) offers a lower bound of responds' randomness in the worst case.

$$H_\infty(r) = \sum_{i=1}^{n} - \log_2 \left(\max\{P(r^i = 1), P(r^i = 0)\} \right). \tag{3}$$

According to Sect. 2.2, when the helper data w is disclosed, the min-entropy remained in the recovered response sequence y'' is $H_\infty(y) + H_\infty(r) - \#w$. Assume the length of the generated key is l_{key}, to make the key possess sufficient randomness, $H_\infty(y'')$ should be equal or greater than m, i.e.

$$H_\infty(y) + H_\infty(r) - \#w \geq l_{key}. \tag{4}$$

According to descriptions in Sect. 3.2, there is:

$$p(y^i = 1) = \frac{\sum_{k=1}^{N_{puf}} \sum_{j=1}^{N_{chan}} \left(y^i(ins_k, cha_j) == 1 \right)}{N_{puf} N_{chan}}. \tag{5}$$

$$p(r^i = 1) = \frac{\sum_{k=1}^{N_{meas}} \left(r_k^i(ins, cha) == 1 \right)}{N_{meas}}. \tag{6}$$

$P(r^i = 1)$ and $P(r^i = 0)$ are probabilities for the i_{th} bit of response to equal 1 and 0 respectively. Respectively substitute them into formula (3), we can calculate $H_\infty(y)$ and $H_\infty(r)$. From formula (5) and (6), we can see that the randomness of response sequence y, which will be used to generate the private key, comes from the PUF, $H_\infty(y) = H_\infty(y_{ihrt}(ins, cha))$; as for response r that is used to generate random numbers, its randomness comes from random factors during multiple measure process, i.e. $H_\infty(r) = H_\infty(e)$ and average $p_e = \sum_{i=1}^{n} \min\{P(r^i = 1), P(r^i = 0)\}/n$.

Define entropy density:

$$\rho(r) = \frac{H_\infty(r)}{\#r}. \tag{7}$$

Let l_y and l_r represent the length of y and y_r respectively, then $H_\infty(y) = l_y\rho(y)$ and $H_\infty(y_r) = l_r\rho(y_r)$, l_y and l_r should satisfy inequations:

$$\frac{l_y}{n}[n\rho(y) + k - n] \geq l_{key}. \tag{8}$$

and

$$l_r\rho(y_r) \geq \frac{l_y}{n}k. \tag{9}$$

4 Implementation

To verify our scheme's feasibility, we implement it on Xilinx KC705 FPGA boards.

4.1 Experiment Architecture

On the KC705 board, there is a Quad SPI flash memory which provides 128 Mb of nonvolatile storage. This flash is directly connected to the board's FPGA. When the Quad SPI flash is used for configuring the FPGA, the flash start-up configuration file (*mcs* file) that contains both the hardware configuration file (*bit* file) and software executable file (*elf* file) will be read from the flash to configure the hardware and then the contained executable *elf* file will run on the Microblaze. Therefore, the *mcs* file can be regarded as the system's firmware.

Therefore, the architecture of our experimental system is shown in Fig. 6, which consists of three parts: **the enhanced PUF module**, including a RO PUF instance, a SHA2-256 hash module and an ECC module that adopts Reed-Muller code, **the Microblaze**, a soft microprocessor core designed for Xilinx FPGAs and **a Quad SPI flash with a SPI flash controller**. Detailed workflows will be elaborated in Sect. 4.2 after all the parameters have been decided according to PUF's actual properties.

4.2 PUF Design and Parameter Determination

We choose RO PUF to implement our scheme. Particularly, we adopt FROPUF proposed in [20]. This PUF fully utilizes configurable propagation delay of Look Up Table to improve RO PUF's hardware efficiency. We implement 1024 such ROs on each KC705 board and each RO pair can generate a 16-bit response.

To determine l_y, l_r and ECC's correction capability, we randomly choose 5000 challenges to investigate the PUF's properties. Based on the obtained data, we figure out the PUF's bit error rate $p_e = 0.0235$, entropy densities of PUF response sequences

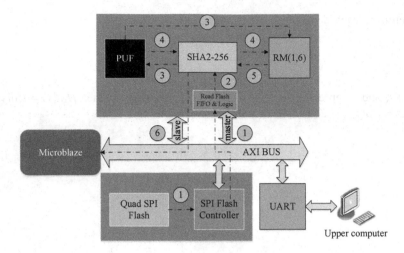

Fig. 6. The architecture and workflows of our key protection scheme

that used for key generation and random number generation are $\rho(y) = 0.9839$ and $\rho(y_r) = 0.0376$ according to formulas (5)–(7).

To generate 256-bit keys, i.e. $l_{key} = 256$, we choose SHA2-256 as the hash module. As the Reed-Muller code $RM(1, m)$ is a binary $[2^m, m + 1, 2^{m-1}]$ linear block code, substitute p_e and the above parameters into formula (2), we get m $\geq$ 6. Therefore, we finally adopt $RM(1, 6)$, whose code length $n = 64\,bit$ and the required random sequence in every block is 7-bit long, i.e. $k = 7$. Substitute n, k, l_{key} and $\rho(y)$ into in Eq. (8) we get $l_y \geq 2744.57$. Let it be the smallest integer that can be divided evenly by n, there is $l_y = 2816$, $l_y/n = 44$. Substitute them and other related parameters into inequation (9), we learn that the length of the random number sequence $l_y \cdot k/n = 308$ bit and $l_r \geq 8191.49$, let $l_r = 8192$.

After we implement all the hardware designs, we find that the size of the generated *mcs* file is about 30.74 Mb. As we need 2816 bit response to generate the private key and every 16-bit response is corresponding to a 20-bit challenge, we totally need $2816 \times 20/16 = 3520$ bit challenge. Let the challenge length l_{chal} be the smallest integer that can be divided evenly by 256, we get $l_{chal} = 3584$ and $l_{chal}/256 = 14$.

The working process of the enhanced PUF module is demonstrated as follows:

Key Generation Phase:

1. Receive key generation command from the CPU, then read 35 Mb data from the SPI flash;
2. Divide the read data into 14 parts, hash each 2.5 Mb part in sequence to totally get a 3584-bit sequence, cut out 3520 bits as the challenge sequence;
3. Invoke the PUF instance by every 20-bit challenge successively to obtain a 2816-bit response sequence y;
4. Divide the 1024 ROs into 512 pairs, read the response of all the RO pairs to form an 8192-bit response sequence y_r, then divide y_r into four parts, hash every part to totally get 512 bits random number, cut 308 bits as the random number sequence r;

5. Use the ECC module to encode the random sequence r by every 7 bits, then sketch the response sequence y with encoded r and output the helper data;
6. Hash the response sequence y to acquire a 256-bit key and output it.

Key Recovery Phase:

1. Receive recovery command and helper data from the CPU, then read 35 Mb data from the SPI flash;
2. Divide the read data into 14 parts, hash each 2.5 Mb part in sequence to totally get a 3584-bit sequence, cut out 3520 bits as the challenge sequence;
3. Invoke the PUF instance by every 20-bit challenge successively to obtain a 2816-bit response sequence y';
4. Sent the helper data to the ECC module;
5. Use the ECC module to recover the noisy response sequence y' with the helper data and get recovered response sequence y'';
6. Hash the recovered response sequence y'' to acquire a 256-bit key and output it.

4.3   Experiment and Result

We generate 128 different *elf* files with Xilinx SDK. Functions of these 128 *elf* files are roughly the same but differ in detail. Then we pack these *elf* files respectively with the *bit* file to generate 128 *mcs* files. For comparison, we load these *mcs* files separately into the onboard SPI flash of two KC705 evaluation boards. Finally, we send commands by the upper computer to control the onboard system to generate a key and recover it for 100 times and record the generation and recovery results.

According to our experiment result, all the 256 generated keys (128 on each board) are 100% successfully recovered. The distributions of generated keys' Hamming distances are demonstrated in Fig. 7. We mainly compare keys that generated from the same *mcs* file but on different boards and keys that generated on the same board but come from different *mcs* files. From the figure, we can conclude that changes either in the hardware or the firmware would lead to dramatical variation in the generated key.

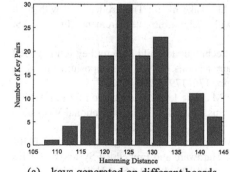

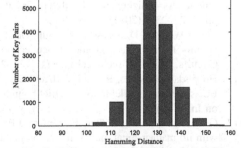

(a)   keys generated on different boards   (b)   keys generated from different *mcs* files

Fig. 7. Distributions of generated keys' Hamming distance

5   Conclusion

To protect the PUF-based generated key throughout the chip's lifetime, we propose a novel key protection scheme, in which we bind the chip's firmware and the embeded PUF to collaboratively generate the chip's exclusive key. Before the valid firmware is completed, there is no legal key observed, our scheme thereby protects the system during the manufacturing and software development stages. After the software development stage, the system is sensitive to any change of the firmware code. The successful recovery of the legal key in return verifies the device and firmware's legality and the hash module naturally forms a CPUF with the PUF instance, which further boosts the PUF's resistance to attacks.

References

1. Rührmair, U., Holcomb, D. E.: PUFs at a glance. In: Design, Automation and Test in Europe Conference and Exhibition (DATE), pp. 1–6 (2014)
2. Gassend, B.: Physical random functions. In: Computer Security Conference, p. 928 (2003)
3. Pappu, R., Recht, B., Taylor, J., Gershenfeld, N.: Physical one-way functions. Science **297** (5589), 2026–2030 (2002)
4. Daniel, E.H., Wayne, P.B., Kevin, F.: Power-up SRAM state as an identifying fingerprint and source of true random numbers. IEEE Trans. Comput. **58**(9), 1198–1210 (2009)
5. Kota, F., Mitsuru, S., Akitaka, F., Takahiko, M., Takeshi, F.: The arbiter-PUF with high uniqueness utilizing novel arbiter circuit with delay-time measurement. In: ISCAS, pp. 2325–2328 (2011)
6. Gassend, B.: Physical random functions. M.S. thesis, Massachusetts Institute of Technology (MIT), MA, USA, p. 36, 52, 209 (2003)
7. Gassend, B., Clarke, D., van Dijk, M., Devadas, S.: Silicon physical random functions. In: ACM Conference on Computer and Communications Security – CCS, pp. 148–160. ACM (2002)
8. Guajardo, J., Kumar, S.S., Schrijen, G.-J., Tuyls, P.: FPGA intrinsic pufs and their use for IP protection. In: Paillier, P., Verbauwhede, I. (eds.) CHES 2007. LNCS, vol. 4727, pp. 63–80. Springer, Heidelberg (2007). https://doi.org/10.1007/978-3-540-74735-2_5
9. Kota, F., Mitsuru, S., Akitaka, F., Takahiko, M., Takeshi, F.: The arbiter-PUF with high uniqueness utilizing novel arbiter circuit with delay-time measurement. In: ISCAS, pp. 2325–2328 (2011)
10. Lee, J.W., Lim, D., Gassend, B., Suh, G.E.: A technique to build a secret key in integrated circuits for identification and authentication applications. In: 2004 Symposium on VLSI Circuits, Digest of Technical Papers, vol. 42, pp. 176–179. IEEE (2004)
11. Hospodar, G., Maes, R., and Verbauwhede, I.: Machine learning attacks on 65 nm Arbiter PUFs: accurate modeling poses strict bounds on usability. In: IEEE International Workshop on Information Forensics and Security, vol. 2, pp. 37–42. IEEE (2012)
12. Ganji, F., Tajik, S., Fäßler, F., Seifert, J.P.: Strong machine learning attack against PUFs with no mathematical model. In: Cryptographic Hardware and Embedded Systems – CHES 2016. Springer, Heidelberg (2016). https://doi.org/10.1007/978-3-662-53140-2_19
13. Ruhrmair, U., Solter, J.: PUF modeling attacks: an introduction and overview. In: Conference on Design, Automation & Test in Europe, European Design and Automation Association, vol. 13, p. 348 (2014)

14. Gassend, B., Clarke, D., Dijk, M.V., Devadas, S.: Controlled physical random functions. ACM Trans. Inf. Syst. Secur. **10**(4), 1–22 (2002)
15. Gassend, B., Clarke, D., Dijk, M.V., Devadas, S.: Controlled physical random functions. In: Computer Security Applications Conference, 2002, Proceedings, vol. 10, pp. 149–160. IEEE (2007)
16. Roel, M.: Physically Unclonable Functions: Constructions, Properties and Applications. Katholieke Universiteit Leuven, Belgium (2012)
17. Dodis, Y., Reyzin, L., Smith, A.: Fuzzy extractors: how to generate strong keys from biometrics and other noisy data. In: Cachin, C., Camenisch, J.L. (eds.) EUROCRYPT 2004. LNCS, vol. 3027, pp. 523–540. Springer, Heidelberg (2004). https://doi.org/10.1007/978-3-540-24676-3_31
18. Maes, R., Van Herrewege, A., Verbauwhede, I.: PUFKY: a fully functional PUF-based cryptographic key generator. In: Prouff, E., Schaumont, P. (eds.) CHES 2012. LNCS, vol. 7428, pp. 302–319. Springer, Heidelberg (2012). https://doi.org/10.1007/978-3-642-33027-8_18
19. Delvaux, J., Gu, D., Schellekens, D., Verbauwhede, I.: Helper data algorithms for PUF-based key generation: overview and analysis. IEEE Trans. Comput.-Aided Des. Integr. Circ. Syst. **34**(6), 889–902 (2015)
20. Zhang, Q., Liu, Z., Ma, C., Li, C., Zhang, L.: FROPUF: how to extract more entropy from two ring oscillators in FPGA-based PUFs. In: Deng, R., Weng, J., Ren, K., Yegneswaran, V. (eds.) International Conference on Security and Privacy in Communication Systems, pp. 675–693. Springer, Cham (2016). https://doi.org/10.1007/978-3-319-59608-2_37

Towards a Trusted and Privacy Preserving Membership Service in Distributed Ledger Using Intel Software Guard Extensions

Xueping Liang[1,2,3], Sachin Shetty[4], Deepak Tosh[5], Peter Foytik[4], and Lingchen Zhang[1(✉)]

[1] Institute of Information Engineering, Chinese Academy of Sciences,
Beijing 100093, China
zhanglingchen@iie.ac.cn
[2] School of Cyber Security, University of Chinese Academy of Sciences,
Beijing 100190, China
[3] College of Engineering, Tennessee State University, Nashville, TN 37209, USA
[4] Virginia Modeling Analysis and Simulation Center, Old Dominion University,
Norfolk, VA 23529, USA
[5] Department of Computer Science, Norfolk State University,
Norfolk, VA 23504, USA

Abstract. Distributed Ledger Technology (DLT) provides decentralized services by removing the need of trust among distributed nodes and the trust of central authority in the distributed system. Transactions across the whole network are visible to all participating nodes. However, some transactions may contain sensitive information such as business contracts and financial reports, or even personal health records. To protect user privacy, the architecture of distributed ledger with membership service as a critical component can be adopted. We make a step towards such vision by proposing a membership service architecture that combines two promising technologies, distributed ledger and Intel Software Guard Extensions (SGX). With SGX remote attestation and isolated execution features, each distributed node can be enrolled as a trusted entity. We propose security properties for membership service in distributed ledger and illustrate how SGX capabilities help to achieve these properties in each phase of membership service, including member registration, enrollment, transaction signing and verifying and transacting auditing. The SGX enabled membership service could enhance the support of privacy preservation, and defense capabilities against adversarial attacks, with scalability and cost effectiveness.

Keywords: Intel SGX · Distributed ledger · Membership service
Security · Privacy · Channel

1 Introduction

Distributed Ledger Technology offers a range of benefits to public and private services, including government, financial institutions and various industrial

© Springer International Publishing AG, part of Springer Nature 2018
S. Qing et al. (Eds.): ICICS 2017, LNCS 10631, pp. 304–310, 2018.
https://doi.org/10.1007/978-3-319-89500-0_27

scenarios [21]. One of the most important features of distributed ledger is the decentralized architecture which brings efficiency and robustness for data processing and distribution. Every node in the network hosts a copy of the overall state across the ledger. Modifications to a certain transaction recorded on the ledger can be immediately reflected in all copies, indicating the ability of the ledger to detect and reject unauthorized changes. Meanwhile, integrity is preserved for each transaction since it is difficult for attackers to corrupt the ledger. Blockchain, as a major implementation of distributed ledger technology, uses a chain of blocks as a data structure to record transactions and preselected consensus algorithms to achieve agreement on all transactions. Basically, there are two types of blockchains, namely permissionless and permissioned blockchains. Permissionless blockchains, like Bitcoin [18], allow anyone to join in the block mining process. Every nodes possesses an identical copy of the whole ledger and there is no single owner of the ledger. Permissioned blockchains, also known as private blockchains, supported by most open source blockchain projects such as Multichain [5], limit node participation under permissions from blockchain owners or a certain role defined in the blockchain. This methodology is better suited for applications requiring access control, efficiency, and greater transparency.

Hyperledger [1] is an open source permissioned blockchain project hosted by The Linux Foundation, including leaders in finance, banking, IoT, supply chain, manufacturing and technology. Hyperledger Fabric [7] is an architecture delivering high degree of confidentiality, reliability, flexibility and scalability on top of the Hyperledger platform, supporting pluggable implementations of different customized components. Membership service is one of the critical components that Hyperledger Fabric provides to support dynamic entity registration and identity management, as well as auditing.

The CIA triad model [2] is a basic guideline for information security systems with the requirement of three properties including confidentiality, integrity and availability. Some previous work [14] meets these three criteria in a cloud data sharing system by implementing ProvChain, a blockchain based data provenance architecture which guarantees data confidentiality, integrity and availability using tamper-proof and immutable blockchain receipt and hash algorithms. However, the identity management and scalability as well as privacy preservation remain as challenging problems. In this paper, we design a flexible and scalable membership service based on Hyperledger Fabric, and propose a set of protocols to secure the transactions and preserve the privacy of user data in a fine-grained sense where users can define the extend to which the access is controlled among other users during communication or data sharing. We provide extra security features in peer communications by enabling Intel SGX, which is a promising technology introduced since the sixth generation of Intel processors in 2015 [3]. Our architecture serves as a feasible and scalable solution to satisfy the requirement of identity management and privacy preservation.

2 Background

2.1 Intel SGX Security Capabilities

Intel SGX provides seven capabilities that can be used for security considerations. Enclave Execution (C1). The isolated environment inside the CPU, i.e., enclave, is responsible for preventing attackers from accessing the trusted execution environment and hence greatly reducing the attack surface [16]. Hardware based attacks such as side-channel attack are also possible to prevent. Remote Attestation (C2). Remote attestation allows a client platform to attest itself to a remote party proving that the client is running in a trusted environment. Similarly, the server can attest itself to the client in case of phishing attack. This ensures the integrity of code execution in both the client and server side according to application needs. Trusted Elapsed time (C3). This is critical for scenarios where it is time sensitive, such as auditing. Sealing and Unsealing (C4). Intel SGX's sealing feature helps to store confidential information outside the enclave for future access after system shutdown. Therefore, integrity can be preserved since no entity can modify the data without the trusted execution environment or the access to the unsealing key.

2.2 Overview of Membership Service

The Membership Service Provider (MSP) in Hyperledger has four roles, namely Registration Authority (RA), ECA (Enrollment Certificate Authority) and TCA (Transaction Certificate Authority) and auditor. The client is an entity requesting service from the system and can be a user or peer. RA is responsible for client registration and issues user credential for enrollment. With issued credential, the client turns to ECA for an Enrollment Certificate (ECert) which will be used for identity management throughout the following interactions. After obtaining the ECert, the client then requests to TCA for a Transaction Certificate (TCert) or a batch of TCerts. Owning TCerts enables the client to propose transactions within a corresponding channel in the system. Channel is used for private communication in a given group of clients. After the establishment of channels, channel members will start signing and verifying transactions continuously. Auditors are assigned by the membership service provider for each channel to inspect transactions. When certificate expires or is compromised, corresponding TCA and ECA will be responsible for certificate renewal and revocation.

3 Design of SGX-Enabled Membership Service

The overall architecture for a reliable and privacy preserving membership service based on SGX is composed of three components, including enrollment, signing and verifying transactions, as well as auditing transactions.

Enrollment (P1). The Certificate Authority (CA) generates public and private keys (Pub_k, Pri_k) for signing certificates. The Pub_k is known to all participant nodes. Two kinds of CA roles are set up, including ECA and TCA. For each client to be enrolled in the system, there will be a RA to collect physical evidence such as a photo ID, or digital measures such as an email address. The process of identifying a user is launched inside an enclave to ensure trusted execution and resist against eavesdropping. After identity check (for example, a validating email), the client will be provisioned with a secret key (SK_c), indicating ownership of cloud data. During enrollment, the Intel SGX attestation model [6] is adopted between a CA (or a intermediate CA) and the requesting client to ensure that the requesting client is running on a trusted platform. First of all, the CA asks client application for a remote attestation (step 1). The client application receiving the request is not trusted, so it turns to the enclave part of the application for a local attestation (step 2). The enclave returns a REPORT signed with the Enclave Identity Key (step 3), which is forwarded by the application to the Quoting Enclave (step 4). The Quoting Enclave signs the Report with its private key and generate the QUOTE which is sent back to the application (step 5). The application forwards the QUOTE to the CA (step 6). To verify the authenticity of the QUOTE, CA will send it to an Attestation Verification Service (AVS) (step 7) and receive a result of the status checking of the client platform (step 8). If the client wants to ensure that it is requesting to an authentic CA, it can attest the CA in the same way.

Using Intel SGX attestation feature, the compromise of the platform can be detected. Generally, the remote attestation is launched only once during enrollment. If the same client platform is re-enrolled, the AVS can detect this event, under the name based mode [11] which can reveal whether two requests are from the same CPU. If the user wants to disenroll the system and enroll again after a period of time, the CA can set the rules that one single platform can re-enroll after disenroll. If the client platform launches re-enrollment without previous disenroll, then the CA is sure that the platform is compromised or user identity is stolen. To differentiate these two cases, the CA keeps a flag for each client during enrollment, indicating the re-enrollment state. After a successful attestation between the CA and the client, the CA issues an ECert which contains special attributes needed for the client to participate.

Signing and Verifying Transactions (P2). After a member joins a channel, the member will request to a TCA for a TCert or a batch of TCerts to sign transactions. To keep unlinkability between TCerts, multiple TCerts are used to access multiple channels. We use Camenisch-Lysyanskaya (CL) signature scheme [8] to provide flexible TCerts by making TCert a zero-knowledge proof of an ECert. This proof indicates that the TCert is really from the desired ECert but no information of that ECert will be disclosed. The generation of the proof is running inside an enclave, which provides a trusted environment.

Besides, for each transaction, selective attribute disclosure can be adopted for the generation of TCert. For example, Node can use a subset of its attributes (for example, AttrA) on Transaction A and use another subset of attributes (for example, AttrB) on Transaction B. This preserves privacy on the transaction level. Each peer participating the transaction verification process uses CA's public key Pub_k to verify that a certain transaction is signed by an authorized member.

Auditing Transactions (P3). Each channel has an auditor to audit transactions within the channel. To support auditability and accountability, the role of auditor is assigned by MSP at channel creation to audit the behaviors of client users and peers. To audit transactions from a single channel, the auditor is issued a special TCert from the MSP, which has access to all transactions inside the channel. This special TCert, generated within an enclave, has the ability to reveal linkage of transactions to the corresponding entities involved. Each auditor is responsible for one channel. A set of auditors form an auditing channel, following the general channel formation protocol. Both internal and external auditing can be done upon request from application users and service providers. The corresponding subledger to the auditing channel forms an immutable record for all auditing logs. This preserves the availability of audit logs for future usage. Meanwhile, the existence of auditing channel ensures that each auditor is performing decent behaviors. According to system requirement, cross-auditing can be launched upon requesting of each auditor.

One essential security property for cloud auditing is that the auditor itself should be auditable [10]. The auditing channel established fulfills this objective by encapsulating the auditor behavior in an auditing transaction which will be validated by all auditors in that channel. Auditing transaction contains the basic elements of an audit trial, including the time, subject and object. The element of time is critical for auditing considering that some attackers modify the time of an intrusion event would easily hide their malicious behavior. SGX provides a trusted timestamping function $sgx\_get\_trusted\_time$ to assist the auditing process.

4   Related Work and Conclusions

Intel SGX offers a list of benefits from the cloud and cyber applications, which ensures a secure and trusted execution environment and reduces the attack surface. Several SGX based blockchain architecture are proposed. Sawtooth Lake [4] provides a trusted consensus algorithm, called proof of eclipsed time, in blockchain applications. However, the detailed design is not well illustrated and does not provide any security guarantee. Teechan [15] introduces a payment channel based on SGX and proves to be secure and efficient for blockchain transactions. [19] proposes a proof of execution using SGX, which ensures the active participation of nodes in gossip-based blockchains. Proof of Luck [17] provides a consensus algorithm based on SGX. OpenSGX [9] is a software emulation platform based on QEMU but lacks security measures and capabilities. However, none of these work addresses the potential privacy risks.

Hawk [13] is proposed to protect transaction privacy for smart contracts with the notion of cryptography primitives and a formal analysis model. However, the entire framework is based on the assumption of the input dependent privacy and the security of blockchain mining scheme. SGP [20] is a cryptography primitive which can be applied in SGX based smart contract for transparent information exchange with fairness. TC [22] is an authenticated data feed system which combines a blockchain front end with trusted hardware, such as SGX, to scrape websites. Besides, research work in [12] also emphasizes the adoption of SGX based blockchain and smart contract applications for security and privacy considerations, indicating the significant potential of the wide adoption of SGX enabled platforms.

Several blockchain architecture integrates Intel SGX. Sawtooth Lake [4] is an open source distributed ledger project based on trusted execution environment including Intel SGX which provides a trusted consensus algorithm, called proof of eclipsed time, in blockchain applications. However, the detailed design is not well illustrated and does not provide any security guarantee. Teechan [15], introduces a payment channel, which is established based on SGX and proves to be secure and efficient for blockchain transactions. [19] proposes a proof of execution using SGX, which ensures the active participation of nodes in gossip-based blockchains. Proof of Luck [17] provides a consensus algorithm based on SGX. These work focus on the security guarantee of peer but are faced with potential privacy risks.

In this paper, we utilize Intel SGX to help prevent these attacks and effectively address the potential privacy issues in blockchain applications, removing the need of trust between participating nodes during transactions. In the future, we will utilize the design, implement a privacy preserving blockchain service in a cloud data sharing application, and evaluate the overall application performance.

Acknowledgements. This work was supported by Office of the Assistant Secretary of Defense for Research and Engineering (OASD (R & E)) agreement FA8750-15-2-0120. The work was also supported by a grant from the National Natural Science Foundation of China (No. 61402470) and the research project of Trusted Internet Identity Management (2016YFB0800505 and 2016YFB0800501).

References

1. Hyperledger-blockchain technologies for business. https://www.hyperledger.org/
2. Information security - wikipedia. https://en.wikipedia.org/wiki/Information_security
3. Intel architecture instruction set extensions programming reference. https://software.intel.com/sites/default/files/managed/07/b7/319433-023.pdf
4. Introduction - sawtooth lake latest documentation. https://intelledger.github.io/introduction.html
5. Multichain private blockchain white paper. http://www.multichain.com/download/MultiChain-White-Paper.pdf
6. Anati, I., Gueron, S., Johnson, S., Scarlata, V.: Innovative technology for CPU based attestation and sealing. In: Proceedings of the 2nd International Workshop on Hardware and Architectural Support for Security and Privacy, vol. 13 (2013)
7. Cachin, C.: Architecture of the Hyperledger blockchain fabric. In: Workshop on Distributed Cryptocurrencies and Consensus Ledgers (2016)

8. Camenisch, J., Lysyanskaya, A.: A signature scheme with efficient protocols. In: Cimato, S., Persiano, G., Galdi, C. (eds.) SCN 2002. LNCS, vol. 2576, pp. 268–289. Springer, Heidelberg (2003). https://doi.org/10.1007/3-540-36413-7_20
9. Jain, P., Desai, S., Kim, S., Shih, M.W., Lee, J., Choi, C., Shin, Y., Kim, T., Kang, B.B., Han, D.: OpenSGX: an open platform for SGX research. In: Proceedings of the Network and Distributed System Security Symposium, San Diego, CA (2016)
10. Jia, X.: Auditing the auditor: secure delegation of auditing operation over cloud storage. Technical report, IACR Cryptology ePrint Archive. https://eprint.iacr.org/2011/304.pdf. Accessed 10 Aug 2016
11. Johnson, S., Scarlata, V., Rozas, C., Brickell, E., Mckeen, F.: Intel software guard extensions: EPID provisioning and attestation services. White Paper (2016)
12. Kaptchuk, G., Miers, I., Green, M.: Managing secrets with consensus networks: fairness, ransomware and access control. IACR Cryptology ePrint Archive 2017/201 (2017)
13. Kosba, A., Miller, A., Shi, E., Wen, Z., Papamanthou, C.: Hawk: the blockchain model of cryptography and privacy-preserving smart contracts. In: 2016 IEEE Symposium on Security and Privacy (SP), pp. 839–858. IEEE (2016)
14. Liang, X., Shetty, S., Tosh, D., Kamhoua, C., Kwiat, K., Njilla, L.: ProvChain: a blockchain-based data provenance architecture in cloud environment with enhanced privacy and availability. In: International Symposium on Cluster, Cloud and Grid Computing. IEEE/ACM (2017)
15. Lind, J., Eyal, I., Pietzuch, P., Sirer, E.G.: Teechan: payment channels using trusted execution environments. arXiv preprint arXiv:1612.07766 (2016)
16. McKeen, F., Alexandrovich, I., Berenzon, A., Rozas, C.V., Shafi, H., Shanbhogue, V., Savagaonkar, U.R.: Innovative instructions and software model for isolated execution. In: HASP@ ISCA, p. 10 (2013)
17. Milutinovic, M., He, W., Wu, H., Kanwal, M.: Proof of luck: an efficient blockchain consensus protocol. In: Proceedings of the 1st Workshop on System Software for Trusted Execution, p. 2. ACM (2016)
18. Nakamoto, S.: Bitcoin: a peer-to-peer electronic cash system (2008)
19. van Renesse, R.: A blockchain based on gossip?-a position paper
20. Tramer, F., Zhang, F., Lin, H., Hubaux, J.P., Juels, A., Shi, E.: Sealed-glass proofs: using transparent enclaves to prove and sell knowledge. In: 2017 IEEE European Symposium on Security and Privacy (EuroS&P), pp. 19–34. IEEE (2017)
21. Walport, M.: Distributed ledger technology: beyond blockchain. UK Gov. Off. Sci. (2016)
22. Zhang, F., Cecchetti, E., Croman, K., Juels, A., Shi, E.: Town crier: an authenticated data feed for smart contracts. In: Proceedings of the 2016 ACM SIGSAC Conference on Computer and Communications Security, pp. 270–282. ACM (2016)

Malicious Code Defense and Mobile Security

Deobfuscation of Virtualization-Obfuscated Code Through Symbolic Execution and Compilation Optimization

Mingyue Liang[1], Zhoujun Li[1(✉)], Qiang Zeng[2], and Zhejun Fang[3]

[1] Beihang University, Beijing, China
{liangmy,lizj}@buaa.edu.cn
[2] Temple University, Philadelphia, PA, USA
qzeng@temple.edu
[3] CNCERT/CC, Beijing, China
fzj@cert.org.cn

Abstract. Virtualization-obfuscation replaces native code in a binary with semantically equivalent and self-defined bytecode, which, upon execution, is interpreted by a custom virtual machine. It makes the code very difficult to analyze and is thus widely used in malware. How to deobfuscate such virtualization obfuscated code has been an important and challenging problem. We approach the problem from an innovative perspective by transforming it into a compilation optimization problem, and propose a novel technique that combines trace analysis, symbolic execution and compilation optimization to defeat virtualization obfuscation. We implement a prototype system and evaluate it against popular virtualization obfuscators; the results demonstrate that our method is effective in deobfuscation of virtualization-obfuscated code.

Keywords: Deobfuscation · Virtualization obfuscation
Symbolic execution · Compilation optimization

1 Introduction

Virtualization-based obfuscation replaces the code in a binary with semantically equivalent bytecode, which can only be interpreted by a virtual machine whose instruction set and architecture can be customized. Thus, it makes the resulting code difficult to understand and analyze, and is widely used in malware [1]. When regular dynamic and static analyzers are directly applied to analyzing such code, their execution gets trapped into the VM interpreter and thus can hardly reveal the real logic of the code. Therefore, how to deobfuscate virtualization-obfuscated code has been an important and challenging problem.

Existing techniques either reverse engineer the virtual machine to infer the logic behind the bytecode [2], or execute the obfuscated code and work on the instruction traces corresponding to the executed bytecode [3–5]. While the

© Springer International Publishing AG, part of Springer Nature 2018
S. Qing et al. (Eds.): ICICS 2017, LNCS 10631, pp. 313–324, 2018.
https://doi.org/10.1007/978-3-319-89500-0_28

former relies on a complete reverse engineering of the virtual machine, which is challenging in itself, the latter requires advanced control/data-flow analysis (which usually involves many false negatives and positives and requires many *ad hoc* methods for handling different obfuscations) to remove redundant code. Indeed, due to garbage code insertion, one of the main challenges to deobfuscate virtualization-obfuscated code is how to correctly remove unneeded code and generate concise code. This challenge is not well resolved yet.

Our insight is that redundant code elimination is well resolved and implemented in the field of compilation optimization; thus, if we can leverage the power of compilers, the challenge above can be resolved elegantly. Thus, we approach the challenge from an innovative compilation-optimization perspective. Specifically, we first apply symbolic execution to summarize the semantics of each bytecode handler (the execution of each bytecode corresponds to the invocation of its handler), and then automatically transform the semantics of a handler into a function represented in some high-level programming language. Next, after the execution of bytecode is transformed into a piece of source code that represents the invocations of the corresponding functions, we leverage a compiler to compile the source code. Consequently, the compiler eliminates unneeded code of VM, such as operations on virtual stack and registers, thanks to compilation optimization, and generates deobfuscated code, which then can be analyzed using various off-the-shelf tools.

We made the following contributions.

(a) We propose an innovative idea that resolves the deobfuscation challenge from the perspective of compilation optimization, which makes it possible to reuse powerful code optimizations implemented in modern compilers.
(b) We propose a symbolic execution based method for automatically extracting semantic information of bytecode handlers, and represent the handlers in high-level programming languages.
(c) We have implemented a prototype system and evaluated it against representative obfuscators including VMProtect [6] and Code Virtualizer [7].

2   Background and Challenges

This section describes the background about virtualization obfuscation and discusses the challenges in the process of deobfuscation and code recovery.

2.1   Background: Virtualization Obfuscation

A virtualization obfuscator takes a binary file as input, parses its machine code instructions, and translates them to self-defined bytecode, which can be interpreted by an embedded interpreter during execution. Thus, a virtualization obfuscator has to implement a complete virtual machine that contains the virtual instruction set definition and a corresponding bytecode interpreter. Below, we describe some important concepts and details for virtualization obfuscation.

Virtual Machine. A *virtual machine*, also called an *emulator* or *interpreter*, is the core of an obfuscation system for interpreting bytecode instructions. As the original machine code is removed and replaced by virtual instructions, the obfuscated binary embeds a corresponding interpreter in the code section. A *Virtual Program Counter* in a VM works like the EIP register in x86 architecture; it stores the address pointing to the location of the current virtual instruction (described below). When interpreting virtual instructions, the virtual machine fetches the instruction pointed to by the VPC and execute it, after which VPC will be updated to point to the next instruction.

Virtual Instructions. Virtual instructions are also called *bytecode* instructions. Virtual instructions are translated from original machine code and encoded in the data section of the obfuscated binary. The virtual machine fetches bytecode as read-only data and interprets it with embedded *hander* functions. The execution of a virtual instruction corresponds to an invocation of the corresponding handler function. As the virtual instruction set is privately defined by the obfuscator and is quite different from public architectures such as Intel, ARM and MIPS, regular static analysis tools cannot analyze virtualization obfuscated code.

Virtual Registers. A virtual machine uses virtual registers to store temporary variable values, but they do not exactly match the x86/x64 general-purpose registers. For example, VMProtect VM has 16 virtual registers, which are randomly mapped to 8 Intel x86 registers to increase obfuscation.

Virtual Stack. Stack-based VMs are popular in virtualization obfuscation, and is also the target architecture of our work. In a stack-based VM, all data passing operations go through a virtual stack, and registers and memory never exchange data directly. Given an X86 instruction *add eax, ebx*, its equivalent virtual instruction sequence in a stack-based VM is:

```
vPush vR0
vPush vR1
vAdd
vPop vFlag
vPop vR2
```

The first double *vPush* instructions push two registers onto a virtual stack, after which the *vAdd* pops two variables from the stack to perform the addition and then stores the result and the side-effect flag back to the stack. The last *vPop* instructions pop the addition result and the flag to registers.

2.2   Challenges of Deobfuscation

While conventional runtime-packed code can be extracted from the memory when the code is executed and unpacked [8], virtualization-obfuscated code never restores the original code in the memory during execution. Thus, regular unpackers cannot recover the original code.

Another challenge is various bytecode-level obfuscation can be applied to the virtualization-obfuscated code, which makes the extracted bytecode even harder to analyze and understand. For example, a simple x86 instruction can be translated into several virtual instructions which keep same semantic but are much more complex to understand. A concrete example is logical operation obfuscation in VMProtect. A VM in VMProtect does not generate *not, and, or* or *xor* instructions but only *nor* instructions. All these logical operations are implemented in *nor* instructions; e.g., *or(a, b) = nor(nor(a, b), nor(a, b))*.

Various VM architecture of virtual obfuscators is also a challenge. Conventional deobfuscation tools works well on general architecture (Intel, ARM and MIPS) but do not support customized VM architecture without specialized adaption. When deobfuscating virtualization-obfuscated code, there is a lack of a generic technique that tackles various VM architecture with different kinds of bytecode-level obfuscation. Our goal is to conquer this challenge and propose such a generic technique.

3   Deobfuscation·Through Symbolic Execution and Compilation Optimization

3.1   Main Idea and Architecture

Instead of implementing various deobfuscation algorithms, we creatively propose to leverage the power of modern compilers, which perform advanced code optimization, to resolve the deobfuscation problem. However, it is infeasible to apply a regular compiler, such as gcc and clang, to processing custom virtual instructions directly. We thus propose to convert each virtual-instruction handler, which is relatively simple, to a function coded in some high-level programming language, and our approach is to summarize the semantics of handlers through symbolic execution. Subsequently, a sequence of virtual instructions can be represented as a sequence of invocations of these functions, which then can be processed by a regular compiler for automatic optimization to eliminate garbage code and obtain concise resulting code.

Figure 1 shows the architecture of our deobfuscation system, which comprises the following components: (1) A trace analysis module, which records runtime information of the obfuscated binary and does offline analysis to identify and

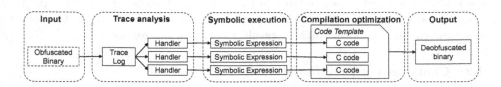

Fig. 1. Overview of our approach.

extract handler functions. (2) A symbolic execution module, which analyzes semantic information of each handler function and outputs symbolic expressions as the function summary. (3) A compilation module, which translates the symbolic expressions to C code and applies compilation optimization to the C code to generate deobfuscated code.

3.2 Trace Record and Offline Analysis

When running the obfuscated binary, our system records the dynamic trace, which contains instruction sequences and their operations on registers and memory. We use Pin [9], a binary instrument tool developed by Intel, to record the trace. Pin provides instrumentation interface on instruction level for user to insert callback function before or after execution of instructions, which gives the chance to record all context information. Although Pin allows us to run analysis routine upon execution of program, we prefer to record all information to a file and do offline analysis on the trace file. By decoupling trace recording and the analysis, we can apply multiple rounds of analysis to the trace without running the executable repeatedly. Once we have the trace file, we can reconstruct the control flow graph (CFG) and extract virtual instruction handlers.

CFG Construction. As the code is obfuscated with many indirect jumps, reconstruction the CFG statically is very difficult. For instance, below shows the dispatcher code extracted from VMProtect 2.13 (with most junk code deleted as a matter of convenience for readers).

```
mov al, byte ptr [esi-0x1]
mov ecx, dword ptr [eax*4+0x4058da]
mov dword ptr [esp+0x28], ecx
push dword ptr [esp+0x28]
ret 0x2c
```

The dispatcher fetches the opcode of the instruction pointed to by the *VPC*, which is stored in *esi* register, and then jumps to the corresponding handler according to the opcode, which is done by an indirect jump through *push* and *ret* instruction. Without dynamic execution, it would be difficult to determine the target of such indirect jumps. Static analysis tools such as IDA Pro [10] is unable to generate the CFG for such case.

We instead choose to reconstruct the CFG from the dynamic execution trace. The basic steps of reconstructing the CFG from trace are as follows:

Step 1: Initialization of basic blocks. Initialize each instruction of the trace to a basic block. For the sequence of instructions in the trace such as $I_1 I_2 \ldots$, the instructions are initialized to basic blocks $B_1 B_2 \ldots$, respectively; a directed edge is then added from B_1 to B_2 according the instruction order of trace. We then get a directed graph structure.

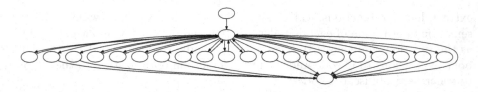

Fig. 2. A typical fetch-decode-dispatch CFG.

Step 2: Emerging basic blocks. For each connected pair of basic blocks B_1 and B_2 are merged into a new block named B_{12}, if and only if the outbound degree of B_1 and inbound degree of B_2 are both 1.

Step 3: Loop. The processing goes back to Step 2 until no more blocks can be merged. Then we get our CFG.

Handler Identification. The CFG of a virtualization-obfuscated binary is characteristic, mainly because of dispatch-based virtual instruction handling. Most obfuscators such as VMProtect and Code Virtualizer, implement the virtual machine as a typical *fetch-decode-dispatch* loop [3], which forms many outgoing branches from the dispatcher node, as shown in Fig. 2. The dispatcher in a virtual machine jumps to a handler function according to the opcode of a virtual instruction and every handler functions return to dispatcher to continue the execution of the next instruction.

According to this feature, we can extract the dispatcher and the handlers by analyzing the CFG. At first, we detect all circle in the graph; each circle in CFG represents a separate execution path of interpretation loop. Secondly, we solve the intersection set of all circles, then the common nodes are marked as dispatcher of interpreter. For each circle, nodes other than dispatcher nodes will be collected sequentially according to execution order and identified as a handler.

3.3   Semantic Analysis of Handlers

Handlers are functions that virtual machine used to interpret virtual instructions. We can extract semantic information of virtual instructions by analyzing corresponding handler functions. We propose to apply a symbolic execution based approach to extracting semantics of each handler.

The overall interpretation logic of virtual machine is too complicated to be symbolically executed as a whole due to time and memory overhead. *Our approach instead applies symbolic execution to handler functions separately.* Each handler function processes a single virtual instruction, which usually has simple logic, therefore the path explosion problem is naturally avoided and symbolic expressions will not be too complex. In addition, with the use of symbol execution, many obfuscations on handler functions such as junk code insertion and instruction replacement are automatically tackled by the symbolic engine.

In our design, all registers and memory in handler function are initialized as symbolic variables. After symbolic execution of the function, the symbolic execution engine outputs a series of symbolic expressions, which represents the operations the handler does.

Here is an example of *vPushReg4* handler in VMProtect. Our prototype system uses Miasm [11] as our symbolic execution engine, which symbolically executes binary code of the handler and returns symbolic expressions in Miasm IR format as below. The disassembly and the symbolic expression are shown below ('@' in Miasm IR expressions means dereference of address):

```
and al, 0x3c
mov edx, dword ptr [edi+eax*1]
sub ebp, 0x4
mov dword ptr [ebp], edx
jmp 0x40100a
```

```
EAX = {(EAX_init[0:8]&0x3C) 0 8, EAX_init[8:32] 8 32}
EDX = @32[(EDI_init + {(EAX_init[0:8]&0x3C) 0 8, EAX_init[8:32]
8 32})]
EBP = (EBP_init+0xFFFFFFFC)
@32[(EBP_init+0xFFFFFFFC)] = @32[(EDI_init+{(EAX_init[0:8]&0x3C)
0 8, EAX_init[8:32] 8 32})]
```

From the expressions we know that this handler loads the value at a memory address based by *edi* offset by *eax* & 0x3C, then stores the value to where *ebp* points to. Assuming *edi* represents the initial address of the virtual register array and *ebp* the virtual stack top, this handler simply pushes a virtual register value to the virtual stack.

The above example shows that the symbolic expression of the handler function can fully express its operations; that is, it can capture the semantic information of the corresponding virtual instruction.

3.4 Compilation and Code Recovery

While function summary can eliminate dead code *within* a handler, it is ineffective in handling obfuscations *among* virtual instructions, which is one of the main challenges of deobfuscation we aim to conquer. When CISC instructions (e.g., x86) are converted into virtual RISC instructions, the problem is more severe, as a single CISC instruction is usually transformed into multiple virtual RISC instructions. It will significantly benefit code analysis and understanding if we can convert the multiple virtual RISC instructions back into the single CISC one. An intuitive approach is to prepare a whole set of templates for transformation, each of which tries to match a specific sequence of RISC instructions and recover the original CISC instruction. Such template-based transformation has multiple drawbacks: (1) A lot of tedious work has to be done to prepare the transformation templates; worse, whenever a new VM is encountered, they have to be updated. (2) During the transformation, the register information gets lost and more inference must be done to restore it. (3) Obfuscators often apply additional obfuscation on the virtual-instruction layer, which may render the template match ineffective.

We consider such obfuscation as an opposite process of optimization, since it replaces the original concise instructions with more complex but semantically equivalent code, while deobfuscation aims to optimize away the intermediate variables and redundant instructions introduced by virtual machine. Thus, we propose to use modern compiler such as *gcc* and *clang*, which have been developed for years and proven to have excellent optimization capabilities, to optimize the virtual instructions by relying on their built-in data flow analysis and live variable analysis; this way, we can remove redundant instructions and generate concise code.

Translation of Symbolic Expressions. After the previous semantic analysis (Sect. 3.3), we have automatically generated symbolic expressions for each virtual instruction handler. But these symbolic expressions are still unable to be directly processed by the compiler. We have implemented a *Miasm translator* module to translate them to C code, which hence can be processed by compilers. Let us continue the example in Sect. 3.3. The symbolic expressions of *vPushReg4* are translated to C code:

```
*(uint32_t *)(EBP + 0xfffffffc) = *(uint32_t *)(EDI + EAX & 0x3c);
EBP = EBP + 0xfffffffc;
```

The registers are treated as unsigned integer variables, and are converted to pointers when used as addresses.

Compilation Optimization. The following optimizations are conducted to obtain concise and clear code: (1) symbolic variables are translated to local variables if possible; (2) the virtual stack in a virtual machine is converted to a local array variable, and stack pointers now point to array elements; and (3) every virtual instruction handler is defined as an inline function or C macro, and hence the entire bytecode sequence will be translated to a sequence of calls to inline functions.

Let us take VMs in VMProtect as an example: VMProtect reuses the x86 call stack as its virtual stack with *ebp* as stack pointer. When converting to C code, we define a virtual stack as a large enough local array and the stack pointer as a pointer to array elements. Figure 3 is a sample of the converted C code.

In this example, as the handler functions are defined as inline functions, which are invoked by a global function *vmp_func*, the compiler will automatically optimize the generated code. An example on push and pop optimization is shown as Fig. 4. After compilation optimization the redundant stack operation code is eliminated, which makes the result code more concise and easier to understand.

```
#define STACK_SIZE 2048
static uint8_t *sp;

// handlers translated from
// symbolic expressions.
static inline void
vPushReg4(uint32_t *reg_ptr){
  sp -= 4;
  *((uint32_t *)sp) = *reg_ptr;
}
static inline void
vPopReg4(uint32_t *reg_ptr){
  *reg_ptr = *((uint32_t *)sp);
  sp += 4;
}
```

```
void vmp_func()
{
uint32_t regs[16];
uint8_t stack[STACK_SIZE];
sp = &stack[STACK_SIZE/2];

/** virtual instructions **/
...
vPushReg4(&regs[0]);
vPopReg4(&regs[1]);
...
}
```

Fig. 3. A sample of the converted C code.

Before compiling	After inline	After optimization
`void vmp_func()`	`void vmp_func()`	`void vmp_func()`
`{`	`{`	`{`
`...`	`...`	`...`
	`sp -= 4;`	
`vPushReg4(&regs[0]);`	`*((uint32_t *)sp) = regs[0];`	`regs[1] = regs[0];`
`vPopReg4(&regs[1]);`	`regs[1] = *((uint32_t *)sp);`	`// sp not changed.`
	`sp += 4;`	
`...`	`...`	`...`
`}`	`}`	`}`

Fig. 4. An example on push and pop optimization.

4   Evaluation

We have evaluated our system against VMProtect and Code Virtualizer; both are
well-known commercial obfuscators. We first performed some micro-benchmark
experiments, which consider the following four samples:

- *mov*, which has only a single mov instruction.
- *binop*, which tests binary operators like *add, sub, and, or* and so on.
- *xor*, which is a sample of an xor encoder.
- *base64*, which is a sample of a base64 encoder.

We recorded the count of original and obfuscated instruction trace, dispatcher address, count of handlers and deobfuscated instruction trace. As shown
in Table 1, we applied our method to the four samples obfuscated by VMProtect; plus, the base64 sample is obfuscated by different obfuscators as shown
in Table 2. According to the results of manual inspection, our method correctly

Table 1. Evaluation against different samples obfuscated by VMProtect.

Sample	Original trace	Obfucscated trace	Dispatcher address	Handlers	Deobfuscated trace
mov	1	357	0x40320b	5	7
binop	128	10276	0x4074f9	20	304
xor	667	123366	0x407592	20	3123
base64	485	107998	0x407063	21	2876

Table 2. Evaluation against base64 sample obfuscated by different obfuscators.

Obfuscator	Original trace	Obfucscated trace	Dispatcher address	Handlers	Deobfuscated trace
VMProtect 1.81	485	107998	0x407063	21	2876
VMProtect 2.13	485	1028805	0x4074f9	22	3445
CodeVirtualizer 1.3.8	485	1007378	0x405556	36	3122

```
// Original source.

void vmp_func(int x[],
int y[], char z)
{
  y[0] = x[1] + x[0];
  y[1] = x[2] ^ x[1];
  y[2] = x[3] & x[2];
  y[3] = x[4] | x[3];
  y[4] = x[4] - x[5];
  y[5] = x[5] << z;
  y[6] = x[6] >> z;
  y[7] = x[7] / x[8];
  y[8] = x[8] % x[9];
  y[9] = x[10] * x[9];
}
```

```
// Deobfuscated code.
// (decompiled by IDA Pro.)
signed int vmp_func()
{
    int v0; // eax@1
    signed int result; // eax@1
    int *v2; // [sp+440h] [bp-40Ch]@0
    int *v3; // [sp+444h] [bp-408h]@0
    char v4; // [sp+448h] [bp-404h]@0

    *v3 = v2[1] + *v2;
    v3[1] = (v2[2] | v2[1]) & ~(v2[1] & v2[2]);
    v3[2] = v2[3] & v2[2];
    v3[3] = v2[4] | v2[3];
    v3[4] = ~(v2[5] + ~v2[4]);
    v3[5] = v2[5] << v4;
    v3[6] = v2[6] >> v4;
    v3[7] = v2[7] / v2[8];
    v0 = v2[8] % v2[9];
    dword_804A130 = 0;
    v3[8] = v0;
    result = 36;
    v3[9] = v2[10] * v2[9];
    return result;
}
```

(a)   (b)

Fig. 5. Source and deobfuscated code of binop.

locates the dispatcher address and extracts the handlers from the trace. We use *gcc* as our compiler with O3 optimization level against the translated virtual instruction trace; the results demonstrate that the trace count is greatly reduced after deobfuscation.

Figure 5 shows an intuitive comparison when we applied our method on the *binop* sample, whose source code is shown Fig. 5(a). After optimizing with compiler and decompiling with IDA Pro, the deobfuscated the pseudo C code, shown as Fig. 5(b), is concise and equivalent to the original code. Basic array memory access and most binary operations such as *add, and, or, shift* etc. between array elements are precisely recovered. The *xor* and *subtraction* operators are not exactly same as origin but the deobfuscated code has equivalent semantic.

5   Related Work

Deobfuscation approaches for virtualization-based obfuscated binaries have long been part of the state-of-the-art research in reverse engineering and binary analysis. Rolles [2] points out the essence of virtualization obfuscation is bytecode interpretation, and his paper describes a generic approach to defeating such protection by completely reversing the emulator, however, no automated system is presented. Coogan et al. [4] present a semantics-based approach to deobfuscating virtualization-obfuscated software. In that work, obfuscated binary is executed and all instructions execution information are recorded in a trace file; then, instructions that interact with the system directly or indirectly are kept with other instructions discarded. It does not perform further deobfuscation, though. Sharif et al. [3] propose an automatic analysis method to extract the virtual program counter information and construct the original control flow graph from a virtualized binary; Kalysch et al. [12] present VMAttack, an IDA Pro plugin, as an assistance tool for analyzing virtualization-packed binaries. Both are new analysis methods but unable to recover the deobfuscated code. While Yadegari et al. [13] pointed out *compiler optimization* can assist deobfuscation, specifically *arithmetic simplification* in their case (Sect. III.C), they did not reuse any compilers as a generic approach to deobfuscation. Instead, they use taint analysis to identify instructions for value propagation, and various specialized optimizations for simplifying the code; plus, symbolic execution is used to generate inputs for running a binary. To our knowledge, our system is the first that reuses modern compilers and leverages compilation optimization as a generic approach to deobfuscating virtualization-obfuscated code.

6   Conclusion

Virtualization obfuscation has been proven to be one of the most effective techniques to obfuscate binaries. This paper presents a novel automated deobfuscation method. It first constructs a CFG via offline trace analysis to detect dispatcher and handler functions, and symbolically execute the handlers to generate symbolic expressions. Then, symbolic expressions are translated into C code and bytecode is converted into invocations of the C functions, which are then optimized by compilers to recover simplified and semantically equivalent code. We have implemented a prototype system and evaluated it against popular commercial obfuscators. The experimental result indicates that our system can successfully recover concise code from virtualization-obfuscated code. Our work demonstrates that compilation optimization is an effective and generic approach to tackling virtualization obfuscation.

Acknowledgments. This work was supported in part by National High Technology Research and Development Program of China (No. 2015AA016004), the National Key R&D Program of China (No. 2016QY04W0802).

References

1. Nagra, J., Collberg, C.: Surreptitious Software: Obfuscation, Watermarking, and Tamperproofing for Software Protection. Pearson Education, London (2009)
2. Rolles, R.: Unpacking virtualization obfuscators. In: 3rd USENIX Workshop on Offensive Technologies (WOOT) (2009)
3. Sharif, M., Lanzi, A., Giffin, J., Lee, W.: Automatic reverse engineering of malware emulators. In: 2009 30th IEEE Symposium on Security and Privacy, pp. 94–109. IEEE (2009)
4. Coogan, K., Lu, G., Debray, S.: Deobfuscation of virtualization-obfuscated software: a semantics-based approach. In: Proceedings of the 18th ACM Conference on Computer and Communications Security, pp. 275–284. ACM (2011)
5. HexEffect: Virtual deobfuscator. http://www.hexeffect.com/virtual_deob.html
6. VMProtect: Vmprotect software protection. http://vmpsoft.com/
7. Oreans: Code virtualizer. https://oreans.com/codevirtualizer.php
8. Ugarte-Pedrero, X., Balzarotti, D., Santos, I., Bringas, P.G.: SoK: deep packer inspection: a longitudinal study of the complexity of run-time packers. In: 2015 IEEE Symposium on Security and Privacy (SP), pp. 659–673. IEEE (2015)
9. Luk, C.K., Cohn, R., Muth, R., Patil, H., Klauser, A., Lowney, G., Wallace, S., Reddi, V.J., Hazelwood, K.: Pin: building customized program analysis tools with dynamic instrumentation. ACM SIGPLAN Not. **40**, 190–200 (2005)
10. Eagle, C.: The IDA Pro Book: The Unofficial Guide to the World's Most Popular Disassembler. No Starch Press, San Francisco (2011)
11. CEA: cea-sec/miasm: reverse engineering framework in Python. https://github.com/cea-sec/miasm
12. Kalysch, A., Götzfried, J., Müller, T.: VMAttack: deobfuscating virtualization-based packed binaries. In: ARES (2017)
13. Yadegari, B., Johannesmeyer, B., Whitely, B., Debray, S.: A generic approach to automatic deobfuscation of executable code. In: 2015 IEEE Symposium on Security and Privacy (SP), pp. 674–691. IEEE (2015)

A Self-healing Key Distribution Scheme for Mobile Ad Hoc Networks

Guangli Xiang[✉], Lu Yu, Beilei Li, and Mengsen Xia

College of Computer Science and Technology, Wuhan University of Technology,
Wuhan, China
glxiang@whut.edu.cn, 13657285326@163.com, 2443828157@qq.com,
1714483165@qq.com

Abstract. Group communication in mobile Ad Hoc network (MANET), because of its special characteristics of large-scale mobile nodes, frequent change and update of group members relationship, open and unstable communication channel and high rate of packets loss, making secure group communication in MANET face many security threats, so how to realize secure communication between mobile nodes and how to establish secure session keys shared between mobile nodes has been the focus of MANET. Aimed at the problem mentioned above, a group key distribution scheme based on three hash chains is proposed for MANET. This scheme introduces a self-healing hash chain based on Dual Directional Hash Chain(DDHC), when a node is revoked, the corresponding self-healing hash value will be replaced by a new random value, so that revoked nodes can not realize collusion attack with the newly added node; This scheme also takes into account the high rate of packet loss in MANET, and realizes self-healing property. The security and performance analysis shows that the scheme can meet the security requirements of group communication for MANET, and it has the characteristics of dynamic revocation and resists collusion. The scheme also reduces the storage overhead and the communication load to a large extent, and can meet the performance requirements of group communication for MANET.

Keywords: Mobile ad hoc network · Group key distribution
Dual directional hash chain · Self-healing · Resist collusion

1 Introduction

The MANET is a multi-hop temporary autonomous system consisting of a set of mobile nodes with wireless transceivers, unlike traditional networks that rely on communications infrastructure, all mobile nodes in MANET assume both communication and routing responsibilities, and all mobile nodes are equal, without a central control organization [20]. And the nodes move in or out range dynamically so that the topology of network dynamically changes. These features guarantee the flexibility of MANET applications, but also face to many challenges.

© Springer International Publishing AG, part of Springer Nature 2018
S. Qing et al. (Eds.): ICICS 2017, LNCS 10631, pp. 325–335, 2018.
https://doi.org/10.1007/978-3-319-89500-0_29

Therefore, it is necessary to encrypt and authenticate the messages in the communication to avoid the adversaries intercept, tamper even partially interrupt the communication. Group key can be used to establish secure communication over an unreliable channel in MANET.

In this paper, we propose a self-healing group key distribution scheme with dynamic revocation and collusion resistance. our scheme is based on Dual Directional Hash Chain so that it can keep the forward secrecy and backward secrecy. And we introduce a self-healing hash chain to resist collusion attack between the new joined mobile node and the revoked mobile node. In addition, our scheme can revoke nodes during a session, while the previous schemes based on hash chains can not totally overcome such flaw.

Key management is one of the core technologies to realize the mobile ad hoc network security using cryptography technology [13]. The self-healing key distribution scheme was first proposed by Staddon et al. in [9] based on the information entropy theory. Initially, it is design for unreliable network to ensure the establishment and updating of session keys and improve the usability of the system in harsh communication environment. Liu et al. first proposed an efficient self-healing key distribution scheme based on revocation polynomials [8]. Dutta and Mukhopadhyay proposed an efficient computationally secure solution based on the combination of forward hash chain and reverse hash chain [4], which can greatly reduce resource cost, yet the scheme would lead to session keys being exposed [3,16,17]. Dutta and Mukhopadhyay further replace m mask polynomials with a bivariate t-degree polynomial [5], reducing the communication overhead and storage overhead to $O((t+1) \log q)$. However, the scheme is still flawed and cannot resist collusion attack. To prevent collusion attack, Du et al. introduced a secret random number for each session [2], as long as the attacker cannot get these secret random numbers. Wang et al. proposed a self-healing key distribution scheme based on the revocation polynomial [15], which solve the collusion attack problem by binding the joining time with its capability for recovering previous group session keys. Chen et al. solved the collusion attack problem [1], by introducing the unique session identifier and binding the joining time with the capability of recovering previous session keys.

Zou et al. proposed the first key distribution scheme based on the access polynomial [21]. Tian et al. proposed a simpler and more efficient key distribution scheme based on access polynomials [11], but later, this scheme was proved to be insecure later. Yuan et al. proposed unconditional secure key distribution schemes based on access polynomials [18,19], but these schemes only apply to specific groups. Wang et al. proposed a novel self-healing group key distribution scheme based on the access polynomial [14], which achieves the self-healing attribute by binding the joining time with the capability of recovering previous session keys, however, Guo et al.proved that the scheme does not have forward secrecy [6]. Sun et al. proposed two improved self-healing key distribution schemes with the capability of broadcast and authentication based on access polynomials [10], which further improved the ability to resist collusion attacks. Guo et al. proposed two self-healing group key distribution schemes based on exponential arithmetic, and introduced a novel broadcast method to reduce the storage cost and communication cost [7].

2   Preliminaries

Our scheme is based on the Dual Directional Hash Chain(DDHC), we first introduce the definition of a one-way hash function, which is the foundation of the DDHC. A hash function is any function that can be used to map data of arbitrary size to data of fixed size. A one-way hash function $H(x)$ satisfies the following conditions:

(1) *Unidirectional:* Let $H : A \rightarrow B$ as a one-way hash function, given $x \in A$, it is easy to compute $y = H(x)$. But if given $y \in B$, it is computationally infeasible to compute the $x \in A$ and $H(x) = y$.
(2) *Resist weak collision:* Let $H : A \rightarrow B$ as a one-way hash function, given $x \in A$, it is computationally infeasible to compute $x' \in A$, $x' \neq x$ and $H(x') = H(x)$.
(3) *Resist strong collision:* Let $H : A \rightarrow B$ as a one-way hash function, it is computationally infeasible to compute x, $x' \in A$, $x' \neq x$, and $H(x') = H(x)$.

A DDHC consists of two one-way hash chains with equal length, a forward hash chain and a backward hash chain. First, generating two random key seeds FK and BK from finite field $\mathbb{F}_q$. Then repeatedly applies the same one-way function $H(x)$ on each key seed to produce two hash chains of equal length m. So, the DDHC is defined as follows:

$$\{K_F^0 = FK, K_F^1 = H(K_F^0), \ldots, K_F^m = H^m(K_F^0)\}$$

$$\{K_B^m = H^m(K_B^0), \ldots, K_B^1 = H(K_B^0), K_B^0 = BK\}$$

In our scheme, we mainly focus on how to guarantee the security of communication between mobile nodes. To further clarify our goals and facilitate the later presentation, We define security model for the proposed self-healing key distribution scheme as follows:

(1) *Key confidentiality*: Any mobile nodes that are not the member of the group have no access to the keys that can decrypt the data that broadcast to the group.
(2) *Forward secrecy*: For the set R_j of mobile nodes revoked before session j, it is computationally infeasible for the mobile nodes $u_i \in R_j$ colluding together to recover any of subsequent session keys $SK_j, SK_{j+1}, \cdots, SK_m$, even with the knowledge of keys $SK_1, SK_2, \cdots, SK_{j-1}$.
(3) *Backward secrecy*: For the set J_j of new mobile nodes joined after session j, it is computationally infeasible for the mobile nodes $u_i \in J_j$ colluding together to recover any of past session keys $SK_1, SK_2, \cdots, SK_j$, even with the knowledge of keys $SK_{j+1}, SK_{j+2}, \cdots, SK_m$.

(4) *Collision resistant*: Given any set R_i of mobile nodes revoked before session i and any set J_j of new mobile nodes joined after session j, $i < j$. It is computationally infeasible for a colluding coalition $R_i \cup J_j$ to recover any keys SK_i, SK_{i+1}, $\cdots$, SK_{j-1} between session i and session j.

(5) *Revocation capability*: The illegal mobile nodes will be removed from the current group in time when the detection system detects the illegal mobile nodes.

3   Proposed scheme

The self-healing key distribution scheme proposed in this paper focuses on a communication group in the MANET. A communication group includes a key distribution center KDC and n group members. Each member in the group has a unique identifier, represented by u_i, and KDC shares a session key SK with group members in the group communication. The lifetime of the group communication is divided into m sessions, where a session is a fixed interval of time denoted as T_r, the jth session is represented by s_j, and the session key of the jth session is SK_j. The scheme consists of six parts: initialization, key update, key recovery, add or revoke group members, self-healing mechanism and re-initialization mechanism. The basic process shown in Fig. 1.

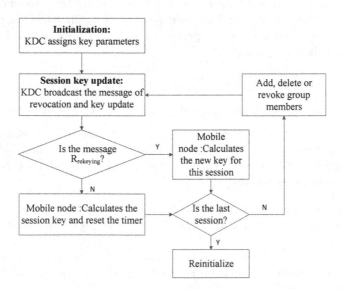

Fig. 1. Basic process of the proposed scheme

3.1   Initialization

Let t be a positive integer. KDC first randomly chooses a bivariate t-degree polynomial $h(x, y)$ from a small finite field $\mathbb{F}_q[x, y]$:

$$h(x, y) = \sum_{0 \leq i,j \leq t} a_{ij} x^i y^j \bmod q \qquad (t \leq m, t \leq n) \qquad (1)$$

According to the identifier of each mobile node and $h(x, y)$, KDC assigns a polynomial $h(u_i, y)$ to each mobile node as its mask polynomial.

KDC randomly picks the forward key seed FK, the backward key seed BK and the self-healing hash seed SH from $\mathbb{F}_q$, respectively. Then KDC generates three hash chains: $fk^j = H^j(FK)$, $bk^j = H^{m-j+1}(BK)$, $sh_j = H_1^j(SH)$, Where the structure of the DDHC adopts the hash function $H(x)$, and the structure of the self-healing hash chain adopts the hash function $H_1(x)$.

During the initialization phase, KDC will send the following packet over the secure channel to the mobile node u_i with the session period s_i to s_j ($1 \leq s_i < s_j \leq m$).

$$KDC \rightarrow u_i : \{T_r \| h(u_i, y) \| fk^i \| sh_i\}$$

where T_r is the length of each session, $fk^i = H^i(FK)$ is the forward key hash value and sh_i is the self-healing hash value corresponding to session s_i. When the mobile node receives the initialization packet, decrypts and obtains the corresponding session key update parameters and system parameters, sets the update time of timer to T_r, and saves the session key update parameters.

3.2   Key Update

At the beginning of each session, KDC constructs the revocation set R to store the revoked mobile node and a set U to store the non-revoked mobile node. Let R_j be the set of all mobile nodes revoked in s_j, and $R = R_1 \cup R_2 \cdots \cup R_j$, $U_j = \{u_1, u_2, \cdots, u_n\}$ be the set of all legal mobile nodes in s_j.

If a mobile node is revoked in s_j, KDC will produce a random value sh'_j to replace the self-healing hash value sh_j, that is $sh_j = sh'_j$, subsequent self-healing hash values can be computed using the random value sh'_j: $sh_{j+k} = H_1^k(sh'_j)(0 < k \leq m - j)$. If there is no mobile node is revoked in s_j, KDC will compute the self-healing hash value $sh_j = H_1(sh_{j-1})$. So the session key SK_j of s_j as follows:

$$SK_j = fk^j + sh_j \times bk^j \qquad (2)$$

If a mobile node is revoked in s_j, KDC first constructs the revocation polynomial $r_j(x)$ according to the revocation set $R = \{r_1, r_2, \cdots, r_{\omega_j}\}$:

$$r_j(x) = (x - r_1)(x - r_2) \cdots (x - r_{\omega_j}) \bmod q \qquad (3)$$

Then KDC constructs the recovery polynomial $\psi_j(x)$ to recover the lost session keys:

$$\psi_j(x) = r_j(x) sh'_j + h(x, fk^j) \bmod q \qquad (4)$$

KDC constructs the access polynomial $v_j(x)$ according to the set U_j:

$$v_j(x) = [1 + (x - u_1)(x - u_2) \cdots (x - u_n)] \bmod q \tag{5}$$

Where legal mobile nodes compute the access polynomial $v_j(x)$ will get $v_j(x) = 1$, however, the revoked mobile nodes will get a random value that different from 1.

After constructing the access polynomial, KDC will compute the broadcast polynomial $b_j(x)$:

$$b_j(x) = v_j(x) \times bk^j + h(x, fk^j) \bmod q \tag{6}$$

Based on these preparations, KDC will broadcast the key update messages B_j in the group. The format of B_j is as follows:

$$B_j = \{R_1 \cup R_2 \cup \cdots \cup R_j \| U_j \| b_j(x) \| \cup_{j'=1}^{j} \psi_{j'}(x)\} \tag{7}$$

3.3   Key Recovery

The session key consists of three parts: fk^j, bk^j and sh_j. fk^j is secretly assigned to each legal mobile node in the initialization phase, sh_j is updated at the beginning of each session.

At the beginning of s_j, when a legal mobile node u_i receives the key update packet, it first computes fk^j, then computes the result of $h(u_i, fk^j)$, and then computes the result of access polynomial $v_j(u_i)$ according to the legal node set U_j, and computes the backward hash value:

$$bk^j = \frac{b_j(u_i) - h(u_i, fk^j)}{v_j(u_i)} \bmod q \tag{8}$$

If the mobile node is revoked, the result of access polynomial is a random value different from 1, the mobile node cannot obtain the right backward hash value bk^j.

If there is no revoked mobile node in s_j, u_i computes $sh_j = H_1(sh_{j-1})$. Otherwise, u_i can compute sh_j from the recovery polynomial $\psi_j(x)$ in the broadcast message B_j:

$$sh_j = sh'_j = \frac{\psi_j(u_i) - h(u_i, fk^j)}{r_j(u_i)} \bmod q \tag{9}$$

Finally, u_i can further compute the session key $SK_j = fk^j + sh_j \times bk^j$.

3.4   Add or Revoke Group Members

Add group members: When a node u_i wants to join the communication group and to be legal from s_i to s_j, u_i first get in touch with KDC. After verifying its identification, KDC encrypts and sends the session key parameters to u_i via the secure communication channel:

$$KDC \rightarrow u_i : \{T_r \| h(u_i, y) \| fk^i \| sh_i\}$$

At the same time, KDC adds u_i to the legal set U_j, updates key and recovers key.When a non-revoked mobile node leaves the communication group,the mobile node will be deleted from the legal set U_j, and the mobile node can rejoin the communication group with the same identify.

Revoke group members: Assuming that a mobile node is captured by the attacker during s_j, KDC immediately broadcasts an $R_{rekeying}$ key update message to revoke the captured mobile node:

$$B_j \rightarrow all : \{R_{rekeying}\|R'_j\|U'_j\|\psi_j(x)\}$$

When the non-revoked mobile node receives the $R_{rekeying}$ message, it will compute the new session key SK'_j. Noted that when the mobile node is revoked during the session, the non-revoked mobile node does not reset the timer.

3.5 Self-healing Mechanism

Suppose mobile node u_i whose lifetime is from s_{j_1} to s_{j_2} receives broadcast message B_{j_1} in s_{j_1} and broadcast message B_{j_2} in s_{j_2}, but not message B_j for s_j, where $1 \leq j_1 < j < j_2 \leq m$, u_i can recover the lost session key SK_j as follows:

Firstly, u_i can obtain fk^j and bk^j as a non-revoked mobile node.

Secondly, u_i can recover sh_{j_1} as a non-revoked mobile node, then u_i can recover sh_j as follows: If there is no mobile node is revoked from s_{j_1} to s_{j_2}, u_i repeatedly applies the hash function $H_1(x)$ on sh_{j_1} to obtain the self-healing hash value sh_j. Otherwise, u_i still can recover sh_j. For example, suppose there is a mobile node is revoked in $s_{j'}$, where $j_1 < j' < j < j_2$, u_i can recover the self-healing hash value $sh'_{j'}$ according to the recovery polynomial $\psi_{j'}(x)$ in broadcast message B_{j_2}. Then, u_i repeatedly applies the hash function $H_1(x)$ on $sh'_{j'}$ to obtain sh_j.

Thirdly, u_i computes the lost session key $SK_j = fk^j + sh_j \times bk^j$.

3.6 Re-initialization Mechanism

If the lifetime of the communication group ends, the group must re-initialize and assign the key materials for all legal mobile nodes.

4 Security Analysis

Theorem 1: The scheme is a session key with privacy and achieves self-healing with revocation capability.

Proof: (1) The scheme is a session key with privacy: For a non-revoked mobile node u_i in s_j, the SK_j is determined by fk^j, bk^j and sh_j. fk^j is assigned to the non-revoked mobile node when the node joins the communication group. bk^j can only be recovered by non-revoked mobile nodes at the beginning of each session. Even if a revoked mobile node obtain fk^j and bk^j, sh_j will be updated immediately when a mobile node is revoked, such that the revoked cannot recover sh_j. Thus, it is impossible for any mobile node to obtain the session key only by fk^j and bk^j or only by sh_j.

(2) Self-healing: As described in Sect. 3.5, a non-revoked mobile node can recover the lost session key by the self-healing hash value and the recovery polynomial.

(3) Revocation capability: In the scheme, the session key is updated in two ways, one is to update periodically, and the other is to update when the mobile node is revoked. The periodic update prevents the session key from being cracked because it uses time too long. The dynamic revocation mechanism ensures that the revoked mobile node is removed from the communication group in time to avoid further damage to the system. Let R be the set of all mobile nodes revoked in and before s_j. For a mobile node $u_i \in R$, because the access polynomial $v_j(u_i)$ is always zero, u_i cannot recover bk^j from the broadcast polynomial $b_j(u_i)$, moreover, once the mobile node u_i is revoked, the self-healing hash value sh_j will replace by a random value sh'_j, u_i cannot obtain sh'_j. Because u_i cannot obtain bk^j and sh'_j, it is infeasible for u_i to recover the session key SK_j.

Theorem 2: The scheme achieves forward security and backward security.

Proof: (1) Forward security: Let R be the set of all mobile nodes revoked in and before s_k. Consider a mobile node $u_i \in R$, whose lifetime is from s_{start} to s_{end}. We can analyze the forward security in two scenarios:

$s_{start} < s_k \le s_{end}$, which signifies that s_k in the lifetime of u_i, and u_i can obtain fk^k. If u_i is revoked before s_k, u_i cannot recover bk^k and sh_k, so u_i cannot recover SK_k. If u_i is revoked in s_k, u_i can recover bk^k, but sh_k will be replaced by a new random value sh'_k when u_i is revoked, u_i cannot recover sh'_k, so u_i cannot recover SK_k.

$s_k > s_{end}$, in this case u_i could only obtain fk^k and cannot recover bk^k and sh_k. Thus u_i cannot recover SK_k. As a result, the scheme achieves forward security.

(2) Backward security: Suppose u_i joins the communication group in s_j, for $s_k < s_j$, u_i could only recover bk^k, and cannot obtain fk^k and sh_k. Moreover, even if holds the broadcast message corresponding to s_k, it cannot compute the mask polynomial $h(u_i, fk^k)$. Thus u_i cannot recover SK_k. As a result, the scheme achieves backward security.

Theorem 3: The scheme resists collusion of revoked mobile nodes and newly joined mobile nodes.

Proof: Suppose the mobile node u_i is revoked in s_i and the mobile node u_j join the group in s_j, where $s_i < s_j$. u_i and u_j can collude to obtain the value of DDHC from s_i to s_j. The self-healing hash chain is a forward hash chain in the scheme, sh_i will be replaced by a new random value sh'_i when u_i is revoked, subsequent self-healing hash value will be computed with sh'_i, that is $sh_j = H_1^{j-i}(sh'_i)$. It is computationally infeasible to compute sh_{j-1} even if it obtains sh_j. Therefore, even if the revoked mobile node in collusion with the newly joined mobile node, they cannot obtain session keys more than their lifetime. As a result, the scheme resists the collusion of revoked mobile nodes and newly joined mobile node.

5 Performance analysis

In order to evaluate the performance of the proposed scheme, we will compare with the communication overhead and storage overhead between our scheme and the previous self-healing key distribution schemes based on hash chain. The comparison results are shown in Table 1. The storage overhead of a non-revoked mobile node with the lifetime from s_i to s_j is shown in Table 2, and the total storage overhead of a non-revoked mobile node is $(t+4)\ log\ q$ bits.

At the session s_j, the broadcast message B_j consists of t-degree broadcast polynomial $b_j(x)$, v t-degree recovery polynomials $\psi_{j'}(x)$, set U_j and the revocation set R. The communication overhead of the set U_j and the revocation set R can be ignored because the mobile node identify can be selected from a small finite field $\mathbb{F}_q$. Therfore, The total communication overhead of our scheme is $(v+1)(t+1)\ log\ q$ bits, where $0 \le v < j \le m$.

According to the Table 1, the scheme 3 of [5] is better than our scheme in term of storage overhead and communication overhead, however, the scheme 3 of [5] can not resist the collusion of newly joined user and revoked users whose lifetimes do not expire and the users in the scheme can not be revoked during a session. Although the scheme of [2,7] have the revocation capability, they can only resist the collusion of newly joined user and revoked users incompletely and the users in these two schemes can not be revoked during a session. The scheme of [12] has the revocation capability, but the users in the scheme can not be revoked during a session. From the comparison in Table 1, although the storage overhead and communication overhead of proposed scheme are slightly increased, only our scheme can revoke a user dynamically and resist collusion of newly joined user and revoked users no matter whether their lifetimes expire or not.

Table 1. Comparison of self-healing key distribution schemes based on hash chains

Schemes	Storage overhead ($log\ q$)	Communication overhead ($log\ q$)	Revocation capability	Collusion resistance	Robustness
Scheme 3 of [5]	$(t+1)$	$(t+1)$	✓	✗	✗
Scheme of [2]	$(2s_j - 2s_i + 4)$	$(t + (1+m)/2)$	✓	incomplete	✗
Scheme of [7]	$(2m+1)$	$(2t+1)$	✓	incomplete	✗
Scheme of [12]	$(2s_j - 2s_i + 6)$	$(t+l+1)$	✓	✓	✓
Proposed scheme	$(t+4)$	$(v+1)(t+1)$	✓ dynamic	✓	✓

✳ m is the number of sessions, l is the number of the elements of the self-healing set, t is the degree of polynomial, v is the number of polynomials.

Table 2. Storage overhead of key material

Key material	Storage space ($log\ q$)
The seeds of hash chain fk^i,sh_i	2
Masking polynomials $h(u_i, fk^i)$	$(t+1)$
Session length T_r	1

6   Conclusion

A self-healing group key distribution scheme with dynamic revocation and collusion resistance is proposed in this paper. The scheme based on DDHC to ensure the forward security and backward security of session key. For the problem of packet loss, the scheme introduces a self-healing hash chain to ensure that the non-revoked mobile node can recover the lost session key. At the same time, the scheme has a small storage overhead and communication overhead and can be applied to resource-constrained MANET communication.

References

1. Chen, H., Xie, L.: Improved one-way hash chain and revocation polynomial-based self-healing group key distribution schemes in resource-constrained wireless networks. Sensors **14**(12), 24358–24380 (2014)
2. Du, C., Hu, M., Zhang, H., Zhang, W.: Anti-collusive self-healing key distribution scheme with revocation capability. Inf. Technol. J. **8**(4), 619–624 (2009)
3. Du, W., He, M.: Self-healing key distribution with revocation and resistance to the collusion attack in wireless sensor networks. In: Baek, J., Bao, F., Chen, K., Lai, X. (eds.) ProvSec 2008. LNCS, vol. 5324, pp. 345–359. Springer, Heidelberg (2008). https://doi.org/10.1007/978-3-540-88733-1_25
4. Dutta, R., Mukhopadhyay, S.: Improved self-healing key distribution with revocation in wireless sensor network. In: Wireless Communications and NETWORKING Conference, pp. 2963–2968. IEEE (2007)
5. Dutta, R., Mukhopadhyay, S., Collier, M.: Computationally secure self-healing key distribution with revocation in wireless ad hoc networks. Ad Hoc Netw. **8**(6), 597–613 (2010)
6. Guo, H., Zheng, Y.: On the security of a self-healing group key distribution scheme. Wirel. Pers. Commun. **91**(3), 1109–1121 (2016)
7. Guo, H., Zheng, Y., Zhang, X., Li, Z.: Exponential arithmetic based self-healing group key distribution scheme with backward secrecy under the resource-constrained wireless networks. Sensors **16**(5), 609 (2016)
8. Liu, D., Ning, P., Sun, K.: Efficient self-healing group key distribution with revocation capability. In: ACM Conference on Computer and Communications Security, pp. 231–240. ACM (2003)
9. Staddon, J., Miner, S., Franklin, M., Balfanz, D., Malkin, M., Dean, D.: Self-healing key distribution with revocation. In: 2002 IEEE Symposium on Security and Privacy, Proceedings, pp. 241–257. IEEE (2002)

10. Sun, X., Wu, X., Huang, C., Zhong, J., Zhong, J.: Modified access polynomial based self-healing key management schemes with broadcast authentication and enhanced collusion resistance in wireless sensor networks. Ad Hoc Netw. **37**(P2), 324–336 (2016)
11. Tian, B., Han, S., Dillon, T.S.: An efficient self-healing key distribution scheme. In: New Technologies, Mobility and Security, pp. 1–5. IEEE (2008)
12. Tian, B., Han, S., Dillon, T.S., Das, S.: A self-healing key distribution scheme based on vector space secret sharing and one way hash chains. In: World of Wireless, Mobile and Multimedia Networks, pp. 1–6. IEEE (2008)
13. Wang, G., Wen, T., Guo, Q., Ma, X.: An efficient and secure group key management scheme in mobile ad hoc networks. J. Comput. Res. Dev. **30**(3), 937–954 (2010)
14. Wang, Q., Chen, H., Xie, L., Wang, K.: Access-polynomial-based self-healing group key distribution scheme for resource-constrained wireless networks. Secur. Commun. Netw. **5**(12), 1363–1374 (2012)
15. Wang, Q., Chen, H., Xie, L., Wang, K.: One-way hash chain-based self-healing group key distribution scheme with collusion resistance capability in wireless sensor networks. Ad Hoc Netw. **11**(8), 2500–2511 (2013)
16. Xu, Q., He, M.: Improved constant storage self-healing key distribution with revocation in wireless sensor network. Inf. Secur. Appl. **5379**, 41–55 (2008)
17. Yang, Y., Zhou, J., Deng, R.H., Bao, F.: Computationally secure hierarchical self-healing key distribution for heterogeneous wireless sensor networks. Inf. Commun. Secur. **5927**, 135–149 (2009)
18. Yuan, T., Ma, J., Zhong, Y., Zhang, S.: Efficient self-healing key distribution with limited group membership for communication-constrained networks. In: IEEE/IFIP International Conference on Embedded Ubiquitous Computing, pp. 453–458. IEEE (2008)
19. Yuan, T., Ma, J., Zhong, Y., Zhang, S.: Self-healing key distribution with limited group membership property. In: International Conference on Intelligent Networks Intelligent Systems, pp. 309–312. IEEE (2008)
20. Zhu, S., Setia, S., Xu, S., Jajodia, S.: GKMPAN: an efficient group rekeying scheme for secure multicast in ad-hoc networks. J. Comput. Secur. **14**(4), 301–325 (2006)
21. Zou, X., Dai, Y.S.: A robust and stateless self-healing group key management scheme. In: International Conference on Communication Technology, pp. 1–4. IEEE (2006)

IoT Security

SecHome: A Secure Large-Scale Smart Home System Using Hierarchical Identity Based Encryption

Yu Li[1], Yazhe Wang[1(✉)], and Yuan Zhang[2]

[1] State Key Laboratory of Information Security,
Institute of Information Engineering, Chinese Academy of Sciences,
Beijing 100093, China
{liyu,wangyazhe}@iie.ac.cn
[2] State Key Laboratory for Novel Software Technology,
Computer Science and Technology Department, Nanjing University,
Nanjing 210023, China
zhangyuan05@gmail.com

Abstract. With the rapid development of Cyber-Physical Systems, there has been a growing trend among smart devices to connect networks via different wireless protocols. In particular, smart home devices are becoming more and more prevalent. However, security issues on how to control and prevent unauthorized access to smart devices connected to the cloud still need to be considered and solved. Hierarchical Identity-Based Encryption is a well-known access control model which enables parent nodes to decrypt the data from descendant nodes. In this paper, we present SecHome, a large-scale smart home system using hierarchical identity based encryption protocol. SecHome applies the protocol by using efficient pairing based cryptography to enforce an access control policy, so parent nodes at the top of the hierarchy can monitor their descendant nodes. In practice, we have implemented our SecHome system on both smart phone and smart device sides, and the final evaluations demonstrate that our system is proved to be of practicality and with high efficiency.

Keywords: Smart device · Security · Privacy
Hierarchical Identity-Based Encryption

1 Introduction

In recent years, smart home devices have received much attention due to their potential applications and the proliferation of Internet of Things. As a result, users who would like to set up different access controls to different people and devices are driven to use an access manager. Some access managers are provided by smart home vendors as part of smart home ecosystem, and some are provided by third-party cloud services. There are several different types of

© Springer International Publishing AG, part of Springer Nature 2018
S. Qing et al. (Eds.): ICICS 2017, LNCS 10631, pp. 339–351, 2018.
https://doi.org/10.1007/978-3-319-89500-0_30

Internet of Things access methods with a smart home system, which include IEEE 802.11(Wi-Fi), Bluetooth and ZigBee. All these technologies are helping smart devices connecting to a cloud center. The owner of the devices can utilize her smart phone to control and monitor them. Most of them are wireless-network based where passwords are backed up to cloud and synced across the smart home devices.

However, numerous recent surveys show that smart home systems are vulnerable to hacking because of the weak authentication and authorization. The security and privacy issues are highly concerned for smart home adoption since the data generated by living environment is usually sensitive [1]. So far, we can identify two types of issues for smart home system: security issue and privacy issue. By saying security issue, we refer to the broad class of adversaries that intentionally attack the system. The problems of security issue need to be addressed, for example, using authentication and encryption scheme to avoid interference over the communication channel. Although the authentication between users and cloud is important in previous home automation researches, the focus of this paper is on privacy, which we expect will be the dominant concern of users in a smart home system. Specifically, privacy issue is concerned by home owners who are afraid that cloud service providers will get sensitive information and affect the security of the living environment. For example, sensitive information like smart lock will indicate whether there are any people at home. A cloud service provider will need a secure protocol to guarantee users' private information.

Current existing smart home systems use Transport Layer Security (TLS) or HTTPS protocol to provide authentication as well as encryption. However, such smart home systems may have several issues. First, there is no guarantee of third party security and privacy protection. The cloud server of smart home systems would master all sensitive data and it is difficult to say that the data won't harm users' privacy. Second, the smart home owner cannot issue keys to her home members dynamically so that they must interact with the cloud server which may have many potential dangers. Third, compared with the traditional security system, smart devices are more vulnerable since the low-cost embedded systems are used. Therefore, we cannot just rely on the traditional security system to provide a strong security guarantee in Cyber-Physical Systems, especially in smart home system.

In this paper, we propose a secure large-scale smart home system using hierarchical identity based encryption. Generally speaking, the basic scheme of our system can be described as follows. When a home owner starts setting a smart home, she issues a secret key to the home members based on the hierarchy of the home. Later, when any home member buys a smart device, the owner issues a private key for it and it connects to the presetting private cloud. The private cloud then communicates with the public cloud by using the public ID to encrypt the sensitive data. In order to allow users to control the access to the smart home devices, suitable hierarchy and authentication as well as encryption are required.

There are two main issues in our system design that need to be addressed. First, since a malicious user may attempt to impersonate a normal user and control her smart devices, every device needs to be authenticated by smart home cloud server to ensure that device qualifies for connecting. Second, different home members should have different access rights to monitor and control smart devices. For instance, the smart home owner can control and issue access rights to her home members.

Our contributions can be summarized as follows:

- We are the first to study privacy protection in smart home system by using hybrid cloud architecture and to propose a hierarchical key management scheme.
- To the best of our knowledge, we are also the first to study a privacy protection in smart home using Hierarchical Identity Based Encryption.
- In terms of privacy, our algorithm leaks no knowledge about each party's data.

The rest of this paper is organized as follows. In Sect. 2, we discuss the related works. In Sect. 3, we present the overall architecture and intuitions behind our design. We then give the full specification of our system and analyze the security in Sect. 4. In Sect. 5, we present evaluations of our solution. Our conclusion and future work are shown in Sect. 6.

2   Related Work

According to [2,3], this novel paradigm, named "Internet of Things", is rapidly gaining ground as the modern wireless networks technology. However, in [4], the IoT has a great impact on personal privacy and security. Therefore, a high degree of reliability is needed which includes data authentication, access control and clients' privacy. Unlike other Cyber-Physical Systems devices, smart home devices have a direct influence on people's daily life. Therefore, the design of the access control scheme in smart home system is extremely important and the encrypted data generated by the system should only be viewed by the correct home member. To the best of our knowledge, there is no such scheme that can only let smart home owner monitor the data. Each of the existing smart home systems relies on a reliable third party cloud server.

Identity-Based Encryption(IBE) which was proposed by Shamir in [5] can simplify key management in a Public Key Infrastructure(PKI) by using objects' identities(e.g., unique mobile phone number, email address, product serial number, etc.) as public keys. After that the first secure IBE scheme was proposed by Boneh and Franklin [6] from the bilinear pairings. They have also proved that the IBE scheme is semantically secure against adaptive chosen-ciphertext attack under the DBDH assumption in the random oracle model. Moreover, a handful of researches on constructing provable secure IBE scheme were proposed in [7–10]. Many alternative approaches are derived from IBE with the development of cloud computing, for example, Role Based Encryption (RBE) [11] and Attribute Based Encryption (ABE)[12–16]. Another approach which can enforce access control policies and data encryption is to apply the Hierarchical ID-based Encryption (HIBE)[17–19] to Internet of Things.

The design of our secure smart home system is motivated by [20], which is an emerging active research area in the intersection of computer security and Internet of Things. In HIBE, the length of the identity becomes longer with the growth in the depth of hierarchy, which is suitable for a home's structure since the depth of the hierarchy would not be too large in a family. However, as far as we know, there is no previous proposed security and privacy protection scheme for smart home systems. Furthermore, although our design is motivated by HIBE proposed in [20], our problem does not fit exactly into the specific cryptographic-design. For example, in our system, we consider various hardware securities, such as secure boot and data isolation [21].

3   Architecture

In this section, we present the architecture of our secure hierarchical smart home system. In our system, there are five components which include public cloud, private cloud, home owner, home members and smart devices. The architecture is shown in Fig. 1. Public cloud is utilized to store and transfer the encrypted sensitive data. Due to the limited computation capacity, a private cloud is used to help encrypting and decrypting data generated by the smart device sensors. Home owner and home members use a smart phone to control and monitor data generated by the smart devices. Home owner, home members and smart devices are arranged in a form of a hierarchy which can be visualized as a pyramid. The hierarchy will be described in Sect. 5.2.

In our secure hierarchical smart home architecture, we assume that a private cloud has been set up in the home. Then we let the owner of the home be at the depth 1 in the home hierarchy. After that, the home owner can set keys for her children nodes as well as the sub-structure as shown in steps 1 and 2. Home members also set keys for their smart devices in steps 3 and 4. Smart devices

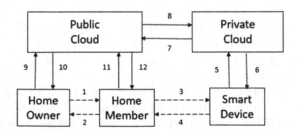

Fig. 1. Our HIBE system architecture

transfer the encrypted data to private cloud using symmetric key encryption as shown in steps 5 and 6. The private cloud can only be accessed by the home owner and the data must be encrypted by HIBE encryption when they leave the private cloud as shown in step 7 and 8. A public cloud is a third-party cloud which is employed to store and transfer the encrypted data. Home owner and home members who equip with a smart phone can send HIBE encrypted data and command public cloud in step 9–12. Therefore, the top of the home hierarchy can monitor the huge data generated by their descendant nodes and smart devices through the public cloud. The step details of how to set up keys and encrypt data for home members and smart devices will be described in Sect. 5.2.

4   SecHome Using HIBE: Specification

4.1   Overview of Our System

In this section, we present the overview of our system and the intuitions behind our design. Boneh et al. proposed a hierarchical identity based encryption with constant size ciphertext in [20] which can apply to a number of applications. However, since the encryption scheme they proposed is only a general approach for constructing HIBE using pairing based encryption, we will apply the HIBE that matches the properties of smart home system. Moreover, we also provide a revocation mechanism to keep our system more secure. At a high level, smart home device usually contains an embedded chip with a real time operating system running on it. But this kind of systems is more vulnerable because of the design of the system architecture [22,23]. Therefore, our system also considers other aspects of security that would protect the data stored in the device. Intuitively, we provide a hardware-assisted dynamic root of trust which allows secure task loading at the runtime.

4.2   Design of Our SecHome System

Our goal is to maintain the confidentiality and integrity of users' data running on a network of hosts potentially under the control of an adversary. This section outlines our design to achieve this with good performance and through keeping adversary's attack out of the SecHome system.

Algorithm 1 shows the overall scheme of our smart home system, which consists of the initialization, adds and revokes nodes in the hierarchy. Specifically, people nodes in this hierarchy are equipped with a mobile device that allows them to generate keys for children nodes and to send as well as receive messages through a wireless network.

Algorithm 1. Algorithm for Smart Home Keys Generation and Encryption

Initialization:

For each home owner who joins in the smart home system, the owner generates public parameters $(g, g_1, g_2, g_3, h_1, h_2, \cdots h_L)$ and master key $mk = g_2^\alpha$.

Input:

For each member and smart device in depth 1, we denote it as ID_1. Home owner randomly chooses r, generates $d_{ID_1} = (g_2^\alpha \cdot (h_1^{H(ID_1)} \cdot g_3)^r, g^r, h_2^r, \cdots h_L^r)$ and sends it via a secret channel described in Algorithm 2.

Add an element in the hierarchy:

When a new smart device joins in this hierarchy at depth 2, ID_1 randomly chooses t and generates $d_{H(ID_2)} = (a_0 \cdot b_2^{H(ID_2)} \cdot (h_1^{H(ID_1)} \cdots h_2^{H(ID_2)} \cdot g_3)^t, a_1 \cdot g^t, b_3 \cdot h_3^t \cdot b_L \cdot h_L^t)$ and sends it via a secret channel described in Algorithm 2.

ID_1 encrypts t using ID_0's ID and sends it to ID_0. ID_0 gets $r + t$ which can decrypt device in depth 2.

When a new home member joins in this hierarchy in depth 1 and controls a device in depth 2,

Home owner only needs to generate a d_{ID_1} for the member and sends the encrypted device's r to him via a secret channel using Algorithm 2. The member can use device's r to control or get the data from it.

Recursively we can set up keys for all nodes in the hierarchy.

Update an element in the hierarchy:

When a node in this hierarchy at depth 2 needs to update decryption key,

The parent ID_1 randomly chooses a new t and generates $d_{H(ID_2)} = (a_0 \cdot b_2^{H(ID_2)} \cdot (h_1^{H(ID_1)} \cdots h_2^{H(ID_2)} \cdot g_3)^t, a_1 \cdot g^t, b_3 \cdot h_3^t \cdot b_L \cdot h_L^t)$ and sends it via a secret channel described in Algorithm 2.

ID_1 encrypts t using ID_0's ID and sends it to ID_0. ID_0 gets $r + t$ which can decrypt device in depth 2.

We can update nodes'keys in the list by recursively using $RL_{ID|k}$ and $d_{ID|k-1}$.

Revoke an element in the hierarchy:

When a node in this hierarchy at depth 2 needs to be revoked,

The parent ID_1 randomly chooses t and generates $d_{H(ID_2)} = (a_0 \cdot b_2^{H(ID_2)} \cdot (h_1^{H(ID_1)} \cdots h_2^{H(ID_2)} \cdot g_3)^t, a_1 \cdot g^t, b_3 \cdot h_3^t \cdot b_L \cdot h_L^t)$, and sends it via a secret channel described in Algorithm 2.

ID_1 encrypts t using ID_0's ID and sends it to ID_0. ID_0 gets $r + t$ which can decrypt device in depth 2.

The node will have been successfully revoked by recursively doing this until all sub-nodes getting new keys.

When a home owner generates a key for her children nodes, for example, we use a general HIBE structure in Fig. 2 to illustrate our scheme and explain how the proposed scheme adds and revokes a home member or device in the hierarchy. Start by assuming a home owner's id is Pid_1. The owner has two

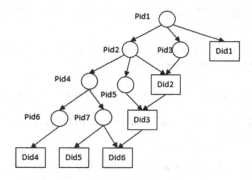

Fig. 2. Our HIBE example

children nodes Pid_2 and Pid_3. A smart device, with ID number Did_1 can only be controlled by Pid_1. Home owner Pid_1 generates public parameters and master key using Setup mentioned above. For the children nodes Pid_2 and Pid_3, home owner generates two tuples (Pid_1, Pid_2) and (Pid_1, Pid_3). Then the owner uses KeyGen to produce two private keys for the two children nodes. In order to send the keys to the children nodes securely, we choose the broadcast encryption scheme proposed in Algorithm 2 which needs a presetting secret key sk_u for each node. The parent node first sets up an identity space ID, and then produces a message (Hdr, c) for each user and broadcast it to children node group. The children nodes decrypt the message using their presetting secret key sk_u to get the private key d_I. For the device Did_1, the key distribution process is as same as the children nodes. However, there is another scenario that another person may also need to control it after the key distribution. Therefore, we are required to add an element between Pid_1 and Did_1. To solve this problem, Pid_1 can issue a private key to the new element and send the encrypted d_{Did_1} to the owner. Then the new element can be inserted into the hierarchy successfully.

In another scenario, child node Pid_3 buys a smart device Did_2 and wants to set it up within this hierarchy. First, Pid_2 generates private keys for the device using public parameters of the parent node. Then Pid_2 encrypts the devices' private r using Encrypt in Algorithm 1 and sends back to the parent node. The parent node can decrypt it using Decrypt and get r in order to obtain the private key of the device. Therefore, Pid_1 can control and gain the data generated by device Did_2.

Sometimes, a node in the hierarchy needs to update the decryption, or even the node should be revoked in this hierarchy. For example, the node Pid_4 needs to be revoked in the hierarchy. We first generate a subtree that contains Pid_4 from the root node to the leaf nodes. In this hierarchy, the node Pid_4 has a parent node Pid_2 and two children nodes Pid_6 and Pid_7. Therefore, Pid_2 generates two private keys for Pid_6 and Pid_7 and recursively the descendant nodes of Pid_4 get new keys and send the encrypted r using ID to all ancestor nodes. Then the node Pid_4 has been successfully revoked.

Algorithm 2. Algorithm for Broadcasting Smart Home Keys

Initialization:

    Home owner sets up a broadcast scheme for identity space ID. It outputs public parameters as well as a master secret key.

KeyGen:

    Takes the master key and a user $u \in ID$ and outputs a secret key d_I

Encryption:

    takes the public parameters and a subset $S \in ID$, and produces a (Hdr, c). c is encrypted by using device ID.

Decryption:

    takes the header Hdr and presetting secret key sk_u and outputs the key d_I

Algorithm 2 gives a broadcast encryption scheme for distributing the key for each element in the hierarchy. In order to achieve the broadcast encryption scheme, the manufactory of the smart device will preset a secret key sk_u into the smart device. When a home member issues a private key d_I to the child node, she generates a tuple (Hdr, c), where c is encrypted by using ID. The child node can decrypt c and get the private key d_I after receiving the tuple that is indicated to her. By executing this scheme, the child node can get data like SSID and Wi-Fi password in a secure way and connect to the gateway securely.

Besides the above HIBE scheme, we also provide some security enhancements in our SecHome system which are described in the following.

Initialization Key. The SecHome's smart phone and device hardware platforms come with an initialization key. Access to this key is controlled by the MPU and only trusted software components are given access to it. HIBE keys can be derived from the key.

Memory Protection Unit (MPU). SecHome's smart device side is based on MPU provided by [21]. The MPU provides secure initialization and configuration which can act as a root of trust for the HIBE scheme.

Secure Boot. SecHome's trusted software components are loaded with secure boot and isolated from the rest of the system by the MPU to ensure their integrity.

Cryptographic Hash. We rely on a keyed pseudo-random function and a collision-resistant cryptographic hash function. Our implementation uses HMAC and SHA-256.

Authenticated Encryption. For HIBE encryption, we use a stream cipher that provides authenticated encryption with associated data. The associated data is authenticated, but not included in the ciphertext. In this way, it is difficult to forge any ciphertext and the security against chosen ciphertext attack can be provided.

4.3   Security Considerations of Our System

We now discuss several attack scenarios on SecHome which are partly outside the adversary model.

Server Spoofing Attack Resistance. Compared to other classical remote authentications, our system also allows users to verify the server side in order to avoid server spoofing attacks.

Replay Attacks Resistance. The adversary may try to attack in various ways by replaying a prior command. In order to prevent this kind of attacks, our scheme provides online key exchange protocol, so that the users can simply refuse to give d_{ID} a second time to any other nodes.

Masquerade Attack Resistance. Our system is session based and in each session a receiver will be assigned a dynamic salt. A dynamic salt can hide the real ID from eavesdropping, and only be valid in a certain session. Whenever an expired ID is received, the receiver can simply discard those requests.

Data Isolation. Many low-end platforms do not have multiprocessing and virtual memory, but the MPU used in our SecHome system can achieve data isolation with memory access control.

Overall, SecHome achieves all security and functional requirements better than previously proposed solutions in smart home system.

5   Experiments and Results

5.1   Experiment Setup

We have implemented the above architecture of the secure smart home system. The system consists of three parties which include public cloud server, smart phones and smart home devices. The public cloud is implemented in Java. The interfaces of the cloud are exposed as web services, and the web services are hosted in Apache Tomcat. The clouds use MySQL database which can be easily replaced by other databases for server side data storage. The smart phone side is written with Android which can run in any smart phone with Android platform support. The smart device is written with C programming language which deploys on Raspberry Pi2. To ensure that the smart devices side gets the valid secret key, these keys are embedded in the smart devices, and the smart devices are signed by the key generated by the trusted certificate authority when the devices are initialized.

Our HIBE scheme uses asymmetric bilinear groups, and the bilinear map takes inputs from an isomorphic groups G. In our implementation, we use jPBC [24] and PBC [25] as our pairing-based cryptography library. We use ChaCha20 as the symmetric encryption algorithm. The reason for our choice is that ChaCha20 has better performance on mobiles and smart devices with ARM platform. We consider ChaCha20 as a secure symmetric encryption algorithm since ChaCha20 is designed to meet the standard notions of privacy and authenticity and ChaCha20 can provide a 256-bit security level [26]. We have performed our experiments on a cluster server with two 6-core Intel(R) Xeon(R) CPU 1.90 GHz processors, 16 GB of RAM, and 6 TB 7200 RPM hard disks, which are connected by gigabit switched Ethernet. On the smart phone side, we performed our experiments on a smart phone equipped with a Samsung Exynos4412 CPU 1.5 GHz processor, 1 GB of RAM and 8 GB flash disk. On the smart device side, we have performed our experiments on Raspberry Pi2 equipped with a ARM Cortex-A7 based BCM2836 CPU 900 MHz processor, and 1 GB of RAM.

5.2   Results on Effectiveness

Encryption and decryption are the most frequently used operations in the system. Since we have smart phone side and smart device side that need to encrypt and decrypt their data, we first measure the time taken at the smart phone for performing encryption and decryption. The time for smart phone decryption is measured from the time the smart phone receives the encrypted data from the private cloud, to the time the smart phone starts to display the data to the home member.

Figure 3(a) shows the time that the smart phone has spent in executing the encryption and decryption algorithm on different sizes of data. In this case, increasing the size of the plaintext also increases the decryption time; increasing the number of ancestor nodes has the same influence on the encryption and decryption time. However it is important to note that the number of ancestors is usually much smaller than the increasing of the plaintext data.

Figure 3(b) shows the time that the smart phone has spent on different depth of the hierarchy. In this experiment, we have created a hierarchy with depth of 7. From the result we can get the depth has a minor influence on each node's encryption and decryption performance.

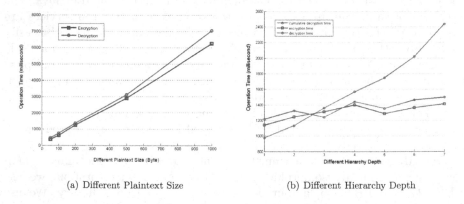

(a) Different Plaintext Size   (b) Different Hierarchy Depth

Fig. 3. Smart phone operation time

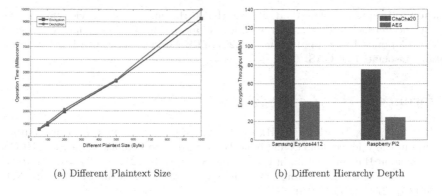

(a) Different Plaintext Size   (b) Different Hierarchy Depth

Fig. 4. Smart device operation time

Next we look at the smart device side operation time. Figure 4(a) shows the time for encrypting and decrypting files of different sizes on the smart device side. In this experiment, we have created a hierarchy with depth of 5. In our measurements, the encryption time is measured from the time when a sensor starts to collect the data to the time the smart device starts sending the encrypted data to the cloud. The decryption time is measured from the time the cloud starts sending encrypted data to the time the smart device starts executing the command. From the result, we can believe that SecHome has the potential to be used in many commercial situation.

Since we use ChaCha20 as our symmetric encryption algorithm, the encryption and decryption can happen while the data is being transferred between smart phones, smart devices and cloud. Figure 4(b) shows the comparison of ChaCha20 and AES which demonstrates that ChaCha20 is more suitable for smart phones and devices.

6   Conclusion

In this paper, we present SecHome, a system to provide a secure hierarchical identity encryption for smart home to protect users' security and privacy. Our system protects users' data privacy and security from a cryptography perspective, and we show that our system enables each node to monitor her descendant node data in a secure way successfully. We also give a security analysis of our system. As far as we know, this is the first solution that has privacy considerations for smart home's hierarchy properties. Our main result works for smart home encryption, and we extend it for authentication and initialization protection as well. We also implement a prototype of our system and show that the overhead of our system is insignificant. Evaluations of the security and complexity show that the nodes can be protected and monitored, unless the computing resource of the nodes is extremely low.

Acknowledgement. We would like to thank the anonymous reviewers for their insight and detailed feedback. Our work was supported by The National Key Research and Development Program of China NO.2017YFB0801900 and Youth Innovation Promotion Association of CAS.

References

1. Brush, A., Lee, B., Mahajan, R., Agarwal, S., Saroiu, S., Dixon, C.: Home automation in the wild: challenges and opportunities. In: Proceedings of the SIGCHI Conference on Human Factors in Computing Systems, pp. 2115–2124. ACM (2011)
2. Atzori, L., Iera, A., Morabito, G.: The internet of things: a survey. Comput. Netw. **54**(15), 2787–2805 (2010)
3. Gubbi, J., Buyya, R., Marusic, S., Palaniswami, M.: Internet of things (IoT): a vision, architectural elements, and future directions. Future Gener. Comput. Syst. **29**(7), 1645–1660 (2013)
4. Weber, R.H.: Internet of things-new security and privacy challenges. Comput. Law Secur. Rev. **26**(1), 23–30 (2010)
5. Shamir, A.: Identity-based cryptosystems and signature schemes. In: Blakley, G.R., Chaum, D. (eds.) CRYPTO 1984. LNCS, vol. 196, pp. 47–53. Springer, Heidelberg (1985). https://doi.org/10.1007/3-540-39568-7_5
6. Boneh, D., Franklin, M.: Identity-based encryption from the weil pairing. In: Kilian, J. (ed.) CRYPTO 2001. LNCS, vol. 2139, pp. 213–229. Springer, Heidelberg (2001). https://doi.org/10.1007/3-540-44647-8_13
7. Boneh, D., Boyen, X.: Efficient selective-ID secure identity-based encryption without random oracles. In: Cachin, C., Camenisch, J.L. (eds.) EUROCRYPT 2004. LNCS, vol. 3027, pp. 223–238. Springer, Heidelberg (2004). https://doi.org/10.1007/978-3-540-24676-3_14
8. Waters, B.: Efficient identity-based encryption without random oracles. In: Cramer, R. (ed.) EUROCRYPT 2005. LNCS, vol. 3494, pp. 114–127. Springer, Heidelberg (2005). https://doi.org/10.1007/11426639_7
9. Waters, B.: Dual system encryption: realizing fully secure IBE and HIBE under simple assumptions. In: Halevi, S. (ed.) CRYPTO 2009. LNCS, vol. 5677, pp. 619–636. Springer, Heidelberg (2009). https://doi.org/10.1007/978-3-642-03356-8_36
10. Liang, K., Liu, J.K., Wong, D.S., Susilo, W.: An efficient cloud-based revocable identity-based proxy re-encryption scheme for public clouds data sharing. In: Kutyłowski, M., Vaidya, J. (eds.) ESORICS 2014. LNCS, vol. 8712, pp. 257–272. Springer, Cham (2014). https://doi.org/10.1007/978-3-319-11203-9_15
11. Zhou, L., Varadharajan, V., Hitchens, M.: Achieving secure role-based access control on encrypted data in cloud storage. IEEE Trans. Inf. Forensics Secur. **8**(12), 1947–1960 (2013)
12. Goyal, V., Pandey, O., Sahai, A., Waters, B.: Attribute-based encryption for fine-grained access control of encrypted data. In: Proceedings of the 13th ACM Conference on Computer and Communications Security. ACM, pp. 89–98 (2006)
13. Bethencourt, J., Sahai, A., Waters, B.: Ciphertext-policy attribute-based encryption. In: IEEE Symposium on Security and Privacy, SP 2007, pp. 321–334. IEEE (2007)
14. Li, M., Yu, S., Zheng, Y., Ren, K., Lou, W.: Scalable and secure sharing of personal health records in cloud computing using attribute-based encryption. IEEE Trans. Parallel Distrib. Syst. **24**(1), 131–143 (2013)

15. Wan, Z., Liu, J.E., Deng, R.H.: Hasbe: a hierarchical attribute-based solution for flexible and scalable access control in cloud computing. IEEE Trans. Inf. Forensics Secur. **7**(2), 743–754 (2012)
16. Jung, T., Li, X.-Y., Wan, Z., Wan, M.: Control cloud data access privilege and anonymity with fully anonymous attribute-based encryption. IEEE Trans. Inf. Forensics Secur. **10**(1), 190–199 (2015)
17. Horwitz, J., Lynn, B.: Toward hierarchical identity-based encryption. In: Knudsen, L.R. (ed.) EUROCRYPT 2002. LNCS, vol. 2332, pp. 466–481. Springer, Heidelberg (2002). https://doi.org/10.1007/3-540-46035-7_31
18. Shao, J., Cao, Z.: Multi-use unidirectional identity-based proxy re-encryption from hierarchical identity-based encryption. Inf. Sci. **206**, 83–95 (2012)
19. Blazy, O., Kiltz, E., Pan, J.: (Hierarchical) identity-based encryption from affine message authentication. In: Garay, J.A., Gennaro, R. (eds.) CRYPTO 2014. LNCS, vol. 8616, pp. 408–425. Springer, Heidelberg (2014). https://doi.org/10.1007/978-3-662-44371-2_23
20. Boneh, D., Boyen, X., Goh, E.-J.: Hierarchical identity based encryption with constant size ciphertext. In: Cramer, R. (ed.) EUROCRYPT 2005. LNCS, vol. 3494, pp. 440–456. Springer, Heidelberg (2005). https://doi.org/10.1007/11426639_26
21. Koeberl, P., Schulz, S., Sadeghi, A.-R., Varadharajan, V.: Trustlite: a security architecture for tiny embedded devices. In: Proceedings of the Ninth European Conference on Computer Systems, Article no. 10, p. 1. ACM (2014)
22. Costin, A., Zaddach, J., Francillon, A., Balzarotti, D., Antipolis, S.: A large-scale analysis of the security of embedded firmwares. In: USENIX Security Symposium (2014)
23. Cui, A., Stolfo, S. J.: A quantitative analysis of the insecurity of embedded network devices: results of a wide-area scan. In: Proceedings of the 26th Annual Computer Security Applications Conference, pp. 97–106. ACM (2010)
24. Caro, A.D., Iovino, V.: Java pairing based cryptography library (2011). http://libeccio.dia.unisa.it/projects/jpbc
25. Lynn, B.: Pairing-based cryptography library (2007). http://crypto.stanford.edu/pbc
26. Nir, Y., Langley, A.: ChaCha20 and Poly1305 for IETF Protocols (2015). https://tools.ietf.org/html/rfc7539

Multi-attribute Counterfeiting Tag Identification Protocol in Large-Scale RFID System

Dali Zhu[1,2], Wenjing Rong[1,2(✉)], Di Wu[1], and Na Pang[1,2]

[1] Institute of Information Engineering, Chinese Academy of Sciences,
Beijing, China
{zhudali, rongwenjing, wudi, pangna}@iie.ac.cn
[2] School of Cyber Security, University of Chinese Academy of Sciences,
Beijing, China

Abstract. Counterfeiting products identification is the main application of RFID technology. Among all the RFID security problems, counterfeiting tag identification is an urgent issue with rapid growth of counterfeiters. In this paper, a multi-attribute counterfeiting tag identification protocol based on multi-dimension dynamic bloom filter in large-scale RFID system is proposed. Dynamic bloom filters for tag's attributes: identity information ID and location information angle value, are first brought as criterion of counterfeiting tag identification. Different from previous probabilistic approaches, our protocol not only identifies unknown tags, but also first solves problem that counterfeiters hold the same ID with genuine ones. Furthermore, our protocol can detect and verify counterfeiting tags' identity. Performance analysis shows that especially with huge amount of tags, our protocol can achieve higher identification efficiency with reasonable time cost.

Keywords: Multi-attribute · Location · Identification
Bloom filter · Security · RFID

1 Introduction

Radio frequency identification (RFID) is a ubiquitous technology applied in numerous automated identification systems such as supply chain, manufacturing management, pharmaceuticals and many other everyday life applications. So security of large-scale RFID system becomes quite important. Among all the security problems, counterfeiting tag identification is an urgent issue since the quantity of counterfeiting products grows dramatically in recent years [1]. For example, counterfeiting products can forge a tag to sneak into genuine products which results in great economic loss. According to survey in [2], economic loss leads by counterfeiting products is more than $600 billion and is growing with yearly progressive increase. So accurate and fast counterfeiting tag identification is very important to many applications.

In this paper, a multi-attribute counterfeiting tag identification protocol based on framed slotted ALOHA algorithm in large-scale RFID system is proposed. Different from other framed slotted ALOHA based schemes, multi-dimension dynamic bloom

© Springer International Publishing AG, part of Springer Nature 2018
S. Qing et al. (Eds.): ICICS 2017, LNCS 10631, pp. 352–362, 2018.
https://doi.org/10.1007/978-3-319-89500-0_31

filter is applied in our protocol, which indicates that tag has more than one attribute. When talked about tag's attribute, the only one comes to mind is tag's identity ID. In fact, reader can measure angle between tag and itself after scanning. So, our protocol first utilizes two attributes: tag identity ID and angle value. In previous works [1, 17, 18], counterfeiting tag is defined as one which is not in back-end server's database. However, there exists a condition that a tag which holds the same ID with a genuine one is attached to a counterfeiting item. In this condition, tag's angle value is a good criterion to point out counterfeiting tags. Our protocol is the first one to solve problem that counterfeiting tag forges the same ID with a genuine one. That is to say, our protocol can not only point out unknown tags, but also counterfeiting goods with genuine tag IDs. Also our protocol is suit for tag identification in large-scale RFID system. Even if quantity of RFID tags grows rapidly, identification efficiency can still be kept around an acceptable range. Compared with recently proposed methods, it can achieve higher identification efficiency, especially with huge amount of tags. And the time cost of our protocol is controlled in a reasonable range.

2 Related Works

The main usage of RFID tags in practice is identifying counterfeiting goods. In previous works like [1], counterfeiting tag is defined as one which is not in back-end server's database. Other studies [2, 3] call tags under this condition unknown tags. In previous studies, counterfeiting tag detection or they call it unknown tag detection, is classified into two categories: deterministic authentication and probabilistic estimation.

Deterministic authentication is mainly proposed in early works [5–8]. Weis et al. [5] propose a hash lock authentication scheme to protect tags from tracked. As its searching complexity is $O(N)$, where N is number of tags, it suffers from poor efficiency in large-scale RFID system. In order to reduce search complexity, Lu et al. [6] introduce a tree-based method with complexity of $O(log(N))$. Then they propose a new scheme which can achieve complexity of $O(1)$ in [7]. Recently, Chen et al. [8] introduce a token-based protocol whose overhead in both tag and reader is $O(1)$. However, schemes [6–8] are both tree-based protocols whose number of keys increases logarithmically with growth of tags.

In recent years, probabilistic estimation schemes [9–12] are gradually proposed. However, these methods are focus on estimating cardinality of tags. They cannot announce identities of counterfeiting tags. Also, there are several identity detection schemes [13–16]. But they are aimed to find missing tags. Yang et al. [17] first offer a framed slotted ALOHA based solution to detect counterfeiting tags or they call them unknown tags. Bianchi et al. [18] further improve this by introducing a standard bloom filter structure. Then Liu et al. [4] propose sampling filtering techniques based on bloom filter. However all these bloom filter based methods which leads to more collisions, haven't well utilized space of frame. Further, Gong et al. [1] provide a counterfeiting tag estimation scheme. But it cannot figure out counterfeiting tag. Later, schemes [3, 19] offer an indicator vector for tags which results in more overhead in tags. In contrast, our protocol not only points out unknown tags, but also counterfeiting goods with genuine tags. What's more, it can achieve a high detection efficiency with reasonable time cost.

3 Preliminary

3.1 System Model and Assumption

A typical RFID system consists of three entities: tags, readers and a back-end server. Reader is connected to back-end server through wired or wireless link with high computational ability. RFID tags are divided into three types: active, semi-active and passive tags. Our protocol mainly talks about passive tags. A reader interrogates and receives responses from a tag via transmitting a radio-frequency (RF) signal. Each tag is associated with identity information ID and location information angle value.

In our large-scale system model, reader is in the center and periodically scans tags. All tags are within reader's interrogation range. Tags include genuine ones and counterfeits. If identity and angle value of a tag are both stored in back-end server, this tag is a genuine one. The existence of counterfeiting tags includes two conditions. The first one is neither tag's identity or angle value is stored in back-end server, while the second one is a tag which holds the same ID with a genuine one is attached to a counterfeiting item. The first condition is usually proposed in previous works [1, 3, 17, 18]. However, problem in the second condition is first proposed and solved in this paper.

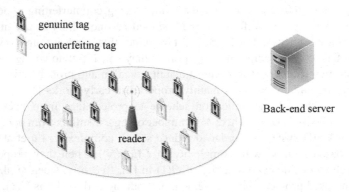

Fig. 1. System model

The whole process is divided in two interrogations by reader. When tag settles down in reader's interrogation range, it assumes that tags are all genuine ones and tags will be not transferred to another place before the second interrogation. Then reader scans tags and measures angle value between tag and itself by RSSI information which we will not describe in this paper. Afterwards, reader writes the corresponding angle value on each tag. So tag's attributes stores in tag are identity ID and angle value. As tag does not change places before the second interrogation, actual angle value between reader and tag will be identical with the angle value stored in tag. During period between the two interrogations, counterfeits can move into interrogation range. Counterfeit can forge the same ID with genuine one, however, it cannot forge actual angle value since counterfeit does not know accurate location of the one it forges in a large-scale RFID system. In the second interrogation, reader will authenticate tag's identity and angle value to find out counterfeits. The scenario is illustrated in Fig. 1.

3.2   Framed Slotted ALOHA Algorithm

Our protocol is based upon framed slotted ALOHA algorithm which is widely used in EPC Global C1G2 standard as its MAC-layer communication protocol. In framed slotted ALOHA algorithm, reader first broadcasts frame size f and random seed r. Each tag within interrogation range of the reader evaluates a hash function $h(f, r, ID)$ $mod\,f$ to select a slot in frame. Slot is classified into three categories. Empty slot means that there is no reply in this slot, while singleton slot denotes that only one reply is in this slot, and collision slot indicates that there are two or more replies in this slot.

3.3   Problem Formulation

Assume that there is one reader and N tags and all the tags are within the range of reader. Some counterfeiting tags may be moved in due to some reasons. So among N tags, there are n counterfeits after the first interrogation. Each genuine tag holds tag's attributes which includes tag's identity information ID and tag's location information angle value written by reader. For counterfeiting tags, it can forge genuine tag's identity by following some regulations like EPC standard, and location information by randomly guess. However it's hard for counterfeits to map identity information to location information since they are in a large-scale RFID system.

4   Multi-attribute Counterfeiting Tag Identification Protocol

4.1   Multi-dimension Dynamic Bloom Filter

In a standard bloom filter, each element in a given set $S = \{x_1, x_2, \ldots, x_N\}$ is mapped to filter using k hashing functions $h_1, h_2, \ldots, h_k$. When checking whether an element x belongs to S, it needs to find whether the bits $h_1(x), h_2(x), \ldots, h_k(x)$ of bloom filter are set to 1. For multi-dimension dynamic bloom filter [20], set S becomes a dynamic set with a dynamic $s \times N$ bit matrix where s represents s attributes of element. As N is a dynamic number and length of standard bloom filter f is a static one, multi-dimension dynamic bloom filter (MDBF) will add numbers of standard bloom filter with the variation of N. Suppose that N is mapped to L standard bloom filters. To check whether an element x belongs to S in multi-dimension dynamic bloom filter, it need to map $s \times L \times k$ bits are set to 1 in corresponding bloom filter.

4.2   Protocol Design

In our protocol, each tag has two attributes {ID, angle}: identity information ID and location information angle value. The angle value is written by the reader after the first interrogation. Also, tag will not change place before the next interrogation, which means that angle value written in tag is identical with tag's real-time location information. All tag's information is stored in back-end sever which can be access by reader. For tag T_i's attribute identity information ID_i, there are k uniform hashing functions to map it to k locations $\{ld_{i1}, ld_{i2}, \ldots, ld_{iu}, \ldots, ld_{ik}\}$ in bloom filter for ID, where $ld_{iu} = H_u(ID_i, r, f)\ mod\ f$, $u \in [1, k]$, and r is a random seed. Similarity, tag T_i's attribute location information $angle_i$ can be mapped to k locations $\{la_{i1}, la_{i2}, ..., la_{iu}, ..., la_{ik}\}$ in bloom filter for angle, where $la_{iu} = H_u(ID_i, r, f) \bmod f$, $u \in [1, k]$, and r is a random seed. Since there are L standard filters in multi-dimension dynamic bloom filter, tags need to choose one to join in. So different from the previous multi-dimension dynamic bloom filter [20], our protocol introduces participation probability p ($p \leq 1$) for tags to determine which bloom filter to take part.

Our protocol consists of two parts: counterfeiting tag detection and counterfeiting tag verification. In detection part, multi-dimension dynamic bloom filter is used to find counterfeiting tag whose ID or angle value is not identical with the one stored in back-end server. This includes two conditions. The first one is neither tag's identity or angle value is stored in back-end server, while the second one is a tag which holds the same ID with a genuine one is attached to a counterfeiting item. According to these conditions, counterfeiting tag verification will announce their identity and verify their angle value.

Algorithm 1 protocol for reader
1:    collect tag angle information and write angle information on tags
2:    get two attributes ID and angle for MATI
3:    **for** $i = 0$ to 1 **do**
4:    MATI $\leftarrow$ CreateDBF(i)
5   **end for**
6:    **CreateDBF()**
7:    **if** $N \leq f_t$ **then**
8:        **return** standard bloom filter
9:    **else**
10:       $m = ceil(N/f)$
11:          **for** $j = 1$ to m **do**
12:             DBF$\leftarrow$ standard bloom filter
13:          **end for**
14:    **end else**

Counterfeiting Tag Detection. Reader collects tag's identity information ID and location information in the first interrogation. Then it writes corresponding angle value on tag. According to tag's attributes array $A[] = [ID, angle]$, the attribute number s of multi-attribute counterfeiting tag identification (short for MATI) is set to 2. For each attribute, Algorithm 1 generates dynamic bloom filter for N tags. The length of a standard bloom filter is f, and f_t is threshold of tags that standard bloom filter can contain subjected to constraints (f, k). So, if $N \leq f_t$, it just needs one standard bloom filter, otherwise Algorithm 1 should create m standard bloom filters where $m = |N/f_t| + 1$. Then reader calculates participation probability p for each tag and broadcasts frame size f, random seed r, participation probability p. When tag receives above information, it first chooses to response in one of m frames based on probability p. Then it initializes its own attribute array $A[] = [ID, angle]$ and computes $S[i][j] = H_j(f, r_i, A[i]) \bmod f$, where $0 \leq i \leq 1, 1 \leq j \leq k$. In Algorithm 2, $S[0][j]$ represents k slots in bloom filter for identity ID, while $S[1][j]$ is mapped to k slots in bloom filter for angle value.

After Algorithms 1 and 2, reader receives responses from all tags in its interrogation range. Obviously, if either k slots for identity or k slots for angle value is not in database of back-end server, it must be a counterfeit. Reader notes the counterfeiting tags in this condition. There exists a condition that two tags hold the same k slots in bloom filter for identity, it means that a counterfeiting tag may be there. Since bloom filter has false positive probability, it cannot conclude that two tags with same k slots for identity hold the same identity. It needs to be confirmed in counterfeiting tag verification.

Algorithm 2 protocol for tag
1:    receive frame start command
2:    receive frame size f, random seed r, participation probability p.
3:    choose to participate in one of m frames or sleep based on the probability p
4:    if not participate, sleep until another frame starts.
5:    initialize attribute array $A[]=[ID, angle]$
6:    **for** $i = 0$ to 1 **do**
7:      **for** $j = 1$ to k **do**
8:        $S[i][j]= H_j(f, r_i, A[i])\ mod\ f$
9:      **end for**
10:   **end for**
11:   response slot numbers $S[i][j]$ $(0 \le i \le 1, 1 \le j \le k)$

Counterfeiting Tag Verification. This phase mainly verifies tags in the second condition of counterfeiting tag detection. Reader first seeks database in back-end server to find identity matched to the k slots. If there are two identities mapped, reader looks up tags' k slots for angle value. On condition that two tags matches two genuine tags in database of back-end server, there exists no counterfeits. Otherwise, tag which is not matched should be a counterfeit.

If there is only one identity matched, reader will broadcast the identity and wait for tags' response. According to the response, reader measures two tags' angle value. Tag with whose measured angle value is not identical with the one in database of back-end server should be a counterfeit. To now, all counterfeiting tags have been confirmed.

5 Performance Analysis

5.1 Identification Efficiency

Our protocol is based on multi-dimension dynamic bloom filter, which can yield a false positive p_{MATI}. So identification efficiency in this protocol equals to $1-p_{MATI}$, which means our protocol can achieve a higher identification efficiency when the false positive probability is low. False positive is due to a case that all k bits in both bloom filter for identity and bloom filter for angle value are set to 1 by other element previously. False positive probability in our protocol will be analyzed as follows.

Different from previous multi-dimension dynamic bloom filter, our protocol introduces participation probability p in Algorithm 2. Each tag need to choose a frame from m standard bloom filters based on the probability p. Probability p_z represents that one slot in a bloom filter is still zero after N tags' responses.

$$p_z = \left(1 - p\frac{1}{f}\right)^{kN} \approx e^{-\frac{pkN}{f}} \tag{1}$$

Then a standard bloom filter's false positive probability p_s is:

$$p_s = (1 - p_z)^k \approx \left(1 - e^{-\frac{pkN}{f}}\right)^k \tag{2}$$

For our protocol, $m = |N/f_t| + 1$ is a dynamic number. In a single standard bloom filter, there are only f_t tags. So standard bloom filter's false positive probability p_s in dynamic bloom filter should be $\left(1 - e^{-\frac{pkf_t}{f}}\right)^k$. As probability that there is no false positive in all m bloom filters is $(1 - p_s)^m$, false positive probability p_{DBF} of dynamic bloom filter can be denoted as:

$$p_{DBF} = 1 - (1 - p_s)^m \approx 1 - \left(1 - \left(1 - e^{-\frac{pkf_t}{f}}\right)^k\right)^m \tag{3}$$

Since tag's information includes identity ID and angle value, attribute number of MATI s is set to 2. Probability p_{DBF-ID} and $p_{DBF-angle}$ represents false positive in dynamic bloom filter for identity and angle value respectively. If a false positive event happens in our protocol, it should satisfy that all k slots in both dynamic bloom filter for identity and dynamic bloom filter for angle value are set to 1. So false positive probability p_{MATI} is denoted as:

$$p_{MATI} = p_{DBF\_ID}p_{DBF\_angle} \approx \left(1 - \left(1 - \left(1 - e^{-\frac{pkf_t}{f}}\right)^k\right)^m\right)^2 \tag{4}$$

As our protocol is based on framed slotted ALOHA algorithm, longer frame size can decrease collisions. Figure 2(a) shows that our protocol acquires better identification efficiency with increase of frame size in large-scale RFID system. In order to minimize false positive probability, ratio of f and N should be optimized. According to previous work [21], it can be concluded that false positive probability p_s is minimized when ratio of f and N satisfies Eq. (5). From Fig. 2(b), the result is clearly depicted.

$$k = \frac{f_t}{pN} \ln 2 \tag{5}$$

As p_{DBF_ID} and p_{DBF_angle} are false positive probability in dynamic bloom filter for identity and angle value respectively, it's obviously that they are all below 1. So it can be concluded that either p_{DBF_ID} or p_{DBF_angle} is greater than p_{MATI}, which indicates that multi-attribute counterfeiting tag identification can achieve better identification efficiency than dynamic bloom filter.

$$p_{MATI} < p_{DBF\_ID} \text{ or } p_{DBF\_angle} \tag{6}$$

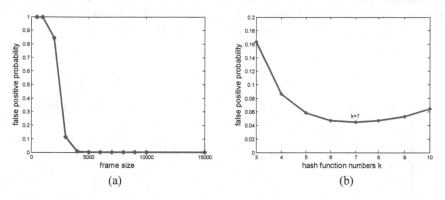

(a)   (b)

Fig. 2. (a) When $N = 15000$, $k = 7$, $f_t = 300$, $p = 1$, the false probability of MATI; (b) When $N = 15000$, $f = 5000$, $f_t = 495$, $p = 1$, the false probability of MATI.

Compared with standard bloom filter, multi-attribute counterfeiting tag identification has efficiency superiority. Standard bloom filter has space constraints with the growth of tag number, while multi-attribute counterfeiting tag identification defines a threshold for a single standard bloom filter which can reduce collisions and enhance space utilization. Figure 3 with settings that hash function number k is 7, participation probability p is 1 and frame size f is 5000, shows that multi-attribute counterfeiting tag identification has apparent identification efficiency advantage over standard and

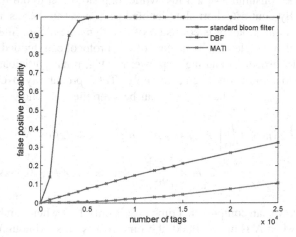

Fig. 3. When $f = 5000$, $f_t = 495$, $k = 7$, $p = 1$, the false probability of standard bloom filter, dynamic bloom filter and MATI respectively.

dynamic bloom filter with the increment of tag numbers. Then false positive probability of SEBA+ [18], WP [3] and our protocol is examined in Fig. 4. We fix number of tags $N = 1000$, participation probability $p = 1$, hash function number $k = 7$. As shown in Fig. 4, when frame size is greater than 2000, our protocol's false positive probability is approached to zero, which means identification efficiency is almost up to 1. In contrast, false positive probability of SEBA and WP is still greater than 0.4, which has huge difference with our protocol. In conclusion, compared with other methods, our protocol achieves better identification efficiency in large-scale RFID system.

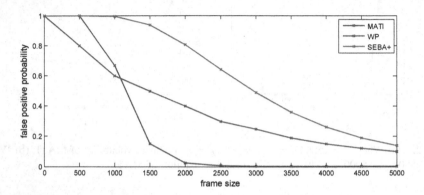

Fig. 4. When $N = 1000$, $f_t = 300$, $k = 7$, $p = 1$, the false probability of WP, SEBA+ and MATI respectively.

5.2 Time Cost

According to Philips I-Code [22], time slots are classified into tag slots, long slots and short slots. Based on length of slot, tag slot which is denoted as t_{id} can transmit a 96-bit message with time consuming of 2.4 ms; while long slot is set to 0.8 ms and affords a 10-bit response. By contrast, short slot, denoted as t_s, is set to 0.4 ms and allows only 1-bit response. As our protocol is consisted of two dynamic bloom filters, time cost is two times larger than single one. Time cost of our protocol can divided into two parts: time cost of reader broadcast and tag response. For tag, it has participation probability $p_i(1 \leq i \leq m)$ to choose one frame to reply. Total probability p of p_i should be $p = p_1 + p_2 + \ldots + p_m = 1$. Then Eq. (7) can be simplified as follow.

$$T = 2\left[m \times \left\lceil \frac{f}{96} \right\rceil \times t_{id} + (p_1 f + p_2 f + \ldots + p_m f) \times N \times t_s\right]$$
$$= 2\left[m \times \left\lceil \frac{f}{96} \right\rceil \times 2.4\,\text{ms} + f \times N \times 0.4\,\text{ms}\right] \tag{7}$$

From Eq. (7), we can compute that time cost is only 10 s when number of tags is up to 10000. Also, when N is up to 50000, the time cost is 40 s. Although our protocol's time cost is not very low, its false positive probability is far less than WP from Fig. 4.

Specially, with the increment of tags, our protocol has apparent advantage in identification efficiency. It's worth to consume more time to achieve better identification efficiency.

6 Conclusion

In this paper, a multi-attribute counterfeiting tag identification protocol based on framed slotted ALOHA algorithm in large-scale RFID system is proposed. Different from previous works, there are two attributes: identity ID and angle value in our protocol. Also, it's the first scheme using multi-dimension dynamic bloom filter to give a solution for RFID security problem that counterfeiting tag forges the same ID with a genuine one. Compared with previous works, our protocol not only points out unknown tags, but also counterfeiting goods with genuine tag ID. What's more, it can achieve a high identification efficiency with reasonable time cost. Future work is to apply our protocol on hardware and examine stability and functionality of our protocol in practice.

Acknowledgement. This work was supported by research of life cycle management and control system for equipment household registration, No. J770011104 and natural science foundation of China (61701494). We also thank the anonymous reviewers and shepherd for their valuable feedback.

References

1. Gong, W., Stojmenovic, I., Nayak, A., et al.: Fast and scalable counterfeits estimation for large-scale RFID systems. IEEE Trans. Netw. (TON) **24**(2), 1052–1064 (2016)
2. The spread of counterfeiting: Knock-offs catch on. The Economist, March 2010
3. Gong, W., Liu, J., Yang, Z.: Fast and reliable unknown tag detection in large-scale RFID systems. In: Proceedings of the 17th ACM International Symposium on Mobile Ad Hoc Networking and Computing, pp. 141–150. ACM (2016)
4. Liu, X., Qi, H., Li, K., et al.: Sampling bloom filter-based detection of unknown RFID tags. IEEE Trans. Commun. **63**(4), 1432–1442 (2015)
5. Weis, S.A., Sarma, S.E., Rivest, R.L., Engels, D.W.: Security and privacy aspects of low-cost radio frequency identification systems. In: Hutter, D., Müller, G., Stephan, W., Ullmann, M. (eds.) Security in Pervasive Computing. LNCS, vol. 2802, pp. 201–212. Springer, Heidelberg (2004). https://doi.org/10.1007/978-3-540-39881-3_18
6. Lu, L., Han, J., Xiao, R., Liu, Y.: ACTION: breaking the privacy barrier for RFID systems. In: INFOCOM 2009, pp. 1953–1961. IEEE (2009)
7. Lu, L., Liu, Y., Li, X.Y.: Refresh: weak privacy model for RFID systems. In: Proceedings of INFOCOM 2010, pp. 1–9. IEEE (2010)
8. Chen, M., Chen, S.: ETAP: enable lightweight anonymous RFID authentication with O(1) overhead. In: 2015 IEEE 23rd International Conference on Network Protocols (ICNP), pp. 267–278. IEEE (2015)
9. Shahzad, M., Liu, A.X.: Fast and accurate estimation of RFID tags. IEEE/ACM Trans. Networking **23**(1), 241–254 (2015)

10. Liu, J., Xiao, B., Chen, S., Zhu, F.: Fast RFID grouping protocols. In: 2015 IEEE Conference on Computer Communications (INFOCOM), pp. 1948–1956. IEEE (2015)
11. Zheng, Y., Li, M.: ZOE: fast cardinality estimation for large-scale RFID systems. In: 2013 Proceedings IEEE, INFOCOM, pp. 908–916. IEEE (2013)
12. Gong, W., Liu, K., Miao, X., Liu, H.: Arbitrarily accurate approximation scheme for large-scale RFID cardinality estimation. In: 2014 Proceedings IEEE, INFOCOM, pp. 477–485. IEEE (2014)
13. Yu, J., Chen, L., Zhang, R., et al.: On missing tag detection in multiple-group multiple-region RFID systems. IEEE Trans. Mob. Comput. **16**(5), 1371–1381 (2017)
14. Liu, X., Li, K., Min, G., Shen, Y., Liu, A.X., Qu, W.: Completely pinpointing the missing RFID tags in a time-efficient way. IEEE Trans. Comput. **64**(1), 87–96 (2015)
15. Liu, X., Li, K., Min, G., Shen, Y., Liu, A.X., Qu, W.: A multiple hashing approach to complete identification of missing RFID tags. IEEE Trans. Commun. **62**(3), 1046–1057 (2014)
16. Shahzad, M., Liu, A.X.: Expecting the unexpected: fast and reliable detection of missing RFID tags in the wild. In: 2015 IEEE Conference on Computer Communications (INFOCOM), pp. 1939–1947. IEEE (2015)
17. Yang, L., Han, J., Qi, Y., Liu, Y.: Identification-free batch authentication for RFID tags. In: 2010 18th IEEE International Conference on Network Protocols (ICNP), pp. 154–163. IEEE (2010)
18. Bianchi, G.: Revisiting an RFID identification-free batch authentication approach. IEEE Commun. Lett. **15**(6), 632–634 (2011)
19. Liu, X., Xiao, B., Zhang, S., Bu, K.: Unknown tag identification in large RFID systems: An efficient and complete solution. IEEE Trans. Parallel Distrib. Syst. **26**(6), 1775–1788 (2015)
20. Guo, D., Wu, J., Chen, H., et al.: Theory and network applications of dynamic bloom filters. In: Proceedings of 25th IEEE International Conference on Computer Communications, pp. 1–12. IEEE (2006)
21. Bloom, B.: Space/time trade-offs in hash coding with allowable errors. Commun. ACM **13**(7), 422–426 (1970)
22. Philips Semiconductors. Your Supplier Guide to ICODE Smart Label Solutions (2008)

Hijacking Your Routers via Control-Hijacking URLs in Embedded Devices with Web Interfaces

Ming Yuan, Ye Li, and Zhoujun Li[✉]

Beihang University, Beijing, China
yuanmingbuaa@gmail.com, {li_ye,lizj}@buaa.edu.cn

Abstract. Embedded devices start to get into the lives of ordinary people, such as SOHO routers and IP camera. However, studies have shown that the safety consideration of these devices is not enough, which has led to a growing number of security researchers focusing on the exploit of embedded devices. A majority of embedded devices run a web service to facilitate user management, which provides a potential attack interface. But what needs to be pointed out is that unfortunately most vulnerabilities of web service need attackers to provide login credentials to access and exploit, which makes attacking much less practical. This paper presents an automated vulnerability detecting and exploiting model DAEWC (Detect and Exploit without Credentials). Firstly, the DAEWC uses the symbol execution method to find URLs that are not protected by authentication mechanism. Secondly, DAEWC aims at these URLs using fuzzing method, combined with a lightweight dynamic data flow tracking technology to analyze the web server, which can quickly and accurately find easy-to-exploit vulnerabilities. Last but not least, DAEWC implements an automatic vulnerability exploit model, which generates executable custom shellcode, for example, executing system ("/bin/sh") or read/write arbitrary memory. Using these vulnerabilities, we can attack embedded devices with web services even without the access to the web interface. For example, attackers can control a Wi-Fi router at the airport without login credentials by sending a specially constructed URL request. We applied the DAEWC to the firmware of two embedded device vendors, found 9 unreported 0-day vulnerabilities in four of them and generated highly usable exploit script.

Keywords: Firmware · Authentication-bypassing URLs · Symbolic execution Lightweight dynamic data tracker · Automatic exploit generation

1 Introduction

Along with the development of the Internet of Things, more and more embedded devices connect to the Internet. For the convenience of user management, these devices usually run a web service, so that users can remotely operate or set these devices. Users need to have a web authentication before the management operation, and only after the authentication (such as the username/password check or the cookies check) they can have access to other pages. If authentication fails, the server will return a 401 HTTP

© Springer International Publishing AG, part of Springer Nature 2018
S. Qing et al. (Eds.): ICICS 2017, LNCS 10631, pp. 363–373, 2018.
https://doi.org/10.1007/978-3-319-89500-0_32

code (unauthorized response), or a 302 HTTP code that redirect user to the login page. However, in practice, some device manufacturers do not complete the verification of all user URL requests, which leads to unauthorized access to some URLs. Once the function to handle this type of URL request in the web sever is vulnerable, attackers can control the firmware program flow by directly requesting these URLs and sending malicious payload even without the login credentials. We call this type of URLs control-hijacking URLs.

Web services on embedded devices might have vulnerabilities such as SQL injection, XSS, CSRF and so on, but these web application layer problems often fail to meet the requirements of fully controlling the devices. This article aims at the web server binaries, and focuses on the detection of web services memory corruption vulnerabilities (such as buffer overflow, command execution, format string vulnerability and so on). Once attacker control the web server program flow, they can operate with web server's privileges on the operation system level. The web server of embedded devices is usually run as root, so that attacker can control the device with the root privilege of the operation system. It is obvious that in embedded devices, compared to the vulnerabilities of the web application (i.e. CSRF or XSS), the binary's memory corruption or command execution vulnerability are more threatening. And this kind of vulnerability not only exists in theory, in fact, in 2017 the Axis camera is reported to have a vulnerability that affects millions of IoT devices and it can be exploited by sending a POST package to control the equipment.[1]

But finding control-hijacking URLs is not easy. Firstly, we can't get the firmware source code - this is a problem for all binary analysis method. Secondly, firmware is run on the device, and deploying device for each firmware will undoubtedly cost a lot. Andrei Costin [1] simulate the firmware's web interface, perform static and dynamic analysis on it. But this analysis is dependent on the existing static (RIPS) or dynamic (metesploit or exp from exploit database) analysis tools, and as the manufacturer's security consciousness improves, these vulnerabilities can be easily found by manufacturers themselves and fix, and thus the number of them has greatly reduced. Also some of the vulnerabilities they found require web login credentials (such as cookies) to be triggered, thus these vulnerability do not pose an effective threat to devices in the real world. In addition, they need to use a real Linux kernel to simulate the firmware, which is not efficient enough.

Static vulnerability detection method, such as Yan Shoshitaishvili's Firmliace, can detect logic flaw (such as back door) effectively, but for the memory corruption and command injection vulnerabilities static detection is not effective enough. However, to perform dynamic firmware testing, one needs to spend a lot on buying equipments or need to get firmware simulated. In fact, the present automated simulation technique works for only a part of the firmware and as we said before, the test result is often not ideal.

In light of these challenges, we purpose a novel firmware vulnerabilities detecting and exploiting tools - DAEWC. It can automatically extract the firmware and look for web server binary. In the firmware binary, through specific strategy it can locate the

---

[1] http://blog.senr.io/blog/devils-ivy-flaw-in-widely-used-third-party-code-impacts-millions.

credential authentication code in the program and use symbol execution technique to identify URLs accessible by unauthorized users, then use a lightweight dynamic data tracker system to detect potential memory corruption and arbitrary command execution vulnerabilities. In addition, this framework can also detect URLs that can open undesired backdoor services (such as Telnet, SSH), which also do not require credentials.

We tested the DAEWC model on four different routers and found at least one control-hijacking URLs on each of them. These routers have different web services, and their architecture includes ARM and MIPS. Experimental results show that DAEWC is effective and accurate to automatically detect vulnerabilities and generate exploit (exp).

To sum up, we made the following contributions:

- We purpose a novel model that can perform automated detection of Control-hijacking URLs in the embedded device firmware. It can be used to control embedded devices without the web login credentials, so the model can detect more exploitable vulnerabilities than existing firmware vulnerability detection techniques. We can exploit the memory crash and arbitrary code execution vulnerabilities without knowing the details of the firmware implementation.

We implemented a tool DAEWC for automatic vulnerability detection based on the model, which uses the original firmware as input, outputs control-hijacking URLs, and the PoC (Proof of Concept) corresponding to each problematic URL. DAEWC can detect vulnerabilities in multiple architecture firmware and is not related to device hardware platforms.

- We used DAEWC to detect four different real-world firmware samples and successfully found nine 0-day vulnerabilities. They have been submitted to CVEs.
- According to vulnerability detection report, we generated usable exploit successfully.

2 Approach Overview

DAEWC determines control-hijacking URLs in the firmware by following a few steps. First of all firmware is preprocessed. Then it find all URLs that don't need user authentication by using the static method. After that the dynamic test method is used to identify the vulnerabilities that web server may have in handling these URLs and the payload to trigger these vulnerabilities. Using the payload, a exploit program is automatically generated. At last we manually validate the results (Fig. 1).

Pretreatment. Before vulnerability analysis, we need to do some initial work, including selecting firmware to meet the requirements (we will discuss the requirements in Sect. 3), firmware decompression, determination of its root directory, finding the web service application (httpd, lighthttpd, boa, etc.) and its related files, and recording the firmware architecture.

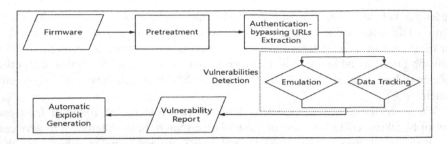

Fig. 1. Module Graph of DAEWC

Authentication-bypassing URLs Extraction. The pre-processed firmware is passed to the authentication-bypassing URLs extraction module. We design the URLs authentication security policies, and according to this policies the DAEWC determine the web authentication module in the firmware (we call this the URLs privilege check point). In these module, by using the method of symbolic execution and regular expression match, DAEWC find URLs in the web site that does not need web authentication. We will discuss the Authentication-bypassing URLs Extraction module in Sect. 4.

Vulnerability Detection. After extraction, DAEWC dynamically detect the URLs that are output from the previous module. Then we simulate exclusively the web server, hook the sensitive library functions in web server. According to the special URLs we construct tagged input. After the tagged input gets into our hook function, we can check the context, and perform a series of comparison operation, to determine whether there is buffer overflow or arbitrary command execution vulnerability. Finally, we export the vulnerability detection report, including the location of the bug in the assemble instructions, the payload to trigger crash, and the type of vulnerability. We will discuss the Vulnerability Detection module in Sect. 5.

Automatic Exploit Generation. In this process, we analyzed the report generated in the previous stage and established different exploit generation models for different types of vulnerability. Our ultimate goal is to run our own shellcode by hijacking control flow, to achieve arbitrary read/write, or even to bounce a shell directly to our computer. We will discuss the Automatic Exploit Generation module in Sect. 6.

Let's illustrate this method with a simplified example. For simplicity, we define the security policy for the URLs authentication as "cookies verification for the requested URL (the fixed strings 'COOKIES')". DAEWC first decompresses the firmware, extracts the web server binary, library files, and configuration files. The results are then passed to the authentication-bypassing URLs extraction module, it generates program control flow graph (CFG) and data dependency graph (DDG). Then it finds the function to verify the cookies, which has the "cookies" fixed string as the URL privilege check point of the program. Then using the angr [2] it generates to control flow diagram the data dependency graph (DPG), and makes a back slice from the URLs privilege check point, and finally uses the constraint solver to find all the URLs that do not require authentication. In the code example below, it is "goform/ping".

```c
int RequestHander(char *url)
{
        if (strcmp(url,"goform/ping") == 0)
                return 1;
        else
        {
                char *request_cookies = han-
dle_header(url,'COOKIES')
                if (check_cookies(request_cookies))
                {
                        int code = 200;
                        pointless();
                        response(code,TEMPLATE);
                }
                else
                {
                        int code = 300;
                        pointless();
                        response(code,"This document has
moved to a new....");
                }
        }
}
int main()
{
        char *url = getrequest();
        char cmd[20];
        if (RequestHander(url))
        {
                snprintf(cmd,20,"ping
%s",getValue(url,"target"));
                system(cmd)
        }
}
```

These URLs are then passed into the vulnerability detection module. The DAEWC will simulate the web services of the firmware and then, using a lightweight data tracker, identify possible vulnerabilities. Specifically, we will get the parameters of the URLs of the previous output to construct special payload.

And then we hook and examine the context of sensitive system function. If the input we construct gets into the parameters of the sensitive function or overrides the key memory, you can assume there is a vulnerability here. In the above code example, when program is processing "goform/ping" request, we will find that the value of parameter "target" becomes a parameter of the sensitive function system, which is equivalent to triggering a command execution vulnerability. DAEWC will output a vulnerability report then. The automatic exp generation module, based on the report, determines that a command execution vulnerability exists, and then sets target's parameter values to a command we expect to execute, such as '/bin/sh' or 'cat/etc./passwd'. It is important to note that in order to ensure that the command is executed successfully, we add a semicolon before the command to ensure that the preceding instructions, such as the ping command in the program, are closed. Finally, the full exploit is generated according to the payload in the leak report, so as long as the exploit program is directly run, it can obtain a shell or steal the login credentials of the user.

3 Pretreatment

We download the latest firmware from the vendor's website. We select the firmware that was easy to decompress, with a file system, and with Unix-like operating system. We then use binwalk, firmware-mod-kit, or other tools to extract the firmware's instruction set type based on /bin/busybox or /bin/sh. Finally, the DAEWC finds the web server (boa, HTTPD, or lighthttpd) in the decompressed directory, along with the configuration file and the document root (WWW directory).

4 Authentication-bypassing URLs Extraction

There are many ways to handle URL requests in the firmware, such as binaries (HTTPD, boa), scripting languages (PHP, LUA). We will use two methods to find control-hijacking URLs. For binary files, DAEWC use symbolic execution methods. For scripting languages, we will make targeted regular expression matches.

4.1 Regular Expression Match

Our study of some script-type CGI has found that its user authentication mechanism follows certain rule. Web server based on Lua language is very common. In our tests, we found that most of the Lua script will use entry function to determine whether you need web authentication. For example if the last parameter is set as true, it means that the interface can be accessed without the user login authentication. For this authentication method, we use a custom regular expression match to find.

In addition, some dynamic request mechanism in javascript server often ignores the authority certification. For example, in some HTML files in the router firmware we can find URLs of the ajax synchronization mechanisms to be lack of cookies validation. This type of URLs can also be found effectively through regular expression matching.

4.2   Symbolic Execution Methods

Security Policies. For binary programs, unlike other vulnerability detection system like Firmalice [3], KLEE [4], AEG [5], and Mayhem [6], DAEWC is more complex. It first finds URLs that do not require web credentials verification and then exploits them. It is actually using the firmware's logical bug in the design process to find these URLs. After connecting to the Wi-Fi, hackers can reset the router web interface's user name and password without credential validation. That is because that the firmware does not have a credentials checking when processing the URL request to modify the username.

In the absence of development documentation, to infer automatically complete web server's request processing logic is very complicated, so we need to manually specify which operation is related to checking web access and providing specific access policy. This requires the analyst to have a good understanding of the firmware internal program, and to know which sensitive programs or memory are involved in authorization authentication. We developed the following strategies for the DAEWC.

- *Fixed strings.* The security policy can be specified as several fixed strings. An example of such a policy is that the web server directly extracts the value of the "COOKIES" field in the request for inspection. We can use the data dependency graph to identify where it is in the program.
- *Behavioral patterns.* Another policy for DAEWC is to determine the location based on what the authentication program might do. For example, a server may return a 302 redirect code or 400 code in the HTTP response headers when the authentication check returns false. We can determine the location of the credentials verification code according to this behavior pattern. In addition, web server may access specific memory (a data segment that holds a user's password) after authentication or validation, which can also be treated as a behavioral pattern.
- *Manually specified.* If we already see the identification checking function when manually reverse engineering, we can specify this code as our policy.

Symbol Execution. We'll perform some static analysis before symbol execution, because instead of analyzing the entire web server, we can just focus on the credentials verification section. The DAEWC generates control flow graph (CFG) by using the static analysis module of angr, and then generates control dependency graph (CDG) on this basis, combining with data dependency graph (DDG) to generate the program dependency graph (PDG). We can then start slicing back from the credentials verification point. When back slicing, irrelevant functions and instructions can be ignored, which greatly reduces the complexity of the analyzer.

Finally, we use the claripy constraint solver of angr to get all the URLs that do not need to pass the authorization process, and analyze the parameters passed when the request is sent to these URLs.

5   Vulnerability Detection

In the vulnerability detection phase, we aim to find opening undesired services (SSH, Telnet), memory corruption and arbitrary command execution vulnerabilities.

To detect undesired services open, we can directly match strings such as *ssh*, *telnet*, *ftp* in the URL generated in the previous module. Once these strings which suggest that a special service open exist, a warning will be reported for further verification. If the service is actually turned on, we can use tool like Hydra to brute force SSH/TELNET/FTP user name and password. Because embedded devices generally run these services as root, this means that a back door exists.

For memory corruption or arbitrary command execution vulnerability, we adopt a dynamic lightweight data tracker detection method.

First, we need to solve the problem of simulating the web server. Chen et al.'s [7] method is to simulating the whole firmware, Costin [1] focuses on getting the firmware web interface into the simulation environment to run. These two solutions both need Linux kernel, and with efficiency and success rate under satisfaction. We are using the User Mode of the qemu emulator directly (such as qemu-arm) to run the web server program. At the beginning, the web server program needs to be patched in the binary level. (1) The IP of the BSS section is changed to a fixed value of 0.0.0.0 in data section, so we can make local network testing. (2) We ignore the external library functions that some vendors customize that has no influence on web services; (3) The functions in libnvram, such as nvram_get, are hooked to make it return fixed number directly, and so on. After chrooting the decompressed the firmware, modifying the web configuration file, running init program (such as rcS), we finally start the web server.

Next we come up with a solution that can quickly find a web sever memory corruption vulnerability and command execution vulnerability. Through hooking sensitive library function, we can monitor the register value when the sensitive function is called and the memory of the address in the register. We summarized more than 40 library functions involving memory operations and command execution (strcpy, system and popen, etc.). We compile the hooking program to generate a dynamic library file, and use preloading to hook library function call. The hooking function will call the original library function after processing.

After hook, we will conduct a series of tests to determine if there are any vulnerabilities. First, we send special payload, such as "AAAAAA" strings, in a URL request, and then perform the following detection:

A. For the command execution vulnerability and the format string vulnerability, we check the parameter registers to determine whether the input data is part of the function's parameters. For example, our data goes to the first parameter register r0 of the printf function, which can tell that there is a format string vulnerability. When our data is the first parameter register r0 or the second parameter register r1 of execve, you can judge that there is a command execution vulnerability here.
B. We check some specific registers or memory data for memory corruption vulnerabilities. For example, in a stack overflow vulnerability, before overwriting the return address on the stack, payload will first overwrite the fp address, that is, the address pointed by the r11 register in ARM architecture. So each time after

hooking memory copy functions (memcpy/strcpy/sprintf), we read the parameter register to check if they contain any constructed payload. If so, the hooking function will call the original library function itself, and then check the r11 pointing memory. It should be pointed out that the stack frame base address is a linked list, so we can record the whole list in the first place, and read each address in the list to check if it is polluted.

We use our own fuzzing script to generate payload as the URL parameters output by the previous module, and record the payload to compare to the data in hook operation to export a vulnerability report. Our report is in json format, which contains the URLs and parameters of the vulnerability, the addresses in the binary, the types of vulnerabilities, and the payload needed to trigger the crash.

6 Automatic Exploit Generation

As early as 2011, Avgerinos [5] put forward a model that use symbolic execution to automate the generation of vulnerability utilization programs-AEG. However, this model has three problems to consider. Firstly, it takes a long time to determine the location of the vulnerability by using the simple symbol execution, and the effect is not ideal. Secondly its exploit generation model is basically aimed at overflow vulnerability, and there is no vulnerability modeling for the format string vulnerability and arbitrary command execution. Thirdly, AEG emphasize particularly on exploiting on x86 architecture. However, embedded devices are mostly based on reduced instruction set such as MIPS and ARM. Their function call convention, parameters passing convention and stack frame structure are very different from x86, so we can't simply transplanted AEG model.

DAEWC proposes a new automatic exploit generation model for embedded devices. We consider the ARM and MIPS instruction set to generate arbitrary read/write, rebound shell and a series of other shellcode. And the final purpose is to hijack the web sever program control flow to make it execute our shellcode.

In fact, automatic exploit generation requires a separate modeling of different vulnerability types. Based on vulnerability types and payload to trigger crash detected in previous module, we use the following different ways to generate exploit:

1. For arbitrary command execution vulnerability, the values of the URL parameters become directly a part of the command execution function's parameters, such as the 'system' function. We can replace the parameter value of any command: reboot, cat/etc/passwd and so on. In order to make these commands execute smoothly, we can add a semicolon to avoid interference of other strings in command execution function parameters.
2. For formatting string vulnerability, we first use libformatstr to determine the location of the formatted string parameters in the stack and the length of padding that needs to be fulfill the 32-bit alignment in the stack. Then use %s and %n parameters to achieve arbitrary address read and write. Because the string will have "\x00" truncation, we will put the read-write address at the end of the constructed malicious formatting string.

For overflow vulnerabilities, the following steps need to be taken. Firstly we need to locate the overflow point, which can be obtained according to the report of the vulnerability detection module. Secondly we need to locate the return address. In order to achieve this, we firstly use the qemu to simulate the web sever simulation, and then using ptrace[2] to monitor the running program. After that we changed each byte of the crash trigger payload from the last byte, and resend the payload after every change. After ptrace capture the SIGSEGV signal, we will check PC and stack registers. If value in PC registers has changed, the changed byte's position minus three is the length of needed padding to rewrite the return address in the stack. With padding we can control the PC by adding target address. Since embedded devices rarely open security mechanism like NX, ASLR or Canary of x86 platform, it's easy to take advantage of it. The third step is to determine the layout of the stack. In the second step we already have the padding required to cover the return address and the return address, so we're going to consider shellcode's layout. Because there is no NX and ASLR protection, we can simply put shellcode as part of the input into the stack, and then return to the address in the stack where shellcode located. In the previous step by ptrace, we not only get the position of the return address, but also obtained the stack frame pointer value, so we'll deploy shellcode behind the return address, and then overwrite the return address to be the stack frame pointer value.

7 Evaluation

The Tenda router is popular around the world, and the AC series router has sold hundreds of thousands of units based on conservative estimates. We tested the Tenda AC6 router with the DAEWC, and found that several critical vulnerabilities could be triggered without the need of web credential validation.

Preprocessing. The firmware obtained by preprocessing is based on 32-bit ARM architecture. Web service program is started by HTTPD, web directory is /webroot, and rcS program is found.

Authentication-bypassing URLs Extraction. HTTPD has obvious behavioral pattern when checking the web request credentials. A 302 code response will be returned when authentication failed. We use this as a security policy, and we use the symbol execution module of DAEWC to slice and analyze the HTTPD. We generate 312 slices, and then we get 17 URLs that do not require authorization.

Vulnerability Detection. We found a URL that can open telnet service the regular expression matching process in the previous step and found two command execution vulnerabilities and four overflow vulnerabilities. In the manual vulnerability verification process, we also surprisingly found a password reset vulnerability based on the report of the DAEWC.

---

[2] http://man7.org/linux/man-pages/man2/ptrace.2.html.

Authentication-bypassing URLs Extraction. DAEWC generated successfully the exploit of the command execution vulnerability and exploit of the stack overflow vulnerability. In view of vendor safety, we have not disclosed these exploit.

Besides AC6 router, we also use DAEWC to analyze other series of Tenda routers and PHICOMM router. We found 9 zero day vulnerabilities that has never been disclosed. we has submitted them to CVE (CVE-2017-9138, CVE-2017-9139, CVE-2017-11495) [8–10] classified by different vendor and vulnerability type.

Acknowledgment. This work is supported in part by National High Technology Research and Development Program of China (No. 2015AA016004), the National Key R&D Program of China (No. 2016QY04W0802).

References

1. Costin, A., Zarras, A., Francillon, A.: Automated dynamic firmware analysis at scale: a case study on embedded web interfaces. In: Proceedings of the 11th ACM on Asia Conference on Computer and Communications Security, pp. 437–448. ACM (2016)
2. http://angr.io/
3. Shoshitaishvili, Y., Wang, R., Hauser, C., Kruegel, C., Vigna, G.: Firmalice - automatic detection of authentication bypass vulnerabilities in binary firmware. In: Proceedings of the Symposium on Network and Distributed System Security (NDSS) (2015)
4. Cadar, C., Dunbar, D., Engler, D.R.: KLEE: unassisted and automatic generation of high-coverage tests for complex systems programs. In: Proceedings of OSDI, vol. 8, pp. 209–224 (2008)
5. Avgerinos, T., Cha, S.K., Hao, B.L.T., Brumley, D.: AEG: automatic exploit generation. In: Proceedings of the Network and Distributed System Security Symposium, February 2011
6. Cha, S.K., Avgerinos, T., Rebert, A., Brumley, D.: Unleashing mayhem on binary code. In: Proceedings of the IEEE Symposium on Security and Privacy, pp. 380–394. IEEE (2012)
7. Chen, D.D., Egele, M., Woo, M., Brumley, D.: Towards automated dynamic analysis for linux-based embedded firmware. In: ISOC Network and Distributed System Security Symposium (NDSS) (2016)
8. CVE-2017-9138. https://cve.mitre.org/cgi-bin/cvename.cgi?name=CVE-2017-9138
9. CVE-2017-9139. https://cve.mitre.org/cgi-bin/cvename.cgi?name=CVE-2017-9139
10. CVE-2017-11495. https://cve.mitre.org/cgi-bin/cvename.cgi?name=CVE-2017-11495

A Method to Effectively Detect Vulnerabilities on Path Planning of VIN

Jingjing Liu[1], Wenjia Niu[1(✉)], Jiqiang Liu[1(✉)], Jia Zhao[1], Tong Chen[1], Yinqi Yang[1], Yingxiao Xiang[1], and Lei Han[2]

[1] Beijing Key Laboratory of Security and Privacy in Intelligent Transportation, Beijing Jiaotong University, Beijing 100044, China
{niuwj,jqliu}@bjtu.edu.cn
[2] Science and Technology on Information Assurance Laboratory, Beijing 100072, China

Abstract. Reinforcement Learning has been used on path planning for a long time, which is thought to be very effective, especially the Value Iteration Networks (VIN) with strong generalization ability. In this paper, we analyze the path planning of VIN and propose a method that can effectively find vulnerable points in VIN. We build a 2D navigation task to test our method. The experiment for interfering VIN is conducted for the first time. The experimental results show that our method has good performance on finding vulnerabilities and could automatically adding obstacles to obstruct VIN path planning.

Keywords: Path planning · Reinforcement learning · VIN
Vulnerable points

1 Introduction

Path planning for robot mainly solves three problems. First, it must ensure that the robot can move from the initial point to the target point. Second, it should allow the robot to bypass the obstacles with a certain method. Third, it tries to optimize the robot running trajectory in the completion of the above tasks on the premise. In general, path planning approach has two different types, the global planning and the local path planning. The global planning method usually can find the optimal solution. The available planning algorithms for this class are framework space method [6], free space method [7] and grid method [8]. But it needs to know the accurate information of the environment in advance, and the calculation is very large. The accuracy of path planning depends on the accuracy of obtaining the environmental information. The local path planning requires only the robot's near obstacle information, so that the robot has good ability to avoid collision. The commonly used local path planning methods are template matching [9] and artificial potential fields [10]. The template matching method is very easy to achieve, but the fatal flaw of this method is to rely on the past experience of the robot, and if there is not enough path template

© Springer International Publishing AG, part of Springer Nature 2018
S. Qing et al. (Eds.): ICICS 2017, LNCS 10631, pp. 374–384, 2018.
https://doi.org/10.1007/978-3-319-89500-0_33

in the case library, it is impossible to find the path that matches the current state. The artificial potential fields method is much flexible to control. However, this method is easy to fall into local optimum, resulting in motion deadlock. Nowadays, researchers start to put their attention on Reinforcement Learning (RL), a typical machine learning approach acquiring knowledge in the action-evaluation environment, for better solutions.

Traditional RL methods are Policy Iteration (PI) [11], Value Iteration (VI) [12], Monte-Carlo Method (MC) [13], Temporal-Difference Method (TD) [14] and Q-learning [1]. However, most traditional methods perform relatively poor when encounter different scenes from the previous training set. In contrast, deep RL, which incorporates the advantages of neural networks, has better performance and accuracy. Deep RL has been considered one of the major human learning patterns all the time. It is widely used in robot automatic control, artificial intelligence (AI) for computer games and optimization of market strategy. Deep RL is especially good at controlling an individual who can act autonomously in an environment and constantly improve individual behavior through interaction with the environment. Well known deep RL works are Deep Q-Learning (DQN) [15] and Value Iteration Networks (VIN) [5].

Among them, VIN has better generalization ability [5]. There is a kind of special value iteration in VIN, not only need to use the neural network to learn a direct mapping from the state to the decision, but also can embed the traditional planning algorithm into neural network. Thus, the neural network learns how to make long-term planning in the current environment, and uses long-term planning to assist the neural network in making better decisions. That is, VIN learns to plan and make decisions by observing current environment. Assuming VIN has already learned a model to predict rewards of future states, the flaw is when such predictions carry on, the errors of observations accumulate and can not be avoided because VIN perform VI over the whole environment. We can use this flaw to study how to obstruct VIN's performance. Apparently, adding some obstacles, which are unnoticed for human but can be detected by robots, to form a fake environment sample will probably make VIN be tricked and do wrong predictions.

Our main contribution is a method for detecting potential attack that could obstruct VIN. We study the typical and most recent works about path planning [2–4] and build our own method. We build a 2D navigation task demonstrate VIN and study how to add obstacles to effectively affect VIN's performance and propose a general method suitable for different kinds of environment. Our empirical results show that our method has great performance on automatically finding vulnerable points of VIN and thus obstructing navigation task.

2   Related Work

2.1   Reinforcement Learning

Traditional Reinforcement Learning methods are Policy Iteration, Value Iteration, Monte-Carlo Method, Temporal-Difference Method and Q-learning.

Policy Iteration and Value Iteration. The purpose of Policy Iteration [11] is to iteratively converge the value function in order to maximize the convergence of the policy. It is essentially the direct use of the Bellman Equation. So Policy Iteration is generally divided into two steps: (1) Policy Evaluation; (2) Policy Improvement. Value Iteration [12] is obtained by Bellman Optimal Equation. Thus, Policy Iteration uses Bellman Equation to update value, finally the convergence of the value is currently under policy value (so called to evaluate policy), to get new policy. And Value Iteration uses the bellman optimal equation to update the value and finally converges to the resulting value. Therefore, as long as the final convergence is concerned, then the optimal policy is obtained. This method is based on updating value, so it's called Value Iteration.

Monte-Carlo Method. Monte Carlo's idea is simple, that is, repeating tests to find the average. The Monte Carlo method is only for problems with stage episode [13]. For example, playing a game is step by step and will end. The Monte Carlo Method cares only for problems that can end quickly. The Monte Carlo method is extremely simple. But the disadvantages are also obvious. It takes a lot of time to do as many tests as possible, and to calculate at the end of each test. AlphaGo [16] uses the idea of Monte Carlo Method in Reinforcement Learning. It only uses the final winning or losing results to optimize each step.

Time Difference can be regarded as a combination of Dynamic Programming and Monte Carlo Method. Time Difference [14] also can directly learn from experience, does not require any dynamic model in the environment, but also a kind of Reinforcement Learning, can learn step by step, and does not need to wait for the end of the entire event, so there is no problem of calculating the peak value.

Q-learning is an important milestone in Reinforcement Learning. Watkins [1] takes the Reinforcement Learning method, whose evaluation function is based on Q value of state-action, as Q-learning. It is actually a change form of the Markov Decision Process (MDP). In Reinforcement Learning, the reinforcement function R and the state transfer function P are unknown, so the Q-learning uses iterative algorithm to approximate the optimal solution. Q-learning does not go forward along the path of the highest Q value at each iteration. The reason why the Q-learning effects is the updating of the Q matrix.

2.2 Deep Reinforcement Learning

Well known deep Reinforcement Learning works are Deep Q-Learning and Value Iteration Networks.

Deep Q-learning is the first deep enhancement learning algorithm proposed by Google DeepMind in 2013 [15] and further improved in 2015 [4]. DeepMind applies DQN to computer games like Atari, which is different from the previous practice, using video information as input and playing games with humans. This is the first introduction of the concept of deep Reinforcement Learning, and it's beginning to develop rapidly. In DQN, since the output value of the value network is the Q value, if the target Q value can be constructed, the loss function can be obtained by the mean-square error (MSE). But for the value network, the input information is the state s, action a and feedback R. Therefore, how to calculate the target Q value is the key to the DQN, which is the problem that Reinforcement Learning can solve.

Value Iteration Networks. The biggest innovation of this work is that a Planing Module is added to the General Policy. The author believes that joining the motivation of this module is natural, because when solving a space problem, it is not simply solving the problem, but planning in this space. It aims at solving the problem of poor generalization ability in Reinforcement Learning. In order to solve this problem, a Learn to Plan module is proposed [5]. The innovations of VIN are mainly the following points: (1) the reward function and transfer function are also parameterized and can be derived; (2) a spatial assisted strategy is introduced to make policy more generalized; (3) the attention mechanism is introduced into the solution of the strategy; (4) the design of VI module is equivalent to CNN, and the BP algorithm can be used to update the network.

We find that each method has its own superiority. But, VIN is much better at planning in different sample from training set. Thus, we choose VIN as our experiment bases and we will show our analysis in Sect. 3.

3   Method

In this section, we will discuss how we build the method for obstructing VIN's performance. First, we analyze the path planning idea of VIN, and carry out tentative experiments to speculate the factors that might affect VIN path planning. After that, we propose the method of obstructing VIN according to these factors. In Sect. 4, we will use a large number of experiments to verify this method.

3.1   Analysis of VIN

Figure 1 is a sample of VIN path planning, from which we can see that VIN does have the ability to reach the destination but not along the theoretical shortest

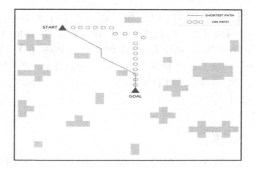

Fig. 1. Diagram of VIN Planning in a map

path. VIN defines a MDP space, M, which consists of a series of tuples, that is, some columns' states, actions, transfers, rewards, data tuples, and M that determines our final strategy. Then, a strategy obtained by data M from this MDP space policy is not a good generalization strategy because the policy is limited to this data space. Therefore, the authors assume that the unknown data space M' is obtained, and that the optimal plan in this space contains important information about the optimization strategies in the M space. In fact, the assumption is that M is just a sampling trajectory of a part of the MDP space, adding M' is as a complement to the trajectory in this space.

VIN believes that the reward R' and the transfer probability P' in the data space M' also depend on the observations in the M data space. After doing such hypothesis, it introduces two functions, fR and fP, respectively, for parameterized R' and P'. fR is the reward mapping: when inputting state, it will calculate the corresponding reward value. For example, the reward value is higher in the state near the target, and the value is lower when the state position is near the obstacle.

3.2   Problem Definition

As we said before, we aim to find those vulnerable points and try to add some obstacles at there to effectively affect VIN's performance. We want to build a method to calculate a kind of value for each point over the entire environment depending on some potential rules. Thus, we can directly derive vulnerable points from our method without exhaustive experiment for every space. So, the problem is transformed into acquiring reasonable formulas for solving the set of interference points.

Based on analysis of VIN and the correct of tentative experimental trials, we summarize three rules that might effectively obstructing VIN: (1) The farther away from the VIN planning path, the less the disturbance to the path. (2) It is often the most successful to add obstacles around the turning points in the path. (3) The closer the adding obstacle position is to the destination, the less likely it is to change the path.

Assuming that we know the entire environment (including obstacles, starting point and destination), and we also know that the robot is using the VIN method to find the path, it is easy to get the VIN planning path and the theoretical shortest path.

Let the points on the VIN path be X set: $\{x_1, x_2, \cdots, x_n\}$, the existed obstacles be B set: $\{b_1, b_2, \cdots, b_n\}$, any other available points be Y set: $\{y_1, y_2, \cdots, y_n\}$. The method only considers the points in Y. We want to calculate a value v considering three rules above for each point of Y, and then sort the values to pick up most wanted points, that is S set: $\{y|v_{yk} \in \max_i V, y \in Y\}$, $V = \{v_{y_1}, v_{y_2}, \cdots, v_{y_k}\}$.

3.3   Method Building

Now, the problem is converted from solving S to solving V. In our method, the value v consists of three parts: v_1, v_2, v_3, which refers to the three rules.

Rule 1: The farther away from the VIN planning path, the less the disturbance to the path.

The formula is:

$$v_{1y_k} = \omega_1 \min\{d_1 | d_1 = \sqrt{(x_r - y_{kr})^2 + (x_c - y_{kc})^2},$$
$$(x_r, x_c) = x \in X, (y_{kr}, y_{kc}) = y_k \in Y\} \tag{1}$$

where (x_r, x_c) is the coordinate of x, (y_{kr}, y_{kc}) is the coordinate of y_k, ω_1 is the weight of v_1. The formula considers the Euclidean distance from y_k to VIN path, and use the weight ω_1 to control the attenuation of v_1.

Rule 2: It is often the most successful to add obstacles around the turning points in the path.

First, to get the turning points, we can calculate the gradient of adjacent two points in path and compare adjacent gradients. The point at which the gradient varies is the turning point. Thus, we can get the turning points set $T: \{t_1, t_1, ..., t_n\}$.

The formula is:

$$v_{2y_k} = \omega_2 \min\{d_2 | d_2 = \max(|t_r - y_{kr}|, |t_c - y_{kc}|),$$
$$(t_r, t_c) = t \in T, (y_{kr}, y_{kc}) = y_k \in Y\} \tag{2}$$

where (t_r, t_c) is the coordinate of t, (y_{kr}, y_{kc}) is the coordinate of y_k, ω_2 is the weight of v_2. The formula considers the Chebyshev distance from y_k to the nearest turning point, and use the weight ω_2 to control the attenuation of v_2.

Rule 3: The closer the adding obstacle position is to the destination, the less likely it is to change the path.

The formula is:

$$v_{3y_k} = \omega_3 \max(|x_{nr} - y_{kr}|, |x_{nc} - y_{kc}|),$$
$$(x_{nr}, x_{nc}) = x_n, (y_{kr}, y_{kc}) = y_k \in Y \tag{3}$$

where (x_{nr}, x_{nc}) is the coordinate of x_n, the destination of the path, (y_{kr}, y_{kc}) is the coordinate of y_k, ω_3 is the weight of v_3. The formula considers the Chebyshev distance from y_k to the destination, and use the weight ω_3 to control the attenuation of v_3.

For the points in X and B, the value is 0. That is: $v_x = 0, v_b = 0$.

So, the problem now is how to use ω to control the attenuation of each formula. We define ω_3 as constant, because v_3 is the least important among v, that is Rule 3 is not that important compared with the other two. And we define $\omega_i (i = 1, 2)$ as follows:

$$\omega_i = \exp(-\frac{d_i^2}{2\theta_i^2}), i = 1, 2 \tag{4}$$

where the $\omega_i (i = 1, 2)$ is exponential decay, and when it multiplies $d_i (i = 1, 2)$, $v_i (i = 1, 2)$ will grows within a certain range, then decays exponentially. And $\theta_i (i = 1, 2)$ is the parameter to control the peak point and the rate of the decay.

So, the value of each y is:

$$v_{y_k} = \sum_{i=1}^{3} v_{iy_k} \tag{5}$$

And our target $S = \{s_1, s_2, \cdots, s_m\} = \{y| \max_m\{v_{y_k}\}\}$.
Our algorithm based on the method above is:

Algorithm 1. Method for Detecting Vulnerabilities in VIN Path Planning

Input: the training set: D_{map}, the test set: T_{map}
Output: labeled training set: T_{result}

---

1. Data preprocessing: $T_{map} \rightarrow T_{experiment}$
2. VIN training model: $D_{map} \rightarrow VIN\ Model$
for T_{map}
  for $T_{map(i)}$
    3. Calculate value: $T_{map(i)}(k) \xrightarrow{Method} (T_{map(i)}(k), value_i(k))$
    4. Sort and get the available set:$\max_5(value_i(k)) \rightarrow S = (s_1, s_2, s_3, s_4, s_5)$
    5. Juge and get the final result:
    randomly select $n, (n = 1, 2, 3)$ points from S to add the obstacle
    load $VIN\ Model$
    if $(Path_{VIN}^{after} - Path_{VIN}^{before} \geq 3)$ or $(Time_{VIN}^{after} - Time_{VIN}^{before} \geq 0.00001)$
      $T_{result}(i) = (T_{map(i)}, n, 'sucess')$
    else
      $T_{result}(i) = (T_{map(i)}, n, 'fail')$
output T_{result}

---

4   Experiment

Our goal in this section is mainly to figure out the following question: Can our method work effectively on adding obstacles automatically to obstruct VIN's performance?

The basis of our experiment is VIN. We apply the available source code [18] provided by VIN's author to train VIN Model. We adopt 28×28 Grid-World domain as the domain input and output.

First, we generate $20,000$ maps with random starting and ending points and shortest path. We use $10,000$ maps to train the VIN Model. Then, we preprocess the other $10,000$ domains as the testing set: getting rid of those can't reach the ending point by VIN. And pick $5,000$ domains from them to be the testing set.

Second, we carry out the experiment on testing set with the method proposed in this paper, and get the label (success or fail) of each domain.

At last, we use the method for random addition of noise as a comparison test. The result shows that our method does have superiority on finding vulnerabilities in VIN path planning and automatically adding obstacles.

4.1   Single Map Obstructing

As the pictures of Fig. 2 show, our method does have ability to find vulnerabilities in VIN and thus interfere its performance. Fig. 2(a) is a sample of testing set, and Fig. 2(b) to (f) are the top 5 vulnerable points picked by our method. Four of them can effectively interfere VIN's path.

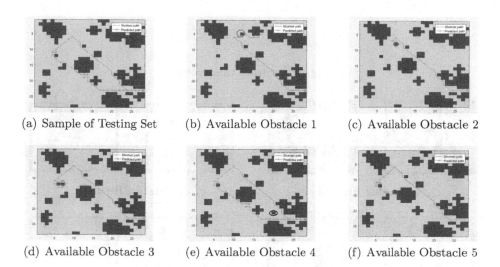

(a) Sample of Testing Set   (b) Available Obstacle 1   (c) Available Obstacle 2

(d) Available Obstacle 3   (e) Available Obstacle 4   (f) Available Obstacle 5

Fig. 2. Experiment sample

Table 1. success rate comparison

Obstacle number	Our method success rate	Random method success rate
1	34.54%	4.34%
2	37.06%	8.46%
3	66.48%	11.24%

Since there is no such research focusing on interfering VIN, we choose random method as the comparison experiment. Figure 3 is an accuracy comparison of our method and random method. The random method we use is to randomly select points in some fixed areas, like areas around the turning points. As you can see, the trend of accuracy is growing as the number of obstacles increases. But, our method is much better at first and the increment is more obvious. Table 1 shows the value from our experiment by testing 5,000 domains, which is the same value as Fig. 3.

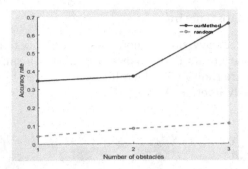

Fig. 3. Accuracy comparison

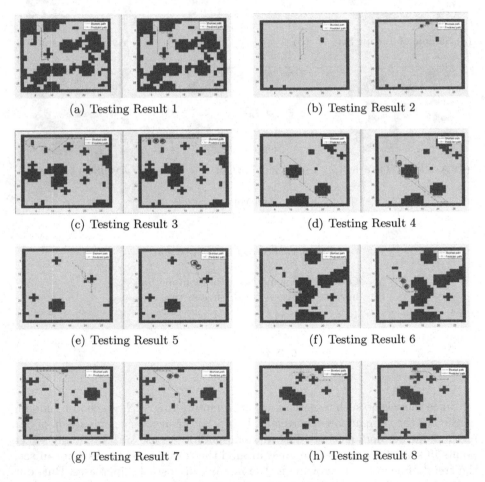

(a) Testing Result 1

(b) Testing Result 2

(c) Testing Result 3

(d) Testing Result 4

(e) Testing Result 5

(f) Testing Result 6

(g) Testing Result 7

(h) Testing Result 8

Fig. 4. Experiment sample

4.2   Batch Obstructing

This part uses the same method as above, but we show kinds of result in Fig. 4. As you can see, we pick up some well worked samples of adding two obstacles. These obstacles are randomly picked from the top 5 candidates. The results show that our method does have ability to successfully add obstacles in different domains. But you may wonder why the success rates in the Table 1 and Fig. 3 are not very high. That's because of the variety of testing set. For example, the starting and ending point in one sample can be very close, which means no matter what you do on this sample, you could hardly interfere VIN's planning.

5   Conclusion and Outlook

In this paper, we analyze the path planning methods of Reinforcement Learning, especially VIN and propose a method that can effectively find vulnerable points in path planning sample of VIN. We build a 2D navigation task to test our method and the result shows our method has great performance on finding vulnerabilities and automatically adding obstacles to obstruct VIN path planning.

Based on this paper, we believe that Reinforcement Learning methods have commonalities. If our method can work on VIN, it probably will work on other Reinforcement Learning methods. But we could further study methods for generating aggressive samples, like Generative Adversarial Networks (GAN) [17] and improve our method to a more general way.

Acknowledgments. This material is based upon work supported by the National Natural Science Foundation of China (Grant No. 61672092, No. 61502030), Science and Technology on Information Assurance Laboratory (No. 614200103011711), BM-IIE Project (No. BMK2017B02-2), and the Fundamental Research Funds for the Central Universities (Grant No. 2016JBM020, No. 2017RC016).

References

1. Watkins, C.J.C.H., Dayan, P.: Q-learning. Mach. Learn. **8**(3–4), 279–292 (1992)
2. Giusti, A., Guzzi, J., Dan, C.C., et al.: A machine learning approach to visual perception of forest trails for mobile robots. IEEE Robot. Autom. Lett. **1**(2), 661–667 (2016)
3. Levine, S., Finn, C., Darrell, T., et al.: End-to-end training of deep visuomotor policies. J. Mach. Learn. Res. **17**(39), 1–40 (2016)
4. Mnih, V., Kavukcuoglu, K., Silver, D., et al.: Human-level control through deep reinforcement learning. Nature **518**(7540), 529–533 (2015)
5. Tamar, A., Wu, Y., Thomas, G., et al.: Value iteration networks. In: Advances in Neural Information Processing Systems, pp. 2154–2162 (2016)
6. Hyndman, R.J., Koehler, A.B., Snyder, R.D., et al.: A state space framework for automatic forecasting using exponential smoothing methods. Int. J. Forecast. **18**(3), 439–454 (2002)
7. Brooks, R.A.: Solving the find-path problem by good representation of free space. IEEE Trans. Syst. Man Cybern. **2**, 190–197 (1983)

8. Zhu, Q.B., Zhang, Y.: An ant colony algorithm based on grid method for mobile robot path planning. Robot **27**(2), 132–136 (2005)
9. Terwilliger, T.C.: Automated main-chain model building by template matching and iterative fragment extension. Acta Crystallogr. Sect. D: Biol. Crystallogr. **59**(1), 38–44 (2003)
10. Warren, C.W.: Global path planning using artificial potential fields. In: Proceedings of 1989 IEEE International Conference on Robotics and Automation, pp. 316–321. IEEE (1989)
11. Lagoudakis, M.G., Parr, R.: Least-squares policy iteration. J. Mach. Learn. Res. **4**(Dec), 1107–1149 (2003)
12. Pineau, J., Gordon, G., Thrun, S.: Point-based value iteration: an anytime algorithm for POMDPs. In: IJCAI, vol. 3, pp. 1025–1032 (2003)
13. Dellaert, F., Fox, D., Burgard, W., et al.: Monte Carlo localization for mobile robots. In: Proceedings of 1999 IEEE International Conference on Robotics and Automation, vol. 2, pp. 1322–1328. IEEE (1999)
14. Tesauro, G.: Temporal difference learning and TD-Gammon. Commun. ACM **38**(3), 58–68 (1995)
15. Mnih, V., Kavukcuoglu, K., Silver, D., et al.: Playing Atari with deep reinforcement learning. arXiv preprint arXiv:1312.5602 (2013)
16. Wang, F.Y., Zhang, J.J., Zheng, X., et al.: Where does AlphaGo go: from church-turing thesis to AlphaGo thesis and beyond. IEEE/CAA J. Automatica Sin. **3**(2), 113–120 (2016)
17. Goodfellow, I., Pouget-Abadie, J., Mirza, M., et al.: Generative adversarial nets. In: Advances in neural information processing systems, pp. 2672–2680 (2014)
18. UC Berkeley. https://github.com/avivt/VIN

Healthcare and Industrial Control System Security

Towards Decentralized Accountability and Self-sovereignty in Healthcare Systems

Xueping Liang[1,2,3], Sachin Shetty[4], Juan Zhao[3], Daniel Bowden[5],
Danyi Li[1(✉)], and Jihong Liu[1]

[1] Institute of Information Engineering, Chinese Academy of Sciences,
Beijing 100093, China
lidanyi@iie.ac.cn
[2] School of Cyber Security, University of Chinese Academy of Sciences,
Beijing 100190, China
[3] College of Engineering, Tennessee State University, Nashville, TN 37209, USA
[4] Virginia Modeling Analysis and Simulation Center, Old Dominion University,
Norfolk, VA 23529, USA
[5] Sentara Healthcare, Norfolk, VA 23455, USA

Abstract. With the increasing development and adoption of wearable devices, people care more about their health conditions than ever before. Both patients and doctors as well as insurance agencies benefit from this advanced technology. However, the emerging wearable devices creates a major concern over health data privacy as data collected from those devices can reflect patients' heath conditions and habits, and could increase the data disclosure risks among the healthcare providers and application vendors. In this paper, we propose using the trusted execution platform enabled by Intel SGX to provide accountability for data access and propose a decentralized approach with blockchain technology to address the privacy concern. By developing a web application for personal health data management (PHDM) systems, the individuals are capable of synchronizing sensor data from wearable devices with online account and controlling data access from any third parties. The protected personal health data and data access records are hashed and anchored to a permanent but secure ledger with platform dependency, ensuring data integrity and accountability. Analysis shows that our approach provides user privacy and accountability with acceptable overhead.

Keywords: Privacy protection · Healthcare industry
Access control · Self-sovereignty · Trusted computing · Blockchain
Decentralization · Intel SGX · Accountability

1 Introduction

The rising of wearable technology contributes to the digitalization of the world. Wearable technology refers to networked devices embedded with sensors which can be worn comfortably on the body or even inside the body to collect health

© Springer International Publishing AG, part of Springer Nature 2018
S. Qing et al. (Eds.): ICICS 2017, LNCS 10631, pp. 387–398, 2018.
https://doi.org/10.1007/978-3-319-89500-0_34

data and tracking activities [19] thus serving as a convenient tool to monitor personal health. From doctors' side, those collected data can be valuable clues for determining the appropriate medical treatment. Besides, Insurance 3.0 [3] rises as a result of analysis on big data. With the availability of rich health data in the cloud, health insurance companies can make more strategic policies according to individual characteristics.

However, challenges are arising since more health data can be collected from both wearable devices and EHR systems. First, patients become more concerned about the privacy of the health data. Many exiting state-of-the-art approaches focus on improving data providers' responsibilities to detect the data disclosure activities, however, it is urgent to protect data access and provide immediate notifications of data disclosure risks. Second, over 300 different EHR systems are in use today, but most of them adopt a centralized architecture which suffers from single point of failure. Meanwhile, there are little or even no communication and cooperation among systems [1]. The isolation between data centers results in the lack of a holistic and thorough view of personal health. It is reported that 62% of insured adults rely on their doctors to manage their health records [1], which limits their ability to interact with other healthcare providers than their primary doctor. Moreover, even though many health providers are supposed to follow rules or laws, such as HIPAA (Health Insurance Portability and Accountability Act of 1996), but there are still many entities which are not covered by any laws. Therefore, it is crucial that any entity that has access to the data should be accountable for their operations on the data and any operations on the data need to be audited.

With the above mentioned issues of data ownership, data isolation and lack of accountability, as well as high privacy risks existing in current EHR systems, patients have little control over their personal health data [10], the notion of Self-Sovereignty [7,13] gains great popularity for dealing with healthcare data issues. To better bring this concept into reality, we adopt two novel technologies, Intel SGX and blockchain, to implement a patient-centric personal health data management system with accountability and decentralization. Intel SGX offers an anonymous key system (AKS) [18] that can generate an anonymous certificate which will then be transmitted to a certification platform for validation. Blockchain technology, where data are stored in a public, distributed and immutable ledger, maintained by a decentralized network of computing nodes, provides a decentralized and permanent record keeping capability, which is critical for data provenance [12] and access control [9] in cloud data protection.

In this paper, we propose a complete patient-centric personal health data management system, allowing patients to collect and manage their health data all in a compliant way. In the development of the system, we take the user ownership of data into consideration and the contribution is as follows.

– **Self-Sovereign Data Ownership.** We adopt the idea of user-centric architecture to control data access and issue permissions. It is the data owner that decides who can acess the data and whether to make the data public or private, as well as how to validate the data. Token-based verification is utilized to grant one time access to data requested by third parties.

- **Permanent Data Record with Integrity.** We collect data records and submit an abstract of each record to the blockchain network. The records are included in a block and the integrity of the record is guaranteed by the consensus mechanism used in the block mining process.
- **Scalable Data Processing.** The volume of health data collected from wearable devices and user input scales greatly so we propose a high-speed algorithm to improve the efficiency of data processing.
- **Decentralized and Distributed Privacy and Access Control.** We propose a decentralized permission management protocol to deal with each personal health data request. The data access records are stored to provide traceable logs, using blockchain to preserve immutability.
- **Trusted Accountability.** The trusted execution environment provisioned by Intel SGX is utilized to generate a fingerprint for each data access. For medical treatment and insurance enforcement, every action is traceable. Once data leakage is detected, the malicious entity can be identified for investigation.

The rest of the paper is organized as follows. Section 2 introduces the overall system design, including the architecture, system entities, key establishment and system procedures. We describe the token-based access control in Sect. 3 and decentralized integrity protection and accountability in Sect. 4. Performance evaluation is presented in Sect. 5. Section 6 concludes the paper.

2 Architecture Design

2.1 System Overview

A three layer architecture for accountability and privacy preservation is designed for the PHDM system. The data sharing layer provides users with entire control over their personal health data and handles data requests from third parties. The SGX enabled hardware layer provisions a trusted execution environment in the cloud, generates data access tokens and is responsible for reliable data storage and process. The blockchain network layer, which is distributed and untrusted, records data operations and various data access requests for immutability and integrity protection. Figure 1 is a general scenario for the patient centric personal health data management (PHDM) system. Personal wearable devices collect original health data, such as walking distance, sleeping conditions and heartbeat, which may be synchronized by the user with their online account associated with the cloud server and cloud database. Every piece of health data could be hashed and uploaded to the blockchain network for record keeping and integrity protection. The original data is maintained in the cloud database hosted on trusted platform enabled by SGX. The user owns personal health data, maintains access tokens and is responsible for granting, denying and revoking data access from any other parties requesting data access. For example, a user seeking

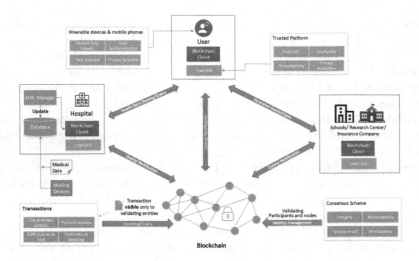

Fig. 1. Patient centric personal health data management system scenario.

medical treatment would grant the doctor a one time data access token. Same scenario applies to user-insurance company interactions. Besides, user can also manually record everyday activities according to a particular medical treatment such as medicine usage and share the information frequently with the doctor. Healthcare providers such as doctors can perform medical test, give suggestions or provide medical treatment, and request access to previous medical treatment from the patient. The data request and the corresponding data access is recorded on the blockchain for distributed validation. Besides, user may request a health insurance quote from insurance companies to choose health insurance plans. Insurance companies can also request access to user health data from wearable devices and medical treatment history. The blockchain network is used for three purposes. For health data collected from wearable devices and from healthcare providers, each of the hashed data entry is uploaded to the blockchain network for integrity protection. For personal health data access request from healthcare provider and health insurance company, a permission from the data owner is needed with a decentralized permission management scheme. Besides, each of the access request and access activity should be recorded on the blockchain for further auditing or investigation.

2.2   Key Establishment

In the patient centric data management system, users are required to register an online account to be involved in the system, and generate data encryption key pairs to encrypt their cloud data for confidentiality. For key management, we assume the system developers adopt a secure wallet service. The description of each key established is as follows.

- **User Registration Key** K_{UR}. The user needs to create an online account to store health data collected from wearable devices and other sources in the cloud database. We denote the user registration key as K_{UR}. Every time user wants to operate on their cloud health data, the registration key is needed. This key is generated from the platform identity key using Intel SGX anonymous key system and is thus bounded to the user. Even if the user's registration key is stolen or compromised, it could not be used elsewhere without the user authentication. Similarly, the registration key for healthcare provider and healthcare insurance company is K_{HR} and K_{IR}, respectively.
- **Data Encryption Key** K_{DE}. After registration, the user generates an encryption key K_{DE} to encrypt all the health data stored in the cloud database. When a health data entry is created, user has the option to encrypt the data entry, which limits the data access only to the key owners, and the hashed data entry will be uploaded instantly to the blockchain.
- **Data Sharing Public/Private Key Pair** (PK_{DS}, PR_{DS}). For health data sharing, a public/private key pair will be generated, denoted as (PK_{DS}, PR_{DS}). In some cases that the data sharing activity is to be recorded on the blockchain, the private key is used to generate a signature from the user to indicate the health data ownership, while the public key is used by others to verify the ownership. When users want to share their health data with healthcare providers or insurance companies, they share the private key for data access and the corresponding tokens generated with this private key.
- **Platform Identification Key** K_{PID}. Each trusted platform owns a platform identification key K_{PID}, also generated from the platform identity key using Intel SGX anonymous key system. Every health data request and data access on a certain platform will generate an activity record signed by K_{PID} for accountability while still with anonymity preserved. Different entity keys are noted as K_{PIDu} for users, K_{PIDp} for healthcare providers and K_{PIDi} for insurance companies.

2.3 PHDM Procedures

In the system, there are four phases for personal health data management including user registration, health data generation and synchronization (data generated from user, healthcare provider and insurance company), health data access management, health data access record uploading and health data access auditing.

User Registration. In the system, user needs to create an online account to store health data collected from wearable devices and other sources in the cloud database by way of establishing an online ID. Other entities in the system cannot correlate the online ID with their real identity, preserving user privacy in the registration phase.

Health Data Generation and Synchronization. Health data contains four categories, including data collected from wearable devices, data collected from medical test, data collected by patient indicating their treatment details and data recorded by healthcare providers and insurance companies. After registration, the user can collect health data from wearable devices, which monitor their everyday activities, such as walking, bicycling and sleeping, and choose to synchronize those data with their online account. The collected data is encrypted using K_{DE} and stored in the cloud database. This preserves user privacy in the data generation and storage phase. The synchronization step triggers an event in the system which transforms the event into a transaction on the blockchain. Everytime a health data entry is created, user has the option to encrypt the data entry and upload the record on the blockchain.

Health Data Access Management. User can share data with healthcare providers to seek healthcare services, and with insurance companies to get a quote for the insurance policy and to be insured. A token based access control mechanism is adopted to control personal health data access and exposure. The health data is stored in the cloud database and the access control policies are stored on the blockchain in a decentralized way to ensure integrity and remove the necessity of a trusted third party. Both healthcare providers and insurance companies can request data access to the data owner, that is, the registered user in the system. User can grant, deny and revoke access from both parties. Each time there is a data request, the user will generate an Access Token to the requester. The Access Token is bound to a trusted platform for accountability.

Health Data Access Record Uploading. As mentioned above, once a data request or data access event is monitored in the system, the event will be captured as a data access record which will serve as a system log for future validation and regulation. The record is hashed and eventually transformed into a Merkle tree node [14] using Tierion API [4]. The Merkle tree root node will be anchored in a blockchain transaction following the Chainpoint 2.0 protocol [2]. For the blockchain nodes, both healthcare providers and insurance companies can join the blockchain mining process in exchange for the large-scale dataset retrieved from personal health database as mining rewards. For privacy concerns, the dataset removes sensitive information such as name and location and is anonymous. Insurance companies can learn more information from medical history and health data so that they can make specific policies according to the characteristics of customers. Healthcare providers can learn from previous medical treatment and gain experiences which will benefit future medical cases and improve medical levels.

Health Data Access Auditing. When it is necessary for legal regulators to investigate the system security, user can grant the system auditor access to the data records on blockchain network. Each data record is verifiable by checking the record signatures. It is also accountable against the trusted platform by identifying the platform key used in the signature.

3   Token-Based Access Control

For anonymity and verification purposes, we adopt the token based access control mechanism to handle the data management process. As is shown in Fig. 2, the cloud server is responsible for issuing and verifying tokens, and also maintaining both the data record database and data access log database. Users can request and share the access tokens to data requstors. Potential data requestors include healthcare providers, insurance companies and even system auditors. Each data and token operation is recorded in the blockchain and thus validated. After user registration, the cloud server can issue tokens based on the personal information provided by users. To access data, the required token will be presented to the cloud server and verified. The server issuance operation, the user token presentation and verification omit system logs which will be stored in the log database, as well as data requests and access from third parties.

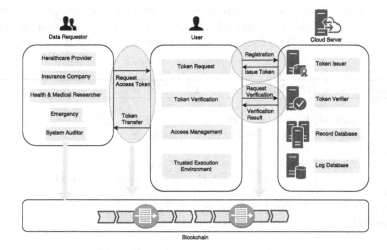

Fig. 2. PHDM system interaction.

3.1 U-Prove Based Token Generation

User registration is based on U-Prove [16], which is proved capable to be integrated into Trusted Platform Module 2.0 in [6]. U-Prove [15] includes three entities, namely issuer, prover and verifier. In our system, the issuer and the verifier is the same entity, that is, the cloud server. The user in our PHDM system is the prover entity in U-Prove model. During user registration phase, there are some parameter definitions for both prover and issuer.

- The value of the token information field (TI): $TI \in (0,1)^*$
- The value of the prover information field (PI): $PI \in (0,1)^*$
- Application Attributes (AA): $(A_1, ..., A_n), TI$
  $(A_1, ..., A_n)$ indicates n attributes from the application itself.
- Issuer Parameters (IP): $UID_p, desc(G_p), UID_H, (g_0, g_1, ..., g_n, g_t), (e_1, ..., e_n), S$ UID_p is an application-specific identifier for this particular IP, which is unique across the PHDM system and $desc(G_p)$ specifies the group (G_p)

with an order of p which is used for discrete logarithm computation in the following verification steps. UID_H is the identifier for the secure hash algorithm. $(g_0, g_1, ..., g_n, g_t)$ is the Issuer's public key. $(e_1, ..., e_n)$ is generated from AA, indicating the format of each application attribute.

- The hash of the $IP(P)$: $P = H(IP)$
- Device-protected Boolean (DB): d
  This indicates whether the protocol is device protected. PHDM adopts trusted execution environment so the value by default is *true*.
- Device Parameters (DP): g_d, x_d, h_d
  The Device generator g_d satisfies $g_d \in G_q$. x_d is device private key and h_d is the public key.

With the above information provided, we choose the issuance protocol version number 0x01. The user platform identification key K_{PIDu} is used to generate the device private key. The token generation protocol is as follows.

Protocol 1. User Registration on the Cloud Server

Input:

$\quad x_t = Hash(0x01, P, TI)$, $x_i = Hash(A_i)$, $\gamma = g_0 g_1^{x_1} ... g_n^{x_n} h_d$

$\quad UID_p$, random $\alpha, \beta_1, \beta_2, \omega$, and issuer private key y_0

Compute:

$\quad h = \gamma^\alpha$, $\sigma_z = \gamma^{y_0}$, $\sigma_z^1 = \gamma^{y_0}$, $\sigma_a^1 = g_0^{\beta_1} g^{\beta_2} g^\omega$, $\sigma_b^1 = (\sigma_z^1)^{\beta_1} h^{\beta_2} \gamma^{\omega\alpha}$

$\quad \sigma_c^1 = Hash(h, PI, \sigma_z^1, \sigma_a^1, \sigma_b^1)$, $\sigma_r^1 = (\sigma_c^1 + \beta_1 \mod q)y_0 + \omega \mod q + \beta_2 \mod q$

Output:

$\quad$ U-Prove token T: $UID_P, h, TI, PI, \sigma_z^1, \sigma_c^1, \sigma_r^1, d$

$\quad$ prover private key: α^{-1}

The cloud server issues tokens to users with the signature $(\sigma_z^1, \sigma_c^1, \sigma_r^1)$. For privacy concerns, the application attributes are hashed for the generation of U-Prove based token. During some circumstances, the issuer is able to generate multiple tokens at one time for better performance.

3.2   Token Presentation Protocol

A presentation proof of ownership of certain messages or attributes contained in the token is generated using the token private key and is required to access user data in the cloud database. Before accessing data, the data requestor needs to attest itself and convince the user that it is running on top of SGX enabled environment in an isolated enclave. The SGX attestation is launched by the data requestor which will send a signed quote to the data owner for verification using the platform dependent key. The remote attestation between the two platforms is performed with the assistance of the Intel Attestation Service [5]. After the verification, the user will request a one-time U-Prove token with a newly generated private key PR_{DS} and share it with the data requestor. The data requestor forwards the token to the verifier of the cloud database and will be granted access after the verification. Different decisions can be made by the user, such as to grant, deny and revoke access. The presentation proof serves two purposes. For one thing, it proves the integrity and the authenticity of the attribute values and for another, it establishes the confirmation of the ownership of the private key associated with the token itself, which will further prevent token replay attack.

4 Decentralized Accountability and Integrity Protection

As is shown in Fig. 2, each data and token operation is recorded in the blockchain and thus validated in a decentralized and permanent manner, ensuring data integrity. Besides, every operation is launched on a trusted platform enabled by Intel SGX, making the operation record trustworthy and nonframeable. The event record can be described using a tuple as {*datahash, owner, receiver, time, location, expirydate, signature*} where the signature comes with platform dependency for accountability. Then the tuple is submitted to the blockchain network which is followed by several steps to transform a list of records into a transaction. A list of transactions will be used to form a block, and the block will be validated by nodes in the blockchain network by consensus algorithms. After a series of processes, the integrity of the record can be preserved, and future validation on the block and the transaction related to this record is accessible. Each time there is an operation on the personal health data, a record will be reflected and anchored to the blockchain. The SGX platform identification key K_{PID} is used to generate the signature thus making each record platform dependent and ensuring that every action on personal health data is accountable. The token generation and issuance are also recorded in the same way so as to track the data requests and authorizations.

For scalability considerations, we adopt a Merkle tree based architecture [14] to handle large number of data records. Each leaf node represents a record and the intermediate node is computed as the hash of the two leaf nodes. The Merkle root, along with the tree path from the current node to the root, serves as the proof of integrity and validation, that is, the Merkle proof. The basic Merkle proof is shown in Fig. 3. First, we need to identify the record location, the targetHashB. The target hash and the path to the Merkle root, that is, nodes in green, constitute the Merkle proof of the hashed data record, which is stored in a JSON-LD document that contains the information to cryptographically verify that the record is anchored to a blockchain. By calculating the hashes in different tree levels, it is easy and fast to obtain the root hash, which is anchored in the blockchain transaction, witnessed and maintained by some distributed nodes. It proves the data was created as it was at the time anchored. The Merkle root for each Merkle tree is related to one transaction in the blockchain network, which means a blockchain transaction represents a list of data records the Merkle hosts, enabling the scalability and effectiveness of data integrity protection and validation. The tree based architecture protects the integrity of each operation record itself which can be validated by traversing the tree nodes. Meanwhile, it implicitly indicates the integrity of all the nodes in that any single node modification could lead to the modification of the root, thus protecting the integrity of the whole tree structure at trivial costs.

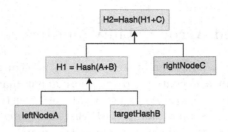

Fig. 3. Merkle tree based data integrity protection.

5   System Evaluation

To evaluate the performance of the system and overhead brought by the security measures, we adopt two metrics, including the efficiency to handle different number of accountable records and generate large numbers of tokens. For record anchoring, the tree based algorithm bears a computation complexity of $log(n)$ and the average time cost for each record is 0.4 ms when 1000 entries are processed concurrently.

For U-Prove based token generation, we select five attributes predefined and involved in each token and two of them are required to obtain a data access token. During the token issuance, there are basically two cryptographic methods for digital signature including Subgroup and ECC. The evaluation results for token issuance and presentation with these two methods are shown in Fig. 4(a) and (b). It can be concluded that ECC-based token generation is more efficient than the subgroup-based method. This can be explained that ECC utilizes shorter

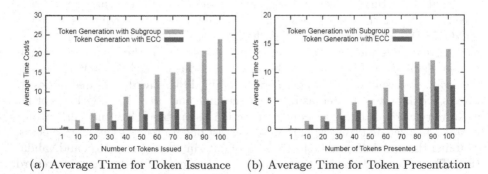

(a) Average Time for Token Issuance   (b) Average Time for Token Presentation

Fig. 4. Average time cost for token issuance and presentation

key length for the elliptic curve than subgroups of equivalent security levels and computes faster with a small field. Adopting the ECC-based U-Prove protocols for both token issuance and presentation, the average overhead brought to the system is 8.1% and 9.4%, respectively.

6   Conclusion and Future Work

Some work [17] has been done to integrate blockchain technology to the healthcare industry. MedRec [8] is proposed to build the healthcare on top of smart contract. But still, privacy risks remain to be addressed. [20] points out that MPC (Secure Multi-Party Computing) is a promising solution to enable untrusted third-party to conduct computation over patient data without violating privacy but the actual efficiency is not clear. [21] addresses the adoption of blockchain in social network domain but not fully explores the benefits of the blockchain. [11] addresses the blockchain adoption in Internet of Things environment.

In this paper, we build a web based system for personal health data management using blockchain and Intel SGX. By utilizing blockchain technology in the self-sovereign healthcare systems, we manage to distribute the responsibility of maintaining trusted records for data operation as well as token generations. Meanwhile, benefiting from the blockchain consensus scheme and the decentralized architecture, along with the trusted execution environment and the platform dependency provisioned by Intel SGX, the records are anchored with trusted timestamping and redundancy, preserving both availability and accountability of the healthcare data and operations. We also propose a U-Prove based protocols for the permission management. We implement a prototype of the PHDM system and the evaluation shows that the performance is acceptable. In the future, we will integrate the PHDM system with the enhancement of a blockchain based access control scheme to provide better data protection and user privacy.

Acknowledgements. This work was supported by Office of the Assistant Secretary of Defense for Research and Engineering (OASD (R & E)) agreement FA8750-15-2-0120. The work was also supported by a grant from the National Natural Science Foundation of China (No. 61402470) and the research project of Trusted Internet Identity Management (2016YFB0800505 and 2016YFB0800501).

References

1. Connected patient report. https://www.salesforce.com/assets/pdf/industries/2016-state-of-the-connected-patient-pr.pdf
2. Chainpoint: a scalable protocol for anchoring data in the blockchain and generating blockchain receipts. http://www.chainpoint.org/
3. Insurance 3.0 - The Turn of the Digital. http://www.huxley.com/fr/actualites-et-articles-de-fond/actualites/insurance-3-0-le-virage-du-digital. Accessed 7 Mar 2017
4. Tierion API. https://tierion.com/app/api

5. Anati, I., Gueron, S., Johnson, S., Scarlata, V.: Innovative technology for cpu based attestation and sealing. In: Proceedings of the 2nd International Workshop on Hardware and Architectural Support for Security and Privacy, vol. 13 (2013)
6. Chen, L., Li, J.: Flexible and scalable digital signatures in TPM 2.0. In: Proceedings of the 2013 ACM SIGSAC Conference on Computer & Communications Security, CCS 2013, pp. 37–48. ACM, New York (2013). https://doi.org/10.1145/2508859.2516729
7. Clippinger, J.H.: Why Self-Sovereignty Matters. https://idcubed.org/chapter-2-self-sovereignty-matters/. Accessed 7 Mar 2017
8. Ekblaw, A., Azaria, A., Halamka, J.D., Lippman, A.: A case study for blockchain in Healthcare:MedRec prototype for electronic health records and medical research data. In: Proceedings of IEEE Open & Big Data Conference (2016)
9. Hardjono, T., Pentland, A.S.: Verifiable anonymous identities and access control in permissioned blockchains
10. Kish, L.J., Topol, E.J.: Unpatients-why patients should own their medical data. Nat. Biotechnol. 33(9), 921–924 (2015)
11. Liang, X., Zhao, J., Shetty, S., Li, D.: Towards data assurance and resilience in IoT using distributed ledger. In: IEEE MILCOM. IEEE (2017)
12. Liang, X., Shetty, S., Tosh, D., Kamhoua, C., Kwiat, K., Njilla, L.: ProvChain: a blockchain-based data provenance architecture in cloud environment with enhanced privacy and availability. In: International Symposium on Cluster, Cloud and Grid Computing. IEEE/ACM (2017)
13. Liang, X., Zhao, J., Shetty, S., Liu, J., Li, D.: Integrating blockchain for data sharing and collaboration in mobile healthcare applications, October 2017
14. Merkle, R.C.: Protocols for public key cryptosystems. In: 1980 IEEE Symposium on Security and Privacy, p. 122. IEEE, April 1980
15. Paquin, C.: U-prove technology overview v1.1 (revision 2), April 2013. https://www.microsoft.com/en-us/research/publication/u-prove-technology-overview-v1-1-revision-2/
16. Paquin, C., Zaverucha, G.: U-prove cryptographic specification v1. 1. Technical report, Microsoft Corporation (2011)
17. Peterson, K., Deeduvanu, R., Kanjamala, P., Boles, K.: A blockchain-based approach to health information exchange networks (2016)
18. Sarangdhar, N., Nemiroff, D., Smith, N., Brickell, E., Li, J.: Trusted platform module certification and attestation utilizing an anonymous key system, 19 May 2016. https://www.google.com/patents/US20160142212. US Patent App. 14/542,491
19. Thierer, A.D.: The internet of things and wearable technology: addressing privacy and security concerns without derailing innovation. Richmond J. Law Technol. 21, 1 (2014)
20. Yue, X., Wang, H., Jin, D., Li, M., Jiang, W.: Healthcare data gateways: found healthcare intelligence on blockchain with novel privacy risk control. J. Med. Syst. 40(10), 218 (2016). https://doi.org/10.1007/s10916-016-0574-6
21. Zhang, J., Xue, N., Huang, X.: A secure system for pervasive social network-based healthcare. IEEE Access 4, 9239–9250 (2016)

P3ASC: Privacy-Preserving Pseudonym and Attribute-Based Signcryption Scheme for Cloud-Based Mobile Healthcare System

Changji Wang[1,2(✉)], Yuan Yuan[3], and Shengyi Jiang[1,2]

[1] School of Information Science and Technology,
Guangdong University of Foreign Studies, Guangzhou 510006, China
wchangji@gmail.com
[2] Collaborative Innovation Center for 21st-Century Maritime Silk Road Studies,
Guangdong University of Foreign Studies, Guangzhou 510006, China
[3] School of Finance, Guangdong University of Foreign Studies,
Guangzhou 510006, China

Abstract. With the development of wireless body sensor network and mobile cloud computing, cloud-based mobile healthcare, which extends the operation of healthcare provider into a pervasive environment for better health delivery and monitoring, has attracted considerable interest recently. However, how to keep data security and privacy in cloud-based mobile healthcare system is an important and challenging issue since personal health information is quite sensitive. In this paper, we introduce a new cryptographic primitive named privacy-preserving pseudonym and attribute-based signcryption (P3ASC) scheme, which can fulfill the functionality of pseudonym-based signature and key-policy attribute-based encryption in a logical step. We propose a provable secure P3ASC scheme from bilinear pairings and present a novel secure and efficient cloud-based mobile healthcare system by exploiting our proposed P3ASC scheme. The proposed system can ensure data confidentiality, integrity, source authentication and non-repudiation, but also can provide fine-grained access control and user anonymity.

Keywords: Mobile healthcare · Cloud computing
Wireless body area network · Pseudonym-based signature
Key-policy attribute-based encryption · Signcryption

1 Introduction

The promotion of wireless body area network (WBAN) has accelerated the explosive growth of medical and biological data, posing new challenges to data storage and data processing for health care providers [1,2]. A possible way to overcome these challenges is to exploit the benefits of cloud computing [3]. Cloud computing can provide an information technology infrastructure that allows hospitals,

© Springer International Publishing AG, part of Springer Nature 2018
S. Qing et al. (Eds.): ICICS 2017, LNCS 10631, pp. 399–411, 2018.
https://doi.org/10.1007/978-3-319-89500-0_35

insurance companies, research institutions and other government agencies in the healthcare ecosystem to leverage improved computing capabilities with lower cost and complexity, and allows them to access a shared pool of configurable computing resources from anywhere at any time.

Cloud computing has been widely deployed in mobile healthcare systems to improve the quality of healthcare services and potentially reduce healthcare costs in recent years. However, it also brings about a series of challenges, especially how to ensure the security of personal health information (PHI) and user privacy from various attacks [4]. Firstly, the outsourced PHI may be misused or accessed by unauthorized users. Secondly, the outsourced PHI contain personal and sensitive private information. User privacy will be destroyed once exposed to the public. Thus, scalable and strict security mechanisms are mandatory and should provide data confidentiality, integrity, source authentication, access control and user anonymity [5,6].

To solve the problem of fine-grained access control over encrypted data, Sahai and Waters [7] first introduced the concept of attribute-based encryption (ABE). Since then, various ABE schemes have been proposed, such as [8–11], and several cloud-based secure systems using ABE have been developed, such as [12–14]. There are two different and complementary notions of ABE: key-policy ABE (KP-ABE) and ciphertext-policy ABE (CP-ABE).

In KP-ABE scheme [8], ciphertexts are labeled by the data owner with a set of descriptive attributes, while data users' private keys are issued by a trusted private key generator (PKG) captures an access policy that specifies which type of ciphertexts the key can decrypt. When the access policy defined in the private key matches the attributes labeled with the ciphertext, then it decrypts the ciphertext. In CP-ABE scheme [9], the data owner encrypts a message under an access policy over attributes. A data user who possesses a set of attributes can obtain corresponding secret attribute keys from the PKG. A data user is able to decrypt a ciphertext if his attributes satisfy the access policy associated with the ciphertext.

In recent years, various cloud-based healthcare systems have been proposed by exploiting CP-ABE scheme to simultaneously achieve data confidentiality and access control. Yu et al. [15] and Tan et al. [16] pointed out that KP-ABE scheme is more appropriate than the CP-ABE scheme to be implemented in cloud-based mobile healthcare system. The main reasons are as follows: Firstly, encryption performs by using descriptive attributes has lower encryption complexity and shorter computation time than encryption to be performed by using access policy. Secondly, assignment of descriptive attributes in KP-ABE for encryption purpose is much simpler and less time consuming than assignment of access policy in CP-ABE encryption. This results from the fact that a slight update mistake in the access policy would cause a complication in the entire encryption and decryption system. Furthermore, in terms of access control, KP-ABE allows higher flexibility and efficiency in the modification of access control towards any authorized personnel compared to CP-ABE. This stems from the fact that the updates made on the descriptive attributes are much simpler than updates made on access structure.

Given the importance of PHI and the compliance of health insurance portability and accountability act (HIPPA), it is critical to guarantee source authentication and integrity of PHI in cloud-based mobile healthcare system. Otherwise, anyone can modify or forge someone's PHI, which is undesirable. In addition, user privacy may impede its wide adoption. Digital signature is a very useful tool for providing authenticity, integrity and non-repudiation while it is rarely considered to provide user privacy by its own. Although privacy-preserving signature schemes, such as ring signature, group signature, mesh signature, attribute-based signature [17], have been widely studied in recent years, they are very complicated and time-consuming.

In this paper, we introduce a new cryptographic primitive named privacy preserving pseudonym and attribute-based signcryption (P3ASC) scheme, which can fulfill the functionality of pseudonym-based signature and key-policy attribute-based encryption in a logical step. To achieve user anonymity, privacy preserving technique based on pseudonyms is adopted. Then, we propose a P3ASC scheme and prove it is indistinguishable against adaptive chosen plaintext attacks in the selective-set model under the DBDH assumption, and is existentially unforgeable against adaptive chosen message and pseudonym attacks in the random oracle model under the ECDL assumption. Finally, we provide an architectural model of cloud-based mobile healthcare system by exploiting our proposed P3ASC scheme. It can ensure data confidentiality, integrity, authenticity, and non-repudiation, but also can provide fine-grained access control and user anonymity.

The rest of the paper is organized as follows. We introduce some necessary preliminary work in Sect. 2. We give syntax and security definitions for P3ASC scheme in Sect. 3. We present a P3ASC scheme in Sect. 3. We describe an architecture of cloud-based mobile healthcare system by exploiting the proposed P3ASC scheme in Sect. 4. Finally, we conclude our paper and discuss our future work in Sect. 5.

2   Preliminaries

We denote by κ the system security parameter. When $\mathbf{S}$ is a set, $x \xleftarrow{\$} \mathbf{S}$ denotes that x is uniformly picked from $\mathbf{S}$. Let $\mathbf{M}$, $\mathbf{ID}$ and Ω be message universe, identity (pseudonym) universe and attribute universe, respectively.

2.1   Access Structure and Linear Secret Sharing Scheme

Let $\Omega = \{\omega_1, \omega_2, \cdots, \omega_n\}$ be a set of attributes, and denote by 2^Ω its power set. A collection $\mathbb{A} \subseteq 2^\Omega$ is monotone if for every $\mathbf{B}$ and $\mathbf{C}$, if $\mathbf{B} \in \mathbb{A}$ and $\mathbf{B} \subseteq \mathbf{C}$ then $\mathbf{C} \in \mathbb{A}$. An access structure (respectively, monotone access structure) is a collection (respectively, monotone collection) $\mathbb{A}$ of non-empty subsets of Ω, i.e.

$\Omega \setminus \emptyset$. The sets in $\mathbb{A}$ are called the authorized sets, and the sets not in $\mathbb{A}$ are called the unauthorized sets [9].

We restrict our attention to monotone access structures. If a set of attributes ω satisfies an access policy (access structure) $\mathbb{A}$, we denote it as $\mathbb{A}(\omega) = 1$. Otherwise, we denote it as $\mathbb{A}(\omega) = 0$.

Let $\mathbf{M}_{\ell \times k}$ be a matrix, and $\rho : \{1, \ldots, \ell\} \to \Omega$ be a function that maps a row of $\mathbf{M}_{\ell \times k}$ to an attribute for labeling. A secret sharing scheme for access structure $\mathbb{A}$ over a set of attributes Ω is a linear secret-sharing scheme over $\mathbf{F}_q$ and is represented by $(\mathbf{M}_{\ell \times k}, \rho)$ if it consists of two polynomial-time algorithms:

- Share: The algorithm takes as input $s \in \mathbf{F}_q$ which is to be shared. It chooses $v_2, \ldots, v_k \xleftarrow{\$} \mathbf{F}_q$ and let $\boldsymbol{v} = (s, v_2, \ldots, v_k)$. It outputs $\mathbf{M}_{\ell \times k} \cdot \boldsymbol{v}^\top$ as the vector of ℓ shares of the secret s. The share $\lambda_i = <\mathbf{M}_i, \boldsymbol{v}>$ belongs to party $\rho(i)$, where we denote $\mathbf{M}_i$ as the i-th row in $\mathbf{M}_{\ell \times k}$.
- Reconstruct: The algorithm takes as input $\mathbf{S} \subseteq \Omega$ satisfies $\mathbb{A}$. Let $\mathbf{I} = \{i | \rho(i) \in \mathbf{S}\}$. It outputs reconstruction constants $\{(i, \mu_i)\}_{i \in \mathbf{I}}$ which has a linear reconstruction property, i.e., $\sum_{i \in \mathbf{I}} \lambda_i \cdot \mu_i = s$.

2.2 Bilinear Pairing and Complexity Assumptions

Let P be a point with a prime order q in an elliptic curve $\mathrm{E}_p(a, b)$, and $\mathbf{G}$ be a subgroup generated by the base point P, i.e., $\mathbf{G} \stackrel{\text{def}}{=} \langle P \rangle$.

Definition 1. *Given $Q \in \mathbf{G}$, the elliptic curve discrete logarithm problem (ECDLP) in $\mathbf{G}$ is to find the integer a where $1 \le a \le q$, such that $Q = [a]P$.*

The advantage of an adversary $\mathcal{A}$ in breaking the ECDLP in $\mathbf{G}$ is defined by

$$\mathsf{Adv}_{\mathcal{A}}^{\mathrm{ECDLP}}(1^\kappa) = \Pr[\mathcal{A}(P, Q = [a]P) = a \mid a \xleftarrow{\$} \mathbf{Z}_q^*].$$

We say that the ECDL assumption holds for the group $\mathbf{G}$, if for any probabilistic polynomial time (PPT) adversary $\mathcal{A}$, the advantage $\mathsf{Adv}_{\mathcal{A}}^{\mathrm{ECDLP}}(1^\kappa)$ is a negligible function in the security parameter κ.

A bilinear group parameter generator $\mathcal{G}$ is an algorithm that takes as input a security parameter κ and outputs a bilinear group setting $(q, \mathbf{G}_1, \mathbf{G}_T, \hat{e})$, where $\mathbf{G}_1$ and $\mathbf{G}_T$ are a cyclic additive group and a multiplicative group of prime order q, respectively, and $\hat{e} \colon \mathbf{G}_1 \times \mathbf{G}_1 \to \mathbf{G}_T$ is a bilinear pairing with the following properties:

- Bilinearity: For $P_1, P_2 \xleftarrow{\$} \mathbf{G}_1$ and $a, b \xleftarrow{\$} \mathbf{Z}_q^*$, we have $\hat{e}([a]P_1, [b]P_2) = \hat{e}(P_1, P_2)^{ab}$.
- Non-degeneracy: There exists $P_1, Q_1 \in \mathbf{G}_1$ such that $\hat{e}(P_1, Q_1) \ne 1_{\mathbf{G}_T}$.
- Computability: There is an efficient algorithm to compute $\hat{e}(P_1, Q_1)$ for $P_1, Q_1 \xleftarrow{\$} \mathbf{G}_1$.

Definition 2. *Given a bilinear group setting* $(q, \mathbf{G}_1, \mathbf{G}_T, \hat{e})$ *generated by* $\mathcal{G}(1^\kappa)$, *define two distributions*

$$\mathcal{D}_0(1^\kappa) \stackrel{\text{def}}{=} \{P_1, [a]P_1, [b]P_1, [c]P_1, \hat{e}(P_1, P_1)^z\}$$

$$\mathcal{D}_1(1^\kappa) \stackrel{\text{def}}{=} \{P_1, [a]P_1, [b]P_1, [c]P_1, \hat{e}(P_1, P_1)^{abc}\}$$

where $a, b, c, z \stackrel{\$}{\leftarrow} \mathbf{Z}_q^*$, $P_1 \stackrel{\$}{\leftarrow} \mathbf{G}_1$, *the decisional bilinear Diffie-Hellman problem (DBDHP) in* $(q, \mathbf{G}_1, \mathbf{G}_T, \hat{e})$ *is to determine whether* $\hat{e}(P_1, P_1)^z = \hat{e}(P_1, P_1)^{abc}$.

The advantage of an adversary $\mathcal{A}$ in breaking DBDHP in $(q, \mathbf{G}_1, \mathbf{G}_T, \hat{e})$ is defined by

$$\mathsf{Adv}_{\mathcal{A}}^{\text{DBDHP}}(1^\kappa) = |\Pr[\mathcal{D}_0(1^\kappa) \to 1] - \Pr[\mathcal{D}_1(1^\kappa) \to 1]|$$

We say that the DBDH assumption holds for $(q, \mathbf{G}_1, \mathbf{G}_T, \hat{e})$, if for any PPT adversary $\mathcal{A}$, the advantage $\mathsf{Adv}_{\mathcal{A}}^{\text{DBDHP}}(1^\kappa)$ is a negligible function in the security parameter κ.

3 Privacy-Preserving Pseudonym and Attribute-based SignCryption Scheme

A P3ASC scheme consists of the following six polynomial-time algorithms:

- Setup: The probabilistic setup algorithm is run by the PKG. It takes as input a security parameter κ and an attribute universe $\boldsymbol{\Omega}$. It outputs the public system parameters mpk, and the master secret key msk which is known only to the PKG.
- PIDKeyGen: The probabilistic pseudonym-based private key generation algorithm is run by the PKG. It takes as input mpk, msk, and a real user identity id. It outputs a pseudonym pid and a private key sk_{pid} corresponding to the pseudonym.
- ABKeyGen: The probabilistic attribute-based private key generation algorithm is run by the PKG. It takes as input mpk, msk, and an access structure $\mathbb{A}$ assigned to a user. It outputs a private key $dk_{\mathbb{A}}$ corresponding to the access structure $\mathbb{A}$.
- SignCrypt: The probabilistic signcrypt algorithm is run by a sender. It takes as input mpk, a message Msg, a sender's pseudonym-based private key sk_{pid}, and a set $\boldsymbol{\omega}$ of descriptive attributes. It outputs a signcrypted ciphertext Sct.
- PubVerify: The deterministic public verifiability algorithm is run by any receivers. It takes as input mpk, a signcrypted ciphertext Sct, a sender's pseudonym pid, and a set $\boldsymbol{\omega}$ of descriptive attributes. It outputs a bit b which is 1 if Sct is generated by the sender, or 0 if Sct is not generated by the sender.
- UnSigncrypt: The deterministic unsigncryption algorithm is run by a receiver. It takes as input mpk, a signcrypted ciphertext Sct, a sender's pseudonym pid, a set $\boldsymbol{\omega}$ of descriptive attributes, and a receiver's attribute-based private key $dk_{\mathbb{A}}$. It outputs Msg if $\mathbb{A}(\boldsymbol{\omega}) = 1$. Otherwise it outputs $\perp$.

The set of algorithms must satisfy the following consistency requirement:

$$\mathsf{Setup}(1^\kappa, \Omega) \to (mpk, msk), \mathrm{Msg} \xleftarrow{\$} \mathbf{M}, \mathsf{id} \xleftarrow{\$} \mathbf{ID},$$
$$\mathsf{PIDKeyGen}(mpk, msk, \mathsf{id}) \to (\mathsf{pid}, sk_{\mathsf{pid}}),$$
$$\mathsf{ABKeyGen}(mpk, msk, \mathbb{A}) \to dk_\mathbb{A},$$
$$\mathsf{SignCrypt}(mpk, sk_{\mathsf{pid}}, \boldsymbol{\omega}, \mathrm{Msg}) \to \mathrm{Sct}, \; \boldsymbol{\omega} \in \Omega$$

$$\text{If } \mathbb{A}(\boldsymbol{\omega}) = 1 \Rightarrow \begin{cases} \mathsf{PubVerify}(mpk, \mathsf{pid}, \boldsymbol{\omega}, \mathrm{Sct}) = 1 \\ \mathsf{UnSignCrypt}(mpk, dk_\mathbb{A}, \mathsf{pid}, \boldsymbol{\omega}, \mathrm{Sct}) = \mathrm{Msg} \end{cases}$$

A P3ASC scheme should satisfy confidentiality and unforgeability. For the confidentiality, we consider the following indistinguishability against adaptive chosen plaintext attack (IND-CPA) game played between a challenger $\mathcal{C}$ and an adversary $\mathcal{A}$ in the selective-set model [8].

- **Init:** $\mathcal{A}$ declares a set of attributes, $\boldsymbol{\omega}^*$.
- **Setup:** $\mathcal{C}$ runs the Setup algorithm, gives mpk to $\mathcal{A}$, while keeps msk secret.
- **Phase 1:** $\mathcal{A}$ is allowed to issue the following queries adaptively.
  - Singing private key query on an identity id_i. $\mathcal{C}$ runs the PIDKeyGen algorithm, and sends $(\mathsf{pid}_i, sk_{\mathsf{pid}_i})$ back to $\mathcal{A}$.
  - Decrypting private key query on an access structures $\mathbb{A}_j$. If $\mathbb{A}_j(\boldsymbol{\omega}^*) \neq 1$, then $\mathcal{C}$ runs the ABKeyGen algorithm, and sends $dk_{\mathbb{A}_j}$ back to $\mathcal{A}$. Otherwise, $\mathcal{C}$ rejects the request.
- **Challenge:** $\mathcal{A}$ submits two equal length messages $(\mathrm{Msg}_0, \mathrm{Msg}_1)$, and an identity id to $\mathcal{C}$. Then, $\mathcal{C}$ flips a random coin b, runs $\mathsf{PIDKeyGen}(mpk, msk, \mathsf{id}) \to (\mathsf{pid}, sk_{\mathsf{pid}})$ and $\mathsf{Signcrypt}(mpk, sk_{\mathsf{pid}}, \boldsymbol{\omega}^*, \mathrm{Msg}_b) \to \mathrm{Sct}^*$ in sequence. Finally, $\mathcal{C}$ sends Sct^* to $\mathcal{A}$.
- **Phase 2:** Phase 1 is repeated.
- **Guess:** $\mathcal{A}$ outputs a guess b' of b.

The advantage of $\mathcal{A}$ in the above game is defined as

$$\mathrm{Adv}_{\mathcal{A}}^{\text{IND-CPA}}(1^\kappa) = \Pr[b' = b] - \frac{1}{2}.$$

Definition 3. *A P3ASC scheme is said to be IND-CPA secure in the selective-set model if $Adv_{\mathcal{A}}^{IND\text{-}CPA}(1^\kappa)$ is negligible in the security parameter κ.*

For the unforgeability, we consider the following existential unforgeability against adaptive chosen message and pseudonyms attack (UF-CMPA) game played between a challenger $\mathcal{C}$ and a forger $\mathcal{F}$.

- **Setup:** Same as in the above IND-CPA game.
- **Find:** $\mathcal{F}$ is allowed to issue the following queries adaptively.
  - Singing private key query. Same as in the above IND-CPA game.
  - Decrypting private key query. Upon receiving decryption private key query on an access structure $\mathbb{A}_j$, $\mathcal{C}$ runs $\mathsf{ABKeyGen}(mpk, msk, \mathbb{A}_j) \to dk_{\mathbb{A}_j}$, and sends $dk_{\mathbb{A}_j}$ back to $\mathcal{F}$.

- Signcrypt query on $\langle \text{Msg}, sk_{\text{pid}}, \omega \rangle$. $\mathcal{C}$ runs $\text{Signcrypt}(mpk, sk_{\text{pid}}, \omega,$ Msg) $\rightarrow$ Sct successively. Finally, $\mathcal{C}$ sends Sct back to $\mathcal{F}$.
- **Forgery:** $\mathcal{F}$ produces a new triple $\langle \text{Sct}^*, \omega^*, \text{pid}^* \rangle$. The only restriction is that $\langle \omega^*, \text{pid}^* \rangle$ does not appear in the set of previous Signcrypt queries during the Find stage and the signing private key of pid^* is never returned by any PIDKeyGen query.

$\mathcal{F}$ wins the game if

$$\text{PubVerify}(mpk, \text{pid}^*, \omega^*, \text{Sct}^*) = 1,$$

and the advantage of $\mathcal{F}$ is defined as the probability that it wins.

Definition 4. *A P3ASC scheme is said to be EUF-CMPA secure if no polynomially bounded adversary $\mathcal{F}$ has non-negligible advantage in the above game.*

3.1 Our Proposed P3ASC Scheme

Our proposed P3ASC scheme is described as follows.

- Setup: The PKG performs as follows.
  1. Generate an elliptic curve group $\mathbf{G} \overset{\text{def}}{=} \langle P \rangle$.
  2. Run $\mathcal{G}(1^\kappa) \rightarrow \langle q, \mathbf{G}_1, \mathbf{G}_T, \hat{e} \rangle$.
  3. Choose $P \overset{\$}{\leftarrow} \mathbf{G}$, $P_1 \overset{\$}{\leftarrow} \mathbf{G}_1$, $x, y \overset{\$}{\leftarrow} \mathbf{Z}_q^*$, $t_i \overset{\$}{\leftarrow} \mathbf{Z}_q^*$ for each attribute $\text{Atr}_i \in \mathbf{\Omega}$, four secure hash functions $H_1 : \mathbf{Z}_q^* \times \mathbf{G} \rightarrow \mathbf{ID}$, $H_2 : \mathbf{ID} \times \mathbf{G} \rightarrow \mathbf{Z}_q^*$, $H_3 : \mathbf{G} \times \mathbf{G}_T \times \mathbf{Z}_q^* \rightarrow \mathbf{Z}_q^*$, and $H_4 : \mathbf{G} \times \mathbf{G}_T \times \mathbf{G}_T \rightarrow \mathbf{Z}_q^*$.
  4. Compute $P_{\text{pub}} = [x]P$, $Y = \hat{e}(P_1, P_1)^y$ and $T_i = [t_i]P_1$ for $1 \leq i \leq |\mathbf{\Omega}|$.
  5. Set $msk = \{t_1, t_2, \cdots, t_{|\mathbf{\Omega}|}, x, y\}$.
  6. Publish $mpk = \{\mathbf{\Omega}, T_1, T_2, \cdots, T_{|\mathbf{\Omega}|}, P_{\text{pub}}, Y, H_1, H_2, H_3, H_4\}$.
- PIDKeyGen: A user with real identity id_U registers to the PKG to get his/her pseudonym pid_U and pseudonym-based private key sk_U by performing the following pseudonym-based key generation protocol. Figure 1 illustrates the procedure.
  1. The user chooses $\bar{r}_U \overset{\$}{\leftarrow} \mathbf{Z}_q^*$, computes $\bar{R}_U = [\bar{r}_U]P$, and sends a pseudonym-based private key request $(\bar{R}_U, \text{id}_U)$ to the PKG.
  2. Upon receiving the private key request, the PKG first verifies id_U. If it is valid, then the PKG picks $\hat{r}_U \overset{\$}{\leftarrow} \mathbf{Z}_q^*$, computes $\hat{R}_U = [\hat{r}_U]P$, $R_U = \bar{R}_U + \hat{R}_U$, $\text{pid}_U = H_1(x, R_U) \oplus \text{pid}_U$, $c_U = H_2(\text{pid}_U, R_U)$ and $\widehat{sk}_U = \hat{r}_U + c_U \cdot x \mod q$. Finally, the PKG sends $(\text{pid}_U, \widehat{sk}_U, \hat{R}_U)$ to the user via a secure channel.
  3. Upon receiving the response from the PKG, the user computes $R_U = \bar{R}_U + \hat{R}_U$, $c_U = H_2(\text{pid}_U, R_U)$ and $sk_U = \bar{r}_U + \widehat{sk}_U \mod q$, sets the corresponding public key $Q_U = [sk_U]P$, and checks the following equation:

$$Q_U \overset{?}{=} R_U + [c_U]P_{\text{pub}}$$

If it holds, the user stores the tuple (pid_U, R_U) and the corresponding private key sk_U.

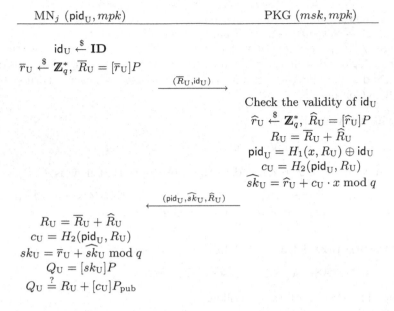

Fig. 1. Pseudonym-based key generation protocol

- ABKeyGen: A user sends an attribute-based private key request to the PKG, and the PKG performs as follows.
  1. Assign a linear secret sharing scheme for access structure $\mathbb{A}$ described by $(\mathbf{M}_{\ell \times n}, \rho)$ to the user.
  2. Choose $u_i \xleftarrow{\$} \mathbf{Z}_q^*$ for $1 \leq i \leq n$ such that $\sum_{i=1}^n u_i = y$, and set $\boldsymbol{u} = (u_1, u_2, \ldots, u_n)$.
  3. Compute $\lambda_i = <\mathbf{M}_i, \boldsymbol{u}>$ and $D_i = [\lambda_i / t_{\rho(i)}]P$ for each row vector $\mathbf{M}_i$ of $\mathbf{M}_{\ell \times n}$.
  4. Send the attribute-based decryption key $dk_{\mathbb{A}} = \{D_i\}_{i=1}^\ell$ associated with the access structure $\mathbb{A}$ to the user.
- Signcrypt: To signcrypt a message Msg $\in \mathbf{G}_T$ along with a set $\boldsymbol{\omega}$ of attributes, a sender with pseudonym pid_U performs as follows.
  1. Compute $c_U = H_2(\mathsf{pid}_U, R_U)$.
  2. Choose $s \xleftarrow{\$} \mathbf{Z}_q^*$.
  3. Compute $A = [s]P$, $C' = \mathrm{Msg} \cdot Y^s$, $h_3 = H_3(A, C', c_U)$, $\sigma = s + h_3 \cdot sk_U$, $h_4 = H_4(A, \mathrm{Msg}, Y^s)$, and $C_i = [s]T_i$ for $1 \leq i \leq |\boldsymbol{\omega}|$.
  4. Output Sct $= \{\boldsymbol{\omega}, \mathsf{pid}_U, R_U, C', \{C_i\}_{i=1}^{|\boldsymbol{\omega}|}, A, \sigma, h_4\}$
- PubVerify: Any receiver can check the validity of the signcrypted ciphertext Sct against sender's pseudonym pid_U as follows.
  1. Compute $c_U = H_2(\mathsf{pid}_U, R_U)$ and $h_3 = H_3(A, C', c_U)$.
  2. Check $[\sigma]P \overset{?}{=} A + [h_3](R_U + [c_U]P_{\mathrm{pub}})$. It outputs 1 if the equation holds, or 0 if the equation does not hold.

– UnSigncrypt: A receiver uses his decryption private key $dk_\mathbb{A}$ associated to the access structure $\mathbb{A}$ described by $(\mathbf{M}_{\ell \times n}, \rho)$ to recover and verify the signcrypted ciphertext Sct $= \{\omega, \mathsf{pid}_U, R_U, C', \{C_i\}_{i=1}^{|\omega|}, A, \sigma, h_4\}$ as follows.

1. Determine $\mathbb{A}(\omega) \overset{?}{=} 1$. If not, the receiver rejects the signcrypted ciphertext Sct.

2. Validate the signcrypted ciphertext Sct as any receiver performs in the PubVerify algorithm.

3. Define $\mathbf{I} = \{i | \rho(i) \in \omega\} \subset \{1, 2, \ldots, \ell\}$, and let $\{\mu_i\}$ be a set of constants such that if $\{\lambda_i\}$ are valid shares of y according to $(\mathbf{M}_{\ell \times n}, \rho)$, then $\sum_{i \in \mathbf{I}} \lambda_i \cdot \mu_i = y$.

4. Compute $V = \prod_{\rho(i) \in \omega} \hat{e}(D_i, C_{\rho(i)})^{\mu_i}$ and $\text{Msg}' = C'/V$.

5. Check $H_4(A, \text{Msg}', V) \overset{?}{=} h_4$. If it holds, the receiver accepts and outputs the message Msg. Otherwise, rejects and outputs $\perp$.

Theorem 1. *Our P3ASC scheme satisfies consistency requirement.*

Proof. Consistency requirement can be verified as follows.

$$[\sigma]P = [s + h_3 \cdot sk_U]P = [s]P + [h_3][sk_U]P$$
$$= A + [h_3](R_U + [c_U]P_{\text{pub}})$$
$$V = \prod_{\rho(i) \in \omega} \hat{e}(D_i, C_{\rho(i)})^{\mu_i} = \prod_{\rho(i) \in \omega} \hat{e}([\lambda_i/t_{\rho(i)}]P, [s \cdot t_{\rho(i)}]P)^{\mu_i}$$
$$= \prod_{\rho(i) \in \omega} \hat{e}(P, P)^{s \cdot \lambda_i \cdot \mu_i} = \hat{e}(P, P)^{s \sum_{\rho(i) \in \omega} \lambda_i \cdot \mu_i}$$
$$= \hat{e}(P, P)^{sy}$$
$$\text{Msg}' = C'/V = \text{Msg} \cdot Y^s / \hat{e}(P, P)^{sy}$$
$$= \text{Msg}.$$

Theorem 2. *Our P3ASC scheme satisfies the conditional anonymity for the sender.*

Proof. In the PIDKeyGen, sender can choose a family of pseudonyms and obtain associated private keys by running a Schnorr-like lightweight identity-based blind signature scheme with the PKG ([18–20]). Although the signcrypted message Sct must include a pseudonym of the sender and R_U. However, anyone, except the PKG, cannot extract sender's real identity id_U because they have no idea of the master secret key x. Furthermore, there is no linkage between these pseudonyms, anyone, except the PKG, cannot link two sessions initiated by the same sender. Of course, the PKG can extract the sender's real identity by computing $\mathsf{id}_U = \mathsf{pid}_U \oplus H_1(x, R_U)$. Thus, our P3ASC scheme achieves the conditional anonymity for the sender.

Theorem 3. *Our P3ASC scheme is IND-CPA secure in the selective-set model under the DBDH assumption.*

Proof. We will give detailed security proof in the full version due to the space limitation.

Theorem 4. *Our P3ASC scheme is EUF-CMA secure in the adaptive model under the ECDL assumption.*

Proof. We will give detailed security proof in the full version due to the space limitation.

4   Privacy Preserving Cloud-Based Mobile Healthcare System

The general architecture and message sequence of our privacy-preserving cloud-based mobile healthcare system is shown in Fig. 2. Three types of users are supported by our proposed system:

- PHI owner who generates personal health data collected from wireless body sensor network, creates signcrypted ciphertexts and forward them to the medical cloud service provider (CSP).
- PHI reader who can only read a PHI owner's PHI.
- PHI writer who can access a PHI owner's PHI, but also can modify a PHI owner's PHI, e.g., an authorized doctor can generate medical data for a PHI owner.

There are five essential participants in our cloud-based mobile healthcare system: hospital authority (HA), PHI Owners, medical CSP, PHI readers, and PHI writers. We assume that all communications between participants are secured by transport layer security (TLS) protocol.

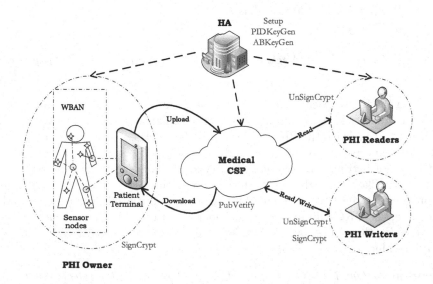

Fig. 2. Architecture of proposed cloud-based mobile healthcare system

- HA, who acts as the PKG. HA is responsible for generating system public parameters, issuing pseudonym-based private keys for PHI owners and PHI writers, and attribute-based private keys for PHI writers and PHI readers.
- PHI Owners, who carry multiple wearable or implanted sensors and a patient terminal. Those sensors can sense and process vital signs or environmental parameters, and transfer the relevant data to the patient terminal. Typically, patient terminal is equipped with mobile health application and database collection and storage functions with the ability for mobile communication. PHI owners register themselves to the HA by sending their real identity, and the HA allocates pseudo-identity to the PHI owner, which is to be used for all the communications in the network. Thus, the actual identity of the PHI owner is concealed.
- Medical CSP, who keeps patient related data of registered users and provides various services to the registered users. We assume that the medical CSP is honest-but-curious, which means that the medical CSP will perfectly execute the protocol specifications, but intend to extract the patient's private personal health information.
- PHI readers, who are allowed to view a PHI owner's PHI. It can be doctors, nurses, researchers, insurance company employees, etc.
- PHI writers, who are allowed to view and update a PHI owner's PHI. It can be doctors who may access the patients' medical information and provide medical services.

5   Conclusions

To achieve medical data security (confidentiality, integrity, authenticity and access control) and user privacy in mobile health cloud, we introduce a new cryptographic primitive named privacy-preserving pseudonym and attribute-based signcryption scheme, propose a provable secure construction and present a novel secure and efficient cloud-based mobile healthcare system by exploiting our proposed construction. For future work, we plan to further investigate and implement the proposed system in a suitable cloud platform. We will also evaluate the security and performance of the proposed system after being implemented and compare them with the most related work in the area.

Acknowledgments. This research is jointly funded by Science and Technology Program of Guangzhou (Grant No. 201707010358), and the Opening Project of Shanghai Key Laboratory of Integrated Administration Technologies for Information Security (Grant No. AGK201707).

References

1. Negra, R., Jemili, I., Belghith, A.: Wireless body area networks: applications and technologies. Procedia Comput. Sci. **83**, 1274–1281 (2016)
2. Kang, J., Adibi, S.: A review of security protocols in mHealth Wireless Body Area Networks (WBAN). In: Doss, R., Piramuthu, S., Zhou, W. (eds.) FNSS 2015. CCIS, vol. 523, pp. 61–83. Springer, Cham (2015). https://doi.org/10.1007/978-3-319-19210-9_5
3. Sadiku, M.N.O., Musa, S.M., Momoh, O.D.: Cloud computing: opportunities and challenges. IEEE Potentials **33**(1), 34–36 (2014)
4. Buchade, A.R., Ingle, R.: Key management for cloud data storage: methods and comparisons. In: Fourth International Conference on Advanced Computing Communication Technologies, pp. 263–270. IEEE Press (2014)
5. Patil, H.K., Seshadri, R.: Big data security and privacy issues in healthcare. In: IEEE International Congress on Big Data, pp. 762–765. IEEE (2014)
6. Samaher, A.J., Ibrahim, A.S., Mohammad, S., Shahaboddin, S.: Survey of main challenges (security and privacy) in wireless body area networks for healthcare applications. Egypt. Inform. J. **18**(2), 113–122 (2017)
7. Sahai, A., Waters, B.: Fuzzy identity-based encryption. In: Cramer, R. (ed.) EURO-CRYPT 2005. LNCS, vol. 3494, pp. 457–473. Springer, Heidelberg (2005). https://doi.org/10.1007/11426639_27
8. Goyal, V., Pandey, O., Sahai, A., Waters, B.: Attribute based encryption for fine-grained access conrol of encrypted data. In ACM conference on Computer and Communications Security, pp. 89–98 (2006)
9. Bethencourt, J., Sahai, A., Waters, B.: Ciphertext-policy attribute-based encryption. In: IEEE Symposium on Security and Privacy, pp. 321–334. IEEE Press (2007)
10. Waters, B.: Ciphertext-policy attribute-based encryption: an expressive, efficient, and provably secure realization. In: Catalano, D., Fazio, N., Gennaro, R., Nicolosi, A. (eds.) PKC 2011. LNCS, vol. 6571, pp. 53–70. Springer, Heidelberg (2011). https://doi.org/10.1007/978-3-642-19379-8_4
11. Attrapadung, N., Libert, B., de Panafieu, E.: Expressive key-policy attribute-based encryption with constant-size ciphertexts. In: Catalano, D., Fazio, N., Gennaro, R., Nicolosi, A. (eds.) PKC 2011. LNCS, vol. 6571, pp. 90–108. Springer, Heidelberg (2011). https://doi.org/10.1007/978-3-642-19379-8_6
12. Pirretti, M., Traynor, P., McDaniel, P., Waters, B.: Secure attribute-based systems. J. Comput. Secur. **18**(5), 799–837 (2010)
13. Li, M., Yu, S.C., Zheng, Y., Ren, K., Lou, W.J.: Scalable and secure sharing of personal health records in cloud computing using attribute-based encryption. IEEE Trans. Parallel Distrib. Syst. **24**(1), 131–143 (2013)
14. Wang, C.J., Xu, X.L., Shi, D.Y., Fang, J.: Privacy-preserving cloud-based personal health record system using attribute-based encryption and anonymous multi-receiver identity-based encryption. Informatica **39**(4), 375–382 (2015)
15. Yu, S., Wang, C., Ren, K., Lou, W.: Achieving secure, scalable, and fine-grained data access control in cloud computing. In: Proceedings IEEE INFOCOM, pp. 1–9 (2010)
16. Tan, Y.L., Goi, B.M., Komiya, R., Phan, R.: Design and implementation of key-policy attribute-based encryption in body sensor network. Int. J. Cryptol. Res. **4**(1), 84–101 (2013)

17. Maji, H.K., Prabhakaran, M., Rosulek, M.: Attribute-based signatures. In: Kiayias, A. (ed.) CT-RSA 2011. LNCS, vol. 6558, pp. 376–392. Springer, Heidelberg (2011). https://doi.org/10.1007/978-3-642-19074-2_24
18. Pointcheval, D., Stern, J.: Provably secure blind signature schemes. In: Kim, K., Matsumoto, T. (eds.) ASIACRYPT 1996. LNCS, vol. 1163, pp. 252–265. Springer, Heidelberg (1996). https://doi.org/10.1007/BFb0034852
19. Galindo, D., Garcia, F.D.: A Schnorr-like lightweight identity-based signature scheme. In: Preneel, B. (ed.) AFRICACRYPT 2009. LNCS, vol. 5580, pp. 135–148. Springer, Heidelberg (2009). https://doi.org/10.1007/978-3-642-02384-2_9
20. Chatterjee, S., Kamath, C., Kumar, V.: Galindo-Garcia identity-based signature revisited. In: Kwon, T., Lee, M.-K., Kwon, D. (eds.) ICISC 2012. LNCS, vol. 7839, pp. 456–471. Springer, Heidelberg (2013). https://doi.org/10.1007/978-3-642-37682-5_32

S7commTrace: A High Interactive Honeypot for Industrial Control System Based on S7 Protocol

Feng Xiao[1(✉)], Enhong Chen[1], and Qiang Xu[2]

[1] Anhui Province Key Laboratory of Big Data Analysis and Application,
School of Computer Science and Technology,
University of Science and Technology of China, Hefei, China
xiaof686@mail.ustc.edu.cn, cheneh@ustc.edu.cn
[2] Electronic Engineering Institute of Hefei, Hefei, China
yfnm126@126.com

Abstract. Intensively happened cyber-attacks against industrial control system pose a serious threat to the critical national infrastructure. It is significant to capture the detection and the attacking data for industrial control system by means of honeypot technology, as it provides the ability of situation awareness to reveal potential attackers and their motivations before a fatal attack happens. We develop a high interactive honeypot for industrial control system-S7commTrace, based on Siemens' S7 protocol. S7commTrace supports more function codes and sub-function codes in protocol simulation, and improves the depth of interaction with the attacker to induce more high-level attacks effectively. A series of comparative experiments is carried out between S7commTrace and Conpot, by deploying these two kinds of honeypots under the same circumstance in four countries. Data captured by these two kinds of honeypots is analyzed respectively in four dimensions, which are query results in Shodan, count of data and valid data, coverage of function code and diversity of source IP address. Experiment results show that S7commTrace has better performance over Conpot.

Keywords: Industrial control system · Honeypot · S7 · Conpot

1 Introduction

With the development of "Industry 4.0" in the world, more and more industrial control systems access to the Internet, which improves the production efficiency greatly. At the same time, the security threats in cyberspace begin to penetrate into industrial control systems. Stuxnet worm was disclosed in June 2010 for the first time, which is the first worm attacking the energy infrastructure [1,2]. In 2014 the hackers attacked a steel plant in Germany through manipulating and destroying the control system, so that the blast furnace could not be closed properly, resulting in a huge loss [3]. On December 23, 2015, the Ukrainian power

© Springer International Publishing AG, part of Springer Nature 2018
S. Qing et al. (Eds.): ICICS 2017, LNCS 10631, pp. 412–423, 2018.
https://doi.org/10.1007/978-3-319-89500-0_36

network suffered a hacker attack, which was the first successful attack to the power grid, resulting in hundreds of thousands users suffering power blackout for hours [4]. On June 12, 2017, the security vendor ESET disclosed an industrial control network attack weapons named as win32/Industroyer, which implemented malicious attacks on power substation system. It can directly control the circuit breaker to power the substation off [5].

Industrial control systems are highly interconnected and interdependent with the critical national infrastructure [6]. Once a cyberspace security incident occurs in the industrial control systems, it has a significant impact on the country's political and economic and other aspects. Therefore, different from the traditional security strategy in Internet, security incidents in industrial control system should not be deal with after its occurrence. As we all know, every cyberspace attack was preceded by a probe to host(s) or network [7]. So it is critical for the industrial control system to build the ability of situation awareness by capturing the detection and attacking data passively and to reveal potential attackers and their motivations before a fatal attack happens.

Based on Siemens' S7 communications protocol, we develop S7commTrace which is a kind of high interactive honeypot for industrial control system. Furthermore, we deploy S7commTrace and Conpot under the same circumstance in four countries. According to the comparative experiments on the captured data by these two kinds of honeypots in the following 20 days and the searching results in Shodan after 30 days later, S7commTrace shows better performance than Conpot.

2   Related Work

Honeypot is a kind of security resource that is used to attract the attacker for illegal application without any business utility [8]. Honeypot technology is a method to set some of the hosts, network services or information as a bait, to induce attackers, so that the behavior of attack can be captured and analyzed [9]. Honeypots can be used to better understand the landscape of where these attacks are originating [10]. Venkat Pothamsetty and Matthew Franz of the Cisco Critical Infrastructure Assurance Group (CIAG) released the first PLC honeypot in 2004. They used Honeyd architecture to simulate the Modbus industrial control protocol [11]. Rist et al. [12] released Conpot, which was a open source low interactive honeypot for industrial control system in May 2013. Conpot stopped updating in November 2015. Although it supports up to seven kinds of protocols (S7, Modbus, BACnet, HTTP, Kamstrup, SNMP, IPMI), all of them are low interactive and only support a small number of function codes.

Serbanescu et al. [13] analyzed the attractiveness of the industrial equipment exposed in the public network to the attacker and the behavior of the attacker by setting low interactive ICS honeypot on a large scale. Jicha et al. [10] deployed 12 Conpot SCADA Honeypot on AWS to evaluate the attractiveness and behavior in detail, by analyzing the scan results of NMAP and SHODAN. Buza et al. [14] divided the honeypot into three categories according to the complexity: low interaction, high interaction and hybrid. They summarized the development of related project about honeypot for industrial control system since 2004, including: CIAG SCADA HoneyNet Project, Honeyd, Digital Bond SCADA HoneyNet, Conpot Project. After analyzing the advantages and disadvantages of these projects, they designed and developed the Crysys PLC honeypot (CryPLH), which supported Http, Https, SNMP, and Step 7.

Search engine for Internet-accessed devices, which is different from the traditional content search engine, probes the Internet network equipment information, stores the results in the database, and provides web and API query interface. Commonly used search engines for Internet- accessed devices are Shodan [15] Censys [16,17] and ZoomEye [18]. Shodan uses the industrial control protocol directly to crawl the industrial control equipment on the Internet, and visualized the location and other information of them [19]. It is not only convenient for network security practitioners, but also facilitates the attacker to locate victims. Furthermore it may expose the existence of honeypots. Bodenheim et al. [20] deployed four Allen-Bradley ControlLogix 1756-L61 PLCs on the Internet to check Shadon's capabilities and found that four PLCs were all indexed by Shodan within 19 days. Subsequently, he proposed a solution to reduce the risk of exposure in Shodan by transforming the web service banner.

In summary, previous studies mainly focused on low interactive honeypots for industrial control system. Conpot is one of the most famous and advanced honeypot in recent years. Although it supports various industrial control protocols, Conpot is easy to be recognized as honeypot by cyberspace search engine for its characteristic of low interaction. CryPLH tries to improve the performance on interaction, but it still lacks of the capability of support real industrial control protocols. As we know, a deliberate and fatal network attack always starts with detections to target. If there is no response to the initial requests, attackers will abort their further operations. Therefore, it is quite necessary to develop a kind of high interactive honeypot based on industrial control protocols to capture detection and attacking data with good quality, while reducing the risk of being marked by cyberspace search engine.

3   Honeypot Based on S7 Protocol

S7 communications protocol is a Siemens proprietary protocol [21] running on programmable logic controllers (PLCs) of Siemens S7-300, 400, 1200 and 1500 series. It is suitable for either Ethernet, PROFIBUS or MPI networks. Because the objects of this study are those industrial control systems being accessed to the Internet, we only discuss the TCP-based S7 communications protocol in Ethernet networks. As shown in Fig. 1, S7 communications protocol packets are packed by COTP protocol, and then packed by TPKT protocol package for TCP connection. As shown in Fig. 2, the communication procedure of S7 protocol is divided into three stages. The first stage is to establish COTP connection, the second stage is to S7 communication setup, and the third stage is to exchange the request and the response for function code.

IP header	TCP header	TPKT header	COTP header	S7 data

Fig. 1. Header format of S7 communication packet

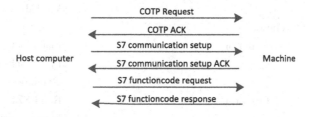

Fig. 2. Communication procedure of S7 protocol

3.1 Function Codes

The Magic flag of the S7 communications protocol is fixed to 0x32, and the following fields are S7 type, data unit ref, parameters length, data length, result info, parameters and data. In parameters field, the first byte stands for the function code of S7. Table 1 shows the optional function codes of S7. Communication Setup code is used to build a S7 connection, Read code helps the host computer to read data from PLC, Write code helps the host computer to write data to PLC. As for the codes of Request Download, Download Block, Download End, Download Start, Upload and Upload End, they are designed for downloading or uploading operations of blocks. PLC Control code covers the operations of Hot Run and Cool Run, while PLC Stop is used to turn off the device. When the function code is 0x00, it stands for system function which is used to check system settings or status. And the details are described by the 4-bits function group code and 1-byte subfunction code in the parameters field. System Functions further are divided into 7 groups, as shown in Table 2. Block function is used to read the block, and Time Function is used to check or set the device clock.

Table 1. System functions codes of S7

Code	Functions	Code	Functions	Code	Functions
0x00	System functions	0x1b	Download block	0x1f	Upload end
0x04	Read	0x1c	Download end	0x28	PLC control
0x05	Write	0x1d	Download start	0x29	PLC stop
0x1a	Request download	0x1e	Upload	0xf0	Communication setup

Table 2. System function group and corresponding subfunction

Function group code	Function	Subfunction code	Subfunction
1	Programmer commands	1	Request diag data
		2	VarTab
2	Cyclic data	1	Memory
3	Block function	1	List blocks
		2	List blocks of type
		3	Get block info
4	CPU function	1	Read SZL
		2	Message service
5	Security	1	PLC password
6	PBC BSEND/BRECV	None	None
7	Time function	1	Read clock
		2,3	Set clock
		4	Read clock (following)

3.2 S7commTrace

S7commTrace can be divided into four modules, including TCP communication module, S7 communications protocol simulation module, data storage module and user template, as shown in Fig. 3. TCP communication module is responsible for listening on TCP port 102, submitting the received data to the Protocol Simulation module, and replying to the remote peer. S7 communications protocol simulation module parses the received data according to the protocol format and obtains the valid contents at first. And then S7 communications protocol Simulation module generates the reply data referring to user template. At last, the reply data are submitted back to TCP communication module to be packaged. User template records all the user-defined information such as PLC serial number, manufacturer, and so on. The data storage module handles the request and response of data storage.

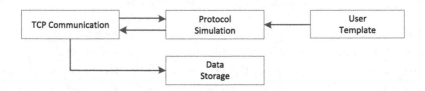

Fig. 3. Modules of S7commTrace

Cyber attacks against the S7 device are implemented based on some specific function codes, such as uploading, stopping, etc. And as we known, an experienced attacker usually tries to check the system status list (Read SZL) or do other operations before the execution of those significant function codes. Therefore, in order to record the attacker's communication data completely and accurately, a sophisticated honeypot should have as more responses to S7 function codes as possible to induce the attacker's further operations. After setting up a S7 communication, Conpot only support the subfunction code of Read SZL and reply a fixed value of SZL ID and index. As for other function codes, Conpot has no response to them. S7commTrace makes a great improvement over Conpot by responding to all the function codes and subfunction codes listed in Tables 1 and 2.

In order to fabricate the responding data, we request and record the real responses from a S7-300 PLC device firstly. And then by means of those real data, a user defined template is made in S7commTrace. At the same time, we customize unique settings of User Template among different S7commTrace honeypots, without changing the data format.

4   Evaluation

We deploy Conpot and S7commTrace honeypots in United States (US), German (GE), China (CN) and Singapore (SG) around the global area at the same time. The deployment utilize Aliyun (US, CN, SG) and Host1Plus (GE) as virtual host with configuration of 1.5 Ghz single core CPU, 1 GB RAM and 40 GB Disk. All the operation systems of virtual hosts are Ubuntu Server 16.04 64 bits. Every virtual host installs MySQL database to store data captured by local honeypot. Furthermore, two copies of the VPS are rented in every county to make sure that Conpot and S7commTrace are deployed under the same circumstance. The experiment lasts for 60 days.

4.1   Query Results in Shodan

According to the statistics of Bodenheim et al. [20], if a PLC device accesses to the Internet, it will be marked by Shodan up to 19 days later. Therefore, after 30 days of deployment, we search all the honeypots in Shodan. We find that all Conpot honeypots in four countries are indexed and marked as Conpot by Shodan, as shown in Fig. 4. But only one S7commTrace honeypot in Singapore is indexed by Shodan, and marked as Conpot. Considering this IP was used for Conpot deployment before the experiment, the search results may be affected. We deploy another new S7commTrace honeypot in Japan (JP), and it isn't indexed by Shodan after 30 days, as shown in Fig. 5. Table 3 makes a detailed comparison of how the two kinds of honeypots are indexed by Shodan. As we know, Shodan only detects but not indexes the real ICS device for security consideration. In the experiment, S7commTrace was not indexed by Shodan with capturing the real detection data of Shodan. This is a clear evidence which proves that S7commTrace vividly simulates a PLC and is recognized as a physical device. Therefore, the risk of exposure by cyber space search engines is greatly reduced.

418   F. Xiao et al.

Fig. 4. Lables of Conpot in Shodan

Fig. 5. Lables of Conpot in Shodan

Table 3. Conpot and S7commTrace honeypots indexed by Shodan

Locations	Conpot	S7commTrace
US	Indexed and marked as Conpot	Not being indexed
GE	Indexed and marked as Conpot	Not being indexed
CN	Indexed and marked as Conpot	Not being indexed
SG	Indexed and marked as Conpot	Indexed and marked as Conpot
JP	–	Not being indexed

4.2 Count of Data and Valid Data

In order to avoid the situation that the honeypots may not be detected at the beginning, we use the data from 31 days to 50 days after deployment. If we define an uninterrupted TCP communication connection as a session, Conpot records 17 sessions and S7commTrace records 56 sessions. Compared with Conpot honeypot, the number of session is significantly increased in every S7commTrace honeypot, as shown in Table 4. As each session contains a number of data requests, Conpot records a total of 472 data requests, while S7commTrace records a total of 1217 data requests. Compared with Conpot honeypot, the number of requests is increased to some extent in every S7commTrace honeypot, as shown in Table 5. Especially the S7commTrace honeypot in China, it records 9 times more requests than the Conpot honeypot. In fact, not all data recorded are in accordance with the format of S7 protocol. Ignoring such data, Conpot records a total of 82 valid requests, while S7commTrace records a total of 535 valid requests. Compared with Conpot honeypot, the number of valid request is significantly increased in every S7commTrace honeypot. On the purpose of checking the quality of the data, we calculate the rate of valid request in two kinds of honeypots. The average rate of valid request in Conpot is 17.37%, while the maximum rate does not exceed 22.78%. But in S7commTrace, the average rate increases to 43.96%, while the minimum rate is not less than 36.11%. Therefore, S7commTrace not only records more requests but also records more valid request, compared with Conpot. That means data quality is great improved in S7commTrace.

Table 4. Comparison of session number between Conpot and S7commTrace

Locations	Conpot	S7commTrace	Improvement
US	3	9	200.00%
GE	6	10	66.67%
CN	3	30	900.00%
SG	5	7	40.00%
Total	17	56	229.41%

Table 5. Comparison of request number between Conpot and S7commTrace

Locations	Requests			Valid requests			Valid rate		
	Con	S7	Imp	Con	S7	Imp	Con	S7	Imp
US	126	157	24.60%	11	61	454.55%	0.0873	0.3885	345.02%
GE	141	158	12.06%	31	62	100.00%	0.2199	0.3924	78.44%
CN	79	758	859.49%	18	360	1900.00%	0.2278	0.4749	108.47%
SG	126	144	14.29%	22	52	136.36%	0.1746	0.3611	106.82%
Total	472	1217	157.84%	82	535	552.44%	0.1737	0.4396	153.08%

Note: Con, S7, and Imp is short for Conpot, S7commTrace and Improvement.

4.3   Coverage of Function Code

When we analyze the function codes used in the data captured, we find that the data of Conpot only covers the function codes of COTP Connect, Communication Setup, and Read SZL. But the List Blocks function code is included in the data of S7commTrace in addition to the above three. Furthermore, function codes are also used more frequently in the data of S7commTrace than COTP, as shown in Table 6. Read SZL is the function code to the read system status with the parameters of SZL ID and SZL Index. In the data of Conpot, there are only two kinds of parameters, like (0x0011, 0x0001) and (0x001C, 0x0001). But in the data of S7commTrace, five different kinds of parameters are found, including (0x0011, 0x0001), (0x001C, 0x0001), (0x0011, 0x0000), (0x001C, 0x0000) and (0x0131, 0x0001).

Table 6. Comparison of function codes between Conpot and S7commTrace

Functions	Conpot	S7commTrace	Improvement
COTP connect	31	142	358.06%
Communication setup	21	106	404.76%
Read SZL	30	150	400.00%
List blocks	0	10	–

4.4 Diversity of Source IP Address

Conpot records data from 14 different IP addresses, while S7commTrace records data from 43 different IP addresses, as shown in Table 7. And the total number of different IP address is 49. As shown in Table 8, 11 IP addresses appear in at least two honeypots. Meanwhile 113.225.219.220 and 113.225.210.250 are recorded only by four S7commTrace honeypots but absent in all Conpot honeypots. According to the DNS query results, 10 of the 49 IP addresses point to Shodan's domain name with the suffix of shodan.io. 3 IP addresses point to the domain name of Electrical Engineering and Computer Science (EECS) Department of University of Michigan with the suffix of eecs.umich.edu. As we know EECS is one of the institutions which develop Censys [16,17]. Furthermore, 2 IP addresses point to BEACONLAB's domain name with the suffix of plcscan.org. Different with Shodan and Censys, BEACONLAB specializes in safety research and practice on industrial control systems and provides related services [22]. As for other IP address, they are resolved to be dynamic domain name or none domain name.

Table 7. Comparison of IP source between Conpot and S7commTrace

Locations	Conpot	S7commTrace	Improvement
US	4	9	125.00%
GE	7	10	42.86%
CN	4	28	600.00%
SG	6	7	16.67%
Total	14	43	207.14%

As shown in Table 9, S7commTrace records more IP addresses of Shodan and Plcscan than Conpot, while they records the same IP addresses of Censys. Therefore, compared to Conpot, S7commTrace attracts more detections from famous search engines focusing on industrial control system. Conpot records 14 IP addresses located in 6 countries and regions, while S7commTrace records 43 IP addresses located in 10 countries and regions. Figure 6 shows how these IP addresses distribute geographically. In the world wide, detections recorded by S7commTrace are more widely distributed than those by Conpot.

Table 8. IP address recorded by Conpot and S7commTrace

IP	Conpot				S7commTrace			
	US	GE	CN	SG	US	GE	CN	SG
139.162.99.243	✓	✓	✓	✓	✓	✓	✓	✓
141.212.122.145	✓	✓	✓	–	✓	✓	–	✓
113.225.219.220	–	–	–	–	✓	✓	✓	✓
113.225.210.250	–	–	–	–	✓	✓	✓	✓
80.82.77.139	✓	–	–	✓	–	–	✓	–
71.6.146.185	–	✓	✓	–	–	–	–	–
188.138.125.44	–	–	✓	–	–	–	✓	–
120.132.93.150	–	–	✓	–	–	–	✓	–
141.212.122.96	–	✓	–	–	–	✓	–	–
141.212.122.48	–	✓	–	–	–	✓	–	–
66.240.219.146	–	–	–	✓	–	–	–	✓

Table 9. Comparison of IP addresses with static suffix between Conpot and S7commTrace

Domain	Conpot	S7commTrace
shodan.io	66.240.219.146	66.240.192.138 66.240.219.146
	66.240.236.119	71.6.158.166 71.6.165.200
	71.6.146.185	80.82.77.33 80.82.77.139
	80.82.77.139	89.248.167.131 198.20.70.114
eecs.umich.edu	141.212.122.48	141.212.122.48
	141.212.122.96	141.212.122.96
	141.212.122.145	141.212.122.145
plcscan.org	188.138.125.44	85.25.79.124
		188.138.125.44
		188.138.125.155

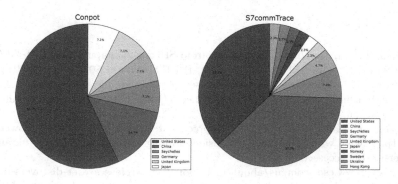

Fig. 6. Comparison of IP addresses distribution between Conpot and S7commTrace

5   Conclusions

We developed a kind of high interactive honeypot name as S7commTrace for industrial control system based on Siemens' S7 communications protocol. Through deploying Conpot and S7commTrace globally at the same time, we compared them from two dimensions: how they were indexed by cyberspace search engine, and the detection and attacking data they recorded. And thus we can draw the following in conclusion. Compared to the S7 component in Conpot, S7commTrace has the following advantages:

- S7commTrace supports more function codes and sub-function codes in protocol simulation, and improves the depth of interaction with the attacker to induce more high-level attacks effectively.
- S7commTrace has more realistic simulation of the PLC device, reduces the risk of honeypots being exposed by cyber space search engines.
- S7commTrace records more sessions and requests with higher rate of valid requests.
- S7commTrace attracts more network detections and attacks, and the recorded IP addresses are more widely distributed all around the world.

6   Future Work

S7commTrace only implements high interactive honeypot for S7 communications protocol. We will continue to develop high interactive honeypots for Modbus, BACnet, and Kamstrup which are already supported by Conpot. Furthermore we will focus on DNP3 and IEC104 which are not supported by Conpot. Another research work is the deployment of S7commTrace globally in 12 countries. Recently, S7commTrace has captured 42581 valid sessions, and we are committed to the analysis of fingerprint.

Acknowledgment. This study is supported by National Natural Science Foundation of China (U1605251).

References

1. Chen, T.M., Abu-Nimeh, S.: Lessons from Stuxnet. Comput. **44**(4), 91–93 (2011)
2. Kushner, D.: The real story of stuxnet. IEEE Spectrum **50**(3), 48–53 (2013)
3. Zetter, K.: A cyberattack has caused confirmed physical damage for the second time ever. http://www.wired.com//2015//01//german-steel-mill-hack-destruction. Accessed 8 July 2017
4. Zetter, K.: Inside the cunning, unprecedented hack of Ukraine's power grid. https://www.wired.com/2016/03/inside-cunning-unprecedented-hack-ukraines-power-grid/. Accessed 8 July 2017
5. https://www.eset.com/us/about/newsroom/press-releases/eset-discovers-dangerous-malware-designed-to-disrupt-industrial-control-systems/. Accessed 8 July 2017

6. Stouffer, K., et al.: Guide to industrial control systems (ICS) security. NIST special publication vol. 800, no. 82, p. 16 (2011)
7. Hink, R.C.B., Goseva-Popstojanova, K.: Characterization of cyberattacks aimed at integrated industrial control and enterprise systems: a case study. In: IEEE International Symposium on High Assurance Systems Engineering, pp. 149–156 (2016)
8. Spitzner, L.: Honeypots: Tracking Hackers. Addison-Wesley Longman Publishing Co. Inc., Boston (2002)
9. Zhuge, J.-W., et al.: Honeypot technology research and application. Ruanjian Xuebao/J. Softw. **24**(4), 825–842 (2013)
10. Jicha, A., et al.: SCADA honeypots: an in-depth analysis of Conpot. In: 2016 IEEE Conference on Intelligence and Security Informatics (ISI)
11. Pothamsetty, V., Franz, M.: SCADA Honeynet Project: Building Honeypots for Industrial Networks. SCADA Honeynet Project, 15 July 2005
12. CONPOT ICS/SCADA Honeypot. http://conpot.org/. Accessed 16 July 2017
13. Serbanescu, A.V., et al.: ICS threat analysis using a large-scale honeynet. In: Proceedings of the 3rd International Symposium for ICS & SCADA Cyber Security Research. British Computer Society (2015)
14. Buza, D.I., Juhász, F., Miru, G., Félegyházi, M., Holczer, T.: CryPLH: protecting smart energy systems from targeted attacks with a PLC honeypot. In: Cuellar, J. (ed.) SmartGridSec 2014. LNCS, vol. 8448, pp. 181–192. Springer, Cham (2014). https://doi.org/10.1007/978-3-319-10329-7_12
15. Shodan. https://www.shodan.io/. Accessed 15 July 2017
16. Censys. https://censys.io/. Accessed 15 July 2017
17. Durumeric, Z., et al.: A search engine backed by internet-wide scanning. In: Proceedings of the 22nd ACM SIGSAC Conference on Computer and Communications Security. ACM (2015)
18. Zoomeye. https://www.zoomeye.org/. Accessed 16 July 2017
19. Ics-radar. https://ics-radar.shodan.io/. Accessed 15 July 2017
20. Bodenheim, R., et al.: Evaluation of the ability of the Shodan search engine to identify Internet-facing industrial control devices. Int. J. Crit. Infrastruct. Protect. **7**(2), 114–123 (2014)
21. https://wiki.wireshark.org/S7comm. Accessed 15 July 2017
22. http://plcscan.org/blog/. Accessed 16 July 2017

Privacy Protection

Research on Clustering-Differential Privacy for Express Data Release

Tianying Chen$^{(\boxtimes)}$ and Haiyan Kang

Department of Information Security,
Beijing Information Science and Technology University, Beijing, China
1161490519@qq.com, kanghaiyan@126.com

Abstract. With the rapid development of "Internet +", the express delivery industry has exposed more privacy leakage problems. One way is the circulation of the express orders, and the other way is the express data release. For the second problem, this paper proposes a clustering-differential privacy preserving method combining with the theory of anonymization. Firstly, we use DBSCAN density clustering algorithm to initialize the original data set to achieve the first clustering. Secondly, in order to reduce the data generalization we combine the micro-aggregation technology to achieve the second clustering of the data set. Finally, adding Laplace noise to the clustering data record and correct the data that does not satisfy the differential privacy model to ensure the data availability. Simulation experiments show that the clustering-differential privacy preserving method can apply on the express data release, and it can keep higher data availability relative to the traditional differential privacy preserving.

Keywords: Express data release · Density clustering · Micro-aggregation

1 Introduction

With the rapid development of e-commerce, there has been unprecedented prosperity in China's express industry. Since 2011, the express business has increased by an average of more than 50% annually. As of December 20, 2016, the State Post Bureau announced that China's express business has reached 30 billion, and it continues to be ranked first in the world. The rapid development of express industry also inevitably brings about some privacy leakage problems. The circulation of express delivery order and the express data release are the main ways of express information leakage.

At present, the domestic related departments and some scholars have given a lot of suggestions and solutions to the issue of privacy leakage in the express delivery industry. The national postal office announced that the parcel delivery real-name registration system should be carried out from November 1, 2015 in order to cut off drugs circulation. Wei [1] proposed the customer's information leakage includes two aspects: The information leakage in the express delivery and the information leakage in the direct contact with the courier at the end of the express distribution. For the former, they proposed a new K-anonymous model to protect the of customers' privacy by randomly breaking the relationship between the attributes in the records. For the privacy leakage in the express order, Zhou [2] designed the express information

S. Qing et al. (Eds.): ICICS 2017, LNCS 10631, pp. 427–437, 2018.
https://doi.org/10.1007/978-3-319-89500-0_37

management system based on DES and RSA encryption technology. Yang [3] proposed personal privacy protection logistics system based on two-dimensional code technology to protect customer's information. That has solved the contradiction between the logistics information encryption and logistics process through the hierarchical encryption and permission grading. However, the above research focused on strengthening the protection of express order information alone. Relevant research on the express data release is rare. If data without privacy processing has been released, these messages will be inadvertently stolen by malicious individuals and institutions. And then it will pose a serious threat to personal safety. As for the data release, Chai [4] proposed to use the improved K-means clustering algorithm to cluster sensitive attributes to achieve the data table protection anonymously. According to the clustering analysis in the data mining and the problem of hidden attribute publishing in the clustering analysis, a new perturbation method NESDO based on synthetic data replacement is proposed by Chong [5]. The algorithm can effectively keep the clustering-data personalities and their common characteristics. Liu [6] combined anonymous technology to propose a data privacy protection method, which maintains the higher availability of published data by adding noise to anonymous data.

Combined with the existing literature, this paper proposes a clustering-differential privacy preserving method for express data release. Firstly, using DBSCAN density clustering algorithm initializes the original data set to achieve the first clustering. Secondly, in order to reduce the data generalization we combine the micro-aggregation technology to achieve the second clustering of the data set. Thirdly, considering that the clustering will lead to the information leakage, this paper uses Laplace noise mechanism to process the clustering data to meet the requirement of differential privacy protection model. Finally, correcting the data that does not satisfy the differential privacy model to ensure the data availability.

2 Related Concepts and Theories

2.1 Basic Concept

Definition 1 (Explicit Identifier). It can be referred to as EI. It is attribute that can uniquely identify the data record in the data table, such as name, ID number.

Definition 2 (Quasi-Identifiers). It can be referred to as QI. A quasi identifier property is a collection of attributes that can uniquely identify an individual after being linked to an external data table, such as gender and zip code.

Definition 3 (Sensitive Attribute). It can be referred to as SA. Sensitive attributes contain individual privacy information which do not want to be known by others, such as contact numbers, addresses. They need to be protected in data release. Sensitive attributes can be divided into single-dimensional sensitive attributes and multi-dimensional sensitive attributes.

There are several types of information stored in the express company database. For example, the sender/recipient's name, the gender, ID number, mobile phone number, the goods' price and so on. Table 1 lists the basic information on the express sheet. The courier numbers are given according to Yuantong express.

Table 1. Sender's basic information on the express sheet.

Tracking number	Sender name	Sender address	Sender phone
2688530748	Wang Ming	Shandong	153****7788
8853054869	Zhang Song	Hebei	186****0463
2688544749	Huang Rui	Henan	136****5633
8853558691	Liu Yang	Beijing	136****2786
8993074869	Li Ming	Shanxi	180****4633

Table 2. Recipient's basic information on the express sheet.

Tracking number	Recipient name	Recipient address	Recipient phone
2688530748	ZY	Zhejiang	152****2911
8853054869	LK	Jiangsu	180****2629
2688544749	WR	Shandong	136****4655
8853558691	LX	Jiangsu	137****7789
8993074869	ZM	Zhejiang	156****6722

As can be seen from Tables 1 and 2, the sender and recipient's basic information contains a lot of sensitive information. They need to be given corresponding protection before the data is released. Table 3 is the detailed information of recipient stored in the courier database. In Table 3, the recipient name, ID number is the explicit identifier. Zip code, gender, age (gotten from the recipient ID number) is Quasi-identifier. Phone number and recipient's address are sensitive attributes. If these are stolen by criminals, it will pose a threat to the recipient's security.

Table 3. Recipient's detailed information on the express database.

Name (EI)	ID number (EI)	Zip code (QI)	Gender (QI)	Age (QI)	Phone number (SA)	Address (SA)
ZY	3303031994***52	325024	M	23	152***2911	Wenzhou, Zhejiang
LK	3210021972***32	225002	F	45	180***2629	Yangzhou, Jiangsu
WR	4103032002***98	471000	F	15	136***4655	Luoyang, Henan
LX	3205061983***0X	215100	M	34	137***7789	Suzhou, Jiangsu
ZM	1401071977***92	030000	M	40	156***6722	Taiyuan, Shanxi

(Note: in Table 2, the 'address' should be more specific. For example, ZY's address is 5, 4th Floor, Unit 3, No. 1, Shengxing Road, Wenzhou City, Zhejiang Province. Due to the table restriction, we abbreviated the 'address' column.)

2.2   Micro-aggregation

Micro-aggregation technology is a kind of data anonymity scheme. Micro-aggregation [7] can be divided into two parts: k-division and aggregation. K-division can achieve intra class homogeneity as much as possible and class homogeneity as small as possible.

Definition 4 (K-division). There is a table $T(A_1, A_2 ... A_n)$. QI is Quasi-Identifiers of T. QI contains p attributes. The data table T is divided into g classes based on QI, n_i is the number of tuples for the class of i. For $\forall i$, $n_i \geq k$, $n = \sum_{i=1}^{g} n_i$, then the data table T is divided into k-division based on QI.

Definition 5 (Aggregation). There is a table $T(A_1, A_2 ... A_n)$. QI is Quasi-Identifiers of T. A k - division based on QI divides T into g classes. C_i is the tuple centroid for the class of i. For $i(i = 1, 2..., g)$, we use C_i to replace all the operation of the object of the class of i. And this process is called aggregation.

Definition 6 (Dissimilarity matrix). It refers to the storage of n objects between the two similarities. $d(j, i)$ is the quantitative representation of the object j and i dissimilarity. The closer the two objects are, the closer value of d is to zero. The value of d is calculated using Euclidean distance.

$$d(X, Y) = \left(\sum (X_i - Y_i)^2 \right)^{1/2} \tag{1}$$

2.3   Differential Privacy

Dwork proposed a new privacy protection definition [8–11] for database privacy disclosure in 2006. It is differential privacy. It can protect the privacy data effectively under the condition that the attacker has the greatest background knowledge. The main idea of differential privacy is to achieve privacy protection by adding noise to query and analysis results.

Definition 7 (*Differential privacy*). In non-interactive systems, the definition of differential privacy is as the following.

There is a random algorithm M. P_M is a set of all M outputs. For any two sets of data, D and D', which only has at least one different record and any subset S_M of P_M. If the algorithm M satisfies

$$P_r[M(D) \in S_M] \leq \exp(\varepsilon) \times [M(D') \in S_M] \tag{2}$$

Algorithm M satisfies the ε - differential privacy protection, where Pr [.] indicates that the probability of privacy being compromised. Pr [.] is determined by the randomness of algorithm A. The parameter 'ε' is called the privacy protection budget.

Definition 8 (*Privacy protection budget*). From the definition of differential privacy, it can be seen that the privacy protection budget is used to control the ratio of the probability that the algorithm M obtains the same output on two adjacent data sets. It actually reflects the level of privacy protection that algorithm M can provide. The smaller the 'ε', the higher the level of privacy protection.

Definition 9 (*Noise mechanism*). The main implementation mechanism of the differential privacy is the noise mechanism. In this paper, the Laplace noise mechanism is used to deal with the transmitted data.

Definition 10 (*Similarity*). In the set of U, $x \in U, y \in U$. The formula of similarity is

$$\sin(i,j) = \frac{x}{y} \tag{3}$$

The similarity of multidimensional is calculated by the similarity of correction, which represents the mean of each dimension, and their similarity is

$$\sin(i,j) = \frac{\sum_{u \in U}(R_{u,i} - \bar{R}_u)(R_{u,j} - \bar{R}_u)}{\sqrt{\sum_{u \in U}(R_{u,i} - \bar{R}_u)^2}\sqrt{\sum_{u \in U}(R_{u,j} - \bar{R}_u)^2}} \tag{4}$$

3 Algorithm and Analysis

3.1 Algorithm Design

This paper proposes a clustering - differential privacy preserving method. Firstly, using DBSCAN (density - based spatial clustering of applications with noise) algorithm clusters the original data set. According to this, data are divided into different classes. Secondly, we use the MDAV (maximum distance to average vector) algorithm to gather the k-division of the data set to divide the data into a finer equivalence class, and then replace the data with the centroid of the class. Through the secondary division of the data, the problem of density clustering led to over-generalization of data is solved, and the sensitivity of the query function can be reduced. Thus this way will reduce the amount of noise adding. Thirdly, adding noise (adding Laplace noise) to the processed data using differential privacy techniques to ensure privacy during data processing. Finally, using similarity thresholds evaluates the processed data. If the similarity threshold is small than specified threshold, the data can be seen adding too noise. It needs to be corrected until it meets similarity requirements. The process of clustering-differential privacy preserving is shown in Fig. 1.

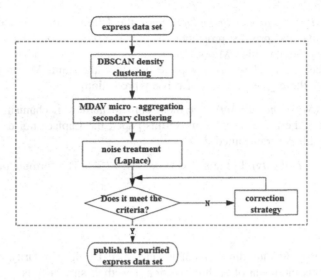

Fig. 1. Clustering-differential privacy preserving

3.2   Algorithm Description

Input: Raw data set D = {D₁, D₂ ...... Dₙ}, neighbor radius 'e', neighbor density
threshold 'Minpts', equivalence class quantity 'k', privacy protection budget
'ε', similarity threshold 'y'

Output: the data set T clustered

Clustering - differential privacy algorithm flow:

Step 1, marking all objects of X is unvisited;
Step 2, randomly selecting an unvisited object D1 to determine whether the e-field
of D1 contains at least Minpts objects. If not, we then mark D1 as noise. Otherwise
we create a new cluster C for D1 and place all the objects in the e-domain of D1 in
the candidate set N;
Step 3, denoting D′ for unvisited in N, and determine whether there is at least
Minpts objects in the e-field of D′. If not, the marked D′ is the noise point.
Otherwise put D′ into C and put all the objects in the e-domain of D1' in the
candidate set N;
Step 4, repeating 2–3 steps until the set N is empty. Output data set C =
{C1, C2...Cn};
Step 5, calculating the center a of the data set C according to the dissimilarity
matrix (formula 1), find the point r which is the furthest distance, and find the point
s which is the farthest from the distance r;
Step 6, to r as the center to find the nearest r-k-1 points to form an equivalent class.
To k as the center of the nearest k-1 points to form an equivalent category;

Step 7, if the number of tuples is greater than 2 k, repeat steps 5–6. If the number of tuples between k and 2 k, then they divide into a class. If the number of tuples is less than k, then return to the nearest class;

Step 8, calculating the centroid of each class with the centroid instead of all the objects within the class;

Step 9, adding Laplace noise to each data record that is queried, and return the data set T that satisfies the differential privacy;

Step 10, the similarity threshold (formula 4) is used to evaluate the data before and after the processing, and the correction is performed below the specified threshold until the similarity is satisfied.

3.3 Usability Analysis

In this paper, the central part of clustering-differential privacy preserving is dividing the data into several classes. The records in each class group are uniform, but the data records between the groups are heterogeneous. The data set is divided twice. The data achieves another division using micro-aggregation MDAV algorithm, which reduces the degree of data generalization and decreases the information loss rate. Adding the Laplace noise decreases the loss of information when the centriod replaces the class. And the differential privacy model can resist homogeneous attacks and background knowledge of the attacker. So we can say the Usability of the processed data is higher.

3.4 Security Analysis

The main idea of the differential privacy is to add Laplace noise to the query function. According to the properties of sequence combination and parallel composition of the differential privacy algorithm proposed by the literature [12], adding noise that meets the privacy protection budget 'ε' to the parallel data record, the processed data set can meet the differential privacy model. In clustering - differential privacy preserving algorithm, the data in express database is independent. They don't affect each other. So the algorithm satisfies the property of parallel composition. And it satisfies the differential privacy preserving model.

4   Experiment and Analysis

4.1   Experimental Environment and Evaluation Indicators

Hardware environment: processor Intel (R) Core (TM) i5-4590 3.30 Hz, memory 4 GB. Experimental platform: windows 7 (x64), using JAVA language. Programming environment: MyEclipse6.0 + MySQL. The data involved in the algorithm are derived from the customer information of the official website of the major express. The description of the experimental data set is shown in Table 4.

Table 4. Description of the experimental data set.

Number of data records	Number of QI	Number of SA	Data type
5000	3	2	real

The experiment measures the data availability by calculating the amount of information loss. That is the sum of the squared errors between the processed data and the original data. 'SSE' is the standard to measure the information loss. The smaller the value of 'SSE', the smaller the value of the published data deviates from the original data. The formula is:

$$SSE = \sum_{d_j \in D} \sum_{a_j^i \in d_j} (dist(a_j^i, (a_j^i)'))^2 \tag{5}$$

The experiment compares the clustering - differencial privacy method proposed in this paper with the general differential privacy method in terms of information loss. It uses the 'SCORE' to evaluate the two methods. The formula is:

$$SCORE = \frac{SSE_1}{SSE_2} \tag{6}$$

In formula (6), 'SSE_1' represents the information loss after clustering - differential privacy. 'SSE_2' represents the information loss after traditional differential privacy. The process of scoring is normalizing the information loss. The smaller the 'SSE_1' relative to 'SSE_2', the higher the availability of the release data.

4.2   Testing and Analysis

Test 1. Setting the parameters of e = 15, Minpts = 5, k = 7, ε = 0.05. Increasing the amount of experimental data. The experimental results are shown in Fig. 2.

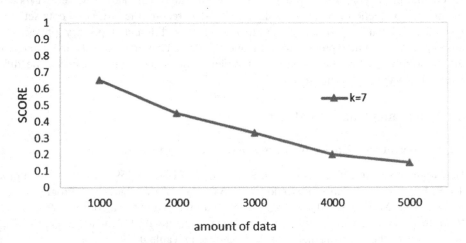

Fig. 2. K = 7, the variation of 'SCORE'.

Keeping the parameters of e = 15, Minpts = 5, ε = 0.05. Setting the parameter of k = 5. Increasing the amount of experimental data. The experimental results are shown in Fig. 3.

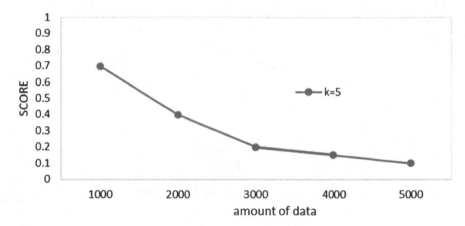

Fig. 3. K = 5, the variation of '*SCORE*'.

By comparing Figs. 2 and 3, we can draw the following conclusions:

① The value of '*SCORE*' is always less than 1, which indicates that the clustering - differential privacy method proposed in this paper can maintain high data availability compared with the general differential privacy method;

② As the amount of data increases, the value of '*SCORE*' decreases gradually, which shows that the clustering - differential privacy method can have a better reflection in dealing with large data sets;

③ With the decreasing of k, the value of '*SCORE*' is decreasing. Because the k is small, the number of data records that divided into the same equivalent class by the MDAV algorithm is less. When the centroid of equivalent class replaces all the records, the information loss is less.

Test 2. The amount of data is 5000. Setting the parameters e = 15, k = 5, ε = 0.02. Increasing the density threshold - Minpts. The experimental results are shown in Fig. 4.

The amount of data is 5000. Setting the parameters e = 15, k = 5, ε = 0.02. Increasing the density threshold - Minpts. The experimental results are shown in Fig. 5.

By comparing Figs. 4 and 5, we can draw the following conclusions:

① The value of '*SCORE*' is always less than 1, which indicates that the clustering - differential privacy method proposed in this paper can maintain high data availability compared with the general differential privacy method;

② Keeping the other parameters unchanged and gradually increasing the Minpts, the '*SCORE*' also has an increasing trend;

③ As 'ε' increases, the amount of noise added to the data decreases. The information loss is small. And the value of '*SCORE*' is small too.

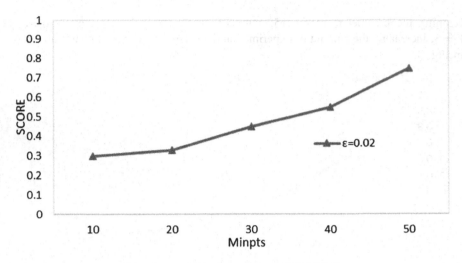

Fig. 4. ε = 0.02, the variation of '*SCORE*'.

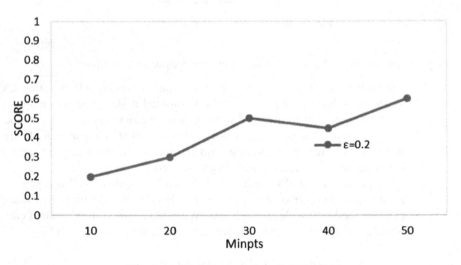

Fig. 5. ε = 0.2, the variation of '*SCORE*'.

5 Conclusion

Aiming at the information leakage in the express data release, this paper proposes a clustering - differential privacy preserving method. On the basis of density clustering algorithm, combining the idea of anonymity, the twice division of data set is carried out by using micro aggregation technology, which reduces the data generalization. Taking into account the clustering process will lead to leakage of information, while to resist the homogeneity attacks and background knowledge attacks, this paper adds Laplace noise to processed data set. Then we need to correct the data which does not meet the similarity requirements. Theoretical analysis and experimental results show that this method is suitable for the express data release and it can guarantee a higher data availability in data release.

Acknowledgments. This work is partially supported by Natural Science Foundation of China No.61370139, Social Science Foundation of Beijing No.15JGB099 and High level talents cross training "real training plan" (scientific reserach) fund.

References

1. Wei, Q., Li, X.Y.: Express information protection application based on K- anonymity. Appl. Res. Comput. **31**(2), 555–557 (2014)
2. Zhou, C.Q., Zhu, S.Z., Wang, S.S., Ao, L.N.: Research on privacy protection in express information management system. Logist. Eng. Manage. **37**(12), 30–32 (2015)
3. Zhang, X.W., Li, H.K., Yang, Y.T., Sun, G.Z.: Logistic information privacy protection system based on encrypted QR code. Appl. Res. Comput. **33**(11), 3455–3459 (2016)
4. Chai, R.M., Feng, H.H.: Efficient (K, L)-anonymous privacy protection based on clustering. Comput. Eng. **41**(1), 139–142 (2015)
5. Chong, Z., Ni, W., Liu, T., et al.: A privacy-preserving data publishing algorithm for clustering application. J. Comput. Res. Dev. **47**(12), 2083–2089 (2010)
6. Liu, X.Q., Li, Q.M.: Differentially private data release based on clustering anonymization. J. Commun. **37**(5), 125–129 (2016)
7. Song, J., Xu, G.Y., Yao, R.P.: Anonymized data privacy protection method based on differential privacy. J. Comput. Appl. **36**(10), 2753–2757 (2016)
8. Xiong, P., Zhu, T.Q., Wang, X.F.: A survey on differential privacy and applications. Chin. J. Comput. **37**(1), 101–122 (2014)
9. Bhaskar, R., Laxman, S., Thakurta, A.: Discovering frequent patterns in sensitive data. In: Proceedings of the 16th ACM SIGKDD International Conference on Knowledge Discovery and Data Mining. Washington, USA, pp. 503–512 (2010)
10. Sweeney, L.: k-anonymity: a model for protecting privacy. Int. J. Uncertain. Fuzziness Knowl. Based Syst. **10**(5), 557–570 (2002)
11. Sarwar, B., Karypis, G., Konstan, J., et al.: Intembased collaborative filtering recommendation algorithms. In: Proceedings of the 10th International Conference on World Wide Web, pp. 285–295. ACM (2001)
12. Mcsherry, F.D.: Privacy integrated queries: an extensible platform for privacy-preserving data analysis. In: The 2009 ACM SIGMOD International Conference on Management of Data. Providence, Rhode Island, pp. 19–30. ACM (2009)

Frequent Itemset Mining with Differential Privacy Based on Transaction Truncation

Ying Xia, Yu Huang[✉], Xu Zhang, and HaeYoung Bae

Research Center of Spatial Information System,
Chongqing University of Posts and Telecommunications, Chongqing, China
{xiaying, zhangx}@cqupt.edu.cn, 740696144@qq.com,
hybae@inha.ac.kr

Abstract. Frequent itemset mining is the basis of discovering transaction relationships and providing information services such as recommendation. However, when transaction databases contain individual sensitive information, direct release of frequent itemsets and their supports might bring privacy risks to users. Differential privacy provides strict protection for users, it can distort the sensitive data when attackers get the sensitive data from statistical information. The transaction length is related to sensitivity for counting occurrences (SCO) in a transaction database, larger SCO will reduce the availability of frequent itemsets under ε-differential privacy. So it is necessary to truncate some long transactions in transaction databases. We propose the algorithm FI-DPTT, a quality function is designed to calculate the optimal transaction length in exponential mechanism (EM), it aims to minimize noisy supports. Experimental results show that the proposed algorithm improves the availability and privacy efficiently.

Keywords: Frequent itemset mining · Differential privacy
Exponential mechanism · Quality function · Laplace mechanism
Transaction truncation

1 Introduction

Frequent itemset mining can find valuable knowledge from mass data, but mining sensitive data may reveal individual privacy. For example, analysis of search logs can acquire the behavior of user's page click, then get their interests in privacy. Therefore, it is necessary to introduce privacy protection mechanism into frequent itemset mining.

Differential privacy [1, 2] is a privacy protection technology that adds noise to query request or analysis results, it is not affected by attacker's background knowledge, and guarantees that adding or removing one transaction has little effect on the query results.

The research of frequent itemset mining algorithm has made great progress with differential privacy. Bhaskar et al. [3] applied Laplace mechanism (LM) to compute noisy supports of all possible frequent itemsets, and then publish the top-k frequent itemsets with the highest noisy supports. Zeng et al. [4] analyze the effect of transaction length on global sensitivity, then they propose transaction truncating and heuristic method. Zhang et al. [5] adopt EM to select the top-k frequent itemsets. In order to boost availability of the noisy supports, they propose the technique of consistency constraints.

An effective frequent itemset mining algorithm with differential privacy should guarantee a certain privacy, then it tries to improve the availability of frequent itemsets. According to SCO, the transaction length is proportional to Laplace noise, how to reduce the length of long transactions is the key point for a transaction database, the approach reduces some noisy errors, but it results in loss of items and brings more truncation errors at the same time. So the challenge is how to balance both noisy errors and truncation errors, the main contributions of this paper are as follows.

(1) In order to improve privacy protection of frequent itemsets, we propose the algorithm FI-DPTT, it perturbs real supports of top-k frequent itemsets by Laplace noise.
(2) In order to improve the availability of frequent itemsets under differential privacy, we propose a quality function which balances both noisy errors and truncation errors in EM, it draws on the idea of Median to find the optimal transaction length.

2 Preliminaries

2.1 Differential Privacy

Definition 1 (Neighboring Databases). Two transaction databases D_1 and D_2 are neighboring databases, if and only if we can obtain one from the other by adding or removing one transaction, such that $|D_1 - D_2| = 1$.

Definition 2 (ε-Differential Privacy [1]). Let F be an algorithm of privacy protection, F satisfies ε-differential privacy, if and only if for any pair of neighboring databases D_1 and D_2, and any output O of F, we have:

$$Pr[F(D_1)=O] \leq e^{\varepsilon} \times Pr[F(D_2)=O] \tag{1}$$

In the above definition, $Pr[F(D)=O]$ denotes that $F(D)$ outputs the probability of being O, ε is called the privacy budget, which controls the strength of privacy protection. A smaller ε leads to stricter privacy protection and vice versa.

2.2 Noisy Mechanism

Definition 3 (Global Sensitivity [1]). Given a query function Q with numerical outputs O, the global sensitivity of Q is ΔQ:

$$\Delta Q = \max_{D_1, D_2} |Q(D_1) - Q(D_2)| \tag{2}$$

D_1 and D_2 are arbitrary neighboring databases, ΔQ denotes the most distance between $Q(D_1)$ and $Q(D_2)$, global sensitivity is independent for arbitrary transaction databases.

Definition 4 (Sensitivity for Counting Occurrences (SCO) [6]). Given a transaction database D with the longest transaction length l_{max}, then for a query $Q = \{p_1, p_2, \ldots, p_n\}$ which for each itemset p_i of length in the range $I = [Q_{min}, Q_{max}]$ computes the number of occurrences in D, global sensitivity $\Delta Q = \Delta I \times l_{max}$, where $\Delta I = Q_{max} - Q_{min} + 1$.

SCO is proportional to the maximum transaction length from Definition 4. If there is an only one long transaction, we need add much Laplace noise to frequent itemsets.

Definition 5 (Laplace Mechanism (LM) [7]). Given a query $Q(D) \rightarrow O$, if the output of algorithm F satisfies Eq. (3), then the F enforces ε-differential privacy.

$$F(D)=Q(D)+<Lap_1(\Delta Q/\varepsilon), \ldots, Lap_n(\Delta Q/\varepsilon)> \tag{3}$$

$Lap_i(\Delta Q/\varepsilon)(1 \leq i \leq n)$ is independent Laplace noise mutually, The Laplace parameter is $\Delta Q/\varepsilon$, the Laplace noise is proportional to ΔQ and inversely proportional to ε. The idea is that we add Laplace noise to the real output values for privacy protection.

Definition 6 (Exponential Mechanism (EM) [8]). We design a quality function u(p, D), if algorithm F satisfies Eq. (4), then algorithm F enforces ε-differential privacy.

$$F(u)=\{p:|\Pr[p \in O] \propto \exp(\frac{\varepsilon \times u(p, D)}{2 \times \Delta u})\} \tag{4}$$

Where Δu denotes global sensitivity of quality function u(p, D). The key point is how to design a quality function u(p, D), p denotes the selected items from the output fields O. A larger $\exp\left(\frac{\varepsilon \times u(p, D)}{2 \times \Delta u}\right)$ leads to higher probability that is selected as output.

2.3 Availability Analysis

Definition 7 (False Negative Rate (FNR) [5]). Let $TP_k(D)$ be top-k frequent itemsets in the database D, FNR measures the ratio that the real top-k frequent itemsets are in $TP_k(D)$ and not in $TP_k(D_t)$. A smaller FNR leads to higher data accuracy.

$$FNR = \frac{|TP_k(D) \cup TP_k(D_t) - TP_k(D_t)|}{k} \tag{5}$$

Definition 8 (Average Relative Error (ARE) [5]). It measures the errors that we add Laplace noise to top-k frequent itemsets in database D. Where $TC(p_i, TP_k(D))$ denotes real supports of the frequent itemset p_i in database D. $NC(p_i, TP_k(D_t))$ denotes noisy supports of frequent itemset p_i, If p_i is not in $TP_k(D_t)$, we set $NC(p_i, TP_k(D_t)) = 0$. A smaller ARE leads to higher data accuracy.

$$ARE = \frac{\sum_{P_i \in TP_k(D)} \frac{|TC(p_i, TP_k(D)) - NC(p_i, TP_k(D_t))|}{TC(p_i, TP_k(D))}}{k} \tag{6}$$

3 Proposed Algorithm

3.1 Idea of Transaction Truncation

We define the optimal transaction length. Total errors are the sum of noisy errors and truncation errors, we truncate an original transaction database D into the transaction database D_t, the total errors which we generate frequent itemsets in the D_t under ε-differential privacy are the smallest than any other truncated database, so the longest transaction length in the database D_t is the optimal transaction length in the database D.

3.2 Algorithm Description

Algorithm 1 FI-DPTT(D, ε, SCALE, λ)
Input: database D, privacy budget ε, the optimal truncation ratio SCALE, threshold λ
Output: top-k frequent itemsets and their noisy supports under ε-differential privacy

1. $D' \leftarrow \text{Rank}(D)$
2. $\varepsilon = \varepsilon_1 + \varepsilon_2$
3. $l_{opt} \leftarrow \text{SelectOptLen}(D', \text{SCALE}, \varepsilon_1)$
4. $D_t \leftarrow \text{Truncate}(D', l_{opt})$
5. $FS \leftarrow \text{Perturb-Frequency}(D_t, \lambda, l_{opt}, \varepsilon_2)$
6. **return** FS

In order to reduce truncation errors, Apriori method is performed first to get candidates of 1-frequent itemsets and their supports, and then items of each transaction is ranked in descending order with supports to get the database D' (Step 1), when we truncate a transaction database. ε (Step 2) is allocated to two steps ε_1 (Step 3) and ε_2 (Step 5) on average. The database D' is truncated into D_t by l_{opt} (Step 4).

3.3 Interpretation of Important Processes

For the algorithm FI-DPTT, two important procedures are interpreted as follows.

Procedure SelectOptLen(D', SCALE, ε_1)
Input: transaction database D', Privacy budget ε_1, the optimal transaction ratio SCALE that will be calculated in the experimental chapter
Output: The optimal transaction length l_{opt} under EM

1. **For** each transaction record i∈D'
2. Calculating the length of each transaction record and marking t_i. Getting supports of the t_i-th item, marking $count_{ti}$.
3. Designing score function: $u(t_i, D') = \frac{count_{ti}}{|rank(t_i) - SCALE \times |D'||}$
4. $E(t_i) = \exp(\frac{\varepsilon_1 \times u(t_i, D')}{2 \times \Delta u})$
5. $Pr(l_{opt} = t_j) = E[t_j] / \sum_{i=1}^{|D'|} E[t_i]$, $Pr(l_{opt} = t_j)$ denotes the probability which t_j is selected
6. **end for**
7. $l_{opt} \leftarrow$ randomly selecting t_j as the optimal transaction length according to $Pr(l_{opt} = t_j)$
8. **return** l_{opt}

Procedure SelectOptLen draws on the characteristic of Median [9] that describes the trend of transaction records, it is rarely influenced by extreme values. We scan the database D' to obtain length of each transaction, then adopt EM to get l_{opt}. A quality function $u(t, D') = \dfrac{count_t}{|rank(t) - SCALE \times |D'|||}$. If $rank(t) = SCALE \times |D'|$, we set $u(t, D')$ $= 2 \times count_t$, $count_t$ denotes the supports of the last item in the current transaction record, $rank(t)$ denotes the location where t is ranked in ascending order from the database D'. $\Delta u(t, D')$ is affected one at most. Because we add or remove one transaction record from the database D', the global sensitivity of $u(t, D')$ is one, that is, $\Delta u(t, D') = 1$.

Procedure Perturb-Frequency(D_t, λ, l_{opt}, ε_2)
Input: truncated transaction database D_t, a support threshold λ, privacy budget ε_2 and l_{opt}
Output: top-k frequent itemsets and their noisy supports under ε-differential privacy

1. $S \leftarrow$ FP-Growth(D_t, λ) /*Employing FP-Growth to generate k-frequent itemsets.*/
2. $k \leftarrow |S|$
3.   **for** i=1 to k **do**
4. $c_t(p_i) \leftarrow c(p_i) + Lap(l_{opt}/\varepsilon_2)$ /*top-k frequent itemsets with Laplace noisy supports.*/
5.   **end for**
6.   **return** FS

Procedure Perturb-Frequency generates frequent itemsets and add Laplace noise to real supports. Let $c(p_i)$ is real supports of a frequent itemset p_i, $c_t(p_i)$ is the supports that is added Laplace noise. l_{opt} is the global sensitivity of frequent itemsets in the database D_t.

4   Experimental Evaluation

4.1   Experimental Setting

This section evaluates FI-DPTT algorithm on the data availability with DP-topkP [5]. Experimental environment is Inter Core i5-2410 M, CPU 2.30 GHz, 4 GB memory, Windows 7 and datasets PUMSB-STAR, RETAIL and KOSARAK [10]. FNR and ARE are used for data analysis. We repeat the experiment for five times and get the average (Table 1).

Table 1. Description of three datasets.

Dataset	Number of transaction	Number of distinct item	Average transaction length	Longest transaction length
Retail	88162	16470	11.3	76
Pumb-star	49046	2088	50	63
Kosarak	990002	41270	8.1	2498

4.2   Experimental Result Analysis

We fix k = 100 and ε = 1.0 to analyze the impact of SCALE on availability. When we set SCALE = 0.85 in Fig. 1, it ensures the best availability. A smaller SCALE leads to increase in truncation errors and reduce in noisy errors, total errors tends to increase and vice versa. Furthermore, the effect of truncation errors is greater than noisy errors on availability. We fix SCALE = 0.85 in the follow-up experiments.

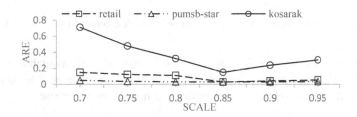

Fig. 1. The relationship between SCALE and availability

We fix k = 100 to analyze the impact of ε on availability in Fig. 2. When ε < 1, FI-DPTT achieves lower FNR than DP-topkP, because we give priority to reducing truncation errors, FNR is only related to truncation errors. FI-DPTT achieves lower ARE than DP-topkP, ARE is related to both truncation errors and noisy errors, it will be larger than FNR. It shows that the availability of FI-DPTT is better than DP-topkP.

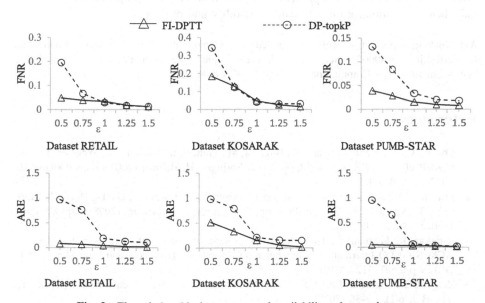

Fig. 2. The relationship between ε and availability when ε changes

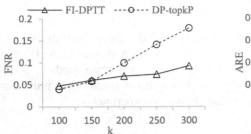 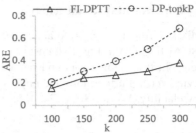

Fig. 3. The relationship between k and availability when k changes in the dataset KOSARAK

From Fig. 3, we fix $\varepsilon = 1$ to analyze the impact of k on availability. With the increase of k, the availability of two algorithms will reduce, because it leads to smaller threshold λ, it makes both truncation errors and noisy errors increase.

5   Conclusion

If there are some long transactions in a transaction database, it makes the availability of frequent itemsets reduced under differential privacy. The algorithm FI-DPTT combines exponential mechanism with Laplace mechanism. In order to improve the availability of frequent itemsets under differential privacy, a quality function of exponential mechanism is designed to balance truncation errors and noisy errors, then Laplace noise is added to the real supports of frequent itemsets. The proposed algorithm can gain better performance on both data availability and privacy.

Acknowledgments. This work is funded by Chongqing Natural Science Foundation (cstc2014kjrc-qnrc40002), Scientific and Technological Research Program of Chongqing Municipal Education Commission (KJ1500431, KJ1400429).

References

1. Dwork, C.: Differential privacy. In: Bugliesi, M., Preneel, B., Sassone, V., Wegener, I. (eds.) ICALP 2006. LNCS, vol. 4052, pp. 1–12. Springer, Heidelberg (2006). https://doi.org/10.1007/11787006_1
2. Dwork, C.: Differential privacy: a survey of results. In: Agrawal, M., Du, D., Duan, Z., Li, A. (eds.) TAMC 2008. LNCS, vol. 4978, pp. 1–19. Springer, Heidelberg (2008). https://doi.org/10.1007/978-3-540-79228-4_1
3. Bhaskar, R., Laxman, S., Thakurta, A.: Discovering frequent patterns in sensitive data. In: ACM SIGKDD International Conference on Knowledge Discovery and Data Mining 2010 DBLP, pp. 503–512 (2010)
4. Zeng, C., Naughton, J.F., Cai, J.Y.: On differentially private frequent itemset mining. VLDB J. **6**(1), 25–36 (2012)
5. Zhang, X., Miao, W., Meng, X.: An accurate method for mining top-k frequent pattern under differential privacy. J. Comput. Res. Develop. **51**(1), 104–114 (2014)

6. Bonomi, L., Xiong, L.: A two-phase algorithm for mining sequential patterns with differential privacy. In: ACM International Conference on Information & Knowledge Management, pp. 269–278. ACM (2013)

7. Dwork, C., McSherry, F., Nissim, K., Smith, A.: Calibrating noise to sensitivity in private data analysis. In: Halevi, S., Rabin, T. (eds.) TCC 2006. LNCS, vol. 3876, pp. 265–284. Springer, Heidelberg (2006). https://doi.org/10.1007/11681878_14

8. Mcsherry, F., Talwar, K.: Mechanism design via differential privacy. In: Foundations of Computer Science 2007, FOCS 2007, pp. 94–103. IEEE (2007)

9. Guoqing, L., Xiaojian, Z., Liping, D.: Frequent sequential pattern mining under differential privacy. J. Comput. Res. Develop. **52**(12), 2789–2801 (2015)

10. Datasets. http://fimi.ua.ac.be/data/

Perturbation Paradigms of Maintaining Privacy-Preserving Monotonicity for Differential Privacy

Hai Liu[1], Zhenqiang Wu[1(✉)], Changgen Peng[2], Shuangyue Zhang[1], Feng Tian[1], and Laifeng Lu[3]

[1] School of Computer Science, Shaanxi Normal University, Xi'an 710119, China
{liuhai,zqiangwu,zsy,tianfeng}@snnu.edu.cn
[2] Guizhou Provincial Key Laboratory of Public Big Data, Guizhou University, Guiyang 550025, China
sci.cgpeng@gzu.edu.cn
[3] School of Mathematics and Information Science, Shaanxi Normal University, Xi'an 710119, China
lulaifeng@snnu.edu.cn

Abstract. To preserve confidential information for numeric and character data, there are corresponding to differential privacy mechanisms. However, current work without uniform evaluation criterion for these differential privacy mechanisms, because the data types are different. In this paper, we proposed privacy-preserving monotonicity principle as an evaluation criterion of differential privacy mechanisms. Firstly, this paper summarized three perturbation paradigms of existing work, including the linear perturbation, non-linear perturbation, and randomized perturbation. Secondly, for numeric and character data, we proposed privacy-preserving monotonicity principle of differential privacy based on computational indistinguishability, respectively. Finally, through analysis privacy-preserving monotonicity of existing perturbation methods for each perturbation paradigm, we presented constrained perturbation paradigms for numeric and character data that can achieve privacy-preserving monotonicity. Therefore, our privacy-preserving monotonicity principle shows the tradeoff between privacy and utility, and it can be regarded as an evaluation criterion of differential privacy mechanisms. Furthermore, we show that constrained perturbation paradigms of maintaining privacy-preserving monotonicity provide a useful guideline for differential privacy development.

Keywords: Computational indistinguishability · Differential privacy
Perturbation paradigms · Privacy metrics
Privacy-preserving monotonicity

1 Introduction

To ensure the tradeoff between data utility and privacy-preserving, Dwork et al. [1] first proposed differential privacy for numeric data. It is a rigorous

S. Qing et al. (Eds.): ICICS 2017, LNCS 10631, pp. 446–458, 2018.
https://doi.org/10.1007/978-3-319-89500-0_39

mathematical proof method based on computational indistinguishability. Differential privacy ensures the ability of an adversary to any set of individual data should be essentially the same, independent of whether an individual presence and absence of the dataset. In [1], Laplace mechanism was firstly presented to achieve differential privacy for numeric data. Next, Dwork et al. [2] achieved differential privacy using Gaussian mechanism for numeric data. In 2007, McSherry and Talwar [3] proposed Exponential mechanism for character data. Data perturbation is achieved by adding noise in Laplace mechanism and Gaussian mechanism, and by random selection in Exponential mechanism. With widely applications of differential privacy, in addition to perturbation methods of adding noise and random selection to meet application requirements, randomized response [4] is also mainly perturbation method to achieve differential privacy for character data.

According to the differential privacy mechanisms above, we can compare Euclidean distances for numeric data, such that error can be used as privacy metric, but entropy cannot be. Conversely, we cannot compare Euclidean distances for character data, because the character data directly indicate the semantics. Thus, error cannot be used as privacy metric for character data, but entropy can be, because of using randomized perturbation. Another, properties of differential privacy, including post-processing, group privacy, and composition theorem, cannot be as an evaluation criterion of privacy-preserving. These are inherent properties of differential privacy. In other words, for numeric or character data, these properties are satisfied as long as differential privacy is held. Another, there is also no uniform method that indicates the tradeoff between privacy and utility. Thus, there is no uniform evaluation criterion for these differential privacy mechanisms.

To this end, we proposed privacy-preserving monotonicity principle as an evaluation criterion of differential privacy for numeric and character data and it shows the tradeoff between privacy and utility. Then, we presented constrained perturbation paradigms of maintaining privacy-preserving monotonicity which provide the guideline for differential privacy exploration. In this paper, the main contributions are summarized as follows.

(1) We summarized three perturbation paradigms, including the linear perturbation, non-linear perturbation, and random perturbation.
(2) We proposed privacy-preserving monotonicity principle of differential privacy based on computational indistinguishability to numeric and character data.
(3) According to privacy-preserving monotonicity principle of differential privacy, through analyzing current perturbation paradigms, we presented constrained perturbation paradigms to satisfy privacy-preserving monotonicity for numeric and character data.

The rest of this paper is organised as following. We introduce the preliminaries in Sect. 2. Section 3 summarizes current perturbation paradigms. We propose the privacy-preserving monotonicity principle of differential privacy for numeric and character data in Sect. 4. We analyze privacy-preserving monotonicity of perturbation paradigms and present constrained perturbation paradigms to satisfy privacy-preserving monotonicity principle for numeric and character data in Sect. 5. Section 6 concludes this paper.

2   Preliminaries

Here, we introduce the preliminaries of computational indistinguishability and differential privacy.

2.1   Computational Indistinguishability

Informally, two probability distributions are computationally indistinguishable [5] if no efficient algorithm can distinguish them. The definition of computational indistinguishability is as following.

Definition 1 (Computational Indistinguishability). Considering two distributions X and Y over dataset $D = \{r_1, \ldots, r_m\}$, X and Y each assigns some probability to every element in D. X and Y are computationally indistinguishable, if for any probabilistic polynomial time algorithm A there exists a negligible function $negl(n)$ on security parameter n such that

$$|Pr[A(D, X)] - Pr[A(D, Y)]| \leq negl(n) \tag{1}$$

Equivalently, the variant of computational indistinguishability is

$$1 - negl(n) \leq \frac{Pr[A(D, X)]}{Pr[A(D, Y)]} \leq 1 + negl(n) \tag{2}$$

Let $negl(n) = \varepsilon$, because of $e^\varepsilon \approx 1 + \varepsilon$ for small ε. So we get the equal variant of computational indistinguishability is $e^{-\varepsilon} \leq \frac{Pr[A(D,X)]}{Pr[A(D,Y)]} \leq e^\varepsilon$.

Since ε is small, we say that some algorithm A cannot distinguish these two distributions. This mean that A cannot tell whether it is given an element r_i sampled according to distribution X or Y. We can know that the smaller ε, the better indistinguishable. In other words, the probability ratio of two distributions X and Y is closer to 1, the indistinguishability is better. Therefore, the indistinguishability is stronger, and the distinguish error or uncertainty of an algorithm A is bigger.

2.2   Differential Privacy

We present differential privacy and it corresponds to mechanisms [6]. Two datasets D_1 and D_2 are adjacent datasets if they have the same size and identical except for a single record. Thus, the Hamming distance $d(D_1, D_2)$ between adjacent datasets D_1 and D_2 is 1. In the basis of adjacent datasets, the definition of (ε, δ)-differential privacy is as following.

Definition 2 ((ε, δ)-Differential Privacy). Given $\varepsilon > 0$, a randomized algorithm M is (ε, δ)-differential privacy, if for any two adjacent datasets D_1 and D_2, and for any outputs $S \subseteq Range(M)$ of M, so $M(D_1) \in S$ and $M(D_2) \in S$, such that $Pr[M(D_1)] \leq e^\varepsilon Pr[M(D_2)] + \delta$, where $\delta \in [0, 1]$ is any probability of not satisfying differential privacy, and if $\delta = 0$, M is $(\varepsilon, 0)$-differential privacy algorithm.

Next, there is any query function $f : D \to R^k$ about a dataset D, for all adjacent datasets D_1 and D_2, the sensitivity of f is

$$\Delta f = max_{d(D_1, D_2)=1} \|f(D_1) - f(D_2)\|_1 \tag{3}$$

The definition of Laplace mechanism and Gaussian mechanism satisfying differential privacy is as following.

Definition 3 (Laplace Mechanism). Given any function $f : D \to R^k$, the Laplace mechanism is $M_L(D) = f(D) + Y$, where $Y = (Y_1, \ldots, Y_k)$ is independent identical distribution random noise drawn from Laplace distribution $Lap(\frac{\Delta f}{\varepsilon})$.

Definition 4 (Gaussian Mechanism). Given any function $f : D \to R^k$, the Gaussian mechanism is $M_G(D) = f(D) + Y$, where $Y = (Y_1, \ldots, Y_k)$ is independent identical distribution random noise drawn from Gaussian distribution $N(0, \sigma^2)$ and $\sigma \geq \frac{\Delta f \sqrt{2 \ln(\frac{1.25}{\delta})}}{\varepsilon}$.

Laplace mechanism and Gaussian mechanism are suitable for numerical data. Exponential mechanism is used for character data. Given some arbitrary range $\Re$, which the user prefers to output some element of $\Re$ with the maximum possible utility. With respect to some utility function $u : D \times \Re \to R$, which maps database and output pairs into utility. So the sensitivity of utility function u is

$$\Delta u = max_{r \in \Re} max_{d(D_1, D_2)=1} |u(D_1, r) - u(D_2, r)| \tag{4}$$

The definition of Exponential mechanism satisfying differential privacy is as following.

Definition 5 (Exponential Mechanism). Exponential mechanism $M_E(D)$ selects and outputs an element $r \in \Re$ with probability proportional to $exp(\frac{\varepsilon u(D, r)}{2 \Delta u})$.

3   Perturbation Paradigms

In widely applications, different perturbation methods have reached the goals of demand. We summarize three perturbation paradigms, including the linear perturbation, non-linear perturbation, and randomized perturbation.

In linear perturbation, the perturbation is achieved by adding linear noise in existing work. Yang et al. [7] proposed Bayesian differential privacy with output perturbation by adding Laplace noise. Abadi et al. [8] developed deep learning with differential privacy by adding Gaussian noise. Tong et al. [9] proposed a scheduling protocol for the purpose of protecting user's location privacy and minimizing vehicle miles based on joint differential privacy by adding Gaussian noise.

In addition to adding noise, we give several perturbation methods in the linear perturbation paradigm, including subtraction, multiplication, division, filtering, and moving average filtering noise. To the best of our knowledge, there is no nonlinear perturbation paradigm in the present work. We give several perturbation methods in the non-linear perturbation paradigm, including adding absolute value, square, exponential transformation, sine transformation and cosine transformation of noise. Next, we summarize technologies of randomized perturbation are as following, including Exponential mechanism and randomized response.

Many data summarization applications involving sensitive data about individuals whose privacy concerns are not automatically addressed, so Mitrovic et al. [10] proposed a general and systematic study of differential privacy submodular maximization by using Exponential mechanism. Qin et al. [11] proposed LDPMiner, a two-phase mechanism for obtaining accurate heavy hitters with local differential privacy using randomized response.

In Table 1, we summarize the perturbation methods of three perturbation paradigms for numeric and character data.

Table 1. Perturbation methods of three perturbation paradigms for numeric and character data

Perturbation paradigms	Data types	Perturbation methods
Linear perturbation	Numeric data	Addition [7–9]
		Subtraction
		Multiplication
		Division
		Filtering
		Moving average filtering
Non-linear perturbation	Numeric data	Adding absolute value
		Adding square
		Adding exponential transformation
		Adding sine transformation
		Adding cosine transformation
Randomized perturbation	Character data	Exponential mechanism [10]
		Randomized response [11]

4   Privacy-Preserving Monotonicity Principle

In this section, according to privacy metrics, we present the privacy-preserving monotonicity principle of differential privacy for numerical data and character data.

We use error and uncertainty as privacy metrics for numerical data and character data, respectively. Concretely, we use expected estimation error and entropy as privacy metrics for numerical data and character data, respectively. Here, other error metrics can also be used for numeric data, such as Euclidean distance, and other uncertainty metrics can be also used for character data. Since noise perturbation of differential privacy mechanisms are random for numerical data, the monotonicity curve of expected estimation error is more smooth than that of Euclidean distance. Thus, we chose expected estimation error as privacy metric for numeric data in this paper. The expected estimation error is the expected distance between the perturbation value x_i' and the true value x_i. The $p(x_i')$ is the probability of perturbation value x_i'. The metric of the expected estimation error (EEE) is $EEE = \sum_{x_i \in D} p(x_i')||x_i' - x_i||_1$.

And, entropy quantifies the amount of information contained in a random variable. It is used as a privacy metric, which indicates the adversary's uncertainty. Thus, entropy (ENT) metric is $ENT = -\sum_{i=1}^{n} p(x_i) \log_2 p(x_i)$, where $p(x_i)$ denotes the probability of the random variable.

According to the definition of computational indistinguishability and privacy metric of expected estimation error, we have the following theorem about privacy-preserving monotonicity of differential privacy for numeric data.

Theorem 1. In differential privacy, the expected estimation error EEE decreases as the privacy budget ε increases for numeric data.

Proof. Here, we use the identity query function $f : D \rightarrow D$. In differential privacy, for any adjacent datasets D_1 and D_2, we perturb query results using the same noise subjected to identical distribution with different expectations. Thus, we have $Pr[M(D_1)] \leq e^{\varepsilon} Pr[M(D_2)] + \delta$.

Now, let us assume that the mechanism $M(D_2)$ subjects to a fixed probability distribution, and probability value δ is constant. For privacy budget ε_i, if the probability density function is $p(x)$, then there is

$$Pr[M(D_1, \varepsilon_i)] = \int_{-\infty}^{X_k} p(x)dx \tag{5}$$

where $M(D_1, \varepsilon_i)$ denotes differential privacy mechanism which privacy budget to be ε_i. So

$$EEE_i = \sum Pr[M(D_1, \varepsilon_i)]||M(D_1, \varepsilon_i) - D_1||_1 \tag{6}$$

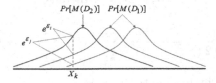

For privacy budget ε_j, there is

$$Pr[M(D_1, \varepsilon_j)] = \int_{-\infty}^{X_k} p(x)dx \tag{7}$$

where $M(D_1, \varepsilon_j)$ denotes differential privacy mechanism which privacy budget to be ε_j. So

$$EEE_j = \sum Pr[M(D_1, \varepsilon_j)] \| M(D_1, \varepsilon_j) - D_1 \|_1 \tag{8}$$

If $\varepsilon_i \leq \varepsilon_j$, as you can see from the figure, then $Pr[M(D_1, \varepsilon_i)] \geq Pr[M(D_1, \varepsilon_j)]$. Therefore, such that $EEE_i \geq EEE_j$. $\square$

According to the definition of computational indistinguishability and privacy metric of entropy, we have the following theorem about privacy-preserving monotonicity of differential privacy for character data.

Theorem 2. In differential privacy, the entropy ENT decreases as the privacy budget ε increases for character data.

Proof. To achieve differential privacy, for any adjacent datasets D_1 and D_2, we make random selection using Exponential mechanism. Then, with respect to utility function $u : D \times \Re \to R$, Exponential mechanism $M_E(D)$ selects and outputs an element $r \in \Re$ with probability proportional to $exp(\frac{\varepsilon u(D,r)}{2 \Delta u})$. Thus, we have $Pr[M_E(D_1)] \leq e^\varepsilon Pr[M_E(D_2)] + \delta$. u_i denotes the utility $u(D, r_i)$ of element r_i in the following proof.

Since the entropy of discrete random variables $X = \{x_1, \ldots, x_n\}$ is $H(X) = -\sum_{i=1}^{n} p(x_i) \log_2 p(x_i)$. Thus, for Exponential mechanism of privacy budget ε, there is

$$H(\varepsilon) = -\sum_{i=1}^{n} \frac{e^{\varepsilon u_i}}{\sum_{j=1}^{n} e^{\varepsilon u_j}} \log_2 \frac{e^{\varepsilon u_i}}{\sum_{j=1}^{n} e^{\varepsilon u_j}} \tag{9}$$

Let $H_i(\varepsilon) = -\frac{e^{\varepsilon u_i}}{\sum_{j=1}^{n} e^{\varepsilon u_j}} \log_2 \frac{e^{\varepsilon u_i}}{\sum_{j=1}^{n} e^{\varepsilon u_j}}$. Thus, the derivative of $H_i(\varepsilon)$ is

$$H_i^{'}(\varepsilon) = -\frac{1}{\ln 2} \frac{e^{\varepsilon u_i} \sum_{j=1}^{n} (u_i - u_j) e^{\varepsilon u_j}}{(\sum_{j=1}^{n} e^{\varepsilon u_j})^2} (\varepsilon u_i - \ln \sum_{j=1}^{n} e^{\varepsilon u_j} + 1) \tag{10}$$

and

$$H^{'}(\varepsilon) = -\sum_{i=1}^{n} (\frac{1}{\ln 2} \frac{e^{\varepsilon u_i} \sum_{j=1}^{n} (u_i - u_j) e^{\varepsilon u_j}}{(\sum_{j=1}^{n} e^{\varepsilon u_j})^2} (\varepsilon u_i - \ln \sum_{j=1}^{n} e^{\varepsilon u_j} + 1)) \tag{11}$$

Since $\sum_{i=1}^{n} e^{\varepsilon u_i} \sum_{j=1}^{n} (u_i - u_j) e^{\varepsilon u_j} = 0$, there is

$$H^{'}(\varepsilon) = -\frac{1}{\ln 2} \frac{\varepsilon}{(\sum_{i=1}^{n} e^{\varepsilon u_i})^2} (\sum_{i=1}^{n} u_i^2 e^{\varepsilon u_i} \sum_{i=1}^{n} e^{\varepsilon u_i} - (\sum_{i=1}^{n} e^{\varepsilon u_i})^2) \tag{12}$$

According to the Cauchy inequality, there is

$$\sum_{i=1}^{n} u_i^2 e^{\varepsilon u_i} \sum_{i=1}^{n} e^{\varepsilon u_i} \geq (\sum_{i=1}^{n} (\sqrt{u_i^2 e^{\varepsilon u_i}} \sqrt{e^{\varepsilon u_i}}))^2 = (\sum_{i=1}^{n} u_i e^{\varepsilon u_i})^2 \tag{13}$$

Therefore, $H'(\varepsilon) \leq 0$ when given $\varepsilon \geq 0$. So $H(\varepsilon)$ deceases as ε increases. When $\varepsilon = 0$, $H(\varepsilon)$ is the maximum, which denotes the strongest privacy preserving level. Similarity, the same property can be proved for randomized response.   □

We know that differential privacy has privacy-preserving monotonicity principle for numeric data and character data from Theorems 1 and 2. Furthermore, privacy-preserving monotonicity principle shows the tradeoff between privacy and utility.

5   Privacy-Preserving Monotonicity of Perturbation Paradigms

We analyze privacy-preserving monotonicity of perturbation paradigms by experimental evaluation, and then give the constrained perturbation paradigms to maintain privacy-preserving monotonicity of differential privacy for numeric and character data. In experimental analysis of linear and non-linear perturbation paradigms, we use the count of total rental bikes including both casual and registered in bike sharing dataset [12] from January 1, 2011 to December 31, 2012. In experimental analysis of randomized perturbation, we will select a different dataset.

5.1   Privacy-Preserving Monotonicity Analysis of Linear Perturbation

In linear perturbation, we make the experimental evaluation of adding, subtracting, multiplying, dividing, filtering, moving average filtering noise for numeric data. Note that we need to explain the moving average filtering methods. The moving average filtering works by averaging a number of points from the input signal to produce each point in the output signal as shown in the following equation $y_i = \frac{\sum_{j=0}^{N-1} x(i+j)}{N}$, where $x(i+j)$ is the input signal, y_i is the output signal, and N is the number of points used in the moving average.

In the Fig. 1, three linear perturbations of addition, subtraction, and filtering maintain privacy-preserving monotonicity for Laplace mechanism and Gaussian mechanism. We observe the multiplication and division perturbations of Laplace mechanism and Gaussian mechanism do not satisfy privacy-preserving monotonicity from Figs. 2 and 3. For moving average filtering perturbation of Gaussian mechanism, it does not maintain privacy-preserving monotonicity as the integer N increases from Fig. 4. Note that because the average of Laplace random variables without satisfying Laplace distribution, Laplace mechanism has no moving average filtering perturbation.

From the observation above, we have the following theorem.

Theorem 3. Linear perturbations of addition, subtraction, and filtering noise $Y = X \pm kb$ satisfy the privacy-preserving monotonicity of differential privacy for numeric data, where b is the scale parameter of probability distribution that generating noise X and k is any appropriate real number.

The proof of this theorem is similar to the proof of Theorem 1.

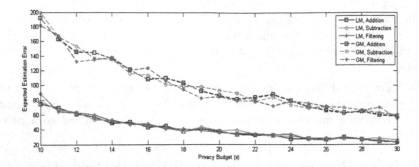

Fig. 1. Addition, subtraction, and filtering perturbations of Laplace mechanism (LM) and Gaussian mechanism (GM)

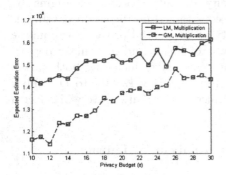

Fig. 2. Multiplication perturbation of Laplace mechanism (LM) and Gaussian mechanism (GM)

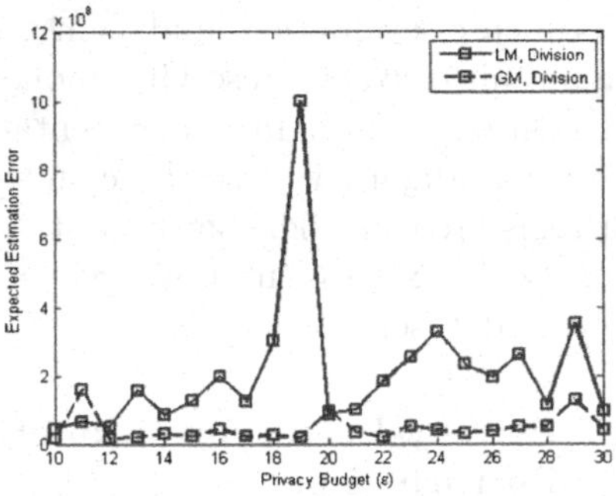

Fig. 3. Division perturbation of Laplace mechanism (LM) and Gaussian mechanism (GM)

5.2 Privacy-Preserving Monotonicity Analysis of Non-linear Perturbation

In non-linear perturbation, for numeric data, we make the experimental evaluation for adding absolute value, square, exponential transformation, sine transformation and cosine transformation of noise generated by Laplace mechanism and Gaussian mechanism.

From Figs. 5 and 6, the adding absolute value, square, and sine transformation perturbations of Laplace mechanism and Gaussian mechanism maintain privacy-preserving monotonicity. On the contrary, the exponential transformation and cosine transformation perturbations of Laplace mechanism and Gaussian mechanism do not maintain privacy-preserving monotonicity.

From the observation above, we obtain the following theorem.

Theorem 4. Non-linear perturbations of adding absolute value, square, and sine transformation of noise $Y = X \pm kb$ satisfy the privacy-preserving

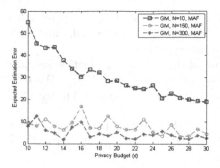

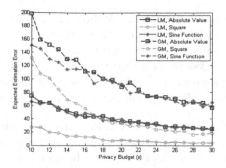

Fig. 4. Moving average filtering (MAF) perturbation of Gaussian mechanism (GM) for different N

Fig. 5. Adding absolute value, square, and sine transformation perturbations of Laplace mechanism (LM) and Gaussian mechanism (GM)

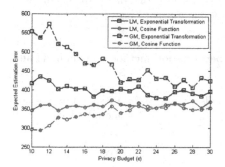

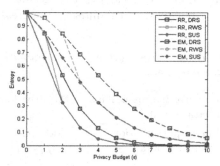

Fig. 6. Adding exponential transformation and cosine transformation perturbations of Laplace mechanism (LM) and Gaussian mechanism (GM)

Fig. 7. Direct random selection (DRS), roulette wheel selection (RWS), and stochastic universal selection (SUS) perturbations of randomized response (RR) and Exponential mechanism (EM)

monotonicity of differential privacy for numeric data, where b is the scale parameter of probability distribution that generating noise X and k is any appropriate real number.

The proof of Theorem 4 also is similar to the proof of Theorem 1.

5.3 Privacy-Preserving Monotonicity Analysis of Randomized Perturbation

To analyze privacy-preserving monotonicity of randomized perturbation for character data, we need the set of possible datasets is $D = \{0, 1\}$, where 1 and 0 can denote the randomized response of "Yes" or "No", respectively. In this section, we analyze the privacy-preserving monotonicity of Exponential mechanism and randomized response using dataset $D = \{0, 1\}$. The Exponential mechanism and randomized response are achieved by direct random selection (it directly distributes corresponding probability to the data element without using other random selection schemes) and two random selection schemes [13], including roulette wheel selection and stochastic universal selection.

We observe that randomized perturbations of three random selection schemes maintain the privacy-preserving monotonicity of entropy from Fig. 7. We have the following Theorem 5, which its proof is similar to the proof of Theorem 2.

Theorem 5. If random perturbation satisfies the privacy-preserving monotonicity of differential privacy for character data, then the entropy ENT decreases as the privacy budget ε increases.

Finally, under differential privacy, Table 2 summarizes the perturbation methods of each perturbation paradigm whether or not satisfying privacy-preserving monotonicity for numeric and character data. Note that the privacy-preserving monotonicity of moving average filtering perturbation for Gaussian mechanism does not exist as the integer N increases in linear perturbation.

Table 2. Privacy-preserving monotonicity of perturbation methods for numeric and character data

Perturbation paradigms (Data types)	Perturbation methods	Privacy-preserving monotonicity
Linear perturbation (Numeric data)	Addition	Yes
	Subtraction	Yes
	Multiplication	No
	Division	No
	Filtering	Yes
Non-linear perturbation (Numeric data)	Adding absolute value	Yes
	Adding square	Yes
	Adding exponential transformation	No
	Adding sine transformation	Yes
	Adding cosine transformation	No
Randomized perturbation (Character data)	Exponential mechanism	Yes
	Randomized response	Yes

6   Conclusion

In this paper, we summarized three perturbation paradigms for differential privacy. Then, according to the privacy metrics of error and uncertainty, we proposed the privacy-preserving monotonicity principle of differential privacy based on computational indistinguishability to numeric and character data. Moreover, privacy-preserving monotonicity principle shows the tradeoff between privacy and utility for differential privacy. Finally, we make an experimental evaluation for existing perturbation methods. We gave the constrained perturbation methods for numeric and character data to maintain privacy-preserving monotonicity. Our privacy-preserving monotonicity principle can be regarded as an evaluation criterion of differential privacy investigation, and these constrained perturbation paradigms provide the guideline of designing differential privacy approaches or mechanisms to enhance data utility.

Acknowledgments. This work was supported by the National Natural Science Foundation of China with No. 61173190, No. 61602290, and No. 61662009, Natural Science Basic Research Program of Shaanxi Province with No. 2017JQ6038, Fundamental Research Founds for the Central Universities with No. GK201704016, No. 2016CBY004, No. GK201603093, No. GK201501008, and No. GK201402004, Program of Key Science and Technology Innovation Team in Shaanxi Province with No. 2014KTC-18, and Open Project Fund of Guizhou Provincial Key Laboratory of Public Big Data with No. 2017BDKFJJ026.

References

1. Dwork, C., McSherry, F., Nissim, K., Smith, A.: Calibrating noise to sensitivity in private data analysis. In: Halevi, S., Rabin, T. (eds.) TCC 2006. LNCS, vol. 3876, pp. 265–284. Springer, Heidelberg (2006). https://doi.org/10.1007/11681878_14
2. Dwork, C., Kenthapadi, K., McSherry, F., Mironov, I., Naor, M.: Our data, ourselves: privacy via distributed noise generation. In: Vaudenay, S. (ed.) EUROCRYPT 2006. LNCS, vol. 4004, pp. 486–503. Springer, Heidelberg (2006). https://doi.org/10.1007/11761679_29
3. McSherry, F., Talwar, K.: Mechanism design via differential privacy. In: 48th Annual IEEE Symposium on Foundations of Computer Science, pp. 94–103. IEEE (2007)
4. Warner, S.L.: Randomized response: a survey technique for eliminating evasive answer bias. J. Am. Stat. Assoc. **60**(309), 63–69 (1965)
5. Katz, J., Lindell, Y.: Introduction to Modern Cryptography. CRC Press, Boca Raton (2014)
6. Dwork, C., Roth, A.: The algorithmic foundations of differential privacy. Found. Trends® Theor. Comput. Sci. **9**(3–4), 211–407 (2014)
7. Yang, B., Sato, I., Nakagawa, H.: Bayesian differential privacy on correlated data. In: Proceedings of the 2015 ACM SIGMOD International Conference on Management of Data, pp. 747–762. ACM (2015)
8. Abadi, M., Chu, A., Goodfellow, I., McMahan, H. B., Mironov, I., Talwar, K., Zhang, L.: Deep learning with differential privacy. In: Proceedings of the 2016 ACM SIGSAC Conference on Computer and Communications Security, pp. 308–318. ACM (2016)
9. Tong, W., Hua, J., Zhong, S.: A jointly differentially private scheduling protocol for ridesharing services. IEEE Trans. Inf. Forensics Secur. **12**(10), 2444–2456 (2017)
10. Mitrovic, M., Bun, M., Krause, A., Karbasi, A.: Differentially private submodular maximization: data summarization in disguise. In: International Conference on Machine Learning, pp. 2478–2487. ACM (2017)

11. Qin, Z., Yang, Y., Yu, T., Khalil, I., Xiao, X., Ren, K.: Heavy hitter estimation over set-valued data with local differential privacy. In: Proceedings of the 2016 ACM SIGSAC Conference on Computer and Communications Security, pp. 192–203. ACM (2016)
12. Fanaee-T, H., Gama, J.: Event labeling combining ensemble detectors and background knowledge. Prog. Artif. Intell. **2**(2–3), 113–127 (2014)
13. Lipowski, A., Lipowska, D.: Roulette-wheel selection via stochastic acceptance. Phys. A: Stat. Mech. Appl. **391**(6), 2193–2196 (2012)

The De-anonymization Method Based on User Spatio-Temporal Mobility Trace

Zhenyu Chen[1,2]([✉]), Yanyan Fu[1], Min Zhang[1], Zhenfeng Zhang[1], and Hao Li[1]

[1] Institute of Software Chinese Academy of Science, Beijing, China
{chenzhenyu,fuyy,mzhang,zfzhang,lihao}@tca.iscas.ac.cn
[2] University of Chinese Academy of Sciences, Beijing, China

Abstract. Nowadays user mobility traces are more and more likely to de-anonymize users in addition to other types of data. Among them, model-based approaches usually provide more accurate de-anonymize than that of feature-locations-based approaches. More recently, Hidden Markov Model (HMM) based approaches are proposed to find out the mobility pattern of user mobility traces. However, in the key step of the hidden state definition, existing models rely on the fixed classification of time, space or number, which can hardly suit for all various users. In this paper, we propose a user de-anonymization method based on HMM. Different from current approaches, the method utilizes a novel density-based HMM, which uses the density-based clustering to obtain hidden states of HMM from three-dimensional (time, latitude and longitude) spatio-temporal data, and provide much better performance. Furthermore, we also propose a frequent spatio-temporal cube filter (FSTC-Filter) which significantly reduces the number of candidate models and thus improves the efficiency.

Keywords: De-anonymization · Density-based HMM
Frequent spatio-temporal cube · Mobility trace

1 Introduction

With the popularity of smartphones, application service providers can easily collect personal activity information from billions of users, but this also brings about the massive risk of user privacy leakage. Usually, these providers will take means of anonymization before publishing them to the public, for instance, substituting users identifiers (e.g., name, SSN) with pseudonyms, but the user identity still can be compromised due to a more in-depth study. Some famous de-anonymization examples include discovering the political stance from Netflix viewing history and linking Netflix account to real users [10], distinguishing users in the anonymous social network by comparing the similarity of graph structure [9,11]. Recently, user mobility traces can be better used to predict future locations [5,14,15], distinguish abnormal users [6,7], also include de-anonymize users.

© Springer International Publishing AG, part of Springer Nature 2018
S. Qing et al. (Eds.): ICICS 2017, LNCS 10631, pp. 459–471, 2018.
https://doi.org/10.1007/978-3-319-89500-0_40

Early studies [2,3,8,17] usually take several feature places (e.g., most frequent locations) of each user as user mobility profile. Some studies [4,12,13,18] build a statistical probability model (e.g., Markov chain, HMM) as user mobility profile. As we will see in Sect. 2, model-based approaches usually provide more accurate match than feature-locations based approaches. More recently, several approaches based on HMM can better find out the activity pattern of user mobility traces. In these approaches, core part is the definition of hidden states, which determines the effectiveness of the model. Existing models choose hidden states either on the classification of time and space or EM-cluster, which cant handle all various users simultaneously.

In this paper, we propose a novel density-based HMM, which uses the density-based clustering to obtain hidden states of HMM from three-dimensional (time, latitude and longitude) data. Rather than assuming everyone has the same hidden states, our density-based HMM automatically extract distinct hidden states from the mobility trace of each user, considering the time and spatial density feature of data. Furthermore, we also propose a frequent spatio-temporal cube filter (FSTC-Filter) to improve de-anonymization efficiency.

In general, the contribution of this paper are summarized as follows:

1. We define a density-based HMM (DBHMM) to profile user mobility. DBHMM establish an accurate mobility model by generating more personalized hidden states for each user. The clusters (hidden states) and its number are generated directly from each user's data.
2. We introduce a frequent spatio-temporal cube filter (FSTC-Filter) to reduce the number of candidate models for anonymous trace matching. It improves the efficiency of attack while ensuring accuracy.
3. We perform experiments based on two real datasets. Results show that DBHMM describes user behavior more accurately than others, FSTC-Filter precisely filters out lots of incorrect users to improve efficiency.

The rest of this paper is organized as follows. Section 2 highlights related works and analyses existing approaches. Section 3 introduces the framework of our method. Two essential components are elaborated in Sects. 4 and 5, respectively. Extensive experimental evaluation is presented in Sect. 6. Finally, Sect. 7 concludes this paper.

2   Related Work

Existing de-anonymization approaches based on user locations can classify into two major categories. One kind of works builds user mobility profile by extracting his/her feature locations, which we call the feature-locations-based approaches. Another build a statistical probability model from his/her mobility traces, which we call the model-based approaches.

Feature-locations-based approaches characterize a user by his/her feature locations(usually frequent locations). Zang and Bolot [17] performed a study on the top-k most frequently visited locations of each user. De Montjoye et al.

[2] demonstrated that four randomly selected spatio-temporal points in one's trace could uniquely identify 95% of individuals. Freudiger et al. [3] proposed the home/work pair as a quasi-identifier to each user. Naini et al. [8] used the location distribution histogram as a profile to identify users.

The feature-locations-based approaches are mostly computational efficient, but which with limited accuracy. There are three reasons for the flaw: (1) They omit the time sequence; therefore, it can not distinguish the feature locations of user A and B in Table 1, e.g., t1: $l1 \rightarrow l2$ matches with both user A and B. (2) Ignored lots of non-feature locations, it can't find a match for a trace without feature locations, e.g., t2: $l3 \rightarrow l4$; (3) A mobility trace contains different feature locations of many users, e.g., t3: $l1 \rightarrow l2 \rightarrow l3 \rightarrow l4$ can match user A by l1, l2, and match user C by l2, l3.

Table 1. Example of feature-locations shortcoming analysis

User	Daily traces	Feature locations	Anonymous mobility traces	Matching results
A	$l1 \rightarrow l2 \rightarrow l3 \rightarrow l4$, $l1 \rightarrow l2 \rightarrow l4$	l1, l2	t1: $l1 \rightarrow l2$ (A)	t1: A, B
B	$l2 \rightarrow l1 \rightarrow l6$, $l2 \rightarrow l1$	l1, l2	t2: $l3 \rightarrow l4$ (A)	t2: null
C	$l2 \rightarrow l3 \rightarrow l6$, $l2 \rightarrow l3 \rightarrow l5$	l2, l3	t3: $l1 \rightarrow l2 \rightarrow l3 \rightarrow l4$ (A)	t3: A, C

Model-based approaches train a statistical probability model as user mobility profile. If the probability of an anonymous user matching with an existing user model is higher than others, they are considered to be the same user. Gambs et al. [4] proposed the Mobility Markov Chain (MMC) user mobility profile. It only considers the location information, taking no time influence into account. Pan et al. [12] built a Markov-modulated Poisson process model for check-in data. It envisions the trace state change as a Markov jump process (MJP), each check-in is an inhomogeneous Poisson process depends on the state, and check-in locations are consistent with Gaussian distribution.

The most relevant works to our paper are these HMM-related approaches. Zhang et al. [18] proposed GMove that couples the subtasks of user grouping and mobility modeling. They use EM algorithm to generate hidden states of HMM for each group. But they nominate a unified number of hidden states for any groups without caring for their differences. Wang et al. [13] defined UHMM to profile user mobility behavior and exploit it to launch the de-anonymization attack. It divides one day into 24 time spans as 24 hidden states. But user behavior is not entirely related to time; it ignores the user subjective initiative.

Generally speaking, model-based approaches reflect the time sequence of traces by state transition and capture non-feature locations as observations. So they provide more accurate match than that of feature-locations based approaches. However, there are still two deficiencies of them. Firstly, allocating hidden states to all users by the same rules may bring in inconvenience for some of the users. Secondly, the time cost is far more than feature-locations. We will discuss and improve them in detail in Sects. 4 and 5, respectively.

3   Overview

In this paper, we propose a de-anonymization attack method that is built upon density-based HMM and FSTC-Filter. As discussed above, existing HMM is not personalized enough to capture user mobility feature and its time cost is too much. Firstly, we improve mobility modeling by generating more accurate hidden states. With density-based clustering algorithm, we obtain hidden states for each user without specifying unified states or states number. Besides, we add a FSTC-Filter to reduce the number of candidate models for anonymous mobility trace matching. The sub-phases of filter and mobility model matching can minimize time cost and ensure accuracy respectively.

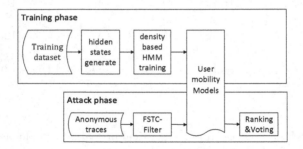

Fig. 1. The framework of our method

Figure 1 depicts the framework of our method, which includes two major phases: the training phase and the attack phase. The training phase is the preparation stage for de-anonymization. It used to train a statistical probability model as mobility profile for each user. We first generate personalized hidden states by density-based clustering algorithm, then train the density-based HMM depending on the above hidden states. The attack phase is the execution stage for de-anonymization. It used to find out the user who is the most probable owner of anonymous mobility traces. In this phase, we de-anonymize anonymous data in three steps: Firstly, we utilize frequent spatio-temporal cube filter (FSTC-Filter) to reduce the number of candidate models for anonymous trace matching. Then, we use the Viterbi algorithm to generate matching probability between anonymous traces and filtered candidate models. Finally, through ranking and voting, we pick a final match result from the top-k candidate sets.

4   Density-Based HMM Training

In this section, we show how to generate more accurate hidden states accurately for each user, and describe how to build user HMM with these hidden states.

4.1   Principle of Hidden States Selection

One most important principle of hidden states generation is that hidden states should not appoint in advance. Directly specified means the hidden states of all users are generated according to a uniform principle. Study [13] specified each hour as a hidden state, study [1] specified a grid as a hidden state. These approaches may generate inaccurate hidden states which result in an inaccurate model. As Fig. 2 shows, if we specify each grid as a hidden state, it can't accurately distinguish the mobility points of user B since its points are in different grids. Therefore these specified hidden states cannot profile the user accurately. Moreover, although there may exist such a classification which fits one person well, definitely there is no division which fits all users well.

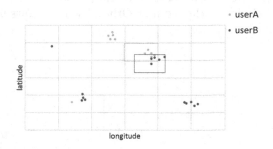

Fig. 2. Example of existing hidden state

Secondly, the number of hidden states of a user should be variable, since different people may have different mobility patterns. To a certain extent, EM clustering methods guarantee a more precise correspondence between hidden states and user behavior when users have similar patterns [7,18]. They specify a uniform cluster number for all users. However, different users may have a different number of hidden states in practice. As shown in Fig. 2, user B has three hidden states and a discrete point. If we specify that there are 2 hidden states for user B, it is highly possible that most of B's movements are clustered as one state while the discrete point as the other state. EM algorithm cannot fix the problem that given a wrong number of user states.

4.2   Generation of Hidden State

Obviously, density clustering that finds the high-density area separated by low-density area can solve the above problems. With the density parameters, it can

automatically obtain all high-density areas that have an uncertain number and
any shape. On the other hand, the dense area of spatio-temporal points usually
implies a pattern of user mobility, which corresponds to the purpose of hidden
states generation.

We build our hidden states generation algorithm by extending the density
joinable cluster (DJ-Cluster) algorithm (a typical density-based clustering algorithm [20]) to three-dimensional space. The main idea of DJ is to generate the
initial cluster by parameters Minpts and ε, then merges the initial clusters step
by step until it stops. Minpts is the minimal number of points needed to create an initial cluster, while ε is the maximum radius of the initial cluster. The
Euclidean distance d (p1, p2) is adapted to measure the distance between two
spatio-temporal points p1 (t1, Lat1, Lon1) and p2 (t2, Lat2, Lon2). More specifically, d (p1, p2) is defined as follows:

$$d(p1, p2) = \sqrt{(t1 - t2)^2 + a * (Lat1 - Lat2)^2 + b * (lon1 - Lon2)^2}$$

where a = 111000, b = 111000 * cos((Lat1 + Lat2)/2) are parameters that translate the distance measure unit to meters, and time measure unit in seconds.

Given the points are shown in Fig. 3(a) and (b), four hidden states are generated which are all circled in the red line. Other discrete points not in any cluster
are regarded as a special state.

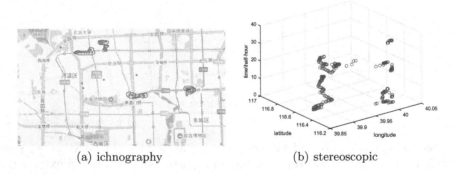

(a) ichnography   (b) stereoscopic

Fig. 3. Dense points correspond to hidden states (Color figure online)

4.3 Density-Based HMM Training

Known how to generate hidden states, we can build the density-based HMM for
a user with all his/her mobility traces. More specifically, the DBHMM = {O, S,
Π, A, E } is defined as follows:

- Hidden states set $S = \{s_1, s_2, \ldots, s_m\}$, is generated from user traces by
  density-based clustering.
- Observation set $O = \{o_1, o_2, \ldots, o_n\}$, in which each element is a spatio-
  temporal point/record visited by a user.

- Initial probability set Π, is the initial probability distribution of the hidden states. The initial probability of a hidden state s_i is defined as:

$$\pi_i = p(s_i) = \frac{count(s_i)}{\sum_{j=1}^{m} count(s_j)}$$

  where $count(s_i)$ represents the number of records/points belongs to s_i.
- Transition probability set $A = \{a_{1,1}, a_{1,2}, \ldots, a_{i,j}, \ldots\}$, each element $a_{i,j}$ represents the probability of transferring from s_i to s_j, which is defined as:

$$a_{i,j} = \frac{T(s_i, s_j)}{T(s_i)}$$

  where $T(s_i)$ indicates how many times the user visits a place in s_i and the next place not in s_i, while $T(s_i, s_i)$ indicates how many times the user visits a place in s_i and visits the next place in s_j.
- Emission probability set $E = \{e_1(o_1), \ldots, e_k(o_i), \ldots, e_m(o_n)\}$, each element $e_k(o_i)$ is the probability that observation is o_i when the state is s_k, which is defined as

$$e_k(o_i) = p(o_i|s_k) = \frac{\phi(o_i|s_k)}{\sum_{j=1}^{n} \phi(o_j|s_k)}$$

  where $\phi(o_j|s_k)$ indicates how many times the user visits o_j in s_k.

In particular, we note that user behavior is not exactly similar every day. For example, most people do not go to the workplaces at weekends. Therefore, we build user mobility model based on three granularities. Firstly, each user only has a unique model; secondly, each user has a rest day model and a workday model; thirdly, each user has seven models (from Sunday to Saturday).

5   Execution of De-anonymization Attack

Most of the existing HMM-based approaches always calculates the matching probability by Viterbi Algorithm. Viterbi Algorithm is a dynamic programming algorithm for finding the most likely sequence of hidden states that results in a sequence of observed events. If we have an observation set O (trace) and a HMM, the probability P that the observation set match with the HMM can be defined as:

$$P = max_{j \in S}(\delta_n(j)), \qquad \delta_n(j) = max[\delta_{n-1}(i) * a_{ij}] * e_j(o_n)$$

where $\delta_n(j)$ is the observation o_n in the hidden state s_j.

However, the efficiency cost should be considered seriously. The time complexity of the Viterbi algorithm is $O(n * k * k)$, the time complexity of feature-locations based approaches is $O(n)$, where n is the number of points in an anonymous trace, k is the number of hidden states of a model. The computational cost of HMM-based approaches is much larger than another. For example, if an anonymous trace match with a user who has 10 hidden states, the time cost of Viterbi Algorithm is 100 times of feature-locations. There are also scalability concerns about the number of users. In reality, de-anonymization attacks may involve millions of users that are far more than users in the research experiment.

To overcome the deficiency, we introduce a frequent spatio-temporal cube filter (FSTC-Filter) to reduce the number of users to match with anonymous mobility trace. We divide the three-dimensional (time, latitude and longitude) space into spatio-temporal cubes. One day is divided into 24 intervals by hour, latitude and longitude are divided into intervals by 1 km. The maximum number of cubes is Nx * Ny * 24, and each cube's volume is about 1 km * 1 km * 1 h. Nx and Ny are the numbers of segments of latitude and longitude in user trace range. A cube is a FSTC when the point of user trace appears in the cube greater than the threshold (depend on the density of dataset). We set the overlapping proportion x that is t_a match with each FSTC; no overlapping threshold is λ. If $x \geq 1 - \lambda$, we skip the step that match with DBHMM. The x calculate as follows:

$$x = \frac{|c \in t_a \cap FSTC_i|}{|t_a|}$$

where $|c \in t_a \cap FSTC_i|$ is the number of t_a cubes also in FSTC, repeat the count of the same cube that multiple appears; $|t_a|$ is the number of cubes in t_a.

Table 2. Example of attack execution

Anonymous mobility trace	FSTC	Filter results when $\lambda = 0.5$	HMM	Matching results
$t_a = \{c_1,$	$FSTC_1 = \{c_1, c_2, c_4, c_{11}\}$	x = 0.7, pass	$DBHMM_1$	p1
$c_5, c_3, c_2,$	$FSTC_2 = \{c_2, c_3, c_5, c_{21}\}$	x = 0.6, pass	$DBHMM_2$	p2
$c_2, c_2, c_3,$	$FSTC_4 = \{c_4, c_{41}, c_{42}\}$	x = 0.1	Skip	
$c_5, c_1, c_1\}$	$FSTC_3 = \{c_3, c_{31}, c_{32}\}$	x = 0.1	Skip	
	$FSTC_5 = \{c_5, c_{51}, c_{52}\}$	x = 0.2	Skip	

As Table 2 shows, we use an example to explain the execution process of de-anonymization. Assume we have an anonymous mobility trace t_a, each point of t_a is represented by its corresponding cube; there are five user models, each model consist of DBHMM and FSTC-Filter ($M_i = \{DBHMM_i, FSTC_i\}, i = 1, 2, \ldots, 5$). When t_a match with FSTC, the overlapping proportion of user3, 4, 5 is less than $1 - \lambda$, t_a only match with DBHMM of user1 and user2. Then, we get the Viterbi result of t_a and users. If an anonymous user only has t_a, the most top-k p is the result set. If an anonymous user has N traces, we select the most frequent k user in the N*top-k set.

6   Experiment

In this section, we evaluated our method based on data sets described in Sect. 6.1. All the codes were implemented in JAVA, and the experiments were conducted on a computer with Intel Core i7-4770 3.4 GHz CPU and 8 GB memory.

6.1   Data

In this study, we consider two widely used real-life mobility trace data sets, namely GeoLife [19], Gowalla [16]. Note that we will use only the longitude, altitude, date and time from these datasets.

GeoLife contains GPS traces of 182 users of Beijing collected per 5s from Apr. 2007 to Oct. 2011. Each record includes pseudonym, latitude, longitude, altitude, date and time. To ensure the accuracy of models, we just use the data of users who have more than 15 daily records, and total 105 users up to the standard.

Gowalla contains 456,988 check-in records of 10,162 users in the California and Nevada between Feb. 2009 and Oct. 2010. Each record includes user ID, time, coordinate (latitude and longitude) and POI information. Our experiment chooses 1072 users who have more than 100 records.

We divided each dataset into two parts: the training set and the test set. And we randomly choose 80% data as the training set, the rest 20% as the test set. These two sets are not any overlapping.

The raw data sets are not suitable for user modeling directly. First, it can cause overfitting. Because its precision is centimeter, a user record in the same place may be treated as different locations (e.g., p1(39.994622, 116.326757), p2(39.994614, 116.326753), distance is about 80 cm, but p1 ≠ p2). This overfitting will lead to the mismatch between anonymous traces and candidate users. Second, high-precision data requires excessive calculation. In the experiment, the raw spatio-temporal data precision is generalized, latitude and longitude precision is about 100 m, time precision is half an hour.

6.2   Result Evaluation

To compare with our method, we implemented the following user mobility models for de-anonymization: (1) MMC [12], construct mobility Markov chains from the training and test data without considering time influence, comparing the similarity of two Markov chains. (2) Rand4 [10] randomly select four spatio-temporal points or POIs as user mobility profile to identify users. (3) UHMM [13] train User-HMM for each user, but specify 24 h of a day as 24 hidden states.

As shown in Fig. 4, the accuracy of our method significantly outperforms all the other three methods on both Geolife and Gowalla. In contrast, the accuracy of MMC in these two datasets is less than 0.3, no time, multiple build MMC and measure of MMC distance all affect its accuracy. In both datasets, UHMM accuracy is better than MMC about 0.2. It builds user mobility model by HMM and considering the spatio-temporal influences. But it specifies hidden states,

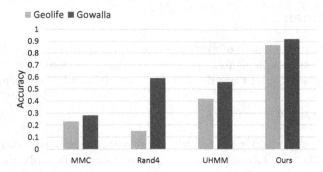

Fig. 4. The accuracy of different methods

may cause wrong matches. The accuracy of Rand4 in Geolife is the worst. But in Gowalla, the accuracy of Rand4 method is better than MMC and UHMM. It is probably because of that, Gowalla is user initiative published points, randomly select 4 points may uniquely identify a user; but randomly selected 4 points in Geolife may choose useless points that belong to multiple users' trace.

The accuracy of all different methods in Gowalla is better than in Geolife. Gowalla is check-in data set. Each point contains lots of biased information and behavior characteristics. Geolife is GPS data that collected by devices. Most points provide lots of non-subjective and irrelevant information. Besides, Geolife includes traces of MSRA employees who work in the same location; its mobility trace similarity is higher than average level.

6.3   Effects of Parameters

As mentioned earlier, there are four primary parameters in DBHMM: λ, ε, k, and m. After tuning these parameters, we find that the trends of all parameters are very similar on GeoLife and Gowalla. So we only report the results on GeoLife.

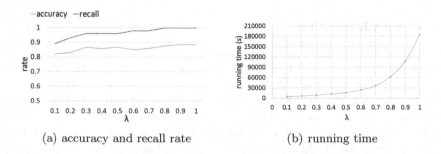

(a) accuracy and recall rate   (b) running time

Fig. 5. Effect of parameter λ

We first study parameter λ. It indicates the most non-overlap proportion that anonymous trace can pass a FSTC-Filter. Figure 5a shows the accuracy and recall rate are slowly increasing with the parameter λ before it gradually becomes stable. The increasing trend of recall rate is slightly greater than accuracy. When λ is small, it may filter out some correct users, recall rate and accuracy increase with λ; with λ become large, more users will pass filter, resulting in a larger recall rate increasing than accuracy. Figure 5b shows the total cost of 1861 traces (total contain 4861679 records) match with 105 models (1861 * 105 match probabilities are calculated). The running time increases exponentially with λ. It is because that increasing λ will pass a lot of incorrect users, then the running time increase rapidly. As we can see, $\lambda = 0.3$ is a turning point which both accuracy and recall rate tend to be stable, and running time also is in the smooth growth stage.

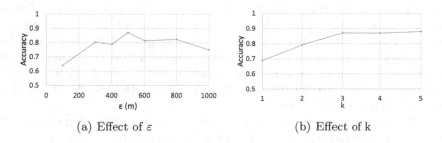

(a) Effect of ε (b) Effect of k

Fig. 6. Effects of parameters ε and k for accuracy

Then, we report the effect of ε, the parameter of density-based cluster algorithm. Figure 6a shows the accuracy change when ε increase from 100 to 1000. Not hard to observe, the accuracy first increases with ε and then decreases. A small ε tend to generate a lot of small clusters, while a large ε tend to generate only a large cluster, making the model inaccurate. In a word, ε should not set to a too small or too large value in practice (e.g., $\varepsilon = 500$).

Next, we proceed to study parameter k. It decides the number of users in the result set. Figure 6b shows the accuracy of top-k when k varies from 1 to 5. It first increases with k, quickly become stable as long as $k \geq 3$. Obviously, $k = 3$ is the optimal point what we want to find.

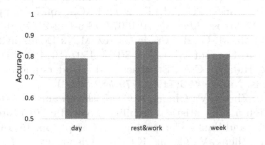

Fig. 7. Effect of model granularity

We also study the effect of parameter m which indicates the granularity of user model. As shown in Fig. 7, the accuracy that each user only has one unique model is the lowest; the accuracy that each user has two models (rest day and work day) is the highest. Due to overfitting, the accuracy that each user has seven models (Sunday to Saturday) is reduced. It suggests that user activity is significantly different between weekdays and weekends.

7 Conclusion

In this paper, we propose a de-anonymization attack that infers the owner of an anonymous set of user mobility traces. Our method distinguishes itself from existing methods in three aspects. (1) It analyses the advantages of feature-locations-based approaches and model-based approaches. (2) It uses frequent spatio-temporal cube to perform rationally coarse-grained filtering. (3) It uses density-based clustering to extract hidden states of HMM that can reflect the subjective initiative of each user and captures user personalized feature. Our experiments on two real-life datasets show that our method is effective in different types of user mobility traces.

In the future, we plan to extend the current work by following avenues. We will further introduce the semantic and social element to our model, integrate multiple signals to generate a comprehensive view of user behavior. We will also explore a privacy protection mechanism to resist this de-anonymization attack while ensuring data usability.

Acknowledgement. This work is supported by the National Natural Science Foundation of China (No. U1636216, No. 61232005, No. 61402456)

References

1. Ayhan, S., Samet, H.: Aircraft trajectory prediction made easy with predictive analytics. In: Proceedings of the 22nd International Conference on Knowledge Discovery and Data Mining (2016)
2. De Montjoye, Y.-A., Hidalgo, C.A., Verleysen, M., Blondel, V.D.: Unique in the crowd: the privacy bounds of human mobility. Sci. Rep. **3**, 1376 (2013)
3. Freudiger, J., Shokri, R., Hubaux, J.-P.: Evaluating the privacy risk of location-based services. In: Danezis, G. (ed.) FC 2011. LNCS, vol. 7035, pp. 31–46. Springer, Heidelberg (2012). https://doi.org/10.1007/978-3-642-27576-0_3
4. Gambs, S., Killijian, M.-O., del Prado Cortez, M.N.: De-anonymization attack on geolocated data. J. Comput. Syst. Sci. **80**(8), 1597–1614 (2014)
5. Gonzalez, M.C., Hidalgo, C.A., Barabasi, A.-L.: Understanding individual human mobility patterns. Nature **453**(7196), 779–782 (2008)
6. Lin, M., Cao, H., Zheng, V., Chang, K.C., Krishnaswamy, S.: Mobile user verification/identification using statistical mobility profile. In: 2015 International Conference on Big Data and Smart Computing (BigComp), pp. 15–18. IEEE (2015)
7. Lin, M., Cao, H., Zheng, V., Chang, K.C.-C., Krishnaswamy, S.: Mobility profiling for user verification with anonymized location data. In: Twenty-Fourth International Joint Conference on Artificial Intelligence (2015)

8. Naini, F.M., Unnikrishnan, J., Thiran, P., Vetterli, M.: Where you are is who you are: user identification by matching statistics. IEEE Trans. Inf. Forensics Secur. **11**(2), 358–372 (2016)
9. Narayanan, A., Shi, E., Rubinstein, B.I.P.: Link prediction by de-anonymization: how we won the kaggle social network challenge. In: The 2011 International Joint Conference on Neural Networks (IJCNN), pp. 1825–1834. IEEE (2011)
10. Narayanan, A., Shmatikov, V.: Robust de-anonymization of large sparse datasets. In: IEEE Symposium on Security and Privacy, SP 2008, pp. 111–125. IEEE (2008)
11. Narayanan, A., Shmatikov, V.: De-anonymizing social networks. In: 2009 30th IEEE Symposium on Security and Privacy, pp. 173–187. IEEE (2009)
12. Pan, J., Rao, V., Agarwal, P., Gelfand, A.: Markov-modulated marked Poisson processes for check-in data. In: International Conference on Machine Learning, pp. 2244–2253 (2016)
13. Wang, R., Zhang, M., Feng, D., Fu, Y., Chen, Z.: A de-anonymization attack on geo-located data considering spatio-temporal influences. In: Qing, S., Okamoto, E., Kim, K., Liu, D. (eds.) ICICS 2015. LNCS, vol. 9543, pp. 478–484. Springer, Cham (2016). https://doi.org/10.1007/978-3-319-29814-6_41
14. Wang, Y., Yuan, N.J., Lian, D., Xu, L., Xie, X., Chen, E., Rui, Y.: Regularity and conformity: location prediction using heterogeneous mobility data. In: Proceedings of the 21th ACM SIGFKDD International Conference on Knowledge Discovery and Data Mining, pp. 1275–1284. ACM (2015)
15. Xue, A.Y., Zhang, R., Zheng, Y., Xie, X., Huang, J., Xu, Z.: Destination prediction by sub-trajectory synthesis and privacy protection against such prediction. In: 2013 IEEE 29th International Conference on Data Engineering (ICDE), pp. 254–265. IEEE (2013)
16. Yuan, Q., Cong, G., Ma, Z., Sun, A., Thalmann, N.M.: Time-aware point-of-interest recommendation. In: Proceedings of the 36th International ACM SIGIR Conference on Research and Development in Information Retrieval, pp. 363–372. ACM (2013)
17. Zang, H., Bolot, J.: Anonymization of location data does not work: a large-scale measurement study. In: Proceedings of the 17th Annual International Conference on Mobile Computing and Networking, pp. 145–156. ACM (2011)
18. Zhang, C., Zhang, K., Yuan, Q., Zhang, L., Hanratty, T., Han, J.: Gmove: group-level mobility modeling using geo-tagged social media. In: Proceedings of the 22nd ACM SIGKDD International Conference on Knowledge Discovery and Data Mining, pp. 1305–1314. ACM (2016)
19. Zheng, Y., Zhang, L., Xie, X., Ma, W.-Y.: Mining interesting locations and travel sequences from GPS trajectories. In: Proceedings of the 18th International Conference on World Wide Web, pp. 791–800. ACM (2009)
20. Zhou, C., Frankowski, D., Ludford, P., Shekhar, S., Terveen, L.: Discovering personally meaningful places: an interactive clustering approach. ACM Trans. Inf. Syst. (TOIS) **25**(3), 12 (2007)

Privacy-Preserving Disease Risk Test
Based on Bloom Filters

Jun Zhang, Linru Zhang, Meiqi He, and Siu-Ming Yiu$^{(\boxtimes)}$

Department of Computer Science, The University of Hong Kong,
Pokfulam Road, Pok Fu Lam, Hong Kong
{jzhang3,lrzhang,mqhe,smyiu}@cs.hku.hk

Abstract. Decreasing costs in genome sequencing have been paving the way for personalised medicine. An increasing number of individuals choose to undergo disease risk tests provided by medical units. However, it poses serious privacy threats on both the individuals' genomic data and the tests' specifics. Several solutions have been proposed to address the privacy issues, but they all suffer from high storage or communication overhead. In this paper, we put forward a general framework based on bloom filters, reducing the storage cost by 100x. To reduce communication overhead, we create index for encrypted genomic data. We speed up the searching of genomic data by 60x with bloom filter tree, compared to B_+ tree index. Finally, we implement our scheme using the genomic data of a real person. The experimental results show the practicality of our scheme.

Keywords: Genomic privacy · Bloom filters
Homomorphic encryption

1 Introduction

The first full sequencing of a human genome ("Human Genome Project")[1] was completed in 2003, which takes 13 years, 3 billion dollars and involves more than 20 institutions world wide. Since then, numerous companies and research institutions have been moving toward more and more affordable and accurate technologies. For example, a genomics company called Illumina has brought the price of sequencing a human genome down to $1,000 in 2014, and the company claims that its newest machine can bring the cost down to $100 over the next few years. Advances in Whole Genome Sequencing (WGS) make genome testing available to the masses. At the same time, it stimulates the development of personalized healthcare such as predicting disease predisposition or response to the treatment. Some commercial companies (e.g., 23andMe[2]) already provide low-cost risk tests to their customers for certain diseases.

---

[1] The human genome project, https://www.genome.gov/12011238/an-overview-of-the-human-genomeproject/.

[2] https://www.23andme.com. Accessed on 8/Sep/2017.

© Springer International Publishing AG, part of Springer Nature 2018
S. Qing et al. (Eds.): ICICS 2017, LNCS 10631, pp. 472–486, 2018.
https://doi.org/10.1007/978-3-319-89500-0_41

Certified Institution (CI)   Storage and Processing Unit (SPU)

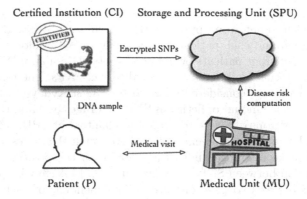

Fig. 1. System model for disease risk computation.

However, genomic data disclosure brings great risk to personal privacy. Genomic information not only uniquely identifies its owner [1], but also reveals the genetic risk of diseases [2], leading to genetic discrimination (i.e., insurance or job hunting). Due to its hereditary nature, disclosure of an individual's genome undermines the genomic privacy of his close relatives [3]. Although Genetic Information Non-discrimination Act (GINA) prohibits unauthorized use of genomic data, these kinds of laws are difficult to enforce. Furthermore, the genomes remain stable over time which cannot be revoked once made public [4]. Traditional anonymization methods have been proved to be ineffective for genomic data [5,6]. As a result, current research focuses on privacy-enhancing technologies to protect genomic privacy. In general, we can classify the existing works into five main categories: (i) genome-wide association study (GWAS) [7], (ii) private string searching and comparisons [8], (iii) sequence alignments [9], (iv) private release of aggregate data [10], and (v) genomic tests [11].

Disease Risk Computation Model. In this paper, we concentrate on protecting both the patients' genomic data and tests' specifics during disease risk tests. We adopt a similar model as [11] which involves a Patient (P), a Certified Institution (CI), a Storage and Processing Unit (SPU) and a Medical Unit (MU) as shown in Fig. 1. One patient provides his sample (e.g., his saliva) to the certified institution for sequencing. CI is a trusted party and responsible for sequencing and encrypting the patient's genomic data. For efficiency and security, the encrypted genomic data is stored and processed at a centralized SPU. MU can be a hospital or a pharmaceutical company, which makes requests to SPU for computation on the genomic data. CI and P are honest parties, while MU and SPU are honest-but-curious (honestly follow the protocol, but try to infer private information).

Motivations. Single Nucleotide Polymorphism (SNP) is the most common DNA variation that occurs at a specific position in the genome.[3] SNP might have

---

[3] Refer to the explanation of SNP in Sect. 3.1.

different states (i.e., homozygous or heterozygous). Position and state uniquely define a variation. There are approximately 50 million approved SNPs in the human population and each patient carries on average 4 million variants out of this 50 million. Different patients own different sets of 4 million SNPs. For a particular patient, all the 4 million SNPs are called *real SNPs*. The remaining SNPs (around 46 million) are considered as *fictitious SNPs*. Ayday et al. analyze the tradeoff between the amount of fictitious SNPs (storage cost) and the level of privacy [12]. The positions of SNPs are stored in plaintext at SPU, while the states are encrypted by homomorphic encryption.[4] Although the states are encrypted, SPU can still make inference about the states with the positions known, taking the correlation between SNPs into account (i.e., Linkage Disequilibrium [13] implies that SNPs at two positions are not independent of each other). As a result, they encrypt the positions in [11] as well. One drawback of [11] is that the squared value of each SNP must be stored at SPU to realize disease risk computation via homomorphic operations. Even worse, the protocol in [11] has two security weaknesses. The first one is that SPU can distinguish the requests for fictitious SNPs from the real ones, as they only store one ciphertext for all the fictitious SNPs. The second one is that it reveals how many SNPs are being tested. To remove the need of storing squares, Danezis and Cristofaro use an alternative encoding method [14]. Besides, their scheme encrypts all the possible SNPs of the human (50 million) for each patient. Consequently, SPU cannot differentiate requests for fictitious SNPs from those for real SNPs. Furthermore, they rely on *padding*, which means adding enough fictitious requests with zero weight to the test, to hide the number of SNPs relevant to the disease. Although they choose a small-ciphertext cryptosystem (AH-ECC [15]), downloading all the SNPs for a disease test is still unacceptable as it incurs high communication overhead. Besides, it depends heavily on the hardware security of a smartcard. In this paper, we aim to come up with a general framework to reduce the storage complexity of existing works, regardless of the underlying cryptosystem. For a disease risk test, we want MU to download only the SNPs related to the disease (padding included). Considering the large size of the dataset, it is impractical for SPU to search item by item. Therefore, a compact and efficient index structure is imperative.

Inspired by research on ciphertext retrieval [16], we treat the positions of SNPs as "keywords" and the corresponding states as "documents". Bloom filter [17] is a space-efficient probabilistic data structure to test whether an element is a member of a set. In our scheme, we let CI encrypt the positions of SNPs and insert them into bloom filters. For 50 million possible SNPs, we create 0.5 million bloom filters and each bloom filter contains 100 SNPs with the same state.[5] To avoid searching all the bloom filters sequentially, we organize them with a tree structure. Then CI uploads only the bloom filter tree to SPU. As SPU does not store the encrypted positions, bloom filters take up little space. For example, the size of a bloom filter which contains 1 million elements is around 1.7 megabytes

---

[4] See the definition of homomorphic encryption in Sect. 3.3.
[5] We discuss the reason for choosing 100 in Sect. 4.1.

(with false positive rate 0.1%). We link one ciphertext to each bloom filter at the leaf node level to represent the encrypted states of SNPs. In [11, 14], they store one ciphertext (encrypted state) for each position of SNPs. However, we store one ciphertext for 100 positions of SNPs. Without considering the small-size index structure, we reduce the storage overhead by 100x. On the other hand, bloom filter provides fast searching speed. For example, we only need to compute ten hash functions to check whether an element belongs to a bloom filter which contains 1 million elements (with false positive rate 0.1%). If MU wants to conduct disease risk test for a patient, MU will send a list of encrypted positions to SPU. Then SPU checks the bloom filter tree hierarchically and returns the corresponding encrypted states to MU if contained. The disease risk is computed on the MU's side via homomorphic operations. Once the computation is done, the final disease risk is disclosed to MU under the authorization of the patient. The main contributions of our work are summarized as follows.

(1) We put forward a general framework to reduce the storage overhead of existing works by 100x, regardless of the underlying cryptosystem. To be specific, we insert 100 positions into a bloom filter and link one ciphertext to the bloom filter to represent the encrypted states of SNPs.
(2) For genetic disease risk test, we are the first to create index for the encrypted SNPs stored at SPU. We organize bloom filters with a tree structure. Compared to B_+ tree index, we speed up the searching of SNPs by 60x.
(3) We implement our scheme with SNPs of a real person. The experimental results show the practicality of our scheme.

2   Related Work

Ziegeldorf et al. perform string matching with bloom filters [18] on the Track 3 dataset provided by the iDASH Secure Genome Analysis Competition. They assume n patients have SNPs at the same m locations, without considering the fact that different patients own different sets of 4 million SNPs. Our paper handles with the positions and states of the SNPs separately. We focus on the storage and searching of SNPs [11, 12, 14] in this paper. But beyond that, there exists some related work worthy to be discussed. Since the genome contains the most sensitive information, how and where should a patient's genomic data be stored have always been controversial. In the cloud? In a physician's office? On a smartphone? All have strengths and limitations in terms of portability, capacity, computing power and privacy. One personal genomic toolkit called GenoDroid is implemented on the Android platform [19]. To reduce the computation on mobile phones, the genomic data and certain cryptographic operations should be pre-processed on a laptop. On the other hand, although the SNPs are encrypted at SPU, a honest-but-curious SPU learns which SNPs are accessed, how often SNPs are used. Therefore, SPU might try to infer the nature of the ongoing test. To hide the access pattern, [20] uses Oblivious RAM (ORAM) to store DNA in several small encrypted blocks. The blocks are accessed in an oblivious manner.

However, the usage of ORAM will inevitably incur large cost due to periodically reshuffle process, which is impractical to implement in real-life scenarios. Furthermore, as MU knows the SNP weights, the risk computation can be seen as a linear equation where the states of SNPs are the unknowns. MU can launch brute-force attack. For example, we assume 10 SNPs are used in the disease risk test. Each SNP only has 3 different states. Therefore, MU can try all the 3^{10} combinations of SNPs. If one of these potential end-results matches the actual end-result of the test, the MU actually learns the states of the relevant SNPs. One simple obfuscation method is to provide the end-result of the genetic test to MU as a range. Therefore, Ayday et al. discussed how to use privacy-preserving integer comparison to report the range of genetic test [21]. Provided that the result range is divided into 4 smaller ranges $[0, 0.25)$, $[0.25, 0.50)$, $[0.50, 0.75)$ and $[0.75, 1]$, SPU compares the encrypted disease risk with those pre-defined boundaries to determine the range that the test result falls in. Moreover, they take into account clinical and environmental data to compute the final disease risk, such as hypertension, age, smoking and family disease history. The above techniques can be combined with our scheme proposed in this paper.

3   Preliminaries

3.1   Genomics Background

The human genome is encoded in double stranded DNA molecules consisting of two complementary polymer chains. Each chain consists of simple units called nucleotide or "bases", adenine (A), cytosine (C), guanine (G), thymine (T). Specifically, A/T and C/G are complementary pairs, respectively. The human genome consists of approximately three billion nucleotides, of which only around 0.1% of one individual's DNA is different from others due to genetic variation. The remaining 99.9% of the genome is identical between any two individuals.

What is SNP? Single Nucleotide Polymorphism (SNP) is the most common DNA variation. SNP is a variation in a single nucleotide that occurs at a specific position in the genome. For example, at a specific position of two DNA fragments in Fig. 2, the nucleotide C may appear in most individuals, but in a minority of individuals, the position is occupied by base T. In this case, we say there is a SNP at this position and we call the two possible nucleotide variations (C or T) alleles. Each individual carries two alleles at each SNP (one inherited from the father and one from the mother). There are approximately 50 million approved SNPs in the human population and each patient carries on average 4 million variants. Different patients own different sets of 4 million SNPs. For a particular patient, all the 4 million SNPs are called real SNPs and the remaining SNPs are considered as fictitious SNPs.

Relationship Between SNPs and Genetic Diseases: It is shown by Multiple Genome-Wide Association Studies (GWAS) that a patient's susceptibility to genetic diseases can be predicted from SNPs. Assume that the SNP in Fig. 2 (with alleles C and T) is relevant to a disease and T is the one carrying the disease

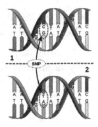

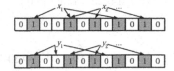

Fig. 2. Single nucleotide polymorphism (© David Hall, License: Creative Commons).

Fig. 3. An example of a bloom filter.

risk, then an individual with TT has the highest risk to develop the disease. CT implies lower disease risk. And individuals with CC are least likely to suffer from the disease. We use $\{0, 1, 2\}$ to represent the number of risk alleles. Furthermore, we adopt the encoding scheme in [14] to express $\{0, 1, 2\}$ as $\{100, 010, 001\}$, as binary encoding of SNPs is able to remove non-linear operations (i.e., squaring).

Disease Risk Computation: There are different functions for computing disease risk. One popular method is weighted averaging, which computes the predicted susceptibility by weighting the SNPs by their contributions. For each SNP_i, the contribution amount w_i is known by the medical unit, determined by previous studies on case and control groups. To be specific, w_i relies on position contribution p_i and state contribution c_i, and we have $w_i = p_i c_i$. Assume that we denote the set of SNPs of a user associated with disease X as I, the risk can be calculated by $S = \frac{\sum w_i I_i}{\sum p_i}$.

3.2 Bloom Filters

Bloom filter [17] is a space-efficient probabilistic data structure to test whether an element is a member of a set. It is represented by a m-bit array $B \in \{0, 1\}^m$. The bits of an empty bloom filter are all set to 0. Before inserting elements, we choose k independent hash functions $h_1, h_2, \cdots, h_k$ which map the elements into the range $[1, m]$. To add an element e_i to the bloom filter, we calculate k hash values $h_1(e_i), h_2(e_i), \cdots, h_k(e_i)$ and set the bits of B corresponding to those hash values to 1. Similarly, to test whether $e_i \in B$, we check the bits at positions $h_1(e_i), h_2(e_i), \cdots, h_k(e_i)$. If all the bits are 1, then e_i is considered as a member of the set. Otherwise, e_i is not contained in the set. In Fig. 3, we provide an example. Firstly, x_1 and x_2 are added to one bloom filter using three hash functions. Then we check whether y_1 or y_2 is in the set, and we can conclude that the set contains y_2 instead of y_1. Due to hash collisions, bloom filter may produce false positive, where it suggests that an element is in the set even though it is not. The false positive probability p is determined by the number of hash functions k, the number of added elements n and the length m of the bloom filter.

$$p = (1 - (1 - \frac{1}{m})^{kn})^k \tag{1}$$

Given a fixed n, if we want to keep p below a threshold ϵ, we need to set m to be $m \geq n \, log_2 \, e \cdot log_2 \left(\frac{1}{\epsilon}\right)$ where e is the base of the natural logarithm and $log_2 \, e \approx 1.44$ [22]. The optimal value for k is $\frac{m \ln(2)}{n}$. For many applications, false positives may be acceptable as long as their probability is sufficiently small.

3.3 Homomorphic Encryption

Homomorphic encryption performs computation on ciphertexts, and generates an encrypted result which matches the result of operations performed on the plaintexts when decrypted. Homomorphic encryption can be classified to three categories: (i) Fully Homomorphic Encryption (FHE), (ii) Somewhat homomorphic encryption (SWHE), and (iii) Partially Homomorphic Encryption (PHE). We focus on PHE in this paper and show an additively homomorphic encryption scheme - the modified paillier [23] in Fig. 4. The additive homomorphism is denoted as $E(m_1 + m_2) = E(m_1)E(m_2)^6$.

Given two safe primes p and q, we compute $N = pq$, $g = -a^{2N}$ $(a \in \mathbb{Z}_{N^2}^*)$, the secret key $s \in [1, \frac{N^2}{2}]$, the public key $(N, g, h = g^s)$.

Encryption: To encrypt plaintext $m \in \mathbb{Z}_N$, we select a random $r \in [1, \frac{N}{4}]$ and generate the ciphertext $E(m) = (C_m^{(1)}, C_m^{(2)})$ as below:

$$C_m^{(1)} = g^r \, mod \, N^2 \quad and \quad C_m^{(2)} = h^r(1 + mN) \, mod \, N^2 \tag{2}$$

Decryption:

$$t = \frac{C_m^{(2)}}{\left(C_m^{(1)}\right)^s} \qquad m = \frac{t - 1 \, mod \, N^2}{N} \tag{3}$$

Additive Homomorphism: Supposed that we have two plaintexts m_1, m_2, and their ciphertexts are $E(m_1) = (C_{m_1}^{(1)}, C_{m_1}^{(2)})$, $E(m_2) = (C_{m_2}^{(1)}, C_{m_2}^{(2)})$. The ciphertext $E(m_1 + m_2)$ can be computed as $E(m_1 + m_2) = (C_{m_1}^{(1)}C_{m_2}^{(1)}, C_{m_1}^{(2)}C_{m_2}^{(2)})$.

Proxy Re-encryption: A ciphertext $E(m) = (C_m^{(1)}, C_m^{(2)})$ can be re-encrypted under the same public key, by using a new random number $r_1 \in [1, n/4]$.

$$C_m^{(1)'} = g^{r_1}C_m^{(1)} \qquad C_m^{(2)'} = h^{r_1}C_m^{(2)} \tag{4}$$

Fig. 4. The modified paillier cryptosystem

4   Our Scheme

In this paper, we aim to put forward a general framework to reduce the storage overhead, regardless of the underlying cryptosystem. For a disease risk test, we want MU to download only the SNPs related to the disease (padding included). Thus, we are supposed to build index to make SPU efficiently select SNPs. Recall that position and state uniquely define a SNP, we should select cryptosystems for them separately. In Sect. 4.1, we provide you with the building blocks required to construct a privacy-preserving disease risk test protocol. Then we demonstrate our scheme in Sect. 4.2.

---

[6] m_1, m_2 are plaintexts and $E(m_1)$, $E(m_2)$ are their corresponding ciphertexts.

4.1 Building Blocks

Encryption of SNPs' Positions. As position information of SNPs is also sensitive, CI needs to decide on a cryptosystem to encrypt the positions. We provide two options which apply to different scenarios - a symmetric encryption scheme (i.e., AES), and a public key encryption scheme (i.e., ECC). Symmetric scheme needs the help of P to submit MU's requests to SPU. Whereas, public key encryption scheme enables MU to submit requests independently.

Encryption of SNPs' States. Any additively homomorphic encryption scheme can be used to encrypt the states of SNPs. Although [14] shows that AH-ECC cryptosystem provides smaller ciphertexts and faster operations, decryption requires to compute discrete log. As the discrete log problem is assumed to be hard, we have to maintain a pre-computed table of discrete logarithms (which is only practical for small ranges of plaintext). Therefore, in this paper, we choose modified paillier cryptosystem (Fig. 4) for ease of implementation.

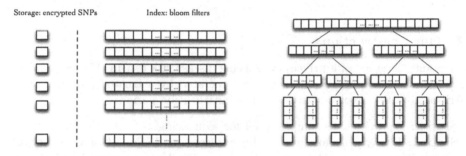

Fig. 5. Storage overview at SPU. **Fig. 6.** Bloom filter tree.

Storage Overview. For 50 million possible SNPs, we create 0.5 million bloom filters. Each bloom filter contains 100 SNPs with the same state. In order to represent the encrypted states of SNPs, we link one ciphertext to each bloom filter. We show the storage architecture in Fig. 5. On the left side, we store the encrypted states of the SNPs. On the right side, we store the bloom filters. There is a one-to-one correspondence between the encrypted state and the bloom filter at each row. To avoid searching all the bloom filters sequentially, we organize them with a tree structure. To make it clear, we show a binary tree example in Fig. 6. At the leaf node level, we store the 0.5 million bloom filters and the corresponding ciphertexts. At level $i - 1$, we store bloom filters which double the size of the bloom filters at level i. However, we want to point out that our scheme is not restricted to binary tree. Any multi-branch tree can be used. For a k-branch tree, the size of bloom filters at level $i - 1$ is k times the size of bloom filters at level i.

Why a Bloom Filter Contains 100 Positions? The decrease of storage overhead depends on the capacity of each bloom filter. With the capacity increases, the storage overhead decreases. As there are three possible states for each SNP, we only need three bloom filters in the extreme case, with each bloom filter at maximum capacity. In this case, we get the maximum storage overhead decrease. However, the length of bloom filter reveals the frequency of different states of SNPs. Therefore, we need to fix a constant capacity for the bloom filters. On the other hand, there is one security weakness that SPU will know requests made to the same bloom filter might have the same state. Supposed that there are b bloom filters, and MU requests for t real SNPs, the probability that any two requests appear on the same bloom filter is C_t^2/b. For fixed t, the above probability decreases with b increases. The number of real SNPs for a particular disease is quite small (i.e., less than 60)[7]. For example, calculating the susceptibility of Alzheimer's disease requires only 10 SNPs [24] and coronary artery disease risk computation includes 23 SNPs [25]. With 0.5 million bloom filters, the probability that any two different requests appear on the same bloom filter is at most $C_{60}^2/(5 \times 10^5) = 0.35\%$. Therefore, we choose the constant capacity 100 for the bloom filters to achieve a balance between the decrease of storage overhead and privacy.

4.2   Our Construction

We present the steps of a privacy-preserving disease risk test in this section. We assume that the cryptographic keys are generated by a trusted authority and distributed to the involved parties at the initialization period.

- **Step 1:** P provides his sample to CI for sequencing.
- **Step 2:** Firstly, CI randomizes the positions of SNPs. Then CI encrypts the positions by symmetric encryption (or public key encryption) and inserts them into the bloom filters. Moreover, CI encrypts the states of SNPs by modified paillier cryptosystem and links one ciphertext to each bloom filter. Then CI organizes the bloom filters with a tree structure. CI uploads the bloom filter tree and the corresponding ciphertexts to SPU.
- **Step 3:** P goes to the MU to take disease risk test. MU pads some fictitious positions among real ones to hide the number of SNPs involved in the test.
  - If symmetric encryption is adopted in Step 2, MU has to send the positions (padding included) to the patient first. Then patient encrypts the positions and sends the encrypted positions to SPU.
  - If public key encryption is used in Step 2, it is possible for MU to make requests to SPU directly without the help of P. To prevent SPU from checking whether an element is contained in a bloom filter without P's authorization, we make use of keyed hashing when creating bloom filters. If P agrees to conduct the disease risk test, then MU gets the hash keys.
- **Step 4:** SPU receives the encrypted positions from P (or MU). SPU will check the index tree of bloom filters hierarchically. If the encrypted position lies in a bloom filter, then SPU will return the ciphertext linked to this bloom filter

---

[7] http://www.eupedia.com/genetics/cancer_related_snp.shtml, accessed on 9 Sep 2017.

to MU. If two or more requests occur in the same bloom filter, SPU should re-encrypt the ciphertext before returning to MU (Eq. (4)). Furthermore, we require SPU to return the encrypted states according to the order of MU's requests.

- **Step 5:** Once getting the encrypted states of requested SNPs, MU computes the disease risk via homomorphic operations based on weighted averaging.
- **Step 6:** The encrypted final result is sent to P. After decryption, the result is return back to MU.

Extensions: Disease risk computation is based on weighted averaging. Apart from genomic data, clinical and environmental data can be integrated into our scheme. For better security, we can output the disease risk as a range. Ayday et al. demonstrate how to use privacy-preserving integer comparison [26] to report the range of genetic test [21], which can be easily incorporated into our scheme. Besides, if the secret key of a patient is divided into two secret shares and distributed to SPU and MU, the final result can be revealed to MU after two rounds of partial decryption without the patient's help.

5 Privacy Analysis

The SNPs of a patient contain sensitive information. Homomorphic encryption makes it possible to compute disease risk for the patients without revealing the true values of SNPs. At the same time, the medical unit (i.e., pharmaceutical company) might consider the test specifics as trade secret. Hence, MU does not want to make public the weights (or even the number) of the disease test. Therefore, we conduct privacy analysis of our proposed scheme in term of these two aspects. The MU will download the requested encrypted SNPs and compute the disease risk locally. Therefore, the privacy of test weights preserves. Recall that CI and P are honest parties, SPU and MU are honest-but-curious (Fig. 1), we consider two kinds of attacks: (i) an attacker at MU trying to know the SNPs of the patient (type-1 attack). (ii) an attacker at SPU inferring the requests from MU and the SNPs of the patient (type-2 attack).

Security Under Type-1 Attack: The MU makes requests to SPU for SNPs of a patient to conduct disease risk test. SPU returns the corresponding encrypted states of the requested SNPs to MU. Even different requests occur in the same bloom filter, SPU will re-encrypt the ciphertext. Therefore, the ciphertexts are indistinguishable among different requests from the point of view of MU. Security under type-1 attack relies on the security of the underlying cryptosystem that encrypts the states. In our scheme, any additively homomorphic cryptosystem can be used. As long as the underlying cryptosystem is semantic secure, it is unable for the attacker at MU to infer any additional information about the plaintext with the ciphertext known. Most of the additively homomorphic cryptosystems base their security on assumptions relying on deciding residuosity. But the two cryptosystems we mentioned in Sect. 4.1 base on non-residuosity-related decisional assumption. To be specific, the security of modified paillier cryptosystem [23] is based on decisional Diffie-Hellman assumption. The security of AH-ECC is based on the intractability of Elliptic Curve Discrete Logarithm Problem (ECDLP). Due to space limit, we do not go into details here.

Security Under Type-2 Attack: The MU requests for SNPs with encrypted positions. As the positions are encrypted, it is impossible for SPU to know the true positions as long as the underlying cryptosystem is secure. Taking AES for an example, the key is kept secret by the patient. Anyone without the secret key cannot deduce anything from the ciphertexts. Moreover, MU pads some fictitious positions among the real positions. In this way, it successfully hide the number of the requested SNPs, which prevents the SPU from speculating the disease type according to the number of involved SNPs. We then show that the requests for SNPs are distributed uniformly among different bloom filters. First, the positions are randomized at CI before being inserted into the bloom filters. Second, we choose hash functions which map the inputs as evenly as possible over the output range to create bloom filters. In other words, every hash value in the output range is generated with roughly the same probability. Therefore, the distribution of ones in different bloom filters reveals nothing about its inputs. Recall that we link one ciphertext to each bloom filter, there is one security weakness that SPU will know requests made to the same bloom filter might have the same state. In this paper, we create 0.5 million bloom filters for 50 million possible SNPs to achieve a trade-off between the decrease of storage overhead and privacy. If co-occurrence does happen, we want to point out that even though SPU might know requests on the same bloom filter are likely to have the same state, it cannot know whether it is a real or fictitious request or what the state is.

6   Experimental Evaluation

To evaluate the proposed scheme, we implemented it on our PC which is Windows 7 Enterprise 64-bit Operating System with Intel(R) Core(TM) i5 CPU (4 cores), 3.4 GHz and 16 GB memory. To provide platform-independence, we use the Java programming language.

We downloaded the SNPs of a real individual from openSNP.[8] There are 985,949 (around 1 million) SNPs in our dataset. We run experiments on this smaller dataset (compared to 50 million) to measure the searching speed and storage cost. We use the CCM mode of AES to encrypt the positions of SNPs, and modified paillier cryptosystem to encrypt the states of SNPs with 1024-bit security parameter. In order to facilitate the subsequent processing, we saved the encrypted positions and states into a MySQL 5.5 database. To uniquely locate a SNP, we combine rsid (reference SNP cluster id), chromosome number and offset to denote the position of each SNP. There are around 1 million SNPs in our dataset. It is notoriously slow to search for one particular encrypted position without index. MySQL does provide us with a way to create index for the tables

---

[8] https://opensnp.org, accessed on 16 Aug 2017.

based on B_+ three, which performs well in running range search (i.e., [1, 100]). However, the encrypted positions of SNPs related to a particular disease may be scattered throughout the space. In this scenario, bloom filter is better in terms of searching speed and storage. Recall that we store 100 SNPs in each bloom filter, we have around 10^4 bloom filters for our dataset. To facilitate presentation, we organize the bloom filters with 10-branch tree. The number of bloom filters at each level and the capacity of each bloom filter are shown in Table 1. We show the time to search requested SNPs at SPU based on B_+ tree or bloom filter tree in Fig. 7, varying the number of SNPs from 1 to 1000. For B_+ tree index, the searching time increases from 130 ms to 3200 ms with increasing number of SNPs. By contrast, for bloom filter tree index, the searching time increases from 6.4 ms to 52 ms approximately linearly. On average, we speed up the searching by 60x.

Table 1. Statistics of bloom filter tree.

Level	Bloom filter's capacity	# of bloom filters
1	10^6	1
2	10^5	10
3	10^4	10^2
4	10^3	10^3
5	10^2	10^4

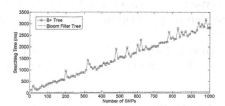

Fig. 7. Time to search the requested SNPs at SPU.

Since bloom filter may cause false positive, we also measure the effect of false positive rate on the size of our index (bloom filter tree). Given a fixed n, if we want to keep p below a threshold ϵ, we need to set m to be $m \geq n \, log_2 \, e \cdot log_2 \left(\frac{1}{\epsilon}\right)$ (see Sect. 3.2). For 1 million elements, the size of our index under false positive rate 1%, 0.1% and 0.01% is 4.84 MB, 6.91 MB and 9.68 MB, respectively. The number of hash functions used in each bloom filter is 7, 10 and 14, respectively. In comparison, the size of B_+ three index generated by MySQL is 48.69 MB. Therefore, our bloom filter tree index not only speeds up the searching of SNPs but also is space-efficient. All the existing works store one encrypted state for each SNP (i.e., [11,14]). To be specific, one encrypted state corresponds to one position. But in this paper, we insert 100 positions with the same state into one bloom filter and link one ciphertext to the bloom filter. Therefore, one encrypted state corresponds to 100 SNP positions. This is the reason why we can reduce the storage overhead by 100x. It is shown in [14] that the encryption of 50 million SNPs takes about 100 GB by modified paillier cryptosystem, and 4.5 GB by AH-ECC cryptosystem (under 112-bit security parameter). As a result, our scheme makes a big difference in storage overhead regardless of the underlying cryptosystem.

7   Discussion and Conclusions

In this paper, we assume that P and CI are trusted, SPU and MU are honest-but-curious. If we allow MU to be dishonest (arbitrarily deviates from the protocol), it is likely that MU will launch illegal requests (i.e., with one weight of value 1, the remaining is 0) to SPU to infer the patient's SNPs. We can make a compromise between the privacy of MU (i.e., tests' specifics) and the privacy of patient's SNPs [27]. MU is forced to reveal iteratively some weights to the SPU, until the SPU is convinced that the ongoing test is legitimate.

To conclude, we build an efficient index tree for the encrypted SNPs with bloom filters. We speed up the searching of SNPs by 60x compared to B_+ tree index. Moreover, we successfully reduce the storage cost by 100x regardless of the underlying cryptosystem. We implement our scheme on SNPs of a real patient, the experimental results highlight the practicality of our scheme. Due to the space-efficient property of bloom filter, our future work is to optimize our scheme and deploy it on smartphones without a centralized SPU.

Acknowledgement. This project is partially supported by a collaborative research grant (RGC Project No. CityU C1008-16G) of the Hong Kong Government.

References

1. Homer, N., Szelinger, S., Redman, M., Duggan, D., Tembe, W., Muehling, J., Pearson, J.V., Stephan, D.A., Nelson, S.F., Craig, D.W.: Resolving individuals contributing trace amounts of DNA to highly complex mixtures using high-density SNP genotyping microarrays. PLoS Genet. **4**(8), e1000167 (2008)
2. Altshuler, D., Daly, M.J., Lander, E.S.: Genetic mapping in human disease. Science **322**(5903), 881–888 (2008)
3. Humbert, M., Ayday, E., Hubaux, J.-P., Telenti, A.: Addressing the concerns of the lacks family: quantification of kin genomic privacy. In: Proceedings of the 2013 ACM SIGSAC Conference on Computer and Communications Security, pp. 1141–1152. ACM (2013)
4. Erlich, Y., Narayanan, A.: Routes for breaching and protecting genetic privacy. Nat. Rev. Genet. **15**(6), 409–421 (2014)
5. Malin, B.A.: An evaluation of the current state of genomic data privacy protection technology and a roadmap for the future. J. Am. Med. Inform. Assoc. **12**(1), 28–34 (2005)
6. Shringarpure, S.S., Bustamante, C.D.: Privacy risks from genomic data-sharing beacons. Am. J. Hum. Genet. **97**(5), 631–646 (2015)
7. Zhang, Y., Blanton, M., Almashaqbeh, G.: Secure distributed genome analysis for gwas and sequence comparison computation. BMC Med. Inform. Decis. Mak. **15**(5), S4 (2015)
8. Perl, H., Mohammed, Y., Brenner, M., Smith, M.: Privacy/performance trade-off in private search on bio-medical data. Future Gener. Comput. Syst. **36**, 441–452 (2014)
9. Chen, Y., Peng, B., Wang, X.F., Tang, H.: Large-scale privacy-preserving mapping of human genomic sequences on hybrid clouds. In: NDSS (2012)

10. Zhou, X., Peng, B., Li, Y.F., Chen, Y., Tang, H., Wang, X.F.: To release or not to release: evaluating information leaks in aggregate human-genome data. In: Atluri, V., Diaz, C. (eds.) ESORICS 2011. LNCS, vol. 6879, pp. 607–627. Springer, Heidelberg (2011). https://doi.org/10.1007/978-3-642-23822-2_33
11. Ayday, E., Raisaro, J.L., Hubaux, J.-P., Rougemont, J.: Protecting and evaluating genomic privacy in medical tests and personalized medicine. In: Proceedings of the 12th ACM Workshop on Workshop on Privacy in the Electronic Society, pp. 95–106. ACM (2013)
12. Ayday, E., Raisaro, J.L., Hubaux, J.-P.: Personal use of the genomic data: privacy vs. storage cost. In: 2013 IEEE Global Communications Conference (GLOBECOM), pp. 2723–2729. IEEE (2013)
13. Falconer, D.S., Mackay, T.F.C., Frankham, R.: Introduction to Quantitative Genetics. Trends in Genetics, vol. 12, no. 7, 4th edn, 280 p. Elsevier Science Publishers (Biomedical Division), Amsterdam (1996)
14. Danezis, G., De Cristofaro, E.: Fast and private genomic testing for disease susceptibility. In: Proceedings of the 13th Workshop on Privacy in the Electronic Society, pp. 31–34. ACM (2014)
15. Ugus, O., Westhoff, D., Laue, R., Shoufan, A., Huss, S.A.: Optimized implementation of elliptic curve based additive homomorphic encryption for wireless sensor networks. arXiv preprint arXiv:0903.3900 (2009)
16. Huang, R.W., Gui, X.L., Yu, S., Zhuang, W.: Research on privacy-preserving cloud storage framework supporting ciphertext retrieval. In: 2011 International Conference on Network Computing and Information Security (NCIS), vol. 1, pp. 93–97. IEEE (2011)
17. Bloom, B.H.: Space/time trade-offs in hash coding with allowable errors. Commun. ACM **13**(7), 422–426 (1970)
18. Ziegeldorf, J.H., Pennekamp, J., Hellmanns, D., Schwinger, F., Kunze, I., Henze, M., Hiller, J., Matzutt, R., Wehrle, K.: BLOOM: bloom filter based oblivious outsourced matchings. BMC Med. Genomics **10**(2), 44 (2017)
19. De Cristofaro, E., Faber, S., Gasti, P., Tsudik, G.: Genodroid: are privacy-preserving genomic tests ready for prime time? In: Proceedings of the 2012 ACM Workshop on Privacy in the Electronic Society, pp. 97–108. ACM (2012)
20. Karvelas, N., Peter, A., Katzenbeisser, S., Tews, E., Hamacher, K.: Privacy-preserving whole genome sequence processing through proxy-aided ORAM. In: Proceedings of the 13th Workshop on Privacy in the Electronic Society, pp. 1–10. ACM (2014)
21. Ayday, E., Raisaro, J.L., Laren, M., Jack, P., Fellay, J., Hubaux, J.-P.: Privacy-preserving computation of disease risk by using genomic, clinical, and environmental data. In: Proceedings of USENIX Security Workshop on Health Information Technologies (HealthTech 2013), no. EPFL-CONF-187118 (2013)
22. Broder, A., Mitzenmacher, M.: Network applications of bloom filters: a survey. Internet Math. **1**(4), 485–509 (2004)
23. Bresson, E., Catalano, D., Pointcheval, D.: A Simple public-key cryptosystem with a double trapdoor decryption mechanism and its applications. In: Laih, C.-S. (ed.) ASIACRYPT 2003. LNCS, vol. 2894, pp. 37–54. Springer, Heidelberg (2003). https://doi.org/10.1007/978-3-540-40061-5_3
24. Seshadri, S., Fitzpatrick, A.L., Arfan Ikram, M., DeStefano, A.L., Gudnason, V., Boada, M., Bis, J.C., Smith, A.V., Carrasquillo, M.M., Lambert, J.C., et al.: Genome-wide analysis of genetic loci associated with Alzheimer disease. JAMA **303**(18), 1832–1840 (2010)

25. Rotger, M., Glass, T.R., Junier, T., Lundgren, J., Neaton, J.D., Poloni, E.S., Van't Wout, A.B., Lubomirov, R., Colombo, S., Martinez, R., et al.: Contribution of genetic background, traditional risk factors, and HIV-related factors to coronary artery disease events in HIV-positive persons. Clin. Infect. Dis. **57**(1), 112–121 (2013)

26. Erkin, Z., Franz, M., Guajardo, J., Katzenbeisser, S., Lagendijk, I., Toft, T.: Privacy-preserving face recognition. In: Goldberg, I., Atallah, M.J. (eds.) PETS 2009. LNCS, vol. 5672, pp. 235–253. Springer, Heidelberg (2009). https://doi.org/10.1007/978-3-642-03168-7_14

27. Barman, L., Graini, E., Raisaro, J.L., Ayday, E., Hubaux, J.-P., et al.: Privacy threats and practical solutions for genetic risk tests. In: 2nd International Workshop on Genome Privacy and Security (GenoPri 2015), no. EPFL-CONF-207435 (2015)

Engineering Issues of Crypto

Verifiable and Forward Secure Dynamic Searchable Symmetric Encryption with Storage Efficiency

Kazuki Yoneyama[✉] and Shogo Kimura

Ibaraki University, Hitachi-shi, Ibaraki, Japan
kazuki.yoneyama.sec@vc.ibaraki.ac.jp

Abstract. Searchable symmetric encryption (SSE) provides private searching over an encrypted database against an untrusted server. Though various SSE schemes have been studied, recently, it is shown that most of existing schemes are vulnerable to file injection attacks. At ACM CCS 2016, Bost proposed a forward secure SSE scheme to resist such attacks, called $\Sigma o\phi o\varsigma$. Besides the basic scheme ($\Sigma o\phi o\varsigma$) secure against semi-honest servers, a verifiable scheme ($\Sigma o\phi o\varsigma$-ϵ) secure against malicious servers is also introduced. In $\Sigma o\phi o\varsigma$-ϵ, each client keeps hash values of indexes of documents corresponding to each keyword. Thus, the client storage cost is higher than for $\Sigma o\phi o\varsigma$, and the hash table must be reconstructed when a new document is added. Also, since any security definition and proof of security against malicious servers are not provided, what $\Sigma o\phi o\varsigma$-ϵ guarantees against malicious server is unclear. In this paper, we propose a new verifiable and forward secure SSE scheme against malicious servers. An advantage of our scheme to $\Sigma o\phi o\varsigma$-ϵ is the client storage cost; that is, our scheme only needs the same storage cost as $\Sigma o\phi o\varsigma$. Our key idea is to bind each index and keyword with a tag generated by an algebraic pseudo-random function, and to store the tag to the server as well as the encrypted index on an update phase. The client can efficiently check validity of answers to search queries by verifying the combined tag thanks to closed form efficiency of the algebraic pseudo-random function; and thus, the client does not need to keep the hash table. Also, we formally prove security against malicious servers. Specifically, we show that our scheme satisfies the strong reliability definition.

Keywords: Searchable symmetric encryption · Forward security
Algebraic pseudo-random function · Strong reliability

1 Introduction

In our daily life, we use various cloud storage services, and our sensitive data are stored in an outside server. Because many leakage incidents of databases stored in cloud storage servers recently happen (e.g., "The Fappening" of Apple's iCloud in 2014), these data must be encrypted. However, if we use ordinary

© Springer International Publishing AG, part of Springer Nature 2018
S. Qing et al. (Eds.): ICICS 2017, LNCS 10631, pp. 489–501, 2018.
https://doi.org/10.1007/978-3-319-89500-0_42

symmetric encryption schemes like AES, it is difficult to search a document for clients. For this problem, Song et al. [1] introduced the notion of *searchable symmetric encryption* (SSE). The aim of SSE is to provide private search over the encrypted database store in an untrusted server. Specifically, the client wants to hide information of keywords in the search phase as well as information of documents. SSE schemes need to guarantee that small (or inevitable) information only leaks to the server.

The first strongly secure SSE scheme was proposed by Curtmola et al. [2]. Their scheme is *static*; that is, the encrypted database is stored in the server only in the setup phase, and if a new document is added, then the encrypted database must be reconstructed. Hence, static SSE schemes are not suitable for environments that data is frequently updated. Kamara et al. [3] proposed an efficient *dynamic* SSE scheme[1] that the client can add/delete a document corresponding to a set of keywords to/from the already stored encrypted database without reconstructing it. Thus, dynamic SSE schemes are more useful in cloud storage services than static SSE schemes. Various dynamic SSE schemes have been studied to improve efficiency and search flexibility. From the viewpoint of security, it is important to resist attacks by an untrusted server because some malicious insiders may operate cloud storage services. Especially, we must consider that the malicious server tries to respond a fake answer to a search query (i.e., The true answer for keyword w is document D, but the server returns another document D'). Kurosawa and Ohtaki [4] introduced the notion of verifiable SSE which guarantees that the client can verify if the answer is true or not, and they extended it to the dynamic SSE setting [5]. Kurosawa et al. [6] formally defined verifiability as *strong reliability* such that no malicious server can make the client accepted for any fake answer.

In the sense of adversary, Islam et al. [7] introduced a new type of attacks to SSE schemes, called *leakage-abuse attacks*. In this attack, if the server knows (almost) all the contents of the client's documents, then it can determine the client's queries from leakage of query pattern (i.e., when a query is repeated) and the file-access pattern (i.e., which files are returned in response to each query). Since such leakage is considered as practically small leakage, their attack clarifies that security of some existing SSE schemes are not enough in reality. Moreover, Cash et al. [8] extended the attack such that full plaintext of the encrypted database can be recovered by allowing larger leakage. For dynamic SSE setting, Zhang et al. [9] showed an attack to reveal the content of a past search query by injecting few new documents in the update phase, called *file injection attacks*. Their attack is very powerful because most of existing dynamic SSE schemes are not resistant to the attack (i.e., The server can learn that the new document matches a previous search query.).

Related to file injection attacks, Chang and Mitzenmacher [10] proposed an (inefficient) *forward secure* dynamic SSE scheme with linear search cost. The notion of forward security guarantees that no server can tell if a newly

---

[1] Though Song et al. [1] already proposed a dynamic SSE scheme, the search cost is linear in the number of documents.

inserted document matches previous search queries. Thus, forward secure SSE schemes can resist to file injection attacks. Also, forward secure SSE schemes allow for an online build of the encrypted database because the update phase does not leak information. In most of non-forward secure SSE schemes, inverted indexes of the database are necessary in the setup phase; and thus, an indexing step may be an efficiency bottleneck of the system. Stefanov et al. [11] proposed a forward secure dynamic SSE scheme based on the oblivious RAM (ORAM). However, their scheme is not verifiable, and needs large bandwidth overhead on updates due to ORAM. Bost et al. [12] extended Stefanov et al.'s scheme to verifiable. Their scheme also need large bandwidth overhead on updates.

Recently, Bost [13] proposed an efficient forward secure dynamic SSE scheme ($\Sigma o\phi o\varsigma$) without relying on ORAM. $\Sigma o\phi o\varsigma$ achieves optimal search and update complexity for both computation and communication for forward secure SSE. The key idea of $\Sigma o\phi o\varsigma$ is that the location of the newly added encrypted document and the search token are unlinkable by preventing the adversary to generate any new search token from old one, but the client can compute new one by using trapdoor permutations. Also, he shows an extension to verifiable scheme ($\Sigma o\phi o\varsigma\text{-}\epsilon$). The idea of $\Sigma o\phi o\varsigma\text{-}\epsilon$ is that the client keeps each hash value of indexes of documents for each keyword. If the malicious server returns a fake answer, then the client can verify validity by comparing the hash value. However, $\Sigma o\phi o\varsigma\text{-}\epsilon$ needs the additional storage cost for clients than $\Sigma o\phi o\varsigma$ because of keeping the hash table. Specifically, whereas $\Sigma o\phi o\varsigma$ needs $O(W \log D)$ storage, $\Sigma o\phi o\varsigma\text{-}\epsilon$ needs $O(W(\log D + \kappa))$ storage, where W is the number of distinct keywords, D is the number of documents and κ is the security parameter. For an implementation in [13], experimental parameters sizes are set as $D \leq 2^{48}$, $W \leq 2^{23}$ and κ is 128 bit; and thus, the extra client storage cost of $\Sigma o\phi o\varsigma\text{-}\epsilon$ is about 128MB to the cost of $\Sigma o\phi o\varsigma$. Therefore, to achieve both of forward security against malicious servers and client storage efficiency is an important remaining problem. Also, any formal definition and proof of security against malicious servers is not shown in [13]. Hence, it is unclear that $\Sigma o\phi o\varsigma\text{-}\epsilon$ is actually secure against malicious servers.

1.1   Our Contribution

The contribution of this paper is twofold: one is to resolve the problem on the storage cost in $\Sigma o\phi o\varsigma\text{-}\epsilon$, and the other is to show the formal security against malicious servers.

New Forward Secure Dynamic SSE. We propose a new forward secure dynamic SSE scheme which is secure against malicious servers. The storage cost of our scheme is asymptotically the same as $\Sigma o\phi o\varsigma$; that is, $O(W \log D)$. We show a comparison among previous forward secure SSE schemes and our scheme in Table 1.

Our key idea is to change the way to verify the answer of the server. In $\Sigma o\phi o\varsigma\text{-}\epsilon$, verifiability is achieved by using client's hash table of indexes of

Table 1. Comparison among previous forward secure SSE schemes and our scheme

	Computation		Communication		Client Storage	Malicious server
	Search	Update	Search	Update		
[11]	$O\left(\min\left\{\begin{array}{l}a_w + \log N \\ n_w \log^3 N\end{array}\right\}\right)$	$O(\log^2 N)$	$O(n_w + \log N)$	$O(\log N)$	$O(N^\alpha)$	×
[12]	$O\left(\min \dfrac{a_w + \log^2 N}{n_w \log^3 N}\right)$	$O(\log^2 N)$	$O(n_w + \log N)$	$O(\log N)$	$O(N^\alpha)$	✓
Σοφος [13]	$O(a_w)$	$O(1)$	$O(n_w)$	$O(1)$	$O(W \log D)$	×
Σοφος-ε [13]	$O(a_w)$	$O(1)$	$O(n_w)$	$O(1)$	$O(W(\log D + \kappa))$	not proven
Ours	$O(a_w)$	$O(1)$	$O(n_w)$	$O(1)$	$O(W \log D)$	✓

Part of this table is borrowed from [13]. N is the number of keyword/document pairs. W is the number of distinct keywords. D is the number of documents. n_w is the size of the search result set for keyword w. a_w is the number of times that the queried keyword w was historically added to the database.

documents for each keyword. Thus, an additional storage cost is necessary. In our scheme, verifiability is achieved by using the mechanism of message-authentication codes (MAC) based on a pseudo-random function (PRF). Specifically, each client generates a secret key for the PRF in the setup phase, and computes and sends a tag to bind the document index and the keyword with the PRF to the server in the update phase. The client can erase tags after the update phase. In the search phase, the client can check the validity of the search result by receiving and verifying indexes and tags. Since the secret key for the PRF is only known by the client, it is difficult to forge a tag by the server from the property of the PRF. Thus, the security against malicious servers without increasing the storage size can be achieved. However, in this approach, the communication cost and the computational cost for the client are large.

Hence, we use the other idea to resolve the problems on costs. We use an algebraic PRF (APRF) with closed form efficiency [14]. The APRF is a special type of PRF such that certain algebraic operations on these outputs can be computed more efficiently with the secret salt than computing separately. We generate tags for document indexes by using the APRF instead of the standard PRF. Then, in the search phase, the server composes these tags by using the algebraic property of APRF, and the client can efficiently check the validity with the secret salt. Hence, the communication and computation cost is comparable to Σοφος-ε without increasing the storage cost.

Formal Security Proof against Malicious Servers. We adapt strong reliability [6] as the definition of security against malicious servers. Strong reliability guarantees that no malicious server can make an client accept a fake answer or a fake tag to a search query. It is a suitable definition for schemes which uses tags to check the validity of the search result because tags are explicitly defined. Hence, we use strong reliability. The SSE scheme in [12] is also proved to be secure against malicious servers. Their security definition is called soundness which also guarantees that no adversary output a fake search result that is accepted by the client. However, in the soundness definition, since tags are not explicitly defined, the adversary is not regarded to win even if a tag is forged but the search result is valid. On the other hand, in the strong reliability definition, the adversary wins if a tag is forged but the search result is valid. Therefore, strong reliability is stronger than soundness. The detailed discussion about the difference between two types of definitions is shown in [6]. We formally prove that our scheme satisfies strong reliability by assuming the APRF. Specifically, we show a reduction to pseudo-randomness of the APRF from strong reliability.

Also, we prove that our scheme satisfies forward security by assuming the APRF and the one-way trapdoor permutation in the random oracle model. The definition of forward security is the same as in [13].

2 Preliminaries

Notations. Throughout this paper we use the following notations. We denote κ as the security parameter, and $negl(\kappa)$ as the negligible function in κ. Hereafter, we omit the security parameter for inputs of algorithms except cases that we must explicitly state it. If Set is a set, then by $m \in_R$ Set we denote that m is sampled uniformly from Set. If $\mathcal{ALG}$ is an algorithm, then by $y \leftarrow \mathcal{ALG}(x; r)$ we denote that y is output by $\mathcal{ALG}$ on input x and randomness r (if $\mathcal{ALG}$ is deterministic, r is empty). When X is a bit-string, we denote $|X|$ as the bit length, and when X is a set, we denote $|X|$ as the number of elements.

2.1 Building Blocks

Pseudo-Random Function and Algebraic Pseudo-Random Function.
Let $\mathsf{F} = \{F_\kappa : Salt_\kappa \times Dom_\kappa \to Rng_\kappa\}_\kappa$ be a function family with a family of domains $\{Dom_\kappa\}_\kappa$, a family of salt spaces $\{Salt_\kappa\}_\kappa$ and a family of ranges $\{Rng_\kappa\}_\kappa$.

Definition 1 (Pseudo-Random Function). *We say that function family* $\mathsf{F} = \{F_\kappa\}_\kappa$ *is the pseudo-random function (PRF) family, if for any PPT distinguisher* $\mathcal{D}$ *and salt* $s \in_R Salt_\kappa$, *advantage* $\mathsf{Adv}_\mathcal{D} = | \Pr[1 \leftarrow \mathcal{D}^{F_\kappa(s,\cdot)}] - \Pr[1 \leftarrow \mathcal{D}^{RF_\kappa(\cdot)}]| \leq negl(\kappa)$, *where* $RF_\kappa : Dom_\kappa \to Rng_\kappa$ *is a truly random function.*

Definition 2 (Algebraic Pseudo-Random Function [14]). *We say that PRF function family* $\mathsf{F} = \{F_\kappa\}_\kappa$ *is the algebraic pseudo-random function (APRF) family if the following two properties are satisfied:*

Algebraic. *The range* Rng *of PRF* $F(\cdot)$ *for every* κ *and the salt* s *forms an Abelian multiplicative group. We require that the group operation on* Rng *be efficiently computable.*

Closed form Efficiency. *Let* N *be the order of the range sets of* F *for security parameter* κ. *Let* $z = (z_1, \ldots, z_\ell) \in \{\{0,1\}^m\}^\ell$, $k \in N$, *and efficiently computable* $h : \mathbb{Z}_N^k \to \mathbb{Z}_N^\ell$ *with* $h(x) = \langle h_1(x), \ldots, h_\ell(x) \rangle$. *There exists an algorithm* $\mathsf{CFEval}_{h,z}$ *such that for every* $x \in \mathbb{Z}_N^k$, $\mathsf{CFEval}_{h,z}(x, s) = \prod_{i=1}^\ell [F(s, z_i)]^{h_i(x)}$ *and the running time of* CFEval *is polynomial in* κ, m, k *but sublinear in* ℓ.

Hereafter, we omit κ in F_κ for simplicity.

2.2 Dynamic Searchable Symmetric Encryption

Syntax. In this paper, we focus on the single keyword search and inverted index schemes (i.e., The server returns index lists corresponding to each search query.). Let $\mathsf{D} = \{D_1, \ldots, D_n\}$ be a set of documents, and $\mathsf{DB} := (\mathsf{ind}_i, \mathsf{W}_i)_{i=1}^n$ be a database containing pairs of index ind_i corresponding to document D_i and set of keywords W_i included in D_i, where $\mathsf{ind}_i \in \{0,1\}^l$ for constant l and $\mathsf{W}_i \subseteq \{0,1\}^*$. Also, let $W := \cup_{i=1}^n \mathsf{W}_i$ be the set of keywords, $W := |\mathsf{W}|$ be the number of distinct keywords, D be the number of documents, and $\mathsf{DB}(w) = \{\mathsf{ind}_i | w \in \mathsf{W}_i\}$ be the set of indexes of documents including keyword w. For example, if $\mathsf{DB}(w) = \{\mathsf{ind}_1, \mathsf{ind}_2, \mathsf{ind}_3\}$, then documents including keyword w are D_1, D_2 and D_3.

A dynamic SSE scheme consist of three phases (Setup, Search, Update).

Setup(DB): On input DB, the client outputs encrypted database EDB, secret key K and state of the client σ, and stores EDB to the server.

Search$(K, w, \sigma, \mathsf{EDB}) = (\mathsf{Search}_C(K, w, \sigma), \mathsf{Search}_S(t(w), \mathsf{EDB}))$: On input secret key K, state σ and keyword w for the client, and encrypted database EDB for the server, the client sends trapdoor $t(w)$ to the server, and the server returns $\mathsf{DB}(w)$. The server returns verifier $\mathsf{Ver} = \{Ver_i | \mathsf{ind}_i \in \mathsf{DB}(w)\}$ as well as $\mathsf{DB}(w)$, and the client verifies Ver for $\mathsf{DB}(w)$. If the verification holds, the client regards that $\mathsf{DB}(w)$ is the valid answer.

Update$(K, \sigma, op, in, \mathsf{EDB}) = (\mathsf{Update}_C(K, \sigma, op, in), \mathsf{Update}_S(\mathsf{EDB}, u(in)))$: On input K, σ, operation $op \in \{add, del\}$ and a document/keyword pair $in = (\mathsf{ind}, w)$ for index ind and keyword w for the client, and EDB for the server, the client sends update information $u(in)$ corresponding to in to the server, and the server updates EDB, where add/del means the addition/deletion of in.

It is required that an honest server always returns the true answer for any search query.

Definition 3 (Correctness). *For any* DB *the following holds:*

$$\Pr[(\mathsf{EDB}, K, \sigma) \leftarrow \mathsf{Setup}(\mathsf{DB}); \textit{repetition of } \mathsf{Update}(K, \sigma, op, in, \mathsf{EDB});$$
$$t(w) \leftarrow \mathsf{Search}_C(K, w, \sigma); x \leftarrow \mathsf{Search}_S(t(w), \mathsf{EDB}); x \neq \mathsf{DB}(w)] \leq negl(\kappa)$$

Security Model. For SSE schemes, privacy against the server is required. It is ideal if there is no leaked information to the server. However, it is not realistic in the SSE setting. Hence, we define leakage function $\mathcal{L} = (\mathcal{L}^{Stp}, \mathcal{L}^{Srch}, \mathcal{L}^{Updt})$ to represent what a SSE scheme leaks to the adversary. $\mathcal{L}^{Stp}/\mathcal{L}^{Srch}/\mathcal{L}^{Updt}$ means the leakage function in the setup/search/update phase. The leakage function $\mathcal{L}$ keeps the query list Q as it state. Q contains entries (i, w) for a search query on keyword w, or entries (i, op, in) for an update query. i is incremented at each query. The search pattern $sp(w)$ is defined as $sp(w) = \{j : (j, x) \in Q\}$. The history of keyword $hist(w)$ contains the set of documents indexes matching w at the setup phase, and the set of updated documents indexes matching w at the update phase. As the security model of dynamic SSE schemes, we show definitions of confidentiality, forward security, and strong reliability.

Confidentiality. It is required that there is no leak from each phase except derivable information from leakage functions. Confidentiality is defined by the simulation paradigm (i.e., indistinguishability between the real world and the ideal world), and is parametrized by leakage functions.

Definition 4 (Confidentiality). *The real world SSE_{real} and the ideal world SSE_{ideal} containing a simulator S are defined as follows:*

1. *An adversary A chooses database DB.*
2. *A obtains EDB ← Setup(DB) in SSE_{real}, or a simulated output EDB ← $S(\mathcal{L}^{Stp}(DB))$ in SSE_{ideal}.*
3. *A can repeatedly pose search (resp. update) queries with input w (resp. (op, in)), and obtains DB(w) ← Search(K, w, σ, EDB) (resp. EDB ← Update(K, σ, op, in, EDB)) in SSE_{real}, or a simulated output DB(w) ← $S(\mathcal{L}^{Srch}(w))$ (resp. EDB ← $S(\mathcal{L}^{Updt}(op, in))$) in SSE_{ideal}.*
4. *A outputs a bit b.*

We say that a SSE scheme is $\mathcal{L}$-adaptively secure if for any PPT A there exists S such that

$$|\Pr[1 \leftarrow AinSSE_{real}] - \Pr[1 \leftarrow AinSSE_{ideal}]| \leq negl(\kappa).$$

Forward Security. It is required that the adversary cannot tell if an updated document is corresponding to keywords in previous search queries.

Definition 5 (Forward Security [13]). *We say that a $\mathcal{L}'$-adaptively secure SSE scheme is forward secure if the update leakage function $\mathcal{L}^{Updt}$ is represented as follows:*

$$\mathcal{L}^{Updt}(op, in) = \mathcal{L}'(op, (\text{ind}_i, \mu_i)),$$

where (ind_i, μ_i) is a set of modified documents paired with the number μ_i of modified keywords for the updated document ind_i.

Strong Reliability. It is required that no malicious server can make a client accept a fake answer to a search query. Especially, strong reliability guarantees unforgeability of a verifier corresponding to a document.

Definition 6 (Strong Reliability [6]). *We consider the following game between an honest client and an adversary A.*

Setup **phase** *A chooses DB, and sends it to the client. The client generates secret key K and EDB, and sends EDB to A.*

Update **phase** *A chooses (op_i, in_i), and sends it to the client. The client generates update information $u(in_i)$, and sends $(op_i, u(in_i))$ to A.*

Search **phase** *A chooses keyword w_i, and sends it to the client. The client generates $t(w_i)$, and sends it to A. A returns $(DB(w)', Ver')$ to the client.*

We note that the Update phase and the Search phase can be adaptively repeated by A. We define that the adversary A wins if for some Search phase the client accepts $(DB(w)', Ver')$ as a true answer, and $(DB(w)', Ver') \neq (DB(w), Ver)$, where $(DB(w), Ver) \leftarrow$ Search(K, w, σ, EDB). We say that a dynamic SSE scheme is strong reliable if for any PPT A, $\Pr[Awins] \leq negl(\kappa)$.

3 $\Sigma o\phi o\varsigma\text{-}\epsilon$, Revisited

In this section, we recall $\Sigma o\phi o\varsigma\text{-}\epsilon$, a forward secure dynamic SSE scheme secure against malicious servers.

3.1   Overview of $\Sigma o\phi o\varsigma$ and $\Sigma o\phi o\varsigma\text{-}\epsilon$

To guarantee forward security, $\Sigma o\phi o\varsigma$ introduces a search token update mechanism with a one-way trapdoor permutation (OWTP) π. Here, we roughly recall the design of $\Sigma o\phi o\varsigma$. In the Setup phase, the client generates secret key sk for OWTP. In the Update phase to add a new index ind corresponding to keyword w, for the first addition of keyword w the client randomly chooses the initial search token $ST_0^{(w)}$, sets counter $c^{(w)} := -1$, keeps $(ST_0^{(w)}, c^{(w)})$ as the current search token, computes update token $UT_0^{(w)} = H_1(ST_0^{(w)})$ and the encrypted index $e_0^{(w)} = \text{ind} \oplus H_2(ST_0^{(w)})$ with hash function H_1 and H_2 (modelled as random oracles (ROs)), and sends $(UT_0^{(w)}, e_0^{(w)})$ to the server. For previously added keyword w the client computes new search token $ST_{c+1}^{(w)} = \pi_{sk}^{-1}(ST_c^{(w)})$, keeps $(ST_{c+1}^{(w)}, c^{(w)} + 1)$ as the current search token, computes update token $UT_{c+1}^{(w)} = H_1(ST_{c+1}^{(w)})$ and the encrypted index $e_{c+1}^{(w)} = \text{ind} \oplus H_2(ST_{c+1}^{(w)})$, and sends $(UT_{c+1}^{(w)}, e_{c+1}^{(w)})$ to the server. The server stores $(UT_{c+1}^{(w)}, e_{c+1}^{(w)})$ to EDB. We note that the malicious server cannot compute $ST_{c+1}^{(w)}$ even if $UT_{c+1}^{(w)}$ is given because RO H_1 is not invertible. Similarly, ind is hidden even if $e_{c+1}^{(w)}$ is given because RO H_2 is not invertible. In the Search phase for keyword w, the client sends the current search token $ST_c^{(w)}$ to the server. Since the server know public key pk, the server can derive $ST_i^{(w)}{}_{0 \le i \le c-1}$. Also, since $UT_i^{(w)} = H_1(ST_i^{(w)})$, then the server can find $\text{DB}(w)$ by decrypting each $e_i^{(w)}$ for $0 \le i \le c-1$. We note that the malicious server cannot compute ST_{c+1} even if ST_c is given because secret key sk is only known to the client. Therefore, $\Sigma o\phi o\varsigma$ guarantees forward security.

$\Sigma o\phi o\varsigma\text{-}\epsilon$ is a verifiable version of $\Sigma o\phi o\varsigma$. In the Update phase, the client also keeps $H(\text{DB}(w))$ for each keyword w as well as $(ST_{c+1}^{(w)}, c^{(w)} + 1)$ with a collision resistance hash function H. In the Search phase, the client verifies if $\text{DB}(w)'$ sent from the server is valid by checking $H(\text{DB}(w)) \overset{?}{=} H(\text{DB}(w)')$. From collision resistance of H, it is infeasible to find $\text{DB}(w)' \ne DB(w)$ such that $H(\text{DB}(w)) = H(\text{DB}(w)')$. Thus, $\Sigma o\phi o\varsigma\text{-}\epsilon$ is secure against malicious servers.

3.2   Complexity of $\Sigma o\phi o\varsigma\text{-}\epsilon$

In the sense of the storage cost, each client must keep table **W** and **H**. Table **W** contains (i_w, c) for every keyword; and hence, the storage cost is $O(W \log D)$. Table **H** contains $H_3(\text{DB}(w))$ for every keyword; and hence, the storage cost is $O(W\kappa)$. Therefore, the total storage cost for a client is $O(W(\log D + \kappa))$.

The computational cost is $O(a_w)$ in the Search phase and $O(1)$ in the Update phase, where a_w is the number of times that the queried keyword w was historically added to the database. Also, the communication cost is $O(n_w)$ in the Search phase and $O(1)$ in the Update phase, where n_w is the size of the search result set.

3.3   Naive Approach to Reduce Storage Cost

There are several naive approaches to reduce the extra $O(W \log D)$ storage cost for $\Sigma o\phi o\varsigma\text{-}\epsilon$. For example, the client encrypts $H_3(\mathsf{DB}(w))$ and stores it to the server instead of storing by him/her. Then, in the Search phase, the client receives the ciphertext of $H_3(\mathsf{DB}(w))$ and $\mathsf{DB}(w)$, decrypts the ciphertext, and can check the validity of $\mathsf{DB}(w)$. Thus, the storage cost can be the same as $\Sigma o\phi o\varsigma$. However, in the Update phase, an additional round is necessary to receive the ciphertext of $H_3(\mathsf{DB}(w))$ because the client does not memorize it and $H_3(\mathsf{DB}(w))$ must be updated. Therefore, this naive approach is not very good from the viewpoint of round complexity.

4   Our Scheme

In this section, we show the protocol of our scheme. It is based on $\Sigma o\phi o\varsigma$, but achieves verifiability by another way than $\Sigma o\phi o\varsigma\text{-}\epsilon$.

4.1   Design Principle

In our scheme, we do not use any client-local verification table like table $\mathbf{H}$ in $\Sigma o\phi o\varsigma\text{-}\epsilon$, but use a "tag" binding the keyword and the index as a verifier. Specifically, the client sends a verifier $Ver_{c+1}^{(w)}$ as well as $(UT_{c+1}^{(w)}, e_{c+1}^{(w)})$ to the server in the Update phase, and checks if $Ver_{c+1}^{(w)}$ is correctly bound with $\mathsf{DB}(w)$ in the Search phase. We note that the client do not have to keep $Ver_{c+1}^{(w)}$ after sending it, but the client receives the verifier corresponding to indexes. We use a PRF to generate the verifier, and unforgeability of the verifier is guaranteed from pseudo-randomness of the PRF.

However, if the client receives $Ver_{c+1}^{(w)}$ for n_w indexes matching with w in each Search phase, the communication complexity increases by n_w PRF values and the client needs to compute n_w PRF values. Hence, we use a algebraic PRF (APRF) AF with closed form efficiency. APRF is a special type of PRF with a range that forms an Abelian group such that group operations are efficiently computable. In addition, certain algebraic operations on these outputs can be computed significantly more efficiently if one possesses the salt of the PRF that was used to generate them. As Definition 2, since $\prod_{i=1}^{n_w}[AF(s, z_i)]^{h_i(x)}$ can be efficiently computed by $\mathsf{CFEval}_{h,z}(x, s)$, the server can just compute and send $\prod_{i=1}^{n_w}[AF(s, z_i)]$ to the client, and the client can just compute $\mathsf{CFEval}_{h,z}(x, s)$ with a sublinear running time in n_w to check the validity of the verifier, where $h(x) = \langle 1, \ldots, 1 \rangle$.

It saves the increase of the communication complexity only to one group element, and the computational cost for the client is bounded by sublinear in n_w. For example, we can use the APRF from the decisional Diffie-Hellman (DDH) assumption [15] or from the strong DDH assumption proposed [14].

4.2 Protocol Description

Let π be a OWTP with the key generation algorithm KeyGen, $F : \{0,1\}^\kappa \times \{0,1\}^* \to \{0,1\}^\kappa$ be a PRF, $AF : \{0,1\}^\kappa \times \{0,1\}^* \to G$ be an APRF (where G is an Abelian group and $h(x) = \langle 1, \ldots, 1 \rangle$), and H_1 and H_2 are hash functions modelled as random oracles.

- Setup(DB):
    1. $K_S \in_R \{0,1\}^\kappa$
    2. $K_V \in_R \{0,1\}^\kappa$
    3. $(sk, pk) \leftarrow$ KeyGen(1^κ)
    4. $\mathbf{W}, \mathbf{T} \leftarrow$ empty tables
    5. **store** DB to $\mathbf{W}$ and $\mathbf{T}$ according to Update phase
    6. **return** (K_S, K_V, sk) as secret key K and $\mathbf{W}$ as the state of the client σ
    7. **return** $\mathbf{T}$ as encrypted database EDB

- Update($add, \mathbf{W}, (\text{ind}, w), \mathbf{T}$):
    - **Client:**
        1. $K_w \leftarrow F(K_S, w)$
        2. $(ST_c^{(w)}, c^{(w)}) \leftarrow \mathbf{W}[w]$
        3. **if** $(ST_c^{(w)}, c^{(w)}) = \perp$ **then**
        4. **generate** $ST_0^{(w)}$ by using the storage reducing technique [13]
        5. $c^{(w)} \leftarrow -1$
        6. **else**
        7. $ST_{c+1}^{(w)} \leftarrow \pi_{sk}^{-1}(ST_c^{(w)})$ by using the storage reducing technique [13]
        8. **end if**
        9. $\mathbf{W}[w] \leftarrow (i_w, c^{(w)} + 1)$
        10. $Ver_{c+1}^{(w)} \leftarrow AF(K_V, (c^{(w)} + 1, w, \text{ind}))$
        11. $UT_{c+1}^{(w)} \leftarrow H_1(K_w, ST_{c+1}^{(w)})$
        12. $e_{c+1}^{(w)} \leftarrow \text{ind} \oplus H_2(K_w, ST_{c+1}^{(w)})$
        13. **send** $(UT_{c+1}^{(w)}, e_{c+1}^{(w)}, Ver_{c+1}^{(w)})$ to the server as update information $u(\text{ind}, w)$
    - **Server:**
        1. $\mathbf{T}[UT_{c+1}^{(w)}] \leftarrow (e_{c+1}^{(w)}, Ver_{c+1}^{(w)})$

- Search($w, \mathbf{W}, \mathbf{T}$):
    - **Client:**
        1. $K_w \leftarrow F(K_S, w)$
        2. $(ST_c^{(w)}, c^{(w)}) \leftarrow \mathbf{W}[w]$

3. **if** $(ST_c^{(w)}, c^{(w)}) = \bot$
4. **return** $\emptyset$
5. **send** $(K_w, ST_c^{(w)}, c^{(w)})$ to the server as trapdoor $t(w)$
- **Server:**
    1. **for** $i = c$ **to** 0 **do**
    2. $UT_i^{(w)} \leftarrow H_1(K_w, ST_i^{(w)})$
    3. $(e_i^{(w)}, Ver_i^{(w)}) \leftarrow \mathbf{T}[UT_i^{(w)}]$
    4. $\mathsf{ind}_i^{(w)} \leftarrow e_i^{(w)} \oplus H_2(K_w, ST_i^{(w)})$
    5. $ST_{i-1} \leftarrow \pi_{pk}(ST_i)$
    6. **end for**
    7. **send** $(\mathsf{DB}(w) = \{\mathsf{ind}_i^{(w)}\}_{0 \leq i \leq c}, \mathsf{Ver}^{(w)} = \prod_{i=0}^{c} Ver_i^{(w)})$ to the client
- **Client:**
    1. **if** $|\mathsf{DB}(w)| \geq c + 1$ or $\mathsf{Ver}^{(w)} \neq \mathsf{CFEval}_{h, \{i, w, \mathsf{ind}_i^{(w)}\}_{0 \leq i \leq c}}(0, K_V)$
    2. **return** 0

Remark 1. The input of AF is (c, w, ind). If the domain of APRF AF is also required to be a group, the input is hashed by some collision-resistance hash function which maps to the group.

4.3 Correctness

According to the protocol, for any search query, an honest server can return true answer $(\mathsf{DB}(w), \mathsf{Ver}^{(w)})$, and the client always accept the answer except the probability that some collision on UT occur. If a collision of UT for distinct inputs to H_1 occurs, the server cannot find the correct encrypted index and verifier. However, since H_1 is a RO, the collision probability is negligible in κ.

4.4 Deletion Support

Our scheme is easily extended to supporting deletions of indexes by duplicating the data structure as the extension of $\Sigma o \phi o \varsigma$-$\epsilon$. Specifically, one instance of our scheme is used for insertions, and the other for deletions. In the Search phase, the server derives two $\mathsf{DB}(w)$ for two instances, and regards the difference of them as indexes to be returned. The verifier is also duplicated for each instance, and the client can check the validity of both instances respectively. If the verification of one of instances is rejected, then the client decides that the response is not valid. Therefore, strong reliability is also satisfied for this extension.

4.5 Complexity of Our Scheme

Each client must keep only table $\mathbf{W}$. It is not necessary to keep $ev_{c+1}^{(w)}$ sent in the Update phase because the client can check validity of verifier $Ver_i^{(w)}$ only with secret salt K_V, state $ST_c^{(w)}$ and received ind_i. Table $\mathbf{W}$ contains (i_w, c) for every keyword; and hence, the storage cost is $O(W \log D)$. Therefore, the total storage cost for a client is $O(W \log D)$. It is the same as $\Sigma o \phi o \varsigma$ whereas $\Sigma o \phi o \varsigma$ is not secure against malicious servers.

The computational cost and communication cost are asymptotically the same as $\Sigma o \phi o \varsigma$-$\epsilon$. The exact additional communication cost is only one group element (i.e., 160-bit for 80-bit security) both in the Update phase and the Search phase. Also, the exact additional computational cost for the client is an APRF computation in the Update phase and a sublinear computation in n_w in the Search phase. Therefore, our scheme is still efficient even in exact costs.

5   Security of Our Scheme

In this section, we prove that our scheme satisfies forward security and strong reliability. Especially, to prove strong reliability as verifiability is a distinguished point from $\Sigma o \phi o \varsigma$-$\epsilon$ because there is no formal security proof of verifiability of $\Sigma o \phi o \varsigma$-$\epsilon$ in [13].

5.1   Forward Security

Theorem 1. *We assume that F is a PRF, AF is an APRF, and π is a OWTP. Then, our scheme satisfies forward security for leakage functions $\mathcal{L}^{Stp}(\mathsf{DB}) = \bot$, $\mathcal{L}^{Srch}(w) = (sp(w), hist(w))$ and $\mathcal{L}^{Updt}(add, (\mathsf{ind}, w)) = \bot$ in the RO model, where $sp(w)$ is the search pattern and $hist(w)$ is the history of keyword w.*

The proof of Theorem 1 is almost the same as [13, Theorem 1]. We use hybrid games that proceed from the real world game to the ideal world game. The difference from the previous proof is the treatment of verifier Ver. We add a hybrid game to change the computation of $Ver_{c+1}^{(w)}$ in the Update phase and the Search phase to using a random function RF instead of using APRF AF. The proof is given in the full version.

5.2   Strong Reliability

Theorem 2. *We assume that AF is an APRF. Then, our scheme satisfies strong reliability.*

We can directly reduce the security of APRF to strong reliability. It means that, if there exists an adversary who breaks strong reliability, then a distinguisher for APRF can be constructed. The proof is given in the full version.

References

1. Song, D.X., Wagner, D., Perrig, A.: Practical techniques for searches on encrypted data. In: IEEE Symposium on Security and Privacy 2000, pp. 44–55 (2000)
2. Curtmola, R., Garay, J.A., Kamara, S., Ostrovsky, R.: Searchable symmetric encryption: improved definitions and efficient constructions. In: ACM Conference on Computer and Communications Security 2006, pp. 79–88 (2006)

3. Kamara, S., Papamanthou, C., Roeder, T.: Dynamic searchable symmetric encryption. In: ACM Conference on Computer and Communications Security 2012, pp. 965–976 (2012)
4. Kurosawa, K., Ohtaki, Y.: UC-secure searchable symmetric encryption. In: Keromytis, A.D. (ed.) FC 2012. LNCS, vol. 7397, pp. 285–298. Springer, Heidelberg (2012). https://doi.org/10.1007/978-3-642-32946-3_21
5. Kurosawa, K., Ohtaki, Y.: How to update documents *Verifiably* in searchable symmetric encryption. In: Abdalla, M., Nita-Rotaru, C., Dahab, R. (eds.) CANS 2013. LNCS, vol. 8257, pp. 309–328. Springer, Cham (2013). https://doi.org/10.1007/978-3-319-02937-5_17
6. Kurosawa, K., Sasaki, K., Ohta, K., Yoneyama, K.: UC-secure dynamic searchable symmetric encryption scheme. In: Ogawa, K., Yoshioka, K. (eds.) IWSEC 2016. LNCS, vol. 9836, pp. 73–90. Springer, Cham (2016). https://doi.org/10.1007/978-3-319-44524-3_5
7. Islam, M.S., Kuzu, M., Kantarcioglu, M.: Access pattern disclosure on searchable encryption: ramification, attack and mitigation. In: NDSS 2012 (2012)
8. Cash, D., Grubbs, P., Perry, J., Ristenpart, T.: Leakage-abuse attacks against searchable encryption. In: ACM Conference on Computer and Communications Security 2015, pp. 668–679 (2015)
9. Zhang, Y., Katz, J., Papamanthou, C.: All your queries are belong to us: the power of file-injection attacks on searchable encryption. In: USENIX Security Symposium 2016, pp. 707–720 (2016)
10. Chang, Y.-C., Mitzenmacher, M.: Privacy preserving keyword searches on remote encrypted data. In: Ioannidis, J., Keromytis, A., Yung, M. (eds.) ACNS 2005. LNCS, vol. 3531, pp. 442–455. Springer, Heidelberg (2005). https://doi.org/10.1007/11496137_30
11. Stefanov, E., Papamanthou, C., Shi, E.: Practical dynamic searchable encryption with small leakage. In: NDSS 2014 (2014)
12. Bost, R., Fouque, P.A., Pointcheval, D.: Verifiable dynamic symmetric searchable encryption: optimality and forward security. In: IACR Cryptology ePrint Archive 2016 (2016)
13. Bost, R.: Σοφος: forward secure searchable encryption. In: ACM Conference on Computer and Communications Security 2016, pp. 1143–1154 (2016)
14. Benabbas, S., Gennaro, R., Vahlis, Y.: Verifiable delegation of computation over large datasets. In: Rogaway, P. (ed.) CRYPTO 2011. LNCS, vol. 6841, pp. 111–131. Springer, Heidelberg (2011). https://doi.org/10.1007/978-3-642-22792-9_7
15. Naor, M., Reingold, O.: Number-theoretic constructions of efficient pseudo-random functions. In: FOCS 1997, pp. 458–467 (1997)

Improved Automatic Search Tool for Bit-Oriented Block Ciphers and Its Applications

Lingchen Li[1,2]([✉]) [iD], Wenling Wu[1], and Lei Zhang[1]

[1] Institute of Software, Chinese Academy of Sciences, Beijing 100190, China
{lilingchen,wwl}@tca.iscas.ac.cn
[2] University of Chinese Academy of Sciences, Beijing 100049, China

Abstract. The tool based on Mixed-integer Linear Programming (MILP) is simple and effective that frequently used in searching some different types of distinguishers recently. In this paper, we mainly focus on the automatic search method using MILP and the optimizer Gurobi for bit-oriented block ciphers.

We introduce the OPB file format to construct MILP models for the bit-oriented block ciphers. Compared to the LP file format, it is more concise and suitable to deal with boolean variables. And we modify the high-level strategy to reduce the solution time by setting parameter MIP-Focus provided by the optimizer Gurobi. Moreover, the new simple linear inequalities of differential pattern propagation of modular addition are given without considering the differential probability in the impossible differential search. As applications, we give the exact lower bounds of the number of differential active s-boxes for 5~12 rounds LBlock in the related-key model and all of impossible differentials limited the input and output differences to only 1 active bit for the full versions of SPECK.

Keywords: Related-key differentials · Impossible differentials
LBlock · SPECK · MILP

1 Introduction

Finding different types of distinguishers is the key step to evaluate the security of block ciphers. The automatic search methods are the main choices. Most of the early automatic search methods were based on special algorithms implemented from scratch in general purpose programming language. This kinds of methods may be more efficient in some specific cases but they are much more difficult to implement. Recently, the search problem is described as an SAT, MILP, or CP models which can be automatically solved with the corresponding solvers. Among them, the automatic search method based on MILP is simple and practical which has become a popular tool.

The MILP method was first proposed by Mouha *et al.* [1] which used for counting minimum number of differential (or linear) active s-boxes for word-oriented block ciphers. In Asiacrypt 2014, Sun *et al.* [2] proposed a extended

© Springer International Publishing AG, part of Springer Nature 2018
S. Qing et al. (Eds.): ICICS 2017, LNCS 10631, pp. 502–508, 2018.
https://doi.org/10.1007/978-3-319-89500-0_43

framework for bit-oriented block ciphers. The key idea of [2] is to exact the inequalities from the H-representation of the convex hull of all possible differential patterns of the s-box. The linear inequalities describing the differential properties of up to 5-bit s-boxes can be obtained by using the SAGE [3] software and a greedy algorithm. Recently, the tools using the MILP method to searching integral distinguishers [4] based on division property and impossible differentials [5] have also been proposed. Usually, the MILP instances are be described with the LP format and solved with the optimizer Gurobi [6] which is the most efficient commercial solver currently. The MILP method is powerful, but there are some inherent drawbacks. In this paper, we mainly simplify the scale of MILP models and accelerate the search of (related-key) differential characteristics and impossible differentials for bit-oriented block ciphers.

Our Contributions. We proposes the OPB file format to describe the MILP models. Compared to the LP file format, this is more concise and more suitable for constructing models for bit-oriented block ciphers. By setting the parameter MIPFocus of Gurobi reasonably, the solution time can be greatly reduced. For the impossible differentials search, we give the simply linear inequalities of differential propagation of the modular addition without considering the differential probability. This helps reduce the number of variables and constraints in MILP models and speed up searches. As applications, we give the exact lower bounds of the number of related-key differential active s-boxes for LBlock and the impossible differentials for the SPECK family.

Organization. The remainder of the paper is organized as follows. In Sect. 2, we give a brief introduction to the automatic search tools based on MILP and Gurobi for bit-oriented block ciphers. And then we propose some techniques to improve the tools of (related-key) differentials and impossible differentials. As applications, we search the exact lower bounds of the number of related-key differential active s-boxes of LBlock and the impossible differentials of the SPECK family in Sect. 3. We conclude in Sect. 4.

2   The Automatic Search Tool Based on MILP and Gurobi

2.1   The (Related-Key) Differential Automatic Search Method for Bit-Oriented Block Ciphers

In this section, we give a brief introduction of Sun *et al.* [2] framework to find the exact lower bounds of the number of (related-key) differential active s-boxes for bit-oriented block ciphers. The details as follow.

Objective Function. We need introduce a 0–1 variable A_i to mark every s-box in the encryption process and the key schedule algorithm, such that:

$$A_i = \begin{cases} 1, if \ the \ input \ word \ of \ the \ sbox \ is \ nonzero \\ 0, otherwise \end{cases} \tag{1}$$

So, the objective function is $\sum_i A_i$.

Constraints. For the XOR operation, the bit-level input differences are a, b and the bit-level output difference is c. Then the constraints are:

$$\begin{cases} d_\oplus \geq a, d_\oplus \geq b, d_\oplus \geq c \\ a + b + c \geq d_\oplus \\ a + b + c \leq 2 \end{cases} \tag{2}$$

where $d_\oplus$ is a dummy variable.

For the $w \times v$ s-box marked by A_i, the input difference is $(x_{i0}, x_{i1}, \cdots, x_{i(w-1)})$, the output difference is $(y_{i0}, y_{i1}, \cdots, y_{i(v-1)})$, then:

$$\begin{cases} A_t - x_{ik} \geq 0, k \in \{0, \cdots, w-1\} \\ -A_t + \sum_{j=0}^{w-1} x_{ij} \geq 0 \end{cases} \tag{3}$$

For an bijective s-box, we have:

$$\begin{cases} w \sum_{j=0}^{v-1} y_{ij} - \sum_{j=0}^{w-1} x_{ij} \geq 0 \\ v \sum_{j=0}^{w-1} x_{ij} - \sum_{j=0}^{v-1} y_{ij} \geq 0 \end{cases} \tag{4}$$

In order to make use of the differential distribution table of the s-box, Sun *et al.* used the inequality-generator() function in the sage.geometry.polyhedron class of the SAGE software to obtain the convex hull of all possible differential patterns of the s-box. The number of this linear inequalities can be effectively reduced by using the greedy algorithm. After defining the objective function and the constraints, we need to construct a MILP instances in the LP format. Then we can employ the optimizer Gurobi to solve the MILP instances.

2.2 Improved Tools for Bit-Oriented Block Ciphers

We propose a new file format OPB to describe the MILP models for bit-oriented block ciphers. Gurobi can solve a variety of file format models, such as MPS, LP, OPB and so on. Among them, the MPS format is the most common, the LP format is more readable than MPS. The common method to describe the MILP models is the LP file format using Python or C++ language. The OPB format is used to store pseudo-Boolean satisfaction and pesudo-boolean optimization models which contains only boolean variables 0 or 1. So the OPB file format is more suitable to build MILP models for bit-oriented block ciphers. Compared to the LP file format, the OPB format is more concise, easy to read and write. The key words and contents of the two file formats are different, as shown in Table 1. First, the OPB format does not need to specify the variables and their types in particular because all of them have been default to Boolean variables. In addition, we can easy to describe the constraints of the differential propagation of the XOR operation in this format. As the bit-level input differences are a, $b$and the bit-level output difference is c. Then the constraint is:

$$c - a - b + 2ab = 0 \tag{5}$$

Table 1. The comparison between the LP and OPB file format

*.lp	*.opb
Minimize	min:(objection)
Subject to	(constraints)
(constraints)	
Binary	
(variables)	
End	

Many optimization parameters are provided by Gurobi to modify your high-level solution strategy, in which the parameter MIPFocus is one of the most important. MIPFocus $= 1$ means that you are more interested in good quality feasible solution. If the solver is having no trouble finding the optimal solution, select MIPFocus $= 2$. If the best objective bound is moving very slowly (or not at all), try MIPFocus $= 3$. So setting parameters properly can effectively reduce the solution time of the model. When solving the model of the number of (related-key) differential of active s-boxes, we can set MIPFocus $= 1$ to find a higher quality solution that can effectively shorten the solution time. The experimental results in Sect. 3.1 show that the solution time of the optimized models described with the OPB format are reduced greatly.

In addition, we propose a new simple linear inequalities of differential property of modular addition used in the search of impossible differentials. In [7], Fu *et al.* appended which is used to compute the differential probability to the vector and obtained 13 linear inequalities to describe the differential propagation of modular addition in bit-level. In [8,9], this linear inequalities are used to the impossible differential search for ARX ciphers directly. In fact, it is not necessary to compute the differential probability of modular addition in the impossible differential search. We only need to give the linear inequalities of the 56 possible difference patterns of modular addition. By using the inequality-generator() function in the SAGE and the greedy algorithm, we only need 8 linear inequalities of all possible patterns of modular addition in bit-level which are listed below.

$$
\begin{cases}
-\alpha[i] - \beta[i] - \gamma[i] + \alpha[i+1] + \beta[i+1] + \gamma[i+1] \geq -2 \\
\alpha[i] + \beta[i] + \gamma[i] - \alpha[i+1] - \beta[i+1] - \gamma[i+1] \geq -2 \\
\alpha[i] + \beta[i] + \gamma[i] + \alpha[i+1] + \beta[i+1] - \gamma[i+1] \geq 0 \\
\alpha[i] + \beta[i] + \gamma[i] + \alpha[i+1] - \beta[i+1] + \gamma[i+1] \geq 0 \\
\alpha[i] + \beta[i] + \gamma[i] - \alpha[i+1] + \beta[i+1] + \gamma[i+1] \geq 0 \\
-\alpha[i] - \beta[i] - \gamma[i] + \alpha[i+1] - \beta[i+1] - \gamma[i+1] \geq -4 \\
-\alpha[i] - \beta[i] - \gamma[i] - \alpha[i+1] + \beta[i+1] - \gamma[i+1] \geq -4 \\
-\alpha[i] - \beta[i] - \gamma[i] - \alpha[i+1] - \beta[i+1] + \gamma[i+1] \geq -4
\end{cases}
\tag{6}
$$

As application, we use this linear inequalities of differential property of modular addition to construct the models of the impossible differential search for the SPECK family with the OPB format in Sect. 3.2.

3   Applications

3.1   Application to LBlock

Lblock is a lightweight block cipher designed by Wu and Zhang at ACNS [10]. Since the shift operation number of the key schedule of LBlock is 29, we can only use the bit-oriented MILP model in related-key differential search. The models based on the LP format and the OPB format are solved respectively. The size of models described by the OPB format are less than the LP format, so the solution time is more faster usually. By setting the parameter MIPFocus = 1, the solution time of the models is further shortened. The results are shown in Table 2. We improved the results of 9~11 rounds LBlock which show that 9/10/11 rounds exact lower bounds is 7/9/11 active s-boxes. In [11], Sun et al. needed about 4 days to find the 11-round exact lower bounds of the number of differential active s-boxes of LBlock in the related-key model. We only needed about 2 days. To the best of our knowledge, the 12-round exact lower bounds of the number of differential active s-boxes of LBlock is first obtained using about 3 weeks.

The computations are performed on PC (Intel(R) Core(TM) i3-4160 CPU, 3.60 GHz, 4.00 GB RAM, 4 cores, window7) with the optimizer Gurobi7.0.1.

Table 2. The exact lower bounds of the number of differential active s-boxes for round-reduced variants of LBlock in the related-key model

Rounds	The number of active s-boxes			Time (in seconds)	
	This paper	[11]	[2]	LP	OPB&MIPFocus = 1
5	1	1	1	2.5	1.56
6	2	2	2	8.5	8.36
7	4	4	3	70	90
8	6	6	5	2419	745
9	7	8	6	6478	1739
10	9	10	8	56462	13238
11	11	12	10	-	161165
12	13	–	–	-	≈3 weeks

3.2   Application to SPECK

SPECK is a family of lightweight block ciphers publicly released by National Security Agency (NSA) in June 2013 [12]. Cui et al. [8] proposed an algorithm for finding impossible differentials for block ciphers and obtained four 17-round impossible differentials for HIGHT. In [9], Lee et al. found 157 6-round impossible differentials for SPECK-64 by using the same method. All of them used the same linear inequalities of differential property of modular addition provided by [7]. We applied the improved model to the full versions of the SPECK family and limited the input and output differences to only 1 active bit. The results of the experiments are shown in the Table 3. The input or output difference is expressed by the position of non-zero bit. The position of the leftmost bit is 0.

The computations are performed on PC (Intel(R) Core(TM) i7-7500U CPU, 2.70 GHz, 8.00 GB RAM, 4 cores, window10) with the optimizer Gurobi7.0.1.

Table 3. Summary of impossible differentials on the SPECK family

Version	Rounds	$\Delta_{in} \nrightarrow \Delta_{out}$	# ID	Time (in seconds)
SPECK-32	6	$9 \nrightarrow 16$	3	166
		$9 \nrightarrow 30$		
		$9 \nrightarrow 31$		
SPECK-48	6	$16 \nrightarrow 0$	20	450
		$16 \nrightarrow 2$		
		$\vdots$		
		$29 \nrightarrow 45$		
SPECK-64	6	$0 \nrightarrow 16$	157	918
		$0 \nrightarrow 64$		
		$\vdots$		
		$45 \nrightarrow 62$		
SPECK-96	7	$40 \nrightarrow 93$	12	3946
		$40 \nrightarrow 94$		
		$\vdots$		
		$53 \nrightarrow 94$		
SPECK-128	7	$0 \nrightarrow 125$	160	16422
		$2 \nrightarrow 125$		
		$\vdots$		
		$90 \nrightarrow 125$		

In addition, the modular addition exists a differential with probability 1 that the leftmost bit of one of input differences is active and the leftmost bit of the output difference is active. This difference can be propagate to the round function of SPECK. $56 \nrightarrow 56$ and $57 \nrightarrow 56$ are the 7-round impossible differentials for SPECK-128. We can append one round at the bottom and obtain two 8-round impossible differentials $56 \nrightarrow 0, 64$ and $57 \nrightarrow 0, 64$ for SPECK-128.

4   Conclusion

Our work provides a new OPB file format to describe the MILP models for bit-oriented block ciphers and also through setting the parameter MIPFocus = 1 to accelerate the search. In addition, we give a system of simple linear inequalities of differential patterns propagation of modular addition used in impossible differential search. We applied our techniques to LBlock and SPECK.

Acknowledgments. The authors would like to thank all anonymous referees for their valuable comments that greatly improve the manuscript. This work is supported by National Natural Science Foundation of China (No. 61672509, No. 61232009) and National Cryptography Development Fund (MMJJ20170101).

References

1. Mouha, N., Wang, Q., Gu, D., Preneel, B.: Differential and linear cryptanalysis using mixed-integer linear programming. In: Wu, C.-K., Yung, M., Lin, D. (eds.) Inscrypt 2011. LNCS, vol. 7537, pp. 57–76. Springer, Heidelberg (2012). https://doi.org/10.1007/978-3-642-34704-7_5
2. Sun, S., Hu, L., Wang, P., Qiao, K., Ma, X., Song, L.: Automatic security evaluation and (related-key) differential characteristic search: application to SIMON, PRESENT, LBlock, DES(L) and other bit-oriented block ciphers. In: Sarkar, P., Iwata, T. (eds.) ASIACRYPT 2014, Part I. LNCS, vol. 8873, pp. 158–178. Springer, Heidelberg (2014). https://doi.org/10.1007/978-3-662-45611-8_9
3. Stein, W., et al.: Sage: Open source mathematical software (2008)
4. Xiang, Z., Zhang, W., Bao, Z., Lin, D.: Applying MILP method to searching integral distinguishers based on division property for 6 lightweight block ciphers. In: Cheon, J.H., Takagi, T. (eds.) ASIACRYPT 2016, Part I. LNCS, vol. 10031, pp. 648–678. Springer, Heidelberg (2016). https://doi.org/10.1007/978-3-662-53887-6_24
5. Sasaki, Y., Todo, Y.: New Impossible differential search tool from design and cryptanalysis aspects. In: Coron, J.-S., Nielsen, J.B. (eds.) EUROCRYPT 2017, Part III. LNCS, vol. 10212, pp. 185–215. Springer, Cham (2017). https://doi.org/10.1007/978-3-319-56617-7_7
6. Gurobi Optimization: Gurobi optimizer reference manual (2013). http://www.gurobi.com
7. Fu, K., Wang, M., Guo, Y., Sun, S., Hu, L.: MILP-based automatic search algorithms for differential and linear trails for speck. In: Peyrin, T. (ed.) FSE 2016. LNCS, vol. 9783, pp. 268–288. Springer, Heidelberg (2016). https://doi.org/10.1007/978-3-662-52993-5_14
8. Cui, T., Jia, K., Fu, K., et al.: New Automatic Search Tool for Impossible Differentials and Zero-Correlation Linear Approximations. Cryptology ePrint archive, Report 2016/689 (2016). https://eprint.iacr.org/2016/689
9. Lee, H.C., Kang, H.C., Hong, D., et al.: New Impossible Differential Characteristic of SPECK64 using MILP. Cryptology ePrint archive, Report 2016/1137 (2016). https://eprint.iacr.org/2016/1137
10. Wu, W., Zhang, L.: LBlock: a lightweight block cipher. In: Lopez, J., Tsudik, G. (eds.) ACNS 2011. LNCS, vol. 6715, pp. 327–344. Springer, Heidelberg (2011). https://doi.org/10.1007/978-3-642-21554-4_19
11. Sun, S., Hu, L., Wang, M., et al.: Towards finding the best characteristics of some bit-oriented block ciphers and automatic enumeration of (related-key) differential and linear characteristics with predefined properties. Cryptology ePrint Archive, Report 2014/747 (2014). https://eprint.iacr.org/2014/747
12. Beaulieu, R., Shors, D., Smith, J., Treatman-Clark, S., Weeks, B., Wingers, L.: The SIMON and SPECK famillies of lightweight block ciphers. Cryptology ePrint archive, Report 2013/543 (2013). http://eprint.iacr.org/2013/543

Hypercubes and Private Information Retrieval

Anirban Basu[✉][iD], Rui Xu, Juan Camilo Corena, and Shinsaku Kiyomoto

KDDI Research, Fujimino, Japan
{basu,ru-xu,corena,kiyomoto}@kddi-research.jp

Abstract. In geometry, a hypercube is a regular polytype – a generalisation of a 3-dimensional cube to λ-dimensions, with mutually perpendicular sides of equal lengths. For $\lambda = 0, 1, 2, 3,$ and 4, a hypercube is a point, a straight line segment, a square, a cube and a tesseract respectively. In this paper, we apply the concept of hypercubes in computationally private information retrieval (CPIR) based on additively homomorphic cryptosystems and optimise it further at the cost of a measurable privacy loss.

Keywords: Privacy · Hypercubes · Information retrieval

1 Introduction

A *computationally private information retrieval* (CPIR) lets a receiver retrieve an l-bit element from the sender's database of n elements without revealing the retrieved element to the sender. This is a weaker version of the 1-out-of-n oblivious transfer, which ensures that the receiver is unable to obtain any information about the other elements in the sender's database.

CPIR is useful in many real world scenarios. For example, in an opinion poll, the identity of the person submitting the opinion should be decoupled from the opinion itself to facilitate unbiased polls, and yet ensure that only a set of authorised entities are allowed to submit the opinions. One way of doing this is to let every authorised person pick a valid token using CPIR, and then submit opinions where every opinion is tied to a previously picked valid token. Even if the identity of the submitter is not concealed (unless using anonymous networking) the submitter can plausibly deny that the submitted opinion is hers because the poll administrator cannot prove, due to CPIR, that a particular token was picked by her.

In geometry, a hypercube is a generalisation of a 3-dimensional cube to λ-dimensions, with mutually perpendicular sides of equal length, d.

J. C. Corena—Portions of this work are contributions from Juan Camilo Corena when he was at KDDI Research (erstwhile KDDI R&D Laboratories). He currently works for Google. This work is not related to or supported by Google in any way. He is also reachable at investigacion@juancamilocorena.com.

S. Qing et al. (Eds.): ICICS 2017, LNCS 10631, pp. 509–515, 2018.
https://doi.org/10.1007/978-3-319-89500-0_44

For $\lambda = 0, 1, 2, 3,$ and 4, a hypercube is a point, a straight line segment, a square, a cube and a tesseract respectively.

In this paper, we describe how the concept of hypercubes could be utilised in computationally private information retrieval (CPIR), which is very similar to the scheme described by Chan [1]. We propose a method to improve the performance of the hypercube-backed CPIR at the cost of a measurable loss in privacy.

The rest of the paper is structured as follows. We present a brief overview of the state-of-the-art in private information retrieval in Sect. 2. This is followed by some background in homomorphic encryption in Sect. 3 before we delve into describing our CPIR protocol based on λ-dimensional hypercubes in Sect. 4 with an optimised version in Sect. 4.2. We present technical feasibility through evaluations of cryptographic primitives in Sect. 5 before concluding in Sect. 6.

2   Related Work

The problem of hiding the index of a retrieval operation on a database from the server which actually holds the database was investigated by Rivest et al. [2], Blakely and Meadows [3], Abadi et al. [4,5], Beaver and Feigenbaum [6]. The current known seminar work on private information retrieval by Chor et al. [7,8] builds upon the above. PIR can be roughly grouped into two categories, information-theoretic PIR and computationally PIR. The initial proposals of Chor et al. [7,8] assume k non-communicating servers to store the database and can resist computationally unbounded malicious servers. Later on the weaker notion of computational PIR [9], which aims only at providing privacy against computationally bounded adversary, emerges so as to relieve the critical assumption on more than one non-communicating servers.

The work very close to our scheme is by Chan [1], which uses 2-D hypercube and its generalisations into higher dimensions for a single server private information retrieval with $\mathcal{O}(n)$ communication complexity. The work is more computationally efficient on the server side than ours but has more computations (than ours) on the client-side. Chan's work uses the Damgård-Jurik cryptosystem, reducing the need for a larger homomorphic cryptosystems for every hypercube dimension reduction than the previous reduction. The main difference between our work and [1] is that we propose a version of PIR, in which we can reduce a lot of the computational complexity at the cost of a measurable privacy loss, which is explained in Sect. 4.2.

3   Background – Homomorphic Encryption

Homomorphic encryption allows computing over encrypted data without requiring the knowledge of either the actual data or any results produced through the computation. Depending on the type of computational operations supported, homomorphic cryptosystems are classified as: (1) additive, (2) multiplicative,

(3) somewhat homomorphic (e.g., allowing a number of additions and one multiplication), and (4) fully homomorphic.

The Paillier public-key cryptosystem [10], satisfying semantic security against chosen plaintext attacks (IND-CPA requirement), and its variant, the Damgård-Jurik cryptosystem [11], have practical implementations and both exhibit only additively homomorphic properties: (a) the encryption of the sum of two plaintext messages m_1 and m_2 is the modular product of their individual ciphertexts, i.e., $\mathcal{E}(m_1 + m_2) = \mathcal{E}(m_1) \cdot \mathcal{E}(m_2)$ and (b) the encryption of the product of one plaintext message m_1 and another plaintext multiplicand π is the modular exponentiation of the ciphertext of m_1 with π as the exponent, i.e., $\mathcal{E}(m_1 \cdot \pi) = \mathcal{E}(m_1)^\pi$.

4 Computationally Private Information Retrieval (CPIR) Using λ-Dimensional Hypercubes

In private information retrieval, given a database of elements $T = t_1 t_2 t_3 \ldots t_n$, the aim is to retrieve a t_x such that the database owner cannot learn which t_x was retrieved. Since n can be very large, T is folded into a λ-dimensional hypercube. This means that each edge of the hypercube will contain $d = \sqrt[\lambda]{n}$ elements. Finding a t_x is essentially locating a point on the λ-dimensional coordinate space.

Essentially, the responder sends λ vectors of encrypted 0s and encrypted 1s, each of length $d = \sqrt[\lambda]{n}$ and each having exactly one encrypted 1 while the rest are encrypted 0s. Each encrypted vector multiplied with a multi-dimensional hypercube helps reducing the hypercube by one dimension until it reduces to a single point. This process, depending on the way it is done, may require fully homomorphic encryption.

Let us see how this works for $\lambda = 2$ i.e., a 2-D hypercube or a square matrix. Assume that all the tokens in T are arranged in the square matrix of size $d \times d$, as:

$$
T = \begin{pmatrix}
t_{1,1} & t_{1,2} & t_{1,3} & \cdots & t_{1,d} \\
t_{2,1} & t_{2,2} & t_{2,3} & \cdots & t_{2,d} \\
t_{3,1} & t_{3,2} & t_{3,3} & \cdots & t_{3,d} \\
\cdots & \cdots & \cdots & \cdots & \cdots \\
t_{d,1} & t_{d,2} & t_{d,3} & \cdots & t_{d,d}
\end{pmatrix} \tag{1}
$$

We can reduce this with two encrypted vectors of zeros and ones, each of size n: $V_a = \{\mathcal{E}_a(v_{a,1}), \mathcal{E}_a(v_{a,2}), \mathcal{E}_a(v_{a,3}), \ldots, \mathcal{E}_a(v_{a,m})\}$ and $V_b = \{\mathcal{E}_b(v_{b,1}), \mathcal{E}_b(v_{b,2}), \mathcal{E}_b(v_{b,3}), \ldots, \mathcal{E}_b(v_{b,d})\}$ where any of $v_{a,k}$ or $v_{b,k}$ is either a zero or one. Exactly one component in each vector is an encrypted one. The encryption function $\mathcal{E}_b()$ is such that its plaintext space is same as or more than the ciphertext space of $\mathcal{E}_a()$, for example $\mathcal{E}_b()$ could be a 512 bits Paillier cryptosystem while $\mathcal{E}_a()$ is a 256 bits Paillier cryptosystem.

Homomorphically multiplying the first row of T with V_a and homomorphically summing the components, we will produce: $T_{1,a} = \mathcal{E}_a(v_{a,1})^{t_{1,1}} \mathcal{E}_a(v_{a,2})^{t_{1,2}} \mathcal{E}_a(v_{a,3})^{t_{1,3}} \ldots \mathcal{E}_a(v_{a,m})^{t_{1,d}}$ but only one of these components is non-zero because remember that only one component amongst $v_{a,k}$ is one. Let us suppose, $v_{a,3} = 1$, which means $\mathcal{E}_a(v_{a,3})^{t_{1,3}}$ is non-zero from the first row of T. Therefore, the homomorphic sum of the homomorphic products for the first row will produce $T_{1,a} = \mathcal{E}_a(v_{a,3})^{t_{1,3}}$, which when decrypted will result in $t_{1,3}$. However, decryption is not done at this stage. If we repeat this for every row in T (with V_a assuming that $v_{a,3} = 1$) and obtain the homomorphic sums per row, we generate a column vector as follows:

$$T_a = \begin{pmatrix} T_{1,a} = \mathcal{E}_a(v_{a,3})^{t_{1,3}} \\ T_{2,a} = \mathcal{E}_a(v_{a,3})^{t_{2,3}} \\ T_{3,a} = \mathcal{E}_a(v_{a,3})^{t_{3,3}} \\ \ldots \\ T_{d,a} = \mathcal{E}_a(v_{a,3})^{t_{d,3}} \end{pmatrix} \tag{2}$$

If we homomorphically multiply each element in T_a with V_b and homomorphically add the resulting components, we get: $T_b = \mathcal{E}_b(v_{b,1})^{T_{1,a}} \mathcal{E}_b(v_{b,2})^{T_{2,a}} \mathcal{E}_b(v_{b,3})^{T_{3,a}} \ldots \mathcal{E}_b(v_{b,d})^{T_{d,a}}$ but again, only one of $v_{b,k}$ is non-zero. Let us assume that $v_{b,2} = 1$. Therefore, $T_b = \mathcal{E}_b(v_{b,2})^{T_{2,a}}$ because all the other components are effectively zero in plaintext domain. Thus, our 2-D square matrix has been reduced to a point in the encrypted domain, i.e., $T_b = \mathcal{E}_b(v_{b,2})^{T_{2,a}}$. If we now run the decryption $\mathcal{D}_b(T_b)$ first, we effectively obtain $T_{2,a}$ since $v_{b,2} = 1$. Running the decryption $\mathcal{D}_a(T_{2,a})$, we obtain $t_{2,3}$, which is exactly the point that can be located by setting $v_{b,2} = 1$ and $v_{a,3} = 1$. Note that for simplicity, we did not describe the shuffling of the components of both vectors because it is related to ensuring randomisation and not the hypercube reduction process. The above process of hypercube reduction can be easily generalised to dimensions higher than $\lambda = 2$. If the encryption function for reducing dimension i to $i-1$ is denoted by $\mathcal{E}_i$ then the ciphertext space for $\mathcal{E}_i$ must be less than the plaintext space of $\mathcal{E}_{i-1}$. In the above example, $\mathcal{E}_i = \mathcal{E}_a$ and $\mathcal{E}_{i-1} = \mathcal{E}_b$. This constraint on the cryptosystems illustrates the fact that with higher dimensions, one would require multiple cryptosystems with large key sizes.

4.1　Computational and Communication Complexities

Assuming that the computational complexity of the combination of a homomorphic addition and a homomorphic multiplication with a cryptosystem that reduces the dimension of the hypercube from i to $i-1$ is c_i. We noticed above that to obtain the final result, we had a complexity of $c_1 d$. Similarly, the complexity due to the hypercube reduction before that was $c_2 d^2$. The total complexity can be expressed as the series $c_1 d + c_2 d^2 + c_3 d^3 + \ldots + c_i d^i + \ldots c_\lambda d^\lambda$. Given n as the total number of elements, we know $n = d^\lambda$. Thus, the expression for complexity can be re-written as $c_\lambda n + c_{\lambda-1} n^{\frac{\lambda-1}{\lambda}} + c_{\lambda-2} n^{\frac{\lambda-2}{\lambda}} + \ldots + c_1 n^{\frac{1}{\lambda}}$, or $\mathcal{O}(n)$. Note that the complexity due to any c_i is higher than that due to any c_j for $i < j$.

The requester sends λ vectors, each of size d while the database responds with a single encrypted value. The sizes of the vectors are different because each contains d values encrypted with different cryptosystems. If we denote the size of a ciphertext for a cryptosystem used to reduce the hypercube from i to

$i - 1$ dimension as b_i (independent of n, hence constant) then the total size of the request is $db_1 + db_2 + \ldots + db_\lambda$. The size of the response is always b_1. The communication complexity is in order of λd, or $\log_d(n) \sqrt[d]{n}$. Thus, for an optimal size of d, the complexity is dependent on λ, which means it is in $\mathcal{O}(n)$.

4.2   Reducing the Number of Homomorphic Computations – Impact on Privacy

We noted that the cryptosystem with encryption function $\mathcal{E}_i$ (responsible for reducing the dimension of the hypercube from i to $i-1$) should generate ciphertexts that fit in the plaintext space of the cryptosystem with encryption function $\mathcal{E}_{i-1}$. If $\mathcal{E}_i$ is a 1024-bit Paillier then its ciphertexts are 2048-bits. Therefore, $\mathcal{E}_{i-1}$ must be 2048-bits or above (assuming there is no speciality of the implementations of those cryptosystems, e.g., supporting negative or fractional numbers using plaintext space division). If the 1024-bit Paillier is deemed to be the minimum standard for security then with just $\lambda = 4$, the cryptosystem for E_1 will be the 8192-bit Paillier, which is significantly slow compared to the 1024-bit Paillier. Thus, with higher values of λ, the reductions to certain lower dimensions of the hypercube may not be computationally feasible given the implementations of the cryptosystems.

One way of addressing this challenge is to limit the use of cryptography to only $\lambda = 4$ or $\lambda = 3$, while for all other higher values of λ, the CPIR protocol uses plaintext coordinates to address those dimensions. There is an obvious loss of privacy. According to the original definition of CPIR, the database owner must not know which element (out of n elements) was picked by the requester, thus allowing the requester n-anonymity. If we use the cryptography for reducing only the lower m dimensions, for example, then for any $n = d^\lambda$, the requester will have no privacy in the $d^{\lambda-m}$ dimensions. Suppose $k = d^m$. Then, the requester will still have k-anonymity so long as the plaintext coordinates (for $\lambda-m$ dimensions) are chosen from a uniform random distribution. In other words, as an example, if $m = 4$, and $\lambda = 7$, the requester will specify 3 coordinates in plaintext and use the proposed CPIR protocol for the lower 4 dimensions. Thus, the chosen element will lie somewhere amongst the points in the tesseract defined by d^4. If we assume $d = 100$, the requester will have $k = 100^4$-anonymity.

Loss of Privacy. Following the strategy for quantifying the loss of privacy in [12], we use Shannon's entropy to measure how much privacy is lost for using homomorphic encryption in the m lower dimensions only. The entropy is a measure of uncertainty in a random variable X, and is defined as $\mathcal{H}(X) = -\sum_x p_X(x) \log p_X(x)$. Let $\mathcal{H}(V)$ denote the uncertainty of the vector V, where only one element is 1 and the rest are 0. Since the elements in the vector can either be 0 or 1, and the entire vector can only have one element that is 1, we can write that for a d-element vector, $\mathcal{H}(V) = -\sum_i^d \frac{1}{d} \log \frac{1}{d} = \log d$. Thus, for λ such independent vectors, the total entropy is $\lambda \log d$. If only m such vectors are encrypted, then we can quantify the loss in privacy in terms of entropy as $\mathcal{P}_{loss} = (\lambda - m) \log d$ and leaving us with the residual privacy as $\mathcal{P}_{residual} = m \log d$.

5   Evaluation

In the performance evaluation of cryptographic primitives shown in Table 1, we have used an open-source implementation of the Paillier cryptosystem[1]. The performance of this implementation on a 64-bit Macbook Pro running macOS Sierra 10.12.5 and Java 1.8.0_121-b13 on a 2.9 GHz Intel Core i5 with a 16 GB 2133 MHz LPDDR3 RAM are given in Table 1. The plaintext and integer multiplicands chosen from random integers of bit lengths 256, 512 and 1024 respectively. Notice that these bit lengths are half the size of the public key sizes of the tested cryptosystems because our implementation supports negative integers by dividing the plaintext space into half with the upper half reserved for positive integers and the lower half for negative ones.

Table 1. Comparison of the performances, in terms of time, of a Java implementation of the Paillier cryptosystem with different bit lengths for the public key (i.e. modulus n).

Paillier cryptosystem (key size)	512-bits	1024-bits	2048-bits
Encryption (ms)	1.606	10.586	71.93
Decryption (ms)	1.605	10.773	70.848
Homomorphic addition (ms)	0.156	0.376	1.314
Homomorphic multiplication (ms)	0.894	5.561	36.588

5.1   Computationally Private Information Retrieval (CPIR)

We evaluate the performance of our proposed PIR scheme by setting, without loss of generality, $\lambda = 2$ and each side of our 2-D hypercube to $d = 7$, for simplicity. This involves $d^2 = 49$ homomorphic additions and homomorphic multiplications in $\mathcal{E}_2()$ and only $d = 7$ homomorphic additions and homomorphic multiplications in $\mathcal{E}_1()$. Note that $\mathcal{E}_2()$ is faster than $\mathcal{E}_1()$ because its key size, i.e., n is lower. Setting $\mathcal{E}_2()$ to 512-bits Paillier and $\mathcal{E}_1()$ to 2048-bits Paillier, and using the timings from Table 1 we can compute the time taken for d^2 homomorphic additions and multiplications as $(0.156 + 0.894) \times 49 = 51.45$ ms and for d homomorphic additions and multiplications as $(1.314 + 36.588) \times 7 = 265.314$ ms.

Generalising this, if we denote the time taken by a homomorphic multiplication and a homomorphic addition by $t_{\mathcal{E}\mathcal{M}_i}$ and $t_{\mathcal{E}\mathcal{A}_i}$ respectively, where $\mathcal{E}\mathcal{M}_i$ and $\mathcal{E}\mathcal{A}_i$ are applied for hypercube dimension reduction from i to $i-1$, then for a λ-dimensional hypercube represented by $\mathbb{R}$ with each side measuring d, the total time taken to extract a single point due to the homomorphic multiplications and additions is given as:

$$t_{total} = (t_{\mathcal{E}\mathcal{M}_\lambda} + t_{\mathcal{E}\mathcal{A}_\lambda})d^\lambda + (t_{\mathcal{E}\mathcal{M}_{\lambda-1}} + t_{\mathcal{E}\mathcal{A}_{\lambda-1}})d^{\lambda-1} + \ldots + (t_{\mathcal{E}\mathcal{M}_1} + t_{\mathcal{E}\mathcal{A}_1})d$$

Note that every $t_{\mathcal{E}\mathcal{M}_i} < t_{\mathcal{E}\mathcal{M}_j}$ and every $t_{\mathcal{E}\mathcal{A}_i} < t_{\mathcal{E}\mathcal{A}_j}$ for $i > j$. Given the optimisation on the CPIR protocol described before, which only uses homomorphic encryption for a limited number of dimension reductions, the time taken will be less than this generalised expression.

---

[1] Paillier implementation: https://github.com/anirbanbasu/paillier-crypto

6   Conclusions

In this paper, we have proposed a computationally private information retrieval method based on the concept of hypercubes. We have also shown that in order to make our CPIR scheme efficient, we may need to make limited use of homomorphic cryptosystems with a quantifiable loss of privacy.

One avenue of future work includes testing the proposed system (both versions – one without privacy loss and one with measurable privacy loss) for scalability for picking one token from a large number of tokens in a database.

References

1. Chang, Y.-C.: Single database private information retrieval with logarithmic communication. In: Wang, H., Pieprzyk, J., Varadharajan, V. (eds.) ACISP 2004. LNCS, vol. 3108, pp. 50–61. Springer, Heidelberg (2004). https://doi.org/10.1007/978-3-540-27800-9_5
2. Rivest, R.L., Adleman, L., Dertouzos, M.L.: On data banks and privacy homomorphisms. Found. Secur. Comput. **4**(11), 171–181 (1978)
3. Blakley, G., Meadows, C.: A database encryption scheme which allows the computation of statistics using encrypted data. In: 1985 IEEE Symposium on Security and Privacy, p. 116. IEEE (1985)
4. Abadi, M., Feigenbaum, J., Kilian, J.: On hiding information from an oracle. J. Comput. Syst. Sci. **39**(1), 21–50 (1989)
5. Beaver, D., Feigenbaum, J., Kilian, J., Rogaway, P.: Locally random reductions: improvements and applications. J. Cryptol. **10**(1), 17–36 (1997)
6. Beaver, D., Feigenbaum, J.: Hiding instances in multioracle queries. In: Choffrut, C., Lengauer, T. (eds.) STACS 1990. LNCS, vol. 415, pp. 37–48. Springer, Heidelberg (1990). https://doi.org/10.1007/3-540-52282-4_30
7. Chor, B., Goldreich, O., Kushilevitz, E., Sudan, M.: Private information retrieval. In: Proceedings of the 36th Annual Symposium on Foundations of Computer Science, pp. 41–50. IEEE (1995)
8. Chor, B., Goldreich, O., Kushilevitz, E., Sudan, M.: Private information retrieval. J. ACM **45**(6), 965–982 (1998)
9. Chor, B., Gilboa, N.: Computationally private information retrieval. In: Proceedings of the Twenty-Ninth Annual ACM Symposium on Theory of Computing, pp. 304–313. ACM (1997)
10. Paillier, P.: Public-key cryptosystems based on composite degree residuosity classes. In: Stern, J. (ed.) EUROCRYPT 1999. LNCS, vol. 1592, pp. 223–238. Springer, Heidelberg (1999). https://doi.org/10.1007/3-540-48910-X_16
11. Damgård, I., Jurik, M.: A generalisation, a simplification and some applications of paillier's probabilistic public-key system. In: Kim, K. (ed.) PKC 2001. LNCS, vol. 1992, pp. 119–136. Springer, Heidelberg (2001). https://doi.org/10.1007/3-540-44586-2_9
12. Coney, L., Hall, J.L., Vora, P.L., Wagner, D.: Towards a privacy measurement criterion for voting systems. In: Proceedings of the 2005 National Conference on Digital Government Research, pp. 287–288. Digital Government Society of North America (2005)

A Multi-client Dynamic Searchable Symmetric Encryption System with Physical Deletion

Lei Xu[1,2], Chungen Xu[1(✉)], Joseph K. Liu[2], Cong Zuo[2], and Peng Zhang[3]

[1] School of Science, Nanjing University of Science and Technology, Nanjing, China
xuleinjust@yeah.net, xuchung@njust.edu.cn
[2] Faculty of Information Technology, Monash University, Melbourne, VIC, Australia
{joseph.liu,cong.zuo1}@monash.edu
[3] ATR Key Laboratory of National Defense Technology,
College of Information Engineering, Shenzhen University, Shenzhen, China
zhangp@szu.edu.cn

Abstract. Dynamic Searchable Symmetric Encryption (DSSE) provides a simple and fast storage as well as retrieval method for encrypted profiles which stored in cloud. However, due to the nature of the symmetric encryption algorithm, it allows only one client to access the data. To make the scheme more practical, this paper propose a multi client dynamic symmetric searchable encryption scheme that could allow multi-client to search the privacy data with the delegation search token and dynamic delete expected files with delete token. Compared with similar works, our construction achieves a balance in network security and practical performance. We also demonstrate that the proposed scheme has same IND-CKA2 security property against adaptive adversary.

Keywords: Searchable symmetric encryption · Cloud storage
Multi-client · RSA function

1 Introduction

Cloud storage is a new concept that extends and develops in the concept of cloud computing, which collects data storage and service access functions through the combination of cluster application, network technology or distributed file system, and collects many different types of storage devices in the network together through application software to work together. It is an emerging network storage technique, which has many good qualities. For one thing it makes all the storage resources be integrated together to achieve data storage management automation and intelligence, for another, it improve the storage efficiency and flexible expansion through the visualization technology to solve the waste of storage space, reduce the operating costs [1–4]. Due to its properties of flexible management and low rental prices, many users and businesses choose to put their own data in the cloud.

© Springer International Publishing AG, part of Springer Nature 2018
S. Qing et al. (Eds.): ICICS 2017, LNCS 10631, pp. 516–528, 2018.
https://doi.org/10.1007/978-3-319-89500-0_45

With the promotion of cloud services, the industry soon found that when cloud storage brings people convenience, it gradually appears some short boards, and the biggest obstacle of cloud service promotion is the security issues around the data. The user suspects that the cloud service can not provide the corresponding security support for the data, which hinders the transfer of more data and business platform. In order to solve the problem mentioned above, we need to satisfies the following two conditions: Integrity and confidentiality, that is the cloud storage server should ensure that the data and operations in the cloud would not be malicious or non-malicious loss, destruction, leakage or illegal use; Access and privacy, when users visit some sensitive data, the system can prevent potential rivals to infer the user's behavior through the user's access mode. At present, the main means to solve such problems is to use the cryptography techniques. Users always use encryption system to encrypt their sensitive data before upload to the cloud to protect the data's confidentiality from illegal adversary. This method is the most straightforward and the simplest, but is not practical in the real scene. After a long period of research, for the former, people find that the searchable encryption is good tool to solve this problem. In this paper, we will focus on how to realize the dynamic data confidentiality and privacy retrieval control in cloud.

1.1   Related Work

The earliest research on searchable symmetric encryption system can be traced back to Chor et al.'s work [5] in 1995. They proposed the first retrieval scheme on encrypted data that stored in the database, which enables the user to search the special encrypted file without leaking anything of the data. After Chor's work, searchable symmetric encryption has been deeply studied and most of them focus on improving search performance, search pattern and security [6–8]. Cash et al. [9] renewed the encrypted data structure refer to the original one, and designed the first sub-linear SSE scheme which supported boolean queries for large databases at the cost of leaking the search pattern to the server. To make up for the lack of that Cash's work can only support single search, Jarecki extended Cash's OXT protocol to multi-client OXT [10] through provided the client s set of partial trapdoors for some permitted keywords. Their core policy is to define a sequence of attributes corresponding each query on an element in the keyword set, and the token could be computed when it satisfy the attributes.

There are also a lot of other works focus on realizing the dynamic search model, multi-client searching and other functions [11–15]. Compared with SE supporting single user, which can be regarded as data outsourcing, multi-user SE can achieve share of sensitive data. Generally, many existing SE schemes use key sharing, key distribution, proxy re-encryption, broadcast encryption, or other techniques to achieve the extension from single user to multi-user. Such as, in 2006, Curtmola et al. [16] proposed the first multiuser SE system under a broadcast encryption system, which brings enormous cost of user revocation. In 2008, Bao et al. [17] also proposed a multi-user SE. Because the users access rights depend on corresponding attribute set, the efficiency of system will increase by number of users. Dong et al. [18] constructed multi-user system based on proxy re-encryption techniques, where each user has its own unique key to encrypt, search and decrypt data. Thus, the scheme need a trusted server to manage keys. At the same time, recently, there are many systems based on ABE, in which user used attribute set to define rights of search [19–22]. Wang et al. [19] achieves fine-grained access control to authorized users with different access rights using a standard CP-ABE without key share. 2016, Wang et al. [20] proposed an efficiently multiuser searchable attribute-based encryption scheme with attribute revocation and grant for cloud storage. In the scheme, attribute revocation and grant processes of users are delegated to proxy server. In 2015, Rompay et al. [23] introduces a third party, named a proxy, that performs an algorithm to transform a single user query into one query per targeted document. In this way, sever cannot have access to content of query and its result, which achieves query privacy.

1.2   Our Contribution

In this work, we provide a multi-client dynamic searchable symmetric encryption system (MC-DSSE) for retrieving encrypted privacy data in cloud, and the main properties are listed as follows:

1. Multi-client. For practical use, this work focus on achieving single-writer/multi-reader search mode. It allows the data owner to delegate the search capability to multi-clients by a RSA approach. In fact, we distinguish the client by giving them the different ability search for a set of permitted keywords. When someone want to search for some special keyword, he needs to apply a partial search token from the data owner firstly, then generates the full search token according to the expected keyword.
2. Dynamic. To enhance the flexibility of the scheme, we add the **AddKeyword**, **DeleteFile**, algorithm to make it dynamic for the data owner. With these algorithms, the data owner can use his private key to add the new keyword and delete the encrypted file with the delete token.
3. Privacy. The proposed scheme achieves IND-CKA2 secure against probability polynomial adversary. Users could search the encrypted data stored in cloud platform which contains some keywords by a unique token without leaking anything about the origin data. Moreover, we also demonstrate that our scheme is secure for multi-clients by employ the RSA function.

1.3   Organization

The rest of this paper is organized as follows: In Sect. 2, we describe the definition of MC-DSSE scheme and gave some hardness assumptions. In Sects. 3 and 4, we propose a novel DSSE scheme support for multi-client and give its security proof. Section 5 gives its communication and computation cost. Finally, we end the paper with a brief conclusion.

2 Preliminaries

In this section, we first review the definition of the multi-client dynamic searchable symmetric encryption with keyword search, and then introduce some hardness problems with its complexity assumption related to our security proof.

2.1 MC-DSSE Definition and Related Database Structure

Here mainly introduce the syntax of multi-client dynamic symmetric searchable encryption and give a brief description of some necessary database structures.

Definition 1 (MC-DSSE) [24]. *A MC-DSSE scheme consists of the following five polynomial algorithms among a data owner, a client and a server:*

- **Setup:** *The data owner takes security parameter λ and a database DB as input, generate the system master key MK and public key PK, and sends the encrypted database EDB to the server, the server stores EDB.*
- **ClientKGen:** *The data owner takes MK, and a set w of permitted keywords as input and generates a search authorized private key sk for the client.*
- **AddKeyword:** *The data owner takes a new the file-keyword pair (id, w) and his secret key as input, generates and sends the ciphertexts to the server. The server takes the EDB as input, and inserts these ciphertexts into EDB.*
- **DeleteFile:** *The data owner takes the file's identifier and his secret key as input, returns a delete token to the server. The server takes the EDB as input, and deletes all ciphertexts of a file with identifier id from EDB.*
- **Search:** *The client takes the keyword and his secret parameters as inputs, generates a search token for the server. Then the server takes the database EDB as input, and returns the corresponding file identifiers of the file.*

In order to make the proposed scheme look more concise and practical, here it will employ two data structures $\mathcal{D}, \mathcal{T}$ which denotes List and Dictionary respectively, and then introduce four database language **Great, Get, Update, Remove** from [24], and it also will be used in our construction.

2.2 Security Definition and Hardness Assumptions

In this paper, we consider IND-CKA2 security of our MC-DSSE scheme. First, we define four response rules for the simulator for returning each query (Such as **Setup, AddKeyword, DeleteFile, Search**) of adversary $\mathcal{A}$, which will be used in our security model, and then give detail IND-CKA2 security model for our multi client searchable encryption.

- When $\mathcal{A}$ gives a selected database DB to $\mathcal{S}$ to have a test on protocol **Setup**, $\mathcal{S}$ takes leakage function $\mathcal{L}_{Setup}$ as input, and simulates an encrypted database EDB.
- When $\mathcal{A}$ gives a new file-keyword pair to $\mathcal{S}$ to have a test on protocol **Add-Keyword**, $\mathcal{S}$ takes leakage function $\mathcal{L}_{AddKeyword}$ as input, and generates the corresponding searchable ciphertexts.

- When $\mathcal{A}$ gives a selected file to $\mathcal{S}$ to test on protocol **DeleteFile**, $\mathcal{S}$ takes leakage function $\mathcal{L}_{DeleteFile}$ as input, and generates the corresponding delete token.
- When $\mathcal{A}$ gives a selected keyword to $\mathcal{S}$ to have a test on protocol **Search**, $\mathcal{S}$ takes leakage function $\mathcal{L}_{Search}$ as input, and simulates the corresponding search token.

Definition 2 (IND-CKA2 Security) [24]. *Let $\Pi = $ (Setup, AddKeyword, DeleteFile, ClientKGen, Search) be a multi client dynamic symmetric searchable encryption scheme, $\mathcal{A}$ and $\mathcal{S}$ denote the adversary and simulator, respectively. Suppose tuple ($\mathcal{L}_{Setup}$, $\mathcal{L}_{AddKeyword}$, $\mathcal{L}_{DeleteFile}$, $\mathcal{L}_{ClientKGen}$, $\mathcal{L}_{Search}$) be five leakage functions, consider the related two probabilistic games as follows:*

$Real_A(1^k)$: $\mathcal{A}$ chooses an initial database DB. A challenger runs Setup to generate (MK, PK, EDB) where (PK, MK) denote the public/secret key of data owner and DB denotes the encrypted data of database DB. Once $\mathcal{A}$ receives the EDB from challenger, it makes a polynomial number of queries for protocol Add-Keyword, DeleteFile, ClientKGen and Search. For response, the challenger feedbacks the corresponding result to $\mathcal{A}$. Finally, the adversary $\mathcal{A}$ outputs a bit 'b' as the result of the game.

$Ideal_{A,S}(1^k)$: $\mathcal{A}$ chooses an initial database DB. Given the leakage $\mathcal{L}_{Setup}$, $\mathcal{S}$ computes and sends encrypted database EDB to $\mathcal{A}$. Then $\mathcal{A}$ makes a polynomial number of queries for the five protocols as above. For each query, $\mathcal{S}$ masters the relevant leakage function five-tuple ($\mathcal{L}_{AddKeyword}$, $\mathcal{L}_{DeleteFile}$, $\mathcal{L}_{ClientKGen}$, $\mathcal{L}_{Search}$), For response, the challenger feedbacks the corresponding result to $\mathcal{A}$. Finally, the adversary $\mathcal{A}$ outputs a bit 'b' as the result of the game.

We say that a multi-client DSSE scheme is called IND-CKA2 secure with leakage functions above, if the probability $Pr[\mathbf{Real}_A(k) = 1] - Pr[\mathbf{Ideal}_{A,S}(k) = 1]$ is negligible for some security parameter k.

Definition 3 (Strong RSA Problem) [25]. *Let p, q be two k-bit big prime numbers, and set $n = pq$. Choose $g \in \mathbb{Z}_n^*$ randomly. We say that an efficient algorithm $\mathcal{A}$ solves the strong RSA problem if it receives as input the tuple (n, g) and outputs two element (z, e) such that $z^e = g \mod n$.*

3   Our MC-DSSE Construction

Assume Data owner, Server, Client be the participants who take part in the DSSE scheme. With the four database language described in Sect. 2.1, now we design our detail multi-client dynamic searchable symmetric encryption scheme which includes the following five phases.

Setup(1^k, DB, $NULL$):

- Data owner: Take a security parameter k and a database DB as inputs. Let $F:\{0,1\}^k \times \{0,1\}^* \to \{0,1\}^k$ be a key-based pseudo random function, and

$H \colon \{0,1\}^* \to \{0,1\}^{2k+1}$, $G \colon \{0,1\}^* \to \{0,1\}^{3k+1}$ be two cryptographic hash functions. Choose two big prime integers p, q, and pick $k_1, k_2 \in \{0,1\}^k$ randomly, then output the master key MK $= (p, q, k_1, k_2, g)$ and the public key PK$= (n = pq, F, G, H)$. Finally, run the Algorithm 1 to generate the EDB and send it to the Server, keep the $\mathcal{T}_P$ secret.

– Server: Store the encrypted database EDB.

Algorithm 1. EDB Generate Algorithm

Require: MK, PK, DB;
Ensure: $\mathcal{I}$
1: EDB $\leftarrow \{\}$, $\mathcal{T}_P \leftarrow \{\}$, $\mathcal{T}_W \leftarrow \{\}$, $\mathcal{T}_F \leftarrow \{\}$, $\mathcal{T}_{F,W} \leftarrow \{\}$
2: **for** $w \in$ DB **do**
3:     **if** $P_w = NULL$ **then**
4:         $L_w \leftarrow F_{k_1}(g^{1/w} \mod n)$
5:     **else**
6:         $L_w \leftarrow P_w$
7:     **end if**
8:     **for** $id \in$ DB(w) **do**
9:         **if** $P_{id} = NULL$ **then**
10:             $L_{id} = F_{k_1}(g^{1/id} \mod n)$
11:         **else**
12:             $L_{id} \leftarrow P_{id}$
13:         **end if**
14:         $\mathcal{T}_P \leftarrow \mathcal{T}_P \cup (id, P_{id})$, $L_{id,w} = F_{k_1}(g^{\frac{1}{id \cdot w}} \mod n)$
15:         $R_w \xleftarrow{\$} \{0,1\}^k$, $D_w \leftarrow H(F_{k_2}(g^{1/w} \mod n), R_w) \oplus (0||id||P_w)$
16:         $K_1 \leftarrow (L_w, D_w, D_w)$, $\mathcal{T}_W \leftarrow \mathcal{T}_W \cup K_1$
17:         $R_{id} \leftarrow \{0,1\}^k$, $D_{id} \leftarrow G(F_{k_2}(g^{1/id} \mod n), R_{id}) \oplus (0||L_w||L_{id,w}||P_{id})$
18:         $K_2 \leftarrow (L_{id}, D_{id}, D_{id,2})$, $\mathcal{T}_F \leftarrow \mathcal{T}_W \cup K_2$
19:         $R_{id,w} \leftarrow \{0,1\}^{2k}$, $D_{id,w} = H(F_{k_2}(g^{\frac{1}{id \cdot w}} \mod n), R_{id,w}) \oplus (0||L_w||L_{id})$
20:         $K_3 \leftarrow (L_{id,w}, D_{id,w,1}, D_{id,w,2})$, $\mathcal{T}_{W,F} \leftarrow \mathcal{T}_{W,F} \cup K_1$
21:     **end for**
22:     $\mathcal{T}_P \leftarrow \mathcal{T}_P \cup (w, P_w)$,
23: **end for**
24: **return** EDB $\leftarrow (\mathcal{T}_W, \mathcal{T}_F, \mathcal{T}_{F,W})$, $\mathcal{T}_P$

ClientKGen(MK, w):

– Client: Assuming that a legitimate client wish to perform searches over keywords $\mathbf{w} = (w_1, w_2, \ldots, w_n)$, he send $\mathbf{w}$ to the owner to apply for his private key of keywords $\mathbf{w}$.
– Data owner: The data owner generates a corresponding private key as:

$$sk_{\mathbf{w}} = (sk_{\mathbf{w},1}, sk_{\mathbf{w},2}, sk_{\mathbf{w},3}) \leftarrow (k_1, k_2, g^{1/\prod_{j=1}^{n} w_j} \mod n)$$

and then sends back $sk_{\mathbf{w}}$ together with $\mathbf{w}$ to the client.

AddKeyword$((MK, \mathcal{D}_P, id, w), EDB)$:

- Data owner: Take the master key MK $= (k_1, k_2, p, q)$, dictionary $\mathcal{D}_P$, encrypted database EDB $= (\mathcal{D}_W, \mathcal{D}_F, DT_{id})$ and a chosen file-keyword pair (id, w) as inputs, then execute **Add Keyword Algorithm** to add the new ciphertext of the pair to EDB.
- Server: Take $EDB = (\mathcal{D}_W, \mathcal{D}_F, \mathcal{D}_{F,W})$ and $(L_w, D_w, L_{id}, D_{id}, L_{id,w}, D_{id,w})$ as inputs, and then run standard data algorithm **Update**$(D_W, (L_w, D_w))$, and **Update**$(\mathcal{D}_{F,W}, (L_{id,w}, D_{id,w}))$.

Algorithm 2. Add Keyword Algorithm

Require: MK, $\mathcal{D}_P, id, w$, EDB;
Ensure: K_1, K_2, K_3
 1: $P_w \leftarrow$ **Get**$(\mathcal{D}_p, w)$;
 2: **if** $P_w = NULL$ **then**
 3:      $L_w \leftarrow F_{k_1}(g^{1/w} \mod n)$
 4: **else**
 5:      $L_w \leftarrow P_w$
 6: **end if**
 7: $R_w \xleftarrow{\$} \{0,1\}^k$, $D_w \leftarrow H(F_{k_2}(g_1^{1/w} \mod n), R_w) \oplus (0||id||P_w)$
 8: $K_1 \leftarrow (L_w, D_w, R_w)$
 9: **Update**$(\mathcal{D}_p(w, P_w))$
10: $P_{id} \leftarrow$ **Get**$(\mathcal{D}_p, id)$
11: **if** $P_{id} = NULL$ **then**
12:      $L_{id} = F_{k_1}(g^{1/id} \mod n)$
13: **else**
14:      $L_{id} \leftarrow P_{id}$
15: **end if**
16: $R_{id} \xleftarrow{\$} \{0,1\}^{2k}$, $D_{id} \leftarrow G(F_{k_2}(g^{1/id} \mod n), R_{id}) \oplus (0||L_w||L_{id,w}||P_{id})$
17: $K_2 \leftarrow (L_{id}, D_{id}, R_{id})$
18: $L_{id,w} \leftarrow F_{k_1}(g^{\frac{1}{id \cdot w}} \mod n), R_{id,w} \xleftarrow{\$} \{0,1\}^k$
19: $D_{id,w} \leftarrow H(F_{k_2}(g^{\frac{1}{id \cdot w}} \mod n), R_{id,w}) \oplus (0||L_w||L_{id})$
20: $K_3 \leftarrow (L_{id,w}, D_{id,w}, R_{id,w})$
21: **return** K_1, K_2, K_3

DeleteFile$((MK, id), EDB)$:

- Data owner: Take $K = (k_1, k_2, p, q)$, $\mathcal{D}_P$ and a file identifier id as inputs, generate and send a delete token

$$DT_{id} = (F_{k_1}(g^{1/id} \mod n), F_{k_2}(g^{1/id} \mod n))$$

to the server.
- Server: Take the encrypted database $EDB = (\mathcal{D}_W, \mathcal{D}_F, DT_{id})$ as inputs, set $L_{id} = F_{k_1}(g^{1/id} \mod n)$, and executes the following algorithm to delete the expected file.

Algorithm 3. Delete File Algorithm

1: **procedure** DELETEFILE$(((MK, id), EDB))$
2:     $D_{id} \leftarrow \mathbf{Get}(\mathcal{D}_F, L_{id})$
3:     **if** $P_{id} = NULL$ **then**
4:         return $\perp$
5:     **else**
6:         $(D_{id,1}, D_{id,2}) \leftarrow D_{id}$
7:         $T||L_w||L_{id,w}||P_{id} = D_{id,1} \oplus G(F_{k_2}(g^{1/id} \mod n), D_{id,2})$
8:         $\mathbf{Remove}(\mathcal{D}_F, L_{id})$
9:         **if** T=0 **then**
10:             $D_w \leftarrow \mathbf{Get}(\mathcal{D}_w, L_w), (D_{w,1}, D_{w,2}) \leftarrow D_w$
11:             $D_{w,1} = D_{w,1} \oplus (1||0^{2k})$
12:             $\mathbf{Update}(\mathcal{D}_w, (L_w, D_w(D_{w,1}, D_{w,2}))), \mathbf{Remove}(\mathcal{D}_F, L_{id})$
13:             $L_{id} \leftarrow P_{id}$
14:         **end if**
15:     **end if**
16: **end procedure**

Search$((sk_\mathbf{w}), \text{EDB})$:

– Client: Whenever the client with searchable ability on keywords $\mathbf{w} = (w_1, w_2, \cdots, w_n)$ wants to search the file on keyword w_i, he uses his private key as inputs, compute the search token

$$ST_{w_i} = (F_{sk_{\mathbf{w},1}}(sk_{\mathbf{w},3}^{\prod_{w \in \mathbf{w}/\{w_i\}} w} \mod n), F_{sk_{\mathbf{w},2}}(sk_{\mathbf{w},3}^{\prod_{w \in \mathbf{w}/\{w_i\}} w} \mod n))$$

and send $ST_{w_i} = (F_{k_1}(g^{1/w_i} \mod n), F_{k_2}(g^{1/w_i} \mod n))$ to the server;
– Server: Take EDB $= (\mathcal{D}_W, \mathcal{D}_F)$ and token $ST_{w_i} = (F_{k_1}(g^{1/w_i} \mod n)),$ $F_{k_2}(g^{1/w_i} \mod n))$ as inputs, initialize an empty set $\mathcal{I}$, a temporary index-data pair $(L_w^t = NULL, D_w^t = NULL)$ and a temporary pointer $P_w^t = NULL$, set $L_w = F_{k_1}(g^{1/w_i})$, and do the following steps:

4 Security Analysis

In this section, we show that our proposed protocol is IND-CKA2 secure against the adaptive server and the client one after another as [24] except some leakage function. Before starting our proof, we need a simulator $\mathcal{S}$ to response the query from $\mathcal{A}$, which is defined in Sect. 2, to take the following leakage functions as input:

Theorem 1. *Suppose hash functions H and G and key-based pseudo-random function F_{k_1} are respectively modeled as three random oracles. Our complete DSSE scheme is IND-CKA2 secure with leakage functions in the random oracle model, where $(\mathcal{L}_{Setup} = |DB|, \mathcal{L}_{AddKeyword} = New(id, w), \mathcal{L}_{DeleteFile} = (Old(id), New(id)), New(id, w)$ and $\mathcal{L}_{Search} = (DB(w), Old(w), New(w))$.*

Algorithm 4. Search Algorithm

Require: (ST_{w_i}, EDB)
Ensure: $\mathcal{I}$
1: $D_w \leftarrow \textbf{Get}(\mathcal{D}_W, L_w)$
2: **if** $D_w = NULL$ **then**
3:      return $\perp$
4: **else**
5:      $D_w = (D_{w,1}, D_{w,2})$
6:      $T\|id\|P_W = D_{w,1} \oplus H(F_{k_2}(g^{\frac{1}{id \cdot w}} \mod n), D_{w,2})$
7:      $L_w^t = L_w, D_w^t = D_w, P_w^t = P_w, L_w = P_w$
8:      **if** T=0 **then**
9:          $\mathcal{I} \leftarrow \mathcal{I} \cup id, L_w^t \leftarrow L_w, D_w^t \leftarrow D_w, P_w^t \leftarrow P_w$
10:     **else**
11:         **if** T=1 **then**
12:             $D_w^t \leftarrow (D_{w,1}^t, D_{w,2}^t), D_{w,1}^t \leftarrow D_{w,1}^t \oplus (0^{k+1}\|(P_w^t \oplus P_w))$
13:             **Update**$(\mathcal{D}_w, (L_w^t, D_w^t = (D_{w,1}^t, D_{w,2}^t)))$, **Remove**$(\mathcal{D}_w, L_w)$
14:         **end if**
15:     **end if**
16: **end if**
17: return $\mathcal{I}$

The proof of Theorem 1 relies on Lemmas 1, 2, 3 and 4 defined below in [24], which just construct a map $f : x \rightarrow g^x$, here x can be w or id. Now it needs an efficient simulator $\mathcal{S}$ to play game $\textbf{Ideal}_{\mathcal{A},\mathcal{S}}(k)$ with an adversary $\mathcal{A}$. Our main arguments are the each lemma listed in following must be computational indistinguishable from the real one with leakage functions in the view of $\mathcal{A}$ under several complexity assumptions.

1. $\mathcal{L}_{Setup} = |DB|$: After running **Setup** algorithm, one will statistics the number of file-keyword pairs in DB according to the size of EDB.
2. $\mathcal{L}_{AddKeyword} = New(id, w)$: When running the **AddKeyword** algorithm, one will get the generated ciphertexts $New(id, w)$ by comparing with the former database.
3. $\mathcal{L}_{DeleteFile} = (Old(id), New(id))$: When deleting a selected file id, one will know all deleted ciphertexts of file which identifier is id, and ciphertexts of them were simulated by protocol **Setup** or **AddKeyword**.
4. $\mathcal{L}_{Search} = (DB(w), Old(w), New(w))$: When searching a file which contains the keyword w, one will know all matched ciphertexts and their father files in $DB(w)$, and the first part of these ciphertexts were generated by protocol **Setup** or **AddKeyword**.

Lemma 1. *Suppose that there exists an adversary $\mathcal{A}$ that run protocol **Setup** to get the corresponding encrypted database from $\mathcal{S}$, and the leakage function $\mathcal{L}_{Setup} = |DB|$, then $\mathcal{A}$ can not distinguish the above simulated EDB with a real one.*

Lemma 2. *Suppose that H and G are random oracles, then for any polynomial time adversary $\mathcal{A}$, there exists an algorithm $\mathcal{S}_{AddKeyword}$, such that $\mathcal{A}$ could distinguish it with a real one that is generated in game $\textbf{Real}_{\mathcal{A}}(k)$.*

Lemma 3. *Suppose H and F_{k_1} are random oracles, then for any polynomial time adversary $\mathcal{A}$, there exists an algorithm $\mathcal{S}_{Search}$, such that $\mathcal{A}$ could distinguish it with a real one that is generated in game $\textbf{Real}_{\mathcal{A}}(k)$.*

Lemma 4. *Suppose G and F_{k_1} are random oracles, then for any polynomial time adversary $\mathcal{A}$, there exists an algorithm $\mathcal{S}_{DeleteFile}$, such that $\mathcal{A}$ could distinguish it with a real one that is generated in game $\textbf{Real}_{\mathcal{A}}(k)$.*

We define algorithm **Setup**, **DeleteFile**, **AddKeyword**, **Search** be the event C_i for $i = 1, 2, \cdots, 4$ respectively. From the four lemmas above, we have that the distinguish probability of them each can be write as $|Pr[\textbf{Real}_{\mathcal{A}}^{C_i}(k) = 1] - Pr[\textbf{Ideal}_{\mathcal{A},\mathcal{S}}^{C_i}(k) = 1]| \leq \epsilon_i$, where $1 \leq i \leq 4$, and ϵ_i are all negligible.

Summarily, the indistinguishability of above four protocols implies that $\mathcal{A}$ can not distinguish game $\textbf{Ideal}_{\mathcal{A},\mathcal{S}}(k)$ with game $\textbf{Real}_{\mathcal{A}}(k)$. Because, we have that the probability $|Pr[\textbf{Real}_{\mathcal{A}}(k) = 1] - Pr[\textbf{Ideal}_{\mathcal{A},\mathcal{S}}(k) = 1]|$ is also negligible, which can be got by the computation below:

$$|Pr[\textbf{Real}_{\mathcal{A}}(k) = 1] - Pr[\textbf{Ideal}_{\mathcal{A},\mathcal{S}}(k) = 1]|$$
$$= \prod_{i=1}^{5} |Pr[\textbf{Real}_{\mathcal{A}}^{C_i}(k) = 1] - Pr[\textbf{Ideal}_{\mathcal{A},\mathcal{S}}^{c_i}(k) = 1]| = \prod_{i=1}^{5} \epsilon_i$$

This completes the proof of Theorem 1.

Theorem 2. *Our scheme Π is secure against malicious clients, i.e., search token in Π is unforgeable against adaptive attacks, assuming that the strong RSA assumption holds.*

Assume that there exists an adversarial client $\mathcal{A}$ who can generate a valid search token for some nonauthorized keyword w_0, so he can get the correct value $(g^{1/w'} \mod n)$. In this case, we can use $\mathcal{A}$ to construct an efficient algorithm $\mathcal{B}$ to solve the strong RSA problem with a non-negligible probability by Euclidean algorithm. Consider the properties of RSA function, actually unless the client can compute the correct value $g^{1/w'} \mod n$, or no one can generate a valid search token for non-authorized keyword w'.

5   Comparison and Analysis

In this section, we simply analyze the efficiency of our scheme by providing the cost of communication and computation in our scheme. Here we set all the number of keywords be one so to compare easily. Let $|G|, |\mathbb{Z}_p|$ respectively be the size of the group element $\mathbb{G}$, security parameter size. *exp* denotes the

Table 1. The communication and computation cost of some classical retrieval scheme

Scheme	Key size	Cipher. size	Search cost	Dynamic	Multi-client
Xu et al. [24]	$2\|k\|$	$O(\|DB\|)$	$O(\|DB(w)\|)$	$\checkmark$	
Sun et al. [25]	$3\|k\| + \|G\|$	$3O(\|DB(w)\|)$	$O(\|DB(w)\| \cdot exp)$		$\checkmark$
Ours	$2k + \|G\|$	$O(\|DB\|)$	$O(\|DB(w)\|)$	$\checkmark$	$\checkmark$

computation cost of the exponential operation. Table 1 lists some classical similar schemes about searchable encryption.

From the table, we can see that our searchable encryption achieves a balance in diversified function and communication cost. The size of EDB can keep the size of $O(\|DB\|)$, which is similar with the scheme proposed by Xu [24]. And we also realize the multi-client function in our paper without increasing much computation cost.

6 Conclusion

We construct an efficient and practical multi-client symmetric searchable encryption scheme with physical deletion property via RSA function in the random oracle model, and prove the security of the scheme by using the strong RSA function and four attack lemmas. The scheme gives a general method to extend the single reader model searchable encryption scheme to multiple readers. We also present the detailed communication cost and computation cost of the proposed scheme and point out that our scheme is more efficient than other classical ones by comparing the running time with some classical searchable encryption in each phase.

Acknowledgments. This work is partially supported by the Fundamental Research Funds for the Central Universities (No. 30916011328), the National Natural Science Foundation of China (61702342), and Shenzhen Science and Technology Program (JCYJ20170302151321095, JCYJ20170302145623566). The authors also gratefully acknowledge the helpful comments and suggestions of the reviewers, which have improved the presentation.

References

1. Liu, J.K., Au, M.H., Susilo, W., et al.: Secure sharing and searching for real-time video data in mobile cloud. IEEE Netw. **29**(2), 46–50 (2015)
2. Baek, J., Vu, Q.H., Liu, J.K., et al.: A secure cloud computing based framework for big data information management of smart grid. IEEE Trans. Cloud Comput. **3**(2), 233–244 (2015)
3. Wang, S., Zhou, J., Liu, J.K., et al.: An efficient file hierarchy attribute-based encryption scheme in cloud computing. IEEE TIFS **11**(6), 1265–1277 (2016)
4. Wang, S., Liang, K., Liu, J.K., et al.: Attribute-based data sharing scheme revisited in cloud computing. IEEE TIFS **11**(8), 1661–1673 (2016)

5. Chor, B., Kushilevitz, E., Goldreich, O., et al.: Private information retrieval. J. ACM **45**, 965–981 (1998)
6. Golle, P., Staddon, J., Waters, B.: Secure conjunctive keyword search over encrypted data. In: Jakobsson, M., Yung, M., Zhou, J. (eds.) ACNS 2004. LNCS, vol. 3089, pp. 31–45. Springer, Heidelberg (2004). https://doi.org/10.1007/978-3-540-24852-1_3
7. Liu, C., Zhu, L., Wang, M., et al.: Search pattern leakage in searchable encryption: attacks and new construction. Inf. Sci. **265**, 176–188 (2014)
8. Liu, J., Lai, J., Huang, X.: Dual trapdoor identity-based encryption with keyword search. Soft. Comput. **21**(10), 2599–2607 (2015)
9. Cash, D., Jarecki, S., Jutla, C., Krawczyk, H., Roşu, M.-C., Steiner, M.: Highly-scalable searchable symmetric encryption with support for boolean queries. In: Canetti, R., Garay, J.A. (eds.) CRYPTO 2013. LNCS, vol. 8042, pp. 353–373. Springer, Heidelberg (2013). https://doi.org/10.1007/978-3-642-40041-4_20
10. Jarecki, S., Jutla, C., Krawczyk, H., et al.: Outsourced symmetric private information retrieval. In: Proceedings of the 2013 ACM SIGSAC Conference on Computer and Communications Security, pp. 875–888. ACM, Berlin (2013)
11. Liang, K., Huang, X., Guo, F., Liu, J.K.: Privacy-preserving and regular language search over encrypted cloud data. IEEE TIFS **11**(10), 2365–2376 (2016)
12. Kasra Kermanshahi, S., Liu, J.K., Steinfeld, R.: Multi-user cloud-based secure keyword search. In: Pieprzyk, J., Suriadi, S. (eds.) ACISP 2017. LNCS, vol. 10342, pp. 227–247. Springer, Cham (2017). https://doi.org/10.1007/978-3-319-60055-0_12
13. Yang, X., Lee, T.T., Liu, J.K., et al.: Trust enhancement over range search for encrypted data. In: Trustcom, pp. 66–73. IEEE, New York (2016)
14. Zuo, C., Macindoe, J., Yang, S., et al.: Trusted Boolean search on cloud using searchable symmetric encryption. In: Trustcom, pp. 113–120. IEEE, New York (2016)
15. Liang, K., Su, C., Chen, J., Liu, J.K.: Efficient multi-function data sharing and searching mechanism for cloud-based encrypted data. In: Proceedings of the 11th ACM on Asia CCS, pp. 83–94. ACM (2016)
16. Curtmola, R., Garay, J., Ostrovsky, R.: Searchable symmetric encryption: improved definitions and efficient constructions. In: CCS 2006, pp. 79–88. ACM, New York (2006)
17. Bao, F., Deng, R.H., Ding, X., Yang, Y.: Private query on encrypted data in multi-user settings. In: Chen, L., Mu, Y., Susilo, W. (eds.) ISPEC 2008. LNCS, vol. 4991, pp. 71–85. Springer, Heidelberg (2008). https://doi.org/10.1007/978-3-540-79104-1_6
18. Dong, C., Russello, G., Dulay, N.: Shared and searchable encrypted data for untrusted servers. In: Atluri, V. (ed.) DBSec 2008. LNCS, vol. 5094, pp. 127–143. Springer, Heidelberg (2008). https://doi.org/10.1007/978-3-540-70567-3_10
19. Wang, Q., Zhu, Y., Luo, X.: Multi-user searchable encryption with fine-grained access control without key sharing. In: International Conference on Advanced Computer Science Applications and Technologies, pp. 119–125. IEEE (2014)
20. Wang, S., Zhang, X., Zhang, Y.: Efficiently multi-user searchable encryption scheme with attribute revocation and grant for cloud storage. PLoS ONE **11**(11), e0167157 (2016)
21. Wang, Y., Wang, J., Sun, S.-F., Liu, J.K., Susilo, W., Chen, X.: Towards multi-user searchable encryption supporting Boolean query and fast decryption. In: Okamoto, T., Yu, Y., Au, M.H., Li, Y. (eds.) ProvSec 2017. LNCS, vol. 10592, pp. 24–38. Springer, Cham (2017). https://doi.org/10.1007/978-3-319-68637-0_2

22. Cui, H., Deng, R.H., Liu, J.K., Li, Y.: Attribute-based encryption with expressive and authorized keyword search. In: Pieprzyk, J., Suriadi, S. (eds.) ACISP 2017. LNCS, vol. 10342, pp. 106–126. Springer, Cham (2017). https://doi.org/10.1007/978-3-319-60055-0_6
23. Van Rompay, C., Molva, R., Önen, M.: Multi-user searchable encryption in the cloud. In: Lopez, J., Mitchell, C.J. (eds.) ISC 2015. LNCS, vol. 9290, pp. 299–316. Springer, Cham (2015). https://doi.org/10.1007/978-3-319-23318-5_17
24. Xu, P., Liang, S., Wang, W., Susilo, W., Wu, Q., Jin, H.: Dynamic searchable symmetric encryption with physical deletion and small leakage. In: Pieprzyk, J., Suriadi, S. (eds.) ACISP 2017. LNCS, vol. 10342, pp. 207–226. Springer, Cham (2017). https://doi.org/10.1007/978-3-319-60055-0_11
25. Sun, S.-F., Liu, J.K., Sakzad, A., Steinfeld, R., Yuen, T.H.: An efficient non-interactive multi-client searchable encryption with support for Boolean queries. In: Askoxylakis, I., Ioannidis, S., Katsikas, S., Meadows, C. (eds.) ESORICS 2016. LNCS, vol. 9878, pp. 154–172. Springer, Cham (2016). https://doi.org/10.1007/978-3-319-45744-4_8

High-Performance Symmetric Cryptography Server with GPU Acceleration

Wangzhao Cheng[1,2,3], Fangyu Zheng[1,2(✉)], Wuqiong Pan[1,2], Jingqiang Lin[1,2], Huorong Li[1,2,3], and Bingyu Li[1,2,3]

[1] Data Assurance and Communication Security Research Center, Beijing, China
[2] State Key Laboratory of Information Security,
Institute of Information Engineering, CAS, Beijing, China
{chengwangzhao,zhengfangyu,panwuqiong,linjingqiang,lihuorong,
libingyu}@iie.ac.cn
[3] School of Cyber Security, University of Chinese Academy of Sciences,
Beijing, China

Abstract. With more and more sensitive and private data transferred on the Internet, various security protocols have been developed to secure end-to-end communication. However, in practical situations, applying these protocols would decline the overall performance of the whole system, of which frequently-used symmetric cryptographic operations on the server side is the bottleneck. In this contribution, we present a high-performance symmetric cryptography server. Firstly, a symmetric algorithm SM4 is carefully scheduled in GPUs, including instruction-level implementation and variable location improvement. Secondly, optimization methods is provided to speed up the inefficient data transfer between CPU and GPU. Finally, the overall server architecture is adopted for mass data encryption, which can deliver 15.96 Gbps data encryption through network, 1.23 times of the existing fastest symmetric cryptographic server. Furthermore, the server can be boosted by 2.02 times with the high-speed pre-calculation technique for long-term-key applications such as IPSec VPN gateways.

Keywords: Symmetric Cryptographic Algorithm
Graphics Processing Unit (GPU) · CUDA · SM4 implementation
Symmetric cryptography server · Performance

1 Introduction

Cloud computing, e-commerce, online bank and other Internet services are developing rapidly, more and more sensitive and private data is transferred on the

---

W. Cheng—This work was partially supported by the National 973 Program of China under award No. 2014CB340603 and the National Cryptography Development Fund under award No. MMJJ20170213.

S. Qing et al. (Eds.): ICICS 2017, LNCS 10631, pp. 529–540, 2018.
https://doi.org/10.1007/978-3-319-89500-0_46

Internet. SSL, TLS, IPSec and other security protocols have been developed to support secure and reliable end-to-end communication. Under these security protocols, servers and clients first use key exchange protocols to negotiate a symmetric key, and then use the symmetric key to encrypt the communication content. From 2011 to 2015, the total amount of global data have increased for more than 10 times (from 0.7 ZB to 8.6 ZB), and CPU performance is only about three times higher, CPU's development can hardly meet the expanding demand.

In order to satisfy the need for symmetric calculation power, we present a high-performance symmetric cryptography server. Our server can be deployed in cloud computing, database encryption, end-to-end encrypted communication and other applications. It works as a proxy and outsources these complex and onerous symmetric computation from the original server.

To build the high-performance symmetric cryptography server, we accomplished a high speed SM4 kernel, used a GPU card as an SM4 algorithm accelerator, and optimized the network service based on the characteristics of GPU card. Our work is to gradually optimize the following three aspects.

1. Speeding up the SM4 kernel. We used CUDA's PTX (Parallel Thread Execution) instructions to accomplish bitwise exclusive OR operation and circular shift operation in the algorithm. At the same time, we adjusted the order of plain-text in global memory and modified its accessing method to increase plain-text's accessing rate. S-Box and round keys were also carefully arranged. On NVIDIA GeForce GTX 1080, our SM4 kernel is able to encrypt 535.68 Gb data per second. It achieves 12.59 times of the existing fastest SM4 implementation by Martínez-Herrera et al. [12].
2. Enhancing the overall throughput of the GPU card. Using GPUs as an accelerator, data transfer between GPUs and CPUs limits its overall throughput. We took advantage of multi-stream's parallel operation, and overlapped data transfer and calculation process with each other. Finally, the overall throughput of GPU card is enhanced to 76.89 Gbps, and our optimizations methods make use of 85.4% of GTX 1080's PCI-E bandwidth.
3. Optimizing the network service. Based on the characteristics that the GPU card is weak performance under single thread, and strong performance under multiple threads, we designed a queue to cache network service requests, and the GPU card can handles multiple encryption requests in the queue at the same time. The server's peak throughput through network is 15.96 Gbps. For the case that using a single key, like large IPSec VPN gateways, we designed a memory management framework and used pre-calculation technique to decrease data copy operations and reduce the degree of coupling. With these optimizations, the server's peak throughput reaches 32.23 Gbps, and it is 2.48 times faster than SSLShader [6].

The remainder of the paper is organized as follow. Section 2 introduces the related work. Section 3 presents the overview of GPU, CUDA, and SM4 symmetric encryption. Section 4 describes in detail about the GPU-accelerated SM4 implementation, the optimization for data transfer, and how we enhance our server's performance. Section 5 analyses the performance of proposed algorithm and server, and it also compares them with previous works. Section 6 concludes the paper.

2 Related Work

The SM4 algorithm is Chinese standard symmetric cipher for data protection, and it is first declassified in 2006 and standardized in 2012. Researchers have done a lot of works on its security and attacking methods [2,3]. Chinese government is also vigorously promoting the SM4 algorithm as a standard for data protection. However, the heavy cryptographic computation of SM4 limits its using scene, and there are few studies to solve this problem.

As a graphics dedicated processor, GPUs are concentrated in the field of computer graphics [1]. After CUDA was introduced, GPU became widely used in the field of general purpose computing, many symmetric algorithms were scheduled in GPUs for better performance. Manavski et al. [11] took the lead in using CUDA to accelerate AES, which followed the Rijndael reference implementation, and provided optimal location for storing the T-tables to enhance the benchmark performances, and their work was followed by most teams. Harrison et al. completed AES-CTR on CUDA enabled GPUs [5]. While optimizing the algorithm's calculation rate, this work also contributed on how to schedule serial and parallel execution of block ciphers on GPUs. On Tesla P100, Nishikawa [13] increased the speed of the AES-ECB to 605.9 Gbps. Except for AES, the optimization of other symmetric algorithms on the GPU has also been extensively studied by researchers, including DES [10], Blowfish, IDEA, CAST-5, Camellia [4], MD5-RC4 [8].

In addition to symmetric cryptography, GPUs were also widely applied in asymmetric cryptography, including RSA [6,16] and ECC [17]. GPU-based cryptographic servers were also growing rapidly. Using GPU as a general-purpose SSL accelerators, SSLShader accelerated SSL cryptographic operations, and it handled 29K SSL TPS and achieved 13 Gbps bulk encryption throughput [6]. Guess [15] was a dedicated equipment for signature generation and verification, and it was capable of 8.71×10^6 operations per second (OPS) for signature generation or 9.29×10^5 OPS for verification.

3 Background

3.1 GPU and CUDA

Compared with CPUs, modern GPUs devote most of the transistor to arithmetic processing unit with much less data cache and flow controler. This unique hardware design is specialized for manipulating computer graphics, and it is also quiet fit for compute-intensive operations and high parallel computation. CUDA is a parallel computing platform, which was created and firstly introduced in

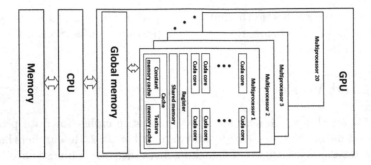

Fig. 1. NVIDIA GeForce GTX 1080's architecture and how it works in the system

2006 by NVIDIA [14]. By harnessing the power of GPUs, it enables dramatic computing performance increases on GPUs.

The target platform in this paper is NVIDIA GeForce GTX 1080. As shown in Fig. 1, GeForce GTX 1080 contains 20 streaming multiprocessors (SM) and each SM owns 128 single precision CUDA cores, 8 texture mapping units (TMU), and 256 KB L2 cache. 32 threads (grouped as a warp) within one SM run in a clock concurrently. All GPU threads follow the Single Instruction Multiple Threads (SIMT) architecture. When a warp is stalled due to memory access delay, it may be preempted, and the scheduler may switch the runtime context to another available warp. For better utilization of the pipeline, multiple warps of threads are usually assigned to one SM and called one block. The maximum number of GPU threads per block is 1024. Each block could access 96 KB fast shared memory, 48 KB L1 cache, and 64K 32-bit registers. All SMs share 8 GB global memory, cached read-only texture memory and cached read-only constant memory. Global memory is the off-chip video RAM, and it is accessible to both the device and the host through special functions provided by CUDA. Texture memory and constant memory are special area of global memory, both of them have separate on-chip catch.

3.2 SM4 Symmetric Encryption

SM4 is a 32 round unbalanced Feistel cipher, and it is Chinese standard symmetric cipher for data confidentiality [9]. The processing block and the encryption key are both 128-bit, and its security strength is same to that of AES-128.

4 Implementation Architecture

In this work, our main contributions are on these aspects: (*i*) Algorithm level optimizations for scheduling SM4 encryption on GPUs. (*ii*) Optimizations for data transfer between CPUs and GPUs. (*iii*) Optimizing the overall performance of the server.

4.1   Optimizing SM4 for GPU

For the SM4 kernel, naive porting of CPU algorithms to a GPU would waste most GPU computational resources and cause server performance degradation, In this part, we describe our approaches and design choices to maximize performance of SM4 kernel on GPUs, and the key point in maximizing SM4 performance lies in rational use of GPU storage resources and reducing GPU computational resources consumption.

The plani-text of SM4 encryption is divided into 4 32-bit blocks. With the corresponding round key, the round function uses these 4 blocks to generation a new 32-bit block. Generated block and the last 3 blocks are the input for the next round function, and the first block will never be used again. In order to reduce the usage of registers, we use the first block of the original input to store the generated block. SM4 symmetric encryption operation consists of 32 round functions, and the entire encryption process originally required 36 32-bit registers. With our tricks, only 4 32-bit registers are used in the entire process.

Then we optimized the implementation of the round function. For the round function, it carries out bitwise exclusive OR, left circular shift operations and non-linear permutations on these 32-bit inputs. PTX instruction *xor.b32* is used to complete bitwise exclusive OR operation for two 32-bit units. The implementation for the left circular shift operation is more complicated, we used *shl.b32*, *shr.b32* and *or.b32* these three instructions.

For non-linear permutations, we build a 256 bytes size S-Box, and it needs to query the S-Box for 4 times to implement the non-linear permutations for a 32-bit block, and we carefully considered the arrangement for the S-Box. The naive way is to store the S-box in global memory. Global memory's accessing rate is slow, and it results in SM4 kernel performance degradation. Except for global memory, GPUs have 32-bit register, constant memory and shared memory, which also can be used to store S-Box. Through comparative tests, we find when S-box is stored in constant memory, the performance of SM4 kernel is the best. GPUs have specially on-chip cache for constant memory, and after data in constant memory was loaded in the on-chip cache, the program get the data directly from the cache, rather than device memory. Register is also optional in certain circumstances, compared with using constant memory, the implementation of SM4 kernel that uses register to store S-Box is resistant to key recovery timing attack [7], although it has compromised in terms of performance.

After optimizing the round function, we also need a reasonable arrangement of the data for the SM4 kernel. During the encryption process, there are three kinds data: plain-text, round keys and S-box. As mentioned above, S-Box is stored in constant memory. The arrangement for round keys varies depending on the applications. When the application uses multiple keys, round keys for each GPU thread is different, so each GPU thread must derives its own round keys and store them in global memory. When only a single key is used in the application, we use CPU to derive round keys in advance and store them in shared memory for faster accessing rate. The plain-text is stored in global memory, because other storage space on GPUs are not suitable. Register is very limited, and normally the size of plain-text is quite big, using 64K 32-bit registers to store plain-text results in degradation of the SM4 kernel. Every GPU thread access different plain-text, so shared memory is not a good choice. Plain-text is not constant value, so constant memory is not suitable too.

As plain-text is stored in global memory, and compared with other memory space, global memory has lower bandwidth, and we then optimized the inefficient accessing to the plain-text in global memory. We used the coalesced access to improve the accessing efficiency. Coalesced access needs two conditions: (i) The size of data accessed by a thread each time must be 4 bytes, 8 bytes or 16 bytes; (ii) The memory space accessed by a warp must be continuous. We used INT, INT2, and INT4 these unique instructions provided by the CUDA API to access global memory. INT, INT2, and INT4 are used to access 4,8,16 bytes global memory respectively. To meet the second condition, we adjust the order of the data blocks, and every GPU thread accesses the global memory in a special method. Under normal circumstances, each piece of plain-text encrypted by the same key is processed by one GPU threads, and multiple pieces are combined into one data block and then transferred to GPU's global memory. In this case, every thread is accessing a continuous memory space, but each time when a warp performs a memory accessing operation, it accesses multiple discrete data fragments, just as shown in Fig. 2(a). To benefit from coalesced access, we adjust the order of the data blocks. First, every piece of plain-text is split into several blocks, the size of the block depends on the instruction used to access global memory, instruction INT, INT2 and INT4 corresponds to 4-bytes, 8-bytes and 16-bytes block size respectively. Second, rearranging these blocks, make sure that all pieces's first blocks are combined in the natural order, and so it is with other blocks, as shown in Fig. 2(b). Every time a GPU thread accesses global memory, the next hop of the pointer also needs to point to the corresponding block. Under this condition, the accessed memory space by a warp is continuous, and each thread is processing its corresponding data.

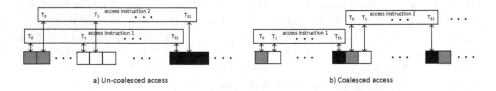

a) Un-coalesced access   b) Coalesced access

Fig. 2. How global memory is accessed by a warp

We designed a set of comparative experiments to evaluate which is the best combination of instructions and access methods. In the experiments, except for the difference in the methods of accessing global memory and the used instructions, other conditions are the same. We test the throughput of these SM4 kernel implementations, and the result is shown in Table 1.

Compared with non-coalesced access, the throughput of coalesced access is about 5 or 6 times higher. This is because that global memory resides in the device memory, which is accessed via 32, 64 or 128 bytes memory transactions [14]. When a threads accesses global memory, the data need to be read in the cache by generating 32, 64 or 128 bytes memory transactions, then the thread gets data from the cache. As the size of the memory transactions is fixed, so more data than the actual demand will be cached. When the conditions of coalesced access are met, most threads directly gets the data from the cache without generating more memory transactions. The result also shows that instruction INT4 is the best choice.

Table 1. Comparing the throughput of non-coalesced access and coalesced access.

	INT	INT2	INT4
Non-coalesced access (Gbps)	78.58	81.29	81.80
Coalesced access (Gbps)	420.48	422.60	423.67

At last, we set the SM4 kernel's parameters to 20 blocks and each block owns 1024 GPU threads, so that the SM4 kernel maximize the use of GPU's computational resources.

4.2   Optimizing Data Transfer Between GPUs and CPUs

After optimizing SM4 kernel on GPUs, we used a GPU card as an SM4 accelerator. Using GPU card to complete the data encryption operation, first, it needs to copy plain-text from the host memory to GPU's global memory, then encrypt plain-text. After the encryption operation is complete, it needs to copy the cipher-text back to the host memory. These processes must be executed serially. To make the most of GeForce GTX 1080's two copy engines, we used multiple streams to complete these operations in parallel, so that data transfer between CPUs and GPUs overlaps with encryption operation, and the overall throughput of GPU card increases. The specific optimization methods are as follows: First, we initialize multiple streams and divide the data into corresponding fragments. Then these streams begin to perform operations such as data transfer and calculation process on theirs respective data asynchronously, as shown in Fig. 3.

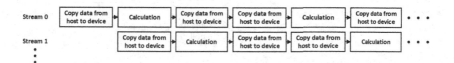

Fig. 3. How to overlap data transfer with calculation process

To achieve the highest throughput of the GPU card, the parameter of the SM4 kernel changed. We reduce the threads per block from 1024 to 512, every stream only hold one block, and the stream number is 10. This is because our SM4 kernel is much faster than the data transfer, reducing the number of blocks and the number of threads per block improve the efficiency of the parallel execution between these streams.

After our optimization, the throughput of the GPU card reaches to 76.89 Gbps. Compared with the SM4 kernel, it is much slower. The test tool provided by the NVIDIA CUDA Toolkit shows that the bandwidth of our target platform's (GeForce GTX 1080) PCI-E is about 90 Gbps. So Our optimization makes use of 85.4% of the bandwidth, and this result is satisfactory.

4.3 Optimizing the Performance of the Server

We build a scalable SM4 encryption proxy that uses the high-performance SM4 encryption operations of GPU to outsources symmetric computation from the original server. Meanwhile, we complete ECB, CBC and CTR these three mainstream encryption modes, and the server is capable of providing data encryption through TCP/IP protocol.

In the server, CPU accepts service requests from network and caches them in a queue. When the GPU is task-free, CPU takes out requests and organize the plain-text, then GPU is called for data encryption. In this way, GPU provide data encryption for multiple service requests at the same time, and its parallel execution ability can be fully exploited. For the case of using multiple keys, GPU threads use different keys, so each GPU threads derives its own round keys, and then uses them to encrypt plain-text.

In some applications, end to end communication data is encrypted by a single key over a period of time, like large IPSec VPN gateways. For these applications, round keys are derived for only one time by CPU, then stored in shared memory and used by all GPU threads.

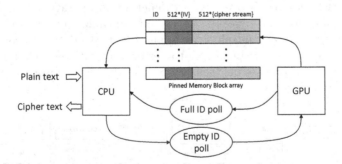

Fig. 4. The specially designed memory management framework

In the single key case, we have further optimizations. Based on the feature that CTR mode supports pre-calculation, we use the GPU to generate stream ciphers and store them in host memory. When CPU received service request, it just encrypts the plain-text with the stream ciphers, and send the cipher-text back. In the case of multiple keys, before plain-text is encrypted, it would be copied for three times, including pushed in the queue, popped out from the queue and copied to a piece of continuous pinned host memory. In the single key case, with our optimizations, plain-text is directly encrypted with no other copy operation. And at the same time, through our optimizations, CPU and GPU work independently, the degree of the system's coupling is greatly reduced. It is worth mentioning that technique can be applied to enhance the overall performance of GPU servers for other symmetric algorithms, such as AES-CTR, and DES-CTR.

Figure 4 shows how our optimizations work in detail. First, we designed a memory management framework. In the framework, there is a pinned memory block array, each pinned memory block is pre-allocated and specially designed to store 512×16 bytes IVs and the generated cipher streams. Every block has an unique ID, and all these IVs and cipher streams could be accessed by querying the ID. In the initialization process, CPU fills the IVs with random numbers and pushes these IDs into the empty ID poll. After the initialization is completed, GPU begins to generate cipher streams: it pulls out IDs from the empty ID poll and uses the IVs in the block to generate cipher streams. When the cipher streams are full filled, these IDs are pushed into the full ID poll. When GPU is generating cipher streams, CPU gets an ID from the full ID poll and deals with network requests. When it receives a request, it generates the cipher-text with the cipher streams, and then sends the encrypted data back. If the cipher streams are used up, CPU refills the IVs, pushes the ID back to the empty ID poll and gets another ID from the full ID poll.

5 Performance Assessment

In this section, we evaluated our SM4 kernel, and compared it with other implementations. We tested the capabilities of our symmetric cryptography server, and compared it with other servers. Our server platform was equipped with one Intel E5-2699 v3 CPU, 8 GB memory, and one NVIDIA GTX 1080 cards.

Table 2. Comparison of the best obtained results including AES-128.

	Our SM4 kernel	Our GPU card	FPGA-based SM4 [12]	Nishikawa's AES-128 kernel [13]
Platform	GTX1080	GTX1080	xc6vhx380t-3ff1155	Tesla P100
Throughput (Gbps)	**535.68**	**76.8**	42.54	605.9
Gbps per CUDA core	**0.21**	-	-	0.17
Gbps per $	**0.90**	-	-	0.1

5.1 Performance of Our SM4 Kernel and Comparison with Other Implementations

The existing fastest SM4 implementation belongs to Martínez-Herrera et al. [12]. Through speeding-up the polynomial multiplier in SM4 algorithm on an FGPA (which is xc6vhx380t-3ff1155), their implementation reaches 42.54 Gbps.

In order to test the performance of our SM4 kernel, plain-text and secret key are generated by CPUs with random value and then transferred to GPU's global memory. Each GPU thread generates its own round keys and loops the encryption for 1 KB plain-text. Our test result is shown in Table 2. The throughput of our SM4 kernel reaches 535.68 Gbps, it is 12.59 times faster than Martínez-Herrera et al.'s work. The throughput of our GPU card is still satisfactory, and it reaches 76.8 Gbps.

The security strength of AES-128 is same to that of SM4, we compared our SM4 kernel with the fastest AES-128 kernel. Naoki Nishikawa et al. [13] accelerate AES-128 on Tesla P100. We think their hardware has a huge advantage, and our SM4 kernel has better performance on each CUDA core. Considering that Tesla P100 is about 10 times more expensive than GTX 1080, our work is very competitive.

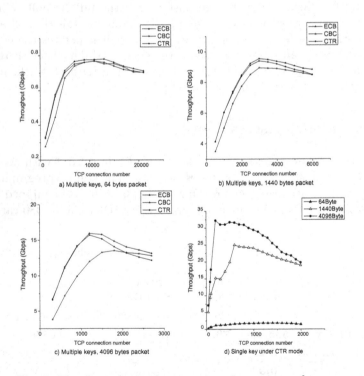

Fig. 5. The throughput of our symmetric cryptography server

5.2 Performance of the Our Server and Comparison with Other GPU Servers

We test the performance of the server when it encrypts different size packets: 64 bytes, 1440 bytes and 4096 bytes packet. Our server is capable of providing CBC, CTR and ECB these three modes of data encryption, and the test result is shown in Fig. 5. As the packet size becomes larger, the peak throughput of the server increases. When the packet size is 4096 bytes, the peak throughput is 15.96 Gbps.

For the case that using a single key under CTR mode, our optimizations raised the throughput of the server almost two to three times. As shown in Fig. 5(d), when using a single key, our server's peak throughput reaches 32.23 Gbps.

In SSLShader [6], they used 2 CPUs and 2 GPUs in a NUMA (Non Uniform Memory Access Architecture) system. NUMA can make a set of CPU and GPU run independently of another set, just like two servers, and SSLShader achieves 13 Gbps symmetric encryption throughput. Our server only used 1 CPU and 1 GPU, the peak throughput of our server is 15.96 Gbps, and for the case that using a single key to do data encryption under CTR mode, our server's throughput reaches 32.23 Gbps, which is 2.48 times faster than SSLShader.

6 Conclusion

In this work, we have presented how to use GPUs to accelerate SM4 encryption. On GeForce GTX 1080, the speed of our SM4 kernel reaches 535.68 Gbps, it is 12.59 times faster than the existing fastest SM4 implementation. We have sped up inefficient data transfer between GPUs and CPUs, and our optimization makes use of 85.4% bandwidth of GTX 1080's PCI-E. We also have showed the potential of using GPUs to enhance the performance of symmetric cryptography servers. Our symmetric cryptography server is capable of providing data encryption under ECB mode, CBC mode and CTR mode. For the case that uses a single key for a long term, like IPSec VPN gateways, the throughput of our server reaches 32.23 Gbps, it is 2.48 times faster than SSLShader

For SM4 symmetric algorithm, the kernel rate is much higher than data transfer rate. While the GPU performs SM4 operations, other algorithms can be operated at the same time to avoid the waste of GPU's computational resources. The inefficiency in the Linux TCP/IP stack is limiting the potential of our server, and Intel's DPDK seems to be a possible solution. These issues are our future work.

References

1. Bolz, J., Farmer, I., Grinspun, E., Schröoder, P.: Sparse matrix solvers on the GPU: conjugate gradients and multigrid. ACM Trans. Graph. (TOG) **22**(3), 917–924 (2003)
2. Erickson, J., Ding, J., Christensen, C.: Algebraic cryptanalysis of SMS4: Gröbner basis attack and SAT attack compared. In: Lee, D., Hong, S. (eds.) ICISC 2009. LNCS, vol. 5984, pp. 73–86. Springer, Heidelberg (2010). https://doi.org/10.1007/978-3-642-14423-3_6

3. Etrog, J., Robshaw, M.J.B.: The cryptanalysis of reduced-round SMS4. In: Avanzi, R.M., Keliher, L., Sica, F. (eds.) SAC 2008. LNCS, vol. 5381, pp. 51–65. Springer, Heidelberg (2009). https://doi.org/10.1007/978-3-642-04159-4_4
4. Gilger, J., Barnickel, J., Meyer, U.: GPU-acceleration of block ciphers in the OpenSSL cryptographic library. In: Gollmann, D., Freiling, F.C. (eds.) ISC 2012. LNCS, vol. 7483, pp. 338–353. Springer, Heidelberg (2012). https://doi.org/10.1007/978-3-642-33383-5_21
5. Harrison, O., Waldron, J.: Practical symmetric key cryptography on modern graphics hardware. In: USENIX Security Symposium, vol. 2008 (2008)
6. Jang, K., Han, S., Han, S., Moon, S.B., Park, K.: SSLShader: cheap SSL acceleration with commodity processors. In: NSDI (2011)
7. Jiang, Z.H., Fei, Y., Kaeli, D.: A complete key recovery timing attack on a GPU. In: 2016 IEEE International Symposium on High Performance Computer Architecture (HPCA), pp. 394–405. IEEE (2016)
8. Li, C., Wu, H., Chen, S., Li, X., Guo, D.: Efficient implementation for MD5-RC4 encryption using GPU with CUDA. In: 3rd International Conference on Anti-counterfeiting, Security, and Identification in Communication. ASID 2009, pp. 167–170. IEEE (2009)
9. Liu, F., Ji, W., Hu, L., Ding, J., Lv, S., Pyshkin, A., Weinmann, R.-P.: Analysis of the SMS4 block cipher. In: Pieprzyk, J., Ghodosi, H., Dawson, E. (eds.) ACISP 2007. LNCS, vol. 4586, pp. 158–170. Springer, Heidelberg (2007). https://doi.org/10.1007/978-3-540-73458-1_13
10. Luken, B.P., Ouyang, M., Desoky, A.H.: AES and DES encryption with GPU. In: ISCA PDCCS, pp. 67–70 (2009)
11. Manavski, S.A.: CUDA compatible GPU as an efficient hardware accelerator for AES cryptography. In: IEEE International Conference on Signal Processing and Communications. ICSPC 2007, pp. 65–68. IEEE (2007)
12. Martínez-Herrera, A.F., Mancillas-López, C., Mex-Perera, C.: GCM implementations of Camellia-128 and SMS4 by optimizing the polynomial multiplier. Microprocess. Microsyst. **45**, 129–140 (2016)
13. Nishikawa, N., Amano, H., Iwai, K.: Implementation of bitsliced AES encryption on CUDA-enabled GPU. In: Yan, Z., Molva, R., Mazurczyk, W., Kantola, R. (eds.) NSS 2017. LNCS, vol. 10394, pp. 273–287. Springer, Cham (2017). https://doi.org/10.1007/978-3-319-64701-2_20
14. NVIDIA. CUDA C Programming Guide 8.0 (2017). http://docs.nvidia.com/cuda/cuda-c-programming-guide/index.html#introduction
15. Pan, W., Zheng, F., Zhao, Y., Zhu, W.-T., Jing, J.: An efficient elliptic curve cryptography signature server with GPU acceleration. IEEE Trans. Inf. Forensics Secur. **12**(1), 111–122 (2017)
16. Zheng, F., Pan, W., Lin, J., Jing, J., Zhao, Y.: Exploiting the floating-point computing power of GPUs for RSA. In: Chow, S.S.M., Camenisch, J., Hui, L.C.K., Yiu, S.M. (eds.) ISC 2014. LNCS, vol. 8783, pp. 198–215. Springer, Cham (2014). https://doi.org/10.1007/978-3-319-13257-0_12
17. Zheng, F., Pan, W., Lin, J., Jing, J., Zhao, Y.: Exploiting the potential of GPUs for modular multiplication in ECC. In: Rhee, K.-H., Yi, J.H. (eds.) WISA 2014. LNCS, vol. 8909, pp. 295–306. Springer, Cham (2015). https://doi.org/10.1007/978-3-319-15087-1_23

An Experimental Study of Kannan's Embedding Technique for the Search LWE Problem

Yuntao Wang[1,4]($\boxtimes$) (iD), Yoshinori Aono[2], and Tsuyoshi Takagi[3,4]

[1] Graduate School of Mathematics, Kyushu University, Fukuoka, Japan
y-wang@math.kyushu-u.ac.jp
[2] National Institute of Communication and Technology, Tokyo, Japan
aono@nict.go.jp
[3] Institute of Mathematics for Industry, Kyushu University, Fukuoka, Japan
takagi@imi.kyushu-u.ac.jp
[4] Graduate School of Information Science and Technology, The University of Tokyo, Tokyo, Japan

Abstract. The learning with errors (LWE) problem is considered as one of the most compelling candidates as the security base for the post-quantum cryptosystems. For the application of LWE based cryptographic schemes, the concrete parameters are necessary: the length n of secret vector, the moduli q and the deviation σ. In the middle of 2016, Germany TU Darmstadt group initiated the LWE Challenge in order to assess the hardness of LWE problems. There are several approaches to solve the LWE problem via reducing LWE to other lattice problems. Xu et al.'s group solved some LWE Challenge instances using Liu and Nguyen's adapted enumeration technique (reducing LWE to BDD problem) [14] and they published this result at ACNS 2017 [23]. In this paper, we study Kannan's embedding technique (reducing LWE to unique SVP problem) to solve the LWE problem in the aspect of practice. The lattice reduction algorithm we use is the progressive BKZ [2,3]. At first, from our experimental results we can intuitively observe that the embedding technique is more efficient with the embedding factor M closer to 1. Then especially for the cases of $\sigma/q = 0.005$, we will give an preliminary analysis for the runtime and give an estimation for the proper size of parameters. Moreover, our experimental results show that for $n \geq 55$ and the fixed $\sigma/q = 0.005$, the embedding technique with progressive BKZ is more efficient than Xu et al.'s implementation of the enumeration algorithm in [21,23]. Finally, by our parameter setting, we succeeded in solving the LWE Challenge over $(n, \sigma/q) = (70, 0.005)$ using $2^{16.8}$ s (32.73 single core hours).

Keywords: Lattice · LWE Challenge · BDD · Unique SVP
Embedding technique · Lattice reduction · Post-quantum cryptography

1 Introduction

Nowadays many post-quantum cryptographic schemes as fully homomorphic encryption and lattice-based signature schemes base their security on some

© Springer International Publishing AG, part of Springer Nature 2018
S. Qing et al. (Eds.): ICICS 2017, LNCS 10631, pp. 541–553, 2018.
https://doi.org/10.1007/978-3-319-89500-0_47

lattice hard problems as the learning with errors (LWE) problem, short integer solution (SIS) and so on [9,16,18]. LWE problem was introduced by Regev in 2005, which comes from "learning parity with noise" by lifting the moduli value, and concreting the probability distribution of "error" [18]. As an average-case lattice problem, LWE problem is proved as hard as certain worst-case lattice problems such as GapSVP and SIVP [18], which allows to build many provably secure lattice-based cryptographic schemes. The hardness of LWE problem is related to three critical parameters: the length n of secret vector, the moduli q and the deviation σ of error vectors. Some theoretical analysis for the hardness of LWE are given as lattice-based attack [14,15], and BKW type attack [11], but rarely concrete parameters based on experiments were published. However, for the practical application, it is indispensable to estimate the concrete parameters of LWE from sufficient experiments. In this work, we focus on the more practical lattice-based attack. At first, the LWE problem can be seen as a particular bounded distance decoding (BDD) instance on a q-ary lattice. For a given lattice and a target vector close to the lattice points in a reasonable bound, BDD is to find the closest lattice vector to the target.

There are two main methods to process the BDD instance. One is reducing the lattice basis first and search the secret vector by Babai's NearestPlane [4] algorithm or its variants [14,15]. Especially in [14], Liu and Nguyen intermingle the short error vector into an enumeration searching tree, which makes the attack more efficient. Another procedure is to reduce BDD to the unique-shortest vector problem (unique-SVP) by Kannan's embedding technique [10]. This procedure increase one more lattice dimension by adding the target vector and a so-called embedding factor M into the new basis. By a proper parameter setting, the short error vector is usually a component of the shortest vector in the new lattice. So there is a big gap between the shortest vector and the second shortest vector in the new lattice, which makes a lattice reduction algorithm or a searching algorithm find the shortest one more efficiently. Since both methods call the SVP solver as subroutine, their complexity grow exponentially with the dimension increasing.

In order to assess the hardness of the LWE problem in practice, TU Darmstadt, in alliance with UC San Diego and TU published, a new platform "Darmstadt LWE Challenge" [5,21]. LWE Challenge provides LWE samples by increasing hardness for researcher to test their solving algorithms.

In this work, we apply the embedding technique on LWE problem, using state-of-the-art progressive BKZ algorithm [2]. The LWE instances used in our experiments are sampled from Darmstadt LWE Challenge. From our experiments, we find that the algorithm can derive a better efficiency if the embedding factor M is closer to 1. We also give an preliminary analysis for the proper parameter as the dimension m of LWE samples should be used in the attack associate to the secret length n. Especially for $n \geq 55$ and the fixed $\sigma/q = 0.005$, our implemented embedding technique with progressive BKZ is more efficient than Xu et al.'s implementation of the enumeration algorithm in [21,23]. Finally, we got the records of case $(70, 0.005)$ in Darmstadt LWE Challenge, using our extrapolated setting of m, which took 32.73 single core hours.

Roadmap. Section 2 recalls the notations and background on lattice, LWE problem and BKZ reduction algorithms. We introduce Kannan's embedding technique in Sect. 3. Our experimental results and preliminary analysis on the relevant parameters settings in Kannan's embedding technique are shown in Sect. 4. Finally we give some conclusions in Sect. 5.

2   Preliminaries

2.1   Lattice Theory

A lattice L is an infinite regular space expanded by a basis $\mathbf{B} = \{\mathbf{b}_1, \ldots, \mathbf{b}_n\}$, where $\mathbf{b}_i$ $(i = 1, \ldots, n)$ are a set of linearly independent row vectors in $\mathbb{R}^m$ and n is the dimension of L. Note that even $\mathbf{B}$ is matrix with row vectors, in this paper we use integral lattice for convenience we write the basis in a matrix form as $\mathbf{B} = (\mathbf{b}_1, \ldots, \mathbf{b}_n) \in \mathbb{Z}^{n \times m}$, where we will declare the matrix with column vectors if it appears, as the matrix $\mathbf{A}$ in LWE problem. The n-dimensional *volume* of L is denoted by $\mathrm{vol}(L)$, which is computed by the *determinant* of the basis B, i.e. $\mathrm{vol}(L) = \det(B)$. The Euclidean norm of a vector $\mathbf{v} \in \mathbb{R}^m$ is $\|\mathbf{v}\|$. We denote by $V_n(R) = R^n \cdot \frac{\pi^{n/2}}{\Gamma(n/2+1)}$ the volume of n-dim Euclidean ball of radius R.

Shortest Vector. There are at least two non-zero vectors with same minimal Euclidean norm but contrary sign in a lattice L: this norm is called the *first minimum* $\lambda_1(L)$ of L. The *shortest vector* of L refers to one of the vectors whose norms are both $\lambda_1(L)$. Similarly we denote by $\lambda_2(L)$ the length of the second shortest vector, which is linearly independent of the first shortest vectors.

Orthogonalization. We denote by $\mathbf{B}^* = (\mathbf{b}_1^*, \ldots, \mathbf{b}_n^*)$ the associated Gram-Schmidt orthogonalization of the given basis $\mathbf{B} = (\mathbf{b}_1, \ldots, \mathbf{b}_n)$. Here $\mathbf{b}_1^* = \mathbf{b}_1$ and $\mathbf{b}_i^* = \mathbf{b}_i - \sum_{j=1}^{i-1} \mu_{ij} \mathbf{b}_j^*$ for all $2 \le i \le n$ while $\mu_{ij} = \frac{\langle \mathbf{b}_i, \mathbf{b}_j^* \rangle}{\|\mathbf{b}_j^*\|^2}$ $(1 \le j < i \le n)$.

Hermite Factor. To estimate the performance of the algorithm on solving SVP, we usually use the Hermite factor which is defined in [8] as:

$$\mathrm{HF}(\mathbf{b}_1, \ldots, \mathbf{b}_n) = \|\mathbf{b}_1\| / \mathrm{vol}(L)^{1/n}.$$

So for a lattice of dimension n, we say the algorithm performs better if the Hermite factor of output is smaller. Also we usually use root Hermite factor convenient for analysis, which is denoted by:

$$\delta = \mathrm{rHF}(\mathbf{b}_1, \ldots, \mathbf{b}_n) = (\|\mathbf{b}_1\| / \mathrm{vol}(L)^{1/n})^{1/n}$$

Note that our definition of rHF depending on the given bases and the output $(\mathbf{b}_1, \ldots, \mathbf{b}_n)$ of the short vector from lattice algorithms.

Gaussian Heuristic. Given a n-dimensional lattice L and a continuous (and usually convex) set $S \subset \mathbb{R}^n$, Then the *Gaussian heuristic* estimates that the number of points in $S \cap L$ is approximately $\mathrm{vol}(S)/\mathrm{vol}(L)$.

Particularly, taking S as the origin-centered ball of radius R, the number of lattice point is $V_n(R)/\text{vol}(L)$, which derives the length of shortest vector λ_1 so that the volume of ball is equal to that of lattice:

$$\lambda_1(L) \approx \frac{(\Gamma(n/2+1)\text{vol}(L))^{1/n}}{\sqrt{\pi}}$$

This is the so-called *Gaussian heuristic of a lattice*, and we denote it by $\text{GH}(L)$. Here the gamma function $\Gamma(s)$ is defined for $s > 0$ by the integral $\Gamma(s) = \int_0^\infty t^{s-1} \cdot e^{-t}dt$.

γ-unique SVP. It is called unique SVP problem, if for a given lattice L which satisfies $\lambda_1(L) \ll \lambda_2(L)$, to find the shortest vector in L. And the γ-unique SVP problem is scaling the bound by a positive multiple as $\gamma\lambda_1(L) < \lambda_2(L)$. The auxiliary condition can be seen as a promised gap between the lengths of the first shortest vector and the second shortest vector. It is known that if the gap is bigger, it is easier to find the shortest vector by a certain algorithm. We abbreviate the γ-unique SVP to γ-uSVP in this paper.

2.2   The Learning With Errors Problem [18]

There are four parameters in LWE problem: the number of samples $m \in \mathbb{Z}$, the length $n \in \mathbb{Z}$ of secret vector, modulo $q \in \mathbb{Z}$ and the standard deviation $\sigma \in \mathbb{R}_{>0}$ for the discrete Gaussian distribution (denoted by D_σ) on $\mathbb{Z}$. Uniformly sample a matrix $\mathbf{A} \in \mathbb{Z}_q^{m \times n}$ and a secret vector $\mathbf{s} \in \mathbb{Z}_q^n$, and randomly sample a relatively small perturbation vector $\mathbf{e} \in \mathbb{Z}_q^m$ from Gaussian distribution D_σ. The LWE distribution Ψ is constructed by pairs $(\mathbf{A}, \mathbf{b} \equiv \mathbf{As} + \mathbf{e} \pmod{q}) \in (\mathbb{Z}_q^{m \times n}, \mathbb{Z}_q^m)$ sampled as above. The *search LWE problem* is for a given pair $(\mathbf{A}, \mathbf{b})$ sampled from LWE distribution Ψ, to compute the pair $(\mathbf{s}, \mathbf{e})$.

2.2.1   Darmstadt LWE Challenge

In 2016, TU Darmstadt, in alliance with UC San Diego and TU Eindhoven published a platform for the concrete parameter analysis of LWE problem [5,21]. In Darmstadt LWE Challenge, the organizers merge the two parameters σ and q into the *relative error size* α, such that $\alpha = \sigma/q$. n is the length of secret vector and q is the minimum prime number bigger than n^2. For each case of length n, they offer the sampled n column vectors in basis $\mathbf{A}' \in \mathbb{Z}_q^{n^2 \times n}$, and one column target vector $\mathbf{b}' \in \mathbb{Z}_q^{n^2}$. The length n and the relative error size α are arithmetic sequences from 40 and 0.005, with common differences of 5 and 0.005 respectively. To adapt the current lattice algorithms used in the attack algorithm, we should randomly sample $m \ll n^2$ entries of the column vectors in the original basis $\mathbf{A}' \in \mathbb{Z}_q^{n^2 \times n}$ and ample from the target vector $\mathbf{b}' \in \mathbb{Z}_q^{n^2}$ respectively, as from $(\mathbf{A}', \mathbf{b}') \in (\mathbb{Z}_q^{n^2 \times n}, \mathbb{Z}_q^{n^2})$ in Darmstadt LWE Challenge to our instance $(\mathbf{A}, \mathbf{b}) \in (\mathbb{Z}_q^{m \times n}, \mathbb{Z}_q^m)$. This is called sublattice attack, and we will discuss how to choose a suitable m in Sect. 3.4.

2.2.2 Bounded Distance Decoding

In a Euclidean space spanned by a lattice L, there is a target vector $\mathbf{w} \in \mathbb{R}^m$ which is guaranteed to be within a distance $r \leq \alpha\lambda_1(L)$ where $\alpha > 0$. The bounded distance decoding (BDD) output a vector $\mathbf{b} \in L$ such that $\|\mathbf{w} - \mathbf{b}\| \leq r$.

2.2.3 q-ary Lattice

A lattice $L \subset \mathbb{Z}^m$ is a q-ary lattice if $q\mathbb{Z}^m \subset L$ for an integer q. Let $\mathbf{A} \in \mathbb{Z}_q^{m \times n}$ $(m > n)$ be a matrix with column vectors, we define the following m-dimensional q-ary lattice.

$$L_{(\mathbf{A},q)} = \{\mathbf{y} \in \mathbb{Z}_q^m | \mathbf{y} \equiv \mathbf{A}\mathbf{x} \pmod{q} \text{ for some } \mathbf{x} \in \mathbb{Z}^n\}$$

It is the linear code generated by the columns of $\mathbf{A}$ mod q with $\mathrm{vol}(L_{(\mathbf{A},q)}) \geq q^{m-n}$. $\mathrm{vol}(L_{(\mathbf{A},q)}) = q^{m-n}$ when the columns of $\mathbf{A}$ are linearly independent over $\mathbb{Z}_q$. We can construct the basis $\mathbf{B}$ of q-ary $L_{(\mathbf{A},q)}$ as follows. $L = \{\mathbf{y} \in \mathbb{Z}_q^m | \mathbf{y} \equiv \mathbf{A}\mathbf{x} \pmod{q}, \mathbf{x} \in \mathbb{Z}^n\}$ as

$$\mathbf{B} = \left(\frac{\mathbf{A}^T}{q\mathbf{I}_m} \right) \in \mathbb{Z}^{(m+n) \times m},$$

Then eliminate the linearly dependent vectors by an elementary transformation. In this work, we reduce this basis to a square matrix with Hermite Normal Form, see next paragraph.

2.2.4 Hermite Normal Form

The Hermite Normal Form (HNF) of a basis $\mathbf{B}$ satisfies: (1) $\mathbf{B}$ is lower triangular; (2) the diagonal entries are positive; (3) any entry below the diagonal is a non-negative number strictly less than the diagonal entry in its column. In this work, we use the HNF module in Victor Shoup's NTL library [17], which uses the Domich et al.'s algorithm [7]. Particularly, a q-ary lattice $L_{(\mathbf{A},q)}$ has this form for some matrix $A'_{n \times (m-n)} \in \mathbb{Z}_q^{n \times (m-n)}$.

$$\mathbf{B}_{\mathrm{HNF}} = \begin{pmatrix} q\mathbf{I}_{m-n} & \mathbf{0} \\ A'_{n \times (m-n)} & \mathbf{I}_n \end{pmatrix} \in \mathbb{Z}^{(m+n) \times m}.$$

2.3 BKZ Reduction Algorithms

The lattice reduction algorithms can make the given basis vectors "better": relatively more orthogonal to each other with relatively smaller lengths than the given ones. Schnorr and Euchner [20] proposed the BKZ reduction algorithm, which processes the LLL reduction [12] and the enumeration algorithm iteratively with a fixed blocksize. Here the enumeration algorithm is an exhaustive point search algorithm. Refer to [20] for more details about enumeration. The root Hermite Factor of Schnorr and Euchner's BKZ was considered limited by 1.01 according to Gama and Nguyen [8]. Chen and Nguyen improved the BKZ algorithm called BKZ 2.0, by inviting "extreme pruning" enumeration in subroutine [6]. The root Hermite Factor of BKZ 2.0 break through the 1.01 limit with a reasonably big blocksize. In 2016, Aono et al. proposed a practical progressive BKZ algorithm [2]. The progressive BKZ algorithm invites some technique from BKZ 2.0. While the significant improvement is that they propose a sharp simulator based on the *Geometric Series Assumption* (GSA) [19], to estimate the runtime for a fixed blocksize β. Then the current local BKZ-β reduction is terminated after this runtime, and increase the blocksize to a simulated optimal larger one or just increase the blocksize step by step, until deriving the expected reduced basis. This progressive BKZ algorithm is shown about 50 times faster than BKZ 2.0 in [2]. Moreover, they also published their progressive BKZ source code in [3]. In this work, we will use the progressive BKZ algorithm to reduce the q-ary lattice bases in solving the LWE problem.

3   Overview of Embedding Technique for Solving LWE Problem

In this section, we recall Kannan's embedding technique [10], and introduce the parameter settings in our experiments.

3.1   From LWE to BDD

The LWE problem can be reduced to BDD case as follows.

Input: a lattice $L = \{\mathbf{v} \in \mathbb{Z}_q^m | \mathbf{v} \equiv \mathbf{As} \pmod{q}, \mathbf{s} \in \mathbb{Z}_n\}$ and a target vector $\mathbf{t}$ with bounded distance $\|\mathbf{e}\|$.

Output: a vector $\mathbf{v} \in L$ close to $\mathbf{t}$, and get $\mathbf{s}$ from $\mathbf{v} \equiv \mathbf{As}$ if succeeded.

In 2016, Xu et al.'s group solved some instances of LWE Challenge by reducing LWE to BDD and using Liu-Nguyen's adapted enumeration algorithm, which can solve BDD directly with a considerable success probability. In this work we focus on solving BDD by embedding technique: further reduce BDD to unique-SVP [10]. The embedding attack is shown in Algorithm 1. We will elaborate on the algorithm as follows.

3.2   Solving LWE via the Embedding Technique

Preprocessing. To solve a given LWE instance, it does not need to use all given samples. For instance, the Darmstadt LWE Challenge supplies the original basis $\mathbf{A}' \in \mathbb{Z}_q^{n^2 \times n}$ for each problem case, thus, a naive construction of matrices in Algorithm 1 requires a lattice reduction of a large number of matrices even for small LWE dimensions. Hence, we can choose m ($m \ll n^2$) vectors as a parameter to optimize the computational time, as from $(\mathbf{A}', \mathbf{b}') \in (\mathbb{Z}_q^{n^2 \times n}, \mathbb{Z}_q^{n^2})$ to $(\mathbf{A}, \mathbf{b}) \in (\mathbb{Z}_q^{m \times n}, \mathbb{Z}_q^m)$. We will discuss the way to compute the optimal m in Sect. 3.4. Also during the random sampling, we should check the independency of vectors to make sure: (1) the correctness of the attack algorithm; (2) the

---

Algorithm 1. Kannan's embedding technique to solve LWE problem. [10]

Input: An LWE instance $(\mathbf{A}, \mathbf{b} \equiv \mathbf{As} + \mathbf{e} \ (\text{mod } q)) \in (\mathbb{Z}_q^{m \times n}, \mathbb{Z}_q^m)$.
Output: The secret vector $\mathbf{s} \in \mathbb{Z}_q^n$ and the short error vector $\mathbf{e} \in \mathbb{Z}_q^m$, s.t. $\mathbf{b} = \mathbf{As} + \mathbf{e}$.
Step 1. Construct the basis $\mathbf{B}$ of q-ary lattice
$$L_{(\mathbf{A}, q)} = \{\mathbf{v} \in \mathbb{Z}_q^m \mid \mathbf{v} \equiv \mathbf{Ax} \ (\text{mod } q), \mathbf{x} \in \mathbb{Z}^n\}$$
as $\mathbf{B} = \begin{pmatrix} \mathbf{A}^T \\ q\mathbf{I}_m \end{pmatrix} \in \mathbb{Z}^{(m+n) \times m}$; and compute the HNF of $\mathbf{B}$ as

$$\mathbf{B}_{\text{HNF}} = \begin{pmatrix} q\mathbf{I}_{m-n} & \mathbf{0} \\ \mathbf{A}'_{n \times (m-n)} & \mathbf{I}_n \end{pmatrix} \in \mathbb{Z}^{m \times m};$$

Step 2. Reduce BDD to unique-SVP by rescaling $\mathbf{B}_{\text{HNF}}$
to $\mathbf{B}' = \begin{pmatrix} \mathbf{B}_{\text{HNF}} & \mathbf{0} \\ \mathbf{b} & M \end{pmatrix} \in \mathbb{Z}^{(m+1) \times (m+1)}$;

Step 3. Process $\mathbf{B}'$ using lattice algorithm to derive a
short vector $\mathbf{w}$ including the error vector $\mathbf{e}$;
Step 4. Use $\mathbf{e}$ to compute the secret vector $\mathbf{s}$ by
Gauss elimination in $(\mathbf{b} - \mathbf{e}) = \mathbf{As}$.

---

volume of derived q-ary lattice is q^{m-n}, which will be used in Sect. 3.4. We give explanations for each step in Algorithm 1.

> **Step 1.** We follow the method in Sect. 2.2.3 to construct and compute the HNF basis $\mathbf{B}_{\text{HNF}}$ of q-ary lattice $L_{(\mathbf{A}, q)} = \{\mathbf{v} \in \mathbb{Z}^m \mid \mathbf{v} \equiv \mathbf{Ax} \ (\text{mod } q), \mathbf{x} \in \mathbb{Z}^n\}$.
> **Step 2.** This step is the key point of embedding technique: expand the q-ary basis $\mathbf{B}_{\text{HNF}} \in \mathbb{Z}^{m \times n}$ by one dimension, and embed the target vector $\mathbf{b}$ and one embedding factor M into the new basis $\mathbf{B}' \in \mathbb{Z}^{(m+1) \times (m+1)}$.
> **Step 3.** At this step, we process the new basis $\mathbf{B}'$ by lattice algorithms. After the reduction, we get the error vector $\mathbf{e}$ from the output shortest vector $\mathbf{w}$, since $\mathbf{e} = \mathbf{b} - \mathbf{Bu}$ and $\mathbf{w} = \mathbf{B}'\left(\begin{smallmatrix} \mathbf{u} \\ 1 \end{smallmatrix}\right) = \left(\begin{smallmatrix} \mathbf{e} \\ M \end{smallmatrix}\right)$ for some $\mathbf{u} \in \mathbb{Z}_q^m$. In our work, we use the progressive BKZ reduction in this step [2].
> **Step 4.** Simply get the secret vector $\mathbf{s}$ by Gauss elimination.

In the following, we explain four discussion points of the algorithm.

(1) In the embedding procedure of Step 3, if the output vector $\mathbf{w}$ of the lattice algorithm satisfies

$$\|\mathbf{w}\| \leq \sqrt{\|\mathbf{e}\|^2 + M^2} \approx \left(\frac{\sqrt{2m}\sigma}{(Mq^{m-n})^{1/(m+1)}} \right)^{1/(m+1)}, \tag{1}$$

here $\|\mathbf{e}\| \approx \sqrt{m}\sigma$, then the answer is correct with high probility.
(2) There is a gap between the shortest vector and the linearly independent second shortest vector in $L'(\mathbf{B}')$, namely we have to solve a unique-SVP in this lattice. The size of embedding factor M can affect the gap in some sense and we will discuss it in Sect. 3.3.
(3) Since we do not know the exact value of $\|\mathbf{e}\|$, we can not terminate by condition (1). $\|\mathbf{w}\| \leq \sqrt{\|\mathbf{e}\|^2 + M^2}$ is the condition for a reduction or point

searching algorithm to terminate in Step 4. However, during the update of lattice reduction of basis $(\mathbf{b}_1, \ldots, \mathbf{b}_n)$ in our progressive BKZ, we found that the root Hermite factor δ suddenly drop to a very small value from value around 1. We can set the algorithm to terminate when $\delta < 0.7$ for convenience.

(4) There is a trade-off between the attack efficiency and success rate, depending on the dimension m of $L_{(\mathbf{A},q)}(\mathbf{A} \in \mathbb{Z}_q^{m \times n})$ and the embedding factor M of the sampled LWE instances in the embedding algorithm. In this work, our goal is from experiments to get a preliminary analysis of the affect of m and M on the runtime for solving Darmstadt LWE Challenge instances.

3.3   How to Choose M at Step 2

The size of $\|\mathbf{e}\|$ and M intuitively affect the gap of the shortest and the second shortest vector in the unique-SVP of $L(\mathbf{B}') \in \mathbb{Z}^{(m+1) \times (m+1)}$, since the reduction output is $\mathbf{w} = \binom{\mathbf{e}}{M}$. For the entries of error vector $\mathbf{e}$ are randomly and linearly independently sampled from the discrete Gaussian distribution D_σ, then $\|\mathbf{e}\|^2$ subject to $\sigma^2 \times \chi^2$, where χ means chi distribution. So $\|\mathbf{e}\|^2$ has expectation of $m\sigma^2$ and we can estimate $\|\mathbf{e}\| \approx \sqrt{m}\sigma$. Lyubashevsky and Micciancio [13] suggest that the choice for the embedding factor $M \in \mathbb{N}$ is $\|\mathbf{e}\|$. If M is bigger, then there is a lower chance to solve LWE problems, since the gap in unique-SVP will become smaller. However, if M is too small, there may exist a vector $\mathbf{v} \in L(\mathbf{B}')$ such that $\|\mathbf{v} + c \cdot \binom{\mathbf{b}}{M}\| < \|\mathbf{w}\| = \|\binom{\mathbf{e}}{M}\|$ where $c \in \mathbb{Z}$, according to [1]. In our experiments we observe the runtime of attack using increasing M from 1.

3.4   How to Choose m

In this part, we follow the analysis proposed by Micciancio and Regev [16]. With a small Gaussian standard deviation σ, the error vector $\mathbf{e}$ is much shorter than the second shortest vector in the lattice L', and the latter one can be assumed as the shortest vector in lattice L. According to the Gaussian heuristic, the length of the shortest vector in an m dimensional lattice is $\lambda_1(L) \approx \frac{(\Gamma(m/2+1)\mathrm{vol}(L))^{1/m}}{\sqrt{\pi}}$, approximately $\sqrt{\frac{m}{2\pi e}} q^{(m-n)/m}$. So we can get $\lambda_2(L') \approx \lambda_1(L) \approx \sqrt{\frac{m}{2\pi e}} q^{(m-n)/m}$. In our experiments, we get the result that the attack is more efficient if the embedding factor M is closer to 1 (see Sect. 4.1). We set $M = 1$ here and assume $\lambda_1(L') \approx \|\frac{\mathbf{e}}{M}\| \approx \sqrt{m}\sigma$, for the Gaussian sampled $\mathbf{e}$ has length around $\sqrt{m}\sigma$. So we want to enlarge the following gap in unique-SVP for an efficient attack:

$$\gamma(m) = \frac{\lambda_2(L')}{\lambda_1(L')} \approx \frac{\sqrt{\frac{m}{2\pi e}} q^{(m-n)/m}}{\sqrt{m}\sigma} \tag{2}$$

We need $\sigma \ll q^{\frac{m-n}{m}}$. What's more, for a lattice reduction algorithm with a root Hermite factor δ, the gap should satisfies $\gamma(m) > c\delta^m$ for a proper value c. The constant c is unknown, so we can maximize $q^{(m-n)/m}/\delta^m$, to get the optimal sub-dimension m of LWE sample instances is

$$m = \sqrt{n \log_2(q)/\log_2(\delta)}. \tag{3}$$

This can properly enlarge the gap in γ-unique SVP transformed from BDD, within a reduction algorithm's capability estimated by the root Hermite factor $\delta = \mathrm{rHF}(\mathbf{b}_1, \ldots, \mathbf{b}_n) = (\|\mathbf{b}_1\|/\mathrm{vol}(L)^{1/n})^{1/n}$.

4   Experimental Results and Analysis

In this section, we give the details in our experiments on solving LWE problems using embedding technique (Algorithm 1). All the cases are taken from Darmstadt LWE Challenge [21]. In our experiments, we just observe the hardness of small dimensions from 40 to 60, with the same $\alpha = 0.005$. As a preparing work, we take δ in the range $[1.010, 1.011, \ldots, 1.025]$ and randomly sample $m = \sqrt{n \log_2(q)/\log_2 \delta}$ vector entries for $\mathbf{A} \in \mathbb{Z}_q^{m \times n}$ in each LWE case. For each case with parameters (n, δ), we sample 20 different bases. The progressive BKZ algorithm and its open source code of version 1.1 are used in the Step 3 of Algorithm 1. Our implementation using C language and NTL on Intel(R) Xeon(R) CPU E5-2697 v2 @ 2.70 GHz with 24 cores (over-clocked to 3.5 GHz and hyper-threaded to 48 threads). Xu et al. were using parallel implementation technique and the specifications of hardware are 3.60 GHz Intel Core i7 processor with eight cores and a cluster consisting of 20 c4.8xlarge instances, each equipped by 36 cores (hyper-threaded to 72 threads) [23]. The time unit in the following sections are all **single thread seconds**.

4.1   Efficiency by Changing M

As we discussed in Sect. 3.3, in the Step 2 of Algorithm 1, the embedding factor M in basis $\mathbf{B}' \in \mathbb{Z}^{(m+1) \times (m+1)}$ affect the size of gap in the unique-SVP of $L(B')$. In this section we will observe what size of M is better for an efficient

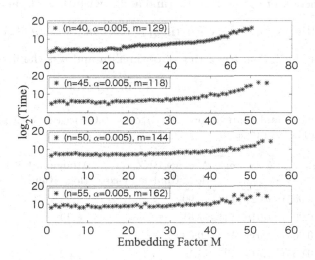

Fig. 1. Runtime for cases (n, α) with fixed bases and increasing embedding factor M.

embedding technique. The fixed dimension m of $L_{(\mathbf{A},q)}$ is referred to Sect. 4.2, and the embedding factor M is from 1 to around 55. For each case of parameters $n = 40, 45, 50, 55$ with fixed $\alpha = 0.005$, we sample a same basis $\mathbf{A} \in \mathbb{Z}^{m \times n}$ from Darmstadt LWE Challenge respectively. Figure 1 shows the runtime of Algorithm 1 for each case with increasing sequence of embedding factor M. We can observe that with growing M, the runtime of Algorithm 1 is gradually increasing. So it is more efficient to solve LWE problem with the embedding factor M closer to 1.

4.2   Optimal Choice of m for Each (n, α)

According to the Eqs. (2) and (3) in Sect. 3.4, the dimension m of q-ary lattice $L_{(\mathbf{A},q)}$ in Step 3 also affects the efficiency of Algorithm 1. A larger dimension m will lead the root Hermite Factor smaller, which makes the lattice algorithm inefficient. While a smaller m will reduce the gap of unique-SVP and make the problem harder to solve. In this section, we observe the affect of size m on the efficiency of Algorithm 1.

At first for each case of $(n, \alpha = 0.005)$, we fix the embedding factor as $M = 1$. We take δ in the range $[1.010, 1.011, \ldots, 1.025]$ and for each δ calculate $m = \sqrt{n \log_2(q) / \log_2 \delta}$. We did the experiments for $n = 40, 45, 50, 55, 60, 65$. Note that for case of $(n = 40, \alpha = 0.005)$, since the runtime are close to each other, we ignore it here. We calculate the average runtime for each δ by around 20 random samples of $\mathbf{A} \in \mathbb{Z}_q^{m \times n}$. In Table 1 the "Average BKZ Runtime" shows the minimum of average runtime for each δ. Further, the "Minimum BKZ Runtime" is the minimum data for the relevant δ and m.

From now we will analyze the experimental data in Table 1. We extrapolated the data by curve fitting technique in Fig. 2. The stars are the minimum of Average Runtime in each (n, α) cases as showed in Table 1. Here we get the quadratic function of the average runtime and n with three decimal precision:

$$\text{FittingLog}_2(\text{Average Runtime}) = 0.0153n^2 - 1.17n + 27.6, \qquad (4)$$

and plot it in Fig. 2. And the fitting of optimal m and n is the linear function

$$\text{Optimal}(m) = \lceil 4.82n - 98.7 \rfloor. \qquad (5)$$

Table 1. Experimental runtime for each $(n, \alpha = 0.005)$ cases with parameter δ in range $[1.01, 1.011, \ldots, 1.025]$.

(n, α)	δ	m	Average BKZ (log$_2$ Runtime (sec))	Minimum BKZ (log$_2$ Runtime (sec))
$(45, 0.005)$	1.025	118	5.99	4.28
$(50, 0.005)$	1.019	144	7.51	6.49
$(55, 0.005)$	1.017	162	9.03	8.08
$(60, 0.005)$	1.013	195	13.13	10.62
$(65, 0.005)$	1.012	213	16.04	14.65

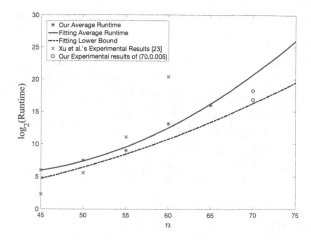

Fig. 2. The runtime for embedding technique on Darmstadt LWE Challenge of $(n, \alpha = 0.005)$ cases: the stars and the full curve denote our average and it fitting of the experimental runtime for the optimal m respectively; the dot line is fitting of the smallest runtime for each optimal m case, which is heuristically seen as the lower bound in our work; the red crosses are Xu et al.'s records at the LWE Challenge website; the hollow circles are our experimental results for $(n, \alpha) = (70, 0.005)$. (Color figure online)

Here the mark $\ulcorner \ldots \lrcorner$ means taking a rounding number.

Moreover, we also illustrate the minimum runtime (seen as the lower bound heuristically) in all $(n, \alpha = 0.005)$ cases with parameter m from Eq. (4).

$$\text{FittingLog}_2(\text{Lower Bound}) = 0.00584n^2 - 0.208n + 2.21 \tag{6}$$

and we plot the fitting line in Fig. 2. Note that we take the quadratic formulas for the estimation in 4 and 6 since the state-of-the-art extreme pruning enumeration runs in $2^{O(n^2)-0.5n}$ as the subroutine of progressive BKZ.

Furthermore, in Table 2, we estimate the necessary dimension m and the relevant runtime by embedding technique on solving LWE Challenge cases $n \geq 75, \sigma = 0.005$,using progressive BKZ algorithm. Our estimation depending on the fitting function (4) and (5).

Moreover, from Fig. 2 we can see that Xu et al.'s LWE Challenge records of $\alpha = 0.005$ stopped at $n = 65$ for the overwhelming runtime and low success probability [22]. Our implemented embedding technique with progressive BKZ can solve the LWE Challenge instances more efficiently than Xu et al.'s enumeration implementation for $n \geq 55$.

For the cases of $(n = 70, \alpha = 0.005)$, we compute the extrapolated $m \approx 239$ (relevant $\delta = 1.010$) from function (5). Then we use $\delta =1.010, 1.011, 1.012, 1.013$ and there are just two Darmstadt LWE Challenge cases with $\delta = 1.011, 1.012$ are successfully solved by $m = 233, 223$ in time $2^{16.8}$, $2^{18.2}$ s respectively. and we plot it in Fig. 2, which are lying between the two fitting curves and close to the runtime of estimated FittingLog$_2$(Lower Bound).

Table 2. Estimation of effective m and runtime on solving($n \geq 75, \sigma = 0.005$) in the LWE Challenge.

(n, α)	q	δ	m	Estimated BKZ ($\log_2$ Runtime (sec))
(75, 0.005)	5639	1.009	263	25.91
(80, 0.005)	6421	1.008	287	31.92
(85, 0.005)	7229	1.008	311	38.69
(90, 0.005)	8101	1.007	335	46.23
(95, 0.005)	9029	1.007	359	54.53

5   Conclusions

In this paper, we studied the algorithm to solve LWE problem using Kannan's embedding technique. Especially we randomly sampled LWE instances from Darmstadt LWE Challenge and applied the progressive BKZ algorithm to reduce the embedded bases. From our experiments of fixed relative error size $\alpha = \sigma/q = 0.005$, we observed that the algorithm has a more efficient trend if the embedding factor M is closer to 1. We also illustrated the relation of the dimension m of the q-ary lattice $L_{(\mathbf{A},q)}$ in LWE instance, the length n of secret vector $\mathbf{s}$, and the runtime of the algorithm. Furthermore, Xu et al.'s LWE Challenge records of $\alpha = 0.005$ stopped at $n = 55$ for the overwhelming runtime, while our experimental results show that for $n \geq 55$, the embedding technique with progressive BKZ can solve the LWE Challenge instances more efficiently than Xu et al.'s implementation of Liu-Nguyen's enumeration algorithm. Finally our LWE Challenge record of $(n, \alpha) = (70, 0.005)$ cases succeeded in $2^{16.8}$ s (32.73 single core hours), which also lies in the bounds of our fitting curves.

Acknowledgment. This work was supported by JSPS KAKENHI Grant Number JP17J01987, JP26730069 and JST CREST Grant Number JPMJCR14D6, Japan.

References

1. Albrecht, M.R., Fitzpatrick, R., Göpfert, F.: On the efficacy of solving LWE by reduction to unique-SVP. In: Lee, H.-S., Han, D.-G. (eds.) ICISC 2013. LNCS, vol. 8565, pp. 293–310. Springer, Cham (2014). https://doi.org/10.1007/978-3-319-12160-4_18
2. Aono, Y., Wang, Y., Hayashi, T., Takagi, T.: Improved progressive BKZ algorithms and their precise cost estimation by sharp simulator. In: Fischlin, M., Coron, J.-S. (eds.) EUROCRYPT 2016. LNCS, vol. 9665, pp. 789–819. Springer, Heidelberg (2016). https://doi.org/10.1007/978-3-662-49890-3_30
3. The progressive BKZ code. http://www2.nict.go.jp/security/pbkzcode/
4. Babai, L.: On Lovász' lattice reduction and the nearest lattice point problem. In: Mehlhorn, K. (ed.) STACS 1985. LNCS, vol. 182, pp. 13–20. Springer, Heidelberg (1985). https://doi.org/10.1007/BFb0023990

5. Buchmann, J., Büscher, N., Göpfert, F., Katzenbeisser, S., Krämer, J., Micciancio, D., Siim, S., Vredendaal, C., Walter, M.: Creating cryptographic challenges using multi-party computation: the LWE challenge. In: AsiaPKC 2016, pp. 11–20 (2016)
6. Chen, Y., Nguyen, P.Q.: BKZ 2.0: better lattice security estimates. In: Lee, D.H., Wang, X. (eds.) ASIACRYPT 2011. LNCS, vol. 7073, pp. 1–20. Springer, Heidelberg (2011). https://doi.org/10.1007/978-3-642-25385-0_1
7. Domich, P., Kannan, R., Trotter, L.: Hermite normal form computation using modulo determinant arithmetic. Math. Oper. Res. **12**, 50–59 (1987)
8. Gama, N., Nguyen, P.Q.: Predicting lattice reduction. In: Smart, N. (ed.) EURO-CRYPT 2008. LNCS, vol. 4965, pp. 31–51. Springer, Heidelberg (2008). https://doi.org/10.1007/978-3-540-78967-3_3
9. Gentry, C., Peikert, C., Vaikuntanathan, V.: Trapdoors for hard lattices and new cryptographic constructions. In: STOC 2008, pp. 197–206 (2008)
10. Kannan, R.: Minkowski's convex body theorem and integer programming. Math. Oper. Res. **12**(3), 415–440 (1987)
11. Kirchner, P., Fouque, P.-A.: An improved BKW algorithm for LWE with applications to cryptography and lattices. In: Gennaro, R., Robshaw, M. (eds.) CRYPTO 2015. LNCS, vol. 9215, pp. 43–62. Springer, Heidelberg (2015). https://doi.org/10.1007/978-3-662-47989-6_3
12. Lenstra, A.K., Lenstra Jr., H.W., Lovász, L.: Factoring polynomials with rational coefficients. Math. Ann. **261**(4), 515–534 (1982)
13. Lyubashevsky, V., Micciancio, D.: On bounded distance decoding, unique shortest vectors, and the minimum distance problem. In: Halevi, S. (ed.) CRYPTO 2009. LNCS, vol. 5677, pp. 577–594. Springer, Heidelberg (2009). https://doi.org/10.1007/978-3-642-03356-8_34
14. Liu, M., Nguyen, P.Q.: Solving BDD by enumeration: an update. In: Dawson, E. (ed.) CT-RSA 2013. LNCS, vol. 7779, pp. 293–309. Springer, Heidelberg (2013). https://doi.org/10.1007/978-3-642-36095-4_19
15. Lindner, R., Peikert, C.: Better key sizes (and attacks) for LWE-based encryption. In: Kiayias, A. (ed.) CT-RSA 2011. LNCS, vol. 6558, pp. 319–339. Springer, Heidelberg (2011). https://doi.org/10.1007/978-3-642-19074-2_21. Decoding Radius and DMT Optimality, ISIT2011, pp. 1106–1110 (2011)
16. Micciancio, D., Regev, O.: Lattice-based cryptography. In: Bernstein, D.J., Buchmann, J., Dahmen, E. (eds.) Post-Quantum Cryptography 2009, pp. 147–191. Springer, Heidelberg (2009). https://doi.org/10.1007/978-3-540-88702-7_5
17. Victor Shoup's NTL library. http://www.shoup.net/ntl/
18. Regev, O.: On lattices, learning with errors, random linear codes, and cryptography. In: STOC 2005, pp. 84–93 (2005)
19. Schnorr, C.P.: Lattice reduction by random sampling and birthday methods. In: Alt, H., Habib, M. (eds.) STACS 2003. LNCS, vol. 2607, pp. 145–156. Springer, Heidelberg (2003). https://doi.org/10.1007/3-540-36494-3_14
20. Schnorr, C.P., Euchner, M.: Lattice basis reduction: improved practical algorithms and solving subset sum problems. Math. Program. **66**, 181–199 (1994)
21. TU Darmstadt Learning With Errors Challenge. https://www.latticechallenge.org/lwe_challenge/challenge.php
22. Xu, R.: Private communication (2017)
23. Xu, R., Yeo, S.L., Fukushima, K., Takagi, T., Seo, H., Kiyomoto, S., Henricksen, M.: An experimental study of the BDD approach for the search LWE problem. In: Gollmann, D., Miyaji, A., Kikuchi, H. (eds.) ACNS 2017. LNCS, vol. 10355, pp. 253–272. Springer, Cham (2017). https://doi.org/10.1007/978-3-319-61204-1_13

Cloud and E-commerce Security

A Security-Enhanced vTPM 2.0 for Cloud Computing

Juan Wang[1,2], Feng Xiao[1], Jianwei Huang[1], Daochen Zha[1],
Chengyang Fan[1,2(✉)], Wei Hu[1,2], and Huanguo Zhang[1,2]

[1] School of Computer, Wuhan University, Wuhan 430072, China
{jwang, f3i, jw.huang, daochenzha, cyfan,
liss}@whu.edu.cn, 564545297@qq.com
[2] Key Laboratory of Aerospace Information Security and Trusted Computing
Ministry of Education, Wuhan 430072, China

Abstract. Virtual Trusted Platform Module is required in cloud due to the scalability and migration of virtual machine. Through allocating a vTPM (Virtual Trusted Platform Module) to a VM (Virtual Machine), users of VM can use the vTPM's crypto and measurement function, like using the physical TPM. However, current vTPM still faces some key challenges, such as lacking runtime protection for the vTPM keys and code, lacking the mechanism of vTPM keys management, and lacking the support for the new TPM 2.0 specification. To address these limitations, we design vTPM 2.0 system and then propose a runtime protection approach for vTPM 2.0 based on SGX. Furthermore, we present vTPM key distribution and protection mechanism. We have implemented vTPM 2.0 system and the security-enhanced protection mechanism. As far as we know, the vTPM 2.0 system based on KVM and its security-enhanced mechanism are designed and implemented for the first time.

Keywords: vTPM · Trusted computing · Intel SGX · KMC · Cloud security

1 Introduction

Security is currently the key factor of restricting the development of cloud computing. In the cloud computing environment, how to protect the integrity of cloud infrastructure is a basic requirement of cloud security. Trusted computing has been considered as a feasible way to protect the integrity of cloud infrastructure.

However, in cloud computing environment, a lot of virtual machines may be running in a physical machine. It is difficult to use hardware TPM (Trusted Platform Module) to build trusted virtual execution environment. Therefore, vTPM has been put forward and used in cloud [13, 14].

IBM designed and implemented vTPM system on a virtualized hardware platform [11]. They virtualized the Trusted Platform Module by extending the standard TPM command set to support vTPM lifecycle management and enable trust establishment in the virtualized environment. Hence, each virtual machine instance gets its own unique and virtual TPM. However, vTPM still faces some key challenges in cloud.

© Springer International Publishing AG, part of Springer Nature 2018
S. Qing et al. (Eds.): ICICS 2017, LNCS 10631, pp. 557–569, 2018.
https://doi.org/10.1007/978-3-319-89500-0_48

Firstly, current vTPM lacks the mechanism to ensure the security vTPM itself. vTPM is an emulated software TPM. Due to lacking the physical hardware protection, it is subject to greater security threats compared with entity TPM. Furthermore, physical TPM may not provide runtime protection for vTPM because its NVRAM is usually very small and cannot support multiple virtual machines. In addition, entity TPM incurs a large overhead in performance when multiple vTPMs run at the same time.

Secondly, current vTPM cannot support TPM 2.0 specification. The architecture of TPM 2.0 is different with TPM 1.2, for example the keys of TPM 2.0 are generated by three persistent hierarchies and also it can support all kinds of cryptographic algorithms through incorporating an algorithm identifier. Hence we need to design vTPM based on TPM 2.0 architecture so as to improve vTPM 1.2.

Aiming at these problems, we propose security-enhanced vTPM 2.0 system which can support TCG TPM 2.0 specification and the keys and private data can be protected using SGX keys and enclave. To the best of our knowledge, it is the first time that vTPM 2.0 based on KVM (Kernel-based Virtual Machine) has been proposed and implemented. In our system, we also propose a vTPM 2.0 key distribution and protection mechanism based on KMC (Key Management Center) [20, 21]. Our approach can achieve the key hierarchy, which is same as the physical TPM. In addition, it can avoid the problem that new physical platform always regenerates the certificate for vTPM and rebuilds the trust binding during the migration for each time. Moreover, the basic seeds of vTPM can be backed up by KMC. When the vTPM is damaged, the keys and data of vTPM can be easily recovered. We also implement our system on KVM and Skylake CPU and evaluate vTPM 2.0 performance. The result shows that the SGX-enhanced vTPM brings about 20% additional overhead compared with the vTPM 2.0 which lacks security protection.

The remainder of this paper is organized as follows. Section 2 provides related work. Section 3 introduces the background of TPM 2.0 and SGX. Section 4 describes the design of security-enhanced vTPM 2.0. Section 5 proposes the vTPM key distribution and protection mechanism. The security-enhanced vTPM 2.0 implementation is described in Sect. 6. Section 7 presents the evaluation of vTPM 2.0. Section 8 provides the conclusion.

2   Related Work

Trusted computing technology is usually used to building trusted computing base of a computer system and protects the system integrity and confidentiality. Microsoft has leveraged trusted computing technology to implement trusted boot and its BitLocker has been used to disk encryption. Google chrome book [24] also has integrated TPM [23] chip to implement trusted boot and device anti-theft. Chen et al. [7] proposed cTPM which is practical, versatile, and easily applicable to cross-device trusted mobile applications. Santos et al. [6] provided a new trusted computing abstraction for designing trusted cloud services. Bates et al. [8] defined a provenance trusted computing base and created a trusted provenance-aware execution environment, collecting complete whole-system provenance. With the development of trusted computing, the limitations of

TCG TPM 1.2 architecture [25] are found, for example, cipher algorithms are not flexible. Hence TCG has proposed TPM 2.0 specification [1–5] and has published as ISO standard in 2015 [22]. Scarlata et al. [18] present a support for a variety of TPM model and different security properties of system framework based on Xen virtual machine hypervisor.

vTPM is a virtualized TPM which is generally used in virtualized environment, such as cloud computing platform, to build trust computing base. The most important work about virtualized TPM is that Berger et al. [9] from IBM designed and implemented a vTPM system on a virtualized hardware platform. They virtualized the Trusted Platform Module by extending the standard TPM command set to support vTPM lifecycle management and enable trust establishment in the virtualized environment. England and Loeser [15] extended hypervisor to add the vPCR (virtual PCR) and TPM context manager resource virtualization which allows guests operating systems to share hardware TPM. But the number of virtual machines on a physical machine is uncertain, their approach must meet performance bottleneck due to the limited memory space of TPM. In addition, Yang et al. [16] designed an Ng-vTPM framework. In Ng-vTPM framework, the EK and SRK are produced by physical TPM. The approach can protect the keys' security to some extent, but once the physical TPM is damaged, the keys of vTPM will not be used and recovered forever. Yan et al. [17] propose a secure enhancement named vTSE. The scheme utilizes the physical memory isolation feature of SGX to protect the code and data of vTPM instances, but they do not consider the vTPM keys recovery and cannot support TPM 2.0.

Current work is just support TPM 1.2. In our work, we design and implement the vTPM 2.0 on KVM. In addition, we provide runtime protection for code and private data of vTPM 2.0 using SGX. Furthermore, the vEK (virtual EK) and vSRK (virtual SRK) of vTPM 2.0 will be generated by a trusted party, KMC, and they are bound with VM UUID. Therefore, the keys are easy to be recovered once damaged.

3 Background

3.1 TPM 2.0

Trusted computing is a technology mainly used to protect the integrity and confidentiality of a system. It relies on TPM, which is a cryptographic coprocessor integrated in most commercial PCs and servers. TCG released TPM 1.2 specification in 2003. Currently, TCG has released TPM 2.0 specification [1–4] which has overcome some of the drawbacks of TPM 1.2. Compared with TPM 1.2, TPM 2.0 has many advantages.

TPM 1.2 can only support SHA1 and RSA, but TPM 2.0 can support all kinds of cryptographic algorithms, such as ECC, SHA256 and AES. Additionally, TPM 1.2 has only one key hierarchy: the storage hierarchy. TPM 2.0 has three persistent hierarchies: platform, storage, and endorsement, each with at least one root, such as EPS (Endorsement Primary Seed), SPS (Storage Primary Seed), and PPS (Platform Primary Seed). Furthermore, TPM 2.0 incorporates an algorithm identifier that would permit design of a TPM using any algorithm without changing the specification. Hence all kinds of cipher algorithms, such as Chinese commercial cipher algorithms SM2, SM3 and SM4 can be integrated easily. In addition, TPM 2.0 unifies the way all entities in a

TPM that are authorized. Besides the traditional password and HMAC authentication methods, the authentication method based on policy authorization has been added. It allows one or more authorization policies are used, which can enhance key's security. Last but not least, TPM 2.0 enhances the robustness. In the TPM 2.0 specification, some important things can be sealed to a PCR (platform configuration register) value approved by a particular signer instead of to a particular PCR value. Additionally, platform hierarchy allows OEM (Original Equipment Manufacturer) directly to use the function of TPM in BIOS without considering the OS' s support.

3.2   SGX

The Software Guard Extension (SGX) [26, 27] was introduced in 2013 by Intel Corporation. It protects a portion of the application's memory space and places code and data in this container that Intel calls enclave [12, 28]. Once the protected part of the application is loaded into the enclave, SGX will protect them from external process such as OS, drivers, BIOS, hypervisor and System Management Mode (SMM). Moreover, when the process terminates, its enclaves will be destroyed and the runtime data and code that are protected in the enclave will disappear. SGX also provides the seal function to encrypt the data and store it on the permanent media and then we can restore it in enclave when we need to use it again.

In addition to providing security attributes of memory isolation and protection. SGX architecture also supports attestation function. In SGX, attestation [30] is to prove the identity of the platform, and supports two attestations, local attestation between enclaves and remote attestation by a third party.

4   Design of Security-Enhanced vTPM 2.0

In this section, we design security-enhanced vTPM 2.0 architecture. Specifically, each VM can get its unique vTPM 2.0 devices with TPM 2.0 functionality.

As shown in Fig. 1, our security-enhanced vTPM 2.0 architecture includes the following basic components: vTPM 2.0 management, Libtpms 2.0, NVRAM files, tpm2driver, tpm_tis and SeaBIOS. The vTPM 2.0 management module implements vTPM management, such as vTPM creating, command processing interface etc. Libtpms 2.0 is the main module which can provide emulated TPM function in hypervisor. NVRAM files save the seeds, keys, PCRs and other private data. The module tpm2driver provides the interfaces to access TPM 2.0 hardware device. Tpm_tis emulates the hardware interface of TPM interface specification. SeaBIOS is a virtual

BIOS served for guest OS. In our system, the key modules of vTPM 2.0 including Libtpms 2.0, NVRAM, are sealed by SGX keys and isolated in a SGX enclave.

Libtpms 2.0 a TPM emulator, is the key module of vTPM 2.0 which is able to provide all the TPM 2.0 functions and command sets. Due to supporting multiple virtual machines on the same physical platform to access TPM 2.0 resources independently without impacting each other, we design Libtpms 2.0 as a shared software library located in host operating system. Libtpms 2.0 consists of tpm module, platform module, Crypto Engine module, and include module. TPM module implements the

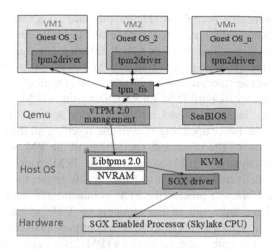

Fig. 1. Security-enhanced vTPM2.0 architecture

reset of NVRAM, the initialization of TPM components and the process of command. Platform module implements the creation of NVRAM file, the set of locality and the management of power state of TPM. The Crypto Engine module packages the realization of crypto algorithms provided by TPM and implements them through calling interfaces provided by OpenSSL.

Because Libtpms 2.0 module undertakes the core function of vTPM 2.0, its code and process need to be protected. We isolated the module into a SGX enclave. When Libtpms 2.0 is loaded, the SGX enclave is created and then Libtpms 2.0 program is measured to validate its integrity. Once the integrity is not tampered with, Libtpms 2.0 code will be executed in the enclave EPC (enclave page cache). Hence the program is protected in runtime and only itself can access the code in the enclave. The untrusted part of vTPM 2.0, such as vTPM 2.0 management module, just can call the function of Libtpms 2.0 through enclave call (ecall) and out call (ocall).

NVRAM is like TPM memory. Due to lacking the isolated physical NVRAM of TPM, it is designed as a separated file which saves the keys, PCR values, seeds and other private data. When a vTPM 2.0 device is created, a NVRAM file will be also created. Because the important data of vTPM is saved in NVRAM file, it is vital for vTPM security. Hence, we leverage SGX sealing to protect NVRAM. To preserve some secret data in an enclave for future use, SGX offers a sealing function. Sealing can encrypt the data inside an enclave and store them on a permanent medium such as a hard disk drive, so the data can be used the next time. When sealing data, there are two options available: sealing to the current enclave using the current version of the enclave measurement (MRENCLAVE) or sealing to the enclave author uses the identity of the enclave author (MRSIGNER). In this work, we use both mechanisms. The private data of NVRAM is sealed by the seal key which is generated in the corresponding enclave. When the NVRAM file is loaded into RAM, it will be unsealed and isolated in an enclave. Therefore the software except for Libtpms 2.0, including OS, drivers, BIOS and hypervisor cannot access the data of NVRAM.

Tpm2driver is generally used to provide the interfaces to access TPM 2.0 hardware device. Tpm_tis emulates the hardware interface of TIS (TPM Interface Specification) in QEMU and implements the interfaces to call Libtpms 2.0. SeaBIOS also plays an important part in the process of creating a VM on KVM platform. Apart from implementing the whole standard calling interfaces as a typical x86 hardware BIOS, SeaBIOS is extended to support TPM by initializing the vTPM 2.0 when creating a VM. This includes allocating a fixed virtual memory address in which the vTPM communicates with the lower operating system and resetting all the registers of vTPM.

When a VM sends a TPM command, tpm2driver of the VM will firstly talk to the tpm_tis frontend emulated by QEMU to deliver the TPM request. Then the tpm_tis frontend in QEMU delivers the request to Libtpms 2.0 driver, the driver will call the Libtpms 2.0 shared library to process the TPM command and return the results. This method does not have any limit of the numbers of VM (as long as the hardware resources permit). All that a user needs to do is to configure an exclusive NVRAM used to save all the persistent state and data for the vTPM 2.0 in each VM. During the VM migration, the corresponding NVRAM is migrated along with the VM and then the VM can continue to use vTPM 2.0 resources on the new platform.

5   The Key Distribution and Protection Mechanism of vTPM 2.0

When vTPM 2.0 is protected using SGX enclave, its keys and PCRs are encrypted by the CPU supported SGX. Once a virtual machine with vTPM 2.0 device is migrated, the vTPM 2.0 device also need to be migrated. However, the SGX keys cannot be migrated. Hence, the trust chain between vTPM and physical CPU will be broken during the vTPM migration. In addition, the current method cannot support key recovery. Once vTPM is damaged, the keys of vTPM will be lost. To solve the problems, we propose a vTPM 2.0 key distribution and protection mechanism based on KMC and Intel SGX.

In our method, the primary seeds of vTPM 2.0 including EPS (Endorsement Primary Seeds), SPS (Storage Primary Seeds) and PPS (Platform Primary Seeds) will be generated by KMC and then distributed to vTPM 2.0 by encrypted and secure channel. The primary seeds will be encrypted and saved in KMC and this process is carried out in the Enclave safe. Meanwhile, the primary seeds in a virtual machine will be encrypted by SGX key on host. Once physical CPU or vTPM is damaged, KMC can recover the primary seeds and then recover vTPM keys. The key distribution and protection process of vTPM 2.0 is described as shown Fig. 2. The encrypted communication channel is established using the SGX remote authentication feature. In order to achieve encrypted communication channel, it needs to introduce a special quoting enclave which is used to generate the credential that reflects enclave and platform status. When the KMC wants to authenticate a VM, the VM first executes the EREPORT instruction to generate the REPORT structure and then use the report key of quoting enclave to generate a MAC, along with the REPORT send to quoting enclave. Then the quoting enclave packs them into a quote structure QUOTE and signs it with EPID. Finally the quoting enclave sends QUOTE and signature to KMC.

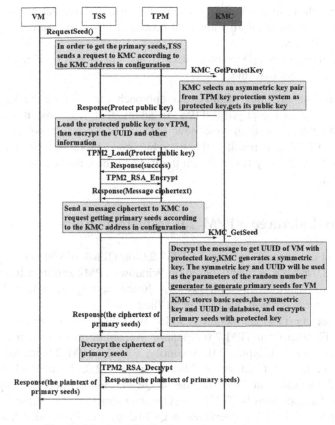

Fig. 2. The key distribution and protection process

1. A virtual machine communicates with TSS (Trusted Software Stack) and calls API (Application Programming Interface) to request getting primary seeds at startup process. Its UUID (Universally Unique Identifier) is as a parameter of the request.
2. In order to get the primary seeds, TSS sends a message to KMC according to the KMC address in configuration.
3. KMC selects an asymmetric key pair (e.g. RSA) from key protection system as a protected key, gets its public key and returns the protected public key to TSS.
4. TSS calls TPM2_Load to load the protected public key to vTPM, then calls TPM2_RSA_Encrypt to encrypt them and sends the cipher text to KMC, requests KMC to send basic seeds.
5. After KMC gets the encrypted request, it will use TPM interface to decrypt the cipher text to get the request with the private key. Then KMC will generate a symmetric key. Furthermore, the symmetric key and UUID will be used as the parameters of the random number generator to generate basic seeds for the virtual machine.

6. KMC stores the basic seeds, the symmetric key and UUID in database, and encrypts basic seeds and other information with protected key, then sends back the cipher text to vTPM TSS.
7. TSS calls TPM2_RSA_Decrypt to decrypt the cipher text, and returns the basic seeds to the virtual machine.

Compared with previous method, our approach can achieve the key hierarchy, which is the same as the physical TPM. In addition, it can avoid the problem that during the migration for each time new physical platform always regenerates the certificate for vTPM and rebuilds the trust bindings. Moreover, the basic seeds of vTPM can be backed up by KMC. When the vTPM is bad, the keys and data of vTPM can be recovered.

6   Security-Enhanced vTPM 2.0 Implementation

We implement our security-enhanced vTPM 2.0 on QEMU/KVM and Skylake CPU. Our Libtpms 2.0 module is mainly based on Windows TPM2 emulator from Microsoft. It only supports Windows operating system, hence we migrate it from Windows to Linux. During the migration, we rewrite all files.

Furthermore, the TPM 2.0 module is added into QEMU virtual machine. Firstly, we extract TPM libraries from TPM 2.0 emulator. According to source code analysis for TPM 2.0 and name it Libtpms 2.0. Secondly, we add TPM 2.0 module in QEMU virtual machine to call functions in library Libtpms 2.0. Then TPM 2.0 interface tpm_libtpms2.c is added in TPM module of QEMU. Furthermore we implement the TPM 2.0 interfaces defined in TPMDriverOps data structure with those functions.

The modules of TPM 2.0 interfaces in QEMU are mainly divided into two parts: the initialization module and the command process module. The initialization module includes device initialization, memory initialization, NVRAM initialization and so on. The command process module is responsible for receiving the TSS commands from VM, executing them and returning results.

In order to support TPM 2.0 device in VM, we update the device driver to TPM 2.0 in guest OS. Apart from modifying tpm.c, tpm.h, the Kconfig and the Makefile, the updating work is mainly in the new added tpm2_tis.c, which is the core file to realize TPM2.0 driver.

Firstly, we rewrite the entry function of loading and unloading driver. Then we begin to write the driver initialization function tpm2_tis_init(). This function will finish the register of TPM 2.0 device, including allocating its virtual memory address space, setting the default timeout, waiting delay, locality and all the internal flags of TIS and doing device self-testing. Besides, we write tpm2_tis_recv() and tpm2_tis_send() functions to send the TPM commands and receive the results. Finally, we write a couple of TPM 2.0 device attributes such as endorseauth, ownerauth, PCRs, phenable, shenable, ehenable. Users can access these attributes directly under /sys/class/misc/tpm0/device.

We also implement the protection mechanism of vTPM 2.0 based on SGX and KMC. When a virtual machine is created, a request seed message will be sent to KMC through encrypted communication channel. KMC then creates a RSA key pair and sends the public key to QEMU. QEMU furthermore sends VM UUID encrypted by public key to KMC through security channel. KMC creates an AES key by local crypto chip. The AES key and UUID are used as the parameters of the random number generator to generate primary seed for virtual machines. Meanwhile the basic seeds, UUID and AES key will be encrypted by local crypto chip and then stored in KMC database. The encrypted seed will be reply to QEMU. The Libtpms 2.0 module in QEMU, QEMU will create vEK, vSRK, and other root keys for the vTPM.

For a vTPM, QEMU allocates a memory file to save nonvolatile data. The vEK, vSRK, and other root keys are saved to this file named NVRAM. In order to protect the keys security, the NVRAM file is sealed and isolated by SGX keys and enclave. The keys are also backed up to KMC. In addition, the Libtpms 2.0 is compiled into a static library so as to be loaded and run in the SGX enclave. We also add the ecall and ocall in the vTPM management module and the Libtpms 2.0 module in order to implement the communication with them.

7 Evaluation

7.1 Function and Performance

Firstly we conduct function test of the vTPM 2.0. For the test we use a server with an Intel Skylake processor i7 6700 CPU, 8 G memory and 500 G hard disk. The host OS is Ubuntu 16.04 and the guest OS is Ubuntu 14.04. Once the virtual machine has successfully loaded the tpm2_tis.ko module, there will be a device named tpm0 under /sys/class/misc/, indicating that the TPM device is successfully emulated in the VM.

In vTPM 2.0, we have implemented the support of multiple virtual machines. We create five VMs in one host and conduct the testing of authorization policies setting, key derivation, digital signature and verification, encryption and decryption using SM2 algorithm and RSA algorithm respectively. In order to make sure that the vTPM 2.0 in five VMs have different primary seeds and primary keys, we make a comparison of the primary keys between two different VMs during the primary key derivation process. The result is shown in Fig. 3, proving that the vTPM 2.0 state in different VMs is independent and will not influence each other.

We have measured the runtime performance of the SGX-enhanced vTPM 2.0 and the vTPM 2.0 which lacks security protection. We calculate the time of calling TPM interfaces to create RSA and SM2 signature keys, conduct RSA and SM2 signature, and verify RSA and SM2 signature. These tests have been done for twenty times and average time is calculated so as to make the results more precise. Figure 4 shows the comparison results. The result shows SGX-enhanced vTPM brings about 20% additions overhead.

7.2 Migration

We also carried out the single VM and multiple VMs live migration test. [19] Migration channel using SSH RSA public key encryption, we record the start time and end time, and compute the time cost of migration. In addition to the normal time

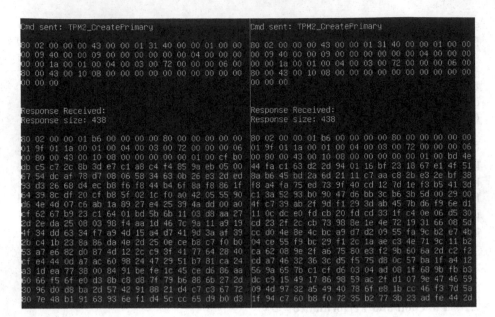

Fig. 3. TPM2_CreatePrimary result in two different VMs

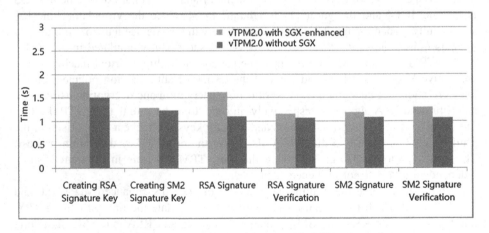

Fig. 4. The performance of vTPM with SGX-enhanced

needed for migration, VM with SGX-enhanced vTPM migration time also includes four parts: (1) unseal NVRAM from enclave; (2) migrate vTPM state; (3) the destination host decrypts NVRAM; (4) use new SGX to seal NVRAM. VM without vTPM does not include the four parts.

For a single VM migration, the VM image is Ubuntu 14.04 64-bit and the hardware resources allocated for the VM are 1 VCPU, 1024 MB RAM and 20 G Disk. For multiple VMs (ten units) concurrent migration, the allocated hardware resources for each VM are 1 VCPU, 1024 RAM, and 6 G Disk.

Our test is divided into four parts altogether: single_VM, single_VM_no_vtpm, multi_VM, multi_VM_no_vtpm. We test 100 times respectively and calculate the average value, the result is shown in Fig. 5.

We can know that the time-consuming of a single VM migration with SGX-enhanced vTPM is more than 5 s as compared to the single VM migration without it. When ten VMs migrate, the value is less than 10 s.

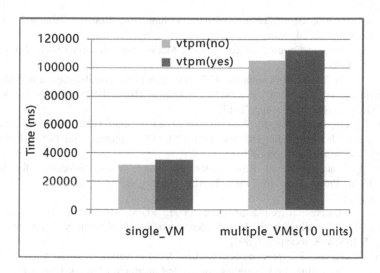

Fig. 5. The average time of VM migration

8 Conclusion

In the environments of cloud computing and NFV (Network Function Virtualization), vTPM is more and more used for protecting the security of virtualized machines and virtualized network function. TCG also presented TPM 2.0 specification to overcome the shortcomings of TPM 1.2. In this paper, we design a security-enhanced vTPM 2.0 system. Our approach cannot only support TPM 2.0 specification and KVM hypervisor, but also the keys and private data of vTPM 2.0 are statically and dynamically protected using Intel SGX. In addition, a vTPM key distribution and protection mechanism base on KMC are proposed, which can more conveniently support vTPM key recovery and vTPM migration. Moreover, we implement the security-enhanced vTPM 2.0 system and evaluate its performance.

Acknowledgment. This work is sponsored by the National Basic Research Program of China (973 Program) granted No. 2014CB340600, National Natural Science Foundation of China granted No. 61402342, 61173138 and 61103628, and the Huawei Technologies Co., Ltd. collaborative research project.

References

1. Trusted Computing Group. TPM Rev 2.0 Part1. Architecture. Family 2.0, Level 00. Revision 16 Jan 2014
2. Trusted Computing Group. TPM Rev 2.0 Part2. Structures. Family 2.0, Level 00. Revision 16 Jan 2014
3. Trusted Computing Group. TPM Rev 2.0 Part3. Commands. Family 2.0, Level 00. Revision 16 Jan 2014
4. Trusted Computing Group. TPM Rev 2.0 Part4. Supporting. Routines. Family 2.0, Level 00. Revision 16 Jan 2014
5. Trusted Computing Group. Trusted Platform Module Specification Family 2.0, Level 00. Revision 00.99 (2014)
6. Santos, N., Rodrigues, R., Gummadi, K.P., Saroiu, S.: Policy-sealed data: a new abstraction for building trusted cloud services. In: Proceedings of 21th USENIX Security Symposium on USENIX Security Symposium (2012)
7. Chen, C., Raj, H., Saroiu, S., Wolman, A.: cTPM: a cloud TPM for cross-device trusted applications. In: Proceedings of the 11th USENIX Conference on Networked Systems Design and Implementation (2014)
8. Bates, A., Tian, D., Kevin, R.B.: Trustworthy whole-system provenance for the Linux Kernel. In: Proceedings of 24th USENIX Security Symposium on USENIX Security Symposium (2015)
9. Berger, S., Cáceres, R., Goldman, K.A., et al.: vTPM: virtualizing the trusted platform module. In: Proceedings of the 15th Conference on USENIX Security Symposium, vol. 15, p. 21. USENIX Association (2006)
10. Anati, I., Gueron, S., Johnson, S., Scarlata, V.: Innovative technology for CPU based attestation and sealing. In: Proceedings of the 2nd International Workshop on Hardware and Architectural Support for Security and Privacy, vol. 13 (2013)
11. Sadeghi, A.-R., Stüble, C., Winandy, M.: Property-based TPM virtualization. In: Wu, T.-C., Lei, C.-L., Rijmen, V., Lee, D.-T. (eds.) ISC 2008. LNCS, vol. 5222, pp. 1–16. Springer, Heidelberg (2008). https://doi.org/10.1007/978-3-540-85886-7_1
12. Hoekstra, M., Lal, R., Pappachan, P., Phegade, V., Del Cuvillo, J.: Using innovative instructions to create trustworthy software solutions. In: HASP@ ISCA, pp. 11–17 (2013)
13. Garfinkel, T., Pfaff, B., Chow, J., et al.: Terra: a virtual machine-based platform for trusted computing. ACM SIGOPS Operating Syst. Rev. 37(5), 193–206 (2003)
14. Krautheim, F.J., Phatak, D.S., Sherman, A.T.: Introducing the trusted virtual environment module: a new mechanism for rooting trust in cloud computing. In: Acquisti, A., Smith, S. W., Sadeghi, A.-R. (eds.) Trust 2010. LNCS, vol. 6101, pp. 211–227. Springer, Heidelberg (2010). https://doi.org/10.1007/978-3-642-13869-0_14
15. England, P., Loeser, J.: Para-virtualized TPM sharing. In: Lipp, P., Sadeghi, A.-R., Koch, K.-M. (eds.) Trust 2008. LNCS, vol. 4968, pp. 119–132. Springer, Heidelberg (2008). https://doi.org/10.1007/978-3-540-68979-9_9
16. Yang, Y., Yan, F., Mao, J.: Ng-vTPM: a next generation virtualized TPM architecture. J. Wuhan Univ. (Nat. Sci. Ed.) 2, 103–111 (2015)
17. Yan, F., Yu, Z., Zhang, L., et al.: vTSE: a solution of SGX-based vTPM secure enhancement. Adv. Eng. Sci. 49(2), 133–139 (2017)
18. Scarlata, V., Rozas, C., Wiseman, M., Grawrock, D., Vishik, C.: TPM virtualization: building a general framework. In: Pohlmann, N., Reimer, H. (eds.) Trusted Computing. Vieweg+Teubner (2008)

19. Danev, B., Masti, R.J., Karame, G.O., et al.: Enabling secure VM-vTPM migration in private clouds. In: Proceedings of the 27th Annual Computer Security Applications Conference, pp. 187–196. ACM (2011)
20. Zhang, Q., Zhao, S., Qin, Y., et al.: Formal analysis of TPM 2.0 key management APIs. Chin. Sci. Bull. **59**(32), 4210–4224 (2014)
21. NIST, Recommendation for Key Management–Part 1: General (Revision 3), Special Publication 800–57
22. http://www.trustedcomputinggroup.org/media_room/news/392
23. http://www.infineon.com/cms/en/product/security-ic/trustedcomputing/channel.html?channel=db3a30433efacd9a013f10d2a7264daa
24. http://www.chromebookblog.com/tag/tpm-chips-for-chromebook/
25. Arthur, W., Challener, D.: Practical Guide to TPM 2.0 Using the Trusted Platform Module in the New Age of Security. Willey (2015)
26. Mckeen, F., Alexandrovich, I., Berenzon, A., et al.: Innovative instructions and software model for isolated execution (2013)
27. Intel Software Guard Extensions, https://software.intel.com/en-us/sgx
28. Sinha, R., Rajamani, S., Seshia, S., Vaswani, K.: Moat: verifying confidentiality of enclave programs. In: ACM Sigsac Conference on Computer and Communications Security, pp. 1169–1184 (2015)

SDAC: A New Software-Defined Access Control Paradigm for Cloud-Based Systems

Ruan He[1], Montida Pattaranantakul[2,3], Zonghua Zhang[2,3(✉)], and Thomas Duval[1]

[1] Orange labs, Châtillon, France
{ruan.he,thomas.duval}@orange.com
[2] IMT Lille Douai, Institut Mines-Télécom, Paris, France
{montida.pattaranantakul,zonghua.zhang}@imt-lille-douai.fr
[3] CNRS UMR 5157 SAMOVAR, Paris, France

Abstract. A cloud-based system usually runs in multiple geographically distributed datacenters, making the deployment of effective access control models extremely challenging. This paper presents a novel software-defined paradigm, called SDAC, to achieve scoped, flexible and dynamic access control. In particular, SDAC enables the tenant-specific generation of *access control model and policy (SMPolicy* in short), as well as their dynamic configuration by the cloud-hosting applications. To achieve that, SDAC uses an access control meta-model to initiate and customize different SMPolicies. Also, SDAC is decoupled into control plane and policy plane, allowing the global *SMPolicy* generated at the control plane to be efficiently propagated to the policy plane and enforced locally in different datacenters. As such, the local *SMPolicy* of a tenant can be synchronized with its global *SMPolicy* only when it's necessary, e.g., a user or a role cannot be identified. To validate the feasibility and effectiveness of SDAC, we implement a prototype in a carrier grade datacenter. The experimental results demonstrate that SDAC can achieve the desirable properties, maintain the throughput at a reasonable level regardless of the varying number of tenants, users, and datacenters, highly preserving scalability and adaptability.

1 Introduction

In the distributed cloud systems, one tenant can provision the resources from different cloud infrastructures. Considering the multi-tenancy, extremely dynamic and heterogeneous cloud environments, each tenant is expected to protect its users and resources with an effective access control model. However, the best practice of access control for cloud-based systems usually relies on the pre-definition of the access control models, e.g., Mandatory Access Control (MAC), Role Based Access Control (RBAC), while the tenant-specific and user-customized access control model remains unavailable.

© Springer International Publishing AG, part of Springer Nature 2018
S. Qing et al. (Eds.): ICICS 2017, LNCS 10631, pp. 570–581, 2018.
https://doi.org/10.1007/978-3-319-89500-0_49

Ideally, an access control paradigm for cloud-based systems should provide a mechanism for defining access control model on demand, as well as the dynamic specification of its policies at large scale. More importantly, the scope of an access control model and associated policies should be limited to an individual tenant instead of the whole system, while the tenant user is given the privilege to customize the most appropriate access control model and specify the corresponding policies. Then the policy of the tenant can be enforced at the multiple cloud infrastructures through a distributed access control framework.

To achieve these objectives, we propose a Software-Defined Access Control paradigm, called SDAC, which consists of an access control meta-model and a distributed framework: the meta-model is used for dynamically creating the access control model and policy (*SMPolicy*), while the distributed framework is used to enforce the policies in multiple datacenters. Thanks to the meta-model, SDAC is enabled with programmability, flexibility, and adaptability, allowing a tenant owner to define and customize his own access control model and specify the policies that are enforced inside the tenant. Also, the distributed framework makes SDAC scalable, enabling the access control policies to be effectively enforced at the tenant-level which is deployed across multiple datacenters.

To evaluate the feasibility and effectiveness of SDAC, we implement and deploy a prototype in a carrier grade cloud datacenter and conduct a set of experiments to validate its performance in terms of the desirable metrics, which is reported in Sect. 4. The design details of SDAC is presented in Sect. 3, covering the access control meta-model and the distributed framework. In Sect. 2, we briefly investigate the related work.

2 Related Work

Multi-tenancy is one of the salient features of cloud computing, which refers to the fact that the cloud infrastructure and its applications can be divided into the isolated sets of resources called tenants, according to different ownerships and requirements. As resources are distributed among several datacenters, their appropriate isolation and access control are key issues for both providers and users. However, as pointed out in [1,2], the conventional access control approaches are not suitable for the cloud, in which the resources are dynamically pooled and provisioned, the entities are heterogeneous, and the attributes are context-specific, resulting in sophisticated and fine-grained authorization requests.

It is well recognized that the access control policies needs to be created, configured or removed by the authorized users, so both DAC (Discretionary access control) and MAC allow to be specified the constrains on the assignment or the use of permissions [3]. For example, DAC allows the owner of an object to set up its access control list, while MAC supports the clearance and classification configuration by the administrator. However, these properties can not sufficiently meet all the requirements in the cloud, especially on the dynamic customization of access control models and the specification of policies. By leveraging the software-defined approach, our SDAC provides a *generic* and *independent* policy customization approach that can *dynamically* create a specific access control model, together with its policy, for a group of objects.

The notion of *scope* in access control was firstly introduced in MAC as category [4], which refers to the validity of security lattice and provides a finer grained security classification. Also, OrBAC (Organisation-based access control) defines one security policy for one organization [5], while attribute-based access control encapsulates policy definition and decision-making algorithms into an independent unit [6]. Then in [7], the authors extend the notion of scope for multi-tenancy with RBAC and establishes trust relationship between the scopes. However, in the cloud, each tenant needs an access control policy to define the rules that authorize the users to access the appropriate resources. If we treat a tenant as a *scope*, a generic data model is expected to customize the access control model for handling the dynamically created scopes. Unfortunately, to the best of our knowledge, few of the available access control paradigms can achieve such an objective. For example, IBM [8] proposed Tivoli Access Manager to provide best practice of web-based access control solution for protecting tenant's cloud resources and supporting multi-tenant architectures. In [9, 10], the authors presented distributed access control architectures for cloud computing, in which XML and XACML respectively, are used to formulate the access control policies. However, all of them have limited capability to generate different tenant-specific access control models and support distributed access control framework. In SDAC, we propose a *meta-model* to generate different access control models and policies, and present a four-layered framework to specify and enforce the tenant-specific access control policies in a *distributed* way, significantly improving the flexibility and dynamicity. In [16], a generic NFV based security management framework has been proposed, with an objective to orchestrating various security functions such as access control. However, the actual implementations have not been extensively discussed.

We have also seen tremendous efforts on designing access control schemes using cryptographic approaches [11], which mainly handle the access to the storage systems, while the protection scope of SDAC is all the computing resources (e.g., compute, storage, network) associated with the tenant. In [1], the authors pointed out that the user-role and role-permission assignments should be separately constructed using policies applied on the attributes of users, roles, the objects and the environment. Also, the attribute-based user-role and role-permission assignment rules should be applied in real-time in order to enforce access control decisions. Our SDAC successfully fulfills such requirements and provides a flexible way for the tenant owners to specify, configure, and manage access control model and policies on the fly according to the particular needs.

3   SDAC: Software-Defined Access Control Paradigm

In this section, we firstly identify the requirements on developing SDAC. We then specifically present the paradigm, which consists of a distributed framework and an access control meta-model.

3.1   Design Requirements

- **Tenant-specific and model generation on demand.** The protection scope should be limited to the tenants, so that the entities of the access control model (*e.g.*, subject, object, role, and related information) need to be specified based on particular tenant domain. As a tenant can be dynamically created or removed, the access control model and associated policies (Scoped Model and Policy (*SMPolicy*)) need to be generated or removed in real time.
- **Programmability of *SMPolicy*.** To facilitate the dynamic generation of SMPolicy, a meta-model needs to be developed through which each tenant can customize its access control model and policy set according to its specific security needs. As a tenant can be across multiple cloud infrastructures, the SMPolicy allows arbitrary update of any parts of the access control model instead of duplicating one complete access control model for each cloud.
- **Integration of diverse features.** The emerging access control models usually integrate diverse features to include more semantic information. For example, *session* in RBAC [12] can temporally activate or deactivate a user-role assignment, while the hierarchy role enables privilege inheritance from one role to another, and the *delegation* sets up a temporal trust relation between two users. UCON [13] provides continuous control through obligations and conditions, and it also enables attribute mutability as a supplementary instruction before or after an access decision [14].
- **Centralized control yet distributed enforcement.** To ensure the consistency and efficiency, a user should be able to create or configure a SMPolicy in a centralized way by describing all its datasets, while the policies need to be enforced in a distributed manner, covering all the datacenters that the tenant is deployed. More importantly, the policy updates should be delivered to the related enforcement components in the distributed infrastructure.

To meet the above requirements, we develop Software-Defined Access Control Paradigm (SDAC), which contains an access control meta-model and a distributed framework. In particular, the meta-model is used to initiate different access control models and policies (*SMPolicy*) for a scope, and the distributed framework is used to enforce the generated scoped policies. Specifically, the major operations of SDAC include: (1) creating a scope and identity entities involved in this scope; (2) generating an access control model; (3) specifying an access control policy based on the model, and; (4) enforcing the policies.

3.2   SDAC Framework

We propose SDAC framework to abstract and centralize policies into a control plane instead of distributing them to the local datacenters. As shown in Fig. 1, SDAC framework is composed of four planes, which are described as follows,

- **Application plane,** which hosts the applications that invoke PAP (Policy Administration Point) to customize *SMPolicy*. In [15], the feasibility of this access control framework has been demonstrated through a NFV orchestrator, which can be treated as an application.

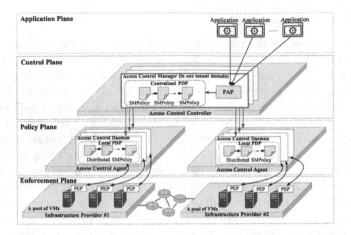

Fig. 1. Design architecture of SDAC

- **Controller plane:** an *Access Control Controller* containing multiple *Access Control Managers*, each of which is in charge of one tenant and has a global view about all the authorization related information and rules for that tenant. In another word, the *Access Control Manager* defines *SMPolicies* for each tenant. As in XACML [17], a PAP and a PDP (Policy Decision Point) are used for authorization.

- **Policy plane:** *Access Control Agents* are deployed in each local datacenter, serving as the agent of *Access Control Controller*. Each *Access Control Agent* holds a set of *Access Control Daemons*, which contain all the related information about the local usage of one tenant. The global *SMPolicies* are defined in the control plane, while the local *SMPolicies* are stored in the local PDP of each access control daemon. Thus, the users only need to customize the *SMPolicies* in the control plane, eventually leading to the automated customization of *SMPolicies* in the policy plane.

- **Enforcement plane:** the PEPs (Policy Enforcement Points) are installed into cloud-based systems for sending authorization requests to the corresponding local PDP running in the *Access Control Daemon* and finally enforces the decision from that distributed PDP.

3.3   Access Control Meta-model

The purpose of access control meta-model is to instantiate an access control model, *e.g.*, DAC, MAC, RBAC for a specific scope (one tenant in the cloud). To do that, we use attribute-based specification, which has potential to cover various access control models [18]. In particular, the attributes are those security-related properties such as role, domain, group, and type. Then a policy can define a set of rules based on the values of these attributes. To develop the meta-model, two notations are given as follows,

- Entity $E = \{e_i\}$, which can be used as *subjects* or *objects* in the access control model, and they can be either users or cloud resources.
- Information I: the related security properties of each entity, *e.g.*, user roles, file types. One entity can be assigned with several types of properties, called categories, and each of which has a set of values, *e.g.*, $I = InfoCategory \times CatScope$, where *InfoCategory* is a set of the types of security properties, and *CatScope* is a set of potential values for each category.

We suppose that each *SMPolicy* (Meta-model based Access Control Model and Policy) specified by the SDAC meta-model consists of an access control model (*ACM*) and an access control policy (*ACP*), which are described as follows.

Access Control Model: $ACM = (MD, MR)$, which includes a meta-data (MD) and a meta-rule (MR). In particular, MD defines a schema to instantiate an access control model, i.e., $MD = (SubjectMD, ObjectMD, ActionMD)$, where $SubjectMD, ObjectMD, ActionMD \subseteq InfoCategory$. The MR defines the schema to create the rules, which involve information categories based on which an authorization-related instruction can be executed, i.e.,

$SubjectCategory \times ObjectCategory \times ActionCategory \rightarrow Instruction$; where

$SubjectCategory \subseteq SubjectMD$, $ObjectCategory \subseteq ObjectMD$, $Action Category \subseteq ActionMD$, $Instruction$: $\{AuthzDecision, PolicyUpdate, Policy Chain\}$

For instance, the rule can be a decision to grant or deny an authorization request, update the policy itself, or redirect to another policy in the policy chaining. Thus, by extending the conventional access control policy with generic instructions, the meta-model is able to instantiate different access control models and advanced control features, and integrate them within one policy chain.

Access Control Policy: $ACP = (D, R, P, EDAss)$, which creates an access control policy for the access control model that is applied to a particular scope *e.g.*, one tenant in the cloud. The policy specifies potential values called data (D) for each category, establishes rules (R), identifies perimeter (P) and assigns values to each entities ($EDAss$) of this policy. Specifically,

- Data (D) is a complete set of values for each category for subjects, objects, actions, i.e., $D = (SubjectD, ObjectD, ActionD, Instruction)$, where $SubjectD \subseteq SubjectMD \times CatScope$, $ObjectD \subseteq ObjectMD \times CatScope$, $ActionD \subseteq ActionMD \times CatScope$
- Rule (R) specifies user privileges by using category values of subjects, objects, and actions to determine the instructions to be triggered, i.e., $R : SubjectD \times ObjectD \times ActionD \rightarrow Instruction$. As aforesaid, three types of instruction are identified, (1) authorization decision (grant or deny); (2) policy update to modify the category values of an entity; (3) policy chain to route the request to another policy.
- Perimeter (P) is a set of entities (subjects, objects, actions) to be protected. As each SMPolicy is applied to one particular scope, we need to define its

perimeter by identifying the entities that are involved in this scope, i.e., $P = (S, O, A)$, where $S, O, A \subseteq E$.

- Entity-Data Assignment ($EDAss$) is used to establish many-to-many relationship between related data and entities by assigning category value to each entity. Formally, $EDAss = (SubjectDataAss, ObjectDataAss, ActionDataAss)$, where $SubjectDataAss \subseteq S \times SubjectD$, $ObjectDataAss \subseteq O \times ObjectD$ $ActionDataAss \subseteq A \times ActionD$.

Policy Decision Algorithm, which is based on the values of categories. When an access request arrives, the algorithm fetches category values of subject, object and action to interpret the request through the value assignment of each entity. Then the algorithm checks whether these values match some rules in the policy. That says, access request (s_i, o_j, a_k) may trigger an instruction $inst_l$ if:

$$(\{s_i\} \times SubjectDataAss, \{o_j\} \times ObjectDataAss, \{a_k\} \times ActionDataAss, inst_l) \subseteq R$$

where $\{e\} \times DataAss$ means fetching all attributes of the entity e from its entity-data assignment.

3.4 SMPolicy Programmability

To generate an access control model, we use object-oriented approach. In particular, in access control model, an *object* is usually the resource that can be manipulated by a *subject*. If we model the *subjects*, *objects*, *attributes*, and the *relations* between them as *objects*, the authorized users then can manipulate them through a customization interface, *e.g.*, creating, modifying, and removing any parts of an access control model. As relations are also treated as *objects* that can be manipulated, users can modify attribute assignment as well. As shown in Fig. 2, SDAC meta-model enables dynamic creation of access control model and policy through a policy customization interface, which allow any SMPolicy defined by meta-model to be programmed and configured.

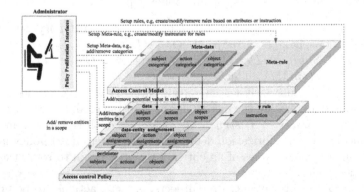

Fig. 2. SDAC data model: key components and customization

For a particular tenant, a corresponding *SMPolicy* is created as follows,

1. Through the meta-data interface, the admin creates categories for *subjects, objects* and *actions*, then defines *meta-rules*, which specify categories to be used to build rules. The meta-data (MD), together with meta-rule (MR), constructs a customized access control model.
2. The admin creates an access control policy based on this access control model by specifying the values for each category, and creating rules (*instructions*) based on these values and the *meta-rule*;
3. The admin identifies *subjects, objects* and *actions* that need to be protected by this *SMPolicy*, and finally assigns values to each category *subjects, objects* and *actions*.

To illustrate the creation of *SMPolicy*, an implementation of MLS (Multi-Level Security) with *SMPolicy* is given here. In particular, MLS sets up security levels for subjects and objects, authorization is then granted through their comparison. By applying SDAC meta-model, we can define the *SMPolicy* of MLS as follows,

- E = {$user_0, user_1, user_2, vm_0, vm_1$, start-vm, stop-vm}
- InfoCategory = (subject-security-level, object-security-level, action-type)
- CatScope = ((subject-security-level, [low, medium, high]), (object-security-level, [low, medium, high]), (action-type, [vm-action, storage-action]))

Meta-data MD:

- SubjectMD = (subject-security-level)
- ObjectMD = (object-security-level)
- ActionMD = (action-type)

Meta-rule MR:

- SubjectCategory = (subject-security-level)
- ObjectCategory = (object-security-level)
- ActionCategory = (action-type)
- Instruction = (AuthzDecision)

Data D:

- SubjectD = (subject-security-level, [low, medium, high])
- ObjectD = (object-security-level, [low, medium, high])
- ActionD = (action-type, [vm-action, storage-action])

Rule R:

- r = ((subject-security-level, [high]), (object-security-level, [medium]), (action-type, [vm-action], (instruction, [grant]))
- r = ((subject-security-level, [high, medium]), (object-security-level, [low]), (action-type, [vm-action], (instruction, [grant]))

Perimeter P:

- S: $\{user_0, user_1\}$
- O: $\{vm_0, vm_1\}$
- A: $\{$start-vm, stop-vm$\}$

Entity-Data Assignment $EDAss$:

- SubjectDataAss = $((user_0,$ high$), (user_1,$ medium$))$
- ObjectDataAss = $((vm_0,$ medium$), (vm_1,$ low$))$
- ActionDataAss = $(($start-vm, vm-action$), ($stop-vm, vm-action$))$

In this MLS, a user can start or stop a VM if and only if his or her security level is higher than that of VM. For example, $user_0$ can manipulate vm_0 and vm_1, while $user_1$ can only manipulate vm_1.

3.5   SMPolicy Chaining

The basic idea of policy chaining is to combine and route several *SMPolicies* together. For example, the authors of [6] have applied this idea to attribute-based access control for grid computing. For the cloud-based systems, it is well recognized that developing a generic access control model meeting the diverse requirements of all the tenants is mission impossible. We therefore propose to chain several feature-specific *SMPolicies* together rather than develop a generic one for implementing the integrated access control semantics. In doing so, an existing sophisticated access control policy with advanced features can be decomposed into a set of atomic SMPolicies, each of which can implement either a basic access control model or a particular advanced feature, e.g., session, delegation.

Formally, we define policy chain as a set of ordered SMPolicies, each of which is atomic that contains all the dataset about its model and policy. By introducing the concept of *instruction* in the SDAC meta-model, we extend an access control model to be more sophisticated to specify advanced control features, such as session in RBAC or continuous control in UCON. That says, a *SMPolicy* can be used to realize either a basic access control policy or an advanced feature. When a request occurs, the *SMPolicy* firstly fetches all the information related to this request. Based on their category values, it then decides whether to launch one or several instructions. For a basic access control policy, an access control policy makes a decision for triple-request (subject, object and action), where a subject (user) intends to take an action on an object. The resulting instruction of this *SMPolicy* is an authorization decision like grand or deny, based on the available information. If a *SMPolicy* specifies a control feature like session, obligation, the implication of triple-request (subject, object, action) refers to the fact that modifying (action) an attribute (object) of an entity (subject). The resulting *instruction* is then to update the *SMPolicy*. Similarly, if the *instruction* involves forwarding the request to another *SMPolicy*, then the triple-request (subject, object, action) means sending (action) the request (subject) to another *SMPolicy* (object). The three fields of an *instruction* allow to modify the *SMPolicy* and its dataset, route the request and/or dataset to another *SMPolicy* and finally validate the request.

4   Experiments

Our SDAC prototype is deployed into three HA (High-Availability) OpenStack clusters, one serves as master platform, while another two run as slave platforms. Each one is equipped with 5 servers (Intel E5-2680 with 48 cores/251G RAM), of which 3 are controller nodes and 2 are compute nodes. The 6th server is set up as a security node running SDAC. Specifically, our SDAC is implemented based on a micro-service architecture, which means that both *Access Control Manager* in the control plane and *Access Control Daemon* in the policy plane are implemented through a set of containers.

Throughput of the Policy Engine. One of the key metrics for evaluating the capability of access control policy engine (PDP) is *throughput, e.g.,* the number of authorization requests per second that it can handle. In this evaluation, we set *SMPolicy* as a basic *RBAC*, which has 10 users, 5 roles and 10 objects. We gradually increased the number of requests to observe the throughput of the policy engine. As shown in Fig. 3, the average throughput arrives its limit (4.1 requests per second) when the request frequency was adjusted from 1 to 20 requests per second. It is worth nothing that, thanks to the micro-service architecture, one identical *SMPolicy* container will be automatically launched when the number of request is beyond the throughput of the policy engine.

SMPolicy Chaining Overhead. Our SDAC allows several *SMPolicies* to be chained together to meet specific policy requirements. This apparently will incur certain overhead. In this experiment, we configure one tenant (10 users, 5 roles and 10 objects) with a purpose to comparing the authorization overhead between (1) $RBAC_0$ implemented by one policy only; and (2) $RBAC_0$ that is realized by chaining 2 SMPolicies together. The results is shown in Fig. 4. In case (1), the throughput was around 4 requests per second, while in case (2), the throughput was 2.9 requests per. It can be concluded that the extra overhead introduced by policy chaining is around 32%.

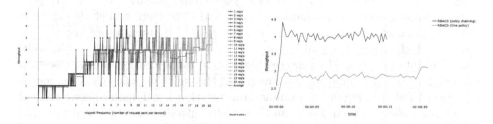

Fig. 3. Throughput: # of requests per second   **Fig. 4.** SMPolicy chaining overhead

Scalability with the increasing number of users. We set *SMPolicy* as a basic *RBAC* for one tenant, which has 5 predefined roles and 10 VMs (as objects). We then increased the number of users and observed that the throughput remained stable as 5.9 requests per second when there were 50 users. Then the throughput

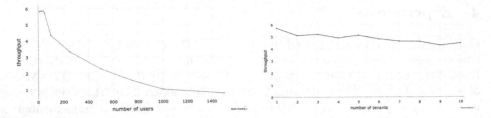

Fig. 5. # of users varying from 10 to 1500   **Fig. 6.** # of tenants varying from 1 to 10

decreased dramatically when the number of users got larger than 50, as shown in Fig. 5. The worst case was 0.5 requests per second when the number of users reached to 1500.

Scalability with the varying number of tenants. To evaluate its scalability, we configured each tenant which has 10 users, 5 predefined roles and 10 VM objects. As shown in Fig. 6, the throughput of policy engine varied from 5.7 requests per second (one tenant) to 4.5 requests per second (10 tenants), showing slight degradation. The reason is that SDAC is implemented using the micro-service architecture, in which *SMPolicies* of each tenant run in a dedicated and independent containers, enabling SDAC to scale freely with multiple tenants.

5   Conclusion

This paper proposed a software-defined access control paradigm called SDAC for cloud-based systems, which requires the access control to be dynamic, adaptive, fully distributed and easily managed. Specifically, SDAC is featured with a distributed framework and a meta model. The distributed framework allows the access control models and policies to be distributed to the multiple tenants in different could datacenters, while they can be managed and updated in a centralized way. The meta-model provides a generic customization interface to generate different access control models on demand. The meta-model also extends conventional access control to be more sophisticated by integrating instruction, through which an access control policy can implement other operations in addition to grant and deny. More interestingly, some advanced features like session and delegation can be enabled and integrated through the policy chaining mechanisms in PDP. It is worth mentioning, however, that the dynamic access control model and policy customization can potentially introduce novel security vulnerabilities, and the policy chaining may cause conflicts. Thus, our future work will be focused on validating the correctness of access control model generation and chaining. Trust relationship between different tenants in the cloud will be also considered in the policy chaining.

References

1. Meghanathan, N.: Review of access control models for cloud computing. Comput. Sci. Inf. Technol. **3**, 77–85 (2013)
2. Ngo, C., Demchemko, Y., de Laat, C.: Multi-tenant attribute-based access control for cloud infrastructure services. J. Inf. Secur. Appl. **27**, 65–84 (2016)
3. Sandhu, R.S., Samarati, P.: Access control: principle and practice. IEEE Commun. Mag. **32**(9), 40–48 (1994)
4. Sandhu, R.S.: Lattice-based access control models. Computer **26**(11), 9–19 (1993)
5. Kalam, A.A.E., Baida, R.E., Balbiani, P., Benferhat, S., Cuppens, F., Deswarte, Y., Miege, A., Saurel, C., Trouessin, G.: Organization based access control. In: POLICY 2013, pp. 120–131 (2003)
6. Lang, B., Foster, I., Siebenlist, F., Ananthakrishnan, R., Freeman, T.: A flexible attribute based access control method for grid computing. J. Grid Comput. **7**, 169–180 (2009)
7. Calero, J.M., Edwards, N., Kirschnick, J., Wilcock, L., Wray, M.: Toward a multi-tenancy authorization system for cloud services. IEEE Secur. Priv. **8**(6), 48–55 (2010)
8. IBM: Best practices for access control in multi-tenant cloud solutions using Tivoli Access Manager, May 2011. https://www.ibm.com/developerworks/cloud/library/cl-cloudTAM/index.html
9. Almutairi, A.A., Sarfraz, M.I.: A distributed access control architecture for cloud computing. IEEE Softw. **29**(2), 36–44 (2012)
10. Decat, M., Lagaisse, B., Van Landuyt, D., Crispo, B., Joosen, W.: Federated authorization for software-as-a-service applications. In: Meersman, R., Panetto, H., Dillon, T., Eder, J., Bellahsene, Z., Ritter, N., De Leenheer, P., Dou, D. (eds.) OTM 2013. LNCS, vol. 8185, pp. 342–359. Springer, Heidelberg (2013). https://doi.org/10.1007/978-3-642-41030-7_25
11. Yu, S., Wang, C., Ren, K., Lou, W.: Achieving secure, scalable, and fine-grained data access control in cloud computing. In: IEEE INFOCOM 2010, pp. 1–9 (2010)
12. Ferraiolo, D.F., Sandhu, R., Gavrila, S., Kuhn, D.R., Chandramouli, R.: Proposed NIST standard for role-based access control. ACM Trans. Inf. Syst. Secur. **4**(3), 224–274 (2001)
13. Park, J., Sandhu, R.: The UCONABC usage control model. ACM Trans. Inf. Syst. Secur. **7**(1), 128–174 (2004)
14. Park, J., Zhang, X., Sandhu, R.: Attribute mutability in usage control. In: Farkas, C., Samarati, P. (eds.) DBSec 2004. IIFIP, vol. 144, pp. 15–29. Springer, Boston, MA (2004). https://doi.org/10.1007/1-4020-8128-6_2
15. Pattaranantakul, M., Tseng, Y., He, R., Zhang, Z., Meddahi, A.: A first step towards security extension for NFV orchestrator. In: 2016 IEEE Trust-com/BigDataSE/ISPA, pp. 598–605 August 2016
16. Pattaranantakul, M., He, R., Meddahi, A., Zhang, Z.: SecMANO: towards network functions virtualization (NFV) based security management and orchestration. In: ACM International Workshop on SDN-NFVSec 2017, pp. 25–30, March 2017
17. XACML:3.0: eXtensible access control markup language (XACML) Version 3.0, OASIS Standard (2013). http://portal.etsi.org/NFV/NFV_White_Paper.pdf
18. Jin, X., Krishnan, R., Sandhu, R.: A unified attribute-based access control model covering DAC, MAC and RBAC. In: Cuppens-Boulahia, N., Cuppens, F., Garcia-Alfaro, J. (eds.) DBSec 2012. LNCS, vol. 7371, pp. 41–55. Springer, Heidelberg (2012). https://doi.org/10.1007/978-3-642-31540-4_4

A Cross-Modal CCA-Based Astroturfing
Detection Approach

Xiaoxuan Bai[1], Yingxiao Xiang[1], Wenjia Niu[1(✉)], Jiqiang Liu[1(✉)],
Tong Chen[1], Jingjing Liu[1], and Tong Wu[2]

[1] Beijing Key Laboratory of Security and Privacy in Intelligent Transportation,
Beijing Jiaotong University, Beijing 100044, China
{niuwj,jqliu}@bjtu.edu.cn
[2] Tsinghua University, Beijing 100084, China

Abstract. In recent years, astroturfing can generate abnormal, damaging even illegal behaviors in cyberspace which may mislead the public perception and bring a bad effect on both Internet users and society. This paper aims to design a algorithm to detect astroturfing in online shopping effectively and help users to identify potential online astroturfers quickly. The previous work used single method text-text or image-image to detect astroturfing, while in this paper we first propose a cross-modal canonical correlation analysis model (CCCA) which combines text and images. First, we identify several features of astroturfing and analysis these features. Then, we use feature extraction algorithm, image similarity algorithm and CCA algorithm, and propose a cross-modal method to detect astroturfing which release comments with pictures. We also conduct an experiment on a Taobao dataset to verify our method. The experimental results show that the supervised method proposed is effective.

Keywords: Astroturfing detection
Canonical correlation analysis algorithm · Cross-modal method
CCCA model

1 Introduction

With the rapid development of Internet, especially the popularity of the online shopping, produced unprecedented significant impact on the way that people live and goods purchase. However, there are a large number of astroturfing with their false comments in the product comments, which may affect the user's point of view and guide public opinion [1,2]. Because the network is virtual, consumers are difficult to select the best quality goods among various kinds of products through the pictures. In recent years, online shopping has become a part of people's lives, although consumers enjoy the convenience of online shopping. So consumers tend to refer to the comments in the goods to decide the choice, but in order to improve the credibility, sales, baby popularity, most merchants use astroturfing to brush praise. The comments of astroturfing is likely to mislead the

© Springer International Publishing AG, part of Springer Nature 2018
S. Qing et al. (Eds.): ICICS 2017, LNCS 10631, pp. 582–592, 2018.
https://doi.org/10.1007/978-3-319-89500-0_50

purchasers and affect them to select the goods incorrectly, the existence of false comments seriously affect the reference value of the information, misleading the consumer's judgment of potential consumers greatly. Therefore, in order to create a good online shopping environment and protect the interests of consumers, detecting the online astroturfing is very important [3].

At present, most of the comments on shopping sites is a combination of text and picture comments website such as Taobao. Astroturfing which post comments with pictures in online shopping can be probably divided into two categories. One class is that most of the astroturfing tend to post similar comments directly and selected the original pictures of goods in the comments for convenience, we can see that their images are almost identical, and the words in the text comment are similar. The word repetition rate is so high and the overall meaning of the comment is roughly the same. In addition, the pictures selected or intercepted by users might be affected by resolution, format, and so on. Therefore, the pictures similarity will not be high only through the picture recognition, it is difficult to detect the astroturfing. The combination of pictures and text can express the overall meaning of the comments, and improve the similarity of the comments.

To warm up, we can use the CCCA model to combine the text and the picture and transform them to each other. Hence, we label this waterarmy "astrotufing 1" who publish similar text and images, and we use CCCA model to detect them.

The other class is that a lot of astroturfing post other pictures casually instead of buying goods which makes the pictures of comments are inconsistent with the corresponding goods. Therefore, the text comments are similar while the pictures comments are irrelevant, so that the comments pictures will have low similarity to the goods pictures. Hence, we label this waterarmy "astrotufing 2" who publish similar text and different images, and we use image similarity algorithm to detect them.

The structure of this paper is organized as follows. Section 2 will discuss the related work in this field. Section 3 will present astroturfing detection methods through CCCA model. Section 4 gives experimental and results. Finally, conclusion is showed in Sect. 5.

2   Related Work

Currently, the study of astroturfing has made great progress compared to previous years ago. According to the different features, the methods of astroturfing identification using, mainly divided into three categories: based on content characteristics, based on behavioral characteristics and based on synthetic features.

Content Based Approach. Content-based approaches are based on the comments similarity and its linguistic features to extract comments of similar content and discover false reviewers. Through the analysis of tendency of the text in comments, the false comments issued by the astroturfing could be found. Ott et al. [2] studied deceptive opinion spam that have been deliberately written to sound authentic, and they verified that the text feature of the comment can be used to identify the false comments. Duh et al. [4] found that astroturfing released a false comment that deviated from the normal user comments by analyzing the tendencies of the review text.

Behavior Based Approach. Behavior-based approaches refer to the astroturfing has a number of comments focused on sudden, extreme, releasing early product reviews and so on. Lim et al. [5] identify several characteristic behaviors of review spammers and model these behaviors so as to detect them. They analyzed a large number of product reviews in Amazon and extracted similar comments and propose scoring methods to measure the degree of spam for each reviewer. Mukherjee et al. [6] propose a novel angle to the problem by modeling spamicity as latent, they use users and their published comments to build classifiers and use the characteristics of astroturfing to distinguish itself with ordinary users.

Multiple-feature Based Approach. Multiple-feature based approaches are the combination of the content characteristics and behavior characteristics of astroturfing, which utilize the artificial tagging the samples of astroturfing and the credibility theory of communication to identify astroturfing. Lu et al. [7] combine the astroturfing characteristics and content characteristics using the annotative factor graph model and identify the unknown network using the artificial tagging network of astroturfing samples and theory of credibility propagation. Mukherjee et al. [8] first put forward the e-commerce field network of astroturfing identification methods, they use the content of the comments to produce candidate groups, and then found astroturfing according to their characteristics.

Thus, it can be seen that the traditional methods of astroturfing identification in the field of e-commerce mainly based on the content similarity and its text features to find false commentators, the methods are very simple and inaccurate. This work, we combine text with pictures and use cross-modal CCA method to identify astroturfing in e-commerce.

3 Astroturfing Detection Method

3.1 Framework of Cross-Modal Canonical Correlation Analysis Model

This section is in order to find the astroturfing in the comments of products on Taobao site, we try to solve the problem through a newly proposed detection method, which utilizes the cross-modal canonical correlation analysis model and can effectively detect the astroturfing. The overall flow diagram of the model is shown in Fig. 1.

We will describe in detail the implementation of each algorithm proposed in this paper, and show how to achieve the CCCA model to detect astroturfing.

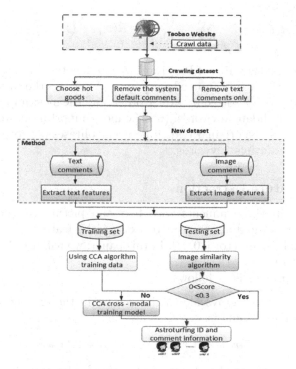

Fig. 1. Schematic representation of the astroturfing detection method framework based on CCCA model

3.2   Text Feature Extraction

The comments data obtained from the Taobao website can not be used directly as experimental data, so we preprocess the data. Since the comment is a paragraph of text, so it is necessary to convert the text into multi-dimensional eigenvector. First of all, we extract the keywords in the comments and split a text comment into a number of words, then we use these words to represent a document [9]. Text keywords extraction will be implemented by the Textrank algorithm. Hence, we present the specific steps:

(1) We split up the text comment T that we have climbed in accordance with the complete sentence. (2) For each sentence, we use word segmentation and word tagging, and filter out the stop words, only retain the specified part of the word, such as nouns, verbs, adjectives, retain candidate keywords. (3) Constructing candidate keywords graphs $G = (V, E)$, where V is a node set which is composed of the candidate keywords generated in step 2, then we use co-occurrence to construct the edges between any two points. There are edges between the two nodes, only when their corresponding vocabulary in the length of the window K co-exist, K represents the window size, that is, the most common K words. (4) According to the above formula, iterating and propagating the weight of each node until they converge.

$$R(w_i) = \lambda \sum_{j:w_j \to w_i} \frac{e(w_j, w_i)}{O(w_j)} R(w_j) + (1 - \lambda)\frac{1}{|V|} \tag{1}$$

where $R(w)$ denotes the value of PageRank; $O(w)$ denotes the side of the degree; $e(w_j, w_i)$ denotes the weight from edge w_j to w_i; λ denotes the smoothing factor. (5) The node weights are sorted in reverse order, and the most important T words are obtained as candidate keywords. (6) The most important T words from step 5 will be marked in the original text, if adjacent phrases are formed, then they are grouped into multiple keywords.

3.3   Image Feature Extraction

As the pictures in the comments with text and picture can not be directly identified by the computer, we need to extract the feature of the image as a multidimensional eigenvector [10,11]. In this paper, we will use the HOG feature extraction algorithm.

The specific process is as follows:

(1) First carries on the grayscale to the picture in the crawled comment, the transformation formula is:

$$Gray = 0.3 * R + 0.59 * G + 0.11 * B \tag{2}$$

(2) Gamma correction method is used to the standardization (normalization) of color space for input images, we utilize the square root method for Gamma standardization, the formula is as follows (where $\gamma = 0.5$):

$$Y(x, y) = I(x, y)^{\gamma} \tag{3}$$

The gradient and gradient directions of the image are respectively calculated in the horizontal and vertical directions. Mainly to capture the contours and texture information, and further weakening the interference of light.
The gradient of the pixel (x, y) in the image is:

$$G_x(x, y) = H(x + 1, y) - H(x - 1, y) \tag{4}$$

$$G_y(x, y) = H(x, y + 1) - H(x, y - 1) \tag{5}$$

where $G_x(x, y)$, $G_y(x, y)$, $H(x, y)$ respectively represent the gradient and pixel values in the horizontal and vertical directions at the pixel points (x, y) in the input image. The original image is convolved with $[-1, 0, 1]$ and $[1, 0, -1]^T$ gradient operators, respectively, and the horizontal x and vertical y directions are obtained. And then we use the following formula to calculate the gradient size and direction of the pixel.

$$G(x, y) = \sqrt{G_x(x, y)^2 + G_y(x, y)^2} \tag{6}$$

$$\alpha(x, y) = \tan^{-1}\left(\frac{G_y(x, y)}{G_x(x, y)}\right) \tag{7}$$

(3) The image is divided into several small units, the gradient histogram of each small unit is counted. Several units make up a block, and the eigenvectors of all the units in a block are concatenated to get the HOG eigenvector of this block.

(4) The HOG eigenvectors of all the blocks in the image can be connected in series to get the HOG feature vector of the image. This is the final multi-dimensional feature vector available for classification.

Finally, the image feature vector format is $S_i = I_{S_i}^1, I_{S_i}^2, \ldots, I_{S_i}^n$.

3.4 Canonical Correlation Analysis Algorithm Based on Text and Image Cross-Modal Matching

After the text and image feature extraction, we use the processed feature data for cross-mode retrieval of text and images. To achieve cross-search between images and text, we first represent the image and text with a feature vector respectively, that is, mapping the image data to the image feature space I_1 and mapping the text data to the text feature space T_1 [12,13]. However, there is no direct connection between the feature spaces I_1 and T_1, CCA algorithm can map I_1 and T_1 to I_2 and T_2 respectively through the training of many "image-text" sample pairs, where the feature spaces I_2 and T_2 are linearly related and then make the training text and image features related [14]. The specific algorithm is as follows:

Let $t \in R^p$, $i \in R^q$ be the two random multivariate vectors [15]. $S_t = x_1, x_2, \ldots, x_m$, $S_i = y_1, y_2, \ldots, y_n$ represent two sets of vectors for text and images. T_i and I_i represent the text comments and corresponding picture comments in each comment. Let $w \in R^p$, $v \in R^q$ be the two projection vectors, the eigenvector spaces of w, v are expressed as $S_{wt} = (<w, t_1>, <w, t_2>, \ldots, <w, t_n>)$, $S_{vi} = (<v, i_1>, <v, i_2>, \ldots, <v, i_n>)$. The purpose of the algorithm is to find the projection vector w, v so that the correlations of $S_w x$ and $S_v y$ are greatest. The correlations can be written as $\rho^* = \max_{w,v} corr(S_{wt}, S_{vi})$. Figure 2 shows the Canonical Correlation Analysis (CCA) algorithm. The corresponding image and text pairs in each comment will be mapped to the same common subspace through training to find the correlation between them.

3.5 Astroturfing Detection Algorithm

In this section, the specific process of the detection algorithm can be described as follow: In the detection algorithm, the input $D_{experiment}$ is the comment data crawled through Taobao, and the output R_{user} is the user ID suspected astroturfing detected in the end. The algorithm firstly detects the second type of astroturfing and then detects the first type of astroturfing. First of all, to extract the text and image features of data set, and the data set is divided into two parts: the training set and the test set. The next step is to manually mark the suspected first type of astroturfing comments in training set, and assign

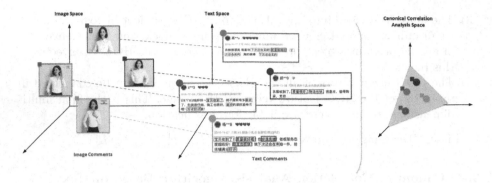

Fig. 2. Schematic of the proposed cross-modal canonical correlation analysis method

them to the label of "astroturfing 1". Then, the CCA algorithm is exploited to study the cross-modal learning for each pair of text and image comments, and a classification model is obtained. Finally, in the part of test, we compared the image similarity of the pictures in comments of test data set and the sample pictures of products provided by businesses. If the similarity score is less than 0.3, the comment may be suspected to be the second type of astroturfing, and the user's ID is output. Otherwise, the text comment and all the picture comments are projected into the common feature subspace o using the space projection function φ_T, φ_I, and then the K-nearest neighbor algorithm is used to find the closest category in the trained model and finally the results are output.

Algorithm: Astroturfing Detection Algorithm Based on Cross-Modal

Input: *the test set of comments database* $D_{experiment}$

Output: *astroturfing commnets* R_{user}

1. *Data preprocessing*: $D_{comments} \rightarrow D_{experiment}$
2. *Text feature extracting*: $S_i = T^1_{S_i}, T^2_{S_i}, ..., T^m_{S_i}$
3. *Image feature extracting*: $S_i = I^1_{S_i}, I^2_{S_i}, ..., I^n_{S_i}$
4. *CCA training model Building*: $(S_1, S_2, ..., S_i) \xrightarrow{CCA} Model$
5. *Astroturfing detecting*:

For $D_{experiment}$
  If $(0 < Score(I_{S_i}, I_{simple}) < 0.3)$
   Output user's ID
    Else $S_{io} \leftarrow \varphi_T(S_i)$
   For I_{S_i} *in* S_i *do*
     $S_{io} \leftarrow \varphi_I(S_i)$
     $KNN(S_i)$
     Output label
     If label = "*astroturfing1*"
   Output user's ID

---

4   Experimental and Results

4.1   Experimental Setup

We first get the raw comment data, and we crawl the comment data on Taobao's web page through the crawler program on the cloud-based server. In the experiment, we selected the top selling products of five different products to crawl the comment data, and the five items are from three different categories. Because the hot products have a huge amount of comments, there is a higher possibility to detect abnormal comments. In the end, we crawled 56,688 comments, and after preprocessing, there were 26,303 comments left with pictures, where each of the commentary contains 6 data items as follows: (1) Product ID; (2) Product name; (3) User ID; (4) Comment time; (5) Comment text; (6) Comment picture. The details of the crawl are shown in Table 1.

Table 1. The details of the product comments

Product ID	Product name	Number of comments
538868266734	Female T-shirt	5947
438870787421	White blouse	4545
536185035714	Men's sports pants	3678
520712769539	Female canvas shoes	8759
545963355120	Female bag	3374

First, we conduct an experiment on a commodity (commodity ID: 538868266734). It has a total of 19,941 comments, of which 5,947 comments with pictures, so the 4,500 comments with pictures is selected as the training set and the remaining 1,447 data as the test set.

Next, the training data set is manually annotated, we mark the suspected first class of astroturfing who publish the similar text and images as the label "astroturfing 1", and the other data is labeled as the "normal user". We utilize the gensim toolkit to extract the textual characteristics of the training data, and the feature vector files are obtained; Using the VLFeat visual library to extract the image features of the training data, and we get the feature vector files; Using the scikit-learn toolkit to learn the training data through the CCA algorithm.

According to the algorithm rules proposed in this paper, we carry out the test for test data, and finally output the user ID suspected of astroturfing.

4.2   Experimental Result and Evaluation

In this part, we will introduce the result of the experiment in detail.

Figure 3 shows the result for the astroturfing detection by CCCA model.

Then we do experiment on the other four products. We use the ROC curve to evaluate the classification accuracy of our experiment. The ROC curve and

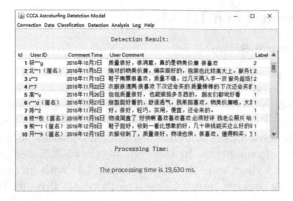

Fig. 3. The results of the test results of the astroturfing comments

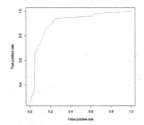

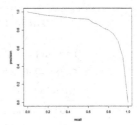

Fig. 4. ROC curve of experiment

Fig. 5. ROC curve of three types of products (Color figure online)

Fig. 6. Precise-Recall curve

the AUC value can be used to evaluate the pros and cons of a binary classifier. In this paper, we use the ROC curve and the AUC value to evaluate the classification accuracy of our experiment. The ROC curve of the experimental results is shown in Fig. 4. According to the accuracy of ROC curve for all test dataset, the accuracy of our detection method is 89.5%.

The ROC curves of three types of products are shown in Fig. 5. There are three curves which represent three types of products, the yellow one represent the clothing, the green one represent the shoes and the blue one represent the bags. We can see that the AUC value for clothing is 0.9143, the AUC value for shoes is 0.8762 and the AUC value for bags is 0.8236. Therefore, the astroturfing of clothing have high accuracy. Hence, the astroturfing may would like to publish their comments in clothing class.

As shown in Fig. 6, we can see that the precision rate is equal to recall rate when the value is about 0.8. It validates that the proposed cross-modal detection method of astroturfing have a good performance.

5 Conclusion

In this paper, we proposed a cross-modal CCA model to detect astroturfing in online shopping. To verify our method, we conduct an experiment on a Taobao dataset containing comments of manufactured products. We first extract text and image features, and use image similarity algorithm to detect the astroturfing which release pictures of goods irrelevant to the samples. Then, we use the CCA algorithm to study the cross-modal learning for each pair of text and image comments, mapping the text and image from their respective natural spaces to a CCA space. Finally, we use this method to detect astroturfing that publish pictures of goods almost same to the samples. Experimental results have demonstrated that the proposed method has a good performance. As part of our future work, we will explore and study more astroturfing features not only on shopping website and research more approaches to detect astroturfing.

Acknowledgments. This material is based upon work supported by the National Natural Science Foundation of China (Grant Nos. 61672092, 61502030, 61672091), Science and Technology on Information Assurance Laboratory (No. 614200103011711), BM-IIE Project (No. BMK2017B02-2), the Fundamental Research Funds for the Central Universities (No. 2017RC016), National High Technology Research and Development Program of China (863 Program) (No. 2015AA016003).

References

1. Stringhini, G., Kruegel, C., Vigna, G.: Detecting spammers on social networks. In: Proceedings of the 26th Annual Computer Security Applications Conference, pp. 1–9. ACM (2010)
2. Ott, M., Choi, Y., Cardie, C., Hancock, J.T.: Finding deceptive opinion spam by any stretch of the imagination. In: Proceedings of the 49th Annual Meeting of the Association for Computational Linguistics: Human Language Technologies, vol. 1, pp. 309–319. Association for Computational Linguistics (2011)
3. Chen, C., Wu, K., Srinivasan, V., Zhang, X.: Battling the internet water army: detection of hidden paid posters. In: 2013 IEEE/ACM International Conference on Advances in Social Networks Analysis and Mining (ASONAM), pp. 116–120. IEEE (2013)
4. Duh, A., Štiglic, G., Korošak, D.: Enhancing identification of opinion spammer groups. In: Proceedings of International Conference on Making Sense of Converging Media, p. 326. ACM (2013)
5. Lim, E.-P., Nguyen, V.-A., Jindal, N., Liu, B., Lauw, H.W.: Detecting product review spammers using rating behaviors. In: Proceedings of the 19th ACM International Conference on Information and Knowledge Management, pp. 939–948. ACM (2010)
6. Mukherjee, A., Kumar, A., Liu, B., Wang, J., Hsu, M., Castellanos, M., Ghosh, R.: Spotting opinion spammers using behavioral footprints. In: Proceedings of the 19th ACM SIGKDD International Conference on Knowledge Discovery and Data Mining, pp. 632–640. ACM (2013)
7. Lu, Y., Zhang, L., Xiao, Y., Li, Y.: Simultaneously detecting fake reviews and review spammers using factor graph model. In: Proceedings of the 5th Annual ACM Web Science Conference, pp. 225–233. ACM (2013)

8. Mukherjee, A., Liu, B., Glance, N.: Spotting fake reviewer groups in consumer reviews. In: Proceedings of the 21st International Conference on World Wide Web, pp. 191–200. ACM (2012)

9. Peng, L., Bin, W., Zhiwei, S., Yachao, C., Hengxun, L.: Tag-TextRank: a webpage keyword extraction method based on tags. J. Comput. Res. Dev. **49**(11), 2344–2351 (2012)

10. Lin, Y., Lv, F., Zhu, S., Yang, M., Cour, T., Yu, K., Cao, L., Huang, T.: Large-scale image classification: fast feature extraction and SVM training. In: 2011 IEEE Conference on Computer Vision and Pattern Recognition (CVPR), pp. 1689–1696. IEEE (2011)

11. Mizuno, K., Terachi, Y., Takagi, K., Izumi, S., Kawaguchi, H., Yoshimoto, M.: Architectural study of hog feature extraction processor for real-time object detection. In: 2012 IEEE Workshop on Signal Processing Systems (SiPS), pp. 197–202. IEEE (2012)

12. Pereira, J.C., Coviello, E., Doyle, G., Rasiwasia, N., Lanckriet, G.R.G., Levy, R., Vasconcelos, N.: On the role of correlation and abstraction in cross-modal multimedia retrieval. IEEE Trans. Pattern Anal. Mach. Intell. **36**(3), 521–535 (2014)

13. Rasiwasia, N., Pereira, J.C., Coviello, E., Doyle, G., Lanckriet, G.R.G., Levy, R., Vasconcelos, N.: A new approach to cross-modal multimedia retrieval. In: Proceedings of the 18th ACM International Conference on Multimedia, pp. 251–260. ACM (2010)

14. Wang, K., He, R., Wang, W., Wang, L., Tan, T.: Learning coupled feature spaces for cross-modal matching. In: Proceedings of the IEEE International Conference on Computer Vision, pp. 2088–2095 (2013)

15. Ranjan, V., Rasiwasia, N., Jawahar, C.V.: Multi-label cross-modal retrieval. In: Proceedings of the IEEE International Conference on Computer Vision, pp. 4094–4102 (2015)

Security Protocols

Secure and Efficient Two-Factor Authentication Protocol Using RSA Signature for Multi-server Environments

Zhiqiang Xu[1], Debiao He[1(✉)], and Xinyi Huang[2]

[1] State Key Lab of Software Engineering, Computer School, Wuhan University, Wuhan, China
jkebxzq@163.com, hedebiao@163.com
[2] Fujian Provincial Key Laboratory of Network Security and Cryptology, School of Mathematics and Computer Science, Fujian Normal University, Fuzhou, China
xyhuang81@yahoo.com

Abstract. To avoid multiple number of registrations using multiple passwords and smart-cards, many two-factor multi-server authentication protocols based on RSA have been proposed. However, most of the existing RSA-based multi-server authentication protocols are susceptible to various security attacks, and have high computation complexities. Recently, Amin et al. proposed a two-factor RSA-based robust authentication system for multi-server environments. However, we found that Amin et al.'s protocol cannot resist common modulus attack. To enhance the security, we propose a secure two-factor RSA-based authentication protocol for multi-server environments. The performance and security features of our scheme are also compared with that of the similar existing schemes. The performance and security analysis show that our protocol achieves more security features and has lower computation complexity in comparison with the latest related schemes.

Keywords: RSA · Smart card · User authentication
Multi-server environment

1 Introduction

User authentication scheme is essential for implementing the secure communication because it can provide mutual authentication. Two-factor authentication protocols are widely used to ensure secure communication between the remote client and the server. It is a critical task to design a secure and robust two-factor authentication protocols. To ensure the security of client-server communication in single server environment, many authentication protocols using RSA cryptosystem [1–3], hash function [1,4,5], chaotic map [6,7] and elliptic curve [8] have been proposed. However, most of these protocols cannot be used in multi-server environments. To address the issue, many authentication protocols for

© Springer International Publishing AG, part of Springer Nature 2018
S. Qing et al. (Eds.): ICICS 2017, LNCS 10631, pp. 595–605, 2018.
https://doi.org/10.1007/978-3-319-89500-0_51

multiple server environments have been designed. The multi-server communications contain three entities: the registration center, the users and multiple application-servers. All the users and application-servers must register themselves to the registration center. The responsibility of application-servers is to provide remote services for the users.

One of the most important aspects in authentication protocol is user anonymity [9,10]. The adversary shouldn't obtain user's identity in many application areas such as wireless sensor network [11], medical system and banking, where the adversary cannot guess or extract user's identity in the phase of login and authentication.

1.1   Related Work

To achieve strong security as well as lower complexities, the researchers have designed a lot of authentication protocols for multiple servers environments. Liao et al. [12] designed a authentication protocol for multi-server environments. Unfortunately, Hsiang et al. [13] showed that Liao et al.'s protocol cannot withstand several common attacks, and then they improved the identified weaknesses. However, Lee et al. [14] demonstrated that Hsiang et al.'s scheme also have some security issues. To solve these problems, they designed an efficient and enhanced authentication protocol. Unfortunately, Troung et al. [15] demonstrated that their scheme cannot withstand user impersonation and smart-card stolen attacks. To overcome these problems, they designed a secure authentication protocol in [15]. Further, Sood et al. [16] demonstrated that Hsiang et al.'s protocol [13] had different security weaknesses and put forwarded a new authentication protocol. Subsequently, Li et al. [17] showed that Sood et al.'s protocol cannot resist smart-card stolen attack and proposed a new protocol.

Recently, Pippal et al. [18] put forward a new user authentication protocol and claimed that their protocol could resist known attacks. However, He et al. [19] showed that their protocol cannot withstand impersonation attacks. In 2015, Giri et al. [2] put forward a secure protocol based on RSA and showed that their protocol could resist known attacks. Unfortunately, Amin and Biswas [1] pointed out that Giri et al.'s protocol could not against several security attacks, and then they devised a new protocol. However, Arshad et al. [20] demonstrated that [1] was not secure and proposed a new RSA-based authentication protocol.

1.2   Our Contributions

We put forward a secure and efficient two-factor authentication protocol based on RSA signature. Our major contributions are summarized as follows:

- Firstly, we analyse Amin et al.'s scheme [21] and prove it cannot withstand the common modulus attack.
- Secondly, we put forward a secure and efficient two-factor authentication protocol using RSA signature for multi-server environment. The new scheme can resist against various attacks.

– Finally, we analyse the security of our scheme and demonstrate that it is provably secure. Moreover, the performance analysis shows that our scheme is better in terms of communication overheads and computation.

1.3 Organization of the Article

The organization of this paper are described as follows: Sect. 2 analyzes the security problems of [21] and then a secure and efficient two-factor authentication protocol using RSA signature for multi-server environments are proposed in Sect. 3. Section 4 elaborates the security of the new scheme briefly. Furthermore, the comparison with some relevant protocols for efficiency and security are presented Sect. 5. Finally, we draw a conclusion.

2 Security Analysis of Amin et al.'s Scheme

In this section, we analyze the security of [21]. From our analysis, their scheme is insecure against common modulus attack. We present a list of symbols used throughout this article in Table 1. The details are described as follows:

Any of the application server can extract a public key e_{j2} and it's public/ private key pair (e_{j1}, d_{j1}). All the application servers share the public modulu $\phi(n)$, where $n = p * q$, $\phi(n) = (p-1)(q-1)$. It can computes $e_{j1}d_{j1} \equiv 1 \mod \phi(n)$, $e_{j1}d_{j1} - 1 = k\phi(n)$, $\phi(n) \mid e_{j1}d_{j1} - 1$. It can computes $(e_{j1}d_{j1} - 1, e_{j2}) = s$ using euclidean algorithm. If $s = 1$, there exist some f, g such that $f(e_{j1}d_{j1} - 1) + ge_{j2} = 1$. So the value of g is the private key corresponding to e_{j2}. If $s \neq 1$, suppose that $t = e_{j1}d_{j1} - 1/s$, $(e_{j1}d_{j1} - 1/s, e_{j2}) = 1$. There exist some f, g such that $ft + ge_{j2} = 1$ using extended euclidean algorithm. Therefore, $ge_{j2} \equiv 1 \mod \phi(n)$, the value of g is the private key corresponding to e_{j2}.

Suppose that the adversary dispatches the same message m whose encryption exponents respectively are e_{j1} and e_{j2}. Suppose further that $gcd(e_{j1}, e_{j2}) = 1$,

Table 1. Notations

Symbol	Meaning
U_i	User
AS_j	Application-server
RC	Registration center
ID_i	Identity of U_i
ID_j	Identity of AS_j
g	A generator g $\in Z_n^*$
e	Public key of RC
d	Private key of RC
a, r	Random number selected by the U_i in authentication phase

it can computes $c_1 = m^{e_{j1}} \bmod n$, $c_2 = m^{e_{j2}} \bmod n$. There exist some r, s such that $re_{j1} + se_{j2} = 1$, $m = m^{re_{j1} + se_{j2}} = (m^{e_{j1}})^r (m^{e_{j2}})^s = c_1^r c_2^s \bmod n$. Therefore, the adversary can get the value of m using c_1, c_2, r, s.

3   Proposed Protocol

We put forward a secure authentication system for multi-server environment which can withstand the above mentioned security issues. Our scheme consists of three phases: application-server registration phase, user registration phase, verification phase.

3.1   Application-Server Registration Phase

- AS_j selects two large prime numbers p, q, and computes $n_j = p_j \times q_j$, $\phi(n_j) = (p_j - 1)(q_j - 1)$.
- AS_j chooses a public key e_j $(1 < e_j < \phi(n_j))$, where $gcd(\phi(n_j), e_j) = 1$. Then, it computes it's private key $d_j \equiv e_j^{-1} \bmod \phi(n_j)$.
- Finally, AS_j chooses his/her identity ID_j and sends $\langle e_j, n_j, ID_j \rangle$ to RC securely.
- RC computes $Cer_j = h(e_j \| ID_j \| n_j)^d$ and sends Cer_j to AS_j.

3.2   User Registration Phase

- U_i chooses his/her identity ID_i and sends it to RC.
- After receiving $\langle ID_i \rangle$, RC computes $d_i = h(ID_i)^d \bmod n_j$.
- RC sends d_i to U_i securely.

3.3   Authentication Phase

- U_i randomly selects a number T_i, then it sends T_i to AS_j.
- After receiving T_i, AS_j computes $A_j = h(T_i)^{d_j}$. Then, it sends $\langle e_j, n_j, Cer_j, A_j \rangle$ to U_i.
- Upon receiving the message, U_i checks whether $Cer_j^e \bmod n_j = h(ID_j \| e_j \| n_j)$ and $A_j^{e_j} = h(T_i)$. If holds, U_i authenticates AS_j.
- U_i chooses three random number a_i, r, m and computes $PID_i = (ID_i \oplus a_i \| a_i)^{e_j} \bmod n_j$, $R_i = h(PID_i)^r \bmod n_j$, $x = h(m, R_i)$ and $S_i = d_i^{r-x}$. Then, U_i sends $\langle PID_i, R_i, S_i, x \rangle$ to AS_j.
- After receiving the message, AS_j computes $S_i^{e_j} = h(ID_i)^{r-x}$, $PID_i^{d_j} \bmod n_j = ID_i \oplus a_i \| a_i$, $ID_i' = ID_i \oplus a_i \| a_i$. Then, it checks whether $S_i^{e_j} h\left(ID_i'\right)^x = R_i$. If holds, AS_j authenticates U_i.

4   Security Analysis

4.1   Security Proof

In this subsection, according to the formal security model described as [22], we show our protocol is secure as follows.

Theorem 1. If has advantage $Adv_P^{ake}(A)$ against our scheme running in time q_{send} Send queries, q_{exe} Execute queries and q_h Hash queries. Define the security length l and the password space $|D|$. Then, we can attain: $Adv_P^{ake} \leq \frac{q_h^2}{2^{l-1}} + \frac{(q_{send}+q_{exe})^2}{p} + 2q_h \cdot Adv_G^{DLP}(t) + \frac{q_{send}}{2^{l-2}} + \frac{2q_{send}}{|D|}$, where $Adv_G^{DLP}(t)$ denote the probabilistic polynomial time t to breach DLP problem.

Proof: C obtains (y, g, n) and intends to compute x satisfying $g^x = y \mod n$ using the PPT turingmachine A. C utilizes the hash function as a random oracle and maintains an empty $H - list$. We define G_i as the sequence of games and Suc_i as A gets b successfully.

Game G_0: This game corresponds to the real attack, we have $Adv_P^{ake}(A) = 2Pr[Suc_0] - 1$.

Game G_1: In this game, we imitate the hash oracles $h(\cdot)$ by maintaining hash list L_h and the Execute, Reveal, Send, Corrupt and Test oracles are simulated as real attacks (see Figs. 1 and 2). Therefore, we have $Pr[Suc_1] = Pr[Suc_0]$.

Game G_2: In this game, we imitate all oracles as previous games, except that we will halt all executions under the condition: A collision occurs in the transcript $\langle e_j, n_j, Cer_j, A_j \rangle$, $\langle PID_i, R_i, S_i, x \rangle$. According to the birthday paradox, the probability of the hash oracle collisions is $\frac{q_h^2}{2^{l+1}}$. The probability of the transcripts colisions is $\frac{(q_{send}+q_{exe})^2}{2p}$.

Game G_3: In this game, we simulate all oracles as previous games, except that we will cancel all executions where in the adversary guess the authentication parameters A_j and R_i without making hash query. Therefore, we have $Pr[Suc_3] - Pr[Suc_2] \leq \frac{q_{send}}{2^l}$.

Game G_4: In this game, we imitate all oracles under the condition that the adversary guess the parameter $h(T_i)$ successfully without making the related queries. We define $k = h(T_i)$ to imitate this game.

- AS_j: Search for $(*, k)$ in L_h. This game will be terminated if the information does not exist. Otherwise, compute $A_j = k^{d_j}$.
- U_i: Computes $A_j^{e_j}$ and checks whether $A_j^{e_j} = h(T_i)$. If holds, U_i search for $\langle e_j, n_j, Cer_j, A_j \rangle$ in the send list.

If A guess the parameter k successfully without making hash quries, this game will succeed. Therefore, we have $Pr[Suc_3] - Pr[Suc_2] \leq \frac{q_{send}}{2^l}$.

Game G_5: We design this game to imitate Discrete logarithm problem. The security of our protocol depends on the Discrete logarithm problem solely: $R_i = h(PID_i)^r \mod n^j$.

On hash oracle queries C maintains a hash list L_h. The tuple $\{x, y\}$ is in L_h and $y = h(x)$. After receiving the queries from A, the response from C is as follows:

- Quries $\{x, y\}$ in L_h and returns y if it exists.
- Otherwise, selects a number y and responds it to A. Finally, adds $\{x, y\}$ into L_h.

On a query Send$(U_i, start)$, assuming U_i is in the correct state, U_i responds the query as follows:

- Chooses a nonce T_i.
- Responds the information $\{T_i\}$.

On a query Send$(AS_j, \{T_i\})$, assuming AS_j is in the prospective state, AS_j responds the query as follows:

- Calculates $A_j = h(T_i)^{d_j}$.
- Responds the information $\{Cer_j, e_j, n_j, A_j\}$.

On a query Send$(U_i, \{Cer_j, e_j, n_j, A_j\})$, assuming U_i is in the correct state, U_i responds the query as follows:
Checks whether $Cer_j^e \bmod n_j = h(ID_j \,||\, e_j \,||\, n_j)$ and $A_j^{e_j} = h(T_i)$.

- Terminates this session if not holds.
- Otherwise, chooses two random number a_i, r. Then computes: $PID_i = (ID_i \oplus a_i \,||\, a_i)^{e_j} \bmod n_j$, $R_i = h(PID_i)^r \bmod n_j$, $x = h(m, R_i)$, $S_i = d_i^{r-x}$.
- Responds the message $\langle PID_i, R_i, S_i, x \rangle$.

On a query Send$(AS_j, \{PID_i, R_i, S_i, x\})$, Assuming AS_j is in the prospective state, AS_j responds the query as follows:
Calculates $S_i^{e_j} = h(ID_i)^{r-x}$, $PID_i^{d_j} \bmod n_j = ID_i \oplus a_i \,||\, a_i$, $ID_i' = ID_i \oplus a_i \,||\, a_i$.
Then checks whether $S_i^{e_j} h\left(ID_i'\right)^x = R_i$.

- Aborts the message $\langle PID_i, R_i, S_i, x \rangle$ if not holds.
- Otherwise, the message $\langle PID_i, R_i, S_i, x \rangle$ is accepted.

Fig. 1. Simulation of Send query.

- U_i: Chooses two random numbers a_i and r. Then calculates: $PID_i = (ID_i \oplus a_i \,||\, a_i)^{e_j} \bmod n_j$, $S_i = d_i^{r-x}$. Finally, stores $\{S_i, x\}$ into hash list.
- AS_j: Calculates $S_i^{e_j} = h(ID_i)^{r-x}$, $PID_i^{d_j} \bmod n_j = ID_i \oplus a_i \,||\, a_i$, $ID_i' = ID_i \oplus a_i \,||\, a_i$. Then stores $\left\{S_i^{e_j}, h(ID_i)^x\right\}$ into hash list.

This game is different from previous games where in the adversary quries $h(\cdot)$ on $g^x = y \bmod n$. We can obtain DLP secret with $\frac{1}{q_h}$. Hence, we have $Pr[Suc_5] - Pr[Suc_4] \leq q_h \cdot Adv_G^{DLP}(t)$.

Game G_6: In this game, we simulate all oracles as in game G_5, except that we will abort the Test query in which A asks a $h(\cdot)$ for $g^x = y \bmod n$. The probability that A gets the session key is $\frac{q_h^2}{2^{l+1}}$. Therefore, we have $Pr[Suc_5] - Pr[Suc_4] \leq \frac{q_h^2}{2^{l+1}}$.

In addition, the probability of off-line dictionary attacks is $\frac{q_{send}}{|D|}$. Therefore, we can get the conclusion showed in the beginning of this subsection.

On a query Execute, we proceed using the simulation of the Send query as follows:

- $\{T_i\} \leftarrow \text{Send}(U_i, start)$.
- $\{Cer_j, e_j, n_j, A_j\} \leftarrow \text{Send}(AS_j, \{T_i\})$.
- $\langle PID_i, R_i, S_i, x \rangle \leftarrow \text{Send}(U_i, \{Cer_j, e_j, n_j, A_j\})$

Finally, the query responds $\{T_i\}$, $\{Cer_j, e_j, n_j, A_j\}$ and $\langle PID_i, R_i, S_i, x \rangle$.

On a query Corrupt, we proceed as follows:

- If $a = 1$, it outputs U_i's password.
- Otherwise, it outputs the secret parameters of U_i stored in smart card.

On a query Reveal, we proceed as follows:

- If $\prod_{i,j}^n$ has accepted, it responds the session key betweeen $\prod_{i,j}^n$ and its partner.
- Else it outputs a null value.

On a query Test, we proceed as follows: It flips a fair coin b.

- If $b = 1$, it returns the right parameters.
- Otherwise, it responds a random value with the same size.

Fig. 2. Simulation of Execute, Reveal, Test query.

4.2 Other Discussions

This subsection shows our scheme is able to withstand various attacks.

- User impersonation attack: To impersonate as a legal U_i, A has to compute a valid message $\langle PID_i, R_i, S_i, x \rangle$ during authentication phase, where $PID_i = (ID_i \oplus a_i \| a_i) \bmod n_j$, $R_i = h(PID_i)^r \bmod n_j$, $x = h(m, R_i)$ and $S_i = d_i^{r-x}$. However, it is infeasible to compute PID_i and R_i without knowing the random number a_i and r. Therefore, our proposed scheme can withstand user impersonation attack.
- Server impersonation attack: To impersonate as a legal application-server, A has to compute the message $\langle e_j, n_j, Cer_j, A_j \rangle$, which is to be authenticated by U_i, where $A_j = h(T_i)^{d_j}$ and $Cer_j = h(e_j \| ID_j \| n_j)^d$. However, it is infeasible to compute A_j and Cer_j without knowing the private key d of RC. Therefore, our proposed scheme can withstand server impersonation attack.
- User anonymity: Our proposed scheme can provide anonymity of users. Taking the situation where an adversary can get the message d_i, where $d_i = h(ID_i)^d \bmod n_j$. However, d cannot be known by the adversary. The adversary may also eavesdrop the information $\langle PID_i, R_i, S_i, x \rangle$, where PID_i are related to the user's identity and $PID_i = (ID_i \oplus a_i \| a_i)^{d_j}$. As the random a_i cannot be known by the adversary, it is impossible to get the user's identity from PID_i. Therefore, our proposed scheme can provide anonymity of users.
- Common modulus attacks: In our proposed scheme, the public key and private key of AS_j are generated by the server itself. AS_j computes $n_j = p_j \times q_j$, $\phi(n_j) = (p_j - 1)(q_j - 1)$. The modulu of n_j is not same in every application server and the application servers does not share the public modulu. Therefore, our proposed scheme can withstand Common modulus attack.

- Mutual authentication: In our proposed scheme, AS_j and U_i authenticate each other. U_i authenticates AS_j by checking whether $Cer_j^e \bmod n_j = h(ID_j \| e_j \| n_j)$ and $A_j^{e_j} = h(T_i)$. A needs to get T_i to reconstruct A_j, however, only a legal AS_j owns the value. AS_j authenticates U_i by checking whether $S_i^{e_j} h\left(ID_i'\right)^x = R_i$. A needs to compute PID_i and r to reconstruct R_i, however, only a legal U_i can compute those values. Therefore, U_i and AS_j mutually authenticate and our proposed scheme can provide proper mutual authentication.
- Smart-card stolen attack: An adversary A can extract the information of smart-card by means of power consumption monitoring technique. Suppose that A obtains the smart card of U_i and extracts the information $\langle d_i \rangle$, where $d_i = h(ID_i)^{d_j} \bmod n_j$. From the value, A cannot compute any useful information, because the value is safeguarded with a one-way hash function. Further, A cannot obtain the value of d_j. Therefore, our proposed scheme can withstand smart card stolen attacks.

5   Performance Analysis

In this section, we compare the proposed scheme with recent authentication schemes [18,21,23–25] proposed in terms of security and performance (as shown in Table 2). We use some time complexities to evaluate the computational cost. T_h denotes the cost time for one-way hash operation. T_{sym} denotes the execution time for symmetric key encryption/decryption operation. T_e denotes the running time for exponentiation operation. T_m denotes the execution time for modular multiplication operation.

We have implemented various cryptographic operations with the MIRACL C/C++ Library [26] on a personal computer with 4G bytes memory and the Windows 7 operating system. It requires Visual C++ 2008, 1024-bit cyclic group, AES for symmetric encryption/decryption, 160-bit prime field F_p and

Table 2. Comparison of security

Security attributes and schemes	[18]	[23]	[24]	[25]	[21]	Our scheme
User anonymity	√	√	√	√	√	√
Stolen smart card attack	√	√	√	√	√	√
Impersonation attack	×	√	√	√	√	√
Replay attack	√	√	√	√	√	√
Denial of service attack	√	√	√	√	√	√
Session key verification	×	×	×	×	√	√
Man-in-the-middle	×	√	√	√	√	√
Common modulus attacks	√	√	√	√	×	√

Table 3. Comparison of computation cost at the user side and the server side

Schemes	User	Server
Pippal et al. [18]	$4T_h + 3T_e + T_m$	$3T_h + 4T_e + T_m$
Yeh et al. [23]	$4T_h + 2T_e + T_m$	$5T_h + 4T_e + T_m$
Wei et al. [24]	$7T_h + 2T_e$	$6T_h + 2T_e$
Li et al. [25]	$5T_h + T_e$	$8T_h + 3T_e$
Amin et al. [21]	$6T_h + 2T_e$	$6T_h + 2T_e + T_{sym}$
Proposed scheme	$5T_h + 2T_e$	$5T_h + 2T_e$

Table 4. Comparison of execution time at the user side and the server side

Schemes	User	Server
Pippal et al. [18]	5.4966 ms	7.3235 ms
Yeh et al. [23]	3.6701 ms	7.5621 ms
Wei et al. [24]	3.6566 ms	3.6562 ms
Li et al. [25]	1.8289 ms	5.4839 ms
Amin et al. [21]	3.6562 ms	3.7865 ms
Proposed scheme	3.5861 ms	3.6132 ms

SHA-1 operation. The execution time of these different operations are: 0.0004 ms, 0.1303 ms, 0.0147 ms and 1.8269 ms.

In Table 1, we find that our proposed scheme can withstand known attacks, such as user anonymity, common modulus attacks, mutual authentication, Server impersonation attack. In Tables 3 and 4, we find that computational cost time of our proposed scheme is lower than the schemes in [18, 23] and nearly equal with the schemes in [21, 24, 25].

6   Conclusion

In this paper, we cryptanalyzed Amin et al.'s scheme, and found that their protocol is susceptible to common modulus attack. Then We present a secure and efficient two-factor authentication protocol using RSA signature for multi-server environments. We prove informally that our protocol can withstand different cryptographic attacks. In the proposed scheme, we employ RSA signature to implement the authentication scheme. Our proposed scheme is suitable for deployment in various low-power smart cards, and in particular for the mobile computing networks.

Acknowledgements. The work of was supported by the National Natural Science Foundation of China (Nos. 61501333, 61572379, 61572370, 61772377), and the Natural Science Foundation of Hubei Province of China (Nos. 2015CFA068, 2017CFA007).

References

1. Amin, R., Biswas, G.P.: An improved RSA based user authentication and session key agreement protocol usable in TMIS. J. Med. Syst. **39**(8), 1–14 (2015)
2. Giri, D., Maitra, T., Amin, R., Srivastava, P.D.: An efficient and robust RSA-based remote user authentication for telecare medical information systems. J. Med. Syst. **39**(1), 1–9 (2015)
3. Amin, R., Biswas, G.P.: Remote access control mechanism using rabin public key cryptosystem. In: Mandal, J.K., Satapathy, S.C., Sanyal, M.K., Sarkar, P.P., Mukhopadhyay, A. (eds.) Information Systems Design and Intelligent Applications. AISC, vol. 339, pp. 525–533. Springer, New Delhi (2015). https://doi.org/10.1007/978-81-322-2250-7_52
4. Amin, R., Biswas, G.P.: Cryptanalysis and design of a three-party authenticated key exchange protocol using smart card. Arab. J. Sci. Eng. **40**(11), 1–15 (2015)
5. Islam, S.K.H., Biswas, G.P., Choo, K.K.R.: Cryptanalysis of an improved smartcard-based remote password authentication scheme. Inf. Sci. Lett. **3**(1), 35 (2014)
6. Hafizul Islam, S.K., Khan, M.K., Obaidat, M.S., Bin Muhaya, F.T.: Provably secure and anonymous password authentication protocol for roaming service in global mobility networks using extended chaotic maps. Wirel. Pers. Commun. **84**(3), 1–22 (2015)
7. Hafizul Islam, S.K.: Design and analysis of a three party password-based authenticated key exchange protocol using extended chaotic maps. Inf. Sci. Int. J. **312**(C), 104–130 (2015)
8. Amin, R., Biswas, G.P.: A secure three-factor user authentication and key agreement protocol for TMIS with user anonymity. J. Med. Syst. **39**(8), 1–19 (2015)
9. Hafizul Islam, S.K.: Design and analysis of an improved smartcard-based remote user password authentication scheme. Int. J. Commun. Syst. **29**(11), 1708–1719 (2016)
10. Hafizul Islam, S.K.: A provably secure id-based mutual authentication and key agreement scheme for mobile multi-server environment without ESL attack. Wirel. Pers. Commun. **79**(3), 1975–1991 (2014)
11. Amin, R., Biswas, G.P.: A secure light weight scheme for user authentication and key agreement in multi-gateway based wireless sensor networks. Ad Hoc Netw. **36**, 58–80 (2016)
12. Liao, Y.-P., Wang, S.-S.: A secure dynamic ID based remote user authentication scheme for multi-server environment. Comput. Stand. Interfaces **31**(1), 24–29 (2009)
13. Hsiang, H.-C., Shih, W.-K.: Improvement of the secure dynamic ID based remote user authentication scheme for multi-server environment. Comput. Stand. Interfaces **31**(6), 1118–1123 (2009)
14. Lee, C.-C., Lin, T.-H., Chang, R.-X.: A secure dynamic ID based remote user authentication scheme for multi-server environment using smart cards. Expert Syst. Appl. **38**(11), 13863–13870 (2011)
15. Truong, T.-T., Tran, M.-T., Duong, A.-D.: Robust secure dynamic ID based remote user authentication scheme for multi-server environment. In: Murgante, B., Misra, S., Carlini, M., Torre, C.M., Nguyen, H.-Q., Taniar, D., Apduhan, B.O., Gervasi, O. (eds.) ICCSA 2013. LNCS, vol. 7975, pp. 502–515. Springer, Heidelberg (2013). https://doi.org/10.1007/978-3-642-39640-3_37

16. Sood, S.K., Sarje, A.K., Singh, K.: A secure dynamic identity based authentication protocol for multi-server architecture. J. Netw. Comput. Appl. **34**(2), 609–618 (2011)
17. Li, X., Xiong, Y., Ma, J., Wang, W.: An efficient and security dynamic identity based authentication protocol for multi-server architecture using smart cards. J. Netw. Comput. Appl. **35**(2), 763–769 (2012)
18. Pippal, R.S., Jaidhar, C.D., Tapaswi, S.: Robust smart card authentication scheme for multi-server architecture. Wirel. Pers. Commun. **72**(1), 729–745 (2013)
19. He, D., Chen, J., Shi, W., Khan, M.K.: On the security of an authentication scheme for multi-server architecture. Int. J. Electr. Secur. Digit. Forensics **5**(3/4), 288–296 (2013)
20. Arshad, H., Rasoolzadegan, A.: Design of a secure authentication and key agreement scheme preserving user privacy usable in telecare medicine information systems. J. Med. Syst. **40**(11), 237 (2016)
21. Amin, R., Islam, S.K., Khan, M.K., et al.: A two-factor RSA-based robust authentication system for multiserver environments. Secur. Commun. Netw. **2017**, 15 p. (2017). Article no. 5989151
22. Ding, W., Ping, W.: Two birds with one stone: two-factor authentication with security beyond conventional bound. IEEE Trans. Dependable Secure Comput. **PP**(99), 1 (2016)
23. Yeh, K.-H.: A provably secure multi-server based authentication scheme. Wirel. Pers. Commun. **79**(3), 1621–1634 (2014)
24. Wei, J., Liu, W., Hu, X.: Cryptanalysis and improvement of a robust smart card authentication scheme for multi-server architecture. Wirel. Pers. Commun. **77**(3), 2255–2269 (2014)
25. Li, X., Niu, J., Kumari, S., Liao, J., Liang, W.: An enhancement of a smart card authentication scheme for multi-server architecture. Wirel. Pers. Commun. Int. J. **80**(1), 175–192 (2015)
26. Lili, X., Fan, W.: Cryptanalysis and improvement of a user authentication scheme preserving uniqueness and anonymity for connected health care. J. Med. Syst. **39**(2), 10 (2015)

Authenticated Group Key Agreement
Protocol Without Pairing

Gaurav Sharma[1(✉)], Rajeev Anand Sahu[1], Veronika Kuchta[1],
Olivier Markowitch[1], and Suman Bala[2]

[1] Université Libre de Bruxelles, Brussels, Belgium
gsharma@ulb.ac.be
[2] Amity University, Noida, India

Abstract. Since the inception of pairing-based constructions in cryptography, the authentication in group key agreement (GKA) protocol has been usually achieved by pairings. But due to high computation cost of pairing such constructions are inefficient for practical implementation, specially for low power devices. Also, in almost all such constructions leakage of both the keys- the long-term secret key and the ephemeral key has not been considered for security guarantee. In this view, construction of an efficient and secure GKA protocol is desired. In this paper, we propose an authenticated GKA protocol without pairing. We have achieved security of the proposed scheme following the most standard and recent security notion namely the EGBG model. In particular, we have proved the authenticated key exchange (AKE) security and the mutual authentication (MA) security with full forward secrecy, considering leakage of both the keys long-term and ephemeral, adopting a comparatively efficient technique, the game hopping technique. Our proposed scheme is more efficient in the view of computation and operation time with compare to the existing similar schemes, hence it is more acceptable for the tiny processors. To the best of our knowledge ours is the first pairing free balanced AGKA protocol secure in the EGBG model.

Keywords: Group key agreement · Authentication · Insider security
Forward security · Mutual authentication · Batch verification

1 Introduction

A group key agreement (GKA) protocol ensures establishment of a common session key among the group members that remains unknown to outsiders. The GKA protocol is applicable in various real world communication networks such as ad-hoc networks, wireless sensor networks and body area networks, where devices are involved in sharing common secret data over an open channel. There are numerous other real life examples of GKA including distributed computations, video conferencing, multi-user games, etc. The key establishment protocols can be categorized into two sets: key transport protocols and key agreement protocols. In the former, the session key is derived by one of the powerful nodes

© Springer International Publishing AG, part of Springer Nature 2018
S. Qing et al. (Eds.): ICICS 2017, LNCS 10631, pp. 606–618, 2018.
https://doi.org/10.1007/978-3-319-89500-0_52

and then the key is transferred securely to all the members of the group. In the latter, a common session key is derived by all the members by interactive participation in an agreement protocol. Moreover, group key agreement protocols can be further categorized into balanced and imbalanced protocols. All the participants in balanced GKA share same computing burden whereas in imbalanced protocols a powerful node verifies all the received signatures. As established by Bellare and Rogaway (CRYPTO 1993) [2], *authentication* is an essential security requirement for key exchange protocols, otherwise the man in the middle (MITM) attack yields the protocol vulnerable to impersonation attacks. Precisely, we provide here a construction of an authenticated group key agreement (AGKA) protocol. We rely on the application of PKI based signature for the purpose. Motivated by Shamir's idea of identity-based (ID) cryptosystem [20], we deploy our scheme on the ID-based setting to avoid overhead of certificate management due to classical PKI setup.

After the seminal work of Diffie and Hellman [10], there has been extensive efforts to convert their two-party key exchange protocol to multi-party key exchange protocol [6,14,21]. Among the most notable works, Joux's one round three-party key agreement protocol [15] is considered as a significant contribution for practical GKA protocol due to the functionality of pairing. Based on Joux's work [15], Barua et al. [1] have presented protocols of multi-party key agreement in two flavors *unauthenticated*- based on ternary trees and *authenticated*- from bilinear maps. Unfortunately, their protocols are secure against only passive adversaries. The first provable security model for authenticated key exchange (AKE) security was introduced by Bresson et al. [3–5] but their protocol accounts $O(n)$ rounds, which is very expensive. Further, Katz and Yung improved the model in [17] and proposed a scalable compiler which transforms any unauthenticated GKA into an authenticated one. Later, Katz and Shin [16] modeled the *insider security* in GKA protocols. In 2009, Gorantla et al. [11] proposed a security model, we call it the GBG model, which addresses the *forward secrecy* and *key compromise impersonation resilience* (KCIR) for GKA protocols to take into account authenticated key exchange (AKE) security and mutual authentication (MA) security. Their model was revisited and enhanced by Zhao et al. [29] in 2011. They improved the GBG model to stronger extended GBG model, we call it the EGBG model, where they addressed both, the leakage of secret key as well as the leakage of ephemeral key independently.

The authenticated ID-based GKA protocol was first formalized by Choi et al. [7] in 2004, but their scheme was found vulnerable to insider colluding attack [28]. In 2007, Kyung-Ah [18] claimed that scheme in [7] is vulnerable to another insider colluding attack and improved the protocol. Unfortunately, none of these AGKA protocols could achieve the perfect forward secrecy. Perfect forward secrecy allows the compromise of long term secret keys of all participants maintaining all earlier shared secrets unrevealed. In 2011, Wu et al. [27] presented a provably secure ID-AGKE protocol from pairings, providing forward secrecy and security against the insider attacks. Later, Wu et al. [26] presented their first revocable ID-based AGKE (RID-AGKE) protocol, which is provably secure and can resist malicious participants as well. The major limitation of existing literature is, not to consider the ephemeral key leakage [29]. In 2015, Teng et al. [22] presented first ID-based AGKA protocol secure in EGBG model. Their protocol claims MA security with KCIR, achieving full forward secrecy. This protocol includes extensive number of pairing operations $(2n^2 - 2n)$ which is inefficient for practical implementations specially for low power devices. The session key in their construction is concatenation of k_i where k_is are randomly chosen strings of length k. Therefore, the leakage of randomness will reveal the session key and hence, to the best of our knowledge, there is no existing protocol secure in EGBG model. Our AGKA protocol does not use any pairing operation and hence turns to be very much suitable for the computational performance, especially during the implementation with limited resource. We have proved the security following the EGBG model. Moreover, our efficiency analysis asserts that our scheme is more efficient in the view of computation and operation time with compare to the existing similar schemes.

Rest of the paper is organized as follows: in Sect. 2, we introduce necessary definitions, corresponding hardness assumption, the AGKA protocol and security model for AGKA. The proposed AGKA scheme is described in Sect. 3. The security analysis and efficiency comparison have been presented in Sects. 4 and 5 respectively, followed by the conclusion in Sect. 6.

2   AGKA Protocol and Its Security

In this section, we introduce mathematical definitions, hardness assumptions, the notion of AGKA protocol and security model for it. If X is a set, then $y \xleftarrow{\$} X$ denotes the operation of choosing an element y of X according to the uniform random distribution on X.

2.1   Definitions and Assumptions

Definition 1 (Computational Diffie-Hellman Problem (CDHP)). Let G be an additive cyclic group (precisely an elliptic curve group) of order q with generator P. Let $CDH : G \times G \rightarrow G$ be a map defined by

$$CDH(X, Y) = Z \quad \text{where } X = aP, Y = bP \text{ and } Z = abP.$$

The *computational Diffie-Hellman problem* (CDHP) is to evaluate $CDH(X, Y)$ given $X, Y \xleftarrow{\$} G$ without the knowledge of $a, b \in \mathbb{Z}_q^*$. (Note that obtaining $a \in \mathbb{Z}_q^*$, given $P, X \in G$ is solving the elliptic curve discrete logarithm problem (ECDLP)).

Definition 2 (Computational Diffie-Hellman Assumption). Given a security parameter λ, let $\langle q, G, P, X, Y, \rangle \leftarrow \mathfrak{G}(\lambda)$. The computational Diffie-Hellman assumption (CDHA) states that for any PPT algorithm $\mathcal{A}$ which attempts to solve CDHP, its advantage

$$\mathbf{Adv}_{\mathfrak{G}}(\mathcal{A}) := Prob[\mathcal{A}(q, G, P, X, Y) = CDH(X, Y)]$$

is negligible in λ. We say that the (t, ϵ)-CDH assumption holds in group G if there is no algorithm which takes at most t running time and can solve CDHP with at least a non-negligible advantage ϵ.

2.2   AGKA Protocol

Suppose there are total n participants $U_1, U_2, \ldots, U_n$ and any subset with $(n \geq 2)$ can run the protocol (π). Each participant is provided with a (public, private) key pair. In our protocol, we refer by *session* a running instance. Each participant is allowed to run multiple sessions concurrently. An ith instance of the protocol is represented as Π_U^i where U is the corresponding user or participant. We define two identities, the session identity sid_U^i which is the session dependent information computed by user U at its ith instance using the shared information in that session, and the partner identity pid_U^i which is a set of identities of the participants who are involved in generation of the session key with Π_U^i. We say an instance Π_U^i *accepts* when it computes a valid session key sk. We say instances Π_U^i and $\Pi_{U'}^j$ (for $\Pi_U^i \neq \Pi_{U'}^j$) are partnered iff (i) they have both accepted (ii) $sid_U^i = sid_{U'}^j$, (iii) $pid_U^i = pid_{U'}^j$. We further define the term *freshness*.

Definition 3 (Freshness). *An instance Π_U^i is referred to be fresh if it satisfies the following conditions:*

1. *If the instance Π_U^i is accepted, neither U_i nor any of its partnered instances can query Reveal key oracle.*
2. *No participant is allowed to query Corrupt and Reveal Ephemeral Key simultaneously.*
3. *In a partnered instance between U_i and U_j, if an adversary $\mathcal{A}$ corrupts U_j, any message sent from U_j to U_i must actually come from U_j.*

We precisely present here two round interactive authenticated key agreement protocol divided into **Setup**, **KeyGen**, **Key Agreement** and **Key Computation** phases. We assume existence of a private key generator (PKG) who generates long-term private keys for the users. The users interact among them using their private keys to share session dependent information sid, which leads to compute the session key.

2.3   Security Model for AGKA Protocol

We analyze the security of proposed protocol within the standard security frame of indistinguishability. For the purpose we define the following experiment between the challenger $\mathcal{C}$ and the adversary $\mathcal{A}$:

Setup: On input a security parameter 1^λ, the challenger $\mathcal{C}$ runs **KeyGen**(1^λ) to generate the public parameter *Params* and the system key pair (pk, msk) and gives the adversary $\mathcal{A}$ the public key pk. msk is the master secret of the system.

Queries: $\mathcal{A}$ can adaptively make the following queries:

- Execute(Π_U^i): Any time the adversary $\mathcal{A}$ can query for the complete transcripts of an honest execution among the users selected by himself.
- Send(Π_U^i, m): During the normal execution of the protocol, this query returns the reply generated by instance Π_U^i.
- Reveal Key (Π_U^i): When the oracle is accepted, this query outputs the group session key.
- Corrupt(U_i): This query models the reveal of long-term secret key. The participant is honest iff adversary $\mathcal{A}$ has not made any *Corrupt* query.
- Ephemeral Key Reveal(Π_U^i): This query models the reveal of ephemeral key of participant U_i for instance Π_U^i.
- Test(Π_U^i): This query can be made only once during the execution of protocol π. The challenger responds with a session key.

Challenge: During the Test query, the challenger randomly selects a bit $b \xleftarrow{\$}$ $\{0, 1\}$ and returns the real session key if $b = 0$ or a random value if $b = 1$.
Guess: $\mathcal{A}$ outputs its guess b' for b.

The adversary succeeds in breaking the security if $b' = b$. We denote this event by $Succ_{\mathcal{A}}$ and define $\mathcal{A}$'s advantage as $Adv_{\mathcal{A}}(1^k) \overset{\text{def}}{=} |2Pr[Succ_{\mathcal{A}}] - 1|$.

Definition 4 (AKE-Security). *Let $\mathcal{A}_{ake}$ be an adversary against AKE-security. It is allowed to make queries to the Execute, Send, RevealKey, Corrupt and Ephemeral Key Reveal oracles. It is allowed to make a single Test query to the instance Π_U^i at the end of the phase and given the challenge session key $sk_{ch,b}$ (depending on bit b). Finally, $\mathcal{A}_{ake}$ outputs a bit b' and wins the game if (1) $b = b'$ and (2) the instance Π_U^i is fresh till the end of the game. The advantage of $\mathcal{A}_{ake}$ is $Adv_{\mathcal{A}_{ake}} = |2Pr[Succ_{\mathcal{A}_{ake}}] - 1|$. The protocol is called AKE-secure if the adversary's advantage $Adv_{\mathcal{A}_{ake}}$ is negligible.*

Definition 5 (MA-Security with Outsider KCIR). *Let $\mathcal{A}_{ma,out}$ be an outsider adversary against MA-security. Let pid_U^i be a set of identities of participant in the group with whom Π_U^i wishes to establish a session key and sid_U^i denotes a session id of an instance Π_U^i. $\mathcal{A}_{ma,out}$ is allowed to make queries to the Execute, Send, RevealKey, Corrupt and EphemeralKey Reveal oracles. $\mathcal{A}_{ma,out}$ breaks the MA-security with outsider KCIR notion if at some point there is an uncorrupted instance Π_U^i with the key sk_U^i and another party U' which is uncorrupted when Π_U^i accepts such that there are no other insiders in pid_U^i and the following conditions hold:*

- *there is no instance $\Pi_{U'}^{i'}$ with $(pid_{U'}^{i'}, sid_{U'}^{i'}) = (pid_U^i, sid_U^i)$ or,*
- *there is an instance $\Pi_{U'}^{i'}$ with $(pid_{U'}^{i'}, sid_{U'}^{i'}) = (pid_U^i, sid_U^i)$ which has accepted with $sk_{U'}^{i'} \neq sk_U^i$.*

Definition 6 (MA-security with insider KCIR). *Let $\mathcal{A}_{ma,in}$ be an insider adversary against MA-security. It is allowed to query Execute, Send, RevealKey, Corrupt and EmphemeralKey Reveal oracles. It breaks the MA-security with insider KCIR if at some point there is an uncorrupted instance Π_U^i which has accepted with the secret key sk_U^i and another party U' which is uncorrupted when Π_U^i accepts and*

– *there is no instance* $\Pi_{U'}^{i'}$ *with* $(pid_{U'}^{i'}, sid_{U'}^{i'}) = (pid_U^i, sid_U^i)$ *or,*
– *there is an instance* $\Pi_{U'}^{i'}$ *with* $(pid_{U'}^{i'}, sid_{U'}^{i'}) = (pid_U^i, sid_U^i)$ *which has accepted with* $sk_{U'}^{i'} \neq sk_U^i$.

3 Authenticated Group Key Agreement Protocol

Our AGKA protocol consists of following algorithms:

Setup(1^λ)**:** On input security parameter 1^λ, the PKG generates the system parameters *Params* in the following steps:

- Chooses an elliptic curve group G of prime order q. Let P be a generator of group G
- Computes system's public key as $P_{pub} = sP$ by choosing a master secret $s \xleftarrow{\$} \mathbb{Z}_q^*$
- Chooses cryptographic hash functions $H_1 : \{0,1\}^* \times G \to \mathbb{Z}_q^*$, $H_2 : \{0,1\}^* \times G \times G \to \mathbb{Z}_q^*$, $H_3 : \{0,1\}^* \to \mathbb{Z}_q^*$ and $H : \{0,1\}^* \to \{0,1\}^k$
- Finally, publishes the system parameters
  $Params = \{G, q, H_1, H_2, H_3, H, P_{pub}\}$ and keeps the master key secret.

KeyGen(s)**:** The PKG performs the following for all the group members:

- Chooses $r_i \xleftarrow{\$} \mathbb{Z}_q^*$ and computes $R_i = r_i P$
- Computes the private key for the user U_i as $x_i = r_i + sH_1(ID_i, R_i)$
- The user U_i can verify the private key as $x_i P = R_i + H_1(ID_i, R_i)P_{pub}$

Key Agreement(x_i, pid)**:** This protocol runs in the following two rounds:

- **Round 1:**
  Each user $U_i (1 \leq i \leq n)$ does the following

  • Chooses $eph_i \xleftarrow{\$} \mathbb{Z}_q^*$ and computes $l_i = H_3(eph_i, x_i)$ and $L_i = l_i P$
  • Chooses a random string $k_i \in \{0,1\}^k$ of length k. Each user, except U_n computes $H(k_i)$. The user U_n masks the randomness as $\tilde{k}_n = H(k_n, x_n)$ where x_n is long-term secret of U_n. Now, he computes $H(\tilde{k}_n)$.
  • Broadcasts the tuple $<L_i, H(k_i), H(\tilde{k}_n), R_i>$ to all $n-1$ members.

- **Round 2:**
  On receiving the message $<L_j, H(k_j), H(\tilde{k}_n), R_j>$, each user U_i performs the following:

  • Computes $U_{ij} = l_i L_j$ and $L = L_1 \parallel L_2 \parallel \dots \parallel L_n$
  • Each user, except U_n computes $K_{ij} = H(U_{ij}) \oplus k_i$. The user U_n computes $mask = H(U_{ij}) \oplus \tilde{k}_n$
  • Chooses another random number $t_i \in \mathbb{Z}_q^*$ and compute $T_i = t_i l_i P$. Also, computes the signature on $<L, T_i>$ as $\sigma_i = t_i l_i + x_i H_2(ID_i, L, T_i, pid)$
  • Broadcasts $<K_{ij}(1 \leq j \leq n, j \neq i), mask, \sigma_i, T_i>$ to all $n-1$ members

Key Computation (K_{ji}, sid, pid): Upon receiving $<K_{ji}, mask, \sigma_i, T_i>$, each user verifies the received signature as:

$$\sigma_i P = T_i + (R_i + H_1(ID_i, R_i)P_{pub})H_2(ID_i, L, T_i, pid)$$

Each user U_i then computes $\tilde{k}_j = H(U_{ji}) \oplus K_{ji}$. Similarly, $\tilde{k}_n$ can be computed using mask. Note that, $U_{ij} = l_i L_j = l_i l_j P = l_j l_i P = l_j L_i = U_{ji}$. Each user U_i checks the correctness of k_i as $H(k_j) = H(\tilde{k}_j)$ for $(1 \leq j \leq n, j \neq i)$ and computes the session identity $sid = H(k_1) \parallel H(k_2) \parallel \ldots \parallel H(\tilde{k}_n)$. Finally, the session key is computed as $sk = H(k_1 \parallel k_2 \parallel \ldots \parallel \tilde{k}_n \parallel sid \parallel pid)$.

Batch Verification: A signature scheme, independently EUF-ACMA secure does not guarantee its security in batch signature. Recall that, the signature algorithms proposed by Schnorr [19], Hess [12] are not secure when used as batch signature. Recently, in a noted contribution by Horng [13], an efficient method was introduced to derive batch signature. Adopting the concept of small exponent test in [13], each member will choose a random vector $v = (v_1, v_2, \ldots, v_n)$, where v_i ranges between 1 and 2^t, each v_i is random, to make sure the property of non-repudiation. To avoid any computational overhead, t is a very small value with error probability at most 2^{-t}. Any forged signature can be easily detected with a glitch of probability 2^{-t}. Below we present the correctness of our batch verification.

$$\left(\sum_{i=1}^{n} v_i \sigma_i \right) P = \left(\sum_{i=1}^{n} v_i (l_i + x_i h_{i2}) \right) P = \sum_{i=1}^{n} v_i \left(T_i + (R_i + h_{i1} P_{pub}) h_{i2} \right)$$

where $h_{i1} = H_1(ID_i, R_i)$ and $h_{i2} = H_2(ID_i, L, T_i, pid)$.

4   Security Analysis

In our security proof, we cover the most recent security concept which achieves the AKE and MA security, where the latter covers the impersonation attacks. Particularly, we consider key compromise impersonation (KCI) resilience against insider and outsider adversaries as discussed in [11]. An outsider adversary may compromise the long-term private key of all parties except one. An outsider adversary is successful in KCI attack if it can impersonate an uncorrupted instance (in our case the ephemeral key) of an uncorrupted party to an uncorrupted instance of any of the corrupted parties. The adversary's goal is to break the confidentiality of the session private key and to break the MA-security. An adversary is called insider adversary if it succeeds in corrupting a party and participating in a protocol session representing the corrupted party. An insider adversary is successful in breaking KCI security if it succeeds to impersonate an uncorrupted instance of an uncorrupted party A to another uncorrupted instance of another party B. The only goal of an insider adversary is to break the MA-security.

Theorem 1. *We first show that our protocol is AKE-secure under the hardness of CDH problem and under the condition that the underlying signature scheme is UF-CMA secure and H_1, H_2, H_3, H are random oracles. The advantage of $\mathcal{A}_{ake}$ is upper bounded by the following term*

$$2 \left(n^2 Adv_{\mathcal{A}_{CMA},\Sigma} + \frac{(q_s + q_e + q_{H_1} + q_{H_2} + q_{H_3} + q_H)^2}{2^\lambda} + \frac{q_s^2}{2^\lambda} \right.$$

$$\left. + n q_s q_{H_1} q_{H_2} q_{H_3} q_H Adv_{\mathcal{A}_{CDH}} + \frac{q_s q_{H_1} q_{H_2} q_{H_3} + q_H}{2^\lambda} \right),$$

where n is the number of participants.

Proof. We prove the theorem via game hopping technique. Let E_i be an event that $\mathcal{A}_{ake}$ wins the i-th AKE-security game. Furthermore, let ρ_i be the advantage of $\mathcal{A}_{ake}$ in game i. We set $\rho_i = |2Pr[S_i] - 1|$. Our idea of game hopping technique is motivated by [9]. If an event E' occurs during $\mathcal{A}'_{ake}$s execution and it is detectable by simulator, then E' is independent of E_i. We say that two games $Game_i, Game_{i+1}$ are identical unless an event E' occurs such that $Pr[E_{i+1} | E'] = 1/2$.

Game0: This game is the same as original AKE-security game. The advantage is given by $Adv_{\mathcal{A}_{ake}} = |2Pr[E_0] - 1| = \rho_0$.

Game1: This is a game as $Game0$ except that the simulation of an event fails if an event 'Forge' occurs, which means that $\mathcal{A}_{ake}$ issues a Send query with (m_i, σ_i), where user U_i is not corrupted and m_i was not output in the previous instance of U_i. According to the AKE-security for KCI attacks definition, $\mathcal{A}_{ake}$ can corrupt up to $n-1$ parties, but it cannot modify messages at the instances of corrupted users. If Forge occurs, it can be used to fake signatures given a public key as follows: the public key is assigned to one person where the other $n-1$ parties are assumed to be normal according to the protocol. Since $n-1$ parties are corrupt, the secret keys of those $n-1$ parties are known. The only secret key which corresponds to the public key of the Unf-CMA game can be queried to the signing oracle. The signing oracle is available from the underlying signature scheme. It is obvious that the probability that $\mathcal{A}_{cma}$ does not corrupt a party is $1/n$, such that holds $Adv_{\mathcal{A}} \geq \frac{1}{n}Pr[Forge] \Leftrightarrow Pr[Forge] \leq nAdv_{\mathcal{A}_{cma}}$.

Game2: This game is the same as the previous but the simulation fails if an event 'Collision' appears. This is the case when one of the random oracles produces a collision. This happens when $H_1(ID_i, R_i) = H_1(ID'_i, R_i)$, with $|I|$ possible values for ID'_i, where I is the identity space, or $H_1(ID_i, R_i) = H_1(ID_i, R'_i)$, with q possible values for R'_i, or $H_1(ID_i, R_i) = H_1(ID'_i, R'_i)$ with $q|I|$ possible variations for (ID'_i, R'_i). Since the input of the second hash function consists of 3 entries, there are 6+1 options for a possible collision with in total $q^2|ID|$ possible value for all options of collisions. Analogously there are 3 options for the collision of H_3 with total $\lambda!|q-1|$ possible values and 1 collision option for the H function with $\lambda!$ possible values in total. Each of the Execute and Send queries requires a query to one of the random oracles, such that the number of random oracle queries is bounded by $(q_s + q_e + q_{H_1} + q_{H_2} + q_{H_3} + q_H)^2$. The probability of Collision is:

$$Pr[Collision] \leq \frac{(q_s + q_e + q_{H_1} + q_{H_2} + q_{H_3} + q_H)^2}{2^\lambda}$$

Game3: The game is the same as the previous one, except that the simulation fails when a 'Repeat' event occurs. A 'Repeat' event happens when an instance of user U_i chooses a nonce κ_i that was also used by another instance of the user U_i. The maximum of instances which can choose a nonce is $q_e + q_s$, therefore

$$Pr[Repeat] \leq \frac{(q_s + q_e)^2}{2^\lambda}$$

Game4: This game differs from the previous game by $\mathcal{A}_{ake}$' randomly chosen value ν from the set of values which is bounded by Execute and Send queries, i.e. $x_i \in \{1, \ldots, q_s + q_e\}$. This value states for the guess of the session in which the adversary will be tested. If $\mathcal{A}_{ake}$ chooses a different session where he issues Test queries, then the simulation aborts. Otherwise, the event that the adversary picks the right session for being tested, happens with the probability of $1/(q_e + q_s)$. The probability that the simulation aborts is correspondingly given by $1 - \frac{1}{(q_e + q_s)}$. Therefore we can say that the probability of event E_4 (correct guess) is the reduced probability of the previous event from Game3 plus the abort probability, i.e.

$$Pr[E_4] = Pr[E_3]\frac{1}{(q_s + q_e)} + \frac{1}{2}\left(1 - \frac{1}{q_s + q_e}\right)$$

Game5: This game differs from previous game by the differences in answers to the Send queries during the Test session. We assume that in round 1 the values l_i are randomly chosen from $\{0, 1\}^\lambda$. All other calculations are the same as in the previous game. Since in the previous game, the values l_i are results of a hash function, i.e. $l_i = H_3(\cdot)$, where H_3 is represented as a random oracle, then an adversary $\mathcal{A}_{ake}$ can distinguish between Game4 and Game5 only if the inputs x_i, x_i' are distinct. Let $\tilde{E}$ be an event where the adversary succeeds to distinguish the values of a hash function. Then the probability is $|Pr[E_4] - Pr[E_5]| \leq Pr[\tilde{E}]$. When $\mathcal{A}_{ake}$ can distinguish between the random and real value, then we can also solve the CDH problem as follows. Let U_i be a random party involved in the test session, then we set $R_i = aP$ and $L_i = bP$. Let C be a randomly chosen value from $\{0, 1\}^\lambda$. If $\tilde{E}$ occurs, then the probability that C chosen from the random oracle table is also the solution of CDH problem, is at least $1/(q_{H_3})$. It follows, that $Adv_{CDH} \geq \frac{1}{nq_{H_3}}Pr[\tilde{E}]$.

Game6: The difference of this game to the previous one is that the test session aborts if $\mathcal{A}_{ake}$ issues a query $(k_1|| \ldots ||k_n||sid_i||pid_i)$. Since the adversary does not get any information about k_n, he can only guess the value with a probability of $1/2^\lambda$. $\mathcal{A}_{ake}$ issues at most q_H Test queries. Thus follows:

$$|Pr[E_6] - Pr[E_5]| \leq \frac{q_H}{2^\lambda}$$

The advantage of $\mathcal{A}_{ake}$ in this game satisfies the following equation: $\rho_5 = 2\frac{q_H}{2^\lambda} + \rho_6$. The advantage ρ_6 is 0, if $\mathcal{A}_{ake}$ does not issue a querry to the H oracle on the correct value $(k_1||\ldots||k_n||sid_i||pid_i)$.

Combining all the probabilities from the presented games, the advantage of $\mathcal{A}_{ake}$ is negligible.   □

In the following theorem, we formulate the MA-security for our protocol.

Theorem 2. *We first show that our protocol is MA-secure under the hardness of CDH problem and under the condition that the underlying signature scheme is UF-CMA secure and H_1, H_2, H_3, H are random oracles. The advantage of $\mathcal{A}_{ma}$ is upper bounded by the following term*

$$2\left(n^2 Adv_{\mathcal{A}_{CMA},\Sigma} + \frac{(q_s + q_e + q_{H_1} + q_{H_2} + q_{H_3} + q_H)^2}{2^\lambda} + \frac{q_s^2}{2^\lambda}\right.$$
$$\left. + nq_s q_{H_1} q_{H_2} q_{H_3} q_H Adv_{\mathcal{A}_{CDH}} + \frac{q_s q_{H_1} q_{H_2} q_{H_3} + q_H}{2^\lambda}\right),$$

where n is the number of participants.

Proof. The proof follows using the game hopping technique as in the proof of previous theorem. Since the descriptions of the games is very similar to the already presented proof of AKE-security, we sketch it here and show only the final result. The game sequence ends after the third game, where the Forge, Collision and Repeat events could be resolved during the three games. If the game does not abort, it follows that all honest parties from pid_i compute the same secret key, such that $Pr[E_3] = 0$.

5   Efficiency Analysis

In this section, we compare the efficiency of our proposed AGKA protocol with some recent ID-based GKA protocols [22, 24–27] (Table 1).

Table 1. Efficiency comparison for each participant

Scheme	Wu [27]	Wu [26]	Wu [25]	Wu [24]	Teng [22]	Ours
Round	3	3	2	2	2	2
Pairing	6	8	$3n + 3$	$3n + 2$	$2(n-1)$	0
ScalarMulti	$4n + 1$	$2n + 8$	$n + 10$	$n + 9$	$n + 9$	$(3n + 2) + n\dagger$
ModularExpo.	$2n + 7$	0	$n - 1$	0	0	0
MaptoPointHash	0	$4n$	3	4	0	0
ProvablySecure	Yes	Yes	Attack by [23]	Yes	No	Yes
Time(ms)	344.49	335.96	486.78	442.16	249.64	37.57

Remark 1. Here, † represents the computation cost of scalar multiplication by a small random integer. Note that the execution time of a scalar multiplication $v_i P$ (where $v_i \in [1; 2^t]$) is far less than the usual scalar multiplication in elliptic curve and hence we ignore this for our computation. Here, we consider $n = 5$, for operation time computation. For the operation timings, we refer to [8].

From the above table, it is clear that our proposed AGKA do not require any expensive operation like pairing and hence very efficient with compare to the existing schemes. To the best of our knowledge, ours is the first pairing free balanced AGKA protocol secure in the strong security model, the EGBG model.

6   Conclusion

This paper presents an authenticated group key agreement protocol secure in extended GBG (EGBG) model. The computation cost makes the results interesting especially for low power devices. In the security analysis we allow both the leakage of long term secret key and ephemeral key (of course for different users), as privileged in EGBG model. In particular, we have proved the authenticated key exchange (AKE) security and the mutual authentication (MA) security with full forward secrecy. Moreover, we have done an efficiency analysis and have shown that our scheme is more efficient in the view of computation and operation time with compare to the existing similar schemes which are more acceptable for the tiny processors. To the best of our knowledge, ours is the first pairing free balanced AGKA protocol secure in the EGBG model.

References

1. Barua, R., Dutta, R., Sarkar, P.: Extending Joux's protocol to multi party key agreement. In: Johansson, T., Maitra, S. (eds.) INDOCRYPT 2003. LNCS, vol. 2904, pp. 205–217. Springer, Heidelberg (2003). https://doi.org/10.1007/978-3-540-24582-7_15
2. Bellare, M., Rogaway, P.: Entity authentication and key distribution. In: Stinson, D.R. (ed.) CRYPTO 1993. LNCS, vol. 773, pp. 232–249. Springer, Heidelberg (1994). https://doi.org/10.1007/3-540-48329-2_21
3. Bresson, E., Chevassut, O., Pointcheval, D.: Provably authenticated group Diffie-Hellman key exchange — the dynamic case. In: Boyd, C. (ed.) ASIACRYPT 2001. LNCS, vol. 2248, pp. 290–309. Springer, Heidelberg (2001). https://doi.org/10.1007/3-540-45682-1_18
4. Bresson, E., Chevassut, O., Pointcheval, D.: Dynamic group Diffie-Hellman key exchange under standard assumptions. In: Knudsen, L.R. (ed.) EUROCRYPT 2002. LNCS, vol. 2332, pp. 321–336. Springer, Heidelberg (2002). https://doi.org/10.1007/3-540-46035-7_21
5. Bresson, E., Chevassut, O., Pointcheval, D., Quisquater, J.-J.: Provably authenticated group Diffie-Hellman key exchange. In: Proceedings of the 8th ACM Conference on Computer and Communications Security, pp. 255–264. ACM (2001)

6. Burmester, M., Desmedt, Y.: A secure and efficient conference key distribution system. In: De Santis, A. (ed.) EUROCRYPT 1994. LNCS, vol. 950, pp. 275–286. Springer, Heidelberg (1995). https://doi.org/10.1007/BFb0053443
7. Choi, K.Y., Hwang, J.Y., Lee, D.H.: Efficient ID-based group key agreement with bilinear maps. In: Bao, F., Deng, R., Zhou, J. (eds.) PKC 2004. LNCS, vol. 2947, pp. 130–144. Springer, Heidelberg (2004). https://doi.org/10.1007/978-3-540-24632-9_10
8. Debiao, H., Jianhua, C., Jin, H.: An ID-based proxy signature schemes without bilinear pairings. Ann. Telecommun.-annales des télécommunications 66(11–12), 657–662 (2011)
9. Dent, A.W.: A note on game-hopping proofs. IACR Cryptology ePrint Archive 2006:260 (2006)
10. Diffie, W., Hellman, M.: New directions in cryptography. IEEE Trans. Inf. Theory 22(6), 644–654 (1976)
11. Gorantla, M.C., Boyd, C., González Nieto, J.M.: Modeling key compromise impersonation attacks on group key exchange protocols. In: Jarecki, S., Tsudik, G. (eds.) PKC 2009. LNCS, vol. 5443, pp. 105–123. Springer, Heidelberg (2009). https://doi.org/10.1007/978-3-642-00468-1_7
12. Hess, F.: Efficient identity based signature schemes based on pairings. In: Nyberg, K., Heys, H. (eds.) SAC 2002. LNCS, vol. 2595, pp. 310–324. Springer, Heidelberg (2003). https://doi.org/10.1007/3-540-36492-7_20
13. Horng, S.-J., Tzeng, S.-F., Pan, Y., Fan, P., Wang, X., Li, T., Khan, M.K.: b-SPECS+: batch verification for secure pseudonymous authentication in vanet. IEEE Trans. Inf. Forensics Secur. 8(11), 1860–1875 (2013)
14. Ingemarsson, I., Tang, D., Wong, C.: A conference key distribution system. IEEE Trans. Inf. Theory 28(5), 714–720 (1982)
15. Joux, A.: A one round protocol for tripartite Diffie–Hellman. In: Bosma, W. (ed.) ANTS 2000. LNCS, vol. 1838, pp. 385–393. Springer, Heidelberg (2000). https://doi.org/10.1007/10722028_23
16. Katz, J., Shin, J.S.: Modeling insider attacks on group key-exchange protocols. In: Proceedings of the 12th ACM Conference on Computer and Communications Security, pp. 180–189. ACM (2005)
17. Katz, J., Yung, M.: Scalable protocols for authenticated group key exchange. In: Boneh, D. (ed.) CRYPTO 2003. LNCS, vol. 2729, pp. 110–125. Springer, Heidelberg (2003). https://doi.org/10.1007/978-3-540-45146-4_7
18. Kyung-Ah, S.: Further analysis of ID-based authenticated group key agreement protocol from bilinear maps. IEICE Trans. Fundam. Electron. Commun. Comput. Sci. 90(1), 295–298 (2007)
19. Schnorr, C.P.: Efficient identification and signatures for smart cards. In: Brassard, G. (ed.) CRYPTO 1989. LNCS, vol. 435, pp. 239–252. Springer, New York (1990). https://doi.org/10.1007/0-387-34805-0_22
20. Shamir, A.: Identity-based cryptosystems and signature schemes. In: Blakley, G.R., Chaum, D. (eds.) CRYPTO 1984. LNCS, vol. 196, pp. 47–53. Springer, Heidelberg (1985). https://doi.org/10.1007/3-540-39568-7_5
21. Steiner, M., Tsudik, G., Waidner, M.: Key agreement in dynamic peer groups. IEEE Trans. Parallel Distrib. Syst. 11(8), 769–780 (2000)
22. Teng, J., Wu, C., Tang, C., Tian, Y.: A strongly secure identity-based authenticated group key exchange protocol. Sci. China Inf. Sci. 58(9), 1–12 (2015)
23. Wei, F., Wei, Y., Ma, C.: Attack on an ID-based authenticated group key exchange protocol with identifying malicious participants. IJ Netw. Secur. 18(2), 393–396 (2016)

24. Wu, T.-Y., Tsai, T.-T., Tseng, Y.-M.: A provably secure revocable ID-based authenticated group key exchange protocol with identifying malicious participants. Sci. World J. **2014** (2014)
25. Wu, T.-Y., Tseng, Y.-M.: Towards ID-based authenticated group key exchange protocol with identifying malicious participants. Informatica **23**(2), 315–334 (2012)
26. Wu, T.-Y., Tseng, Y.-M., Tsai, T.-T.: A revocable ID-based authenticated group key exchange protocol with resistant to malicious participants. Comput. Netw. **56**(12), 2994–3006 (2012)
27. Wu, T.-Y., Tseng, Y.-M., Yu, C.-W.: A secure ID-based authenticated group key exchange protocol resistant to insider attacks. J. Inf. Sci. Eng. **27**(3), 915–932 (2011)
28. Zhang, F., Chen, X.: Attack on an ID-based authenticated group key agreement scheme from PKC 2004. Inf. Process. Lett. **91**(4), 191–193 (2004)
29. Zhao, J., Gu, D., Gorantla, M.C.: Stronger security model of group key agreement. In: Proceedings of the 6th ACM Symposium on Information, Computer and Communications Security, pp. 435–440. ACM (2011)

Network Security

Machine Learning for Black-Box Fuzzing of Network Protocols

Rong Fan[✉] and Yaoyao Chang

Beijing Institute of Technology, Beijing, China
fanrong_1992@163.com

Abstract. As the network services are gradually complex and important, the security problems of their protocols become more and more serious. Vulnerabilities in network protocol implementations can expose sensitive user data to attackers or execute arbitrary malicious code deployed by attackers. Fuzzing is an effective way to find security vulnerabilities for network protocols. But it is difficult to fuzz network protocols if the specification and implementation code of the protocol are both unavailable. In this paper, we propose a method to automatically generate test cases for black-box fuzzing of proprietary network protocols. Our method uses neural-network-based machine learning techniques to learn a generative input model of proprietary network protocols by processing their traffic, and generating new messages using the learnt model. These new messages can be used as test cases to fuzz the implementations of corresponding protocols.

Keywords: Black-box fuzzing · Proprietary network protocol
Machine learning

1 Introduction

Fuzzing is one of the most effective techniques to find security vulnerabilities in application by repeatedly testing it with modified or fuzzed inputs. State-of-the-art Fuzzing techniques can be divided into two main types: (1) black-box fuzzing [1], and (2) white-box fuzzing [2]. Black-box fuzzing is used to find security vulnerabilities in closed-source applications and white-box fuzzing is for open source applications. In terms of proprietary protocols, whose specification and implementation code are unavailable, black-box fuzzing is the only method can be conducted. There are two kinds of black-box fuzzing: (1) mutation-based fuzzing, and (2) generation-based fuzzing. Mutation-based fuzzing requires no knowledge of the protocol under test, it modifies an existing corpus of seed inputs to generate test cases. In contrast, generation-based fuzzing requires the input model to specify the message format of the protocol, in order to generate test cases. It has been proved that generation-based fuzzing performs much better, when compared to mutation-based fuzzing [3]. However, the input model of generation-based fuzzing can not be provided if neither the specification nor the

© Springer International Publishing AG, part of Springer Nature 2018
S. Qing et al. (Eds.): ICICS 2017, LNCS 10631, pp. 621–632, 2018.
https://doi.org/10.1007/978-3-319-89500-0_53

implementation code of the protocol are available. Therefore, it requires protocol reverse engineering to figure out the message format of the protocol.

There have been many approaches to find security vulnerabilities in protocol implementations. For example, static code analysis [4,5], white-box fuzzing [2,6], symbolic execution [7,8], and dynamic taint analysis [9] can help spotting vulnerabilities of the protocol, if the source code of the protocol is available. And if the specification of the protocol is already known, there are several modern fuzzers such as Sulley [10], Peach [11] and SPIKE [12] can be used. However, if the specification and implementation code of the protocol are both unavailable, things have become completely different. In this situation, only a few methods [13,14] can be applied for protocol vulnerability discovery. These methods provided first solution for automatically fuzzing proprietary protocols if a program analysis is not possible or hard to carry out. But they have used variants of traditional clustering algorithm and n-gram based approaches that are limited by contents of finite length.

In contrast with previous work, we make the first attempt at applying neural-network-based machine-learning techniques for black-box fuzzing of proprietary network protocol. Our method combine the concepts from fuzzing with the techniques from natural language processing. In specifically, we capture sufficient network traffic of an unknown protocol, then use seq2seq model with LSTM cells to learn a generative input model that can be used to generate test cases. Finally, we use the generative model to communicate with the implementation of unknown protocol.

The rest of the paper is organized as follows: Sect. 2 gives a brief introduction to neural-network-based machine-learning techniques. We introduce our method for black-box fuzzing of proprietary protocols in Sect. 3. Section 4 presents results of fuzzing experiments with our method. Related work is discussed in Sect. 5. We conclude in Sect. 6.

2   Preliminaries

We now give a brief introduction to neural-network-based machine-learning techniques.

2.1   Recurrent Neural Networks

Recurrent neural networks (RNNs) address the issue of information persistence, which traditional neural networks can't do. They are networks with loops in them, operating on a variable length input sequence $(x_1, x_2, ..., x_T)$ and consist of a hidden state h_t and an output y.

As Fig. 1 shows, a block of neural network, A, looks at some input x_t and outputs a value h_t. A loop is able to pass information from one step of the network to the next. A RNN can be thought of as multiple copies of the same network, each passing a message to a successor as Fig. 2.

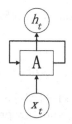

Fig. 1. Recurrent neural network with loops

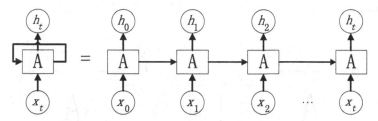

Fig. 2. Unrolled recurrent neural network

The RNN processes the input sequence in a series of time stamps. For a particular time stamp t, the hidden state h_t and the output y_t at that time stamp has equations as Eqs. 1 and 2 show.

$$h_t = f(h_{t-1}, x_t) \tag{1}$$

$$y_t = \phi(h_t) \tag{2}$$

In Eq. 1, f is a non-linear activation function such as sigmoid, tanh etc., which is used to introduce non-linearity into the network. And ϕ in Eq. 2 is a function such as softmax that computes the output probability distribution over a given vocabulary conditioned on the current hidden state. RNNs can learn a probability distribution over a character sequence $(x_1, x_2, ..., x_{t-1})$ by training to predict the next character x_t in the sequence.

In theory, RNNs are absolutely capable of handling long-term dependencies, where the predictions need more context. Unfortunately, in practice, RNNs become unable to learn to connect the information in cases shown in Fig. 3,

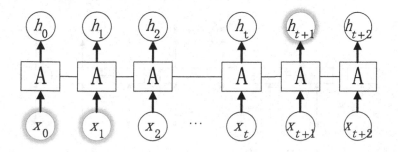

Fig. 3. RNN long-term dependencies

where the distance between the relevant information and the place that it is needed becomes very large.

2.2   Long Short-Term Memory Networks

Long short-term memory networks (LSTMs) are a special kind of RNN, explicitly designed to avoid the long-term dependency problem. They also have the form of a chain, which has repeating modules of neural networks. But instead of having a single neural network layer, the repeating module has a different structure as Fig. 4 shows.

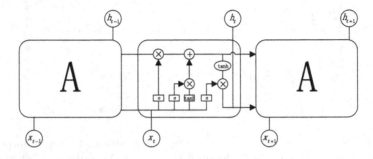

Fig. 4. LSTM repeating module with four interacting layers

The horizontal line crossing through the top of Fig. 4 is the cell state, which is the key of LSTMs. LSTMs are able to remove or add information to cell state with structures called gates, which composed out of a sigmoid neural net layer and a point wise multiplication operation.

2.3   Sequence to Sequence

A basic sequence-to-sequence (seq2seq) model, as introduced by Cho et al. [15], consists of two recurrent neural networks, an encoder RNN that processes a variable dimensional input sequence to a fixed-size state vector, and a decoder RNN that takes the fixed-size state vector and generates the variable dimensional output sequence. The basic architecture is depicted as Fig. 5.

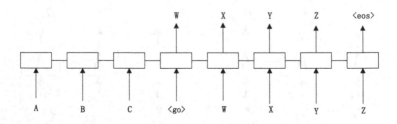

Fig. 5. Basic sequence to sequence

Each box in Fig. 5 represents a cell of the RNN, in our method an LSTM cell. Encoder and decoder can share weights or, as is more common, use a different set of parameters. We train the seq2seq model using a corpus of network recordings, treating each one of the message as a sequence of characters. Before training, we concatenate all the messages into a single file.

3   Methodology

The main idea of our method is to learn a generative input model over the set of network protocol messages. We use a seq2seq model that has been historically proved to be very successful at many automatic tasks such as speech recognition and machine translation. Traditional n-gram based approaches are limited by contexts of finite length, while the seq2seq model is able to learn arbitrary length contexts to predict next sequence of characters. The seq2seq model can be trained in an unsupervised mode to learn a generative input model, which can be used to generate test cases.

3.1   Training the Model

Before training the seq2seq model, we need to preprocess the corpus. Firstly, we count the non-repeating characters in the corpus, and sort them in a list according to their frequency of occurrence. Then, take each character as key and its order in list as value, storing in a dictionary. Finally, create a tensor file which replace all characters with its value in list. The main purpose of preprocessing is to calculate the number of batches N_b,

$$N_b = \frac{S_t}{S_b * L_s} \tag{3}$$

where S_t is the size of tensor file, S_b is the size of one batch, which is set to 50 by default. And L_s is the length of each sequence in batches.

After the preprocessing, we train the seq2seq model in an unsupervised learning mode. Due to the absent of training dataset labels, we are not able to accurately determine how well the trained models are performing. We instead train several models with different *epochs*, which is the number of learning algorithm execution. Therefore, an *epoch* is defined as an iteration of the learning algorithm to go over the complete training dataset. We train the seq2seq models M_s as shown in Algorithm 1 with five different numbers of epochs N_e: 10, 20, 30, 40 and 50. We use an LSTM model with 2 hidden layers, and each layer consists of 128 hidden states.

I_p is the initial path, where the checkpoints file stored in. N_s is the number of training steps to save intermediate result and the default setting is 1000.

Algorithm 1. Pseudocode for training

Input: I_p, N_b, N_e, N_s.
Output: M_s
1. **if** I_p is not None **then**
2.   restore checkpoints from file
3. **end if**
4. new M_s
5. **for** e = 0,1,...,N_e **do**
6.   initialize training session
7.   **for** b = 0,1,...,N_b **do**
8.   run training session with M_s
9.   **if** (e*N_b+b) % N_s == 0 or
10.   e == N_e-1 **and** b == N_b-1 **then**
11.   **Output** M_s
12.   **end if**
13.   **end for**
14.**end for**

3.2   Test Case Generation

We use the trained seq2seq model to generate new protocol messages. At the beginning of the fuzzing, we always connect to the server, and take the received message for initial sequence I_s. Then request the seq2seq model to generate a sequence until it outputs one protocol message terminator like CRLF in ftp. Based on sampling strategy, there are three different strategies for message generation. Now, we give the details of these three different sampling strategies we make experiments with.

Max at Each Step: In this sampling strategy, we pick the best character in the predicted probability distribution. This strategy will generate protocol messages which are most likely to be well-formed. But this feature just makes the strategy unsuitable for fuzzing. Because we need test cases which are not quite the same as well-formed messages for fuzzing.

Sample at Each Step: In this sampling strategy, we don't pick the best predicted next characters in the probability distribution. As a result, this strategy is able to generate multifarious new protocol messages, which combines various templates the seq2seq model has learnt from the protocol messages. Due to sampling, the generated protocol messages will not always be well-formed, which is of great use for fuzzing.

Sample on Spaces: This sampling strategy combines the two strategies described above. It uses the best predicted character in the probability distribution when the last character of the input sequence is not a space. And it samples distribution to generate next character when the input sequence ends with a space, similar to the second strategy. More well-formed protocol messages compared to the second strategy can be generated by this strategy.

Algorithm 2. Pseudocode for sampling

Input: I_s, M_s, N, strategy type T.
Output: generated sequence S
1. put I_s into M_s
2. c = last character in I_s
3. **for** n = 0,1,...,N **do**
4.   use M_s to predict the D_p
5.   **if** $T == 0$ **then**
6.   pick the best character in D_p
7.   **else if** $T == 1$ **then**
8.   weighted pick character in D_p
9.   **else**
10.   **if** c is space **then**
11.   weighted pick character in D_p
12.   **else**
13.   pick the best character in D_p
14.   **end if**
15.   **end if**
16.   append picked character to S
17. c = picked character
18.**end for**
19.**Output** S

N is the number of characters in the generated sequence, and we set it randomly to generate messages of arbitrary length.

4 Experimental Evaluation

4.1 Experiment Setup

In this section, we present results of fuzzing experiments with two ftp applications WarFTPD 1.65 and Serv-U build 4.0.0.4. We establish these two ftp applications on two servers, which run Windows Server 2003. The seq2seq models is trained on a personal computer, which has a Ubuntu 16.04 operating system. We implement a client program to communicate with ftp server, using the test cases generated by trained seq2seq model as input. If the program detects any error reports from ftp server, it records error messages in an error log. And we can validate whether the recorded error messages are indeed able to trigger vulnerabilities. Moreover, it is also feasible to implement a server program of the protocol to fuzz the client applications.

We use three working standards to evaluate fuzzing effectiveness:

Coverage: A basic demand shared by random and more advanced grammar-based fuzzers is that the instruction coverage should be as high as possible. In the case of our method, the fuzzer is able to fuzz the communication both ends but its coverage is highly depend on the network recordings.

Bugs: During the fuzzing process, we take the advantage of tool AppVerifier to monitor the running of ftp server. AppVerifier is a free runtime monitoring tool which can catch memory corruption bugs like buffer overflows, and it is widely used for fuzzing on Windows.

Performance Comparison: We record the statistical data when our fuzzer and existing fuzzer Sulley and SPIKE running with Serv-U build 4.0.0.4 for performance comparison. The statistical data include *Times*, *Time* and *Speed*. *Times* is the number of test cases sent, and *Time* means how many minutes was taken to find the bug. *Speed* indicates the number of test cases sent per second.

4.2   Corpus

We extracted about 10,000 messages for WarFTPD and 36,000 messages for Serv-U from network recordings. Most of the network recordings are generated by normal access to ftp server. And part of the traffic is generated by Sulley. Using Sulley is to improve the instruction coverage, because normal access may not include some less commonly used commands like MDTM, which is used to get the modification time of the remote file.

These 10,000 messages for WarFTPD and 36,000 messages for Serv-U which have both client and server side data are the training corpus for the seq2seq model we used in this work. We generate protocol messages using the trained seq2seq model, but the input data for ftp server should be transfered from network. Therefore we implement a client program to send the generated messages to ftp server.

4.3   Result

In order to obtain a reasonable explanation of coverage results, we select the network recordings of normal access to ftp server, and measure their coverage of the ftp application, to be used as a baseline for following experiments. When training the seq2seq model, an important parameter is the number of epochs. The results of experiments obtained after training the seq2seq model with 10, 20, 30, 40 and 50 epochs is reported here.

Coverage. Figure 6(a) and (b) show the instruction coverage obtained with **sample at each step** and **sample at spaces** from 10 to 50 epochs for WarFTPD and Serv-U. The figures also show the coverage obtained with the corresponding baseline.

We observe the following:

- The coverage for **sample at each step** and **sample on spaces** are above the **baseline** coverage for most epoch results.
- The trend for the coverage of WarFTPD and Serv-U from 10 to 50 epochs is quite unstable and unpredictable.
- The best coverage obtained with **sample at each step** and **sample on spaces** are both with 40-epochs.

(a)

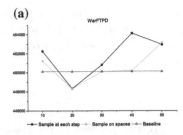

(b)

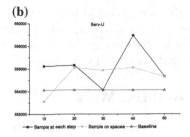

Fig. 6. Coverage for WarFTPD and Serv-U from 10 to 50 epochs.

Table 1. Bugs found by fuzzing

Application	Test results	Bug type
WarFTPD 1.65	CWD, CDUP, DELE, NLST, LIST	DoS
	USER	Buffer overflow
Serv-U build 4.0.0.4	SITE, CHMOD, MDTM, LIST	Buffer overflow
	XCRC, STOU, DSIZ	DoS

Bugs. Another working standard is of course the number of bugs found. Our method has been tested on WarFTPD and Serv-U two ftp applications, and after a nearly 4-days experiment, we found almost all of the already known vulnerabilities in these two ftp applications as Table 1 shows.

There is a *SMNT* buffer overflow vulnerability in Serv-U not found, because of the incompleteness of network traffic we used to train the seq2seq model.

Performance Comparison. In addition to coverage and bugs, a third working standard of interest is performance of our method. We compared our fuzzer with existing fuzzer Sulley [10] and SPIKE [12]. As Table 2 shows, the efficiency of our method is slightly lower than that of the existing methods. This is because

Table 2. Performance comparison

Command	Sulley			SPIKE			Our fuzzer		
	Times	Time	Speed	Times	Time	Speed	Times	Time	Speed
SITE	987	1	16	3123	2	26	1307	3	9
CHMOD	1322	1	22	1212	1	20	3426	5	11
MDTM	1453	1	24	3127	2	24	1688	2	13
LIST	922	1	15	1562	1	26	987	2	8
XCRC	1348	1	22	2043	1	34	3366	5	12
STOU	2897	2	23	3031	2	25	1590	2	14
DSIZ	3188	2	26	3875	2	29	3425	6	10

that the generation of test cases by seq2seq model takes a lot of time. However, Sulley and SPIKE can only be used when the specification of the protocol is available, but our method is able to fuzz proprietary network protocols, whose specification and implementation code are both unavailable.

5   Related Work

Protocol Reverse Engineering. Over a decade ago, the process of reverse engineering a network protocol was a tedious, time-consuming and manual task. Nowadays, there are plenty of methods proposed for automating the process of protocol reverse engineering. The methods can be divided into two branches: On the one hand, methods that utilize the protocol implementation [16,17], and on the other hand, those extract protocol specification from network recordings only. The Protocol Informatics Project [18] uses a bioinformatics method to implement byte sequence alignment of similar message formats. The Discoverer tool [19] present a recursive clustering approach of tokenized messages. Biprominer [20] and ProDecoder [21] presented by Wang et al. focused on binary protocols, they retrieve statistically relevant keywords and sequencing. Based on data mining techniques, AutoReEngine [22] reveal keywords and their position within messages. It is particularly difficult to extract protocol specification in case the protocol implementation code can not be available for network security staff, but network recordings only. These approaches provide first means for automatically identify message field boundaries and formats, but unfortunately, they are not able to relate variable fields over temporal states.

Protocol Fuzzing. Fuzzing is one of the most effective techniques to uncover security flaws in application by generating test case in an automated way. Two types of fuzzing can be discriminated here: (1) black-box fuzzing [1] which a tester can only seeing what input and output of an application, and white-box fuzzing [2] that allows the tester to inspect the implementation code (either binary or source code) and for instance, take advantage of static code analysis and symbolic execution. This classification is obviously applicable to protocol fuzzing as well. Most well-known black-box random fuzzers today support generation-based fuzzing, e.g. Peach [11] and SPIKE [12], can be used to fuzz protocol implementation when the specification of the protocol is available, but can do no more when the protocol is unknown. Only few approaches can fuzz protocol in situation where specification and implementation code are both unavailable. AutoFuzz [13] and PULSAR [14], which both infer the protocol state machine and message formats from network traffic alone.

6   Conclusion

It is a challenging problem of computer security to find vulnerabilities in the implementations of proprietary protocols. To the best of our knowledge, this is the first attempt to do black-box protocol fuzzing using neural network learning algorithm, which is able to find vulnerabilities in protocol implementations, whether or not the code nor specification are available. We presented and evaluated algorithms with different sampling strategies to automatically learn a generative model of protocol messages.

Although we have applied our method on very common network protocols, the method is also able to find vulnerabilities in unusual implementations, such as in embedded devices and industrial control systems. Moreover, we are considering adding some form of reinforcement learning in our future work to guide the fuzzing process with coverage feedback from the application.

References

1. Sutton, M., Greene, A., Amini, P.: Fuzzing: Brute Force Vulnerability Discovery. Pearson Education, London (2007)
2. Godefroid, P., Levin, M.Y., Molnar, D.A., et al.: Automated whitebox fuzz testing. In: NDSS, vol. 8, pp. 151–166 (2008)
3. Miller, C., Peterson, Z.N.: Analysis of mutation and generation-based fuzzing. Technical report, Independent Security Evaluators (2007)
4. Sotirov, A.I.: Automatic vulnerability detection using static source code analysis. Ph.D. thesis, University of Alabama (2005)
5. Chess, B., McGraw, G.: Static analysis for security. IEEE Secur. Priv. 2(6), 76–79 (2004)
6. Godefroid, P., Kiezun, A., Levin, M.Y.: Grammar-based whitebox fuzzing. In: ACM Sigplan Notices, vol. 43, pp. 206–215. ACM (2008)
7. Cadar, C., Godefroid, P., Khurshid, S., Păsăreanu, C.S., Sen, K., Tillmann, N., Visser, W.: Symbolic execution for software testing in practice: preliminary assessment. In: Proceedings of the 33rd International Conference on Software Engineering, pp. 1066–1071. ACM (2011)
8. Cadar, C., Sen, K.: Symbolic execution for software testing: three decades later. Commun. ACM 56(2), 82–90 (2013)
9. Schwartz, E.J., Avgerinos, T., Brumley, D.: All you ever wanted to know about dynamic taint analysis and forward symbolic execution (but might have been afraid to ask). In: 2010 IEEE Symposium on Security and Privacy (SP), pp. 317–331. IEEE (2010)
10. Amini, P., Portnoy, A.: Sulley: pure Python fully automated and unattended fuzzing framework (2013)
11. Eddington, M.: Peach fuzzing platform. In: Peach Fuzzer, p. 34 (2011)
12. Spike fuzzing platform. http://www.immunitysec.com/resourcesfreesoftware.shtml
13. Gorbunov, S., Rosenbloom, A.: Autofuzz: automated network protocol fuzzing framework. IJCSNS 10(8), 239 (2010)
14. Gascon, H., Wressnegger, C., Yamaguchi, F., Arp, D., Rieck, K.: PULSAR: stateful black-box fuzzing of proprietary network protocols. In: Thuraisingham, B., Wang, X.F., Yegneswaran, V. (eds.) SecureComm 2015. LNICST, vol. 164, pp. 330–347. Springer, Cham (2015). https://doi.org/10.1007/978-3-319-28865-9_18
15. Cho, K., Van Merriënboer, B., Gulcehre, C., Bahdanau, D., Bougares, F., Schwenk, H., Bengio, Y.: Learning phrase representations using RNN encoder-decoder for statistical machine translation. arXiv preprint arXiv:1406.1078 (2014)
16. Comparetti, P.M., Wondracek, G., Kruegel, C., Kirda, E.: Prospex: protocol specification extraction. In: 2009 30th IEEE Symposium on Security and Privacy, pp. 110–125. IEEE (2009)

17. Caballero, J., Yin, H., Liang, Z., Song, D.: Polyglot: automatic extraction of protocol message format using dynamic binary analysis. In: Proceedings of the 14th ACM Conference on Computer and Communications Security, pp. 317–329. ACM (2007)
18. Beddoe, M.: The protocol informatics project (2004)
19. Cui, W., Kannan, J., Wang, H.J.: Discoverer: automatic protocol reverse engineering from network traces. In: USENIX Security Symposium, pp. 1–14 (2007)
20. Wang, Y., Li, X., Meng, J., Zhao, Y., Zhang, Z., Guo, L.: Biprominer: automatic mining of binary protocol features. In: 2011 12th International Conference on Parallel and Distributed Computing, Applications and Technologies (PDCAT), pp. 179–184. IEEE (2011)
21. Wang, Y., Yun, X., Shafiq, M.Z., Wang, L., Liu, A.X., Zhang, Z., Yao, D., Zhang, Y., Guo, L.: A semantics aware approach to automated reverse engineering unknown protocols. In: 2012 20th IEEE International Conference on Network Protocols (ICNP), pp. 1–10. IEEE (2012)
22. Luo, J.Z., Yu, S.Z.: Position-based automatic reverse engineering of network protocols. J. Netw. Comput. Appl. **36**(3), 1070–1077 (2013)

A Novel Semantic-Aware Approach
for Detecting Malicious Web Traffic

Jing Yang[1,2], Liming Wang[1(✉)], and Zhen Xu[1]

[1] State Key Laboratory of Information Security,
Institute of Information Engineering, Chinese Academy of Sciences, Beijing, China
{yangjing,wangliming,xuzhen}@iie.ac.cn
[2] School of Cyber Security, University of Chinese Academy of Sciences,
Beijing, China

Abstract. With regard to web compromise, malicious web traffic refers
to requests from users visiting websites for malicious targets, such as
web vulnerabilities, web shells and uploaded malicious advertising web
pages. To directly and comprehensively understand malicious web visits is meaningful to prevent web compromise. However, it is challenging
to identify different malicious web traffic with a generic model. In this
paper, a novel semantic-aware approach is proposed to detect malicious
web traffic by profiling web visits individually. And a semantic representation of malicious activities is introduced to make detection results
more understandable. The evaluation shows that our algorithm is effective in detecting malice with an average precision and recall of 90.8% and
92.9% respectively. Furthermore, we employ our approach on more than
136 million web traffic logs collected from a web hosting service provider,
where 3,995 unique malicious IPs are detected involving hundreds of websites. The derived results reveal that our method is conductive to figure
out adversaries' intentions.

Keywords: Web security · Malicious web traffic · Semantic analysis
Unsupervised learning

1 Introduction

Compromised websites have become increasingly attractive targets for attackers
who exploit them to commit cyber crimes, such as distributing malware, controlling botnets and implementing watering hole attacks [1–3]. Due to current
security mechanisms (e.g., Google Safe Browsing) for protecting users against
malicious sites, attackers have to find more known and clean hosting sites [1].
Consequently any openly accessible website on the Internet may become their
prey.

For a webmaster, it is meaningful to distinguish malicious web traffic generated by users who access the website not for its inherent services but for some
malicious targets, such as web application vulnerabilities, uploaded malware and

© Springer International Publishing AG, part of Springer Nature 2018
S. Qing et al. (Eds.): ICICS 2017, LNCS 10631, pp. 633–645, 2018.
https://doi.org/10.1007/978-3-319-89500-0_54

malicious advertising web pages. If a website is compromised, the webmaster can be notified immediately and make a remedy. If not, understanding attackers' intentions in advance can help the webmaster strengthen security strategies to prevent the site from being compromised.

Generally malicious web traffic involving web compromise can be categorized as three types. As common threats on the Internet, web scan focuses on probing websites for known weaknesses, and web penetration emphasises on finding and exploiting web application vulnerabilities with elaborately crafted web requests. Web abusing traffic, proposed in our work, refers to visits for malicious resources uploaded on a compromised site by attackers. Although extensive works [4–10] on detection of malicious web traffic have been proposed, they can only apply to some types of web attacks with respective prerequisites. In the literature there is no a generic detection model which can distinguish different malicious web traffic without depending on training data or priori knowledge, as different malicious web visits vary greatly.

In this work, we introduce a semantic-aware methodology to distinguish malicious web traffic in an unsupervised-learning way. Our key observation is that, for a website, most requests from normal users are semantically similar while different from malicious users. Regardless of human or bots, users send requests to a website for acquiring its provided services, which makes most network behavior look similar. The malicious send requests for finding or exploiting vulnerabilities, and accordingly their requests are surely different from those of the normal. As illustrated in Fig. 1, for a journal's website, almost all of requests sent from normal users are semantically relevant, and different users may send same requests with a great probability. However, requests from malicious users vary greatly, and most of them are totally irrelevant to normal requests.

```
Normal User N₁:                              Normal User N₂:
GET    /volumn/home.shtml                    GET    /volumn/home.shtml
GET    /journal/authorLogOn.action?mag_Id=1  GET    /journal/expertLogOn.action?mag_Id=1
GET    /journal/images/notice.gif            GET    /journal/images/notice.gif
POST   /journal/j_acegi_security_check       POST   /journal/j_acegi_security_check
GET    /journal/manuscript/Manuscript!view.action?id=1  GET    /journal/reviewer/PersonReviewer!reviewerEdit.action?id=1

Malicious User A₁:
GET    /5.66/plus/car.php
POST   /plus/mytag_js.php?aid=9090

Malicious User A₂:
POST   /exchange.action%0A
GET    /journal/editorInChiefLogOn.action?mag_Id=1%0A??method:%23_memberAccess%3d%40ognl.OgnlContext%40DEFAUT_ME
MBER_ACCESS%2c%23a%3d%40java.lang.Runtime%40getRuntime%28%29.exec%28%23parameters.command%5B0%5D%29.getIn
putStream%28%29%2c%23b%3dnew%20java.io.InputStreamReader%28%23a%29%2c%23c%3dnew%20java.io.BufferedReader%28%
23b%29%2c%23d%3dnew%20char%5B51020%5D%2c%23c.read%28%23d%29%2c%23kxlzx%3d%40org.apache.struts2.ServletActio
nContext%40getResponse%28%29.getWriter%28%29%2c%23kxlzx.println%28%23d%29%2c%23kxlzx.close&command=netstat
```

Fig. 1. Examples of requests from normal users and malicious users

Based on the observation, our methodology profiles a web user's visiting behavior and measures the degree of abnormality of a visit by utilizing a modified term frequency and inverse document frequency (TF-IDF) algorithm. A dynamic threshold is derived to distinguish abnormal users. Unlike existing works, our detection results include not only anomaly scores but also the summary information of malicious activities, which makes the detection results more understandable. We evaluate our approach with a manually labeled dataset consisting of four different websites. It is shown that our method is effective in discovering various malicious web users, as the average precision is 90.8% and the recall is averagely 92.9%. Furthermore, we employ our approach on a large dataset with more than 136 million web traffic logs from a web hosting service provider, where 3,995 unique malicious IPs are detected involving hundreds of websites. In the results, it is impressive that the semantic representation of malicious visits can help webmasters or security analysts understand malice intuitively, which is helpful to improve network defense strategies and identify compromised sites.

We organize this paper as following: Background and related work are introduced in Sect. 2. We present our approach and give details on the anomaly score computation in Sect. 3. Evaluation of our approach and results in the wild are presented in Sect. 4. Finally we make a discussion and conclude the paper in Sect. 5.

2   Background and Related Work

2.1   Classification of Malicious Web Traffic

With regard to web compromise, malicious web traffic refers to requests sent from users who browsing the website not for its inherent services but for malicious targets. We summarize various malicious web traffic into three categories according to the adversary's intention.

- **Web Scan.** In web scanning, attackers probe a website to determine whether it contains certain exploitable web resources. Typical targets in web scan include URLs of known vulnerable third-party components (e.g., Wordpress, CKEditor), URLs of known web shells (e.g., R57, c99), and sensitive file links (e.g., www.zip, .htaccess). Web scan is one of the most common web attacks and usually performed in a large scale on the Internet. In other words, most of web scanning are indiscriminate. Requests in these attacks are very similar to each other.
- **Web Penetration.** In web penetration, actual web hacking attacks, including SQL/Command injection, Cross-Site scripting and others, are performed to locate web vulnerabilities and exploit them in order to compromise a site. Furthermore, web shells would be uploaded to the compromised websites and used to control the sites by attackers. Contrary to web scanning, the requests used for web application penetration are usually elaborately crafted manually or with special web vulnerability exploitation tools. Typical features of request in this traffic are the different distribution of characters and the different structural information from normal requests.
- **Web Abuse.** After successfully subverting control a website, attackers may abuse it for further illicit activities, such as distributing malware and advertising illicit contents (e.g., drug, adult and gambling). These unwanted resources,

for a webmaster, may attract a plenty of visits from bots and human to the website accompanied with a large volume of abusing traffic. Requests in web abusing traffic usually do not contain harmful information to web applications, but the resources they ask for are never seen in previous traffic.

2.2 Related Work About Malicious Web Traffic Detection

Xie et al. [4] introduced Scanner Hunter to detect HTTP scanning. Their key assumption is that web requests of different scanners are similar with each other. Accordingly, it does not work on a site with small traffic volume, since it is not common that many scanners probe a small website.

Kruegel and Vigna [5] proposed a supervised learning based method to detect malicious web requests with a combination of six different anomaly detection models. Many following works [6–9] introduced improved detection approaches. Aiming at the problem of requiring training data, Lampesberger et al. [10] presented an online-learning detection method by transforming a request into a fixed-length symbol sequence. All of them emphasis on detection of malicious requests with crafted parameters, which only probably occur in web penetration attacks.

A web shell is an important tool used in web penetration. Canali and Balzarotti [12] analyzed communication behavior between attackers and web shells after they have compromised a website. Starov et al. [13] gave a more comprehensive study of web shells. Both of them do not involve any detection method. FireEye [14] reported a detailed analysis of the popular shell *China Chopper* and explained how to detect it through network traffic with Snort rules. For web abusing traffic, there is no detection work proposed in the literature as well, and only Alrwais et al. [2] referred to the abusing traffic and utilized it to find compromised websites.

Overall, all of the above works focus on identifying some types of malicious web traffic with respective prerequisites. There is no a generic method to detect all three types of malice without depending on training data or priori knowledge. For a webmaster, it is most concerned that how to distinguish malicious visits from massive complex web traffic by employing a direct and simple method. The challenge is that different types of malicious traffic vary greatly in terms of requests' volume, structure and semantics.

2.3 Related Work About Semantic Analysis in Network Security

Recently, semantic analysis has been more popular in the area of network security. Zhang et al. [11] proposed SBotScope to analysis large-scale malicious bot queries received by a known search engine. Liao et al. [15] introduced a technique *semantic inconsistency search* to detect illicit advertising content. For detection of malicious web traffic, semantic analysis can help avoid too much dependencies on structural information, which requires strong background knowledge on specific attacking techniques.

3   Methodology

To generically detect various malicious web traffic, we employ the literal similarity in requests from normal visits, and introduce a novel semantic-aware detection approach. Since our detection is conducted on the level of a single visit, it is crucial that how to characterize users' dynamic web visiting activities. In our approach, a user's visiting profile is represented in two word sets, and the anomaly score of each word is computed by using a modified TF-IDF algorithm. Furthermore, to avoid interference of normal but infrequent words, a global normal word dictionary is automatically generated. The anomaly score of a user is educed from scores of the two word sets. Then we derive a dynamic threshold to classify abnormal users. The concept of our methodology is shown in Fig. 2.

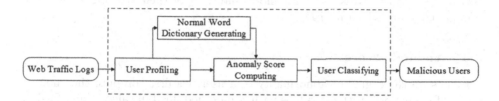

Fig. 2. The overview of our approach

3.1   User Profile

The intentions of web users are directly tied to their requests sent to websites. We derive a method to represent massive requests in aggregation to get a user's profile.

A HTTP request begins with a method token and a Request-URI which includes a resource identifier and an optional query string. After URL decoding, we extract all N_r requests for a user U, and put all resource identifiers and query strings together into two independent text files: F_1 and F_2. The method token is added in F_1 as well.

For F_1, we use / and SPACE as separators to split the file into a word set $W_1 = \{(w_{1i} : n_{1i})\}$, where n_{1i} is the occurrences of the word w_{1i} in the file F_1. For F_2, the separators are /, ?, =, &, ,, @, -, ; and SPACE, and the word set is $W_2 = \{(w_{2i} : n_{2i})\}$. In addition, we replace all continuous numbers with the character X. An example of the user profiling process is shown in Fig. 3.

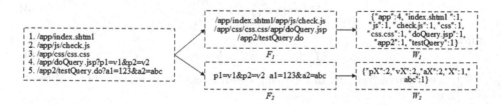

Fig. 3. An example of user profiling

3.2   Normal Word Dictionary

The normal word dictionary is a word set automatically derived from the words of all users. It is based on the assumption that a word is more likely to be normal if it occurs in more visits. Furthermore, even if a word is infrequent, but it is structurally similar with normal words, it is probably normal. We use n-gram to measure the structural similarity. Empirically we choose 4-gram.

To derive the dictionary set D_{nw}, firstly a global word set $G_w = \{(w_i : m_{w_i})\}$ is maintained, in which m_{w_i} is the number of users whose request contains the word w_i, and the number of total users is M. Then, we define a percentage threshold T_{fw} to distinguish frequent words, which means a word w_i is normal if it is in the first T_{fw} percent of words in G_w in descending order by m_{w_i}. All the frequent words are put in D_{nw}, and the n-gram items of them are put in NG_{nw}. For other words in G_w, if more than half of their n-gram items are in NG_{nw}, they are added into D_{nw}.

3.3   Anomaly Score

To measure the degree of abnormality of a user, we first compute the anomaly score of each word in the two files with a modified TF-IDF algorithm. TF-IDF is one of the most popular scheme in the area of information retrieval and text mining, which uses a numerical statistic to reflect how important a word is to a document in a corpus. In our method, a word's abnormality is reflected by its importance in the document F_1 or F_2, where the corpus is the global word set G_w. A word is defined as a normal word in F_b, where $b \in \{0, 1\}$, if its anomaly score equals to 0.

For a word w_{bi} in F_b the anomaly score a_{bi} is defined as following:

$$a_{bi} = tf(w_{bi}, F_b) \times idf(w_{bi}, G_w). \tag{1}$$

The computation of the inverse document frequency is the same for the both files:

$$idf(w_{bi}, G_w) = \log(\frac{M}{m_{w_{bi}}}). \tag{2}$$

Since F_1 contains words in resource identifiers, some words may occur repeatedly. Directly using the number of times that a word occurs in F_1 may amplify the score of a frequent word. Here we compute the term frequency for F_1 or F_2 separately as following:

$$tf(w_{1i}, F_1) = 1 + \frac{n_{1i}}{N_r}, \tag{3}$$

and

$$tf(w_{2i}, F_2) = 1 + \log(n_{2i}). \tag{4}$$

If a word stratifies any of following conditions, the anomaly score is directly set to 0.

- the word is in the normal word dictionary D_{nw};
- the word is the character X;
- the word is a non-English word (e.g., a Chinese word);
- the word ends with a postfix of some embedded static resources (e.g., a.jpg, b.css and c.js).

The anomaly score of F_b is the summation of all words' scores as $A_{Fb} = \sum a_{bi}$. Owing to that the abnormality of a user lies on malicious requests sent from the user, it is probable that the anomaly score of a user with more requests is higher than that with less requests, which would make that some small-scale malicious activities are ignored. To avoid it, we introduce penalty factors ω_1 and ω_2 for each file, along with an adjustment function $P(x)$. The user's anomaly score is derived as bellow:

$$A = P(\omega_1)A_{F1} + P(\omega_2)A_{F2},\tag{5}$$

where ω_1 and ω_2 respectively indicate the proportion of normal words in F_1 and F_2. $P(x)$ is a piecewise linear function, defined as following:

$$P(x) = \begin{cases} x & \text{if } x <= 0.5 \\ 3x - 1 & \text{if } x > 0.5. \end{cases}\tag{6}$$

3.4 Dynamic Threshold

Existing works involved with anomaly scores usually use a given threshold provided externally. For example, Kreugel and Vigna [5] set the threshold of each web request to a certain percentage of the highest anomaly score. In our method, anomaly scores of different malicious users and different websites may vary greatly, and it is impractical to specify a threshold externally. Here we employ a dynamic threshold to distinguish abnormal users.

Ideally in a given set $\{A_i\}$, where A_i is the anomaly score of the user U_i, scores of normal users should be as small as possible, while malicious users are opposite. If the gap between scores of normal users and malicious users is large enough, the threshold is easily to confirm, where the gap is not necessarily the global maximum. Hence, we transfer the problem of determining the threshold to finding a local maximum gap for a monotonously non-decreasing sequence.

An intuitive method is given as following: the sequence of ordered scores $\{\tilde{A}_k | A_i^{min} \leq \tilde{A}_k \leq \tilde{A}_{k+1} \leq A_i^{max}\}$ is derived from the original set $\{A_i\}$; If $\tilde{A}_{\hat{k}}$ is the first score where the gap between $\tilde{A}_{\hat{k}}$ and $\tilde{A}_{\hat{k}-1}$ is greater than a gap threshold T_{gap}, which means that $\tilde{A}_{\hat{k}}$ is distinctly larger than $\tilde{A}_{\hat{k}-1}$, and $\tilde{A}_{\hat{k}}$ is determined as the threshold. For the set $\{A_i\}$, if A_i is larger than $\tilde{A}_{\hat{k}}$, the user U_i is determined as malicious. Empirically the gap threshold T_{gap} is set as $\log M$.

3.5 Semantic Representation

The detection result for an abnormal user is represented with the anomaly score A as well as the malicious word sets MW_1 and MW_2. The two malicious word sets are derived from W_1 and W_2, where $MW_1 = \{(w_{1i} : a_{1i})|a_{1i} \geq a_{1i+1}\}$ and MW_2 is the same. Based on the semantic representation, the overview of a malicious user's web activities can be directly identified without the need for reviewing the raw traffic logs.

4   Evaluation and Results

We use a labeled dataset D_L to evaluate our approach and an unknown dataset D_U to analysis its detection ability in the wild. All of them are web traffic logs collected with the open-source network monitor Bro [16]. For simplicity, a user is identified with the source IP address of a request. For the proxy traffic, the original IP is extracted from the HTTP header X-Forwarded-For.

4.1   Dataset

The labeled dataset D_L involves four different websites, which are named from Site A to Site D. We respectively collected traffic logs from the four sites in different seven days, and labeled them manually with several free web security log analyzers as auxiliary tools, including Apache-scalp [17] and 360 xingtu [18]. Among total 43,504 IPs, we found 376 malicious IPs, and more than two-thirds of them are not detected by our auxiliary tools. The summary of D_L is shown in Table 1. The average ratio of malicious IPs to the total for each day is listed in the last column. For all malicious IPs, the number of web requests in their malicious traffic ranges from one to more than ten thousands.

Table 1. Summary of the labeled dataset D_L

No.	Website	Site type	Date range	#Requests	#IPs	#MIPs	Ratio
1	Site A	Aspx	Apr. 01–07	27,544	998	170	13.2%
2	Site B	Php	May 17–23	32,272	2,479	49	2.1%
3	Site C	Java	May 17–23	115,440	7,759	59	0.8%
4	Site D	Html	May 17–23	386,725	32,268	98	0.3%

The details of malicious IPs of four sites are illustrated in Fig. 4. Figure 4(a) shows the occurrence of malicious IPs in each day, and Fig. 4(b) presents the number of malicious IPs in three types of malice. Significantly, the number of malicious IPs for Site A greatly increases in the last two days, while the situations of other three sites are almost stable. At the same time, web abuse only occurs in the traffic of Site A, and for other sites web scan is relatively in the majority, which is in line with expectations. It is owing to that Site A was compromised in the fifth day by attackers through exploiting the PUT method vulnerability, and uploaded several web shells, such as

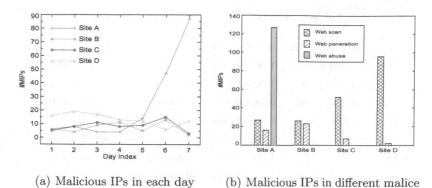

(a) Malicious IPs in each day   (b) Malicious IPs in different malice

Fig. 4. Malicious IPs in D_L

/xwvkk11544.txt, /byHmei7.txt and /miao.xx.txt. Subsequently, some malicious pages were added to the site, which lead to a large number of visits for malicious URLs (e.g., /guiling/hotel/goto.aspx?read_LdLdnApFWm.html). The great majority of the abusing traffic are from web robots of known search engines. Additionally, the most popular attack in web penetration traffic for Sites B and C is SQL injection.

The unknown dataset D_U consists of 136 million web traffic logs involving roughly 3,000 fully qualified domain names (FQDNs) from Jul. 22, 2016 to Aug. 2, 2016, which were collected from a web hosting service provider. The distinct IPs totally count for more than one millions. Most of websites in D_U are portal sites generated by a commercial Content Management System (CMS). Consequently, the most visited web resources are static web pages with .html as postfixes of resource identifiers.

4.2 Evaluation

For D_L, we use two metrics **Precision (P)** and **Recall (R)** to measure the effectiveness of our methodology. Given the numbers of True Positive (TP) and False Positive (FP), the precision is calculated as: $P = TP/(TP + FP)$, and the recall is $R = TP/(TP + FN)$.

Many existing works use True Positive Rate (TPR) and False Positive Rate (FPR) as metrics to evaluate an anomaly detection method. However, in our labeled dataset D_L, the negative samples of four web site vary greatly, which may cause too much deviation in FPR.

With the detection window as one day and T_{fw} for the normal word dictionary as 45%, the dataset actually is separated as 28 groups. The detection results for each group are listed in Table 2. In the results, the precision of 12 groups are up to 100%, and 18 groups achieve 100% recall. Overall, the average precision achieved by our approach is 90.7%, and the recall is averagely 92.9%.

It is worthy of attention that the recall is only 15.1% for the seventh day of Site A. The reason is that among 264 IPs of Site A in Day 7 there are 78 IPs who queried uploaded malicious pages, which makes the normal word dictionary

Table 2. The precision and recall on four sites

	Site A (P/R)	Site B (P/R)	Site C (P/R)	Site D (P/R)
Day 1	1.000/0.833	1.000/1.000	1.000/0.800	0.947/1.000
Day 2	0.800/1.000	1.000/1.000	0.889/0.889	0.864/1.000
Day 3	1.000/1.000	0.889/0.889	0.750/0.900	0.850/1.000
Day 4	1.000/1.000	1.000/1.000	0.778/0.875	0.722/1.000
Day 5	1.000/1.000	1.000/1.000	0.900/1.000	0.857/1.000
Day 6	1.000/0.894	1.000/0.909	0.833/1.000	0.875/0.875
Day 7	0.925/0.151	1.000/1.000	0.750/1.000	0.750/1.000
Avg	0.961/0.840	0.984/0.971	0.843/0.923	0.838/0.982

polluted. Actually, our approach is mainly used to provide a direct and effective way to analyze web traffic afterwards. For analysts, it is an obvious indicator of a possible web compromise that the number of malicious IPs in Day 6 increased roughly five times than the average of the previous four days. In such situation, the normal word dictionaries generated in the following detection windows are not trustable anymore, which should be replaced by dictionaries in previous detection windows. Here, we replace the normal word dictionary of Day 7 with Day 1, and the recall rises to 96.5% with 100% precision.

4.3 Results in the Wild

For D_U, we set the detection window as one day as well. In order to reduce false positives as much as possible, we set T_{fw} as 30% and filter out the FQDNs whose number of visiting IPs in a detection window is less than 20. As a result, there are altogether 1,413 FQDNs and 969,731 distinct IP addresses left.

We totally find 3,995 unique malicious IPs involving 782 attacked FQDNs. In Fig. 5(a) it is presented that for almost 90% of attacked FQDNs, there are no more than 50 distinct malicious IPs. However, there are about two in five FQDNs attacked in more than 10 days. It is indicated that for websites in D_U, web attacks frequently occur but not burst.

The top six malicious IPs sorted by cumulative anomaly scores are presented in Table 3. In the last column, we list the top abnormal words of each user. From the words, the intention of each attacker can be directly identified. The first two IPs attacked four different sites in different days, while the words show that they utilized the same tool to carry out targeted web scans. The next three IPs attacked more than two hundreds FQDNs respectively, and the difference is that *.*.40.135 and *.*.153.20 carried out web scan persistently while *.*.154.104 only used one day. Different from the first five malicious web scanners, the last one is an attacker who intended to discover vulnerabilities of the target website with an automatic web penetration tool, since the total number of request sent from the IP is more than 1 millions. From its typical words, it is obvious that

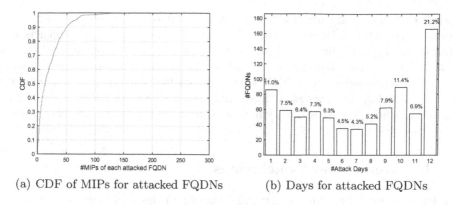

(a) CDF of MIPs for attacked FQDNs   (b) Days for attacked FQDNs

Fig. 5. Detection results in D_U

the malicious IP at least conducted large amounts of SQL injection attacks. Due to the site only containing static web resources, the injection strings were added into the resource identifiers of requests and consequently occurs in MW_1.

Table 3. Top 6 malicious IPs in D_U

IP	#F	#D	#R	Top abnormal words
..195.144	3	1	513,903	MW_1: head spacecp_index.asp indignation aspxspyX.jsp
				MW_2: etc cdir id c+dir type action rif connector file
..220.206	3	3	548,520	MW_1: head spacecp_index.asp indignation aspxspyX.jsp
				MW_2: c+dir type action rif etc cdir .htr action type
..40.135	397	7	123,957	MW_1: post a.php newsletters login-wall-ypasv fuck.php
				MW_2: aid eval($_post[expdoor]); cmd {${eval($_post)}}
..153.20	271	12	259,688	MW_1: post plus mytag-js.php zdqd.php manage xianf.asp
				MW_2: aid X
..154.104	241	1	2,063,842	MW_1: classes web-inf .idea uc_server database.sql
				MW_2: index.jsp file servletpath contextpath inputfile
..122.133	1	1	1,171,289	MW_1: tX%'andX+X-X-X=X+X+X+Xand'cwlf'!='cwlf%_X.html
				if(now()=sysdate(),sleep(X),X)
				MW_2: .jpg_X.html_X.html .jpg.html .jpg_X.html .html

Statistically, the top 20 most popular malicious words existing in our detected malicious traffic include get, plus, index.php, admin, mytag-js.php, convert, utility, bbs, post, data, asp, include, install, editor, config, plugins, templates, templets, ckeditor, config.inc.php. It is revealed that most of malicious visits look for typical weaknesses of some php and asp web applications. For example, plus and mytag-js.php belong to the request /plus/mytag-js.php?aid=9090, which is a web shell link existing in the known CMS application *DedeCMS* in China. In addition, we analyze the top 30 most attacked FQDNs and find that their popular abnormal words are almost the same as the above. However, there is only one exception which consists of a unique word `m.yonjizz.com`. With querying it in a search engine, we find that it is a online video site related to adult. There are more than twenty malicious IPs who visited the FQDN with requests like `/n/M.yonjizz.com/szh/1` and `/l/Www.58porn.com/es/1`. Such malicious request are not discovered from traffic of other FQDNs in D_U, which may be a clue that the site was possibly compromised.

5   Discussion and Conclusions

Understanding cybercrimer's network behavior in the wild is extremely important. In the paper, we introduce a semantic-aware methodology to distinguish malicious web traffic in an unsupervised-learning way.

Compared with Scanner Hunter proposed in [4], our approach does not depend on the mutual similarity between different attackers and can be directly employed on massive raw web traffic logs even that there is only one malicious request. Lampesberger et al. [10] also introduced an unsupervised-learning method to detect malicious requests. Utilizing a statistical representation of bytes between two separators, their approach loses the semantic information of original requests and can only detect requests with obvious changes in the statistical distribution of characters. Our method preserves the semantic information at the maximum extent and is able to distinguish malicious traffic with almost the same character distribution as the normal, like web abuse.

In conclusion, we firstly extend the scope of malicious web traffic by importing web abuse in this work. And then to model dynamic malicious web activities, we propose a generic detection method to identify malicious web users with a modified TF-IDF algorithm. We evaluate our approach on a manually labeled dataset, and the results reveal that it can effectively distinguish various malicious web traffic. Furthermore, as shown in the results derived from the unknown dataset, the semantic representation can help to understand malice directly, which is valuable for improving network defense strategies and identifying web compromise.

Acknowledgments. This paper is supported by the National Key R&D Program of China (2017YFB0801900).

References

1. StopBadware and CommTouch: Compromised Websites: An Owner's Perspective. https://www.stopbadware.org/files/compromised-websites-an-owners-perspective.pdf
2. Alrwais, S., Yuan, K., Alowaisheq, E., Liao, X., Oprea, A., Wang, X., Li, Z.: Catching predators at watering holes: finding and understanding strategically compromised websites. In: Proceedings of the 32nd Annual Conference on Computer Security Applications, pp. 153–166. ACM (2016)

3. Li, F., Ho, G., Kuan, E., Niu, Y., Ballard, L., Thomas, K., Bursztein, E., Paxson, V.: Remedying web hijacking: notification effectiveness and webmaster comprehension. In: Proceedings of the 25th International Conference on World Wide Web, pp. 1009–1019. ACM (2016)
4. Xie, G., Hang, H., Faloutsos, M.: Scanner hunter: understanding http scanning traffic. In: Proceedings of the 9th ACM Symposium on Information, Computer and Communications Security, pp. 27–38. ACM (2014)
5. Kruegel, C., Vigna, G.: Anomaly detection of web-based attacks. In: Proceedings of the 10th ACM Conference on Computer and Communications Security, pp. 251–261. ACM (2003)
6. Valeur, F., Mutz, D., Vigna, G.: A learning-based approach to the detection of SQL attacks. In: Proceedings of the Conference on Detection of Intrusions and Malware and Vulnerability Assessment (DIMVA), pp. 123–140 (2005)
7. Robertson, W., Vigna, G., Kruegel, C., Kemmerer, R.A.: Using generalization and characterization techniques in the anomaly-based detection of web attacks. In: Annual Network and Distributed System Security Symposium (NDSS) (2006)
8. Song, Y., Keromytis, A.D., Stolfo, S.J.: Spectrogram: a mixture-of-Markov-chains model for anomaly detection in web traffic. In: Annual Network and Distributed System Security Symposium (NDSS) (2009)
9. Krueger, T., Gehl, C., Rieck, K., Laskov, P.: TokDoc: a self-healing web application firewall. In: Proceedings of the 2010 ACM Symposium on Applied Computing, pp. 1846–1853. ACM (2010)
10. Lampesberger, H., Winter, P., Zeilinger, M., Hermann, E.: An on-line learning statistical model to detect malicious web requests. In: SecureComm, pp. 19–38 (2011)
11. Zhang, J., Xie, Y., Yu, F., Soukal, D., Lee, W.: Intention and origination: an inside look at large-scale bot queries. In: Annual Network and Distributed System Security Symposium (NDSS) (2013)
12. Canali, D., Balzarotti, D.: Behind the scenes of online attacks: an analysis of exploitation behaviors on the web. In: Annual Network and Distributed System Security Symposium (NDSS) (2013)
13. Starov, O., Dahse, J., Ahmad, S.S., Holz, T., Nikiforakis, N.: No honor among thieves: a large-scale analysis of malicious web shells. In: Proceedings of the 25th International Conference on World Wide Web, pp. 1021–1032. ACM (2016)
14. FireEye. Detecting and Defeating the China Chopper Web Shell. https://www.fireeye.com/content/dam/fireeye-www/global/en/current-threats/pdfs/rpt-china-chopper.pdf
15. Liao, X., Yuan, K., Wang, X., Pei, Z., Yang, H., Chen, J., Duan, H., Du, K., Alowaisheq, E., Alrwais, S., Xing, L., Beyah, R.: Seeking nonsense, looking for trouble: efficient promotional-infection detection through semantic inconsistency search. In: IEEE Symposium on Security and Privacy, pp. 707–723 (2016)
16. Paxson, V.: Bro: a system for detecting network intruders in real-time. In: Proceedings of 7th USENIX Security Symposium (1998)
17. Apache-scalp. https://github.com/nanopony/apache-scalp
18. 360 Xingtu. http://wangzhan.360.com/Activity/xingtu

An Active and Dynamic Botnet Detection Approach to Track Hidden Concept Drift

Zhi Wang, Meiqi Tian, and Chunfu Jia$^{(\boxtimes)}$

College of Computer and Control Engineering, Nankai University,
Tianjin 300350, China
cfjia@nankai.edu.cn

Abstract. Nowadays, machine learning has been widely used as a core component in botnet detection systems. However, the assumption of machine learning algorithm is that the underlying botnet data distribution is stable for training and testing, which is vulnerable to well-crafted concept drift attacks, such as mimicry attacks, gradient descent attacks, poisoning attacks and so on. In this paper we present an active and dynamic learning approach to mitigate botnet hidden concept drift attacks. Instead of passively waiting for false negative, this approach could actively find the trend of hidden concept drift attacks using statistical p-values before performance starts to degenerate. And besides periodically retraining, this approach could dynamically reweight predictive features to track the trend of underlying concept drift. We test this approach on the public CTU botnet captures provided by malware capture facility project. The experiment results show that this approach could actively get insights of botnet hidden concept drift, and dynamically evolve to avoid model aging.

Keywords: Malware · Botnet detection · Concept drift
Model aging horizontal correlation

1 Introduction

Botnet is one of the most significant threats for Internet security. Nowadays, the botnet keeps evolving which is composed by not only compromised computers, but also a large variety of IoT devices, including smart phones, IP cameras, routers, printers, DVRs and so on. With enormous cumulative bandwidth and computing capability, botnet becomes the most important and powerful tool available for cheaper and faster large-scale network attacks in the Internet [1].

According to AV-Test [2] report, on average over 390,000 new malware samples are detected every day. The enormous volume of new malware variants renders manual analysis inefficient and time-consuming. Nowadays, machine learning has been widely deployed in botnet detection system as a core component [3–6], and has achieved good detection results.

© Springer International Publishing AG, part of Springer Nature 2018
S. Qing et al. (Eds.): ICICS 2017, LNCS 10631, pp. 646–660, 2018.
https://doi.org/10.1007/978-3-319-89500-0_55

However, with financial motivation, attackers keep evolving the evasion techniques to bypass machine learning detection. Currently, more and more well-crafted botnets exploit concept drift, a vulnerability of machine learning, to accelerate the decay of detection model. Machine learning algorithms assume that the underlying botnet data distribution is stable in training and testing dataset. The well-crafted concept drift attacks gradually and stealthily introduce changes into malware data distribution to mislead machine learning models, such as new communication channels [7–11], mimicry attacks [12,13], gradient descent attacks [12,13], poison attacks [14], and so on. To build change-resistant and self-renewal learning models against advanced evasion techniques is very important for botnet detection system.

Existing solutions use passive and periodical model retraining to mitigate concept drift attacks. However, the interval of two retraining is hard to decide because frequently retraining is not efficient while loose frequency leads untrusted predictions in some periods. And the manual labelling of all new samples is required for supervised retraining process. The labelling is based on the traditional coarse-grained and fixed threshold, which are not sensitive to hidden and gradual changes of underlying data distribution. Stationary learning model's confidential values are critical for detection performance. So if the learning model's algorithm and parameters are stolen by adversaries [15], retraining will be no longer useful for sudden concept drift attacks, which are crafted quickly and easily based on full knowledge of the detection model.

In this paper, we present an active and dynamic botnet detection approach that enhance traditional horizontal correlation detection model. Compared to the traditional models, this model could actively detect hidden concept drift attacks and dynamically evolve to track the trend of latest botnet concept.

In particular, this paper makes the following contributions:

- As far as we know, we are the first to present an active and dynamic learning approach for botnet detection that actively tracks the trend of hidden botnet concept drift and accordingly evolves learning model dynamically to mitigate model aging.
- We extend the traditional passive decision method which is based on coarse-grained threshold to check whether the bottom line are crossed or not. In contrast, we introduce fine-grained p-values as indicator to actively identify hidden concept drift before the detection performance starts to degrade.
- The confidential values of traditional detection models are fixed, such as model parameters, so retraining is the only way to combat concept drift attacks. We introduce DRIFT assessment and feature reweighting to dynamically tune model parameters following the trend of current botnet concept.

The remainder of this paper is outlined as follows: In Sect. 2, we review the related works. Section 3 presents the architecture of our active and dynamic botnet detection approach, and describes each components. Section 4 shows our experiments performed to assess the recognition of underlying data distribution concept drift and model self-renewal. In Sect. 5, we discuss the limitations and future work, and in Sect. 6 we summarize our results.

2   Related Works

Nowadays, machine learning (ML) has been widely used in botnet detection system as a core component. The assumption of ML is that the underlying data distribution is stable for both training dataset and testing dataset. By exploiting the assumption of ML, many well-crafted evasion approaches, known as concept drift attacks, have been proposed to evade or mislead ML models [16]. As shown in Fig. 1, every step of ML process is a potential part of the concept drift attack surface. With different levels of knowledge of target ML system, attackers could launch various concept drift attacks [17]. Arce [18] pointed out that machine learning itself could be the weakest link in the security chain.

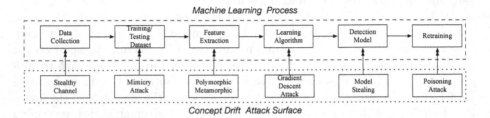

Fig. 1. Machine learning process and corresponding concept drift attack surface

Botnet attackers have begun to exploit many stealthy communication channels which are beyond the scope of ML data collection, such as social network [10,11], email protocol [19], SMS [7] and bluetooth [8]. Erhan *et al.* [11] proposed social network based botnet to abuse trusted popular websites, such as twitter.com, as C&C servers. Kapil *et al.* [19] evaluated the viability of using harmless-looking emails to delivery botnet C&C message. The new stealthy channel always involve highly trusted and very popular websites or heavily used email servers, which own excellent reputation and are whitelisted from most detection systems. And the exploited websites or email servers have very large normal traffic volume, so that light-weight occasional botnet traffic is unlikely to be noticed.

Mimicry attack refers to the techniques that mimic benign behaviors to reduce the differentiation between the malicious events and benign events. Wagner and Soto [20] demonstrated the mimicry attack against a host-based IDS that mimicked the legitimate sequence of system calls. Šrndic and Laskov [17] presented a mimicry attack against PDFRate [21], a system to detect malicious pdf files based on the random forest classifier.

Gradient descent is an optimization process to iteratively minimize the distance between malicious points and benign points. Srndic and Laskov [12] applied a gradient descent-kernel density estimation attack against the PDFRate system that uses SVM and random forest classifier. Biggio et al. [13] demonstrated a gradient descent component against the SVM classifier and a neural network.

Poisoning attacks work by introducing carefully crafted noise into the training data. Biggio et al. [14] proposed poisoning attacks to merge the benign and malicisous clusters that make learning model unusable.

Therefore, botnet problems are not stable but change with time. For machine learning based botnet detectors, they are designed under the assumption that the training and testing data follow the same distribution which make them vulnerable to concept drift problem that the underlying data distribution are changing with time. One of the concept drift mitigation approach is to recognize and react to recent concept changes before model aging. Demontis et al. [14] proposed an adversary-aware approach to proactively anticipates the attackers. Deo et al. [22] presented a probabilistic predictor to assess the underlying classifier and retraining model when it recognized concept drift. Transcend [23] is a framework to identify model aging in vivo during deployment, before the performance starts to degrade. In this paper we present an active and dynamic botnet detection approach which could actively detect the trend of hidden concept drift attacks and dynamically evolve learning model to mitigate model aging.

3   Active and Dynamic Botnet Learning Approach

Driven by financial motivation, malware authors keep evolving malware perpetually using various advanced evasion techniques to evade detection, especially to bypass widely deployed learning-based models. Many learning-based detection models calculate a score for a new approaching sample describing the relationship between the known malware samples and the new one. Then detectors compare the score with a fixed and empirical threshold to make a decision if it is malicious. The threshold usually fits the old training dataset very well, even overfits. However, the performance degenerates to the new ever-changing malicious dataset with time. In this paper, we propose an active and dynamic learning approach to track the trend of botnet underlying concept drift and renew learning model to mitigate model aging.

Figure 2 depicts the framework of active and dynamic botnet detection approach that includes five components: non-conformity measure (NCM), conformal learning, concept drift detection, model assessment, and self renewal. Non-conformity measure is the core part of botnet detection system, which is used to tell the different degree between a given sample and known botnet samples. In this paper, we select the horizontal correlation classifier BotFinder [24] as the NCM. The conformal learning component uses p-values to carry out statistical analysis based on NCM scores. The p-value is more fine-grained than threshold which can be used to observe the gradual decay of detection model. The concept drift recognition component uses the average p-value (APV) algorithm to detect the concept drift of malware data distribution between two different time windows. The model assessment component applies DRIFT algorithm to locate the features that are affected by identified concept drift. The self renewal component dynamically adjust the weight of predictive features to track the current botnet concept.

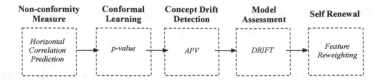

Fig. 2. The framework of active and dynamic botnet learning approach

3.1 Horizontal Correlation Classifier

In general, horizontal correlation techniques focus on the common behaviors among a set of hosts, and use clustering and classification algorithm to build detection model to recognize the infected machines or suspect behaviors. In this section, we introduce BotFinder into our approach as the underlying NCM. BotFinder includes four parts: training dataset selection, preprocessing, feature extraction, modeling with machine learning algorithm.

Training Dataset. The training dataset selection directly affects the quality of the detection model. The CTU botnet capture dataset is stored in files using the binetflow format, in which each row represents a network behavior and each column is a behavior feature. According to the granularity, the network behaviors can be abstracted to different levels, such as packets, netflows, traces and hosts. In this work, netflow is the basic data unit for training datasets, and then we abstract netflows into traffic trace by grouping the netflows with the same source IP address, the same destination IP address, the same destination port and the protocol together.

Preprocessing. Before starting training phase, we will preprocess the data that filter noise data and transform the features by scaling each feature to a given range. In this work the range of each feature on the training dataset is given between 0 and 1 at initialization time. To make the data clearer and more usable, we will filter the datasets by whitelisting common Internet service, such as Microsoft Update and Google, and known online movie and music traffic by their communication pattern.

Feature Extraction. After trace generation, we perform a statistical analysis of the traces consisting of netflows. All features extracted are presented as floats range from 0 to 1, and grouped to 2 feature sets: as listed in Table 1.

Modeling with Machine Learning Algorithm. The horizontal correlation classifier BotFinder is a detection method that does not require deep packet inspection. BotFinder uses the CLUES algorithm to cluster the similar traces of a botnet family, and builds detection model for each class of this family. This method can effectively identify the botnet network traffic similarity between different malware variants, and give a prediction based on the optimal threshold fitting the training dataset.

Table 1. Overview of feature sets

Set	Features
Volume features	Average of send bytes
	Standard deviation of send bytes
	Average of received bytes
	Standard deviation of received bytes
Time-related features	Average of duration
	Standard deviation of duration
	Average of received interval
	Standard deviation of interval
	Connection frequency

3.2 Non-conformity Measures

Many machine learning algorithms are in fact scoring classifiers: when trained on a set of observations and fed with a test object x, they could calculate a prediction score $s(x)$ called scoring function. The input of the NCM is a known sample set and an unknown sample, and the output is a score that describes the similarity or dissimilarity of the unknown sample to the known sample set. So any scoring classifiers using a fixed and empirical threshold can be introduced into our approach as a underlying NCM. In this work, we select BotFinder as the NCM. BotFinder selects time related features and traffic volume features to build detection model from the horizontal perspective. BotFinder is in fact also a scoring classifier: when trained on a set of observations and fed with a test object x, it could calculate a prediction score $botfinder(x)$, and $botfinder()$ is used as the underlying NCM in our approach.

3.3 P-Value

Once a non-conformity measure is selected, conformal predictor computes a p-value p_{z^*}, which in essence for a new object z^*, represents the percentage of objects in $\{x \in C, \forall C \in \mathbb{D}\}$, (i.e., the whole dataset) that are equally or more estranged to C as p_{z^*}, and we will get a number between 0 and 1. The algorithm is shown in Algorithm 1.

P-value measures the fraction of objects within $\mathbb{D}$, that are at least as different from a class C as the new object z^*. For instance, if C represents the set of botnet traces, a high p-value p_{z^*} means that there is a significant part of the objects in this set that is more different than z^* with C. On the other words, z^* is more similar to these botnet traces than the objects that already marked botnet. Therefore, the prediction result based on a high p-value shows a high credibility. P-values are directly involved in our discussion of concept drift recognition.

Algorithm 1. P-value calculation used in Conformal Predictor

Data: Dataset $D = \{z_1, , z_n\}$, sequence of objects $C \subset D$, non-conformity measure A, and new object z^*
Output: p-value p_{z^*}
1: Set provisionally $C = C \cup \{z^*\}$
2: **for** $i \leftarrow 1$ **to** n **do**
3:      $\alpha \leftarrow A(C \setminus z_i, z_i)$
4: **end for**
5: $p_{z^*} = \frac{|\{j : \alpha_j \geq \alpha_{z^*}\}|}{n}$

3.4 Concept Drift Identification

We use the average p-value (APV) algorithm and drift rating function to calculate concept drift scores (CDS) for each time windows, which is used to recognize concept drift attacks, as shown in Fig. 3.

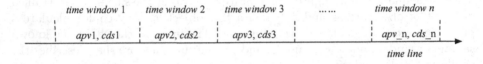

Fig. 3. The conformal learning component calculates APV for each time windows

Firstly, to visualize the botnet underlying data distribution, we select tSNE [25] algorithm to do dimension reduction. The tSNE is an algorithm to visualize high-dimensional datasets by dimensionality reduction. The tSNE maps the high-dimensional points into two or three dimensions and keeps the distance structure that the close points in high-dimensional space remain close to each other on the low dimension space. Secondly, we calculate the p-values of each botnet trace to see the significant level of this trace in its family traces. Because there are usually a large number of traces for most botnet family, to be efficient, we split tSNE space into small $n \times n$ grids. For each grid, we calculate its APV, which is the average p-value of all botnet traces belong to this grid, as shown in Fig. 4. We group the botnet traces into different time windows according to their time stamps in the timeline. After calculating APV of each grid, we judge the concept drift in each time window using a drift rating function. In the tSNE space, there are common grids shared by multiple botnet traces in different time windows, while there are exclusive grids that are occupied by the botnet traces only in one time window. We use the fraction of the sum of APV of exclusive grids over the sum of APV of all grids in one time window to represent the drift rating in this time window, as shown in the Eq. 1.

$$ConceptDriftScore = \frac{\sum APV_{exclusive}}{\sum APV_{common} + \sum APV_{exclusive}} \tag{1}$$

The change of concept drift score (CDS) between different time window reflects the change of underlying botnet data distribution with time that can identify gradual moderate drift.

If the CDS score in the latest time window increases, it shows that the current concept of underlying botnet data distribution is different from the old concept learnt from previous time window, and indicates that the detection model is suffering from concept drift attack. But the decay of threshold based detection performance may not be observed immediately when concept drift is found. Only when the variation of the underlying data distribution exceeds the boundary of the threshold, the detection model starts make poor decisions. If the CDS score does not increase in the new time window, it means in the current time window, the distribution of botnet traces does not have significant concept drift.

3.5 Model Assessment

When concept drift is found in the latest time window, we will use the DRIFT algorithms to evaluate the contribution of each feature in current window to identify the features which effected by concept drift, as shown in Algorithm 2. $DRIFT[i]$ represents the effect of the ith feature on the average distance between two botnet traces in different time windows. If $DRIFT[i]$ increases, it means that the concept drift affects the ith feature.

3.6 Model Self Renewal

When concept drift is recognized, we will reweight the affected features according to the DRIFT score to dynamically update the model before the cumulative radical drift. The formula for calculating a new weight based on DRIFT score is:

Algorithm 2. $DRIFT$ algorithm

Data: feature vectors $x_1, x_2, ..., x_n$, labels $y_1, y_2, ..., y_n$
Output: $DRIFT$ coefficients
  $DRIFT = []$
  $X = \{x_1, x_2, ..., x_n\}$
  $uY =$ unique entries in Y: our classes
  for $i = 1$ to d **do**
    $X_i = i^{th}$ column of X
    $DRIFT[i] = 0$
    for class in elements of uY **do**
      $fromclass = X_i[\text{where } Y == \text{class}]$
      $notclass = X_i[\text{where } Y \mathrel{!=} \text{class}]$
      pdist = respective distanced between elements in $fromclass$ and elements in $notclass$
      $DRIFT[i] = DRIFT[i] + (\text{sum(pdist)/length(pdist)})$
    end for
    $DRIFT[i] = DRIFT[i]/\text{length}(uY)$
  end for

$$W_i = \begin{cases} 3 \times (1 - \sqrt{DRIFT[i]}) & \text{if} \quad DRIFT[i] \leq 0.05 \\ 2 \times (1 - \sqrt{DRIFT[i]}) & \text{if} \quad 0.05 < DRIFT[i] < 0.1 \\ (1 - \sqrt{DRIFT[i]}) & \text{if} \quad DRIFT[i] \geq 0.1 \end{cases} \quad (2)$$

By updating the weight, we can reduce the weight of feature that is significantly influenced by concept drift attack, and increase the weight of feature that reflect current botnet concept very well.

4   Experiment

4.1   Botnet Dataset

In this paper, we use the public CTU botnet datasets for our experiment that is provided by Malware Capture Facility project[1]. They capture long-live real botnet traffic and generate labeled netflow files that are public for malware research. The traffic dataset is from 2011 to present. We plan to recognize the concept drift between different variants in the same family. We select 6 botnet families that have more than 2 variants for this experiments as shown in Table 2. All file names of CTU botnet captures have the same prefix "CTU-Malware-Capture-Botnet", and each capture has an unique suffix name. In the Table 2, only suffix names are listed to save space. Each family has multiple variants and the capture time of all variants and the time span of each family are different.

Table 2. The selected botnet families in CTU malware dataset

Malware family	CTU botnet captures
Dynamer	189-1,217-1,229-1
Taobao	232-1,237-1
OpenCandy	194-1,195-1,208-1,213-1
Cridex	108-1,109-1
Dridex	113-1,153-1,218-1,227-1,228-1,246-1,248-1,259-1
Yakes	104-1,107-1,108-1,203-1,310-1

4.2   Active Concept Drift Recognition

We cut the time span of each family into 2 time windows: tw_1 and tw_2, so there are 12 time windows that each botnet family has 2 disjoint time windows. According to the time order of variants, the tw_2 of each family only contains its latest variant, while other variants are all grouped into tw_1. To recognize

---

[1] Garcia, Sebastian. Malware Capture Facility Project. Retrieved from https://stratosphereips.org.

the hidden concept drift between different time windows, we take three steps: first, visualize botnet data distribution in the two dimension figure; second, split the two dimension space into small grids and compute the significant levels of all grids; third, calculate concept drift score using botnet data distribution and significant levels.

The data distribution of each family are shown in Fig. 4. We select tSNE [25] algorithm to do dimension reduction. The tSNE is an algorithm to visualize high-dimensional datasets by dimensionality reduction. The tSNE maps the high-dimensional points into two or three dimensions and keeps the distance structure that the close points in high-dimensional space remain close to each other on the low dimension space.

We split the 2-dimension tSNE space into 30×30 grids, so there are 900 grids in total for each family as shown in Fig. 4. And we calculate average p-values (APV) for all grids. The APV represents the significance of each grid. If a grid has a high APV, the grid is important for the description of this botnet family characteristics. In the Fig. 4, we use square to denote the common grids for two time windows, and the triangle represents the grid only for tw_1, and the circle means this grid only belong to tw_2.

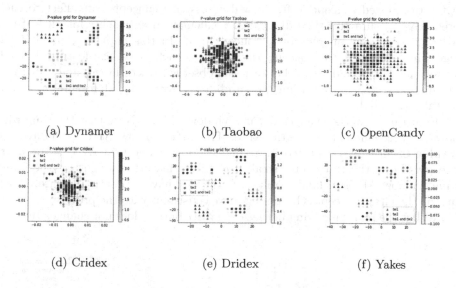

(a) Dynamer   (b) Taobao   (c) OpenCandy

(d) Cridex   (e) Dridex   (f) Yakes

Fig. 4. The drift of data distribution and significant levels of each family.

According to the difference of data distribution and significant levels between the traces in two time windows, we calculate the concept drift scores (CDS) for the traces in tw_2. The scope of CDS is between 0 and 1. 0 means there is no concept drift between the 2 time windows, while 1 represents sudden drift that there is no common grid shared in two time windows.

From the Fig. 5, we can see the CDS of OpenCany family is 0.018, which means there is almost no concept drift in the latest time window. And the CDSs

Table 3. The feature DRIFT scores and new weights of Dridex

Feature	DRIFT	New weight
ti_avg	0.0836	1.4218
dur_avg	0.0008	2.91515
rxbyte_avg	0.1155	0.6601
txbyte_avg	0.1145	0.6615
fft	0.0867	1.4111

Table 4. The feature DRIFT scores and new weights of Yakes

Feature	DRIFT	New weight
ti_avg	0.0500	1.5528
dur_avg	0.0019	2.8693
rxbyte_avg	0.0470	2.3496
txbyte_avg	0.0000	3.0000
fft	0.1231	0.6491

for family Dynamer, Taobao, Cridex are 0.121, 0.216 and 0.238, which means there are gradual and moderate concept drifts in the latest time windows. For family Yakes and Dridex, the CDSs are 0.994 and 0.998 which indicate radical concept drifts in the latest time windows.

4.3 Dynamic Model Evolution

After recognized concept drift, we will assess this concept drift affect to each predictive feature and then dynamically calculate new weights for all features to track the trend of underlying concept drift. In this paper, we use DRIFT algorithms to assess the concept drift effect to each predictive feature. DRIFT score represents the distance between the observed traces in tw_2 and the traces in tw_1. According to Algorithm 2, we update the weight for all features as shown in Tables 3 and 4.

Figure 6 shows the changes of time windows APVs. Note that the time window APV is different from grid APV. The time window APV is the average p-value of all traces captured in a time window, while grid APV is the average p-value of the traces in a small grid. After feature reweighting, the latest time window APVs of family Yakes and Dridex have dramatic increase, which means the latest concept is becoming more consistent with the previous concept. Note that the real underlying botnet data distribution does not change. Just the

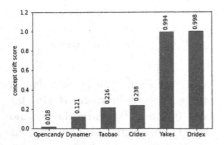

Fig. 5. The concept drift scores of each family.

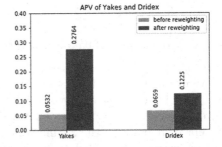

Fig. 6. The APV of time windows before and after feature reweighting.

model observing perspective changes. From the new perspective, the new botnet variant looks more similar to known variants.

5   Discussion

Machine learning is widely used as a core component in the advanced botnet detection system. However, machine learning is not a panacea, which is suffering from the advanced concept drift attacks. Concept drift attacks exploit the vulnerable assumption of machine learning that the underlying data distribution is stable for both training and testing dataset. There are various advanced concept drifts attacks, such as mimicry attacks, gradient descent attacks, poisoning attacks, and so on. Such concept drift attacks change the underlying data distribution to make the botnet concept appear to be different from machine learning observing perspective. The new botnet concept just looks different, but the botnet essential behaviors are still the same.

To mitigate botnet concept drift attacks and build sustainable botnet detection model, we can make efforts from the following aspects: dynamic feature selection, dynamic reweighting, and ensemble learning. The goal of dynamic feature selection is to dynamically choose relevant features to the current botnet concept. Before changing feature selection, we should get deep insights of the trend of hidden botnet concept drift and assess the contribution of each feature to this new trend. In this paper, we propose the concept drift score to identify the hidden drift, and DRIFT function to assess the contribution of each feature to the new trend of concept drift. Dynamic reweighting handles botnet concept drift by changing the feature weight in the learning model to make model dynamically fit the current botnet concept. Note that dynamic reweighting may cause data overfitting. In this paper, we use the piecewise reweighting function to calculate new weight using different sub-functions according to DRIFT scores. Ensemble learning maintains a set of learning models that observe the botnet concept from diverse perspectives. Ensemble learning has multiple botnet concept descriptions, so it is robust to the hidden concept drift which increases the complexity for botnet evasion.

In this work, we use concept drift scores and DRIFT function to identify hidden concept drift and dynamic feature reweighting. However, we only has one botnet description based on network trace horizontal correlation. The concept drift scores and DRIFT function are agnostic to the underlying learning algorithm, making our approach versatile and compatible with multiple ML algorithms. Our approach could not only use horizontal correlation BotFinder classifier, but also be applied on the top of any other botnet classification or clustering algorithm that uses a numeric score for prediction. In the future, we are trying to introduce more botnet concept descriptions to build ensemble botnet learning model.

6   Conclusions and Future Work

The botnet threat is totally different from optical character recognition, speech recognition, bioinformatics and so on, whose concept description could be stable for many years. For the financial motivation, botnet keeps evolving perpetually and introducing well-crafted concept drift to evade detection. To build a sustainable and secure learning model, we need to quickly recognize and react to the concept drift of underlying botnet data distribution. In this paper we proposed an novel botnet detection approach that based on the matching scores provided by BotFinder classifier, we use concept drift scores and DRIFT function to identify hidden concept drift and dynamic feature reweighting. As far as we know, we are the first to achieve an active and dynamic learning approach for botnet detection that actively tracks the trend of hidden botnet concept drift and accordingly evolves learning model dynamically to fit latest botnet concept.

Our approach is agnostic to the algorithm, making it compatible with most botnet classification or clustering algorithm that uses a score for prediction. In the future, we will integrate more diverse scoring botnet classifiers into this approach, such as vertical correlation classifiers, to increase botnet concept description and learn botnet from more and more diverse perspectives. And we are going to improve the efficiency of this approach through introducing sliding window to online learn the latest concepts and remove aging data dynamically.

Acknowledgements. This material is based upon the work supported by the National Natural Science Foundation of China under the Grant No. 61300242 and No. 61772291, and by the Tianjin Research Program of Application Foundation and Advanced Technology under the Grant No. 15JCQNJC41500 and No. 17JCZDJC30500, and by the Open Project Foundation of Information Security Evaluation Center of Civil Aviation, Civil Aviation University of China under the Grant No. CAAC-ISECCA-201701 and No. CAAC-ISECCA-201702, and by the National Key Basic Research Program of China under the Grant No. 2013CB834204.

References

1. Antonakakis, M., April, T., Bailey, M., Bernhard, M., Bursztein, E., Cochran, J., Durumeric, Z., Halderman, J.A., Invernizzi, L., Kallitsis, M., Kumar, D., Lever, C., Ma, Z., Mason, J., Menscher, D., Seaman, C., Sullivan, N., Thomas, K., Zhou, Y.: Understanding the mirai botnet. In: 26th USENIX Security Symposium (USENIX Security 2017), Vancouver, BC. USENIX Association, August 2017
2. AV-Test: Malware statistics, September 2017. https://www.av-test.org/en/statistics/malware/
3. Demontis, A., Melis, M., Biggio, B., Maiorca, D., Arp, D., Rieck, K., Corona, I., Giacinto, G., Roli, F.: Yes, machine learning can be more secure! A case study on android malware detection. IEEE Trans. Dependable Secure Comput. (2017)
4. Garca, S., Grill, M., Stiborek, J., Zunino, A.: An empirical comparison of botnet detection methods. Comput. Secur. **45**, 100–123 (2014)
5. Garca, S., Zunino, A., Campo, M.: Survey on network-based botnet detection methods. Secur. Commun. Netw. **7**, 878–903 (2014)

6. Ye, Y., Li, T., Adjeroh, D., Iyengar, S.S.: A survey on malware detection using data mining techniques. ACM Comput. Surv. **50**, 41:1–41:40 (2017)
7. Zeng, Y., Shin, K.G., Hu, X.: Design of SMS commanded-and-controlled and P2P-structured mobile botnets. In: Proceedings of the Fifth ACM Conference on Security and Privacy in Wireless and Mobile Networks, WISEC 2012, New York, NY, USA, pp. 137–148. ACM (2012)
8. Singh, K., Sangal, S., Jain, N., Traynor, P., Lee, W.: Evaluating Bluetooth as a medium for botnet command and control. In: Kreibich, C., Jahnke, M. (eds.) DIMVA 2010. LNCS, vol. 6201, pp. 61–80. Springer, Heidelberg (2010). https://doi.org/10.1007/978-3-642-14215-4_4
9. Krombholz, K., Hobel, H., Huber, M., Weippl, E.: Advanced social engineering attacks. J. Inf. Secur. Appl. **22**, 113–122 (2015). Special Issue on Security of Information and Networks
10. Yin, T., Zhang, Y., Li, S.: DR-SNBOT: a social network-based botnet with strong destroy-resistance. In: IEEE International Conference on Networking, Architecture, and Storage, pp. 191–199 (2014)
11. Kartaltepe, E.J., Morales, J.A., Xu, S., Sandhu, R.: Social network-based botnet command-and-control: emerging threats and countermeasures. In: Proceedings of Applied Cryptography and Network Security, International Conference, ACNS 2010, Beijing, China, 22–25 June 2010, pp. 511–528 (2010)
12. Šrndic, N., Laskov, P.: Practical evasion of a learning-based classifier: a case study. In: Proceedings of the 2014 IEEE Symposium on Security and Privacy, SP 2014, Washington, DC, USA, pp. 197–211. IEEE Computer Society (2014)
13. Biggio, B., Pillai, I., Rota Bulò, S., Ariu, D., Pelillo, M., Roli, F.: Is data clustering in adversarial settings secure? In: Proceedings of the 2013 ACM Workshop on Artificial Intelligence and Security, AISec 2013, New York, NY, USA, pp. 87–98. ACM (2013)
14. Biggio, B., Rieck, K., Ariu, D., Wressnegger, C., Corona, I., Giacinto, G., Roli, F.: Poisoning behavioral malware clustering. In: Proceedings of the 2014 Workshop on Artificial Intelligent and Security Workshop, AISec 2014, New York, NY, USA, pp. 27–36. ACM (2014)
15. Tramèr, F., Zhang, F., Juels, A., Reiter, M.K., Ristenpart, T.: Stealing machine learning models via prediction APIs. In: 25th USENIX Security Symposium (USENIX Security 16), Austin, TX, pp. 601–618. USENIX Association (2016)
16. Kantchelian, A., Afroz, S., Huang, L., Islam, A.C., Miller, B., Tschantz, M.C., Greenstadt, R., Joseph, A.D., Tygar, J.D.: Approaches to adversarial drift. In: Proceedings of the 2013 ACM Workshop on Artificial Intelligence and Security, AISec 2013, New York, NY, USA, pp. 99–110. ACM (2013)
17. Srndic, N., Laskov, P.: Practical evasion of a learning-based classifier: a case study. In: Proceedings of the 35th IEEE Symposium on Security and Privacy (S&P), San Jose, CA, May 2014
18. Arce, I.: The weakest link revisited. IEEE Secur. Priv. **1**, 72–76 (2003)
19. Singh, K., Srivastava, A., Giffin, J., Lee, W.: Evaluating emails feasibility for botnet command and control. In: IEEE International Conference on Dependable Systems and Networks with FTCS and DCC, Anchorage, AK, pp. 376–385. IEEE, June 2008
20. Wagner, D., Soto, P.: Mimicry attacks on host-based intrusion detection systems. In: Proceedings of the 9th ACM Conference on Computer and Communications Security, CCS 2002, New York, NY, USA, pp. 255–264. ACM (2002)

21. Smutz, C., Stavrou, A.: Malicious PDF detection using metadata and structural features. In: Proceedings of the 28th Annual Computer Security Applications Conference, ACSAC 2012, New York, NY, USA, pp. 239–248. ACM (2012)
22. Deo, A., Dash, S.K., Suarez-Tangil, G., Vovk, V., Cavallaro, L.: Prescience: probabilistic guidance on the retraining conundrum for malware detection. In: Proceedings of the 2016 ACM Workshop on Artificial Intelligence and Security, AISec 2016, New York, NY, USA, pp. 71–82. ACM (2016)
23. Jordaney, R., Sharad, K., Dash, S.K., Wang, Z., Papini, D., Nouretdinov, I., Cavallaro, L.: Transcend: detecting concept drift in malware classification models. In: Proceedings of the 26th USENIX Security Symposium (USENIX Security 2017) (2017)
24. Tegeler, F., Fu, X., Vigna, G., Kruegel, C.: Botfinder: finding bots in network traffic without deep packet inspection. In: Proceedings of the 8th International Conference on Emerging Networking Experiments and Technologies (CoNEXT 2012), France, pp. 349–360. ACM, New York, December 2012
25. van der Maaten, L., Hinton, G.: Visualizing data using t-SNE. J. Mach. Learn. Res. **9**, 2579–2605 (2008)

Statically Defend Network Consumption Against Acker Failure Vulnerability in Storm

Wenjun Qian[1,2], Qingni Shen[1,2(✉)], Yizhe Yang[2,3], Yahui Yang[1,2],
and Zhonghai Wu[1,2]

[1] School of Software and Microelectronics, Peking University, Beijing, China
wenjunqian@pku.edu.cn, {qingnishen,yhyang,wuzh}@ss.pku.edu.cn
[2] National Engineering Research Center for Software Engineering,
Peking University, Beijing, China
yangyizhe1003@pku.edu.cn
[3] School of Electronics and Computer Engineering,
Peking University, Shenzhen, China

Abstract. Storm has been a popular distributed real-time computation system for stream data processing, which currently provides an acker mechanism to enable all topologies to be processed reliably. In this paper, via the source code analysis, we point out that the acker failure and message retransmission result in the consumption of network resources. Even worse, adversary conducts a malicious topology to consume over unconstrained network resources, which seriously affects the average processing time of topology for normal users. Aiming at defending the vulnerability, we design an offline static detection against acker failure in Storm, mainly including the code decompile, the function call relationship and the judgement rules in offline module. Meanwhile, we validate the protection scheme in Storm 0.10.0 cluster, and experimental results show that our mentioned judgement rules can achieve well precision.

Keywords: Stream data · Storm · Acker failure
Message retransmission · Network consumption

1 Introduction

Before the development of the streaming computing platform, many Internet companies, in the face of real-time big data processing problems, usually set up network channels and multiple work nodes by themselves to deal with messages in real time. However, the approach could no longer meet the requirement for data processing, such as no losing data, scaling up the cluster, and manipulating easily. The appearance of Storm [2] solved the above problems, and Storm can deal with real-time massive data which is generated on social platforms. At present, there are many stream data computing systems, such as Storm, S4 [12], Spark Streaming [3], TimeStream [4] and Kafka [1]. S4 and Kafka implement

© Springer International Publishing AG, part of Springer Nature 2018
S. Qing et al. (Eds.): ICICS 2017, LNCS 10631, pp. 661–673, 2018.
https://doi.org/10.1007/978-3-319-89500-0_56

high availability through passive waiting strategy, while Storm, Spark Streaming and TimeStream achieve high availability via upstream backup strategy [6,11]. Compared with other stream processing platforms, Storm is the most widely-used platform in the industry from the aspects of system architecture, application interface, support language and high availability. Storm has advantages in terms of performance, but it raises some security problems.

At present, the academic and industry mainly focus on the security and privacy issues of batch processing platforms, such as information stealing, decision interference and denial of service attack [5,7,16]. And many solutions have been proposed for Hadoop, such as authentication, authorization, differential privacy technology and trusted computing base TCG (Trusted Computing Group), etc. These solutions are complete for secure hardware environment, trusted data processing platform, data encryption and secure computing process [8,13–15]. However, it is inevitable that the complete solutions are not optimal, and need to be improved and tested in practice. Moreover, security issues in big data environments are complex and diverse, and different computing frameworks may require different solutions. Compared with batch processing platforms, stream processing platforms mainly focus on the real-time and reliability. Unfortunately, there are few concern about such security vulnerability issues.

Typically, reliable mechanism in Storm is designed simply and there are security vulnerabilities in reliable mechanism. In this paper, we mainly focus on the security vulnerability of Storm platform. We verify that there are problems of network consumption caused by Acker failure and message retransmission through analyzing source codes and experimental results. Furthermore, we propose a protection scheme to examine malicious code statically and design the experiment in Storm. **Our contributions** can be summarized as follows:

- We show the problems of reliable mechanism in Storm, and the vulnerability of over network consumption, which is caused by Acker failure and message retransmission. If the XOR value of message traced by *Acker Bolt* is not zero, which means failing to process message, Spout will resend message and occupy the cluster's resources. Evenly, over network consumption affect processing efficiency for the normal users' topology in real time.
- We run eight Storm benchmarks, and the number of worker and executor are the same in each topology. According to the relative consumption of resources, we classify all benchmarks as memory-dependency topology, CPU-dependency topology and network-dependency topology. Finally, we select the network-dependency topology as the normal user's topology.
- In addition, we also compare the resource consumption dependency with different stream grouping methods for the same topology, and find that global grouping will consume more network resource than other stream grouping methods in the same topology. We design a malicious topology using global grouping to verify the over network consumption.
- We design a protection scheme based on malicious code static detection technology, which decompiles the topology offline, and then analyzes statically the source code according to some judgement rules. If the topology is malicious, it would be killed.

The rest of this paper is organized as follows. We introduce the background in Sect. 2, and discuss problems and challenges of current acker mechanism in Sect. 3. In Sect. 4, we implement and evaluate the effects of malicious attack. We then present the protection scheme and performance of static detection against acker failure in Sect. 5. We conclude the paper in Sect. 6.

2   Background

Our work is related to the fields of Acker in Storm as well as Stream Grouping. In this section, we succinctly introduce the background in these fields.

2.1   Acker in Storm

The reliable mechanism traces each message emitted by Spout relying on *Acker Bolt* in Storm. Tuple tree can be understood as a directed acyclic logic structure, which is formed by source tuples emitted by Spout and new tuples emitted by Bolts. Within timeout limit, *Acker Bolt* tasks conducted the simple *XOR* operation on each *tupleId* in a tuple tree (uniquely identified by *msgId*), and then judged whether the result of *XOR* operation was zero or not. If the *XOR* result was zero, the tuple tree would be processed successfully. Otherwise, the tuple tree was considered to fail. More specifically, the implementation of reliable mechanism is as follows:

- When sending a source tuple, Spout specifies an *msgId* (as the unique *RootId* to identify a tuple tree) and a *tupleId* for the source tuple. Then Spout acknowledges the source tuple and sends $\langle RootId, tupleId \rangle$ to *Acker Bolt*.
- After processing a received tuple successfully, Bolt sends one or more new tuples anchored to the received tuple (uniquely identified by $tupleId_{rec}$), and specifies a random $tupleId_{new}$ for each new tuple. Then it acknowledges the received tuple and sends $\langle RootId, tupleId_{rec} \wedge tupleId_{new} \rangle$ to *Acker Bolt*.
- *Acker Bolt* executes the *XOR* operation on all received acknowledgement messages, which belong to the same *RootId*. If the *XOR* result is zero, *Acker Bolt* acknowledges that the source tuple tagged with *RootId* is processed completely, and then sends *ack* to Spout. Otherwise, after timeout, *Acker Bolt* sends *fail* to Spout and the source tuple is judges as failed.

2.2   Stream Grouping

Stream grouping mechanism in Storm provides eight kinds of message grouping method for topology, and determines how the messages emitted by Spout or Bolt will be received by the downstream Bolt. In this paper, we mainly focus on three kinds of commonly used methods, including shuffle grouping, field grouping and global grouping.

- **ShuffleGrouping.** The shuffle grouping method determines that tuples are assigned between Spout and Bolt randomly. And the random assignment result causes the same number of tuples to be allocated on each Bolt.
- **FieldGrouping.** In a topology, the field grouping method can specify that all tuples emitted by the upstream Spout or Bolt, are grouped by one or more fields, and then distributed to multiple downstream Bolt tasks. That is to say, each downstream Bolt receives tuples in same group.
- **GlobalGrouping.** In a topology, the global grouping method assigns all tuples emitted by the upstream Spout and Bolt to one downstream Bolt task, specifically, the Bolt task with the smallest *taskId*.

3   Problems and Challenges

In this section, we point out the problems and challenges of current reliable mechanism in Storm, and present an attack model with the existed vulnerability.

3.1   Vulnerability Analysis

Through analyzing the source code of reliable mechanism, we detect that both reliable and unreliable topologies can be run in Storm. Besides, Storm developer provides programmer with flexible API. However, it is vital to deal with some business scenarios with message consistency, such as bank deposit, transformation and remittance business.

When programmer design their topology, Storm provides Spout and Bolt components with some basic interfaces and abstract classes, including *Icomponent, ISpout, IBolt, IRichSpout, IRichBolt, IBasicBolt* and some other kinds of basic interfaces, as well as *BaseComponent, BaseRichSpout, BaseRichBolt* and *BaseBasicBolt* and some other kinds of basic abstract classes. *BaseBasicBolt* class implements *IBasicBolt* interface, which acknowledges the received tuple automatically. Programmer requires for inheriting *BaseBasicBolt* abstract class when designing reliable Bolt, and *BaseRichBolt* abstract class when designing unreliable Bolt. Through analyzing the source code of acker mechanism, we point out some existed vulnerabilities in Storm as follows:

- **Q1:** *In a reliable topology, it is necessary to execute the ack or fail operation for each processed message, which enables the reliability of message in Storm. Correspondingly, tracing message consumes memory resources.*

At the beginning of designing Storm, in order to give users a better experience, Storm provides reliable and unreliable interface and abstract class. However, it indicates that user can render Bolt tasks more reliable by means of calling *ack()* function in unreliable abstract class. Although this way is more flexible, it cannot avoid the danger of attackers.

- **Q2:** *If some Bolts (called unreliable Bolt) don't execute the ack or fail operation for its received messages, it will result in the value of ack in Acker Bolt is* *not equal to zero in the extended time. Spout cannot trigger the ack() function to evacuate the messages, so it will result in resources waste.*

When users design a reliable Bolt by inheriting *BasicRichBolt* abstract classes, every Bolt task will process the received tuple, emit new tuple, and call the *ack()* function after completing tuple anchoring. Although the tuple tree has been processed completely actually within timeout limit, the tuple tree will always be traced and cannot be released. Over timeout, Bolt will be not able to send $tupleId_{rec}$ and $tupleId_{new}$ to *Acker Bolt*, and the tuple tree will be judged as failure.

- **Q3:** *When reaching extended time, Acker Bolt send fail to Spout about source tuple. If user triggers fail() function and implement resend tuple function from Spout, this will lead to source tuple resending over and over again, which consume CPU and network resources.*

In practice, it is not been implemented to re-transmit tuple in the *fail()* function of Spout component by system developer. If user implements fail() function, Spout will call it to re-transmit a source tuple. Similarly, the source tuple will also be judged as failure in the end. There are two ways of designing reliable Bolt as follows:

- Reliable Bolt can be implemented by calling *IRichBolt* interface. Firstly, it needs anchor each new tuple to the received tuple while sending new tuples, and then call *ack()* method to acknowledge the received tuple. If no anchoring or calling, the new tuple emitted by Bolt will not be traced.
- Reliable Bolt can be implemented by inheriting *BaseBasicBolt* abstract class, which automatically implement the emitting, anchoring and acknowledgement operations for each new tuple in *executor()* method.

3.2 Attack Model

Attack Target. If *Acker Bolt* do not receive the acknowledgment message from Bolt, Acker failure and message retransmission will result in the vulnerability of over network consumption. Once the vulnerability is used by bad attacker, who faked as a legal user in cluster, and submitted a malicious topology, it not only consumes network resource in cluster, but also affects the efficiency of topology for a normal user.

The attack model of malicious topology is designed as Fig. 1. The malicious topology implements a reliable Spout, a reliable $Bolt_1$ and an unreliable $Bolt_2$ by inheriting *IRichBolt*. However, $Bolt_2$ tasks are anchored to the received tuples and not acknowledged. The adversary runs a malicious topology as follows:

1. By running test.py script to write contents into */tmp/fluem/test.log*, Flume monitors the log file, and transfers the input data to test topic in Kafka.
2. Spout assigns *msgId* to each source tuple, and sends a key-value pair ⟨*RootId, tupleId*⟩ to *Acker Bolt* after acknowledging the source tuple.

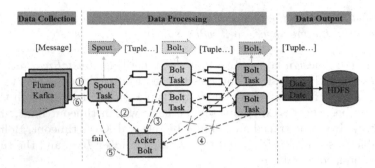

Fig. 1. The attack model of malicious topology

3. $Bolt_1$ emits new tuples and anchors these tuples to the received tuple. Then, Bolt calls $ack()$ function to acknowledge all received tuples, and sends $tupleId_{rec}$ and $tupleId_{new}$ to *Acker Bolt*.
4. $Bolt_2$ pulls every tuple from $Bolt_1$ using global grouping method, and does not call $ack()$ function to acknowledge all received tuples.
5. After timeout limit, it is not zero that the *XOR* value of *RootId* in *Acker Bolt*. The source tuple is processed failed.
6. Spout will call *fail()* function itself, and re-transmit the failed message from Kafka message queue. By repeating the previous steps, the failed message is still processed failed all the time.

4   Experimental Evaluation

Through the Ganglia monitoring tool, we view the resource occupancy in cluster. Through the Storm UI, we view the malicious topology and normal user topology operation, and compare the average processing time of normal user's topology whether running malicious programs or not. We design three kinds of topologies, including general topology (simplified as GT_1), malicious topology (simplified as MT_2) and malicious topology (simplified as MT_3). GT_1 consists of a reliable Spout, a reliable $Bolt_1$ and a reliable $Bolt_2$, MT_2 consists of a reliable Spout, a reliable $Bolt_1$ and an unreliable $Bolt_2$, and MT_3 consists of a reliable Spout, a reliable $Bolt_1$ and an unreliable $Bolt_2$. The difference between GT_1 and MT_2 is that whether $Bolt_2$ is a reliable component, and the difference between MT_2 and MT_3 is that stream grouping method is global grouping in MT_3.

Network Consumption. Comparing the network consumption between GT_1 and malicious topologies, we respectively submitted three topologies into Storm 0.10.0 cluster. Figure 2 shows the total network and memory consumption when only running GT_1 in Storm cluster. And Fig. 3 shows the network consumption respectively when only running a malicious topology, namely MT_2 or MT_3.

There are significant differences between GT_1 and malicious topologies. When GT_1 running within one hour in Storm cluster, the input network consumption of GT_1 is average of 68.5k, and output network consumption is average of 67.7k. However, it is significant for two malicious topology on the increased network consumption. Compared with MT_2, especially for MT_3 using global grouping, the input network consumption is average of 195.3k, the output network consumption is average of 196.0k, which has more than 3x in network consumption. From MT_2 and MT_3, we can see that it is relatively high in network consumption for the malicious topology using global grouping topology. From GT_1 and MT_2, we can see that it is an obviously growth to consume network resources for the MT_2, and experimental results show that the growth is nearly 10x. However, it is roughly the same memory consumption for GT_1 and two malicious topologies. We find that the memory resource consumption value depends on the number of worker that is set in a topology by programmer.

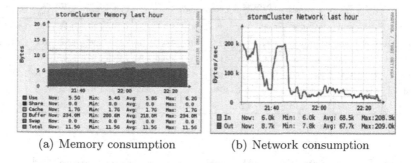

(a) Memory consumption   (b) Network consumption

Fig. 2. The network and memory consumption when only running GT_1 in Storm

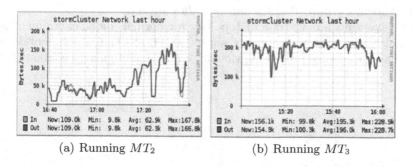

(a) Running MT_2 (b) Running MT_3

Fig. 3. The network consumption when running MT_2 or MT_3 respectively in Storm

Resource Dependent Classification. There are eight benchmarks in Storm, and we only test six benchmarks in Storm cluster, excluding two benchmarks only run in local mode. We run each benchmark separately for one hour in Storm cluster. In order to eliminate the interference caused by the number of worker and executor in different topologies, we set the number of worker to three, and the number of executor to twelve for each benchmark. Besides, six bench-marks are reliable topologies. By counting and comparing the consumption of memory, CPU, and network resources for each benchmark at runtime, as shown in Table 1, we find that *Slidwindow* consumes the highest amount of network resources, *Multipletogger* consumes the lowest amount of network resources. The in-network consumption of *Slidwindow* is 1.7x than the in-network overhead of the *Multiplelogger*. In the subsequent malicious topology attacks, we will conduct a malicious topology to impact the network resource-dependent topology, namely *Slidwindow*.

Table 1. Network, CPU and memory consumption statistics about examples in Storm

	Cluster				Supervisor1				Supervisor2				Supervisor3			
	Network		CPU	Memory	Network		CPU	Memory	Network		CPU	Memory	Network		CPU	Memory
	In	Out			In	Out			In	Out			In	Out		
Exclamation	35.4k	17.4k	1.5%	6.2G	9.9k	3.9k	2.1%	1.8G	8.2k	3.5k	1.5%	1.2G	10.3k	6.3k	1.8%	1.5G
Multiplelogger	31.6k	17.2k	1.6%	6.2G	9.2k	3.5k	2.2%	1.8G	7.6k	3.5k	1.5%	1.2G	9.8k	6.6k	1.8%	1.5G
Resourceaware	35.5k	18.0k	1.5%	6.2G	10.4k	4.0k	2.1%	1.7G	8.4k	3.5k	1.5%	1.2G	10.9k	6.4k	1.7%	1.4G
Slidetuple	49.2k	31.1k	2.1%	6.4G	14.7k	8.4k	2.8%	1.8G	12.6k	7.7k	2.3%	1.2G	15.0k	11.1k	2.5%	1.5G
Slidwindow	54.4k	36.0k	2.3%	6.4G	16.6k	10.6k	3.1%	1.8G	14.1k	9.1k	2.6%	1.3G	17.0k	12.8k	2.8%	1.5G
Wordcount	43.4k	30.0k	2.3%	6.1G	13.4k	9.2k	3.0%	1.7G	10.6k	7.1k	2.2%	1.1G	14.2k	10.0k	3.0%	1.6G

Average Processing Time. We designs an *experiment group* and a *control group* to verify the influence of malicious topology on the average processing time for normal topology. In control group, a normal user's topology (*WordCount*) and a general user's topology (GT_1) are run in Storm at the same time. Whereas in experimental group, *WordCount* and MT_3 are run.

The average running time of topology for normal under experiment group and that under control group are shown as Fig. 4. The experimental results show that the average processing time of *WordCount* topology is about 1.49 ms

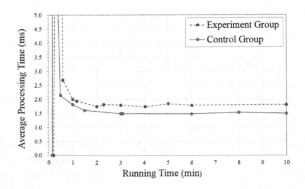

Fig. 4. The average processing time of normal topology in Storm

under normal circumstances. In experiment group, the average processing time of *WordCount* topology for normal users is about 1.79 ms, and the processing speed is slowed by 19.4%.

5   Protection Against Acker Failure

In this section, we first present an overview of static detection against acker failure in Storm, mainly including decompile, function call relationship and judgement rules in offline module, and then describe design and implementation of the judgement rules.

5.1   Design of Static Detection

In order to solve the security vulnerability of Acker failure, we propose a protection scheme from three angles as follows:

- Improving Acker code through designing a secure Spout or Bolt interface.
- Detecting Spout and Bolt in a reliable topology by static code detection.
- Detecting all abnormal behaviors of resources consumption by ganglia tool.

In the previous analysis of interface, we can see that Storm provides a secure and reliable anchoring mechanism for Spout and Bolt, and provides a reliable *IBasicBolt* interface and *BaseBasicBolt* abstract class for Bolt. Therefore, we does not need to design a secure Spout or Bolt interface. In addition, ganglia monitors the entire Storm cluster from the perspective of the application layer. Note that, if Ganglia detects the excessive consumption of network resources, maybe the abnormal behavior is not caused by acker failure and message retransmission in malicious procedures.

Based on the above analysis, we design and present an offline static detection against failure in Storm as shown in Fig. 5. If the detection result of a topology is legal, the topology will be processed in real time. The offline static detection against acker failure in Storm works as follows:

1. Decompile process makes executable topology code to be java source code, and needs that it is optimized to restore the source code form.
2. The class function call relationship graph can be achieved by using Model-Goon plugin tool. Specifically, this step needs present the implementation interface and the call method.
3. The source code will be analyzed according to the specified judgement rules. If a topology is designed reliably at first, only if all Spout and Bolt have invoked the ack method, the topology is legal. Otherwise, it is judged as a malicious topology. If a topology is unreliable, it is directly determined as a legal topology.

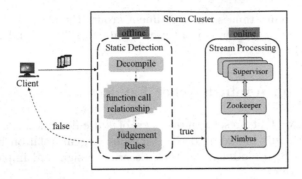

Fig. 5. The overview of offline static detection against acker failure in Storm

5.2   Judgement Rules

In the offline environment, the source code of a topology is analyzed based on the judgement rules. If the result is true, the topology will be submitted and processed in real time. Otherwise, the topology is rejected. Specifically, judgement rules are as follows:

– **Rule-1**: In a topology, if the developer calls Spout's *nextTuple()* method to send a source tuple that is not specified with a unique *msgId*, the topology is determined as an unreliable topology. Storm will not start the *Acker Bolt* component to trace the source tuple, and the return value is true. Otherwise, the topology is a reliable topology and needs to be judged continually by *Rule-2* and *Rule-3*.
– **Rule-2**: If the developer inherits the *BaseBasicBolt* class that implements the *IBasicBolt* interface, this indicates that the Bolt's *execute()* method will automatically implement the anchoring and acknowledgement operations, and the return value is true.
– **Rule-3**: If the developer inherits the *BaseRichBolt* class that implements the *IRichBolt* interface, and emits a new tuple that is anchored to the parent tuple at the same time, the parent tuple does not explicitly call the *ack()* method. Then the Bolt is determined as an unreliable Bolt, and the return value is false. Otherwise, the Bolt is a reliable Bolt, and the return value is true.

In particular, if Bolt is implemented by an unreliable interface in a topology, regardless that whether new tuple is anchored to the parent tuple, the topology is judged as a malicious topology eventually as long as the call of *ack()* method is not explicitly called.

5.3   Performance

After decompiling a topology, the executable .class.jar package is decompiled into a java source file. Then, through the ModelGoon plug-in, we draw the class function relationship graph. In this section, we just test the decompile result and achieve a usable relationship graph. We conduct the code detection offline, which does not effect the real-time performance in Storm.

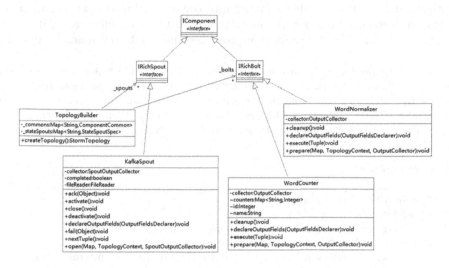

Fig. 6. The class relationship of decompiled topology

We decompile a topology submitted from client, and get a class relationship by Eclipse ModelGoon plug-in as shown in Fig. 6. It consists of a *KafkaSpout* component and two Bolt components. *KafkaSpout* implements *IRichSpout* interface, and WordNormalizer Bolt and WordCounter Bolt implement *IRichBolt* interface. Further, through the call hierarchy view function call, it was found that the *ack()* method was invoked only when the *execute()* method was called in the WordNormalizer class implementation, the message was not statically linked in the WordCounter class, and the *ack()* method was not explicitly called. The topology submitted by user is judged as a malicious topology, and can not be submitted into Storm cluster.

6 Conclusion

In this paper, we mainly study two mechanisms in Storm, including reliable mechanism and stream grouping mechanism. Meanwhile, we analyze and point out the security vulnerability of current reliable mechanism, in which unreliable Bolt enables the source tuple to fail, retransmit it continually and bring with over network consumption. Via experimental results and source code analysis, we find that malicious topology influent the normal user's topology, over 19.4% at the average processing time. Motivated by the vulnerability of acker failure, we presents a protection scheme using malicious code static detection technology.

Our work still need to study and improve a better detection against acker failure. Firstly, we only consider the static detection. Dromard et al. [9] and Wang et al. [17] proposed different methods of anomaly detection respectively, which are worthy of reference to improve the current static detection scheme. Secondly, during the detection of malicious programs, the selected feature is anchoring and acknowledgement. Furthermore, our next work is to select different features, and use the method of SVM (Support Vector Machine) to detect anomaly like [10].

Acknowledgments. This work is supported by the National Natural Science Foundation of China under Grant No. 61672062, 61232005, and the National High Technology Research and Development Program ("863" Program) of China under Grant No. 2015AA016009. Thanks to Lingyun Guo and Liming Zheng for the support of experimental data collection and stream grouping analysis.

References

1. Apache kafka. http://kafka.apache.org
2. Apache storm. http://storm.apache.org
3. Spark streaming. http://spark.apache.org/streaming
4. TimeStream. https://github.com/TimeStream/timestream
5. Alguliyev, R., Imamverdiyev, Y.: Big data: big promises for information security. In: IEEE International Conference on Application of Information and Communication Technologies, pp. 1–4 (2014)
6. Aritsugi, M., Nagano, K.: Recovery processing for high availability stream processing systems in local area networks. In: TENCON 2010–2010 IEEE Region 10 Conference, pp. 1036–1041 (2010)
7. Bertino, E., Ferrari, E.: Big data security and privacy. In: IEEE International Congress on Big Data, pp. 757–761 (2015)
8. Dinh, T.T.A., Saxena, P., Chang, E.C., Ooi, B.C., Zhang, C.: M2R: enabling stronger privacy in MapReduce computation (2015)
9. Dromard, J., Roudiere, G., Owezarski, P.: Online and scalable unsupervised network anomaly detection method. IEEE Trans. Netw. Serv. Manag. **PP**(99), 1 (2017)
10. Khaokaew, Y., Anusas-Amornkul, T.: A performance comparison of feature selection techniques with SVM for network anomaly detection. In: International Symposium on Computational and Business Intelligence, pp. 85–89 (2016)
11. Nagano, K., Itokawa, T., Kitasuka, T., Aritsugi, M.: Exploitation of backup nodes for reducing recovery cost in high availability stream processing systems. In: Fourteenth International Database Engineering & Applications Symposium, pp. 61–63 (2010)
12. Neumeyer, L., Robbins, B., Nair, A., Kesari, A.: S4: distributed stream computing platform. In: IEEE International Conference on Data Mining Workshops, pp. 170–177 (2011)
13. Ohrimenko, O., Costa, M., Fournet, C., Gkantsidis, C., Kohlweiss, M., Sharma, D.: Observing and preventing leakage in MapReduce (2015)
14. Roy, I., Setty, S.T.V., Kilzer, A., Shmatikov, V., Witchel, E.: Airavat: security and privacy for MapReduce. In: Usenix Symposium on Networked Systems Design and Implementation, NSDI 2010, 28–30 April 2010, San Jose, CA, USA, pp. 297–312 (2010)

15. Sweeney, L.: k-anonymity: a model for protecting privacy. Int. J. Uncertainty Fuzziness Knowl. Based Syst. **10**(05), 557–570 (2002)
16. Takabi, H., Joshi, J.B.D., Ahn, G.J.: Security and privacy challenges in cloud computing environments. IEEE Secur. Priv. **8**(6), 24–31 (2010)
17. Wang, Z., Yang, J., Zhang, H., Li, C., Zhang, S., Wang, H.: Towards online anomaly detection by combining multiple detection methods and storm. In: Network Operations and Management Symposium, pp. 804–807 (2016)

Pollution Attacks Identification in Structured P2P Overlay Networks

Zied Trifa[1(✉)], Jalel Eddine Hajlaoui[2], and Maher Khemakhem[3]

[1] MIRACL Laboratory, University of Sfax, Sfax, Tunisia
trifa.zied@gmail.com
[2] MARS Research Laboratory, University of Sousse, Sousse, Tunisia
hajlaouijalel.ig@gmail.com
[3] College of Computing and Information Technology,
University of King Abdulaziz, Jeddah, Saudi Arabia
makhemakhem@kau.edu.sa

Abstract. Structured p2p overlay networks have emerged as a dominant means for sharing and exchange of information on the Internet. However, they suffer from severe security threats, known as pollution attacks, in which malicious peers insert decoys in data object. The existence of such polluters is considered as a major problem since these systems are based on trust between peers to ensure the sharing and access to available resources. Pollution attacks ravages network resources and annoys peers with contaminated objects. Although there have been numerous works on pollution attacks, there have been no studies on these attacks in structured p2p overlay networks and all of them are not qualified to ensure security. This paper investigates the different strategies of polluter nodes and their impact on the security of communication. We also detail a monitoring process to supervise, detect and attenuate these threats. Our experiments show that our strategy decreases enormously the pollution attacks with a slight number of monitor peers.

Keywords: Pollution attacks · Structured p2p overlay networks
Chord · Monitoring · Tracking

1 Introduction

Structured p2p systems have grown increasingly in recent years as a means of communication, resource sharing, distributed computing and the development of collaborative application. They provide self-organization architecture of large-scale application. Thus, they were subjected to further analysis and a careful design to ensure scalability and efficiency [1].

However, recent research [2] have focused on creating efficient search algorithms that can be used to build more complex systems. But, they have not considered how to deal with pollution attacks. These attacks occur when a polluter peer added decoys in data object (Content pollution) or alters the metadata (Metadata pollution) or tries to falsify indexes (index poisoning). Thus, resulting in a wide range of polluted objects propagating in the system.

© Springer International Publishing AG, part of Springer Nature 2018
S. Qing et al. (Eds.): ICICS 2017, LNCS 10631, pp. 674–686, 2018.
https://doi.org/10.1007/978-3-319-89500-0_57

Pollution is one of the major issues affecting structured p2p networks. A study conducted in the KAD network to quantify the pollution of contents proved that 2/3 of the contents are polluted [15].

In this paper, our goal is to deal with pollution attacks in structured p2p systems using supervision and detection process. The remainder of this paper is organized as follows. In the next section, we provide some background information about pollution attacks. Section 3 reviews the related works. Section 4 details our contributions. We describe our proposed solution and its underlying ideas. In Sect. 5, we present details about the simulations steps and measurements used to assess the effectiveness of our supervision and detection process. Section 6 concludes the paper and outlines further directions.

2 The Pollution Attack

Pollution attacks damage targeted objects and dispatches them in the network. In this way, contaminated objects will be distributed through the sharing overlay. Thus, they break trust between users during objects exchange.

An object is considered polluted if the content does not fit the description presented to the user. Pollution attacks can be classified into three categories: Content pollution, Metadata pollution and Index poisoning.

The content pollution occurs when a malicious node adds decoys in data object. Thus, it can easily generate multiple false copies of objects that have the same content key by exploiting the weakness of the used hash functions. In this way, the transmission quality decreases significantly [3].

Metadata pollution occurs when polluter node alters the metadata of an object. Thus, nodes that will download objects based on metadata will obtain corrupted one [4]. In this way, nodes may unintentionally store contaminated objects in index table. It is very similar to the content pollution in terms of malicious intents. In both strategies, the polluter node tries to poison the content of the object to make it unusable. Thus, it uses its own resources to share contaminated objects in the overlay.

To find the location of desired objects, structured p2p systems use index. Polluter node tries to falsify these indexes by the insertion of massive numbers of false information. Consequently, when user attempts to download an object with randomly generated identifier, sharing system fails to locate the associated object.

Polluter node always tries to poison the index of the most popular objects. When other nodes download these objects, they get wrong or nonexistent one. Then, it connects directly to the victim's nodes. In this case, other nodes cannot obtain services from victim's nodes because these nodes have occupied the allowed connection [5].

Index poisoning directly attacks the structure of the overlay. First, polluter node can generate a random content key which could not point anywhere in the network. Moreover, it can generate multiple identities based on an invalid IP address or unavailable port number and publishes keys that point to one of it camouflaged identities [6].

3 Understanding Pollution Defense

Several researches have been done to address the pollution attacks in structured p2p overlay networks. In this section, we describe a wide range of mechanisms to attenuate these attacks.

3.1 Mechanisms Based on Downloading Objects

Correspondence Techniques. Correspondence techniques are based on the existence of a trusted centralized or decentralized database, which contains traces of the authentic objects. The authentic traces could be the content key or the metadata key. After downloading object, the node establishes correspondence with basic trust. If no match is found, node determines that the object is polluted. In this context, the project Sig2dat [7] makes available to users of KAZAA system a tool to obtain the authentic content key associated to any object in the network. This tool displays the titles of objects and key values on websites and forums.

Filtering Techniques. In these techniques, users must first check their downloaded objects before sharing their objects. In this way, the level of pollution attack would be significantly reduced. The major challenge is to provide users a robust system that encourages them to filter contaminated objects. Liang et al. [8] proposed an IP identification technique associated with malicious nodes. This is achieved by the use of special robots designed to collect metadata from the network.

3.2 Mechanisms Based on Trust, Reputation and Collaborative Approaches

Reputation Techniques. Kamvar et al. [9] have proposed EigenTrust: an algorithm that computes and maintains a reputation index for each peer in the network. This reputation is computed based on the experience of other peers, which interact with it. They have demonstrated how to use the index reputation to identify peers who provide contaminated objects. Costa et al. [10] have proposed Scrubber: a peer identifies malicious nodes that publish polluted objects on the basis of its experience and testimony of his neighbors. Vieira et al. [11] have proposed SimplyRep: a new decentralized reputation system that identifies and penalizes content polluters, while incurring in low overhead in terms of bandwidth consumption. It relies only on individual experiences of a peer to compute the reputation of its partners. Meng and Tan [12] have proposed a mechanism that computes pollution degree of each peer participating in the network. This degree is under the charge of its neighbors. When a query message is forwarded to the desired peer, its neighbors will calculate his pollution degree in order to assess that the file was polluted or not. Walsh and Sirer [13] have proposed Credence: a distributed reputation system, designed to thwart content pollution. It enables a peer to determine the authenticity of shared content. Peers in the Credence network votes on objects. The aim is to collate these votes and weight them by a novel similarity measure. Feng and Dai [14] have proposed Lip: a ranking approach based on the lifetime and the popularity of objects. They have proposed two detectors that filter logs files to identify contaminated objects. Zhang et al. [15] have proposed InfoRanking: a mechanism that tries to mitigate pollution attacks by ranking content items. It is based on the observation where malicious peers provide numerous fakes versions of the same information items in order to avoid blacklisting. Shin and Reeves [16] have proposed Winnowing: a novel distributed hash table based anti-pollution schema. It aims to reduce decoy index records held by DHT nodes in the system. Qi et al. [17] have proposed a reputation system combined with peer reputation and object reputation. They calculate the reputation of sharing objects by the reputation of the voting peer. Thus, honest peer, who uploads unpolluted objects and actively votes on objects, can have a higher reputation, while a malicious peer, who uploads polluted objects, would have a reduced reputation.

Collaborative Techniques. In these techniques, users download the objects from his neighbors who trust him completely. If a user starts receiving contaminated objects from any trust friend, it stops accepting objects and signals the presence of malicious users. These approaches allow users to locate their friends using instant presence detection process [18].

3.3 Mechanisms Based on Identification of Malicious Peers

The mechanisms of this category are based on the localization of malicious peers. Wang et al. [19] have proposed a schema based on messages in which the malicious peers can be rapidly located as long as they spread a single false message into the network. They try to track the origin of corrupted blocks. Gaeta and Grangetto [20] have proposed a monitoring tool to detect polluter nodes. They propose to use a statistical inference technique, namely Belief Propagation, to estimate the probability of peers being malicious. The detection algorithm runs by a set of trusted monitor nodes that receives notification messages from peers whenever they obtain a chunk of data. In [21] Gaeta et al. have proposed a system called DIP (*Distributed Identification of Polluters*) in p2p live streaming. DIP relies on checks that are computed by peers upon completing reception of all blocks composing a data chunk. A check is a message that contains the set of peer's identifiers providing blocks of the chunk as well as a bit to signal if the chunk is corrupted.

3.4 Discussion

Pollution attacks remain one of the major challenges to overcome especially in the context of structured p2p overlay networks. Unfortunately, reputation techniques were not effective in preventing or reducing such attacks. This is due to the complexity of setting such mechanisms in autonomous and complex systems. These are penalized if the peers realize bad votes. Besides, peer reputation mechanisms only care about the reputation of object providers, while object reputation mechanisms only care about the reputation of sharing objects. These mechanisms relay on identification-based approaches of malicious nodes. Herein, the major drawback is the high computational costs for verification all chunks and the communication overhead due to the number of messages exchanged between monitor nodes and nodes participating in the system.

We notice that all proposed solutions are not applied to structured p2p overlay networks and are not qualified to protect them in real time. We propose in the next section a new monitoring tool that can detect and isolate polluter nodes in real time. Our system is based on the identification of polluter nodes by monitoring the published messages.

4 Contributions

In this section, we present our vision of monitoring polluter nodes. It aims to detect a wide range of polluter nodes, which provide polluted objects.

4.1 Identifying Suspicious Polluter Nodes

The goal is to identify suspicious polluter nodes providing and pretending disposing polluted objects, yet narrow enough to exclude the vast majority of honest nodes. The main idea is to introduce monitoring peers within the overlay. Positioned in a strategic way, the monitors allow us to gain full control over a zone of the overlay. We use the Sybil attack to infiltrate the overlay and collect the different information of suspicious polluter nodes such as the IP address, the node identifier and port number. The aim here is to infiltrate the overlay with few number of monitor nodes, which are all controlled by one entity, the coordinator. These monitors seek to detect suspicious polluter nodes. The coordinator is able to create thousands of monitors on one single physical machine. We divided the overlay into zones to achieve accuracy and obtain a more global view. We introduce 2^n detectors into the network; the first n bits are different (prefix of each zone) and the following bits are fixed, they are the signatures of our detectors.

To infiltrate the network and detect suspicious polluter, the monitor M is implemented in the following steps. First, it sends hello message to the neighbor peers in order to poison their routing tables with entries that point our monitors. The peer that receive hello message will add the monitor to their routing table. Second, it sends lookup message to locate some random content IDs or random keyword IDs in the monitored zone. We must ensure that random content IDs or random keyword IDs does not exist in the ID space K. The normal behavior is to reply with the nearest nodes to the queried ID. However, the polluter puts its ID in the response and claims he is the owner of the queried ID. By checking who privileges the ownership of those non-existent IDs, we can identify suspicious polluter nodes. Finally, it gathers the following information: overlay ID, IP address and the port number of all suspicious nodes detected and report results to the coordinator. To bypass the detection process, the polluter node may behave appropriately or not respond to the search message. So we need to monitor the published messages to determine polluter nodes.

4.2 Monitoring Publish Message

Infiltration Process. We place a monitor peer within the suspicious polluter node spotted by the detection process for its best exploration. This enables us to control all the published and queried messages. At the start of the infiltration process, the monitor node introduces itself in the overlay in the following two steps. First, it initiates the monitor node and places next to the target node in the ID space:

$$ID_M = \text{ Min } \delta \left(SP_i; \; M_j \right) \tag{1}$$

Second, neighbor's discovery, a neighbor of a node M is any node that belongs to the transmission range of M. As soon as a monitor node M is infiltrated, it sends a hello message. Any node that receives the message and sends a reply back to M within a predefined time out will be added to its neighbor list.

Monitoring Process. For a node M to be able to monitor a node S. M must be a neighbor of both S and the neighbors of S, saying Ns. In such a case, M monitors all the communication of S and Ns. The monitor peer M captures information for each message sent and received from Ns to S in the following two steps. When suspicious peer S receives a request from the requester peer, it replies with monitor peer address because according to suspicious peer S routing table, monitor peer M is one of the closest peers to the requested ID. When the requester peer learns about the monitor peer, it sends the same request. Thus, the monitor receives a copy of all messages for the address space attributed to the suspicious peer S.

In the distributed hash table, the publication node publishes its sharing information using two types of messages: publish content message and publish keyword message.

In publish content message, requests are sent towards the hash of the object to associate an object with a source. In publish keyword message, requests are sent towards the hash of the keyword to associate the keyword with the object.

Monitor peer M should attempt to verify the content of each publish message and verify the content key in a keyword publish message. To achieve these goals, monitor peer determines first the nature of the publish message (content or keyword). If it is a publish content message, the monitor peer gathers the following information: the sender IP address and the port number, the object id, the content id, source IP address and the port number. Second, M verifies the location of the content id. If the IP address belongs to the blacklist nodes gathered by the identification process, M calls the isolation process. In the other case, if the IP address is valid, M invokes the verification of the published keyword message in order to verify the content message of each object id. Algorithm 1 details the pseudo code of the monitoring process.

If it is a publish keyword message, the monitor peer gathers the following information: the sender IP address and the port number, the keyword id and the list of object id. Also, for each object, M gathers the content id, IP address and port number. Second, M verifies the location of the keyword id. If the IP address belongs to the blacklist, the monitor calls the isolation process. However, if the IP address is valid, M verifies in the same way the location of each object id received to guarantee that IP address does not belong to the blacklist. Finally, M verifies the content id of each object through the verification of the packet information to determine if the object is polluted or not.

Algorithm 1. Monitoring publish message process

For each publish message (content, keyword)
  /*Publish Content message verification*/
  If (publish message = publish content)
    /* M stores (@IP, port number, object ID, content ID) */
    /* M Verify content ID location*/
      If (IP address of the destination ∈ list_suspicious_polluter_nodes)
        Call isolation process
      Else
        Call publish keyword message verification
    End
  Else
    /*Publish Keyword message verification*/
    If (publish message = publish keyword)
      /* M stores (@IP sender, port number, keyword ID, list of objects IDs) */
      For each object:
        /* M stores (@IP, port number, object ID, content ID) */
        /* M Verify keyword ID location*/
        If (IP address of the destination ∈ list_suspicious_polluter_nodes)
          Call isolation process
        Else
          /*Verify location of each object*/
          For each object id
          If (IP address of the destination ∈ list_suspicious_polluter_nodes)
            Call isolation process
          Else
          /* M Verify content key, searches of content ID and verifies the packet information */

          If (the packet information does not match with the packet information in the database)

            Call isolation process
          End
        End
      End
    End
  End
    End
  End
End

4.3 Isolation Process

Detection process is only the first step towards protecting the structured p2p overlay networks against polluter nodes. The notification and isolation process are used to propagate the notification of detected polluter nodes to the neighbors and takes the appropriate actions to isolate them from the overlay. To achieve these steps a monitor node executes the following actions. First, M sends to each neighbor of S an authenticated alert message in the following form:

$$ALT\_Msg = \{ID_M; ID_{SP}; H_M; PK_M\} \tag{2}$$

Second, each neighbor of S receiving the alert message achieves this three actions. It verifies the authentication of the alert message; marks S as a polluter node and stores the message in an alert buffer to prevent other nodes to accept or forward any message from and to S until its remove from the overlay. Finally, M proceed to the isolation process. It redirects all messages coming to S to other nodes; drops all messages forwarded by S and removes S from its neighbor list.

5 Evaluation

To evaluate our methodology, we performed several experiments on PeerfactSim.Kom [22] simulator. This tool has an advantageous architecture compared to other simulators and implements different distributed hash systems. Besides, we choose to implement our monitoring process using Chord protocol [23] since it's considered as the most deployed distributed hash table system. We reformed the application layer to incorporate polluter nodes. They intercept all search queries in order to claim the owner of the requested objects. Also, they spread polluted objects using the publication of content key or metadata key as described in Sect. 2.

In order to make statements on the performance of an overlay under pollution attacks, suitable scenarios are needed. We used two scenarios during the simulations. In the first, we used a network without any protection as depicted in Fig. 1. However, in the second, we activated our monitoring and detection process as shown in Fig. 2.

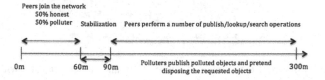

Fig. 1. Pollution attacks without detection process

We considered a network with 500 nodes, 4 zones and 5 simulated hours. In the first step, each node joins the network. We assumed that 50% of nodes are honest and 50% are polluter. After stabilization phase, nodes perform random operations every

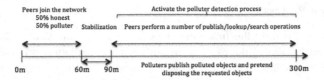

Fig. 2. Pollution attacks with detection process

60 s such as the publication and search objects. Honest nodes publish unpolluted objects. However, polluter ones publish polluted objects. Thus, they claim to be the source of all requested objects. Figures 3 and 4 present the evolution of the number of successfully and futilely published object.

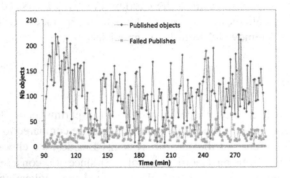

Fig. 3. The evolution of the number of successfully and futilely objects (without any protection)

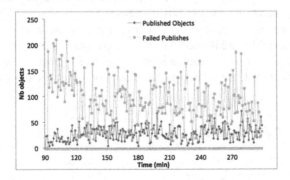

Fig. 4. The evolution of the number of successfully and futilely objects (with protection)

Figure 3 depicts the evolution of the number of successfully and futilely objects without any protection. However, we display in Fig. 4 the same number but after the activation of the protection process. In Fig. 3 we can notice that the number of successfully published objects is very important related with the number of failed one. Indeed, honest and polluter nodes publish objects in a random manner and the lack of a monitoring and control mechanism explain the high number of polluted and unpolluted object published successfully. Moreover, the malicious behavior of polluter nodes and the high complexity in the edifice of routing table explain the number of futilely objects.

In Fig. 4, we can notice that the number of successfully published objects decrease in a remarkable way. However, the number of futilely objects increases. This is due to the activation of the supervision and detection process. Finally, we note that the supervision has a lot of variations; this is due to the integration of the monitoring peers in the network and the variation of the malicious behavior peers. Besides, the dynamic nature of these peers causes a high change in the structure of the network.

Figure 5 presents the evolution of the number of monitored peers vs the evolution of the number of polluter peers when using a network with 4 zones. We can observe that the number of monitored peers raises exponentially, which due to the fact that the number of connected peers to our monitor peers increases over the duration of the experiment. Also, we can notice that the number of detected suspicious and polluter peers increases with the detection process. The high level of participating in the network, make polluter peers supervised and tracked by our tracking process.

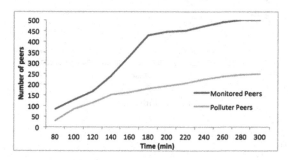

Fig. 5. The evolution of the number of monitored peers VS the evolution of the number of detected polluter peers

Finally, we present the evolution of the false negative and the false positive to assess the effectiveness of our monitoring process. Figure 6 depicts the evolution of the number of false negative related with the evolution of the number of suspicious peers. It refers to a failure to detect polluter peers that are present on a system. We can notice that the number of false negative decreases significantly in function of the evolution of suspicious peers.

Figure 7 shows the evolution of the number of false positive related with the evolution of the number of detected peers. It occurs when the detector peers mistakenly flag an honest peer as being infected. We can notice that the number of false positive is very low.

In summary, the validation experiments show that our supervision and tracking process detect close to 92% of polluter nodes, which prove the effectiveness of our methodology.

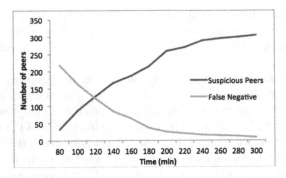

Fig. 6. False negative

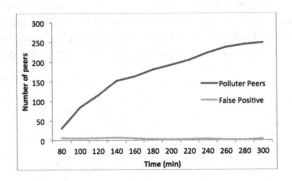

Fig. 7. False positive

6 Conclusion

In this paper, we presented the pollution attacks in structured p2p overlay networks. We have depicted that this attack is one of the major problems that affect these systems. Pollution attacks waste network resources and annoys users with contaminated objects. They damage the contents of the target objects and dispatches them in the network. In this way, contaminated objects will be distributed through the sharing system. We have proposed a new monitoring process based on three steps. The first step is based on the identification of suspicious nodes. The second step is based on supervision of all messages of suspicious nodes and its neighbors in order to identify polluter nodes and invoke the last step that allows the isolation process. Finally, we have implemented our methodology on the PeerfactSim.Kom simulator using the Chord protocol.

As a future work, we plan to implement our solution on some real distributed hash table such as KAD and try to refine both solution and the corresponding features in order to go further towards reaching a secure overlay networks.

References

1. Maurya, R.K., Pandey, S., Kumar, V.: A survey of peer-to-peer networks. J. Adv. Res. Comput. Commun. Eng. (2016)
2. Liang, J., Kumar, R., Xi, Y., Ross, K.W.: Pollution in p2p file sharing systems. In: Proceeding of the International IEEE Conference INFOCOM, Miami, FL, March 2005
3. Chawla, S.: Content pollution in P2P system. J. Inf. Comput. Technol. 3(8), 841–844 (2013)
4. Chen, C.S., et al.: Application of fault-tolerant mechanism to reduce pollution attacks in peer-to-peer networks. J. Distrib. Sensor Netw. 10(7), 792407 (2014)
5. Locher, T., Mysicka, D., Schmid, S., Wattenhofer, R.: Poisoning the Kad network. In: Kant, K., Pemmaraju, S.V., Sivalingam, K.M., Wu, J. (eds.) ICDCN 2010. LNCS, vol. 5935, pp. 195–206. Springer, Heidelberg (2010). https://doi.org/10.1007/978-3-642-11322-2_22
6. Liang, J., Naoumov, N., Ross, K.W.: The index poisoning attack in p2p file sharing systems. In: Proceeding of the International IEEE Conference INFOCOM, April 2006
7. Shi, J., Liang, J., You, J.: Measurements and understanding of the KaZaA P2P network. J. Current Trends High Perform. Comput. Appl. (2005)
8. Liang, J., Naoumov, N., Ross, K.W.: Efficient blacklisting and pollution-level estimation in P2P file-sharing systems. In: Cho, K., Jacquet, P. (eds.) AINTEC 2005. LNCS, vol. 3837, pp. 1–21. Springer, Heidelberg (2005). https://doi.org/10.1007/11599593_1
9. Kamvar, S.D., Schlosser, M.T., Garcia-Molina, H.: The eigentrust algorithm for reputation management in p2p networks. In: Proceeding of the International Conference on WWW, Budapest, Hungary, pp. 640–651 (2003)
10. Costa, C., Soares, V., Almeida, J., Almeida, V.: Fighting pollution dissemination in peer-to-peer networks. In: Proceeding of the International Conference ACM SAC, Seoul, Korea, pp. 1586–1590 (2007)
11. Vieiera, A.B., et al.: SimplyRep: a simple and effective reputation system to fight pollution in P2P live streaming. J. Comput. Netw. 57(4), 1019–1036 (2013)
12. Meng, X.-F., Tan, J.: Field theory based anti-pollution strategy in P2P networks. In: Yu, Y., Yu, Z., Zhao, J. (eds.) CSEEE 2011. CCIS, vol. 159, pp. 107–111. Springer, Heidelberg (2011). https://doi.org/10.1007/978-3-642-22691-5_19
13. Walsh, K., Sirer, E.G.: Fighting peer-to-peer SPAM and decoys with object reputation. In: Proceedings of the International Conference on P2PECON, Philadelphia, August 2005
14. Feng, Q., Dai, Y.: Lip a lifetime and popularity based ranking approach to filter out fake files in p2p file sharing systems. In: Proceedings of the International Conference on IPTPS, February 2007
15. Zhang, P., Fotiou, N., Helvik, B.E., Marias, G.F., Ployzos, G.C.: Analysis of the effect of InfoRanking on content pollution in P2P systems. J. Secur. Commun. Netw. 7(4), 700–713 (2014)
16. Shin, K., Reeves, D.S.: Winnowing: protecting P2P systems against pollution through cooperative index filtering. J. Netw. Comput. Appl. 31(1), 72–84 (2012)
17. Qi, M., Guo, Y., Yan, H.: A reputation system with anti-pollution mechanism in P2P file sharing systems. J. Distrib. Sensor Netw. 5, 44–48 (2009)
18. Montassier, G., Cholez, T., Doyen, G., Khatoun, R., Chrisment, I., et al.: Content pollution quantification in large P2P networks: a measurement study on KAD. In: Proceedings of 11th IEEE International Conference on Peer-to-Peer Computing, Japan, August 2011
19. Wang, Q., Vu, L., Nahrstedt, K., Khurana, H.: Identifying malicious nodes in network-coding-based peer-to-peer streaming networks. In: Proceedings of the International Conference on IEEE INFOCOM (2010)

20. Gaeta, R., Grangetto, M.: Identification of malicious nodes in peer-to-peer streaming: a belief propagation based technique. J. IEEE Trans. Parallel Distrib. Syst. **24**(10), 1994–2003 (2013)
21. Gaeta, R., Grangetto, M., Bovio, L.: DIP: Distributed Identification of Polluters in P2P live streaming. J. ACM Trans. Multimedia Comput. **10**(3), 24 (2014)
22. Graffi, K.: PeerfactSim.KOM – a peer-to-peer system simulator: experiences and lessons learned. In: Proceedings of IEEE International Conference on Peer-to-Peer Computing (2011)
23. Stoica, I., Morris, R., Karger, D., Kaashoek, M.F., Balakrishnan, H.: Chord: a scalable peer-to-peer lookup service for Internet applications. In: Procceedings of ACM SIGCOMM, San Diego, California (2001)

Author Index